ScottForesman
LITERATURE
AND INTEGRATED STUDIES

Middle School: Grade Six

Middle School: Grade Seven

Middle School: Grade Eight

Forms in Literature

World Literature

American Literature

English Literature

The cover features a detail of James Bama's *Portrait of a Sioux,*
which appears in full on this page. After a distinguished career
as a sports illustrator, Bama (born 1926) decided that what he
most wanted to do was paint Western subjects.

ScottForesman
LITERATURE
AND INTEGRATED STUDIES

American Literature

Senior Consultants

Alan C. Purves
State University of New York at Albany

Carol Booth Olson
University of California, Irvine

Carlos E. Cortés
University of California, Riverside (Emeritus)

ScottForesman

A Division of HarperCollins*Publishers*

Editorial Offices: Glenview, Illinois
Regional Offices: San Jose, California • Tucker, Georgia
Glenview, Illinois • Oakland, New Jersey • Dallas, Texas

Visit ScottForesman's Home Page at http://www.scottforesman.com

Acknowledgments

Texts

xxvi "Harrison Bergeron" from *Welcome to the Monkey House* by Kurt Vonnegut, Jr. Copyright © 1961 by Kurt Vonnegut, Jr. Reprinted by permission of Delacorte Press/Seymour Lawrence, a division of Bantam Doubleday Dell Publishing Group, Inc. **9** "This Newly Created World" by Paul Radin from *The Road of Life and Death: A Ritual Drama of the American Indians.* Copyright 1945 by Princeton University Press, renewed 1972. Reprinted by permission of Princeton University Press. **10** "I Have Killed the Deer" from *Hollering Sun* by Nancy Wood. Copyright 1972 by Nancy Wood. Reprinted by permission. **14** Excerpt from *Castaways* by Enrique Pupo-Walker. Reprinted by permission of the University of California Press and the author. **18** "Before They Got Thick" from "The White People Who Came in a Boat" by M.E. Opler from *Memoirs of the American Folklore Society.* Reproduced by permission of the American Folklore Society from the *Journal of American Folklore* 63:247, 1950. Not for further reproduction. **22** From *Great Slave Narratives* by Arna Bontemps. Copyright 1969 by Arna W. Bontemps. Reprinted by permission of Beacon Press. **31** From *Of Plymouth Plantation* by William Bradford, edited by Samuel Eliot Morison. Copyright 1952 by Samuel Eliot Morison and renewed 1980 by Emily M. Beck. Reprinted by permission of Alfred A. Knopf, Inc. **34** From *A Narrative of the Life of Mrs. Mary Jemison,* by James E. Seaver, with an introduction by June Namias. Copyright 1992 by June Namias. Published by the University of Oklahoma Press. Reprinted by permission. **42** "Corn: Builder of Cities" by Mary Talbot from *Newsweek, Columbus Special Issue,* Fall/Winter 1991, page 61. Copyright © 1991 by Newsweek, Inc. All rights reserved. **43** "The Animal That Changed History" from *U.S. News & World Report,* July 8, 1991. Copyright © 1991 by U.S. News & World Report. Reprinted by permission of U.S. News & World Report.

44 From "The Buzzard and the Hawk" by Mr. Ted Williams. Reprinted by permission of The University of Georgia Press. **44** From *When Roots Die: Endangered Traditions on the Sea Islands* by Patricia Jones-Jackson. Reprinted by permission of The University of Georgia Press. **62** From *The Crucible* by Arthur Miller. Copyright 1952, 1953, 1954, renewed 1980 by Arthur Miller. Used by permission of Viking Penguin, a division of Penguin Books USA Inc. **136** "Witchcraft in Salem: A Fungus in the Rye" from *Science News.* Reprinted by permission. **205** "Lost" by David Wagoner. Reprinted by permission of the author. **205** "The Gift Outright" by Robert Frost from *The Poetry of Robert Frost,* edited by Edward Connery Lathem. Copyright © 1942 by Robert Frost. Copyright © 1970 by Lesley Frost Ballantine. Copyright © 1969 by Henry Holt and Company, Inc. Reprinted by permission of Henry Holt and Company, Inc. **207** From "This Land Is Your Land," words and music by Woody Guthrie. TRO-©-Copyright 1956 (Renewed) 1958 (Renewed) 1970 Ludlow Music, Inc., New York, New York. Reprinted by permission of The Richmond Organization. **213** "A Fable for Tomorrow" from *Silent Spring* by Rachel Carson. Copyright © 1962 by Rachel L. Carson, renewed © 1990 by Roger Christie. Reprinted by permission of Houghton Mifflin Company. All rights reserved. **214** "Return" from *Selected Poetry* by Robinson Jeffers. Copyright 1935 and renewed © 1963 by Donnan Jeffers and Garth Jeffers. Reprinted by permission of Random House, Inc. **288** From *Danse Macabre* by Stephen King. Reprinted by permission. **290** "The Thrill of Chills" by Ellen Blum Barish from *Current Health 2,* Vol. 18, No. 7, March 1992, pages 24–25. Reprinted by permission. **332** From *Behind the Blue and the Gray: The Soldier's Life in the Civil War* by Delia Ray, pages 50–56. Reprinted by permission.

continued on page 1015

Senior Consultants

Alan C. Purves
Professor of Education and Humanities, State University of New York at Albany; Director of the Center for Writing and Literacy. Dr. Purves developed the concept and philosophy of the literature lessons for the series, consulted with editors, reviewed tables of contents and lesson manuscript, wrote the Assessment Handbooks, and oversaw the development and writing of the series testing strand.

Carol Booth Olson
Director, California Writing Project, Department of Education, University of California, Irvine. Dr. Olson conceptualized and developed the integrated writing strand of the program, consulted with editors, led a team of teachers in creating literature-based Writing Workshops, and reviewed final manuscript.

Carlos E. Cortés
Professor Emeritus, History, University of California, Riverside. Dr. Cortés designed and developed the multicultural strand embedded in each unit of the series and consulted with grade-level editors to implement the concepts.

Series Consultants

Visual and Media Literacy/Speaking and Listening/Critical Thinking
Harold M. Foster. Professor of English Education and Secondary Education, The University of Akron, Akron. Dr. Foster developed and wrote the Beyond Print features for all levels of the series.

ESL and LEP Strategies
James Cummins. Professor, Modern Language Centre and Curriculum Department, Ontario Institute for Studies in Education, Toronto.

Lily Wong Fillmore. Professor, Graduate School of Education, University of California at Berkeley.

Drs. Cummins and Fillmore advised on the needs of ESL and LEP students, helped develop the Building English Proficiency model for the program, and reviewed strategies and manuscript for this strand of the program.

Fine Arts/Humanities
Neil Anstead. Coordinator of the Humanitas Program, Cleveland Humanities Magnet School, Reseda, California. Mr. Anstead consulted on the fine art used in the program.

Reviewers and Contributors

Pupil and Teacher Edition
Jay Amberg, Glenbrook South High School, Glenview, Illinois **Edison Barber,** St. Anne Community High School, St. Anne, Illinois **Lois Barliant,** Albert G. Lane Technical High School, Chicago, Illinois **James Beasley,** Plant City Senior High School, Plant City, Florida **Linda Belpedio,** Oak Park/River Forest High School, Oak Park, Illinois **Richard Bruns,** Burges High School, El Paso, Texas **Kay Parks Bushman,** Ottawa High School, Ottawa, Kansas **Jesús Cardona,** John F. Kennedy High School, San Antonio, Texas **Marlene Carter,** Dorsey High School, Los Angeles, California **Patrick Cates,** Lubbock High School, Lubbock, Texas **Timothy Dohrer,** New Trier Township High School, Winnetka, Illinois **Margaret Doria,** Our Lady of Perpetual Help High School, Brooklyn, New York **Lucila Dypiangco,** Bell Senior High School, Bell, California **Judith Edminster,** Plant City Senior High School, Plant City, Florida **Mary Alice Fite,** Columbus School for Girls, Columbus, Ohio **Montserrat Fontes,** Marshall High School, Los Angeles, California **Diane Fragos,** Turkey Creek Middle School, Plant City, Florida **Joan Greenwood,** Thornton Township High School, Harvey, Illinois **William Irvin,** Pittsfield Public Schools, Pittsfield, Massachusetts **Carleton Jordan,** Montclair High School, Montclair, New Jersey **Mark Kautz,** Chapel Hill High School, Chapel Hill, North Carolina **Elaine Kay,** Bartow High School, Bartow, Florida **Roslyn Kettering,** West Lafayette Junior/Senior High School, West Lafayette, Indiana **Kristina Kostopoulos,** Lincoln Park High School, Chicago, Illinois **Julia Lloyd,** Harwood Junior High School, Bedford, Texas **John Lord,** Ocean Township High School, Oakhurst, New Jersey **Dolores Mathews,** Bloomingdale High School, Valrico, Florida **Jim McCallum,** Milford High School, Milford, Massachusetts **Monette Mehalko,** Plant City Senior High School, Plant City, Florida **Lucia Podraza,** DuSable High School, Chicago, Illinois **Frank Pool,** Anderson High School, Austin, Texas **Alice Price,** Latin School, Chicago, Illinois **Anna J. Roseboro,** The Bishop's School, La Jolla, California **Peter Sebastian,** Granite Hills High School, El Cajon, California **Rob Slater,** East Forsyth High School, Winston-Salem, North Carolina **Catherine Small,** Nicolet High School, Glendale, Wisconsin **Dennis Symkowiak,** Mundelein High School, Mundelein, Illinois **Rosetta Tetteh,** Senn High School, Chicago, Illinois **Pamela Vetters,** Harlandale High School, San Antonio, Texas **Polly Walwark,** Oak Park High School, Oak Park, Illinois **Karen Wrobleski,** San Diego High School, San Diego, California **Dru Zimmerman,** Chapel Hill High School, Chapel Hill, North Carolina

Contents

▶ MODEL FOR ACTIVE READING AND DISCUSSION

Kurt Vonnegut, Jr.   **Harrison Bergeron**   xxvi

Unit 1   American Beginnings
Part One: A Collision of Cultures

▶ HISTORICAL OVERVIEW: A COLLISION OF CULTURES   2

Cherokee	**How the World Was Made** ◆ creation story	6
Winnebago	**This Newly Created World** ◆ song	9
Chippewa	**Dream Song** ◆ song	9
Taos Pueblo Indian	**I Have Killed the Deer** ◆ song	10
Álvar Núñez Cabeza de Vaca	from **La Relación** ◆ memoir	14
Percy Bigmouth	**Before They Got Thick** ◆ folk tale	18
Olaudah Equiano	from **The Interesting Narrative of the Life of Olaudah Equiano** ◆ autobiography	22
William Bradford	from **Of Plymouth Plantation** ◆ history	31
Canassatego	**Offer of Help** ◆ speech	33
Mary Jemison	from **The Life of Mary Jemison** ◆ memoir	34

INTEGRATED STUDIES   INTERDISCIPLINARY STUDY: The Great Exchange

The Great Exchange ◆ *social studies*   41
Corn: Builder of Cities ◆ *social studies*   42
The Animal That Changed History ◆ *social studies*   43
Old-Time Talk We Still de Talkem Here! ◆ *language*   44

LANGUAGE HISTORY   45
The Language Exchange

WRITING WORKSHOP: Narrative Focus   46
Assignment Earth—A Strange New World
Revising Strategy Using Vivid Language
Editing Strategy Keeping Consistent Tense

BEYOND PRINT: Visual Literacy   51
Looking at Art

Part Two: A Tragedy at Salem

▶ HISTORICAL OVERVIEW: A TRAGEDY AT SALEM   52

Samuel Sewall   from **The Diary of Samuel Sewall** ◆ diary   56
Jonathan Edwards   from **Sinners in the Hands of an Angry God** ◆ sermon   58
Arthur Miller   **The Crucible** ◆ play   62

INTEGRATED STUDIES   INTERDISCIPLINARY STUDY: Mass Hysteria
Witchcraft in Salem: A Fungus in the Rye ◆ *science*   136
A Climate of Fear ◆ *social studies*   137

WRITING WORKSHOP: Persuasive Focus   142
Assignment Reacting Under Pressure
Revising Strategy Being Clear and Specific
Editing Strategy Clarifying Pronoun References

BEYOND PRINT: Technology   148
Speaking the Language of Technology

LOOKING BACK   150
Multicultural Connections
Independent and Group Projects

Unit 2 A New Nation

A Spirit of Independence

▶ HISTORICAL OVERVIEW: A SPIRIT OF INDEPENDENCE   154

Dekanawidah | from **The Iroquois Constitution** ◆ oral tradition   158

Benjamin Franklin | from **The Autobiography of Benjamin Franklin** ◆ autobiography   162

Thomas Paine | from **The American Crisis** ◆ essay   170

Patrick Henry | from **Speech in the Virginia Convention** ◆ speech   172

Thomas Jefferson | **The Declaration of Independence** ◆ historical document   178

Abigail Adams | **Letter to John Adams** ◆ letter   184

Prince Hall | **Petition to the Massachusetts General Assembly** ◆ petition   186

INTEGRATED STUDIES | INTERDISCIPLINARY STUDY: The Quest for Freedom
Freedom Fighters Around the World ◆ *multicultural connection*   188
Preamble by Mike Wilkins ◆ *fine art*   190
A Sailor Works for Freedom ◆ *career connection*   191

LANGUAGE HISTORY   192
Noah Webster and American English

WRITING WORKSHOP: Persuasive Focus   193
Assignment Taking A Stand
Revising Strategy Repetition as Persuasive Technique
Editing Strategy Using Pronouns Correctly

BEYOND PRINT: Visual Literacy   199
Looking at Heroes

LOOKING BACK   201
Multicultural Connections
Independent and Group Projects

THEMES IN AMERICAN
LITERATURE: THE WILDERNESS

Song of the Sky Loom Tewa Indian   204

The Gift Outright by Robert Frost   205

Lost by David Wagoner   205

Song of the Red Bird by Charles Burchfield   206

This Land Is Your Land by Woody Guthrie   207

The Falls of Niagara by Edward Hicks   208

Niagara Falls by Albert Bierstadt   209

Cabins in the Wilderness by William James   210

A Mountain Forest by Isabella Bird   211

The Impact of the Frontier by Frederick Jackson Turner   211

Dead Pine Over Canyonlands by Carol Hoy   212

A Fable for Tomorrow by Rachel Carson   213

Return by Robinson Jeffers   215

America the Beautiful by Katherine Lee Bates   215

Also featuring John Locke, George Catlin, William Bradford, Mary
Rowlandson, Tecumseh, Thomas Cole, Erik H. Erikson, William Cullen
Bryant, Charles Kuralt, Herbert Johnson and Henry David Thoreau

Unit 3 American Classic

Part One: Romantic Truths and Terrors

▶ HISTORICAL OVERVIEW: AMERICAN ROMANTICISM — 218

Ralph Waldo Emerson — from **Self-Reliance** ◆ essay — 222

Henry David Thoreau — from **Walden** ◆ essay — 226

from **Civil Disobedience** ◆ essay — 231

Sojourner Truth — **Ain't I a Woman** ◆ speech — 237

Washington Irving — **The Devil and Tom Walker** ◆ short story — 240

Edgar Allan Poe — **The Pit and the Pendulum** ◆ short story — 253

The Raven ◆ poem — 268

Nathaniel Hawthorne — **Dr. Heidegger's Experiment** ◆ short story — 276

INTEGRATED STUDIES — INTERDISCIPLINARY STUDY: An Appetite for Fright

An Appetite for Fright ◆ *pop culture* — 286

from **Danse Macabre** by Stephen King ◆ *pop culture* — 288

That Which I Should Have Done I Did Not Do by Ivan Albright ◆ *fine art* — 289

The Thrill of Chills by Ellen Blum Barish ◆ *health* — 290

LANGUAGE HISTORY — 291
The Language of Gothic Horror

WRITING WORKSHOP: Narrative Focus — 292
Assignment Writing in Style
Revising Strategy Using Contrast to Develop Mood
Editing Strategy Using Too Few Letters

BEYOND PRINT: Media Literacy — 296
Looking at Horror Movies

Part Two: The Civil War

▶ HISTORICAL OVERVIEW: THE CIVIL WAR ... 298

Mary Chesnut — **The Attack on Fort Sumter** ◆ diary ... 302

Abraham Lincoln — **The Gettysburg Address** ◆ speech ... 304

Herman Melville — **Shiloh** ◆ poem ... 308

The Portent ◆ poem ... 308

Ambrose Bierce — **An Occurrence at Owl Creek Bridge** ◆ short story ... 312

Ulysses S. Grant — from **Personal Memoirs of U. S. Grant** ◆ memoir ... 322

Robert E. Lee — **Farewell Order to the Army of Northern Virginia** ◆ historical document ... 325

Frederick Douglass — from **What the Black Man Wants** ◆ speech ... 328

INTEGRATED STUDIES

INTERDISCIPLINARY STUDY: Behind the Lines

from **Behind the Blue and the Gray** by Delia Ray ◆ *science* ... 332

from **Hospital Sketches** by Louisa May Alcott ◆ *history* ... 334

from **"Co. Aytch"** by Sam R. Watkins ◆ *history* ... 335

from **Reminiscences of My Life in Camp** by Susie King Taylor ◆ *history* ... 336

Park Ranger Brings the Civil War to Life ◆ *career connection* ... 337

WRITING WORKSHOP: Expository Focus ... 338
Assignment You Are There
Revising Strategy Making Smooth Transitions
Editing Strategy Citing Works in Correct Form

BEYOND PRINT: Technology ... 344
Electronic Research

LOOKING BACK ... 346
Multicultural Connections
Independent and Group Projects

Unit 4 Expanding America

Part One: Letters to the World

	▶ HISTORICAL OVERVIEW: A CHANGING SOCIETY	350
Emily Dickinson	**This is my letter to the World** ◆ poem	354
	Much Madness is divinest Sense ◆ poem	354
	The Soul selects her own Society ◆ poem	354
	Because I could not stop for Death ◆ poem	357
	A Bird came down the Walk ◆ poem	357
Walt Whitman	**I Hear America Singing** ◆ poem	361
	What is the Grass? from **Song of Myself** ◆ poem	362
	There Was a Child Went Forth ◆ poem	364
Paul Laurence Dunbar	**Sympathy** ◆ poem	370
	We Wear the Mask ◆ poem	371
Stephen Crane	**To the Maiden** ◆ poem	374
	The Wayfarer ◆ poem	374
	I Saw a Man Pursuing the Horizon ◆ poem	375
	A Man Said to the Universe ◆ poem	375
INTEGRATED STUDIES	INTERDISCIPLINARY STUDY: American Visionaries	
	Paintings by Frederic Edwin Church, Albert Pinkham Ryder, William Rimmer, Elihu Vedder, Erastus Salisbury Field, and William Holbrook Beard ◆ *fine art*	377
	WRITING WORKSHOP: Expository Focus	381
	Assignment Dear World,	
	Revising Strategy Being Concise	
	Editing Strategy Avoiding Run-Ons	
	BEYOND PRINT: Visual Literacy	385
	Looking at Paintings	

Part Two: The Frontier

| | ▶ HISTORICAL OVERVIEW: THE FRONTIER | 386 |
| Mark Twain | **The Celebrated Jumping Frog of Calaveras County** ◆ short story | 390 |

Américo Paredes	**El Corrido de Gregorio Cortez** ◆ ballad	398
Anonymous	**Gold Mountain Poems** ◆ poetry	400
Satanta	**My Heart Feels Like Bursting** ◆ speech	403
Willa Cather	**A Wagner Matinée** ◆ short story	407

INTEGRATED STUDIES

INTERDISCIPLINARY STUDY: Frontier Adventures and Tragedies

Legends of the Wild West ◆ *pop culture*	416
from **Black Hawk, an Autobiography** ◆ *history*	418
from **Thousand Pieces of Gold** by Ruthanne Lum McCunn ◆ *literature*	420
from **Down the Santa Fe Trail** by Susan Shelby Magoffin ◆ *history*	421

LANGUAGE HISTORY   422
The Many Flavors of American English

WRITING WORKSHOP: Expository Focus   423
Assignment Bringing History to Life
Revising Strategy Using Spatial Order Terms
Editing Strategy Avoiding Homophone Errors

BEYOND PRINT: Media Literacy   427
Watching Westerns

LOOKING BACK   429
Multicultural Connections
Independent and Group Projects

THEMES IN AMERICAN LITERATURE:

THE JOURNEY

Night Journey by Theodore Roethke	432
Madam Knight Travels to New York by Sarah Kemble Knight	434
Dust Bowl Migrants Move Westward by John Steinbeck	435
The Cowards Never Started, and the Weak Died Along the Way by Lydia Allen Rudd	436
The Heirloom by Tom Lovell	437
Lost Travelers by Ronald Reagan	437
The Steerage by Alfred Stieglitz	438
The Moth and the Star by James Thurber	440
Speed by May Swenson	440
Pearblossom Hwy., 11–18th April 1986 by David Hockney	441
Homesick Blues by Langston Hughes	442
The Migration of the Negro series, No. 1 by Jacob Lawrence	442
Indian Boarding School: The Runaways by Louise Erdrich	443

Also featuring N. Scott Momaday, Abraham Lincoln, Thomas Hart Benton, William Least Heat Moon, Eddy Harris, Mark Twain, Cesar Chavez, Anne Morrow Lindbergh, James Lovell, and Emma Lazarus

Unit 5 Breaking the Mold

Part One: Beyond the Limits

▶ HISTORICAL OVERVIEW: STRETCHING THE LIMITS — 446

Kate Chopin — **The Story of an Hour** ◆ short story — 450

Susan Glaspell — **Trifles** ◆ play — 455

Mary E. Wilkins Freeman — **The Revolt of "Mother"** ◆ short story — 468

Ida B. Wells-Barnett — from **Crusade for Justice** ◆ autobiography — 483

Edna St. Vincent Millay — **The Spring and the Fall** ◆ poem — 492

On Thought in Harness ◆ poem — 493

INTEGRATED STUDIES — INTERDISCIPLINARY STUDY: Within Limits

The Uprising of Women ◆ *history* — 495

Teaching by the Rules ◆ *history* — 497

from **For Her Own Good** by Barbara Ehrenreich and Deirdre English ◆ *science* — 498

LANGUAGE HISTORY — 500

The Language of Gender

WRITING WORKSHOP: Expository Focus — 501

Assignment Update: Women Then and Now

Revising Strategy Orienting Your Audience

Editing Strategy Using Apostrophes Correctly

BEYOND PRINT: Visual Literacy — 506

Looking at Photographs

Part Two: The Harlem Renaissance

▶ HISTORICAL OVERVIEW: A CULTURAL REVOLUTION — 508

James Weldon Johnson — **Harlem: The Culture Capital** ◆ essay — 512

Arna Bontemps — **A Black Man Talks of Reaping** ◆ poem — 524

Claude McKay — **If We Must Die** ◆ poem — 525

Langston Hughes	**The Negro Speaks of Rivers** ◆ poem	526
Countee Cullen	**Harlem Wine** ◆ poem	526
Langston Hughes	**Youth** ◆ poem	527
Sterling A. Brown	**Ma Rainey** ◆ poem	528
Zora Neale Hurston	**How It Feels to Be Colored Me** ◆ essay	533

INTEGRATED STUDIES

INTERDISCIPLINARY STUDY: An Artistic Awakening

Artworks by Meta Warrick Fuller, Richmond Barthé, Augusta Savage, Archibald J. Motley, Jr., Palmer Hayden, and Aaron Douglas ◆ *fine art* 538

Tour Director Shows Off Harlem Treasures ◆ *career connection* 542

WRITING WORKSHOP: Persuasive Focus 543

Assignment Calling All Artists

Revising Strategy Using Appropriate Tone

Editing Strategy Using Adjectives and Adverbs Correctly

BEYOND PRINT: Effective Speaking 548

Speaking Your Mind

LOOKING BACK 549

Multicultural Connections

Independent and Group Projects

THEMES IN AMERICAN LITERATURE:

THE SEARCH FOR EQUALITY

15th, 19th, and 26th amendments	552
Stump Speaking by George Caleb Bingham	553
Follow the Drinking Gourd	554
The Price of Freedom by Lewis Douglass	554
Tragic Prelude by John Steuart Curry	555
There Are No Laundries in China	556
Booker T. Washington and W. E. B. DuBois Debate	556
The Promised Land by Mary Antin	557
Raise Less Corn and More Hell! by Mary Elizabeth Lease	558
Which Side Are You On? by Florence Reece	558
The American Working Man of the Future by Frederick Opper	558
The Feeling of Solidarity by Roberto Acuna	559
Viva Chavez by Paul Davis	559
The Indian and the Buffalo by Jim Domke	560
Return to Wounded Knee by Mary Crow Dog	560
Affirmative Action: Pro and Con by Roger Wilkins and Shelby Steele	561

Also featuring Thomas Jefferson, Elizabeth Cady Stanton, Alexis de Tocqueville, Hector St. Jean de Crèveçoeur, and Eleanor Roosevelt

Unit 6 Modern Dilemmas

Part One: Lost in a Crowd

▶ HISTORICAL OVERVIEW: BETWEEN THE WARS   564

T. S. Eliot   **The Love Song of J. Alfred Prufrock** ◆ poem   568

Edwin Arlington Robinson   **Richard Cory** ◆ poem   576

E. E. Cummings   **l(a** ◆ poem   577

Ernest Hemingway   **In Another Country** ◆ short story   580

F. Scott Fitzgerald   **Winter Dreams** ◆ short story   586

Richard Wright   from **Black Boy** ◆ autobiography   605

Katherine Anne Porter   **The Jilting of Granny Weatherall** ◆ short story   611

INTEGRATED STUDIES   INTERDISCIPLINARY STUDY: The Roaring Twenties
The Younger Generation Runs Wild ◆ *pop culture*   620
Roaring Twenties Glossary ◆ *pop culture*   622

LANGUAGE HISTORY   624
What's New in Language

WRITING WORKSHOP: Expository Focus   625
Assignment Analyzing Alienation
Revising Strategy Revising a Thesis Statement
Editing Strategy Using Commas Correctly

BEYOND PRINT: Technology   631
The Wonders of Word Processing

Part Two: The Strength of Tradition

▶ HISTORICAL OVERVIEW: THE STRENGTH OF TRADITION — 632

Robert Frost — **Stopping by Woods on a Snowy Evening** ◆ poem — 636

Mending Wall ◆ poem — 637

Birches ◆ poem — 639

William Faulkner — **The Tall Men** ◆ short story — 644

Thomas S. Whitecloud — **Blue Winds Dancing** ◆ essay — 658

Eudora Welty — **A Worn Path** ◆ short story — 667

John Steinbeck — **The Leader of the People** ◆ short story — 676

Tennessee Williams — **Lord Byron's Love Letter** ◆ play — 690

INTEGRATED STUDIES — INTERDISCIPLINARY STUDY: Life on the Home Front

New Opportunities for African Americans and Women: Sybil Lewis ◆ *history* — 699

Children of the Home Front: Sheril Jankovsky Cunning ◆ *history* — 700

Japanese Americans are "Relocated": Henry Murakami ◆ *history* — 702

WRITING WORKSHOP: Expository Focus — 704

Assignment Point-Counterpoint

Revising Strategy Signaling Comparisons and Contrasts

Editing Strategy Punctuating Quotations from Literature

BEYOND PRINT: Critical Thinking — 710

Propaganda

LOOKING BACK — 712

Multicultural Connections

Independent and Group Projects

Unit 7 Years of Change

Part One: Person to Person

▶ HISTORICAL OVERVIEW: POSTWAR CULTURE   716

Flannery O'Connor   **The Life You Save May Be Your Own** ◆ short story   720

Tillie Olsen   **I Stand Here Ironing** ◆ short story   732

John Updike   **Separating** ◆ short story   742

Maxine Hong Kingston   from **The Woman Warrior** ◆ essay   754

Alice Walker   **Everyday Use** ◆ short story   760

Sylvia Plath   **Mirror** ◆ poem   771

Elizabeth Bishop   **One Art** ◆ poem   772

Nikki Giovanni   **Legacies** ◆ poem   773

Sam Hamod   **Leaves** ◆ poem   774

Alma Luz Villanueva   **To Jesus Villanueva, with Love** ◆ poem   775

INTEGRATED STUDIES   INTERDISCIPLINARY STUDY: Television Comes of Age

Life After Television by John Brooks ◆ *pop culture*   779

What's on TV? ◆ *pop culture*   781

WRITING WORKSHOP: Persuasive Focus   784

Assignment You Be the Judge

Revising Strategy Writing in the Active Voice

Editing Strategy Comparative Forms of Adjectives and Adverbs

BEYOND PRINT: Media Literacy   789

Looking at Television

Part Two: In the Midst of Struggle . . .

▶ HISTORICAL OVERVIEW: A STORMY ERA   790

Lorraine Hansberry   from **To Be Young, Gifted and Black** ◆ autobiographical essay   794

Martin Luther King, Jr.   from **Letter from a Birmingham Jail** ◆ letter   800

Malcolm X   from **The Autobiography of Malcolm X** ◆ autobiography   806

Tim O'Brien   **On the Rainy River** ◆ short story   812

Nguyên Qúi Dú'c   from **Where the Ashes Are** ◆ autobiography   828

Estela Portillo Trambley   **Village** ◆ short story   838

INTEGRATED STUDIES   INTERDISCIPLINARY STUDY: Time of Turmoil: 1955–1975
The Pace of Change ◆ *history*   846

LANGUAGE HISTORY: Euphemisms:
Polite and Deadly Language   851

WRITING WORKSHOP: Narrative Focus   852
Assignment Reflecting on the Sixties
Revising Strategy When to Quote Directly
and When to Paraphrase
Editing Strategy Punctuating Direct Quotations

BEYOND PRINT: Technology   857
Multimedia Presentations

LOOKING BACK   858
Multicultural Connections
Independent and Group Projects

Unit 8 American Voices Today
Citizens of Tomorrow

▶ HISTORICAL OVERVIEW: BALANCING UNITY AND DIVERSITY   862

Anne Tyler	**Teenage Wasteland** ◆ short story	866
Garrison Keillor	**Gary Keillor** ◆ short story	876
Sandra Cisneros	**Salvador Late or Early** ◆ short story	888
Martín Espada	**Coca-Cola and Coco Frío** ◆ poem	893
Cathy Song	**Lost Sister** ◆ poem	894
Barbara Kingsolver	**Naming Myself** ◆ poem	896
Ana Castillo	**Red Wagons** ◆ poem	898
Amy Tan	**Mother Tongue** ◆ essay	902
Sherman Alexie	**This Is What It Means to Say Phoenix, Arizona** ◆ short story	911
T. Coraghessan Boyle	**Top of the Food Chain** ◆ short story	923
Pam Houston	**A Blizzard Under Blue Sky** ◆ short story	930
August Wilson	**The Janitor** ◆ play	936

INTEGRATED STUDIES   INTERDISCIPLINARY STUDY: A Glimpse Into the Future   939
The Way We Will Be ◆ *futurist connection*
**Future Technology: Dream Word
or Nightmare?** ◆ *futurist connection*
**Future Fashions by Donna Karan and
Tim Burton** ◆ *futurist connection*

LANGUAGE HISTORY: Computerese   945

WRITING WORKSHOP: Narrative Focus   946
Assignment Poetic Insights
Revising Strategy Using Imagery and Figures of Speech
Editing Strategy Avoiding Careless Spelling Mistakes

BEYOND PRINT: Critical Thinking   951
Analyzing Advertising

LOOKING BACK   953
Multicultural Connections
Independent and Group Projects

THEMES IN AMERICAN
LITERATURE: THE MEDIA
Ballyhoo by Frederick Lewis Allen   956
Media Blitz by Rubén Martínez   957
Yellow Journalism and the Spanish-American War
by James Creelman   958
William Randolph Hearst as "The Yellow Kid"   959
Let Us Prey by Thomas Nast   959
Newsstand in Omaha, Nebraska, 1938 by James Vauhon   960
Supermarket Tabloids   961
Fanzines   962
Talk Shows   963
Video Games   964
The Internet   965

Also featuring Andy Warhol, William Lloyd Garrison, Will Rogers,
1st Amendment, Pagan Kennedy, and Geraldo Rivera

Glossaries, Handbooks, and Indexes

Glossary of Literary Terms. 968
Glossary of Vocabulary Words 975
Language and Grammar Handbook 985
Index of Skills and Strategies 1003
Index of Fine Art and Artists 1011
Index of Authors and Titles 1013
Text Acknowledgments. 1015
Illustration Acknowledgments. 1017

Genre Overview

Short Stories

Harrison Bergeron xxviii
The Devil and Tom Walker. 240
The Pit and the Pendulum. 253
Dr. Heidegger's Experiment. 276
An Occurrence at Owl Creek Bridge. 312
The Celebrated Jumping Frog of
Calaveras County 390
Wagner Matinée 407
The Story of an Hour. 450
The Revolt of "Mother" 468
In Another Country 580
Winter Dreams. 586
The Jilting of Granny Weatherall 611
The Tall Men 644
A Worn Path 667
The Leader of the People 676
The Life You Save May Be Your Own 720
I Stand Here Ironing 732
Separating. 742
Everyday Use 760
On the Rainy River 812
Village 838
Teenage Wasteland. 866
Gary Keillor 876
Salvador Late or Early 888
This Is What It Means to Say
Phoenix, Arizona 911
Top of the Food Chain. 923
A Blizzard Under Blue Sky 930

Poetry

This Newly Created World. 9
Dream Song 9
I Have Killed the Deer 10
The Raven 268
Shiloh 308
The Portent 308
This is my letter to the World. 354
Much Madness is divinest Sense 354
The Soul selects her own Society 354
Because I could not stop for Death 357
A Bird came down the Walk 357
I Hear America Singing 361
What is the Grass? from
Song of Myself 362
There Was a Child Went Forth. 364
Sympathy 370
We Wear the Mask 371
To the Maiden 374
The Wayfarer 374
I Saw a Man Pursuing the Horizon 375
A Man Said to the Universe. 375
El Corrido de Gregorio Cortez. 398
Gold Mountain Poems 400
The Spring and the Fall. 492
On Thought in Harness. 493
A Black Man Talks of Reaping. 524
If We Must Die. 525
The Negro Speaks of Rivers 526
Harlem Wine 526
Youth 527
Ma Rainey 528
The Love Song of J. Alfred Prufrock 568

Richard Cory 576

I(a 577

Stopping by Woods on a
Snowy Evening 636

Mending Wall 637

Birches 639

Mirror 771

One Art 772

Legacies 773

Leaves 774

To Jesus Villanueva, with Love 775

Coca-Cola and Coco Frío 893

Lost Sister 894

Naming Myself 896

Red Wagons 898

Plays

The Crucible 62

Trifles 455

Lord Byron's Love Letter 690

The Janitor 936

Nonfiction

from La Relación 14

from The Interesting Narrative of
the Life of Olaudah Equiano 22

from Of Plymouth Plantation 31

Offer of Help 33

from The Life of Mary Jemison 34

from The Diary of Samuel Sewall 56

from Sinners in the Hands
of an Angry God 58

from The Iroquois Constitution 158

from The Autobiography of
Benjamin Franklin 162

from The American Crisis 170

from Speech in the Virginia Convention . . . 172

The Declaration of Independence 178

Letter to John Adams 184

Petition to the Massachusetts
General Assembly 186

from Self-Reliance 222

from Walden 226

from Civil Disobedience 231

Ain't I a Woman 237

The Attack on Fort Sumter 302

The Gettysburg Address 304

from Personal Memoirs of U. S. Grant 322

Farewell Order to the Army of
Northern Virginia 325

from What the Black Man Wants 328

My Heart Feels Like Bursting 403

from Crusade for Justice 483

Harlem: The Culture Capital 512

How It Feels to Be Colored Me 533

from Black Boy 605

Blue Winds Dancing 658

from The Woman Warrior 754

from To Be Young, Gifted and Black 794

from Letter from a Birmingham Jail 800

from The Autobiography of Malcolm X 806

from Where the Ashes Are 828

Mother Tongue 902

Folk Tales

How the World Was Made 6

Before They Got Thick 18

Feature Overview

Historical Overviews

A Collision of Cultures 2

A Tragedy at Salem 52

A Spirit of Independence 154

American Romanticism 218

The Civil War 298

A Changing Society 350

The Frontier 386

Stretching the Limits 446

A Cultural Revolution 508

Between the Wars. 564
The Strength of Tradition. 632
Postwar Culture. 716
A Stormy Era. 790
Balancing Unity and Diversity 862

Interdisciplinary Studies

The Great Exchange 41
Mass Hysteria 136
The Quest for Freedom. 188
An Appetite for Fright 286
Behind the Lines 332
American Visionaries. 377
Frontier Adventures and Tragedies 416
Within Limits 495
An Artistic Awakening 538
The Roaring Twenties 620
Life on the Home Front 699
Television Comes of Age. 779
Time of Turmoil: 1955–1975 846
A Glimpse Into the Future 939

Language History

The Language Exchange. 45
Noah Webster and American English 192
The Language of Gothic Horror 291
The Many Flavors of American English. . . . 422
The Language of Gender 500
What's New in Language. 624
Euphemisms: Polite and
Deadly Language 851
Computerese. 945

Writing Workshops

Earth—A Strange New World (Narrative) . . . 46
Reacting Under Pressure (Persuasive) 142
Taking a Stand (Persuasive) 193
Writing in Style (Narrative). 292
You Are There (Expository) 338
Dear World, (Expository) 381
Bringing History to Life (Expository) 423
Update: Women Then and Now
(Expository) 501
Calling All Artists (Persuasive). 543
Analyzing Alienation (Expository) 625
Point-Counterpoint (Expository) 704
You Be the Judge (Persuasive) 784
Reflecting on the Sixties (Narrative) 852
Poetic Insights (Narrative) 946

Beyond Print

Looking at Art (Visual Literacy) 51
Speaking the Language of Technology
(Technology) 148
Looking at Heroes (Visual Literacy). 199
Looking at Horror Movies
(Media Literacy). 296
Electronic Research (Technology) 344
Looking at Paintings (Visual Literacy) 385
Watching Westerns (Media Literacy). 427
Looking at Photographs
(Visual Literacy) 506
Speaking Your Mind
(Effective Speaking). 548
The Wonders of Word
Processing (Technology) 631
Propaganda (Critical Thinking) 710
Looking at Television (Media Literacy) 789
Multimedia Presentations (Technology). . . . 857
Analyzing Advertising (Critical Thinking) . . . 951

Themes in American Literature

The Wilderness 203
The Journey. 431
The Search for Equality 551
The Media 955

Model for Active Reading

Good readers read actively. They become involved in what they read, relating the characters and situations to people and events in their own lives. They question, predict, evaluate, and in other ways think about the story or article they are reading. Three students, Kelly Horvath, Pratik Patel, and Abigail Baim-Lance, agreed to let us in on their thoughts as they read "Harrison Bergeron." You might have different ideas and questions about the story than they did. However, their responses may give you some ideas for how you can get actively engaged as you read literature.

KELLY HORVATH I enjoy playing sports and being active, and also working on my computer. The kinds of books I like to read are mystery novels and collections of short stories. In the future I might become a lawyer.

PRATIK PATEL I enjoy sports, too, because they're a way to escape from the pressures of schoolwork. I like to read short stories and poetry. I especially like poetry because you get a lot out of a little—poetry is efficient. When I grow up I want to be a doctor.

ABIGAIL BAIM-LANCE My friends call me Abby. I like tennis, and I'm kind of getting into soccer. I like to read. I don't know what I want to be when I grow up—there are so many different possibilities. I want to keep an open mind.

Six Reading Terms Explained

The following are some of the techniques that good readers use, often without being aware of them.

Question Ask questions that arise as you read.

Example: Was this society a democracy at one time?

Predict Make reasoned guesses, based on what's happened so far, about what might happen next.

Example: I think Harrison will overthrow the government and outlaw handicaps.

Clarify Clear up confusion and answer questions.

Example: I guess the Handicapper General can do whatever she wants—even kill people.

Summarize Review some of the main ideas or events.

Example: No one in the society can think long thoughts and draw conclusions or make judgments.

Evaluate Reason from common sense, established guidelines, and evidence to arrive at sound opinions and valid conclusions.

Example: Initiative in this society is illegal; laziness applauded. This doesn't sound like a "progressive" society; it's a "backward" one.

Connect Compare the text with something in your own experience, with another text, or with ideas within the text.

Example: Most people in this society have rejected excellence and have committed themselves to mediocrity. The same seems to be true of many people in our own society.

HARRISON BERGERON

KURT VONNEGUT, JR.

▲ What message do you think George Tooker is trying to convey in his painting, *Landscape With Figurines* (1966)? After you've read Harrison Bergeron, decide whether there is any kind of a theme connection between this painting and the story.

The year was 2081, and everybody was finally equal. They weren't only equal before God and the law. They were equal every which way. Nobody was smarter than anybody else. Nobody was better looking than anybody else. Nobody was stronger or quicker than anybody else. All this equality was due to the 211th, 212th, and 213th Amendments to the Constitution, and to the unceasing vigilance of agents of the United States Handicapper General.

Some things about living still weren't quite right, though. April, for instance still drove people crazy by not being springtime. And it was in that clammy month that the H-G men took George and Hazel Bergeron's fourteen-year-old son, Harrison, away.

It was tragic, all right, but George and Hazel couldn't think about it very hard. Hazel had a perfectly average intelligence, which meant she couldn't think about anything except in short bursts. And George, while his intelligence was way above normal, had a little mental handicap radio in his ear. He was required by law to wear it at all times. It was tuned to a government transmitter. Every twenty seconds or so, the transmitter would send out some sharp noise to keep people like George from taking unfair advantage of their brains.

George and Hazel were watching television. There were tears on Hazel's cheeks, but she'd forgotten for the moment what they were about.

On the television screen were ballerinas.

A buzzer sounded in George's head. His thoughts fled in panic, like bandits from a burglar alarm.

"That was a really pretty dance, that dance they just did," said Hazel.

"Huh?" said George.

"That dance—it was nice," said Hazel.

"Yup," said George. He tried to think a little about the ballerinas. They weren't really very good—no better than anybody else would have been, anyway. They were burdened with sashweights and bags of birdshot, and their faces were masked, so that no one, seeing a free and graceful gesture or a pretty face, would feel like something the cat drug in. George was toying with the vague notion that maybe dancers shouldn't be handicapped. But he didn't get very far with it before another noise in his ear radio scattered his thoughts.

George winced. So did two out of the eight ballerinas.

Hazel saw him wince. Having no mental handicap herself, she had to ask George what the latest sound had been.

"Sounded like somebody hitting a milk bottle with a ball peen hammer," said George.

PRATIK   This is a futuristic, controlled society—kind of a "Brave New World." (connect)

ABIGAIL   These two sentences are interesting. They show that some things can't be changed, no matter how hard you try to make them conform. (evaluate)

KELLY   If people aren't allowed to elaborate or continue their thoughts, they can't react to what happens. (evaluate)

ABIGAIL   It's ironic that they're showing ballerinas on the screen, because they're a symbol of beauty and possess special talents most people don't possess. (evaluate)

PRATIK   Here you can see that George is above average in intelligence. He questions why one situation has to be the way it is. But every time he does this, a sound in his head disturbs him, and so nothing will change. All the citizens are programmed so they can't make a difference. (summarize)

"I'd think it would be real interesting, hearing all the different sounds," said Hazel, a little envious. "All the things they think up."

"Um," said George.

"Only, if I was Handicapper General, you know what I would do?" said Hazel. Hazel, as a matter of fact, bore a strong resemblance to the Handicapper General, a woman named Diana Moon Glampers. "If I was Diana Moon Glampers," said Hazel, "I'd have chimes on Sunday—just chimes. Kind of in honor of religion."

"I could think, if it was just chimes," said George.

"Well—maybe make 'em real loud," said Hazel. "I think I'd make a good Handicapper General."

"Good as anybody else," said George.

"Who knows better'n I do what normal is?" said Hazel.

"Right," said George. He began to think glimmeringly about his abnormal son who was now in jail, about Harrison, but a twenty-one-gun salute in his head stopped that.

"Boy!" said Hazel, "that was a doozy, wasn't it?"

It was such a doozy that George was white and trembling, and tears stood on the rims of his red eyes. Two of the eight ballerinas had collapsed to the studio floor, were holding their temples.

"All of a sudden you look so tired," said Hazel. "Why don't you stretch out on the sofa, so's you can rest your handicap bag on the pillows, honeybunch." She was referring to the forty-seven pounds of birdshot in a canvas bag, which was padlocked around George's neck. "Go on and rest the bag for a little while," she said. "I don't care if you're not equal to me for a while."

George weighed the bag with his hands. "I don't mind it," he said. "I don't notice it anymore. It's just a part of me."

"You been so tired lately—kind of wore out," said Hazel. "If there was just some way we could make a little hole in the bottom of the bag, and just take out a few of them lead balls. Just a few."

"Two years in prison and two thousand dollars fine for every ball I took out," said George. "I don't call that a bargain."

"If you could just take a few out when you came home from work," said Hazel. "I mean—you don't compete with anybody around here. You just set around."

"If I tried to get away with it," said George, "then other people'd get away with it—and pretty soon we'd be right back to the dark ages again, with everybody competing against everybody else. You wouldn't like that, would you?"

"I'd hate it," said Hazel.

"There you are," said George. "The minute people start cheating on laws, what do you think happens to society?"

If Hazel hadn't been able to come up with an answer to this

ABIGAIL Notice how Hazel has this curiosity about George's pain. She doesn't just accept the pain—she's also "a little envious" of it. So they haven't succeeded in doing away with competition. (connect)

KELLY I think it's good that they're trying for a perfect society—but what good is that if everybody is unhappy? Why would you want to live like this? They use all these devices to make people stop thinking—like the twenty-one-gun salute that makes George cry and makes two ballerinas fall to the floor. It has to be nerve-wracking. (summarize, evaluate)

PRATIK This kind of thinking is going to get them in trouble. (predict)

KELLY George has to wear a handicap bag so he's equal to everybody else. But I don't see anything wrong with competition. It doesn't have to be excessive, but competition brings some spice to life. That way you don't just sit around the house watching TV. (evaluate)

ABIGAIL I think Vonnegut is satirizing socialism. (connect)

question, George couldn't have supplied one. A siren was going off in his head.

"Reckon it'd fall all apart," said Hazel.

"What would?" said George blankly.

"Society," said Hazel uncertainly. "Wasn't that what you just said?"

"Who knows?" said George.

The television program was suddenly interrupted for a news bulletin. It wasn't clear at first as to what the bulletin was about, since the announcer, like all announcers, had a serious speech impediment. For about half a minute, and in a state of high excitement, the announcer tried to say, "Ladies and gentlemen—"

He finally gave up, handed the bulletin to a ballerina to read.

"That's all right—" Hazel said of the announcer, "he tried. That's the big thing. He tried to do the best he could with what God gave him. He should get a nice raise for trying so hard."

"Ladies and gentlemen—" said the ballerina, reading the bulletin. She must have been extraordinarily beautiful, because the mask she wore was hideous. And it was easy to see that she was the strongest and most graceful of all the dancers, for her handicap bags were as big as those worn by two-hundred-pound men.

And she had to apologize at once for her voice, which was a very unfair voice for a woman to use. Her voice was a warm, luminous, timeless melody. "Excuse me—" she said, and she began again, making her voice absolutely uncompetitive.

"Harrison Bergeron, age fourteen," she said in a grackle squawk, "has just escaped from jail, where he was held on suspicion of plotting to overthrow the government. He is a genius and an athlete, is under-handicapped, and should be regarded as extremely dangerous."

A police photograph of Harrison Bergeron was flashed on the screen, upside down, then sideways, upside down again, then right side up. The picture showed the full length of Harrison against a background calibrated in feet and inches. He was exactly seven feet tall.

The rest of Harrison's appearance was Halloween and hardware. Nobody had ever borne heavier handicaps. He had outgrown hindrances faster than the H-G men could think them up. Instead of a little ear radio for a mental handicap, he wore a tremendous pair of earphones, and spectacles with thick wavy lenses. The spectacles were intended to make him not only half blind, but to give him whanging headaches besides.

Scrap metal was hung all over him. Ordinarily, there was a certain symmetry, a military neatness to the handicaps issued to strong

PRATIK A broadcaster with a speech impediment, ballerinas who can't dance well—there's a lot of irony here. (connect)

KELLY The ballerina even has to apologize for her voice—it's too beautiful. (clarify)

KELLY Now I think I know how the story will end. Harrison will change everything. He'll get rid of all the handicaps. He'll show everyone that a society without handicaps will still be OK. (predict)

people, but Harrison looked like a walking junkyard. In the race of life, Harrison carried three hundred pounds.

And to offset his good looks, the H-G men required that he wear at all times a red rubber ball for a nose, keep his eyebrows shaved off, and cover his even white teeth with black caps at snaggletooth random.

"If you see this boy," said the ballerina, "do not—I repeat, do not—try to reason with him."

There was the shriek of a door being torn from its hinges.

Screams and barking cries of consternation came from the television set. The photograph of Harrison Bergeron on the screen jumped again and again, as though dancing to the tune of an earthquake.

George Bergeron correctly identified the earthquake, and well he might have—for many was the time his own home had danced to the same crashing tune. "Oh, no—" said George, "that must be Harrison."

The realization was blasted from his mind instantly by the sound of an automobile collision in his head.

When George could open his eyes again, the photograph of Harrison was gone. A living, breathing Harrison filled the screen.

Clanking, clownish, and huge, Harrison stood in the center of the studio. The knob of the uprooted studio door was still in his hand. Ballerinas, technicians, musicians, and announcers cowered on their knees before him, expecting to die.

"I am the Emperor!" cried Harrison. "Do you hear? I am the Emperor! Everybody must do what I say at once!" He stamped his foot and the studio shook.

"Even as I stand here—" he bellowed, "crippled, hobbled, sickened—I am a greater ruler than any man who ever lived! Now watch me become what I *can* become!"

Harrison tore the straps of his handicap harness like wet tissue paper, tore straps guaranteed to support five thousand pounds.

Harrison's scrap-iron handicaps crashed to the floor.

Harrison thrust his thumbs under the bar of the padlock that secured his head harness. The bar snapped like celery. Harrison smashed his headphones and spectacles against the wall.

He flung away his rubber-ball nose, revealed a man that would have awed Thor, the god of thunder.

"I shall now select my Empress!" he said, looking down on the cowering people. "Let the first woman who dares rise to her feet claim her mate and her throne!"

A moment passed, and then a ballerina arose, swaying like a willow. Harrison plucked the mental handicap from her ear,

---

PRATIK I guess Harrison is the perfect man without his handicaps—strong, good-looking, intelligent. (clarify)

KELLY The society tries so hard to keep Harrison down. But he realizes that all of this is wrong. (evaluate)

ABIGAIL Harrison is breaking the conformity of this society. (clarify)

KELLY Harrison wants to reach his full potential. The other people just accept society as it is and don't try to change it. (summarize)

PRATIK It's interesting the way Vonnegut decides that Harrison will be the Emperor. That's kind of an ancient theme—in the past, all the emperors were strong men, like Harrison. (connect)

ABIGAIL Harrison is arrogant. This is individual supremacy versus government supremacy. (evaluate)

snapped off her physical handicaps with marvelous delicacy. Last of all, he removed her mask.

She was blindingly beautiful.

"Now—" said Harrison, taking her hand, "shall we show the people the meaning of the word dance? Music!" he commanded.

The musicians scrambled back into their chairs, and Harrison stripped them of their handicaps, too. "Play your best," he told them, "and I'll make you barons and dukes and earls."

The music began. It was normal at first—cheap, silly, false. But Harrison snatched two musicians from their chairs, waved them like batons as he sang the music as he wanted it played. He slammed them back into their chairs.

The music began again and was much improved.

Harrison and his Empress merely listened to the music for a while—listened gravely, as though synchronizing their heartbeats with it.

They shifted their weight to their toes.

Harrison placed his big hands on the girl's tiny waist, letting her sense the weightlessness that would soon be hers.

And then, in an explosion of joy and grace, into the air they sprang!

Not only were the laws of the land abandoned, but the law of gravity and the laws of motion as well.

They reeled, whirled, swiveled, flounced, capered, gamboled, and spun.

They leaped like deer on the moon.

The studio ceiling was thirty feet high, but each leap brought the dancers nearer to it.

It became their obvious intention to kiss the ceiling.

They kissed it.

And then, neutralizing gravity with love and pure will, they remained suspended in air inches below the ceiling, and they kissed each other for a long, long time.

It was then that Diana Moon Glampers, the Handicapper General, came into the studio with a double-barreled ten-gauge shotgun. She fired twice, and the Emperor and the Empress were dead before they hit the floor.

Diana Moon Glampers loaded the gun again. She aimed it at the musicians and told them they had ten seconds to get their handicaps back on.

It was then that the Bergerons' television tube burned out.

Hazel turned to comment about the blackout to George. But George had gone out into the kitchen for a can of beer.

George came back in with the beer, paused while a handicap

ABIGAIL As an individual, Harrison is not the greatest person. Yet he seems great because he's the only one breaking the conformity. (evaluate)

PRATIK Dance is being used as a symbol here. Dance represents freedom of movement and expression—just freedom in general. (connect)

KELLY Defying gravity also shows the freedom they have. They don't have anything to hold them down. (connect)

KELLY This society is not truly equal, because the Handicapper General has the right to kill people. She's like a dictator. (evaluate)

signal shook him up. And then he sat down again. "You been crying?" he said to Hazel.

"Yup," she said.

"What about?" he said.

"I forget," she said. "Something real sad on television."

"What was it?" he said.

"It's all kind of mixed up in my mind," said Hazel.

"Forget sad things," said George.

"I always do," said Hazel.

"That's my girl," said George. He winced. There was the sound of a riveting gun in his head.

"Gee—I could tell that one was a doozy," said Hazel.

"You can say that again," said George.

"Gee—" said Hazel, "I could tell that one was a doozy."

PRATIK   You can see how family life hardly exists in this society. George and Hazel don't even know what has happened to their son—they can't remember. (summarize)

ABIGAIL   Without individuality, there would be this mass conformity. I think we take many things for granted, such as our personal liberties, which the characters in this story don't have. (connect)

Discussion After Reading

General Comments

ABIGAIL   What do you think of Vonnegut's writing style? (question)

KELLY   All of the sentences were very easy to read, and the vocabulary wasn't very complex. (evaluate)

ABIGAIL   I think the writing style represents the society. Like in the first paragraph, where three sentences in a row begin with *Nobody.* There's not much variation here—it's like the exactness and lack of variation in this society. (connect)

PRATIK   I agree. Reading this story is not like reading Faulkner, where you read something and ask, Where did that come from? With this story, you can stay focused on it—it's easy to follow. So you get a clear message. (connect)

KELLY   I think the message is that there's no perfect society. No matter how hard you try, there's always going to be something wrong.

So there's no point in trying to create a perfect society. (evaluate)

PRATIK   They're striving for equality, but actually they're producing inequality. (clarify)

ABIGAIL   I agree. They try to create equality by reforming everybody, but there really is no equality. (summarize)

KELLY   I wouldn't like living in this society. I don't like to be just average—I always like to try for more. (connect)

PRATIK   This society seems to be saying that people are not rational or good, and that if you let them think for themselves it will cause a disaster. But this idea is reversed in the theme of the story, which is that individuality is good, variation is good. We're all different from one another. (summarize, evaluate)

After reading "Harrison Bergeron," these students reveal their personal reactions (Shaping Your Response) and literary responses (Analyzing the Story), along with the connections they have made to their own experiences (Extending the Ideas). These are the types of questions you will find in this book.

Shaping Your Response

What "handicaps" would you be given if you were a character in this story?

KELLY   I'm outgoing, so I'd probably have a handicap that would make me more shy.

PRATIK   I consider myself intelligent, so I'd probably have a mental handicap radio in my ear.

ABIGAIL   Maybe they'd blind me, so I couldn't read books. I also think they would some- how block my sensitivity to other people. If people knew about other people's pain and got together, it would be eas- ier to rebel against society.

Analyzing the Story

What do you think Vonnegut is satirizing in this story?

ABIGAIL   I think he's satirizing the role government should have in society. Harrison talks about himself as the Emperor— he doesn't say, "I'll be your leader." It's almost like a throw- back to an earlier time.

PRATIK   I think he's satirizing society.

ABIGAIL   Well, I suppose that society would have had to allow this to happen.

KELLY   I don't think they knew it would be this extreme. Everybody wanted equality, but after they realized how extreme it would be, it was too late—they no longer had the ability to think.

Extending the Ideas

What pressures are there in the world today for people to be all the same?

KELLY   The big thing now is peer pressure. If everybody's doing something, you're expected to do it also. Sometimes that's good and sometimes it's not—it's up to you to decide.

PRATIK   The pressure in our society against interracial marriage—that's a pressure for conformity.

ABIGAIL   Our parents influence us a lot. If I wanted to be a dancer or an artist, my parents would be pretty open about it. Some teenagers have parents who tell them they have to make a lot of money—that can limit their opportunities.

American Beginnings

A Collision of Cultures
Part One, pages 2–51

A Tragedy at Salem
Part Two, pages 52–151

A Collision

HISTORICAL OVERVIEW

The earth was much larger than Columbus imagined, and its population far more diverse. A watershed in the history of cross-cultural contact occurred when Europeans first arrived in the Western Hemisphere and encountered hundreds of Native American cultures of tremendous variety and richness. For the first European settlers, America proved to be much more than a single new world: it was an unimagined universe—strange and threatening. Another group experiencing profound cultural shocks was Africans, sometimes free, but more often enslaved. The illustration on the right, combining the faces of these different peoples, suggests the complexity of the Western Hemisphere's cultural mosaic.

They are artless and generous with what they have. . . . Of anything they have, if it be asked for, they never say no, but do rather invite the person to accept it, and show as much lovingness as though they would give their hearts.
1492 ~ Columbus's account of the Arawaks

Their trappings and arms are all made of iron. They dress in iron and wear iron casques on their heads. . . . Their deer carry them on their backs wherever they wish to go.
1519 ~ Aztec account of the Spanish

At last they brought me to . . . Powhatan their Emperor. Here more than two hundred of those grim courtiers stood wondering at me, as I had been a monster.
1608 ~ John Smith describing his captivity

# of Cultures

*They are of a gentle and tractable disposition . . . .
Their bodies are shapely; they are very active
and very skillful with bows and arrows.*
1673 ~ Father Marquette's description
of the Illinois people

*Brothers, these people from the
unknown world will cut down our
groves, spoil our hunting and
planting grounds, and . . .
our women and children
will be enslaved.*
1675 ~ Metacomet's speech
to the Wampanoags

*I was now persuaded that
I had gotten into a world of
bad spirits, and that they
were going to kill me. Their
complexions too differing so
much from ours, their long hair,
and the language they spoke . . .
confirmed me in this belief.*
Mid-1750s ~ Olaudah Equiano's
description of European slave traders

Key Dates

1492
*Christopher
Columbus arrives
in the West Indies
and meets the
Arawaks.*

1521
*Cortés conquers
the Aztec empire.*

1607
*The English
settle Jamestown.*

1608
*Samuel de
Champlain claims
Quebec for France.*

1610
*Spanish found
Sante Fe, New
Mexico.*

1616
*Smallpox wipes
out most of the
New England
Indians.*

1619
*A Dutch ship
brings the first
Africans to
Virginia.*

3

Part One

A Collision of Cultures

America has always been a region of great cultural diversity, beginning with its hundreds of American Indian peoples. The arrival of Europeans and Africans increased both the cultural richness and the social frictions that can result from dramatic cultural encounters.

Multicultural Connection What insights into the **interactions** of peoples of vastly different cultures and experiences do the following selections provide?

Literature

Cherokee	**How the World Was Made** ◆ creation story	6
Winnebago	**This Newly Created World** ◆ song	9
Chippewa	**Dream Song** ◆ song	9
Taos Pueblo	**I Have Killed the Deer** ◆ song	10
Álvar Núñez Cabeza de Vaca	*from* **La Relación** ◆ memoir	14
Percy Bigmouth	**Before They Got Thick** ◆ folk tale	18
Olaudah Equiano	*from* **The Interesting Narrative of the Life of Olaudah Equiano** ◆ autobiography	22
William Bradford	*from* **Of Plymouth Plantation** ◆ history	31
Canassatego	**Offer of Help** ◆ speech	33
Mary Jemison	*from* **The Life of Mary Jemison** ◆ memoir	34

Interdisciplinary Study The Great Exchange

The Great Exchange ◆ social studies 41
Corn: Builder of Cities ◆ social studies 42
The Animal That Changed History ◆ social studies 43
Old-Time Talk We Still de Talkem Here! ◆ language 44

Language History

The Language Exchange 45

Writing Workshop Narrative Writing

Earth—A Strange New World 46

Beyond Print Visual Literacy

Looking at Art 51

Before Reading

How the World Was Made Cherokee   **Dream Song** Chippewa

This Newly Created World Winnebago   **I Have Killed the Deer** Taos Pueblo

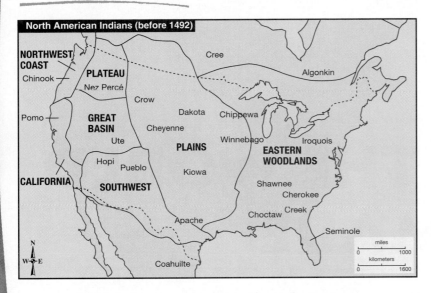

Building Background

Land of Diversity Long before Columbus arrived, hundreds of diverse American Indian peoples flourished across what is now the United States. The map on the left indicates just a few of these societies. "How the World Was Made," "This Newly Created World," "Dream Song," and "I Have Killed the Deer" represent some of the **oral traditions** that have been maintained for generations by American Indian cultures.

The Cherokee

The Cherokee originally had more than sixty villages throughout the southern Appalachian and Great Smoky Mountains. When European settlers arrived, the Cherokee farmed alongside them, built schools and libraries, and had a constitutional government. However, in the 1830s the U. S. government forced them to resettle on lands beyond the Mississippi River. About one fourth of the Cherokee died on this march, known today as the Trail of Tears. Today most Cherokee live in Oklahoma and North Carolina. "How the World Was Made" is a version of the Cherokee creation story, and was first written down in the late 1800s.

Literary Focus

Theme As you read the following four selections, think about whether each work seems to have a main idea or underlying meaning. If so, this will be the work's **theme.** Then, think about the four of them together. Is there a common thread or idea that connects them all in some way? What theme or themes do the story and songs share?

Writer's Notebook

Take a Good Look "How the World Was Made" is an **origin story**— it explains how something came to be. Take a good look at the things you encounter in the world around you, whether you live in the country, in a town, or in a large city. Are there parts of your world—unusual buildings, strange rock formations, interesting plants or animals— whose origins you wonder about? Write a list of things from your world that would be good candidates for an origin story.

Creation Legend (1946), by Tom Two-Arrows depicts an Iroquois creation story in which white water birds met Skywoman as she descended onto a turtle—the Earth. When you finish reading the story, decide how the two depictions of creation stories—one a painting and one a story—are similar and different from each other. ➤

HOW THE WORLD WAS MADE

CHEROKEE CREATION STORY

The earth is a great island floating in a sea of water, and suspended[1] at each of the four cardinal points[2] by a cord hanging down from the sky vault,[3] which is of solid rock. When the world grows old and worn out, the people will die and the cords will break and let the earth sink down into the ocean, and all will be water again. The Indians are afraid of this.

When all was water, the animals were above in Galunlati[4] beyond the arch; but it was very much crowded, and they were wanting more room. They wondered what was below the water, and at last Dayunisi,[5] "Beaver's Grandchild," the little Water-beetle, offered to go and see if it could learn. It darted in every direction over the surface of the water, but could find no firm place to rest. Then it dived to the bottom and came up with some soft mud, which began to grow and spread on every side until it became the island which we call the earth. It was afterward fastened to the sky with four cords, but no one remembers who did this.

At first the earth was flat and very soft and wet. The animals were anxious to get down, and sent out different birds to see if it was yet dry, but they found no place to alight[6] and came back again to Galunlati. At last it seemed to be

---

1. **suspended** (sə spend′ed), *adj.* hung down by attaching to something above.
2. cardinal points, *n.* the four main points of a compass.
3. vault (vôlt), *n.* something like an arched roof.
4. **Galunlati** (gä lün lä′ti).
5. **Dayunisi** (tä yü ni′si).
6. alight (ə līt′), *v.* descend and lightly settle.

time, and they sent out the Buzzard and told him to go and make ready for them. This was the Great Buzzard, the father of all the buzzards we see now. He flew all over the earth, low down near the ground, and it was still soft. When he reached the Cherokee country, he was very tired, and his wings began to flap and strike the ground, and wherever they struck the earth there was a valley, and where they turned up again there was a mountain. When the animals saw this, they were afraid that the whole world would be mountains, so they called him back, but the Cherokee country remains full of mountains to this day.

When the earth was dry and the animals came down, it was still dark, so they got the sun and set it in a track to go every day across this island from east to west, just overhead. It was too hot this way, and Tsiskagili,[7] the Red Crawfish, had his shell scorched a bright red, so that his meat was spoiled; and the Cherokee do not eat it. The conjurers[8] put the sun another handbreadth higher in the air, but it was still too hot. They raised it another time, and another, until it was seven handbreadths high and just under the sky arch. Then it was right, and they left it so. This is why the conjurers call the highest place Gulkwagine Digalunlatiyun,[9] "the seventh height," because it is seven handbreadths above the earth. Every day the sun goes along under this arch, and returns at night on the upper side to the starting place.

There is another world under this, and it is like ours in everything—animals, plants, and people—save that the seasons are different. The streams that come down from the mountains are the trails by which we reach this underworld,[10] and the springs at their heads are the doorways by which we enter it, but to do this one must fast and go to water and have one of the underground people for a guide. We know that the seasons in the underworld are different from ours, because the water in the springs is always warmer in winter and cooler in summer than the outer air.

When the animals and plants were first made—we do not know by whom—they were told to watch and keep awake for seven nights, just as young men now fast and keep awake when they pray to their medicine.[11] They tried to do this, and nearly all were awake through the first night, but the next night several dropped off to sleep, and the third night others were asleep, and then others, until, on the seventh night, of all the animals only the owl, the panther, and one or two more were still awake. To these were given the power to see and to go about in the dark, and to make prey of the birds and animals which must sleep at night. Of the trees only the cedar, the pine, the spruce, the holly, and the laurel were awake to the end, and to them it was given to be always green and to be greatest for medicine, but to the others it was said: "Because you have not endured to the end you shall lose your hair every winter."

Men came after the animals and plants. At first there were only a brother and sister until he struck her with a fish and told her to multiply, and so it was. In seven days a child was born to her, and thereafter every seven days another, and they increased very fast until there was danger that the world could not keep them. Then it was made that a woman should have only one child in a year, and it has been so ever since.

---

7. **Tsiskagili** (tsi skä gil′e).
8. conjurer (kon′jər ər), *n.* person who practices magic.
9. **Gulkwagine Digalunlatiyun** (gül kwä gin′o ti gä lŭn lä′ti yŭn).
10. **underworld** (un′dər wėrld′), *n.* in various mythologies, a world that exists below the ground, sometimes considered a dwelling-place for the dead.
11. **medicine** (med′ə sən), *n.* guiding spirit.

This Newly Created World

Pleasant it looked,
this newly created world.
Along the entire length and breadth
of the earth, our grandmother,
5 extended the green reflection
of her covering
and the escaping odors
were pleasant to inhale.

Dream Song

CHIPPEWA SONG

as my eyes
    search the prairie
        I feel the summer in the spring

The Winnebago

The Winnebago originally lived in what is now Wisconsin. In the Revolutionary War and the War of 1812, the Winnebago fought with the British. The U.S. government moved them to Minnesota, but white settlers, frightened by the 1862 Sioux uprising, drove them out again. The Winnebago Indian Reservation is in northeastern Nebraska, while some Winnebagos continue to live in southern Wisconsin.

The Chippewa

The Chippewa were originally made up of independent bands living in the Great Lakes area. They hunted and fished, and later traded furs with the French. After the French surrendered to the British, the Chippewa joined forces to fight the British. The uprising was unsuccessful, and the Chippewa were pushed westward. Now many Chippewa live on reservations in Minnesota.

I Have Killed the Deer

TAOS PUEBLO SONG

I have killed the deer.
I have crushed the grasshopper
And the plants he feeds upon.
I have cut through the heart
5 Of trees growing old and straight.
I have taken fish from water
And birds from the sky.
In my life I have needed death
So that my life can be.
10 When I die I must give life
To what has nourished me.
The earth receives my body
And gives it to the plants
And to the caterpillars
15 To the birds
And to the coyotes
Each in its own turn so that
The circle of life is never broken.

The Pueblo Indians

Pueblo Indians are thought to be the descendants of the Anasazi, a people that built magnificent cliff-dwellings in the canyons of the Southwest. There are six languages among the Pueblo Indians, and each pueblo, or community, is independent, having its own government and identity. Two Pueblo towns are the oldest continually inhabited towns in the United States.

▲ Hopi Kachina dolls like this Deer Kachina represent benevolent spirit beings and are used in Hopi ceremonies having to do with the well-being of the community and for teaching children.

After Reading

Making Connections

Shaping Your Response

1. As you think back over the origin story and the poems, write down the first five words that come to mind. Explain how these words relate to the works.

2. If you were going to illustrate the story or one of the songs, which would you choose? Why?

Analyzing the Selections

3. What important characteristics of the world does "How the World Was Made" try to explain?

4. Poems or songs often help readers create **images** in their minds by appealing to one of the senses. To what senses do "This Newly Created World" and "Dream Song" appeal?

5. A **paradox** is a statement or situation in which two opposites somehow exist together. Does "I Have Killed the Deer" contain a paradox? Explain your answer.

Extending the Ideas

6. 👣 Many people are familiar with the Bible story of creation, in which God creates the world in six days and rests on the seventh. How is the Cherokee story of creation similar and different?

7. "When the world grows old and worn out, the people will die and the cords will break and let the earth sink down into the ocean, and all will be water again. The Indians are afraid of this." People today have many concerns about the earth as well. Do you think today's concerns are similar in any way to the concern expressed in this passage?

Literary Focus: Theme

It's easy to get the **theme,** or underlying idea of a work, and the topic confused. For instance, the topic of the origin story might be the creation of the world with its animals, plants, and people, but its theme is something else. The topic of the songs may be the new earth, spring, and consuming plants and animals, but what are the story and poems saying *about* these topics? What kinds of main ideas are contained in these works?

   With a small group of your classmates, discuss what the main ideas, or themes, for these works might be. Choose the ones that seem the most powerful or relate best to these works.

Vocabulary Study

Use the words in the list at the left to complete the sentences below. You can use one item twice.

cardinal points
vault
alight
conjurer

1. The stars seem like holes punctured in the dark ____ of the night sky.

2. The birds in the legend had to wait until the ground dried before they could ____ upon the new land.

3. North, south, east, and west are the ____ of a compass.

4. Our words echoed back to us from the arched ____ of the cave's ceiling.

5. The sun rose every morning as if called forth by the magic of a ____.

Expressing Your Ideas ____

Writing Choices

Writer's Notebook Update Now that you have read the origin story, reread the list of things in your world that you wrote in your notebook. Choose one item and write a paragraph giving the basic plot for an origin story.

Sensational Seasons What is your favorite time of year? Choose your favorite season and make a list of sensations you enjoy about it. When you complete your list, use your notes to write a short **poem** expressing your feelings about your favorite season.

Outside Influences When cultures come into contact, their traditions—including stories— are sometimes changed by the encounter. What aspects of "How the World Was Made" do you think may have been influenced by contact with Europeans? Write a **paragraph** telling why you think so.

Other Options

A Well-Told Tale American Indians, like people in other cultures around the world, passed their stories from generation to generation by telling them—not by writing them. Select another American Indian story, or a story from another tradition. Read it, rehearse how you think it should be told, and present it to the class. In your introduction, tell about the people from which the story originated. Join with others in your class and arrange a **storytelling festival.**

Circle of Life Draw a **chart** to illustrate the circle of life described in "I Have Killed the Deer."

A Legend in Art On page 7, Tom Two-Arrows has depicted a creation legend in art. Use his work as an example, or strike out in your own direction to retell "How the World Was Made" in some other art form, such as a **poster** or **mobile.**

Before Reading

from La Relación by Álvar Núñez Cabeza de Vaca
Before They Got Thick by Percy Bigmouth

Álvar Núñez Cabeza de Vaca
1490–1560

In 1527 Cabeza de Vaca (kä-bā′sä de vä′kä) set out for Florida, and was eventually shipwrecked off the coast of Texas. For eight years he and his few surviving companions wandered the Southwest, living with many Indian peoples and learning their languages and their customs.

Percy Bigmouth

Percy Bigmouth, a Lipan Apache, related the tale "Before They Got Thick" in 1935. The Lipan Apaches lived in Louisiana and Texas until the Indian wars of the mid 1800s, when the official policy in Texas called for the extermination of all Indians. They fled to Mexico, then later moved to New Mexico. The tale was told to Bigmouth by his grandmother.

Building Background

The Travels of Cabeza de Vaca Cabeza de Vaca traveled through territory never before seen by Europeans. The map below shows the route he took during his eight years of travel.

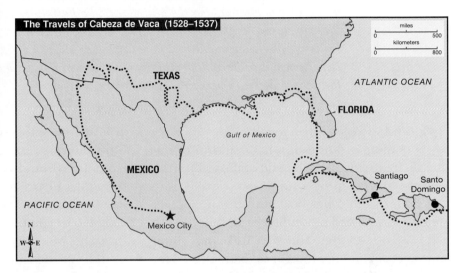

Literary Focus

Point of View In conversation, people often use **point of view** to tell whose opinion is being represented. In literary terms, however, *point of view* refers to the narrator. A *first-person narrator* is a character in a selection. The reader can only know what that character observes and thinks. *Third-person narrators* are outside a story. As you read each selection, identify the narrator. What point of view is used? How would the selection change if another point of view were used?

Writer's Notebook

Facing the Unknown If you were a young Spaniard in the 1500s, would you have signed on to a ship to explore places known as the "New World"? If you were an American Indian who came across a shipload of Europeans landing on a beach, would you want to be the first one to approach them? Before reading the next two selections, jot down your feelings about these situations.

La Relación

ÁLVAR NÚÑEZ CABEZA DE VACA

Álvar Núñez Cabeza de Vaca left Spain on June 17, 1527, as treasurer of an expedition that consisted of five ships and 600 men. Their goal was to "conquer and govern the provinces that lie between the River Las Palmas and the tip of Florida." For the next year and a half the expedition suffered through storms, shipwrecks, starvation, disease, and battles with American Indians. The following excerpt from Cabeza de Vaca's La Relación (The Report) *begins as he and about forty other men in a handmade boat sail in the Gulf of Mexico looking for land.*

And so we sailed on together for four days, eating a ration of a half-handful of raw maize[1] daily. At the end of these four days we were overtaken by a storm that caused us to lose sight of the other boat, and through God's great mercy toward us we did not all founder,[2] so bad was the weather, and with its being winter and very cold and the hunger we had suffered for so many days. As a result of the buffeting we received from the sea, next day the men began to fail very much, so that by sunset all those in my boat were lying heaped upon one another, so near to death that few of them were conscious, and by this time not five men among them were fit to stand. And when night fell only the mate and I were capable of sailing the boat, and two hours after nightfall the mate told me to take over, for he was in such a condition that he thought he would die that night. And so I took the helm,[3] and after midnight I went to see if the mate was dead, and he told me that he was in fact better and that he would steer until morning.

At that moment I would surely have much preferred to accept death than see so many people before my eyes in such a condition. And after the mate took charge of the boat I rested a little, but very restlessly, and nothing was further from my thoughts than sleep. Near dawn I thought I heard breakers,[4] for as the coast was low the waves made a great deal of noise, and called to the mate in alarm; he answered that he thought we were near land, and we made soundings and found a depth of seven fathoms,[5] and he thought we ought to stay at sea until daylight. And so I took an oar and rowed parallel to the land, for we were a league[6] away from it, and then turned our stern[7] to the sea. And when we were near land a wave took us that tossed the boat out of the water a good horseshoe's cast; and with the great jolt it gave, almost all the

---

1. **maize** (māz), *n.* corn.
2. founder (foun′dər), *v.* fill with water and sink.
3. helm (helm), *n.* the steering apparatus of a ship.
4. breaker (brā′kər), *n.* wave that breaks into foam on the shore, rocks, etc.
5. fathom (faᴛн′əm), *n.* unit for measuring depth of water; a fathom is six feet.
6. **league** (lēg), *n.* measure of distance, usually about three miles.
7. stern (stėrn), *n.* rear part of a ship or boat.

A *Cabeza de Vaca in the Desert* (1906) by American artist Frederic Remington shows the explorer in his later travels. Does the mood of the painting match that of the narrative? Why or why not?

men in the boat who were half dead came to themselves. And as they saw that land was near, they began to slip over the side and crawl on hands and feet, and as they came ashore where there were some gullies, we made a fire and cooked some maize that we had with us and found some rainwater; and with the heat of the fire the men revived and began to recover their spirits somewhat. The day we arrived there was the sixth of November.

After the men had eaten I sent Lope de Oviedo, who was stronger and hardier than anyone else, to go to some trees that were nearby and climb one of them, to find out what sort of country we were in and try to gain some idea of it. He did this and realized that we were on an island and saw that the earth on the mainland was trampled like the ground where livestock have often passed, and this made him think that it was Christian territory, and he told us so. I told him to go and look again more carefully, and to see if there were paths there that could be followed, but not to go too far away because of possible danger. He went and, finding a path, walked along it for about half a league and found some Indian huts that were empty because the Indians had gone out into the countryside; and he took one of their pots and a little dog and a few mullet and came back to us.

And as we thought him long in returning, I sent two other Christians to look for him and find out what had happened to him, and they caught sight of him nearby and saw that three Indians with bows and arrows were following him and calling to him, and he was answering them by signs.

And so he reached the place where we were and the Indians stayed a short distance behind, seated right on the shore; and after half an hour a hundred other Indians armed with arrows came, who whether they were large or not seemed like giants owing to our fear, and they stopped near us, where the first three were. As for us, it was useless to think that anyone could defend himself, for there were scarcely half a dozen who could get up from the ground. The inspector and I went toward them and called to them and they came closer to us; and as best we could we tried to reassure them and ourselves and gave them beads and hawk's bells, and each of them gave me an arrow, which is a sign of friendship; and they told us by signs that they would return in the morning and bring us food, for at the moment they had none.

Next day as the sun was rising, which was the hour that the Indians had indicated to us, they came to us as they had promised and brought us a large quantity of fish and some roots that they eat and that resemble nuts, some larger and some smaller; most of them are gathered under-

water, and with much effort. In the afternoon they returned and brought us more fish and the same roots and had their women and children come to see us, and so they returned rich with the bells and beads that we gave them, and on other days they visited us again with the same things as before. As we saw that we were well supplied with fish and roots and water and the other things that we asked them for, we decided to launch the boats again and continue on our way; and we dug the boat out of the sand in which it was half buried, and we all had to strip and expend a great deal of effort to get it into the water, for we were in such a sorry plight that even much lighter tasks exhausted us. And so, having launched the boat, we were a distance of two crossbow shots into the sea when there came a wave so huge that it soaked us all, and as we were naked and the cold was so great, we let go of the oars, and another wave from the sea overturned the boat. The inspector and two others clung to it to escape death: but quite the opposite happened, for the boat carried them under and they were drowned.

As the coast there is very rugged, the sea in one lurch threw all the others, submerged in the waves and half drowned, onto the shore of the same island, and the only ones missing were the three whom the boat had carried under.

. . . we looked like the very image of death.

The rest of us who escaped were naked as the day we were born and had lost all that we had with us, which though it was not worth much, was everything to us at that time. And since by then it was November and the cold was very great and we were in such a plight that one could have counted our bones without difficulty, we looked like the very image of death. Of myself I can say that I had eaten nothing but roasted maize since the month of May, and sometimes I had to eat it raw, for though the horses were slaughtered during the time the boats were being built, I was never able to eat them and did not eat fish as many as ten times.

I say this to avoid entering into further explanations, for anyone can imagine the sorry state we were in. And in addition to everything I have said, a north wind had started to blow, so that we were closer to death than to life. But it pleased Our Lord that, as we searched among the embers of the fire we had made there, we found fire, with which we made great bonfires, and thus we were imploring[8] Our Lord for mercy and pardon for our sins, shedding many tears,

. . . they had built a house for us with many fires in it.

each one bewailing not only his own plight but that of all the others whom he saw in the same state. And at the hour of sunset the Indians, believing that we had not left, came looking for us again to bring us food; but when they saw us in such different circumstances as at first, and in such a strange condition, they were so frightened that they turned back. I went toward them and called them and they came, in great consternation;[9] I gave them to understand by signs how a boat had sunk and three of our number had drowned, and there before them they saw two corpses and saw that those of us who were left were on the way to becoming corpses too. When the Indians saw the disaster that had come upon us and the disaster we were in, with so much ill luck and misery, they sat down among us and, with the great grief and pity they felt on seeing us in such a desperate plight, all of them began to weep loudly, and so sincerely that they could be heard a long way off, and this lasted more than half an hour; and certainly, to see that those uncivilized and savage men, like brutes, were so sorry for us, caused me and others in our company to feel still more grief and the full realization of our misfortune.

When this weeping had subsided I questioned the Christians and said that if they were in agreement I would ask those Indians to take us to their houses; and some of them, who had been in New Spain, answered that there could be no question of it, for if they took us to their houses they would sacrifice us to their idols.[10] But in view of the fact that there was no other solution, and that if we took any other course death would be closer and more certain, I paid no heed[11] to what they were saying; rather, I implored the Indians to take us to their houses, and they showed great pleasure at the prospect and told us to wait for a little while and they would do as we wished; and then thirty of them loaded themselves with firewood and went to their houses, which were a good distance away; and we stayed with the others until near nightfall, when they seized us, and holding us closely and in great haste, went with us to their houses. And because it was very cold, and fearing that some of us might die or collapse on the way, they provided four or five very large bonfires placed at intervals and warmed us at each one; and as soon as they saw that we had acquired some strength and warmth they took us to the next fire, so quickly that they scarcely allowed our feet to touch the ground, and in this way we went to their houses, where we found that they had built a house for us with many fires in it; and by an hour after the time we arrived they began to dance and make great revelry[12] (which lasted all night), though for us there was neither pleasure nor revelry nor sleep, waiting to know when they were going to sacrifice us; and next morning they again gave us fish and roots and such good treatment that we felt a little safer and lost to some degree our fear of sacrifice.

---

8. **implore** (im plôr′), *v.* beg or pray earnestly for.
9. **consternation** (kon′stər nā′shən), *n.* great dismay.
10. **idols** (ī′dlz), *n.* images or other objects worshipped as gods.
11. **paid no heed**, ignored.
12. **revelry** (rev′əl rē), *n.* a noisy good time.

BEFORE THEY GOT THICK

Percy Bigmouth

This Lipan Apache tale, like Cabeza de Vaca's narrative, describes an early encounter between American Indians and European explorers. The painting above is Camp of the Lipans *(1896) by Theodore Gentilz. What can you tell about the life of the people depicted?*

My grandmother used to tell this story; she told it to my mother. It is about the time when they lived near the gulf. She says that they lived at a place called "Beside the Smooth Water." They used to camp there on the sand. Sometimes a big wave would come up and then they would pick up many seashells. Sometimes they used to find water turtles. They used to find fish too and gather them and eat them.

One time they had a big wave. It was very bad. They thought the ocean was going to come right up. It came up a long way. Living things from the water covered the bank, were washed up. Then, when the sun came out and it was hot all these things began to swell and smelled bad.

One day they looked over the big water. Then someone saw a little black dot over on the water. He came back and told that he had seen that strange thing. Others came out. They sat there and looked. It was getting larger. They waited. Pretty soon it came up. It was a boat. The boat came to the shore. The Indians went back to the big camp. All the Indians came over and watched. People were coming out. They looked at those people coming out. They saw that the people had blue eyes and were white. They thought these people might live in the water all the time.

They held a council that night. They were undecided whether they should let them live or kill them.

One leader said, "Well, they have a shape just like ours. The difference is that they have light skin and hair."

Another said, "Let's not kill them. They may be a help to us some day. Let's let them go and see what they'll do."

So the next day they watched them. "What shall we call them?" they asked. . . .

Some still wanted to kill them. Others said no. So they decided to let them alone.

The Lipan went away. After a year they said, "Let's go back and see them."

They did so. Only a few were left. Many had starved to death. Some said, "Let's kill them now; they are only a few." But others said, "No, let us be like brothers to them."

It was spring. The Lipan gave them some pumpkin seed and seed corn and told them how to use it. The people took it and after that they got along all right. They raised a little corn and some pumpkins. They started a new life. Later on the Lipan left for a while. When they returned, the white people were getting along very well. The Lipan gave them venison.[1] They were getting along very well. After that, they began to get thick.

---

1. **venison** (ven′ə sən), *n.* deer meat.

After Reading

Making Connections

Shaping Your
Response

1. Rate Cabeza de Vaca as a leader on a scale of one to five, one being poor and five being very capable. Explain your rating.

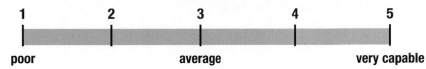

1 — poor   2   3 — average   4   5 — very capable

2. Put yourself in the Spanish explorers' or the Lipan Apaches' place. You are meeting a group of people you know nothing about. Would you have done anything differently than either the Spanish explorers or the Lipan Apaches did?

Analyzing the
Selections

3. What does Cabeza de Vaca's account reveal about his **character** and the qualities that enable him to survive?

4. What does Percy Bigmouth mean when he says the white men "began to get thick"?

5. Compare Cabeza de Vaca and his companions' experience with that of the settlers in "Before They Got Thick." In what ways are the experiences the same and in what ways are they different?

Extending the
Ideas

6. The newcomers at the end of Percy Bigmouth's tale are "getting along very well." Extend the story. What do you think happened in the next year? in five years? in ten years?

7. 🐾 The Lipan Apaches had no idea who the newcomers were. They had no prior experience on which to base their **interactions,** or ways of relating with this new group. What if strangers, perhaps from another planet, suddenly arrived in your area. How would people react?

Literary Focus: Point of View

Point of view in literature refers to who is narrating a story. A first-person narrator is a character in the narrative, and a third-person narrator is not. How would these selections be different if they were told in third-person point of view, perhaps by a modern historian? Choose one of these selections and try to retell it from a third-person point of view, presenting both sides of the situation. Fill in the gaps with plausible events. Remember, as a third-person narrator, you can't know for sure what either group is thinking or feeling. How does the tone and the presentation of the events change?

stern
helm
fathom
breaker
founder

Vocabulary Study

Define these nautical terms: *stern, helm, fathom, breaker,* and *founder.* Then make a drawing that "pictures" these terms. Label each term.

Expressing Your Ideas

Writing Choices

Writer's Notebook Update Now that you've read about these early encounters between American Indians and European explorers, review your Writer's Notebook notes about how you would feel as a Spanish explorer or as an Indian meeting one of the explorers. Then write a diary entry as either one of the explorers or one of the Lipan Apaches. Record your feelings, thoughts, and actions on the day of the first encounter as you faced the unknown.

Help Wanted It is 1527, and you are a wealthy Spaniard organizing an expedition to the New World. How do you get people to sign on as part of the crew? What qualities are you looking for in your employees? Write a **want ad** that describes the positions you want to fill and makes the job sound exciting and adventurous.

Survival Guide You and a few of Cabeza de Vaca's companions believe the awful rumors you have heard about human sacrifice. You reject Cabeza de Vaca's plan to return with the Indians to their homes. Write a **step-by-step plan** outlining your alternative plans for survival.

Other Options

To Be or Not to Be The Lipan Apaches could not agree on what to do about the explorers who arrived by boat. With several of your classmates, re-create the **debate** that might have taken place to decide the fate of the newcomers. Present it to the class.

Lessons Learned Read the last few chapters from a complete edition of the travels of Cabeza de Vaca to find out what happens when he finally meets up with the other Spaniards. What has he learned from his experiences? Prepare a **summary** of the events and present it to the class.

The Way We Were Before Europeans arrived in North America, a huge variety of cultures thrived in the land, from the Mississippian mound-builders in Illinois to the Aztecs of Mexico, from the Iroquois of the Northeast to the Pueblo peoples of the Southwest. Choose a Native American group to research, then create your own 10-minute videotaped **documentary** on the group, including both historical and up-to-date information.

Before Reading

from The Interesting Narrative of the Life of Olaudah Equiano

Olaudah Equiano
1745–1797

Olaudah means "fortunate" in the author's native African language. The life of Olaudah Equiano (ō lou′dä ā′kwē - ä′nō) seems quite the opposite, however. He was kidnapped from his home in Benin (now part of Nigeria), sold as a slave to other Africans, sold to European slave traders, shipped to Barbados, and then sold to a succession of owners, one of whom named him Gustavus Vassa after a famous Swedish king. During this time he learned to read and write, and he became a Christian. Equiano finally earned enough money to buy his freedom, and he moved to England where he worked in the anti-slavery movement.

Building Background

Let My People Go! From the 1500s to the mid-1800s, as many as one of every six people shipped from Africa to the Western Hemisphere as slaves died during the terrible voyage across the Atlantic Ocean, known as the **Middle Passage.** That's about two million deaths and ten million enslaved Africans delivered to the plantations of the Americas. Most of the Africans who survived the trip were brought to the West Indies. While only 6% of African captives went to North America, by 1860 there were four million slaves in the southern United States.

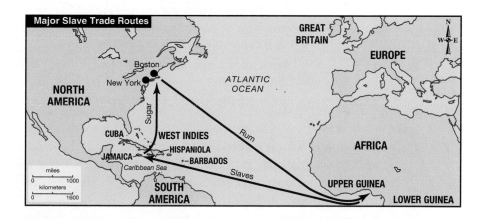

Literary Focus

Imagery A writer uses **imagery,** or sensory details, to help readers relate to a topic. As Equiano describes his experiences on the slave ship, can you see what he sees, smell what he smells, hear what he hears? How do his descriptions bring the details to life?

Writer's Notebook

Break the Chains Olaudah Equiano probably was younger than you are now when he suffered the trauma of being kidnapped from his home in Africa and sold into slavery. As you read the narrative, jot down details and incidents from his life that can be used as evidence in an argument against the institution of slavery.

The Interesting Narrative of the Life of Olaudah Equiano

While the adults were out tending the fields, a young African boy, Olaudah Equiano, and his sister were stolen from their home, separated, and sold into slavery in a distant village. Sold repeatedly, Equiano was taken farther from his inland home toward the coast, where he was eventually sold to European slave traders. The following excerpt from his narrative describes his experiences aboard a slave ship traveling from the west coast of Africa to the West Indies island of Barbados.

The first object which saluted my eyes when I arrived on the coast, was the sea, and a slave ship, which was then riding at anchor, and waiting for its cargo. These filled me with astonishment, which was soon converted into terror, when I was carried on board. I was immediately handled, and tossed up to see if I were sound, by some of the crew; and I was now persuaded that I had gotten into a world of bad spirits, and that they were going to kill me. Their complexions, too, differing so much from ours, their long hair, and the language they spoke (which was very different from any I had ever heard), united to confirm me in this belief. Indeed, such were the horrors of my views and fears at the moment, that, if ten thousand worlds had been my own, I would have freely parted with them all to have exchanged my condition with that of the meanest slave in my own country. When I looked round the ship too, and saw a large furnace of copper boiling, and a multitude of black people of every description chained together, every one of their countenances[1] expressing dejection and sorrow, I no longer doubted of my fate; and quite overpowered with horror and anguish, I fell motionless on the deck and fainted. When I recovered a little, I found some black people about me, who I believed were some of those who had brought me on board, and had been receiving their pay; they talked to me in order to cheer me, but all in vain.[2] I asked them if we were not to be eaten by those white men with

---

1. **countenances** (koun′tə nəns ez), *n.* faces; features.
2. **in vain,** without effect or success.

horrible looks, red faces, and long hair. They told me I was not, and one of the crew brought me a small portion of spirituous liquor in a wine glass; but, being afraid of him, I would not take it out of his hand. One of the blacks, therefore, took it from him and gave it to me, and I took a little down my palate,[3] which, instead of reviving me, as they thought it would, threw me into the greatest consternation at the strange feeling it produced, having never tasted any such liquor before. Soon after this, the blacks who brought me on board went off, and left me abandoned to despair.

CLARIFY: What were Equiano's initial fears upon being taken aboard the ship?

I now saw myself deprived of all chance of returning to my native country, or even the least glimpse of hope of gaining the shore, which I now considered as friendly; and I even wished for my former slavery in preference to my present situation, which was filled with horrors of every kind, still heightened by my ignorance of what I was to undergo. I was not long suffered to indulge my grief; I was soon put down under the decks, and there I received such a salutation in my nostrils as I had never experienced in my life: so that, with the loathsomeness[4] of the stench, and crying together, I became so sick and low that I was not able to eat, nor had I the least desire to taste anything. I now wished for the last friend, death, to relieve me; but soon, to my grief, two of the white men offered me eatables; and, on my refusing to eat, one of them held me fast by the hands, and laid me across, I think, the windlass,[5] and tied my feet, while the other flogged[6] me severely. I had never experienced anything of this kind before, and, although not being used to the water, I naturally feared that element the first time I saw it, yet, nevertheless, could I have got over the nettings, I would have jumped over the side, but I could not; and besides, the crew used to watch us very closely who were not chained down to the decks, lest we should leap into the water; and I have seen some of these poor African prisoners most severely cut, for attempting to do so, and hourly whipped for not eating. This indeed was often the case with myself. In a little time after, amongst the poor chained men, I found some of my own nation, which in a small degree gave ease to my mind. I inquired of these what was to be done with us? They gave me to understand, we were to be carried to these white people's country to work for them. I then was a little revived, and thought, if it were no worse than working, my situation was not so desperate; but still I feared I should be put to death, the white people looked and acted, as I thought, in so savage a manner; for I had never seen among any people such instances of brutal cruelty; and this

. . . could I have got over the nettings, I would have jumped over the side . . .

not only shown towards us blacks, but also to some of the whites themselves. One white man in particular I saw, when we were permitted to be on deck, flogged so unmercifully with a large rope near the foremast, that he died in consequence of it; and they tossed him over the side as they would have done a brute. This made me fear these people the more; and I expected nothing less than to be treated in the same manner. I could not help expressing my fears and apprehensions to some of my countrymen;

---

3. **palate** (pal′it), *n.* roof of the mouth.
4. loathsomeness (lōŦH′səm nəs), *n.* cause of disgust.
5. **windlass** (wind′ləs), *n.* a kind of winch for pulling an anchor out of the water.
6. **flogged** (flogd), *v.* beat with a whip.

I asked them if these people had no country, but lived in this hollow place (the ship)? They told me they did not, but came from a distant one. "Then," said I, "how comes it in all our country we never heard of them?" They told me because they lived so very far off. I then asked where were their women? had they any like themselves? I was told they had. "And why," said I, "do we not see them?" They answered, because they were left behind. I asked how the vessel could go? They told me they could not tell; but that there was cloth put upon the masts by the help of the ropes I saw, and then the vessel went on; and the white men had some spell or magic they put in the water when they liked, in order to stop the vessel. I was exceedingly amazed at this account, and really thought they were spirits. I therefore wished much to be from amongst them, for I expected they would sacrifice me; but my wishes were vain—for we were so quartered that it was impossible for any of us to make our escape.

CLARIFY: Why does Equiano think the white men are spirits?

While we stayed on the coast I was mostly on deck; and one day, to my great astonishment, I saw one of these vessels coming in with the sails up. As soon as the whites saw it, they gave a great shout, at which we were amazed; and the more so, as the vessel appeared larger by approaching nearer. At last, she came to an anchor in my sight, and when the anchor was let go, I and my countrymen who saw it, were lost in astonishment to observe the vessel stop—and were now convinced it was done by magic. Soon after this the other ship got her boats out, and they came on board of us, and the people of both ships seemed very glad to see each other. Several of the strangers also shook hands with us black people, and made motions with their hands, signifying I suppose, we were to go to their country, but we did not understand them.

In his 1956 painting *The Slave Ship,* artist Robert Riggs uses a cutaway to reveal the conditions of the prisoners below decks. What words would you use to characterize the **interactions** between cultural groups depicted in this painting?

At last, when the ship we were in, had got in all her cargo, they made ready with many fearful noises, and we were all put under deck, so that we could not see how they managed the vessel. But this disappointment was the least of my sorrow. The stench of the hold while we were on the coast was so intolerably loathsome, that it was dangerous to remain there for any time, and some of us had been permitted to stay on the deck for the fresh air; but now that the whole ship's cargo were confined together, it became absolutely pestilential.[7] The closeness of the place, and the heat of the climate, added to the number in the ship, which was so crowded that each had scarcely room to turn himself, almost suffocated us. This produced copious perspirations, so that the air soon became unfit for respiration, from a variety of loathsome smells, and brought on a sickness among the slaves, of which many died—thus falling victims to the improvident avarice,[8] as I may call it, of their purchasers. This wretched situation was again aggravated by the galling of the chains, now became insupportable, and the filth of the necessary tubs,[9] into which the children often fell, and were almost suffocated. The shrieks of the women, and the groans of the dying, rendered the whole a scene of horror almost inconceivable. Happily perhaps, for myself, I was soon reduced so low here that it was thought necessary to keep me almost always on deck; and from my extreme youth I was not put in fetters. In this situation I expected every hour to share the fate of my companions, some of whom were almost daily brought upon deck at the point of death, which I began to hope would soon put an end to my miseries. Often did I think many of the inhabitants of the deep much more happy than myself. I envied them the freedom they enjoyed, and as often wished I could change my condition for theirs. Every circumstance I met with, served only to render my state more painful, and heightened my apprehensions, and my opinion of the cruelty of the whites.

*D*uring our passage, I first saw flying fishes, which surprised me very much; they used frequently to fly across the ship, and many of them fell on the deck. I also now first saw the use of the quadrant; I had often with astonishment seen the mariners make observations with it, and I could not think what it meant. They at last took notice of my surprise; and one of them, willing to increase it, as well as to gratify my curiosity, made me one day look through it. The clouds appeared to me to be land, which disappeared as they passed along. This heightened my wonder; and I was now more persuaded than ever,

I was now more persuaded than ever, that I was in another world, and that every thing about me was magic.

that I was in another world, and that every thing about me was magic. At last, we came in sight of the island of Barbadoes, at which the whites on board gave a great shout, and made many signs of joy to us. We did not know what to think of this; but as the vessel drew nearer, we plainly saw the harbor, and other ships of different kinds and sizes, and we soon anchored amongst them, off Bridgetown. Many merchants and planters now came on board, though it was in the evening. They put us in separate parcels, and examined us attentively. They also made us jump, and pointed to the land, signifying we were to go there. We thought by this, we should

---

7. pestilential (pĕs′tl en′shəl), *adj.* causing or likely to cause disease or death.
8. avarice (av′ər is), *n.* greed.
9. **necessary tubs,** containers for bodily waste.

be eaten by these ugly men, as they appeared to us; and, when soon after we were all put down under the deck again, there was much dread and trembling among us, and nothing but bitter cries to be heard all the night from these apprehensions, insomuch, that at last the white people got some old slaves from the land to pacify us. They told us we were not to be eaten, but to work, and were soon to go on land, where we should see many of our country people. This report eased us much. And sure enough, soon after we were landed, there came to us Africans of all languages.

We were conducted immediately to the merchant's yard, where we were all pent up together, like so many sheep in a fold, without regard to sex or age. As every object was new to me, everything I saw filled me with surprise. What struck me first, was, that the houses were built with bricks and stories, and in every other respect different from those I had seen in Africa; but I was still more astonished on seeing people on horseback. I did not know what this could mean; and, indeed, I thought these people were full of nothing but magical arts. While I was in this astonishment, one of my fellow prisoners spoke to a countryman of his, about the horses, who said they were the same kind they had in their country. I understood them, though they were from a distant part of Africa; and I thought it odd I had not seen any horses there; but afterwards, when I came to converse with different Africans, I found they had many horses amongst them, and much larger than those I then saw.

We were not many days in the merchant's custody, before we were sold after their usual manner, which is this: On a signal given (as the beat of a drum), the buyers rush at once into the yard where the slaves are confined, and make choice of that parcel they like best. The noise and clamor with which this is attended, and the eagerness visible in the countenances of the buyers, serve not a little to increase the apprehension of terrified Africans, who may well be supposed to consider them as the ministers of that destruction to which they think themselves devoted. In this manner, without scruple,[10] are relations and friends separated, most of them never to see each other again. I remember, in the vessel in which I was brought over, in the men's apartment, there were several brothers, who, in the sale, were sold in different lots; and it was very moving on this occasion, to see and hear their cries at parting. O, ye nominal[11] Christians! might not an African ask you— Learned you this from your God, who says unto you, Do unto all men as you would men should do unto you? Is it not enough that we are torn from our country and friends, to toil for your luxury and lust of gain? Must every tender feeling be likewise sacrificed to your avarice? Are the dearest friends and relations, now rendered more dear by their separation from their kindred, still to be parted from each other, and thus prevented from cheering the gloom of slavery, with the small comfort of being together, and mingling their sufferings and sorrows? Why are parents to lose their children, brothers their sisters, or husbands their wives? Surely, this is a new refinement in cruelty, which, while it has no advantage to atone for it, thus aggravates distress, and adds fresh horrors even to the wretchedness of slavery.

---

10. scruple (skrü′pəl), *n.* a feeling of uneasiness that keeps a person from doing something.
11. nominal (nom′ə nəl), *adj.* in name only.

After Reading

Making Connections

Shaping Your Response

1. Equiano describes many of the horrors involved with the slave trade. Choose one passage from the narrative that had the biggest impact on you. Be prepared to discuss your choice.

2. What do you think motivates the slave traders to behave so cruelly?

Analyzing the Narrative

3. Although terrified as a captive on the slave ship, Equiano's curiosity still surfaces. What marvels does he encounter, and how do they affect him?

4. Equiano suggests that the cruelty he and his fellow captives experienced are "hardships which are inseparable from this accursed trade" of slavery. What do you suppose he means by this?

5. Surviving in such harsh circumstances is difficult, and many African captives died aboard the ships. What have you learned about Equiano that may have helped him survive his ordeal?

Extending the Ideas

6. As a free man, Equiano became an abolitionist and worked to end slavery. If he could travel in time and see American society today, what would he say? What would he take pride in? What would he want changed?

Literary Focus: Imagery

Imagery is description that appeals to the senses. Authors use imagery to create vivid settings and to make characters come to life. Jot down a list of ten words or phrases that Equiano uses to show what life was like on the ship. To what senses do they appeal?

Vocabulary Study

Use your Glossary and text to answer the following questions which include italicized vocabulary words.

**loathsomeness
pestilential
avarice
scruple
nominal**

1. What conditions contributed to the *loathsomeness* of the journey?

2. The *pestilential* state in which the captives lived aboard ship caused what kinds of problems for them?

3. Who was guilty of *avarice?* Why?

4. If the slave traders had not been without *scruple,* how might their behavior have been different?

5. Why does Equiano say the slave traders were *nominal* Christians?

Expressing Your Ideas

Writing Choices

Writer's Notebook Update Look back at the evidence you've gathered against the slave trade from Olaudah Equiano's narrative. Use the evidence to argue against slavery in a newspaper article that might have been written by an abolitionist of the time.

If You Were There The drawing below depicts the plan slave traders used to maximize the number of enslaved Africans transported in a ship. Put yourself in the place of one of the people shown in the drawing. What do you feel? What do you see? What do you hear? What do you smell? Write a **poem or a prose description** capturing the experience.

Other Options

Money Talks Do a bit of research, then prepare a **chart** or illustration that shows the major economic factors in the colonies and in Europe that fueled the slave trade. Explain the chart to your classmates.

The Real Story Research the history of enslavement of Africans, focusing on one of the following topics: How did slavery become an accepted institution in European societies and in the Americas? How did slavery differ in the Americas and in Africa or Europe? How was slavery finally abolished in various countries? Present your findings in an **oral report** to your classmates.

After Reading

from **Of Plymouth Plantation** by William Bradford

Offer of Help by Canassatego

from **The Life of Mary Jemison**

William Bradford
1590–1657

In 1620, William Bradford set out on the *Mayflower* and landed in Massachusetts in December. There the Pilgrims started the Plymouth Plantation. In the following selection, the Pilgrims have just endured the two-month trip across the Atlantic.

Canassatego
died 1750

Canassatego (kä´näs sä tā´gō), an Onondaga (on´ən dô´gə) leader, was a member of the Iroquois League that united six Indian nations of upstate New York. Long before the colonists decided to unite, Canassatego suggested they would be stronger if they formed a league like that of the Iroquois.

Mary Jemison
1742?–1833

Captured in her youth by Shawanee Indians and Frenchmen, Mary Jemison was adopted by a Seneca family, married, and raised a large family. More than once, Jemison was offered the opportunity to return to her white relatives, but she chose to stay with her Indian family.

Building Background

Experience Is the Best Teacher Often we have preconceived notions about people and groups of people, and our attitudes about them may change as we get to know them personally. The next three selections tell of encounters between individuals and groups of people. In each selection, what does the speaker learn from the encounter? You may want to fill out a chart like the one shown here to keep track of the speakers' attitudes.

	Possible preconceived notions	What is learned from the encounter
William Bradford		
Mary Jemison		
Canassatego		

Literary Focus

Style Language is the tool of writers. How they use it is their **style.** One author may use dialogue to give a realistic feel to a piece of writing. Another may use vivid imagery to describe a setting or to create a mood. Style involves an author's choice and arrangement of words, as well as the tone, mood, and imagery that may or may not appear in a work. After you read each of the next three selections, identify the purpose of each author. How does the style of writing help to achieve that purpose?

Writer's Notebook

It's a Paradox Europeans thought themselves more civilized than the native peoples in the colonies. Yet civilizations had flourished for centuries in the Americas, and some of the colonists' actions seem less than civilized to people today. Before reading the next selections, write your personal definition of *civilized.* How do civilized people behave? What are their values?

Of Plymouth Plantation

William Bradford

William Formby Halsall's *Mayflower in Plymouth Harbor* (1880) portrays what the scene at Plymouth Harbor might have looked like to the pilgrims. Based on Bradford's narrative and this painting, what five words would you use to describe the pilgrims' first experiences in their new homeland?

Being thus arrived in a good harbor, and brought safe to land, they fell upon their knees and blessed the God of Heaven who had brought them over the vast and furious ocean, and delivered them from all the perils[1] and miseries thereof, again to set their feet on the firm and stable earth, their proper element. And no marvel if they were thus joyful, seeing wise Seneca[2] was so affected with sailing a few miles on the coast of his own Italy, as he affirmed, that he had rather remain twenty years on his way by land than pass by sea to any place in a short time, so tedious[3] and dreadful was the same unto him.

But here I cannot but stay and make a pause, and stand half amazed at this poor people's present condition; and so I think will the reader, too, when he well considers the same. Being thus passed the vast ocean, and a sea of troubles before in their preparation (as may be remembered by that which went before), they had now no friends to welcome them nor inns to entertain or refresh their weatherbeaten bodies; no houses or much less towns to repair to, to seek for succour. It is recorded in Scripture as a mercy to the Apostle and his shipwrecked company, that the barbarians showed them no small kindness in refreshing them, but these savage barbarians, when they met with them (as after will appear) were readier to fill their sides full of arrows than otherwise. And for the season it was winter, and they that know the winters of that country know them to be sharp and violent, and subject to cruel and fierce storms, dangerous to travel to known places, much more to search an

---

1. peril (per′əl), *n.* chance of harm or loss.
2. **Seneca,** ancient Roman statesman, playwright, and philosopher.
3. tedious (tē′dē əs), *adj.* long and tiring.

unknown coast. Besides, what could they see but a hideous and desolate wilderness, full of wild beasts and wild men—and what multitudes there might be of them they knew not. . . .

But that which was most sad and lamentable was, that in two or three months' time half of their company died, especially in January and February, being the depth of winter, and wanting houses and other comforts; being infected with the scurvy[4] and other diseases which this long voyage and their inaccommodate condition had brought upon them. So as there died sometimes two or three of a day in the foresaid time, that of one hundred and odd persons scarce fifty remained. . . .

All this while the Indians came skulking about them, and would sometimes show themselves aloof off,[5] but when any approached near them, they would run away; and once they stole away their tools where they had been at work and were gone to dinner. But about the 16th of March, a certain Indian came boldly amongst them and spoke to them in broken English, which they could well understand but marveled at it. At length they understood by discourse with him, that he was not of these parts, but belonged to the eastern parts where some English ships came to fish, with whom he was acquainted and could name sundry of them by their names, amongst whom he had got his language. He became profitable to them in acquainting them with many things concerning the state of the country in the east parts where he lived, which was afterwards profitable unto them; as also of the people here, of their names, number and strength, of their situation and distance from this place, and who was chief amongst them. His name was Samoset. He told them also of another Indian whose name was Squanto, a native of this place, who had been in England and could speak better English than himself.

Being, after some time of entertainment and gifts dismissed, a while after he came again, and five more with him, and they brought again all the tools that were stolen away before, and made way for the coming of their great Sachem,[6] called Massasoit. Who, about four or five days after, came with the chief of his friends and other attendance, with the aforesaid Squanto. With whom, after friendly entertainment and some gifts given him, they made a peace with him (which hath now continued this 24 years) in these terms:

1
That neither he nor any of his should injure or do hurt to any of their people.

2
That if any of his did hurt to any of theirs, he should send the offender, that they might punish him.

3
That if anything were taken away from any of theirs, he should cause it to be restored; and they should do the like to his.

4
If any did unjustly war against him, they would aid him; if any did war against them, he should aid them.

5
He should send to his neighbours confederates to certify them of this, that they might not wrong them, but might be likewise comprised in the conditions of peace.

6
That when their men came to them, they should leave their bows and arrows behind them.

After these things he returned to his place called Sowams, some 40 miles from this place, but Squanto continued with them and was their interpreter and was a special instrument sent of God for their good beyond their expectation. He directed them how to set their corn, where to take fish, and to procure other commodities, and was also their pilot to bring them to unknown places for their profit, and never left them till he died.

---

4. **scurvy** (skėr′vē), *n.* disease caused by lack of Vitamin C in the diet.
5. **aloof off,** away at some distance, but within view.
6. **Sachem** (sā′chəm), *n.* the chief of a tribe.

Offer of Help

Canassatego

At treaty talks between members of the Iroquois League and colonists in 1744, Canassatego made the following reply to an offer from the Virginia government to educate some Iroquois youths at the College of William and Mary.

We know you highly esteem the kind of Learning taught in these Colleges, and the maintenance of our young Men, while with you, would be very expensive to you. We are convinced, therefore, that you mean to do us Good by your Proposal; and we thank you heartily. But you who are so wise must know that different Nations have different Conceptions of things; and you will not therefore take it amiss, if our Ideas of this kind of Education happens not to be the same with yours. We have had some experience of it. Several of our young People were formerly brought up in the Colleges of the Northern Provinces; they were instructed in all your Sciences; but, when they came back to us, they were bad Runners, ignorant of every means of living in the Woods, unable to bear either Cold or Hunger, knew neither how to build a Cabin, take a deer, or kill an enemy, spoke our language imperfectly, were therefore neither fit for Hunters, Warriors, nor Counsellors, they were totally good for nothing. We are however not the less obliged for your kind Offer, tho' we decline accepting it; and to show our grateful Sense of it, if the Gentlemen of Virginia shall send us a Dozen of their Sons, we will take great care of their Education, instruct them in all we know, and make Men of them.

The Life of Mary Jemison

👣 In the person of Mary Jemison, two very different cultures come together. *Two Canoes* (1988), by Jolene Rickard presents two cultures coming together in another way, through a marriage. What do you think the artist is trying to say by bringing these two images together? ➤

One spring morning in 1755 young Mary Jemison and her family were captured by a band of Shawanee Indians and Frenchmen. Although her family members were killed when the kidnappers discovered they were being pursued, Jemison was spared. The following excerpt begins after Jemison and other young captives have been separated from their families and taken to a French fort.

The night was spent in gloomy forebodings.[1] What the result of our captivity would be, it was out of our power to determine or even imagine.—At times we could almost realize the approach of our masters to butcher and scalp us;—again we could nearly see the pile of wood kindled on which we were to be roasted; and then we would imagine ourselves at liberty: alone and defenseless in the forest, surrounded by wild beasts

---

1. foreboding (fōr bō′ding), *n.* feeling that something bad is going to happen.

that were ready to devour us. The anxiety of our minds drove sleep from our eyelids; and it was with a dreadful hope and painful impatience that we waited for the morning to determine our fate.

The morning at length arrived, and our masters came early and let us out of the house, and gave the young man and boy to the French, who immediately took them away. Their fate I never learned; as I have not seen nor heard of them since.

I was now left alone in the fort, deprived of my former companions, and of every thing that was near or dear to me but life. But it was not long before I was in some measure relieved by the appearance of two pleasant looking squaws of the Seneca tribe, who came and examined me attentively for a short time, and then went out. After a few minutes absence they returned with my former masters, who gave me to them to dispose of as they pleased.

The Indians by whom I was taken were a party of Shawanees, if I remember right, that lived, when at home, a long distance down the Ohio.

My former Indian masters, and the two squaws, were soon ready to leave the fort, and accordingly embarked; the Indians in a large canoe, and the two squaws and myself in a small one, and went down the Ohio. . . .

At night we arrived at a small Seneca Indian town, at the mouth of a small river, that was called by the Indians, in the Seneca language, She-nan-jee, where the two squaws to whom I belonged resided. There we landed, and the Indians went on; which was the last I ever saw of them.

Having made fast to the shore, the squaws left me in the canoe while they went to their wigwam[2] or house in the town, and returned with a suit of Indian clothing, all new and very clean and nice. My clothes, though whole and good

. . . they seemed to rejoice over me as over a long lost child.

. . . .

when I was taken, were now torn in pieces, so that I was almost naked. They first undressed me and threw my rags into the river; then washed me clean and dressed me in the new suit they had just brought, in complete Indian style; and then led me home and seated me in the center of their wigwam.

I had been in that situation but a few minutes, before all the squaws in the town came in to see me. I was soon surrounded by them, and they immediately set up a most dismal howling, crying bitterly, and wringing their hands in all the agonies of grief for a deceased relative.

Their tears flowed freely, and they exhibited all the signs of real mourning. At the commencement of this scene, one of their number began, in a voice somewhat between speaking and singing, to recite some words to the following purport, and continued the recitation till the ceremony was ended; the company at the same time varying the appearance of their countenances, gestures and tone of voice, so as to correspond with the sentiments expressed by their leader:

"Oh our brother! Alas! He is dead—he has gone; he will never return! Friendless he died on the field of the slain, where his bones are yet lying unburied! Oh, who will not mourn his sad fate? No tears dropped around him; oh, no! No tears of his sisters were there! He fell in his prime, when his arm was most needed to keep us from danger! Alas! he has gone! and left us in sorrow, his loss to bewail. . . . Though he fell on the field of the slain, with glory he fell, and his

---

2. **wigwam** (wig′wom), *n.* structure made of bark or mats laid over a dome-shaped frame of poles, used by the Algonquian Indians of the eastern woodlands of North America.

spirit went up to the land of his fathers in war! Then why do we mourn? With transports of joy they received him, and fed him, and clothed him, and welcomed him there! Oh friends, he is happy; then dry up your tears! His spirit has seen our distress, and sent us a helper whom with pleasure we greet. Dickewamis has come: then let us receive her with joy! She is handsome and pleasant! Oh! she is our sister, and gladly we welcome her here. In the place of our brother she stands in our tribe. With care we will guard her from trouble; and may she be happy till her spirit shall leave us."

In the course of that ceremony, from mourning they became serene[3]—joy sparkled in their countenances, and they seemed to rejoice over me as over a long lost child. I was made welcome amongst them as a sister to the two squaws before mentioned, and was called Dickewamis; which being interpreted, signifies a pretty girl, a handsome girl, or a pleasant, good thing. That is the name by which I have ever since been called by the Indians.

I afterwards learned that the ceremony I at that time passed through, was that of adoption. The two squaws had lost a brother in Washington's war, sometime in the year before, and in consequence of his death went up to Fort Pitt, on the day on which I arrived there, in order to receive a prisoner or an enemy scalp, to supply their loss. . . .

It was my happy lot to be accepted for adoption; and at the time of the ceremony I was received by the two squaws, to supply the place of their brother in the family; and I was ever considered and treated by them as a real sister, the same as though I had been born of their mother.

During my adoption, I sat motionless, nearly terrified to death at the appearance and actions of the company, expecting every moment to feel their vengeance, and suffer death on the spot. I was, however, happily disappointed, when at the close of the ceremony the company retired, and my sisters went about employing every means for my consolation and comfort.

Being now settled and provided with a home, I was employed in nursing the children, and doing light work about the house. Occasionally I was sent out with the Indian hunters, when they went but a short distance, to help them carry their game. My situation was easy; I had no particular hardships to endure. But still, the recollection of my parents, my brothers and sisters, my home, and my own captivity, destroyed my happiness, and made me constantly solitary, lonesome and gloomy.

My sisters would not allow me to speak English in their hearing; but remembering the charge that my dear mother gave me at the time I left her, whenever I chanced to be alone I made a business of repeating my prayer, catechism, or something I had learned in order that I might not forget my own language. By practicing in that way I retained it till I came to Genesee flats, where I soon became acquainted with English people with whom I have been almost daily in the habit of conversing.

My sisters were diligent in teaching me their language; and to their great satisfaction I soon learned so that I could understand it readily, and speak it fluently. I was very fortunate in falling into their hands; for they were kind good natured women; peaceable and mild in their dispositions; temperate and decent in their habits, and very tender and gentle towards me. I have great reason to respect them, though they have been dead a great number of years. . . .

About planting time, our Indians all went up to Fort Pitt, to make peace with the British, and took me with them. We landed on the opposite side of the river from the fort, and encamped for the night. Early the next morning the Indians took me over to the fort to see the white people that were there. It was then that my heart bounded to be liberated from the Indians and to be restored to my friends and my country. The

---

3. serene (sə rēn′), *adj.* peaceful; calm.

white people were surprised to see me with the Indians, enduring the hardships of a savage life, at so early an age, and with so delicate a constitution[4] as I appeared to possess. They asked me my name; where and when I was taken—and appeared very much interested on my behalf. They were continuing their inquiries, when my sisters became alarmed, believing that I should be taken from them, hurried me into their canoe and recrossed the river—took their bread out of the fire and fled with me, without stopping, till they arrived at the river Shenanjee. So great was their fear of losing me, or of my being given up in the treaty, that they never once stopped rowing till they got home.

Shortly after we left the shore opposite the fort, as I was informed by one of my Indian brothers, the white people came over to take me back; but after considerable inquiry, and having made diligent[5] search to find where I was hid, they returned with heavy hearts. Although I had then been with the Indians something over a year, and had become considerably habituated to their mode of living, and attached to my sisters, the sight of white people who could speak English inspired me with an unspeakable anxiety to go home with them, and share in the blessings of civilization. My sudden departure and escape from them, seemed like a second captivity, and for a long time I brooded the thoughts of my miserable situation with almost as much sorrow and dejection as I had done those of my first sufferings. Time, the destroyer of every affection, wore away my unpleasant feelings, and I became as contented as before. . . .

Not long after the Delawares came to live with us, at Wiishto, my sisters told me that I must go and live with one of them, whose name was She-nin-jee. Not daring to cross them, or disobey their commands, with a great degree of reluctance I went; and Sheninjee and I were married according to Indian custom.

Sheninjee was a noble man; large in stature;[6] elegant in his appearance; generous in his conduct; courageous in war; a friend to peace, and a great lover of justice. He supported a degree of dignity far above his rank, and merited and received the confidence and friendship of all the tribes with whom he was acquainted. Yet, Sheninjee was an Indian. The idea of spending my days with him, at first seemed perfectly irreconcilable to my feelings; but his good nature, generosity, tenderness, and friendship towards me, soon gained my affection; and, strange as it may seem, I loved him!—To me he was ever kind in sickness, and always treated me with gentleness; in fact, he was an agreeable husband, and a comfortable companion.

---

4. **constitution** (kon′stə tü′ shən), *n.* way in which a person or thing is organized; makeup; nature.
5. diligent (dil′ə jənt), *adj.* hard-working; industrious.
6. **stature** (stach′ər), *n.* height.

After Reading

Making Connections

Shaping Your
Response

1. You are a modern-day career advisor, and Bradford, Jemison, and Canassatego are three of your clients. What careers would you suggest for each of these individuals? Why?

2. Which of the three selections did you find most interesting? Explain your choice.

Analyzing the
Selections

3. Is William Bradford's first impression of the Indians accurate? Why or why not?

4. Mary Jemison's life was completely disrupted by her captivity. Why do you suppose she decided to stay with the Seneca when she had the opportunity to leave?

5. " . . . strange as it may seem, I loved him!" Why might Mary Jemison have felt she needed to explain her reasons for loving her husband?

6. 🐾 Canassatego points out some basic cultural differences between the Iroquois and the colonists. Does he seem to be respectful of the differences in culture, or is he implying that one culture is better than the other? Explain your answer.

Extending the
Ideas

7. William Bradford and Mary Jemison use certain words, such as "savages" and "skulking," which perpetuate stereotypes. If these events were told by the Indians involved, how might the narratives be different?

8. 🐾 All three of these selections depict situations in which individuals or groups of different cultures relate to one another. What can be learned about such **interactions** from these selections that might be useful to people today?

Literary Focus: Style

The **style** of a piece of writing—the way writers use words and sentences to suit their ideas—can have a great effect on how the reader reacts. Tone, mood, imagery, formal or informal language, are all part of style. Take a look back at the styles of William Bradford, Mary Jemison, and Canassatego, then answer the following questions.

- Which individual's style would work best in a letter to a friend about an exciting mountain climbing trip? Why?

- Which individual's style would work best for a written argument explaining why students should be allowed to leave school early on Fridays? Why?

Vocabulary Study

Choose the letter of the word that is most nearly *opposite* the numbered vocabulary word.

peril
tedious
serene
foreboding
diligent

1. peril   **a.** danger   **b.** loss   **c.** safety   **d.** cooperation

2. tedious   **a.** time-consuming   **b.** fascinating   **c.** repetitive   **d.** boring

3. serene   **a.** frantic   **b.** calm   **c.** asleep   **d.** heavenly

4. foreboding   **a.** fear   **b.** eagerness   **c.** sadness   **d.** dejection

5. diligent   **a.** careful   **b.** careless   **c.** complete   **d.** uninterested

Expressing Your Ideas

Writing Choices

Writer's Notebook Update Look back at the definition you wrote for *civilized.* Has your definition changed at all since reading the selections? Based on the selections, chart any general similarities and differences you noticed between the colonial and the American Indian cultures.

American Indians and Colonists	
similarities	differences

Role Reversal You are the president of the College of William and Mary. Canassatego has offered to educate some of your students in the ways of the Iroquois. What do you think of his suggestion? Write a **letter** responding to the invitation.

Other Options

Old-fashioned Cruise Director In 1620, 102 Pilgrims set out for North America. Two months later, in December, they arrived at Plymouth. Since it was winter, they had to wait until late summer until they could harvest any crops they planted. Clearly the Pilgrims weren't well-prepared for their journey. If you had planned the trip, what would you have done differently? What would you have packed to ensure that the colony would be successful? Work with a group to determine the supplies that would be needed for such an undertaking, and what quantities would be necessary to insure survival in the harsh new land. Present your findings in a **chart or graph.**

A Sticky Situation Canassatego's people had different notions than the colonists about what makes an educated man, but they did not want to offend the colonists. Analyze Canassatego's speech. How do you suppose he said each sentence? Rehearse how he might have delivered his words. Then be Canassatego and deliver his **speech** to the class.

A Collision of Cultures

The Great Exchange

Social Studies Connection

Many selections in Part One describe cultural exchanges—when one culture influences another. The most dramatic cultural exchange in history began when, one year after his first voyage, Columbus returned with 17 ships packed with items never before seen in the Americas. This marked the beginning of a hemispheric swap of people, plants, animals, and diseases.

A FOOD SUPERHIGHWAY

It might be hard to imagine pasta without tomato sauce, but before the Great Exchange many now familiar dishes simply weren't on the menu. Trades in food caused revolutions in cooking on both sides of the Atlantic. However, rather than cooking the same way, the cultures of the world used the same ingredients to create unique dishes. For example, beef, corn and chilies might become a taco in Mexico, meatballs and polenta in Italy, or a spicy stir-fry in China.

"NEW WORLD" TO OLD

TO NEW

"OLD WORLD"

The Great Exchange

Corn

Turkey

Chili Pepper

Tomato

Tobacco

Pumpkin

Peach

Wheat

Pig

Honey Bee

Chicken

Dandelion

A DEADLY EXCHANGE

One tragic aspect of the Exchange was exposure to new diseases. Native American communities across the western hemisphere lost 50-90% of their people to epidemics of small pox, measles, and other diseases brought over with the Europeans. Dangerous diseases such as syphilis also returned to Europe with the explorers, resulting in deadly outbreaks there.

CORN: BUILDER OF CITIES

Were it not for corn, archeologists say, the Spaniards would have been mightily disappointed when they arrived in the Americas. There would have been no Aztecs with floating cities and carved pyramids to conquer, no vast Indian armies with whom to do battle. The conquistadors likely would have left Peru empty-handed, for there would have been no Incan empire offering temples paneled in gold and stocked with jeweled icons. Corn was what made the great civilizations of Central and South America possible: it supplied the calories that nourished the thriving populations required to build complex societies.

Christopher Columbus first sampled corn in Cuba. He was impressed, declaring it "most tasty boiled, roasted or ground into flour." When he returned to Spain, he took along a few specimen Indians, some handfuls of gold dust and a packet of corn kernels. Those first seeds may not have made a big impression on Ferdinand and Isabella, but they quickly proved their value. Within a few years the Spaniards had introduced maize around the Mediterranean. By the mid-16th century corn was so familiar in the Southern European diet that it formed the basis of such national dishes as Italian polenta and the Romanian staple mamaliga (a sort of cornmeal mush). Corn also traveled to the Philippines and the rest of Asia; by 1560 it was a fixture in Chinese cooking, in everything from porridge to stir fry.

Portuguese traders, who used corn as slave-ship stores, carried the grain to Africa. It was an instant success there: corn grew more rapidly than other grains, and it needed very little cultivation. You could plant it and then pretty much ignore it until harvest time. Corn weathered drought and the harsh African sun better than other staple foods. But its advent in Africa was not an unmixed blessing. It produced something of a population boom, which may in turn have fed the slave trade. In addition, says historian Robert Hall, "Europeans used slave labor in Africa for cultivating New World crops like corn, yams and cassava to provision the slave ships." And it led to a serious imbalance in the African diet. By the late 18th century, many Africans ate almost nothing but corn, and suffered from vitamin deficiency as a result. Africans today are still afflicted by pellagra or "mealie disease," a sickness related to malnutrition from overreliance on corn.

In the Americas, Indians who depended on maize combined it with tomatoes, capsicum peppers and sometimes fish—all of which contain the necessary vitamins to make up for the deficit in corn. In fact, corn on its own provided only about a third of the calories of Old World staples like sorghum and millet. In Europe, humans never really took to corn, but it became a major source of fodder for animals and helped improve nutrition by making meat cheaper.

Today, corn continues to relieve the planet's hunger—and slake its thirst. Any portrayal of the Pilgrims' first Thanksgiving would be incomplete without the requisite display of Indian maize, but what probably made the meal so jolly was a native brew of fermented corn. Later, less puritan immigrants took the process a few steps further to make that most American of liquors, bourbon whisky. Corn is the staple food of 200 million people in Africa and Latin America, and Americans consume an average of three pounds of corn a day in the form of meat, poultry and dairy products. And it's not just food: corn is used in products from baby powder to embalming fluid—the cradle to the grave.

from Newsweek

The Animal That Changed History

The Indians took one look at the strange creatures and decided they were the biggest dogs they had ever seen. Only dogs walked on four legs and got along with people, the islanders reasoned as Columbus unloaded his two dozen mares and stallions.

Actually, horses were not totally new to the Western Hemisphere. They had roamed America during the Pleistocene era but vanished along with mastadons and saber-toothed tigers. From the Spanish horses that Columbus 10,000 years later took to Hispaniola descended those that Hernando Cortés brought to Mexico in 1519. Cortés's animals terrified the Aztecs, who thought each rider and his steed were one gigantic god.

The "sky dogs," as the Aztecs called them, propagated swiftly. Within a century, herds ran wild from northern Mexico to the pampas of Argentina. By 1690, Apaches and Comanches were breaking mustangs north of the Rio Grande. By 1750, herds reached Canada, and the Great Plains abounded with Indians on horseback.

Tribes that existed for centuries on small game and nuts in Missouri and Minnesota moved west to the plains to harvest buffaloes—a task the horse made easy. Diets and lifestyles improved, as did the Indians' ability to raid other Indians and, more important, to resist the steady westward advance of the white man.

The image of the warrior on horseback endures in popular culture and in the legends of the Indians themselves. Yet it represents merely a blink of Native American history. People inhabited the continent for millenniums, but the plains horsemen rode unimpeded for little more than a century. Their era ended at the Battle of Wounded Knee.

from *U.S. News and World Report*

Responding

1. How would you evaluate the effects of the Great Exchange? Consider the perspectives of all involved, including African, European, Asian, and Native American peoples.

2. What were the advantages of having horses?

3. How might history have been different without corn?

Language Connection

When cultures collide, each side tries to communicate. In this process, words from each culture's language often become integrated into the other. Some languages, called *creoles*, preserve the features of vocabulary, grammar, and idioms from several different languages. This page focuses on Gullah—the only creole English still in use in the United States.

"THE BUZZARD AND THE HAWK"

A GULLAH FOLKTALE AS TOLD BY
MR. TED WILLIAMS

YOU KNOW THE BUZZARD ALWAYS WAS A—A NICE EDUCATED ANIMAL, YOU KNOW! E TAKE E TIME—JUST LIKE HE DONE WITH THE HAWK.

HIM AND THE HAWK WAS SITTING DOWN ON THE LIMB ONE DAY, AND HE SAID—HIM AND THE HAWK HAD A CONSOLATION [CONSULTATION].

SAY, "I'M VERY HUNGRY!!!"

THE HAWK SAY, "I'M HUNGRY TOO! LORD—O LORD! MY STOMACH! I TOO HUNGRY!"

THE BUZZARD SAY, "WAIT ON THE LORD—" AND E LOOK UP—NOTHING FOR DEAD—NOTHING, YOU KNOW

SO THE BUZZARD SAY, "MAN!!!"

THE HAWK SAY, "I CAN'T WAIT NO LONGER!"

SO WHEN HE LOOK, A LITTLE SPARROW COME ALONG. AND—AND—AND THE HAWK GET UP AND RUN AT THE SPARROW AND HIT A TREE *UH HUH!*

AND THE BUZZARD SIT ON HE LIMB AND LOOK AT THE HAWK, LOOK AT THE HAWK, WHEN HE RUN INTO TREE. THE BUZZARD SAY, "I TELL YOU WAIT ON THE LORD. NOW I GONE EAT YOU NOW!"

OLD-TIME TALK WE STILL DE TALKEM HERE!
(WE STILL SPEAK GULLAH HERE!)

Gullah is spoken chiefly on the Sea Islands located off the coast of South Carolina and Georgia. Large numbers of West Africans were enslaved and brought to raise cotton and rice on these marshy islands. Words from their native languages combined with English to form Gullah. Later, black settlements on the islands were isolated from the mainland, allowing Gullah to thrive as the primary language, sheltered from the influence of American English.

Many old words and expressions are still in use among the Gullah speakers of the Sea Islands. For example:

DAY CLEAN: DAYBREAK
UGLY TOO MUCH: VERY UGLY
THIS SIDE: THIS ISLAND
SWEETHMOUTH: FLATTER
ONE DAY MONG ALL!: FINALLY!
LONG EYE: ENVY
SMALL SMALL: VERY SMALL
SMALL SMALL SMALL: TINY
I DE SHELL EM: I AM SHELLING THEM
I BEN SHELL EM: I SHELLED THEM
I BINA SHELL EM: I HAVE BEEN SHELLING THEM
I BEN DON SHELL EM: I SHELLED THEM SOME TIME AGO

Hundreds of words derived from West African languages occur in Gullah, and some have crossbred with English to become common expressions. Here are a few of them, with the languages from which they may have come:

GOOBER: "PEANUT" (KIMBUNDU)
GUMBO: "OKRA" (TSHILUBA)
HEH: "YES" (VAI)
HOODOO: "BAD LUCK" (HAUSA)
YAMBI: "YAM" (VAI)
CHIGGER: "SMALL FLEA" (WOLOF)
NANA: "GRANDMOTHER" (TWI)
TOTE: "TO CARRY" (KONGO)
BIDDY: "SMALL CHICKEN" (KONGO)
BUCKRA: "WHITE MAN" (IBO)

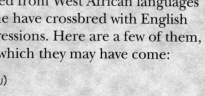

Responding

1. Translate the tale into standard American English. How does the tone and sound of the tale change?

2. Do you think you could communicate with someone who spoke only Gullah? Why or why not?

Language History

The Language Exchange

 The skunk is almost as big as a raccoon, perfect black and white or piebald, with a bush-tail like a fox [and] of so strong a scent that if it light upon anything, there is no abiding of it.

This is the way an English traveler named John Josselyn described an unfamiliar animal he encountered when he visited America in the 1600s. Since this animal was unknown in Europe, he used its American Indian name, *skunk*. European travelers and settlers needed words to describe and communicate what they found in their new American surroundings. One solution was to borrow words from American Indian languages. Thus, there was a language exchange between the "Old World" and the "New," as well as an exchange of plants and animals such as corn and the horse. (See "The Great Exchange," pages 41–44)

Many English words today originally came from American Indian languages. Names such as *raccoon, opossum, moose,* and *chipmunk* were incorporated into English to communicate about these unfamiliar creatures. Likewise, the words *hickory, pecan, persimmon,* and *squash* were added to English vocabulary to name plants unknown in Europe. Numerous American place names also came from the American Indian names for these areas. Over half of the state names in the United States are Native American words. For example, the name *Arizona* comes from the Papago word meaning "place of the little springs," and the name *Idaho* is Shoshone for "the sun is coming up." City names including *Chicago, Kalamazoo,* and *Cheyenne* also have American Indian sources.

It should be noted that not all of the English words with Native American origins sound like they do in the languages they came from. Many were changed to make their sounds easier for English speakers to pronounce. For example, the American Indian words *otcheck* and *seganku* became the English words *woodchuck* and *skunk*.

Writing Workshop

Earth—A Strange New World

Assignment Selections in this part were written by people living in places that were new and strange to them. Some of these writers reacted with surprise and wonder, others with shock and confusion. Now write your own version of someone's reactions to a strange new place.

WRITER'S BLUEPRINT

Product   Starship captain's log entry
Purpose   To react to a familiar place as if it were new to you
Audience   People on the captain's home planet
Specs   To write a successful paper, you should:

❑ Use first-person ("I") point of view, writing as if you were the captain of a starship from a distant planet, to whom Earth is a strange new place.

❑ In order to give your log an air of authenticity, report the date, time, and place at the beginning of your entry. Also, identify yourself and your mission.

❑ Describe your experiences during your first morning on Earth in chronological order. Include your personal reactions, but keep in mind that you are writing a historical account and must strive for completeness and accuracy.

❑ Use vivid language to show the people back home how things on this strange new planet look, sound, smell, and so on.

❑ Conclude by trying to make sense of your experiences. You might offer theories about what you've seen or compare life on Earth to life on your home planet.

❑ Follow the rules of grammar, usage, spelling, and mechanics. Don't shift verb tenses unnecessarily.

The instructions that follow are designed to lead you to a successful paper.

PREWRITING

Learn from the literature. You have read literature by writers living in places that were new and strange to them. Look back through the selections and make notes on their observations and reactions in a chart like this one.

Author	Place	Observations	Reactions
Olaudah Equiano	slave ship at sea	sailors using a quadrant flying fish	curious, amazed, sees ship as magic place

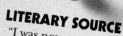

LITERARY SOURCE
"I was now more persuaded than ever, that I was in another world, and that every thing about me was magic."
from *The Interesting Narrative of the Life of Olaudah Equiano*

Keep your notes handy as you plan your paper. They should help you come up with ideas.

Chart your journey. Choose places and events to describe that are familiar to you. Make notes in a chart like this one.

Event or Place	Sights—Reactions	Sounds, etc.—Reactions
Indoor shopping mall	crowds of people moving in all directions puzzle him, he's used to quiet, orderly public life	noise of so many voices all at once puzzles him, tries to make sense of it.

OR . . .
If you can, visit the places you're describing and make notes on your first-hand observations and reactions.

Plan the entry. You might make your plan in the form of a time line, like the one that follows.

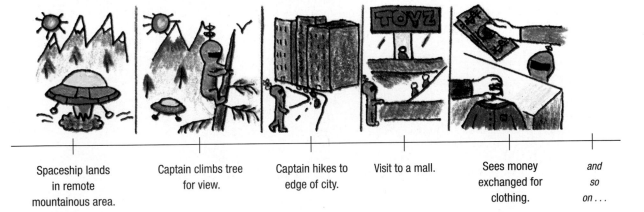

Spaceship lands in remote mountainous area.

Captain climbs tree for view.

Captain hikes to edge of city.

Visit to a mall.

Sees money exchanged for clothing.

and so on . . .

2 DRAFTING

Before you draft, review the Writer's Blueprint and look over your chart and writing plan to make sure you know exactly what you'll be writing about.

As you draft, concentrate on getting your ideas down on paper. You can clean up spelling and punctuation mistakes later on. If you have trouble getting started, these drafting tips might help.

- Decide exactly where you are as the journey begins—inside your ship looking out a window, stepping out of your ship down a stairway to the earth—and describe what you see.

- Describe your reaction to something you see—horror, wonder, amusement—and then describe the scene that caused you to react this way.

- Use vivid language to liven up your descriptions. See the Revising Strategy in Step 3.

OR . . .
You don't have to start at the very beginning of your journey. You could open with the meatiest, most interesting part of the trip. Then, later on, you could tell about the earlier part of your trip in flashback.

3 REVISING

Ask a partner to look over your draft and comment before you revise.

✔ Do my reactions to things sound like the reactions of someone who is seeing life on planet Earth for the first time?

✔ Have I given an accurate description of places and events?

✔ Have I tried to make sense of what I've seen?

✔ Have I used vivid language to make lively descriptions?

Revising Strategy

Using Vivid Language

Vivid language can liven up descriptions. In your writing, use imagery—words that tell how things look, sound, feel, smell, and taste. Notice the strong imagery in this passage.

LITERACY SOURCE

The *stench of the hold* while we were on the coast was so intolerably loathsome, that it was dangerous to remain there . . . The *closeness of the place*, and the *heat of the climate*, added to the number in the ship, . . . almost suffocated us. This produced copious perspirations, so that *the air soon became unfit for respiration* . . .

from *The Interesting Narrative of the Life of Olaudah Equiano*

Notice how this writer used a partner's comment to liven up the description.

What do you mean by "strange"?

This thing called a "dollar bill" feels ~~strange~~ *soft and wrinkly* to my fingers. The smell of it is ~~strange also.~~ *old and musty.* The drawings and lettering upon its surface *are* ~~appear to be very old and~~ worn ~~out.~~ *and faded and its edges are rough and torn.* How then could such an object be of such value to these people?

STUDENT MODEL

4 EDITING

Ask a partner to look over your revised draft before you begin to edit. When you edit, look for errors in grammar, usage, spelling, and mechanics. Pay special attention to errors with unnecessary shifts in verb tense.

Editing Strategy

Keeping Consistent Tense

When a writer shifts verb tenses in a narrative for no apparent reason, the result is confusion. Unless you have a good reason to change, it's best to stick with one tense.

Unnecessary Shift   I was lost now. I turned in circles, looking for a way out of this labyrinth. "Where am I?" I ask myself.

The writer needs to change present-tense *ask* to past-tense *asked* because the story is being narrated in past tense, but the present-tense verb *am* is fine because it's part of a direct quotation.

OR . . .
Consider turning your log entry into a radio play complete with sound effects. You might want to rewrite it as a play or movie.

5 PRESENTING

Here are some ideas for presenting your log entry.

- Get together in small groups and read your entries to each other. Beforehand, draw a map of your journey and display it as you read.

- Publish all the log entries in a collection entitled "Journeys to Planet Earth." Illustrate it and keep it on hand for other students to read.

6 LOOKING BACK

Self-evaluate. What grade do *you* think your log entry deserves? Look back at the Writer's Blueprint and evaluate yourself on each point, using a scale from 6 (superior) to 1 (inadequate).

Reflect. Think about what you've learned from writing this log entry. Write answers to these questions:

✔ Was it fun to describe familiar things as if you'd never seen them before? Why or why not?

✔ How has writing this log entry helped you see what it might be like to be a stranger in a strange new land?

For Your Working Portfolio Add your log entry and your reflection responses to your working portfolio.

Beyond Print

Looking at Art

Whether artworks are paintings, sculpture, everyday objects, collage, photographs, movies, or textiles, they all share one common characteristic—they are a form of communication. Here are some hints that may help you "get" what an artwork may be communicating:

1. **Art is created for a purpose.** Some works of art are designed to illustrate a story or an event—such as a painting of a battle. Some are designed as tributes or memorials—such as a sculpted monument. Others are created for everyday use, such as pottery or furniture. Some art is created for use in religious ceremonies. As you look at a work of art, try to figure out the purpose the artist had in mind.

2. **Art comes in many styles.** The most important thing about a work might be its realistic details, its shape, or the combination of colors. An artwork may represent an object or event, or may focus on a mood, feeling, or idea. If you can't tell what a work is about, ask yourself if it reminds you of any experiences, sights, sounds, or feelings.

3. **Every artist has a point of view.** Like all of us, artists are influenced by their times, and by cultural attitudes, which will be reflected in their works. When you look at a work of art, it's worthwhile to think about the artist's culture, times, personality, and experiences.

4. **The "message" is in the eye of the beholder.** Depending on your tastes and experiences, you may get an entirely different message from a work of art than another observer will. Always pay attention to your own reactions and feelings about an artwork.

Activity Options

Review the Art Choose any piece of art from the first unit of this book to analyze. What purpose does it serve? What thoughts or feelings does it evoke? How might the artist's times and culture have impacted the work? Finally, include your personal reaction.

Re-creation Creation Re-create a moment, event, feeling, idea, mood, or sound in art. What medium and style will you choose, and how will you communicate your message?

A †RAGEDY

HISTORICAL OVERVIEW

One of the most bizarre chapters in American history began in the winter of 1692 in Salem, Massachusetts, when several girls started exhibiting strange behavior. They were diagnosed as being "under an evil hand" and accused three "witches" of casting spells on them. The arrest of the "witches" panicked the town. In the months that followed, everyone seemed to be at the mercy of the "afflicted girls." When they claimed to know the identities of other witches, the accused were arrested and made to stand trial. In the end, 75 people were arrested for suspicion of witch-craft and 20 were executed. By October of 1692 the trials stopped. While most of the town fell victim to the delusion, some were more instrumental than others in fanning the hysteria. Here are some who figured most prominently in the Salem witchcraft trials.

COTTON MATHER
1663–1728

Puritan clergyman Cotton Mather believed strongly in the presence of the devil and witches. In 1689 Mather published a book of his observances of a child believed to be the victim of witchcraft. Some believe that his writings coupled with his warnings from the pulpit helped create the atmosphere of hysteria that led to the tragedy at Salem.

TITUBA
BIRTH AND DEATH UNKNOWN

Tituba was a West Indian slave that mesmerized a group of girls with forbidden tales of the supernatural and fortune telling. When the girls started acting strangely, Tituba was blamed for "bewitching" them. She was the first to be arrested and in her testimony "confessed" that she was a witch. Tituba was thrown in jail but her confession saved her life.

AT SALEM

GILES COREY
1612–1692

Giles Corey was the only victim that wasn't hanged. Because he refused to plead, Corey was sentenced to be crushed to death. As rocks were piled on a board across his chest he was told to confess. He only cried out for more weight. Two days later his wife Martha Corey was found guilty of witchcraft and hanged.

WILLIAM STOUGHTON
1630?–1701

Deputy Governor William Stoughton was responsible for organizing and running the trials. As chief justice for the court, Stoughton insisted that "spectral evidence," testimony about a witch's ghost, be allowed. Some disagreed, including one justice who resigned when it was found acceptable. In the aftermath of the trials, Stoughton was the only justice who refused to express remorse.

ANN PUTNAM
1680?–1716

Her screams, fits, and bizarre behavior convinced many that young Ann was indeed bewitched. One of the first to be diagnosed, she saw more ghosts of witches or *spectres*, as they were called, than the other "afflicted girls" and sent many accused to the hangman's noose. Later, she was the only girl to publicly apologize for her part in the witch hunts.

Key Dates

1647
Massachusetts Bay Colony forbids witchcraft under penalty of death.

1692
January
Three Salem Village girls are stricken with a mysterious illness and accuse three local "witches" of tormenting them.

May
Governor William Phips appoints a special court to hear the witchcraft cases.

June 2
The Salem witchcraft trials begin.

June 10
Bridget Bishop is the first "witch" to be hanged.

October
Governor Phips stops the trials and pardons the remaining accused.

1697
January 14
Judge Samuel Sewall publicly asks forgiveness for his part in the trials.

Part Two

A Tragedy at Salem

Shared traditions and beliefs are a large part of what holds a society together. This is certainly true for the early Puritan colonists, whose unity and conformity helped them survive in an unfamiliar and sometimes dangerous land. But as the wilderness was tamed and the colonists prospered, conformity seemed less important. Ministers began to lose some of their power over the society. Then, a clergyman's daughter and niece began accusing Salem citizens of witchcraft . . .

👣 **Multicultural Connection** All of us are members of different kinds of **groups.** Family, social, cultural, and other groups help us define who we are and give us a sense of belonging. Every group has its own set of norms and beliefs, and members are expected to live according to them. In the following selections, how do the group beliefs and expectations of the Puritans both unify their society and wreak havoc for those who are perceived as different?

Literature

Samuel Sewall   *from* **The Diary of Samuel Sewall** ◆ diary 56
Jonathan Edwards   *from* **Sinners in the Hands of an Angry God**
         ◆ sermon 58
Arthur Miller   **The Crucible** ◆ play 62

Interdisciplinary Study   Mass Hysteria

Witchcraft in Salem: A Fungus in the Rye ◆ science 136
A Climate of Fear ◆ social studies 137

Writing Workshop   Persuasive Writing

Reacting Under Pressure 142

Beyond Print   Technology

Speaking the Language of Technology 148

Before Reading

from **The Diary of Samuel Sewall**

from **Sinners in the Hands of an Angry God** by Jonathan Edwards

Samuel Sewall
1652–1730

Samuel Sewall was the only judge who presided at the Salem witch trials to ask publicly for forgiveness. Prominent in Boston society, Sewall was a wealthy, religious, family man.

Jonathan Edwards
1703–1758

Jonathan Edwards was a famous Puritan preacher and a believer in Calvinism, which teaches that people are innately corrupt, and that they cannot win salvation by good works since God has already determined their fate. Edwards's dynamic preaching helped spark a major religious revival in New England.

Building Background

The Puritans in America In 1630 a group of about 1000 Puritans, disillusioned with the Church of England and persecuted by the government, left for New England, where they created a highly structured, patriarchal society based on their beliefs. With the growth of commerce, religious leaders lost some of their power. Jealousies over wealth and community control may have played a large part in the **Salem witch trials** of 1692. Salem Town, the port, was involved in commerce, while the more traditional settlers around Salem Village considered it a sin to pursue wealth rather than God's grace. The lasting effect of the trials was to diminish the power of the church by discrediting those holding traditional Puritan beliefs.

Some forty years later, a major religious revival called the **Great Awakening** spread through New England. This revival was due in large part to the preaching of ministers like Jonathan Edwards, who became famous for his fire-and-brimstone sermons.

Literary Focus

Simile and Metaphor As you read Edwards's sermon, look for **similes,** comparisons using *like* or *as,* and **metaphors,** implied comparisons. In a chart like the one below, record the comparisons.

X is compared to	Y	simile or metaphor	literary effect
the wrath of God	dammed waters	simile	emphasis on God's powerful and deep anger

Writer's Notebook

What's the Point? Writers often have a specific audience in mind when they write, and a specific purpose for writing. Before you read the next two selections, jot down in your notebook the audience and purpose for these two kinds of writing: a diary entry and a sermon.

The Diary of Samuel Sewall

APRIL 11TH, 1692. Went to Salem, where, in the meeting-house, the persons accused of witchcraft were examined. Was a very great assembly. 'Twas awful to see how the afflicted persons[1] were <u>agitated</u>.[2] . . .

AUGUST 19TH, 1692. This day George Burroughs, John Willard, John Proctor, Martha Carrier, and George Jacobs were executed at Salem, a very great number of spectators being present. Mr. Cotton Mather, Mr. Sims, Hale, Noyes, Cheever, and others. All of them said they were innocent. Carrier and all. Mr. Mather said they all died by a righteous sentence. Mr. Burroughs, by his speech, prayer, protestations of innocence, did much move unthinking persons, which occasions their speaking hardly [severely] concerning his execution.

MONDAY, SEPT. 19, 1692. About noon, at Salem, Giles Cory was pressed to death for standing mute;[3] much pains was used with him two days, one after another, by the court and Capt. Gardner of Nantucket who had been of his acquaintance, but all in vain.

SEPT. 21. A petition is sent to town in behalf of Dorcas Hoar, who now confesses. Accordingly an order is sent to the sheriff to <u>forbear</u>[4] her execution, notwithstanding her being in the warrant to die tomorrow. This is the first condemned person who has confessed.

THURSDAY, SEPT. 22, 1692. William Stoughton, Esq., John Hathorne, Esq., Mr. Cotton Mather, and Capt. John Higginson, and my brother, were at my house, speaking about publishing some trials of the witches. Mr. Stoughton went away and left us, it began to rain and was very dark, so that, getting some way beyond the fortification, was fain to come back again, and lodged here in Capt. Henchman's room. Has been a plentiful rain, blessed be God.

OCT. 26, 1692. A bill is sent in about calling a fast, and convocation of ministers, that may be led in the right way as to the witchcrafts. . . .

NOV. 22, 1692. I prayed that God would pardon all my sinful wanderings and direct me for the future; that God would bless the Assembly in their debates, and that he would choose and assist our judges, etc., and save New England as to enemies and witchcrafts and <u>vindicate</u>[5] the late judges, consisting [compatible] with his justice and holiness, etc., with fasting.

---

1. **afflicted persons,** those who claimed they were bewitched.
2. agitated (aj′ə tāt əd), *adj.* disturbed; very upset.
3. **standing mute,** Cory, 81 years old, refused to plead to an indictment on the charge of witchcraft, believing his estate would be confiscated if he pleaded guilty.
4. forbear (fôr bar′), *v.* hold back; keep from doing.
5. vindicate (vin′də kāt), *v.* justify or support

▲ Painted in 1855, T. H. Matteson's painting, *Trial of George Jacobs, August 5, 1692* depicts George Jacobs being accused by a group of Salem girls. Why do you suppose Sewall's description of George Jacobs' execution is calmer and more matter-of-fact than the trial scene represented in the painting?

DECEMBER 24 [1694]. Sam[6] recites to me in Latin, Matthew 12 from the 6th to the end of the 12th verse. The 7th verse[7] did awfully bring to mind the Salem tragedy.

[**JANUARY 15, 1697**]. Copy of the bill I put up on the fast day, giving it to Mr. Willard as he passed by, and standing up at the reading of it, and bowing when finished; in the Afternoon.

Samuel Sewall, sensible of the reiterated[8] strokes of God upon himself and family, and being sensible, that as to the guilt contracted[9] upon the opening of the [judicial proceedings] at Salem (to which the order for this day relates) he is, upon many accounts, more concerned than any that he knows of, dcsircs to take the blame and shame of it, asking pardon of men, and especially desiring prayers that God, who has an unlimited authority, would pardon that sin and all other his sins. . . .

---

6. **Sam,** one of Sewall's children.
7. **7th verse,** "And if you had understood the meaning of the words: 'What I want is mercy, not sacrifice,' you would not have condemned the blameless."
8. **reiterated** (rē it′ə rāt′əd), *adj.* repeated.
9. **contract** (kən′trakt), *v.* bring on oneself; get.

Sinners in the hands of an Angry God

Jonathan Edwards

▲ This woodcut pictures Richard Mather (1596–1669), a famous Puritan preacher who was the first in a distinguished line of clergymen. 🐾 Based on this image and on what you already know about the Puritans, what values do you think were most important to this cultural **group**?

The wrath[1] of God is like great waters that are dammed for the present; they increase more and more and rise higher and higher, till an outlet is given; and the longer the stream is stopped, the more rapid and mighty is its course when once it is let loose. 'Tis true that judgment against your evil work has not been executed hitherto; the floods of God's vengeance have been withheld; but your guilt in the meantime is constantly

---

1. **wrath** (rath), *n.* very great anger; rage.

increasing, and you are every day treasuring up more wrath; the waters are continually rising and waxing more and more mighty; and there is nothing but the mere pleasure of God that holds the waters back, that are unwilling to be stopped, and press hard to go forward. If God should only withdraw his hand from the floodgate, it would immediately fly open, and the fiery floods of the fierceness and wrath of God would rush forth with inconceivable fury, and would come upon you with omnipotent power; and if your strength were ten thousand times greater than it is, yea, ten thousand times greater than the strength of the stoutest, sturdiest devil in hell, it would be nothing to withstand or endure it.

The bow of God's wrath is bent, and the arrow made ready on the string, and justice bends the arrow at your heart and strains the bow, and it is nothing but the mere pleasure of God, and that of an angry God, without any promise or obligation at all, that keeps the arrow one moment from being made drunk with your blood.

Thus are all you that never passed under a great change of heart by the mighty power of the Spirit of God upon your souls; all that were never born again and made new creatures, and raised from being dead in sin to a state of new and before altogether unexperienced light and life (however you may have reformed your life in many things, and may have had religious affections, and may keep up a form of religion in your families and closets and in the house of God, and may be strict in it), you are thus in the hands of an angry God; 'tis nothing but his mere pleasure that keeps you from being this moment swallowed up in everlasting destruction.

However unconvinced you may now be of the truth of what you hear, by and by you will be fully convinced of it. Those that are gone from being in the like circumstances with you, see that it was so with them; for destruction came suddenly upon most of them; when they expected nothing of it, and while they were saying, Peace and Safety. Now they see that those things that they depended on for peace and safety were nothing but thin air and empty shadows.

The God that holds you over the pit of hell much as one holds a spider or some loathsome insect over the fire, abhors you, and is dreadfully provoked; his wrath toward you burns like fire; he looks upon you as worthy of nothing else but to be cast into the fire; he is of purer eyes than to bear to have you in his sight; you are ten thousand times so abominable in his eyes as the most hateful and venomous serpent is in ours. You have offended him infinitely more than ever a stubborn rebel did his prince; and yet it is nothing but his hand that holds you from falling into the fire every moment. 'Tis ascribed to nothing else, that you did not go to hell the last night; that you were suffered to awake again in this world after you closed your eyes to sleep and there is no other reason to be given why you have not dropped into hell since you arose in the morning, but that God's hand has held you up. There is no other reason to be given why you have not gone to hell since you have sat here in the house of God, provoking his pure eyes by your sinful wicked manner of attending his solemn worship. Yea, there is nothing else that is to be given as a reason why you don't this very moment drop down into hell.

O sinner! Consider the fearful danger you are in. 'Tis a great furnace of wrath, a wide and bottomless pit, full of the fire of wrath, that you are held over in the hand of that God whose wrath is provoked and incensed as much against you as against many of the damned in hell. You hang by a slender thread, with the flames of divine wrath flashing about it, and ready every moment to singe it and burn it asunder; and you have no interest in any Mediator, and nothing to lay hold of to save yourself, nothing to keep off the flames of wrath, nothing of your own, nothing that you ever have done, nothing that you can do, to induce God to spare you one moment. . . .

After Reading

Making Connections

Shaping Your Response

1. What do the diary entries tell you about Sewall as a person?
2. How does the description of God in Jonathan Edwards's sermon compare with those of religions you are familiar with?

Analyzing the Selections

3. What indications can you find in Sewall's diary that he had good intentions?
4. Edwards introduces two **comparisons** for God's wrath in paragraphs two and five. Describe what is being compared in each.

Extending the Ideas

5. If you were a family member of one of the people tried and executed as a witch, what would you want to say to Sewall?
6. Would Edwards be a popular preacher today? Why or why not?

Vocabulary Study

Choose the word or phrase that is most nearly a *synonym* for each numbered vocabulary word.

agitated
forbear
vindicate
reiterated
wrath

1. agitated   **a.** troubled **b.** lying **c.** deceived **d.** accused
2. forbear   **a.** speed up **b.** hold back **c.** discuss **d.** carry
3. vindicate   **a.** clear of suspicion **b.** punish **c.** banish **d.** approve of
4. reiterated   **a.** repeated **b.** emblazoned **c.** holy **d.** indelible
5. wrath   **a.** majesty **b.** breadth **c.** anger **d.** depth

Expressing Your Ideas

Writing Choices

Writer's Notebook Update Which form did you prefer, the diary entry or the sermon? Tell which selection you liked best, and why.

Formal to Normal The notice Samuel Sewall posted in 1697 is written in the formal language used in those times. Write a **paraphrase** of the notice so that it can be easily understood by contemporary readers.

Another Option

Mercy! The wrath of God is described with frightening clarity in "Sinners in the Hands of an Angry God." Choose one of the descriptions and illustrate the scene. Caption your **drawing** with an appropriate line from the text of the sermon.

Before Reading

The Crucible

by Arthur Miller

Arthur Miller
born 1915

In the early 1950s, fear of communism (fueled by the Soviet Union's development of an atomic bomb) reached near-hysterical proportions in the United States. It was during this time that Arthur Miller wrote *The Crucible,* his play about the Salem witch trials. In 1956 Miller was himself called to testify before the House Un-American Activities Committee. Though not a Communist himself, he admitted to attending meetings sponsored by the Communist Party but refused to inform on his friends, resisting what many saw as a modern "witch hunt." Among Miller's other well-known works are *All My Sons, A View from the Bridge,* and the Pulitzer Prize winning *Death of a Salesman.*

Building Background

Plea Bargaining Imagine this scene. You have been called to the office of the Dean of Students. You are puzzled. You don't know what you could have possibly done. When you arrive, the dean explains that widespread cheating on final exams has been discovered, and you have been implicated in the crime. The dean describes your alternatives. You can confess and name the others involved. In that case you would be placed on probation, but you would not be expelled from school. If you deny your part in the cheating scandal, you will be sent before the school board and most likely be expelled for the semester. You are innocent! You have never cheated, nor do you know of anyone who has! How do you feel at this moment? What will you do?

The Crucible explores a similar dilemma with more severe consequences. In 1692 in Salem, Massachusetts, 75 people were accused of witchcraft and jailed. Before the witchcraft trials ended, twenty people were executed.

Literary Focus

Theme Although first performed in 1953, *The Crucible* continues to be popular. This is due in part to the enduring **theme,** or underlying meaning, of the play. When you finish each act, look for the message the playwright is attempting to communicate through the words and actions of the people in Salem, Massachusetts, in 1692.

Writer's Notebook

You Be the Judge The people of Salem believe they are routing out the devil and his evil influence when they begin their witch hunt. However, mass hysteria prevails and the notions of "good" and "evil" become more and more complicated and difficult to sort out. The accused can either remain silent and face execution, or they can choose to give false confessions to save themselves. In your notebook jot down your notions of "good" and "evil" and examples of "good" and "evil" people. Then, as you read each act of the play, evaluate the characters. Who is "good"? Who is "evil"? Who is struggling? Who is just swept up in the mass hysteria?

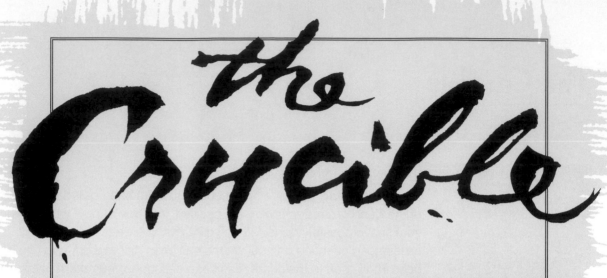

the Crucible

Arthur Miller

CHARACTERS

REVEREND PARRIS

BETTY PARRIS

TITUBA

ABIGAIL WILLIAMS

SUSANNA WALCOTT

MRS. ANN PUTNAM

THOMAS PUTNAM

MERCY LEWIS

MARY WARREN

JOHN PROCTOR

REBECCA NURSE

GILES COREY

REVEREND JOHN HALE

ELIZABETH PROCTOR

FRANCIS NURSE

EZEKIEL CHEEVER

MARSHAL HERRICK

JUDGE HATHORNE

DEPUTY GOVERNOR
DANFORTH

SARAH GOOD

HOPKINS

▲ In this engraving, two women are being accused of witchcraft. How does the style of this work differ from that of Matteson's painting on page 57?

Act One

Occasionally throughout Act One, Miller interrupts his play to provide background information about the characters and events. To indicate that these sections would not be part of a performance, they have been identified by the following symbol: ◆

(An overture)

(A small upper bedroom in the home of REVEREND SAMUEL PARRIS, *Salem, Massachusetts, in the spring of the year 1692.*

There is a narrow window at the left. Through its leaded panes the morning sunlight streams. A candle still burns near the bed, which is at the right. A chest, a chair, and a small table are the other furnishings. At the back a door opens on the landing of the stairway to the ground floor. The room gives off an air of clean spareness. The roof rafters are exposed, and the wood colors are raw and unmellowed.

As the curtain rises, REVEREND PARRIS *is discovered kneeling beside the bed, evidently in prayer. His daughter,* BETTY PARRIS, *aged ten, is lying on the bed, inert.)*

◆ At the time of these events Parris was in his middle forties. In history he cut a villainous[1] path, and there is very little good to be said for him. He believed he was being persecuted[2] wherever he went, despite his best efforts to win people and God to his side. In meeting, he felt insulted if someone rose to shut the door without first asking his permission. He was a widower with no interest in children, or talent with them. He regarded them as young adults, and until this strange crisis he, like the rest of Salem, never conceived that the children were anything but thankful for being permitted to walk straight, eyes slightly lowered, arms at the sides, and mouths shut until bidden to speak.

His house stood in the "town"—but we today would hardly call it a village. The meeting house was nearby, and from this point outward—toward the bay or inland—there were a few small-windowed, dark houses snuggling against the raw Massachusetts winter. Salem had been established hardly forty years before. To the European world the whole province was a barbaric frontier inhabited by a sect of fanatics who, nevertheless, were shipping out products of slowly increasing quantity and value.

No one can really know what their lives were like. They had no novelists—and would not have permitted anyone to read a novel if one were handy. Their creed forbade anything resembling a theater or "vain enjoyment." They did not celebrate Christmas, and a holiday from work meant only that they must concentrate even more upon prayer.

Which is not to say that nothing broke into this strict and somber way of life. When a new farmhouse was built, friends assembled to "raise the roof," and there would be special foods cooked and probably some potent cider passed around. There was a good supply of ne'er-do-wells in Salem, who dallied at the shovelboard[3] in Bridget Bishop's tavern. Probably more than the creed, hard work kept the morals of the

---

1. **villainous** (vil′ə nəs), *adj.* very wicked; depraved.
2. **persecuted** (pèr′sə kyüt əd), *adj.* oppressed because of one's principles or beliefs.
3. **shovelboard,** *n.* a table on which players push coins from the edge into marked scoring areas.

place from spoiling, for the people were forced to fight the land like heroes for every grain of corn, and no man had very much time for fooling around.

That there were some jokers, however, is indicated by the practice of appointing a two-man patrol whose duty was to "walk forth in the time of God's worship to take notice of such as either lye about the meeting house, without attending to the word and ordinances, or that lye at home or in the fields without giving good account thereof, and to take the names of such persons, and to present them to the magistrates, whereby they may be accordingly proceeded against." This predilection[4] for minding other people's business was time-honored among the people of Salem, and it undoubtedly created many of the suspicions which were to feed the coming madness. It was also, in my opinion, one of the things that a John Proctor would rebel against, for the time of the armed camp had almost passed, and since the country was reasonably—although not wholly—safe, the old disciplines were beginning to rankle. But, as in all such matters, the issue was not clear-cut, for danger was still a possibility, and in unity still lay the best promise of safety.

The edge of the wilderness was close by. The American continent stretched endlessly west, and it was full of mystery for them. It stood, dark and threatening, over their shoulders night and day, for out of it Indian tribes marauded from time to time, and Reverend Parris had parishioners who had lost relatives to these heathen.

The parochial[5] snobbery of these people was partly responsible for their failure to convert the Indians. Probably they also preferred to take land from heathens rather than from fellow Christians. At any rate, very few Indians were converted, and the Salem folk believed that the virgin forest was the Devil's last preserve, his home base and the citadel[6] of his final stand. To the best of their knowledge the American forest was the last place on earth that was not paying homage to God.

For these reasons, among others, they carried about an air of innate resistance, even of persecution. Their fathers had, of course, been persecuted in England. So now they and their church found it necessary to deny any other sect its freedom, lest their New Jerusalem be defiled and corrupted by wrong ways and deceitful ideas.

They believed, in short, that they held in their steady hands the candle that would light the world. We have inherited this belief, and it has helped and hurt us. It helped them with the discipline it gave them. They were a dedicated folk, by and large, and they had to be to survive the life they had chosen or been born into in this country.

The proof of their belief's value to them may be taken from the opposite character of the first Jamestown settlement, farther south, in Virginia. The Englishmen who landed there were motivated mainly by a hunt for profit. They had thought to pick off the wealth of the new country and then return rich to England. They were a band of individualists, and a much more ingratiating group than the Massachusetts men. But Virginia destroyed them. Massachusetts tried to kill off the Puritans, but they combined; they set up a communal society which, in the beginning, was little more than an armed camp with an autocratic and very devoted leadership. It was, however, an autocracy by consent, for they were united from top to bottom by a commonly held ideology whose perpetuation was the reason and justification for all their sufferings. So their self-denial, their purposefulness, their suspicion of all vain pursuits, their hardhanded justice, were altogether perfect instruments for the conquest of this space so antagonistic to man.

But the people of Salem in 1692 were not quite the dedicated folk that arrived on the

---

4. **predilection** (pred′ə lek′shən), *n.* a liking; preference.
5. **parochial** (pə rō′kē əl), *adj.* narrowly restricted.
6. **citadel** (sit′ə dəl), *n.* a strongly fortified place; stronghold.

Mayflower. A vast differentiation had taken place, and in their own time a revolution had unseated the royal government and substituted a junta which was at this moment in power. The times, to their eyes, must have been out of joint, and to the common folk must have seemed as insoluble and complicated as do ours today. It is not hard to see how easily many could have been led to believe that the time of confusion had been brought upon them by deep and darkling forces. No hint of such speculation appears on the court record, but social disorder in any age breeds such mystical suspicions, and when, as in Salem, wonders are brought forth from below the social surface, it is too much to expect people to hold back very long from laying on the victims with all the force of their frustration.

The Salem tragedy, which is about to begin in these pages, developed from a paradox.[7] It is a paradox in whose grip we still live, and there is no prospect yet that we will discover its resolution. Simply, it was this: for good purposes, even high purposes, the people of Salem developed a theocracy,[8] a combine of state and religious power whose function was to keep the community together, and to prevent any kind of disunity that might open it to destruction by material or ideological enemies. It was forged for a necessary purpose and accomplished that purpose. But all organization is and must be grounded on the idea of exclusion and prohibition, just as two objects cannot occupy the same space. Evidently the time came in New England when the repressions of order were heavier than seemed warranted by the dangers against which the order was organized. The witch-hunt was a perverse manifestation of the panic which set in among all classes when the balance began to turn toward greater individual freedom.

When one rises above the individual villainy displayed, one can only pity them all, just as we shall be pitied someday. It is still impossible for man to organize his social life without

repressions, and the balance has yet to be struck between order and freedom.

The witch-hunt was not, however, a mere repression. It was also, and as importantly, a long overdue opportunity for everyone so inclined to express publicly his guilt and sins, under the cover of accusations against the victims. It suddenly became possible—and patriotic and holy—for a man to say that Martha Corey had come into his bedroom at night, and that, while his wife was sleeping at his side, Martha laid herself down on his chest and "nearly suffocated him." Of course it was her spirit only, but his satisfaction at confessing himself was no lighter than if it had been Martha herself. One could not ordinarily speak such things in public.

Long-held hatreds of neighbors could now be openly expressed, and vengeance[9] taken, despite the Bible's charitable injunctions. Land-lust which had been expressed before by constant bickering over boundaries and deeds, could now be elevated to the arena of morality; one could cry witch against one's neighbor and feel perfectly justified in the bargain. Old scores could be settled on a plane of heavenly combat between Lucifer and the Lord; suspicions and the envy of the miserable toward the happy could and did burst out in the general revenge. ◆

(REVEREND PARRIS *is praying now, and, though we cannot hear his words, a sense of his confusion hangs about him. He mumbles, then seems about to weep; then he weeps, then prays again; but his daughter does not stir on the bed.*
The door opens, and his Negro slave enters. TITUBA *is in her forties.* PARRIS *brought her with him from Barbados, where he spent some years as a merchant before entering the ministry. She enters as one does who*

---

7. **paradox** (par′ə doks), *n.* person or thing that seems to be full of contradictions.
8. **theocracy** (thē ok′rə sē), *n.* government in which God is recognized as the supreme civil ruler.
9. vengeance (ven′jəns), *n.* revenge.

can no longer bear to be barred from the sight of her beloved, but she is also very frightened because her slave sense has warned her that, as always, trouble in this house eventually lands on her back.)

TITUBA *(already taking a step backward).* My Betty be hearty soon?

PARRIS. Out of here!

TITUBA *(backing to the door).* My Betty not goin' die . . .

PARRIS *(scrambling to his feet in a fury).* Out of my sight! *(She is gone.)* Out of my—*(He is overcome with sobs. He clamps his teeth against them and closes the door and leans against it, exhausted.)* Oh, my God! God help me! *(Quaking with fear, mumbling to himself through his sobs, he goes to the bed and gently takes* BETTY'S *hand.)* Betty. Child. Dear child. Will you wake, will you open up your eyes! Betty, little one . . .

(He is bending to kneel again when his niece, ABIGAIL WILLIAMS, *seventeen, enters—a strikingly beautiful girl, an orphan, with an endless capacity for* dissembling.[10] *Now she is all worry and apprehension and propriety.)*

ABIGAIL. Uncle? *(He looks to her.)* Susanna Walcott's here from Doctor Griggs.

PARRIS. Oh? Let her come, let her come.

ABIGAIL *(leaning out the door to call to* SUSANNA, *who is down the hall a few steps).* Come in, Susanna.

*(*SUSANNA WALCOTT, *a little younger than* ABIGAIL, *a nervous, hurried girl, enters.)*

PARRIS *(eagerly).* What does the doctor say, child?

SUSANNA *(craning around* PARRIS *to get a look at* BETTY*).* He bid me come and tell you, reverend sir, that he cannot discover no medicine for it in his books.

PARRIS. Then he must search on.

SUSANNA. Aye, sir, he have been searchin' his books since he left you, sir. But he bid me tell you, that you might look to unnatural things for the cause of it.

PARRIS *(his eyes going wide).* No—no. There be no unnatural cause here. Tell him I have sent for Reverend Hale of Beverly, and Mr. Hale will surely confirm that. Let him look to medicine and put out all thought of unnatural causes here. There be none.

SUSANNA. Aye, sir. He bid me tell you. *(She turns to go.)*

ABIGAIL. Speak nothin' of it in the village, Susanna.

PARRIS. Go directly home and speak nothing of unnatural causes.

SUSANNA. Aye, sir. I pray for her. *(She goes out.)*

ABIGAIL. Uncle, the rumor of witchcraft is all about; I think you'd best go down and deny it yourself. The parlor's packed with people, sir. I'll sit with her.

PARRIS *(pressed, turns on her).* And what shall I say to them? That my daughter and my niece I discovered dancing like heathen in the forest?

ABIGAIL. Uncle, we did dance; let you tell them I confessed it—and I'll be whipped if I must be. But they're speakin' of witchcraft. Betty's not witched.

PARRIS. Abigail, I cannot go before the congregation when I know you have not opened with me. What did you do with her in the forest?

ABIGAIL. We did dance, uncle, and when you leaped out of the bush so suddenly, Betty was frightened and then she fainted. And there's the whole of it.

PARRIS. Child. Sit you down.

ABIGAIL *(quavering, as she sits).* I would never hurt Betty. I love her dearly.

PARRIS. Now look you, child, your punishment will come in its time. But if you trafficked with spirits in the forest I must know it now, for surely my enemies will, and they will ruin me with it.

ABIGAIL. But we never conjured[11] spirits.

PARRIS. Then why can she not move herself since midnight? This child is desperate! *(*ABIGAIL *lowers her eyes.)* It must come out—my enemies will bring it out. Let me know what you done there. Abigail, do you understand that I have many enemies?

ABIGAIL. I have heard of it, uncle.

---

10. **dissemble** (di sem′bəl), *v.* hide (one's real feelings, thoughts, plans, etc.); conceal one's motives.

11. **conjure** (kon′jər), *v.* summon a devil, spirit, etc.

▲ The photographs accompanying this play are from the National Actors Theatre production of *The Crucible* starring Martin Sheen, Michael York, Maryann Plunkett, Fritz Weaver, Madeleine Potter, and Martha Scott.

PARRIS. There is a faction that is sworn to drive me from my pulpit. Do you understand that?

ABIGAIL. I think so, sir.

PARRIS. Now then, in the midst of such disruption, my own household is discovered to be the very center of some obscene practice. Abominations are done in the forest—

ABIGAIL. It were sport,[12] uncle!

PARRIS (*pointing at* BETTY). You call this sport? (*She lowers her eyes. He pleads.*) Abigail, if you know something that may help the doctor, for God's sake tell it to me. (*She is silent.*) I saw Tituba waving her arms over the fire when I came on you. Why was she doing that? And

---

12. **sport** (spōrt), *n.* playful joking; fun.

I heard a screeching and gibberish coming from her mouth. She were swaying like a dumb beast over that fire!

ABIGAIL. She always sings her Barbados songs, and we dance.

PARRIS. I cannot blink what I saw, Abigail, for my enemies will not blink it. I saw a dress lying on the grass.

ABIGAIL *(innocently).* A dress?

PARRIS *(it is very hard to say).* Aye, a dress. And I thought I saw—someone naked running through the trees!

ABIGAIL *(in terror).* No one was naked! You mistake yourself, uncle!

PARRIS *(with anger).* I saw it! *(He moves from her. Then, resolved.)* Now tell me true, Abigail. And I pray you feel the weight of truth upon you, for now my ministry's at stake, my ministry and perhaps your cousin's life. Whatever abomination you have done, give me all of it now, for I dare not to be taken unaware when I go before them down there.

ABIGAIL. There is nothin' more. I swear it, uncle.

PARRIS *(studies her, then nods, half convinced).* Abigail, I have fought here three long years to bend these stiff-necked people to me, and now, just now when some good respect is rising for me in the parish, you compromise my very character. I have given you a home, child, I have put clothes upon your back—now give me upright answer. Your name in the town—it is entirely white, is it not?

ABIGAIL *(with an edge of resentment).* Why, I am sure it is, sir. There be no blush about my name.

PARRIS *(to the point).* Abigail, is there any other cause than you have told me, for your being discharged from Goody Proctor's service? I have heard it said, and I tell you as I heard it, that she comes so rarely to the church this year for she will not sit so close to something soiled. What signified this remark?

ABIGAIL. She hates me, uncle, she must, for I would not be her slave. It's a bitter woman, a lying, cold, sniveling[13] woman, and I will not work for such a woman!

PARRIS. She may be. And yet it has troubled me that you are now seven month out of their house, and in all this time no other family has ever called for your service.

ABIGAIL. They want slaves, not such as I. Let them send to Barbados for that. I will not black my face for any of them! *(With ill-concealed resentment at him.)* Do you begrudge[14] my bed, uncle?

PARRIS. No—no.

ABIGAIL *(in a temper).* My name is good in the village! I will not have it said my name is soiled! Goody Proctor is a gossiping liar!

(Enter MRS. ANN PUTNAM. She is a twisted soul of forty-five, a death-ridden woman, haunted by dreams.)

PARRIS *(as soon as the door begins to open).* No—no, I cannot have anyone. *(He sees her, and a certain deference springs into him, although his worry remains.)* Why, Goody Putnam, come in.

MRS. PUTNAM *(full of breath, shiny-eyed).* It is a marvel. It is surely a stroke of hell upon you.

PARRIS. No, Goody Putnam, it is—

MRS. PUTNAM *(glancing at BETTY).* How high did she fly, how high?

PARRIS. No, no, she never flew—

MRS. PUTNAM *(very pleased with it).* Why, it's sure she did. Mr. Collins saw her goin' over Ingersoll's barn, and come down light as bird, he says!

PARRIS. Now, look you, Goody Putnam, she never—*(Enter THOMAS PUTNAM, a well-to-do, hard-handed landowner, near fifty.)* Oh, good morning, Mr. Putnam.

PUTNAM. It is a providence[15] the thing is out now! It is a providence. *(He goes directly to the bed.)*

PARRIS. What's out, sir, what's—?

(MRS. PUTNAM goes to the bed.)

PUTNAM *(looking down at BETTY).* Why, *her* eyes is closed! Look you, Ann.

MRS. PUTNAM. Why, that's strange. *(To PARRIS).* Ours is open.

---

13. **sniveling** (sniv′əl ing), *adj.* pretending grief; whining.
14. **begrudge** (bi gruj′), *v.* be reluctant to give or allow (something).
15. **providence** (prov′ə dəns), *n.* instance of God's help.

PARRIS *(shocked)*. Your Ruth is sick?

MRS. PUTNAM *(with vicious certainty)*. I'd not call it sick; the Devil's touch is heavier than sick. It's death, y'know, it's death drivin' into them, forked and hoofed.

PARRIS. Oh, pray not! Why, how does Ruth ail?

MRS. PUTNAM. She ails as she must—she never waked this morning, but her eyes open and she walks, and hears naught, sees naught, and cannot eat. Her soul is taken, surely.

(PARRIS is struck.)

PUTNAM *(as though for further details)*. They say you've sent for Reverend Hale of Beverly?

PARRIS *(with dwindling conviction now)*. A precaution only. He has much experience in all demonic arts, and I—

MRS. PUTNAM. He has indeed; and found a witch in Beverly last year, and let you remember that.

PARRIS. Now, Goody Ann, they only thought that were a witch, and I am certain there be no element of witchcraft here.

PUTNAM. No witchcraft! Now look you, Mr. Parris—

PARRIS. Thomas, Thomas, I pray you, leap not to witchcraft. I know that you—you least of all, Thomas, would ever wish so disastrous a charge laid upon me. We cannot leap to witchcraft. They will howl me out of Salem for such corruption in my house.

◆ A word about Thomas Putnam. He was a man with many grievances, at least one of which appears justified. Some time before, his wife's brother-in-law, James Bayley, had been turned down as minister of Salem. Bayley had all the qualifications, and a two-thirds vote into the bargain, but a faction stopped his acceptance, for reasons that are not clear.

Thomas Putnam was the eldest son of the richest man in the village. He had fought the Indians at Narragansett, and was deeply interested in parish affairs. He undoubtedly felt it poor payment that the village should so blatantly disregard his candidate for one of its more important offices, especially since he regarded himself as the intellectual superior of most of the people around him.

His vindictive nature was demonstrated long before the witchcraft began. Another former Salem minister, George Burroughs, had had to borrow money to pay for his wife's funeral, and, since the parish was remiss in his salary, he was soon bankrupt. Thomas and his brother John had Burroughs jailed for debts the man did not owe. The incident is important only in that Burroughs succeeded in becoming minister where Bayley, Thomas Putnam's brother-in-law, had been rejected; the motif of resentment is clear here. Thomas Putnam felt that his own name and the honor of his family had been smirched by the village, and he meant to right matters however he could.

Another reason to believe him a deeply embittered man was his attempt to break his father's will, which left a disproportionate amount to a stepbrother. As with every other public cause in which he tried to force his way, he failed in this.

So it is not surprising to find that so many accusations against people are in the handwriting of Thomas Putnam, or that his name is so often found as a witness corroborating[16] the supernatural testimony, or that his daughter led the crying-out at the most opportune junctures of the trials, especially when—but we'll speak of that when we come to it. ◆

PUTNAM *(at the moment he is intent upon getting* PARRIS, *for whom he has only contempt, to move toward the abyss)*. Mr. Parris, I have taken your part in all contention here, and I would continue; but I cannot if you hold back in this. There are hurtful, vengeful spirits layin' hands on these children.

PARRIS. But, Thomas, you cannot—

PUTNAM. Ann! Tell Mr. Parris what you have done.

---

16. **corroborate** (kə robʹə rāt'), *v.* confirm; support.

MRS. PUTNAM. Reverend Parris, I have laid seven babies unbaptized in the earth. Believe me, sir, you never saw more hearty babies born. And yet, each would wither in my arms the very night of their birth. I have spoke nothin', but my heart has clamored intimations. And now, this year, my Ruth, my only— I see her turning strange. A secret child she has become this year, and shrivels like a sucking mouth were pullin' on her life too. And so I thought to send her to your Tituba—

PARRIS. To Tituba! What may Tituba—?

MRS. PUTNAM. Tituba knows how to speak to the dead, Mr. Parris.

PARRIS. Goody Ann, it is a formidable[17] sin to conjure up the dead!

MRS. PUTNAM. I take it on my soul, but who else may surely tell us what person murdered my babies?

PARRIS (*horrified*). Woman!

MRS. PUTNAM. They were murdered, Mr. Parris! And mark this proof! Mark it! Last night my Ruth were ever so close to their little spirits; I know it, sir. For how else is she struck dumb now except some power of darkness would stop her mouth? It is a marvelous sign, Mr. Parris!

PUTNAM. Don't you understand it, sir? There is a murdering witch among us, bound to keep herself in the dark. (PARRIS *turns to* BETTY, *a frantic terror rising in him*). Let your enemies make of it what they will, you cannot blink it more.

PARRIS (*to* ABIGAIL). Then you were conjuring spirits last night.

ABIGAIL (*whispering*). Not I, sir—Tituba and Ruth.

PARRIS (*turns now, with new fear, and goes to* BETTY, *looks down at her, and then, gazing off*). Oh, Abigail, what proper payment for my charity! Now I am undone.

PUTNAM. You are not undone! Let you take hold here. Wait for no one to charge you— declare it yourself. You have discovered witchcraft—

PARRIS. In my house? In my house, Thomas?

They will topple me with this! They will make of it a—

(*Enter* MERCY LEWIS, *the Putnams' servant, a fat, sly, merciless girl of eighteen.*)

MERCY. Your pardons. I only thought to see how Betty is.

PUTNAM. Why aren't you home? Who's with Ruth?

MERCY. Her grandma come. She's improved a little, I think—she give a powerful sneeze before.

MRS. PUTNAM. Ah, there's a sign of life!

MERCY. I'd fear no more, Goody Putnam. It were a grand sneeze; another like it will shake her wits together, I'm sure. (*She goes to the bed to look.*)

PARRIS. Will you leave me now, Thomas? I would pray a while alone.

ABIGAIL. Uncle, you've prayed since midnight. Why do you not go down and—

PARRIS. No—no. (*To* PUTNAM). I have no answer for that crowd. I'll wait till Mr. Hale arrives. (*To get* MRS. PUTNAM *to leave*). If you will, Goody Ann . . .

PUTNAM. Now look you, sir. Let you strike out against the Devil, and the village will bless you for it! Come down, speak to them—pray with them. They're thirsting for your word, Mister! Surely you'll pray with them.

PARRIS (*swayed*). I'll lead them in a psalm, but let you say nothing of witchcraft yet. I will not discuss it. The cause is yet unknown. I have had enough contention[18] since I came; I want no more.

MRS. PUTNAM. Mercy, you go home to Ruth, d'y'hear?

MERCY. Aye, mum.

(MRS. PUTNAM *goes out.*)

PARRIS (*to* ABIGAIL). If she starts for the window, cry for me at once.

ABIGAIL. I will, uncle.

PARRIS (*to* PUTNAM). There is a terrible power in her arms today. (*He goes out with* PUTNAM.)

---

17. **formidable** (fôr′mə də bəl), *adj.* hard to overcome.
18. **contention** (kən ten′shən), *n.* struggle; competition.

ABIGAIL (*with hushed trepidation*). How is Ruth sick?

MERCY. It's weirdish, I know not—she seems to walk like a dead one since last night.

ABIGAIL (*turns at once and goes to* BETTY, *and now, with fear in her voice*). Betty? (BETTY *doesn't move. She shakes her.*) Now stop this! Betty! Sit up now!

(BETTY *doesn't stir.* MERCY *comes over.*)

MERCY. Have you tried beatin' her? I gave Ruth a good one and it waked her for a minute. Here, let me have her.

ABIGAIL (*holding* MERCY *back*). No, he'll be comin' up. Listen, now; if they be questioning us, tell them we danced—I told him as much already.

MERCY. Aye. And what more?

ABIGAIL. He knows Tituba conjured Ruth's sisters to come out of the grave.

MERCY. And what more?

ABIGAIL. He saw you naked.

MERCY (*clapping her hands together with a frightened laugh*). Oh, Jesus!

(*Enter* MARY WARREN, *breathless. She is seventeen, a subservient, naive, lonely girl.*)

MARY WARREN. What'll we do? The village is out! I just come from the farm; the whole country's talkin' witchcraft! They'll be callin' us witches, Abby!

MERCY (*pointing and looking at* MARY WARREN). She means to tell, I know it.

MARY WARREN. Abby, we've got to tell. Witchery's a hangin' error, a hangin' like they done in Boston two year ago! We must tell the truth, Abby! You'll only be whipped for dancin', and the other things!

ABIGAIL. Oh, *we'll* be whipped!

MARY WARREN. I never done none of it, Abby. I only looked!

MERCY (*moving menacingly toward* MARY). Oh, you're a great one for lookin', aren't you, Mary Warren? What a grand peeping courage you have!

(BETTY, *on the bed, whimpers.* ABIGAIL *turns to her at once.*)

ABIGAIL. Betty? (*She goes to* BETTY.) Now, Betty, dear, wake up now. It's Abigail. (*She sits* BETTY up and furiously shakes her.*) I'll beat you, Betty! (BETTY *whimpers.*) My, you seem improving. I talked to your papa and I told him everything. So there's nothing to—

BETTY (*darts off the bed, frightened of* ABIGAIL, *and flattens herself against the wall*). I want my mama!

ABIGAIL (*with alarm, as she cautiously approaches* BETTY). What ails you, Betty? Your mama's dead and buried.

BETTY. I'll fly to Mama. Let me fly! (*She raises her arms as though to fly, and streaks for the window, gets one leg out.*)

ABIGAIL (*pulling her away from the window*). I told him everything, he knows now, he knows everything we—

BETTY. You drank blood, Abby! You didn't tell him that!

ABIGAIL. Betty, you never say that again! You will never—

BETTY. You did, you did! You drank a charm to kill John Proctor's wife! You drank a charm to kill Goody Proctor!

ABIGAIL (*smashes her across the face*). Shut it! Now shut it!

BETTY (*collapsing on the bed*). Mama, Mama! (*She dissolves into sobs.*)

ABIGAIL. Now look you. All of you. We danced. And Tituba conjured Ruth Putnam's dead sisters. And that is all. And mark this. Let either of you breathe a word, or the edge of a word, about the other things, and I will come to you in the black of some terrible night and I will bring a pointy reckoning that will shudder you. And you know I can do it; I saw Indians smash my dear parents' heads on the pillow next to mine, and I have seen some reddish work done at night, and I can make you wish you had never seen the sun go down! (*She goes to* BETTY *and roughly sits her up.*) Now, you—sit up and stop this!

(*But* BETTY *collapses in her hands and lies inert*[19] *on the bed.*)

---

19. **inert** (in ėrt′), *adj.* having no power to move or act.

MARY WARREN (*with hysterical fright*). What's got her? (ABIGAIL *stares in fright at* BETTY.) Abby, she's going to die! It's a sin to conjure, and we—

ABIGAIL (*starting for* MARY). I say shut it, Mary Warren!

(*Enter* JOHN PROCTOR. *On seeing him,* MARY WARREN *leaps in fright.*)

◆ Proctor was a farmer in his middle thirties. He need not have been a partisan of any faction in the town, but there is evidence to suggest that he had a sharp and biting way with hypocrites.[20] He was the kind of man—powerful of body, even-tempered, and not easily led—who cannot refuse support to partisans without drawing their deepest resentment. In Proctor's presence a fool felt his foolishness instantly—and a Proctor is always marked for calumny[21] therefore.

But as we shall see, the steady manner he displays does not spring from an untroubled soul. He is a sinner, a sinner not only against the moral fashion of the time, but against his own vision of decent conduct. These people had no ritual for the washing away of sin. It is another trait we inherited from them, and it has helped to discipline us as well as to breed hypocrisy among us. Proctor, respected and even feared in Salem, has come to regard himself as a kind of fraud. But no hint of this has yet appeared on the surface, and as he enters from the crowded parlor below it is a man in his prime we see, with a quiet confidence and an unexpressed, hidden force. Mary Warren, his servant, can barely speak for embarrassment and fear. ◆

MARY WARREN. Oh! I'm just going home, Mr. Proctor.

PROCTOR. Be you foolish, Mary Warren? Be you deaf? I forbid you leave the house, did I not? Why shall I pay you? I am looking for you more often than my cows!

MARY WARREN. I only come to see the great doings in the world.

PROCTOR. I'll show you a great doin' on your arse one of these days. Now you get home; my wife is waitin' with your work! (*Trying to retain a shred of dignity, she goes slowly out.*)

MERCY LEWIS (*both afraid of him and strangely titillated*). I'd best be off. I have my Ruth to watch. Good morning, Mr. Proctor.

(MERCY *sidles out. Since* PROCTOR'S *entrance,* ABIGAIL *has stood as though on tiptoe, absorbing his presence, wide-eyed. He glances at her, then goes to* BETTY *on the bed.*)

ABIGAIL. Gah! I'd almost forgot how strong you are, John Proctor!

PROCTOR (*looking at* ABIGAIL *now, the faintest suggestion of a knowing smile on his face*). What's this mischief here?

ABIGAIL (*with a nervous laugh*). Oh, she's only gone silly somehow.

PROCTOR. The road past my house is a pilgrimage to Salem all morning. The town's mumbling witchcraft.

ABIGAIL. Oh, posh! (*Winningly she comes a little closer, with a confidential, wicked air.*) We were dancin' in the woods last night, and my uncle leaped in on us. She took fright, is all.

PROCTOR (*his smile widening*). Ah, you're wicked yet, aren't y'! (*A trill of expectant laughter escapes her, and she dares come closer, feverishly looking into his eyes.*) You'll be clapped in the stocks[22] before you're twenty.

(*He takes a step to go, and she springs into his path.*)

ABIGAIL. Give me a word, John. A soft word. (*Her concentrated desire destroys his smile.*)

PROCTOR. No, no, Abby. That's done with.

ABIGAIL (*tauntingly*). You come five mile to see a silly girl fly? I know you better.

PROCTOR (*setting her firmly out of his path*). I come to see what mischief your uncle's brewin' now. (*With final emphasis*). Put it out of mind, Abby.

---

20. **hypocrite** (hip′ə krit), *n.* person who is not sincere.
21. **calumny** (kal′əm nē), *n.* a false statement made to injure someone's reputation; slander.
22. **stocks** (stoks), *n.* heavy wooden frame with holes to put a person's feet and sometimes hands through.

ABIGAIL (*grasping his hand before he can release her*). John—I am waitin' for you every night.

PROCTOR. Abby, I never give you hope to wait for me.

ABIGAIL (*now beginning to anger—she can't believe it*). I have something better than hope, I think!

PROCTOR. Abby, you'll put it out of mind. I'll not be comin' for you more.

ABIGAIL. You're surely sportin' with me.

PROCTOR. You know me better.

ABIGAIL. I know how you clutched my back behind your house and sweated like a stallion whenever I come near! Or did I dream that? It's she put me out, you cannot pretend it were you! I saw your face when she put me out, and you loved me then and you do now!

PROCTOR. Abby, that's a wild thing to say—

ABIGAIL. A wild thing may say wild things. But not so wild, I think. I have seen you since she put me out; I have seen you nights.

PROCTOR. I have hardly stepped off my farm this sevenmonth.

ABIGAIL. I have a sense for heat, John, and yours has drawn me to my window, and I have seen you looking up, burning in your loneliness. Do you tell me you've never looked up at my window?

PROCTOR. I may have looked up.

ABIGAIL (*now softening*). And you must. You are no wintry man. I know you, John. I *know* you. (*She is weeping.*) I cannot sleep for dreamin'; I cannot dream but I wake and walk about the house as though I'd find you comin' through some door. (*She clutches him desperately.*)

PROCTOR (*gently pressing her from him, with great sympathy but firmly*). Child—

ABIGAIL (*with a flash of anger*). How do you call me child!

PROCTOR. Abby, I may think of you softly from time to time. But I will cut off my hand before I'll ever reach for you again. Wipe it out of mind. We never touched, Abby.

ABIGAIL. Aye, but we did.

PROCTOR. Aye, but we did not.

ABIGAIL (*with a bitter anger*). Oh, I marvel how such a strong man may let such a sickly wife be—

PROCTOR (*angered—at himself as well*). You'll speak nothin' of Elizabeth!

ABIGAIL. She is blackening my name in the village! She is telling lies about me! She is a cold, sniveling woman, and you bend to her! Let her turn you like a—

PROCTOR (*shaking her*). Do you look for whippin'?
(*A psalm is heard being sung below.*)

ABIGAIL (*in tears*). I look for John Proctor that took me from my sleep and put knowledge in my heart! I never knew what pretense Salem was, I never knew the lying lessons I was taught by all these Christian women and their covenanted men! And now you bid me tear the light out of my eyes? I will not, I cannot! You loved me, John Proctor, and whatever sin it is, you love me yet! (*He turns abruptly to go out. She rushes to him.*) John, pity me, pity me!

(*The words "going up to Jesus" are heard in the psalm, and* BETTY *claps her ears suddenly and whines loudly.*)

ABIGAIL. Betty? (*She hurries to* BETTY, *who is now sitting up and screaming.* PROCTOR *goes to* BETTY *as* ABIGAIL *is trying to pull her hands down, calling "Betty!"*)

PROCTOR (*growing unnerved*). What's she doing? Girl, what ails you? Stop that wailing!

(*The singing has stopped in the midst of this, and now* PARRIS *rushes in.*)

PARRIS. What happened? What are you doing to her? Betty! (*He rushes to the bed, crying, "Betty, Betty!"* MRS. PUTNAM *enters, feverish with curiosity, and with her* THOMAS PUTNAM *and* MERCY LEWIS. PARRIS, *at the bed, keeps lightly slapping* BETTY'S *face, while she moans and tries to get up.*)

ABIGAIL. She heard you singin' and suddenly she's up and screamin'.

MRS. PUTNAM. The psalm! The psalm! She cannot bear to hear the Lord's name!

PARRIS. No, God forbid. Mercy, run to the doctor!

Tell him what's happened here! (MERCY LEWIS *rushes out.*)

MRS. PUTNAM. Mark it for a sign, mark it!

(REBECCA NURSE, *seventy-two, enters. She is white-haired, leaning upon her walking-stick.*)

PUTNAM (*pointing at the whimpering* BETTY). That is a notorious sign of witchcraft afoot, Goody Nurse, a prodigious sign!

MRS. PUTNAM. My mother told me that! When they cannot bear to hear the name of—

PARRIS (*trembling*). Rebecca, Rebecca, go to her, we're lost. She suddenly cannot bear to hear the Lord's—

(GILES COREY, *eighty-three, enters. He is knotted with muscle, canny, inquisitive,*[23] *and still powerful.*)

REBECCA. There is hard sickness here, Giles Corey, so please to keep the quiet.

GILES. I've not said a word. No one here can testify I've said a word. Is she going to fly again? I hear she flies.

PUTNAM. Man, be quiet now!

(*Everything is quiet.* REBECCA *walks across the room to the bed. Gentleness exudes from her.* BETTY *is quietly whimpering, eyes shut.* REBECCA *simply stands over the child, who gradually quiets.*)

◆ And while they are so absorbed, we may put a word in for Rebecca. Rebecca was the wife of Francis Nurse, who, from all accounts, was one of those men for whom both sides of the argument had to have respect. He was called upon to arbitrate[24] disputes as though he were an unofficial judge, and Rebecca also enjoyed the high opinion most people had for him. By the time of the delusion, they had three hundred acres, and their children were settled in separate homesteads within the same estate. However, Francis had originally rented the land, and one theory has it that, as he gradually paid for it and raised his social status, there were those who resented his rise.

Another suggestion to explain the systematic campaign against Rebecca, and inferentially against Francis, is the land war he fought with his neighbors, one of whom was a Putnam. This squabble grew to the proportions of a battle in the woods between partisans of both sides, and it is said to have lasted for two days. As for Rebecca herself, the general opinion of her character was so high that to explain how anyone dared cry her out for a witch—and more, how adults could bring themselves to lay hands on her—we must look to the fields and boundaries of that time.

As we have seen, Thomas Putnam's man for the Salem ministry was Bayley. The Nurse clan had been in the faction that prevented Bayley's taking office. In addition, certain families allied to the Nurses by blood or friendship, and whose farms were contiguous[25] with the Nurse farm or close to it, combined to break away from the Salem town authority and set up Topsfield, a new and independent entity whose existence was resented by old Salemites.

That the guiding hand behind the outcry was Putnam's is indicated by the fact that, as soon as it began, this Topsfield-Nurse faction absented themselves from church in protest and disbelief. It was Edward and Jonathan Putnam who signed the first complaint against Rebecca; and Thomas Putnam's little daughter was the one who fell into a fit at the hearing and pointed to Rebecca as her attacker. To top it all, Mrs. Putnam—who is now staring at the bewitched child on the bed—soon accused Rebecca's spirit of "tempting her to iniquity,"[26] a charge that had more truth in it than Mrs. Putnam could know. ◆

MRS. PUTNAM (*astonished*). What have you done?

(REBECCA, *in thought, now leaves the bedside and sits.*)

PARRIS (*wondrous and relieved*). What do you make of it, Rebecca?

PUTNAM (*eagerly*). Goody Nurse, you will go to my Ruth and see if you can wake her?

---

23. **inquisitive** (in kwiz′ə tiv), *adj.* curious.
24. **arbitrate** (är′bə trāt), *v.* give a decision in a debate.
25. **contiguous** (kən tig′yü əs), *adj.* adjoining.
26. **iniquity** (in ik′wə tē), *n.* wickedness; sin.

REBECCA *(sitting)*. I think she'll wake in time. Pray calm yourselves. I have eleven children, and I am twenty-six times a grandma, and I have seen them all through their silly seasons, and when it come on them they will run the Devil bowlegged keeping up with their mischief. I think she'll wake when she tires of it. A child's spirit is like a child, you can never catch it by running after it; you must stand still, and, for love, it will soon itself come back.

PROCTOR. Aye, that's the truth of it, Rebecca.

MRS. PUTNAM. This is no silly season, Rebecca. My Ruth is bewildered, Rebecca; she cannot eat.

REBECCA. Perhaps she is not hungered yet. (*To* PARRIS.) I hope you are not decided to go in search of loose spirits, Mr. Parris. I've heard promise of that outside.

PARRIS. A wide opinion's running in the parish that the Devil may be among us, and I would satisfy them that they are wrong.

PROCTOR. Then let you come out and call them wrong. Did you consult the wardens before you called this minister to look for devils?

PARRIS. He is not coming to look for devils!

PROCTOR. Then what's he coming for?

PUTNAM. There be children dyin' in the village, Mister!

PROCTOR. I seen none dyin'. This society will not be a bag to swing around your head, Mr. Putnam. (*To* PARRIS.) Did you call a meeting before you—?

PUTNAM. I am sick of meetings; cannot the man turn his head without he have a meeting?

PROCTOR. He may turn is head, but not to Hell!

REBECCA. Pray, John, be calm. (*Pause. He defers to her.*) Mr. Parris, I think you'd best send Reverend Hale back as soon as he come. This will set us all to arguin' again in the society, and we thought to have peace this year. I think we ought rely on the doctor now, and good prayer.

MRS. PUTNAM. Rebecca, the doctor's baffled!

REBECCA. If so he is, then let us go to God for the cause of it. There is prodigious danger in the seeking of loose spirits. I fear it, I fear it. Let us rather blame ourselves and—

PUTNAM. How may we blame ourselves? I am one of nine sons; the Putnam seed have peopled this province. And yet I have but one child left of eight—and now she shrivels!

REBECCA. I cannot fathom that.

MRS. PUTNAM (*with a growing edge of sarcasm*). But I must! You think it God's work you should never lose a child, nor grandchild either, and I bury all but one? There are wheels within wheels in this village, and fires within fires.

PUTNAM (*to* PARRIS). When Reverend Hale comes, you will proceed to look for signs of witchcraft here.

PROCTOR (*to* PUTNAM). You cannot command Mr. Parris. We vote by name in this society, not by acreage.

PUTNAM. I never heard you worried so on this society, Mr. Proctor. I do not think I saw you at Sabbath meeting since snow flew.

PROCTOR. I have trouble enough without I come five mile to hear him preach only hellfire and bloody damnation. Take it to heart, Mr. Parris. There are many others who stay away from church these days because you hardly ever mention God any more.

PARRIS (*now aroused*). Why, that's a drastic charge!

REBECCA. It's somewhat true; there are many that quail to bring their children—

PARRIS. I do not preach for children, Rebecca. It is not the children who are unmindful of their obligations toward this ministry.

REBECCA. Are there really those unmindful?

PARRIS. I should say the better half of Salem village—

PUTNAM. And more than that!

PARRIS. Where is my wood? My contract provides I be supplied with all my firewood. I am waiting since November for a stick, and even in November I had to show my frostbitten hands like some London beggar!

GILES. You are allowed six pound a year to buy your wood, Mr. Parris.

PARRIS. I regard that six pound as part of my salary. I am paid little enough without I spend six pound on firewood.

PROCTOR. Sixty, plus six for firewood—

PARRIS. The salary is sixty-six pound, Mr. Proctor! I am not some preaching farmer with a book under my arm; I am a graduate of Harvard College.

GILES. Aye, and well instructed in arithmetic!

PARRIS. Mr. Corey, you will look far for a man of my kind at sixty pound a year! I am not used to this poverty; I left a thrifty business in the Barbados to serve the Lord. I do not fathom it, why am I persecuted here? I cannot offer one proposition but there be a howling riot of argument. I have often wondered if the Devil be in it somewhere; I cannot understand you people otherwise.

PROCTOR. Mr. Parris, you are the first minister ever did demand the deed to this house—

PARRIS. Man! Don't a minister deserve a house to live in?

PROCTOR. To live in, yes. But to ask ownership is like you shall own the meeting house itself; the last meeting I were at you spoke so long on deeds and mortgages I thought it were an auction.

PARRIS. I want a mark of confidence, is all! I am your third preacher in seven years. I do not wish to be put out like the cat whenever some majority feels the whim. You people seem not to comprehend that a minister is the Lord's man in the parish; a minister is not to be so lightly crossed and contradicted—

PUTNAM. Aye!

PARRIS. There is either obedience or the church will burn like Hell is burning!

PROCTOR. Can you speak one minute without we land in Hell again? I am sick of Hell!

PARRIS. It is not for you to say what is good for you to hear!

PROCTOR. I may speak my heart, I think!

PARRIS (in a fury). What, are we Quakers? We are not Quakers here yet, Mr. Proctor. And you may tell that to your followers!

PROCTOR. My followers!

PARRIS (now he's out with it). There is a party in this church. I am not blind; there is a faction and a party.

PROCTOR. Against you?

PUTNAM. Against him and all authority!

PROCTOR. Why, then I must find it and join it.

(There is shock among the others.)

REBECCA. He does not mean that.

PUTNAM. He confessed it now!

PROCTOR. I mean it solemnly, Rebecca; I like not the smell of this "authority."

REBECCA. No, you cannot break charity with your minister. You are another kind, John. Clasp his hand, make your peace.

PROCTOR. I have a crop to sow and lumber to drag home. (He goes angrily to the door and turns to COREY with a smile.) What say you, Giles, let's find the party. He says there's a party.

GILES. I've changed my opinion of this man, John. Mr. Parris, I beg your pardon. I never thought you had so much iron in you.

PARRIS (surprised). Why, thank you, Giles!

GILES. It suggests to the mind what the trouble be among us all these years. (To all.) Think on it. Wherefore is everybody suing every-body else? Think on it now, it's a deep thing, and dark as a pit. I have been six time in court this year—

PROCTOR (familiarly, with warmth, although he knows he is approaching the edge of GILES' tolerance with this). Is it the Devil's fault that a man cannot say you good morning without you clap him for defamation? You're old, Giles, and you're not hearin' so well as you did.

GILES (he cannot be crossed). John Proctor, I have only last month collected four pound damages for you publicly sayin' I burned the roof off your house, and I—

PROCTOR (laughing). I never said no such thing, but I've paid you for it, so I hope I can call you deaf without charge. Now come along, Giles, and help me drag my lumber home.

PUTNAM. A moment, Mr. Proctor. What lumber is that you're draggin', if I may ask you?

PROCTOR. My lumber. From out my forest by the riverside.

PUTNAM. Why, we are surely gone wild this year. What anarchy is this? That tract is in my bounds, it's in my bounds, Mr. Proctor.

PROCTOR. In your bounds! (Indicating REBECCA). I bought that tract from Goody Nurse's husband five months ago.

PUTNAM. He had no right to sell it. It stands clear in my grandfather's will that all the land between the river and—

PROCTOR. Your grandfather had a habit of willing land that never belonged to him, if I may say it plain.

GILES. That's God's truth; he nearly willed away my north pasture but he knew I'd break his fingers before he'd set his name to it. Let's get your lumber home, John. I feel a sudden will to work coming on.

PUTNAM. You load one oak of mine and you'll fight to drag it home!

GILES. Aye, and we'll win too, Putnam—this fool and I. Come on! (He turns to PROCTOR and starts out.)

PUTNAM. I'll have my men on you, Corey! I'll clap a writ on you!

(Enter REVEREND JOHN HALE *of Beverly.)*

◆ Mr. Hale is nearing forty, a tight-skinned, eager-eyed intellectual. This is a beloved errand for him; on being called here to ascertain witchcraft he felt the pride of the specialist whose unique knowledge has at last been publicly called for. Like almost all men of learning, he spent a good deal of his time pondering the invisible world, especially since he had himself encountered a witch in his parish not long before. That woman, however, turned into a mere pest under his searching scrutiny, and the child she had allegedly been afflicting recovered her normal behavior after Hale had given her his kindness and a few days of rest in his own house. However, that experience never raised a doubt in his mind as to the reality of the underworld or the existence of Lucifer's many-faced lieutenants. And his belief is not to his discredit. Better minds than Hale's were—and still are—convinced there is a society of spirits beyond our ken. One cannot help noting that one of his lines has never yet raised a laugh in any audience that has seen this play; it is his assurance that "We cannot look to superstition in this. The Devil is precise." Evidently we are not quite certain even now whether diabolism[27] is holy and not to be scoffed at. And it is no accident that we should be so bemused.

Like Reverend Hale and the others on this stage, we conceive the Devil as a necessary part of a respectable view of cosmology. Ours is a divided empire in which certain ideas and emotions and actions are of God, and their opposites are of Lucifer. It is as impossible for most men to conceive of a morality without sin as of an earth without "sky." Since 1692 a great but superficial change has wiped out God's beard and the Devil's horns, but the world is still gripped between two diametrically opposed absolutes. The concept of unity, in which positive and negative are attributes of the same force, in which good and evil are relative, ever-changing, and always joined to the same phenomenon—such a concept is still reserved to the physical sciences and to the few who have grasped the history of ideas. When it is recalled that until the Christian era the underworld was never regarded as a hostile area, that all gods were useful and essentially friendly to man despite occasional lapses; when we see the steady and methodical inculcation into humanity of the idea of man's worthlessness—until redeemed—the necessity of the Devil may become evident as a weapon, a weapon designed and used time and time again in every age to whip men into a surrender to a particular church or church-state.

Our difficulty in believing the—for want of a better word—political inspiration of the Devil is due in great part to the fact that he is called up and damned not only by our social antagonists but by our own side, whatever it may be. The Catholic Church, through its Inquisition, is famous for cultivating Lucifer as the arch-fiend, but the Church's enemies relied no less upon the Old Boy to keep the human mind enthralled. Luther was himself accused of alliance with the Devil and had argued theology with him. I am not surprised at this, for at my own university a professor of history—a Lutheran, by the way—used to assemble his graduate students, draw the shades, and commune in the classroom with Erasmus. He was never, to my knowledge, officially scoffed at for this, the reason being that the university officials, like most of us, are the children of a history which still sucks at the Devil's teats. At this writing, only England has held back before the temptations of contemporary diabolism. In the countries of the Communist ideology, all resistance of any import is linked to the totally malign capitalist succubi, and in America any man who is not reactionary in his views is open to the charge of alliance with the Red hell. Political opposition, thereby, is given an inhumane overlay which then justifies the

---

27. **diabolism** (dī ab′ə liz′əm), *n.* having to do with the Devil or devils.

abrogation of all normally applied customs of civilized intercourse. A political policy is equated with moral right, and opposition to it with diabolical malevolence. Once such an equation is effectively made, society becomes a congerie of plots and counterplots, and the main role of government changes from that of the arbiter to that of the scourge of God.

The results of this process are no different now from what they ever were, except sometimes in the degree of cruelty inflicted, and not always even in that department. Normally the actions and deeds of a man were all that society felt comfortable in judging. The secret intent of an action was left to the ministers, priests, and rabbis to deal with. When diabolism rises, however, actions are the least important manifests of the true nature of a man. The Devil, as Reverend Hale said, is a wily one, and, until an hour before he fell, even God thought him beautiful in Heaven.

The analogy, however, seems to falter when one considers that, while there were not witches then, there are Communists and capitalists now, and in each camp there is certain proof that spies of each side are at work undermining the other. But this is a snobbish objection and not at all warranted by the facts. I have no doubt that people *were* communing with, and even worshiping, the Devil in Salem, and if the whole truth could be known in this case, as it is in others, we should discover a regular and conventionalized propitiation of the dark spirit. One certain evidence of this is the confession of Tituba, the slave of Reverend Parris, and another is the behavior of the children who were known to have indulged in sorceries with her.

There are accounts of similar *klatches* in Europe, where the daughters of the towns would assemble at night and, sometimes with fetishes, sometimes with a selected young man, give themselves to love, with some bastardly results. The Church, sharp-eyed as it must be when gods long dead are brought to life, condemned these orgies as witchcraft and interpreted them, rightly, as a resurgence of the Dionysiac forces it had crushed long before. Sex, sin, and the Devil were early linked, and so they continued to be in Salem, and are today. From all accounts there are no more puritanical mores in the world than those enforced by the Communists in Russia, where women's fashions, for instance, are as prudent and all-covering as any American Baptist would desire. The divorce laws lay a tremendous responsibility on the father for the care of his children. Even the laxity of divorce regulations in the early years of the revolution was undoubtedly a revulsion from the nineteenth-century Victorian immobility of marriage and the consequent hypocrisy that developed from it. If for no other reasons, a state so powerful, so jealous of the uniformity of its citizens, cannot long tolerate the atomization of the family. And yet, in American eyes at least, there remains the conviction that the Russian attitude toward women is lascivious. It is the Devil working again, just as he is working within the Slav who is shocked at the very idea of a woman's disrobing herself in a burlesque show. Our opposites are always robed in sexual sin, and it is from this unconscious conviction that demonology gains both its attractive sensuality and its capacity to infuriate and frighten.

Coming into Salem now, Reverend Hale conceives of himself much as a young doctor on his first call. His painfully acquired armory of symptoms, catchwords, and diagnostic procedures are now to be put to use at last. The road from Beverly is unusually busy this morning, and he has passed a hundred rumors that make him smile at the ignorance of the yeomanry in this most precise science. He feels himself allied with the best minds of Europe—kings, philosophers, scientists, and ecclesiasts of all churches. His goal is light, goodness and its preservation, and he knows the exaltation of the blessed whose intelligence, sharpened by minute examinations of enormous tracts, is finally called upon to face what may be a bloody fight with the Fiend himself. ◆

(He appears loaded down with half a dozen heavy books.)

HALE. Pray you, someone take these!

PARRIS *(delighted)*. Mr. Hale! Oh! it's good to see you again! *(Taking some books)*. My, they're heavy!

HALE *(setting down his books)*. They must be; they are weighted with authority.

PARRIS *(a little scared)*. Well, you do come prepared!

HALE. We shall need hard study if it comes to tracking down the Old Boy. *(Noticing* REBECCA*)*. You cannot be Rebecca Nurse?

REBECCA. I am, sir. Do you know me?

HALE. It's strange how I knew you, but I suppose you look as such a good soul should. We have all heard of your great charities in Beverly.

PARRIS. Do you know this gentleman? Mr. Thomas Putnam. And his good wife Ann.

HALE. Putnam! I had not expected such distinguished company, sir.

PUTNAM *(pleased)*. It does not seem to help us today, Mr. Hale. We look to you to come to our house and save our child.

HALE. Your child ails too?

MRS. PUTNAM. Her soul, her soul seems flown away. She sleeps and yet she walks . . .

PUTNAM. She cannot eat.

HALE. Cannot eat! *(Thinks on it. Then, to* PROCTOR *and* GILES COREY*)*. Do you men have afflicted children?

PARRIS. No, no, these are farmers. John Proctor—

GILES COREY. He don't believe in witches.

PROCTOR *(to* HALE*)*. I never spoke on witches one way or the other. Will you come, Giles?

GILES. No—no, John, I think not. I have some few queer questions of my own to ask this fellow.

PROCTOR. I've heard you to be a sensible man, Mr. Hale. I hope you'll leave some of it in Salem.

*(*PROCTOR *goes.* HALE *stands embarrassed for an instant.)*

PARRIS *(quickly)*. Will you look at my daughter, sir? *(Leads* HALE *to the bed.)* She has tried to leap out the window; we discovered her this morning on the highroad, waving her arms as though she'd fly.

HALE *(narrowing his eyes)*. Tries to fly.

PUTNAM. She cannot bear to hear the Lord's name, Mr. Hale; that's a sure sign of witchcraft afloat.

HALE *(holding up his hands)*. No, no. Now let me instruct you. We cannot look to superstition in this. The Devil is precise; the marks of his presence are definite as stone, and I must tell you all that I shall not proceed unless you are prepared to believe me if I should find no bruise of hell upon her.

PARRIS. It is agreed, sir—it is agreed—we will abide by your judgment.

HALE. Good then. *(He goes to the bed, looks down at* BETTY. *To* PARRIS*)*. Now, sir, what were your first warning of this strangeness?

PARRIS. Why, sir—I discovered her—*(indicating* ABIGAIL*)*—and my niece and ten or twelve of the other girls, dancing in the forest last night.

HALE *(surprised)*. You permit dancing?

PARRIS. No, no, it were secret—

MRS. PUTNAM *(unable to wait)*. Mr. Parris's slave has knowledge of conjurin', sir.

PARRIS *(to* MRS. PUTNAM*)*. We cannot be sure of that, Goody Ann—

MRS. PUTNAM *(frightened, very softly)*. I know it, sir. I sent my child—she should learn from Tituba who murdered her sisters.

REBECCA *(horrified)*. Goody Ann! You sent a child to conjure up the dead?

MRS. PUTNAM. Let God blame me, not you, not you, Rebecca! I'll not have you judging me any more! *(To* HALE*)*. Is it a natural work to lose seven children before they live a day?

PARRIS. Sssh!

*(*REBECCA, *with great pain, turns her face away. There is a pause.)*

HALE. Seven dead in childbirth.

MRS. PUTNAM *(softly)*. Aye. *(Her voice breaks; she looks up at him. Silence.* HALE *is impressed.* PARRIS *looks to him. He goes to his books, opens one, turns pages, then reads. All wait, avidly.)*

PARRIS *(hushed)*. What book is that?

MRS. PUTNAM. What's there, sir?

HALE (*with a tasty love of intellectual pursuit*). Here is all the invisible world, caught, defined, and calculated. In these books the Devil stands stripped of all his brute disguises. Here are all your familiar spirits—your incubi and succubi;[28] your witches that go by land, by air, and by sea; your wizards of the night and of the day. Have no fear now—we shall find him out if he has come among us, and I mean to crush him utterly if he has shown his face! (*He starts for the bed.*)

REBECCA. Will it hurt the child, sir?

HALE. I cannot tell. If she is truly in the Devil's grip we may have to rip and tear to get her free.

REBECCA. I think I'll go, then. I am too old for this. (*She rises.*)

PARRIS (*striving for conviction*). Why, Rebecca, we may open up the boil of all our troubles today!

REBECCA. Let us hope for that. I go to God for you, sir.

PARRIS (*with trepidation*[29]*—and resentment*). I hope you do not mean we go to Satan here! (*Slight pause.*)

REBECCA. I wish I knew. (*She goes out; they feel resentful of her note of moral superiority.*)

PUTNAM (*abruptly*). Come, Mr. Hale, let's get on. Sit you here.

GILES. Mr. Hale, I have always wanted to ask a learned man—what signifies the readin' of strange books?

HALE. What books?

GILES. I cannot tell; she hides them.

HALE. Who does this?

GILES. Martha, my wife. I have waked at night many a time and found her in a corner, readin' of a book. Now what do you make of that?

HALE. Why, that's not necessarily—

GILES. It discomfits me! Last night—mark this—I tried and tried and could not say my prayers. And then she close her book and walks out of the house, and suddenly—mark this—I could pray again!

◆ Old Giles must be spoken for, if only because his fate was to be so remarkable and so different from that of all the others. He was in his early eighties at this time, and was the most comical hero in the history. No man has ever been blamed for so much. If a cow was missed, the first thought was to look for her around Corey's house; a fire blazing up at night brought suspicion of arson to his door. He didn't give a hoot for public opinion, and only in his last years—after he had married Martha—did he bother much with the church. That she stopped his prayer is very probable, but he forgot to say that he'd only recently learned any prayers and it didn't take much to make him stumble over them. He was a crank and a nuisance, but withal a deeply innocent and brave man. In court once, he was asked if it were true that he had been frightened by the strange behavior of a hog and had then said he knew it to be the Devil in an animal's shape. "What frighted you?" he was asked. He forgot everything but the word "frighted," and instantly replied, "I do not know that I ever spoke that word in my life." ◆

HALE. Ah! The stoppage of prayer—that is strange. I'll speak further on that with you.

GILES. I'm not sayin' she's touched the Devil, now, but I'd admire to know what books she reads and why she hides them. She'll not answer me, y' see.

HALE. Aye, we'll discuss it. (*To all*). Now mark me, if the Devil is in her you will witness some frightful wonders in this room, so please to keep your wits about you. Mr. Putnam, stand close in case she flies. Now, Betty, dear, will you sit up? (PUTNAM *comes in closer, ready-handed.* HALE *sits* BETTY *up, but she hangs limp in his hands.*) Hmmm. (*He observes her carefully. The others watch breathlessly.*) Can you

---

28. **incubi** (ing′kyə bī) and **succubi** (sək′kyə bī), *n.* evil spirits and demons.

29. **trepidation** (trep′ə dā′shən), *n.* nervous dread.

hear me? I am John Hale, minister of Beverly. I have come to help you, dear. Do you remember my two little girls in Beverly? (*She does not stir in his hands.*)

PARRIS (*in fright*). How can it be the Devil? Why would he choose my house to strike? We have all manner of licentious people in the village!

HALE. What victory would the Devil have to win a soul already bad? It is the best the Devil wants, and who is better than the minister?

GILES. That's deep, Mr. Parris, deep, deep!

PARRIS (*with resolution now*). Betty! Answer Mr. Hale! Betty!

HALE. Does someone afflict you, child? It need not be a woman, mind you, or a man. Perhaps some bird invisible to others comes to you—perhaps a pig, a mouse, or any beast at all. Is there some figure bids you fly? (*The child remains limp in his hands. In silence he lays her back on the pillow. Now, holding out his hands toward her, he intones*). In nomine Domini, Sabaoth sui filiique ite ad infernos. (*She does not stir. He turns to* ABIGAIL, *his eyes narrowing.*) Abigail, what sort of dancing were you doing with her in the forest?

ABIGAIL. Why—common dancing is all.

PARRIS. I think I ought to say that I—I saw a kettle in the grass where they were dancing.

ABIGAIL. That were only soup.

HALE. What sort of soup were in this kettle, Abigail?

ABIGAIL. Why, it were beans—and lentils, I think, and—

HALE. Mr. Parris, you did not notice, did you, any living thing in the kettle? A mouse, perhaps, a spider, a frog—?

PARRIS (*fearfully*). I—do believe there were some movement—in the soup.

ABIGAIL. That jumped in, we never put it in!

HALE (*quickly*). What jumped in?

ABIGAIL. Why, a very little frog jumped—

PARRIS. A frog, Abby!

HALE (*grasping* ABIGAIL). Abigail, it may be your cousin is dying. Did you call the Devil last night?

ABIGAIL. I never called him! Tituba, Tituba . . .

PARRIS (*blanched*). She called the Devil?

HALE. I should like to speak with Tituba.

PARRIS. Goody Ann, will you bring her up? (MRS. PUTNAM *exits.*)

HALE. How did she call him?

ABIGAIL. I know not—she spoke Barbados.

HALE. Did you feel any strangeness when she called him? A sudden cold wind, perhaps? A trembling below the ground?

ABIGAIL. I didn't see no Devil! (*Shaking* BETTY). Betty, wake up. Betty! Betty!

HALE. You cannot evade me, Abigail. Did your cousin drink any of the brew in that kettle?

ABIGAIL. She never drank it!

HALE. Did you drink it?

ABIGAIL. No, sir!

HALE. Did Tituba ask you to drink it?

ABIGAIL. She tried, but I refused.

HALE. Why are you concealing? Have you sold yourself to Lucifer?

ABIGAIL. I never sold myself! I'm a good girl! I'm a proper girl!

(MRS. PUTNAM *enters with* TITUBA, *and instantly* ABIGAIL *points at* TITUBA.)

ABIGAIL. She made me do it! She made Betty do it!

TITUBA (*shocked and angry*). Abby!

ABIGAIL. She makes me drink blood!

PARRIS. Blood!!

MRS. PUTNAM. My baby's blood?

TITUBA. No, no, chicken blood. I give she chicken blood!

HALE. Woman, have you enlisted these children for the Devil?

TITUBA. No, no, sir, I don't truck with no Devil!

HALE. Why can she not wake? Are you silencing this child?

TITUBA. I love me Betty!

HALE. You have sent your spirit out upon this child, have you not? Are you gathering souls for the Devil?

ABIGAIL. She sends her spirit on me in church; she makes me laugh at prayer!

PARRIS. She have often laughed at prayer!

ABIGAIL. She comes to me every night to go and drink blood!

TITUBA. You beg *me* to conjure! She beg *me* make charm—

ABIGAIL. Don't lie! (*To* HALE). She comes to me while I sleep; she's always making me dream corruptions!

TITUBA. Why you say that, Abby?

ABIGAIL. Sometimes I wake and find myself standing in the open doorway and not a stitch on my body! I always hear her laughing in my sleep. I hear her singing her Barbados songs and tempting me with—

TITUBA. Mister Reverend, I never—

HALE (*resolved now*). Tituba, I want you to wake this child.

TITUBA. I have no power on this child, sir.

HALE. You most certainly do, and you will free her from it now! When did you compact with the Devil?

TITUBA. I don't compact with no Devil!

PARRIS. You will confess yourself or I will take you out and whip you to your death, Tituba!

PUTNAM. This woman must be hanged! She must be taken and hanged!

TITUBA (*terrified, falls to her knees*). No, no, don't hang Tituba! I tell him I don't desire to work for him, sir.

PARRIS. The Devil?

HALE. Then you saw him! (TITUBA *weeps.*) Now Tituba, I know that when we bind ourselves to Hell it is very hard to break with it. We are going to help you tear yourself free—

TITUBA (*frightened by the coming process*). Mister Reverend, I do believe somebody else be witchin' these children.

HALE. Who?

TITUBA. I don't know, sir, but the Devil got him numerous witches.

HALE. Does he! (*It is a clue.*) Tituba, look into my eyes. Come, look into me. (*She raises her eyes to his fearfully.*) You would be a good Christian woman, would you not, Tituba?

TITUBA. Aye, sir, a good Christian woman.

HALE. And you love these little children?

TITUBA. Oh, yes, sir. I don't desire to hurt little children.

HALE. And you love God, Tituba?

TITUBA. I love God with all my bein'.

HALE. Now, in God's holy name—

TITUBA. Bless Him. Bless Him. (*She is rocking on her knees, sobbing in terror.*)

HALE. And to His glory—

TITUBA. Eternal glory. Bless Him—bless God . . .

HALE. Open yourself, Tituba—open yourself and let God's holy light shine on you.

TITUBA. Oh, bless the Lord.

HALE. When the Devil comes to you does he ever come—with another person? (*She stares up into his face.*) Perhaps another person in the village? Someone you know.

PARRIS. Who came with him?

PUTNAM. Sarah Good? Did you ever see Sarah Good with him? Or Osburn?

PARRIS. Was it man or woman came with him?

TITUBA. Man or woman. Was—was woman.

PARRIS. What woman? A woman, you said. What woman?

TITUBA. It was black dark, and I—

PARRIS. You could see him, why could you not see her?

TITUBA. Well, they was always talking; they was always runnin' round and carryin' on—

PARRIS. You mean out of Salem? Salem witches?

TITUBA. I believe so, yes, sir.

(*Now* HALE *takes her hand. She is surprised.*)

HALE. Tituba. You must have no fear to tell us who they are, do you understand? We will protect you. The Devil can never overcome a minister. You know that, do you not?

TITUBA (*kisses* HALE'S *hand*). Aye, sir, oh, I do.

HALE. You have confessed yourself to witchcraft, and that speaks a wish to come to Heaven's side. And we will bless you, Tituba.

TITUBA (*deeply relieved*). Oh, God bless you, Mr. Hale!

HALE (*with rising exaltation*). You are God's instrument put in our hands to discover the Devil's agents among us. You are selected, Tituba, you are chosen to help us cleanse our village.

So speak utterly, Tituba, turn your back on him and face God—face God, Tituba, and God will protect you.

TITUBA (*joining with him*). Oh, God, protect Tituba!

HALE (*kindly*). Who came to you with the Devil? Two? Three? Four? How many?

(TITUBA *pants, and begins rocking back and forth again, staring ahead.*)

TITUBA. There was four. There was four.

PARRIS (*pressing in on her*). Who? Who? Their names, their names!

TITUBA (*suddenly bursting out*). Oh, how many times he bid me kill you, Mr. Parris!

PARRIS. Kill me!

TITUBA (*in a fury*). He say Mr. Parris must be kill! Mr. Parris no goodly man, Mr. Parris mean man and no gentle man, and he bid me rise out of my bed and cut your throat! (*They gasp.*) But I tell him "No! I don't hate that man. I don't want kill that man." But he say, "You work for me, Tituba, and I make you free! I give you pretty dress to wear, and put you way high up in the air, and you gone fly back to Barbados!" And I say, "You lie, Devil, you lie!" And then he come one stormy night to me, and he say, "Look! I have *white* people belong to me." And I look—and there was Goody Good.

PARRIS. Sarah Good!

TITUBA (*rocking and weeping*). Aye, sir, and Goody Osburn.

MRS. PUTNAM. I knew it! Goody Osburn were midwife to me three times. I begged you, Thomas, did I not? I begged him not to call Osburn because I feared her. My babies always shriveled in her hands!

HALE. Take courage, you must give us all their names. How can you bear to see this child suffering? Look at her, Tituba! (*He is indicating* BETTY *on the bed.*) Look at her God-given innocence; her soul is so tender; we must protect her, Tituba; the Devil is out and preying on her like a beast upon the flesh of the pure lamb. God will bless you for your help.

(ABIGAIL *rises, staring as though inspired, and cries out.*)

ABIGAIL. I want to open myself! (*They turn to her, startled. She is enraptured, as though in a pearly light.*) I want the light of God, I want the sweet love of Jesus! I danced for the Devil; I saw him; I wrote in his book; I go back to Jesus; I kiss His hand. I saw Sarah Good with the Devil! I saw Goody Osburn with the Devil! I saw Bridget Bishop with the Devil!

(*As she is speaking,* BETTY *is rising from the bed, a fever in her eyes, and picks up the chant.*)

BETTY (*staring too*). I saw George Jacobs with the Devil! I saw Goody Howe with the Devil!

PARRIS. She speaks! (*He rushes to embrace* BETTY.) She speaks!

HALE. Glory to God! It is broken, they are free!

BETTY (*calling out hysterically and with great relief*). I saw Martha Bellows with the Devil!

ABIGAIL. I saw Goody Sibber with the Devil! (*It is rising to a great glee.*)

PUTNAM. The marshal, I'll call the marshal!

(PARRIS *is shouting a prayer of thanksgiving.*)

BETTY. I saw Alice Barrow with the Devil!

(*The curtain begins to fall.*)

HALE (*as* PUTNAM *goes out*). Let the marshal bring irons!

ABIGAIL. I saw Goody Hawkins with the Devil!

BETTY. I saw Goody Bibber with the Devil!

ABIGAIL. I saw Goody Booth with the Devil!

(*On their ecstatic cries*)

THE CURTAIN FALLS

After Reading

Making Connections

Shaping Your Response

1. Retell the main events of Act One as though you were talking to someone who has never read or seen the play. Which events are most important to include in your retelling?

2. What grade would you give Reverend Parris's parenting skills? Explain.

Analyzing the Play

3. Why did Arthur Miller present three accounts of the events of the night in question in Act One? Which account do you believe?

4. List the **conflicts** that are introduced in Act One. Which do you think is the major conflict?

5. Make a list of the **characters** introduced in Act One, identify each one, and write a one-sentence description of his or her personality.

6. What special tools can a playwright use to develop **character** that are not available to a writer of stories or novels?

Extending the Ideas

7. 👣 The norms and beliefs of the Puritan **group** were clearly different than those of Tituba's culture. This led to prejudices and misunderstandings that may have played a large role in the events at Salem. Brainstorm five ways to help prevent the prejudices and misunderstandings that can occur when an individual doesn't fit into a group's norms.

Vocabulary Study

The listed words from the play are being used to describe two of the play's main characters. On a separate sheet of paper, write the word from the list that best fits each blank below. Use your Glossary if necessary.

**persecuted
parochial
vengeance
dissemble
begrudge
corroborate
hypocrite
predilection
contention
trepidation**

Abigail seems to __(1)__ Elizabeth Proctor her marriage, and to want to take __(2)__ for being rejected. She also seems to have a __(3)__ for lying, and she manages to __(4)__ her hopes to win over John Proctor, so that her uncle isn't suspicious. When Abigail accuses people of witchcraft, the other girls __(5)__ her story.

Reverend Parris feels he is being __(6)__ when the people of Salem fail to show him enough respect. Yet, because of his narrow-minded, __(7)__ attitude, he shows his parishioners very little respect, and could be called a __(8)__ . He is filled with __(9)__ when he learns of the licentious behavior of his daughter and niece, because he fears a scandal might fuel the __(10)__ in the parish.

Act Two

(The common room of PROCTOR'S *house, eight days later. At the right is a door opening on the fields outside. A fireplace is at the left, and behind it a stairway leading upstairs. It is the low, dark, and rather long living room of the time. As the curtain rises, the room is empty. From above,* ELIZABETH *is heard softly singing to the children. Presently the door opens and* JOHN PROCTOR *enters, carrying his gun. He glances about the room as he comes toward the fireplace, then halts for an instant as he hears her singing. He continues on to the fireplace, leans the gun against the wall as he swings a pot out of the fire and smells it. Then he lifts out the ladle and tastes. He is not quite pleased. He reaches to a cupboard, takes a pinch of salt, and drops it into the pot. As he is tasting again, her footsteps are heard on the stair. He swings the pot into the fireplace and goes to a basin and washes his hands and face.* ELIZABETH *enters.)*

ELIZABETH. What keeps you so late? It's almost dark.

PROCTOR. I were planting far out to the forest edge.

ELIZABETH. Oh, you're done then.

PROCTOR. Aye, the farm is seeded. The boys asleep?

ELIZABETH. They will be soon. *(And she goes to the fireplace, proceeds to ladle up stew in a dish.)*

PROCTOR. Pray now for a fair summer.

ELIZABETH. Aye.

PROCTOR. Are you well today?

ELIZABETH. I am. *(She brings the plate to the table, and, indicating the food).* It is a rabbit.

PROCTOR *(going to the table).* Oh, is it! In Jonathan's trap?

ELIZABETH. No, she walked into the house this afternoon; I found her sittin' in the corner like she come to visit.

PROCTOR. Oh, that's a good sign walkin' in.

ELIZABETH. Pray God. It hurt my heart to strip her, poor rabbit. *(She sits and watches him taste it.)*

PROCTOR. It's well seasoned.

ELIZABETH *(blushing with pleasure).* I took great care. She's tender?

PROCTOR. Aye. *(He eats. She watches him.)* I think we'll see green fields soon. It's warm as blood beneath the clods.

ELIZABETH. That's well.

*(*PROCTOR *eats, then looks up.)*

PROCTOR. If the crop is good I'll buy George Jacob's heifer. How would that please you?

ELIZABETH. Aye, it would.

PROCTOR *(with a grin).* I mean to please you, Elizabeth.

ELIZABETH *(it is hard to say).* I know it, John.

(He gets up, goes to her, kisses her. She receives it. With a certain disappointment, he returns to the table.)

PROCTOR *(as gently as he can).* Cider?

ELIZABETH *(with a sense of reprimanding herself for having forgot).* Aye! *(She gets up and goes and pours a glass for him. He now arches his back.)*

PROCTOR. This farm's a continent when you go foot by foot droppin' seeds in it.

ELIZABETH *(coming with the cider).* It must be.

PROCTOR *(drinks a long draught, then, putting the glass down).* You ought to bring some flowers in the house.

ELIZABETH. Oh! I forgot! I will tomorrow.

PROCTOR. It's winter in here yet. On Sunday let you come with me, and we'll walk the farm together; I never see such a load of flowers on the earth. *(With good feeling he goes and*

looks up at the sky through the open doorway.)
Lilacs have a purple smell. Lilac is the smell
of nightfall, I think. Massachusetts is a beauty
in the spring!

ELIZABETH. Aye, it is.

(*There is a pause. She is watching him from the table
as he stands there absorbing the night. It is as though
she would speak but cannot. Instead, now, she takes
up his plate and glass and fork and goes with them to
the basin. Her back is turned to him. He turns to her
and watches her. A sense of their separation rises.*)

PROCTOR. I think you're sad again. Are you?

ELIZABETH (*she doesn't want friction, and yet she
must*). You come so late I thought you'd gone
to Salem this afternoon.

PROCTOR. Why? I have no business in Salem.

ELIZABETH. You did speak of going, earlier this
week.

PROCTOR (*he knows what she means*). I thought
better of it since.

ELIZABETH. Mary Warren's there today.

PROCTOR. Why'd you let her? You heard me forbid her to go to Salem any more!

ELIZABETH. I couldn't stop her.

PROCTOR (*holding back a full condemnation of her*).
It is a fault, it is a fault, Elizabeth—you're the
mistress here, not Mary Warren.

ELIZABETH. She frightened all my strength away.

PROCTOR. How may that mouse frighten you,
Elizabeth? You—

ELIZABETH. It is a mouse no more. I forbid her
go, and she raises up her chin like the
daughter of a prince and says to me, "I must
go to Salem, Goody Proctor; I am an official
of the court!"

PROCTOR. Court! What court?

ELIZABETH. Aye, it is a proper court they have
now. They've sent four judges out of Boston,
she says, weighty magistrates of the General
Court, and at the head sits the Deputy
Governor of the Province.

PROCTOR (*astonished*). Why, she's mad.

ELIZABETH. I would to God she were. There be
fourteen people in the jail now, she says.
(PROCTOR *simply looks at her, unable to grasp it.*)

And they'll be tried, and the court have
power to hang them too, she says.

PROCTOR (*scoffing,*[1] *but without conviction*). Ah,
they'd never hang—

ELIZABETH. The Deputy Governor promise
hangin' if they'll not confess, John. The
town's gone wild, I think. She speak of
Abigail, and I thought she were a saint, to
hear her. Abigail brings the others girls into
the court, and where she walks the crowd
will part like the sea for Israel. And folks are
brought before them, and if they scream
and howl and fall to the floor—the person's
clapped in the jail for bewitchin' them.

PROCTOR (*wide-eyed*). Oh, it is a black mischief.

ELIZABETH. I think you must go to Salem, John.
(*He turns to her.*) I think so. You must tell
them it is a fraud.[2]

PROCTOR (*thinking beyond this*). Aye, it is, it is
surely.

ELIZABETH. Let you go to Ezekiel Cheever—he
knows you well. And tell him what she said
to you last week in her uncle's house. She
said it had naught to do with witchcraft, did
she not?

PROCTOR (*in thought*). Aye, she did, she did.
(*Now, a pause.*)

ELIZABETH (*quietly, fearing to anger him by prod-
ding*). God forbid you keep that from the
court, John. I think they must be told.

PROCTOR (*quietly, struggling with his thought*). Aye,
they must, they must. It is a wonder they do
believe her.

ELIZABETH. I would go to Salem now, John—let
you go tonight.

PROCTOR. I'll think on it.

ELIZABETH (*with her courage now*). You cannot
keep it, John.

PROCTOR (*angering*). I know I cannot keep it. I
say I will think on it!

---

1. **scoff** (skof), *v.* to show one does not believe something; mock.
2. **fraud** (frôd), *n.* any deliberate misrepresentation of
the truth; a dishonest act, statement, etc.

ELIZABETH (*hurt, and very coldly*). Good, then, let you think on it. (*She stands and starts to walk out of the room.*)

PROCTOR. I am only wondering how I may prove what she told me, Elizabeth. If the girl's a saint now, I think it is not easy to prove she's fraud, and the town gone so silly. She told it to me in a room alone—I have no proof for it.

ELIZABETH. You were alone with her?

PROCTOR (*stubbornly*). For a moment alone, aye.

ELIZABETH. Why, then, it is not as you told me.

PROCTOR (*his anger rising*). For a moment, I say. The others come in soon after.

ELIZABETH (*quietly—she has suddenly lost all faith in him*). Do as you wish, then. (*She starts to turn.*)

PROCTOR. Woman. (*She turns to him.*) I'll not have your suspicion any more.

ELIZABETH (*a little loftily*). I have no—

PROCTOR. I'll not have it!

ELIZABETH. Then let you not earn it.

PROCTOR (*with a violent undertone*). You doubt me yet?

ELIZABETH (*with a smile, to keep her dignity*). John, if it were not Abigail that you must go to hurt, would you falter now? I think not.

PROCTOR. Now look you—

ELIZABETH. I see what I see, John.

PROCTOR (*with solemn warning*). You will not judge me more, Elizabeth. I have good reason to think before I charge fraud on Abigail, and I will think on it. Let you look to your own improvement before you go to judge your husband any more. I have forgot Abigail, and—

ELIZABETH. And I.

PROCTOR. Spare me! You forget nothin' and forgive nothin'. Learn charity, woman. I have gone tiptoe in this house all seven month since she is gone. I have not moved from there to there without I think to please you, and still an everlasting funeral marches round your heart. I cannot speak but I am doubted, every moment judged for lies, as though I come into a court when I come into this house!

ELIZABETH. John, you are not open with me. You saw her with a crowd, you said. Now you—

PROCTOR. I'll plead my honesty no more, Elizabeth.

ELIZABETH (*now she would justify herself*). John, I am only—

PROCTOR. No more! I should have roared you down when first you told me your suspicion. But I wilted, and, like a Christian, I confessed. Confessed! Some dream I had must have mistaken you for God that day. But you're not, you're not, and let you remember it! Let you look sometimes for the goodness in me, and judge me not.

ELIZABETH. I do not judge you. The magistrate[3] sits in your heart that judges you. I never thought you but a good man, John—(*with a smile*)—only somewhat bewildered.

PROCTOR (*laughing bitterly*). Oh, Elizabeth, your justice would freeze beer! (*He turns suddenly toward a sound outside. He starts for the door as* MARY WARREN *enters. As soon as he sees her, he goes directly to her and grabs her by the cloak, furious.*) How do you go to Salem when I forbid it? Do you mock me? (*Shaking her.*) I'll whip you if you dare leave this house again!

(*Strangely, she doesn't resist him, but hangs limply by his grip.*)

MARY WARREN. I am sick, I am sick, Mr. Proctor. Pray, pray, hurt me not. (*Her strangeness throws him off, and her evident pallor[4] and weakness. He frees her.*) My insides are all shuddery; I am in the proceedings all day, sir.

PROCTOR (*with draining anger—his curiosity is draining it*). And what of these proceedings here? When will you proceed to keep this house, as you are paid nine pound a year to do—and my wife not wholly well?

(*As though to compensate,* MARY WARREN *goes to* ELIZABETH *with a small rag doll.*)

---

3. **magistrate** (maj′ə strāt), *n.* judge in a minor court.
4. **pallor** (pal′ər), *n.* lack of normal color from fear, illness, or death.

MARY WARREN. I made a gift for you today, Goody Proctor. I had to sit long hours in a chair, and passed the time with sewing.

ELIZABETH (perplexed, looking at the doll). Why, thank you, it's a fair poppet.

MARY WARREN (with a trembling, decayed voice). We must all love each other now, Goody Proctor.

ELIZABETH (amazed at her strangeness). Aye, indeed we must.

MARY WARREN (glancing at the room). I'll get up early in the morning and clean the house. I must sleep now. (She turns and starts off.)

PROCTOR. Mary. (She halts.) Is it true? There be fourteen women arrested?

MARY WARREN. No, sir. There be thirty-nine now—(She suddenly breaks off and sobs and sits down, exhausted.)

ELIZABETH. Why, she's weepin'! What ails you, child?

MARY WARREN. Goody Osburn—will hang!

(There is a shocked pause, while she sobs.)

PROCTOR. Hang! (He calls into her face.) Hang, y'say?

MARY WARREN (through her weeping). Aye.

PROCTOR. The Deputy Governor will permit it?

MARY WARREN. He sentenced her. He must. (To ameliorate[5] it). But not Sarah Good. For Sarah Good confessed, y'see.

PROCTOR. Confessed! To what?

MARY WARREN. That she—(in horror at the memory)—she sometimes made a compact with Lucifer, and wrote her name in his black book—with her blood—and bound herself to torment Christians till God's thrown down—and we all must worship Hell forevermore.

(Pause.)

PROCTOR. But—surely you know what a jabberer she is. Did you tell them that?

MARY WARREN. Mr. Proctor, in open court she near to choked us all to death.

PROCTOR. How, choked you?

MARY WARREN. She sent her spirit out.

ELIZABETH. Oh, Mary, Mary, surely you—

MARY WARREN (with an indignant[6] edge). She tried to kill me many times, Goody Proctor.

ELIZABETH. Why, I never heard you mention that before.

MARY WARREN. I never knew it before. I never knew anything before. When she come into the court I say to myself, I must not accuse this woman, for she sleep in ditches, and so very old and poor. But then—then she sit there, denying and denying, and I feel a misty coldness climbin' up my back, and the skin on my skull begin to creep, and I feel a clamp around my neck and I cannot breathe air; and then—(entranced)—I hear a voice, a screamin' voice, and it were my voice—and all at once I remembered everything she done to me!

PROCTOR. Why? What did she do to you?

MARY WARREN (like one awakened to a marvelous secret insight). So many time, Mr. Proctor, she come to this very door, beggin' bread and a cup of cider—and mark this: whenever I turned her away empty, she mumbled.

ELIZABETH. Mumbled! She may mumble if she's hungry.

MARY WARREN. But what does she mumble? You must remember, Goody Proctor. Last month—a Monday, I think—she walked away, and I thought my guts would burst for two days after. Do you remember it?

ELIZABETH. Why—I do, I think, but—

MARY WARREN. And so I told that to Judge Hathorne, and he asks her so. "Sarah Good," says he, "what curse do you mumble that this girl must fall sick after turning you away?" And then she replies—(mimicking an old crone)—"Why, your excellence, no curse at all. I only say my commandments; I hope I may say my commandments," says she!

ELIZABETH. And that's an upright answer.

MARY WARREN. Aye, but then Judge Hathorne say, "Recite for us your commandments!"—(leaning avidly toward them)—and of all the

_____

5. ameliorate (ə mē′lyə rāt), v. to make better or improve.
6. indignant (in dig′nənt), adj. angry at something unworthy, unjust, unfair.

ten she could not say a single one. She never knew no commandments, and they had her in a flat lie!

PROCTOR. And so condemned[7] her?

MARY WARREN (*now a little strained, seeing his stubborn doubt*). Why, they must when she condemned herself.

PROCTOR. But the proof, the proof!

MARY WARREN (*with greater impatience with him*). I told you the proof. It's hard proof, hard as rock, the judges said.

PROCTOR (*pauses an instant, then*). You will not go to court again, Mary Warren.

MARY WARREN. I must tell you, sir, I will be gone every day now. I am amazed you do not see what weighty work we do.

PROCTOR. What work you do! It's strange work for a Christian girl to hang old women!

MARY WARREN. But, Mr. Proctor, they will not hang them if they confess. Sarah Good will only sit in jail some time—(*recalling*)—and here's a wonder for you; think on this. Goody Good is pregnant!

ELIZABETH. Pregnant! Are they mad? The woman's near to sixty!

MARY WARREN. They had Doctor Griggs examine her, and she's full to the brim. And smokin' a pipe all these years, and no husband either! But she's safe, thank God, for they'll not hurt the innocent child. But be that not a marvel? You must see it, sir, it's God's work we do. So I'll be gone every day for some time. I'm—I am an official of the court, they say, and I—

---

7. **condemn** (kən dem′), *v.* pronounce guilty of a crime or wrong.

(She has been edging toward offstage.)

PROCTOR. I'll official you! *(He strides to the mantel, takes down the whip hanging there.)*

MARY WARREN *(terrified, but coming erect, striving for her authority)*. I'll not stand whipping any more!

ELIZABETH *(hurriedly, as* PROCTOR *approaches)*. Mary, promise now you'll stay at home—

MARY WARREN *(backing from him, but keeping her erect posture, striving, striving for her way)*. The Devil's loose in Salem, Mr. Proctor; we must discover where he's hiding!

PROCTOR. I'll whip the Devil out of you! *(With whip raised he reaches out for her, and she streaks away and yells.)*

MARY WARREN *(pointing at* ELIZABETH*)*. I saved her life today!

(Silence. His whip comes down.)

ELIZABETH *(softly)*. I am accused?

MARY WARREN *(quaking)*. Somewhat mentioned. But I said I never see no sign you ever sent your spirit out to hurt no one, and seeing I do live so closely with you, they dismissed it.

ELIZABETH. Who accused me?

MARY WARREN. I am bound by law, I cannot tell it. *(To* PROCTOR*)*. I only hope you'll not be so sarcastical no more. Four judges and the King's deputy sat to dinner with us but an hour ago. I—I would have you speak civilly to me, from this out.

PROCTOR *(in horror, muttering in disgust at her)*. Go to bed.

MARY WARREN *(with a stamp of her foot)*. I'll not be ordered to bed no more, Mr. Proctor! I am eighteen and a woman, however single!

PROCTOR. Do you wish to sit up? Then sit up.

MARY WARREN. I wish to go to bed!

PROCTOR *(in anger)*. Good night, then!

MARY WARREN. Good night. *(Dissatisfied, uncertain of herself, she goes out. Wide-eyed, both,* PROCTOR *and* ELIZABETH *staring.)*

ELIZABETH *(quietly)*. Oh, the noose, the noose is up!

PROCTOR. There'll be no noose.

ELIZABETH. She wants me dead. I knew all week it would come to this!

PROCTOR *(without conviction)*. They dismissed it. You heard her say—

ELIZABETH. And what of tomorrow? She will cry me out until they take me!

PROCTOR. Sit you down.

ELIZABETH. She wants me dead, John, you know it!

PROCTOR. I say sit down! *(She sits, trembling. He speaks quietly, trying to keep his wits.)* Now we must be wise, Elizabeth.

ELIZABETH *(with sarcasm, and a sense of being lost)*. Oh, indeed, indeed!

PROCTOR. Fear nothing. I'll find Ezekiel Cheever. I'll tell him she said it were all sport.

ELIZABETH. John, with so many in the jail, more than Cheever's help is needed now, I think. Would you favor me with this? Go to Abigail.

PROCTOR *(his soul hardening as he senses . . .)*. What have I to say to Abigail?

ELIZABETH *(delicately)*. John—grant me this. You have a faulty understanding of young girls. There is a promise made in any bed—

PROCTOR *(striving against his anger)*. What promise!

ELIZABETH. Spoke or silent, a promise is surely made. And she may dote on it now—I am sure she does—and thinks to kill me, then to take my place.

*(*PROCTOR'S *anger is rising; he cannot speak.)*

ELIZABETH. It is her dearest hope, John, I know it. There be a thousand names; why does she call mine? There be a certain danger in calling such a name—I am no Goody Good that sleeps in ditches, nor Osburn, drunk and half-witted. She'd dare not call out such a farmer's wife but there be monstrous profit in it. She thinks to take my place, John.

PROCTOR. She cannot think it! *(He knows it is true.)*

ELIZABETH *("reasonably")*. John, have you ever shown her somewhat of contempt? She cannot pass you in the church but you will blush—

PROCTOR. I may blush for my sin.

ELIZABETH. I think she sees another meaning in that blush.

PROCTOR. And what see you? What see you, Elizabeth?

ELIZABETH (*"conceding"*). I think you be somewhat ashamed, for I am there, and she so close.

PROCTOR. When will you know me, woman? Were I stone I would have cracked for shame this seven month!

ELIZABETH. Then go and tell her she's a whore. Whatever promise she may sense—break it, John, break it.

PROCTOR (*between his teeth*). Good, then. I'll go. (*He starts for his rifle.*)

ELIZABETH (*trembling, fearfully*). Oh, how unwillingly!

PROCTOR (*turning on her, rifle in hand*). I will curse her hotter than the oldest cinder in hell. But pray, begrudge me not my anger!

ELIZABETH. Your anger! I only ask you—

PROCTOR. Woman, am I so base? Do you truly think me base?

ELIZABETH. I never called you base.

PROCTOR. Then how do you charge me with such a promise? The promise that a stallion gives a mare I gave that girl!

ELIZABETH. Then why do you anger with me when I bid you break it?

PROCTOR. Because it speaks deceit, and I am honest! But I'll plead no more! I see now your spirit twists around the single error of my life, and I will never tear it free!

ELIZABETH (*crying out*). You'll tear it free—when you come to know that I will be your only wife, or no wife at all! She has an arrow in you yet, John Proctor, and you know it well!

(*Quite suddenly, as though from the air, a figure appears in the doorway. They start slightly. It is* MR. HALE. *He is different now—drawn a little, and there is a quality of deference,*[8] *even of guilt, about his manner now.*)

HALE. Good evening.

PROCTOR (*still in his shock*). Why, Mr. Hale! Good evening to you, sir. Come in, come in.

HALE (*to* ELIZABETH). I hope I do not startle you.

ELIZABETH. No, no, it's only that I heard no horse—

HALE. You are Goodwife Proctor.

PROCTOR. Aye; Elizabeth.

HALE (*nods, then*). I hope you're not off to bed yet.

PROCTOR (*setting down his gun*). No, no. (HALE *comes further into the room. And* PROCTOR, *to explain his nervousness*). We are not used to visitors after dark, but you're welcome here. Will you sit down, sir?

HALE. I will. (*He sits.*) Let you sit, Goodwife Proctor. (*She does, never letting him out of her sight. There is a pause as* HALE *looks about the room.*)

PROCTOR (*to break the silence*). Will you drink cider, Mr. Hale?

HALE. No, it rebels my stomach; I have some further traveling yet tonight. Sit you down, sir. (PROCTOR *sits.*) I will not keep you long, but I have some business with you.

PROCTOR. Business of the court?

HALE. No—no, I come of my own, without the court's authority. Hear me. (*He wets his lips.*) I know not if you are aware, but your wife's name is—mentioned in the court.

PROCTOR. We know it, sir. Our Mary Warren told us. We are entirely amazed.

HALE. I am a stranger here, as you know. And in my ignorance I find it hard to draw a clear opinion of them that come accused before the court. And so this afternoon, and now tonight, I go from house to house—I come now from Rebecca Nurse's house and—

ELIZABETH (*shocked*). Rebecca's charged!

HALE. God forbid such a one be charged. She is, however—mentioned somewhat.

ELIZABETH (*with an attempt at a laugh*). You will never believe, I hope, that Rebecca trafficked with the Devil.

HALE. Woman, it is possible.

PROCTOR (*taken aback*). Surely you cannot think so.

HALE. This is a strange time, Mister. No man may longer doubt the powers of the dark are gathered in monstrous attack upon this village. There is too much evidence now to deny it. You will agree, sir?

PROCTOR (*evading*). I—have no knowledge in that line. But it's hard to think so pious a woman be secretly a Devil's bitch after

---

8. **deference** (def′ər əns), *n.* respect.

seventy year of such good prayer.

HALE. Aye. But the Devil is a wily [9] one, you cannot deny it. However, she is far from accused, and I know she will not be. *(Pause.)* I thought, sir, to put some questions as to the Christian character of this house, if you'll permit me.

PROCTOR *(coldly, resentful).* Why, we—have no fear of questions, sir.

HALE. Good, then. *(He makes himself more comfortable.)* In the book of record that Mr. Parris keeps, I note that you are rarely in the church on Sabbath Day.

PROCTOR. No, sir, you are mistaken.

HALE. Twenty-six time in seventeen month, sir. I must call that rare. Will you tell me why you are so absent?

PROCTOR. Mr. Hale, I never knew I must account to that man for I come to church or stay at home. My wife were sick this winter.

HALE. So I am told. But you, Mister, why could you not come alone?

PROCTOR. I surely did come when I could, and when I could not I prayed in this house.

HALE. Mr. Proctor, your house is not a church; your theology must tell you that.

---

9. **wily** (wī′ lē), *adj.* sly; deceitful; tricky.

PROCTOR. It does, sir, it does; and it tells me that a minister may pray to God without he have golden candlesticks upon the altar.

HALE. What golden candlesticks?

PROCTOR. Since we built the church there were pewter candlesticks upon the altar; Francis Nurse made them, y'know, and a sweeter hand never touched the metal. But Parris came, and for twenty week he preach nothin' but golden candlesticks until he had them. I labor the earth from dawn of day to blink of night, and I tell you true, when I look to heaven and see my money glaring at his elbows—it hurt my prayer, sir, it hurt my prayer. I think, sometimes, the man dreams cathedrals, not clapboard meetin' houses.

HALE (*thinks, then*). And yet, Mister, a Christian on Sabbath Day must be in church. (*Pause.*) Tell me—you have three children?

PROCTOR. Aye. Boys.

HALE. How comes it that only two are baptized?

PROCTOR (*starts to speak, then stops, then, as though unable to restrain this*). I like it not that Mr. Parris should lay his hand upon my baby. I see no light of God in that man. I'll not conceal it.

HALE. I must say it, Mr. Proctor; that is not for you to decide. The man's ordained, therefore the light of God is in him.

PROCTOR (*flushed with resentment but trying to smile*). What's your suspicion, Mr. Hale?

HALE. No, no. I have no—

PROCTOR. I nailed the roof upon the church, I hung the door—

HALE. Oh, did you! That's a good sign, then.

PROCTOR. It may be I have been too quick to bring the man to book, but you cannot think we ever desired the destruction of religion. I think that's in your mind, is it not?

HALE (*not altogether giving way*). I—have—there is a softness in your record, sir, a softness.

ELIZABETH. I think, maybe, we have been too hard with Mr. Parris. I think so. But sure we never loved the Devil here.

HALE (*nods, deliberating this. Then, with the voice of one administering a secret test*). Do you know

your Commandments, Elizabeth?

ELIZABETH (*without hesitation, even eagerly*). I surely do. There be no mark of blame upon my life, Mr. Hale. I am a covenanted Christian woman.

HALE. And you, Mister?

PROCTOR (*a trifle unsteadily*). I—am sure I do, sir.

HALE (*glances at her open face then at* JOHN, *then*). Let you repeat them, if you will.

PROCTOR. The Commandments.

HALE. Aye.

PROCTOR (*looking off, beginning to sweat*). Thou shalt not kill.

HALE. Aye.

PROCTOR (*counting on his fingers*). Thou shalt not steal. Thou shalt not covet thy neighbor's goods, nor make unto thee any graven image. Thou shalt not take the name of the Lord in vain; thou shalt have no other gods before me. (*With some hesitation*). Thou shalt remember the Sabbath Day and keep it holy. (*Pause. Then*). Thou shalt honor thy father and mother. Thou shalt not bear false witness. (*He is stuck. He counts back on his fingers, knowing one is missing.*) Thou shalt not make unto thee any graven image.

HALE. You have said that twice, sir.

PROCTOR (*lost*). Aye. (*He is flailing for it.*)

ELIZABETH (*delicately*). Adultery, John.

PROCTOR (*as though a secret arrow had pained his heart*). Aye. (*Trying to grin it away—to* HALE). You see, sir, between the two of us we do know them all. (HALE *only looks at* PROCTOR, *deep in his attempt to define this man.* PROCTOR *grows more uneasy.*) I think it be a small fault.

HALE. Theology, sir, is a fortress;[10] no crack in a fortress may be accounted small. (*He rises; he seems worried now. He paces a little, in deep thought.*)

PROCTOR. There be no love for Satan in this house, Mister.

HALE. I pray it, I pray it dearly. (*He looks to both of them, an attempt at a smile on his face, but his*

---

10. **fortress** (fôr′tris), *n*. a large, permanently fortified place or building.

misgivings are clear.) Well, then—I'll bid you good night.

ELIZABETH (*unable to restrain herself*). Mr. Hale. (*He turns.*) I do think you are suspecting me somewhat? Are you not?

HALE (*obviously disturbed—and evasive*[11]). Goody Proctor, I do not judge you. My duty is to add what I may to the godly wisdom of the court. I pray you both good health and good fortune. (*To* JOHN). Good night, sir. (*He starts out.*)

ELIZABETH (*with a note of desperation*). I think you must tell him, John.

HALE. What's that?

ELIZABETH (*restraining a call*). Will you tell him? (*Slight pause.* HALE *looks questioningly at* JOHN.)

PROCTOR (*with difficulty*). I—I have no witness and cannot prove it, except my word be taken. But I know the children's sickness had naught to do with witchcraft.

HALE (*stopped, struck*). Naught to do—?

PROCTOR. Mr. Parris discovered them sportin' in the woods. They were startled and took sick. (*Pause.*)

HALE. Who told you this?

PROCTOR (*hesitates, then*). Abigail Williams.

HALE. Abigail!

PROCTOR. Aye.

HALE (*his eyes wide*). Abigail Williams told you it had naught to do with witchcraft!

PROCTOR. She told me the day you came, sir.

HALE (*suspiciously*[12]). Why—why did you keep this?

PROCTOR. I never knew until tonight that the world is gone daft with this nonsense.

HALE. Nonsense! Mister, I have myself examined Tituba, Sarah Good, and numerous others that have confessed to dealing with the Devil. They have *confessed* it.

PROCTOR. And why not, if they must hang for denyin' it? There are them that will swear to anything before they'll hang; have you never thought of that?

HALE. I have. I—I have indeed. (*It is his own suspicion, but he resists it. He glances at* ELIZABETH, *then at* JOHN.) And you—would you testify to this in court?

PROCTOR. I—I had not reckoned with goin' into court. But if I must I will.

HALE. Do you falter here?

PROCTOR. I falter nothing, but I may wonder if my story will be credited in such a court. I do wonder on it, when such a steady-minded minister as you will suspicion such a woman that never lied, and cannot, and the world knows she cannot! I may falter somewhat, Mister; I am no fool.

HALE (*quietly—it has impressed him*). Proctor, let you open with me now, for I have a rumor that troubles me. It's said you hold no belief that there may even be witches in the world. Is that true, sir?

PROCTOR (*he knows this is critical, and is striving against his disgust with* HALE *and with himself for even answering*). I know not what I have said, I may have said it. I have wondered if there be witches in the world—although I cannot believe they come among us now.

HALE. Then you do not believe—

PROCTOR. I have no knowledge of it; the Bible speaks of witches, and I will not deny them.

HALE. And you, woman?

ELIZABETH. I—I cannot believe it.

HALE (*shocked*). You cannot!

PROCTOR. Elizabeth, you bewilder him!

ELIZABETH (*to* HALE). I cannot think the Devil may own a woman's soul, Mr. Hale, when she keeps an upright way, as I have. I am a good woman, I know it; and if you believe I may do only good work in the world, and yet be secretly bound to Satan, then I must tell you, sir, I do not believe it.

HALE. But, woman, you do believe there are witches in—

ELIZABETH. If you think that I am one, then I say there are none.

---

11. **evasive** (i vā′siv i vā′ziv), *adj.* tending or trying to evade.
12. **suspiciously** (sə spish′əs lē), *adv.* in a mistrustful manner.

The Crucible—Act Two **97**

HALE. You surely do not fly against the Gospel, the Gospel—

PROCTOR. She believe in the Gospel, every word!

ELIZABETH. Question Abigail Williams about the Gospel, not myself!

(HALE *stares at her.*)

PROCTOR. She do not mean to doubt the Gospel, sir, you cannot think it. This be a Christian house, sir, a Christian house.

HALE. God keep you both; let the third child be quickly baptized, and go you without fail each Sunday in to Sabbath prayer; and keep a solemn, quiet way among you. I think—

(GILES COREY *appears in doorway.*)

GILES. John!

PROCTOR. Giles! What's the matter?

GILES. They take my wife.

(FRANCIS NURSE *enters.*)

GILES. And his Rebecca!

PROCTOR (*to* FRANCIS). Rebecca's in the *jail!*

FRANCIS. Aye, Cheever come and take her in his wagon. We've only now come from the jail, and they'll not even let us in to see them.

ELIZABETH. They've surely gone wild now, Mr. Hale!

FRANCIS (*going to* HALE). Reverend Hale! Can you not speak to the Deputy Governor? I'm sure he mistakes these people—

HALE. Pray calm yourself, Mr. Nurse.

FRANCIS. My wife is the very brick and mortar of the church, Mr. Hale—(*indicating* GILES)—and Martha Corey, there cannot be a woman closer yet to God than Martha.

HALE. How is Rebecca charged, Mr. Nurse?

FRANCIS (*with a mocking, half-hearted laugh*). For murder, she's charged! (*Mockingly quoting the warrant*). "For the marvelous and supernatural murder of Goody Putnam's babies." What am I to do, Mr. Hale?

HALE (*turns from* FRANCIS, *deeply troubled, then*). Believe me, Mr. Nurse, if Rebecca Nurse be tainted, then nothing's left to stop the whole green world from burning. Let you rest upon the justice of the court; the court will send her home, I know it.

FRANCIS. You cannot mean she will be tried in court!

HALE (*pleading*). Nurse, though our hearts break, we cannot flinch; these are new times, sir. There is a misty plot afoot so subtle we should be criminal to cling to old respects and ancient friendships. I have seen too many frightful proofs in court—the Devil is alive in Salem, and we dare not quail to follow wherever the accusing finger points!

PROCTOR (*angered*). How may such a woman murder children?

HALE (*in great pain*). Man, remember, until an hour before the Devil fell, God thought him beautiful in Heaven.

GILES. I never said my wife were a witch, Mr. Hale; I only said she were reading books!

HALE. Mr. Corey, exactly what complaint were made on your wife?

GILES. That bloody mongrel Walcott charge her. Y'see, he buy a pig of my wife four or five year ago, and the pig died soon after. So he come dancin' in for his money back. So my Martha, she says to him, "Walcott, if you haven't the wit to feed a pig properly, you'll not live to own many," she says. Now he goes to court and claims that from that day to this he cannot keep a pig alive for more than four weeks because my Martha bewitch them with her books!

(*Enter* EZEKIEL CHEEVER. *A shocked silence.*)

CHEEVER. Good evening to you, Proctor.

PROCTOR. Why, Mr. Cheever. Good evening.

CHEEVER. Good evening, all. Good evening, Mr. Hale.

PROCTOR. I hope you come not on business of the court.

CHEEVER. I do, Proctor, aye. I am clerk of the court now, y'know.

(*Enter* MARSHAL HERRICK, *a man in his early thirties, who is somewhat shamefaced at the moment.*)

GILES. It's a pity, Ezekiel, that an honest tailor might have gone to Heaven must burn in Hell. You'll burn for this, do you know it?

CHEEVER. You know yourself I must do as I'm

told. You surely know that, Giles. And I'd as lief[13] you'd not be sending me to Hell. I like not the sound of it, I tell you; I like not the sound of it. *(He fears* PROCTOR, *but starts to reach inside his coat.)* Now believe me, Proctor, how heavy be the law, all its tonnage I do carry on my back tonight. *(He takes out a warrant.[14])* I have a warrant for your wife.

PROCTOR *(to* HALE*).* You said she were not charged!

HALE. I know nothin' of it. *(To* CHEEVER*).* When were she charged?

CHEEVER. I am given sixteen warrant tonight, sir, and she is one.

PROCTOR. Who charged her?

CHEEVER. Why, Abigail Williams charge her.

PROCTOR. On what proof, what proof?

CHEEVER *(looking about the room).* Mr. Proctor, I have little time. The court bid me search your house, but I like not to search a house. So will you hand me any poppets that your wife may keep here?

PROCTOR. Poppets?

ELIZABETH. I never kept no poppets, not since I were a girl.

CHEEVER *(embarrassed, glancing toward the mantel where sits* MARY WARREN'S *poppet).* I spy a poppet, Goody Proctor.

ELIZABETH. Oh! *(Going for it).* Why, this is Mary's.

CHEEVER *(shyly).* Would you please give it to me?

ELIZABETH *(handing it to him, asks* HALE*).* Has the court discovered a text in poppets now?

CHEEVER *(carefully holding the poppet).* Do you keep any others in this house?

---

13. **as lief,** as soon.
14. **warrant** (wôr′ənt), *n.* written order giving authority to do something.

PROCTOR. No, nor this one either till tonight. What signifies a poppet?

CHEEVER. Why, a poppet—*(he gingerly turns the poppet over)*—a poppet may signify—Now, woman, will you please to come with me?

PROCTOR. She will not! (*To* ELIZABETH). Fetch Mary here.

CHEEVER (*ineptly*[15] *reaching toward* ELIZABETH). No, no, I am forbid to leave her from my sight.

PROCTOR (*pushing his arm away*). You'll leave her out of sight and out of mind, Mister. Fetch Mary, Elizabeth. (ELIZABETH *goes upstairs.*)

HALE. What signifies a poppet, Mr. Cheever?

CHEEVER (*turning the poppet over in his hands*). Why, they say it may signify that she—*(He has lifted the poppet's skirt, and his eyes widen in astonished fear.)* Why, this, this—

PROCTOR (*reaching for the poppet*). What's there?

CHEEVER. Why—*(He draws out a long needle from the poppet)*—it is a needle! Herrick, Herrick, it is a needle!

(HERRICK *comes toward him.*)

PROCTOR (*angrily, bewildered*). And what signifies a needle!

CHEEVER (*his hands shaking*). Why, this go hard with her, Proctor, this—I had my doubts, Proctor, I had my doubts, but here's calamity. (*To* HALE, *showing the needle*). You see it, sir, it is a needle!

HALE. Why? What meanin' has it?

CHEEVER (*wide-eyed, trembling*). The girl, the Williams girl, Abigail Williams, sir. She sat to dinner in Reverend Parris's house tonight, and without word nor warnin' she falls to the floor. Like a struck beast, he says, and screamed a scream that a bull would weep to hear. And he goes to save her, and, stuck two inches in the flesh of her belly, he draw a needle out. And demandin' of her how she come to be so stabbed, she—*(to* PROCTOR *now)*—testify it were your wife's familiar spirit pushed it in.

PROCTOR. Why, she done it herself! (*To* HALE). I hope you're not takin' this for proof, Mister!

(HALE, *struck by the proof, is silent.*)

CHEEVER. 'Tis hard proof! (*To* HALE). I find here a poppet Goody Proctor keeps. I have found it, sir. And in the belly of the poppet a needle's stuck. I tell you true, Proctor, I never warranted to see such proof of Hell, and I bid you obstruct me not, for I—

(*Enter* ELIZABETH *with* MARY WARREN. PROCTOR, *seeing* MARY WARREN, *draws her by the arm to* HALE).

PROCTOR. Here now! Mary, how did this poppet come into my house?

MARY WARREN (*frightened for herself, her voice very small*). What poppet's that, sir?

PROCTOR (*impatiently, pointing at the doll in* CHEEVER's *hand*). This poppet, this poppet.

MARY WARREN (*evasively, looking at it*). Why, I—I think it is mine.

PROCTOR. It is your poppet, is it not?

MARY WARREN (*not understanding the direction of this*). It—is, sir.

PROCTOR. And how did it come into this house?

MARY WARREN (*glancing about at the avid*[16] *faces*). Why—I made it in the court, sir, and—give it to Goody Proctor tonight.

PROCTOR (*to* HALE). Now, sir—do you have it?

HALE. Mary Warren, a needle have been found inside this poppet.

MARY WARREN (*bewildered*). Why, I meant no harm by it, sir.

PROCTOR (*quickly*). You stuck that needle in yourself?

MARY WARREN. I—I believe I did, sir, I—

PROCTOR (*to* HALE). What say you now?

HALE (*watching* MARY WARREN *closely*). Child, you are certain this be your natural memory? May it be, perhaps, that someone conjures you even now to say this?

MARY WARREN. Conjures me? Why, no, sir, I am entirely myself, I think. Let you ask Susanna Walcott—she saw me sewin' it in court. *Or better still.* Ask Abby, Abby sat beside me when I made it.

PROCTOR (*to* HALE, *of* CHEEVER). Bid him begone.

---

15. **ineptly** (in ept′lē), *adv.* in an awkward or clumsy manner.
16. **avid** (av′id), *adj.* extremely eager.

Your mind is surely settled now. Bid him out, Mr. Hale.

ELIZABETH. What signifies a needle?

HALE. Mary—you charge a cold and cruel murder on Abigail.

MARY WARREN. Murder! I charge no—

HALE. Abigail were stabbed tonight; a needle were found stuck into her belly—

ELIZABETH. And she charges me?

HALE. Aye.

ELIZABETH (*her breath knocked out*). Why—! The girl is murder! She must be ripped out of the world!

CHEEVER (*pointing at* ELIZABETH). You've heard that, sir! Ripped out of the world! Herrick, you heard it!

PROCTOR (*suddenly snatching the warrant out of* CHEEVER's *hands*). Out with you.

CHEEVER. Proctor, you dare not touch the warrant.

PROCTOR (*ripping the warrant*). Out with you!

CHEEVER. You've ripped the Deputy Governor's warrant, man!

PROCTOR. Damn the Deputy Governor! Out of my house!

HALE. Now, Proctor, Proctor!

PROCTOR. Get y'gone with them! You are a broken minister.

HALE. Proctor, if she is innocent, the court—

PROCTOR. If *she* is innocent! Why do you never wonder if Parris be innocent, or Abigail? Is the accuser always holy now? Were they born this morning as clean as God's fingers? I'll tell you what's walking Salem—vengeance is walking Salem. We are what we always were in Salem, but now the little crazy children are jangling the keys of the kingdom, and common vengeance writes the law! This warrant's vengeance! I'll not give my wife to vengeance!

ELIZABETH. I'll go, John—

PROCTOR. You will not go!

HERRICK. I have nine men outside. You cannot keep her. The law binds me, John, I cannot budge.

PROCTOR (*to* HALE, *ready to break him*). Will you see her taken?

HALE. Proctor, the court is just—

PROCTOR. Pontius Pilate! God will not let you wash your hands of this!

ELIZABETH. John—I think I must go with them. (*He cannot bear to look at her.*) Mary, there is bread enough for the morning; you will bake, in the afternoon. Help Mr. Proctor as you were his daughter—you owe me that, and much more. (*She is fighting her weeping. To* PROCTOR). When the children wake, speak nothing of witchcraft—it will frighten them. (*She cannot go on.*)

PROCTOR. I will bring you home. I will bring you soon.

ELIZABETH. Oh, John, bring me soon!

PROCTOR. I will fall like an ocean on that court! Fear nothing, Elizabeth.

ELIZABETH (*with great fear*). I will fear nothing. (*She looks about the room, as though to fix it in her mind.*) Tell the children I have gone to visit someone sick.

(*She walks out the door,* HERRICK *and* CHEEVER *behind her. For a moment,* PROCTOR *watches from the doorway. The clank of chain is heard.*)

PROCTOR. Herrick! Herrick! don't chain her! (*He rushes out the door. From outside*). Damn you, man, you will not chain her! Off with them! I'll not have it! I will not have her chained!

(*There are other men's voices against his.* HALE, *in a fever of guilt and uncertainty, turns from the door to avoid the sight;* MARY WARREN *bursts into tears and sits weeping.* GILES COREY *calls to* HALE.)

GILES. And yet silent, minister? It is fraud, you know it is fraud! What keeps you, man?

(PROCTOR *is half braced, half pushed into the room by two deputies and* HERRICK.)

PROCTOR. I'll pay you, Herrick, I will surely pay you!

HERRICK (*panting*). In God's name, John, I cannot help myself. I must chain them all. Now let you keep inside this house till I am gone! (*He goes out with his deputies.*)

(PROCTOR *stands there, gulping air. Horses and a wagon creaking are heard.*)

HALE (*in great uncertainty*). Mr. Proctor—

PROCTOR. Out of my sight!

HALE. Charity, Proctor, charity. What I have heard in her favor, I will not fear to testify in court. God help me, I cannot judge her guilty or innocent—I know not. Only this consider: the world goes mad, and it profit nothing you should lay the cause to the vengeance of a little girl.

PROCTOR. You are a coward! Though you be ordained in God's own tears, you are a coward now!

HALE. Proctor, I cannot think God be provoked so grandly by such a petty cause. The jails are packed—our greatest judges sit in Salem now—and hangin's promised. Man, we must look to cause proportionate. Were there murder done, perhaps, and never brought to light? Abomination? Some secret blasphemy that stinks to Heaven? Think on cause, man, and let you help me to discover it. For there's your way, believe it, there is your only way, when such confusion strikes upon the world. (*He goes to* GILES *and* FRANCIS.) Let you counsel among yourselves; think on your village and what may have drawn from heaven such thundering wrath upon you all. I shall pray God open up our eyes.

(HALE *goes out.*)

FRANCIS (*struck by* HALE'S *mood*). I never heard no murder done in Salem.

PROCTOR (*he has been reached by* HALE'S *words*). Leave me, Francis, leave me.

GILES (*shaken*). John—tell me, are we lost?

PROCTOR. Go home now, Giles. We'll speak on it tomorrow.

GILES. Let you think on it. We'll come early, eh?

PROCTOR. Aye. Go now, Giles.

GILES. Good night, then.

(GILES COREY *goes out. After a moment*).

MARY WARREN (*in a fearful squeak of a voice*). Mr. Proctor, very likely they'll let her come home once they're given proper evidence.

PROCTOR. You're coming to the court with me, Mary. You will tell it in the court.

MARY WARREN. I cannot charge murder on Abigail.

PROCTOR (*moving menacingly*[17] *toward her*). You will tell the court how that poppet come here and who stuck the needle in.

MARY WARREN. She'll kill me for sayin' that! (PROCTOR *continues toward her.*) Abby'll charge lechery on you, Mr. Proctor.

PROCTOR (*halting*). She's told you!

MARY WARREN. I have known it, sir. She'll ruin you with it, I know she will.

PROCTOR (*hesitating, and with deep hatred of himself*). Good. Then her saintliness is done with. (MARY *backs from him.*) We will slide together into our pit; you will tell the court what you know.

MARY WARREN (*in terror*). I cannot, they'll turn on me—

(PROCTOR *strides and catches her, and she is repeating, "I cannot, I cannot!"*)

PROCTOR. My wife will never die for me! I will bring your guts into your mouth but that goodness will not die for me!

MARY WARREN (*struggling to escape him*). I cannot do it, I cannot!

PROCTOR (*grasping her by the throat as though he would strangle her*). Make your peace with it! Now Hell and Heaven grapple on our backs, and all our old pretense is ripped away— make your peace! (*He throws her to the floor, where she sobs, "I cannot, I cannot . . ." And now, half to himself, staring, and turning to the open door*). Peace. It is a providence, and no great change; we are only what we always were, but naked now. (*He walks as though toward a great horror, facing the open sky.*) Aye, naked! And the wind, God's icy wind, will blow!

(*And she is over and over again sobbing, "I cannot, I cannot, I cannot," as*

THE CURTAIN FALLS

---

17. **menacingly** (men′is ing lē), *adv.* in a threatening manner.

After Reading

Making Connections

Shaping Your Response

1. What advice do you have for John and Elizabeth Proctor to improve their marriage?

2. Write three words that describe Abigail, and tell why they fit her.

Analyzing the Play

3. Why do you think John Proctor is reluctant to appear before the court and repeat what Abigail told him about the night in the forest?

4. In your opinion, what is the **climax** of Act Two?

5. John Proctor has a way with words. Find examples of **figurative language** that he uses that are especially vivid.

Extending the Ideas

6. ✋ Consider the reasons why Goody Good and Goody Osburn are more likely to be accused within the Puritan **group** than Elizabeth Proctor. Are the reasons just? Explain your answer.

Vocabulary Study

scoff, ameliorate, pallor, avid, indignant, deference, evasive, suspiciously, ineptly, menacingly

Playwrights describe how characters are to speak their lines in stage directions. Use the Glossary to determine the meaning of each of the words at the left. Find the words in Act Two (they are underlined) and read the lines the way Arthur Miller wanted them to be spoken. Then write an original dialogue between two people using these words to describe the speakers' attitudes.

Expressing Your Ideas—

Writing Choices

Writer's Notebook Update Much of the guilt in Salem has nothing to do with witchcraft. Choose one of the following characters: John Proctor, Abigail, Reverend Parris, Mary Warren, or Goody Putnam. Write a paragraph explaining a reason or reasons for his or her guilt.

What's the Big Idea? Jot down the major conflict in the play. At this point, what do you think Arthur Miller wants the audience to learn? Then write a sentence that expresses what you think is the **theme** of the play. As you read on, you may want to refine your theme statement.

Good Riddance Abigail called Elizabeth Proctor a bitter, cold, sniveling woman. How does Elizabeth feel about Abigail? Be Elizabeth and write your feelings about her in a personal **diary entry**.

Act Three

(The vestry room of the Salem meeting house, now serving as the anteroom of the General Court.

As the curtain rises, the room is empty, but for sunlight pouring through two high windows in the back wall. The room is solemn,[1] even forbidding. Heavy beams jut out, boards of random widths make up the walls. At the right are two doors leading into the meeting house proper, where the court is being held. At the left another door leads outside.

There is a plain bench at the left, and another at the right. In the center a rather long meeting table, with stools and a considerable armchair snugged up to it.

Through the partitioning wall at the right we hear a prosecutor's[2] voice, JUDGE HATHORNE'S, *asking a question; then a woman's voice,* MARTHA COREY'S, *replying.)*

HATHORNE'S VOICE. Now, Martha Corey, there is abundant evidence in our hands to show that you have given yourself to the reading of fortunes. Do you deny it?

MARTHA COREY'S VOICE. I am innocent to a witch. I know not what a witch is.

HATHORNE'S VOICE. How do you know, then, that you are not a witch?

MARTHA COREY'S VOICE. If I were, I would know it.

HATHORNE'S VOICE. Why do you hurt these children?

MARTHA COREY'S VOICE. I do not hurt them. I scorn it!

GILES' VOICE *(roaring).* I have evidence for the court!

(Voices of townspeople rise in excitement.)

DANFORTH'S VOICE. You will keep your seat!

GILES' VOICE. Thomas Putnam is reaching out for land!

DANFORTH'S VOICE. Remove that man, Marshal!

GILES' VOICE. You're hearing lies, lies!

(A roaring goes up from the people.)

HATHORNE'S VOICE. Arrest him, excellency!

GILES' VOICE. I have evidence. Why will you not hear my evidence?

(The door opens and GILES *is half carried into the vestry room by* HERRICK.*)*

GILES. Hands off, damn you, let me go!

HERRICK. Giles, Giles!

GILES. Out of my way, Herrick! I bring evidence—

HERRICK. You cannot go in there, Giles; it's a court!

(Enter HALE *from the court.)*

HALE. Pray be calm a moment.

GILES. You, Mr. Hale, go in there and demand I speak.

HALE. A moment, sir, a moment.

GILES. They'll be hangin' my wife!

*(JUDGE HATHORNE *enters. He is in his sixties, a bitter, remorseless Salem judge.)*

HATHORNE. How do you dare come roarin' into this court! Are you gone daft,[3] Corey?

GILES. You're not a Boston judge yet, Hathorne. You'll not call me daft!

(Enter DEPUTY GOVERNOR DANFORTH *and, behind him,* EZEKIEL CHEEVER *and* PARRIS. *On his appearance, silence falls.* DANFORTH *is a grave man in his sixties, of some humor and sophistication that does not, however, interfere with an exact loyalty to his position and his cause. He comes down to* GILES, *who awaits his wrath.[4])*

DANFORTH *(looking directly at* GILES). Who is this man?

---

1. **solemn** (sol'əm), *adj.* gloomy; dark; somber in color.
2. **prosecutor** (pros'ə kyü'tər), *n.* the lawyer in charge of the government's case against an accused person.
3. **gone daft,** crazy; insane.
4. **wrath** (rath), *n.* punishment caused by anger.

PARRIS. Giles Corey, sir, and a more contentious—

GILES (*to* PARRIS) I am asked the question, and I am old enough to answer it! (*To* DANFORTH, *who impresses him and to whom he smiles through his strain*). My name is Corey, sir, Giles Corey. I have six hundred acres, and timber in addition. It is my wife you be condemning now. (*He indicates the courtroom.*)

DANFORTH. And how do you imagine to help her cause with such contemptuous riot? Now be gone. Your old age alone keeps you out of jail for this.

GILES (*beginning to plead*). They be tellin' lies about my wife, sir, I—

DANFORTH. Do you take it upon yourself to determine what this court shall believe and what it shall set aside?

GILES. Your Excellency, we mean no disrespect for—

DANFORTH. Disrespect, indeed! It is disruption, Mister. This is the highest court of the supreme government of this province, do you know it?

GILES (*beginning to weep*). Your Excellency, I only said she were readin' books, sir, and they come and take her out of my house for—

DANFORTH (*mystified*). Books! What books?

GILES (*through helpless sobs*). It is my third wife, sir; I never had no wife that be so taken with books, and I thought to find the cause of it, d'y'see, but it were no witch I blamed her for. (*He is openly weeping.*) I have broke charity with the woman. I have broke charity with her. (*He covers his face, ashamed.* DANFORTH *is respectfully silent.*)

HALE. Excellency, he claims hard evidence for his wife's defense. I think that in all justice you must—

DANFORTH. Then let him submit his evidence in proper affidavit.[5] You are certainly aware of our procedure here, Mr. Hale. (*To* HERRICK). Clear this room.

HERRICK. Come now, Giles. (*He gently pushes* COREY *out.*)

FRANCIS. We are desperate, sir; we come here three days now and cannot be heard.

DANFORTH. Who is this man?

FRANCIS. Francis Nurse, Your Excellency.

HALE. His wife's Rebecca that were condemned this morning.

DANFORTH. Indeed! I am amazed to find you in such uproar. I have only good report of your character, Mr. Nurse.

HATHORNE. I think they must both be arrested in contempt,[6] sir.

DANFORTH (*to* FRANCIS). Let you write your plea, and in due time I will—

FRANCIS. Excellency, we have proof for your eyes; God forbid you shut them to it. The girls, sir, the girls are frauds.

DANFORTH. What's that?

FRANCIS. We have proof of it, sir. They are all deceiving you.

(DANFORTH *is shocked, but studying* FRANCIS.)

HATHORNE. This is contempt, sir, contempt!

DANFORTH. Peace, Judge Hathorne. Do you know who I am, Mr. Nurse?

FRANCIS. I surely do, sir, and I think you must be a wise judge to be what your are.

DANFORTH. And do you know that near to four hundred are in the jails from Marblehead to Lynn, and upon my signature?

FRANCIS. I—

DANFORTH. And seventy-two condemned to hang by that signature?

FRANCIS. Excellency, I never thought to say it to such a weighty judge, but you are deceived.

(*Enter* GILES COREY *from left. All turn to see as he beckons in* MARY WARREN *with* PROCTOR. MARY *is keeping her eyes to the ground;* PROCTOR *has her elbow as though she were near collapse.*)

PARRIS (*on seeing her, in shock*). Mary Warren! (*He goes directly to bend close to her face.*) What are you about here?

PROCTOR (*pressing* PARRIS *away from her with a gentle*

---

5. **affidavit** (af/ə dā/vit), *n.* statement written down and sworn to be true, usually before an authorized official.

6. **contempt** (kən tempt/), *n.* open disrespect for the rules or decisions of a court of law.

but firm motion of protectiveness). She would speak with the Deputy Governor.

DANFORTH (*shocked by this, turns to* HERRICK). Did you not tell me Mary Warren were sick in bed?

HERRICK. She were, Your Honor. When I go to fetch her to the court last week, she said she were sick.

GILES. She has been strivin' with her soul all week, Your Honor; she comes now to tell the truth of this to you.

DANFORTH. Who is this?

PROCTOR. John Proctor, sir. Elizabeth Proctor is my wife.

PARRIS. Beware this man, Your Excellency, this man is mischief.

HALE (*excitedly).* I think you must hear the girl, sir, she—

DANFORTH (*who has become very interested in* MARY WARREN *and only raises a hand toward* HALE). Peace. What would you tell us, Mary Warren?

(PROCTOR *looks at her, but she cannot speak.)*

PROCTOR. She never saw no spirits, sir.

DANFORTH (*with great alarm and surprise, to* MARY). Never saw no spirits!

GILES (*eagerly).* Never.

PROCTOR (*reaching into his jacket).* She has signed a deposition,[7] sir—

DANFORTH (*instantly).* No, no, I accept no depositions. (*He is rapidly calculating this; he turns from her to* PROCTOR). Tell me, Mr. Proctor, have you given out this story in the village?

PROCTOR. We have not.

PARRIS. They've come to overthrow the court, sir! This man is—

DANFORTH. I pray you, Mr. Parris. Do you know, Mr. Proctor, that the entire contention of the state in these trials is that the voice of Heaven is speaking through the children?

PROCTOR. I know that, sir.

DANFORTH (*thinks, staring at* PROCTOR, *then turns to* MARY WARREN). And you, Mary Warren, how came you to cry out people for sending their spirits against you?

MARY WARREN. It were pretense, sir.

DANFORTH. I cannot hear you.

PROCTOR. It were pretense, she says.

DANFORTH. Ah? And the other girls? Susanna Walcott, and—the others? They are also pretending?

MARY WARREN. Aye, sir.

DANFORTH (*wide-eyed).* Indeed. (*Pause. He is baffled by this. He turns to study* PROCTOR'S *face.)*

PARRIS (*in a sweat).* Excellency, you surely cannot think to let so vile a lie be spread in open court?

DANFORTH. Indeed not, but it strike hard upon me that she will dare come here with such a tale. Now, Mr. Proctor, before I decide whether I shall hear you or not, it is my duty to tell you this. We burn a hot fire here; it melts down all concealment.

PROCTOR. I know that, sir.

DANFORTH. Let me continue. I understand well, a husband's tenderness may drive him to extravagance in defense of a wife. Are you certain in your conscience, Mister, that your evidence is the truth?

PROCTOR. It is. And you will surely know it.

DANFORTH. And you thought to declare this revelation in the open court before the public?

PROCTOR. I thought I would, aye—with your permission.

DANFORTH (*his eyes narrowing).* Now, sir, what is your purpose in so doing?

PROCTOR. Why, I—I would free my wife, sir.

DANFORTH. There lurks nowhere in your heart, nor hidden in your spirit, any desire to undermine this court?

PROCTOR (*with the faintest faltering).* Why, no, sir.

CHEEVER (*clears his throat, awakening).* I—Your Excellency.

DANFORTH. Mr. Cheever.

CHEEVER. I think it be my duty, sir—(*Kindly, to* PROCTOR.) You'll not deny it, John. (*To* DANFORTH.) When we come to take his wife, he damned the court and ripped your warrant.

PARRIS. Now you have it!

---

7. **deposition** (dep/ə zish/ən), *n.* testimony, especially a sworn statement in writing.

DANFORTH. He did that, Mr. Hale?

HALE (*takes a breath*). Aye, he did.

PROCTOR. It were a temper, sir. I knew not what I did.

DANFORTH (*studying him*). Mr. Proctor.

PROCTOR. Aye, sir.

DANFORTH (*straight into his eyes*). Have you ever seen the Devil?

PROCTOR. No, sir.

DANFORTH. You are in all respects a Gospel Christian?

PROCTOR. I am, sir.

PARRIS. Such a Christian that will not come to church but once in a month!

DANFORTH (*restrained—he is curious*). Not come to church?

PROCTOR. I—I have no love for Mr. Parris. It is no secret. But God I surely love.

CHEEVER. He plow on Sunday, sir.

DANFORTH. Plow on Sunday!

CHEEVER (*apologetically*). I think it be evidence, John. I am an official of the court, I cannot keep it.

PROCTOR. I—I have once or twice plowed on Sunday. I have three children, sir, and until last year my land give little.

GILES. You'll find other Christians that do plow on Sunday if the truth be known.

HALE. Your Honor, I cannot think you may judge the man on such evidence.

DANFORTH. I judge nothing. (*Pause. He keeps watching* PROCTOR, *who tries to meet his gaze.*) I tell you straight, Mister—I have seen marvels in this court. I have seen people choked before my eyes by spirits; I have seen them stuck by pins and slashed by daggers. I have until this moment not the slightest reason to suspect that the children may be deceiving me. Do you understand my meaning?

PROCTOR. Excellency, does it not strike upon you that so many of these women have lived so long with such upright reputation, and—

PARRIS. Do you read the Gospel, Mr. Proctor?

PROCTOR. I read the Gospel.

PARRIS. I think not, or you should surely know that Cain were an upright man, and yet he did kill Abel.

PROCTOR. Aye, God tells us that. (*To* DANFORTH). But who tells us Rebecca Nurse murdered seven babies by sending out her spirit on them? It is the children only, and this one will swear she lied to you.

(DANFORTH *considers, then beckons* HATHORNE *to him.* HATHORNE *leans in, and he speaks in his ear.* HATHORNE *nods.*)

HATHORNE. Aye, she's the one.

DANFORTH. Mr. Proctor, this morning, your wife send me a claim in which she states that she is pregnant now.

PROCTOR. My wife pregnant!

DANFORTH. There be no sign of it—we have examined her body.

PROCTOR. But if she say she is pregnant, then she must be! That woman will never lie, Mr. Danforth.

DANFORTH. She will not?

PROCTOR. Never, sir, never.

DANFORTH. We have thought it too convenient to be credited. However, if I should tell you now that I will let her be kept another month; and if she begin to show her natural signs, you shall have her living yet another year until she is delivered—what say you to that? (JOHN PROCTOR *is struck silent.*) Come now. You say your only purpose is to save your wife. Good, then, she is saved at least this year, and a year is long. What say you, sir? It is done now. (*In conflict,* PROCTOR *glances at* FRANCIS *and* GILES.) Will you drop this charge?

PROCTOR. I—I think I cannot.

DANFORTH (*now an almost imperceptible[8] hardness in his voice*). Then your purpose is somewhat larger.

PARRIS. He's come to overthrow this court, Your Honor!

PROCTOR. These are my friends. Their wives are also accused—

---

8. **imperceptible** (im′pər sep′tə bəl), *adj.* cannot be perceived or felt.

DANFORTH (*with a sudden briskness of manner*). I judge you not, sir. I am ready to hear your evidence.

PROCTOR. I come not to hurt the court; I only—

DANFORTH (*cutting him off*). Marshal, go into the court and bid Judge Stoughton and Judge Sewall declare recess for one hour. And let them go to the tavern, if they will. All witnesses and prisoners are to be kept in the building.

HERRICK. Aye, sir. (*Very deferentially*). If I may say it, sir, I know this man all my life. It is a good man, sir.

DANFORTH (*it is the reflection on himself he resents*). I am sure of it, Marshal. (HERRICK *nods, then goes out.*) Now, what deposition do you have for us, Mr. Proctor? And I beg you to be clear, open as the sky, and honest.

PROCTOR (*as he takes out several papers*). I am no lawyer, so I'll—

DANFORTH. The pure in heart need no lawyers. Proceed as you will.

PROCTOR (*handing* DANFORTH *a paper*). Will you read this first, sir? It's a sort of testament. The people signing it declare their good opinion of Rebecca, and my wife, and Martha Corey. (DANFORTH *looks down at the paper.*)

PARRIS (*to enlist* DANFORTH'S *sarcasm*). Their good opinion! (*But* DANFORTH *goes on reading, and* PROCTOR *is heartened.*)

PROCTOR. These are all landholding farmers, members of the church. (*Delicately, trying to point out a paragraph*). If you'll notice, sir—they've known the women many years and never saw no sign they had dealings with the Devil.

(PARRIS *nervously moves over and reads over* DANFORTH'S *shoulder.*)

DANFORTH (*glancing down a long list*). How many names are here?

FRANCIS. Ninety-one, Your Excellency.

PARRIS (*sweating*). These people should be summoned. (DANFORTH *looks up at him questioningly.*) For questioning.

FRANCIS (*trembling with anger*). Mr. Danforth, I gave them all my word no harm would come to them for signing this.

PARRIS. This is a clear attack upon the court!

HALE (*to* PARRIS, *trying to contain himself*). Is every defense an attack upon the court? Can no one—?

PARRIS. All innocent and Christian people are happy for the courts in Salem! These people are gloomy for it. (*To* DANFORTH *directly*). And I think you will want to know, from each and every one of them, what discontents them with you!

HATHORNE. I think they ought to be examined, sir.

DANFORTH. It is not necessarily an attack, I think. Yet—

FRANCIS. These are all covenanted Christians, sir.

DANFORTH. Then I am sure they may have nothing to fear. (*Hands* CHEEVER *the paper.*) Mr. Cheever, have warrants drawn for all of these—arrest for examination. (*To* PROCTOR). Now, Mister, what other information do you have for us? (FRANCIS *is still standing, horrified.*) You may sit, Mr. Nurse.

FRANCIS. I have brought trouble on these people. I have—

DANFORTH. No, old man, you have not hurt these people if they are of good conscience. But you must understand, sir, that a person is either with this court or he must be counted against it, there be no road between. This is a sharp time, now, a precise time—we live no longer in the dusky afternoon when evil mixed itself with good and befuddled the world. Now, by God's grace, the shining sun is up, and them that fear not light will surely praise it. I hope you will be one of those. (MARY WARREN *suddenly sobs.*) She's not hearty, I see.

PROCTOR. No, she's not, sir. (*To* MARY, *bending to her, holding her hand, quietly*). Now remember what the angel Raphael said to the boy Tobias. Remember it.

MARY WARREN (*hardly audible*). Aye.

PROCTOR. "Do that which is good, and no harm shall come to thee."

MARY WARREN. Aye.

DANFORTH. Come, man, we wait you.

(MARSHAL HERRICK *returns, and takes his post at the door.*)

GILES. John, my deposition, give him mine.

PROCTOR. Aye. (*He hands* DANFORTH *another paper.*) This is Mr. Corey's deposition.

DANFORTH. Oh? (*He looks down at it. Now* HATHORNE *comes behind him and reads with him.*)

HATHORNE (*suspiciously*). What lawyer drew this, Corey?

GILES. You know I never hired a lawyer in my life, Hathorne.

DANFORTH (*finishing the reading*). It is very well phrased. My compliments. Mr. Parris, if Mr. Putnam is in the court, will you bring him in? (HATHORNE *takes the deposition, and walks to the window with it.* PARRIS *goes into the court.*) You have no legal training, Mr. Corey?

GILES (*very pleased*). I have the best, sir—I am thirty-three time in court in my life. And always plaintiff, too.

DANFORTH. Oh, then you're much put-upon.

GILES. I am never put-upon; I know my rights, sir, and I will have them. You know, your father tried a case of mine—might be thirty-five years ago, I think.

DANFORTH. Indeed.

GILES. He never spoke to you of it?

DANFORTH. No, I cannot recall it.

GILES. That's strange, he give me nine pound damages. He were a fair judge, your father. Y'see, I had a white mare that time, and this fellow come to borrow the mare—(*Enter* PARRIS *with* THOMAS PUTNAM. *When he sees* PUTNAM, GILES' *ease goes; he is hard.*) Aye, there he is.

DANFORTH. Mr. Putnam, I have here an accusation by Mr. Corey against you. He states that you coldly prompted your daughter to cry witchery upon George Jacobs that is now in jail.

PUTNAM. It is a lie.

DANFORTH (*turning to* GILES). Mr. Putnam states your charge is a lie. What say you to that?

GILES (*furious, his fists clenched*). A fart on Thomas Putnam, that is what I say to that!

DANFORTH. What proof do you submit for your charge, sir?

GILES. My proof is there! (*Pointing to the paper.*) If Jacobs hangs for a witch he forfeit[9] up his property—that's law! And there is none but Putnam with the coin to buy so great a piece. This man is killing his neighbors for their land!

DANFORTH. But proof, sir, proof.

GILES (*pointing at his deposition*). The proof is there! I have it from an honest man who heard Putnam say it! The day his daughter cried out on Jacobs, he said she'd given him a fair gift of land.

HATHORNE. And the name of this man?

GILES (*taken aback*). What name?

HATHORNE. The man that give you this information.

GILES (*hesitates, then*). Why, I—I cannot give you his name.

HATHORNE. And why not?

GILES (*hesitates, then bursts out*). You know well why not! He'll lay in jail if I give his name!

HATHORNE. This is contempt of court, Mr. Danforth!

DANFORTH (*to avoid that*). You will surely tell us the name.

GILES. I will not give you no name. I mentioned my wife's name once and I'll burn in hell long enough for that. I stand mute.

DANFORTH. In that case, I have no choice but to arrest you for contempt of this court, do you know that?

GILES. This is a hearing; you cannot clap me for contempt of a hearing.

DANFORTH. Oh, it is a proper lawyer! Do you wish me to declare the court in full session here? Or will you give me good reply?

GILES (*faltering*). I cannot give you no name, sir, I cannot.

DANFORTH. You are a foolish old man. Mr. Cheever, begin the record. The court is now in session. I ask you, Mr. Corey—

PROCTOR (*breaking in*). Your Honor—he has the story in confidence, sir, and he—

---

9. **forfeit** (fôr′fit), *v.* giving up of something as a penalty.

PARRIS. The Devil lives on such confidences! (*To* DANFORTH). Without confidences there could be no conspiracy,[10] Your Honor!

HATHORNE. I think it must be broken, sir.

DANFORTH (*to* GILES). Old man, if your informant tells the truth let him come here openly like a decent man. But if he hide in anonymity I must know why. Now sir, the government and central church demand of you the name of them who reported Mr. Thomas Putnam a common murderer.

HALE. Excellency—

DANFORTH. Mr. Hale.

HALE. We cannot blink it more. There is a prodigious fear of this court in the country—

DANFORTH. Then there is a prodigious guilt in the country. Are *you* afraid to be questioned here?

HALE. I may only fear the Lord, sir, but there is fear in the country nevertheless.

DANFORTH (*angered now*). Reproach me not with the fear in the country; there is fear in the country because there is a moving plot to topple Christ in the country!

HALE. But it does not follow that everyone accused is part of it.

DANFORTH. No uncorrupted man may fear this court, Mr. Hale! None! (*To* GILES). You are under arrest in contempt of this court. Now sit you down and take counsel with yourself, or you will be set in the jail until you decide to answer all questions.

(GILES COREY *makes a rush for* PUTNAM. PROCTOR *lunges and holds him.*)

PROCTOR. No, Giles.

GILES (*over* PROCTOR'S *shoulder at* PUTNAM). I'll cut your throat, Putnam, I'll kill you yet!

PROCTOR (*forcing him into a chair*). Peace, Giles, peace. (*Releasing him.*) We'll prove ourselves. Now we will. (*He starts to turn to* DANFORTH.)

GILES. Say nothin' more, John. (*Pointing at* DANFORTH). He's only playin' you! He means to hang us all!

(MARY WARREN *bursts into sobs.*)

DANFORTH. This is a court of law, Mister. I'll have no effrontery here!

PROCTOR. Forgive him, sir, for his old age. Peace, Giles, we'll prove it all now. (*He lifts up* MARY'S *chin.*) You cannot weep, Mary. Remember the angel, what he say to the boy. Hold to it, now; there is your rock. (MARY *quiets. He takes out a paper, and turns to* DANFORTH.) This is Mary Warren's deposition. I—I would ask you remember, sir, while you read it, that until two week ago she were no different than the other children are today. (*He is speaking reasonably, restraining all his fears, his anger, his anxiety.*) You saw her scream, she howled, she swore familiar spirits choked her; she even testified that Satan, in the form of women now in jail, tried to win her soul away, and then when she refused—

DANFORTH. We know all this.

PROCTOR. Aye, sir. She swears now that she never saw Satan; nor any spirit, vague or clear, that Satan may have sent to hurt her. And she declares her friends are lying now.

(PROCTOR *starts to hand* DANFORTH *the deposition, and* HALE *comes up to* DANFORTH *in a trembling state.*)

HALE. Excellency, a moment. I think this goes to the heart of the matter.

DANFORTH (*with deep misgivings*). It surely does.

HALE. I cannot say he is an honest man; I know him little. But in all justice, sir, a claim so weighty cannot be argued by a farmer. In God's name, sir, stop here; send him home and let him come again with a lawyer—

DANFORTH (*patiently*). Now look you, Mr. Hale—

HALE. Excellency, I have signed seventy-two death warrants; I am a minister of the Lord, and I dare not take a life without there be a proof so immaculate[11] no slightest qualm[12] of conscience may doubt it.

DANFORTH. Mr. Hale, you surely do not doubt my justice.

---

10. **conspiracy** (kən spir′ə sē), *n.* secret planning with others to do something unlawful or wrong.
11. **immaculate** (i mak′yə lit), *adj.* without fault or errors.
12. **qualm** (kwäm, kwälm), *n.* disturbance of conscience.

HALE. I have this morning signed away the soul of Rebecca Nurse, Your Honor. I'll not conceal it, my hand shakes yet as with a wound! I pray you, sir, *this* argument let lawyers present to you.

DANFORTH. Mr. Hale, believe me; for a man of such terrible learning you are most bewildered—I hope you will forgive me. I have been thirty-two year at the bar, sir, and I should be confounded were I called upon to defend these people. Let you consider, now— *(To* PROCTOR *and the others).* And I bid you all do likewise. In an ordinary crime, how does one defend the accused? One calls up witnesses to prove his innocence. But witchcraft is *ipso facto,* on its face and by its nature, an invisible crime, is it not? Therefore, who may possibly be witness to it? The witch and the victim. None other. Now we cannot hope the witch will accuse herself; granted? Therefore, we must rely upon her victims—and they do testify, the children certainly do testify. As for the witches, none will deny that we are most eager for all their confessions. Therefore, what is left for a lawyer to bring out? I think I have made my point. Have I not?

HALE. But this child claims the girls are not truthful, and if they are not—

DANFORTH. That is precisely what I am about to consider, sir. What more may you ask of me? Unless you doubt my probity?

HALE *(defeated).* I surely do not, sir. Let you consider it, then.

DANFORTH. And let you put your heart to rest. Her deposition, Mr. Proctor.

*(*PROCTOR *hands it to him.* HATHORNE *rises, goes beside* DANFORTH, *and starts reading.* PARRIS *comes to his other side.* DANFORTH *looks at* JOHN PROCTOR, *then proceeds to read.* HALE *gets up, finds position near the judge, reads too.* PROCTOR *glances at* GILES. FRANCIS *prays silently, hands pressed together.* CHEEVER *waits placidly, the sublime official, dutiful.* MARY WARREN *sobs once.* JOHN PROCTOR *touches her head reassuringly. Presently* DANFORTH *lifts his eyes, stands up, takes out a kerchief and blows his nose. The others stand aside as he moves in thought toward the window.)*

PARRIS *(hardly able to contain his anger and fear).* I should like to question—

DANFORTH *(his first real outburst, in which his contempt for* PARRIS *is clear).* Mr. Parris, I bid you be silent! *(He stands in silence, looking out the window. Now, having established that he will set the gait).* Mr. Cheever, will you go into the court and bring the children here? (CHEEVER *gets up and goes out upstage.* DANFORTH *now turns to* MARY.) Mary Warren, how came you to this turnabout? Has Mr. Proctor threatened you for this deposition?

MARY WARREN. No, sir.

DANFORTH. Has he ever threatened you?

MARY WARREN *(weaker).* No, sir.

DANFORTH *(sensing a weakening).* Has he threatened you?

MARY WARREN. No, sir.

DANFORTH. Then you tell me that you sat in my court, callously lying, when you knew that people would hang by your evidence? *(She does not answer.)* Answer me!

MARY WARREN *(almost inaudibly).* I did, sir.

DANFORTH. How were you instructed in your life? Do you not know that God damns all liars? *(She cannot speak.)* Or is it now that you lie?

MARY WARREN. No, sir—I am with God now.

DANFORTH. You are with God now.

MARY WARREN. Aye, sir.

DANFORTH *(containing himself).* I will tell you this—you are either lying now, or you were lying in the court, and in either case you have committed perjury[13] and you will go to jail for it. You cannot lightly say you lied, Mary. Do you know that?

MARY WARREN. I cannot lie no more. I am with God, I am with God.

(But she breaks into sobs at the thought of it, and the right door opens, and enter SUSANNA WALCOTT, MERCY LEWIS, BETTY PARRIS, *and finally* ABIGAIL. CHEEVER *comes to* DANFORTH.)

---

13. **perjury** (pėr′jər ē), *n.* crime of willfully giving false testimony or withholding evidence while under oath.

CHEEVER. Ruth Putnam's not in the court, sir, nor the other children.

DANFORTH. These will be sufficient. Sit you down, children. *(Silently they sit.)* Your friend, Mary Warren, has given us a deposition. In which she swears that she never saw familiar spirits, apparitions, nor any manifest of the Devil. She claims as well that none of you have seen these things either. *(Slight pause.)* Now, children, this is a court of law. The law, based upon the Bible, and the Bible, writ by Almighty God, forbid the practice of witchcraft, and describe death as the penalty thereof. But likewise, children, the law and Bible damn all bearers of false witness. *(Slight pause.)* Now then. It does not escape me that this deposition may be devised to blind us; it may well be that Mary Warren has been conquered by Satan, who sends her here to distract our sacred purpose. If so, her neck will break for it. But if she speaks true, I bid you now drop your guile and confess your pretense, for a quick confession will go easier with you. *(Pause.)* Abigail Williams, rise. (ABIGAIL *slowly rises.*) Is there any truth in this?

ABIGAIL. No, sir.

DANFORTH *(thinks, glances at* MARY, *then back to* ABIGAIL*).* Children, a very augur bit[14] will now be turned into your souls until your honesty is proved. Will either of you change your positions now, or do you force me to hard questioning?

ABIGAIL. I have naught to change, sir. She lies.

DANFORTH *(to* MARY*).* You would still go on with this?

MARY WARREN *(faintly).* Aye, sir.

DANFORTH *(turning to* ABIGAIL*).* A poppet were discovered in Mr. Proctor's house, stabbed by a needle. Mary Warren claims that you sat beside her in the court when she made it, and that you saw her make it and witnessed how she herself stuck her needle into it for safe-keeping. What say you to that?

ABIGAIL *(with a slight note of indignation).* It is a lie, sir.

DANFORTH *(after a slight pause).* While you worked for Mr. Proctor, did you see poppets in that house?

ABIGAIL. Goody Proctor always kept poppets.

PROCTOR. Your Honor, my wife never kept no poppets. Mary Warren confesses it was her poppet.

CHEEVER. Your Excellency.

DANFORTH. Mr. Cheever.

CHEEVER. When I spoke with Goody Proctor in that house, she said she never kept no poppets. But she said she did keep poppets when she were a girl.

PROCTOR. She has not been a girl these fifteen years, Your Honor.

HATHORNE. But a poppet will keep fifteen years, will it not?

---

14. **a very auger bit** (ô′gər), *n.* tool for boring holes in wood or the earth.

PROCTOR. It will keep if it is kept, but Mary Warren swears she never saw no poppets in my house, nor anyone else.

PARRIS. Why could there not have been poppets hid where no one ever saw them?

PROCTOR (*furious*). There might also be a dragon with five legs in my house, but no one has ever seen it.

PARRIS. We are here, Your Honor, precisely to discover what no one has ever seen.

PROCTOR. Mr. Danforth, what profit this girl to turn herself about? What may Mary Warren gain but hard questioning and worse?

DANFORTH. You are charging Abigail Williams with a marvelous cool plot to murder, do you understand that?

PROCTOR. I do, sir. I believe she means to murder.

DANFORTH (*pointing at* ABIGAIL, *incredulously*[15]). This child would murder your wife?

PROCTOR. It is not a child. Now hear me, sir. In the sight of the congregation she were twice this year put out of this meetin' house for laughter during prayer.

DANFORTH (*shocked, turning to* ABIGAIL). What's this? Laughter during—!

PARRIS. Excellency, she were under Tituba's power at that time, but she is solemn now.

GILES. Aye, now she is solemn and goes to hang people!

DANFORTH. Quiet, man.

HATHORNE. Surely it have no bearing on the question, sir. He charges contemplation of murder.

DANFORTH. Aye. (*He studies* ABIGAIL *for a moment, then*). Continue, Mr. Proctor.

PROCTOR. Mary. Now tell the Governor how you danced in the woods.

PARRIS (*instantly*). Excellency, since I come to Salem this man is blackening my name. He—

DANFORTH. In a moment, sir. (*To* MARY WARREN, *sternly, and surprised*). What is this dancing?

MARY WARREN. I—(*She glances at* ABIGAIL, *who is staring down at her remorselessly. Then, appealing to* PROCTOR). Mr. Proctor—

PROCTOR (*taking it right up*). Abigail leads the girls to the woods, Your Honor, and they have danced there naked—

PARRIS. Your Honor, this—

PROCTOR (*at once*). Mr. Parris discovered them himself in the dead of night! There's the "child" she is!

DANFORTH (*It is growing into a nightmare, and he turns, astonished, to* PARRIS). Mr. Parris—

PARRIS. I can only say, sir, that I never found any of them naked, and this man is—

DANFORTH. But you discovered them dancing in the woods? (*Eyes on* PARRIS, *he points at* ABIGAIL.) Abigail?

HALE. Excellency, when I first arrived from Beverly, Mr. Parris told me that.

DANFORTH. Do you deny it, Mr. Parris?

PARRIS. I do not, sir, but I never saw any of them naked.

DANFORTH. But she have *danced*?

PARRIS (*unwillingly*). Aye, sir.

(DANFORTH, *as though with new eyes, looks at* ABIGAIL.)

HATHORNE. Excellency, will you permit me? (*He points at* MARY WARREN.)

DANFORTH (*with great worry*). Pray, proceed.

HATHORNE. You say you never saw no spirits, Mary, were never threatened or afflicted by any manifest of the Devil or the Devil's agents.

MARY WARREN (*very faintly*). No, sir.

HATHORNE (*with a gleam of victory*). And yet, when people accused of witchery confronted you in court, you would faint, saying their spirits came out of their bodies and choked you—

MARY WARREN. That were pretense, sir.

DANFORTH. I cannot hear you.

MARY WARREN. Pretense, sir.

PARRIS. But you did turn cold, did you not? I myself picked you up many times, and your skin were icy. Mr. Danforth, you—

DANFORTH. I saw that many times.

PROCTOR. She only pretended to faint, Your Excellency. They're all marvelous pretenders.

---

15. **incredulously** (in krej′ə ləs lē), *adv.* in a doubting or skeptical manner.

HATHORNE. Then can she pretend to faint now?

PROCTOR. Now?

PARRIS. Why not? Now there are no spirits attacking her, for none in this room is accused of witchcraft. So let her turn herself cold now, let her pretend she is attacked now, let her faint. (*He turns to* MARY WARREN.) Faint!

MARY WARREN. Faint?

PARRIS. Aye, faint. Prove to us how you pretended in the court so many times.

MARY WARREN (*looking to* PROCTOR). I—cannot faint now, sir.

PROCTOR (*alarmed, quietly*). Can you not pretend it?

MARY WARREN. I—(*She looks about as though searching for the passion to faint.*) I—have no *sense* of it now, I—

DANFORTH. Why? What is lacking now?

MARY WARREN. I—cannot tell, sir, I—

DANFORTH. Might it be that here we have no afflicting spirit loose, but in the court there were some?

MARY WARREN. I never saw no spirits.

PARRIS. Then see no spirits now, and prove to us that you can faint by your own will, as you claim.

MARY WARREN (*stares, searching for the emotion of it, and then shakes her head*). I—cannot do it.

PARRIS. Then you will confess, will you not? It were attacking spirits made you faint!

MARY WARREN. No, sir, I—

PARRIS. Your Excellency, this is a trick to blind the court!

MARY WARREN. It's not a trick! (*She stands.*) I—I used to faint because I—I thought I saw spirits.

DANFORTH. *Thought* you saw them!

MARY WARREN. But I did not, Your Honor.

HATHORNE. How could you think you saw them unless you saw them?

MARY WARREN. I—I cannot tell how, but I did. I—I heard the other girls screaming, and you, Your Honor, you seemed to believe them, and I—It were only sport in the beginning, sir, but then the whole world cried spirits,

spirits, and I—I promise you Mr. Danforth, I only thought I saw them but I did not.

(DANFORTH *peers at her.*)

PARRIS (*smiling, but nervous because* DANFORTH *seems to be struck by* MARY WARREN'S *story*). Surely Your Excellency is not taken by this simple lie.

DANFORTH (*turning worriedly to* ABIGAIL). Abigail. I bid you now search your heart and tell me this—and beware of it, child, to God every soul is precious and His vengeance is terrible on them that take life without cause. Is it possible, child, that the spirits you have seen are illusion only, some deception that may cross your mind when—

ABIGAIL. Why, this—this—is a base question, sir.

DANFORTH. Child, I would have you consider it—

ABIGAIL. I have been hurt, Mr. Danforth; I have seen my blood runnin' out! I have been near to murdered every day because I done my duty pointing out the Devil's people—and this is my reward? To be mistrusted, denied, questioned like a—

DANFORTH (*weakening*). Child, I do not mistrust you—

ABIGAIL (*in an open threat*). Let *you* beware, Mr. Danforth. Think you to be so mighty that the power of Hell may not turn *your* wits? Beware of it! There is—(*Suddenly, from an accusatory attitude, her face turns, looking into the air above—it is truly frightened.*)

DANFORTH (*apprehensively*). What is it, child?

ABIGAIL (*looking about in the air, clasping her arms about her as though cold*). I—I know not. A wind, a cold wind, has come. (*Her eyes fall on* MARY WARREN.)

MARY WARREN (*terrified, pleading*). Abby!

MERCY LEWIS (*shivering*). Your Honor, I freeze!

PROCTOR. They're pretending!

HATHORNE (*touching* ABIGAIL'S *hand*). She is cold, Your Honor, touch her!

MERCY LEWIS (*through chattering teeth*). Mary, do you send this shadow on me?

MARY WARREN. Lord, save me!

SUSANNA WALCOTT. I freeze, I freeze!

ABIGAIL (*shivering visibly*). It is a wind, a wind!

MARY WARREN. Abby, don't do that!

DANFORTH (*himself engaged and entered by* ABIGAIL). Mary Warren, do you witch her? I say to you, do you send your spirit out?

(*With a hysterical cry* MARY WARREN *starts to run.* PROCTOR *catches her.*)

MARY WARREN (*almost collapsing*). Let me go, Mr. Proctor, I cannot, I cannot—

ABIGAIL (*crying to Heaven*). Oh, Heavenly Father, take away this shadow!

(*Without warning or hesitation,* PROCTOR *leaps at* ABIGAIL *and, grabbing her by the hair, pulls her to her feet. She screams in pain.* DANFORTH, *astonished, cries, "What are you about?" and* HATHORNE *and* PARRIS *call, "Take your hands off her!" and out of it all comes* PROCTOR'S *roaring voice.*)

PROCTOR. How do you call Heaven! Whore! Whore!

(HERRICK *breaks* PROCTOR *from her.*)

HERRICK. John!

DANFORTH. Man! Man, what do you—

PROCTOR (*breathless and in agony*). It is a whore!

DANFORTH (*dumfounded*). You charge—?

ABIGAIL. Mr. Danforth, he is lying!

PROCTOR. Mark her! Now she'll suck a scream to stab me with, but—

DANFORTH. You will prove this! This will not pass!

PROCTOR (*trembling, his life collapsing about him*). I have known her, sir. I have known her.

DANFORTH. You—you are a lecher?

FRANCIS (*horrified*). John, you cannot say such a—

PROCTOR. Oh, Francis, I wish you had some evil in you that you might know me! (*To* DANFORTH). A man will not cast away his good name. You surely know that.

DANFORTH (*dumfounded*). In—in what time? In what place?

PROCTOR (*his voice about to break, and his shame great*). In the proper place—where my beasts are bedded. On the last night of my joy, some eight months past. She used to serve me in my house, sir. (*He has to clamp his jaw to keep from weeping.*) A man may think God sleeps, but God sees everything, I know it now. I beg you,

sir, I beg you—see her what she is. My wife, my dear good wife, took this girl soon after, sir, and put her out on the highroad. And being what she is, a lump of vanity, sir—(*He is being overcome.*) Excellency, forgive me, forgive me. (*Angrily against himself, he turns away from the Governor for a moment. Then, as though to cry out is his only means of speech left*). She thinks to dance with me on my wife's grave! And well she might, for I thought of her softly. God help me, I lusted, and there *is* a promise in such sweat. But it is a whore's vengeance, and you must see it; I set myself entirely in your hands. I know you must see it now.

DANFORTH (*blanched, in horror, turning to* ABIGAIL). You deny every scrap and tittle of this?

ABIGAIL. If I must answer that, I will leave and I will not come back again!

(DANFORTH *seems unsteady.*)

PROCTOR. I have made a bell of my honor! I have rung the doom of my good name—you will believe me, Mr. Danforth! My wife is innocent, except she knew a whore when she saw one!

ABIGAIL (*stepping up to* DANFORTH). What look do you give me? (DANFORTH *cannot speak.*) I'll not have such looks! (*She turns and starts for the door.*)

DANFORTH. You will remain where you are! (HERRICK *steps into her path. She comes up short, fire in her eyes.*) Mr. Parris, go into the court and bring Goodwife Proctor out.

PARRIS (*objecting*). Your Honor, this is all a—

DANFORTH (*sharply to* PROCTOR). Bring her out! And tell her not one word of what's been spoken here. And let you knock before you enter. (PARRIS *goes out.*) Now we shall touch the bottom of this swamp. (*To* PROCTOR). Your wife, you say, is an honest woman.

PROCTOR. In her life, sir, she have never lied. There are them that cannot sing, and them that cannot weep—my wife cannot lie. I have paid much to learn it, sir.

DANFORTH. And when she put this girl out of your house, she put her out for a harlot?

PROCTOR. Aye, sir.

DANFORTH. And knew her for a harlot?

PROCTOR. Aye, sir, she knew her for a harlot.

DANFORTH. Good then. (*To* ABIGAIL). And if she tell me, child, it were for harlotry, may God spread His mercy on you! (*There is a knock. He calls to the door.*) Hold! (*To* ABIGAIL). Turn your back. Turn your back. (*To* PROCTOR). Do likewise. (*Both turn their backs—*ABIGAIL *with indignant slowness.*) Now let neither of you turn to face Goody Proctor. No one in this room is to speak one word, or raise a gesture aye or nay. (*He turns toward the door, calls*). Enter! (*The door opens.* ELIZABETH *enters with* PARRIS. PARRIS *leaves her. She stands alone, her eyes looking for* PROCTOR.) Mr. Cheever, report this testimony in all exactness. Are you ready?

CHEEVER. Ready, sir.

DANFORTH. Come here, woman. (ELIZABETH *comes to him, glancing at* PROCTOR'S *back.*) Look at me only, not at your husband. In my eyes only.

ELIZABETH (*faintly*). Good, sir.

DANFORTH. We are given to understand that at one time you dismissed your servant, Abigail Williams.

ELIZABETH. That is true, sir.

DANFORTH. For what cause did you dismiss her? (*Slight pause. Then* ELIZABETH *tries to glance at* PROCTOR.) You will look in my eyes only and not at your husband. The answer is in your memory and you need no help to give it to me. Why did you dismiss Abigail Williams?

ELIZABETH (*not knowing what to say, sensing a situation, wetting her lips to stall for time*). She— dissatisfied me. (*Pause.*) And my husband.

DANFORTH. In what way dissatisfied you?

ELIZABETH. She were—(*She glances at* PROCTOR *for a cue.*)

DANFORTH. Woman, look at me! (ELIZABETH *does.*) Were she slovenly? Lazy? What disturbance did she cause?

ELIZABETH. Your Honor, I—in that time I were sick. And I—My husband is a good and righteous man. He is never drunk as some are, nor wastin' his time at the shovelboard, but always at his work. But in my sickness—you see, sir, I were a long time sick after my last baby, and I thought I saw my husband somewhat turning from me. And this girl—(*She turns to* ABIGAIL.)

DANFORTH. Look at me.

ELIZABETH. Aye, sir. Abigail Williams—(*She breaks off.*)

DANFORTH. What of Abigail Williams?

ELIZABETH. I came to think he fancied her. And so one night I lost my wits, I think, and put her out on the highroad.

DANFORTH. Your husband—did he indeed turn from you?

ELIZABETH (*in agony*). My husband—is a goodly man, sir.

DANFORTH. Then he did not turn from you.

ELIZABETH (*starting to glance at* PROCTOR). He—

DANFORTH (*reaches out and holds her face, then*). Look at me! To your own knowledge, has John Proctor ever committed the crime of lechery? (*In a crisis of indecision she cannot speak.*) Answer my question! Is your husband a lecher!

ELIZABETH (*faintly*). No, sir.

DANFORTH. Remove her, Marshal.

PROCTOR. Elizabeth, tell the truth!

DANFORTH. She has spoken. Remove her!

PROCTOR (*crying out*). Elizabeth, I have confessed it!

ELIZABETH. Oh, God! (*The door closes behind her.*)

PROCTOR. She only thought to save my name!

HALE. Excellency, it is a natural lie to tell; I beg you, stop now before another is condemned! I may shut my conscience to it no more— private vengeance is working through this testimony! From the beginning this man has struck me true. By my oath to Heaven, I believe him now, and I pray you call back his wife before we—

DANFORTH. She spoke nothing of lechery, and this man has lied!

HALE. I believe him! (*Pointing at* ABIGAIL). This girl has always struck me false! She—

(ABIGAIL, *with a weird, wild, chilling cry, screams up to the ceiling.*)

ABIGAIL. You will not! Begone! Begone, I say!

DANFORTH. What is it, child? (*But* ABIGAIL, *pointing with fear, is now raising up her frightened eyes, her awed face, toward the ceiling—the girls are doing the same—and now* HATHORNE, HALE, PUTNAM, CHEEVER, HERRICK, *and* DANFORTH *do the same.*) What's there? (*He lowers his eyes from the ceiling, and now he is frightened; there is real tension in his voice.*) Child! (*She is transfixed—with all the girls, she is whimpering open-mouthed, agape at the ceiling.*) Girls! Why do you—?

MERCY LEWIS (*pointing*). It's on the beam! Behind the rafter!

DANFORTH (*looking up*). Where!

ABIGAIL. Why—? (*She gulps.*) Why do you come, yellow bird?

PROCTOR. Where's a bird? I see no bird!

ABIGAIL (*to the ceiling*). My face? My face?

PROCTOR. Mr. Hale—

DANFORTH. Be quiet!

PROCTOR (*to* HALE). Do you see a bird?

DANFORTH. Be quiet!!

ABIGAIL (*to the ceiling, in a genuine conversation with the "bird," as though trying to talk it out of attacking her*). But God made my face; you cannot want to tear my face. Envy is a deadly sin, Mary.

MARY WARREN (*on her feet with a spring, and horrified, pleading*). Abby!

ABIGAIL (*unperturbed, continuing to the "bird"*). Oh, Mary, this is a black art to change your shape. No, I cannot, I cannot stop my mouth; it's God's work I do.

MARY WARREN. Abby, I'm *here!*

PROCTOR (*frantically*). They're pretending, Mr. Danforth!

ABIGAIL (*now she takes a backward step, as though in fear the bird will swoop down momentarily*). Oh, please, Mary! Don't come down.

SUSANNA WALCOTT. Her claws, she's stretching her claws!

PROCTOR. Lies, lies.

ABIGAIL (*backing further, eyes still fixed above*). Mary, please don't hurt me!

MARY WARREN (*to* DANFORTH). I'm not hurting her!

DANFORTH (*to* MARY WARREN). Why does she see this vision?

MARY WARREN. She sees nothin'!

ABIGAIL (*now staring full front as though hypnotized, and mimicking the exact tone of* MARY WARREN'S *cry*). She sees nothin'!

MARY WARREN (*pleading*). Abby, you mustn't!

ABIGAIL AND ALL THE GIRLS (*all transfixed*). Abby, you mustn't!

MARY WARREN (*to all the girls*). I'm here, I'm here!

GIRLS. I'm here! I'm here!

DANFORTH (*horrified*). Mary Warren! Draw back your spirit out of them!

MARY WARREN. Mr. Danforth!

GIRLS (*cutting her off*). Mr. Danforth!

DANFORTH. Have you compacted with the Devil? Have you?

MARY WARREN. Never, never!

GIRLS. Never, never!

DANFORTH (*growing hysterical*). Why can they only repeat you?

PROCTOR. Give me a whip—I'll stop it!

MARY WARREN. They're sporting. They—!

GIRLS. They're sporting!

MARY WARREN (*turning on them all hysterically and stamping her feet*). Abby, stop it!

GIRLS (*stamping their feet*). Abby, stop it!

MARY WARREN. Stop it!

GIRLS. Stop it!

MARY WARREN (*screaming it out at the top of her lungs, and raising her fists*). Stop it!!

GIRLS (*raising their fists*). Stop it!!

(MARY WARREN, *utterly confounded, and becoming overwhelmed by* ABIGAIL'S—*and the girls'—utter conviction, starts to whimper, hands half raised, powerless, and all the girls begin whimpering exactly as she does.*)

DANFORTH. A little while ago you were afflicted. Now it seems you afflict others; where did you find this power?

MARY WARREN (*staring at* ABIGAIL). I—have no power.

GIRLS. I have no power.

PROCTOR. They're gulling you, Mister!

DANFORTH. Why did you turn about this past two weeks? You have seen the Devil, have you not?

HALE (*indicating* ABIGAIL *and the girls*). You cannot believe them!

MARY WARREN. I—

PROCTOR *(sensing her weakening).* Mary, God damns all liars!

DANFORTH *(pounding it into her).* You have seen the Devil, you have made compact with Lucifer, have you not?

PROCTOR. God damns liars, Mary!

(MARY utters something unintelligible, staring at ABIGAIL, who keeps watching the "bird" above.)

DANFORTH. I cannot hear you. What do you say? *(MARY utters again unintelligibly.)* You will confess yourself or you will hang! *(He turns her roughly to face him.)* Do you know who I am? I say you will hang if you do not open with me!

PROCTOR. Mary, remember the angel Raphael— do that which is good and—

ABIGAIL *(pointing upward).* The wings! Her wings are spreading! Mary, please, don't, don't—!

HALE. I see nothing, Your Honor!

DANFORTH. Do you confess this power! *(He is an inch from her face.)* Speak!

ABIGAIL. She's going to come down! She's walking the beam!

DANFORTH. Will you speak!

MARY WARREN *(staring in horror).* I cannot!

GIRLS. I cannot!

PARRIS. Cast the Devil out! Look him in the face! Trample him! We'll save you, Mary, only stand fast against him and—

ABIGAIL (*looking up*). Look out! She's coming down!

(*She and all the girls run to one wall, shielding their eyes. And now, as though cornered, they let out a gigantic scream, and* MARY, *as though infected, opens her mouth and screams with them. Gradually* ABIGAIL *and the girls leave off, until only* MARY *is left there, staring up at the "bird," screaming madly. All watch her, horrified by this evident fit.* PROCTOR *strides to her.*)

PROCTOR. Mary, tell the Governor what they— (*He has hardly got a word out, when, seeing him coming for her, she rushes out of his reach, screaming in horror.*)

MARY WARREN. Don't touch me—don't touch me! (*At which the girls halt at the door.*)

PROCTOR (*astonished*). Mary!

MARY WARREN (*pointing at* PROCTOR). You're the Devil's man!

(*He is stopped in his tracks.*)

PARRIS. Praise God!

THE GIRLS. Praise God!

PROCTOR (*numbed*). Mary, how—?

MARY WARREN. I'll not hang with you! I love God, I love God.

DANFORTH (*to* MARY). He bid you do the Devil's work?

MARY WARREN (*hysterically, indicating* PROCTOR). He come at me by night and every day to sign, to sign, to—

DANFORTH. Sign what?

PARRIS. The Devil's book? He come with a book?

MARY WARREN (*hysterically, pointing at* PROCTOR, *fearful of him*). My name, he want my name. "I'll murder you," he says, "if my wife hangs! We must go and overthrow the court," he says!

(DANFORTH'S *head jerks toward* PROCTOR, *shock and horror in his face.*)

PROCTOR (*turning, appealing to* HALE). Mr. Hale!

MARY WARREN (*her sobs beginning*). He wake me every night, his eyes were like coals and his fingers claw my neck, and I sign, I sign . . .

HALE. Excellency, this child's gone wild!

PROCTOR (*as* DANFORTH'S *wide eyes pour on him*). Mary, Mary!

MARY WARREN (*screaming at him*). No, I love God; I go your way no more. I love God, I bless God. (*Sobbing she rushes to* ABIGAIL.) Abby, Abby, I'll never hurt you more! (*They all watch, as* ABIGAIL, *out of her infinite charity, reaches out and draws the sobbing* MARY *to her, and then looks up to* DANFORTH.)

DANFORTH (*to* PROCTOR). What are you? (PROCTOR *is beyond speech in his anger.*) You are combined with anti-Christ, are you not? I have seen your power; you will not deny it! What say you, Mister?

HALE. Excellency—

DANFORTH. I will have nothing from you, Mr. Hale! (*To* PROCTOR). Will you confess yourself befouled with Hell, or do you keep that black allegiance yet? What say you?

PROCTOR (*his mind wild, breathless*). I say—I say—God is dead!

PARRIS. Hear it, hear it!

PROCTOR (*laughs insanely, then*). A fire, a fire is burning! I hear the boot of Lucifer,[16] I see his filthy face! and it is my face, and yours, Danforth! For them that quail to bring men out of ignorance, as I have quailed, and as you quail now when you know in all your black hearts that this be fraud—God damns our kind especially, and we will burn, we will burn together!

DANFORTH. Marshal! Take him and Corey with him to the jail!

HALE (*starting across to the door*). I denounce[17] these proceedings!

PROCTOR. You are pulling Heaven down and raising up a whore!

HALE. I denounce these proceedings, I quit this court! (*He slams the door to the outside behind him.*)

DANFORTH (*calling to him in a fury*). Mr. Hale! Mr. Hale!

THE CURTAIN FALLS

---

16. **Lucifer** (lü′sə fər), Satan; the Devil.
17. **denounce** (di nouns′), *v.* to condemn openly; censure.

After Reading

Making Connections

Shaping Your Response

1. To which of the characters does the phrase "no-win situation" apply?
2. Do you think Elizabeth was right or wrong to lie for her husband? Why?

Analyzing the Play

3. "You're the Devil's man!" Why does Mary Warren change sides again and accuse John Proctor?
4. "I denounce these proceedings . . . " Why does Reverend Hale storm out of the courtroom?
5. Consider the **theme** or underlying meaning of the play. What might Arthur Miller be trying to say through the events and characters in Salem?

Extending the Ideas

6. What do you think Reverend Hale would have said to Samuel Sewall if he had gone to see him after the arrest of John Proctor?
7. Clearly justice was not done in Salem. Can you think of other examples of injustices fueled by mass hysteria?

Vocabulary Study

prosecutor
affidavit
contempt
perjury
deposition

Courtrooms, like other places of business, have a specialized vocabulary. Use your Glossary to learn the meanings of the vocabulary words listed at the left. Prepare a brief oral summary of Act Three using these words and present it to the class.

Expressing Your Ideas

Writing Choices

Writer's Notebook Update Look back in your Writer's Notebook to see how you classified the characters in the story: "good," "evil," influenced by others, or struggling with their consciences. Do you still agree with your initial assessment of the characters? Choose a character that you think has changed and write a few paragraphs describing how he or she has changed and what brought about that change.

The Last Hope Reverend Hale storms out of the courtroom in anger and frustration when John Proctor, Giles Corey, and Francis Nurse are arrested. When he cools down, he decides to try once more to convince Deputy Governor Danforth of the huge hoax that the girls of Salem are staging. Write a **letter** to Danforth from Hale presenting evidence to clear the men as well as the many townspeople who have been falsely accused of witchcraft.

Act Four

(A cell in Salem jail, that fall.

At the back is a high barred window; near it, a great, heavy door. Along the walls are two benches. The place is in darkness but for the moonlight seeping through the bars. It appears empty. Presently footsteps are heard coming down a corridor beyond the wall, keys rattle, and the door swings open. MARSHAL HERRICK *enters with a lantern.*

He is nearly drunk, and heavy-footed. He goes to a bench and nudges a bundle of rags lying on it.)

HERRICK. Sarah, wake up! Sarah Good! *(He then crosses to the other bench.)*

SARAH GOOD *(rising in her rags).* Oh, Majesty! Comin', comin'! Tituba, he's here, His Majesty's come!

HERRICK. Go to the north cell; this place is wanted now. *(He hangs his lantern on the wall.* TITUBA *sits up.)*

TITUBA. That don't look to me like His Majesty; look to me like the marshal.

HERRICK *(taking out a flask).* Get along with you now, clear this place. *(He drinks, and* SARAH GOOD *comes and peers up into his face.)*

SARAH GOOD. Oh, is it you, Marshal! I thought sure you be the devil comin' for us. Could I have a sip of cider for me goin'-away?

HERRICK *(handing her the flask).* And where are you off to, Sarah?

TITUBA *(as* SARAH *drinks).* We goin' to Barbados, soon the Devil gits here with the feathers and the wings.

HERRICK. Oh? A happy voyage to you.

SARAH GOOD. A pair of bluebirds wingin' southerly, the two of us! Oh, it be a grand transformation, Marshal! *(She raises the flask to drink again.)*

HERRICK *(taking the flask from her lips).* You'd best give me that or you'll never rise off the ground. Come along now.

TITUBA. I'll speak to him for you, if you desires to come along, Marshal.

HERRICK. I'd not refuse it, Tituba; it's the proper morning to fly into Hell.

TITUBA. Oh, it be no Hell in Barbados. Devil, him be pleasureman in Barbados, him be singin' and dancin' in Barbados. It's you folks—you riles him up 'round here; it be too cold 'round here for that Old Boy. He freeze his soul in Massachusetts, but in Barbados he just as sweet and—*(A bellowing cow is heard, and* TITUBA *leaps up and calls to the window).* Aye, sir! That's him, Sarah.

SARAH GOOD. I'm here, Majesty! *(They hurriedly pick up their rags as* HOPKINS, *a guard, enters.)*

HOPKINS. The Deputy Governor's arrived.

HERRICK *(grabbing* TITUBA*).* Come along, come along.

TITUBA *(resisting him).* No, he comin' for me. I goin' home!

HERRICK *(pulling her to the door).* That's not Satan, just a poor old cow with a hatful of milk. Come along now, out with you!

TITUBA *(calling to the window).* Take me home, Devil! Take me home!

SARAH GOOD *(following the shouting* TITUBA *out).* Tell him I'm goin', Tituba! Now you tell him Sarah Good is goin' too!

(In the corridor outside TITUBA *calls on—"Take me home, Devil; Devil take me home!" and* HOPKINS' *voice orders her to move on.* HERRICK *returns and begins to push old rags and straw into a corner. Hearing footsteps, he turns, and enter* DANFORTH

and JUDGE HATHORNE. *They are in greatcoats and wear hats against the bitter cold. They are followed in by* CHEEVER, *who carries a dispatch case and a flat wooden box containing his writing materials.)*

HERRICK. Good morning, Excellency.

DANFORTH. Where is Mr. Parris?

HERRICK. I'll fetch him. *(He starts for the door.)*

DANFORTH. Marshal. (HERRICK *stops.)* When did Reverend Hale arrive?

HERRICK. It were toward midnight, I think.

DANFORTH *(suspiciously).* What is he about here?

HERRICK. He goes among them that will hang, sir. And he prays with them. He sits with Goody Nurse now. And Mr. Parris with him.

DANFORTH. Indeed. That man have no authority to enter here, Marshal. Why have you let him in?

HERRICK. Why, Mr. Parris command me, sir. I cannot deny him.

DANFORTH. Are you drunk, Marshal?

HERRICK. No, sir; it is a bitter night, and I have no fire here.

DANFORTH *(containing his anger).* Fetch Mr. Parris.

HERRICK. Aye, sir.

DANFORTH. There is a prodigious stench in this place.

HERRICK. I have only now cleared the people out for you.

DANFORTH. Beware hard drink, Marshal.

HERRICK. Aye, sir. *(He waits an instant for further orders. But* DANFORTH, *in dissatisfaction, turns his back on him, and* HERRICK *goes out. There is a pause.* DANFORTH *stands in thought.)*

HATHORNE. Let you question Hale, Excellency; I should not be surprised he have been preaching in Andover lately.

DANFORTH. We'll come to that; speak nothing of Andover. Parris prays with him. That's strange. *(He blows on his hands, moves toward the window, and looks out.)*

HATHORNE. Excellency, I wonder if it be wise to let Mr. Parris so continuously with the prisoners. (DANFORTH *turns to him, interested.)* I think, sometimes, the man has a mad look these days.

DANFORTH. Mad?

HATHORNE. I met him yesterday coming out of his house, and I bid him good morning— and he wept and went his way. I think it is not well the village sees him so unsteady.

DANFORTH. Perhaps he have some sorrow.

CHEEVER *(stamping his feet against the cold).* I think it be the cows, sir.

DANFORTH. Cows?

CHEEVER. There be so many cows wanderin' the highroads, now their masters are in the jails, and much disagreement who they will belong to now. I know Mr. Parris be arguin' with farmers all yesterday—there is great contention, sir, about the cows. Contention make him weep, sir; it were always a man that weep for contention. *(He turns, as do* HATHORNE *and* DANFORTH, *hearing someone coming up the corridor.* DANFORTH *raises his head as* PARRIS *enters. He is gaunt,[1] frightened, and sweating in his greatcoat.)*

PARRIS *(to* DANFORTH, *instantly).* Oh, good morning, sir, thank you for coming, I beg your pardon wakin' you so early. Good morning, Judge Hathorne.

DANFORTH. Reverend Hale have no right to enter this—

PARRIS. Excellency, a moment. *(He hurries back and shuts the door.)*

HATHORNE. Do you leave him alone with the prisoners?

DANFORTH. What's his business here?

PARRIS *(prayerfully holding up his hands).* Excellency, hear me. It is a providence. Reverend Hale has returned to bring Rebecca Nurse to God.

DANFORTH *(surprised).* He bids her confess?

PARRIS *(sitting).* Hear me. Rebecca have not given me a word this three month since she came. Now she sits with him, and her sister and Martha Corey and two or three others, and he pleads with them, confess their crimes and save their lives.

---

1. **gaunt** (gônt), *adj.* very thin and bony; with hollow eyes and a starved look.

DANFORTH. Why—this is indeed a providence. And they soften, they soften?

PARRIS. Not yet, not yet. But I thought to summon you, sir, that we might think on whether it be not wise, to—(*He dares not say it.*) I had thought to put a question, sir, and I hope you will not—

DANFORTH. Mr. Parris, be plain, what troubles you?

PARRIS. There is news, sir, that the court—the court must reckon with. My niece, sir, my niece—I believe she has vanished.

DANFORTH. Vanished!

PARRIS. I had thought to advise you of it earlier in the week, but—

DANFORTH. Why? How long is she gone?

PARRIS. This be the third night. You see, sir, she told me she would stay a night with Mercy Lewis. And next day, when she does not return, I send to Mr. Lewis to inquire. Mercy told him she would sleep in *my* house for a night.

DANFORTH. They are both gone?!

PARRIS (*in fear of him*). They are, sir.

DANFORTH (*alarmed*). I will send a party for them. Where may they be?

PARRIS. Excellency, I think they be aboard a ship. (DANFORTH *stands agape.*) My daughter tells me how she heard them speaking of ships last week, and tonight I discover my—my strongbox is broke into. (*He presses his fingers against his eyes to keep back tears.*)

HATHORNE (*astonished*). She have robbed you?

PARRIS. Thirty-one pound is gone. I am penniless. (*He covers his face and sobs.*)

DANFORTH. Mr. Parris, you are a brainless man! (*He walks in thought, deeply worried.*)

PARRIS. Excellency, it profit nothing you should blame me. I cannot think they would run off except they fear to keep in Salem any more. (*He is pleading.*) Mark it, sir, Abigail had close knowledge of the town, and since the news of Andover has broken here—

DANFORTH. Andover is remedied. The court returns there on Friday, and will resume examinations.

PARRIS. I am sure of it, sir. But the rumor here speaks rebellion in Andover, and it—

DANFORTH. There is no rebellion in Andover!

PARRIS. I tell you what is said here, sir. Andover have thrown out the court, they say, and will have no part of witchcraft. There be a faction here, feeding on that news, and I tell you true, sir. I fear there will be riot here.

HATHORNE. Riot! Why at every execution I have seen naught but high satisfaction in the town.

PARRIS. Judge Hathorne—it were another sort that hanged till now. Rebecca Nurse is no Bridget that lived three year with Bishop before she married him. John Proctor is not Isaac Ward that drank his family to ruin. (*To* DANFORTH). I would to God it were not so, Excellency, but these people have great weight yet in the town. Let Rebecca stand upon the gibbet[2] and send up some righteous prayer, and I fear she'll wake a vengeance on you.

HATHORNE. Excellency, she is condemned a witch. The court have—

DANFORTH (*in deep concern, raising a hand to* HATHORNE). Pray you. (*To* PARRIS). How do you propose, then?

PARRIS. Excellency, I would postpone these hangin's for a time.

DANFORTH. There will be no postponement.[3]

PARRIS. Now Mr. Hale's returned, there is hope, I think—for if he bring even one of these to God, that confession surely damns the others in the public eye, and none may doubt more that they are all linked to Hell. This way, unconfessed and claiming innocence, doubts are multiplied, many honest people will weep for them, and our good purpose is lost in their tears.

DANFORTH (*after thinking a moment, then going to* CHEEVER). Give me the list.

(CHEEVER *opens the dispatch case, searches.*)

---

2. **gibbet** (jib′it), *n.* an upright post with a projecting arm from which bodies are hung as execution.

3. **postponement** (pōst pōn′mənt), *n.* delay.

PARRIS. It cannot be forgot, sir, that when I summoned the congregation for John Proctor's excommunication[4] there were hardly thirty people come to hear it. That speak a discontent, I think, and—

DANFORTH (*studying the list*). There will be no postponement.

PARRIS. Excellency—

DANFORTH. Now, sir—which of these in your opinion may be brought to God? I will myself strive with him till dawn. (*He hands the list to* PARRIS, *who merely glances at it.*)

PARRIS. There is not sufficient time till dawn.

DANFORTH. I shall do my utmost. Which of them do you have hope for?

PARRIS (*not even glancing at the list now, and in a quavering voice, quietly*). Excellency—a dagger— (*He chokes up.*)

DANFORTH. What do you say?

PARRIS. Tonight, when I open my door to leave my house—a dagger clattered to the ground. (*Silence.* DANFORTH *absorbs this. Now* PARRIS *cries out*). You cannot hang this sort. There is danger for me. I dare not step outside at night!

(REVEREND HALE *enters. They look at him for an instant in silence. He is steeped in sorrow, exhausted, and more direct than he ever was.*)

DANFORTH. Accept my congratulations, Reverend Hale; we are gladdened to see you returned to your good work.

HALE (*coming to* DANFORTH *now*). You must pardon them. They will not budge.

(HERRICK *enters, waits.*)

DANFORTH (*conciliatory*). You misunderstand, sir; I cannot pardon these when twelve are already hanged for the same crime. It is not just.

PARRIS (*with failing heart*). Rebecca will not confess?

HALE. The sun will rise in a few minutes. Excellency, I must have more time.

DANFORTH. Now hear me, and beguile yourselves no more. I will not receive a single plea for pardon or postponement. Them that will not confess will hang. Twelve are already executed; the names of these seven are given out, and the village expects to see them die this morning. Postponement now speaks a floundering on my part; reprieve[5] or pardon must cast doubt upon the guilt of them that died till now. While I speak God's law, I will not crack its voice with whimpering. If retaliation[6] is your fear, know this—I should hang ten thousand that dared to rise against the law, and an ocean of salt tears could not melt the resolution of the statutes. Now draw yourselves up like men and help me, as you are bound by Heaven to do. Have you spoken with them all, Mr. Hale?

HALE. All but Proctor. He is in the dungeon.

DANFORTH (*to* HERRICK). What's Proctor's way now?

HERRICK. He sits like some great bird; you'd not know he lived except he will take food from time to time.

DANFORTH (*after thinking a moment*). His wife—his wife must be well on with child now.

HERRICK. She is, sir.

DANFORTH. What think you, Mr. Parris? You have closer knowledge of this man; might her presence soften him?

PARRIS. It is possible, sir. He have not laid eyes on her these three months. I should summon her.

DANFORTH (*to* HERRICK). Is he yet adamant?[7] Has he struck at you again?

HERRICK. He cannot, sir, he is chained to the wall now.

DANFORTH (*after thinking on it*). Fetch Goody Proctor to me. Then let you bring him up.

HERRICK. Aye, sir. (HERRICK *goes. There is silence.*)

HALE. Excellency, if you postpone a week and publish to the town that you are striving for

---

4. **excommunication** (ek′skə myü′nə kā′shən), *n.* a formal cutting off from membership in the church.
5. **reprieve** (ri prēv′), *n.* delay in carrying out a punishment, especially the death penalty.
6. **retaliation** (ri tal′ē ā′shən), *n.* pay back for a wrong, injury, etc.
7. **adamant** (ad′ə mənt), *adj.* firm and unyielding; immovable.

their confessions, that speak mercy on your part, not faltering.

DANFORTH. Mr. Hale, as God have not empowered me like Joshua to stop this sun from rising, so I cannot withhold from them the perfection of their punishment.

HALE *(harder now)*. If you think God wills you to raise rebellion, Mr. Danforth, you are mistaken!

DANFORTH *(instantly)*. You have heard rebellion spoken in the town?

HALE. Excellency, there are orphans wandering from house to house; abandoned cattle bellow on the highroads, the stink of rotting crops hangs everywhere, and no man knows when the harlots' cry will end his life—and you wonder yet if rebellion's spoke? Better you should marvel how they do not burn your province!

DANFORTH. Mr. Hale, have you preached in Andover this month?

HALE. Thank God they have no need of me in Andover.

DANFORTH. You baffle me, sir. Why have you returned here?

HALE. Why, it is all simple. I come to do the Devil's work. I come to counsel Christians they should belie themselves. *(His sarcasm collapses.)* There is blood on my head! Can you not see the blood on my head!!

PARRIS. Hush! *(For he has heard footsteps. They all face the door.* HERRICK *enters with* ELIZABETH. *Her wrists are linked by heavy chain, which* HERRICK *now removes. Her clothes are dirty; her face is pale and gaunt.* HERRICK *goes out.)*

DANFORTH *(very politely)*. Goody Proctor. *(She is silent.)* I hope you are hearty?

ELIZABETH *(as a warning reminder)*. I am yet six month before my time.

DANFORTH. Pray be at your ease, we come not for your life. We—*(uncertain how to plead, for he is not accustomed to it.)* Mr. Hale, will you speak with the woman?

HALE. Goody Proctor, your husband is marked to hang this morning.

(Pause.)

ELIZABETH *(quietly)*. I have heard it.

HALE. You know, do you not, that I have no connection with the court? *(She seems to doubt it.)* I come of my own, Goody Proctor. I would save your husband's life, for if he is taken I count myself his murderer. Do you understand me?

ELIZABETH. What do you want of me?

HALE. Goody Proctor, I have gone this three month like our Lord into the wilderness. I have sought a Christian way, for damnation's doubled on a minister who counsels men to lie.

HATHORNE. It is no lie, you cannot speak of lies.

HALE. It is a lie! They are innocent!

DANFORTH. I'll hear no more of that!

HALE *(continuing to* ELIZABETH*)*. Let you not mistake your duty as I mistook my own. I came into this village like a bridegroom to his beloved, bearing gifts of high religion; the very crowns of holy law I brought, and what I touched with my bright confidence, it died; and where I turned the eye of my great faith, blood flowed up. Beware, Goody Proctor—cleave to no faith when faith brings blood. It is mistaken law that leads you to sacrifice. Life, woman, life is God's most precious gift; no principle, however glorious, may justify the taking of it. I beg you, woman, prevail upon your husband to confess. Let him give his lie. Quail not before God's judgment in this, for it may well be God damns a liar less than he that throws his life away for pride. Will you plead with him? I cannot think he will listen to another.

ELIZABETH *(quietly)*. I think that be the Devil's argument.

HALE *(with a climactic desperation)*. Woman, before the laws of God we are as swine! We cannot read His will!

ELIZABETH. I cannot dispute with you, sir; I lack learning for it.

DANFORTH *(going to her)*. Goody Proctor, you are not summoned here for disputation. Be there no wifely tenderness within you? He will die with the sunrise. Your husband. Do

you understand it? *(She only looks at him.)* What say you? Will you contend with him? *(She is silent.)* Are you stone? I tell you true, woman, had I no other proof of your unnatural life, your dry eyes now would be sufficient evidence that you delivered up your soul to Hell! A very ape would weep at such calamity! Have the Devil dried up any tear of pity in you? *(She is silent.)* Take her out. It profit nothing she should speak to him!

ELIZABETH *(quietly).* Let me speak with him, Excellency.

PARRIS *(with hope).* You'll strive with him? *(She hesitates.)*

DANFORTH. Will you plead for his confession or will you not?

ELIZABETH. I promise nothing. Let me speak with him.

(A sound—the sibilance[8] of dragging feet on stone. They turn. A pause. HERRICK enters with JOHN PROCTOR. His wrists are chained. He is another man, bearded, filthy, his eyes misty as though webs had overgrown them. He halts inside the doorway, his eye caught by the sight of ELIZABETH. The emotion flowing between them prevents anyone from speaking for an instant. Now HALE, visibly affected, goes to DANFORTH and speaks quietly.)

HALE. Pray, leave them, Excellency.

DANFORTH *(pressing HALE impatiently aside).* Mr. Proctor, you have been notified, have you not? *(PROCTOR is silent, staring at ELIZABETH.)*

---

8. **sibilance** (sib′ə lens), *n.* a hissing sound.

I see light in the sky, Mister; let you consel with your wife, and may God help you turn your back on Hell. (PROCTOR *is silent, staring at* ELIZABETH.)

HALE (*quietly*). Excellency, let—

(DANFORTH *brushes past* HALE *and walks out.* HALE *follows.* CHEEVER *stands and follows,* HATHORNE *behind.* HERRICK *goes.* PARRIS, *from a safe distance, offers.*)

PARRIS. If you desire a cup of cider, Mr. Proctor, I am sure I—(PROCTOR *turns an icy stare at him, and he breaks off.* PARRIS *raises his palms toward* PROCTOR.) God lead you now. (PARRIS *goes out.*)

(*Alone.* PROCTOR *walks to her, halts. It is as though they stood in a spinning world. It is beyond sorrow, above it. He reaches out his hand as though toward an embodiment not quite real, and as he touches her, a strange soft sound, half laughter, half amazement, comes from his throat. He pats her hand. She covers his hand with hers. And then, weak, he sits. Then she sits, facing him.*)

PROCTOR. The child?

ELIZABETH. It grows.

PROCTOR. There is no word of the boys?

ELIZABETH. They're well. Rebecca's Samuel keeps them.

PROCTOR. You have not seen them?

ELIZABETH. I have not. (*She catches a weakening in herself and downs it.*)

PROCTOR. You are a—marvel, Elizabeth.

ELIZABETH. You—have been tortured?

PROCTOR. Aye. (*Pause. She will not let herself be drowned in the sea that threatens her.*) They come for my life now.

ELIZABETH. I know it.

(*Pause.*)

PROCTOR. None—have yet confessed?

ELIZABETH. There be many confessed.

PROCTOR. Who are they?

ELIZABETH. There be hundred or more, they say. Goody Ballard is one; Isaiah Goodkind is one. There be many.

PROCTOR. Rebecca?

ELIZABETH. Not Rebecca. She is one foot in Heaven now; naught may hurt her more.

PROCTOR. And Giles?

ELIZABETH. You have not heard of it?

PROCTOR. I hear nothin', where I am kept.

ELIZABETH. Giles is dead.

(*He looks at her incredulously.*)

PROCTOR. When were he hanged?

ELIZABETH (*quietly, factually*). He were not hanged. He would not answer aye or nay to his indictment;[9] for if he denied the charge they'd hang him surely, and auction out his property. So he stand mute, and died Christian under the law. And so his sons will have his farm. It is the law, for he could not be condemned a wizard without he answer the indictment, aye or nay.

PROCTOR. Then how does he die?

ELIZABETH (*gently*). They press him, John.

PROCTOR. Press?

ELIZABETH. Great stones they lay upon his chest until he plead aye or nay. (*With a tender smile for the old man*). They say he give them but two words. "More weight," he says. And died.

PROCTOR (*numbed—a thread to weave into his agony*). "More weight."

ELIZABETH. Aye. It were a fearsome man, Giles Corey.

PROCTOR (*with great force of will, but not quite looking at her*). I have been thinking I would confess to them, Elizabeth. (*She shows nothing.*) What say you? If I give them that?

ELIZABETH. I cannot judge you, John.

(*Pause.*)

PROCTOR (*simply—a pure question*). What would you have me do?

ELIZABETH. As you will, I would have it. (*Slight pause*). I want you living, John. That's true.

PROCTOR (*pauses, then with a flailing of hope*). Giles' wife? Have she confessed?

ELIZABETH. She will not.

(*Pause.*)

PROCTOR. It is a pretense, Elizabeth.

ELIZABETH. What is?

PROCTOR. I cannot mount the gibbet like a saint.

---

9. **indictment** (in dīt′mənt), *n.* accusation.

It is a fraud. I am not that man. *(She is silent.)* My honesty is broke, Elizabeth; I am no good man. Nothing's spoiled by giving them this lie that were not rotten long before.

ELIZABETH. And yet you've not confessed till now. That speak goodness in you.

PROCTOR. Spite[10] only keeps me silent. It is hard to give a lie to dogs. *(Pause, for the first time he turns directly to her.)* I would have your forgiveness, Elizabeth.

ELIZABETH. It is not for me to give, John, I am—

PROCTOR. I'd have you see some honesty in it. Let them that never lied die now to keep their souls. It is pretense for me, a vanity that will not blind God nor keep my children out of the wind. *(Pause.)* What say you?

ELIZABETH *(upon a heaving sob that always threatens).* John, it come to naught that I should forgive you, if you'll not forgive yourself. *(Now he turns away a little, in great agony.)* It is not my soul, John, it is yours. *(He stands, as though in physical pain, slowly rising to his feet with a great immortal longing to find his answer. It is difficult to say, and she is on the verge of tears.)* Only be sure of this, for I know it now. Whatever you will do, it is a good man does it. *(He turns his doubting, searching gaze upon her.)* I have read my heart this three month, John. *(Pause.)* I have sins of my own to count. It needs a cold wife to prompt lechery.

PROCTOR *(in great pain).* Enough, enough—

ELIZABETH *(now pouring out her heart).* Better you should know me!

PROCTOR. I will not hear it! I know you!

ELIZABETH. You take my sins upon you, John—

PROCTOR *(in agony).* No, I take my own, my own!

ELIZABETH. John, I counted myself so plain, so poorly made, no honest love could come to me! Suspicion kissed you when I did; I never knew how I should say my love. It were a cold house I kept! *(In fright, she swerves, as HATHORNE enters.)*

HATHORNE. What say you, Proctor? The sun is soon up.

(PROCTOR, his chest heaving, stares, turns to ELIZABETH. She comes to him as though to plead, her voice quaking.)

ELIZABETH. Do what you will. But let none be your judge. There be no higher judge under Heaven than Proctor is! Forgive me, forgive me, John—I never knew such goodness in the world! *(She covers her face, weeping.)*

(PROCTOR, turns from her to HATHORNE; he is off the earth, his voice hollow.)

PROCTOR. I want my life.

HATHORNE *(electrified, surprised).* You'll confess yourself?

PROCTOR. I will have my life.

HATHORNE *(with a mystical tone).* God be praised! It is a providence! *(He rushes out the door, and his voice is heard calling down the corridor).* He will confess! Proctor will confess!

PROCTOR *(with a cry, as he strides to the door).* Why do you cry it? *(In great pain he turns back to her.)* It is evil, is it not? It is evil.

ELIZABETH *(in terror, weeping).* I cannot judge you, John, I cannot!

PROCTOR. Then who will judge me? *(Suddenly clasping his hands).* God in Heaven, what is John Proctor, what is John Proctor? *(He moves as an animal, and a fury is riding in him, a tantalized search.)* I think it is honest, I think so; I am no saint. *(As though she had denied this he calls angrily at her).* Let Rebecca go like a saint; for me it is fraud!

(Voices are heard in the hall, speaking together in suppressed [11] excitement.)

ELIZABETH. I am not your judge, I cannot be. *(As though giving him release).* Do as you will, do as you will!

PROCTOR. Would you give them such a lie? Say it. Would you ever give them this? *(She cannot answer.)* You would not; if tongs of fire were singeing you you would not! It is evil. Good, then—it is evil, and I do it!

(HATHORNE enters with DANFORTH, and, with them,

---

10. **spite** (spīt), *n.* desire to annoy or harm another.
11. **suppressed** (sə presd′), *adj.* kept in; held back.

CHEEVER, PARRIS, *and* HALE. *It is a businesslike, rapid entrance, as though the ice had been broken.*)

DANFORTH (*with great relief and gratitude*). Praise to God, man, praise to God; you shall be blessed in Heaven for this. (CHEEVER *has hurried to the bench with pen, ink, and paper.* PROCTOR *watches him.*) Now then, let us have it. Are you ready, Mr. Cheever?

PROCTOR (*with a cold, cold horror at their efficiency*). Why must it be written?

DANFORTH. Why, for the good instruction of the village, Mister; this we shall post upon the church door! (*To* PARRIS, *urgently*). Where is the marshal?

PARRIS (*runs to the door and calls down the corridor*). Marshal! Hurry!

DANFORTH. Now, then, Mister, will you speak slowly, and directly to the point, for Mr. Cheever's sake. (*He is on record now, and is really dictating to* CHEEVER, *who writes.*) Mr. Proctor, have you seen the Devil in your life? (PROCTOR'S *jaws lock.*) Come, man, there is light in the sky; the town waits at the scaffold;[12] I would give out this news. Did you see the Devil?

PROCTOR. I did.

PARRIS. Praise God!

DANFORTH. And when he come to you, what were his demand? (PROCTOR *is silent.* DANFORTH *helps.*) Did he bid you to do his work upon the earth?

PROCTOR. He did.

DANFORTH. And you bound yourself to his service? (DANFORTH *turns, as* REBECCA NURSE *enters, with* HERRICK *helping to support her. She is barely able to walk.*) Come in, come in, woman!

REBECCA (*brightening as she sees* PROCTOR). Ah, John! You are well, then, eh?

(PROCTOR *turns his face to the wall.*)

DANFORTH. Courage, man, courage—let her witness your good example that she may come to God herself. Now hear it, Goody Nurse! Say on, Mr. Proctor. Did you bind yourself to the Devil's service?

REBECCA (*astonished*). Why, John!

PROCTOR (*through his teeth, his face turned from* REBECCA). I did.

DANFORTH. Now, woman, you surely see it profit nothin' to keep this conspiracy any further. Will you confess yourself with him?

REBECCA. Oh, John—God send his mercy on you!

DANFORTH. I say, will you confess yourself, Goody Nurse?

REBECCA. Why, it is a lie, it is a lie; how may I damn myself? I cannot, I cannot.

DANFORTH. Mr. Proctor. When the Devil came to you did you see Rebecca Nurse in his company? (PROCTOR *is silent.*) Come, man, take courage—did you ever see her with the Devil?

PROCTOR (*almost inaudibly*). No.

(DANFORTH, *now sensing trouble, glances at* JOHN *and goes to the table, and picks up a sheet—the list of condemned.*)

DANFORTH. Did you ever see her sister, Mary Easty, with the Devil?

PROCTOR. No, I did not.

DANFORTH. (*his eyes narrow on* PROCTOR). Did you ever see Martha Corey with the Devil?

PROCTOR. I did not.

DANFORTH (*realizing, slowly putting the sheet down*). Did you ever see anyone with the Devil?

PROCTOR. I did not.

DANFORTH. Proctor, you mistake me. I am not empowered to trade your life for a lie. You have most certainly seen some person with the Devil. (PROCTOR *is silent.*) Mr. Proctor, a score of people have already testified they saw this woman with the Devil.

PROCTOR. Then it is proved. Why must I say it?

DANFORTH. Why "must" you say it! Why, you should rejoice to say it if your soul is truly purged[13] of any love for Hell!

PROCTOR. They think to go like saints. I like not to spoil their names.

---

12. **scaffold** (skaf′əld), *n.* a raised platform on which criminals are put to death, especially by hanging.
13. **purge** (pèrj), *v.* clear or free of an undesired thing or person.

DANFORTH (*inquiring, incredulous*). Mr. Proctor, do you think they go like saints?

PROCTOR (*evading*). This woman never thought she done the Devil's work.

DANFORTH. Look you, sir. I think you mistake your duty here. It matters nothing what she thought—she is convicted of the unnatural murder of children, and you for sending your spirit out upon Mary Warren. Your soul alone is the issue here, Mister, and you will prove its whiteness or you cannot live in a Christian country. Will you tell me now what persons conspired with you in the Devil's company? (PROCTOR *is silent*.) To your knowledge was Rebecca Nurse ever—

PROCTOR. I speak my own sins; I cannot judge another. (*Crying out, with hatred*). I have no tongue for it.

HALE (*quickly to* DANFORTH). Excellency, it is enough he confess himself. Let him sign it, let him sign it.

PARRIS (*feverishly*). It is a great service, sir. It is a weighty name; it will strike the village that Proctor confess. I beg you, let him sign it. The sun is up, Excellency.

DANFORTH (*considers; then with dissatisfaction*). Come, then, sign your testimony. (*To* CHEEVER.) Give it to him. (CHEEVER *goes to* PROCTOR, *the confession and a pen in hand.* PROCTOR *does not look at it*.) Come, man, sign it.

PROCTOR (*after glancing at the confession*). You have all witnessed it—it is enough.

DANFORTH. You will not sign it?

PROCTOR. You have all witnessed it; what more is needed?

DANFORTH. Do you sport with me? You will sign your name or it is no confession, Mister! (*His breast heaving with agonized breathing,* PROCTOR *now lays the paper down and signs his name*.)

PARRIS. Praise be to the Lord!

(PROCTOR *has just finished signing when* DANFORTH *reaches for the paper. But* PROCTOR *snatches it up, and now a wild terror is rising in him, and a boundless anger*.)

DANFORTH (*perplexed, but politely extending his hand*). If you please, sir.

PROCTOR. No.

DANFORTH (*as though* PROCTOR *did not understand*). Mr. Proctor, I must have—

PROCTOR. No, no. I have signed it. You have seen me. It is done! You have no need for this.

PARRIS. Proctor, the village must have proof that—

PROCTOR. Damn the village! I confess to God, and God has seen my name on this! It is enough!

DANFORTH. No, sir, it is—

PROCTOR. You came to save my soul, did you not? Here! I have confessed myself; it is enough!

DANFORTH. You have not con—

PROCTOR. I have confessed myself! Is there no good penitence but it be public? God does not need my name nailed upon the church! God sees my name; God knows how black my sins are! It is enough!

DANFORTH. Mr. Proctor—

PROCTOR. You will not use me! I am no Sarah Good or Tituba, I am John Proctor! You will not use me! It is no part of salvation that you should use me!

DANFORTH. I do not wish to—

PROCTOR. I have three children—how may I teach them to walk like men in the world, and I sold my friends?

DANFORTH. You have not sold your friends—

PROCTOR. Beguile me not! I blacken all of them when this is nailed to the church the very day they hang for silence!

DANFORTH. Mr. Proctor, I must have good and legal proof that you—

PROCTOR. You are the high court, your word is good enough! Tell them I confessed myself; say Proctor broke his knees and wept like a woman; say what you will, by my name cannot—

DANFORTH (*with suspicion*). It is the same, is it not? If I report it or you sign to it?

PROCTOR (*he knows it is insane*). No, it is not the same! What others say and what I sign to is not the same!

DANFORTH. Why? Do you mean to deny this confession when you are free?

PROCTOR. I mean to deny nothing!

DANFORTH. Then explain to me, Mr. Proctor, why you will not let—

PROCTOR *(with a cry of his whole soul).* Because it is my name! Because I cannot have another in my life! Because I lie and sign myself to lies! Because I am not worth the dust on the feet of them that hang! How may I live without my name? I have given you my soul; leave me my name!

DANFORTH *(pointing at the confession in* PROCTOR'S *hand).* Is that document a lie? If it is a lie I will not accept it! What say you? I will not deal in lies, Mister! (PROCTOR *is motionless.*) You will give me your honest confession in my hand, or I cannot keep you from the rope. (PROCTOR *does not reply.*) Which way do you go, Mister?

(His breast heaving, his eyes staring, PROCTOR *tears the paper and crumples it, and he is weeping in fury, but erect.)*

DANFORTH. Marshal!

PARRIS *(hysterically, as though the tearing paper were his life).* Proctor, Proctor!

HALE. Man, you will hang! You cannot!

PROCTOR *(his eyes full of tears).* I can. And there's your first marvel, that I can. You have made your magic now, for now I do think I see some shred of goodness in John Proctor. Not enough to weave a banner with, but white enough to keep it from such dogs. (ELIZABETH, *in a burst of terror, rushes to him and weeps against his hand.*) Give them no tear! Tears pleasure them! Show honor now, show a stony heart and sink them with it! *(He has lifted her, and kisses her now with great passion.)*

REBECCA. Let you fear nothing! Another judgment waits us all!

DANFORTH. Hang them high over the town! Who weeps for these, weeps for corruption! *(He sweeps out past them.* HERRICK *starts to lead* REBECCA, *who almost collapses, but* PROCTOR *catches her, and she glances up at him apologetically.)*

REBECCA. I've had no breakfast.

HERRICK. Come, man.

(HERRICK *escorts them out,* HATHORNE *and* CHEEVER *behind them.* ELIZABETH *stands staring at the empty doorway.)*

PARRIS *(in deadly fear, to* ELIZABETH). Go to him, Goody Proctor! There is yet time!

(From outside a drumroll strikes the air. PARRIS *is startled.* ELIZABETH *jerks about toward the window.)*

PARRIS. Go to him! *(He rushes out the door, as though to hold back his fate.)* Proctor! Proctor!

(Again, a short burst of drums.)

HALE. Woman, plead with him! *(He starts to rush out the door, and then goes back to her.)* Woman! It is pride, it is vanity. *(She avoids his eyes, and moves to the window. He drops to his knees.)* Be his helper!—What profit him to bleed? Shall the dust praise him? Shall the worms declare his truth? Go to him, take his shame away!

ELIZABETH *(supporting herself against collapse, grips the bars of the window, and with a cry).* He have his goodness now. God forbid I take it from him!

(The final drumroll crashes, then heightens violently. HALE *weeps in frantic prayer, and the new sun is pouring in upon her face, and the drums rattle like bones in the morning air.)*

After Reading

Making Connections

1. If you were to audition for a part in this play, what part would you try out for? Why?

2. Reverend Hale says, ". . . God damns a liar less than he that throws his life away for pride." Do you agree with him? Is it ever acceptable to lie?

3. For which character do you have the most sympathy? Why?

4. Abigail steals her uncle's money and runs off. What **conclusion** can you draw from her behavior?

5. What do you think Danforth's motivations are for refusing to pardon the accused or at least postpone their hangings?

6. Why do you think John Proctor first decides to lie and confess to witchcraft and then changes his mind?

7. The townspeople of Salem who were accused of witchcraft faced death by hanging if they did not confess. Some chose not to confess, based on their principles. Do you think there are causes important enough to put your life on the line for them? If so, what are they?

8. ☝ *The Crucible* explores a clash between individual and **group** values, where some people choose death rather than compromise their integrity. What events in recent history have put individuals in similar situations?

Literary Focus: Theme

The **theme,** or underlying meaning of a piece of literature, is usually not stated; the reader infers it. To understand what theme is, it is helpful to understand what it is not. Theme is *not* a topic. The topic of *The Crucible* is the Salem witch trials. Theme is *not* a conflict. The basic conflict in the play is good versus evil.

To determine the theme, review the events of the play. Who was put to the test in the play? What was the outcome? Write a single sentence that expresses what you think Arthur Miller wants his readers to learn from *The Crucible.* That sentence is a **statement of theme.**

Vocabulary Study

Salem is a town turned upside down. Use your Glossary and text to answer the following questions about Act Four.

reprieve
postponement
excommunication
retaliation
indictment

1. For what purpose does Hale desire a *reprieve* for the prisoners' punishment?

2. Why does Danforth think that *postponement* "speaks a floundering on my part"?

3. Few people attended John Proctor's *excommunication*. What happens at an excommunication?

4. Why doesn't Danforth fear *retaliation*?

5. What was Giles Corey's response to his *indictment*?

Expressing Your Ideas

Writing Choices

Writer's Notebook Update The Salem witch trials tested the character of the townspeople. After reading the entire play, look over your notes about the characters in the play. Draft a letter to the character you admire the most. Explain what he or she did to earn your respect.

Extra! Extra! Imagine you are a newspaper reporter visiting the colonies. You are amazed at the events taking place in Salem. Write an **editorial** for your newspaper explaining the witch trials and taking a stand about them.

Choosing a Leader Your are in charge of choosing a new minister for a church. Two people have applied for the position, Reverend Parris and Reverend Hale. Write a **dialogue** for the interviews you have with both men.

Other Options

Last Words John Proctor and Rebecca Nurse are to be hanged for witchcraft. What if they were allowed to speak before their executions? What would each one say? Be John or Rebecca. Stand before the class and **speak** your last words from your heart.

Judging the Judges In a **mock trial,** put the Salem witch trial judges on trial. Work with a group or the whole class. Choose individuals to be Samuel Sewall, Judge Hathorne, Deputy Governor Danforth, and other figures from the trials, then choose a lawyer for each side to present evidence. Finally, select jury members to decide whether the judges are guilty or not guilty for the part they played in the Salem trials.

American Beginnings

Mass Hysteria

Science Connection

Over the years, several theories have been advanced to explain the strange behavior of the Salem girls of 1692. A former Salem mayor claimed that the girls were merely clever actresses. Freudian psychologists have interpreted the girls' behavior as a severe reaction to Puritan repression. The following article discusses a modern theory in which the culprit is a once common fungus with hallucinogenic properties.

In December 1691, the eight girls were all afflicted with unknown "distempers." Their behavior was characterized by disorderly speech, odd postures and gestures and convulsive fits. Local physicians could find no explanation for the illness, but in February, one doctor finally suggested that the girls might be bewitched.

contaminated rye bread. The symptoms of ergotism include crawling sensations of the skin, tingling in the fingers, vertigo, buzzing in the ears, hallucinations and convulsions. All these symptoms were mentioned in the trials and blamed on witchcraft. Caporael's research points out that growing conditions were favorable for ergot just prior to the outbreak, and that the girls could easily have eaten contaminated bread (with 10 percent of the activity of LSD).

Witchcraft in Salem: A Fungus in the Rye

from *Science News*

The first arrests were made in February, and by June the jails for miles around were crowded with prisoners awaiting trial. By September, 19 men and women had been sent to the gallows, and one man had been pressed to death. This grisly chain of events, generally known as the Salem Witch Trials, shook Massachusetts in 1692. But not until now has there been a comprehensive explanation of what may have caused the witch hunt. According to Linda R. Caporael of the University of California at Santa Barbara, it was not Satan but ergot, a fungus with LSD-like properties, that bewitched eight young Salem girls.

Shortly thereafter, explains Caporael in the April 2 *Science*, the girls made accusations of witchcraft against several women in the village. A flood of accusations followed.

Repeated attempts to explain the ghastly goings on in Salem have failed. Fraud, politics, Freudian psychodynamics, clinical hysteria and even the existence of witchcraft have all been proposed, but no one explanation has been able to account for all of the facts as well as Caporael's ergot hypothesis does.

Ergot grows on rye, a well-established cereal crop in 17th-century New England, and ergotism (long-term ergot poisoning) was once a common condition resulting from eating

"The utmost caution is necessary in assessing the physical and mental states of people dead for hundreds of years," Caporael warns, but her physiological explanation certainly answers more questions than does either demonic possession or witchcraft.

Responding

1. Are you convinced by the ergotism explanation? Why or why not?

2. If people living during the Salem witch hunts had known about ergotism, do you think events would have been different? If so, how? If not, why?

Social Studies Connection

Examples of mass hysteria in America did not end at Salem in the 1690s. In fact, Arthur Miller's play, *The Crucible,* was not inspired by the Salem witch hunts themselves, but rather by the more recent "witch hunts" of the 1950s McCarthy era. A decade of mounting hostility between the United States and the communist government of the former Soviet Union set the stage for anti-communist paranoia in the 1950s. The following pages explore the signs of mass hysteria during this era.

For several years after World War II, the United States was the only country to possess nuclear weapons. When the Soviet Union exploded an atomic bomb in 1949, it helped to generate widespread anxiety and suspicion in the United States. Americans were frightened by the possibility of a Soviet nuclear attack and many wondered whether communist traitors in the U.S. had given atomic bomb secrets to the Soviets. Senator Joseph McCarthy exploited this climate of fear.

A CLIMATE OF FEAR

Arthur Miller is pictured here on the right testifying before the House Un-American Activities Committee in 1956. He was fined $500 and sentenced to 30 days in jail for refusing to name communist sympathizers at his hearing. He said later of his lonely and unpopular stand, "I just didn't believe that the minuscule American Communist Party was a menace to this country."

HOW PREPARED ARE WE IF RUSSIA SHOULD ATTACK?

Visions of Soviet bombs dropping on American cities haunted the imaginations of many during the postwar era and fueled the mass hysteria behind the anti-communist crusade and arms build-up.

This cartoon, created in reaction to the **paranoia of the McCarthy era,** cautions that there will be a price to pay for feeding the appetites of hysteria and fear. How do the symbols chosen by the cartoon's artist contribute to its message and tone?

A CLIMATE OF FEAR

This film was based on the life of Cardinal Mindszenty, a religious leader in Hungary who became a symbol of resistance to communism. Mindszenty was given a life sentence after being convicted of treason by the Communist government. He was later liberated by Hungarian rebels and took refuge in the U.S. Embassy in Budapest for 15 years. Why might members of the movie industry have been interested in portraying his story?

Senator Joseph McCarthy, pictured above, attracted national attention with his claims of a widespread communist conspiracy at the heart of the United States government. His anti-communist crusade, known as McCarthyism, was an enormous success until 1954, when he carried it too far and accused the U.S. Army of harboring communists.

The communist scare even reached the entertainment industry, as screenwriters, producers, directors, and actors were called to testify about their political beliefs before the House Un-American Activities Committee. Here, picketers convinced that movies were produced by communists call for a boycott. In Hollywood, studios responded by blacklisting those who would not fully disclose their political past. Why might anti-communist politicians be particularly concerned about communists in the entertainment industry?

A mother and her children take a practice run to the family fallout shelter. Home bomb shelters made their first appearance in 1951, but had a real boom after the United States and the Soviet Union came to the brink of war during the Berlin Crisis of 1961. Why do you think it is no longer common for families to build their own fallout shelters?

A CLIMATE OF FEAR

The postwar atmosphere in America has been described as the "Age of Anxiety" and "The Lonely Crowd." In his painting *Government Bureau,* how does American artist George Tooker capture the hopelessness and impersonality that some people feel characterized this era?

Responding

1. How are the Salem witch hunts of 1692 similar to the mass hysteria of the 1950s and 60s? How are they different?

2. Can you name an example of mass hysteria that has happened in your lifetime? If so, how does it compare with the situations you've read about here?

Writing Workshop

Reacting Under Pressure

Assignment A major theme in *The Crucible* is fear and its effects on decision-making. The characters must make crucial personal decisions in an atmosphere of mass hysteria. Writing as if you were one of the characters, defend and support a decision you made in the play.

WRITER'S BLUEPRINT

Product   A persuasive paper written in the voice of a character from *The Crucible*

Purpose   To justify a personal decision

Audience The writer's choice

Specs   As the writer of a successful paper, you should:

❑ Write as if you were one of the characters in *The Crucible*—whomever you choose.

❑ Write in an identifiable form (letter, journal entry, testimony, prayer, etc.) to an appropriate audience of your choice (another character, a court, a minister, etc.).

❑ Begin by introducing yourself to your readers. Tell who you are and what your relationships are to other key characters in the play.

❑ Go on to describe the crucial moment of decision: what you did and your thoughts and feelings as you did it.

❑ Give the reasons behind your decision, justifying it as the best possible thing you could have done at the time. Include specific examples of events from the play that support your decision. Make sure your reasons are both clear and specific.

❑ Follow the rules of grammar, usage, spelling, and mechanics. Pay special attention to pronouns and antecedents.

The instructions that follow are designed to lead you to a successful paper.

1 PREWRITING

Gather information. Choose a character with whom you sympathize. Revisit the play and list the decisions made by your chosen character and the reasons behind them. Include important quotes from the play. You might use a chart like the one below.

Character	Decisions	Reasons	Quote from the Play
Abigail Williams	to withhold the truth about how she and the other girls tried to cast a spell in the woods	feels threatened by Parris and Betty; afraid of being called a witch	"We danced. And Tituba conjured . . . And that is all." (Act 1)

OR . . .
For a challenge, choose a character for whom you have little or no sympathy. Write from this character's point of view even though you disagree with it.

Try a quickwrite. Make sure you've picked a character you can work with. Then use your chart to select a crucial decision your character makes. Spend a few minutes writing from your character's point of view about what might have gone through his or her mind before, during, and after this crucial decision.

Consider your purpose and audience. To help select a form and audience for your writing, fill in a table like the one below for the character you chose and for at least one other character. After you've listed as many choices as you can think of, look them over and circle the form and audience you'll be using. Save your chart in case you change your mind later.

Character	Form – Audience
Reverend Hale	Sermon – Congregation Prayer – God
Abigail Williams	Letter – Susanna Speech – the people of Salem

Make a plan. Use your prewriting materials to help make a plan for writing. Use whatever kind of plan works best for the form and audience you've chosen. Make sure your plan addresses these points from the Writer's Blueprint:

- Who you are
- Your relationship to the other characters
- Your crucial moment of decision
- Your thoughts and feelings at the moment of decision
- One reason for your decision
- An event from the play to support it
- Another reason for your decision
- An event from the play to support it

and so on . . .

OR . . .
Draw a web showing all the reasons your character may have considered when making this decision. Circle the most important reasons and find quotes from the play to support them.

Ask a partner to read your plan and answer the following questions. Use your partner's comments to help you revise your plan.

✔ Did I choose an appropriate form and audience for my paper?

✔ Am I following the Specs in the Writer's Blueprint?

2 DRAFTING

Before you draft, review your prewriting materials and writing plan. Also, reread the Writer's Blueprint to be sure the Specs are clear in your mind.

As you draft, don't spend time tracking down errors in spelling or punctuation. Concentrate on getting your persuasive points down on paper. Here are some ideas for getting started.

OR . . .
Speak your character's arguments before you write them. Have a classmate or family member act as audience.

- Just before you start drafting, get into the mind of your character by rereading some passages spoken by that character in the play.

- Begin by addressing your audience by name and making a plea for understanding.

- Begin by telling where you are at the moment and how you feel.

3 REVISING

Ask a partner for comments on your draft before you revise. Then incorporate the most helpful comments. Use the questions at the top of the next page as a guide.

✔ Have I followed the Specs in the Writer's Blueprint?

✔ Does what I wrote sound as if it were written by my character?

✔ Have I written in an identifiable form to an appropriate audience?

✔ Have I given clear, specific reasons for my character's decisions?

Revising Strategy

Being Clear and Specific

Never assume that your readers know all that you know about your topic, as this writer did:

> I, Abigail Williams, did not tell the whole truth about what
>
> happened that night. I was afraid so I lied about it. This caused a lot of
>
> trouble for a lot of other people.

STUDENT MODEL

This is vague writing. It leaves the reader wondering: What happened that night? What is this *whole truth* that Abigail's not telling? What were her reasons for being afraid? Who were these *other people* who got into trouble? What kind of trouble did they get into?

When you revise, always ask yourself: *If I were the reader, would I know what the writer means here?*

Notice how the writer of the passage below, reacting to a partner's comment, added specific information to clear up questions about what Abigail was going to give Proctor's wife and why.

STUDENT MODEL

> *a charm that might kill*
> I asked Tituba for ~~something I could give to~~ John Proctor's wife! I
>
> had to drink the blood of a chicken. I would usually have found the
>
> thought of a chicken's blood in my body revolting, but if it was going to
>
> make me truly happy, I'd dare do it! And I would have done it ten times
>
> *the death of*
> more if I had to, for ~~Elizabeth Proctor's sake!~~ *Sounds like she's helping E.P!*

Ask a partner to review your revised draft before you edit. When you edit, look for errors in grammar, usage, spelling, and mechanics. Take special care to clarify pronoun references.

Editing Strategy

FOR REFERENCE
See the Language and Grammar Handbook for more information on pronoun reference.

Clarifying Pronoun References

As you proofread your essay, be sure that the reader can tell to what or whom each pronoun refers. Don't leave the reader confused about who's who.

Unclear
You see, Goody Ann wished to conjure up the dead, so she went to Ruth. *She* has lost many a child before they reach a day old and wished to know what their cause of dying was. (*Who lost many a child, Goody Ann or Ruth?*)

Clear
You see, Goody Ann wished to conjure up the dead, so she went to Ruth. *Goody Ann* has lost many a child before they reach a day old and wished to know what their cause of dying was.

Notice how this writer has cleared up a confusing pronoun reference.

Well, the morning after, as coincidence would have it, Betty and Ruth became ill. They were motionless and seemed unhearing. When I did get ~~her~~ *Betty* to wake out of her trance, the girl cried for her dead mother and tried to fly! To fly, the silly girl!

STUDENT MODEL

5 PRESENTING

Here are three ideas for presenting your paper.

- Read your paper aloud and ask for comments on how convincing your classmates found it. Are there things you could have done to make it more convincing?

- Work with a partner who chose another character and create a scene in which the two characters explain their decisions to each other. Present your scene live to the class.

- Add illustrations or comments to your paper that suit the form you have chosen. A sermon might have marginal notes about volume or tone of voice; a journal entry might have squiggles and doodles in the margin that the character might have made.

6 LOOKING BACK

Self-evaluate. What kind of grade would *you* give your paper? Look back at the Writer's Blueprint and evaluate yourself on each point, from 6 (superior) down to 1 (inadequate).

Reflect. Think about the experience of writing this essay. Write in response to these questions.

✔ Looking back at your paper, do you, yourself, find it convincing? Why or why not?

✔ If you could do this assignment over, knowing what you know now, what form and audience would you choose?

For Your Working Portfolio Add your essay and reflection responses to your working portfolio.

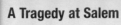
Beyond Print

Speaking the Language of Technology

Computers are changing the way people work, play, study, and even how they talk! Not long ago, few people would have considered keeping a *mouse* on their desk, and most *surfing* was done in water. Read this Technology Glossary and see how many terms you already know.

Application: A particular computer program or piece of software.

Bulletin Board Service (BBS): An individual or company that allows users to connect to their server to download or upload information, usually for a fee.

CD ROM: Compact Disc Read Only Memory; this is used to store information such as text, sounds, pictures, and movies. While these look like audio CDs, they are only readable with a computer.

Database: An organized collection of information.

Desktop: The area on a computer screen that contains icons, menus, and windows.

Document: A file that is created by using a particular application.

Download: Copying a file from a server or network.

Electronic Mail (E-mail): Messages sent over the Internet from one user to another.

Hard Drive: A storage device usually found inside your computer.

Home Page: The first screen that appears when accessing a server on the World Wide Web. It can contain text, graphics, and sound.

Hypertext: Words that can be selected and clicked on which will access further information; used on the World Wide Web.

Internet: A series of computer servers connected together across the country and world, allowing a user who is connected to the Internet to access any information stored on those servers.

Menu: A pull-down list of items at the top of a computer screen.

Modem: A device that allows your computer to use phone lines to connect to a variety of online services or other computers.

Monitor: A screen used to project the information from a computer or video player.

Mouse: An input device with a small ball and buttons that controls an arrow or cursor on a computer screen.

Multimedia: Any combination of media types, including text, sound, pictures, and video.

Network: Two or more computers connected together by cables, allowing them to communicate with each other.

Online: Information available to a user through a network or telephone connection.

Scrolling: The act of moving text on a screen, usually by pressing arrows on the screen.

Server: A computer that operates a network.

Surfing the Net: The act of moving from one server to another on the Internet.

Upload: Copying a file onto a server or network.

User: Any person who is using a computer or similar device.

Window: A rectangular or square area on a computer screen where information is presented.

World Wide Web: A particular way to access the Internet by allowing users to click on words or graphics to gather information.

Activity Options

Personalized Glossary To keep up with the ever-changing world of technology, create a technology glossary of your own in your notebook or in a computer document. Add to it as you come across new terms.

ComputerSpeak With a partner, create a dialogue between two people using the terms in this glossary. Try to see how many you can use and still make sense! Perform your dialogue for your class.

Multicultural Connections

Interactions

Part One: A Collision of Cultures Cabeza de Vaca didn't know what to expect from the American Indian groups he encountered, nor did the Lipan Apaches know what to do about the European newcomers. Olaudah Equiano couldn't fathom the cruelty and seeming magic of the European slave traders. The Pilgrims at Plymouth Plantation had both frustrating and rewarding interactions with local Indian groups. Canassatego analyzed the offer made by colonists to educate Indian youths, and concluded that the cultures were too different. Mary Jemison eventually adopted another culture as her own.

■ Which individual or group from the selections did the best job of interacting with the people they encountered? Explain your choice.

Group

Part Two: A Tragedy at Salem The Puritans had very strong group values, which helped them survive in a strange and threatening land. On the other hand, straying outside the group's rules and beliefs had some dangerous consequences.

■ What were some of the various cultural expectations that might have made people like Tituba, John Proctor, Rebecca Nurse, Martha Corey, and Sarah Good easier than others to accuse?

Activities

Work in small groups on the following activities.

1. Based on what you've learned from the selections in Part One, write up a list of recommendations for your student government that suggest ways to promote positive interactions between students of different cultures.

2. Every group has norms or expectations that it encourages its members to live up to. The effect can be positive or negative, or a little of both. Think of situations in which group expectations caused someone to do something he or she might not otherwise have done. Reenact one of these situations.

Independent and Group Projects

Research

Many Nations Hundreds of American Indian groups existed across North America before the Europeans arrived. Find out who was living where, and what their lives, dwellings, food, and art were like. You may want to work in a group and split up the different areas of the country, each taking a different part to research. Then, bring your information together to build a map, book, or HyperCard stack that provides an overview of life in North America before 1492.

Oral Presentation

Recipe of Exchange What's your favorite food? Choose a favorite recipe that uses four or more ingredients. Identify the ingredients, then make an illustrated diagram that indicates where each ingredient originated. Present your recipe to your class, including an explanation of why your recipe would or would not have been possible before the cultural exchanges that began in 1492.

Art

Who Are They? Choose the perspective of one of the individuals you read about in this unit who encountered other cultures. It could be one of the Lipan Apaches in Percy Bigmouth's tale, it could be Mary Jemison's early impressions of her Indian family, or it might even be Tituba, the sole member of her cultural group in Salem. Taking the individual's perspective, create a piece of art that depicts her or his impressions of the cultural group he or she encountered.

Media

Documentary on Early America With a group of students, plan and create a ten-minute video documentary that tells of some of the events involved in America's beginnings. Include information from each of the selections in this unit. You may want to make a "video slide-show," videotaping paintings and other images to support a brief narrative history of early America.

A NEW NATION

A Spirit of Independence
Pages 154–202

THEMES IN AMERICAN LITERATURE

The Wilderness
Theme Portfolio, pages 203–215

HISTORICAL OVERVIEW

In the 1760s, a tightening of England's control over her American possessions divided opinion among the colonists. Loyalists wishing to remain faithful to the mother country complied with the new taxes and other regulations. Patriots, on the other hand, protested and retaliated with shouts of "no taxation without representation." In 1776 the 13 colonies declared their independence, launching a new experiment in representative government. In the late 1780s, the newly-formed United States drafted a Constitution to structure its government and guarantee the rights of its citizens. The young nation soon doubled its size with the Louisiana Purchase and as it reached westward toward the Pacific coast, it became clear that the United States was evolving into a major world presence.

A SPIRIT

British Canada

Area claimed by U.S., Britain, Spain, and Russia

Rocky Mountains

In 1804 Meriwether Lewis and William Clark led an expedition to explore the Louisiana Territory and to find a water route to the Pacific Ocean. They reached the coast in 18 months with the help of their Shoshone guide Sacajawea.

Colorado River

New Spain

In the late 1700s, Spanish settlements throughout the southwest and Florida centered on a presidio, or fort, for protection and a mission to convert local Indians to Christianity.

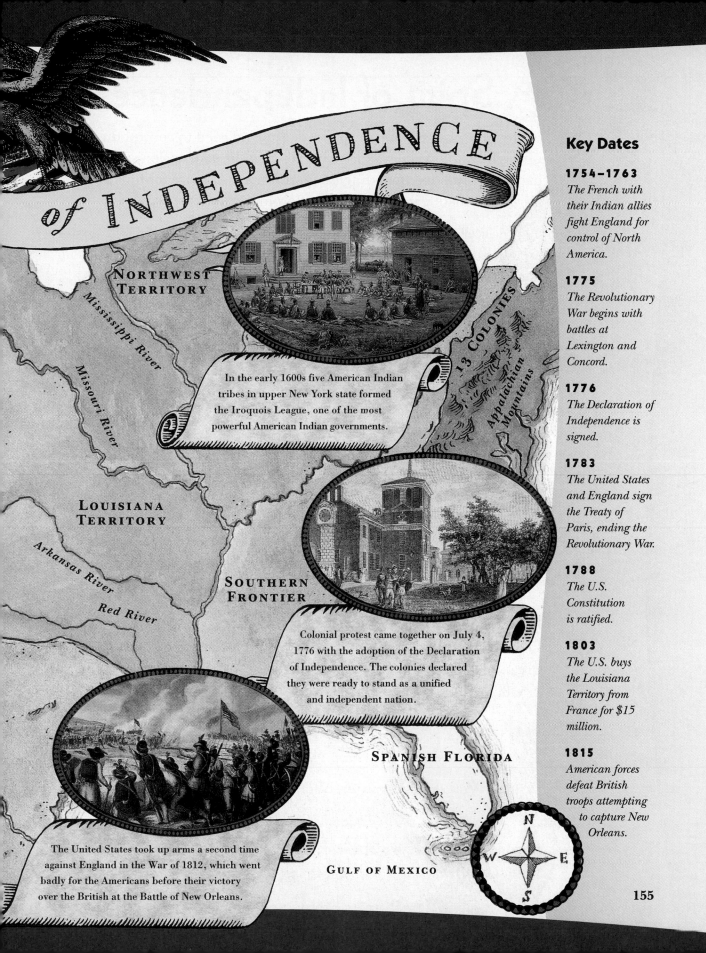

of INDEPENDENCE

NORTHWEST TERRITORY

Mississippi River

Missouri River

13 COLONIES

Appalachian Mountains

In the early 1600s five American Indian tribes in upper New York state formed the Iroquois League, one of the most powerful American Indian governments.

LOUISIANA TERRITORY

Arkansas River

Red River

SOUTHERN FRONTIER

Colonial protest came together on July 4, 1776 with the adoption of the Declaration of Independence. The colonies declared they were ready to stand as a unified and independent nation.

SPANISH FLORIDA

The United States took up arms a second time against England in the War of 1812, which went badly for the Americans before their victory over the British at the Battle of New Orleans.

GULF OF MEXICO

N
W E
S

Key Dates

1754–1763
The French with their Indian allies fight England for control of North America.

1775
The Revolutionary War begins with battles at Lexington and Concord.

1776
The Declaration of Independence is signed.

1783
The United States and England sign the Treaty of Paris, ending the Revolutionary War.

1788
The U.S. Constitution is ratified.

1803
The U.S. buys the Louisiana Territory from France for $15 million.

1815
American forces defeat British troops attempting to capture New Orleans.

A Spirit of Independence

As the American Colonies expanded, England tried to control them through laws and taxes, which were resented by many colonists because they had no representation in English government. A desire for independence grew, culminating in the American Revolutionary War.

 Multicultural Connection The **choices** we make in life—big and small—are often influenced by the cultural values of our society. What can you deduce about the cultural values of the individuals and groups in the following selections based on their choices?

Literature

Dekanawidah   *from* **The Iroquois Constitution**
◆ oral tradition 158

Benjamin Franklin   *from* **The Autobiography** ◆ autobiography 162

Thomas Paine   *from* **The American Crisis** ◆ essay 170

Patrick Henry   *from* **Speech in the Virginia Convention**
◆ speech 172

Thomas Jefferson   **The Declaration of Independence**
◆ historical document 178

Abigail Adams   **Letter to John Adams** ◆ letter 184

Prince Hall   **Petition to the Massachusetts General Assembly**
◆ petition 186

Interdisciplinary Study The Quest for Freedom

Freedom Fighters Around the World ◆ multicultural connection 188

Preamble by Mike Wilkins ◆ fine art 190

A Sailor Works for Freedom ◆ career connection 191

Language History

Noah Webster and American English 192

Writing Workshop Persuasive Writing

Taking a Stand 193

Beyond Print Effective Speaking

Looking at Heroes 199

Before Reading

from The Iroquois Constitution

by Dekanawidah

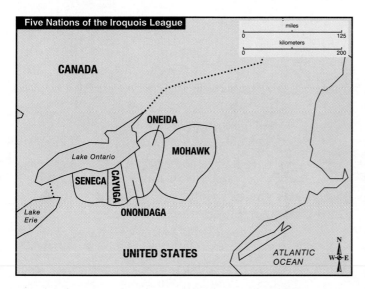

Five Nations of the Iroquois League

miles
0 — 125
kilometers
0 — 200

CANADA

ONEIDA

MOHAWK

Lake Ontario

SENECA CAYUGA

ONONDAGA

Lake Erie

UNITED STATES

ATLANTIC OCEAN

N W—E S

Dekanawidah
1500s

According to Indian tradition, Dekanawidah (de ́kä nä we ́-dä) was a healing spirit in human form. In one story about his life, he appeared to the legendary Indian leader and hero Hiawatha, who was grieving for the death of his family. Dekanawidah said, "I wipe away the tears from your face using the white fawn skin of pity. I make the day light for you." His gracious words soothed Hiawatha and forged a new friendship. The two men set out together to teach the laws of peace to their people. Together, they invited the chiefs of five nations to join their Great League of Peace.

Building Background

The Rise of the Iroquois League
Dekanawidah, along with Hiawatha, is considered the founder of the Iroquois Confederation or League, a group of five (later six) Indian tribes living primarily in what is now northern New York State. The Confederation was governed by a council of fifty men who were selected by women clan leaders, and met each fall. The Confederation was most powerful during the 1600s and 1700s and originally comprised five nations: the Mohawk, the Oneida, the Cayuga, the Seneca, and the Onondaga. Dekanawidah's Iroquois Constitution, regarded as law by these five nations, may also have had a profound effect on another American leader. Thomas Jefferson is said to have been influenced by the Iroquois League's ideas on government structure.

Literary Focus

Symbol A **symbol** is an object or event that represents something other than itself, such as an idea or concept. As you read the Iroquois Constitution, consider what the "Tree of Great Peace" symbolizes to the Iroquois League.

Writer's Notebook

Rules of Government In the Iroquois Constitution, Dekanawidah presents a series of guidelines for the new rulers. Imagine your school has just elected a student body president. What are some of the guidelines your president should follow? What must he or she do in order to govern effectively? In your notebook, jot down a few guidelines that you feel a good student body leader must abide by.

The IROQUOIS CONSTITUTION

DEKANAWIDAH

 I am Dekanawidah, and with the Five Nations confederate lords I plant the Tree of the Great Peace. . . . I name the tree the Tree of the Great Long Leaves. Under the shade of this Tree of the Great Peace we spread the soft white feather down of the globe thistle[1] as seats for you, Atotarho and your cousin lords. There you sit and watch the council fire of the confederacy of the Five Nations. Roots have spread out from the Tree, and the name of these roots is the Great White Roots of Peace. If any man of any nation shall show a desire to obey the laws of the Great Peace, they shall trace the roots to their source, and they shall be welcomed to take shelter beneath the Tree of the Long Leaves. The smoke of the confederate council fire shall pierce the sky so that all nations may discover the central council fire of the Great Peace. I, Dekanawidah, and the confederate lords now uproot the tallest pine tree and into the cavity[2] thereby made we cast all weapons of war. Into the depth of the earth, down into the deep under-earth currents of water flowing into unknown regions; we cast all weapons of war. We bury them from sight forever and plant again the Tree.

We do now crown you with the sacred emblem[3] of the antlers, the sign of your lordship. You shall now become a mentor[4] of the people of the Five Nations. The thickness of your skin will be seven spans, for you will be proof against anger, offensive action, and criticism. With endless patience you shall carry out your duty, and your firmness shall be tempered with compassion for your people. Neither anger nor fear shall find lodgment in your mind, and all your words and actions shall be tempered with calm deliberation. In all your official acts, self-interest shall be cast aside. You shall look and listen to the welfare of the whole people, and have always in view, not only the present but the coming generations—the unborn of the future Nation.

The Onondaga lords shall open each council by expressing their gratitude to their cousin lords, and greeting them, and they shall make an address and offer thanks to the earth where men dwell, to the streams of water, the pools, the springs, the lakes, to the maize[5] and the fruits, to the medicinal herbs and the trees, to the forest trees for their usefulness, to the animals that serve as food and who offer their pelts as clothing, to the great winds and the lesser winds, to the Thunderers, and the Sun, the mighty warrior, to the moon, to the messengers of the Great Spirit who dwells in the skies above, who gives all things useful to men, who is the source and the ruler of health and life.

Then shall the Onondaga lords declare the council open.

---

1. thistle (this′əl), *n.* any of various composite plants with prickly stalks and leaves.
2. cavity (kav′ə tē), *n.* hollow place; hole.
3. emblem (em′bləm), *n.* object or symbol that represents an idea.
4. mentor (men′tər), *n.* a wise and trusted advisor.
5. maize (māz), *n.* corn.

John Verelst's 1710 portrait of Sa Ga Yeath Qua Piet Tow was painted from life when the Mohawk leader was visiting London. Which of the leadership qualities mentioned in the Iroquois Constitution are suggested by this portrait?

After Reading

Making Connections

Shaping Your Response

1. Choose a favorite passage and read it aloud in a way you imagine Dekanawidah might sound.

Analyzing the Selection

2. What **themes** does Dekanawidah stress in his speech?

3. Why do you think Dekanawidah feels it's important that the rulers open each council by offering a sign of gratitude?

Extending the Ideas

4. 🐾 In the Iroquois Constitution, Dekanawidah expresses **choices** about the kinds of leaders the Iroquois rulers should be. In a group of three or four, brainstorm a list of personal qualities, then choose the ones that you feel are most important in a leader. Do your priorities agree with those expressed by Dekanawidah?

Vocabulary Study

Word analogy tests require you to understand the relationship between a pair of words and then choose another pair of words with the same relationship. Analogies may reflect relationships such as the following:

- synonyms (*beige : tan*)
- general kind and specific example (*clothing : sweater*)
- type and characteristic (*scream : loud*)

Determine the relationship between the first word pair in each exercise, then choose the word that best completes the second pair.

thistle
cavity
mentor
maize
emblem

1. plant : *thistle* : : animal :

    a. mammal   **b.** fish   **c.** reptile   **d.** mouse

2. *cavity* : hole : : mound :

    a. climb   **b.** hill   **c.** monument   **d.** tooth

3. *mentor* : wise : : firefighter :

    a. brave   **b.** fire   **c.** danger   **d.** police officer

4. hound : dog : : *maize* :

    a. puzzle   **b.** corn   **c.** shock   **d.** rope

5. *emblem* : symbol : : tan :

    a. confused   **b.** burn   **c.** beige   **d.** hide

Before Reading

from The Autobiography of Benjamin Franklin

Benjamin Franklin
1706–1790

From politics to printing, from making soap to growing cabbages, from making music to inventing things, Benjamin Franklin pursued his interests with a passion, all the while cultivating a reputation for wit and charm. Perhaps most important of all, Franklin was a key player in building the government of the United States. He was the only person to have signed the Declaration of Independence, the Treaty of Alliance with France, the Treaty of Peace with Great Britain, and the Constitution of the United States.

Building Background

Let Us All Hang Together! It is the spring of 1754, and a war has just begun over land disputes between the British and the French and the Indians in America. Like most American colonists, Franklin is eager to defend his home against French troops, but Great Britain has so far refused to follow the colonists' advice on how to defend the thirteen colonies. From Franklin's perspective, it is the colonists who know the land, who can anticipate problems with the Indians, and who can outmaneuver the French as needed. What the colonies really need, Franklin believes, is a central government to coordinate defense efforts. In great excitement, Franklin presents a plan for a new government at a conference in Albany, New York. His Plan of Union recommends that the 13 colonies join together in "one general government" to defeat the French and the Indians.

Literary Focus

Characterization In his *Autobiography,* Benjamin Franklin offers the reader a most interesting **character** sketch of British general Edward Braddock. As you read Franklin's description of the general's activities, ask yourself two questions:

- What is Franklin's opinion of Braddock?
- What is Braddock's opinion of himself?

Writer's Notebook

The British, the Colonists, the Indians Think of what you know about early American history. What was the British government's attitude toward the American colonists? How did the British troops treat the American Indians? How did the colonists act toward the American Indians? How did American Indians react to the British government and the colonists? In your notebook, make some brief notes reviewing what you know about the relationships between the British government, the colonists, and the American Indians.

THE AUTOBIOGRAPHY OF
Benjamin Franklin

Benjamin Franklin wrote The Autobiography *in four different install-ments over a period of nineteen years. Before he died, Franklin had carried his life up to the year 1758. The following is an excerpt from the last part of his* Autobiography. *Here Franklin, new to his role as statesman, describes his difficulties in dealing with the British government.*

In 1754, war with France being again apprehended,[1] a congress of commissioners from the different colonies was by an order of the Lords of Trade to be assembled at Albany, there to confer with the chiefs of the Six Nations concerning the means of defending both their country and ours. Governor Hamilton having received this order acquainted the House with it, requesting they would furnish proper presents for the Indians, to be given on this occasion; and naming the Speaker (Mr. Norris) and myself to join Mr. John Penn and Mr. Secretary Peters as commissioners to act for Pennsylvania. The House approved the nomination and provided the goods for the presents, though they did not much like treating out of the province; and we met the other commissioners at Albany about the middle of June.

In our way thither I projected and drew up a plan for the union of all the colonies under one government, so far as might be necessary for defense, and other important general purposes. As we passed through New York I had there shown my project to Mr. James Alexander and Mr. Kennedy, two gentlemen of great knowledge in public affairs; and being fortified by the approbation,[2] I ventured to lay it before the congress. It then appeared

---

1. **apprehend** (ap′ri hend′), *v.* look forward to with anxiety.
2. **approbation** (ap′rə bā′shən), *n.* approval.

that several of the commissioners had formed plans of the same kind. A previous question was first taken, whether a union should be established, which passed in the affirmative unanimously. A committee was then appointed, one member from each colony, to consider the several plans and report. Mine happened to be preferred and, with a few amendments, was accordingly reported.

By this plan the general government was to be administered by a president-general, appointed and supported by the crown, and a grand council was to be chosen by the representatives of the people of the several colonies met in their respective assemblies.

CONNECT: How is Franklin's plan similar to our system of government today?

The debates upon it in the congress went on daily, hand in hand with the Indian business. Many objections and difficulties were started; but at length they were all overcome and the plan was unanimously agreed to, and copies ordered to be transmitted to the Board of Trade and to the Assemblies of the several provinces. Its fate was singular;[3] the Assemblies did not adopt it, as they all thought there was too much *prerogative* [4] in it; and in England it was judged to have too much of the *democratic*. The Board of Trade did not approve it nor recommend it for the approbation of his majesty; but another scheme was formed, supposed to answer the same purpose better, whereby the governors of the provinces, with some members of their respective councils, were to meet and order the raising of troops, building of forts, etc., and to draw on the treasury of Great Britain for the expense, which was afterward to be refunded by an act of Parliament laying a tax on America. My plan, with my reasons in support of it, is to be found among my political papers that were printed.

Being the winter following in Boston, I had much conversation with Governor Shirley upon both the plans. Part of what passed between us on this occasion may also be seen among those papers. The different and contrary reasons of dislike to my plan make me suspect that it was really the true medium, and I am still of opinion it would have been happy for both sides if it had been adopted. The colonies so united would have been sufficiently strong to have defended themselves; there would then have been no need of troops from England; of course the subsequent pretext for taxing America and the bloody contest it occasioned would have been avoided. But such mistakes are not new; history is full of the errors of states and princes. . . .

The British government, not choosing to permit the union of the colonies as proposed at Albany and to trust that union with their defense, lest they should thereby grow too military and feel their own strength, suspicion and jealousies at this time being entertained of them, sent over General Braddock, with two regiments of regular English troops for that purpose.

This general was, I think, a brave man, and might probably have made a figure as a good officer in some European war. But he had too much self-confidence, too high an opinion of the validity[5] of regular troops, and too mean a one of both Americans and Indians. George Croghan, our Indian interpreter, joined him on his march with one hundred of those people, who might have been of great use to his army as guides and scouts if he had treated them kindly; but he slighted[6] and neglected them and they gradually left him.

---

3. **singular** (sing′gyə lər), *adj.* peculiar.
4. **prerogative** (pri rog′ə tiv), *n.* an exclusive right or priveledge held by a person or group.
5. **validity** (və lid′ə tē), *n.* effectiveness.
6. **slight** (slīt), *v.* overlook; neglect.

In conversation with him one day, he was giving me some account of his intended progress. "After taking Fort Duquesne,"[7] said he, "I am to proceed to Niagara;[8] and having taken that, to Frontenac,[9] if the season will allow time, and I suppose it will; for Duquesne can hardly detain me above three or four days, and then I see nothing that can obstruct my march to Niagara." Having before revolved in my mind the long line his army must make in their march by a very narrow road, to be cut for them through the woods and bushes, and also what I had read of a former defeat of fifteen hundred French who invaded the Illinois country, I had conceived[10] some doubts and some fears for the event of the campaign. But I ventured only to say: "To be sure, sir, if you arrive well before Duquesne with these fine troops, so well provided with artillery, the fort, though completely fortified and assisted with a very strong garrison, can probably make but a short resistance. The only danger I apprehend of obstruction to your march is from the ambuscades of the Indians, who by constant practice are dexterous[11] in laying and executing them; and the slender line, near four miles long, which your army must make, may expose it to be attacked by surprise in its flanks and to be cut like a thread into several pieces, which from their distance cannot come up in time to support each other."

He smiled at my ignorance and replied: "These savages may indeed be a formidable[12] enemy to your raw American militia, but upon the king's regular and disciplined[13] troops, sir, it is impossible they should make any impression."

EVALUATE: What does Braddock's use of the word "savages" tell about his feelings toward the Indians?

I was conscious of an impropriety in my disputing with a military man in matters of his profession, and said no more. The enemy, however, did not take the advantage of his army which I apprehended its long line of march exposed it to, but let it advance without interruption till within nine miles of the place; and then, when more in a body (for it had just passed a river, where the front had halted till all were come over) and in a more open part of the woods than any it had passed, attacked its advance-guard by a heavy fire from behind trees and bushes, which was the first intelligence the general had of an enemy's being near him. This guard being disordered, the general hurried the troops up to their assistance, which was done in great confusions through wagons, baggage, and cattle, and presently the fire came upon their flank. The officers being on horseback were more easily distinguished, picked out as marks, and fell very fast; and the soldiers were crowded together in a huddle, having or hearing no orders and standing to be shot at till two-thirds of them were killed, and then, being seized with a panic, the remainder fled with precipitation.[14]

The wagoners took each a horse out of his team and scampered. Their example was immediately followed by others, so that all the wagons, provisions, artillery, and stores were left to the enemy. The general being wounded was brought

7. **Fort Duquesne** (dü kān′), Fort Duquesne was built by the French in 1754 in the middle of what is now Pittsburgh, Pennsylvania. The French burned the fort in 1758 and fled northward when they learned that a British force was approaching.
8. **Niagara** (nī ag′rə), Fort Niagara was constructed by the French in 1726 on the eastern shore of the Niagara River.
9. **Frontenac** (fron′tn ak), Fort Frontenac was near the present site of Kingston, Ontario. It was built by the French in 1673. British forces captured the fort in 1758.
10. **conceive** (kən sēv′), v. form in the mind; think up.
11. **dexterous** (dek′stər əs), adj. skillful.
12. **formidable** (fôr′mə də bəl), adj. hard to overcome.
13. **disciplined** (dis′ə plind), adj. well-trained.
14. **precipitation** (pri sip′ə tā′shən), n. a hurrying.

▲ Does this painting, *Braddock's Defeat, July 9, 1755* (1903) by Edwin W. Deming convey the same tone about this battle as Franklin's autobiography? Why or why not?

off with difficulty; his secretary, Mr. Shirley, was killed by his side, and out of eighty-six officers sixty-three were killed or wounded, and seven hundred and fourteen men killed of eleven hundred. These eleven hundred had been picked men from the whole army; the rest had been left behind with Colonel Dunbar, who was to follow with the heavier part of the stores, provisions, and baggage. The flyers, not being pursued, arrived at Dunbar's camp, and the panic they bought with them instantly seized[15] him and all his people. And though he had now above one thousand men, and the enemy who had beaten Braddock did not at most exceed four hundred Indians and French together, instead of proceeding and endeavoring to recover some of the lost honor, he ordered all the stores, ammuni-

tion, etc., to be destroyed, that he might have more horses to assist his flight toward the settlements and less lumber to remove. He was there met with requests from the governors of Virginia, Maryland, and Pennsylvania that he would post his troops on the frontiers, so as to afford some protection to the inhabitants, but he continued his hasty march through all the country, not thinking himself safe till he arrived at Philadelphia, where the inhabitants could protect him. This whole transaction gave us Americans the first suspicion that our exalted ideas of the prowess[16] of British regular troops had not been well founded.

---

15. **seize** (sēz′), *v.* take hold of suddenly.
16. prowess (prou′is), *n.* bravery; daring.

CLARIFY: Why does Franklin conclude that the colonists can no longer trust in the powers of the British military?

In their first march, too, from their landing till they got beyond the settlements, they had plundered[17] and stripped the inhabitants, totally ruining some poor families, besides insulting, abusing, and confining the people if they remonstrated.[18] This was enough to put us out of conceit of such defenders if we had really wanted any. How different was the conduct of our French friends in 1781, who during a march through the most inhabited part of our country, from Rhode Island to Virginia, near seven hundred miles, occasioned not the smallest complaint for the loss of a pig, a chicken, or even an apple.

Captain Orme, who was one of the general's aids-de-camp, and being grievously wounded was brought off with him and continued with him to his death, which happened in a few days, told me that he was totally silent all the first day, and at night only said: "Who would have thought it?" That he was silent again the following day, saying only at last, "We shall better know how to deal with them another time," and died in a few minutes after.

The secretary's papers, with all the general's orders, instructions, and correspondence, falling into the enemy's hands, they selected and translated into French a number of the articles, which they printed, to prove the hostile intentions of the British court before the declaration of war. Among these I saw some letters of the general to the ministry, speaking highly of the great service I had rendered to the army and recommending me to their notice. David Hume, who was some years afterward secretary to Lord Hertford when minister in France, and afterward to General Conway when Secretary of State, told he had seen among the papers in that office letters from Braddock highly recommending me. But the expedition having been unfortunate, my service, it seems, was not thought of much value, for those recommendations were never of any use to me.

---

17. **plunder** (plun′dər), *v.* rob.
18. **remonstrate** (ri mon′strāt), *v.* plead in protest.

Benjamin Franklin's Thirteen Virtues

Beyond being an influential politician, an inventor, and a writer, Benjamin Franklin set for himself the lofty goal of achieving moral perfection. To do so he invented the following list of virtues, and kept a record every day of his successes and failures in acquiring these virtues.

1. TEMPERENCE. Eat not to dullness: drink not to elevation.
2. SILENCE. Speak not but what may benefit others or yourself; avoid trifling conversation.
3. ORDER. Let all your things have their places; let each part of your business have its time.
4. RESOLUTION. Resolve to perform what you ought; perform without fail what you resolve.
5. FRUGALITY. Make no expense but to do good to others or yourself, i.e., waste nothing.
6. INDUSTRY. Lose no time; be always employed in something useful; cut off all unnecessary action.
7. SINCERITY. Use no hurtful deceit; think innocently and justly, and, if you speak, speak accordingly.
8. JUSTICE. Wrong none by doing injuries, or omitting the benefits that are your duty.
9. MODERATION. Avoid extremes; forbear resenting injuries so much as you think they deserve.
10. CLEANLINESS. Tolerate no uncleanliness in body, clothes, or habitation.
11. TRANQUILITY. Be not disturbed at trifles, or at accidents common or unavoidable.
12. CHASTITY. Rarely use venery but for health or offspring, never to dullness, weakness, or the injury of your own or another's peace or reputation.
13. HUMILITY. Imitate Jesus and Socrates.

After Reading

Making Connections

Shaping Your Response

1. Based on your reading of the selection, what three adjectives would you use to describe Benjamin Franklin? Why?

Analyzing the Autobiography

2. Why do you suppose the British government doesn't want the American colonies to have a unified central government?

3. Find three passages in which Franklin's opinion of General Braddock and the British army is expressed indirectly. Explain how he manages to convey his opinion in these passages.

4. To what is Franklin referring when he says "the subsequent pretext for taxing America and the bloody contest it occasioned"?

5. What is the **irony** of Franklin's discovery that he had been highly recommended by Braddock?

Extending the Ideas

6. 🐾 General Braddock makes important **choices** based on misjudgments about other cultural groups. If history teaches us lessons, what lesson might be learned from his defeat?

7. How do Benjamin Franklin's Thirteen Virtues compare to the personal qualities described as desirable by Dekanawidah? Use a Venn diagram to show the differences and commonalities.

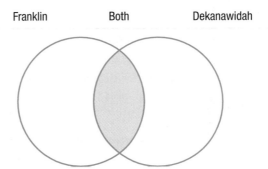

Franklin   Both   Dekanawidah

Literary Focus: Characterization

An author can reveal **characterization** in a number of different ways: through description, dialogue, or the reaction of one character to another. Since Franklin's work is nonfiction, his descriptions of the people involved in the events are based on opinions, knowledge, prejudices, and so on. How does Franklin portray General Braddock? Write a character sketch of Braddock that draws some conclusions about the kind of man he was and the kind of leader he was.

Vocabulary Study

formidable
disciplined
precipitation
prowess
plunder

Benjamin Franklin uses the words in the list when relating the story of General Braddock's march to Fort Duquesne. Demonstrate your knowledge of these words by using them in a paragraph that summarizes Braddock's march.

Expressing Your Ideas

Writing Choices

Writer's Notebook Update Choose one of these relationships—the British government and the colonists, the British troops and the Indians, the colonists and the Indians and the French— that Franklin refers to in his *Autobiography.* In your notebook, write a summary of the relationship based on your previous knowledge and information you gained from the reading.

Will He Listen *This* Time? Imagine Benjamin Franklin was at General Braddock's bedside as he lay dying. What would Franklin have said to Braddock? How would the general have replied? With a classmate, write the **dialogue** you think the two might have had, and then perform it for the class.

Other Options

Re-create the Scene Do a re-creation of General Braddock's famous battle near Fort Duquesne. Choose your art materials, and choose the aspect of the conflict you'd like to depict. Perhaps you'd like to make a **diorama**—with cardboard or construction paper cutouts—that shows Braddock's advance guard on the march before they were attacked. Or maybe you'd like to draw a **map** that marks the course Braddock's troops took on their way to Duquesne.

Join, or Die Benjamin Franklin published this cartoon in his newspaper in the spring of 1754, advertising his plan to unite the colonies. What does the cartoon tell you about the political climate of the time? Think about today's politics. If Franklin were to draw a newspaper cartoon today, what might his subject be? Try your hand at drawing a **cartoon** that makes a political statement.

Before Reading

The American Crisis by Thomas Paine

Speech in the Virginia Convention by Patrick Henry

Thomas Paine
1737–1809

Thomas Paine immigrated to America from England at the age of 37 and soon began working for the cause of American independence. His pamphlets arguing for the colonists' rights became a source of inspiration during the Revolutionary War.

Patrick Henry
1736–1799

A statesman and lawyer during the Revolutionary War, Patrick Henry was considered one of the most brilliant speakers of his time. His fiery orations won him fame in his home state of Virginia, where he served as governor for 5 years.

Building Background

Setting the Stage for Revolution Tensions between the American colonies and the British government had been running high for over ten years before the **Revolutionary War** began in 1775. As colonial agriculture and trade gained importance in the English economy, the British government began passing laws aimed at increasing its control over the colonies. However, many colonists, who had grown accustomed to a large measure of self-government, did not welcome tighter English rule and strongly resisted the new laws. The following two selections were written in a climate of rebellion and protest as these opposing forces came to the brink of war.

Literary Focus

Style The way in which writers shape words and sentences to express their ideas is called **style.** Style is reflected in the choice and arrangement of words, as well as the tone, mood, imagery, sound effects, and other literary devices. As you read the following selections, take note of the styles adopted by revolutionary patriots Thomas Paine and Patrick Henry that were designed to arouse their audience. How do their choices contribute to the force of their arguments?

Writer's Notebook

Powers of Persuasion Think about times that others tried to persuade you to see their point of view. What techniques did they use to try to convince you? What techniques have you used on others to persuade them? Before reading the selections, take a moment to write a list of persuasive strategies in your notebook.

THE AMERICAN CRISIS

THOMAS PAINE

These are the times that try men's souls: The summer soldier and the sunshine patriot will in this crisis, shrink from the service of his country; but he that stands it NOW, deserves the love and thanks of man and woman. Tyranny, like hell, is not easily conquered; yet we have this consolation with us, that the harder the conflict, the more glorious the triumph. What we obtain too cheap, we esteem[1] too lightly:—'Tis dearness only that gives everything its value. Heaven knows how to put a proper price upon its goods; and it would be strange indeed, if so celestial an article as FREEDOM should not be highly rated. Britain, with an army to enforce her tyranny, has declared that she has a right *(not only to)* TAX but "to BIND *us in* ALL CASES WHATSOEVER," and if being *bound in that manner* is not slavery, then is there not such a thing as slavery upon earth. Even the expression is impious,[2] for so unlimited a power can belong only to GOD. . . .

I have as little superstition in me as any man living, but my secret opinion has ever been, and still is, that God Almighty will not give up a people to military destruction, or leave them unsupportedly to perish, who have so earnestly and so repeatedly sought to avoid the calamities of war, by every decent method which wisdom could invent. Neither have I so much of the infidel[3] in me, as to suppose that he has

---

1. **esteem** (e stēm′), *v.* value; consider.
2. impious (im′pē əs), *adj.* not showing reverence to God; wicked; profane.
3. **infidel** (in′fə dəl), *n.* person who does not believe in religion.

relinquished the government of the world, and given us up to the care of devils; and as I do not, I cannot see on what grounds the king of Britain can look up to Heaven for help against us; a common murderer, a highwayman, or a housebreaker, has as good a pretense as he. . . .

I once felt all that kind of anger, which a man ought to feel against the mean principles that are held by the Tories:[4] A noted one, who kept a tavern at Amboy, was standing at his door, with as pretty a child in his hand, about eight or nine years old, as I ever saw, and after speaking his mind as freely as he thought was prudent, finished with this unfatherly expression, *"Well! give me peace in my day."* Not a man lives on the continent but fully believes that a separation must some time or other finally take place, and a generous parent should have said, *"If there must be trouble, let it be in my day, that my child may have peace,"* and this single reflection, well applied, is sufficient to awaken every man to duty. Not a place upon earth might be so happy as America. Her situation is remote from all the wrangling[5] world, and she has nothing to do but to trade with them. A man can distinguish himself between temper and principle, and I am as confident, as I am that GOD governs the world, that America will never be happy till she gets clear of foreign dominion.[6] Wars, without ceasing, will break out till that period arrives, and the continent must in the end be conqueror; for though the flame of liberty may sometimes cease to shine, the coal can never expire. . . .

The heart that feels not now is dead; the blood of his children will curse his cowardice, who shrinks back at a time when a little might have saved the whole, and made *them* happy. I love the man that can smile in trouble, that can gather strength from distress, and grow brave by reflection. 'Tis the business of little minds to shrink; but he whose heart is firm, and whose conscience approves his conduct, will pursue his principles unto death. My own line of reasoning is to myself as straight and clear as a ray of light. Not all the treasures of the world, so far as I believe, could have induced me to support an offensive war, for I think it murder; but if a thief breaks into my house, burns and destroys my property, and kills or threatens to kill me, or those that are in it, and to *"bind me in all cases whatsoever"* to his absolute will, am I to suffer it? What signifies it to me, whether he who does it is a king or a common man; my countryman or not my countryman; whether it be done by an individual villain, or an army of them? If we reason to the root of things, we shall find no difference; neither can any just cause be assigned why we should punish in the one case and pardon in the other. . . .

---

4. **Tories,** American colonists who favored British rule of the colonies.
5. **wrangling** (rang′gəl ing), *adj.* disputatious; arguing.
6. dominion (də min′yən), *n.* power or right of governing.

SPEECH IN THE
Virginia
CONVENTION

Patrick Henry

Mr. President: No man thinks more highly than I do of the patriotism, as well as abilities, of the very worthy gentlemen who have just addressed the house. But different men often see the same subject in different lights: and, therefore, I hope it will not be thought disrespectful to those gentlemen, if, entertaining, as I do, opinions of a character very opposite to theirs, I shall speak forth my sentiments freely and without reserve. This is no time for ceremony. The question before the house is one of aweful moment to this country. For my own part, I consider it as nothing less than a question of freedom or slavery. And in proportion to the magnitude of the subject ought to be the freedom of the debate. It is only in this way that we can hope to arrive at truth, and fulfill the great responsibility which we hold to God and our country. Should I keep back my opinions at such a time, through fear of giving offense, I should consider myself as guilty of treason toward my country, and of an act of disloyalty toward the Majesty of Heaven, which I revere above all earthly kings.

Mr. President, it is natural to man to indulge in the illusions of hope. We are apt to shut our eyes against a painful truth, and listen to the song of that siren till she transforms us into beasts. Is this the part of wise men, engaged in a great and arduous struggle for liberty? Are we disposed to be of the number of those who having eyes see not, and having ears hear not, the things which so nearly concern their temporal salvation? For my part, whatever anguish of spirit it may cost, I am willing to know the whole truth: to know the worst and to provide for it.

I have but one lamp by which my feet are guided, and that is the lamp of experience. I know of no way of judging of the future but by the past. And judging by the past, I wish to know what there has been in the conduct of the British ministry for the last ten years to justify those hopes with which gentlemen have been pleased to solace[1] themselves and the house? Is it that insidious[2] smile with which our petition has been lately received? Trust it not, sir; it will prove a snare to your feet. Suffer not yourselves to be betrayed with a kiss. Ask yourselves how this gracious reception of our petition comports[3] with those warlike preparations which cover our waters and darken our land. Are fleets and armies necessary to a work of love and reconciliation? Have we shown ourselves so unwilling to be reconciled that force must be called in to win back our love? Let us not deceive ourselves, sir. These are the implements of war and subjugation[4]— the last arguments to which kings resort.

I ask gentlemen, sir, what means this martial array, if its purpose be not to force us to

---

1. solace (sol′is), *v.* to give comfort or relief.
2. insidious (in sid′ē əs), *adj.* wily; sly.
3. comport (kəm pôrts′), *v.* agree; suit.
4. subjugation (sub′jə gā shən), *n.* the act of bringing under control; making submissive.

◄ How powerful are speeches such as Henry's? Can they help bring about actions like the one depicted in this painting, *The Nation Makers* (1903) by Howard Pyle, or do they simply reflect how people already feel? Explain your answer.

submission? Can gentlemen assign any other possible motive for it? Has Great Britain any enemy in this quarter of the world, to call for all this accumulation of navies and armies? No, sir, she has none. They are meant for us; they can be meant for no other. They are sent over to bind and rivet upon us those chains which the British ministry have been so long forging.

And what have we to oppose to them? Shall we try argument? Sir, we have been trying that for the last ten years. Have we anything new to offer upon the subject? Nothing. We have held the subject up in every light of which it is capable; but it has been all in vain. Shall we resort to entreaty[5] and humble supplication?[6] What terms shall we find which have not been already exhausted? Let us not, I beseech you, sir, deceive ourselves longer.

Sir, we have done everything that could be done to avert the storm which is now coming on. We have petitioned; we have remonstrated;[7] we have supplicated; we have prostrated[8] ourselves before the throne, and have implored its interposition[9] to arrest the tyrannical hands of the ministry and Parliament. Our petitions have been slighted; our remonstrances have produced additional violence and insult; our supplications have been disregarded; and we have been spurned with contempt from the foot of the throne! In vain, after these things, may we indulge the fond hope of peace and reconciliation. There is no longer any room for hope. If we wish to be free, if we mean to preserve inviolate[10] those inestimable privileges for which we have been so long contending, if we mean not basely to abandon the noble struggle in which we have been so long engaged, and which we have pledged ourselves never to abandon until the glorious object of our contest shall be obtained—we must fight! I repeat it, sir, we must fight! An appeal to arms and to the God of Hosts is all that is left us!

They tell us, sir, that we are weak—unable to cope with so formidable an adversary. But when shall we be stronger? Will it be the next week, or the next year? Will it be when we are totally disarmed, and when a British guard shall be sta-

tioned in every house? Shall we gather strength by irresolution and inaction? Shall we acquire the means of effectual resistance by lying supinely on our backs and hugging the delusive[11] phantom of hope until our enemies shall have bound us hand and foot? Sir, we are not weak, if we make a proper use of those means which the God of nature hath placed in our power. Three millions of people, armed in the holy cause of liberty, and in such a country as that which we possess, are invincible by any force which our enemy can send against us. Besides, sir, we shall not fight our battles alone. There is a just God who presides over the destinies of nations and who will raise up friends to fight our battles for us. The battle, sir, is not to the strong alone; it is to the vigilant, the active, the brave. Besides, sir, we have no election. If we were base enough to desire it, it is now too late to retire from the contest. There is no retreat but in submission and slavery! Our chains are forged! Their clanging may be heard on the plains of Boston! The war is inevitable—and let it come! I repeat it, sir, let it come!

It is in vain, sir, to extenuate the matter. Gentlemen may cry, "Peace, peace"—but there is no peace. The war is actually begun! The next gale that sweeps from the north will bring to our ears the clash of resounding arms! Our brethren[12] are already in the field! Why stand we here idle? What is it that gentlemen wish? What would they have? Is life so dear, or peace so sweet, as to be purchased at the price of chains and slavery? Forbid it, Almighty God! I know not what course others may take; but as for me, give me liberty or give me death!

---

5. entreaty (en trē′tē), *n.* an earnest request or appeal.
6. **supplication** (sup′lə kā′shən), *n.* begging.
7. remonstrate (ri mon′strāt), *v.* reason in protest.
8. prostrate (pros′trāt), *v.* to bow down low in submission, worship, or respect.
9. **interposition** (in′tər pə zish′ən), *n.* intervention.
10. **inviolate** (in vī′ə lit), *adj.* not violated; unbroken.
11. **delusive** (di lü′siv), *adj.* deceptive.
12. **brethren** (breŦн′rən), *n.* fellow members of a church, society, or profession.

After Reading

Making Connections

Shaping Your Response

1. In your opinion, how persuasive were Paine and Henry in their arguments for the Revolution? Rate each of them on a scale from 1 to 5, then explain your ratings.

| 1 | 2 | 3 | 4 | 5 |

not very persuasive　　　　　　　　　　　　　　very persuasive

2. You are a colonist who just attended Henry's speech. What will you do in response to his words?

Analyzing the Selections

3. Paine argues that "Give me peace in my day" is an "unfatherly expression." Do you agree? Why or why not?

4. What would Patrick Henry say is the "painful truth" he mentions in paragraph two of his speech?

5. 🐾 Both Paine and Henry chose war as the means of confronting the issues of their day. Based on the two works, what cultural values do you think influenced the **choices** of each?

Extending the Ideas

6. What recent events have led to debate over whether Americans should go to war? Compare the relevant points made in recent debates to those made in the selections.

7. How have attitudes toward war stayed the same since the American Revolution? How have they changed?

Literary Focus: Style

Paine writes, "What we obtain too cheaply, we esteem too lightly." Imagine he had instead written, "Things that we don't work for are not valued." What qualities of the original does this paraphrase lack? Choose another example from either selection that reflects the author's **style**. Try rewriting the example in another style by experimenting with different word choices, sentence structures, or imagery.

Vocabulary Study

Use the words in the list to fill in the blanks below. Refer to the Glossary, if necessary. You will use some words more than once.

impious
dominion
solace
insidious
entreaty
remonstrate
prostrate

1. Patrick Henry cautioned the colonists not to trust Britain's ____ smile.

2. King George III showed no mercy despite the colonists' ____.

3. Defacing the church was a(n) ____ act.

4. It did the colonists no good to ____ with Britain.

5. British actions offered little ____ for the colonists.

6. The British held ____ over the colonies.

7. Prisoners of war sometimes ____ themselves before their captors.

8. Congress passed a new law after the Senator's passionate ____.

9. The prospect of short-term peace held little ____ for Paine and Henry, who seemed to think that a conflict with Britain was inevitable.

10. Thomas Paine seemed to ____ against those who want to delay the conflict.

Expressing Your Ideas

Writing Choices

Writer's Notebook Update Paine and Henry used a variety of techniques to persuade their audiences to agree with their arguments. Make a list of the techniques that you noticed while reading. How does this list compare to the list of techniques you have used?

On the Other Hand Paine and Henry make strong arguments for going to war, but there is another side to the argument. Do some research to find out more about the Tories' position and then write a **pamphlet** in response to either or both of the authors defending the alternative view.

Other Options

The Bottom Line You are a spy for King George. After reading Paine's pamphlet and secretly attending Henry's speech, give an **oral summary** of what you know about the colonists' activities, and advise the king on a prudent course of action.

Revolutionary Sound Bytes "These are the times that try men's souls" and "Give me liberty or give me death" are among the most famous quotations of the American Revolution. Using a quotation dictionary, create a **collection of famous sayings** of the period.

The Declaration of Independence

by Thomas Jefferson

Thomas Jefferson
1743–1826

At a dinner honoring America's Nobel Prize winners, President John F. Kennedy observed, "This is the most extraordinary collection of talent . . . that has ever been gathered together at the White House, with the possible exception of when Thomas Jefferson dined alone." Although best remembered as the author of the Declaration of Independence and as president, Thomas Jefferson was also one of the leading architects of his time, and a student of art and music. He was an inventor, a scholar, a philosopher, and a talented violinist.

Building Background

The Road to Independence After tensions between the American colonists and the British government led to the outbreak of war in 1775, the next year Richard Henry Lee of Virginia proposed independence. The proposal sparked an intense debate in the **Continental Congress,** but in the end a committee—including Thomas Jefferson, John Adams, and Benjamin Franklin, among others—was appointed to draft a formal declaration. Jefferson was chosen to be on the committee because he was a Virginian and a recognized writer. The task of drafting the Declaration fell to Jefferson, and in just over two weeks, Jefferson had completed a first draft which was approved by his committee with only minor changes. After a brief debate, Congress adopted the Declaration on July 4, which is still celebrated as American Independence Day.

Literary Focus

Tone You can tell a lot about what an author thinks of a subject through his or her **tone.** For example, the tone of a biography about Thomas Jefferson will let you know what the author really thinks about Jefferson. Is he someone to be admired? If the author thinks so, you'll be able to pick up on that by looking at the author's word choices and style. As you read the Declaration, notice Jefferson's tone. What does it reveal about his attitude toward King George III? What does his tone reveal about his attitude toward the colonists' fight for freedom?

Writer's Notebook

With Careful Planning The American colonists are so frustrated with British rule that they decide to declare their independence, and they ask you to write the declaration. The way the declaration is written will have serious ramifications later, so it will take careful planning. What grievances will you include in your statement? How will you organize it? Based on your knowledge of the colonists' situation in 1776, jot down some notes on what should be included in a declaration of independence.

The Declaration of Independence

Thomas Jefferson

When, in the course of human events, it becomes necessary for one people to dissolve the political bands which have connected them with another, and to assume, among the Powers of the earth, the separate and equal station to which the Laws of Nature and of Nature's God entitle them, a decent respect to the opinions of mankind requires that they should declare the causes which impel them to the separation.

We hold these truths to be self-evident: that all men are created equal; that they are endowed by their Creator with certain unalienable[1] Rights; that among these are Life, Liberty, and the pursuit of Happiness. That, to secure these Rights, Governments are instituted among Men, deriving their just powers from the consent of the governed—That, whenever any Form of Government becomes destructive of these ends, it is the Right of the People to alter or abolish it, and to institute new Government, laying its foundation on such Principles, and organizing its Powers in such form, as to them shall seem most likely to effect their Safety and Happiness. Prudence, indeed, will dictate that Governments long established should not be changed for light and transient[2] causes; and, accordingly, all experience hath shown that mankind are more disposed to suffer, while evils are sufferable, than to right themselves by abolishing the forms to which they are accustomed. But, when a long train of abuses and usurpations,[3]

---

1. **unalienable** (un ā′lyə nə bəl), *adj.* permanent; non-transferable.
2. **transient** (tran′shənt), *adj.* passing soon; fleeting.
3. **usurpation** (yū′zər pā′shən), *n.* the seizing and holding of the places or powers of another by force or without right.

pursuing invariably the same Object, evinces a design to reduce them under absolute Despotism,[4] it is their right, it is their duty, to throw off such Government, and to provide new Guards for their future security. Such has been the patient sufferance of these Colonies, and such is now the necessity which constrains[5] them to alter their former Systems of Government. The history of the present King of Great Britain is a history of repeated injuries and usurpations, all having in direct object the establishment of an absolute Tyranny over these States. To prove this, let Facts be submitted to a candid world:

*H*e has refused his Assent to Laws the most wholesome and necessary for the public good.

He has forbidden his Governors to pass Laws of immediate and pressing importance, unless suspended in their operation till his Assent should be obtained; and, when so suspended, he has utterly neglected to attend to them.

He has refused to pass other Laws for the accommodation of large districts of people, unless those people would relinquish the rights of Representation in the Legislature; a right inestimable to them, and formidable to tyrants only.

He has called together legislative bodies at places unusual, uncomfortable, and distant from the depository of their Public Records, for the sole purpose of fatiguing them into compliance with his measures.

He has dissolved Representative Houses repeatedly for opposing, with manly firmness, his invasions on the rights of the people.

He has refused for a long time after such dissolutions[6] to cause others to be elected; whereby the Legislative Powers, incapable of Annihilation, have returned to the People at large for their exercise; the State remaining, in the meantime, exposed to all the dangers of invasions from without, and convulsions within.

He has endeavored to prevent the Population of these States; for that purpose obstructing the Laws for Naturalization of Foreigners; refusing to pass others to encourage their migrations hither, and raising the conditions of new Appropriations of Lands.

He has obstructed the Administration of Justice by refusing his Assent to Laws for establishing Judiciary Powers.

He has made Judges dependent on his Will alone for the tenure of their offices, and the amount and Payment of their salaries.

He has erected a multitude of New Offices, and sent hither swarms of Officers to harass[7] our People and eat out their substance.

He has kept among us, in times of Peace, Standing Armies, without the Consent of our legislatures.

He has affected to render the Military independent of and superior to the Civil Power.

He has combined with others to subject us to a jurisdiction foreign to our constitution, and unacknowledged by our laws: giving his Assent to their Acts of pretended Legislation:

For quartering large bodies of armed troops among us;

For protecting them, by a mock Trial, from Punishment for any Murders which they should commit on the Inhabitants of these States;

For cutting off our Trade with all parts of the world;

For imposing Taxes on us without our Consent;

For depriving us, in many cases, of the benefits of Trial by Jury;

For transporting us beyond Seas to be tried for pretended offenses;

For abolishing the free System of English Laws in a neighboring Province, establishing

---

4. **despotism** (des′pə tiz′əm), *n.* government by a despot; tyranny or oppression.
5. constrain (kən strān′), *v.* force; compel.
6. **dissolution** (dis′ə lü′shən), *n.* a breaking up or ending of an association.
7. **harass** (har′əs, hə ras′), *v.* trouble by repeated attacks; harry.
8. **arbitrary** (är′bə trer′ē), *adj.* based on one's own wishes, notions or will; not going by rule or law.

therein an Arbitrary[8] government, and enlarging its Boundaries, so as to render it at once an example and fit instrument for introducing the same absolute rule into these Colonies;

For taking away our Charters, abolishing our most valuable Laws, and altering, fundamentally, the Forms of our Governments;

For suspending our own Legislatures, and declaring themselves invested with Power to legislate for us in all cases whatsoever.

He has abdicated[9] Government here by declaring us out of his Protection, and waging War against us.

He has plundered our seas, ravaged our Coasts, burnt our towns, and destroyed the Lives of our People.

He is, at this time, transporting large Armies of foreign Mercenaries[10] to complete the works of death, desolation, and tyranny, already begun with circumstances of Cruelty and Perfidy[11] scarcely paralleled in the most barbarous[12] ages, and totally unworthy the Head of a civilized nation.

He has constrained our fellow Citizens, taken Captive on the high Seas, to bear Arms against their Country, to become the executioners of their friends and Brethren, or to fall themselves by their Hands.

He has excited domestic insurrections amongst us, and has endeavored to bring on the inhabitants of our frontiers the merciless Indian Savages, whose known rule of warfare is an undistinguished destruction of all ages, sexes, and conditions.

In every stage of these Oppressions, We have Petitioned for Redress, in the most humble terms: Our repeated Petitions have been answered only by repeated injury. A Prince, whose character is thus marked by every act which may define a Tyrant, is unfit to be the ruler of a free People.

Nor have We been wanting in attentions to our British brethren. We have warned them, from time to time, of attempts by their legislature to extend an unwarrantable jurisdiction over us. We have reminded them of the circumstances of our emigration and settlement here. We have appealed to their native justice and magnanimity,[13] and we have conjured them, by the ties of our common kindred, to disavow these usurpations, which would inevitably interrupt our connections and correspondence. They, too, have been deaf to the voice of justice and of consanguinity.[14] We must, therefore, acquiesce in the necessity which denounces our Separation, and hold them, as we hold the rest of mankind—Enemies in War—in Peace, Friends.

WE, THEREFORE, the REPRESENTATIVES of the UNITED STATES OF AMERICA, in GENERAL CONGRESS Assembled, appealing to the Supreme Judge of the world for the rectitude of our intentions, Do, in the Name and by the Authority of the good People of these Colonies, solemnly PUBLISH and DECLARE, That these United Colonies are, and of Right ought to be, FREE AND INDEPENDENT STATES; that they are Absolved from all Allegiance to the British Crown, and that all political connection between them and the State of Great Britain is, and ought to be, totally dissolved; and that, as FREE AND INDEPENDENT STATES, they have full Power to levy War, conclude Peace, contract Alliances, establish Commerce, and to do all other Acts and Things which INDEPENDENT STATES may of right do. And, for the support of this Declaration, with a firm reliance on the Protection of Divine Providence, we mutually pledge to each other our Lives, our Fortunes, and our Sacred Honor.

---

9. **abdicate** (ab′də kāt), *v.* give up or relinquish formally.
10. **mercenary** (mėr′sə ner′ē), *n.* soldier serving for pay in a foreign army.
11. **perfidy** (pėr′fə dē), *n.* being false to a trust; base treachery.
12. **barbarous** (bär′bər əs), *adj.* not civilized; savage.
13. **magnanimity** (mag′nə nim′ə tē), *n.* nobility of soul or mind.
14. **consanguinity** (kon′sang gwin′ə tē), *n.* relationship by descent from the same parent or ancestor.

After Reading

Making Connections

Shaping Your Response

1. You may have heard the Declaration of Independence recited before, but perhaps this is the first time you've actually read the document. What did you notice about the Declaration when reading it?

Analyzing the Selection

2. Whom do you suppose is the Declaration's intended **audience?**

3. What is the **tone** of the final paragraph?

Extending the Ideas

4. How do you think Americans today would react to the Declaration of Independence if they were reading it for the first time?

5. By writing the Declaration of Independence, Jefferson put himself on the line to stand up for something he believed in. When have you or someone you know been in a similar situation? What happened?

Literary Focus: Tone

The **tone** of a piece conveys the emotional significance of a work and is essential to understanding the total meaning. How does Jefferson's tone convey his belief that a break from Great Britain is an absolute necessity?

Vocabulary Study

unalienable, transient, usurpation, constrain, harass, abdicate, perfidy, barbarous, magnanimity, consanguinity

It's hard to imagine the Declaration of Independence written in any other way. Jefferson's word choices are memorable. Write synonyms for the words in the list. How would using your synonyms change the overall effect of the Declaration?

Expressing Your Ideas

Writing Choice

Writer's Notebook Update Now that you have read the Declaration, review your notes to see whether Jefferson's ideas agree with yours. Does he include the kinds of information you expected? Is it organized as you would have done? Write a brief review in which you evaluate Jefferson's writing of the Declaration.

Another Option

Once More with Feeling The Declaration of Independence is an impassioned work that is frequently recited. Choose a section to present to your class as a **dramatic reading.**

Before Reading

Letter to John Adams by Abigail Adams

Petition to the Massachusetts General Assembly by Prince Hall

Abigail Adams
1744–1818

Abigail Adams was the wife of John Adams, second President of the United States, and mother of John Quincy Adams, sixth president. A gifted writer, she corresponded with her husband during the absences necessitated by his public career. In her letters to her husband, Adams states her controversial opinion that women should be treated as equals in the home and in government matters.

Prince Hall
1735?–1807

Prince Hall was held as a slave until 1770. After he was freed, he organized fourteen African American Bostonians into a society that became an official Masonic order. Hall also wrote a series of petitions on behalf of free and enslaved African Americans. He eloquently petitioned for abolitionism, public education for African American children, and assistance to African Americans who wanted to emigrate to Africa.

Building Background

Something in Common Two people, one white, the other black; one a woman, the other a man, make two memorable pleas for freedom. The first, Abigail Adams, writes to her husband John Adams, future President of the United States, and urges that the new government of the United States recognize women as equal citizens. The second, Prince Hall, makes an appeal to the Massachusetts General Assembly that African Americans be granted equal rights as citizens. Although Abigail Adams and Prince Hall never met, their circumstances were similar in one important regard: they both were determined to speak out to gain their rights.

Literary Focus

Maxims In her letter to John Adams, Abigail Adams uses **maxims** to help convey her ideas. A maxim is a short rule of conduct that suggests a general truth. For example, "Look before you leap" and "A penny saved is a penny earned" are maxims. As you read her letter to her husband, watch for Adams's maxims.

While Prince Hall doesn't use maxims in his petition, he expresses thoughts that might make good maxims. As you read his Petition, look for thoughts that might be good material for creating maxims.

Writer's Notebook

Pleas for Freedom "Letter to John Adams" and "Petition to the Massachusetts General Assembly" are similar in that they are both pleas for freedom. Abigail Adams makes her plea in one way; Prince Hall makes his in another. Take notes on the ways each author presents her or his argument. Later, compare their methods.

LETTER TO JOHN ADAMS

ABIGAIL ADAMS

This pastel portrait of Abigail Adams was made in 1766 by Benjamin Blyth, two years after her marriage to future-president John Adams. What information can you learn about Adams from the portrait that you might not know from her letter?

Braintree
MAY 7, 1776

How many are the solitary hours I spend, ruminating[1] upon the past and anticipating the future whilst you, overwhelmed with the cares of state, have but few moments you can devote to any individual. All domestic pleasures and enjoyments are absorbed in the great and important duty you owe your country "for our country is, as it were, a secondary god and the first and greatest parent. It is to be preferred to parents, wives, children, friends and all things; the gods only excepted. For if our country perishes, it is as impossible to save an individual as to preserve one of the fingers of a mortified hand." Thus do I suppress every wish and silence every murmur, acquiescing in a painful separation from the companion of my youth and the friend of my heart.

I believe it is near ten days since I wrote you a line. I have not felt in a humor to entertain you. If I had taken up my pen, perhaps some unbecoming invective[2] might have fallen from it; the eyes of our rulers have been closed and a lethargy has seized almost every member. I fear

---

1. **ruminate** (rü′mə nāt), *v.* think or ponder; meditate; reflect.
2. **invective** (in vek′tiv), *n.* violent verbal attack.

a fatal security has taken possession of them. Whilst the building is in flame, they tremble at the expense of water to quench it. In short, two months have elapsed since the evacuation of Boston, and very little has been done in that time to secure it or the harbor from future invasion until the people are all in a flame, and no one among us that I have heard of even mentions expense. They think universally that there has been an amazing neglect somewhere. Many have turned out as volunteers to work upon Nodles Island, and many more would go upon Nantasket if it was once set on foot. "It is a maxim of state that power and liberty are like heat and moisture; where they are well mixed everything prospers; where they are single, they are destructive."

A government of more stability is much wanted in this colony, and they are ready to receive it from the hands of the Congress, and since I have begun with maxims of state, I will add another: A people may let a king fall, yet still remain a people, but if a king lets his people slip from him, he is no longer a king. And as this is most certainly our case, why not proclaim to the world in decisive[3] terms your own importance?

Shall we not be despised by foreign powers for hesitating so long at a word?

I cannot say that I think you very generous to the ladies, for whilst you are proclaiming peace and goodwill to men, emancipating[4] all nations, you insist upon retaining an absolute power over wives. But you must remember that arbitrary[5] power is like most other things which are very hard, very liable to be broken—and notwithstanding all your wise laws and maxims, we have it in our power not only to free ourselves but to subdue our masters, and without violence throw both your natural and legal authority at our feet—

Charm by accepting, by submitting sway
Yet have our humor most when we obey

I thank you for several letters which I have received since I wrote last. They alleviate a tedious absence, and I long earnestly for a Saturday evening and experience a similar pleasure to that which I used to find in the return of my friend upon that day after a week's absence. The idea of a year dissolves all my philosophy.

Our little ones, whom you so often recommend to my care and instruction, shall not be deficient in virtue or probity[6] if the precepts of a mother have their desired effect, but they would be doubly enforced could they be indulged with the example of a father constantly before them; I often point them to their sire

Engaged in a corrupted state
Wrestling with vice and faction.

Abigail Adams

---

3. **decisive** (di sī′siv), *adj.* settling something beyond question or doubt.
4. **emancipate** (i man′sə pāt), *v.* release from slavery or restraint; set free.
5. **arbitrary** (är′bə trer′ē), *adj.* based on one's own wishes, notions or will.
6. **probity** (prō′bə tē, prob′ə tē), *n.* high principle; uprightness.

Petition to the Massachusetts General Assembly

Prince Hall

That your Petitioners apprehend that they have, in common with all other Men, a natural and unalienable right to that freedom, which the great Parent of the Universe hath bestowed equally on all Mankind and which they have never forfeited by any compact or agreement whatever—But they were unjustly dragged by the cruel hand of Power, from their dearest friends and some of them even torn from the embraces of their tender Parents. From a populous, pleasant and plentiful Country—and in Violation of the Laws of Nature and of Nation and in defiance of all the tender feelings of humanity, brought hither to be sold like Beasts of Burden, and like them condemned[1] to slavery for Life—Among a People professing the mild Religion of Jesus—A People not insensible[2] of the sweets of rational freedom—Nor without spirit to resent the unjust endeavours of others to reduce them to a State of Bondage and Subjection—Your Honors need not to be informed that a Life of Slavery, like that of your petitioners, deprived of every social privilege, of every thing requisite to render Life even tolerable, is far worse that Non-Existence—In imitation of the laudable[3] example of the good People of these States, your Petitioners have long and patiently waited the event of Petition after Petition by them presented to the legislative Body of this State, and can not but with grief reflect that their success has been but too similar—They can not but express their astonishment, that it has never been considered, that every principle from which America has acted in the course of her unhappy difficulties with Great Britain, pleads stronger than a thousand arguments in favor of your Petitioners. They therefore humbly beseech[4] your Honors, to give this Petition its due weight and consideration, and cause an Act of the Legislature to be passed, whereby they may be restored to the enjoyment of that freedom which is the natural right of all Men—and their Children (who were born in this Land of Liberty) may not be held as Slaves after they arrive at the age of twenty-one years—So may the Inhabitants of this State (no longer chargeable with the inconsistency[5] of acting, themselves, the part which they condemn and oppose in others) be prospered in their present glorious struggles for Liberty; and have those blessings secured to them by Heaven, of which benevolent[6] minds can not wish to deprive their fellow Men.

---

1. **condemn** (kən dem′), *v.* denounce.
2. **insensible** (in sen′sə bəl), *adj.* not sensitive; not able to feel or notice.
3. laudable (lo′də bəl), *adj.* worthy of praise.
4. **beseech** (bi sēch′), *v.* beg; implore.
5. inconsistency (in′kən sis′tən sē), *n.* act that is lacking in agreement, harmony.
6. benevolent (bə nev′ə lənt), *adj.* wishing to promote the happiness of others.

After Reading

Making Connections

Shaping Your Response

1. Think about the two selections you've just read. How persuasive were the pleas for freedom made by Abigail Adams and Prince Hall?

Analyzing the Selections

2. What changes does Abigail Adams imply that her husband must make in his attitude toward women?

3. Consider Abigail Adams's **tone** in her letter. Would you call it assertive, gentle, complaining, or matter-of-fact? Why?

4. How does Prince Hall use **allusions** to the American Revolution to support his argument?

Extending the Ideas

5. 👣 Both of these works address the fact that at the time of the American Revolution the laws limited the **choices** of some groups at the same time they granted freedom to others. Do such inequities still occur today? Explain your answer.

6. How can Americans today fight for changes they believe are needed in government policy?

Literary Focus: Maxims

In "Letter to John Adams," Abigail Adams writes this **maxim**: " . . . power and liberty are like heat and moisture; where they are well mixed everything prospers; where they are single, they are destructive." What other maxims and maxim-like thoughts did you find? For each selection, choose one example of a maxim or maxim-like thought to study. Write the maxim at the top of a page, and then answer these questions:

- What rule of conduct does the maxim suggest?

- Does the maxim express a universal truth? How so?

- Is the thought expressed in the maxim still relevant today? Why or why not?

- Why is using a maxim sometimes better than just saying the thought outright?

Vocabulary Study

emancipate
arbitrary
inconsistency
benevolent
laudable

Both Abigail Adams and Prince Hall recognize the power of government to address their pleas. They convey that recognition to the reader by using forceful words such as those in the list. Using your Glossary if necessary, write a sentence of your own for each word.

A Spirit of Independence

The Quest for Freedom

Multicultural Connection

The famous "shot heard 'round the world" fired at the Battle of Lexington in 1775 may have signaled the beginning of America's fight for independence, but it wasn't the only call ever sounded in the name of freedom. The voices of oppressed peoples have resounded throughout history demanding revolutionary change. Here are some freedom fighters who have led the way.

On page 190 you'll find *Preamble*, artist Mike Wilkins's interpretation of the Preamble of the United States Constitution.

In the United States **women** struggled in the early 1800s to win the right to vote, a right known as suffrage. However, women would have to wait for full voting rights until the passage of the 19th Amendment in 1920.

On September 16, 1810 Mexican priest **Miguel Hidalgo** led a peasant uprising against Spanish rule before being captured and executed in 1811. Pictured in this Diego Rivera mural, Hidalgo started a revolution that led to Mexico's independence in 1821.

In 1791 **Toussaint L'Ouverture** led a slave revolt against occupying France and became the ruler of Haiti and the Dominican Republic. Although L'Ouverture's government was soon overthrown by Napoleon, his actions inspired Haitians to continue their fight for independence, which they achieved in 1804.

Mohandas Gandhi led a revolution to free his native India from British rule. Using only nonviolent protest and civil disobedience, Gandhi and his followers won India's independence in 1947.

In Beijing, China, thousands of **student protesters** rallied in Tiananmen Square from April to June of 1989, demanding social and political reform. On June 4, troops sent in to break up the demonstration killed over 700 protesters. The next day a lone protester stood against oncoming tanks before being pulled to safety.

Nelson Mandela led a movement against South Africa's system of segregation known as apartheid, and was imprisoned in 1962. He was freed in 1990 and helped to end the apartheid system. In 1994 black South Africans were allowed to vote for the first time and Mandela became the first black president of that nation.

Preamble (1987) by Mike Wilkins

Responding

1. Why is the quest for freedom and basic rights so often associated with struggle?

2. Does Wilkins's *Preamble* seem like an appropriate way of celebrating one of the most important documents in U.S. history? Why or why not?

3. Think about what the word "freedom" means to you. What freedoms would you be willing to fight for?

Career Connection

Seven sailors of the United States Navy worked continually during the Persian Gulf War of 1991, shipping supplies from the Navy base at Norfolk, Virginia, to aircraft carriers. The ships and the aircraft that flew missions from them were carrying out Operation Desert Storm, a campaign by the United States and dozens of other countries to free Kuwait, a country that had been invaded by Iraq.

A Sailor Works for Freedom

Petty Officer Maureen Sims, the United States Navy's 1995 Atlantic Fleet Shore Sailor of the Year, was shipping supplies in 1991.

"During Operation Desert Storm, the war, I supplied the parts for all the aircraft that flew the missions," says Sims. "Supply is the most important link in any kind of war." She believes the American military effort during the 1991 Persian Gulf War was part of a modern campaign to safeguard freedom.

"I worked with a supply team in Norfolk, Virginia. We took care of every aircraft carrier based on the East Coast. I was one of seven people, and all we did—day and night, twelve hours on and twelve off—was supplying the parts." She explains that the Navy's successful air-war missions could not have been carried out without the supplies her team provided.

Sims believes that the quest for freedom "definitely is still going on." An Aviation Store Keeper First Class, she has traveled to many places in the world for the Navy. Seeing people struggle for freedom or for improved standards of living in areas of Asia, the Middle East, and the Caribbean has helped Sims appreciate life in the United States.

"I realize how lucky we are as Americans," she says. "When I was sitting in a classroom in high school, I didn't realize how fortunate we are." Her attitudes changed when, earlier in her naval career, she was posted at a United States Navy base in Guantanamo, Cuba, at a time when people from Haiti were arriving as refugees at the base. They had fled their homeland during the rule of a military government, seeking freedom in the United States. Many had risked their lives, making dangerous voyages on stormy seas in small boats. Some of the refugees had died at sea. Others reached Cuba in poor health, injured, starving, or in misery.

"It really was a tragedy to see some of the families when they showed up in boats," Sims recalls. She has seen poor people in various lands with little chance to improve their circumstances. She tells of people in Cuba, the Philippines, and Haiti "doing everything they can, risking their lives, to come to America." In contrast, she notes, there are people in the United States who take freedom and comfortable living for granted.

Petty Officer Sims's most recent assignment has been Aviation Store Keeper First Class at a Navy base in Keflavik, Iceland. Along with her work, Sims is taking college courses to learn more history, to see the "big picture," as she thinks of it. It's a picture that includes freedom for people throughout the world— and the need to defend it.

"History is so important," she says, "because it keeps repeating itself. I think we need to learn from mistakes that we have made, to avoid them in the future."

Responding

In your opinion, should the United States be willing to fight for the freedom of people in other countries? Explain your answer.

Language History

Noah Webster's American English

 The reasons for American English being different from English English are simple: As an independent nation our honor requires us to have a system of our own, in language as well as government.

In this way Noah Webster (1758–1843) argued for the independence of Americans from England in language as well as government. Even after the United States gained political freedom from England, America's language remained English. However, as the new nation began to establish its own identity, American English began to take on unique characteristics that set it apart from the English of England.

No one was more influential in defining the new American language than Noah Webster, who saw a national language as a way to deepen the bonds among a widely scattered and strongly individualistic citizenry. To this end, Webster published in 1783 *The American Spelling Book,* in which he clarified pronunciation with a new system of syllable division, and simplified American spelling by eliminating British elements and silent letters. Thus, Americans use *color* for *colour*, *wagon* for *waggon*, *fiber* for *fibre*, *tire* for *tyre*, and *risk* for *risque*. Later, in 1828, Webster compiled a prescriptive American counterpart to the English lexicographer Samuel Johnson's *Dictionary,* called *American English,* which recorded and standardized the developing language.

Webster's dictionary and spellers made a particularly significant impact on the standardization of American English through the schools. With the ready availability of printed material and increasing literacy through public education, generations of Americans were taught to read and write based on the standards prescribed by Webster.

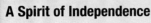

Writing Workshop

Taking a Stand

Assignment To what degree do you think we have lived up to the ideals stated in the Declaration of Independence? Imagine that you are running for public office, and address this question in a persuasive essay, from which you will deliver a persuasive speech.

WRITER'S BLUEPRINT

Product   A persuasive essay and speech

Purpose   To convince voters of your opinions

Audience   A gathering of voters

Specs   To create an effective essay and speech, you should:

❏ Begin your essay by greeting the voters and stating your position on this question: To what extent have we achieved the ideals stated in the Declaration of Independence?

❏ Present your position point by point. Support each point with sound reasoning based on evidence gathered from current events and from personal experience. Be sure to address and counter, point by point, any opposition others might have to your position.

❏ Conclude by suggesting what course you think the United States should follow in the future and how the voters can help keep the country on that course.

❏ Write with a tone of authority. Use rhetorical questions, repetition of key words, and other techniques of persuasive writing.

❏ Make note cards from your essay and use them to deliver a speech.

❏ Follow the rules of grammar, usage, spelling, and mechanics. Pay special attention to correct pronoun usage.

Review the main points of the Declaration of Independence. Work in a small group. Also, read Abigail Adams' letter to John Adams and other relevant selections from the literature. Together, list important words and phrases that represent ideals of early American democracy, such as "all men are created equal" and "the pursuit of happiness."

Chart current issues related to the ideals from your list. Work in a small group. You might want to review TV news shows and articles in magazines and newspapers to help you get caught up on current events. Create a chart similar to the one that follows.

Ideals	Current Issues	Triumphs	Defeats
Equality ("all men are created equal")	Women's rights	• right to vote • can own property • own their own businesses	• no Equal Rights Amendment • unequal salaries and opportunities in the workplace
Liberty			

Evaluate triumphs and defeats. Review your chart and think about how close Americans have come to realizing the early American ideals you've examined. Formulate an overall opinion that takes all these ideals into account. You might use a scale of one to ten, with ten being the perfect realization of all of them.

Try a quickwrite. Write about your position for five minutes. State your overall position on the ideals in your chart and explain it briefly, as if you were trying to convince a friend. Don't write much—just enough to satisfy yourself that your position is sound and that you can defend it effectively. Be prepared to alter your position if your quickwrite takes you in another direction.

Revise your chart. Add the following three new columns: **Position** (summarizing your position on the extent to which this ideal has been achieved), **Opposition** (noting any opposing views), and **Counterarguments** (noting your response to opposing views). Fill in these columns. Use your quickwrite for ideas.

Plan your essay. Make an outline like the one on the next page. Note phrases or sentences you could use for each point.

Introduction
- Greet your audience
- State your overall position

Body
- First point
  Supporting evidence
- Opposing position
  Counter-arguments
- Second point
  Supporting evidence
- Opposing position
  Counter-arguments

and so on . . .

Conclusion
- What you think ought to be done now
- How voters can help

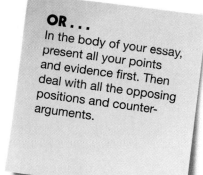

OR . . .
In the body of your essay, present all your points and evidence first. Then deal with all the opposing positions and counter-arguments.

 DRAFTING

Before you draft, reread your chart and quickwrite, as well as your writing plan and the Writer's Blueprint. You'll want to have your arguments and your plan clearly in mind as you write.

As you draft, don't slow the process by worrying about mistakes in spelling and punctuation. Concentrate on getting your ideas down on paper and developing an argument that flows smoothly. Here are some drafting tips.

- Begin your first draft with a series of rhetorical questions—questions that you yourself are prepared to answer ("Have we achieved equality for women?"). Then start answering those questions for your audience ("In my view, we . . .").

- Use a tone of authority, but take care not to appear as an arrogant know-it-all and alienate your audience. Let them know that you have arrived at your position only after a great deal of thought.

- Use repetition of key words and phrases as a way of holding your audience's attention and pounding your points home. See the Revising Strategy in Step 3 of this lesson.

3 REVISING

Ask a partner for comments on your draft before you revise it.

✔ Have I followed the Specs in the Writer's Blueprint?

✔ Have I supported my position with sound reasoning and relevant examples?

✔ Have I used persuasive techniques such as rhetorical questions and repetition of key words and phrases?

Revising Strategy

Repetition as Persuasive Technique

Repetition can create a sense of rhythm and emphasis. It can also make the line of argument clearer and easier to follow. By repeating key words or phrases, the writer can hold an audience's attention and emphasize important ideas, as in the Literary Source below.

LITERARY SOURCE

". . . That these United Colonies are, and of Right ought to be, FREE AND INDEPENDENT STATES . . . and that, as FREE AND INDEPENDENT STATES, they have full Power to levy War, conclude Peace, contract Alliances, establish Commerce, and to do all other Acts and Things which INDEPENDENT STATES may of right do."
 from the Declaration of Independence

As you revise, consider strengthening your argument with repetition of key words and phrases.

4 EDITING

Ask a partner to review your revised draft before you edit. When you edit, look for errors in grammar, usage, spelling, and mechanics. Check carefully for errors in pronoun usage.

Editing Strategy

Using Pronouns Correctly

A subject pronoun *(I, you, he, she, it, we, they)* is used as the subject of a sentence. An object pronoun *(me, you, him, her, us, them)* is used as the object in a sentence. Don't use one form in place of the other. Be especially careful when the pronoun is part of a compound subject or object.

FOR REFERENCE
You'll find more information about pronoun usage in the Language and Grammar Handbook at the back of this book.

Wrong	You may believe *Jefferson and I* when we say that liberty is precious.
Corrected	You may believe *Jefferson and me* when we say that liberty is precious.
Wrong	*The framers of the Constitution and us* agree.
Corrected	*The framers of the Constitution and we* agree.

Strategy: Say the sentence to yourself with just the one pronoun alone *(You may believe I . . . , us agree . . .)*. If you've used the wrong form of the pronoun, the sentence will sound wrong to your ear.

Notice how two sentences in the student model have been edited to correct mistakes with pronouns.

In my view, the current government is obstructing our forefathers' vision of paradise. Thomas Jefferson would be saddened to see the current state of affairs. ~~Him~~ *He,* and others who fought for independence intended for all American citizens to enjoy life, liberty, and the pursuit of happiness. But in today's society, many factors threaten the rights intended for us and those who follow us.

For one, high crime rates have caused many families to restrict their activities and fortify their homes. Some people are virtual captives in their own homes, afraid to venture out after dark. Even my friends and *me,* I have to be careful going out at night or just walking home from school.

STUDENT MODEL

FOR REFERENCE
You'll find more information on preparing and presenting a speech on page 548.

Make note cards for your speech. Review your essay and list the main ideas and details. Use these note cards to deliver your speech—instead of simply reading the essay. Notice how the writer of the student model on page 197 listed main ideas with a few additional notes.

> *Introduction-State position*
>
> *Our government obstructing forefathers' vision*
>
> *Jefferson disappointed*
>
> *Intended "life, liberty, pursuit of happiness"*
>
> *Not in today's society*

Consider these ideas for presenting your speech:

- Deliver your speech in point-counterpoint style, paired with a student who took a position very different from yours.

- Hold a question-answer session after you deliver your speech, in which classmates ask you questions as if they were voters.

STEP 6 LOOKING BACK

Self-evaluate. What grade would you give your essay and speech? Look back at the Writer's Blueprint and give yourself a score for each item, from 6 (superior) to 1 (inadequate).

Reflect. Think about what you learned while working on this assignment.

✔ How was your position changed by listening to the ideas of your classmates?

✔ Do you notice any of the persuasive techniques you used in writing your essay being used in TV commercials to persuade you to buy products? Which commercials do you feel are especially persuasive and why?

For Your Working Portfolio Add your essay, note cards, and reflection responses to your working portfolio.

Beyond Print

Looking at Heroes

In the last 150 years, technological innovations such as photography, motion pictures, and television have made the faces of celebrities widely familiar. But in the long centuries that went before, artists have often had a major role in shaping the historic images of famous people. From the earliest times, rulers (who were about the only people who succeeded in becoming famous) made sure they were represented in a fashion that matched their sense of their own importance. The artworks pictured here illustrate a few characteristics of such heroic images. The examples are drawn from likenesses of George Washington, the first American hero.

Supercolossal

Great size is frequently a characteristic of heroic images, from the time of the Egyptian pharaoh Rameses (who had dozens of colossal statues of himself placed throughout his kingdom) to modern America, where sculptor Gutzon Borglum used dynamite and jackhammers to carve the likenesses of George Washington and three other American presidents into the side of Mount Rushmore (shown above).

Grace Under Pressure

Rulers, who were frequently great military leaders (or wanted history to think they had been) often had themselves depicted on the field of battle, looking very cool under fire. Washington apparently was quite fearless, modestly admitting that he found "something charming in the sound of bullets." He certainly looks relaxed leaning against a cannon in *George Washington at the Battle of Trenton* by Charles Willson Peale, pictured at the right.

All in the Family

Domestic settings were also popular for images of famous people, who wanted the rest of us to know that they had a kinder, gentler side than the historical record might suggest. In 1796, after he had retired from the presidency, Washington was painted with his family by Edward Savage.

The Great Beyond

The admirers of famous people often wish to depict their heroes in the hereafter. After Washington's death in 1800, John James Barralet painted *Sacred to the Memory of Washington.* Escorted by an angel and Father Time and mourned by Columbia (the personification of the United States) and an American Indian, the hero is shown departing for the celestial realm.

Activities

1. Create a collage of images of some American hero—past or present—that reflects a number of different aspects of his or her career.

2. An incumbent President is among the most widely depicted of Americans, appearing on everything from political campaign buttons to the covers of news magazines. With other students, discuss whether and how this material affects the American public's attitude toward the office of the presidency.

Multicultural Connections

Choices

A Spirit of Independence The individuals and groups in this unit are faced with some very important **choices.** Dekanawidah outlines those characteristics the Iroquois League has chosen as most important in a good leader. In the excerpt from Benjamin Franklin's autobiography, General Braddock makes some very poor choices based on cultural biases about the colonists and American Indians. Both Thomas Paine and Patrick Henry explain the values they think should lead others to choose revolution rather than inaction, and Thomas Jefferson explains why the American colonists have chosen to sever their ties with England. Abigail Adams and Prince Hall point out the necessity of being able to make independent choices.

■ Compare the arguments Thomas Paine, Patrick Henry, and Thomas Jefferson use to justify their choice to sever ties with England. Which individual would you say has the best reasons to support the choice he made?

Activities

Work in small groups on the following activities.

1. Think of times when you or someone you know has had to face a difficult decision. Choose one situation to dramatize, presenting both the situation and the factors that led to the decision. Then, explain whether or not your group thinks society or cultural values influenced the choice.

2. Create a *Then and Now* chart like the one below that tells what you think Americans valued most at the time of the American Revolution. You can get clues to their values from the arguments of Jefferson, Paine, Henry, Adams, and Hall. Then, fill out the other side of the chart, telling what you think Americans value—what they base their choices on—today. Compare your chart with other groups' charts.

What Americans Value	
Then (the American Revolution)	Now

Independent and Group Projects

Debate

The Greatest Leader Which of the individuals represented in this unit—Dekanawidah, Franklin, Paine, Henry, Jefferson, Adams, or Hall—would make the best President of the United States? Form groups based on your choices, and with your group, come up with arguments to support your choice. Put your arguments in order and present them to your class.

Media

What the Founding Fathers Forgot The colonists fought for their freedom from England, and in doing so created a whole new government that did its best to secure the rights of its people. Of course, they weren't perfect. Based on this premise, work with a group to interview on videotape people you know—students, relatives, teachers, or others—to get their opinion on what the "Founding Fathers" could have done, if anything, to better secure the rights of all Americans. Present your video, documentary-style, to your class.

Art

Inspiration Creation Which of the selections captured your attention or sparked your imagination more than the others? Was it a memorable quote, a telling passage, or the entire work that stirred your thoughts? Using that selection for inspiration, create a work of art that somehow reflects the piece. You may want to create a mural, compose lyrics for a song or rap, write a poem, or make a collage. Present your work to the class, explaining how it relates to the selection you chose, then gather all of the works into a class gallery.

Drama

Talk About It Dekanawidah, Benjamin Franklin, Thomas Paine, Patrick Henry, Thomas Jefferson, Abigail Adams, and Prince Hall are all on a committee together. They have been assigned the job of forming a new government. With a group, create a dialogue for their first committee meeting, in which each member gets to share his or her opinion about what should be considered in this new government. Then, dramatize your dialogue for the class.

THE WILDERNESS

THEMES
IN AMERICAN
LITERATURE

THE WILDERNESS

IN THE BEGINNING,
ALL THE WORLD
WAS AMERICA.

JOHN LOCKE (1600s)

The question of whether to conquer or cherish the wilderness which was their home would have made little sense to the Indian peoples living in the Americas. The Indians did not see the wilderness as something separate from themselves to be feared or tamed. But to many later settlers the wilderness was a threat that must be overcome if a European-style civilization was to be established in America. In this section you will explore a variety of responses to the American wilderness and the relationship between people and the land.

SONG OF THE SKY LOOM

Oh our Mother the Earth oh
our Father the Sky
Your children are we
        with tired backs we bring you the gifts you love

So weave for us a garment of brightness

May the warp be the white light of morning
May the weft be the red light of evening
May the fringes be the falling rain
May the border be the standing rainbow

Weave for us this bright garment
that we may walk where birds sing
        where grass is green

Oh our Mother the Earth oh our Father the Sky

Tewa Indian (translated by Herbert Spinden)

George Catlin, *River Bluffs, 1320 Miles Above St. Louis* (1832)

THE GIFT OUTRIGHT

The land was ours before we were the land's.
She was our land more than a hundred years
Before we were her people. She was ours
In Massachusetts, in Virginia,
But we were England's, still colonials,
Possessing what we still were unpossessed by,
Possessed by what we now no more possessed.
Something we were withholding made us weak
Until we found out that it was ourselves
We were withholding from our land of living,
And forthwith found salvation in surrender.
Such as we were we gave ourselves outright
(The deed of gift was many deeds of war)
To the land vaguely realizing westward,
But still unstoried, artless, unenhanced,
Such as she was, such as she would become.

Robert Frost (1942)

LOST

Stand still. The trees ahead and bushes beside you
Are not lost. Wherever you are is called Here,
And you must treat it as a powerful stranger,
Must ask permission to know it and be known.
The forest breathes. Listen. It answers,
I have made this place around you.
If you leave it, you may come back again, saying Here.
No two trees are the same to Raven.
No two branches are the same to Wren.
If what a tree or a bush does is lost on you,
You are surely lost. Stand still. The forest knows
Where you are. You must let it find you.

David Wagoner (1976)

205

THE PILGRIMS SIGHT NEW ENGLAND

. . . What could they see but a hideous and desolate wilderness, full of wild beasts and wild men. . . . For summer being done, all things stand upon them with a weather beaten face, and the whole country, full of woods and thickets, represented a wild and savage hue.

William Bradford (1620)

WANDERING IN THE WILDERNESS

I went along that day mourning and lamenting, leaving farther my own country, and traveling into the vast and howling wilderness, and I understood something of Lot's Wife's temptation,[1] when she looked back.

Mary Rowlandson (1682)

Charles Burchfield, *Song of the Red Bird* (1917–60)

1. **Lot's Wife's temptation.** In the Bible, Lot and his wife were ordered by God to flee the wicked city of Sodom, which was to be destroyed by fire from heaven. When Lot's wife looked back at her home, she was turned into a pillar of salt.

THIS LAND IS YOUR LAND

This land is your land, this land is my land
From California to the New York Island,
From the redwood forest to the Gulf Stream Waters;
This land was made for you and me.

As I was walking that ribbon of highway
I saw above me that endless skyway;
I saw below me that golden valley;
This land was made for you and me.

I've roamed and rambled and I followed my footsteps
To the sparkling sands of her diamond deserts;
And all around me a voice was sounding:
This land was made for you and me.

When the sun came shining, and I was strolling,
And the wheat fields waving and the dust clouds rolling.
As the fog was lifting a voice was chanting:
This land was made for you and me.

As I went walking, I saw a sign there,
And on the sign it said, "No Trespassing,"
But on the other side it didn't say nothing,
That side was made for you and me.

In the shadows of the steeple, I saw my people,
By the Relief Office I seen my people;
As they stood there hungry, I stood there asking;
Is this land made for you and me?

Nobody living can ever stop me,
As I go walking that freedom highway;
Nobody living can ever make me turn back,
This land was made for you and me.

Woody Guthrie (1940)

SELL A COUNTRY!
WHY NOT SELL
THE AIR, THE
GREAT SEA, AS
WELL AS THE
EARTH? DID NOT
THE GREAT
SPIRIT MAKE
THEM ALL FOR
THE USE OF HIS
CHILDREN?

TECUMSEH (1810)

T H E   W O N D E R
O F   N I A G A R A

And Niagara! that wonder of the world!—where the sublime and beautiful are bound together in an indissoluble chain. In gazing on it we feel as though a great void had been filled in our minds—our conceptions expand—and we become a part of what we behold!

Thomas Cole (1835)

IN AMERICA
NATURE IS
AUTOCRATIC,
SAYING "I AM
NOT ARGUING,
I AM TELLING
YOU."
ERIK H. ERIKSON
(1950)

Edward Hicks, *The Falls of Niagara* (1825)

Albert Bierstadt, *Niagara Falls* (1869–70)

CABINS IN THE WILDERNESS

A frontier cabin is shown in a painting done by an English visitor in 1822.

Some years ago, while journeying in the mountains of North Carolina, I passed by a large number of "coves," as they call them there, or heads of small valleys between the hills, which had been newly cleared and planted. The impression on my mind was one of unmitigated squalor. The settler had in every case cut down the more manageable trees, and left their charred stumps standing. The larger trees he had girdled and killed, in order that their foliage should not cast a shade. He had then built a log cabin, plastering its chinks with clay, and had set up a tall zigzag rail fence around the scene of his havoc to keep the pigs and cattle out. Finally, he had irregularly planted the intervals between the stumps and trees with Indian corn, which grew among the chips; and there he dwelt with his wife and babes—an axe, a gun, a few utensils, and some pigs and chickens feeding in the woods, being the sum total of his possessions.

The forest had been destroyed; and what had "improved" it out of existence was hideous, a sort of ulcer, without a single element of artificial grace to make up for the loss of Nature's beauty. Ugly, indeed, seemed the life of the squatter scudding, as the sailors say, under bare poles,[1] beginning again away back where our first ancestors started, and by hardly a single item the better off for all the achievements of the intervening generations. Talk about going back to nature! I said to myself, oppressed by the dreariness, as I drove by. Talk of a country life for one's old age and for one's children! Never thus, with nothing but the bare ground and one's bare hands to fight the battle! Never, without the best spoils of culture woven in! The beauties and commodities gained by the centuries are sacred. They are our heritage and birthright. No modern person ought to be willing to live a day in such a state of rudimentariness and denudation.

Then I said to the mountaineer who was driving me, "What sort of people are they who have to make these new clearings?" "All of us," he replied. "Why, we ain't happy here unless we are getting one of these coves under cultivation." I instantly felt that I had been losing the whole inward significance of the situation. Because to me the clearings spoke of naught but denudation, I thought that to those whose sturdy arms and obedient axes had made them they could tell no other story. But, when they looked on the hideous stumps, what they thought of was personal victory. The chips, the girdled trees, and the vile split rails spoke of honest sweat, persistent toil and final reward. The cabin was a warrant of safety for self and wife and babes. In short, the clearing, which to me was a mere ugly picture on the retina, was to them a symbol redolent[2] with moral memories and sang a very paean[3] of duty, struggle, and success.

William James (1898)

---

1. **scudding . . . bare poles,** running before a storm with no sails set.
2. **redolent** (red′l ənt) *adj.* strongly suggesting.

3. **paean** (pē′ən), *n.* song of praise.

THE PRAIRIES

THESE ARE THE GARDENS OF THE DESERT, THESE
THE UNSHORN FIELDS, BOUNDLESS AND BEAUTIFUL,
FOR WHICH THE SPEECH OF ENGLAND HAS NO NAME—
THE PRAIRIES.

WILLIAM CULLEN BRYANT (1833)

A MOUNTAIN FOREST

. . . We ascended into the purple gloom of great pine forests which clothe the skirts of the mountains up to a height of about 11,000 feet and from their chill and solitary depths we had glimpses of golden atmosphere and rose-lit summits, not of "the land very far off," but of the land nearer now in all its grandeur, gaining in sublimity by nearness—glimpses, too, through a broken vista of purple gorges, of the illimitible Plains lying idealized in the late sunlight, their baked, brown expanse transfigured into the likeness of a sunset sea rolling infinitely in waves of misty gold.

We rode upwards through the gloom on a steep trail blazed through the forest, all my intellect concentrated on avoiding being dragged off my horse by impending branches, or having the blankets badly torn, as those of my companions were, by sharp dead limbs, between which there was hardly room to pass—the horses breathless, and requiring to stop every few yards, though their riders, except myself, were afoot. The gloom of the dense, ancient silent forest is to me awe inspiring. On such an evening it is soundless, except for the branches creaking in the soft wind, the frequent snap of decayed timber, and a murmur in the pine tops as of a not distant waterfall, all tending to produce eeriness and a sadness "hardly akin to pain."

Isabella Bird (1879)

THE IMPACT OF THE FRONTIER

The frontier is the line of most rapid and effective Americanization. The wilderness masters the colonist. It finds him a European in dress, industries, tools, modes of travel, and thought. It takes him from the railroad car and puts him in the birch canoe. It strips off the garments of civilization and arrays him in the hunting shirt and the mocassin. It puts him in the log cabin of the Cherokee and Iroquois and runs an Indian palisade around him. . . . Little by little he transforms the wilderness, but the outcome is not the old Europe. . . . The fact is, that here is a new product that is American. At first, the frontier was the Atlantic Coast. It was the frontier of Europe in a very real sense. Moving westward, the frontier became more and more American.

Frederick Jackson Turner (1894)

A HARSH LANDSCAPE

MOST OF THOSE OLD SETTLERS TOLD IT LIKE IT WAS,
ROUGH AND ROCKY. THEY NAMED THEIR TOWNS RIMROCK,
ROUGH ROCK, ROUND ROCK, AND WIDE RUINS, SKULL
VALLEY, BITTER SPRINGS, WOLF HOLE, TOMBSTONE. IT'S A
TOUGH COUNTRY. THE NAMES OF ARIZONA TOWNS TELL YOU
ALL YOU NEED TO KNOW.

CHARLES KURALT (1979)

Carol Hoy, *Dead Pine Over Canyonlands* (1991)

NATIONAL PARK
AS THE PEOPLE INHERITED IT—

THE LOGICAL FINISH
IF WE LET DOWN THE BARS

Herbert Johnson cartoon (1920)

A FABLE FOR TOMORROW

There was once a town in the heart of America where all life seemed to live in harmony with its surroundings. The town lay in the midst of a checkerboard of prosperous farms, with fields of grain and hillsides of orchards where, in spring, white clouds of bloom drifted about the green fields. In autumn, oak and maple and birch set up a blaze of color that flamed and flickered across a backdrop of pines. Then foxes barked in the hills and deer silently crossed the fields, half hidden in the mists of the fall mornings.

Along the roads, laurel, viburnum and alder, great ferns and wildflowers delighted the traveler's eye through much of the year. Even in winter the roadsides were places of beauty, where countless birds came to feed on the berries and on the seed heads of the dried weeds rising above the snow. The countryside was, in fact, famous for the abundance and variety of its bird life, and when the flood of migrants was pouring through in spring and fall people traveled from great distances to observe them. Others came to fish the streams, which flowed clear and cold out of the hills and contained shady pools where trout lay. So it had been from the days many years ago when the first settlers raised their houses, sank their wells, and built their barns.

Then a strange blight crept over the area and everything began to change. Some evil spell had settled on the community: mysterious maladies swept the flocks of chickens; the cattle and sheep sickened and died. Everywhere was a shadow of death. The farmers spoke of much illness among their families. In the town the doctors had become more and more puzzled by new kinds of sickness appearing among their patients. There had been several sudden and unexplained deaths, not only among adults but even among children, who would be stricken suddenly while at play and die within a few hours.

There was a strange stillness. The birds, for example—where had they gone? Many people spoke of them, puzzled and disturbed. The feeding stations in the backyards were deserted. The few birds seen anywhere were moribund;[1] they trembled violently and could not fly. It was a spring without voices. On the mornings that had once throbbed with the dawn chorus of robins, catbirds, doves, jays, wrens, and scores of other bird voices there was now no sound; only silence lay over the fields and woods and marsh.

On the farms the hens brooded, but no chicks hatched. The farmers complained that they were unable to raise any pigs—the litters were small and the young survived only a few days. The apple trees were coming into bloom but no bees droned among the blossoms, so there was no pollination and there would be no fruit.

The roadsides, once so attractive, were now lined with browned and withered vegetation as though swept by fire. These, too, were silent, deserted by all living things. Even the streams were now lifeless. Anglers no longer visited them, for all the fish had died.

In the gutters under the eaves and between the shingles of the roofs, a white granular powder still showed a few patches; some weeks before it had fallen like snow upon the roofs and the lawns, the fields and streams.

No witchcraft, no enemy action had silenced the rebirth of new life in this stricken world. The people had done it themselves.

Rachel Carson (1962)

---

1. **moribund** (mor′ə bund), *adj.* dying.

RETURN

A little too abstract, a little too wise,
It is time for us to kiss the earth again,
It is time to let the leaves rain from the skies,
Let the rich life run to the roots again.
I will go down to the lovely Sur Rivers
And dip my arms in them up to the shoulders.
I will find my accounting where the alder leaf quivers
In the ocean wind over the river boulders.
I will touch things and things and no more thoughts,
That breed like mouthless May-flies darkening the sky,
The insect clouds that blind our passionate hawks
So that they cannot strike, hardly can fly.
Things are the hawk's food and noble is the mountain,
    Oh noble
Pico Blanco, steep sea-wave of marble.

Robinson Jeffers (1935)

America the Beautiful

O Beautiful for spacious skies,

For amber waves of grain,

For purple mountain majesties

Above the fruited plain!

America! America!

God shed His grace on thee

And crown thy good with brotherhood

From sea to shining sea!

Katherine Lee Bates (1893)

RESPONDING

1. If you had to select one American scene glimpsed by these writers and artists as most characteristic of this country, which one would you choose? Why?

2. What different qualities do Edward Hicks, Albert Bierstadt, and Thomas Cole find in Niagara Falls?

3. Should wilderness areas in the United States be developed for recreation or left in their natural state? Explain your answer.

4. What impression of the deserts of the Southwest is conveyed by Carol Hoy's landcape?

American Classic

Romantic Truths and Terrors
Part One, pages 218–297

The Civil War
Part Two, pages 298–347

American

HISTORICAL OVERVIEW

In the 1830s, America began to experience the impact of the Romantic Movement that was transforming European civilization. Like the European movement of which it was an offshoot, American Romanticism was in a broad sense a new attitude toward nature, humanity, and society that espoused individualism and freedom. Many trends characterized American Romanticism. Among the most important are the following:

- an impulse toward reform
- a celebration of individualism
- a reverence for nature
- a concern with the impact of new technology
- an idealization of women
- a fascination with death and the supernatural

A View of the Rocky Mountains by American painter Albert Bierstadt conveys Romanticism's delight in the beauty and mystery of nature.

This era's reform movements included temperance, women's rights, and the abolition of slavery, as indicated by this emblem of the American Anti-Slavery Society.

AM I NOT A MAN AND A BROTHER?

Ralph Waldo Emerson, sculpted here in bronze by artist Daniel Chester French, emphasized the role of imagination and intuition in revealing the individual human spirit.

Romanticism

Romantics were concerned with how new technology, such as this locomotive, built in 1856, was changing people's lives.

The era's concern with mortality is suggested by these pieces of mourning jewelry, which preserved the hair of the deceased.

In the early 1800s America both idealized and exploited women, as suggested by the delicate silhouette of a woman's head and the view of women workers toiling in a textile mill.

Key Dates

1831
The American Anti-Slavery Society is founded.

1838
The Trail of Tears: 15,000 Cherokee Indians are forcibly relocated west of the Mississippi River.

1840
2,800 miles of railroad are in operation in the U.S.

1845
Henry David Thoreau lives alone at Walden Pond.

1846
The United States and Mexico go to war over territory disputes.

1848
The first women's rights convention is held at Seneca Falls, New York.

1849
Speculators rush to California after gold is discovered in 1848.

1855
Walt Whitman publishes Leaves of Grass.

219

Romantic Truths and Terrors

The Romantic movement of the early 1800s optimistically proclaimed that any determined individual could better society. Yet, there was an ominous side to Romanticism as well—a fascination with death and an interest in the unknown, unpredictable parts of the human psyche.

👣 **Multicultural Connection Individuality** may mean either accepting or rejecting cultural norms or group standards. How do the narrators and characters in the following selections express their individuality?

Literature

Ralph Waldo Emerson	*from* **Self-Reliance** ◆ essay	222
Henry David Thoreau	*from* **Walden** ◆ essay	226
	from **Civil Disobedience** ◆ essay	231
Sojourner Truth	**Ain't I a Woman?** ◆ speech	237
Washington Irving	**The Devil and Tom Walker** ◆ short story	240
Edgar Allan Poe	**The Pit and the Pendulum** ◆ short story	253
	The Raven ◆ poem	268
Nathaniel Hawthorne	**Dr. Heidegger's Experiment** ◆ short story	276

Interdisciplinary Study A Romance with Horror

An Appetite for Fright ◆ pop culture 286
from Danse Macabre by Stephen King ◆ pop culture 288
That Which I Should Have Done I Did Not Do
    by Ivan Albright ◆ fine art 289
The Thrill of Chills by Ellen Blum Barish ◆ health 290

Language History

The Language of Gothic Horror 291

Writing Workshop Narrative Writing

Writing in Style 292

Beyond Print Media Literacy

Looking at Horror Movies 296

Before Reading

from Self-Reliance

by Ralph Waldo Emerson

Ralph Waldo Emerson
1803–1882

When Ralph Waldo Emerson was 17 years old, he wrote in his journal, "I find myself often idle, vagrant, stupid. . . . I am indolent and shall be insignificant." In fact, until he was 30, Emerson was unsure of what he wanted to do with his life. An overwhelming tragedy—the death of his wife—launched him into a deep depression. In his grief, he booked passage to Europe. It was there he encountered the Romantic movement, a new direction in art and thought that celebrated individualism and freedom of expression. Renewed in spirit, he returned home and devoted the rest of his life to writing and lecturing.

Building Background

Emerson's Big Ideas Ralph Waldo Emerson was a champion of the individual. He believed that we must look toward ourselves, not to society, in the search for happiness. Emerson presents an eloquent statement of these ideals in the essay "Self-Reliance," which he wrote not to offer a set of rules by which others should live, but to provoke thought about the ways in which we might *want* to live. Although his ideas were considered provocative at the time, they were also received with enthusiasm and acclaim. As writer Herman Melville once said, "Emerson is more than a brilliant fellow. Be his stuff begged, borrowed, or stolen, or of his own domestic manufacture, he is an uncommon man."

Literary Focus

Figurative Language Emerson makes use of figurative language throughout "Self-Reliance" in order to help his readers see things in new ways and to add vividness, clarity, and impact to his writing. Figurative language uses words apart from their literal meaning in order to furnish new effects or fresh insights. For example, in the second paragraph of the selection, Emerson warns, "imitation is suicide." Imitating others, of course, isn't literally suicide, rather this **metaphor,** or comparison between two unlike things, uses **hyperbole** (exaggeration) to emphasize the importance of originality. As you read "Self-Reliance," keep a list of the examples you find of figurative language—language that's used for effect rather than for its literal meaning.

Writer's Notebook

Happiness Is . . . "Self-Reliance" is full of ideas about what leads to human happiness. What do *you* think contributes to happiness? Jot down in your notebook a few of the ideas that make the most sense to you.

How does the composition of this painting, *Men Are Square* (1919) by Gerrit A. Beneker, reflect the cultural values of **individuality** and self-reliance? ➤

Self-Reliance

RALPH WALDO EMERSON

To believe your own thought, to believe that what is true for you in your private heart is true for all men,—that is genius. Speak your latent conviction, and it shall be the universal sense; for the inmost in due time becomes the outmost, and our first thought is rendered[1] back to us by the trumpets of the Last Judgment. Familiar as the voice of the mind is to each, the highest merit we ascribe to Moses, Plato and Milton is that they set at naught books and traditions, and spoke not what men, but what *they* thought. A man should learn to detect and watch that gleam of light which flashes across his mind from within, more than the lustre of the firmament[2] of bards and sages. Yet he dismisses without notice his thought, because it is his. In every work of genius we recognize our own rejected thoughts; they come back to us with a certain alienated majesty. . . .

---

1. **render** (ren′dər), *v.* give in return.
2. **firmament** (fér′mə mənt), *n.* arch of the heavens; sky.

There is a time in every man's education when he arrives at the conviction that envy is ignorance; that imitation is suicide; that he must take himself for better for worse as his portion; that though the wide universe is full of good, no kernel of nourishing corn can come to him but through his toil bestowed[3] on that plot of ground which is given to him to till. The power which resides in him is new in nature, and none but he knows what that is which he can do, nor does he know until he has tried. . . .

Trust thyself: every heart vibrates to that iron string. Accept the place the divine providence has found for you, the society of your contemporaries, the connection of events. Great men have always done so, and confided themselves childlike to the genius of their age, betraying their perception that the absolutely trustworthy was seated at their heart, working through their hands, predominating in all their being. . . .

Whoso would be a man, must be a nonconformist.[4] He who would gather immortal palms must not be hindered[5] by the name of goodness, but must explore if it be goodness. Nothing is at last sacred but the integrity of your own mind. Absolve you to yourself, and you shall have the suffrage of the world. I remember an answer which when quite young I was prompted to make to a valued adviser who was wont to importune[6] me with the dear old doctrines of the church. On my saying, "What have I to do with the sacredness of traditions, if I live wholly from within?" my friend suggested,—"But these impulses may be from below, not from above." I replied, "They do not seem to me to be such; but if I am the Devil's child, I will live then from the Devil." No law can be sacred to me but that of my nature. Good and bad are but names very readily transferable to that or this; the only right is what is after my constitution; the only wrong what is against it. A man is to carry himself in the presence of all opposition as if every thing were titular[7] and ephemeral[8] but he. I am ashamed to think how easily we capitulate[9] to badges and names, to large societies and dead institutions. . . .

The other terror that scares us from self-trust is our consistency; a reverence for our past act or word because the eyes of others have no other data for computing our orbit than our past acts, and we are loath to disappoint them. . . .

A foolish consistency is the hobgoblin of little minds, adored by little statesmen and philosophers and divines. With consistency a great soul has simply nothing to do. He may as well concern himself with his shadow on the wall. Speak what you think now in hard words and tomorrow speak what tomorrow thinks in hard words again, though it contradict every thing you said today.—"Ah, so you shall be sure to be misunderstood."—Is it so bad then to be misunderstood? Pythagoras was misunderstood, and Socrates, and Jesus, and Luther, and Copernicus, and Galileo, and Newton, and every pure and wise spirit that ever took flesh. To be great is to be misunderstood. . . .

Insist on yourself; never imitate. Your own gift you can present every moment with the cumulative force of a whole life's cultivation; but of the adopted talent of another you have only an extemporaneous half possession. . . .

A political victory, a rise of rents, the recovery of your sick or the return of your absent friend, or some other favorable event raises your spirits, and you think good days are preparing for you. Do not believe it. Nothing can bring you peace but yourself. Nothing can bring you peace but the triumph of principles.

---

3. **bestow** (bi stō'), *v.* give as a gift.
4. **nonconformist** (non'kən fôr'mist), *n.* person who refuses to be bound by established customs.
5. **hinder** (hin'dər), *v.* get in the way; make difficult.
6. **importune** (im'pôr tün'), *v.* ask urgently or repeatedly.
7. **titular** (tich'ə lər), *adj.* in title or name only.
8. **ephemeral** (i fem'ər əl), *adj.* lasting only for a very short time.
9. **capitulate** (kə pich'ə lāt), *v.* surrender.

After Reading

Making Connections

Shaping Your Response

1. Emerson believes that it is vital for all people to be nonconformists. Do you agree? Why or why not?

Analyzing the Essay

2. Emerson does not accept conventional ways of judging whether something is "good" or "bad." What system does he use to judge?

3. Some of Emerson's readers were upset by his ideas. What ideas in this excerpt do you think might have shocked people or made them angry? Explain your answer.

Extending the Ideas

4. Which of Emerson's principles do you try to follow in your life? Which do you feel would be too difficult or undesirable to follow? Why?

5. 👣 Being a noncomformist, or expressing one's **individuality,** can sometimes mean going against the norms of one's community or culture. How do you think people in your school or community react to nonconformists?

Literary Focus: Figurative Language

Look over the list of examples of **figurative language** you made while reading "Self-Reliance." Rewrite three of them using literal language. How does this change the meaning or feel of the passage?

Vocabulary Study

render
bestow
importune
capitulate
hinder

List the five numbered words on a piece of paper, then write the letter of each word's synonym next to it.

1. render	4. capitulate	a. ask	d. surrender
2. bestow	5. hinder	b. give	e. return
3. importune		c. obstruct	

Expressing Your Ideas ——————

Writing Choice

Writer's Notebook Update Compare the ideas you wrote about happiness to Emerson's ideas. Tell why living according to Emerson's suggestions would or would not make you a happier person.

Another Option

Emerson Meets the Press In groups, prepare a list of five questions that you'd like to ask Emerson. Then, elect an "Emerson" to **interview,** who can base the answers on the ideas discussed in the essay.

Before Reading

from Walden and Civil Disobedience

by Henry David Thoreau

Henry David Thoreau
1817–1862

Henry David Thoreau faithfully kept a journal after his neighbor, Ralph Waldo Emerson, suggested he use diary entries as an outlet for the thoughts that swirled around in his head. For the next twenty years, while working various odd jobs—he even served as a handyman for Emerson, where his tasks included making gloves for his chickens to protect the garden from their claws—Thoreau recorded his observations, thoughts, opinions, and activities. From his journal entries, he composed his most famous work, *Walden*.

Building Background

Writer and Rebel During the two years that Thoreau lived at Walden Pond (from 1845 to 1847), it was an isolated spot; he had few neighbors and certainly none that he could see from his cabin in the woods. Thoreau used the pond for drinking water and washing and occasionally relied on its fish to provide him with dinner. It was while living here that Thoreau completed his first book, *A Week on the Concord and Merrimack Rivers,* and began writing *Walden.* His solitude and productivity were interrupted briefly in 1846, however, when he was jailed for refusing to pay his poll tax. Thoreau had stopped paying this tax in protest of the war with Mexico. His eventual arrest inspired the famous essay, "Civil Disobedience."

Literary Focus

Allusion You may have heard the saying, "A picture is worth a thousand words." An **allusion** does the same thing because it allows an author to suggest an entire philosophy or line of thought with just a few words. For example, if you were to refer to your friend as a "major league in-line skater" it would conjure up images of someone who is a serious professional and has reached the top of his or her field. As you read the selections, watch for the allusions Thoreau uses.

Writer's Notebook

Getting Away from It All If you were given the chance to get away from your everyday life—school, homework, and any other responsibilities you have—and be alone for a while, what would you do? Where would you go? Jot down a few ideas, and then outline some of the pros and cons of taking a solitary journey. Later, you'll want to compare your imagined journey to Thoreau's life in the woods.

In 1845 Thoreau built a cabin in the woods by Walden Pond and lived there for two years. He wanted to simplify his life to the point where he could learn what the true essentials in life were. While there, he planned to write and study nature. Thoreau began his book, Walden, *after he left the pond, and finished it in 1854. Modern photographer Elliot Porter, who took the photo on the right, has found inspiration for his work in Thoreau's writings.*

Walden

HENRY DAVID THOREAU

When first I took up my abode in the woods, that is, began to spend my nights as well as days there, which, by accident, was on Independence Day, or the fourth of July, 1845, my house was not finished for winter, but was merely a defense against the rain, without plastering or chimney, the walls being of rough weather-stained boards, with wide chinks, which made it cool at night. The upright white hewn studs and freshly planed door and window casings gave it a clean and airy look, especially in the morning, when its timbers were saturated with dew, so that I fancied that by noon some sweet gum would exude from them. To my imagination it retained throughout the day more or less of this auroral character, reminding me of a certain house on a mountain which I had visited the year before. This was an airy and unplastered cabin, fit to entertain a traveling god, and where a goddess might trail her garments. The winds which passed over my dwelling were such as sweep over the ridges of mountains, bearing the broken strains, or celestial parts only, of terrestrial music. The morning wind forever blows, the poem of creation is uninterrupted; but few are the ears that hear it. Olympus[1] is but the outside of the earth every where. . . .

I was seated by the shore of a small pond, about a mile and a half south of the village of Concord and somewhat higher than it, in the midst of an extensive wood between that town and Lincoln, and about two miles south of that our only field known to fame, Concord Battle Ground; but I was so low in the woods that the opposite shore, half a mile off, like the rest, covered with wood, was my most distant horizon. For the first week, whenever I looked out on the pond it impressed me like a tarn high up on the side of a mountain, its bottom far above the surface of other lakes, and, as the sun arose, I saw it throwing off its nightly clothing of mist, and here and there, by degrees, its soft ripples or its smooth reflecting surface was revealed, while the mists, like ghosts, were stealthily[2] withdrawing in every direction into the woods, as at the breaking up of some nocturnal conventicle.

---

1. **Olympus** (ō lim′pəs), mountain home of the gods in Greek mythology.
2. stealthily (stelth′ə lē), *adv.* secretly; slyly.

The very dew seemed to hang upon the trees later into the day than usual, as on the sides of mountains. . . .

I went to the woods because I wished to live deliberately, to front only the essential facts of life, and see if I could not learn what it had to teach, and not, when I came to die, discover that I had not lived. I did not wish to live what was not life, living is so dear; nor did I wish to practice resignation, unless it was quite necessary. I wanted to live deep and suck out all the marrow of life, to live so sturdily and Spartanlike[3] as to put to rout all that was not life, to cut a broad swath and shave close, to drive life into a corner, and reduce it to its lowest terms, and, if it proved to be mean, why then to get the whole and genuine meanness of it, and publish its meanness to the world; or if it were sublime, to know it by experience, and be able to give a true account of it in my next excursion. For most men, it appears to me, are in a strange uncertainty about it, whether it is of the devil or of God, and have *somewhat hastily* concluded that it is the chief end of man here to "glorify God and enjoy him forever."

CLARIFY: What kind of life does Thoreau want to live?

Still we live meanly,[4] like ants; though the fable tells us that we were long ago changed into men; like pygmies we fight with cranes; it is error upon error, and clout upon clout, and our best virtue has for its occasion a superfluous[5] and evitable wretchedness. Our life is frittered away by detail. An honest man has hardly need to count more than his ten fingers, or in extreme cases he may add his ten toes, and lump the rest. Simplicity, simplicity, simplicity! I say, let your affairs be as two or three, and not a hundred or a thousand; instead of a million count half a dozen, and keep your accounts on your thumb nail. In the midst of this chopping sea of civilized life, such are the clouds and storms and quicksands and thousand-and-one items to be allowed for, that a man has to live, if he would not founder and go to the bottom and not make his port at all, by dead reckoning, and he must be a great calculator indeed who succeeds. Simplify, simplify. Instead of three meals a day, if it be necessary eat but one; instead of a hundred dishes, five; and reduce other things in proportion. Our life is like a German Confederacy, made up of petty states, with its boundary forever fluctuating, so that even a German cannot tell you how it is bounded at any moment. The nation itself, with all its so called internal improvements, which, by the way, are all external and superficial, is just such an unwieldy and overgrown establishment, cluttered with furniture and tripped up by its own traps, ruined by luxury and heedless expense, by want of calculation and a worthy aim, as the million households in the land; and the only cure for it as for them is in a rigid economy, a stern and more than Spartan simplicity of life and elevation of purpose. It lives too fast. Men think that it is essential that the *Nation* have commerce, and export ice, and talk through a telegraph, and ride thirty miles an hour, without a doubt, whether *they* do or not; but whether we should live like baboons or like men, is a little uncertain. If we do not get out sleepers, and forge rails, and devote days and nights to the work, but go to tinkering upon our *lives* to improve *them*, who will build railroads? And if railroads are not built, how shall we get to heaven in season? But if we stay at home and mind our business, who will want railroads? We do not ride on the railroad; it rides upon us. . . .

I left the woods for as good a reason as I went there. Perhaps it seemed to me that I had several more lives to live, and could not spare any more time for that one. It is remarkable how easily and

---

3. **Spartanlike,** *adj.* simply; without frills. In ancient Greece, the inhabitants of the city of Sparta were known for their simple and severe manner of living.
4. meanly (mēn′lē), *adv.* of a small-minded nature.
5. superfluous (su̇ pėr′flü əs), *adj.* more than is needed.

insensibly[6] we fall into a particular route, and make a beaten track for ourselves. I had not lived there a week before my feet wore a path from my door to the pond-side; and though it is five or six years since I trod it, it is still quite distinct. It is true, I fear that others may have fallen into it, and so helped to keep it open. The surface of the earth is soft and impressible by the feet of men; and so with the paths which the mind travels. How worn and dusty, then, must be the highways of the world, how deep the ruts of tradition and conformity! I did not wish to take a cabin passage, but rather to go before the mast and on the deck of the world, for there I could best see the moonlight amid the mountains. I do not wish to go below now.

I learned this, at least, by my experiment; that if one advances confidently in the direction of his dreams, and endeavors to live the life which he has imagined, he will meet with a success unexpected in common hours. He will put some things behind, will pass an invisible boundary; new, universal, and more liberal laws will begin to establish themselves around and within him; or the old laws be expanded, and interpreted in his favor in a more liberal sense, and he will live with the license of a higher order of beings. In proportion as he simplifies his life, the laws of the universe will appear less complex, and solitude will not be solitude, nor poverty poverty, nor weakness weakness. If you have built castles in the air, your work need not be lost; that is where they should be. Now put the foundations under them. . . .

Why should we be in such desperate haste to succeed, and in such desperate <u>enterprises</u>?[7] If a man does not keep pace with his companions, perhaps it is because he hears a different drummer. Let him step to the music which he hears, however measured or far away. . . .

If a man does not keep pace with his companions, perhaps it is because he hears a different drummer.

However mean your life is, meet it and live it; do not shun it and call it hard names. It is not so bad as you are. It looks poorest when you are richest. The fault-finder will find faults even in paradise. Love your life, poor as it is. You may perhaps have some pleasant, thrilling, glorious hours, even in a poorhouse. The setting sun is reflected from the windows of the alms-house as brightly as from the rich man's abode; the snow melts before its door as early in the spring. I do not see but a quiet mind may live as contentedly there, and have as cheering thoughts, as in a palace. The town's poor seem to me often to live the most independent lives of any. Maybe they are simply great enough to receive without misgiving. Most think that they are above being supported by the town; but it oftener happens that they are not above supporting themselves by dishonest means, which should be more disreputable. Cultivate poverty like a garden herb, like sage. Do not trouble yourself much to get new things, whether clothes or friends. Turn the old; return to them. Things do not change; we change. Sell your clothes and keep your thoughts. God will see that you do not want society. If I were confined to a corner of a <u>garret</u>[8] all my days, like a spider, the world would be just as large to me while I had my thoughts about me. The philosopher said: "From an army of three divisions one can take away its general, and put it in disorder; from the man the most abject and vulgar one cannot take away his thought." Do not seek so anxiously to be developed, to subject yourself to

---

6. **insensibly** (in sen′sə blē), *adv.* not aware; unmoved; indifferent.
7. enterprise (en′tər prīz), *n.* any undertaking, project, or venture.
8. garret (gar′it), *n.* a space in a house just below a sloping roof.

many influences to be played on; it is all dissipation.[9] Humility like darkness reveals the heavenly lights. The shadows of poverty and meanness gather around us, "and lo! creation widens to our view." We are often reminded that if there were bestowed on us the wealth of Croesus,[10] our aims must still be the same, and our means essentially the same. Moreover, if you are restricted in your range by poverty, if you cannot buy books and newspapers, for instance, you are but confined to the most significant and vital experiences; you are compelled to deal with the material which yields the most sugar and the most starch. It is life near the bone where it is sweetest. You are defended from being a trifler. No man loses ever on a lower level by magnanimity on a higher. Superfluous wealth can buy superfluities only. Money is not required to buy one necessary of the soul. . . .

*R*ather than love, than money, than fame, give me truth. I sat at a table where were rich food and wine in abundance, and obsequious[11] attendance, but sincerity and truth were not; and I went away hungry from the inhospitable board. The hospitality was as cold as the ices. I thought that there was no need of ice to freeze them. They talked to me of the age of the wine and the fame of the vintage; but I thought of an older, a newer, and purer wine, of a more glorious vintage, which they had not got, and could not buy. The style, the house and grounds and "entertainment" pass for nothing with me. I called on the king, but he made me wait in his hall, and conducted like a man incapacitated for hospitality. There was a man in my neighborhood who lived in a hollow tree. His manners were truly regal. I should have done better had I called on him. . . .

CLARIFY: Why is Thoreau so scornful of his host?

The life in us is like the water in the river. It may rise this year higher than man has ever known it, and flood the parched uplands; even this may be the eventful year, which will drown out all our muskrats. It was not always dry land where we dwell. I see far inland the banks which the stream anciently washed, before science began to record its freshets. Everyone has heard the story which has gone the rounds of New England, of a strong and beautiful bug which came out of the dry leaf of an old table of apple-tree wood, which had stood in a farmer's kitchen for sixty years, first in Connecticut, and afterward in Massachusetts,—from an egg deposited in the living tree many years earlier still, as appeared by counting the annual layers beyond it; which was heard gnawing out for several weeks, hatched perchance by the heat of an urn. Who does not feel his faith in a resurrection and immortality strengthened by hearing of this? Who knows what beautiful and winged life, whose egg has been buried for ages under many concentric layers of woodenness in the dead dry life of society, deposited at first in the alburnum of the green and living tree, which has been gradually converted into the semblance of its well-seasoned tomb,—heard perchance gnawing out now for years by the astonished family of man, as they sat round the festive board,—may unexpectedly come forth from amidst society's most trivial and hand-selled furniture, to enjoy its perfect summer life at last!

I do not say that John or Jonathan[12] will realize all this; but such is the character of that morrow which mere lapse of time can never make to dawn. The light which puts out our eyes is darkness to us. Only that day dawns to which we are awake. There is more day to dawn. The sun is but a morning star.

---

9. **dissipation** (dis′ə pā′shən), *n.* a scattering in different directions.
10. **Croesus** (krē′səs), a king of Lydia in the 6th century B.C. renowned for his wealth.
11. **obsequious** (əb sē′kwē əs), *adj.* polite or obedient from hope of gain.
12. **John or Jonathan,** John refers to an Englishman; Jonathan refers to an American.

CIVIL DISOBEDIENCE

HENRY DAVID THOREAU

Disgusted by a government that permitted slavery and sought territorial expansion in the Mexican War (1846–1848), Thoreau allowed himself to be jailed. In his essay, he aligned himself with the abolitionists and the Mexican people, who were desperately fighting the United States for control of over half of Mexico.

I do not hesitate to say, that those who call themselves abolitionists[1] should at once effectually withdraw their support, both in person and property, from the government of Massachusetts, and not wait till they constitute a majority of one,[2] before they suffer the right to prevail through them. I think that it is enough if they have God on their side, without waiting for that other one. Moreover, any man more right than his neighbors constitutes a majority of one already.

I meet this American government, or its representative, the State government, directly, and face to face, once a year—no more—in the person of its tax-gatherer; this is the only mode in which a man situated as I am necessarily meets it; and it then says distinctly, Recognize me; and the simplest, the most effectual, and, in the present posture of affairs, the indispensablest mode of treating with it on this head, of expressing your little satisfaction with and love for it, is to deny it then. My civil neighbor, the tax-gatherer, is the very man I have to deal with,—for it is, after all, with men and not with parchment that I quarrel,—and he has voluntarily chosen to be an agent of the government. How shall he ever know well what he is and does as an officer of the government, or as a man, until he is obliged to consider whether he shall treat me, his neighbor, for whom he has respect, as a neighbor and well-disposed man, or as a maniac and disturber of the peace, and see if he can get over this obstruction to his neighborliness without a ruder and more impetuous thought or speech corresponding with his action. I know this well, that if one thousand, if one hundred, if ten men whom I could name,—if ten *honest* men only,—ay, if *one* HONEST man, in this State of Massachusetts, *ceasing to hold slaves,* were actually to withdraw from this copartnership, and be locked up in the county jail therefor, it would be the abolition of slavery in America. For it matters not how small the beginning may seem to be: what is once well done is done forever. . . .

I have paid no poll-tax for six years. I was put into a jail once on this account, for one night; and, as I stood considering the walls of solid stone, two or three feet thick, the door of wood and iron, a foot thick, and the iron grating which strained the light, I could not help being struck with the foolishness of that institution which treated me as if I were mere flesh and

---

1. **abolitionist,** person who advocates doing away with an institution or custom, such as slavery.
2. **a majority of one,** "A majority of one" was a popular saying among the abolitionists. It dates back to Scottish theologian John Knox (1505–1572), who declared that "a man with God is always in the majority."

blood and bones, to be locked up. I wondered that it should have concluded at length that this was the best use it could put me to, and had never thought to avail itself of my services in some way. I saw that, if there was a wall of stone between me and my townsmen, there was a still more difficult one to climb or break through before they could get to be as free as I was. I did not for a moment feel confined, and the walls seemed a great waste of stone and mortar. I felt as if I alone of all my townsmen had paid my tax. They plainly did not know how to treat me, but behaved like persons who are underbred.[3] In every threat and in every compliment there was a blunder; for they thought that my chief desire was to stand the other side of that stone wall. I could not but smile to see how industriously they locked the door on my meditations, which followed them out again without let or hindrance,[4] and *they* were really all that was dangerous. As they could not reach me, they had resolved to punish my body; just as boys, if they cannot come at some person against whom they have a spite, will abuse his dog. I saw that the State was half-witted,[5] that it was timid as a lone woman with her silver spoons, and that it did not know its friends from its foes, and I lost all my remaining respect for it, and pitied it. . . .

When I came out of prison,—for someone interfered,[6] and paid that tax,—I did not perceive that great changes had taken place on the common, such as he observed who went in a youth and emerged a tottering and gray-headed man; and yet a change had to my eyes come over the scene,—the town, and State, and country,—greater than any that mere time could effect. I saw yet more distinctly the State in which I lived. I saw to what extent the people among whom I lived could be trusted as good neighbors and friends; that their friendship was for summer weather only; that they did not greatly propose to do right; that they were a distinct race from me by their prejudices and superstitions, as the Chinamen and Malays are; that in their sacrifices to humanity they ran no risks, not even to their

property; that after all they were not so noble but they treated the thief as he had treated them, and hoped, by a certain outward observance and a few prayers, and by walking in a particular straight though useless path from time to time, to save their souls. This may be to judge my neighbors harshly; for I believe that many of them are not aware that they have such an institution as the jail in their village. . . .

If others pay the tax which is demanded of me, from a sympathy with the State, they do but what they have already done in their own case, or rather they abet[7] injustice to a greater extent than the State requires. If they pay the tax from a mistaken interest in the individual taxed, to save his property, or prevent his going to jail, it is because they have not considered wisely how far they let their private feelings interfere with the public good. . . .

The authority of government, even such as I am willing to submit to,—for I will cheerfully obey those who know and can do better than I, and in many things even those who neither know nor can do so well,—is still an impure[8] one; to be strictly just, it must have the sanction and consent of the governed. It can have no pure right over my person and property but what I concede to it. The progress from an absolute to a limited monarchy,[9] from a limited monarchy to a democracy, is a progress toward a true respect for the individual. Even the Chinese philosopher was wise enough to regard the individual as the basis of the empire. Is a

3. **underbred** (un′dər bred′), *adj.* of inferior breeding or manners.
4. hindrance (hin′drəns), *n.* person or thing that hinders; an obstacle.
5. **half-witted,** feeble-minded; very stupid; foolish.
6. **someone interfered,** According to legend, Ralph Waldo Emerson paid the tax, but according to Thoreau family reminiscence, it was paid by Thoreau's Aunt Maria.
7. abet (ə bet′), *v.* urge or assist in any way.
8. **impure** (im pyur′), *adj.* not pure; dirty; unclean.
9. **limited monarchy** (mon′ər kē), monarchy in which the ruler's powers are limited by the laws of the nation.

◄ Choose five adjectives that describe the feelings evoked by this painting *Trodden Weeds*, (1951) by Andrew Wyeth. What is it about the painting that creates these feelings in the viewer?

democracy, such as we know it, the last improvement possible in government? Is it not possible to take a step further towards recognizing and organizing the rights of man? There will never be a really free and enlightened State until the State comes to recognize the individual as a higher and independent power, from which all its own power and authority are derived, and treats him accordingly. I please myself with imagining a State at last which can afford to be just to all men, and to treat the individual with respect as a neighbor; which even would not think it inconsistent with its own repose, if a few were to live aloof from it, not meddling with it, nor embraced by it, who fulfilled all the duties of neighbors and fellow-men. A State which bore this kind of fruit and suffered it to drop off as fast as it ripened, would prepare the way for a still more perfect and glorious State, which also I have imagined, but not yet anywhere seen.

Civil Disobedience   **233**

After Reading

Making Connections

Shaping Your Response

1. Thoreau believes that we must "simplify, simplify, simplify" our lives. Do you agree that getting rid of unnecessary luxuries, material goods, and responsibilities leads to happiness? Why or why not?

2. What is your opinion of Thoreau's act of civil disobedience? Do you approve or disapprove? Why?

Analyzing the Essays

3. What does Thoreau mean when he says, "Our life is frittered away by detail"?

4. Using a scale like the one below, rate Thoreau's confidence in the development of an "enlightened state." Explain your rating.

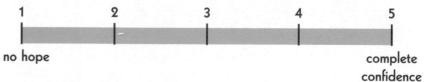

no hope   complete confidence

5. From the **tone** of "Civil Disobedience," does Thoreau seem to feel satisfied or dissatisfied with his action? Why?

6. How does Thoreau use **imagery** to make his arguments more vivid? Give examples from both selections.

Extending the Ideas

7. Thoreau says, "We do not ride upon the railroad; it rides upon us." Think about our society. What inventions seem to have gotten the better of us?

8. 👣 Thoreau was willing to defy his culture's expectations and be an **individual** even when the consequence was going to jail. What other historical figures can you think of that have been jailed for carrying out their beliefs?

Literary Focus: Allusion

Using the footnote at the bottom of page 231, explain this **allusion**: "Moreover, any man more right than his neighbors constitutes a majority of one already." What other allusions can you find in Thoreau's writings?

Vocabulary Study

On a separate sheet of paper, write *correct* next to the number of the italicized word that is used correctly. If the sentence is incorrect, write your own sentence using the word correctly.

stealthily
meanly
superfluous
enterprise
garret
dissipation
obsequious
abolitionist
hindrance
abet

1. Thoreau lived *stealthily* in the woods, with few possessions.

2. According to Thoreau, people tend to live *meanly,* focusing on life's details rather than on the things that are truly important.

3. While food, clothing, and shelter are necessary, video games might be considered *superfluous* possessions.

4. The extra-credit project was so difficult, few students chose to pursue the *enterprise.*

5. Digging a *garret* is the first step in building a house.

6. If you light a candle in the woods, you can watch the *dissipation* of insects toward the flame.

7. The gambler's *obsequious* friends disappeared when she ran out of money.

8. Thoreau's *abolitionist* beliefs caused him to own very little furniture.

9. To reach the roof, Gladys needed the *hindrance* of a ladder.

10. Thoreau's goal was to *abet* the government in the war against Mexico.

Expressing Your Ideas

Writing Choices

Writer's Notebook Update Thoreau chooses to remove himself from society for a period of time, and talks about his reasons for doing so. If you chose to spend a month by yourself, what would you want to accomplish? What essentials besides food, shelter, and clothing would you need?

Thoreau on Trial Thoreau has been charged with tax evasion and has pleaded not guilty. You are his attorney and you are about to present his case before a judge. What will you say in his defense? Prepare an **opening statement** for the jury and present it to your class.

Other Options

Visualizing Make a **sketch** of Thoreau's cabin on Walden Pond as it might have looked in 1845. Use your imagination, or do some research to find out more about the setting. If you have time, add color to your sketch, choosing watercolors or another medium that will fit the mood of the scene.

The Whole Truth Some recent biographies on Thoreau have suggested that he did not lead as difficult or lonely a life as *Walden* suggests. Do more research on Thoreau's life at Walden and report your findings in an **oral report.** Use graphic aids to compare what Thoreau says to what critics say.

Before Reading

Ain't I a Woman?

by Sojourner Truth

Sojourner Truth
1797?–1883

Until her early thirties, Sojourner Truth lived a life of extreme hardship. Born into slavery in New York, Truth worked in the fields or in the slave owner's house from sunup to sundown, with never enough food and rarely enough sleep. In 1826, a year before slavery was abolished in New York, Truth escaped her captivity. At age forty-six, responding to what she felt was divine inspiration, she changed her slave name of Isabella to Sojourner Truth and spent the next thirty years traveling throughout the country speaking in support of abolitionist and feminist causes.

Building Background

Imagine the Scene The time is 1851. The place is Akron, Ohio. Women's rights advocates from all over the country have gathered at a great convention. Speakers have championed the cause of greater freedom for women, yet there are a number of ministers present who loudly oppose women's rights. One of them claims that men have greater intellect than women. Another asserts that Christ's manhood makes men superior. A third points out that the sin of Eve brought evil into the world. The male members of the audience have been enjoying the spectacle. Then Sojourner Truth walks in and addresses the convention with an effect described as "magical, . . . turning the whole tide in our favor."

Literary Focus

Tone When we speak, we convey our thoughts through inflection and facial expression, and through the words we choose. Think of the way you tell your friends about your weekend. You add your own "thumbprint" to the story with your gestures, your smiles and grimaces, your body language. A writer's thumbprint is called **tone**. The tone of a piece can reveal the author's attitude toward a subject, whether it's sympathetic, sarcastic, serious, aloof, and so on.

Writer's Notebook

In Her Own Words "Ain't I a Woman?" is written as it was presented—in everyday familiar language. The use of informal language, or the **vernacular,** makes Truth's message more accessible while preserving its powerful impact. As you read the selection, jot down examples of Truth's use of informal language in a chart like the one below.

Examples of Vernacular	Formal Language	Compare the Effect
racket	noise	"Racket" gives the speech an everyday, practical, common-sense tone.

AIN'T I A WOMAN?

SOJOURNER TRUTH

Well, children, where there is so much racket there must be something out of kilter. I think that 'twixt the Negroes of the South and the women at the North, all talking about rights, the white men will be in a fix pretty soon. But what's all this here talking about?

That man over there says that women need to be helped into carriages, and lifted over ditches, and to have the best place everywhere. Nobody ever helps me into carriages, or over mud-puddles, or gives me any best place! And ain't I a woman? Look at me! Look at my arm! I have ploughed and planted, and gathered into barns, and no man could head me! And ain't I a woman? I could work as much and eat as much as a man—when I could get it—and bear the lash as well! And ain't I a woman? I have borne thirteen children, and seen them most all sold off to slavery, and when I cried out with my mother's grief, none but Jesus heard me! And ain't I a woman?

Then they talk about this thing in the head; what's this they call it? [Intellect, someone whispers.] That's it honey. What's that got to do with women's rights or Negro's rights? If my cup won't hold but a pint, and yours holds a quart, wouldn't you be mean not to let me have my little half-measure full?

Then that little man in black there, he says women can't have as much rights as men, 'cause Christ wasn't a woman! Where did your Christ come from? Where did your Christ come from? From God and a woman! Man had nothing to do with Him.

If the first woman God ever made was strong enough to turn the world upside down all alone, these women together ought to be able to turn it back, and get it right side up again! And now they is asking to do it, the men better let them.

Obliged to you for hearing me, and now old Sojourner ain't got nothing more to say.

◄ 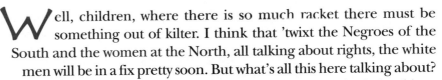 What kinds of cultural values might artist Sargent Johnson be portraying in his 1933 sculpture, *Forever Free?*

After Reading

Shaping Your
Response

Analyzing the
Speech

Extending the
Ideas

Making Connections

1. As you think back over Truth's speech, what five words come to mind? How do these relate to the selection?

2. Truth asks the question, "Ain't I a Woman?" over and over again. What affect does this **repetition** have?

3. What arguments against women's rights does Truth react to in her speech?

4. Explain the **allusion** Truth makes in the fifth paragraph.

5. When was the last time you or someone you know spoke out to right a wrong? Tell about it.

Literary Focus: Tone

In a group, brainstorm a list of adjectives that describe Truth's **tone,** or attitude toward her subject. Then determine how Truth conveys her tone. Is it through her choice of words? imagery? style? the sound of her words? all of these?

Expressing Your Ideas

Writing Choices

Writer's Notebook Update Finish the chart you began before reading the speech. Translate each example of vernacular you found in Truth's speech into more formal language, then compare the two versions. What is the effect of each? Which is more interesting? persuasive? powerful?

Truth in the White House Imagine that Sojourner Truth were alive today and running for President of the United States. What kinds of concerns do you think she would address in her campaign speeches? Write an **outline** of issues for Truth to present.

Another Option

A Meeting of Minds In groups of three, create a **round table discussion** with each student playing the part of Truth, Emerson, or Thoreau. Choose a topic for discussion from among the three works you've read by these authors. Each student should stay in character during the discussion. You may want to videotape your discussion to share with the class later.

Before Reading

The Devil and Tom Walker

by Washington Irving

Washington Irving
1783–1859

Young Washington Irving used to sneak out of his house and go to the nearby John Street Theater against his father's wishes. He would watch the drama until nine o'clock and then leave to be home for evening prayers. Afterward he would escape through a bedroom window to see the end of the performance. As an adult Irving became a lawyer but soon quit. Next he became a partner in his family's hardware business, but it went bankrupt. At that point he turned to writing to support himself. His first book written in his professional career, *The Sketch Book of Geoffrey Crayon,* was a success in both America and England. Two classic Irving stories were included in it, "The Legend of Sleepy Hollow" and "Rip Van Winkle."

Building Background

An American Original Washington Irving is often considered to be the United States's first successful short story writer. To create his tales, Irving took a number of European literary themes and gave them American settings. One of these is the theme of a person who is enchanted and, when the spell is broken, discovers that an enormous amount of time has passed. Irving used this theme as the basis for his "Rip Van Winkle" tale. The theme of a person making a bargain with the devil is another common one in European folklore and literature. The most famous version of this theme is the **Faust legend**, which had its origin in Germany in the late Middle Ages. It describes how a man of great learning named Faust agrees to surrender his soul to the devil in exchange for wealth, power, and sensual pleasures. The legend concludes with Faust being dragged off to Hell. Irving gave the Faust legend an American twist in "The Devil and Tom Walker."

Literary Focus

Stereotype A **stereotype** is a fixed, generalized idea about a character or situation. Stereotyped characters, sometimes called stock characters or flat characters, are not well-developed. They conform to a standardized mental picture and behave in predictable patterns. Some stereotypes you may have encountered in reading, movies, or even television sitcoms are the starving poet, wicked stepmother, clever detective, spoiled child, and absent-minded professor. As you read "The Devil and Tom Walker," decide if the characters are stereotypes or well-rounded characters. What "label" would you attach to the characters you think are stereotypes?

Writer's Notebook

Money! Money! Money! How important is money? What would you be willing to do to get it? In the story you're about to read, one man gets an opportunity to find out just how far he'll go to be wealthy . . . but in the meantime, what about you? Write a paragraph telling where you draw the line when it comes to pursuing money.

THE
Devil
AND
Tom Walker

WASHINGTON IRVING

A few miles from Boston in Massachusetts, there is a deep inlet, winding several miles into the interior of the country from Charles Bay, and terminating in a thickly wooded swamp or morass. On one side of this inlet is a beautiful dark grove; on the opposite side the land rises abruptly from the water's edge into a high ridge, on which grow a few scattered oaks of great age and immense size.

Under one of these gigantic trees, according to old stories, there was a great amount of treasure buried by Kidd the pirate. The inlet allowed a facility to bring the money in a boat secretly and at night to the very foot of the hill; the elevation of the place permitted a good lookout to be kept that no one was at hand; while the remarkable trees formed good landmarks by which the place might easily be found again. The old stories add, moreover, that the devil presided at the hiding of the money, and took it under his guardianship; but this, it is well known, he always does with buried treasure, particularly when it has been ill-gotten. Be that as it may, Kidd never returned to recover his wealth, being shortly after seized at Boston, sent out to England, and there hanged for a pirate.

About the year 1727, just at the time that earthquakes were prevalent[1] in New England, and shook many tall sinners down upon their

---

1. **prevalent** (prev′ ə lənt), *adj.* widespread; common.

Details such as boarded windows, broken shutters, and missing siding indicate that the house in Billy Morrow Jackson's painting, *Philo Bound* (1965), is neglected and poorly maintained. What details in the story lead you to the same conclusion about Tom Walker's home?

knees, there lived near this place a meager, miserly fellow, of the name of Tom Walker. He had a wife as miserly as himself; they were so miserly that they even conspired to cheat each other. Whatever the woman could lay hands on, she hid away; a hen could not cackle but she was on the alert to secure the new-laid egg. Her husband was continually prying about to detect her secret hoards, and many and fierce were the conflicts that took place about what ought to have been common property.

They lived in a forlorn-looking house that stood alone, and had an air of starvation. A few straggling savin trees, emblems of sterility, grew near it; no smoke ever curled from its chimney; no traveler stopped at its door. A miserable horse, whose ribs were as articulate as the bars of a gridiron, stalked about a field, where a thin carpet of moss, scarcely covering the ragged beds of pudding stone, tantalized and balked his hunger; and sometimes he would lean his head over the fence, look piteously at the passer-by, and seem to petition deliverance from this land of famine.

The house and its inmates had altogether a bad name. Tom's wife was a tall termagant,[2] fierce of temper, loud of tongue, and strong of arm. Her voice was often heard in wordy warfare with her husband; and his face sometimes showed signs that their conflicts were not

---

2. **termagant** (tėr′ mə gənt), *n.* a violent, quarreling, scolding woman.

confined to words. No one ventured, however, to interfere between them. The lonely wayfarer shrunk within himself at the horrid clamor and clapper-clawing;[3] eyed the den of discord askance; and hurried on his way rejoicing, if a bachelor, in his celibacy.

One day that Tom Walker had been to a distant part of the neighborhood, he took what he considered a shortcut homeward, through the swamp. Like most shortcuts, it was an ill-chosen route. The swamp was thickly grown with great gloomy pines and hemlocks, some of them ninety feet high, which made it dark at noonday and a retreat for all the owls of the neighborhood. It was full of pits and quagmires, partly covered with weeds and mosses, where the green surface often betrayed the traveler into a gulf of black, smothering mud; there were also dark and stagnant pools, the abodes of the tadpole, the bullfrog, and the water snake, where the trunks of pines and hemlocks lay half-drowned, half-rotting, looking like alligators sleeping in the mire.

Tom had long been picking his way cautiously through this treacherous forest, stepping from tuft to tuft of rushes and roots, which afforded precarious footholds among deep sloughs; or pacing carefully, like a cat, along the prostrate trunks of trees, startled now and then by the sudden screaming of the bittern, or the quacking of wild duck rising on the wing from some solitary pool. At length he arrived at a firm piece of ground, which ran out like a peninsula into the deep bosom of the swamp. It had been one of the strongholds of the Indians during their wars with the first colonists. Here they had thrown up a kind of fort, which they had looked upon as almost impregnable,[4] and had used as a place of refuge for their squaws and children. Nothing remained of the old Indian fort but a few embankments, gradually sinking to the level of the surrounding earth and already overgrown in part by oaks and other forest trees, the foliage of which formed a contrast to the dark pines and hemlocks of the swamp.

It was late in the dusk of evening when Tom Walker reached the old fort, and he paused there awhile to rest himself. Anyone but he would have felt unwilling to linger in this lonely, melancholy[5] place, for the common people had a bad opinion of it, from the stories handed down from the time of the Indian wars, when it was asserted that the savages held incantations here and made sacrifices to the evil spirit.

Tom Walker, however, was not a man to be troubled with any fears of the kind. He reposed himself for some time on the trunk of a fallen hemlock, listening to the boding cry of the tree toad, and delving with his walking staff into a mound of black mold at his feet. As he turned up the soil unconsciously, his staff struck against something hard. He raked it out of the vegetable mold, and lo! a cloven skull, with an Indian tomahawk buried deep in it, lay before him. The rust on the weapon showed the time that had elapsed since this deathblow had been given. It was a dreary memento of the fierce struggle that had taken place in this last foothold of the Indian warriors. "Humph!" said Tom Walker as he gave it a kick to shake the dirt from it.

"Let that skull alone!" said a gruff voice. Tom lifted up his eyes and beheld a great black man seated directly opposite him, on the stump of a tree. He was exceedingly surprised, having neither heard nor seen anyone approach; and he was still more perplexed[6] on observing, as well as the gathering gloom would permit, that the stranger was neither Negro nor Indian. It is true he was dressed in a rude half-Indian garb, and had a red belt or sash swathed around his body;

---

3. **clapper-clawing,** argument accompanied by scratching and slapping.
4. impregnable (im preg′nə bəl), *adj.* able to resist attack.
5. melancholy (mel′ən kol′ē), *adj.* sad; gloomy.
6. perplexed (pər pleksd′), *adj.* puzzled; bewildered.

but his face was neither black nor copper color, but swarthy and dingy, and begrimed with soot, as if he had been accustomed to toil among fires and forges. He had a shock of coarse black hair that stood out from his head in all directions, and bore an ax on his shoulder.

He scowled for a moment at Tom with a pair of great red eyes.

"What are you doing on my grounds?" said the black man, with a hoarse, growling voice.

"Your grounds!" said Tom, with a sneer, "no more your grounds than mine; they belong to Deacon Peabody."

"Deacon Peabody be damned," said the stranger, "as I flatter myself he will be, if he does not look more to his own sins and less to those of his neighbors. Look yonder, and see how Deacon Peabody is faring."

Tom looked in the direction that the stranger pointed and beheld one of the great trees, fair and flourishing without, but rotten at the core, and saw that it had been nearly hewn through, so that the first high wind was likely to blow it down. On the bark of the tree was scored the name of Deacon Peabody, an eminent[7] man who had waxed wealthy by driving shrewd bargains with the Indians. He now looked around, and found most of the tall trees marked with the name of some great man of the colony, and all more or less scored by the ax. The one on which he had been seated, and which had evidently just been hewn down, bore the name of Crowninshield; and he recollected a mighty rich man of that name, who made a vulgar display of wealth, which it was whispered he had acquired by buccaneering.

"He's just ready for burning!" said the black man, with a growl of triumph. "You see I am likely to have a good stock of firewood for winter."

"But what right have you," said Tom, "to cut down Deacon Peabody's timber?"

"The right of a prior claim," said the other. "This woodland belonged to me long before one of your white-faced race put foot upon the soil."

"And pray, who are you, if I may be so bold?" said Tom.

"Oh, I go by various names. I am the wild huntsman in some countries; the black miner in others. In this neighborhood I am known by the name of the black woodsman. I am he to whom the red men consecrated this spot, and in honor of whom they now and then roasted a white man, by way of sweet-smelling sacrifice. Since the red men have been exterminated by you white savages, I amuse myself by presiding at the persecutions of Quakers and Anabaptists;[8] I am the great patron and prompter of slave dealers, and the grand master of the Salem witches."

"The upshot of all which is, that, if I mistake not," said Tom sturdily, "you are he commonly called Old Scratch."

"The same, at your service!" replied the black man, with a half-civil nod.

> QUESTION: What do you think might have been different in this story if it was written by an American Indian or African American writer?

Such was the opening of this interview, according to the old story; though it has almost too familiar an air to be credited. One would think that to meet with such a singular personage, in this wild, lonely place, would have shaken any man's nerves; but Tom was a hardminded fellow, not easily daunted, and he had lived so long with a termagant wife that he did not even fear the devil.

It is said that after this commencement they had a long and earnest conversation together, as Tom returned homeward. The black man told him of great sums of money buried by Kidd the pirate, under the oak trees on the high ridge, not far from the morass. All these were under his

---

7. **eminent** (em′ə nənt), *adj.* above most others; outstanding; distinguished.

8. **Anabaptists,** members of a Protestant sect that originated in the 1500s. Quakers and Anabaptists were persecuted in the Massachusetts colony.

command, and protected by his power, so that none could find them but such as propitiated his favor. These he offered to place within Tom Walker's reach, having conceived an especial kindness for him; but they were to be had only on certain conditions. What these conditions were may be easily surmised, though Tom never disclosed them publicly. They must have been very hard, for he required time to think of them, and he was not a man to stick at trifles when money was in view.

When they had reached the edge of the swamp, the stranger paused. "What proof have I that all you have been telling me is true?" said Tom. "There's my signature," said the black man, pressing his finger on Tom's forehead. So saying, he turned off among the thickets of the swamp, and seemed, as Tom said, to go down, down, down, into the earth, until he totally disappeared.

When Tom reached home, he found the black print of a finger burned, as it were, into his forehead, which nothing could obliterate.

The first news his wife had to tell him was the sudden death of Absalom Crowninshield, the rich buccaneer. It was announced in the papers with the usual flourish that "A great man had fallen in Israel."

Tom recollected the tree which his black friend had just hewn down and which was ready

How does the scene depicted in *The Pledge* (1851), by John Gibson Dunn, remind you of the situation in "The Devil and Tom Walker"?

for burning. "Let the freebooter roast," said Tom; "who cares!" He now felt convinced that all he had heard and seen was no illusion.

He was not prone to let his wife into his confidence; but as this was an uneasy secret, he willingly shared it with her. All her avarice was awakened at the mention of hidden gold, and she urged her husband to comply with the black man's terms, and secure what would make them wealthy for life. However Tom might have felt disposed to sell himself to the devil, he was determined not to do so to oblige his wife; so he flatly refused, out of the mere spirit of contradiction. Many were the quarrels they had on the subject; but the more she talked, the more res- olute[9] was Tom not to be damned to please her.

CLARIFY: What proof does Tom Walker have that his meeting with the devil was real and not imagined?

At length she determined to drive the bargain on her own account, and if she succeeded, to keep all the gain to herself. Being of the same fearless temper as her husband, she set off for

9. (rez′ə lüt), *adj.* determined; firm.

the old Indian fort toward the close of a summer's day. She was many hours absent. When she came back, she was reserved and sullen in her replies. She spoke something of a black man, whom she met about twilight hewing at the root of a tall tree. He was sulky, however, and would not come to terms; she was to go again with a propitiatory offering, but what it was she forbore to say.

The next evening she set off again for the swamp, with her apron heavily laden. Tom waited and waited for her, but in vain; midnight came, but she did not make her appearance; morning, noon, night returned, but still she did not come. Tom now grew uneasy for her safety, especially as he found she had carried off in her apron the silver teapot and spoons, and every portable article of value. Another night elapsed, another morning came; but no wife. In a word, she was never heard of more.

What was her real fate nobody knows, in consequence of so many pretending to know. It is one of those facts which have become confounded by a variety of historians. Some asserted that she lost her way among the tangled mazes of the swamp, and sank into some pit or slough; others, more uncharitable, hinted that she had eloped with the household booty, and made off to some other province; while others surmised that the tempter had decoyed her into a dismal quagmire, on the top of which her hat was found lying. In confirmation of this, it was said a great black man, with an ax on his shoulder, was seen late that very evening coming out of the swamp, carrying a bundle tied in a check apron, with an air of surly triumph.

The most current and probable story, however, observed that Tom Walker grew so anxious about the fate of his wife and his property that he set out at length to seek them both at the Indian fort. During a long summer's afternoon he searched about the gloomy place, but no wife was to be seen. He called her name repeat-

edly, but she was nowhere to be heard. The bittern alone responded to his voice, as he flew screaming by; or the bullfrog croaked dolefully from a neighboring pool. At length, it is said, just in the brown hour of twilight, when the owls began to hoot, and the bats to flit about, his attention was attracted by the clamor of carrion crows hovering about a cypress tree. He looked up and beheld a bundle tied in a check apron and hanging in the branches of the tree, with a great vulture perched hard by, as if keeping watch upon it. He leaped with joy; for he recognized his wife's apron and supposed it to contain the household valuables.

"Let us get hold of the property," said he consolingly to himself, "and we will endeavor to do without the woman."

As he scrambled up the tree, the vulture spread its wide wings and sailed off screaming into the deep shadows of the forest. Tom seized the checked apron, but, woeful sight! found nothing but a heart and liver tied up in it!

EVALUATE: Why do you think the narrator gives these different versions of the events of the story?

Such, according to this most authentic old story, was all that was to be found of Tom's wife. She had probably attempted to deal with the black man as she had been accustomed to deal with her husband; but though a female scold is generally considered a match for the devil, yet in this instance she appears to have had the worst of it. She must have died game, however; for it is said Tom noticed many prints of cloven feet deeply stamped upon the tree, and found handfuls of hair that looked as if they had been plucked from the coarse black shock of the woodsman. Tom knew his wife's prowess by experience. He shrugged his shoulders as he looked at the signs of a fierce clapper-clawing. "Egad," said he to himself, "Old Scratch must have had a tough time of it!"

Tom consoled himself for the loss of his property with the loss of his wife, for he was a man of fortitude. He even felt something like gratitude toward the black woodsman, who, he considered, had done him a kindness. He sought, therefore, to cultivate a further acquaintance with him, but for some time without success; the old blacklegs played shy, for whatever people may think, he is not always to be had for calling for; he knows how to play his cards when pretty sure of his game.

. . . everybody was dreaming of making sudden fortunes for nothing.

At length, it is said, when delay had whetted Tom's eagerness to the quick, and prepared him to agree to anything rather than not gain the promised treasure, he met the black man one evening in his usual woodsman's dress, with his ax on his shoulder, sauntering along the swamp and humming a tune. He affected to receive Tom's advances with great indifference, made brief replies, and went on humming his tune.

By degrees, however, Tom brought him to business, and they began to haggle about the terms on which the former was to have the pirate's treasure. There was one condition which need not be mentioned, being generally understood in all cases where the devil grants favors; but there were others about which, though of less importance, he was inflexibly obstinate. He insisted that the money found through his means should be employed in his service. He proposed, therefore, that Tom should employ it in the black traffic; that is to say, that he should fit out a slave ship. This, however, Tom resolutely refused; he was bad enough in all conscience, but the devil himself could not tempt him to turn slave trader.

Finding Tom so squeamish on this point, he did not insist upon it, but proposed, instead, that he should turn usurer,[10] the devil being extremely anxious for the increase of usurers, looking upon them as his peculiar people.

To this no objections were made, for it was just to Tom's taste.

"You shall open a broker's shop in Boston next month," said the black man.

"I'll do it tomorrow, if you wish," said Tom Walker.

"You shall lend money at two percent a month."

"Egad, I'll charge four!" replied Tom Walker.

"You shall extort bonds, foreclose mortgages, drive the merchants to bankruptcy——"

"I'll drive them to the devil," cried Tom Walker.

"You are the usurer for my money!" said blacklegs with delight. "When will you want the rhino?[11]

"This very night."

"Done!" said the devil.

"Done!" said Tom Walker. So they shook hands and struck a bargain.

> QUESTION: What was the one thing Tom Walker refused to do for the Devil? What inference can you make from Tom's firm stand on this issue?

A few days' time saw Tom Walker seated behind his desk in a countinghouse in Boston.

His reputation for a ready-moneyed man, who would lend money out for a good consideration, soon spread abroad. Everybody remembers the time of Governor Belcher,[12] when money was particularly scarce. It was a time of

---

10. **usurer** (yü′zhər ər), *n.* a person who lends money at an extremely high or unlawful rate of interest.

11. **rhino** (rī′nō), *n.* money [*Slang*].

▲ Tom Walker is a stereotypical miser brought to life through Washington Irving's writing. What stereotypical characteristics does VonBlaas use in his engraving *The Miser*?

paper credit.[13] The country had been deluged with government bills, the famous Land Bank[14] had been established; there had been a rage for speculating; the people had run mad with schemes for new settlements, for building cities in the wilderness; land jobbers went about with maps of grants, and townships, and El Dorados,[15] lying nobody knew where, but which everybody was ready to purchase. In a word, the great speculating fever which breaks out every now and then in the country had raged to an alarming degree, and everybody was dreaming of making sudden fortunes from nothing. As usual the fever had subsided; the dream had gone off, and the imaginary fortunes with it; the

patients were left in doleful plight, and the whole country resounded with the consequent cry of "hard times."

At this propitious[16] time of public distress

---

12. **Governor Belcher,** Jonathan Belcher, who governed Massachusetts from 1730 to 1741.
13. **paper credit,** assets that existed on paper but were actually of little or no value.
14. **Land Bank,** a scheme to relieve the shortage of gold in Massachusetts by establishing a bank whose resources rested on real-estate mortgages.
15. **El Dorado** (el də rä′dō), imaginary country, abounding in gold, searched for by Spaniards in the sixteenth century. The name now applies to any place where it is thought riches can be had easily and quickly.
16. **propitious** (prə pish′ əs), *adj.* favorable.

The Devil and Tom Walker **247**

did Tom Walker set up as usurer in Boston. His door was soon thronged by customers. The needy and adventurous, the gambling speculator, the dreaming land jobber, the thriftless tradesman, the merchant with cracked credit—in short, everyone driven to raise money by desperate means and desperate sacrifices hurried to Tom Walker.

Thus Tom was the universal friend of the needy, and acted like a "friend in need;" that is to say, he always exacted good pay and good security. In proportion to the distress of the applicant was the hardness of his terms. He accumulated bonds and mortgages; gradually squeezed his customers closer and closer; and sent them at length, dry as a sponge, from his door.

In this way he made money hand over hand; became a rich and mighty man, and exalted his cocked hat upon 'Change.[17] He built himself, as usual, a vast house, out of ostentation;[18] but left the greater part of it unfinished and unfurnished, out of parsimony.[19] He even set up a carriage in the fullness of his vainglory, though he nearly starved the horses which drew it; and as the ungreased wheels groaned and screeched on the axletrees, you would have though you heard the souls of the poor debtors he was squeezing.

As Tom waxed old, however, he grew thoughtful. Having secured the good things of this world, he began to feel anxious about those of the next. He thought with regret on the bargain he had made with his black friend, and set his wits to work to cheat him out of the conditions. He became, therefore, all of a sudden, a violent churchgoer. He prayed loudly and strenuously, as if heaven were to be taken by force of lungs. Indeed, one might always tell when he had sinned most during the week by the clamor of his Sunday devotion. The quiet Christians who had been modestly and steadfastly traveling Zionward, were struck with self-reproach at seeing themselves so suddenly outstripped in their career by this new-made convert. Tom was as

rigid in religious as in money matters; he was a stern supervisor and censurer of his neighbors, and seemed to think every sin entered up to their account became a credit on his own side of the page. He even talked of the expediency of reviving the persecution of Quakers and Anabaptists. In a word, Tom's zeal became as notorious[20] as his riches.

Still, in spite of all this strenuous attention to forms, Tom had a lurking dread that the devil, after all, would have his due. That he might not be taken unawares, therefore, it is said he always carried a small Bible in his coat pocket. He had also a great folio Bible on his countinghouse desk, and would frequently be found reading it when people called on business; on such occasions he would lay his green spectacles in the book, to mark the place, while he turned round to drive some usurious bargain.

Some say that Tom grew a little crack-brained in his old days, and that, fancying his end approaching, he had his horse new shod, saddled and bridled, and buried with his feet uppermost; because he supposed that at the last day the world would be turned upside down in which case he should find his horse standing ready for mounting, and he was determined at the worst to give his friend a run for it. This, however, is probably a mere old wives' fable. If he really did take such a precaution, it was totally superfluous; at least so says the authentic old legend, which closes his story in the following manner.

One hot summer afternoon in the dog days, just as a terrible black thundergust was coming up, Tom sat in his countinghouse in his white

---

17. **'Change,** the Exchange, or the financial center of Boston, where merchants, traders, and brokers do business.
18. ostentation (os′ ten tā′ shən), *n.* display intended to impress others.
19. parsimony (pär′ sə mō′ nē), *n.* extreme economy; stinginess.
20. notorious (nō tōr′ ē əs), *adj.* well-known, especially for something bad.

cap and India silk morning gown. He was on the point of foreclosing a mortgage, by which he would complete the ruin of an unlucky land speculator for whom he had professed the greatest friendship. The poor land jobber begged him to grant a few months' indulgence. Tom had grown testy and irritated, and refused another day.

"My family will be ruined and brought upon the parish," said the land jobber.

"Charity begins at home," replied Tom; "I must take care of myself in these hard times."

"You have made so much money out of me," said the speculator.

Tom lost his patience and his piety. "The devil take me," said he, "if I have made a farthing!"

Just then there were three loud knocks at the street door. He stepped out to see who was there. A black man was holding a black horse, which neighed and stamped with impatience.

"Tom, you're come for," said the black fellow, gruffly. Tom shrank back, but too late. He had left his little Bible at the bottom of his coat pocket, and his big Bible on the desk buried under the mortgage he was about to foreclose; never was sinner taken more unawares. The black man whisked him like a child into the saddle, gave the horse the lash, and away he galloped, with Tom on his back, in the midst of the thunderstorm. The clerks stuck their pens behind their ears, and stared after him from the windows. Away went Tom Walker, dashing down the streets, his white cap bobbing up and down, his morning gown fluttering in the wind, and his steed striking fire out of the pavement at every bound. When the clerks turned to look for the black man, he had disappeared.

Tom Walker never returned to foreclose the mortgage. A countryman, who lived on the border of the swamp, reported that in the height of the thundergust he had heard a great clattering of hoofs and a howling along the road, and running to the window caught sight of a figure, such as I have described, on a horse that galloped like mad across the fields, over the hills, and down into the black hemlock swamp toward the old Indian fort; and that shortly after, a thunderbolt falling in that direction seemed to set the whole forest in a blaze.

The good people of Boston shook their heads and shrugged their shoulders, but had been so much accustomed to witches and goblins and tricks of the devil in all kinds of shapes, from the first settlement of the colony, that they were not so much horror-struck as might have been expected. Trustees were appointed to take

> **"The devil take me," said he, "if I have made a farthing!"**

charge of Tom's effects. There was nothing, however, to administer upon. On searching his coffers, all his bonds and mortgages were found reduced to cinders. In place of gold and silver, his iron chest was filled with chips and shavings; two skeletons lay in his stable instead of his half-starved horses, and the very next day his great house took fire and burned to the ground.

Such was the end of Tom Walker and his ill-gotten wealth. Let all griping money brokers lay this story to heart. The truth of it is not to be doubted. The very hole under the oak trees whence he dug Kidd's money is to be seen to this day; and the neighboring swamp and old Indian fort are often haunted on stormy nights by a figure on horseback, in morning gown and white cap, which is doubtless the troubled spirit of the usurer. In fact, the story has resolved itself into a proverb, and is the origin of that popular saying, so prevalent throughout New England, of "The Devil and Tom Walker."

After Reading

Making Connections

Shaping Your
Response

1. Think about the ending of this folk tale. Do you believe Tom got what he deserved? Explain.

2. If you were producing a made-for-TV movie of "The Devil and Tom Walker," who would you cast in the roles of Tom, his wife, and the devil? Why?

Analyzing the
Story

3. Washington Irving uses the color black as a **symbol**. What does it seem to symbolize to Irving? Find examples in the text to support your opinion.

4. What do you think the names carved into the trees represent?

5. Irving describes land speculation as a "fever" and the speculators as "patients." What do you think he is saying through these **metaphors** about the love of money?

6. What do you think is the "one condition which need not be mentioned" that is understood in folklore to be part of all contracts made with the devil?

7. "The Devil and Tom Walker" is told as a **folk tale**. In such tales, the **tone** is frequently humorous; the main characters are generally types rather than individual personalities; and many events are unbelievable or attributed to hearsay ("it is said," "some asserted"). Find examples of these three characteristics in Irving's story.

Extending the
Ideas

8. An evil tempter, a shrewish wife, and a greedy miser. Think about the **stereotyped** characters that appear in the story. What contemporary books, movies, or television programs feature characters like these?

9. How do you maintain a balance between the desire to earn money and an unhealthy preoccupation with material wealth?

Literary Focus: Stereotype

Folk tales like "The Devil and Tom Walker" often use flat characters or **stereotypes.** Plots and settings also can be stereotypical. For example, many cowboy books and movies have predictable plots. A bad guy rides into town to disrupt things, a good guy tries to set things right, and the good guy wins the shoot-out on Main Street. A stereotypical setting for a ghost story would be a deserted mansion on a dark, stormy night. Discuss the use of stereotypes for the characters, the plot, and the settings in "The Devil and Tom Walker."

Vocabulary Study

Each word in the first column below has an **antonym,** or a word with an opposite meaning, in the second column. Copy each word in the first column on a sheet of paper; then choose the best antonym for each from the second column.

propitious
prevalent
melancholy
eminent
parsimony
ostentation
perplexed
resolute
notorious
impregnable

1. propitious
2. prevalent
3. melancholy
4. eminent
5. parsimony
6. ostentation
7. perplexed
8. resolute
9. notorious
10. impregnable

a. joyous
b. humbleness
c. anonymous
d. flimsy
e. rare
f. lowly
g. unfavorable
h. certain
i. unsure
j. generosity

Expressing Your Ideas

Writing Choices

Writer's Notebook Update You find a wallet with a thousand dollars laying in the street and no name in it—what will you do? A friend will pay you one hundred dollars to go on a double-date, but you don't like your date at all. Will you go? Create a story plot with yourself as the protagonist, in which you face a dilemma about money.

Man Disappears on Horseback! Imagine you are a reporter for a newspaper in Boston when Tom Walker worked there. Write a **news story** of at least three paragraphs about Tom's disappearance. Answer the questions *who, what, why, where, when,* and *how.* Maintain an objective tone and use a headline and a lead sentence that attract attention.

Other Options

Tom Walker Comics Work with a group to create a **comic book** version of Tom Walker's story. Choose the text and dialogue you'll need to tell the story, then plan the scenes you'll want to illustrate. The illustrations should accurately represent details about the setting and characters, and reflect the story's mood.

It's All in How You Say It Work with two other students and prepare a **reader's theater** of the dialogue between the devil and Tom Walker in their first encounter on pages 242–244. How would each character sound? How would each line be spoken? How would the narrator set up the scene? Present the reading to the class.

Before Reading

The Pit and the Pendulum

by Edgar Allan Poe

Edgar Allan Poe
1809–1849

Poe's life often was as nightmarish as his stories. He was orphaned when not yet three years of age, was abandoned by his father, and his wife died at a young age. Poe was obsessed with success, but never made much money at his writing and his family sometimes went hungry. To make matters worse, Poe drank very heavily, which often left him unable to work. During the bad times, when he was drunk almost constantly, he had horrible dreams in which he was pursued by various types of madmen. It is from his nightmares that Poe got the inspiration for his most macabre—and famous—tales.

Building Background

Imagine the Scene During the second half of the 1400s, King Ferdinand and Queen Isabella ruled over much of what we now call Spain. Determined to create a strong, unified country, Ferdinand and Isabella established the **Spanish Inquisition,** a special court that imprisoned or killed people suspected of not following Roman Catholic teachings. Prisoners of the Inquisition were often tortured brutally and thrown into dungeons. Think for a moment about how these prisoners felt. Imprisoned for their religious beliefs, they were alone, hungry, and frightened. Would they be set free, or would they be executed? In "The Pit and the Pendulum," Poe describes the final hours of a man imprisoned during the Spanish Inquisition.

Literary Focus

Mood Edgar Allan Poe is a master at establishing **mood**—the overall atmosphere of a work. Mood is created through details of the setting, objects, and images. As you read "The Pit and the Pendulum," watch for the ways Poe sets up a mood. How does he use mood to pull you, the reader, into his work?

Writer's Notebook

A Good Scare Before reading "The Pit and the Pendulum," think about what you expect from a good horror story. What should the characters and setting be like? What are good topics? How should a reader feel while reading a horror story? Make a web like the one below to describe your vision of a good horror story.

THE PIT AND THE PENDULUM

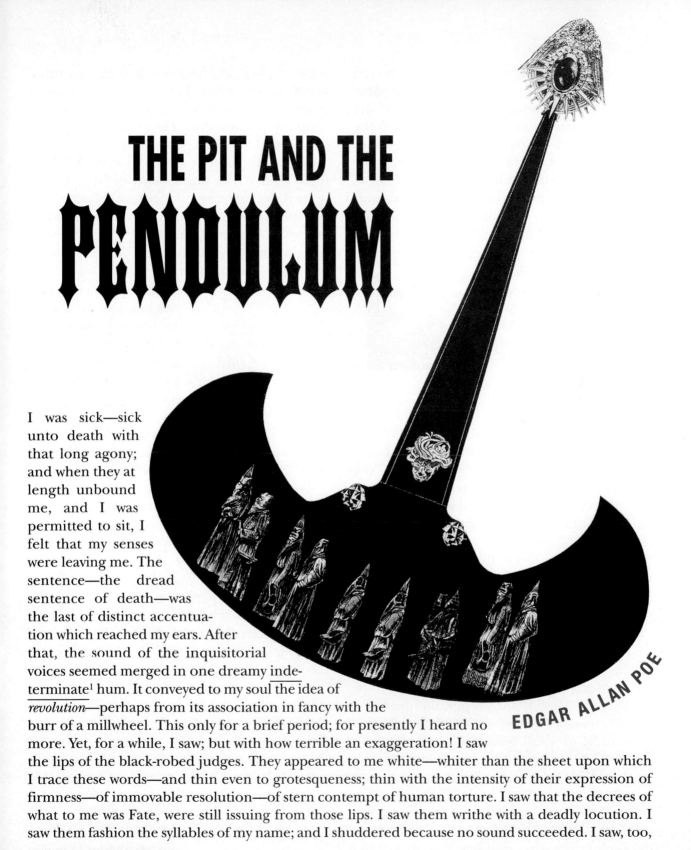

EDGAR ALLAN POE

I was sick—sick unto death with that long agony; and when they at length unbound me, and I was permitted to sit, I felt that my senses were leaving me. The sentence—the dread sentence of death—was the last of distinct accentuation which reached my ears. After that, the sound of the inquisitorial voices seemed merged in one dreamy indeterminate[1] hum. It conveyed to my soul the idea of *revolution*—perhaps from its association in fancy with the burr of a millwheel. This only for a brief period; for presently I heard no more. Yet, for a while, I saw; but with how terrible an exaggeration! I saw the lips of the black-robed judges. They appeared to me white—whiter than the sheet upon which I trace these words—and thin even to grotesqueness; thin with the intensity of their expression of firmness—of immovable resolution—of stern contempt of human torture. I saw that the decrees of what to me was Fate, were still issuing from those lips. I saw them writhe with a deadly locution. I saw them fashion the syllables of my name; and I shuddered because no sound succeeded. I saw, too,

---

1. **indeterminate** (in′di tèr′mə nit), *adj.* not definite or fixed.

for a few moments of delirious horror, the soft and nearly imperceptible waving of the sable draperies which enwrapped the walls of the apartment. And then my vision fell upon the seven tall candles upon the table. At first they wore the aspect of charity, and seemed white slender angels who would save me; but then, all at once, there came a most deadly nausea over my spirit, and I felt every fibre in my frame thrill as if I had touched the wire of a galvanic battery, while the angel forms became meaningless spectres, with heads of flame, and I saw that from them there would be no help. And then there stole into my fancy, like a rich musical note, the thought of what sweet rest there must be in the grave.

. . . no! even in the grave all is not lost.

The thought came gently and stealthily, and it seemed long before it attained full appreciation; but just as my spirit came at length properly to feel and entertain it, the figures of the judges vanished, as if magically, from before me; the tall candles sank into nothingness; their flames went out utterly; the blackness of darkness supervened; all sensations appeared swallowed up in a mad rushing descent as of the soul into Hades. Then silence, and stillness, and night were the universe.

I had swooned;[2] but still will not say that all of consciousness was lost. What of it there remained I will not attempt to define, or even to describe; yet all was not lost. In the deepest slumber—no! In delirium—no! In a swoon—no! In death—no! even in the grave all *is not* lost. Else there is no immortality for man. Arousing from the most profound of slumbers, we break the gossamer web of *some* dream. Yet in a second afterward, (so frail may that web have been) we remember not that we have dreamed. In the return to life from the swoon there are two stages; first, that of the sense of mental or spiritual; secondly, that of the sense of physical, existence. It seems probable that if, upon reaching the second stage, we could recall the impressions of the first, we should find these impressions eloquent in memories of the gulf beyond. And that gulf is—what? How at least shall we distinguish its shadows from those of the tomb? But if the impressions of what I have termed the first stage, are not, at will, recalled, yet, after long interval, do they not come unbidden, while we marvel whence they come? He who has never swooned, is not he who finds strange palaces and wildly familiar faces in coals that glow; is not he who beholds floating in mid-air the sad visions that the many may not view; is not he who ponders over the perfume of some novel flower—is not he whose brain grows bewildered with the meaning of some musical cadence which has never before arrested his attention.

Amid frequent and thoughtful endeavors to remember; amid earnest struggles to regather some token of the state of seeming nothingness into which my soul had lapsed, there have been moments when I have dreamed of success; there have been brief, very brief periods when I have conjured up remembrances which the lucid reason of a later epoch assures me could have had reference only to that condition of seeming unconsciousness. These shadows of memory tell, indistinctly, of tall figures that lifted and bore me in silence down—down—still down—till a hideous dizziness oppressed me at the mere idea of the interminableness[3] of the descent. They tell also of a vague horror at my heart, on account of that heart's unnatural stillness. Then comes a sense of sudden motionlessness throughout all things; as if those who

---

2. **swoon** (swŭn), *v.* faint.
3. interminableness (in tèr′mə nə bəl nes), *n.* endlessness.

bore me (a ghastly train!) had outrun, in their descent, the limits of the limitless, and paused from the wearisomeness of their toil. After this I call to mind flatness and dampness; and that all is *madness*—the madness of a memory which busies itself among forbidden things.

Very suddenly there came back to my soul motion and sound—the tumultuous motion of the heart, and, in my ears, the sound of its beating. Then a pause in which all is blank. Then again sound, and motion, and touch—a tingling sensation pervading my frame. Then the mere consciousness of existence, without thought—a condition which lasted long. Then, very suddenly, *thought,* and shuddering terror, and earnest endeavor to comprehend my true state. Then a strong desire to lapse into insensibility. Then a rushing revival of soul and a successful effort to move. And now a full memory of the trial, of the judges, of the sable draperies, of the sentence, of the sickness, of the swoon. Then entire forgetfulness of all that followed; of all that a later day and much earnestness of endeavor have enabled me vaguely to recall.

So far, I had not opened my eyes. I felt that I lay upon my back, unbound. I reached out my hand, and it fell heavily upon something damp and hard. There I suffered it to remain for many minutes, while I strove to imagine where and *what* I could be. I longed, yet dared not to employ my vision. I dreaded the first glance at objects around me. It was not that I feared to look upon things horrible, but that I grew aghast lest there should be *nothing* to see. At length, with a wild desperation at heart, I quickly unclosed my eyes. My worst thoughts, then, were confirmed. The blackness of eternal light encompassed me. I struggled for breath. The intensity of the darkness seemed to oppress and stifle me. The atmosphere was intolerably close.[4] I still lay quietly, and made effort to exercise my reason. I brought to mind the inquisitorial proceedings, and attempted from that point to deduce my real condition. The sentence had passed; and it appeared to me that a very long interval of time had since elapsed. Yet not for a moment did I suppose myself actually dead. Such a supposition, notwithstanding what we read in fiction, is altogether inconsistent with real existence;—but where and in what state was I? The condemned to death, I knew, perished usually at the *autos-da-fé,* and one of these had been held on the very night of the day of my trial. Had I been remanded to my dungeon, to await the next sacrifice, which would not take place for many months? This I at once saw could not be. Victims had been in immediate demand. Moreover, my dungeon, as well as all the condemned cells at Toledo,[5] had stone floors, and light was not altogether excluded.

A fearful idea now suddenly drove the blood in torrents upon my heart, and for a brief period, I once more relapsed into insensibility. Upon recovering, I at once started to my feet, trembling convulsively in every fibre. I thrust my arms wildly above and around me in all directions. I felt nothing; yet dreaded to move a step, lest I should be impeded by the walls of the *tomb.* Perspiration burst from every pore and stood in cold big beads on my forehead. The agony of suspense grew at length intolerable, and I cautiously moved forward, with my arms extended, and my eyes straining from their sockets, in the hope of catching some faint ray of light. I proceeded for many paces; but still all was blackness and vacancy. I breathed more freely. It seemed evident that mine was not, at least, the most hideous of fates.

And now, as I still continued to step cautiously onward, there came thronging upon my recollection a thousand vague rumors of the horrors of Toledo. Of the dungeons there had been strange things narrated—fables I had always deemed them—but yet strange, and too

---

4. **close,** having little fresh air; stuffy.
5. **Toledo** (tə lē′dō), Toledo, Spain: the headquarters of the Inquisition.

ghastly to repeat, save in a whisper. Was I left to perish of starvation in the subterranean world of darkness; or what fate, perhaps even more fearful, awaited me? That the result would be death, and a death of more than customary bitterness, I knew too well the character of my judges to doubt. The mode and the hour were all that occupied or distracted me.

My outstretched hands at length encountered some solid obstruction. It was a wall, seemingly of stone masonry—very smooth, slimy, and cold. I followed it up; stepping with all the careful distrust with which certain antique narratives had inspired me. This process, however, afforded me no means of ascertaining the dimensions of my dungeon; as I might make its circuit, and return to the point whence I set out, without being aware of the fact; so perfectly uniform seemed the wall. I therefore sought the knife which had been in my pocket, when led into the inquisitorial chamber; but it was gone; my clothes had been exchanged for a wrapper of coarse serge. I had thought of forcing the blade in some minute crevice of the masonry, so as to identify my point of departure. The difficulty, nevertheless, was but trivial; although, in the disorder of my fancy, it seemed at first insuperable.[6] I tore a part of the hem from the robe and placed the fragment at full length, and at right angles to the wall. In groping my way around the prison I could not fail to encounter this rag upon completing the circuit. So, at least I thought: but I had not counted upon the extent of the dungeon, or upon my own weakness. The ground was moist and slippery. I staggered onward for some time, when I stumbled and fell. My excessive fatigue induced me to remain prostrate; and sleep soon overtook me as I lay.

Upon awakening, and stretching forth an arm, I found beside me a loaf and a pitcher with water. I was too much exhausted to reflect upon this circumstance, but ate and drank with avidity. Shortly afterward, I resumed my tour around

This illustration by Satty depicts a scene from the Spanish Inquisition. Based on the information given in the story, what do you think is happening in this scene? What might the characters be saying? ➤

the prison, and with much toil, came at last upon the fragment of the serge. Up to the period when I fell I had counted fifty-two paces, and upon resuming my walk, I counted forty-eight more;—when I arrived at the rag. There were in all, then, a hundred paces; and admitting two paces to the yard, I presumed the dungeon to be fifty yards in circuit. I had met, however, with many angles in the wall, and thus I could form no guess at the shape of the vault; for vault I could not help supposing it to be.

I had little object—certainly no hope—in these researches; but a vague curiosity prompted me to continue them. Quitting the wall, I resolved to cross the area of the enclosure. At first I proceeded with extreme caution, for the floor, although seemingly of solid material, was treacherous[7] with slime. At length, however, I took courage, and did not hesitate to step firmly; endeavoring to cross in as direct a line as possible. I had advanced some ten or twelve paces in this manner, when the remnant of the torn hem of my robe became entangled between my legs. I stepped on it, and fell violently on my face.

In the confusion attending my fall, I did not immediately apprehend a somewhat startling circumstance, which yet, in a few seconds afterward, and while I still lay prostrate, arrested my attention. It was this—my chin rested upon the floor of the prison, but my lips and the upper portion of my head, although seemingly at a less elevation than the chin, touched nothing. At the same time my forehead seemed bathed in a

---

6. **insuperable** (in sŭ′pər ə bəl), *adj.* unable to overcome.
7. **treacherous** (trech′ər əs), *adj.* not reliable.

clammy vapor, and the peculiar smell of decayed fungus arose to my nostrils. I put forward my arm, and shuddered to find that I had fallen at the very brink of a circular pit, whose extent, of course, I had no means of ascertaining at the moment. Groping about the masonry just below the margin, I succeeded in dislodging a small fragment, and let it fall into the abyss. For many seconds I hearkened[8] to its reverberations as it dashed against the sides of the chasm in its descent; at length there was a sullen plunge into water, succeeded by loud echoes. At the same moment there came a sound resembling the quick opening, and as rapid closing of a door overhead, while a faint gleam of light flashed suddenly through the gloom, and as suddenly faded away.

I saw clearly the doom which had been prepared for me, and congratulated myself upon the timely accident by which I had escaped. Another step before my fall, and the world had seen me no more. And the death just avoided, was of that very character which I had regarded as fabulous and frivolous in the tales respecting the Inquisition. To the victims of its tyranny, there was the choice of death with its direst physical agonies, or death with its most hideous moral horrors. I had been reserved for the latter. By long suffering my nerves had been unstrung, until I trembled at the sound of my own voice, and had become in every respect a fitting subject for the species of torture which awaited me.

Shaking in every limb, I groped my way back to the wall; resolving there to perish rather than risk the terrors of the wells, of which my imagination now pictured many in various positions about the dungeon. In other conditions of mind I might have had courage to end my misery at once by a plunge into one of these abysses; but now I was the veriest of cowards. Neither could I forget what I had read of these pits—that the *sudden* extinction of life formed no part of their most horrible plan.

Agitation of spirit kept me awake for many long hours; but at length I again slumbered. Upon arousing, I found by my side as before, a loaf and a pitcher of water. A burning thirst consumed me, and I emptied the vessel at a draught. It must have been drugged; for scarcely had I drunk, before I became irresistibly drowsy. A deep sleep fell upon me—a sleep like that of death. How long it lasted of course, I know not; but when, once again, I unclosed my eyes, the objects around me were visible. By a wild sulphurous lustre, the origin of which I could not at first determine, I was enabled to see the extent and aspect of the prison.

In its size I had been greatly mistaken. The whole circuit of its walls did not exceed twenty-five yards. For some minutes this fact occasioned me a world of vain trouble; vain indeed! for what could be of less importance, under the terrible circumstances which environed me, than the mere dimensions of my dungeon? But my soul took a wild interest in trifles, and I busied myself in endeavors to account for the error I had committed in my measurement. The truth at length flashed upon me. In my first attempt at exploration I had counted fifty-two paces, up to the period when I fell; I must then have been within a pace or two of the fragments of serge; in fact, I had nearly performed the circuit of the vault. I then slept, and upon awaking, I must have returned upon my steps—thus supposing the circuit nearly double what it actually was. My confusion of mind prevented me from observing that I began my tour with the wall to the left, and ended it with the wall to the right.

I had been deceived, too, in respect to the shape of the enclosure. In feeling my way around I had found many angles, and thus deduced an idea of great irregularity; so potent is the effect of total darkness upon one arousing from lethargy or sleep! The angles were simply those of a few slight depressions, or niches, at odd intervals. The general shape of the prison was square. What I had taken for masonry seemed now to be

---

8. **hearken** (här′kən), *v.* listen to attentively.

iron, or some other metal, in huge plates, whose sutures or joints occasioned the depression. The entire surface of this metallic enclosure was rudely daubed in all the hideous and repulsive devices to which the charnel[9] superstitions of the monks has given rise. The figures of fiends in aspects of menace, with skeleton forms, and other more really fearful images, overspread and disfigured[10] the walls. I observed that the outlines of these monstrosities were sufficiently distinct, but that the colors seemed faded and blurred, as if from the effects of a damp atmosphere. I now noticed the floor, too, which was of stone. In the center yawned the circular pit from whose jaws I had escaped; but it was the only one in the dungeon.

All this I saw distinctly and by much effort: for my personal condition had been greatly changed during slumber. I now lay upon my back, and at full length, on a species of low framework of wood. To this I was securely bound by a long strap resembling a surcingle.[11] It passed in many convolutions about my limbs and body, leaving at liberty only my head, and my left arm to such extent that I could, by dint of much exertion, supply myself with food from an earthen dish which lay by my side on the floor. I saw, to my horror, that the pitcher had been removed. I say to my horror; for I was consumed with intolerable thirst. This thirst it appeared to be the design of my persecutors to stimulate: for the food in the dish was meat pungently seasoned.

Looking upward I surveyed the ceiling of my prison. It was some thirty or forty feet overhead, and constructed much as the side walls. In one of its panels a very singular figure riveted my whole attention. It was the painted figure of Time as he is commonly represented, save that, in lieu of a scythe, he held what, at a casual glance, I supposed to be the pictured image of a huge pendulum such as we see on antique clocks. There was something, however, in the appearance of this machine which caused me to regard it more attentively. While I gazed directly upward at it (for its position was immediately over my own) I fancied that I saw it in motion. In an instant afterward the fancy was confirmed. Its sweep was brief, and of course slow. I watched it for some minutes, somewhat in fear, but more in wonder. Wearied at length with observing its dull movement, I turned my eyes upon the other subjects in the cell.

A slight noise attracted my notice, and, looking to the floor, I saw several enormous rats traversing it. They had issued from the well, which lay just within view to my right. Even then, while I gazed, they came up in troops, hurriedly, with ravenous eyes, allured by the scent of the meat. From this it required much effort and attention to scare them away.

It might have been half an hour, perhaps even an hour, (for I could take but imperfect note of time) before I again cast my eyes upward. What I then saw confounded and amazed me. The sweep of the pendulum had increased in extent by nearly a yard. As a natural consequence, its velocity was also much greater. But what mainly disturbed me was the idea that it had perceptibly *descended*. I now observed— with what horror it is needless to say—that its nether extremity[12] was formed of a crescent of glittering steel, about a foot in length from horn to horn; the horns upward, and the under edge

. . . looking to the floor, I saw several enormous rats traversing it.

---

9. **charnel** (chär′nl), *adj.* deathlike; ghastly.
10. **disfigure** (dis fig′yər), *v.* spoil the appearance of.
11. **surcingle** (sėr′sing gəl), *n.* a strap or belt.
12. **nether extremity** (neŦH′ər ek strem′ə tē), *n.* lower end.

evidently as keen as that of a razor. Like a razor also, it seemed massy and heavy, tapering from the edge into a solid and broad structure above. It was appended to a weighty rod of brass, and the whole *hissed* as it swung through the air.

I could no longer doubt the doom prepared for me by monkish ingenuity in torture. My cognizance[13] of the pit had become known to the inquisitorial agents—*the pit* whose horrors had been destined for so bold a recusant[14] as myself—*the pit,* typical of hell, and regarded by rumor as the Ultima Thule of all their punishments. The plunge into this pit I had avoided by the merest of accidents, and I knew that surprise, or entrapment into torment, formed an important portion of all the grotesquerie of these dungeon deaths. Having failed to fall, it was no part of the demon plan to hurl me into the abyss; and thus (there being no alternative) a different and a milder destruction awaited me. Milder! I half smiled in my agony as I thought of such application of such a term.

What boots it to tell of the long, long hours of horror more than mortal, during which I counted the rushing vibrations of the steel! Inch by inch—line by line—with a descent only appreciable at intervals that seemed ages—down and still down it came! Days passed—it might have been that many days passed—ere it swept so closely over me as to fan me with its acrid breath. The odor of the sharp steel forced itself into my nostrils. I prayed—I wearied heaven with my prayer for its more speedy descent. I grew frantically mad, and struggled to force myself upward against the sweep of the fearful scimitar. And then I fell suddenly calm, and lay smiling at the glittering death, as a child at some rare bauble.

There was another interval of utter insensibility; it was brief; for, upon again lapsing into life there had been no perceptible descent in the pendulum. But it might have been long; for I knew there were demons who took note of my

Satty chose an interesting perspective for this illustration of the prisoner trapped beneath the pendulum. How does this perspective relate to the point of view taken by Poe in his narrative? What effect does it have? ➤

swoon, and who could have arrested the vibration at pleasure. Upon my recovery, too, I felt very—oh, inexpressibly sick and weak, as if through long inanition. Even amid the agonies of that period, the human nature craved food. With painful effort I outstretched my left arm as far as my bonds permitted, and took possession of the small remnant which had been spared me by the rats. As I put a portion of it within my lips, there rushed to my mind a half formed thought of joy—of hope. Yet what business had *I* with hope? It was, as I say, a half formed thought—man has many such which are never completed. I felt that it was of joy—of hope; but I felt also that it had perished in its formation. In vain I struggled to perfect—to regain it. Long suffering had nearly annihilated all my ordinary powers of mind. I was an imbecile—an idiot.

The vibration of the pendulum was at right angles to my length. I saw that the crescent was designed to cross the region of the heart. It would fray the serge of my robe—it would return and repeat its operations—again—and again. Notwithstanding its terrifically wide sweep (some thirty feet or more) and the hissing vigor of its descent, sufficient to sunder these very walls of iron, still the fraying of my robe would be all that, for several minutes, it would accomplish. And at this thought I paused. I dared not go farther than this reflection. I dwelt upon it with a pertinacity of attention—as if, in so dwelling, I could arrest *here* the descent of the steel. I forced myself to ponder upon the sound of the crescent as it should pass across the garment—upon the peculiar thrilling sensation which the friction of

---

13. cognizance (kog′nə zəns), *n.* awareness.
14. recusant (ri kyü sənt), *n.* one who refuses to submit or comply.

cloth produces on the nerves. I pondered upon all this frivolity until my teeth were on edge.

Down—steadily down it crept. I took a frenzied pleasure in contrasting its downward with its lateral velocity. To the right—to the left—far and wide—with the shriek of a damned spirit; to my heart with the stealthy pace of the tiger! I alternately laughed and howled as the one or the other idea grew prominent.

Down—certainly, relentlessly down! It vibrated within three inches of my bosom! I struggled violently, furiously, to free my left arm. This was free only from the elbow to the hand. I could reach the latter, from the platter beside me, to my mouth, with great effort, but no farther. Could I have broken the fastenings above the elbow, I would have seized and attempted to arrest the pendulum. I might as well have attempted to arrest an avalanche!

Down—still unceasingly—still inevitably down! I gasped and struggled at each vibration. I shrunk convulsively at its every sweep. My eyes followed its outward or upward whirls with the eagerness of the most unmeaning despair; they closed themselves spasmodically at the descent, although death would have been a relief, oh! how unspeakable! Still I quivered in every nerve to think how slight a sinking of the machinery would precipitate that keen, glistening axe upon my bosom. It was *hope* that prompted the nerve to quiver—the frame to shrink. It was *hope*—the hope that triumphs on the rack—that whispers to the death-condemned even in the dungeons of the Inquisition.

I saw that some ten or twelve vibrations would bring the steel in actual contact with my robe, and with this observation there suddenly came over my spirit all the keen, collected calmness of despair. For the first time during many

. . . there suddenly came over my spirit all the keen, collected calmness of despair.

hours—or perhaps days—I *thought*. It now occurred to me that the bandage, or surcingle, which enveloped me, was *unique*. I was tied by no separate cord. The first stroke of the razor-like crescent athwart[15] any portion of the band, would so detach it that it might be unwound from my person by means of my left hand. But how fearful, in that case, the proximity of the steel! The result of the slightest struggle how deadly! Was it likely, moreover, that the minions of the torturer had not foreseen and provided for this possibility! Was it probable that the bandage crossed my bosom in the track of the pendulum? Dreading to find my faint, and, as it seemed, my last hope frustrated, I so far elevated my head as to obtain a distinct view of my breast. The surcingle enveloped my limbs and body close in all directions—*save in the path of the destroying crescent.*

Scarcely had I dropped my head back into its original position, when there flashed upon my mind what I cannot better describe than as the unformed half of that idea of deliverance to which I have previously alluded, and of which a moiety[16] only floated indeterminately through my brain when I raised food to my burning lips. The whole thought was now present—feeble, scarcely sane, scarcely definite,—but still entire. I proceeded at once, with the nervous energy of despair, to attempt its execution.

For many hours the immediate vicinity of the low framework upon which I lay, had been literally swarming with rats. They were wild, bold, ravenous; their red eyes glaring upon me as if they waited but for motionlessness on my part to make me their prey. "To what food," I thought, "have they been accustomed in the well?"

---

15. **athwart** (ə thwôrt′), *adj.* from side to side; crosswise.
16. **moiety** (moi′ə tē), *n.* a portion.

They had devoured, in spite of all my efforts to prevent them, all but a small remnant of the contents of the dish. I had fallen into an habitual seesaw, or wave of the hand about the platter: and, at length, the unconscious uniformity of the movement deprived it of effect. In their voracity the vermin frequently fastened their sharp fangs into my fingers. With the particles of the oily and spicy viand which now remained, I thoroughly rubbed the bandage wherever I could reach it; then, raising my hand from the floor, I lay breathlessly still.

At first the ravenous animals were startled and terrified at the change—at the cessation[17] of movement. They shrank alarmedly back; many sought the well. But this was only for a moment. I had not counted in vain upon their voracity. Observing that I remained without motion, one or two of the boldest leaped upon the frame-work, and smelt at the surcingle. This seemed the signal for a general rush. Forth from the well they hurried in fresh troops. They clung to the wood—they overran it, and leaped in hundreds upon my person. The measured movement of the pendulum disturbed them not at all. Avoiding its strokes they busied themselves with the anointed bandage. They pressed—they swarmed upon me in ever accumulating heaps. They writhed upon my throat; their cold lips sought my own; I was half stifled by their thronging pressure; disgust, for which the world has no name, swelled my bosom, and chilled, with a heavy clamminess, my heart. Yet one minute, and I felt that the struggle would be over. Plainly I perceived the loosening of the bandage. I knew that in more than one place it must be already severed. With a more than human resolution I lay *still*.

Nor had I erred in my calculations—nor had I endured in vain. I at length felt that I was *free*. The surcingle hung in ribands from my body. But the stroke of the pendulum already pressed upon my bosom. It had divided the serge of the robe. It had cut through the linen beneath. Twice again it swung, and a sharp sense of pain shot through every nerve. But the moment of escape had arrived. At a wave of my hand my deliverers hurried tumultuously away. With a steady movement—cautious, sidelong, shrinking, and slow—I slid from the embrace of the bandage and beyond the reach of the scimitar. For the moment, at least, *I was free*.

Free!—and in the grasp of the Inquisition! I had scarcely stepped from my wooden bed of horror upon the stone floor of the prison, when the motion of the hellish machine ceased and I beheld it drawn up, by some invisible force through the ceiling. This was a lesson which I took desperately to heart. My every motion was undoubtedly watched. Free!—I had but escaped death in one form of agony, to be delivered unto worse than death in some other. With that thought I rolled my eyes nervously around the barriers of iron that hemmed me in. Something unusual—some change which at first I could not appreciate distinctly—it was obvious, had taken place in the apartment. For many minutes in a dreamy and trembling abstraction, I busied myself in vain, unconnected conjecture.[18] During this period, I became aware, for the first time, of the origin of the sulphurous light which illuminated the cell. It proceeded from a fissure, about half an inch in width, extending entirely around the prison at the base of the walls, which thus appeared, and were completely separated from the floor. I endeavored, but of course in vain, to look through the aperture.

As I arose from the attempt, the mystery of the alteration in the chamber broke at once upon my understanding. I have observed that, although the outlines of the figures upon the walls were sufficiently distinct, yet the colors seemed blurred and indefinite. These colors had now assumed, and were momentarily assuming, a startling and most intense brilliancy, that gave to the spectral and fiendish por-

---

17. **cessation** (se sā′shən), *n.* a ceasing, stopping.
18. **conjecture** (kən jek′chər), *n.* formation of opinion without sufficient evidence or proof.

traitures an aspect that might have thrilled even firmer nerves than my own. Demon eyes, of a wild and ghastly vivacity, glared upon me in a thousand directions, where none had been visible before, and gleamed with the lurid lustre of a fire that I could not force my imagination to regard as unreal.

Unreal!—Even while I breathed there came to my nostrils the breath of the vapour of heated iron! A suffocating odor pervaded the prison! A deeper glow settled each moment in the eyes that glared at my agonies! A richer tint of crimson diffused itself over the pictured horrors of blood. I panted! I gasped for breath! There could be no doubt of the design of my tormentors—oh! most unrelenting! oh! most demoniac of men! I shrank from the glowing metal to the centre of the cell. Amid the thought of the fiery destruction that impended, the idea of the coolness of the well came over my soul like balm. I rushed to its deadly brink. I threw my straining vision below. The glare from the enkindled roof illumined its inmost recesses. Yet, for a wild moment, did my spirit refuse to comprehend the meaning of what I saw. At length it forced— it wrestled its way into my soul—it burned itself in upon my shuddering reason.—Oh! for a voice to speak! oh! horror!—oh! any horror but this! With a shriek, I rushed from the margin, and buried my face in my hands—weeping bitterly.

The heat rapidly increased, and once again I looked up, shuddering as with a fit of the ague. There had been a second change in the cell— and now the change was obviously in the *form*. As before, it was in vain that I, at first, endeavoured to appreciate or understand what was tak-

ing place. But not long was I left in doubt. The Inquisitorial vengeance had been hurried by my two-fold escape, and there was to be no more dallying with the King of Terrors. The room had been square. I saw that two of its iron angles were now acute—two, consequently, obtuse. The fearful difference quickly increased with a low rumbling or moaning sound. In an instant the apartment had shifted its form into that of a lozenge. But the alteration stopped not here—I neither hoped nor desired it to stop. I could have clasped the red walls to my bosom as a garment of eternal peace. "Death," I said, "any death but that of the pit!" Fool! might I have not known that *into the pit* it was the object of the burning iron to urge me? Could I resist its glow? or, if even that, could I withstand its pressure? And now, flatter and flatter grew the lozenge, with a rapidity that left me no time for contemplation. Its centre, and of course, its greatest width, came just over the yawning gulf. I shrank back—but the closing walls pressed me resistlessly onward. At length for my seared and writhing body there was no longer an inch of foothold on the firm floor of the prison. I struggled no more, but the agony of my soul found vent in one loud, long, and final scream

I struggled no more, but the agony of my soul found vent in one loud, long, and final scream . . .

of despair. I felt that I tottered upon the brink— I averted my eyes—

There was a discordant hum of human voices! There was a loud blast of many trumpets! There was a harsh grating as of a thousand thunders! The fiery walls rushed back! An outstretched arm caught my own as I fell, fainting, into the abyss. It was that of General Lasalle. The French army had entered Toledo. The Inquisition was in the hands of its enemies.

After Reading

Making Connections

Shaping Your Response

1. Which strikes you as a more dreadful death—the pit or the pendulum?

2. How did you react to the ending of "The Pit and the Pendulum?" Write down five words that describe your reaction and explain your choices.

Analyzing the Story

3. How would you describe the **setting** for "The Pit and the Pendulum"?

4. Why do you think the pit inspires such terror in the narrator, particularly after he is able to look into it?

5. The main character never sees or interacts with his captors. What effect does this lend to the story?

6. Throughout the story, Poe uses **imagery** to help establish **mood.** Find an example of imagery and describe the effect that it creates. Does the image make the scene seem more vivid? How so?

Extending the Ideas

7. "The Pit and the Pendulum" is based on an actual historical event— the Spanish Inquisition. If Poe were alive today, what contemporary events might inspire his writing? Why?

Literary Focus: Mood

Authors create mood through setting, characters, events, and descriptive details. The mood of a selection can be romantic, sad, eerie, lighthearted, dreamlike—the possibilities cover the range of emotions. What is the mood of "The Pit and the Pendulum"? List ten words from the story that contribute to the **mood.**

Vocabulary Study

indeterminate
interminableness
insuperable
treacherous
charnel
disfigure
cognizance
recusant
cessation
conjecture

Imagine that the story, "The Pit and the Pendulum," has just been published for the first time, and it is your job to review it for your local paper. Use the listed words from the story to write a review that captures your readers' interest, without giving the whole plot away. When you're finished, underline the vocabulary words and check to see that you've used them correctly. Use your Glossary if necessary.

Expressing Your Ideas

Writing Choices

Writer's Notebook Update Look back at the web you created before reading "The Pit and the Pendulum." Now that you've read the story, would you like to add anything to your original ideas? In your notebook, tell whether "The Pit and the Pendulum" meets your expectations for a good horror story.

Every Picture Tells a Story As Edgar Allan Poe is a master of **mood** in literature, Edvard Munch is a master of mood in art. His works cover a huge range of emotions—from joy to gloom, from peace to hysteria. Create a story based on Munch's painting, *The Scream*. What are the people in the painting doing? What's the situation? Write a **description** of the characters, setting and plot that reflects the mood of the painting. Or write the whole story!

Other Options

Gallery of Horrors Horror has been a popular theme in the visual arts just as it has been in stories. As a class, create an **art gallery** in the classroom displaying the horror theme in fine art. Each student can find one or more fine art pieces to contribute to the collection, or they can contribute their own creations. You may want to look in a library for books about your favorite well-known artists, to see if they have ever picked up on the horror theme.

Dangerous Differences Thoreau took a stand for what he believed, and, in consequence, he spent a night in jail. Those who took a stand against the Spanish Inquisition suffered much greater consequences. Unfortunately, similar instances of oppression of **individuals** by groups in power have occurred throughout history. Research a historical or current situation in which a group in power oppressed others for their beliefs or other differences. When and where did it take place, who was behind it, and what groups of people were persecuted? Present your findings in an **oral report** to the class, including ideas about how to prevent such occurrences.

Before Reading

The Raven

by Edgar Allan Poe

Building Background

Raven Facts As the largest member of the crow family, ravens occupy a distinguished place in the animal kingdom as well as the world's literature. These black birds can grow to over two feet in length, and their deep rumbling croak can be heard all across the Northern Hemisphere. Poe's poem, "The Raven," is not the first literary work to feature this bird prominently. Ravens are mentioned in various mythologies, they appear in the Bible, and they are often seen in folklore as a sign of bad luck or an omen of death.

Literary Focus

Sound Devices Poets can create an impression through sound by using **sound devices**. Sound devices are the use of words for their auditory effect. Some common ones include **alliteration,** the repetition of consonant sounds; **assonance,** the repetition of similar vowel sounds; **onomatopoeia,** the use of words whose sound suggests the natural sound of an object or activity; and **repetition,** the repeating of a word or phrase. Watch for Poe's use of these sounds devices as you read and jot down examples when you come across them. Use a diagram like the one shown here to organize your notes.

Sound Device	Examples
Alliteration	"weak and weary" (line 1)
Assonance	
Onomatopoeia	
Repetition	
Rhyme	

Writer's Notebook

Things that Go Bump in the Night Many writers of suspense and horror stories use night as a backdrop to create a sense of mystery and fear. Do you remember ever being afraid at night? What aspects of nighttime can be frightening or unsettling? Before reading the next selection, jot down some features of the night that can make it a good setting for a horror tale.

◄ 🐾 Artist Tony Angell believes that the color change in his sculpture, *Transformation* (1987), reflects the transformable spirit of the trickster Raven in American Indian legends. Would you call Poe's raven a trickster? Why or why not?

The Raven

EDGAR ALLAN POE

Once upon a midnight dreary, while I pondered, weak and weary,
Over many a quaint and curious volume of forgotten lore—
While I nodded, nearly napping, suddenly there came a tapping,
As of someone gently rapping, rapping at my chamber door.
5 "'Tis some visitor," I muttered, "tapping at my chamber door—
       Only this and nothing more."

Ah, distinctly I remember it was in the bleak December,
And each separate dying ember wrought its ghost upon the floor.
Eagerly I wished the morrow; vainly I had sought to borrow
10 From my books surcease[1] of sorrow—sorrow for the lost Lenore—
For the rare and radiant maiden whom the angels name Lenore—
       Nameless here forevermore.

And the silken, sad, uncertain rustling of each purple curtain
Thrilled me—filled me with fantastic terrors never felt before;
15 So that now, to still the beating of my heart, I stood repeating,
"'Tis some visitor entreating[2] entrance at my chamber door—
Some late visitor entreating entrance at my chamber door—
       That it is and nothing more."

Presently my soul grew stronger; hesitating then no longer,
20 "Sir," said I, "or Madam, truly your forgiveness I implore;
But the fact is I was napping, and so gently you came rapping,
And so faintly you came tapping, tapping at my chamber door,
That I scarce was sure I heard you"—here I opened wide the door—
       Darkness there and nothing more.

---

1. **surcease** (sėr´sēs´), *n.* end; cessation.
2. **entreat** (en trēt´), *v.* to ask earnestly; to beg or pray.

25 Deep into that darkness peering, long I stood there wondering, fearing,
   Doubting, dreaming dreams no mortal ever dared to dream before;
   But the silence was unbroken, and the stillness gave no token,
   And the only word there spoken was the whispered word, "Lenore?"
   This I whispered, and an echo murmured back the word "Lenore!"
30   Merely this and nothing more.

   Back into the chamber turning, all my soul within me burning,
   Soon again I heard a tapping somewhat louder than before.
   "Surely," said I, "surely that is something at my window lattice;³
   Let me see, then, what thereat is, and this mystery explore—
35 Let my heart be still a moment and this mystery explore;
                                        'Tis the wind and nothing more!"

   Open here I flung the shutter, when, with many a flirt and flutter,
   In there stepped a stately Raven of the saintly days of yore;
   Not the least obeisance⁴ made he; not a minute stopped or stayed he;
40 But, with mien⁵ of lord or lady, perched above my chamber door—
   Perched upon a bust of Pallas just above my chamber door—
                                        Perched, and sat, and nothing more.

   Then this ebony bird beguiling my sad fancy into smiling,
   By the grave and stern decorum of the countenance⁶ it wore,
45 "Though thy crest be shorn and shaven, thou," I said, "art sure no craven,⁷
   Ghastly grim and ancient Raven wandering from the Nightly shore—
   Tell me what thy lordly name is on the Night's Plutonian shore!"
                                        Quoth the Raven, "Nevermore."

   Much I marveled this ungainly fowl to hear discourse so plainly,
50 Though its answer little meaning—little relevancy bore;
   For we cannot help agreeing that no living human being
   Ever yet was blessed with seeing bird above his chamber door—
   Bird or beast upon the sculptured bust above his chamber door,
                                        With such name as "Nevermore."

---

   3. **lattice** (lat′is), *n.* structure of crossed wooden or metal strips with open spaces between them.
   4. obeisance (ō bā′sns, ō bē′sns), *n.* show of deference or respect.
   5. **mien** (mēn), *n.* demeanor; bearing.
   6. countenance (koun′tə nəns), *n.* expression of the face.
   7. craven (krā′vən), *adj.* cowardly.

55 But the Raven, sitting lonely on the placid bust, spoke only
That one word, as if his soul in that one word he did outpour.
Nothing further then he uttered, not a feather then he fluttered—
Till I scarcely more than muttered, "Other friends have flown before;
On the morrow *he* will leave me, as my hopes have flown before."
60   Then the bird said, "Nevermore."

Startled at the stillness broken by reply so aptly[8] spoken,
"Doubtless," said I, "what it utters is its only stock and store,
Caught from some unhappy master whom unmerciful disaster
Followed fast and followed faster till his songs one burden bore—
65 Till the dirges[9] of his hope that melancholy burden bore
                                        Of 'Never—nevermore.'"

But the Raven still beguiling[10] all my fancy into smiling,
Straight I wheeled a cushioned seat in front of bird and bust and door;
Then, upon the velvet sinking, I betook myself to linking
70 Fancy unto fancy, thinking what this ominous bird of yore—
What this grim, ungainly, ghastly, gaunt, and ominous bird of yore
                                        Meant in croaking "Nevermore."

This I sat engaged in guessing, but no syllable expressing
To the fowl, whose fiery eyes now burned into my bosom's core;
75 This and more I sat divining,[11] with my head at ease reclining
On the cushion's velvet lining that the lamplight gloated o'er,
But whose velvet violet lining with the lamplight gloating o'er,
                                        She shall press, ah, nevermore!

Then, methought, the air grew denser, perfumed from an unseen censer[12]
80 Swung by seraphim[13] whose footfalls tinkled on the tufted floor.
"Wretch," I cried, "thy God hath lent thee—by these angels he hath sent thee
Respite—respite and nepenthe[14]—from thy memories of Lenore!
Quaff,[15] oh Quaff this kind nepenthe and forget this lost Lenore!"
                                        Quoth the Raven, "Nevermore."

---

8. aptly (apt′lē), *adv.* intelligently.
9. dirge (dėrj), *n.* funeral song or tune.
10. beguile (bi gīl′), *v.* entertain; amuse. Also deceive; delude.
11. divine (də vīn′), *v.* guess; predict.
12. censer (sen′sər), *n.* container in which incense is burned.
13. seraphim (ser′ə fim), *n.* members of the highest order of angels.
14. nepenthe (ni pen′thē), *n.* a mythological potion thought to relieve sorrow.
15. quaff (kwäf, kwaf, kwôf), *v.* drink in large swallows; drink freely and deeply.

85 "Prophet!" said I, "thing of evil! prophet still, if bird or devil!
   Whether Tempter sent, or whether tempest tossed thee here ashore,
   Desolate yet all undaunted, on this desert land enchanted—
   On this home by Horror haunted—tell me truly, I implore;
   Is there—*is* there balm in Gilead?—tell me—tell me, I implore!"
90   Quoth the Raven, "Nevermore."

   "Prophet!" said I, thing of evil! prophet still, if bird or devil!
   By that Heaven that bends above us, by that God we both adore,
   Tell this soul with sorrow laden if, within the distant Aidenn,
   It shall clasp a sainted maiden whom the angels name Lenore—
95 Clasp a rare and radiant maiden whom the angels name Lenore."
                                         Quoth the Raven, "Nevermore."

   "Be that word our sign of parting, bird or fiend!" I shrieked, upstarting.
   "Get thee back into the tempest and the Night's Plutonian shore!
   Leave no black plume as a token of that lie thy soul hath spoken!
100 Leave my loneliness unbroken!—quit the bust above my door!
   Take thy beak from out my heart, and take thy form from off my door!"
                                         Quoth the Raven, "Nevermore."

   And the Raven, never flitting, still is sitting, *still* is sitting
   On the pallid[16] bust of Pallas just above my chamber door;
105 And his eyes have all the seeming of a demon's that is dreaming,
   And the lamplight o'er him streaming throws his shadow on the floor;
   And my soul from out that shadow that lies floating on the floor
                                         Shall be lifted—nevermore!

---

17. **pallid** (pal′id), *adj.* lacking normal color; wan; pale.

After Reading

Making Connections

Shaping Your
Response

1. How would you describe the narrator's frame of mind? Draw a silhouette of the narrator and fill it with words that describe his inner state.

Analyzing the
Poem

2. Based on the information provided in the poem, what can you **infer** about the narrator's relationship to Lenore?

3. At what point does the poem's **tone** shift from melancholy to anger?

4. What effect do you think the **repetitions** have in this poem?

5. Reread the final stanza. Why is it significant that the narrator, and not the raven, uses the word "nevermore"?

Extending the
Ideas

6. How does the **mood** of "The Raven" compare to Poe's story, "The Pit and the Pendulum"? Use a diagram like the one below to organize your response. Fill in the circles with elements from both works that contribute to the mood.

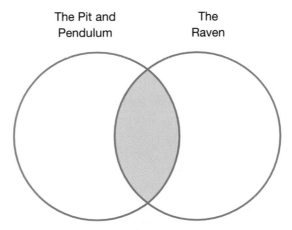

Literary Focus: Sound Devices

The use of **sound devices** can add a rich dimension to writing by conveying mood, establishing meaning, creating a musical sound, or unifying a work. Poe uses several sound devices in "The Raven" that lend a musical quality to the poem and contribute to its ominous, oppressive mood. Look over your notes and reread the poem to generate examples of sound devices used by Poe. Choose one of your examples and try rewriting the stanza without the sound device. How does this change the sound of the stanza? What effect does it have on the mood, the tone, or the meaning?

Vocabulary Study

Decide whether each italicized word is used correctly in the sentence. If not, write a new sentence that uses the word correctly. Use your Glossary if necessary.

beguile
countenance
obeisance
aptly
craven

1. After entering the room, the raven proceeded to *beguile* the narrator with its speech.

2. The narrator was angered by the discouraging *countenance* the raven came to deliver.

3. Lenore's *obeisance* left the narrator melancholy.

4. The narrator was impressed when the raven's reply was *aptly* spoken.

5. The narrator's cushioned seat was a *craven* velvet.

Expressing Your Ideas

Writing Choices

Writer's Notebook Update Now that you've read "The Raven," review your notes on scary aspects of the night. Were any of your ideas reflected in the poem? Did Poe introduce some features that you hadn't thought about? Write a description of a night scene in which you incorporate some or all of these features. Experiment with word choices that either intensify or weaken the menacing effect.

Imitating Poe Edgar Allan Poe has a very distinctive poetic style that some writers find easy to imitate. Try writing a stanza of your own Poe-inspired **poetry.** You might try writing a parody of "The Raven," or a serious stanza that matches the mood of the original. Notice that in each stanza of "The Raven," the middle and end of lines 1 and 3 rhyme. Also, the end of lines 2, 3, and 5 rhyme with "more." In your stanza, try to preserve this rhyme scheme.

Other Options

"The Raven" Comes Alive Poe was often asked to recite "The Raven" and it has been said that his delivery was so dramatic that soon everyone in the room could hear the flutter of wings and the shutter being flung open. Work in small groups to do your own **dramatic reading**. Take turns reading stanzas using intonation and emphasis to capture the narrator's state of mind and the ambiance of the scene, as well as the musical cadence of the rhythm and rhyme.

Ideas Taking Shape "The Raven" is a poem that expresses profound feelings of sadness and loss, as well as a man's descent into madness. Design an abstract **sculpture** that captures the feelings of the poem in its shape and texture. You can either make a drawing of the sculpture, or if you have time, actually produce it out of clay or other materials.

Before Reading

Dr. Heidegger's Experiment

by Nathaniel Hawthorne

Nathaniel Hawthorne
1804–1864

Nathaniel Hawthorne's family tree included several Puritan ancestors who were an embarrassment to him. William, the first Hathorne to emigrate to America, was notorious for his persecution of the Quakers. His son John was equally notorious; he served as a judge in the Salem witchcraft trials in 1692. To distance himself from his embarassing ancestors, Hawthorne changed the spelling of his name, but his feelings about his Puritan heritage show up often in his writing, especially in the novels *The Scarlet Letter* and *The House of the Seven Gables*.

Building Background

Young at Heart Cosmetic manufacturers and plastic surgeons make fortunes helping people try to reverse the effects of aging and keep their youthful appearance. However, the quest for youth is not peculiar to our times. As early as the 1500s, Juan Ponce de Leon, the Spanish explorer, searched Florida to find the legendary Fountain of Youth, the waters of which were said to keep a person from aging. Dr. Heidegger's Experiment explores what might happern if such a Fountain of Youth really existed.

Literary Focus

Foreshadowing When writers give readers hints of what is to come in a story, they are using a technique called **foreshadowing.** Foreshadowing creates suspense and builds expectations. It also sets the stage for future events by making them seem reasonable or inevitable. As you read "Dr. Heidegger's Experiment," look for instances of foreshadowing in the story.

Writer's Notebook

The Scientific Method Before undertaking an experiment, scientists state a purpose for the experiment and a hypothesis, or prediction about what they think will happen. During the experiment they make observations using predetermined procedures, and then they draw conclusions about the results in a report. Dr. Heidegger is about to conduct an experiment to see what will happen to his four old friends when they drink water that is supposedly from the Fountain of Youth. Predict what Dr. Heidegger is up to, and fill out a chart like following in your notebook.

Dr. Heidegger's Experiment	
Purpose:	
Hypothesis:	
Materials:	
Procedures:	

Dr. Heidegger's Experiment

NATHANIEL HAWTHORNE

That very singular man, old Dr. Heidegger, once invited four venerable friends to meet him in his study. There were three white-bearded gentlemen, Mr. Medbourne, Colonel Killigrew, and Mr. Gascoigne, and a withered gentlewoman, whose name was the Widow Wycherly. They were all melancholy old creatures, who had been unfortunate in life, and whose greatest misfortune it was that they were not long ago in their graves. Mr. Medbourne, in the vigor of his age, had been a prosperous merchant, but had lost his all by a frantic speculation, and was now little better than a mendicant.[1] Colonel Killigrew had wasted his best years, and his health and substance, in the pursuit of sinful pleasures, which had given birth to a brood of pains, such as the gout, and divers other torments of soul and body. Mr. Gascoigne was a ruined politician, a man of evil fame, or at least had been so till time had buried him from the knowledge of the present generation, and made him obscure[2] instead of infamous.[3] As for the Widow Wycherly, tradition tells us that she was a great beauty in her day; but, for a long while past, she had lived in deep seclusion, on account of certain scandalous stories which had prejudiced the gentry[4] of the town against her. It is a circumstance worth mentioning that each of these three old gentlemen, Mr. Medbourne, Colonel Killigrew, and Mr. Gascoigne, were early lovers of the Widow Wycherly, and had once been on the point of cutting each other's throats for her sake. And, before proceeding further, I will merely hint that Dr. Heidegger and all his four guests were sometimes thought to be a little beside themselves,—as is not unfrequently the case with old people, when worried either by present troubles or woeful recollections.

"My dear old friends," said Dr. Heidegger, motioning them to be seated, "I am

---

1. **mendicant** (men′də kənt), *n.* beggar.
2. **obscure** (əb skyùr′), *adj.* not well known; attracting no notice.
3. **infamous** (in′fə məs), *adj.* well-known, but with a very bad reputation.
4. **gentry** (jen′trē), *n.* people belonging to the upper class of society.

▲ Does Charles Wilson Peale's portrait *James Peale (The Lamplight Portrait)* portray the same mood as the story of Dr. Heidegger? Explain your answer.

desirous of your assistance in one of those little experiments with which I amuse myself here in my study."

SUMMARIZE: Describe each of Dr. Heidegger's friends.

If all stories were true, Dr. Heidegger's study must have been a very curious place. It was a dim, old-fashioned chamber, festooned with cobwebs, and besprinkled with antique dust. Around the walls stood several oaken bookcases, the lower shelves of which were filled with rows of gigantic folios and black-letter quartos, and the upper with little parchment-covered duodecimos.[5] Over the central bookcase was a bronze bust of

---

5. **. . . folios . . . quartos . . . duodecimos. . . ,** books with certain size pages. A folio is a book made from single pages of paper folded in half; a quarto is made from single pages of paper folded into fourths; and a duodecimo made from single pages of paper folded into twelfths.

Hippocrates,[6] with which, according to some authorities, Dr. Heidegger was accustomed to hold consultations in all difficult cases of his practice. In the obscurest corner of the room stood a tall and narrow oaken closet, with its door ajar, within which doubtfully appeared a skeleton. Between two of the bookcases hung a looking-glass, presenting its high and dusty plate within a tarnished gilt frame. Among many wonderful stories related of this mirror, it was fabled that the spirits of all the doctor's deceased patients dwelt within its verge,[7] and would stare him in the face whenever he looked thitherward. The opposite side of the chamber was ornamented with the full-length portrait of a young lady, arrayed in the faded magnificence of silk, satin, and brocade, and with a visage as faded as her dress. Above half a century ago, Dr. Heidegger had been on the point of marriage with this young lady; but, being affected with some slight disorder, she had swallowed one of her lover's prescriptions, and died on the bridal evening. The greatest curiosity of the study remains to be mentioned; it was a ponderous folio volume, bound in black leather, with massive[8] silver clasps. There were no letters on the back, and nobody could tell the title of the book. But it was well known to be a book of magic; and once, when a chambermaid had lifted it, merely to brush away the dust, the skeleton had rattled in its closet, the picture of the young lady had stepped one foot upon the floor, and several ghastly faces had peeped forth from the mirror; while the brazen head of Hippocrates frowned, and said,—"Forbear!"

Such was Dr. Heidegger's study. On the summer afternoon of our tale a small round table, as black as ebony, stood in the centre of the room, sustaining a cut-glass vase of beautiful form and elaborate workmanship. The sunshine came through the window between the heavy festoons of two faded damask curtains, and fell directly across this vase; so that a mild splendor was reflected from it on the ashen visages[9] of the five old people who sat around. Four champagne glasses were also on the table.

"My dear old friends," repeated Dr. Heidegger, "may I reckon on your aid in performing an exceedingly curious experiment?"

Now Dr. Heidegger was a very strange old gentleman, whose eccentricity[10] had become the nucleus for a thousand fantastic stories. Some of these fables, to my shame be it spoken, might possibly be traced back to my own veracious[11] self; and if any passages of the present tale should startle the reader's faith, I must be content to bear the stigma of a fiction monger.

When the doctor's four guests heard him talk of his proposed experiment, they anticipated nothing more wonderful than the murder of a mouse in an air pump, or the examination of a cobweb by the microscope, or some similar nonsense, with which he was constantly in the habit of pestering his intimates. But without waiting for a reply, Dr. Heidegger hobbled across the chamber, and returned with the same ponderous folio, bound in black leather, which common report affirmed to be a book of magic. Undoing the silver clasps, he opened the volume, and took from among its black-letter pages a rose, or what was once a rose, though now the green leaves and crimson petals had assumed one brownish hue, and the ancient flower seemed ready to crumble to dust in the doctor's hands.

"This rose," said Dr. Heidegger, with a sigh, "this same withered and crumbling flower, blossomed five and fifty years ago. It was given me by Sylvia Ward, whose portrait hangs yonder; and I meant to wear it in my bosom at our wedding. Five and fifty years it has been treasured between the leaves of this old volume. Now, would you

---

6. **Hippocrates,** (hi pok′ rə tēz′) 460-377 B.C., Greek physician, called the father of medicine.
7. **verge** (vėrj), *n.* border.
8. **massive** (mas′iv), *adj.* bulky and heavy; huge.
9. **visage** (viz′ij), *n.* face, appearance or aspect.
10. **eccentricity** (ek′sen tris′ə tē), *n.* oddity; peculiarity.
11. **veracious** (və rā′shəs), *adj.* truthful.

◄ Find the passages that describe the Widow Wycherly. Which of the passages does John Singleton Copley's portrait, *Mrs. Ezekial Goldthwait* (1771), best match? Why?

deem it possible that this rose of half a century could ever bloom again?"

"Nonsense!" said the Widow Wycherly, with a peevish toss of her head. "You might as well ask whether an old woman's wrinkled face could ever bloom again."

"See!" answered Dr. Heidegger.

He uncovered the vase, and threw the faded rose into the water which it contained. At first, it lay lightly on the surface of the fluid, appearing to imbibe[12] none of its moisture. Soon, however, a singular change began to be visible. The crushed and dried petals stirred, and assumed a deepening tinge of crimson,[13] as if the flower were reviving from a deathlike slumber; the slender stalk and twigs of foliage became green; and there was the rose of half a century, looking as fresh as when Sylvia Ward had first given it to her lover. It was scarcely full blown; for some of its delicate red leaves curled modestly around its moist bosom, within which two or three dewdrops were sparkling.

"That is certainly a very pretty deception," said the doctor's friends; carelessly, however, for they had witnessed greater miracles at a conjurer's show; "pray how was it effected?"

"Did you never hear of the 'Fountain of Youth?'" asked Dr. Heidegger, "which Ponce De Leon, the Spanish adventurer, went in search of two or three centuries ago?"

"But did Ponce De Leon ever find it?" said the Widow Wycherly.

"No," answered Dr. Heidegger, "for he never

---

12. **imbibe** (im bīb′), *v.* absorb; drink in.
13. **crimson** (krim′zən), *adj.* a deep red.

sought it in the right place. The famous Fountain of Youth, if I am rightly informed, is situated in the southern part of the Floridian peninsula, not far from Lake Macaco. Its source is overshadowed by several gigantic magnolias, which though numberless centuries old, have been kept as fresh as violets by the virtues of this wonderful water. An acquaintance of mine, knowing my curiosity in such matters, has sent me what you see in the vase."

"Ahem!" said Colonel Killigrew, who believed not a word of the doctor's story; "and what may be the effect of this fluid on the human frame?"

"You shall judge for yourself, my dear colonel," replied Dr. Heidegger; "and all of you, my respected friends, are welcome to so much of this admirable fluid as may restore to you the bloom of youth. For my own part, having had much trouble in growing old, I am in no hurry to grow young again. With your permission, therefore, I will merely watch the progress of the experiment."

While he spoke, Dr. Heidegger had been filling the four champagne glasses with the water of the Fountain of Youth. It was apparently impregnated with an effervescent gas, for little bubbles were continually ascending from the depths of the glasses, and bursting in silvery spray at the surface. As the liquor diffused a pleasant perfume, the old people doubted not that it possessed cordial[14] and comfortable properties; and though utter sceptics as to its rejuvenescent power, they were inclined to swallow it at once. But Dr. Heidegger besought them to stay a moment.

"Before you drink, my respectable old friends," said he, "it would be well that, with the experience of a lifetime to direct you, you should draw up a few general rules for your guidance, in passing a second time through the perils of youth. Think what a sin and shame it would be, if, with your peculiar advantages, you should not become patterns of virtue and wisdom to all the young people of the age!"

The doctor's four venerable friends made him no answer, except by a feeble and tremulous laugh; so very ridiculous was the idea that, knowing how closely repentance treads behind the steps of error, they should ever go astray again.

"Drink, then," said the doctor, bowing: "I rejoice that I have so well selected the subjects of my experiment."

PREDICT: What do you think will happen to the four friends when they drink the water of the Fountain of Youth? Why?

With palsied hands, they raised the glasses to their lips. The liquor, if it really possessed such virtues as Dr. Heidegger imputed to it, could not have been bestowed on four human beings who needed it more woefully. They looked as if they had never known what youth or pleasure was, but had been the offspring of Nature's dotage, and always the gray, decrepit, sapless, miserable creatures, who now sat stooping round the doctor's table, without life enough in their souls or bodies to be animated even by the prospect of growing young again. They drank off the water, and replaced their glasses on the table.

Assuredly there was an almost immediate improvement in the aspect of the party, not unlike what might have been produced by a glass of generous wine, together with a sudden glow of cheerful sunshine brightening over all their visages at once. There was a healthful suffusion on their cheeks, instead of the ashen hue that had made them look so corpse-like. They gazed at one another, and fancied that some magic power had really begun to smooth away the deep and sad inscriptions which Father Time had been so long engraving on their brows. The Widow Wycherly adjusted her cap, for she felt almost like a woman again.

"Give us more of this wondrous water!" cried they, eagerly. "We are younger—but we are still too old! Quick—give us more!"

---

14. **cordial** (kôr′jəl), *adj.* strengthening; stimulating.

"Patience, patience!" quoth Dr. Heidegger, who sat watching the experiment with philosophic coolness. "You have been a long time growing old. Surely, you might be content to grow young in half an hour! But the water is at your service."

Again he filled their glasses with the liquor of youth, enough of which still remained in the vase to turn half the old people in the city to the age of their own grandchildren. While the bubbles were yet sparkling on the brim, the doctor's four guests snatched their glasses from the table, and swallowed the contents at a single gulp. Was it delusion? Even while the draught was passing down their throats, it seemed to have wrought a change on their whole systems. Their eyes grew clear and bright; a dark shade deepened among their silvery locks, they sat around the table, three gentlemen of middle age, and a woman, hardly beyond her buxom[15] prime.

"My dear widow, you are charming!" cried Colonel Killigrew, whose eyes had been fixed upon her face, while the shadows of age were flitting from it like darkness from the crimson daybreak.

The fair widow knew, of old, that Colonel Killigrew's compliments were not always measured by sober truth; so she started up and ran to the mirror, still dreading that the ugly visage of an old woman would meet her gaze. Meanwhile, the three gentlemen behaved in such a manner as proved that the water of the Fountain of Youth possessed some intoxicating qualities; unless, indeed, their exhilaration of spirits were merely a lightsome dizziness caused by the sudden removal of the weight of years. Mr. Gascoigne's mind seemed to run on political topics, but whether relating to the past, present, or future, could not easily be determined, since the same ideas and phrases have been in vogue these fifty years. Now he rattled forth full-throated sentences about patriotism, national glory, and the people's right; now he muttered some perilous stuff or other, in a sly

and doubtful whisper, so cautiously that even his own conscience could scarcely catch the secret; and now, again, he spoke in measured accents, and a deeply deferential tone, as if a royal ear were listening to his well-turned periods. Colonel Killigrew all this time had been trolling forth a jolly bottle song, and ringing his glass in symphony with the chorus, while his eyes wandered toward the buxom figure of the Widow Wycherly. On the other side of the table, Mr. Medbourne was involved in a calculation of dollars and cents, with which was strangely intermingled a project for supplying the East Indies with ice, by harnessing a team of whales to the polar icebergs.

As for the Widow Wycherly, she stood before the mirror courtesying and simpering to her own image, and greeting it as the friend whom she loved better than all the world beside. She thrust her face close to the glass, to see whether some long-remembered wrinkle or crow's foot had indeed vanished. She examined whether the snow had so entirely melted from her hair that the venerable cap could be safely thrown aside. At last, turning briskly away, she came with a sort of dancing step to the table.

"My dear old doctor," cried she, "pray favor me with another glass!"

"Certainly, my dear madam, certainly!" replied the complaisant doctor; "see I have already filled the glasses."

There, in fact, stood the four glasses, brimful of this wonderful water, the delicate spray of which, as it effervesced from the surface, resembled the tremulous glitter of diamonds. It was now so nearly sunset that the chamber had grown duskier than ever; but a mild and moonlike splendor gleamed from within the vase, and rested alike on the four guests and on the doctor's venerable figure. He sat in a high-backed, elaborately-carved, oaken arm-chair, with a gray dignity of aspect that might have

---

15. **buxom** (buk′sǝm), *adj.* attractively and healthily plump.

well befitted that very Father Time, whose power had never been disputed, save by this fortunate company. Even while quaffing the third draught of the Fountain of Youth, they were almost awed by the expression of his mysterious visage.

CLARIFY: Why is Dr. Heidegger compared to Father Time?

But, the next moment, the exhilarating gush of young life shot through their veins. They were now in the happy prime of youth. Age, with its miserable train of cares and sorrows and diseases, was remembered only as the trouble of a dream, from which they had joyously awoke. The fresh gloss of the soul, so early lost, and without which the world's successive scenes had been but a gallery of faded pictures, again threw its enchantment over all their prospects. They felt like new-created beings in a new-created universe.

"We are young! We are young!" they cried exultingly.

Youth, like the extremity of age, had effaced the strongly-marked characteristics of middle life, and mutually assimilated them all. They were a group of merry youngsters, almost maddened with the exuberant[16] frolicsomeness of their years. The most singular effect of their gayety was an impulse to mock the infirmity[17] and decrepitude of which they had so lately been the victims. They laughed loudly at their old-fashioned attire, the wide-skirted coats and flapped waistcoats of the young men, and the ancient cap and gown of the blooming girl. One limped across the floor like a gouty grandfather; one set a pair of spectacles astride of his nose, and pretended to pore over the black-letter pages of the book of magic; a third seated himself in an arm-chair, and strove to imitate the venerable dignity of Dr. Heidegger. Then all shouted mirthfully, and leaped about the room. The Widow Wycherly—if so fresh a damsel could be called a widow—tripped up to the doctor's chair, with a mischievous merriment in her rosy face.

"Doctor, you dear old soul," cried she, "get up and dance with me!" And then the four young people laughed louder than ever, to think what a queer figure the poor old doctor would cut.

"Pray excuse me," answered the doctor quietly. "I am old and rheumatic, and my dancing days were over long ago. But either of these gay young gentlemen will be glad of so pretty a partner."

"Danced with me, Clara!" cried Colonel Killigrew.

"No, no, I will be her partner!" shouted Mr. Gascoigne.

"She promised me her hand, fifty years ago!" exclaimed Mr. Medbourne.

They all gathered round her. One caught both her hands in his passionate grasp—another threw his arm about her waist—the third buried his hand among the glossy curls that clustered beneath the widow's cap. Blushing, panting, struggling, chiding, laughing, her warm breath fanning each of their faces by turns, she strove to disengage herself, yet still remained in their triple embrace. Never was there a livelier picture of youthful rivalship, with bewitching beauty for the prize. Yet, by a strange deception, owing to the duskiness of the chamber, and the antique dresses which they still wore, the tall mirror is said to have reflected the figures of the three old, gray, withered grandsires, ridiculously contending for the skinny ugliness of a shrivelled grandam.

But they were young; their burning passions proved them so. Inflamed to madness by the coquetry[18] of the girl-widow, who neither granted nor quite withheld her favors, the three rivals began to interchange threatening glances. Still keeping hold of the fair prize, they grappled fiercely at one another's throats. As they struggled to and fro, the table was overturned,

---

16. **exuberant** (eg zü′bər ənt), *adj.* abounding in health and good spirits.
17. **infirmity** (in fėr′mə tē), *n.* sickness, illness.
18. **coquetry** (kō′kə trē), *n.* flirting.

and the vase dashed into a thousand fragments. The precious Water of Youth flowed in a bright stream across the floor, moistening the wings of a butterfly, which, grown old in the decline of summer, had alighted there to die. The insect fluttered lightly through the chamber, and settled on the snowy head of Dr. Heidegger.

EVALUATE: Are the four friends behaving the way you would expect them to behave? Explain.

"Come, come, gentlemen!—come, Madam Wycherly," exclaimed the doctor, "I really must protest against this riot."

They stood still and shivered; for it seemed as if gray Time were calling them back from their sunny youth, far down into the chill and darksome vale of years. They looked at old Dr. Heidegger, who sat in his carved arm-chair, holding the rose of half a century, which he had rescued from among the fragments of the shattered vase. At the motion of his hand, the four rioters resumed their seats; the more readily, because their violent exertions had wearied them, youthful though they were.

"My poor Sylvia's rose!" ejaculated Dr. Heidegger, holding it in the light of the sunset clouds; "it appears to be fading again."

And so it was. Even while the party were looking at it, the flower continued to shrivel up, till it became as dry and fragile as when the doctor had first thrown it into the vase. He shook off the few drops of moisture which clung to its petals.

"I love it as well thus as in its dewy freshness," observed he, pressing the withered rose to his withered lips. While he spoke, the butterfly fluttered down from the doctor's snowy head, and fell upon the floor.

His guests shivered again. A strange chilliness, whether of the body or spirit they could not tell, was creeping gradually over them all. They gazed at one another, and fancied that each fleeting moment snatched away a charm, and left a deepening furrow where none had been before. Was it an illusion? Had the changes of a lifetime been crowded into so brief a space, and were they now four aged people, sitting with their old friend, Dr. Heidegger?

"Are we grown old again, so soon?" cried they, dolefully.

In truth they had. The Water of Youth possessed merely a virtue more transient than that of wine. The delirium which it created had effervesced away. Yes! they were old again. With a shuddering impulse, that showed her a woman still, the widow clasped her skinny hands before her face, and wished that the coffin lid were over it, since it could be no longer beautiful.

"Yes, friends, ye are old again," said Dr. Heidegger, "and lo! the Water of Youth is all lavished on the ground. Well—I bemoan it not; for if the fountain gushed at my very doorstep, I would not stoop to bathe my lips in it—no, though its delirium were for years instead of moments. Such is the lesson ye have taught me!"

But the doctor's four friends had taught no such lesson to themselves. They resolved forthwith to make a pilgrimage to Florida, and quaff at morning, noon, and night from the Fountain of Youth.

After Reading

Making Connections

Shaping Your Response

1. Do you agree or disagree with Dr. Heidegger's decision about using the water from the Fountain of Youth?

2. Would you have been willing to take part in Dr. Heidegger's experiment if he asked you to participate? Why or why not?

Analyzing the Story

3. Make a chart contrasting the words and phrases used to describe the four friends before and during the experiment.

	Before	During
All		
Mr. M.		
Col. K.		
Mr. G.		
Widow W.		

4. How does Dr. Heidegger's reaction to the results of the experiment differ from the reaction of his friends?

5. How does the **setting** foreshadow the events that take place?

6. Why do you suppose Dr. Heidegger wanted to establish rules of behavior before he began the experiment?

Extending the Ideas

7. Dr. Heidegger was an observer, not a participant. How do you think the story might change if he, too, had drunk the water?

8. Along with the difficulties aging can bring, there are many benefits. With a group, brainstorm a list of ten possible benefits of being an older person.

Literary Focus: Foreshadowing

The author of "Dr. Heidegger's Experiment" uses **foreshadowing** to create suspense and to help the reader accept the unrealistic idea of a fountain of youth as plausible. Write two or three paragraphs identifying and explaining instances of foreshadowing in this story. Cite quotations from the text to support your statements.

mendicant
infirmity
visage
obscure
veracious
massive
infamous
coquetry
gentry
crimson
imbibe
eccentricity
cordial
exuberant
buxom

Vocabulary Study

Fifteen words from the story have been paired with other words. Decide if the pairs of words are synonyms or antonyms. Be prepared to explain your answer.

1. mendicant – beggar
2. infirmity – health
3. visage – face
4. obscure – prominent
5. veracious – truthful
6. massive – huge
7. infamous – notorious
8. coquetry – flirting
9. gentry – commoners
10. crimson – red
11. imbibe – drink
12. eccentricity – oddity
13. cordial – stimulating
14. exuberant – depressed
15. buxom – scrawny

Expressing Your Ideas

Writing Choices

Writer's Notebook Update Did Dr. Heidegger's experiment turn out the way he thought it would? Write up the results of the experiment. Write a conclusion for the lab report in which you summarize the results of the experiment and compare its observed results with the hypothesis you made before the experiment was begun.

Say "No" to H$_2$O Dr. Heidegger's friends told everyone they knew about the marvelous experience they had. The doctor has been deluged with requests for the water, and he has decided to go into seclusion. Imagine that you are Dr. Heidegger and write a **letter** to post on your office door explaining why you will not repeat the experiment.

Other Options

Mirror, Mirror, on the Wall According to the narrator, the mirror on Dr. Heidegger's wall reflected the aged bodies of the four people in the story even though they looked youthful in person during the experiment. Choose either Mr. Medbourne, Colonel Killigrew, Mr. Gasciogne, or the Widow Wycherly and make an **illustration** of him or her looking into the mirror during the experiment.

Youth for Sale Imagine that Dr. Heidegger's friends have found the Fountain of Youth, and Mr. Medbourne wants to bottle the water and sell it. Working with a group, plan a marketing campaign. Choose a name for the product, then produce a **television commercial** on videotape.

Romantic Truths and Terrors

An Appetite for Fright

Pop Culture Connection

Eerie tales and horror stories like those of Irving, Poe, and Hawthorne have long been a popular form of entertainment. When motion pictures were invented in the 1890s, horror stories were among the first films to be produced. The films pictured here represent some of the types of horror that have thrilled movie goers. On pages 288-289, a modern master of the horror story, Stephen King, talks about why this type of fiction remains popular.

This house may seem innocent enough, but in Psycho (1960), nothing is as it first appears. In this classic thriller, like many other Hitchcock films, subtle details and plot twists keep audiences on the edge of their seats. When you take a closer look, what subtleties of the house and its surroundings contribute to its ominous atmosphere?

The producer of Creature from the Black Lagoon (1954) borrowed the swamp idea from previous Frankenstein and mummy movies. This film about a lovelorn half-man half-fish may be light on plot, but the special effects earned it a loyal following at the time. Do you think audiences today would find it as appealing? Why or why not?

INDESCRIBABLE... INDESTRUCTIBLE! NOTHING CAN STOP IT!

THE BLOB

STEVEN McQUEEN

ANETA CORSEAUT · EARL ROWE

PRODUCED BY JACK H. HARRIS · IRVIN S. YEAWORTH, JR. · THEODORE SIMONSON AND KATE

The Blob *(1958) was one of many space-age creature features that flourished in the fifties and sixties. This story of shapeless goo from outer space that absorbed everything in its path was so popular that it spawned a sequel called* Son of the Blob. *Why do you think there was such a fascination with space aliens during this era?*

FRIGHT

Released in 1986, Friday the 13th Part VI was one in a long series of Friday the 13th movies that started in 1980. These extremely violent slasher films ushered in, along with others, what critics have called a "depressing trend in American films." How is the horror portrayed in these movies different from earlier films?

JASON LIVES

FRIDAY THE 13TH PART VI

KILL OR BE KILLED

This climactic scene from King Kong (1933) depicts the gigantic gorilla battling airplanes high above New York City. In reality, most scenes were shot using a 16 inch-high model that was filmed against special backdrops. What other special effects tricks have been used to bring horror to life on film?

What's on the Other Side of the Door?

from **Danse Macabre**
STEPHEN KING

I want to say something about imagination purely as a tool in the art and science of scaring people. The idea isn't original with me; I heard it expressed by William F. Nolan at the 1979 World Fantasy Convention. Nothing is so frightening as what's behind the closed door, Nolan said. You approach the door in the old, deserted house, and you hear something scratching at it. The audience holds its breath along with the protagonist as she or he (more often she) approaches that door. The protagonist throws it open, and there is a ten-foot-tall bug. The audience screams, but this particular scream has an oddly relieved sound to it. "A bug ten feet tall is pretty horrible," the audience thinks, "but I can deal with a ten-foot-tall bug. I was afraid it might be a *hundred* feet tall." . . .

Bill Nolan was speaking as a screenwriter when he offered the example of the big bug behind the door, but the point applies to all media. What's behind the door or lurking at the top of the stairs is never as frightening as the door or the staircase itself. And because of this, comes the paradox: the artistic work of horror is almost always a disappointment. It is the classic no-win situation. You can scare people with the unknown for a long, long time (the classic example, as Bill Nolan also pointed out, is the Jacques Tourneur film with Dana Andrews, *Curse of the Demon*), but sooner or later, as in poker, you have to turn your down cards up. You have to open the door and show the audience what's behind it. And if what happens to be behind it is a bug, not ten but a hundred feet tall, the audience heaves a sigh of relief (or utters a scream of relief) and thinks, "A bug a hundred feet tall is pretty horrible, but I can deal with that. I was afraid it might be a *thousand* feet tall." . . .

The *danse macabre* is a waltz with death. This is a truth we cannot afford to shy away from. Like the rides in the amusement park which mimic violent death, the tale of horror is a chance to examine what's going on behind doors which we usually keep double-locked. Yet the human imagination is not content with locked doors. Somewhere there is another dancing partner, the imagination whispers in the night—a partner in a rotting

The theme of horror is not limited to books and films— it also shows up in fine art, such as this painting, That Which I Should Have Done I Did Not Do (1931-41) by American artist Ivan Albright. What techniques does Albright use to create a feeling of dread?

ball gown, a partner with empty eye sockets, green mold growing on her elbow-length gloves, maggots squirming in the thin remains of her hair. To hold such a creature in our arms? Who, you ask me, would be so mad? Well . . . ?

"You will not want to open this door," Bluebeard tells his wife in the most horrible of all horror stories, "because your husband has forbidden it." But this, of course, only makes her all the more curious . . . and at last, her curiosity is satisfied.

"You may go anywhere you wish in the castle," Count Dracula tells Jonathan Harker, "except where the doors are locked, where of course you will not wish to go." But Harker goes soon enough.

And so do we all. Perhaps we go to the forbidden door or window willingly because we understand that a time comes when we must go whether we want to or not . . . and not just to look but to be pushed through. Forever.

Responding

1. How is reading a scary book different from watching a scary movie? Which do you prefer?

2. Which of the selections you read would translate best into a horror movie? Why?

3. Do you agree with King's explanation of the continuing appeal of horror in films and literature?

Health Connection

Horror has a reputation of being somehow less than respectable. Yet some health experts believe that horror, in moderate doses, might actually be good for you! Read the following article, and decide whether you agree.

The Thrill of Chills

by Ellen Blum Barish

Does the idea of riding a roller coaster at an amusement park excite you or terrify you? How about watching Freddy Krueger in *Nightmare on Elm Street* in a dark theater? Do you ever pick up a Stephen King novel, or do you stick with drama and romance?

Lots of teens say there is nothing like a good scare from the thrill of an amusement park ride or a tense moment from a horror story. In fact, there are so many who think so, that the "chill industry" is doing very well, thank you.

According to a recent survey of young people age 10 to 13, 89 percent had seen at least one movie in the *Friday the 13th* or *Nightmare on Elm Street* series; 62 percent had seen at least four of them. *Friday the 13th* grossed a total of $200 million dollars. Horror fans have made horror writer Stephen King a millionaire many times over.

In spite of the evidence showing that the chill industry is anything but frozen, there are people who would rather stay far away from scary rides and hold-your-breath movies. But, is one approach better than the other? Is seeking chills a healthy pursuit for teens?

Experts say yes . . . and no. For example, going to a horror movie is experiencing a safe and some-times much-needed escape, says horror critic Douglas E. Winter. "We love to see something so grotesque and unexpected that it makes us scream or laugh . . . secure in the knowledge that in the fun house of fear, such behavior is not only accepted but encouraged," Winter wrote in 1985, the year he published a book of interviews with horror writers called *The Faces of Fear*.

"Every horror story," Winter writes, "has a happy ending. We have a simple escape—we can just wake up and say it was all a dream."

The "dream" can also be a way of preparing for life, according to Dr. Lenore Terr, a San Francisco child psychologist. Dr. Terr says that going to a hor-ror movie or riding a roller coaster can help us feel in control. "It is a way for us to confront our fears," Dr. Terr says, "and gain mastery over our feelings."

There is a feeling of reassurance, notes Dr. Terr, "when you come out (of the movie) alive." . . .

But there is a downside to too much chill seeking. Long-term viewing of the creep shows and horror flicks may lead to violent or aggressive behavior in some young people, says a 1990 American Academy of Pediatrics statement.

Other experts point out that too much horror movie watching or roller coaster riding is like too much of anything—unhealthy—and can keep a teen from experiencing a variety of other activities. . . . Chill seekers should keep in mind that the chill seeking is a temporary, fun, thrill-like experience. . . .

Almost everyone is afraid of something, even if it isn't ghostly. You may steer clear of roller coasters but enjoy in-line skating because it's fast. Or you may change the TV channel if a horror movie comes on but not fear jumping from the high diving board at the pool.

It's healthy to try new things every once in a while—like taking a well-thought-out risk. It's worth finding out what you like, what you dislike, and what you want to avoid. A good scare now and then can help you sort out those feelings.

Responding

1. Do you agree that reading or viewing horror stories can, in moderation, be healthy for you? Explain your answer.

Language History

The Language of Gothic Horror

 The entire surface of this metallic enclosure was rudely daubed in all the hideous and repulsive devices to which the charnel superstitions of the monks has given rise.

In his description of the walls of the torture chamber in "The Pit and the Pendulum," Edgar Allan Poe uses words—such as *hideous, repulsive,* and *charnel*—that create the strange and menacing atmosphere of Gothic fiction. The word *Gothic*, meaning "medieval," was used in the 1700s to described overly dramatic or poorly written works. Later it was used to describe a literary genre that began with Horace Walpole's *The Castle of Otranto* (1764), set in a medieval castle complete with underground passages, trap doors, dark stairways, and mysterious rooms.

Walpole's enormously popular novel began the fashion for strange tales full of weird landscapes, haunted ruins, sinister noblemen, and innocent heroines. Although Gothic novels were not considered good literature, they were a big hit and the genre has thrived for centuries, influencing many American writers, from Poe and Hawthorne to H. P. Lovecraft and Stephen King. In addition to employing exotic words such as *macabre, spectral,* and *eldritch,* Gothic horror shares several common characteristics that set it apart from other kinds of fiction:

- The settings are usually eerie and threatening.

- The plots often involve a fair maiden who is pursued by an evil villain.

- They sometimes involve encounters with otherworldly characters who defy natural laws.

- Inanimate objects often take on mysterious powers.

- There is an atmosphere of fear and dread that evil will prevail over good.

- The main character is at risk of going mad from the extreme pressures of the threatening situation.

Writing Workshop

Writing in Style

Assignment After reading stories by Poe and Hawthorne, you know that each author has his own distinctive style. Now see if you can imitate one of these author's styles.

WRITER'S BLUEPRINT

Product	A scene from a story
Purpose	To explore the ominous side of American Romanticism through the styles of Poe and Hawthorne
Audience	People who are familiar with Poe and Hawthorne
Specs	As the writer of a successful paper, you should:

❏ Analyze the style of "The Pit and the Pendulum" and "Dr. Heidegger's Experiment." Imitate the style of one of these authors in a scene from a story of your own. Set your scene in modern times with your own original plot and characters.

❏ Take care not to copy anything directly, but to imitate your author's style so skillfully that your audience will recognize your source.

❏ Use the technique of contrast to help develop mood.

❏ Follow the rules of grammar, usage, mechanics, and spelling. Take special care to avoid spelling mistakes in which you use too few letters.

 PREWRITING

style (stīl), *n.* characteristic way in which a writer uses language.

Analyze style. To imitate Poe or Hawthorne, you'll first need to examine their work closely. To get started, look at the Literary Source.

Notice how Poe uses a semicolon to combine sentences—he does this often. These and other observations about Poe's style are noted in the chart below. You'll find that they hold true for Poe's other stories as well.

Poe—"The Pit and the Pendulum"

Elements of Style	Observations	Examples
Sentence structure (length, variety)	—uses semicolons to combine sentences —likes exclamations	"My eyes followed its outward . . . unspeakable!"
Vocabulary	—lots of long, physical modifiers	—spasmodically,
Imagery	—shows people in the grip of terror	—"Still I quivered in every nerve . . ."
Figurative language		

LITERARY SOURCE
"My eyes followed its outward or upward whirls with the eagerness of the most unmeaning despair; they closed themselves spasmodically at the descent, although death would have been a relief, oh! how unspeakable! Still I quivered in every nerve . . ."
from "The Pit and the Pendulum" by Edgar Allan Poe

Use a chart like this one to analyze the Poe and Hawthorne selections. Then decide which author's style you'd rather work with.

Brainstorm scene ideas. With a group of people who've chosen the same author as you, discuss ideas for a scene. Remember that your scene will be set in today's world, and that the plot and characters will be your own original creations.

OR . . .
Look through more stories by these authors. Check to see that your observations hold true for them as well, and add new observations to your chart.

Plan your scene by making notes on the setting, characters, action, dialogue, and mood. For tips on creating a strong mood, see the Revising Strategy on page 294.

  DRAFTING

Before you draft, review the Writer's Blueprint, your style chart, and writing plan.

As you draft, here are some things to keep in mind.

- Remember that you're imitating the author's style only. The plot and characters must be your own original creations.

- Use vivid verbs to make the action come alive for the reader.

Ask a **partner** for comments on your draft before you revise it.

✔ Have I imitated the author's style successfully?

✔ Have I developed a strong mood?

— Revising Strategy —

Using Contrast to Develop Mood

Contrast is one technique that writers use to develop a mood. In the Literary Model, notice how Hawthorne contrasts images of old age with images of youth to create a mood of miraculous joy and exhilaration. In the Student Model below, notice how the writer used contrast to help develop a mood of doom. Can you tell which author this writer is imitating?

Was this then to be my ironical fate? Was I, a fisherman, to be put to death in the depths of the very ocean from which I had made my living? My wrists wriggled and squirmed in the padlocked chains like nightcrawlers on a hook; in two parallel column's, bubbles from my *black and murky* nostrils, life! rose from the depths to which I had plummeted, escaping ever upward toward the *brilliant sunlit* surface of the sea.

STUDENT MODEL

STEP 4 EDITING

Ask a **partner** to review your revised draft before you edit. When you edit, look for errors in grammar, usage, spelling, and mechanics. In addition, check for spelling errors that come from leaving certain letters out of words.

Editing Strategy

Using Too Few Letters

If you don't hear certain letters when you pronounce a word, you may misspell it. Practice saying each word below carefully, being sure to pronounce the underlined part. Look for mistakes with words like these when you edit your work.

prob<u>ab</u>ly   fav<u>o</u>rite   des<u>pe</u>rate   dif<u>fe</u>rent

as<u>pi</u>rin   re<u>mem</u>bered   temp<u>e</u>rature   sep<u>a</u>rate

STEP 5 PRESENTING

Here are some suggestions for presenting your narrative.

- Have a Poe/Hawthorne imitator contest. Appoint a panel of judges to decide who did the best job, and present the winners with certificates.

- Turn your scene into a radio play with music and sound effects.

STEP 6 LOOKING BACK

Self-evaluate. What grade would *you* give your paper? Look back at the Writer's Blueprint and give yourself a score for each point, from 6 (superior) down to 1 (inadequate).

Reflect. What have you learned about the ominous side of American Romanticism and about the writer's craft from doing this assignment? Write responses to these questions.

✔ From looking at the styles, characters, and plots of Poe and Hawthorne, what sorts of conclusions could you draw about the society in which they lived?

✔ In the future, when people look back on literature, movies, and television shows of the 1990s, what are some conclusions you think they will draw about our society?

For Your Working Portfolio Add your narrative and your reflection responses to your working portfolio.

Beyond Print

Looking at Horror Movies

America's fascination with horror continues unabated in the forms of books, movies, and television. Why do so many of us find horror movies so fascinating? How do directors of horror movies use film techniques to create fear that is real enough to scare an audience, but entertaining enough to keep them coming back?

Elements of Horror Films

Here are some of the film techniques which are used in horror movies to create the scary effects:

Composition The term refers to the people, places, and objects that are seen within the camera shot. In horror films, a typical composition shows a powerless victim with a menacing force framing and dominating the victim.

Movement In horror movies, cameras typically move slowly through rooms revealing objects that may or may not be important or deadly. Whether a camera is tracking a soon-to-be victim or is showing the point of view of the killer, the slow, methodical movement keeps the viewer in suspense and fear.

Editing This is the process of cutting images and scenes and merging them with others. In a murder scene, you may see a knife, then a screaming face, then dripping blood, then the knife again. The murder will appear to happen quickly with several images spliced together to create an intense and disturbing impact.

Sound Often it is the absence of sound in a horror film that is terrifying as a victim is being stalked. Or it is the grating music that will precede a murder. And, of course, screams in horror movies are a work of art.

Color and Lighting Darkness and shadow are common in horror movies. But when the moment arrives to see the monster, filmmakers frequently use lighting from below, casting a ghastly light on the lower parts of the face, the chin, the lips, the nose.

Make-up Horror films are known for their creative use of life-like make-up and masks to create frightening creatures. Make-up and masks such as the ones used for Freddy Krueger in the *Nightmare on Elm Street* movies can take hours to apply.

Technology Many horror films today are made with technological help such as morphing techniques (transforming faces or objects) and computer animation. One of the most dramatic uses of computer-generated morphing thus far occurs in *Terminator II,* in which Arnold Schwartzenegger morphs through prison bars, into other people, and even shatters into hundreds of pieces.

Close-up on a Master of Horror

Today's scariest movies rely heavily on techniques created by an earlier generation of horror film directors. Among the greatest of these is Alfred Hitchcock, considered a master of suspense. One of his many well-known films is *The Birds,* released in 1963, in which Hitchcock made his viewers terrified of creatures that surround us unnoticed all the time—birds. The movie starts like a romantic comedy and just as the viewer relaxes, Hitchcock unleashes his killer birds.

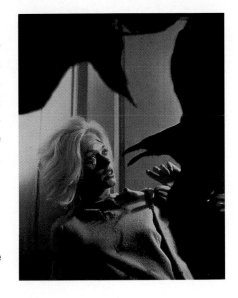

Look closely at the film still from *The Birds*.

- How does this picture make a viewer feel trapped?

- How does the lighting in this picture work to create a sense of fear?

Activity Options

The Next Frame What is happening in the frame pictured from *The Birds,* and what do you think happens next in the movie? Draw one or two frames that show what you think happens next.

You're the Director Plan a scene for a horror movie. What will your topic be? What kinds of lighting and sound will you use? Will you use computer animation to enhance your scene? Describe your horror scene in a paragraph or two, including directions for how you would create the affect you want to achieve.

HISTORICAL OVERVIEW

In the first half of the 1800s, tension grew between the free states of the North and the Southern slave states. Slave owners feared that as western territories became states, the free states would outnumber the slave states. Opposition to slavery in the West grew, and so did the South's fear of becoming a minority in the national government. The delicate balance between North and South was finally broken when Abraham Lincoln, a candidate from Illinois who opposed the expansion of slavery, was elected President in 1860. A month after the election, Southern states began seceding from the union. The rebel states formed their own government, called the Confederacy. The North refused to recognize the Confederacy and a civil war began. It cost four years of struggle and over 600,000 American lives to make the United States one nation again.

Northerners like Daniel Webster (top) argued that federal power was supreme over the states. Southerners like John C. Calhoun (bottom) believed states could ignore federal laws they opposed.

War

$1200 TO **1250 DOLLARS!** FOR NEGROES!!

THE undersigned wishes to purchase a large lot of NEGROES for the New Orleans market. I will pay $1200 to $1250 for No. 1 young men, and $850 to $1000 for No. 1 young women. In fact I will pay more for likely

NEGROES,

Than any other trader in Kentucky. My office is adjoining the Broadway Hotel, on Broadway, Lexington, Ky., where I or

By the 1850s the North's industrial economy (top) was thriving due to cheap labor and new technology. The South's farming economy (bottom), based on staples like cotton, grew more slowly, chiefly enriching plantation owners.

The 1852 novel Uncle Tom's Cabin by Harriet Beecher Stowe (top) on the horrors of slavery fueled Northern antislavery feeling. Many white Southerners didn't own slaves (bottom), but most believed that freeing them would destroy their society.

Key Dates

1793
Eli Whitney invents the cotton gin.

1820
The Missouri Compromise preserves the balance of slave and free states.

1852
Uncle Tom's Cabin is published.

1859
John Brown attacks Harpers Ferry.

1861
Confederate troops fire on Fort Sumter and the Civil War begins.

1863
January 1
Lincoln's Emancipation Proclamation frees slaves in rebel states.

July 1–3
Battle of Gettysburg is fought.

November 19
Lincoln delivers Gettysburg Address.

1865
April 9
Lee surrenders at Appomattox.

April 14
Lincoln is assassinated.

Part Two

The Civil War

Few people, North or South, believed the Civil War would last long. But what began as an effort by the North to preserve the Union ended four years later with fundamental and far-reaching changes to the nation. By the end of the war slavery was abolished, the Confederacy was defeated, 600,000 soldiers were dead, and the way Americans thought about their country had changed forever.

Multicultural Connection **Change** forces people to reevaluate their lives and societies. How people react to change depends to a great degree on their cultural values. In what ways do the following works reveal culturally based perspectives on the changes brought about by the Civil War?

Literature

Mary Chesnut	**The Attack on Fort Sumter** ◆ diary	.302
Abraham Lincoln	**The Gettysburg Address** ◆ speech	.304
Herman Melville	**Shiloh** *and* **The Portent** ◆ poems	.308
Ambrose Bierce	**An Occurrence at Owl Creek Bridge**	
	◆ short story	.312
Ulysses S. Grant	*from* **Personal Memoirs** ◆ memoir	.322
Robert E. Lee	**Farewell Order** ◆ historical document	.325
Frederick Douglass	*from* **What the Black Man Wants** ◆ speech	.328

Interdisciplinary Study Behind the Lines

from Behind the Blue and Gray by Delia Ray ◆ science 332
from Hospital Sketches by Louisa May Alcott ◆ history 334
from "Co. Aytch" by Sam R. Watkins ◆ history 335
from Reminiscences of My Life in Camp
      by Susie King Taylor ◆ history 336
Park Ranger Brings Civil War to Life ◆ career connection 337

Writing Workshop Expository Writing

You Are There 338

Beyond Print Technology

Electronic Research 344

Before Reading

The Attack on Fort Sumter by Mary Boykin Chesnut
The Gettysburg Address by Abraham Lincoln

Mary Boykin Chesnut
1823–1886

When it appeared war between the North and South would be inevitable, Mary Boykin Chesnut's husband James was the first Southern senator to resign and return home. Chesnut's diary provides a vivid account of the Confederate home front.

Abraham Lincoln
1809–1865

During the Civil War, President Abraham Lincoln was both hated and loved—to some he was a visionary, to others, a fool. His grief over the bloodshed had a profound effect on all he said and wrote, including The Gettysburg Address.

Building Background

Sumter and Gettysburg President Lincoln once said that all the hardships he endured in his life were nothing compared to the anxiety he felt about Fort Sumter. When South Carolina seceded from the Union in 1860, its government demanded that Fort Sumter on the Charleston Harbor be given up to the Confederacy. The Union refused. In April 1861, Lincoln ordered a supply fleet to set sail for Fort Sumter. As the Union ships approached the city on April 12, Confederate cannons surrounding the harbor opened fire on Sumter. The American Civil War had begun.

As the attack on Fort Sumter marked the opening of Civil War hostilities, Lincoln's speech at Gettysburg might be seen as the beginning of the process of healing the nation. In November 1863, Lincoln traveled to Gettysburg to dedicate a cemetery on a battlefield where thousands of men had died. Lincoln was displeased with his own speech, calling it "a flat failure." Yet his words have been a source of inspiration for generations since.

Literary Focus

Tone is the author's attitude toward his or her subject and audience. Tone may be revealed by the author's word choice, the details included, or the arrangement of ideas and descriptions. After you've read Chesnut's and Lincoln's words, answers these four questions:

- What is Chesnut's tone?
- What does her tone reveal about her attitude toward the attack and the impending war?
- How would you describe Lincoln's tone?
- Judging from his tone, how does he feel about the Civil War?

Writer's Notebook

Watching the Attack How might a diary entry that describes an event differ from a historian's description of the same event? As you read "The Attack on Fort Sumter," write down the details that tell you this is a diary entry rather than a historical account.

The Attack on Fort Sumter

Mary Boykin Chesnut

In the following excerpts from her diary, Mary Chesnut describes the bombardment of Fort Sumter on April 12–13, 1861, the event that began the Civil War.

12th. — Anderson[1] will not capitulate.[2] Yesterday's was the merriest, maddest dinner we have had yet. Men were audaciously[3] wise and witty. We had an unspoken foreboding that it was to be our last pleasant meeting. . . .

I do not pretend to go to sleep. How can I? If Anderson does not accept terms at four, the orders are he shall be fired upon. I count four, St. Michael's bells chime out, and I begin to hope. At half past four the heavy booming of a cannon. I sprang out of bed, and on my knees prostrate I prayed as I never prayed before.

There was a sound of stir all over the house, pattering of feet in the corridors. All seemed hurrying one way. I put on my double gown and a shawl and went too. It was to the housetop. The shells were bursting. In the dark I heard a man say, "Waste of ammunition." I knew my husband was rowing a boat somewhere in that dark bay. If Anderson was obstinate,[4] Colonel Chesnut[5] was to order the fort on one side to open fire. Certainly fire had begun. The regular roar of the cannon, there it was. And who could tell what each volley accomplished of death and destruction?

The women were wild there on the housetop. Prayers came from the women and imprecations[6] from the men. And then a shell would light up the scene. Tonight they say the forces are to attempt to land. We watched up there, and everybody wondered that Fort Sumter did not fire a shot. . . .

We hear nothing, can listen to nothing: boom, boom, goes the cannon all the time. The nervous strain is awful, alone in this darkened room. "Richmond and Washington ablaze," say the papers—blazing with excitement. Why not? To us these last days' events seem frightfully great. We were all women on that iron balcony. Men are only seen at a distance now. . . .

---

1. **Anderson,** Major Robert Anderson, commander of the Federal troops at Fort Sumter.
2. **capitulate** (kə pich′ə lāt), *v.* surrender.
3. **audaciously** (ô dā′shəs lē), *adv.* bold; impudent.
4. **obstinate** (ob′stə nit), *adj.* not giving in; stubborn.
5. **Colonel Chesnut,** Mary Chesnut's husband. After the vote to secede in 1860, he joined the Confederate army.
6. **imprecation** (im′prə kā′shən), *n.* curse.

A This illustration appeared on the cover of *Harper's Weekly* in May of 1861, about a month after Fort Sumter was attacked. Does the illustration convey the same tone as Chesnut's diary? Why or why not?

13th.—Nobody has been hurt after all. How gay we were last night! Reaction after the dread of all the slaughter we thought those dreadful cannon were making. Not even a battery the worse for wear. Fort Sumter has been on fire. Anderson has not yet silenced any of our guns. So the aides, still with swords and red sashes by way of uniform, tell us. But the sound of those guns makes regular meals impossible. None of us goes to table. Tea trays pervade the corridors, going everywhere. Some of the anxious hearts lie on their beds and moan in solitary misery. Mrs. Wigfall and I solace ourselves with tea in my room. These women have all a satisfying faith. "God is on our side," they say. When we are shut in Mrs. Wigfall and I ask, "Why?" "Of course, He hates the Yankees," we are told, "You'll think that well of Him."

Not by one word or look can we detect any change in the demeanor[7] of these Negro servants. Lawrence sits at our door, sleepy and respectful, and profoundly[8] indifferent. So are they all, but they carry it too far. You could not tell that they even heard the awful roar going on in the bay, though it has been dinning in their ears night and day. People talk before them as if they were chairs and tables. They make no sign. Are they stolidly stupid? or wiser than we are; silent and strong, biding their time?

---

7. **demeanor** (di mē'nər), *n.* way a person looks and acts, manner.
8. **profoundly** (prə found'lē), *adv.* deeply felt; very greatly.

The Gettysburg

One of the bloodiest and most decisive battles of the Civil War was fought near Gettysburg, Pennsylvania, in July, 1863. In November of that year, people gathered for the dedication of a cemetery on the spot where thousands of men had died. Unlike the orator who preceded him and spoke for almost two hours, Lincoln's speech lasted only slightly more than two minutes. In his remarks, now known as the Gettysburg Address, President Lincoln emerges as a national leader deeply grieved by the tragic conflict between North and South and firmly resolved in his commitment to a better future.

Timothy O'Sullivan took this photograph of dead Union soldiers at Gettysburg. In the distance a burial detail gathers the dead. This photograph has been titled *A Harvest of Death*. Discuss why this is or is not an appropriate title for this photo. ➤

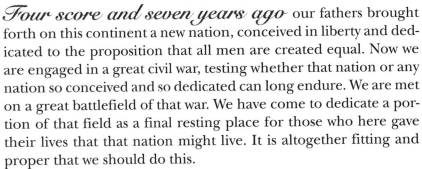

Address

November 19, 1863

Abraham Lincoln

Abraham Lincoln.

Four score and seven years ago our fathers brought forth on this continent a new nation, conceived in liberty and dedicated to the proposition that all men are created equal. Now we are engaged in a great civil war, testing whether that nation or any nation so conceived and so dedicated can long endure. We are met on a great battlefield of that war. We have come to dedicate a portion of that field as a final resting place for those who here gave their lives that that nation might live. It is altogether fitting and proper that we should do this.

But, in a larger sense, we cannot dedicate—we cannot consecrate—we cannot hallow—this ground. The brave men, living and dead, who struggled here have consecrated it far above our poor power to add or detract. The world will little note nor long remember what we say here, but it can never forget what they did here. It is for us, the living, rather to be dedicated here to the unfinished work which they who fought here have thus far so nobly advanced.

It is rather for us to be here dedicated to the great task remaining before us—that from these honored dead we take increased devotion to that cause for which they gave the last full measure of devotion; that we here highly resolve that these dead shall not have died in vain; that this nation, under God, shall have a new birth of freedom, and that government of the people, by the people, for the people shall not perish from the earth.

After Reading

Making Connections

Shaping Your Response

1. If you could speak with Mary Chesnut or Abraham Lincoln, whom would you choose, and what would you ask that person?

Analyzing the Selections

2. What would you say is Mary Chesnut's chief emotion as she writes in her diary?

3. Based on what she writes, what can you **infer** about Mary Chesnut's attitude toward slavery and about the "servants" themselves?

4. What emotional affect do you think Lincoln is trying to create with his speech?

5. What do you think is the **purpose** of the final paragraph of the Address?

Extending the Ideas

6. 👁 The issue of slavery literally tore the country in two. Is there any issue today with the power to produce such social **change?** Explain.

Vocabulary Study

**audaciously
obstinate
imprecation
demeanor
profoundly**

Using your Glossary if necessary, make a word web of synonyms for each of the listed words. An example is provided.

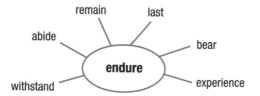

Expressing Your Ideas

Writing Choice

Writer's Notebook Update How does Mary Chesnut's account of the attack on Fort Sumter differ from what you might find if you looked up "Fort Sumter" in the encyclopedia? In your notebook, explain how Mary Chesnut's perspective is unique.

Another Option

You Are There Research the battle of Gettysburg and give an **oral report** to the class as if you were there. You may want to create a three-dimensional **topographical map** as a visual aid for describing the battle.

Before Reading

Shiloh and The Portent

by Herman Melville

Herman Melville
1819–1891

When his father went bankrupt and then died soon after, Herman Melville had to go to work when he was only 13 to help support his family. He left home at age 19, hiring on a ship as a cabin boy. His greatest works—*Moby Dick, Redburn, Typee*—are based on his travels. At age 44, Melville decided he was tired of writing and tired of traveling. He retreated to his home in New York and devoted much of his time to his correspondence and poetry. "The Portent" and "Shiloh" are from *Battle-Pieces* (1866)—a volume of poetry that Melville wrote in an attempt to speak to and reason with all parties involved in the Civil War.

Building Background

Key Players, Key Places John Brown was an abolitionist whose attempt to end slavery helped bring on the Civil War. In 1859, he and twenty-one followers stormed the United States arsenal at **Harpers Ferry,** Virginia. Brown planned to capture the arsenal and then lead his group southward, using force to abolish slavery in the South. Instead, Brown was wounded, captured, and brought to trial. Found guilty of treason, he was hanged on December 2, 1859.

Inexperienced Union and Confederate armies fought at the battle of **Shiloh** in western Tennessee on April 6–7, 1862, producing nearly 24,000 casualties. Ironically, the word "Shiloh" means "place of peace" in Hebrew.

Literary Focus

Sound Devices In both poems, Melville uses **sound devices** to establish mood. Copy the chart below in your notebook. As you read, use the chart to track examples of sound devices you find in each poem.

Sound Devices	Shiloh	The Portent
Rhyme: exact repetition of sounds in the final syllables of two or more words.		
Alliteration: the repetition of consonant sounds at the beginning of words or within words.		
Onomatopoeia: use of a word or words whose sounds imitate the sound of the thing spoken about. *Hiss, mumble, caw,* and *meow* are onomatopoeic words.		
Repetition: a sound, word, or phrase that is repeated for emphasis.		

Writer's Notebook

The Horror of War When you think of war, what words come to mind? Make a list of ten words that you associate with war. You may want to add to your list after you have finished reading the two poems.

Shiloh

A REQUIEM

Herman Melville

Skimming lightly, wheeling still,
    The swallows fly low
Over the field in clouded days,
    The forest-field of Shiloh—
5 Over the field where April rain
Solaced[1] the parched[2] ones stretched
      in pain
Through the pause of night
That followed the Sunday fight
    Around the church of Shiloh—
10 The church so lone, the log-built one,
That echoed to many a parting groan
      And natural prayer
Of dying foemen[3] mingled there—
Foemen at morn, but friends at eve—
15   Fame or country least their care:
(What like a bullet can undeceive!)
    But now they lie low,
While over them the swallows skim,
    And all is hushed at Shiloh.

---

1. solace (sol′is), v. comfort; relieve.
2. parched (pärcht), adj. hot and dry; thirsty.
3. foeman (fō′mən), n. enemy in war; adversary.

The Portent

Herman Melville

Hanging from the beam,
    Slowly swaying (such the law),
Gaunt[1] the shadow on your green,
    Shenandoah![2]
5 The cut is on the crown
    (Lo, John Brown),
And the stabs shall heal no more.

Hidden in the cap
    Is the anguish[3] none can draw;
10 So your future veils its face,
    Shenandoah!
But the streaming beard is shown
    (Weird John Brown),
The meteor[4] of the war.

---

1. gaunt (gônt), adj. very thin and bony.
2. **Shenandoah** (shen′ən dō′ə), The Shenandoah Valley is a hilly area in northern Virginia, and is drained by the Shenandoah River.
3. anguish (ang′gwish), n. great suffering.
4. **meteor** (mē′tē ər), n. falling star; shooting star. Meteors were traditionally believed to be omens of disasters to come.

How does Thomas Hovenden's 1884 painting, *The Last Moments of John Brown*, depict this famous man? As a hero? a criminal? a madman? a martyr? How does the poem depict him? ➤

After Reading

Making Connections

Shaping Your Response

1. Which of the two Civil War poems—"The Portent" or "Shiloh"—do you think better captures the violence of this era? Why?

Analyzing the Poems

2. Based on your reading of the two poems, what would you say is Melville's attitude toward war?

3. What do you think the swallows **symbolize** in "Shiloh"?

4. Why do you think Melville employs **repetition** of the word *Shenandoah* in "The Portent"?

Extending the Ideas

5. John Brown's beliefs were in contrast to a large portion of the population. What individual today might be compared to him? Explain.

Literary Focus: Sound Devices

In groups of three or four, discuss the examples of **sound devices** you found, and decide how you think the sound devices contribute to the overall feel of each poem.

Vocabulary Study

Look back at the poems and use your Glossary if necessary to answer each of the questions.

gaunt
anguish
solace
parched
foeman

1. What does a *gaunt* person look like?

2. What does someone in *anguish* feel?

3. How did the April rain *solace* the soldiers?

4. How can the soldiers overcome being *parched*?

5. What is a synonym for *foeman*?

Expressing Your Ideas

Writing Choice

Writer's Notebook Update Try writing a short poem of your own about the Civil War or a more recent conflict. To help you get started, review the list of words that you made before reading the poems.

Another Option

Emotion Through Music Choose a musical work that could be played as accompaniment to an oral reading of the poems. Find a recording of the work, and do a **dramatic reading** of the poems for your class. Explain your choice of music.

Before Reading

An Occurrence at Owl Creek Bridge

by Ambrose Bierce

Ambrose Bierce
1842–1914?

Ambrose Bierce was born into a large, poverty-stricken family. Bierce had little education, having had to quit school at a young age and go to work. When the Civil War broke out, Bierce enlisted, fought bravely in some of the bloodiest battles, and was repeatedly promoted. After the war, Bierce began writing short satiric pieces for a San Francisco weekly. At the age of 71, after years of being a journalist and fiction writer, he left to cover the Mexican revolution and disappeared, never to return.

Building Background

Bitter Bierce During the Civil War, Bierce served with honor in the 9th Indiana Infantry. He twice risked his life by rescuing fallen companions from the battlefield and was himself severely wounded at Kenesaw Mountain. Bierce's brutal war experiences intensified his naturally gloomy temperament. Known as "Bitter Bierce," he wrote many tales of death, dying, and the supernatural. In "An Occurrence at Owl Creek Bridge," he examines one man's reaction to the knowledge he is about to die. For this well-known death scene, Bierce creates a dimension in which reality is heightened, time is rearranged, and the dream life of the imagination is woven into physical events.

Literary Focus

Flashback The opening scene of "An Occurrence at Owl Creek Bridge" is interrupted with a **flashback**—a break in the narrative—that provides information about a previous episode. As you read the story, pay attention to the flashback. What information does it provide? Why is that information essential?

Writer's Notebook

Building Suspense "An Occurrence at Owl Creek Bridge" may be one of those stories you don't want to put down, because you *have* to know how it ends. Think about books, movies, and television shows you have read and seen that were suspenseful—that kept you on the edge of your seat wanting to know what would happen next. How do the writers and producers create the **suspense**? Jot down a list of five to ten ways to build suspense in a story.

An Occurrence at Owl Creek Bridge

Ambrose Bierce

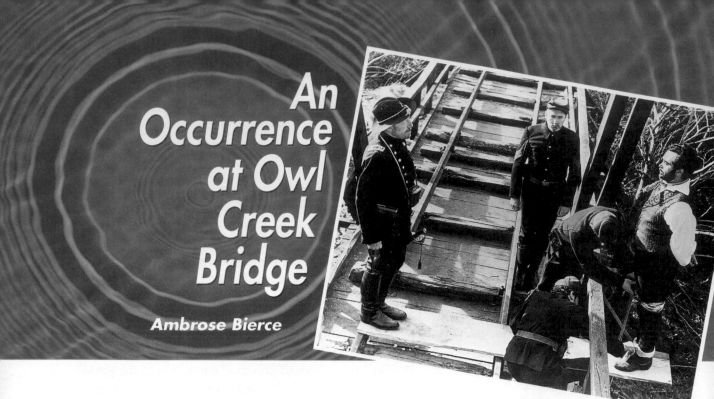

A man stood upon a railroad bridge in northern Alabama, looking down into the swift water twenty feet below. The man's hands were behind his back, the wrists bound with a cord. A rope closely encircled his neck. It was attached to a stout cross-timber above his head and the slack fell to the level of his knees. Some loose boards laid upon the sleepers supporting the metals of the railway supplied a footing for him and his executioners—two private soldiers of the Federal army, directed by a sergeant who in civil life may have been a deputy sheriff. At a short remove upon the same temporary platform was an officer in the uniform of his rank, armed. He was a captain. A sentinel at each end of the bridge stood with his rifle in the position known as "support," that is to say, vertical in front of the left shoulder, the hammer resting on the forearm thrown straight across the chest—a formal and unnatural position, enforcing an erect carriage of the body. It did not appear to be the duty of these two men to know what was occurring at the center of the bridge; they merely blockaded the two ends of the foot planking that traversed it.

Beyond one of the sentinels nobody was in sight; the railroad ran straight away into a forest for a hundred yards, then, curving, was lost to view. Doubtless there was an outpost farther along. The other bank of the stream was open ground—a gentle acclivity[1] topped with a stockade of vertical tree trunks, loopholes for rifles, with a single embrasure[2] through which protruded the muzzle of a brass cannon commanding the bridge. Midway of the slope between bridge and fort were the spectators—a single company of infantry in line, at "parade rest," the butts of the rifles on the ground, the barrels inclining slightly backward against the right shoulder, the hands crossed upon the stock. A lieutenant stood at the right of the line, the point of his sword upon the ground, his left hand resting upon his right. Excepting the group of four at the center of the bridge, not a man moved. The company faced the bridge, staring stonily, motionless. The sentinels, facing the banks of the stream, might have been statues to adorn the bridge. The captain stood with folded arms, silent, observing the work of his

---

1. **acclivity** (ə kliv′ə tē), *n.* an upward slope of ground.
2. **embrasure** (em brā′zhər), *n.* an opening in a wall for a gun, with sides that spread outward to permit the gun to fire through a greater arc.

subordinates, but making no sign. Death is a dignitary who when he comes announced is to be received with formal manifestations of respect even by those most familiar with him. In the code of military etiquette silence and fixity are forms of deference.

The man who was engaged in being hanged was apparently about thirty-five years of age. He was a civilian, if one might judge from his habit, which was that of a planter. His features were good—a straight nose, firm mouth, broad forehead, from which his long, dark hair was combed straight back, falling behind his ears to the collar of his well-fitting frock coat. He wore a mustache and pointed beard, but no whiskers; his eyes were large and dark gray, and had a kindly expression which one would hardly have expected on one whose neck was in the hemp.[3] Evidently this was no vulgar assassin. The liberal military code makes provision for hanging many kinds of persons, and gentlemen are not excluded.

The preparations being complete, the two private soldiers stepped aside and each drew away the plank upon which he had been standing. The sergeant turned to the captain, saluted and placed himself immediately behind that officer, who in turn moved apart one pace. These movements left the condemned man and the sergeant standing on the two ends of the same plank, which spanned three of the crossties of the bridge. The end upon which the civilian stood almost, but not quite, reached a fourth. This plank had been held in place by the weight of the captain; it was now held by that of the sergeant. At a signal from the former the latter would step aside, the plank would tilt and the condemned man go down between two ties. The arrangement commended itself to his judgment as simple and effective. His face had not been covered nor his eyes bandaged. He looked

a moment at his "unsteadfast footing," then let his gaze wander to the swirling water of the stream racing madly beneath his feet. A piece of dancing driftwood caught his attention and his eyes followed it down the current. How slowly it appeared to move! What a sluggish stream!

He closed his eyes in order to fix his last thoughts upon his wife and children. The water, touched to gold by the early sun, the brooding mists under the banks at some distance down the stream, the fort, the soldiers, the piece of drift-all had distracted him. And now he became conscious of a new disturbance. Striking though the thought of his dear ones was a sound which he could neither ignore nor understand, a sharp, distinct, metallic percussion like the stroke of a blacksmith's hammer upon the anvil; it had the same ringing quality. He wondered what it was, and whether immeasurably distant or nearby—it seemed both. Its recurrence was regular, but as slow as the tolling of a death knell.[4] He awaited each stroke with impatience and—he knew not why—apprehension. The intervals of silence grew progressively longer; the delays became maddening. With their greater infrequency the sounds increased in strength and sharpness. They hurt his ear like the thrust of a knife; he feared he would shriek. What he had heard was the ticking of his watch.

QUESTION: Why do you suppose the man thinks the intervals between each tick of his watch grows longer?

He unclosed his eyes and saw again the water below him. "If I could free my hands," he thought, "I might throw off the noose and spring into the stream. By diving I could evade the bullets and swimming vigorously, reach the

---

3. **hemp** (hemp), *n.* tough fibers from the hemp plant, used for rope, twine, cloth.
4. **knell** (nel), *n.* sound of a bell rung slowly after a death or at a funeral.

bank, take to the woods, and get away home. My home, thank God, is as yet outside their lines; my wife and little ones are still beyond the invader's farthest advance."

As these thoughts, which have here to be set down in words, were flashed into the doomed man's brain rather than evolved from it the captain nodded to the sergeant. The sergeant stepped aside.

SUMMARIZE: What has happened to the man up to this point?

II

Peyton Farquhar was a well-to-do planter, of an old and highly respected Alabama family. Being a slave owner and like other slave owners a politician, he was naturally an original secessionist[5] and ardently devoted to the Southern cause. Circumstances of an imperious nature, which it is unnecessary to relate here, had prevented him from taking service with the gallant army that had fought the disastrous campaigns ending with the fall of Corinth, and he chafed under the inglorious restraint, longing for the release of his energies, the larger life of the soldier, the opportunity for distinction. That opportunity, he felt, would come, as it comes to all in wartime. Meanwhile he did what he could. No service was too humble for him to perform in aid of the South, no adventure too perilous for him to undertake if consistent with the character of a civilian who was at heart a soldier, and who in good faith and without too much qualification assented to at least a part of the frankly villainous dictum that all is fair in love and war.

One evening while Farquhar and his wife were sitting on a rustic bench near the entrance to his grounds, a gray-clad soldier[6] rode up to the gate and asked for a drink of water. Mrs. Farquhar was only too happy to serve him with her own white hands. While she was fetching the water, her husband approached the dusty horseman and inquired eagerly for news from the front.

"The Yanks are repairing the railroads," said the man, "and are getting ready for another advance. They have reached the Owl Creek bridge, put it in order, and built a stockade on the north bank. The commandant has issued an order, which is posted everywhere, declaring that any civilian caught interfering with the railroad, its bridges, tunnels or trains will be summarily hanged. I saw the order."

"How far is it to the Owl Creek bridge?" Farquhar asked.

"About thirty miles."

"Is there no force on this side of the creek?"

"Only a picket post half a mile out, on the railroad, and a single sentinel at this end of the bridge."

"Suppose a man—a civilian and student of hanging—should elude the picket post and perhaps get the better of the sentinel," said Farquhar, smiling, "what could he accomplish?"

The soldier reflected. "I was there a month ago," he replied. "I observed that the flood of last winter had lodged a great quantity of driftwood against the wooden pier at this end of the bridge. It is now dry and would burn like tow."[7]

The lady had now brought the water, which the soldier drank. He thanked her ceremoniously, bowed to her husband and rode away. An hour later, after nightfall, he repassed the plantation, going northward in the direction from which he had come. He was a Federal scout.

III

As Peyton Farquhar fell straight downward through the bridge he lost consciousness and was as one already dead. From this state he was awakened—ages later, it seemed to him—by the pain of a sharp pressure upon his throat,

---

5. **secessionist** (si sesh′ə nist), *n.* a person who favored secession from the Union in 1860–1861, which resulted in the Civil War.

6. **gray-clad soldier,** Confederate soldiers wore gray uniforms.

7. **tow** (tō), *n.* the coarse, broken fibers of flax, hemp, or jute.

followed by a sense of suffocation. Keen, poignant[8] agonies seemed to shoot from his neck downward through every fiber of his body and limbs. These pains appeared to flash along well-defined lines of ramification and to beat with an inconceivably rapid periodicity. They seemed like streaks of pulsating fire heating him to an intolerable temperature. As to his head, he was conscious of nothing but a feeling of fullness—of congestion. These sensations were unaccompanied by thought. The intellectual part of his nature was already effaced;[9] he had power only to feel, and feeling was torment. He was conscious of motion. Encompassed in a luminous cloud, of which he was now merely the fiery heart, without material substance, he swung through unthinkable arcs of oscillation, like a vast pendulum. Then all at once, with terrible suddenness, the light about him shot upward with the noise of a loud plash; a frightful roaring was in his ears, and all was cold and dark. The power of thought was restored; he knew that the rope had broken and he had fallen into the stream. There was no additional strangulation; the noose about his neck was already suffocating him and kept the water from his lungs. To die of hanging at the bottom of a river!—the idea seemed to him ludicrous. He opened his eyes in the darkness and saw above him a gleam of light, but how distant, how inaccessible! He was still sinking for the light became fainter and fainter until it was a mere glimmer. Then it began to grow and brighten, and he knew that he was rising toward the surface—knew it with reluctance, for he was now very comfortable. "To be hanged and drowned," he thought, "that is not so bad; but I do not wish to be shot. No; I will not be shot; that is not fair."

He was not conscious of an effort, but a sharp pain in his wrist apprised him that he was trying to free his hands. He gave the struggle his attention, as an idler might observe the feat of a juggler, without interest in the outcome. What splendid effort!—what magnificent, what superhuman strength! Ah, that was a fine endeavor!

Bravo! The cord fell away; his arms parted and floated upward, the hands dimly seen on each side in the growing light. He watched them with a new interest as first one and then the other pounced upon the noose at his neck. They tore it away and thrust it fiercely aside, its undulations resembling those of a water snake. "Put it back, put it back!" He thought he shouted these words to his hands, for the undoing of the noose had been succeeded by the direst pang that he had yet experienced. His neck ached horribly; his brain was on fire; his heart, which had been fluttering faintly, gave a great leap, trying to force itself out at his mouth. His whole body was racked and wrenched with an insupportable[10] anguish! But his disobedient hands gave no heed to the command. They beat the water vigorously with quick, downward strokes, forcing him to the surface. He felt his head emerge; his eyes were blinded by the sunlight; his chest expanded convulsively,[11] and with a supreme and crowning agony his lungs engulfed a great draught of air, which instantly he expelled in a shriek!

He was now in full possession of his physical senses. They were, indeed, preternaturally keen and alert. Something in the awful disturbance of his organic system had so exalted and refined them that they made record of things never before perceived. He felt the ripples upon his face and heard their separate sounds as they struck. He looked at the forest on the bank of the stream, saw the individual trees, the leaves and the veining of each leaf—saw the very insects upon them: the locusts, the brilliant-bodied flies, the gray spiders stretching their webs from twig to twig. He noted the prismatic[12] colors in all the dewdrops upon a million blades

---

8. **poignant** (poi′nyənt), *adj.* very distressing; deeply felt.
9. **effaced** (ə fāsd′), *adj.* rubbed out; blotted out; wiped out.
10. **insupportable** (in′sə pôr′tə bəl), *adj.* unbearable.
11. **convulsively** (kən vul′siv lē), *adv.* in a violently disturbing way.
12. **prismatic** (priz mat′ik), *adj.* varied in color; brilliant.

An Occurrence at Owl Creek Bridge   **315**

of grass. The humming of the gnats that danced above the eddies of the stream, the beating of the dragonflies' wings, the strokes of the water-spiders' legs, like oars which had lifted their boat—all these made audible music. A fish slid along beneath his eyes and he heard the rush of its body parting the water.

He had come to the surface facing down the stream; in a moment the visible world seemed to wheel slowly round, himself the pivotal point, and he saw the bridge, the fort, the soldiers upon the bridge, the captain, the sergeant, the two privates, his executioners. They were in silhouette against the blue sky. They shouted and gesticulated, pointing at him. The captain had drawn his pistol, but did not fire; the others were unarmed. Their movements were grotesque and horrible, their forms gigantic.

Suddenly he heard a sharp report and something struck the water smartly[13] within a few inches of his head, spattering his face with spray. He heard a second report, and saw one of the sentinels with his rifle at his shoulder, a light cloud of blue smoke rising from the muzzle. The man in the water saw the eye of the man on the bridge gazing into his own through the sights of the rifle. He observed that it was a gray eye and remembered having read that gray eyes were keenest, and that all famous marksmen had them. Nevertheless, this one had missed.

A counter-swirl had caught Farquhar and turned him half round; he was again looking into the forest on the bank opposite the fort. The sound of a clear, high voice in a monotonous singsong now rang out behind him and came across the water with a distinctness that pierced and subdued all other sounds, even the beating of the ripples in his ears. Although no soldier, he had frequented camps enough to know the dread significance of that deliberate, drawling, aspirated chant; the lieutenant on shore was taking a part in the morning's work. How coldly and pitilessly—with what an even, calm intonation, presaging,[14] and enforcing tranquility in the men—with what accurately measured intervals fell those cruel words:

"Attention, company! . . . Shoulder arms! . . . Ready! . . . Aim! . . . Fire!"

Farquhar dived—dived as deeply as he could. The water roared in his ears like the voice of Niagara, yet he heard the dulled thunder of the volley and, rising again toward the surface, met shining bits of metal, singularly flattened, oscillating slowly downward. Some of them touched him on the face and hands, then fell away, continuing their descent. One lodged between his collar and neck; it was uncomfortably warm and he snatched it out.

As he rose to the surface, gasping for breath, he saw that he had been a long time underwater; he was perceptibly farther down stream—nearer to safety. The soldiers had almost finished reloading; the metal ramrods flashed all at once in the sunshine as they were drawn from the barrels, turned in the air, and thrust into their sockets. The two sentinels fired again, independently and ineffectually.

The hunted man saw all this over his shoulder: he was now swimming vigorously with the current. His brain was as energetic as his arms and legs; he thought with the rapidity of lightning.

"The officer," he reasoned, "will not make that martinet's[15] error a second time. It is as easy to dodge a volley as a single shot. He has probably already given the command to fire at will. God help me, I cannot dodge them all!"

An appalling plash within two yards of him was followed by a loud, rushing sound, *diminuendo*,[16] which seemed to travel back through the air to the fort and died in an explosion which stirred the very river to its deeps! A rising sheet of water curved over him, fell down upon him, blinded him, strangled him! The cannon had

---

13. smartly (smärt lē), *adv.* in a lively, keen way.
14. presage (pres′ij), *v.* give warning of.
15. martinet (märt′n et′), *n.* a person who upholds and enforces very strict discipline.
16. **diminuendo** (də min′yŭ en′dō), *adv.* with gradually diminishing volume.

taken a hand in the game. As he shook his head free from the commotion of the smitten water, he heard the deflected shot humming through the air ahead, and in an instant it was cracking and smashing the branches in the forest beyond.

"They will not do that again," he thought; "the next time they will use a charge of grape. I must keep my eye upon the gun; the smoke will apprise me—the report arrives too late; it lags behind the missile. That is a good gun."

Suddenly he felt himself whirled round and round—spinning like a top. The water, the banks, the forests, the now distant bridge, fort and men—all were commingled and blurred. Objects were represented by their colors only; circular horizontal streaks of color—that was all he saw. He had been caught in a vortex and was being whirled on with a velocity of advance and gyration[17] that made him giddy and sick. In a few moments he was flung upon the gravel at the foot of the left bank of the stream—the southern bank—and behind

a projecting point which concealed him from his enemies. The sudden arrest of his motion, the abrasion of one of his hands on the gravel, restored him, and he wept with delight.

CLARIFY: What helps Farquhar reach the shore?

He dug his fingers into the sand, threw it over himself in handfuls and audibly blessed it. It looked like diamonds, rubies, emeralds; he could think of nothing beautiful which it did not resemble. The trees upon the bank were giant garden plants; he noted a definite order in their arrangement, inhaled the fragrance of their blooms. A strange, roseate[18] light shone through the spaces among their trunks and the

17. **gyration** (jī rā′shən), *n.* a circular or spiral motion; whirling.
18. **roseate** (rō′zē it), *adj.* rose-colored; rosy.

wind made in their branches the music of aeolian harps.[19] He had no wish to perfect his escape—was content to remain in that enchanting spot until retaken.

A whiz and rattle of grapeshot among the branches high above his head roused him from his dream. The baffled cannoneer had fired him a random farewell. He sprang to his feet, rushed up the sloping bank, and plunged into the forest.

All that day he traveled, laying his course by the rounding sun. The forest seemed interminable;[20] nowhere did he discover a break in it, not even a woodman's road. He had not known that he lived in so wild a region. There was something uncanny in the revelation.

By nightfall he was fatigued, footsore, famishing. The thought of his wife and children urged him on. At last he found a road which led him in what he knew to be the right direction. It was as wide and straight as a city street, yet it seemed untraveled. No fields bordered it, no dwelling anywhere. Not so much as the barking of a dog suggested human habitation. The black bodies of the trees formed a straight wall on both sides, terminating on the horizon in a point, like a diagram in a lesson in perspective. Overhead, as he looked up through this rift in the wood, shone great golden stars looking unfamiliar and grouped in strange constellations. He was sure they were arranged in some order which had a secret and malign[21] significance. The wood on either side was full of singular noises, among which—once, twice, and again—he distinctly heard whispers in an unknown tongue.

His neck was in pain and lifting his hand to it he found it horribly swollen. He knew that it had a circle of black where the rope had bruised it. His eyes felt congested; he could no longer close them. His tongue was swollen with thirst; he relieved its fever by thrusting it forward from between his teeth into the cold air. How softly the turf had carpeted the untraveled avenue—he could no longer feel the roadway beneath his feet!

SUMMARIZE: What seems strange about Farquhar's surroundings?

Doubtless, despite his suffering, he had fallen asleep while walking, for now he sees another scene—perhaps he has merely recovered from a delirium. He stands at the gate of his own home. All is as he left it, and all bright and beautiful in the morning sunshine. He must have traveled the entire night. As he pushes open the gate and passes up the wide white walk, he sees a flutter of female garments; his wife, looking fresh and cool and sweet, steps down from the veranda to meet him. At the bottom of the steps she stands waiting, with a smile of ineffable[22] joy, an attitude of matchless grace and dignity. Ah, how beautiful she is! He springs forward with extended arms. As he is about to clasp her, he feels a stunning blow upon the back of the neck; a blinding white light blazes all about him with a sound like the shock of a cannon—then all is darkness and silence!

Peyton Farquhar was dead; his body, with a broken neck, swung gently from side to side beneath the timbers of the Owl Creek bridge.

---

19. **aeolian harp** (ē ō′lē ən), *n.* musical instrument consisting of a box across which strings are stretched. It is placed at open windows where the wind can produce harmonic, sweet tones.
20. **interminable** (in tėr′mə nə bəl), *adj.* unceasing; endless.
21. **malign** (mə līn′), *adj.* evil; injurious.
22. **ineffable** (in ef′ə bəl), *adj.* too great to be described in words.

After Reading

Making Connections

Shaping Your Response

1. Were you surprised by the end of the story? Why or why not?

2. Did you sympathize with Farquhar as you read the story? Explain.

Analyzing the Story

3. If you had been Bierce's editor, would you have suggested that he remove the **flashback** and tell the story in sequential order? Why or why not?

4. Decide what actually occurred in the **plot.** Which events do you think were real, and which were imagined?

5. How does the title contribute to the ambiguity of the story's **conclusion?** Explain your answer.

Extending the Ideas

6. This story is told from Farquhar's perspective. Try retelling the events from the perspective of one of the soldiers. How does the story change?

7. Think of someone you know who might enjoy reading "An Occurrence at Owl Creek Bridge." Write a note to that person, listing at least three reasons why you'd recommend this story.

Literary Focus: Flashback

A **flashback** is an interruption in the action of a story to portray an event or events that occurred at an earlier time. Think about the flashback in "An Occurrence at Owl Creek Bridge." List the events of the story in a straightforward chronological sequence. What effect is created by Bierce's arrangement of time?

Vocabulary Study

poignant
effaced
prismatic
smartly
presage
gyration
interminable
ineffable
malign
martinet

Use your Glossary if necessary to pair each of the numbered words below with its synonym or antonym from the lettered list. Write the word pairs on your paper. Then write an *A* or an *S* to indicate whether the words are antonyms or synonyms.

1. poignant
2. effaced
3. prismatic
4. smartly
5. presage

6. gyration
7. interminable
8. ineffable
9. malign
10. martinet

a. good
b. temporary
c. disciplinarian
d. rotation
e. describable

f. pleasant
g. obliterated
h. sluggishly
i. foreshadow
j. colorful

Expressing Your Ideas

Writing Choices

Writer's Notebook Update Review the list you made of ways to create suspense. Did "An Occurrence at Owl Creek Bridge" use any of them? Would you call this a suspenseful short story? Compare this story to some of the most suspenseful movies and books you've seen and read. How does it compare?

Did He Forget Something? In some ways, it feels as if there's a chunk of text missing from "An Occurrence at Owl Creek Bridge." Write an addition to Part II that describes Farquhar's attempt to destroy the railroad bridge. When you've finished, share your added **story scene** with the class.

Farquhar, Peyton Imagine that you've been assigned to write a **biographical blurb** about Peyton Farquhar to be included in an encyclopedia of fictional characters. Your space will be limited, of course, perhaps one column or less. What will you write? When you've finished, compare your entry to another student's. Is there anything you'd like to change? Make revisions and submit your final copy.

Other Options

Farquhar's Dream Reread the passage from "An Occurrence at Owl Creek Bridge" that describes Farquhar's struggles underwater. How can you best capture the surreal, or dreamlike, feeling of this scene? Paint a picture of Farquhar underwater, paying special attention to the colors you use for the background. Keep in mind that the finished **painting** should have the same dreamlike feel as the narrative.

Surreal Images A writer like Ambrose Bierce relies on words to create a surreal or dreamlike feel; an artist relies on color and form to do the same thing. Look carefully at *The Persistence of Memory* by Spanish artist Salvador Dalí. How is this painting surreal or dreamlike? In an **oral report,** compare the effect of the painting to the effect of Bierce's description of Farquhar's dream. Do they both have the same feel? Why or why not?

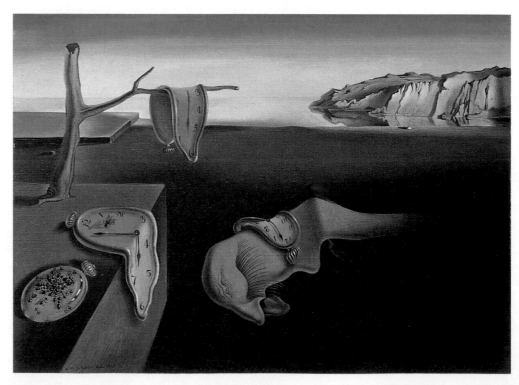

Before Reading

from Personal Memoirs of U. S. Grant by Ulysses S. Grant
Farewell Order to the Army of Northern Virginia by Robert E. Lee

Ulysses S. Grant
1822–1885

When the Civil War broke out, Grant was a clerk. Three years later, he was supreme commander of all Union armies; five years after that, he became President. His *Personal Memoirs* has become a classic of American autobiography.

Robert E. Lee
1807–1870

Robert E. Lee forms a striking contrast to his great opponent, Ulysses S. Grant. Lee was elegant, gentlemanly, and a bold risk-taker, where Grant was often shabby, gruff, and grimly methodical. Among Civil War heroes, Lee has come to represent unblemished gallantry.

Building Background

Endgame Through the latter half of 1864 and into the spring of 1865, Union general Ulysses S. Grant successfully used the North's superior numbers to wear down the forces of Confederate general Robert E. Lee. Grant's army suffered enormous losses but moved relentlessly on toward Richmond. On April 3, 1865, Union forces entered the Confederate capital and then went in pursuit of Lee's army, which was attempting to escape westward. Finding his way blocked to the west, his exhausted army without rations, Lee sent a horseman bearing a white flag. The two generals met on April 9 in the home of the McLean family in the tiny Virginia town of Appomattox Court House.

Literary Focus

Style In literature, style refers to the stamp of a writer's distinctive personality. Style is created through specific decisions involving such things as word choice, syntax, and the use of figurative language. A writer's style can be familiar or formal, lyrical or matter-of-fact. As you read the following two selections, notice how the personalities of Ulysses S. Grant and Robert E. Lee emerge through their writing.

Writer's Notebook

Face to Face As the army of the South finally surrendered, emotions were running high on both sides. As leaders, Grant and Lee set the tone for their followers. What do you think the two talked about when they met after being enemies for so long? Write a dialogue between the two leaders reflecting what you think they might have said at the surrender.

Personal Memoirs of U.S. Grant

Ulysses S. Grant

Appomattox. . . . When I had left camp that morning I had not expected so soon the result that was then taking place, and consequently was in rough garb. I was without a sword, as I usually was when on horseback on the field, and wore a soldier's blouse for a coat, with the shoulder straps of my rank to indicate to the army who I was. When I went into the house I found General Lee. We greeted each other, and after shaking hands took our seats. I had my staff with me, a good portion of whom were in the room during the whole interview.

What General Lee's feelings were I do not know. As he was a man of much dignity, with an impassible[1] face, it was impossible to say whether he felt inwardly glad that the end had finally come, or felt sad over the result, and was too manly to show it. Whatever his feelings, they were entirely concealed from my observation; but my own feelings, which had been quite jubilant[2] on the receipt of his letter, were sad and depressed. I felt like anything rather than rejoicing at the downfall of a foe who had fought so long and valiantly, and had suffered so much for a cause, though that cause was, I believe, one of the worst for which a people ever fought, and one for which there was the least excuse. I do not question, however, the sincerity of the great mass of those who were opposed to us.

General Lee was dressed in a full uniform which was entirely new, and was wearing a sword of considerable value, very likely the sword which had been presented by the State of Virginia; at all events, it was an entirely different sword from the one that would ordinarily be worn in the field. In my rough traveling suit, the uniform of a private with the straps of a lieutenant-general, I must have contrasted very strangely with a man so handsomely dressed, six feet high and of faultless form. But this was not a matter that I thought of until afterwards.

We soon fell into a conversation about old army times. He remarked that he remembered me very well in the old army; and I told him that as a matter of course I remembered him perfectly, but from the difference in our rank and years (there being about sixteen years' difference in our ages), I had thought it very likely that I had not attracted his attention sufficiently to be remembered by him after such a long interval. Our conversation grew so pleasant that I almost forgot the object of our meeting. After the conversation had run on in this style for some time, General Lee called my attention to the object of our meeting, and said that he had asked for this interview for the purpose of getting from me the terms I proposed to give his army. I said that I meant merely that his army should lay down their arms, not to take them up again during the continuance of the war unless duly and properly exchanged. He said that he had so understood my letter.

Then we gradually fell off again into conversation about matters foreign to the subject which had brought us together. This continued for some little time, when General Lee again interrupted the course of the conversation by suggesting that the terms I proposed to give his army ought to be

---

1. **impassible** (im pas′ə bəl), *adj.* not expressing feeling or emotion.
2. **jubilant** (jü′bə lənt), *adj.* joyful.

▲ *Furling the Flag* (1872) by Richard Norris Brooke shows defeated Confederate troops rolling up their flag. What five words would you use to describe the emotions presented in this painting?

written out. I called to General Parker, secretary on my staff, for writing materials, and commenced writing out the following terms:

Appomattox C. H., Va.,
Ap 19th, 1865.

Gen. R. E. Lee,
Comd'g C.S.A.

Gen: In accordance with the substance of my letter to you of the 8th inst., I propose to receive the surrender of the Army of N. Va. on the following terms, to wit: Rolls of all the officers and men to be made in duplicate. One copy to be given to an officer designated by me, the other to be retained by such officer or officers as you may designate. The officers to give their individual paroles[3] not to take up arms against the Government of the United States until properly exchanged, and each company or regimental commander sign a like parole for the men of their commands. The arms, artillery and public property to be parked and stacked, and turned over to the officer appointed by me to receive them. This will not embrace the side-arms of the officers, nor their private horses or baggage. This done, each officer and man will be allowed to return to their homes, not to be disturbed by United States authority so long as they observe their paroles and the laws in force where they may reside.

Very respectfully,
U. S. Grant,
Lt. Gen.

When I put my pen to the paper I did not know the first word that I should make use of in writing the terms. I only knew what was in my

---

3. **parole** (pə rōl′), *n.* words of honor.

mind, and I wished to express it clearly, so that there could be no mistaking it. As I wrote on, the thought occurred to me that the officers had their own private horses and effects, which were important to them, but of no value to us: also that it would be an unnecessary humiliation to call upon them to deliver their side arms.

No conversation, not one word, passed between General Lee and myself, either about private property, side arms, or kindred[4] subjects. He appeared to have no objections to the terms first proposed; or if he had a point to make against them he wished to wait until they were in writing to make it. When he read over that part of the terms about side arms, horses and private property of the officers, he remarked, with some feeling, I thought, that this would have a happy effect upon his army.

Then, after a little further conversation, General Lee remarked to me again that their army was organized a little differently from the army of the United States (still maintaining by implication[5] that we were two countries); that in their army the cavalrymen and artillerists owned their own horses; and he asked if he was to understand that the men who so owned their horses were to be permitted to retain them. I told him that as the terms were written they would not; that only the officers were permitted to take their private property. He then, after reading over the terms a second time, remarked that that was clear.

I then said to him that I thought this would be about the last battle of the war—I sincerely hoped so; and I said further I took it that most of the men in the ranks were small farmers. The whole country had been so raided by the two armies that it was doubtful whether they would be able to put in a crop to carry themselves and their families through the next winter without the aid of the horses they were then riding. The United States did not want them and I would, therefore, instruct the officers I left behind to receive the paroles of his troops to let every man of the Confederate army who claimed to own a horse or mule take the animal to his home. Lee remarked again that this would have a happy effect. . . .

The much talked of surrendering of Lee's sword and my handing it back, this and much more that has been said about it is the purest romance. The word sword or side arms was not mentioned by either of us until I wrote it in the terms. There was no premeditation,[6] and it did not occur to me until the moment I wrote it down. If I had happened to omit it, and General Lee had called my attention to it, I should have put it in the terms precisely as I acceded to the provision about the soldiers retaining their horses.

General Lee, after all was completed and before taking his leave, remarked that his army was in a very bad condition for want of food, and that they were without forage;[7] that his men had been living for some days on parched[8] corn exclusively, and that he would have to ask me for rations and forage. I told him "certainly," and asked for how many men he wanted rations. His answer was "about twenty-five thousand" and I authorized him to send his own commissary and quartermaster to Appomatox Station, two or three miles away, where he could have, out of the trains we had stopped, all the provisions wanted. As for forage, we had ourselves depended almost entirely on the country for that. . . .

When the news of the surrender first reached our lines our men commenced firing a salute of a hundred guns in honor of the victory. I at once sent word, however, to have it stopped. The Confederates were now our prisoners, and we did not want to exult over their downfall. . . .

---

4. **kindred** (kin′drid), *adj.* related.
5. **implication** (im′plə kā′shən), *n.* indirect suggestion; hint.
6. **premeditation** (prē′med ə tā′shən), *n.* previous deliberation or planning.
7. **forage** (fôr′ij), *n.* food for horses, cattle, etc.
8. **parched** (pärchd), *adj.* dried by heating.

FAREWELL ORDER
TO THE ARMY OF NORTHERN VIRGINIA

Robert. E. Lee

After four years of arduous[1] service, marked by unsurpassed courage and fortitude, the Army of Northern Virginia has been compelled to yield to overwhelming numbers and resources. I need not tell the survivors of so many hard-fought battles, who have remained steadfast to the last, that I consented to this result from no distrust of them; but feeling that valor and devotion could accomplish nothing that would compensate[2] for the loss that would have attended the continuation of the contest, I determined to avoid the useless sacrifice of those whose past services have endeared them to their countrymen.

By the terms of the agreement, officers and men can return to their homes and remain there until exchanged. You will take with you the satisfaction that proceeds from the consciousness of duty faithfully performed; and I earnestly pray that a merciful God will extend to you His blessing and protection.

With an increasing admiration of your constancy and devotion to your country, and a grateful remembrance of your kind and generous consideration of myself, I bid you an affectionate farewell.

---

1. arduous (är′jü əs), *adj.* hard to do.
2. compensate (kom′pən sāt), *v.* make an equal return.

After Reading

Making Connections

Shaping Your Response

Analyzing the Selections

Extending the Ideas

1. After reading these selections, what are your immediate impressions of Ulysses S. Grant and Robert E. Lee?

2. Grant's surrender terms for the Southern army were generous. What might have been the consequences if Grant's terms had been harsh and humiliating to the South?

3. What do you feel must have been the atmosphere of the surrender scene as reflected in these two selections?

4. In recent years, the display of symbols of the Confederacy, such as the battle flag, or the "Stars and Bars," has been debated in many American forums—from high schools to the United States Senate. Do you think that the use of the symbols of the Confederacy should be discouraged? Why or why not?

Vocabulary Study

On a separate piece of paper, use the listed words to complete the paragraph below. Use your Glossary if necessary.

impassible
jubilant
premeditation
arduous
compensate

   When the Civil War began, enthusiastic youngsters rushed off with little __(1)__ to join the armies. When the war finally ended, the soldiers were exhausted from years of harsh and __(2)__ service. When they heard the news, they may have felt __(3)__ at the thought that they could return to their homes, or they may have felt only sorrow for the many losses they had endured, losses for which nothing could possibly __(4)__ . Either way, no feelings showed in their __(5)__ faces.

Expressing Your Ideas

Writing Choice

Not Again! The Confederate surrender was negotiated in the home of the McLean family. Four years earlier, after the first battle of the war had been fought practically in their backyard, the McLeans had moved to escape the fighting. Now at its close the war revisited them. Write a **journal entry** in which one of the McLeans reflects on the war reentering their lives.

Another Option

You Are There With other students, research the surrender scene at Appomattox Court House and present a **dramatization** of what took place at the McLean House.

Before Reading

from What the Black Man Wants

by Frederick Douglass

Frederick Douglass
1817–1895

Born into slavery, Frederick Douglass knew firsthand of its horrors. In what he would later call the most important move he ever made, Douglass escaped from slavery in 1838. Free at last, he worked shoveling coal, sawing wood, as a shipyard laborer, and as a brass foundry laborer. In 1841, at a Massachusetts antislavery meeting, Douglass spoke for the first time about what freedom meant to him. From that moment on, he knew his destiny: he would speak out, at any cost, for freedom and justice for all African American people.

Building Background

Historical Notes When Abraham Lincoln signed the Emancipation Proclamation in 1862, Frederick Douglass rejoiced: "We shout for joy that we live to record this righteous decree." Douglass knew, though, that the war for freedom and justice for African Americans had barely begun. Although the Emancipation Proclamation promised that ". . . all persons held as slaves within said designated States . . . are, and henceforward shall be, free . . ." there were many who would continue to deny African Americans their rights. Douglass maintained that his people would never be treated as equals until they were granted equal rights of citizenship—especially the right to vote. Douglass began a fierce campaign for black suffrage that would outrage much of the South and give fresh hope to African American people all over the country.

Literary Focus

Figurative Language An author uses **figurative language**—words used apart from their ordinary, literal meanings—to bring freshness and emphasis to an idea. Frederick Douglass doesn't use figurative language as often as some writers, but his instances of figurative language help emphasize his arguments. As you read "What the Black Man Wants," look for three examples of figurative language.

Writer's Notebook

The Right to Vote The right to vote is something we often take for granted. Some people don't vote; others vote in an uninformed way. Why is it important to exercise the right to vote? List several reasons in your notebook.

What the Black Man Wants

Frederick Douglass

"What the Black Man Wants," excerpted here, is a speech that Frederick Douglass delivered at the annual meeting of the Massachusetts Antislavery Society in Boston, 1865.

. . . I have had but one idea for the last three years to present to the American people, and the phraseology in which I clothe it is the old Abolition phraseology. I am for the "immediate, unconditional, and universal" enfranchisement[1] of the black man, in every state in the Union. Without this, his liberty is a mockery; without this, you might as well almost retain the old name of slavery for his condition; for, in fact, if he is not the slave of the individual master, he is the slave of society, and holds his liberty as a privilege, not as a right. He is at the mercy of the mob, and has no means of protecting himself.

It may be objected, however, that this pressing of the Negro's right to suffrage is premature. Let us have slavery abolished, it may be said, let us have labor organized, and then, in the natural course of events, the right of suffrage will be extended to the Negro. I do not agree with this. The constitution of the human mind is such, that if it once disregards the conviction forced upon it by a revelation of truth, it requires the exercise of a higher power to produce the same conviction afterward. The American people are now in tears. The Shenandoah has run blood, the best blood of the North. All around Richmond, the blood of New England and of the North has been shed, of your sons, your brothers, and your fathers. We all feel, in the existence of this rebellion, that judgments terrible, widespread, far-reaching, overwhelming, are abroad in the land; and we feel, in view of these judgments, just now, a disposition[2] to learn righteousness. This is the hour. Our streets are in mourning, tears are falling at every fireside, and under the chastisement[3] of this rebellion we have almost come up to the point of conceding this great, this all-important right of suffrage. I fear that if we fail to do it now, if Abolitionists fail to press it now, we may not see, for centuries to come, the same disposition that exists at this moment. Hence, I say, now is the time to press this right.

It may be asked, "Why do you want it? Some men have got along very well without it. Women have not this right." Shall we justify one wrong by another? That is a sufficient answer. Shall we at this moment justify the deprivation[4] of the Negro of the right to vote, because some one else is deprived of that privilege? I hold that women, as well as men, have the right to vote, and my heart and my voice go with the movement to extend suffrage to woman; but that question rests upon another basis than that on which our right rests. We may be asked, I say, why we want it. I will tell you why we want it. We want it because it is our right, first of all. No class of men can, without insulting their own nature, be content with any deprivations of their rights. We want it, again, as a means for educating our race. Men are so constituted that they derive their conviction of their own possibilities largely from the estimate formed of them by others. If nothing is expected of a people, that people will find it difficult to contradict that expectation. By depriving us of suffrage, you affirm[5] our incapacity to form an intelligent

◄ What qualities or characteristics does this 1850s photograph of Frederick Douglass present?

---

1. **enfranchisement** (en fran′chīz mənt), *n.* the rights of citizenship, especially the right to vote.
2. **disposition** (dis′pə zish′ən), *n.* one's habitual ways of acting toward others or of thinking about things.
3. **chastisement** (cha stīz′mənt), *n.* punishment.
4. **deprivation** (dep′rə vā′shən), *n.* act of depriving; loss.
5. **affirm** (ə fėrm′), *v.* declare positively to be true.

judgment respecting public men and public measures; you declare before the world that we are unfit to exercise the elective franchise, and by this means lead us to undervalue ourselves, to put a low estimate upon ourselves, and to feel that we have no possibilities like other men. Again, I want the elective franchise, for one, as a colored man, because ours is a peculiar government, based upon a peculiar idea, and that idea is universal suffrage. If I were in a monarchical government, or an autocratic or aristocratic government, where the few bore rule and the many were subject, there would be no special stigma resting upon me, because I did not exercise the elective franchise. It would do me no great violence. Mingling with the mass, I should partake of the strength of the mass, and I should have the same incentives[6] to endeavor with the mass of my fellow men; it would be no particular burden, no particular deprivation; but here, where universal suffrage is the rule, where that is the fundamental idea of the government, to rule us out is to make us an exception, to brand us with the stigma[7] of inferiority, and to invite to our heads the missiles of those about us; therefore, I want the franchise for the black man. . . .

I ask my friends who are apologizing for not insisting upon this right, where can the black man look in this country for the assertion of this right, if he may not look to the Massachusetts Anti-Slavery Society? Where under the whole heavens can he look for sympathy in asserting this right, if he may not look to this platform? Have you lifted us up to a certain height to see that we are men, and then are any disposed[8] to leave us there, without seeing that we are put in possession of all our rights? We look naturally to this platform for the assertion of all our rights, and for this one especially. I understand the antislavery societies of this country to be based on two principles—first the freedom of the blacks of this country; and, second, the elevation of them. Let me not be misunderstood here. I am not asking for sympathy at the hands of Abolitionists, sympathy at the hands of any. I think the American people are disposed[8] often to be generous rather than just. I look over this country at the present time, and I see educational societies, sanitary commissions, freedmen's associations and the like—all very good: but in regard to the colored people there is always more that is benevolent, I perceive, than just, manifested towards us. What I ask for the Negro is not benevolence, not pity, not sympathy, but simple justice. The American people have always been anxious to know what they shall do with us. . . .

Everybody has asked the question, and they learned to ask it early of the Abolitionist, "What shall we do with the Negro?" I have had but one answer from the beginning. Do nothing with us! Your doing with us has already played the mischief with us. Do nothing with us! If the apples will not remain on the tree of their own strength, if they are worm-eaten at the core, if they are early ripe and disposed to fall, let them fall! I am not for tying or fastening them on the tree in any way, except by nature's plan, and if they will not stay there, let them fall. And if the Negro can not stand on his own legs, let him fall also. All I ask is, give him a chance to stand on his own legs! Let him alone! If you see him on his way to school, let him alone—don't disturb him. If you see him going to the dinner table at a hotel, let him go! If you see him going to the ballot box, let him alone—don't disturb him! If you see him going into a workshop, just let him alone—your interference is doing him a positive injury. . . . Let him fall if he can not stand alone! If the Negro can not live by the line of eternal justice, . . . the fault will not be yours; it will be his who made the Negro, and established that line for his government. Let him live or die by that. If you will only untie his hands, and give him a chance, I think he will live. . . .

---

6. **incentive** (in sen′tiv), *n.* something that urges a person on; motive.
7. stigma (stig′mə), *n.* mark of disgrace.
8. **disposed** (dis pōzd′), *adj.* inclined; willing.

After Reading

Making Connections

1. Now that you've read the speech, write the first five words that come to mind about it. Discuss your reactions as a class.

Analyzing the Speech

2. In your own words, explain Douglass's argument that suffrage for African Americans must be achieved at the same time as abolition of slavery.

3. Why does Douglass believe that the right to vote is so important?

4. What does Douglass mean when he says, "What I ask for the Negro is not benevolence, not pity, not sympathy, but simple justice"?

Extending the Ideas

5. 👆 What would Douglass's opinion be of American society today? What advice would he have about **changes** that should be made?

Literary Focus: Figurative Language

Did you spot three examples of **figurative language** in Douglass's speech? Choose one example to analyze by answering the following:

- What type of figurative language is it? Is it a metaphor? a personification? a simile?

- How does Douglass's use of figurative language bring emphasis to his ideas?

Vocabulary Study

**enfranchisement
deprivation
affirm
disposition
stigma**

All of the listed words have multiple meanings. For each word, write two sentences, one that uses the meaning Douglass used, and one that uses a different meaning. Use a dictionary if you need help.

Expressing Your Ideas

Writing Choices

Writer's Notebook Update In his speech, Douglass lists several reasons why African Americans must be given the right to vote. How do his ideas compare to the list you made in your notebook before reading the selection? Using what you've read and what you know, write a paragraph about the importance of the right to vote.

In Honor of Frederick Douglass Imagine that you are in charge of lining up speakers for an event that will honor Frederick Douglass. The speakers can be from any era, past or present. Write a **letter** of invitation to each of your speakers that explains the event.

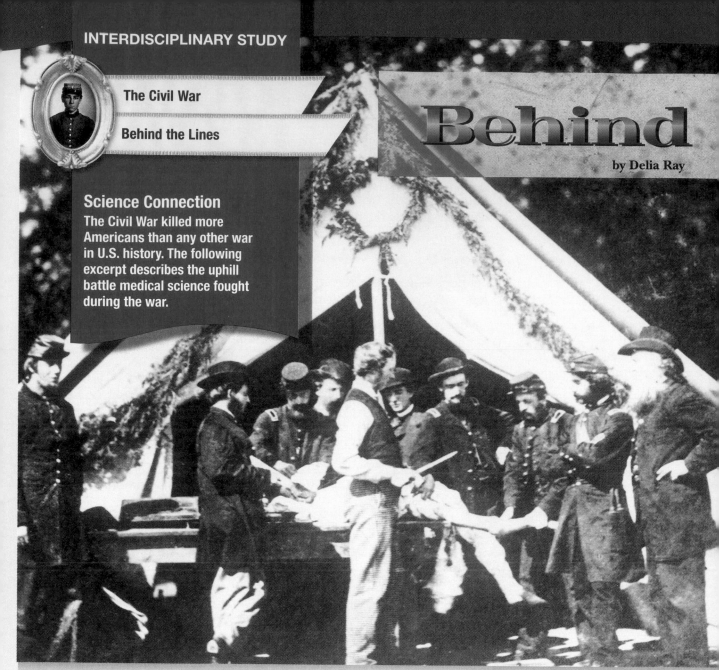

The Civil War

Behind the Lines

Behind

by Delia Ray

Science Connection
The Civil War killed more Americans than any other war in U.S. history. The following excerpt describes the uphill battle medical science fought during the war.

Most doctors during the Civil War did not know what caused the diseases that plagued thousands of soldiers. This lack of medical knowledge had deadly effects. In the Union Army, four men died of sickness for every one killed in battle. In the Confederate Army, death from disease was even more common.

Both sides were totally unprepared to take care of the ever-growing number of sick soldiers. Medical efforts were hindered not only by scientific ignorance, but by a severe shortage of hospitals, doctors, and supplies. At the beginning of the war, the U.S. Medical Department owned just twenty thermometers and no more than six stethoscopes. Neither side had guessed that their worst enemy would be invisible. Now the armies had bitter lessons to learn in the war against mysterious germs. . . .

Although the soldiers could not identify the exact causes of their ailments, they

the Blue and Gray

gradually learned that there was a definite link between dirt and disease. In the last two years of the war, sanitation improved. But not before thousands of men drank contaminated water and died from typhoid fever. Thousands more were bitten by infected mosquitoes and stricken with malaria. Of all wartime diseases, the most common was dysentery, an intestinal disorder causing severe diarrhea. In 1862, the Army of the Potomac reported that 995 out of every 1,000 men suffered from diarrhea and dysentery. . . .

The true test of the Civil War surgeon's abilities came after each battle, when hundreds of wounded soldiers were dragged into the crude, outdoor field hospitals for treatment. Here behind the bloody lines of the battlefield, the soldiers suffered the most. Some had been hit by the rifle bullets called minie balls, which splintered the bones of arms and legs like driftwood. Others had been caught in the path of cannon shells, and their wounds were deep and jagged. Tortured with pain, the soldiers often had to wait hours before a tired, overworked surgeon looked at their injuries. By this time, the dirty wounds had usually become infected. . . .

The wounded endured more misery as they watched what happened to those who reached the operating table before them. The surgeons worked in plain view—on front porches, under trees, or in open tents. Two-thirds of their cases were patients whose arms or legs were so badly mangled that they had to be removed. Using an old door or wagon boards for an operating platform, the surgeons performed these grisly amputations with factory-line speed. First, they

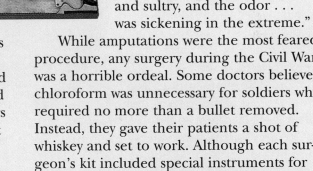

held a cloth soaked with an anaesthetic called chloroform over the patient's nose and mouth. But sometimes this drug was unavailable or simply not strong enough to put the patient to sleep. On these occasions, the surgeon ordered his assistants to hold down the squirming soldier while he pushed ahead with the operation.

Shrieks of pain rang through the woods around the outdoor hospitals. Passing soldiers who wandered over to the surgeon's tent to investigate stumbled upon a gruesome scene. As one private described: "A large hole was dug in the yard about the size of a small cellar, and into this the legs and arms were thrown as they were lopped off by the surgeons . . . The day was hot and sultry, and the odor . . . was sickening in the extreme."

While amputations were the most feared procedure, any surgery during the Civil War was a horrible ordeal. Some doctors believed chloroform was unnecessary for soldiers who required no more than a bullet removed. Instead, they gave their patients a shot of whiskey and set to work. Although each surgeon's kit included special instruments for operating on gunshot wounds, the physicians preferred the faster technique of using their fingers to probe for the bullets.

Responding
Why do you suppose the armies were so unprepared to cope with the wounded and sick soldiers?

INTERDISCIPLINARY STUDY

History Connection

On the following pages you'll read firsthand accounts by some of the people that experienced the Civil War and lived to tell their stories.

Hospital Sketches

by Louisa May Alcott

In 1862 author Louisa May Alcott, best known for her novel Little Women, *volunteered to nurse at a hospital in Washington, D.C. In this passage she recalls her first reactions to working with the wounded soldiers.*

THERE THEY WERE! "Our brave boys," as the papers justly call them, for cowards could hardly have been so riddled with shot and shell, so torn and shattered, nor have borne suffering for which we have no name, with an uncomplaining fortitude, which made one glad to cherish each as a brother. In they came, some on stretchers, some in men's arms, some feebly staggering along propped on rude crutches, and one lay stark and still with covered face, as a comrade gave his name to be recorded before they carried him away to the dead house. . . .

Presently, Miss Blank tore me from my refuge behind piles of one-sleeved shirts, odd socks, bandages and lint; put basin, sponge, towels, and a block of brown soap into my hands, with these appalling directions:

"Come, my dear, begin to wash as fast as you can. Tell them to take off socks, coats and shirts, scrub them well, put on clean shirts, and the attendants will finish them off, and lay them in bed."

If she had requested me to shave them all, or dance a hornpipe on the stove funnel, I should have been less staggered; but to scrub some dozen lords of creation at a moment's notice, was really—really—. However, there was no time for nonsense, and, having resolved when I came to do everything I was bid, I drowned my scruples in my washbowl, clutched my soap manfully, and, assuming a businesslike air, made a dab at the first dirty specimen I saw, bent on performing my task *vi et armis* (by strength and by arms) if necessary. I chanced to light on a withered old Irishman, wounded in the head, which caused that portion of his frame to be tastefully laid out like a garden, the bandages being the walks, his hair the shrubbery. He was so overpowered by the honor of having a lady wash him, as he expressed it, that he did nothing but roll up his eyes, and bless me, in an irresistible style which was too much for my sense of the ludicrous; so we laughed together, and when I knelt down to take off his shoes, he "flopped" also and wouldn't hear of my touching "them dirty craters. May your bed above be aisy darlin', for the day's work ye are doon!—Woosh! There ye are, and bedad, it's hard tellin' which is the dirtiest, the fut or the shoe." It was; and if he hadn't been to the fore, I should have gone on pulling, under the impression that the "fut" was a boot, for trousers, socks, shoes and legs, were a mass of mud. This comical tableau produced a general grin, at which propitious beginning I took heart and scrubbed away like any tidy parent on a Saturday night.

After the Battle

from "Co. Aytch" by Sam R. Watkins

Sam Watkins wrote about his experiences as a private in the Confederate Army. In the following excerpt he describes the gruesome aftermath of the Battle of Chickamauga.

We remained upon the battlefield of Chickamauga all night. Everything had fallen into our hands. We had captured a great many prisoners and small arms, and many pieces of artillery and wagons and provisions. The Confederate and Federal dead, wounded, and dying were everywhere scattered over the battlefield. Men were lying where they fell, shot in every conceivable part of the body. Some with their entrails torn out and still hanging to them and piled up on the ground beside them, and they still alive. Some with their under jaw torn off, and hanging by a fragment of skin to their cheeks, with their tongues lolling from their mouth, and they trying to talk. Some with both eyes shot out, with one eye hanging down on their cheek. In fact, you might walk over the battlefield and find men shot from the crown of the head to the tip end of the toe. . . .

We rested on our arms where the battle ceased. All around us everywhere were the dead and wounded, lying scattered over the ground, and in many places piled in heaps. Many a sad and heart-rending scene did I witness upon this battlefield of Chickamauga.

Our men died the death of heroes. I sometimes think that surely our brave men have not died in vain. It is true, our cause is lost, but a people who loved those brave and noble heroes should ever cherish their memory as men who died for them. I shed a tear over their memory. They gave their all to their country. . . .

One scene I now remember, that I can imperfectly relate. While a detail of us were passing over the field of death and blood, with a dim lantern, looking for our wounded soldiers to carry to the hospital, we came across a group of ladies, looking among the killed and wounded for their relatives, when I heard one of the ladies say, "There they come with their lanterns." I approached the ladies and asked them for whom they were looking. They told me the name, but I have forgotten it. We passed on, and coming to a pile of our slain, we had turned over several of our dead, when one of the ladies screamed out, "O, there he is! Poor fellow! Dead, dead, dead!" She ran to the pile of slain and raised the dead man's head and placed it on her lap and began kissing him and saying, "O, O, they have killed my darling, my darling, my darling! O, mother, mother, what must I do! My poor, poor darling! O, they have killed him, they have killed him!" I could witness the scene no longer. I turned and walked away, and William A. Hughes was crying, and remarked, "O, law me; this war is a terrible thing." We left them and began again hunting for our wounded. All through that long September night we continued to carry off our wounded, and when the morning sun arose over the eastern hills, the order came to march . . .

Reminiscences of My Life in Camp

by Susie King Taylor

Born into slavery in 1848, Susie King Taylor escaped at the age of fourteen and went to work for an African American regiment at Camp Saxton in Georgia. In the following excerpt she tells about the treatment of African American troops and her own experiences working with the wounded.

The first colored troops did not receive any pay for eighteen months, and the men had to depend wholly on what they received from the commissary, established by General Saxton. A great many of these men had large families, and as they had no money to give them, their wives were obliged to support themselves and children by washing for the officers of the gunboats and the soldiers, and making cakes and pies which they sold to the boys in camp. Finally, in 1863, the government decided to give them half pay, but the men would not accept this. They wanted "full pay" or nothing. They preferred rather to give their services to the state, which they did until 1864, when the government granted them full pay, with all the back pay due. . . .

While at Camp Shaw, Chaplain Fowler, Robert Defoe, and several of our boys were captured while tapping some telegraph wires. Robert Defoe was confined in the jail at Walterborough, S.C., for about twenty months. When Sherman's army reached Pocotaligo he made his escape and joined his company (Company G). He had not been paid, as he had refused the reduced pay offered by the government. Before we got to camp, where the payrolls could be made out, he sickened and died of smallpox and was buried at Savannah, never having been paid one cent for nearly three years of service. . . .

The following passage relates events after the regiment has received orders to attack Fort Gregg on James Island, South Carolina.

About four o'clock, July 2, the charge into battle was made. The first of the wounded to be brought in was Samuel Anderson of our company; then others of our boys, some with their legs off, arm gone, foot off, and wounds of all kinds imaginable. . . .

My work now began. I gave my assistance to try to alleviate their sufferings. I asked the doctor at the hospital what I could get for them to eat. They wanted soup, but that I could not get; but I had a few cans of condensed milk and some turtle eggs, so I thought I would try to make some custard. I had doubts as to my success, for cooking with turtle eggs was something new to me, but the adage has it, "Nothing ventured, nothing done," so I made a venture and the result was a very delicious custard. This I carried to the men, who enjoyed it very much. My services were given at all times for the comfort of these men. I was on hand to assist whenever needed. I was enrolled as company laundress, but I did very little of it, because I was always busy doing other things through camp, and was employed all the time doing something for the officers and comrades."

Career Connection
The Civil War continues to be an event that fascinates many Americans. Here you'll meet a man who has made a career out of America's interest in the Civil War.

Park Ranger Brings the Civil War to Life

Dennis Kelly is a Park Ranger at Georgia's Kennesaw Mountain park, the site of a famous Civil War battle.

To add a touch of authenticity to the recreation of a Civil War scene, Dennis Kelly wears a Confederate uniform instead of his ranger uniform as he shoots a cannon at Kennesaw Mountain National Battlefield Park, northwest of Atlanta. Of the park staff, he is most knowledgeable about Kennesaw Mountain, the Atlanta campaign in the Civil War, and the park itself. While he talks about events that happened more than a hundred years ago, he believes we're still living with the effects of the Civil War today.

Dennis Kelly

"The Civil War has never truly left us," Kelly explains. "It was fought over two issues, and these have never been entirely settled. One was states' rights versus federal rights. This issue was particularly important to Southerners. They wanted only a few decisions to be made by the federal government. States' rights were primary, including even the right to secede from the Union. States' rights is an issue still being contested. But today, instead of blue and gray soldiers shooting bullets at each other, politicians and voters continue the struggle.

"However much the strength of government power swings between Washington and the states, the importance of the Northern victory and the maintenance of the Union should never be taken for granted. We are one nation, indivisible. The rise of the United States to superpower status would have been impossible without a Union victory.

"The second issue was slavery. The Civil War helped to broaden the concept of freedom for all. The seed of the modern civil rights movement is in the 1776 Declaration of Independence, but the action that transformed that idea into a dynamic reality was the Civil War.

"Another legacy of the war was the modern approach to warfare by William Tecumseh Sherman, the Union general who led the march across Georgia to the sea and up through South Carolina to victory for the North. Sherman was not much interested in winning or losing battles. An army can win battles and lose a war. His contribution to Union victory was in destroying enemy morale. His capture of Atlanta in 1864 boosted the confidence of the North. The burning of Atlanta and the destructive march to the sea finished off the South's will to resist. General Sherman recognized that beyond the violence and bloodshed and destruction of armies, wars are contests between peoples' ideas, a principle that modern military leaders still hold."

Responding
Do you agree with Dennis Kelly when he says, "The Civil War has never truly left us"? Explain.

Writing Workshop

You Are There

Assignment A saturation research paper is a special kind of research report that uses both fictional and nonfictional techniques to report factual information in a vivid, dramatic manner. Write a saturation research paper on a topic of your choice that focuses on an event from the American Civil War as seen through the eyes of a person of the time.

WRITER'S BLUEPRINT

Product   A saturation research paper

Purpose   To explore in depth a topic from the American Civil War

Audience   Anyone interested in the American Civil War

Specs   To write a successful paper, you should:

❑ Saturate yourself in your topic—gather information about your person and event from every possible source: museum exhibits, battlefield sites, battle re-enactments, interviews with experts, videos, diaries, history books, magazine and newspaper articles, and online sources.

❑ Use first-person ("I") point of view to narrate your event, as if you actually were this person from the Civil War living out these moments in time.

❑ Begin by setting the scene, using strong imagery, including sights, sounds, and smells, to give your reader a vivid picture of where you are. (You might begin with a third-person introduction to set the stage for your first-person account.)

❑ Go on to narrate your event in present tense. Use imagery to keep giving the reader a vivid picture of the action as it unfolds. Take care to make smooth transitions between paragraphs.

❑ Follow the rules of punctuation, spelling, grammar, and mechanics. Make sure your facts are based on reliable sources documented in a Works Cited list.

---

1 PREWRITING

Choose a topic. Working with a small group, brainstorm potential topics. Use anything you've read or seen about the Civil War, including the literature in this part of the unit. Each topic on your list should consist of a person and an event in that person's life from the Civil War era. From the list, choose the person and event that interests you most. Here are some examples:

—Abraham Lincoln writing "The Gettysburg Address"

—a Civil War soldier fighting in a battle

—an event from the life of Harriett Tubman or Frederick Douglass

—Louisa May Alcott tending to wounded soldiers

—an escaped slave fighting with the Union Army

Put your event into perspective. Make a time line that notes historical events that occurred immediately before and after your topic event. Concentrate on events that influenced your topic event or were influenced by it. Use your time line to help guide your research.

Make a list of questions. Working alone now, ask yourself: *What do I need to find out about my topic*? Make a list of numbered questions like these and use them to guide your research.

1. What was Gettysburg like—landscape, weather, climate?

2. Who were the commanders and prominent officers?

3. What was a typical soldier of the North like?
and so on . . .

Brainstorm research sources. With your group now, make a list of sources for gathering information in your school and community, including:

• people (history teachers, librarians, video store clerks)

• places (museums, libraries, historical societies)

• titles (short stories, novels, history books, encyclopedia and magazine articles, films, videos)

Do your research. Use your questions to guide you, and be ready to add new questions as you move along.

Look for **primary sources** (material from eyewitnesses, such as letters, photos, and news accounts of the time) as well as **secondary sources**, such as history textbooks, biographies, and historical fiction.

Write down each source on a numbered **source card**. Number your sources in the order you find them. Then number each **note card** with the number of the source it comes from and the question it relates to.

As you research, look for answers to your questions.

Try a quickwrite. After completing your research, try writing for a few minutes in the voice of the person you chose. Describe what is happening around you, as if you were there, using vivid images that give a *you are there* feel to the writing. Include details about:

—sights
—sounds
—smells
—movements

If you find that you can't describe your surroundings because you don't have enough information, do some more research. Here is part of one student's quickwrite. Notice that the writer has used fragments as well as complete sentences.

> OR . . .
> Instead of writing about your surroundings, draw sketches that illustrate what you see. You might even include a sketch of yourself at the time.

It's July, 1863. Just arrived from Virginia with Lee's army. Near a tiny town in Pennsylvania—Gettysburg. A battle started when our brigade ran into Union cavalry. We were really taken by surprise. Now the battle is raging. I've never seen so many men in one battle. We're trying to get some rest tonight but it's hard to sleep. It's hot, humid. It's dark but you can still hear shooting. Explosions from the battlefield light up the sky over Cemetery Ridge. My feet are sore and swollen from marching without shoes. Tired—exhausted. Last night, bad dreams. Cannons exploding all around. The bitter smell of gunpowder. Men running screaming in all directions. Armies scattered all over the battlefield, crawling around like ants.

STUDENT MODEL

Plan the narrative. Look over your note cards and make an outline like the one shown. For each point on your outline, write phrases to remind yourself of key facts and details from your research.

I. Set the scene
   A. Introduce yourself
   B. Describe the setting
      1. sights
      2. sounds
      3. smells
      4. movements

II. Narrate the event
   A. What happened first
   B. What happened next
   and so on. . .

> **OR . . .**
> Spread out your note cards and arrange them in the order you want your research report to follow. Arrange and rearrange the note cards until you have them in a logical order to serve as your outline.

  **STEP 2 DRAFTING**

Before you draft, review your note cards, quickwrite, and writing plan as well as the Writer's Blueprint.

As you draft, concentrate on getting the events and details down on paper. The following tips may help you get started:

- Spend a few minutes getting into the voice of your first-person narrator. Visualize yourself in your surroundings as the event begins. Then start drafting by introducing yourself and describing your surroundings.

- Begin with a quotation from your research that leads you directly into the scene.

- Begin at the very end of the event or at sometime after the event has taken place, and relate things in flashback.

STEP 3 REVISING

Ask a partner for comments on your draft before you revise.

✔ Have I set the scene at the beginning?

✔ Have I narrated the event in first person?

✔ Have I made things flow with smooth transitions between paragraphs?

Revising Strategy

Making Smooth Transitions

To make writing flow for the reader, build connecting bridges from paragraph to paragraph. One way you can connect paragraphs is to repeat words, ideas, or patterns. Notice how Abraham Lincoln uses repetition of the phrase *It is for us* as a connecting pattern, in addition to repeating the word *dedicated*.

As you revise, try to build bridges between paragraphs. Notice how the two paragraphs in this revised student model flow smoothly together.

Yesterday was the worst day so far. Our troops launched a major attack. We tried to break through the Union lines by charging up the slopes of Cemetery Ridge. As soon as we marched onto the field the Union troops opened fire. We ignored the shooting and kept going, but men were dropping all around me. It's a miracle I'm still here to tell about it.

I didn't come out of it completely untouched, though.

Cousin Jack says that the cuts to my feet are infected. He says I'd better get to a doctor soon. Even though I found a pair of shoes yesterday, it was too late. My feet were already badly injured. I heard that we'll be heading back to Virginia. I hope I can make it that far.

4 EDITING

Ask a partner to review your revised draft before you edit. When you edit, look for errors in grammar, usage, spelling, and mechanics. Look especially for correct form in your Works Cited list.

Editing Strategy

Citing Works in Correct Form

A research paper includes a list called *Works Cited* to tell the reader what sources you used in your research. The correct form changes slightly for different types of sources, as shown in the following student model.

Works Cited List

Brown, Jane. Personal Interview. October, 1997.

Davis, Reed. <u>Faces of the Civil War.</u> Harper, 1961.

Long, Everett B. <u>The Civil War Day by Day: An Almanac, 1861-1865.</u>

Doubleday, 1971.

STUDENT MODEL

 PRESENTING

- Videotape yourself reading your paper as background to a visual collage of the best pictures and original documents you found.

- Organize a display for the library of your historical sources, documents, pictures, and books, to motivate others to explore your topic.

6 LOOKING BACK

Self-evaluate. Look back at the Writer's Blueprint and give yourself a point for each item, from 6 (superior) down to 1 (inadequate).

Reflect. Think about what you learned from writing your paper as you write answers to these questions.

✔ What was something I learned about my topic that surprised me?

✔ What useful advice can I give myself for the next time I write a research paper?

For Your Working Portfolio Add your saturation research paper and reflection responses to your working portfolio.

Beyond Print

Literature Databases

If you're looking for information about an author, the **Author Works** CD ROM offers information, photos, and video about the lives and times of a variety of influential authors. The **Custom Literature Database** CD ROM allows you to search for the works of an author, or to search for works that share a theme.

Electronic Research

Imagine the scene: You've just been assigned to do a research paper on the Civil War. You know there's a world of information "out there," but how do you find it? The easiest, fastest way to locate the information you need is to let technology work for you. Here are some strategies that can help.

1. Know Your Database

A database is any collection of information or data. Electronic databases come in two basic categories: self-contained and online.

A self-contained database is accessed through a computer terminal. The following are some common examples of self-contained databases:

- **Electronic Card Catalogues** Many libraries have transferred their traditional card catalogue systems to computer systems. You simply type in the name of the author, title, or subject and the information source and location will be displayed.

- **Electronic Reference Materials** Entire encyclopedias, dictionaries, thesauruses, atlases, almanacs, and collections of famous quotations can be written onto CD ROM. Many include sound and even movies.

- **Periodical Databases** You can also find databases that list magazine and newspaper articles. Some provide abstracts or entire articles.

Going online means connecting to a database via the telephone line and modem. Here are some ways to go online:

- **Individual Memberships** Many companies operate consumer on-line services. For a fee, members can access online encyclopedias, magazines, reviews, interviews, and subject-specific databases. Members can also post questions and receive advice or ideas.

- **Library Memberships** Libraries often purchase online memberships to a variety of research services. Ask a librarian for information.

- **Library Networks** Many libraries can now search online for resources at other libraries, and can access the materials through inter-library loan.

- **The Internet** The Internet is a world-wide series of computers hooked together through telephone lines. It is accessed via modem through government or educational institutions, as well as consumer online services. The Internet can be used to access databases and resources around the world. Discussion areas or *Newsgroups* allow you to ask questions of other researchers and even Nobel Prize-winning scholars.

2. Beginning the Search

Remember, the computer can't read your mind, so it is crucial to give it clear directions.

Author/Title Search The most accurate way to begin a search is with a specific author's name or title. Be sure your spelling is accurate.

Subject Search In doing a subject search, you will need to enter *keywords* corresponding to the subject. If your topic is, for example, medical practices during the Civil War, the information you seek could be found under *Civil War, medical history, medicine, military, army,* and so on. Before beginning a search, brainstorm a list of subject keywords.

3. Downloading

In doing electronic research there are several ways to move the information off the screen and into your hands. The easiest way is to **print out** the information. Information can also be downloaded directly onto a **terminal or disk.** Finally, you may be able to **order additional information** to be sent to you directly.

Activity Options

Data Tour Ask your school or local librarian for a tour of the library's electronic research resources.

Keyword Search Create a list of keywords on a topic. Try a prewriting technique such as listing or clustering to generate the keywords. Then, use these keywords on several different databases to search for your topic. Print out your results. Did you get the information you hoped for?

Multicultural Connections

Individuality

Part One: Romantic Truths and Terrors "Whoso would be a man," says Emerson, "must be a nonconformist." Thoreau echoes this sentiment, saying, "If a man does not keep pace with his companions, perhaps it is because he hears a different drummer. Let him step to the music which he hears . . ." Clearly both of these writers value individualism over allowing cultural norms to dominate one's life. Sojourner Truth took a stand as an individual against injustices, and the character in Poe's "The Pit and the Pendulum" was persecuted for not conforming to his society's expectations.

■ Which selection presents the most powerful argument for the importance of individuality?

Change

Part Two: The Civil War The Civil War was a powerful agent for change in this country, and reactions to these changes varied. Mary Chesnut's diary reveals a white Southerner's perspective on the war, and she wonders about the reaction of the African American "servants" who await possible change. Abraham Lincoln and Herman Melville reflect on some of the war's events and the cost of change in lost lives. Grant and Lee each have a different perspective on the changes brought about by the end of the war, and Frederick Douglass sees a need for continued change.

■ Which selection do you think reflects the most positive reaction to change?

Activities

Work in small groups on the following activities.

1. Based on what you've learned about the importance of individuality from the "Romantic Truths and Terrors" selections, to what people, both historical or contemporary, would you want to give an "individuality award"? Make a list, and explain your choices.

2. What great cultural changes are happening today? How are people reacting? Create a dramatization that captures some of the biggest changes to society today, and also a variety of reactions from people. Perform your scene for the class.

Independent and Group Projects

Media

Video Literature Create a short video (ten or fifteen minutes at the longest) using one of the selections from this unit for inspiration. Work with a group, and plan carefully how you'll create your video. Will it capture the atmosphere and mood of the selection with music and still pictures, or will you re-create an important event from the selection to capture on video?

Drama

Testimonial In his essay *Self-Reliance* Emerson says, "Trust yourself . . . nothing can bring you peace but the triumph of principles." Pick an author or character from this unit that you think exemplifies someone who lived according to their own principles and write a monologue from that individual's perspective. Relate experiences that would encourage others to follow the path of "self-reliance." Memorize and present the monologue to your class, paying attention to details such as how your individual would speak and dress.

Literature

Rewrite History What if the South had won the Civil War? How would the history of the United States be different? Discuss this idea with a small group and make a list of major events that might have occurred if the South had won the war. Write a report that describes the consequences of this "new" chapter in American history. Finally, make a time line of the major events in the form of a banner to display to your class as you read your report. Discuss your results with the class.

Entertainment

A Modern Classic With a small group, decide which selection from this unit would best translate into a video game. Design a game with a story line that incorporates events from the selection as well as your own ideas. Make an outline that details how to play the game, and draw pictures that show the game's characters and levels. Present your game to the class.

Expanding America

Letters to the World
Part One, pages 350–385

The Frontier
Part Two, pages 386–430

THEMES IN AMERICAN LITERATURE

The Journey
Theme Portfolio, pages 431–443

The use of structural steel permitted the rise of the skyscrapers— such as New York's Flatiron Building—that quickly became one of the most characteristic features of the rapidly growing American cities.

HISTORICAL OVERVIEW

The four writers in this section—Emily Dickinson, Walt Whitman, Paul Laurence Dunbar, and Stephen Crane— lived in a society on the brink of the modern world. The Civil War had changed America forever. The economic, social, and cultural impact of the war was felt differently by different regions and groups, but the changes overall were profound. Between the end of the war and the early 1900s, the United States was transformed from a developing nation into a world power. Some of the most important trends that shaped this era were the following:

• the growth of cities
• new technology
• rapid industrialization
• a global U.S. political role
• increased immigration
• new forms of popular culture
• growth of the labor movement

A Changing

A flood of new inventions, including the electric light, telephone, phonograph, automobile, and airplane, ushered in the modern world.

The United States took on a larger, more dynamic role in world politics, signaled by a swift, decisive victory in the Spanish-American War.

Huge numbers of immigrants from southern and eastern Europe began to alter the cultural character of the American population.

Labor unions, such as the International Ladies' Garment Workers Union, struggled to gain recognition for workers' rights to organize.

The U.S. economy became dominated by huge new corporations, such as the Standard Oil Company, creating both vast wealth and the fear of monopolies (as suggested by this newspaper cartoon).

New forms of popular entertainment—baseball, bicycling, dime novels, nickelodeon movies—changed America's leisure habits.

Key Dates

1869
First professional baseball team—the Cincinnati Red Stockings—is organized.

1877
During the first national labor walkout—the Great Railroad Strike—workers battle federal troops.

1879
Thomas Alva Edison invents the incandescent light bulb.

1882
John D. Rockefeller forms the Standard Oil Trust.

1884
The first steel-frame skyscraper is built.

1898
Spanish American war is fought.

1900
Decade of peak immigration begins.

Letters to the World

Every person has a unique way of looking at the world, and poets have a way of capturing that world-view and putting it into words. In the following pages you'll read the works of four poets, each of whom is sending his or her messages to the world.

 Multicultural Connection **Perspective** involves the way a person interprets the world. As you read the following poems, consider how the poets' cultures and experiences may have influenced their attitudes toward themselves, toward society, and toward life in general.

Literature

Emily Dickinson   **This is my letter to the World** ♦ poem 354

Much Madness is divinest Sense ♦ poem 354

The Soul selects her own Society ♦ poem . . .354

Because I could not stop for Death ♦ poem . . .357

A Bird came down the Walk ♦ poem 357

Walt Whitman   **I Hear America Singing** ♦ poem 361

What Is the Grass? ♦ poem 362

There Was a Child Went Forth ♦ poem 364

Paul Laurence Dunbar   **Sympathy** ♦ poem 370

We Wear the Mask ♦ poem 371

Stephen Crane   **To the Maiden** ♦ poem 374

The Wayfarer ♦ poem 374

I Saw a Man Pursuing the Horizon ♦ poem . .375

A Man Said to the Universe ♦ poem 375

Interdisciplinary Study   American Visionaries

Paintings by Frederic Edwin Church, Albert Pinkham Ryder, William Rimmer, Elihu Vedder, Erastus Salisbury Field, and William Holbrook Beard ♦ fine art 377

Writing Workshop   Expository Writing

Dear World, ...381

Beyond Print   Visual Literacy

Reading a Painting 385

Before Reading

This is my letter to the World
Much Madness is divinest Sense

by Emily Dickinson

The Soul selects her own Society
Because I could not stop for Death
A Bird came down the Walk

Emily Dickinson
1830–1886

Of the 1,775 poems Emily Dickinson wrote, only seven were published during her lifetime—and they were published anonymously. On the topic of publishing her poems she said: "How can you print a piece of your own soul?" Born into a prominent family of Amherst, Massachusetts, Dickinson attended the Mount Holyoke Female Seminary, then dropped out after a year and spent much of her time writing letters to friends, reading, writing poetry, and walking in the gardens and meadows of her family's estate. She was a very private person who rarely left the family home, and shared her poetry with only a few people.

Building Background

An Unconventional Woman Though Dickinson might appear to have been an eccentric woman, she was in fact an independent thinker and quite a rebel for her time. She refused to conform to the religious views held at the Mount Holyoke Female Seminary, in spite of public pressures. She fell in love with a married minister. She chose not to marry and became a recluse, partly to allow herself the independence to develop her own thoughts. Her originality and independence show through in her poetry.

Literary Focus

Personification Emily Dickinson makes extensive use of personification, the attribution of human qualities to inanimate objects or ideas, in her poetry. For example, she personifies nature as a majestic but kind woman in "This is my letter to the World." The web below diagrams the references Dickinson makes to nature as a person.

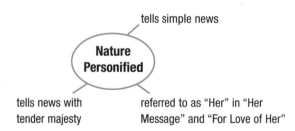

After reading "The Soul selects her own Society" and "Because I could not stop for Death," make webs showing what is personified and the details Dickinson uses in the personification.

Writer's Notebook

Close to Home Emily Dickinson's inspiration for her poetry came from within herself, from reading and reflection, and from observation of her home and yard. Take a mental walk through your home and neighborhood. Then consider what you think about when you are alone. Make a list of topics that you might write poems about.

This is my letter to the World

Emily Dickinson

This is my letter to the World
That never wrote to Me—
The simple News that Nature told—
With tender Majesty

5 Her Message is committed
To Hands I cannot see—
For love of Her—Sweet—countrymen—
Judge tenderly—of Me

Much Madness is divinest Sense

Emily Dickinson

Much Madness is divinest Sense—
To a discerning[1] Eye—
Much Sense—the starkest Madness—
'Tis the Majority
5 In this, as All, prevail—
Assent—and you are sane—
Demur[2]—you're straightway dangerous—
And handled with a Chain—

---

1. **discerning** (də zėrn′ing), *adj.* seeing clearly, perceiving the difference between two or more things.
2. **demur** (di mėr′), *v.* show disapproval or dislike, take exception, object.

The Soul selects her own Society

Emily Dickinson

The Soul selects her own Society—
Then—shuts the Door—
To her divine Majority—
Present no more—

5 Unmoved—she notes the Chariots—
          pausing—
At her low Gate—
Unmoved—an Emperor be kneeling
Upon her Mat—

I've known her—from an ample[1] nation—
10 Choose One—
Then—close the Valves of her attention—
Like Stone—

---

1. **ample** (am′pəl), *adj.* more than enough, abundant.

In this painting, *Woman at the Window* (1822) by Caspar David Friedrich, what do you suppose the woman is thinking as she gazes outside? ➤

In Dickinson's poem, "Because I could not stop for Death," the carriage is headed "toward Eternity." If you were to write a poem about Jamie Wyeth's 1975 painting, *And Then into the Deep Gorge,* what would be the carriage's destination, and why?

Because I could not stop for Death

Emily Dickinson

Because I could not stop for Death—
He kindly stopped for me—
The Carriage held but just Ourselves—
And Immortality.[1]

5 We slowly drove—He knew no haste
And I had put away
My labor and my leisure too,
For His Civility—

We passed the School, where Children strove
10 At Recess—in the Ring—
We passed the Fields of Gazing Grain—
We passed the Setting Sun—

Or rather—He passed Us—
The Dews drew quivering and chill—
15 For only Gossamer, my Gown—
My Tippet—only Tulle[2]—

We paused before a House that seemed
A Swelling of the Ground—
The Roof was scarcely visible—
20 The Cornice[3]—in the Ground—

Since then—'tis Centuries—and yet
Feels shorter than the Day
I first surmised[4] the Horses' Heads
Were toward Eternity—

---

1. **immortality** (im′ôr tal′ə tē), *n.* life without death, a living forever.
2. **Tippet . . . Tulle** (tip′it, tŭl), The speaker's shawl, or tippet, was made of tulle, a fine net cloth.
3. **cornice** (kôr′nis), *n.* an ornamental molding along the top of a wall, pillar, building, etc.
4. **surmise** (sər mīz′), *v.* infer or guess.

A Bird came down the Walk

Emily Dickinson

A Bird came down the Walk—
He did not know I saw—
He bit an Angleworm in halves
And ate the fellow, raw,

5 And then he drank a Dew
From a convenient Grass—
And then hopped sidewise to the Wall
To let a Beetle pass—

He glanced with rapid eyes
10 That hurried all around—
They looked like frightened Beads, I thought—
He stirred his Velvet Head

Like one in danger, Cautious,
I offered him a Crumb
15 And he unrolled his feathers
And rowed him softer home—

Than Oars divide the Ocean,
Too silver for a seam—
Or Butterflies, off Banks of Noon
20 Leap, plashless as they swim.

After Reading

Making Connections

Shaping Your Response

1. Dickinson's poems don't follow the rules of capitalization and punctuation. Why do you suppose she wrote the way she did?

2. Choose one of these five poems to recite aloud to the class. How will you recite it—in whispers? loudly? seriously? with humor? Afterward, tell why you recited it as you did.

Analyzing the Poems

3. What might the "letter to the World" **symbolize** in "This is my letter to the World"?

4. Explain how "The Soul selects her own Society" might be autobiographical.

5. Dickinson uses an **extended metaphor** in "Because I could not stop for Death." What is the metaphor, and what mystery is Dickinson trying to explain?

6. Paraphrase the observations Dickinson makes in "A Bird came down the Walk."

7. 🐾 What **perspective** does "Much Madness is divinest Sense" express about an individual in our world?

Extending the Ideas

8. Emily Dickinson lived over one hundred years ago. Are her poems still timely today? Why or why not?

9. Compare your idea of friendship to Dickinson's in "The Soul selects her own Society." How do they differ?

Literary Focus: Personification

In "Because I could not stop for Death," Dickinson personifies death as a kindly gentleman who stops his carriage for her and then drives her slowly toward eternity. She uses these details in the poem: "He kindly stopped for me," "He knew no haste," "His Civility," "We paused." Look at the web you made for "The Soul selects her own Society." Dickinson personified the soul as a woman unmoved by worldly power. How would you personify death, the soul, or nature? Make a **details web** illustrating the details you would use.

Vocabulary Study

Choose the word from the list that best completes each sentence.

immortality
cornice
surmise
discerning
demur

1. The ____ book dealer could tell the difference between the authentic first edition of the Dickinson poetry collection and the fake one.
2. Famous poets like Dickinson achieve a kind of ____ through their poetry—they are remembered long after their death.
3. A ____ might be found on an older home like Dickinson's.
4. If your friend suggests that writing poetry is easy and you ____, you really don't agree.
5. Would you ____ that Emily Dickinson enjoyed her own company?

Expressing Your Ideas

Writing Choices

Writer's Notebook Update Look over the topics you listed in your notebook before reading Emily Dickinson's poetry. Choose one and write a poem or journal entry about it.

From Dickinson's Window Study John James Audubon's painting *House Wren.* Emily Dickinson might have enjoyed a similar sight in her yard. What might this sight have inspired her to write? What does it inspire you to write? Write a **poem** or a **prose reflection** about the wrens.

Other Options

From Word to Image Choose one of the five poems included here and create some kind of an artwork that reflects the mood and feel of the poem. Be creative—you may want to make a **model,** a **collage,** or **T-shirt design.**

Produce a Tape You are in the business of producing books on tape, and you want to venture into the area of poetry. Your first project is a **tape recording** of Emily Dickinson's poetry. First, tape a brief biography of Dickinson. Then choose ten of her poems, rehearse reading them, and tape your performance. Finally, design a jacket for the tape with appropriate art on the front and a list of the poems on the back.

Before Reading

I Hear America Singing
What Is the Grass?
There Was a Child Went Forth

by Walt Whitman

Walt Whitman
1819–1892

When Walt Whitman's first book of poetry, *Leaves of Grass,* appeared in 1855, it drew mixed reviews. "A gathering of muck," sneered one critic; another pronounced it "the most extraordinary piece of wit and wisdom America has yet produced." Poet John Greenleaf Whittier supposedly burned his copy of the book, and William Cullen Bryant broke off his friendship with Whitman. Whitman did have a few supporters, however, Ralph Waldo Emerson and Henry David Thoreau among them. Although the book was at first a financial failure, Whitman continued to add to, refine, and reissue *Leaves of Grass.*

Building Background

Celebrate Walt Whitman celebrates the American people and their work. He celebrates the spirit of the growing nation, and he celebrates the wonder of life itself. Although Whitman was a romantic at heart, his poetry did not fit the mold of other romantic writers. He rejected the common rhyme and meter of the day and chose to write long lines of free verse to express his themes of democracy and individuality. He wrote about common people and about both pleasant and unpleasant aspects of nature with admiration. While his style and subjects earned him much criticism in his time, today many critics see him as the father of modern poetry in America.

Literary Focus

Symbolism Poetry can be meaningful on both a literal level and a symbolic level. Symbolism is the use of a concrete object to represent an abstract quality or concept. In the poem "What Is the Grass?" the narrator could give a literal reply to the child and say that grass is a plant with green blades. Instead the narrator explores the symbolic meanings of grass. As you read "What Is the Grass?" reflect on the symbolic meanings that the grass might have throughout the poem.

Writer's Notebook

And . . . And . . . And One of Walt Whitman's poetic techniques used in his longer poems is "cataloging," or listing things. Peek ahead at "There Was a Child Went Forth" and notice all of the lines that begin with "And the . . ." If you were to write a poem about sports heroes or movie stars or popular musicians, what images would you list together? Choose a topic and write phrases that you might use in a poem about it.

I Hear America Singing

WALT WHITMAN

I hear America singing, the varied carols I hear,
Those of mechanics, each one singing his as it should be
    blithe[1] and strong,
The carpenter singing his as he measures his plank or beam,
The mason singing his as he makes ready for work, or leaves
    off work,
5 The boatman singing what belongs to him in his boat, the
    deckhand singing on the steamboat deck,
The shoemaker singing as he sits on his bench, the hatter
    singing as he stands,
The woodcutter's song, the ploughboy's on his way in the
    morning, or at noon intermission or at sundown,
The delicious singing of the mother, or of the young wife at
    work, or of the girl sewing or washing,
Each singing what belongs to him or her and to none else,
10 The day what belongs to the day—at night the party of young
    fellows, robust,[2] friendly,
Singing with open mouths their strong melodious songs.

List five adjectives you would use to describe the spirit of Whitman's poem. Do the same five adjectives describe the above painting, George Caleb Bingham's *The Jolly Flatboatmen* (1846)? Why or why not?

---

1. **blithe** (blīŦH), *adj.* happy and cheerful, joyous.
2. **robust** (rō bust′), *adj.* strong and healthy, sturdy.

WHAT IS THE GRASS?

FROM *Song of Myself*

WALT WHITMAN

A child said *What is the grass?* fetching[1] it to me with full hands,
How could I answer the child? I do not know what it is any more than he.

I guess it must be the flag of my disposition,[2] out of hopeful green stuff woven.

Or I guess it is the handkerchief of the Lord,
5 A scented gift and remembrancer designedly dropped,
Bearing the owner's name someway in the corners, that we may see and remark,
     and say *Whose?*

Or I guess the grass is itself a child, the produced babe of the vegetation.

Or I guess it is a uniform hieroglyphic,[3]
And it means, sprouting alike in broad zones and narrow zones,
10 Growing among black folks as among white,
Canuck, Tuckahoe, Congressman, Cuff,[4] I give them the same, I receive
     them the same.

And now it seems to me the beautiful uncut hair of graves.

Tenderly will I use you curling grass,
It may be you transpire[5] from the breasts of young men,
15 It may be if I had known them I would have loved them,
It may be you are from old people, or from offspring taken soon out of
     their mothers' laps,
And here you are the mothers' laps.

---

1. **fetch** (fech), *v.* go to another place and bring back.
2. **disposition** (dis′pə zish′ən), *n.* one's nature or attitude.
3. **hieroglyphic** (hī′ər ə glif′ik), *n.* symbol standing for a word, idea, or sound.
4. **Canuck . . . Cuff,** Canuck is slang for a Canadian. Tuckahoe is a nickname for an inhabitant of eastern Virginia. Cuff, from the African word *cuffee* meaning "a black person," is slang for an African American.
5. **transpire** (tran spīr′), *v.* pass off or send off moisture in the form of vapor, through a membrane or surface, as from the human body or from leaves.

This grass is very dark to be from the white heads of old mothers,
Darker than the colorless beards of old men,
20 Dark to come from under the faint red roof of mouths.

O I perceive after all so many uttering tongues,
And I perceive they do not come from the roofs of mouths for nothing.

I wish I could translate the hints about the dead young men and women,
And the hints about old men and mothers, and the offspring taken soon
     out of their laps.

25 What do you think has become of the young and old men?
And what do you think has become of the women and children?

They are alive and well somewhere,
The smallest sprout shows there is really no death,
And if ever there was it led forward life, and does not wait at the end to
     arrest it,
30 And ceased the moment life appeared.

All goes onward and outward, nothing collapses,
And to die is different from what anyone supposed, and luckier.

A Why do you suppose
William A. Smith
chose this setting
for his painting of
Walt Whitman?

What Is the Grass?   **363**

THERE WAS A Child WENT FORTH

WALT WHITMAN

There was a child went forth every day,
And the first object he look'd upon, that object he became,
And that object became part of him for the day or a certain part
    of the day,
Or for many years or stretching cycles of years.

5 The early lilacs became part of this child,
And grass and white and red morning-glories, and white and red
    clover, and the song of the phoebe-bird,
And the Third-month[1] lambs and the sow's pink-faint litter, and the
    mare's foal and the cow's calf,
And the noisy brood of the barnyard or by the mire of the pond-side,
And the fish suspending themselves so curiously below there, and
    the beautiful curious liquid,
10 And the water-plants with their graceful flat heads, all became part
    of him.

The field-sprouts of Fourth-month and Fifth-month became part
    of him,
Winter-grain sprouts and those of the light-yellow corn, and the
    esculent[2] roots of the garden,
And the apple-trees cover'd with blossoms and the fruit afterward,
    and woodberries, and the commonest weeds by the road,

Apply the fresh **perspective** of childhood that Whitman expresses in his poem to the setting in Claude Monet's *Garden at Vétheuil.* If everything the child in the painting encounters becomes part of the child, what can you say about the youngster based on the surroundings? ➤

---

1. **Third-month,** March. Whitman uses the Quaker method of referring to months.
2. **esculent** (es′kyə lənt), *adj.* suitable for food, edible.

And the old drunkard staggering home from the outhouse of the
    tavern whence he had lately risen,
15 And the schoolmistress that pass'd on her way to the school,
And the friendly boys that pass'd, and the quarrelsome boys,
And the tidy and fresh-cheek'd girls, and the barefoot Negro boy
    and girl,
And all the changes of city and country wherever he went.

His own parents, he that had father'd him and she that had conceiv'd
    him in her womb and birth'd him
20 They gave this child more of themselves than that,
They gave him afterward every day, they became part of him.

The mother at home quietly placing the dishes on the supper-table,
The mother with mild words, clean her cap and gown, a wholesome
    odor falling off her person and clothes as she walks by,
The father, strong, self-sufficient, manly, mean, anger'd, unjust,
25 The blow, the quick loud word, the tight bargain, the crafty lure,
The family usages, the language, the company, the furniture, the
    yearning and swelling heart,
Affection that will not be gainsay'd, the sense of what is real, the
    thought if after all it should prove unreal,
The doubts of day-time and the doubts of night-time, the curious
    whether and how,
Whether that which appears so is so, or is it all flashes and specks?
30 Men and women crowding fast in the streets, if they are not flashes
    and specks what are they?
The streets themselves and the facades of houses, and goods in the
    windows,
Vehicles, teams, the heavy-plank'd wharves, the huge crossing at the
    ferries,
The village on the highland seen from afar at sunset, the river
    between,
Shadows, aureola and mist, the light falling on roofs and gables of
    white or brown two miles off,
35 The schooner near by sleepily dropping down the tide, the little boat
    slack-tow'd astern,
The hurrying tumbling waves, quick-broken crests, slapping,
The strata of color'd clouds, the long bar of maroon-tint away solitary
    by itself, the spread of purity it lies motionless in,
The horizon's edge, the flying sea-crow, the fragrance of salt marsh
    and shore mud,
These became part of that child who went forth every day, and who
    now goes, and will always go forth every day.

After Reading

Making Connections

Shaping Your Response

1. What do you think about Walt Whitman's free verse style? Do you like it, or do you prefer metered, rhymed poetry? Why?

2. Choose five lines from Whitman's poems that stood out as you read them. Tell what it is about the lines that called your attention to them.

Analyzing the Poems

3. Describe what you think is Walt Whitman's attitude about death in "What Is the Grass?" Use quotations from the poem to support your opinion.

4. Whitman was the great poet of selfhood and individuality. What, according to "There Was a Child Went Forth," is the source of a person's identity and individuality?

5. Whitman uses vivid **images** in his poetry. Classify the images in "There Was a Child Went Forth." To which sense does each appeal?

Sight	Sound	Taste	Touch	Smell

6. Whitman does not use a regular line length or rhyme, but the use of **repetition** and **alliteration** in "I Hear America Singing" provide a rhythm. Find examples of these techniques in the poem.

Extending the Ideas

7. If Walt Whitman were alive today, he might want to update his poem "I Hear America Singing." Who would he add to his list of working Americans?

8. Both Walt Whitman and Emily Dickinson explored the topic of death in their poetry. Compare the different **perspectives** of death presented in "What Is the Grass?" and "Because I could not stop for Death." Where do you think their ideas about death may have come from?

Literary Focus: Symbolism

How many different symbolic meanings for "grass" did Walt Whitman discuss in "What Is the Grass?" Make a list of them. Then write a paragraph that sums up the use of symbolism in the poem.

Vocabulary Study

Use your Glossary to help you choose the correct answer for each item.

disposition
blithe
robust
fetch
transpire

1. Using his poetry as an indication, what would be an accurate description of Walt Whitman's *disposition?*

   a. dreary   **b.** sad

   c. silly   **d.** optimistic

2. Describe a *blithe* disposition.

   a. sad and weary   **b.** bored and irritable

   c. happy and cheerful   **d.** shy and quiet

3. Choose a *robust* luncheon dish from this menu.

   a. hearty beef stew   **b.** tasty chicken broth

   c. spring salad greens   **d.** fruit and jello salad

4. Your teacher might have you *fetch* your schoolbooks if you:

   a. forgot them   **b.** damaged them

   c. read them   **d.** translated them

5. For matter to *transpire* from something, it must:

   a. stay within it   **b.** disappear

   c. go through its surface   **d.** expire

Expressing Your Ideas

Writing Choices

Writer's Notebook Update Using one of Whitman's poems as a model, try writing an original poem using the "cataloging" technique. Check the phrases you wrote in your notebook for ideas to get started. For example, you might develop the idea of "I see America playing . . ." or "The music of America rings out forever. . . ."

The Traveling Whitman Walt Whitman is alive and well and just won a trip to Disney World or Six Flags or any other place you choose to send him. Keeping in mind his writing style and enthusiasm for life, write a **journal entry** for Whitman telling about his experiences.

Other Options

Picture It Walt Whitman presents a string of images in "There Was a Child Went Forth" to describe the richness of life. Find visual images to accompany the poem and create a **slide show.** Work with a partner and project the slides as you read the poem. As an alternate activity, make a **collage** to accompany the poem.

Together at Last Imagine Dickinson and Whitman are having lunch together at Dickinson's home. What will the two talk about? With a partner, create a **dialogue** between the two to perform for your class.

Before Reading

Sympathy

We Wear the Mask

by Paul Laurence Dunbar

Paul Laurence Dunbar
1872–1906

The son of former slaves who escaped via the Underground Railroad, Paul Laurence Dunbar dreamed of becoming a lawyer. Without the money to attend college, however, he became an elevator operator for four dollars a week. While working at this job he was also writing poetry. His first book, *Oak and Ivy,* was published in 1893. He didn't make a big impression in the literary world until William Dean Howells, a noted novelist and editor, took notice of his second book of poetry, *Majors and Minors.* Howells convinced Dunbar to choose the best poems from his first two books and publish them in one volume. Dunbar followed his advice, and the resulting book, *Lyrics of a Lowly Life,* launched his literary career.

Building Background

Perspectives What you see is what you get. Or is it? We all perceive things differently. Is a glass half empty or half full? Is a parent who disciplines a teenager for a curfew violation mean-spirited and insensitive or caring and concerned? Dunbar's poems "Sympathy" and "We Wear the Mask" challenge the reader's perspectives. A singing bird is a happy bird, isn't it? A smile is worn by a happy person, isn't it? As you read the poems, notice the contrasts Dunbar uses to develop the theme of each.

Literary Focus

Theme What do the words in a poem say? What message can you read between the lines? A deeper, underlying meaning of a poem is its **theme.** A theme is usually not stated; it is inferred from the characterization, action, images, and tone used in a poem. Before reading the two Dunbar poems, think about how the titles may be hinting at the themes.

Writer's Notebook

Poet Power Poets are economical; most poets make the most of the words they use to make impressions on readers' minds. After you read Dunbar's poems, jot down the words and phrases that create powerful sensations for you as a reader. For example, in the first line of "We Wear the Mask," the phrase "the mask that grins and lies" may be perplexing and unsettling. How can a mask lie?

Sympathy

PAUL LAURENCE DUNBAR

I know what the caged bird feels, alas!
When the sun is bright on the upland slopes;
When the wind stirs soft through the springing grass,
And the river flows like a stream of glass;
5 When the first bird sings and the first bud opes,
And the faint perfume from its chalice[1] steals——
I know what the caged bird feels!

I know why the caged bird beats his wing
Till its blood is red on the cruel bars;
10 For he must fly back to his perch and cling
When he fain would be on the bough a-swing;
And a pain still throbs in the old, old scars
And they pulse again with a keener sting——
I know why he beats his wing!

15 I know why the caged bird sings, ah me,
When his wing is bruised and his bosom sore——
When he beats his bars and he would be free;
It is not a carol of joy or glee,
But a prayer that he sends from his heart's deep core,
20 But a plea, that upward to Heaven he flings——
I know why the caged bird sings!

---

1. chalice (chal′is), *n.* a cup-shaped blossom of a flower.

We Wear the Mask

PAUL LAURENCE DUNBAR

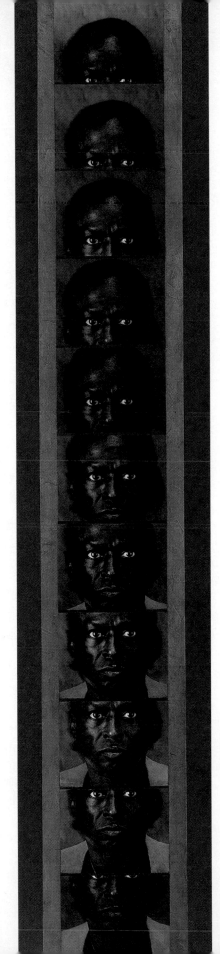

We wear the mask that grins and lies,
    It hides our cheeks and shades our eyes,—
This debt we pay to human guile;[1]
With torn and bleeding hearts we smile,
5 And mouth with myriad[2] subtleties.[3]

Why should the world be over-wise,
In counting all our tears and sighs?
Nay, let them only see us, while
      We wear the mask.

10 We smile, but, O great Christ, our cries
To thee from tortured souls arise.
We sing, but oh the clay is vile[4]
Beneath our feet, and long the mile;
But let the world dream otherwise,
15   We wear the mask!

---

1. guile (gīl), *n.* crafty deceit, sly tricks, cunning.
2. myriad (mir′ē əd), *adj.* countless; innumerable.
3. subtlety (sut′l tē), *n.* fine-drawn distinction, refinement of reasoning.
4. vile (vīl), *adj.* very bad; foul, disgusting, obnoxious.

This work by Gilles Larrain is a photo montage, collage, and painting. Write one word for each photograph in the montage that somehow describes the feeling of the particular photograph. Do your words change or stay the same? Why? ➤

After Reading

Making Connections

Shaping Your Response

1. Both of these poems by Dunbar are written from a first-person point of view. Who do you think is the "I" in "Sympathy"? Who do you think is the "We" in "We Wear the Mask"? Why do you think so?

Analyzing the Poems

2. What do you think the **title** "Sympathy" means?

3. What might the cage, the bird, and the outdoor scene **symbolize?**

4. ☝ Compare the **tone** of these poems by Dunbar to those you have read by Whitman. How do you think the life experiences and **perspectives** of these two poets might be reflected in their poetry?

Extending the Ideas

5. Can wearing a "mask" be useful? When is it good to wear a mask? When is it harmful? Make a pros and cons chart of wearing a mask.

Literary Focus: Theme

Choose either "Sympathy" or "We Wear the Mask" and write a paragraph discussing **theme.** State a theme of the poem. How does Dunbar develop that theme in each stanza?

Vocabulary Study

Use your Glossary to help answer these questions.

chalice
vile
subtlety
myriad
guile

1. What part of a plant might be called a *chalice?*

2. According to your taste buds, what food has a *vile* taste?

3. Which would more likely be called a *subtlety* of poetry, rhyme or theme? Explain your answer.

4. If a painter uses a *myriad* of colors, how many colors are used?

5. What words describe what you do to someone when you use *guile?*

Expressing Your Ideas

Writing Choice

Writer's Notebook Update Write one line of poetry about either a cage or a mask in five different ways. Be an economical poet and use powerful words and phrases. Reread your lines. Which one expresses your thought best?

Another Option

Mask Yourself Draw a series of **masks** that illustrate the faces you wear for different occasions. Label each mask.

Before Reading

To the Maiden
The Wayfarer

I Saw a Man Pursuing the Horizon
A Man Said to the Universe

by Stephen Crane

Stephen Crane
1871–1900

Stephen Crane was sickly as a youngster, and his father and sister both died young. Crane predicted that he wouldn't live past 35. A fast writer, Crane wrote the draft of his first novel, *Maggie, a Girl of the Streets,* in a few days. He couldn't find a publisher, so he paid to have it printed himself. To support himself he wrote for the *New York Tribune,* and at the same time managed to write several volumes of poetry and *The Red Badge of Courage,* a novel about the Civil War. The success of that novel led to his job as a war correspondent. On a trip to Cuba to cover a rebellion, his ship sank, and he was one of the few survivors. He based his short story "The Open Boat" on this experience. Crane was accurate in his prediction about his death—he died of tuberculosis at age 28.

Building Background

Naturalism Stephen Crane wrote this about his literary style: "If I had kept to my clever Rudyard-Kipling style, the road might have been shorter but, ah, it wouldn't be the true road." Crane is considered the first naturalistic writer, meaning a writer who depicts events as rigidly determined by the forces of heredity and environment. Crane wrote about the grimness of life, the indifference of nature, and the individual as a victim. His pessimistic view of life was not well-received in the literary world. Neither was the unorthodox form of his poetry. Crane used no rhyme or meter. Instead he used vivid imagery and irony to make his points.

Literary Focus

Irony Stephen Crane is known for his use of **irony,** which is the contrast between what appears to be and what really is. As you read Crane's poetry, look for examples of irony in two of the poems. Based on the chart below, decide what kind of irony is being used in the poems.

Verbal irony	"Oh, great, I have a flat tire," is an example of verbal irony; the words say the opposite of what the speaker really means.
Irony of situation	Irony of situation occurs when events turn out contrary to what is expected. For example, it is ironic that Crane, never having been in a battle, wrote such a realistic account of war that he was made a war correspondent.
Dramatic irony	A third kind of irony is dramatic irony, which occurs in fiction or drama when the reader or viewer knows more than the characters do.

Writer's Notebook

Get In Style Stephen Crane's poetry is simply written in clear, almost sparse, language. Also, even the shortest of his poems often includes dialogue. Write ideas for dialogue poetry in your notebook. What might be the topic of conversation? Who would the speakers be?

TO THE MAIDEN

STEPHEN CRANE

To the maiden
The sea was blue meadow,
Alive with little froth-people
Singing.
5 To the sailor, wrecked,
The sea was dead grey walls
Superlative[1] in vacancy,
Upon which nevertheless at fateful time
Was written
10 The grim[2] hatred of nature.

THE WAYFARER

STEPHEN CRANE

The wayfarer
Perceiving the pathway to truth
Was struck with astonishment.
It was thickly grown with weeds.
5 "Ha," he said,
"I see that none has passed here
In a long time."
Later he saw that each weed
Was a singular knife.
10 "Well," he mumbled at last,
"Doubtless there are other roads."

---

1. **superlative** (sə pėr′lə tiv), *adj.* of the highest kind; above all others; supreme.
2. **grim** (grim), *adj.* without mercy; stern, harsh, or fierce.

Reread Crane's poem, "To the Maiden." Does Reginald Cleveland Coxe's *The Coming Wind* (1890) depict the maiden's **perspective,** the wrecked sailor's perspective, or yet another perspective on the sea? Explain your answer.

I SAW A MAN PURSUING THE HORIZON

STEPHEN CRANE

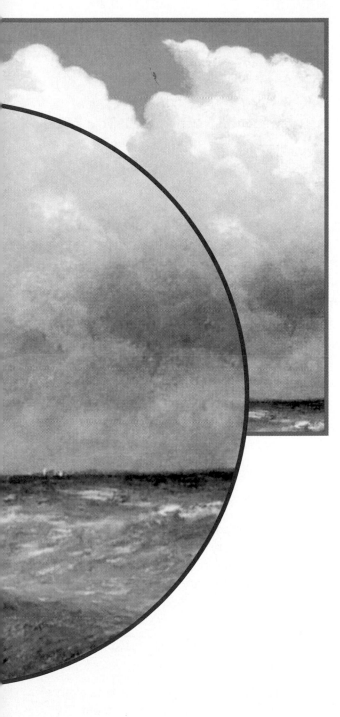

I saw a man pursuing[1] the horizon;[2]
Round and round they sped.
I was disturbed at this;
I accosted[3] the man.
5 "It is futile,"[4] I said,
"You can never——"

"You lie," he cried,
And ran on.

A MAN SAID TO THE UNIVERSE

STEPHEN CRANE

A man said to the universe:
"Sir, I exist!"
"However," replied the universe,
"The fact has not created in me
5 A sense of obligation."

---

1. pursue (pər sü′), v. follow to catch, chase.
2. horizon (hə rī′zn), n. line where the earth and sky seem to meet.
3. accost (ə kôst′), v. approach and speak to.
4. futile (fyü′tl), adj. not successful, useless.

After Reading

Making Connections

Shaping Your Response

1. What do you visualize as you read these poems? Choose one of the poems and explain how you would illustrate it.

Analyzing the Poems

2. Why does the wayfarer's attitude change?

3. **Paraphrase** "I Saw a Man Pursuing the Horizon." Explain your interpretation of the poem.

4. 👣 Crane creates two very different images of the sea in "To the Maiden." What is he saying about the relationship between people's experiences and their **perspectives** on things?

Extending the Ideas

5. Stephen Crane's poem "A Man Said to the Universe" suggests that nature is indifferent. What occurrences in the world today support or contradict that **theme?**

6. Dickinson, Whitman, Dunbar, and Crane each project an attitude toward life in their poetry. Where would you place each poet on this continuum? Explain your choices.

optimistic   **pessimistic**

Literary Focus: Irony

Discuss the **irony** in "The Wayfarer." What do you expect of the wayfarer? Why? What is ironic about his behavior? Which other poem by Crane in this section contains irony of situation?

Vocabulary Study

pursue
horizon
futile
superlative
accost

Try your hand at one of the writing forms that Crane never tried—a cartoon or comic strip. Use the vocabulary words on the left in either speech balloons or captions. The illustrations should provide the context to define the words. Use your Glossary for help.

Expressing Your Ideas

Writing Choice

Writer's Notebook Update Naturalism is writing that depicts events as rigidly determined by the forces of heredity and environment. Try your hand at being a naturalistic writer. Create a prose conversation or a poem in the style of Stephen Crane between two people or between a person and nature.

Letters to the World

American Visionaries

Fine Art Connection
The paintings in this section were created by artists who were contemporaries of Dickinson, Whitman, Dunbar, and Crane. Like these poets, each of these artists expresses a highly personal vision, often employing unusual symbolism or elements of fantasy.

American Visionaries

FREDERIC EDWIN CHURCH
Our Banner in the Sky (1861)
Combining patriotism and nature mysticism, this visionary landscape, painted in the first year of the Civil War, seems to express a hope in heavenly protection for the American union.

American

Visionaries

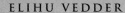

American Visionaries

Responding

1. All of these paintings have an element of strangeness. In which do you find this element the most appealing? the least appealing?

2. Do you think one of these paintings would make an interesting illustration for one of the poems in this section? If so, which poem and why?

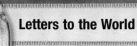
Writing Workshop

Dear World,

Assignment You've read selections that present four different writers' perspectives on the world—their world views. Now present your own world view.

WRITER'S BLUEPRINT

Product   A collage and letter
Purpose   To present in words and pictures your world view
Audience Everyone
Specs   As the creator of a successful presentation, you should:

❑ Assemble a collage of images and quotations that represents the world as you see it. For images, look in magazines and newspapers. For quotations, consider song lyrics, bumper stickers, ads, political slogans, and other sources.

❑ Write a letter to the world that comments on the various elements in your collage and tells how they reflect your world view. Use friendly-letter format.

❑ Conclude by looking back at your work and summarizing your world view.

❑ Be concise.

❑ Follow the rules of grammar, usage, spelling, and mechanics. Pay special attention to avoiding run-ons.

 PREWRITING

Examine a poet's world view. In a small group, analyze one of the poems in this part of the unit as if the images in it were part of a collage representing the poet's world view. Use an image chart like the one shown on the next page to guide your analysis.

Image	Ideas it suggests. Questions it raises.	World view
bird in a cage	people who are capable of great things being held back?	The poet feels that nature is carefree but people are not.

Examine your own world view. Jot down images that come to mind when you think of how you view the world, and analyze them in a personal image chart like the one above. You might also jot down quotes from song lyrics, poems, and other sources.

Make your world-view collage. Use sketches, pictures from magazines, photographs of friends and family, song lyrics, bumper stickers, lines of poetry, single words—whatever works for you. Use your personal image chart as a guide.

Quickwrite for five minutes or so about how the images in your collage illustrate your world view. Then exchange collages with a partner and discuss each other's work. Your partner may give you new insights on your view of the world.

Plan your letter to the world. Look back at your personal image chart, collage, and your partner's quickwrite comments. Underline those sentences in your quickwrite and your partner's comments that you think best explain your collage. Number your comments in the order you plan to use them.

2 DRAFTING

As you draft, use your chart and quickwrites as guides. Here are some tips to help you.

- You don't have to comment on every item in your collage.

- It's easy to go on and on about the things that interest you—and end up boring the reader. Try to be concise. See the Revising Strategy in Step 3 of this lesson.

- When you finish writing about your collage, look back at what you've written and make notes on phrases and ideas you see repeated. Use these repeated ideas and phrases as the main points in your concluding paragraph or two: a summary of your world view.

3 REVISING

Ask a partner for comments on your draft before you revise it. Use the blueprint as a guide. Then see the Revising Strategy below.

Revising Strategy

Being Concise

Think of every single word you write as having its own unique function. It should add meaning, interest, or emphasis to the sentence. If it does not, change it or cut it. Similarly, if you find you can say the same thing in fewer words, do it.

WORDY   The activity I most like to do in my spare time when I'm not working at my job ever since the time when I was a small child is growing plants outside.

CONCISE   My favorite hobby ever since I was little has been gardening.

When you revise, see if you can be more concise. Notice in the student model that needless words and phrases have been removed to make the writing more concise.

> I also notice that people spend a ~~great deal~~ *lot* of their time talking about ~~the subjects and ideas of~~ *world* peace ~~in the world~~ and ~~about violence~~ *racial violence, but people don't* ~~that happens because of race differences.~~ Nobody does anything to change the way they act. ~~They just keep on acting the same.~~

STUDENT MODEL

4 EDITING

Ask a partner to review your revised draft before you edit. When you edit, look for errors in grammar, usage, spelling, and mechanics. Look especially for errors with run-on sentences.

Editing Strategy

FOR REFERENCE
You'll find more tips for avoiding run-ons in the Language and Grammar Handbook at the back of this book.

Avoiding Run-ons

Run-ons are independent clauses that are not joined properly:

> This song lyric is easy to remember it expresses how I feel.

You can correct run-ons by joining the independent clauses with a subordinating conjunction or a comma followed by a coordinating conjunction:

> These lyrics are easy to remember **because** they express how I feel.

> These lyrics are easy to remember**, and** they express how I feel.

You can also split them into separate sentences:

> These lyrics are easy to remember. They express how I feel.

Look for run-ons when you revise.

5 PRESENTING

- Organize a class exhibit of your work and invite members of the school and community to view it.

- Arrange to exchange letters and collages with a class in another city, state, or country.

6 LOOKING BACK

Self-evaluate. Look back at the Writer's Blueprint and give your presentation a score for each item, from 6 (superior) to 1 (inadequate).

Reflect. Which poet most closely reflects your world view? Which one seems the most different? Explain your choices in writing.

For Your Working Portfolio Add your letter and your reflection responses to your working portfolio.

Beyond Print

Reading a Painting

What did you think of the paintings of the American Visionaries on pages 377–380? Your reaction to the paintings will depend largely on the *way* you look at them. Take a closer look at William Holbrook Beard's 1882 painting, *The Lost Balloon,* on page 380, and consider the following elements:

Context What is the time period depicted? Why are those people on the rock? What relationship, if any, do they have to the balloon? What is the mood of the painting? Is this painting set before or after a storm? You will probably have to guess to answer most of these questions, but thinking about them will help you appreciate the work. Does the mysterious nature of this painting work for you, or would you prefer a clearer story line?

Color What colors are used in the painting? What are the brightest colors depicting? What are the darkest colors used for? How do the colors contribute to the painting's overall mood?

Composition Focus on the objects, shapes, and lines in the painting. Notice how the cave and the rock it is in point toward the dark and ominous cloud which leads you toward the lighter sky on the left. Notice how the people are all pointing toward the sky. Finally, look at the water between the bottom trees and the sky. The sun, reflected on the water, once again draws your eyes upward. Eventually all of the elements of this painting seem to lead your gaze to the small and distant lost balloon.

Activity Options

Getting What You Ask For Imagine you have contracted the artist to have *The Lost Balloon* painted. You want a colorful piece showing picnickers out enjoying nature and noticing a hot air balloon on the horizon. When the painting arrives you think it is too moody, dark, and strange. You return the work to the artist, along with suggestions to the artist for making the painting more upbeat and cheerful. What are your suggestions?

Art Review Choose one of the other five American Visionary paintings to analyze. Consider context, color, and composition in your analysis. When you're done, compare your analysis to a classmate's analysis of the same work. Did you reach the same conclusions?

HISTORICAL OVERVIEW

By the 1840s Americans saw it as their "manifest destiny" to expand to the Pacific and become a transcontinental power. Driven by this sense of mission, the United States fought a war with Mexico to gain Texas, the Southwest, and California. Pioneers in wagon trains settled the Oregon Country and later the railroads led the migration west into the Great Plains toward the Pacific Coast. Miners from the California Gold Rush worked their way east, over the Rocky Mountains and into the Black Hills of South Dakota. The men and women who created the new American West suffered many hardships but they also caused suffering as they destroyed traditional ways of life for thousands of American Indians and Mexicans.

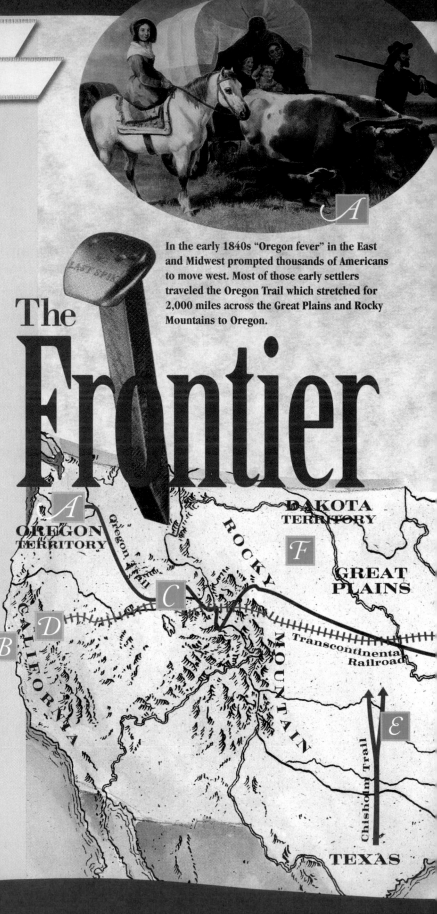

The Frontier

In the early 1840s "Oregon fever" in the East and Midwest prompted thousands of Americans to move west. Most of those early settlers traveled the Oregon Trail which stretched for 2,000 miles across the Great Plains and Rocky Mountains to Oregon.

News of the California gold rush brought thousands of Chinese immigrants to the United States in the early 1850s. Anti-Chinese prejudice culminated with Congress' passage of the Chinese Exclusion Act of 1882, which prohibited the immigration of Chinese workers into the U.S.

On May 10, 1869 the transcontinental railroad was completed at Promontory Point, Utah and the nation was physically united for the first time.

Gold was first discovered in California in 1848 at Sutter's Mill, near Sacramento. By the next year thousands of gold seekers, called "Forty-niners," had arrived in California from across the United States and around the world seeking their fortunes.

Using techniques developed by Spanish vaqueros in the early 1800s, American cowboys in the 1860s guided herds of cattle along the Chisholm Trail from Texas to Abilene, Kansas where they were put on railroad cars and sent to markets in the East.

On June 25, 1876 at the Battle of the Little Bighorn chiefs Sitting Bull and Crazy Horse led 2,500 Sioux and Cheyenne against Lieutenant Colonel George Custer and his 264 U.S. troops. Custer and his men were killed in the battle that came to be known as "Custer's Last Stand."

Key Dates

1840s
Americans travel west on the Oregon Trail.

1849
Gold is discovered in California.

1860s
Cattle drives from Texas begin.

1869
Transcontinental Railroad is completed in Promontory Point, Utah.

1876
The Sioux Indians defeat Custer at the Little Bighorn.

1882
The Chinese Exclusion Act bans the immigration of Chinese workers into the United States.

1910-1940
Angel Island in San Francisco Bay is used to detain and process Asian immigrants.

Part Two

The Frontier

The history of the American West is multifaceted, involving people of different backgrounds and experiences facing difficulties and challenges in a land that held both promise and tragedy. Some of the traditions, experiences, and flavor of the West are captured in the following selections.

👣 **Multicultural Connection Communication** pertains to the many ways we express ourselves—through language, music, art, literature, and in more informal ways, such as the clothing we wear. In the American West of the 1800s, many cultural groups converged, bringing with them their unique styles and forms of communication. What do the communication styles of the following works have in common, and how do they differ?

Literature

Mark Twain	**The Celebrated Jumping Frog of Calaveras County** ◆ short story	390
Américo Paredes	**El Corrido de Gregorio Cortez** ◆ ballad	398
Anonymous	**Gold Mountain Poems** ◆ poetry	400
Satanta	**My Heart Feels Like Bursting** ◆ speech	403
Willa Cather	**A Wagner Matinée** ◆ short story	407

Interdisciplinary Study Frontier Adventures and Tragedies

Legends of the Wild West ◆ pop culture 416

from Black Hawk, an Autobiography ◆ history 418

from Thousand Pieces of Gold
    by Ruthanne Lum McCunn ◆ literature 420

from Down the Santa Fe Trail by Susan Shelby Magoffin ◆ history 421

Language History

The Many Flavors of American English 422

Writing Workshop Expository

Bringing History to Life 423

Beyond Print Media Literacy

Watching Westerns 427

Before Reading

The Celebrated Jumping Frog of Calaveras County

by Mark Twain

Mark Twain
1835–1910

Samuel Clemens was raised in Missouri. His father died when he was twelve, forcing Clemens to quit school and go to work. Apprenticed to a printer, he became an expert at his trade. As a young man, Clemens traveled widely. In 1857, he was apprenticed to a river pilot and began a series of journeys on the Mississippi River. When the outbreak of the Civil War closed the Mississippi, he went to Carson City, Nevada, looking for silver. When he failed at prospecting, he took up journalism, using the pseudonym Mark Twain, a river call meaning "two fathoms," or that the water was twelve feet deep, enough for safe passage.

Building Background

Twain the Prospector While working as a journalist in California, Twain spent some time at his friend Jim Gillis's mining camp at Jackass Gulch in Calaveras County. One night, while Twain and Gillis were sitting around the stove at the Angel Camp saloon, they met storyteller Ben Coon, who told a tale of a champion frog who could out-jump any frog in the West. Twain took Coon's story, embellished it with his own humor and enthusiasm for life in the Old West, and published it as "The Celebrated Jumping Frog of Calaveras County." Although the story of this talented frog was well-known long before Twain published it, nobody had ever told it or written it as Mark Twain had. Twain's career as a humorist had begun.

Literary Focus

Dialect In the following story, Simon Wheeler tells his story in his own **dialect**—the language of the American frontier in the middle and late 1800s. As you read, take note of Wheeler's unique way of saying things. What effect does the dialect have on the tone of the story?

Writer's Notebook

The Art of Exaggerating
Look carefully at the cartoon. What's funny about this scene? Cartoonists sometimes use **exaggeration** for comic effect. Writers will often do the same. For example, the following story describes a dog who was so determined to win fights that he would hang on to his

"Popcorn's done, honey."

opponent for as long as necessary, *even if it took a year.* Before you read, write a list of five humorous exaggerations you've read or heard, or make up your own. Or, if you'd rather, draw a cartoon using exaggeration.

THE CELEBRATED JUMPING FROG OF CALAVERAS COUNTY

Mark Twain

In compliance with the request of a friend of mine, who wrote me from the East, I called on good-natured, garrulous[1] old Simon Wheeler, and inquired after my friend's friend, Leonidas W. Smiley, as requested to do, and I hereunto append[2] the result. I have a lurking suspicion that *Leonidas W.* Smiley is a myth; that my friend never knew such a personage; and that he only conjectured that if I asked old Wheeler about him, it would remind him of his infamous *Jim* Smiley, and he would go to work and bore me to death with some exasperating reminiscence of him as long and as tedious as it should be useless to me. If that was the design, it succeeded.

I found Simon Wheeler dozing comfortably by the barroom stove of the dilapidated[3] tavern in the decayed mining camp of Angel's, and I noticed that he was fat and baldheaded, and had an expression of winning gentleness and simplicity upon his tranquil countenance. He roused up, and gave me good day. I told him a friend of mine had commissioned me to make some inquiries about a cherished companion of his boyhood named *Leonidas W. Smiley—Rev. Leonidas W.* Smiley, a young minister of the Gospel, who he had heard was at one time a resident of Angel's Camp. I added that if Mr. Wheeler could tell me anything about this Rev. Leonidas W. Smiley, I would feel under many obligations to him.

Simon Wheeler backed me into a corner and blockaded me there with his chair, and then sat down and reeled off the monotonous narrative which follows this paragraph. He never smiled, he never frowned, he never changed his voice from the gentle-flowing key to which he tuned his initial sentence, he never betrayed the slightest suspicion of enthusiasm; but all through the interminable narrative there ran a vein of impressive earnestness and sincerity which showed me plainly that, so far from his imagining that there was anything ridiculous or funny about his story, he regarded it as a really important matter, and admired its two heroes as men of transcendent genius in finesse. I let him go on in his own way, and never interrupted him once.

---

1. **garrulous** (gar′ə ləs), *adj.* talkative.
2. **append** (ə pend′), *v.* attach as a supplement.
3. **dilapidated** (də lap′ə dā′tid), *adj.* fallen into disrepair.

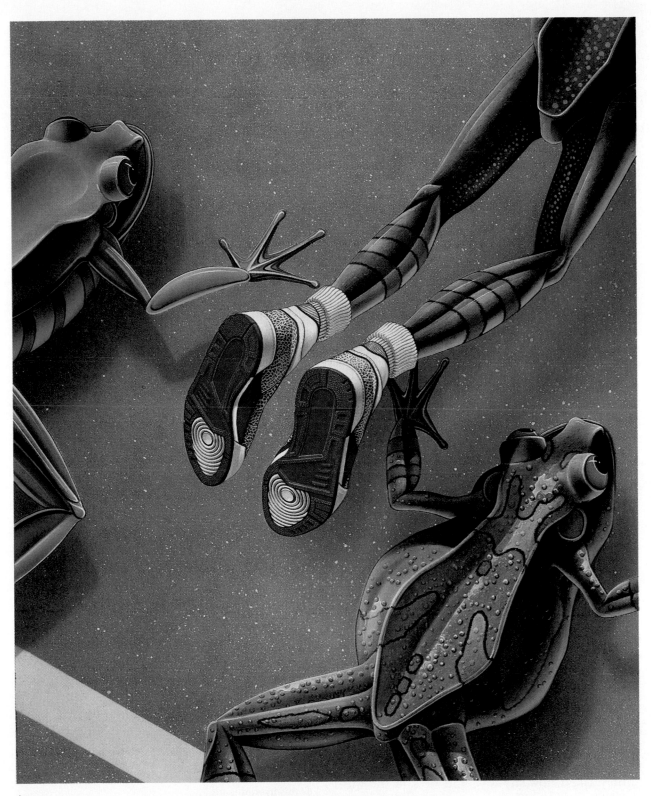

▲ How does the tone of this illustration by Laura Phillips compare with the tone of Mark Twain's story? Is this modern image a good match for Twain's classic published in 1865? Explain.

"Rev. Leonidas W. H'm, Reverend Le—well, there was a feller here once by the name of *Jim Smiley*, in the winter of '49—or maybe it was the spring of '50—I don't recollect exactly, somehow, though what makes me think it was one or the other is because I remember the big flume wasn't finished when he first came to the camp. But anyway, he was the curiousest man about always betting on anything that turned up you ever see, if he could get anybody to bet on the other side; and if he couldn't, he'd change sides. Any way that suited the other man would suit *him*—any way just so's he got a bet, *he* was satisfied. But still he was lucky, uncommon lucky; he most always come out winner. He was always ready and laying for a chance; there couldn't be no solit'ry thing mentioned but that feller'd offer to bet on it, and take any side you please, as I was just telling you. If there was a horse race, you'd find him flush or you'd find him busted at the end of it; if there was a dogfight, he'd bet on it; if there was a cat fight, he'd bet on it; if there was a chicken fight, he'd bet on it. Why, if there was two birds setting on a fence, he would bet you which one would fly first; or if there was a camp meeting, he would be there reg'lar to bet on Parson Walker, which he judged to be the best exhorter about there, and so he was too, and a good man. If he even see a straddlebug start to go any-wheres, he would bet you how long it would take him to get wherever he was going to, and if you took him up, he would foller that straddlebug to Mexico but what he would find out where he was bound for and how long he was on the road.

Lots of the boys here has seen Smiley, and can tell you about him. Why, it never made no differ-ence to *him*—he'd bet on *anything*—the dangdest feller. Parson Walker's wife laid very sick once, for a good while, and it seemed as if they warn't going to save her; but one morning he come in, and Smiley asked how she was, and he said she was considerable better—thank the Lord for His inf'nite mercy—and coming on so smart that with the blessing of Prov'dence she'd get well yet; and Smiley, before he thought, says, 'Well, I'll resk two-and-a-half that she don't anyway.'

"This-hyer[4] Smiley had a mare—the boys called her the fifteen-minute nag, but that was only in fun, you know, because of course she was faster than that—and he used to win money on that horse, for all she was so slow and always had the asthma, or the distemper, or the consump-tion, or something of that kind. They used to give her two or three hundred yards' start, and then pass her underway; but always at the fag end[5] of the race she'd get excited and desperatelike, and come cavorting and straddling up, and scattering her legs around limber, sometimes in the air, and sometimes out to one side among the fences, and kicking up m-o-r-e dust and raising m-o-r-e racket with her coughing and sneezing and blowing her nose—and *always* fetch up at the stand just about a neck ahead, as near as you could cipher it down.

"And he had a little small bull pup, that to look at him you'd think he wan't worth a cent but to set around and look ornery and lay for a chance to steal something. But as soon as money was up on him, he was a different dog; his under jaw'd begin to stick out like the fo'castle of a steamboat, and his teeth would uncover and shine like the furnaces. And a dog might tackle him and bullyrag him, and bite him, and throw him over his shoulder two or three times, and Andrew Jackson—which was the name of the pup—Andrew Jackson would never let on but what *he* was satisfied, and hadn't expected noth-ing else—and the bets being doubled and dou-bled on the other side all the time, till the money was all up; and then all of a sudden he would grab that other dog jest by the j'int of his hind leg and freeze to it—not chaw, you understand, but only just grip and hang on till they throwed up the sponge, if it was a year.

"Smiley always come out winner on that pup,

---

4. **this-hyer,** this here.
5. **fag end,** the last part or remnant of anything, after the best part has been used up.

till he harnessed a dog once that didn't have no hind legs, because they'd been sawed off by a circular saw, and when the thing had gone along far enough, and the money was all up, and he come to make a snatch for his pet holt,[6] he saw in a minute how he'd been imposed on, and how the other dog had him in the door,[7] so to speak, and he 'peared surprised, and then he looked sorter discouraged like, and didn't try no more to win the fight, and so he got shucked out[8] bad. He give Smiley a look, as much as to say his heart was broke, and it was *his* fault, for putting up a dog that hadn't no hind legs for him to take holt of, which was his main dependence in a fight, and then he limped off a piece and laid down and died. It was a good pup, was that Andrew Jackson, and would have made a name for hisself if he'd lived, for the stuff was in him and he had genius—I know it, because he hadn't had no opportunities to speak of, and it don't stand to reason that a dog could make such a fight as he could under them circumstances if he hadn't no talent. It always makes me feel sorry when I think of that last fight of his'n, and the way it turned out.

"Well, this-hyer Smiley had rat terriers, and chicken cocks, and tomcats and all them kind of things, till you couldn't rest, and you couldn't fetch nothing for him to bet on but he'd match you. He ketched a frog one day, and took him home, and said he calk'lated to edercate him; and so he never done nothing for three months but set in his backyard and learn that frog to jump. And you bet he *did* learn him, too. He'd give him a little punch behind, and the next minute you'd see that frog whirling in the air like a doughnut—see him turn one summer-set, or maybe a couple, if he got a good start, and come down flat-footed and all right, like a cat. He got him up so in the matter of catching flies, and kep' him in practice so constant, that he'd

> **Smiley said all a frog wanted was education, and he could do 'most anything—and I believe him.**

nail a fly every time as far as he could see him.

"Smiley said all a frog wanted was education, and he could do 'most anything—and I believe him. Why, I've seen him set Dan'l Webster down here on this floor—Dan'l Webster was the name of the frog—and sing out, 'Flies, Dan'l, flies!' and quicker'n you could wink he'd spring straight up and snake a fly off'n the counter there, and flop down on the floor ag'in as solid as a gob of mud, and fall to scratching the side of his head with his hind foot as indifferent as if he hadn't no idea he'd been doin' any more'n any frog might do. You never see a frog so modest and straightfor'ard as he was, for all he was so gifted. And when it came to fair and square jumping on a dead level, he could get over more ground at one straddle than any animal of his breed you ever see. Jumping on a dead level was his strong suit, you understand; and when it come to that, Smiley would ante up[9] money on him as long as he had a red.[10] Smiley was monstrous proud of his frog, and well he might be, for fellers that had traveled and been everywheres all said he laid over any frog that ever *they* see.

"Well, Smiley kept the beast in a little lattice box, and he used to fetch him downtown sometimes and lay for a bet. One day a feller—a stranger in the camp, he was—come across him with his box, and says:

"'What might it be that you've got in the box?'

"And Smiley says, sorter indifferentlike, 'It might be a parrot, or it might be a canary, maybe, but it ain't—it's only just a frog.'

"And the feller took it, and looked at it careful,

---

6. **pet holt,** pet hold, or favorite hold.
7. **had him in the door,** had him at a disadvantage.
8. **shucked out,** *v.* beaten.
9. **ante up** (en'ē up), *v.* pay one's share.
10. **a red,** a red cent, or any money at all.

The Celebrated Jumping Frog of Calaveras County   **393**

and turned it around this way and that, and says, 'H'm—so 'tis. Well, what's *he* good for?'

"'Well,' Smiley says, easy and careless, 'he's good enough for *one* thing, I should judge—he can out-jump any frog in Calaveras County.'

"The feller took the box again, and took another long, particular look, and give it back to Smiley, and says, very deliberate, 'Well, I don't see no p'ints[11] about that frog that's any better'n any other frog.'

"'Maybe you don't,' Smiley says. 'Maybe you understand frogs and maybe you don't understand 'em; maybe you've had experience, and maybe you ain't only a amature, as it were. Anyways, I've got *my* opinion, and I'll resk forty dollars that he can outjump any frog in Calaveras County.'

"And the feller studied a minute, and then says, kinder sadlike, 'Well, I'm only a stranger here, and I ain't got no frog; but if I had a frog, I'd bet you.'

"And then Smiley says, 'That's all right—that's all right—if you'll hold my box a minute, I'll go and get you a frog.' And so the feller took the box, and put up his forty dollars along with Smiley's, and set down to wait.

"So he set there a good while thinking and thinking to himself, and then he got the frog out and prized his mouth open and took a teaspoon and filled him full of quail shot—filled him pretty near up to his chin—and set him on the floor.

"Smiley he went to the swamp and slopped around in the mud for a long time, and finally he ketched a frog, and fetched him in, and give him to this feller, and says:

"'Now, if you're ready, set him alongside of Dan'l, with his forepaws just even with Dan'l's, and I'll give the word.' Then he says, 'One—two—three—jump!' and him and the feller touched up the frogs from behind, and the new frog hopped off, but Dan'l give a heave and hysted up his shoulders—so—like a Frenchman, but it wan't no use—he couldn't budge; he was planted as solid as an anvil, and he couldn't no more stir than if he was anchored out. Smiley was a good deal surprised, and he was disgusted too, but he didn't have no idea what the matter was, of course.

"The feller took the money and started away; and when he was going out at the door, he sorter jerked his thumb over his shoulder—this way—at Dan'l, and says again, very deliberate, 'Well, *I* don't see no p'ints about that frog that's any better'n any other frog.'

"Smiley he stood scratching his head and looking down at Dan'l a long time, and at last he says, 'I do wonder what in the nation that frog throw'd off for—I wonder if there ain't something the matter with him—he 'pears to look mighty baggy somehow.' And he ketched Dan'l by the nap of the neck, and lifted him up, and says, 'Why blame my cats if he don't weight five pound!' and turned him upside down, and he belched out a double handful of shot. And then Smiley see how it was, and he was the maddest man—he set the frog down and took out after that feller, but he never ketched him. And——"

[Here Simon Wheeler heard his name called from the front yard, and got up to see what was wanted.] And turning to me as he moved away, he said: "Just set where you are, stranger, and rest easy—I ain't going to be gone a second."

But, by your leave, I did not think that a continuation of the history of the enterprising vagabond *Jim* Smiley would be likely to afford[12] me much information concerning the Rev. *Leonidas W.* Smiley, and so I started away.

At the door I met the sociable Wheeler returning, and he buttonholed me and recommenced:[13]

"Well, this-hyer Smiley had a yaller one-eyed cow that didn't have no tail, only just a short stump like a bannanner, and——"

However, lacking both time and inclination, I did not wait to hear about the afflicted cow, but took my leave.

---

11. **p'ints,** points.
12. **afford** (ə fôrd′), *v.* manage to give or spare.
13. **recommence** (rē kə mens′), begin again.

After Reading

Making Connections

Shaping Your Response

1. On a scale of one to ten, how would you rate Simon Wheeler as a storyteller?

1   10

a gifted storyteller   **a terrible storyteller**

2. What three adjectives would you use to describe Jim Smiley? What three adjectives would you use to describe Simon Wheeler?

Analyzing the Story

3. In what ways is "The Celebrated Jumping Frog" a humorous story?

4. If you were able to ask Mark Twain to rank his three **characters**—the narrator, Simon Wheeler, or Jim Smiley—from most favorite to least, what do you think he would reply? Be prepared to explain your response.

5. 👣 Twain chooses a narrator who tells his story in frontier **dialect**. How does the narrator's style of **communication** reflect the society and culture of the West of the 1800s?

Extending the Ideas

6. A common plot in literature involves the situation of "the trickster tricked." Think of another story that uses this plot device.

Literary Focus: Dialect

Dialects deviate from the norms of standard language in vocabulary, pronunciation, and usage. Think about Simon Wheeler's frontier dialect. How does it differ from formal English?

- Reread the fourth paragraph of the story. On a piece of paper, jot down a few examples of Wheeler's peculiar vocabulary and pronunciation. How does Wheeler's dialect contribute to the humor of the story? Does his use of dialect make him a more authentic character? Why or why not?

- In your notebook, "translate" this paragraph into formal English. Compare your translation to the original. Which version do you prefer? Why? If you were to replace all of the dialect in the story with formal English, what would be the overall effect?

Vocabulary Study

garrulous
append
dilapidated
afford
recommence

Use the listed words from the story to write your own tall tale. Unless you're feeling ambitious, a paragraph or two will do. Use your Glossary, if necessary.

Expressing Your Ideas _____

Writing Choices

Writer's Notebook Update You've read Twain's exaggerations, now try a little exaggeration of your own. Write a short paragraph that describes an everyday situation in your life—your trip to school today, perhaps, or the time you spent at the dinner table last night. Then rewrite the paragraph, this time adding exaggeration. For example, your ride on the school bus might become an "endless, terrifying journey, fraught with danger and intrigue."

More About the Frog Some stories never end. With this in mind, get together in small groups and write a **short story** entitled "The Further Adventures of Dan'l Webster." Begin by brainstorming a new adventure for Jim Smiley's frog. Then, in round-robin fashion, dictate the story to your group's secretary. When you've finished, have one group member read the story aloud to the rest of the class. Which group has the funniest or most ridiculous story?

Other Options

Simon Wheeler: Master Storyteller Much to everyone's great surprise, Simon Wheeler has won the prestigious "Storyteller of the Year Award." You've been chosen to give the introductory **speech** at the awards ceremony. What will you say about Simon Wheeler and his storytelling abilities?

Academy Award Material? Imagine that you've been asked to make an animated short film of "The Celebrated Jumping Frog of Calaveras County." To give your staff of animators a starting point, you need to make some quick **sketches** of Simon Wheeler, Jim Smiley, and Dan'l Webster. If you have trouble drawing figures, make a sketch of the setting and include with it a description of how you think the characters (and the frog) should look.

The Jumping Frog Game Imagine that "The Celebrated Jumping Frog of Calaveras County" has become a successful cartoon, and now manufacturers want a game based on the story. It's your job to create it. Design a **game** that picks up on the topics and themes of the story.

Before Reading

El Corrido de Gregorio Cortez by Américo Paredes

Gold Mountain Poems Anonymous

My Heart Feels Like Bursting by Satanta

Américo Paredes
born 1915

Born in Brownsville, Texas, Américo Paredes grew up hearing the ballads and stories of the Lower Rio Grande border. During the 1950s and 1960s, Paredes began to collect and publish the tales. "El Corrido de Gregorio Cortez" is a ballad that has been sung by Mexican Americans for generations.

Gold Mountain Poets

In the early 1850s, many Chinese immigrants arrived in California, a land they'd heard was filled with gold. What they found instead was discrimination and backbreaking work. Some wrote about their experiences in anonymous poems.

Satanta
1830?–1878

Satanta diligently fought U.S. government efforts to move the Kiowa and Comanches onto reservations. Eventually forced onto a reservation, Satanta led raiding parties into Texas and Mexico to look for food and supplies. In 1874, he was imprisoned; four years later, officials announced that he had committed suicide. The people of the Kiowa nation, however, were convinced that Satanta had been murdered.

Building Background

The United States Expands Westward As you read the following selections, keep in mind the events that were taking place at the time.

1830s	The U.S. government, in order to free land for white settlers, forces American Indians to move to the Indian Territory, in what is now Oklahoma.
1845	The United States annexes Texas.
1846	The Mexican War begins. At the end of the war, Mexico agrees to give up all claims to Texas.
1848	Gold is discovered in California.
1849–1850	Thousands of Chinese immigrate to California, looking for gold.
1863	Construction on the Union Pacific Railroad begins. Railroad companies employ Chinese immigrants because they are willing to work for less pay.
late 1860s	Soldiers force American Indians off their western lands.
1876	Plains Indians defeat General George Custer at the Little Bighorn River in Montana. In retaliation, the U.S. government sends more soldiers west.
early 1880s	Nearly all American Indians have been moved onto reservations.
1882	The Chinese Exclusion Act halts the influx of immigrants from China.
1890	The U.S. Bureau of Census declares that no frontiers remain open.

Literary Focus

Tone By recognizing **tone,** a reader can determine whether a writer views a subject with sympathy, aloofness, anger, or admiration. Any of the following might provide a clue to the tone of the following works: point of view, word choice, style, choice of images, even sound and rhythm.

Writer's Notebook

A Frontier Dilemma Choose one of the events listed above and write everything you know about it. Then, write any questions or comments you have about the event.

El Corrido de Gregorio Cortez   397

EL CORRIDO DE
Gregorio Cortez

Américo Paredes

Gregorio Cortez was born in Mexico on June 22, 1875, and emigrated to Texas in 1887. On June 13, 1901, Sheriff W. T. Morris came to his house while looking for a Mexican who had stolen a horse. After asking Gregorio Cortez several questions, Morris mistakenly concluded that Cortez was defying his authority. He gave orders for his men to arrest both Cortez and his brother. In the ensuing fight, Morris shot and killed Cortez's brother, then Cortez shot and killed Morris. Cortez fled, and a posse led by Sheriff Robert M. Glover set out after him.

Glover's posse caught up with Cortez on June 16, 1901. Cortez killed Glover in the gun battle that followed. In spite of the overwhelming odds against Cortez, he escaped and fled toward Mexico. As he approached the border, Cortez was apprehended. He was taken back to Corpus Christi, where a jury determined that he had killed Sheriff Morris in self-defense. However, when tried for killing Sheriff Glover, Cortez was found guilty and given a life sentence in prison. Sixteen years later, Texas Governor Oscar B. Colquitt pardoned him. Could the above 1877 painting, Gauchos in a Horse Corral *by James Walker, be used to portray part of the story of Gregorio Cortez's life? If so, what part of the story?*

In the county of El Carmen
What a misfortune occurred,
The Major Sheriff[1] died,
It is not known who killed him.

5 It must have been two in the afternoon,
About half an hour afterward,
They found that the wrongdoer
Had been Gregorio Cortez.

They let loose the bloodhounds
10 So they could follow the trail,
But trying to overtake Cortez
Was like following a star.

Those rangers of the county
Rode so fast they almost flew,
15 Because they wanted to get
Three thousand dollars they were offered.

In the county of Kansas
They succeeded in overtaking him,
Something more than three hundred,
20 And there he jumped their corral.

Then the Major Sheriff said,
As if he was going to cry,
"Cortez, hand over your weapons;
We are not going to kill you."

25 Then said Gregorio Cortez,
With his pistol in his hand,
"Ah, how many mounted rangers
Against one lone Mexican!"

Now with this I say farewell,
30 In the shade of a cypress tree,
This is the end of the ballad
Of Don Gregorio Cortez.

---

1. **Major Sheriff,** Sheriff Robert Glover, the
sheriff who pursued Cortez after the gunfight
with Sheriff Morris.

En el condado del Carmen
tal desgracia sucedió,
murió el Cherife Mayor,
no saben quién lo mató.

5 Serían las dos de la tarde,
como media hora después,
supieron que el malhechor
era Gregorio Cortez.

Soltaron los perros jaunes
10 pa' que siguieran la juella
pero alcanzar a Cortez
era seguir a una estrella.

Esos rinches del condado
iban que casi volaban
15 porque se querían ganar
tres mil pesos que les daban.

En el condado de Kiancer
lo llegaron a alcanzar,
a poco más de trescientos
20 y allí les brincó el corral.

Decía el Cherife Mayor
como queriendo llorar:
—Cortez, entrega tus armas,
no te vamos a matar.

25 Decía Gregorio Cortez
con su pistola en la mano:
—¡Ah, cuánto rinche montado
para un solo mexicano!

Ya con ésta me despido
30 a la sombra de un ciprés,
aquí se acaba el corrido
de don Gregorio Cortez.

Gold Mountain Poems

Anonymous

亞卿呀。莫作夫情寡。

難夢與儂同講話。遊魂夜夜話交加 ○

In the early 1850s, thousands of Chinese emigrated to California. Their passage to Gum Shan, ("Mountain of Gold"), their name for America, was difficult; many did not survive the 7,000-mile trip. Once they reached San Francisco, hundreds were turned away by immigration officials. Of those who were allowed into the country, many were forced to work backbreaking jobs to earn enough money for food. Disillusioned and embittered, some of them gave vent to their frustration by writing poetry.

What mood, thoughts, or feelings does the image, *Portrait of a Chinese Man* by Isaac Wallace Baker, **communicate** to you?

1

Ever since I've arrived in Gold Mountain,
Not one day have I dared forget my family.
My mind is <u>chaotic</u>,[1] like hemp fibers,
    with <u>constant</u> thoughts of home;
Each meal is hard to swallow, because of sorrow.
5 My dear woman:
Don't ever think your husband has betrayed your love.
It's hard enough to share my words with you in dreams;
My soul is wandering, every night, my tongue tightened.

---

1. **chaotic** (kā ot′ik), *adj.* very confused; completely disordered.

2

The moment I hear
    Wc've entered the port,
I am all ready:
    my belongings wrapped in a bundle.
5 Who would have expected joy to
        become sorrow:
Detained in a dark, crude, filthy room?
What can I do?
Cruel treatment, not one restful
        breath of air,
Scarcity of food, severe restrictions—all unbearable.
10 Here even a proud man bows his head low.

3

America, I have come and landed,
And am stranded here, for more than a year.
Suffering thousands upon thousands of mistreatments.
Is it in retribution for a past life that I deserve such defilement?[1]
5 It is outrageous—
Being humiliated[2] repeatedly by them.
I pray my country will
        become strong
        and even the score:
Send out troops, like
        Japan's war
        against Russia![3]

---

1. **defilement** (di fīl′ mənt), *n.* an act of dishonoring.
2. **humiliate** (hyū mil′ē āt), *v.* cause to feel ashamed.
3. **Japan's war against Russia,** the Russo-Japancsc War (1903–1905) which Japan won.

一聞入港口。打起個伏包(一)。
誰知歡喜反為愁。闇室受困更濁陋。
冇能較(二)。殘酷氣難哮。
缺食不堪嚴掣肘。英雄到此也垂頭。

(一)伏::作「袱」
(二)冇能較::沒法計較，無可奈何

來美經抵步。被困年有多。
個中萬折又千磨。前世吾修折太墮(二)。
真可惡。屢逢佢欺負。
但願國強仇報復。興兵恰似日戰俄。

(一)吾::作「唔」;;前世唔修::前生沒有好德行，今生受苦
(二)折墮::折磨委屈

自抵金山也。無日敢忘家。
心懷桑梓亂如蔴。每飯因愁難咽下。

4

So, liberty is your national principle;
Why do you practice autocracy?[1]
You don't uphold justice, you Americans,
You detain me in prison, guard me closely.
5 Your officials are wolves and tigers,
All ruthless, all wanting to bite me.
An innocent man implicated,[2] such an
　　injustice!
When can I get out of this prison and free
　　my mind?

自由爲國例。何事學專制。
不持公理美人兮。困我監牢嚴密睇 (一)
狼虎差。橫行更欲噬。
罪及無辜眞惡抵 (二) 。幾時出獄開心懷。

（一）睇∴參看歌
（二）惡抵∴難以抵受；參看歌

5

In search of a pin-head gain,
I was idle in an impoverished village.
I've risked a perilous journey to come to
　　the Flowery Flag[3] Nation.
Immigration officers interrogated me:
5 And, just for a slight lapse of memory,
I am deported, and imprisoned in this
　　barren[4] mountain.
A brave man cannot use his might here,
And he can't take one step beyond the
　　confines.

欲覓蠅頭利。窮鄉沒作置。
乘危履險走花旗 (一) 。遇着稅員盤詰汝 (二)
稍忘記。撥禁荒島裡 (三) 。
好漢眞無用武地。不能一步越雷池。

（一）花旗∴美國
（二）稅員∴參看歌
（三）撥∴驅逐

---

1. **autocracy** (ô tok′rə sē), *n.* supreme power of government exerted by one person.
2. implicate (im′plə kāt), *v.* show to have a part or be connected; involved.
3. **Flowery Flag,** Chinese perception of the American flag.
4. barren (bar′ən), *adj.* infertile or sterile; empty.

My Heart Feels Like Bursting

SATANTA

In 1867, the United States government called together the tribes of the Southern Plains to a meeting at Medicine Lodge Creek, Kansas. There government officials announced that two large reservations had been set aside for the Plains Indians. Several Indian chiefs spoke in protest to the plan. The following is the speech that Satanta—the "Orator of the Plains"—delivered.

I love the land and the buffalo and will not part with it. I want you to understand well what I say. Write it on paper. . . . I hear a great deal of good talk from the gentlemen whom the Great Father[1] sends us, but they never do what they say. I don't want any of the medicine lodges[2] within the country. I want the children raised as I was. . . .

I have heard that you intend to settle us on a reservation near the mountains. I don't want to settle. I love to roam over the prairies. There I feel free and happy, but when we settle down, we grow pale and die. I have laid aside my lance, bow, and shield, and yet I feel safe in your presence. I have told you the truth. I have no little lies hid about me, but I don't know how it is with the commissioners. Are they as clear as I am? A long time ago this land belonged to our fathers; but when I go up to the river, I see camps of soldiers on its banks. These soldiers cut down my timber; they kill my buffalo; and when I see that, my heart feels like bursting; I feel sorry. I have spoken.

▲ After seeing how his land has been invaded and destroyed, Satanta says that his heart "feels like bursting." Does his portrait convey that emotion? Explain your answer.

---

1. **Great Father,** President Andrew Jackson.
2. **medicine lodges,** Satanta is referring to schools and churches like those of the white people.

After Reading

Making Connections

Shaping Your Response

1. Which of these selections did you feel was most powerful or moving? Explain why.

Analyzing the Selections

2. What do you think Satanta longs for most? Explain your answer using evidence from the text.

3. How does the ballad **characterize** Gregorio Cortez?

4. Reread the third and the fourth Gold Mountain poems. How do the speakers feel about America? What do you think causes them to feel this way?

5. 👣 What can you learn about the three cultures represented in these works based on the content and chosen forms of their **communications**?

Extending the Ideas

6. With a small group, make a list of the difficulties faced by immigrants to the United States. You may want to include your own experiences or those of an ancestor in the list.

Literary Focus: Tone

Write one sentence for each of the three selections that summarizes its tone. (Consider the Gold Mountain poems as one selection.) Then, write a sentence that compares the three works. How are the three selections similar in tone? How are they different? Finally, choose one selection to examine more closely. Summarize the tone of the piece, then list and explain three clues that helped you decide on the tone. Your clues might fall into categories such as word choice, imagery, point of view, style, and rhythm.

Vocabulary Study

barren
defilement
humiliate
implicate
chaotic

Copy the chart below, supplying a synonym and the best antonym you can for each of the listed words. Use your Glossary if necessary.

Word	Synonym	Antonym
barren		
defilement		
humiliate		
implicate		
chaotic		

Expressing Your Ideas

Writing Choices

Writer's Notebook Update Look back to the questions and comments you wrote about one of the events in the time line on page 397. Add any new thoughts you have after reading the selections.

Cortez's Plea for Freedom Read again the background information about Gregorio Cortez on page 398. Now imagine you are Cortez, desperate for freedom after 16 years in prison. Write a **letter** to the governor that makes a strong plea for your freedom.

Were They Heroic? Write an **essay** that explains why you think Satanta and Cortez were or were not heroes. You may want to begin your essay by offering your own definition of what it takes to be a hero.

Other Options

A Timely Event Choose one of the dates from the time line on page 397 to investigate further. If, for example, you choose to study the Mexican War, find information about the causes, the key players, and the effects on U.S. and Mexican relations. Present a five-minute **oral report** to your class.

Immigration Today In groups, research about U.S. immigration policies. Some questions to consider: What does the government do to try to make immigrants feel welcome? Why does the U.S. put limits on immigration? Are there any policies you would like to see changed? Choose a group spokesperson to **report** on the strengths and weaknesses you found in U.S. immigration policies.

The Wild West
Downing the Nigh Leader by Frederic Remington is typical of the way many artists portrayed the conflicts between settlers and American Indians. What do you suppose was the effect of paintings like this on a world eager for information about America's Western frontier? In a small group **discussion,** determine how such art may have helped perpetuate "Wild West" stereotypes.

Before Reading

A Wagner Matinée

by Willa Cather

Willa Cather
1873–1947

Willa Cather once said to an aspiring writer, "Let your fiction grow out of the land beneath your feet." Cather's remark explains a lot about her own fiction: at age nine, she and her family moved from genteel Virginia to the awesome, empty prairie lands of Nebraska. There she witnessed the effects of pioneer life on settlers who dug their own sod houses out of the hard, dense dirt and coaxed a living out of a reluctant, though hauntingly beautiful, environment. Cather's awe for the western frontier and the pioneers who settled there are themes that she returns to again and again in her short stories and novels.

Building Background

Cather's World Willa Cather once wrote that for her the world broke in two in 1922. Although she never fully explained what she meant, she may have been referring to the fact that the old world she cherished, the world of the frontier struggle for survival on the Great Plains, with all the old-fashioned values the struggle inspired, had given way to the decline in idealism that followed World War I and the new urban culture of the Jazz Age. If you had been alive then, would you have chosen life on the open prairie or the amenities of city life?

Literary Focus

Characterization As you'll see in the story you're about to read, Willa Cather is very subtle in developing **characterization**. There are two central characters in "A Wagner Matinée," neither of which Cather fully describes. As you read, watch how these characters interact. How would you describe their personalities? How would you describe their behavior? How do they feel about each other?

Writer's Notebook

The Western Frontier You may have an idea of what the American frontier was like from watching movies and reading about it. Before reading "A Wagner Matinée," write down your impressions of what it was like to be a pioneer in the Old West. Later, you may want to compare your impressions to Cather's description of life on a Nebraska homestead.

A Wagner Matinée

WILLA CATHER

I received one morning a letter, written in pale ink on glassy, blue-lined notepaper, and bearing the postmark of a little Nebraska village. This communication, worn and rubbed, looking as if it had been carried for some days in a coat pocket that was none too clean, was from my uncle Howard, and informed me that his wife had been left a small legacy by a bachelor relative, and that it would be necessary for her to go to Boston to attend to the settling of the estate. He requested me to meet her at the station and render[1] her whatever services might be necessary. On examining the date indicated as that of her arrival, I found it to be no later than tomorrow. He had characteristically delayed writing until, had I been away from home for a day, I must have missed my aunt altogether.

The name of my Aunt Georgiana opened before me a gulf of recollection so wide and deep that, as the letter dropped from my hand, I felt suddenly a stranger to all the present conditions of my existence, wholly ill at ease and out of place amid the familiar surroundings of my study. I became, in short, the

---

1. **render** (ren′dər), v. give; do.

gangling[2] farmer boy my aunt had known, scourged[3] with chilblains[4] and bashfulness, my hands cracked and sore from the cornhusking. I sat again before her parlor organ, fumbling the scales with my stiff, red fingers, while she, beside me, made canvas mittens for the huskers.

The next morning, after preparing my landlady for a visitor, I set out for the station. When the train arrived, I had some difficulty in finding my aunt. She was the last of the passengers to alight, and it was not until I got her into the carriage that she seemed really to recognize me.

She had come all the way in a day coach; her linen duster had become black with soot and her black bonnet gray with dust during the journey. When we arrived at my boardinghouse, the landlady put her to bed at once and I did not see her again until the next morning.

Whatever shock Mrs. Springer experienced at

---

2. **gangling** (gang′gling), *adj.* thin, tall, and awkward.
3. **scourged** (skėrjd), *v.* afflicted; tormented.
4. **chilblains** (chil′blān′z), an itching sore or redness on the hands or feet caused chiefly by exposure to cold.

◀ How does this painting, *The Homesteader's Wife* (1916) by Harvey Dunn illustrate the difficulties women had to face living on the frontier?

For thirty years my aunt had not been farther than fifty miles from the homestead.

my aunt's appearance, she considerately concealed. As for myself, I saw my aunt's battered figure with that feeling of awe and respect with which we behold explorers who have left their ears and fingers north of Franz Josef Land,[5] or their health somewhere along the Upper Congo. My Aunt Georgiana had been a music teacher at the Boston Conservatory, somewhere back in the latter sixties. One summer, while visiting in the little village among the Green Mountains where her ancestors had dwelt for generations, she had kindled the callow[6] fancy of my uncle, Howard

Carpenter, then an idle, shiftless boy of twenty-one. When she returned to her duties in Boston, Howard followed her, and the upshot of this infatuation was that she eloped with him, eluding the reproaches of her family and the criticism of her friends by going with him to the Nebraska frontier. Carpenter, who, of course, had no money, took up a homestead in Red Willow County, fifty miles from the railroad. There they had measured off their land themselves, driving across the prairie in a wagon, to the wheel of which they had tied a red cotton handkerchief, and counting its revolutions. They built a dugout in the red hillside, one of those cave dwellings whose inmates so often reverted to primitive conditions. Their water they got from the lagoons where the buffalo drank, and their slender stock of provisions was always at the mercy of bands of roving Indians. For thirty years my aunt had not been farther than fifty miles from the homestead.

I owed to this woman most of the good that ever came my way in my boyhood, and had a reverential[7] affection for her. During the years

---

5. **Franz Josef Land,** Arctic archipelago of about eighty islands, uninhabited and mostly ice-covered.
6. callow (kal′ō), *adj.* young and inexperienced.
7. reverential (rev′ə ren′shəl), *adj.* feeling deeply respectful, mixed with wonder.

A Wagner Matinée **409**

when I was riding herd for my uncle, my aunt, after cooking the three meals—the first of which was ready at six o'clock in the morning—and putting the six children to bed, would often stand until midnight at her ironing board, with me at the kitchen table beside her, hearing me recite Latin declensions[8] and conjugations, gently shaking me when my drowsy head sank down over a page of irregular verbs. It was to her, at her ironing or mending, that I read my first Shakespeare, and her old textbook on mythology was the first that ever came into my empty hands. She taught me my scales and exercises on the little parlor organ which her husband had bought her after fifteen years during which she had not so much as seen a musical instrument. She would sit beside me by the hour, darning and counting, while I struggled with the "Joyous Farmer." She seldom talked to me about music, and I understood why. Once when I had been doggedly beating out some easy passages from an old score of *Euryanthe* I had found among her music books, she came up to me and, putting her hands over my eyes, gently drew my head back upon her shoulder, saying tremulously, "Don't love it so well, Clark, or it may be taken from you."

> **EVALUATE: Why do you think Georgiana tells the narrator not to love music so well?**

When my aunt appeared on the morning after her arrival in Boston, she was still in a semi-somnambulant state. She seemed not to realize that she was in the city where she had spent her youth, the place longed for hungrily half a lifetime. She had been so wretchedly trainsick throughout the journey that she had no recollection of anything but her discomfort and, to all intents and purposes, there were but a few hours of nightmare between the farm in Red Willow County and my study on Newbury Street. I had planned a little pleasure for her that afternoon, to repay her for some of the glorious moments she had given me when we used to milk together

in the straw-thatched cowshed and she, because I was more than usually tired, or because her husband had spoken sharply to me, would tell me of the splendid performance of the *Huguenots* she had seen in Paris, in her youth.

At two o'clock the Symphony Orchestra was to give a Wagner[9] program, and I intended to take my aunt; though as I conversed with her, I grew doubtful about her enjoyment of it. I suggested our visiting the Conservatory and the Common before lunch, but she seemed altogether too timid to wish to venture out. She questioned me absently about various changes in the city, but she was chiefly concerned that she had forgotten to leave instructions about feeding half-skimmed milk to a certain weakling calf, "old Maggie's calf, you know, Clark," she explained, evidently having forgotten how long I had been away. She was further troubled because she had neglected to tell her daughter about the freshly-opened kit of mackerel in the cellar, which would spoil if it were not used directly.

I asked her whether she had ever heard any of the Wagnerian operas, and found that she had not, though she was perfectly familiar with their respective situations, and had once possessed the piano score of *The Flying Dutchman.*[10] I began to think it would be best to get her back to Red Willow County without waking her, and regretted having suggested the concert.

From the time we entered the concert hall, however, she was a trifle less passive and inert and for the first time seemed to perceive her surroundings. I had felt some trepidation[11] lest she might become aware of her queer, country

---

8. **declensions** (di klen′shənz), *n.* the inflections of nouns, pronouns, and adjectives.
9. **Wagner** (väg′nər), Richard Wagner (1813–1883) was a German composer who believed that the theater should be more than just a place of entertainment— it should be the center of a community's culture.
10. ***The Flying Dutchman,*** an early opera by Wagner.
11. trepidation (trep′ə dā′shən), *n.* nervous dread; fear.

Could Mary Cassatt's *At the Opera* (1879) work as a portrait of Aunt Georgiana? Why or why not? ➤

clothes, or might experience some painful embarrassment at stepping suddenly into the world to which she had been dead for a quarter of a century. But, again, I found how superficially I had judged her. She sat looking about her with eyes as impersonal, almost as stony, as those with which the granite Rameses in a museum watches the froth and fret that ebbs and flows about his pedestal. I have seen this same aloofness in old miners who drift into the Brown Hotel at Denver, their pockets full of bullion, their linen soiled, their haggard faces unshaven; standing in the thronged corridors as solitary as though they were still in a frozen camp on the Yukon.

The matinée audience was made up chiefly of women. One lost the contour of faces and figures, indeed any effect of line whatever, and there was only the color of bodices past counting, the shimmer of fabrics soft and firm, silky and sheer; red, mauve, pink, blue, lilac, purple, écru, rose, yellow, cream, and white, all the colors that an impressionist finds in a sunlit landscape, with here and there the dead shadow of a frock coat. My Aunt Georgiana regarded them as though they had been so many daubs of tube paint on a palette.

When the musicians came out and took their places, she gave a little stir of anticipation, and looked with quickening interest down over the rail at that invariable grouping, perhaps the first wholly familiar thing that had greeted her eye since she had left old Maggie and her weakling calf. I could feel how all those details sank into her soul, for I had not forgotten how they had sunk into mine when I came fresh from ploughing forever and forever between green aisles of corn, where, as in a treadmill, one might walk from daybreak to dusk without perceiving a shadow of change. The clean profiles of the musicians, the gloss of their linen, the dull black of their coats, the beloved shapes of the instruments, the patches of yellow light on the smooth, varnished bellies of the cellos and the bass viols in the rear, the restless, wind-tossed forest of fiddle necks and bows—I recalled how, in the first orchestra I ever heard, those long bow strokes seemed to draw the heart out of me, as a conjurer's stick reels out yards of paper ribbon from a hat.

The first number was the *Tannhäuser*[12]

---

12. ***Tannhäuser*** (tän′hoi zər), In *Tannhäuser*, Venusberg is an enchanted land of sensual pleasure.

A Wagner Matinée   **411**

overture. When the horns drew out the first strain of the Pilgrim's chorus, Aunt Georgiana clutched my coat sleeve. Then it was I first realized that for her this broke a silence of thirty years. With the battle between the two motives, with the frenzy of the Venusberg theme and its ripping of strings, there came to me an overwhelming sense of the waste and wear we are so powerless to combat; and I saw again the tall, naked house on the prairie, black and grim as a wooden fortress; the black pond where I had learned to swim, its margin pitted with sun-dried cattle tracks; the rain gullied clay banks about the naked house; the four dwarf ash seedlings where the dishcloths were always hung to dry before the kitchen door. The world there was the flat world of the ancients; to the east, a cornfield that stretched to daybreak; to the west, a corral that reached to sunset; between, the conquests of peace, dearer bought than those of war.

> **CLARIFY:** What does the narrator mean when he says that Georgiana had lived for thirty years with a silence?

The overture closed, my aunt released my coat sleeve, but she said nothing. She sat staring dully at the orchestra. What, I wondered, did she get from it? She had been a good pianist in her day, I knew, and her musical education had been broader than that of most music teachers of a quarter of a century ago. She had often told me of Mozart's operas and Meyerbeer's, and I could remember hearing her sing, years ago, certain melodies of Verdi.[13] When I had fallen ill with a fever in her house, she used to sit by my cot in the evening—when the cool, night wind blew in through the faded mosquito netting tacked over the window and I lay watching a certain bright star that burned red above the cornfield—and sing "Home to our mountains, O, let us return!" in a way fit to break the heart of a Vermont boy near dead of homesickness already.

I watched her closely through the prelude to

Tristan and Isolde,[14] trying vainly to conjecture what that seething turmoil of strings and winds might mean to her, but she sat mutely staring at the violin bows that drove obliquely downward, like the pelting streaks of rain in a summer shower. Had this music any message for her? Had she enough left to at all comprehend this power which had kindled the world since she had left it? I was in a fever of curiosity, but Aunt Georgiana sat silent upon her peak in Darien.[15] She preserved this utter immobility throughout the number from *The Flying Dutchman,* though her fingers worked mechanically upon her black dress, as if, of themselves, they were recalling the piano score they had once played. Poor hands! They had been stretched and twisted into mere tentacles to hold and lift and knead with—on one of them a thin, worn band that had once been a wedding ring. As I pressed and gently quieted one of those groping hands, I remembered with quivering eyelids their services for me in other days.

Soon after the tenor began the "Prize Song," I heard a quick drawn breath and turned to my aunt. Her eyes were closed, but the tears were glistening on her cheeks, and I think, in a moment more, they were in my eyes as well. It never really died, then—the soul which can suffer so <u>excruciatingly</u>[16] and so <u>interminably</u>;[17] it withers to the outward eye only; like that strange moss which can lie on a dusty shelf half a century and yet, if placed in water, grows green again. She wept so throughout the development and elaboration of the melody.

---

13. **Mozart . . . Meyerbeer . . . Verdi** Mozart (mōt′särt) 1756–1791, Austrian composer; Meyerbeer (mī′ər-bir) 1791–1864, German composer of opera; Verdi (ver′dē) 1813–1901, Italian composer of opera.
14. *Tristan and Isolde* (tris′ten, isōl′də) an opera by Wagner in which the title characters are lovers.
15. **peak in Darien.** This phrase from the last line of John Keats's sonnet, "On First Looking into Chapman's Homer," refers to a mountain in Panama from which the Pacific was contemplated in silence and awe.
16. excruciatingly (ek skrü′shē ā′ting lē), *adv.* very painfully; torturously.
17. interminably (in tėr′mə nə blē), *adv.* endlessly.

During the intermission before the second half, I questioned my aunt and found that the "Prize Song" was not new to her. Some years before there had drifted to the farm in Red Willow County a young German, a tramp cowpuncher, who had sung in the chorus at Bayreuth[18] when he was a boy, along with the other peasant boys and girls. Of a Sunday morning he used to sit on his gingham-sheeted bed in the hands' bedroom which opened off the kitchen, cleaning the leather of his boots and saddle, singing the "Prize Song" while my aunt went about her work in the kitchen. She had hovered over him until she had prevailed upon him to join the country church, though his sole fitness for this step, in so far as I could gather, lay in his boyish face and his possession of this divine melody. Shortly afterward, he had gone to town on the Fourth of July, been drunk for several days, lost his money at a faro[19] table, ridden a saddled Texas steer on a bet, and disappeared with a fractured collarbone. All this my aunt told me huskily, wanderingly, as though she were talking in the weak lapses of illness.

"Well, we have come to better things than the old *Trovatore*[20] at any rate, Aunt Georgie?" I queried, with a well-meant effort at jocularity.[21]

Her lips quivered and she hastily put her handkerchief up to her mouth. From behind it she murmured, "And you have been hearing this ever since you left me, Clark?" Her question was the gentlest and saddest of reproaches.

The second half of the program consisted of four numbers from the *Ring*, and closed with Siegfried's funeral march. My aunt wept quietly, but almost continuously, as a shallow vessel overflows in a rainstorm. From time to time her dim eyes looked up at the lights, burning softly under their dull glass globes.

The deluge of sound poured on and on; I never knew what she found in the shining current of it; I never knew how far it bore her, or past what happy islands. From the trembling of her face I could well believe that before the last number she had been carried out where the myriad[22] graves are, into the gray, nameless burying grounds of the sea; or into some world of death vaster yet, where, from the beginning of the world, hope has lain down with hope and dream with dream and, renouncing, slept.

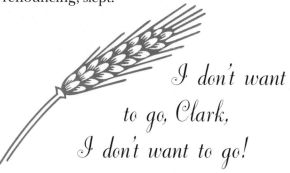

I don't want to go, Clark, I don't want to go!

The concert was over; the people filed out of the hall chattering and laughing, glad to relax and find the living level again, but my kinswoman made no effort to rise. The harpist slipped the green felt cover over his instrument; the flute players shook the water from their mouthpieces; the men of the orchestra went out one by one, leaving the stage to the chairs and music stands, empty as a winter cornfield.

I spoke to my aunt. She burst into tears and sobbed pleadingly. "I don't want to go, Clark, I don't want to go!"

I understood. For her, just outside the concert hall, lay the black pond with the cattle-tracked bluffs; the tall, unpainted house, with weather-curled boards, naked as a tower; the crook-backed ash seedlings where the dishcloths hung to dry; the gaunt, molting turkeys picking up refuse about the kitchen door.

---

18. **Bayreuth** (bī roit′), town in Bavaria, Germany, which has been the home of the annual Richard Wagner Festival since 1876.
19. **faro** (fer′ō), a gambling game played by betting on the order in which certain cards will appear.
20. *Trovatore* (trō vé tôr′e) This popular opera contained "The Anvil Chorus," the hammer blows of which are perhaps a reminder of life on the farm.
21. **jocularity** (jok′yə lar′ə tē), *n.* with a jocular (funny, joking) quality.
22. **myriad** (mir′ē əd), *n.* a very great number; countless.

After Reading

Making Connections

Shaping Your Response

1. What, for you, is the most memorable scene of the story? Sketch the scene in your notebook.

2. What advice would you give to Aunt Georgiana if she asked you whether or not she should return home?

Analyzing the Short Story

3. Using a Venn diagram similar to the one shown, compare the two worlds that Cather describes in "A Wagner Matinée." List any characteristics they share where the circles overlap.

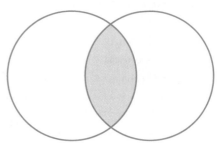

Life on the Nebraska Prairie   **City Life in Boston**

4. What do you suppose Aunt Georgiana was thinking as she looked around at the matinée audience?

5. 👣 Cather describes two completely different worlds—that of Boston and the Nebraska prairie. Why do you think it's so difficult for one person to move back and forth between the two?

6. Would you say Aunt Georgiana enjoyed her day at the opera? Why or why not?

Extending the Ideas

7. Aunt Georgiana is very moved by Wagner's music, and she misses the life she has given up. Think about your own life. If you were going to move to a remote, isolated place, what would you have a hard time giving up?

Literary Focus: Characterization

In "A Wagner Matinée," the reader must draw conclusions about Aunt Georgiana and the narrator by watching what they say and do. Think for a moment about the two characters and then answer the following questions:

- How would you describe the narrator's personality?

- What is his opinion of Aunt Georgiana?

- Do the narrator's feelings for Aunt Georgiana change during the course of the story? Explain.

- How would you describe Aunt Georgiana's personality?

Vocabulary Study

Using your Glossary if necessary, write the word from the list that best matches the context of each sentence. Use each word at least once, and you will need to use one word twice.

render
gangling
callow
reverential
trepidation
excruciatingly
interminably
jocularity
myriad

1. Georgiana's husband, an immature and ____ young man, was immediately attracted to Georgiana's sophistication.

2. With some ____, Clark suggested that he and Georgiana go to the matinée.

3. As a boy, Clark had a ____ love for Georgiana—everything she did and said was wonderful.

4. By the time Clark left home, he was no longer awkward and ____ .

5. Clark's attempt to speak with ____ failed because he was so upset.

6. Although her emotions were ____ painful, Georgiana actually cried for only a short time.

7. The wait for the curtain to rise was ____ long.

8. In his letter to Clark, Georgiana's husband requested that Clark ____ any services necessary to make her stay enjoyable.

9. As they looked around the theater, Clark and Georgiana saw a ____ of colors in every shade imaginable.

10. Georgiana seemed to have a ____ regard for Wagner and his music.

Expressing Your Ideas

Writing Choices

Writer's Notebook Update Now that you've read "A Wagner Matinée," how have your impressions of life on the western frontier changed? Compare the ideas you have now to the impressions you recorded before reading the selection. How does Hollywood's version of the frontier differ from Cather's description? Write several paragraphs that compare the two.

Georgiana's Journal What might Aunt Georgiana write in her diary about her visit to the opera? Write a **diary entry** for her that records her response to the Wagner program.

Other Options

Designing the Backdrop If you were an artist assigned to create the scenery for a play based on Cather's short story, what would you design? Sketch a **scene design** for both the Boston and Nebraska settings.

A Night at the Opera Cather mentions several operas in "A Wagner Matinée": *Euryanthe, Les Huguenots, The Flying Dutchman, Tristan and Isolde,* and *Trovatore.* With a classmate, research one of these operas and then create a two-page **playbill.** On the first page, summarize the story line. On the facing page, sketch an illustration for the opera.

The Frontier

Frontier Adventures and Tragedies

History Connection

When the United States expanded its borders westward, it gained a wealth of natural resources and open spaces for land-hungry settlers. The "Wild West" captured the imagination of Easterners and Europeans alike as a place where tough, larger-than-life individuals thrived on adventure, free from the bounds of "civilized" society. Here are some of the real-life heroes and heroines who helped create and perpetuate the legendary "Wild West."

Davy Crockett

David Crockett (1786-1836) was a frontiersman from Tennessee whose humorous speeches and rugged image helped elect him to three terms in the U.S. Congress. In 1836 Crockett traveled to Texas where he fought and died at the Alamo in Texas's struggle for independence from Mexico.

LEGENDS OF THE WILD WEST

Crazy Horse

Crazy Horse (1842?-1877) was a chief of the Oglala Sioux. Regarded as a great tactician, he led his people in many battles to defend their traditional lands. His greatest victory came in 1876 when he joined forces with Chief Sitting Bull and wiped out a force of U.S. cavalry under Colonel George Custer at the Battle of the Little Bighorn.

Joaquín Murieta

Joaquín Murieta (1830?-1853?) moved from Mexico to California in 1848 looking for gold but instead encountered laws aimed at driving Mexicans away from the gold mines. In retaliation Murieta turned outlaw and led raids robbing miners until he was reportedly captured in 1853 and his decapitated head was put on display. Murieta's legend was secured with John Rollin Ridge's popular 1854 novel, *The Life and Adventures of Joaquín Murieta.*

Calamity Jane

Martha Jane Canary (1852?-1903), later called "Calamity Jane," was orphaned at an early age and wandered the West in the late 1800s. She earned a reputation as a foul-mouthed, hard-drinking gunslinger who sought notoriety with the tales she told about her exploits in the West. Among these were stories of her days scouting for General George Custer and her romance with Wild Bill Hickok.

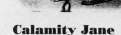

Bill Pickett

Texan Bill Pickett (1870?-1932) was a famous rodeo cowboy who introduced bulldogging, or steer wrestling, in the early 1900s. He would wrestle a running steer to the ground and then bite into the animal's lip to hold it down while he raised his hands in triumph. Pickett became a box-office draw in the U.S. and abroad working for Buffalo Bill's Wild West Show.

Annie Oakley

Phoebe Ann Moses (1860-1926), later known as Annie Oakley, gained national fame as a sharpshooter in 1875 when she defeated professional marksman Frank Butler in a shooting contest. The two married soon after. In 1885 they joined Buffalo Bill's Wild West Show and Annie became a star. She amazed audiences in the U.S. and Europe with her shooting skills for 17 years.

Responding

1. Why do you think these legendary Western figures held such an appeal for people in the Eastern United States and Europe?

2. Who are the modern day larger-than-life heroes? What do you think is their appeal?

History Connection

While the image of the "Wild West" captured the imaginations of those back East, real-life experiences often held less adventure and more heartbreak. Settlers built homes from whatever materials they could find and farmed land that was often hard and unyielding. Immigrants, attracted by tales of easy wealth, often encountered discrimination instead. And with newcomers arriving every day, American Indians found their homelands disappearing before their very eyes.

from

Black Hawk
An Autobiography

For generations the people of the Sauk nation lived in the Mississippi River Valley. Then, in 1828 Sauk Chief Black Hawk and his people were ordered by the U.S. government to leave the valley to make room for the growing numbers of white settlers. In this excerpt from his autobiography, Black Hawk tells his reaction to the news that his people will be forced to leave their homeland.

Our village was situate on the north side of Rock River, at the foot of its rapids, and on the point of land between Rock River and the Mississippi. In its front, a prairie extended to the bank of the Mississippi; and in our rear, a continued bluff, gently ascending from the prairie. On the side of this bluff we had our corn-fields, extending about two miles up, running parallel with the Mississippi; where we joined those of the Foxes whose village was on the bank of the Mississippi, opposite the lower end of Rock Island, and three miles distant from ours. We had about eight hundred acres in cultivation, including what we had on the islands of Rock River. The land around our village, uncultivated, was covered with blue-grass, which made excellent pasture for our horses. Several fine springs broke out of the bluff, near by, from which we were supplied with good water. The rapids of Rock River furnished us with an abundance of excellent fish, and the land, being good, never failed to produce good crops of corn, beans, pumpkins, and squashes. We always had plenty —our children never cried with hunger, nor our people were never in want. Here our village had stood for more than a hundred years, during all which time we were the undisputed possessors of the valley of the Mississippi, from the Ouisconsin to the Portage des Sioux, near the mouth of the Missouri, being about seven hundred miles in length.

At this time we had very little intercourse with the whites, except our traders. Our village was healthy, and there was no place in the country possessing such advantages, nor no hunting grounds better than those we had in possession. If another prophet had come to our village in those days, and told us what has since taken place, none of our people would have believed him. What! to be driven from our village and hunting grounds, and not even permitted to visit the graves of our forefathers, our relations, and friends? . . .

This summer our agent came to live at Rock Island. He treated us well, and gave us

Sauk Chief Black Hawk and his son, Whirling Thunder (1833) by John Jarvis.

good advice. I visited him and the trader very often during the summer, and, for the first time, heard talk of our having to leave my village. The trader explained to me the terms of the treaty that had been made, and said we would be obliged to leave the Illinois side of the Mississippi, and advised us to select a good place for our village, and remove to it in the spring. . . .

I had an interview with Ke-o-kuck, to see if this difficulty could not be settled with our Great Father—and told him to propose to give other land, (any that our Great Father might choose, even our *lead mines,*) to be peaceably permitted to keep the small point of land on which our village and fields were situate. I was of opinion that the white people had plenty of land, and would never take our village from us. Ke-o-kuck promised to make an exchange if possible; and applied to our agent, and the great chief at St. Louis, (who has charge of all the agents,) for permission to go to Washington to see our Great Father for that purpose. This satisfied us for some time. We started to our hunting grounds, in good hopes that something would be done for us. During the winter, I received information that three families of whites had arrived at our village, and destroyed some of our lodges, and were making fences and dividing our corn-fields for their own use—*and were quarreling among themselves about their lines, in the division!* I immediately started for Rock River, a distance of ten day's travel, and on my arrival, found the report to be true. I went to my lodge, and saw a family occupying it. I wished to talk with them, but they could not understand me. I then went to Rock Island, and (the agent being absent,) told the interpreter what I wanted to say to those people, viz: "Not to settle on our lands—nor trouble our lodges or fences—that there was plenty of land in the country for them to settle upon—and they must leave our village, as we were coming back to it in the spring." The interpreter wrote me a paper, and I went back to the village, and showed it to the intruders, but could not understand their reply. I expected, however, that they would remove, as I requested them. . . .

I returned to my hunting ground, after an absence of one moon, and related what I had done. In a short time we came up to our village, and found that the whites had not left it—but that others had come, and that the greater part of our corn-fields had been enclosed. . . . What *right* had these people to our village, and our fields, which the Great Spirit had given us to live upon?

My reason teaches me that *land cannot be sold.* The Great Spirit gave it to his children to live upon, and cultivate, as far as is necessary for their subsistence; and so long as they occupy and cultivate it, they have the right to the soil—but if they voluntarily leave it, then any other people have a right to settle upon it. Nothing can be sold, but such things as can be carried away.

from
Thousand Pieces of Gold
by Ruthanne Lum McCunn

Kidnapped in the early 1800s, Lalu Nathoy was sent from China to the United States where she was sold to a saloon-keeper. In this fictionalized account of her life, she travels with a guide toward her new and unknown home.

Nine days' travel through thickly wooded trails brought them to Lewiston, a strange town made up of tents, makeshift houses of canvas stretched across wood frames, and buildings so new Lalu could smell the rawness of the wood.

"All mining camps look the same," Jim said, . . . "Warrens, the mining camp where you will live, is just like that." His arm made a sweeping movement. "Like this. Only smaller."

Languidly, Lalu's eyes followed the sweep of Jim's hand. Hogs rooted in piles of empty tins, potato peelings, old hambones, eggshells, and cabbage leaves. Chickens, pecking and clucking, strutted on and off the boardwalks and around broken pots, shovels, worn-out kettles, boots, and other rubbish, breaking up clouds of flies that covered clumps of stinking manure. A rat burrowed in the spilled-out entrails of a dead dog. From the buildings and tents lining the street came music, raucous laughter, bursts of gunfire, and breaking glass.

"Those are saloons," Jim said. "Wine shops. Like your master's. Only his is empty of customers. That's why he bought you.

"There are sixteen hundred men in Warrens, twelve hundred Chinese, four hundred or so whites. And there are eleven women. Three are wives, two are widows, and a half dozen are hurdy gurdy girls. But they're all white. You'll be the only Chinese woman, an attraction that will bring men, Chinese and white, from miles around."

From the hitching rack edging the boardwalk, between horses patiently waiting for their masters, she could clearly see the demons [Chinese immigrants called white Americans ghosts or demons] inside the saloons. Some simply smoked and drank or competed at squirting streams of brown tobacco juice. Others crowded around gaming tables or hopped and bounded like performing monkeys, their arms around short-skirted, painted demon women whose heeled boots pounded rhythms on crude plank floors.

Did her master expect her to dress like these half-naked, painted demon women? To dance with hairy, unwashed demon men? . . .

Abruptly, Lalu kicked her mule and urged it forward, galloping past the string of mules and Jim, out of town, and across the meadow, splashing across shallow streams, snapping off low hanging branches in groves of cottonwoods edging the banks, frightening unsuspecting red squirrels, birds, a deer. Finally, the mule staggered, wheezing, blowing, and hollow eyed, its sweat-caked flanks dripping foam. Ashamed, Lalu slowed to a walk.

When the mule's breathing evened, she stopped. Dropping her reins over the pommel so it could drink from the creek, she looked back across the blue green sea of meadow grass and camas. There was no sign of the packstring, not even a faint tinkling of the lead mule's bells. She glanced up at the fiery sun. It would be dark before the pack mules, each one loaded down with five hundred pounds of freight, covered the same length of ground her mule had galloped, and Jim would never dare risk leaving them to pursue her. She could ride on alone, away from the future that waited for her in her master's saloon.

Where would she go? To return to Lewiston or Portland or San Francisco would mean capture. . . . Yet she could not stay out here on the open prairie or in the mountains skirted and crowned with pines. She had no food and no means to obtain it. . . .

She could not escape her fate. Slowly, she wound her reins around the pommel of the saddle and dismounted so the mule could graze while she waited for Jim.

from

Down The Santa Fe Trail

by Susan Shelby Magoffin

In 1846 Susan Shelby Magoffin accompanied her husband on an expedition through the American Southwest. The following passage from her journal reveals some of her initial experiences on the open prairie.

Camp No. 22. Bank of the Arkansas River. Prairie scenes are rather changing today. We are coming more into the buffalo regions. The grass is much shorter and finer. The plains are cut up by winding paths and every thing promises a buffalo dinner on the 4th.

We left our last night's camp quite early this morning. About 9 o'clock we came upon "Dog City." This curiosity is well worth seeing. The Prairie dog, not much larger than a well grown rat, burrows in the ground. They generally make a regular town of it, each one making his house by digging a hole, and heaping the dirt around the mouth of this. Two are generally built together in a neighborly way. They of course visit as regularly as man. When we got into this one, which lays on both sides of the road occupying at least a circle of some hundred yards, the little fellows like people ran to their doors to see the passing crowd. They could be seen all around with their heads poked out, and expressing their opinions I supposed from the loud barking I heard . . .

Came to camp tonight before sunset. Col. Owens' Company, which got before us this morning, were just starting after performing the last office to the dead body of a Mexican. He had consumption. Poor man, 'twas but yesterday that we sent him some soup from our camp, which he took with relish and today he is in his grave!

The manner of interring on the plains is necessarily very simple. The grave is dug very deep, to prevent the body from being found by the wolves. The corpse is rolled in a blanket—lowered and stones put on it. The earth is then thrown in, the sod replaced and it is well beat down. Often the corral is made over it, to make the earth still more firm, by the tromping of the stock. The Mexicans always place a cross at the grave.

Our camp is on the bank of the Arkansas tonight. Its dark waters remind me of the Mississippi. It makes me sad to look upon it. I am reminded of home. Though the Mississippi is a vast distance from there—it seems to me a near neighbor, compared with the distance I am from it—now three hundred miles from Independence. The time rolls on so fast I can scarcely realize it's three weeks out. . . .

Started this P.M. about 4 o'clock traveled well till 6 o'clock, when a very hard thunder storm came up and detained us in the road till after eight. A thunder storm at sunset on the Prairie is a sublime and awing scene indeed. The vivid and forked lightning quickly succeeded by the hoarse growling thunder impresses one most deeply of his own weakness and the magnanimity of his God. With nothing before or near us in sight, save the wide expanse of Prairie resembling most fully in the pale light of the moon, as she occasionally appeared from under a murky cloud and between the vivid lightning, the wide sea.

Responding

How are these three experiences of the American frontier similar? How do they differ?

Language History

The Many Flavors of American English

 What do you call those long, oval-shaped sandwiches sold for lunch in cafeterias? Are they *hoagies, heroes, submarines, grinders, garibaldis,* or *poor boys?* What about the lumpy white cheese you find in your supermarket? Is it *cottage cheese, pot cheese, Dutch cheese, smearcase, clabber cheese,* or *curd cheese?*

Why do different people in different regions of the country have different ways of pronouncing the same word, or even have different names for the same thing? The answer to this question lies in the history of each region, and of the people who inhabit the region. The roots of many regional dialects can be traced back to the period in American History from 1870 to 1914. Because of rapid technological developments, tremendous population expansion, and an explosive push westward, the sound and lexicon—or vocabulary—of American English changed dramatically at this time.

In the West, settlers coined words to describe their new experiences. From cowboys came *stampede, ranch, maverick,* and *hot under the collar.* Gambling terminology lent colorful phrases such as *put up* or *shut up, hit the jackpot,* and *pass the buck.* Writers such as Mark Twain began using the new words and phrases in their writing, which helped move the vocabulary into general use.

The tremendous influx of European immigrants to America during this period also had a profound effect on the sound and vocabulary of American English. Although immigrants settled in many parts of the country, most came to the Northeast first, and had a greater influence on the speech there. From Germans came words such as *delicatessen, hoodlum, spiel,* and *kindergarten.* From Italians, new food words were introduced: *pizza, broccoli, Parmesan, pasta,* and *spaghetti.* From Eastern and Central European Jews came words like *kosher* (all right, fine, legitimate), *schlemiel* (a clumsy person), and *schlep* (move awkwardly).

By this time, African Americans had already been influencing American English—especially in the South—for centuries, introducing African speech patterns, and words such as *gumbo* and *goober.*

Writing Workshop

Bringing History to Life

Assignment You read about life on the American frontier during the mid-1800s. Now collaborate with a group to write a proposal for a museum exhibit that portrays frontier life.

WRITER'S BLUEPRINT

Product A proposal for a museum exhibit

Purpose As a group: (1) propose an idea for a museum exhibit that deals with the American frontier; (2) persuade a museum director to fund your idea

Audience Museum directors

Specs To create an effective proposal, your group should:

❑ Include a cover sheet listing the title of your proposed exhibit and names of team members.

❑ Begin by introducing your idea and describing your exhibit. Use spatial organization to guide your audience. Include:

—its location (outdoors, indoors, or both)

—a diagram of the exhibit and its major components: the larger spaces that will house the exhibit's contents

—a list of the exhibit's contents, such as dioramas, wax figures, animatronic figures, paintings, furniture, clothing, audiotaped or videotaped information.

❑ Include any sketches that might help your audience visualize your exhibit.

❑ End by explaining clearly and convincingly how your exhibit will enrich your community's understanding of life in frontier America.

❑ Follow the rules of grammar, usage, spelling, and mechanics. Take special care to avoid spelling mistakes with homophones.

1 PREWRITING

Find images in the literature that portray frontier life. With a group, review the selections to find images of the frontier. Then group similar images around three or four motifs, such as mining camps, homesteads, and Native Americans. These motifs will be the major components in your exhibit.

Diagram the exhibit. With your group, decide how you'll present the major components you've chosen. Sketch a diagram with labels and notes.

List the items you'll be including in each component. Describe their size and what they'll be made of. For example, you might note that the sod house will be a life-size model constructed from clay and artificial turf. For each item, make notes on the reasons why it will enrich people's understanding of frontier life.

List the most compelling reasons for why a museum director should fund your proposal. Draw on the notes you've made on the reasons why components and items will enrich people's understanding of frontier life. Circle the five most compelling reasons and number them in order, from most significant (5) to least (1).

Read the Beyond Print article on page 951. It deals with persuasive advertising techniques. Draw upon them to help sell your idea.

Divide up tasks. Each group member should take on or share at least one of these tasks:

- Coordinator: Coordinates and edits materials; writes transitions to connect different parts; writes cover page; makes sure group members take responsibility for their tasks

- Designer: Designs, draws, and labels a formal diagram of the exhibit

- Writer: Writes descriptions of the exhibit's major components

- Marketing specialist: Writes the introduction and conclusion in a way that "sells" the idea.

2 DRAFTING

As you draft, give completed sections to the group coordinator, who will assemble the proposal into an organized document.

- As you describe the various components, use spatial organization to guide your readers from place to place. See the Revising Strategy in Step 3 of this lesson.

- As you draft the introduction and conclusion, use some of the advertising techniques mentioned in the Beyond Print article on page 951.

3 REVISING

Ask another group for comments on your draft before revising.

✔ Have we included a complete diagram of the exhibit?

✔ Have we given compelling reasons why our proposal should be funded?

✔ Did we use spatial organization to guide readers through our proposal?

Revising Strategy

Using Spatial Order Terms

Help readers visualize the layout of your exhibit by using spatial order terms that indicate distance *(beyond, near, far)*, direction *(left, right, ahead, behind)* and position *(in front of, below, over)*, as in the student model below.

○   There will be a tee-pee in ^*the middle of* the exhibit. The ^tee-pee will be ^*outside of the*

made of buffalo hides as the Indians made theirs. The tee-pees

○   will be painted with pictures. ^*Inside the tee-pee* There will be a fire and the sleeping

blankets of the family along with their other personal belongings.

STUDENT MODEL

4 EDITING

Ask another group to review the revised draft before editing. When editing, look for errors in grammar, usage, spelling, and mechanics. Look closely for spelling errors with homophones.

Editing Strategy

COMPUTER TIP
If your computer has a spell checker, use it—but don't rely on it to give you perfect spelling. A spell checker won't catch a homophone mistake, like substituting *it's* for *its*. Proofread your writing carefully for spelling.

Avoiding Homophone Errors

Homophones are words that sound alike but have different meanings and usually different spellings. To catch spelling errors with homophones when you edit, pay close attention to their meanings:

it's, its	It's (it is) the first room in the exhibit. Its theme is cross-country travel.
your, you're	Take your time. You're going to know a lot about the frontier when you're through.

5 PRESENTING

- Do a mock presentation of your proposal for a museum board meeting held in your classroom. Classmates can ask questions while playing the roles of board members.

- Build a model of one or more of the components of your proposed exhibit, such as a scale-model of a sod house, to use in your presentation or to display in your school library.

6 LOOKING BACK

Self-evaluate. Look back at the Writer's Blueprint and give yourself a score for each item you worked on, from 6 (superior) to 1 (inadequate).

Reflect. Write your thoughts about working with a group compared to working alone.

For Your Working Portfolio Add your historical exhibit proposal and your reflection responses to your working portfolio.

Beyond Print

Watching Westerns

The American West is one of the all-time favorite topics of movie makers. The first American film that told a story was a western, *The Great Train Robbery,* directed by Edwin S. Porter in 1903. Since this film, the "Old West" has been the subject of too many films to name. Over the years, western movies have both added to and disputed the stereotype of the "Wild West." The following are some of the themes that have been portrayed in western movies. Which types have you seen?

"Civilizing" the West Many of the movies director John Ford made are about bringing "civilization" to the frontier. The settlers in Ford's movies carve a just and law-governed society out of a raw and wild land. His movies include *Stagecoach* (1939), *She Wore a Yellow Ribbon* (1949), and *The Horse Soldiers* (1959).

Only the Strong Survive Film director Howard Hawk's westerns are often about toughness. Only the strong and independent in these films will survive the harshness of the American west. In *Red River* (1948) and *The Big Sky* (1952) the tough persevere.

Where Men and Women Can Be Free Westerns like Sam Peckinpah's *The Wild Bunch* (1969), *Silverado* (1985) directed by Lawrence Kasdan, and the TV miniseries *Lonesome Dove* (1989) convey the idea that the frontier is the last place where the human spirit can be free. Cities are places of confinement and conformity. The West is where men and women reveal a primal nature, and live a simplified lifestyle free from the trappings of modern urban living.

Destroying the West Early westerns portrayed American Indians as savages intent on destroying civilization, and western lands as wild places that need to be subdued and conquered. The modern western has changed this formula, as in Kevin Costner's *Dances with Wolves* (1990). Many of these more recent westerns portray American Indians as victims of the savagery of white settlers who overrun Indian lands and generally destroy the beauty and nature of the West.

Activity Options

Themes of the West Draw, sketch, or paint a picture of a western scene that picks up on one of the themes mentioned on page 427. Consider the composition of your work. Will you draw vast plains with huge skies to convey a sense of loneliness? Will you draw mountains that create a sense of majesty, or a sense of enclosure? Consider carefully the colors you will use. The Great Plains may be the color of wild grasses or wheat, the mountains may be many different colors depending on the time of day, and deserts are often tans and browns. Finally, make something happen in your scene which connects it to one of the themes.

The Story Goes On Westerns are still being made today, in the form of television series, movies, and novels. Choose two or three modern westerns to consider, and decide what themes of the West they portray. Are they the same or different? Are westerns developing a new theme not mentioned here?

The movie poster shown here advertises Howard Hawk's 1952 movie, *The Big Sky*. What image of or stereotypes about the West does the poster portray?

➤

Multicultural Connections

Perspectives

Part One: Letters to the World Emily Dickinson seems to look at the world as a place where lessons can be learned from nature, and where one should carefully choose one's own thoughts and companions. Walt Whitman, on the other hand, seems to see the world as an awesome place in which every experience one encounters becomes part of one. Paul Laurence Dunbar adds a third perspective—the world is a place of cages and restrictions, where one must hide one's true self in order to survive. Finally, Stephen Crane sees a world in which the path to truth is full of knives and nature is alternately beautiful or terrifying, depending on your perspective.

■ Which of these poets' world view most closely matches the way you see the world?

Communication

Part Two: the Frontier Simon Wheeler in "The Celebrated Jumping Frog of Calaveras County" has his own unique way of communicating, filled with the dialect of an Old West mining town. Different cultural groups in the West found different ways to communicate their experiences—"El Corrido de Gregorio Cortez" is a Mexican border ballad, the Gold Mountain Poems are anonymous expressions of the experiences of Chinese immigrants, and Satanta communicates his thoughts in a speech.

■ As you read these selections, which form of communication struck you as the most powerful? Explain.

Activities

Work in small groups on the following activities.

1. How do you see the world—as friendly and safe? frightening and difficult? interesting and mysterious? Write a group "Letter to the World" of one or two pages that tells what your group thinks of the world around you.

2. What are the greatest obstacles to communication? What helps people to communicate? Write a list of the factors that cause communication to break down between people. Then, for each obstacle, write a recommendation for getting around the obstacle.

Independent and Group Projects

Debate

How the West Was "Won"? The United States became a transcontinental nation at the expense of hundreds of thousands of people—namely American Indians. Did the U.S. leaders of the day have a right to advance the country in the name of progress through the lands of those who called it home for generations? Was there another way? Form two groups—one that supports the United States' actions and one that opposes them. Each side should develop and present arguments for its position. Then the two sides can debate the issue.

Research

Evolution of a Town What was your city or town like a century ago? How long has it existed? Form a research committee and investigate the history of the area in which you live. Find information about its origin, including who founded it and when, milestones, and if the area is home to American Indian and immigrant groups or any "unusual" or "colorful" characters. Make a book of your findings and if possible include maps and pictures of its evolution.

Oral Presentation

Interpretation of the Past Do you relate with any of the feelings expressed by the poets and authors in this unit? What is your interpretation of their works? Memorize the selections that are the most meaningful for you and present your interpretations to your class.

Drama

Voice of the Past From Emily Dickinson to Satanta, the individuals in this unit left a lasting impression on American history. With a partner, research the life of one of the individuals in this unit. Then present the information in the form of an interview with the person. You may want to use costumes and field questions your audience might have about this individual.

The Journey

THEMES
IN AMERICAN
LITERATURE

The Journey

From the wanderings of the American Indian peoples to the voyages of the space shuttle, the American story has always been a traveler's tale. Viking longships, Spanish caravels, the Middle Passage, French voyageurs, steamboats and keelboats and rafts on the Mississippi, the Underground Railroad, wagon trains, cattle drives, the building of the transcontinental railroad, immigrant jouneys ending at Ellis Island or Angel Island, the Great Migration, pioneering air flights, civil rights marches—all kinds of travels and all kinds of travelers have been part of our story. In this section you will encounter a few of these American journeys.

NIGHT JOURNEY

THE SETTING OUT

You know, everything had to begin, and this is how it was: the Kiowas came one by one into the world through a hollow log. There were many more than now, but not all of them got out. There was a woman whose body was swollen up with child, and she got stuck in the log. After that, no one could get through, and that is why the Kiowas are a small tribe in number. They looked all around and saw the world. It made them glad to see so many things. They called themselves Kwuda, "coming out."

N. Scott Momaday (1969)

Now as the train bears west,
Its rhythm rocks the earth,
And from my Pullman berth
I stare into the night
While others take their rest.
Bridges of iron lace,
A suddenness of trees,
A lap of mountain mist
All cross my line of sight,
Then a bleak wasted place,
And a lake below my knees.
Full on my neck I feel
The straining at a curve;

THE PILOTS ON OUR WESTERN RIVERS STEER FROM POINT TO POINT AS THEY CALL IT—SETTING THE COURSE OF THE BOAT NO FARTHER THAN THEY CAN SEE.

Abraham Lincoln

My muscles move with steel,
I wake in every nerve.
I watch a beacon swing
From dark to blazing bright;
We thunder through ravines
And gullies washed with light.
Beyond the mountain pass
Mist deepens on the pane;
We rush into a rain
That rattles double glass.
Wheels shake the roadbed stone,
The pistons jerk and shove,
I stay up half the night
To see the land I love.

Theodore Roethke (1940)

Thomas Hart Benton, The Boy *(1950)*

I reckon I got to light out for the Territory, because Aunt Sally she's going to adopt me and civilize me and I can't stand it. I been there before.

Mark Twain,
Huckleberry Finn
(1885)

THE OPEN ROAD

On the old highway maps of America, the main routes were red and the back roads blue. Now even the colors are changing. But in those brevities just before dawn and a little after dark—times neither day nor night—the old roads return to the sky some of its color. Then, in truth, they cast a mysterious shadow of blue, and it's that time when the pull of the blue highway is strongest, when the open road is a beckoning, a strangeness, a place where a man can lose himself.

William Least Heat Moon,
Blue Highways *(1982)*

River Dreams

The Mississippi. Mighty, muddy, dangerous, rebellious, and yet a strong, fathering kind of river. The river captured my imagination when I was young and has never let go. Since I can remember I have wanted to be somehow a part of the river as much as I wanted to be a hero, strong and brave and relentless like the river, looming so large in the life and world around me that it could not be ignored or forgotten. I used to sit on the levee and watch the murkiness lumber down to the sea and I'd dream of the cities and towns the river had passed, the farms and fields and bridges, the magic in the debris picked up here, deposited there, and the other rivers along the way: Ohio, Illinois, Arkansas, taking all on a beautiful voyage to the Gulf of Mexico and beyond. I wanted to go too. I wanted to dip first my toes in the water to test, then all of me, hanging onto whatever and floating along with it, letting the river drop me off wherever and pick me up later and take me on again. I didn't care where. I just wanted to go.

Eddy Harris, Mississippi Solo *(1988)*

Madam Knight Travels to New York

Tuesday, October the third . . . about three, afternoon, went on with my third guide, who rode very hard: and having crossed Providence Ferry, we come to a river which they generally ride through. But I dare not venture; so the post[1] got a lad and canoe to carry me to t'other side, and he rid through and led my horse. The canoe was very small and shallow, so that when we were in, she seemed ready to take in water, which greatly terrified me, and caused me to be very circumspect, sitting with my hands fast on each side, my eyes steady, not daring so much as to lodge my tongue a hair's breadth more on one side of my mouth than t'other, nor so much as think on Lot's wife,[2] for a wry thought would have overset our wherry.[3] But was soon out of this pain, by feeling the canoe on shore, which I as soon almost saluted with my feet; and rewarding my sculler, again mounted and made the best of our way forwards. The road here was very even and the day pleasant, it being now near sunset. But the post told me we had near fourteen miles to ride to the next stage (where we were to lodge). I asked him of the rest of the road, foreseeing we must travel in the night. He told me there was a bad river we were to ride through, which was so very fierce a horse could sometimes hardly stem it: but it was very narrow, and we should soon be over. I cannot express the concern of mind this relation set me in: no thoughts but those of the dangerous river could entertain my imagination; and they were as formidable as various, still tormenting me with blackest ideas of my approaching fate—sometimes seeing myself drowning, otherwhiles drowned, and at the best like a holy sister just come out of a spiritual bath in dripping garments. . . .

Thus, absolutely lost in thought, and dying with the very thoughts of drowning, I come up with the post, who I did not see till even with his horse: he told me he stopped for me; and we rode on very deliberately a few paces, when he entered a thicket of trees and shrubs, and I perceived by the horse's going we were on the descent of a hill, which, as we come nearer the bottom, 'twas totally dark with the trees that surrounded it. But I knew by the going of the horse we had entered the water, which my guide told me was the hazardous river he had told me of; and he, riding up close to my side, bid me not fear—we should be over immediately. I now rallied all the courage I was mistress of, knowing that I must either venture my fate of drowning, or be left like the Children in the Wood.[4] So, as the post bid me, I gave my reins to my nag; and sitting as steady as just before in the canoe, in a few minutes got safe to the other side, which he told me was the Narragansett country.

Sarah Kemble Knight (1704)

AND OH, AUNTIE EM, THERE'S NO PLACE LIKE HOME!

Dorothy Gale,
The Wizard of Oz *(1939)*

---

1. **post,** *n.* messenger who delivers the mail.

2. **Lot's wife,** in the Bible, turned into a pillar of salt when she looked back at the destruction of Sodom.

3. **wherry** (hwer′ē), *n.* small boat.
4. **Children . . . Wood,** abandoned children in a folktale.

Dust Bowl Migrants Move Westward

The cars of the migrant people crawled out of the side roads onto the great cross-country highway, and they took the migrant way to the West. In the daylight they scuttled like bugs to the westward; and as the dark caught them, they clustered like bugs near to shelter and to water. And because they were lonely and perplexed, because they had all come from a place of sadness and worry and defeat, and because they were all going to a new mysterious place, they huddled together; they talked together; they shared their lives, their food, and the things they hoped for in the new country. Thus it might be that one family camped near a spring, and another camped for the spring and for company, and a third because two families had pioneered the place and found it good. And when the sun went down, perhaps twenty families and twenty cars were there.

In the evening a strange thing happened: the twenty families became one family, the children were the children of all. The loss of home became one loss, and the golden time in the West was one dream. And it might be that a sick child threw despair into the hearts of twenty families, of a hundred people, that a birth there in a tent kept a hundred people quiet and awestruck through the night and filled a hundred people with the birth-joy in the morning. A family which the night before had been lost and fearful might search its goods to find a present for a new baby. In the evening, sitting about the fires, the twenty were one. They grew to be units of the camps, units of the evenings and the nights. A guitar unwrapped from a blanket and tuned—and the songs, which were all of the people, were sung in the nights. Men sang the words, and women hummed the tunes.

Every night a world created, complete with furniture—friends made and enemies established; a world complete with braggarts and with cowards, with quiet men, with humble men, with kindly men. Every night relationships that make a world, established; and every morning the world torn down like a circus. . . .

There grew up government in the worlds, with leaders, with elders. A man who was wise found that his wisdom was needed in every camp; a man who was a fool could not change his folly with his world. And a kind of insurance developed in these nights. A man with food fed a hungry man, and thus insured himself against hunger. And when a baby died a pile of silver coins grew at the door flap, for a baby must be well buried, since it has had nothing else of life. An old man may be left in a potter's field,[1] but not a baby.

John Steinbeck, The Grapes of Wrath *(1939)*

The Grape-Workers March to Delano

. . . In every religion-oriented culture "the pilgrimage" has had a place: a trip made with sacrifice and hardship as an expression of penance and commitment—and often involving a petition to the patron of the pilgrimage for some sincerely sought benefit of body and soul. Pilgrimage has not passed from Mexican culture. Daily at any of the major shrines of the country . . . there arrive pilgrims from all points. . . . Many of the "pilgrims" of Delano will have walked such pilgrimages themselves in their lives—perhaps as very small children even—and cling to the memory of the day-long marches, the camps at night, streams forded, hills climbed, the sacral aura of the sanctuary, and the "fiesta" that followed. . . .

Cesar Chavez (1966)

---

1. **potter's field,** *n.* a public cemetery used for burying the poor, unidentified persons, and criminals.

Delano. In 1966 Cesar Chavez led a march from Delano, California to the state capitol at Sacramento to dramatize the plight of migrant farm workers.

"The Cowards Never Started, and the Weak Died Along the Way"

MAY 6, 1852. Left the Missouri river for our long journey across the wild uncultivated plains and unhabitated except by the red man. As we left the river bottom and ascended the bluffs the view from them was handsome! In front of us as far as vision could reach extended the green hills covered with fine grass. . . . Behind us lay the Missouri with its muddy water hurrying past as if in great haste to reach some destined point ahead all unheeding the impatient emigrants on the opposite shore at the ferrying which arrived faster than they could be conveyed over. About half a mile down the river lay a steamboat stuck fast on a sandbar. Still farther down lay the busy village of St. Joseph looking us a good bye and reminding us that we were leaving all signs of civilised life for the present. But with good courage and not one sigh of regret I mounted my pony (whose name by the way is Samy) and rode slowly on. In going some two miles, the scene changed from bright sunshine to drenching showers of rain, This was not quite agreeable for in spite of our good blankets and intentions otherwise we got some wet. The rain detained us so that we have not made but ten miles today. . . .

MAY 11. . . Our men are not any of them very well this morning We passed another grave today which was made this morning. The board stated that he died of cholera. He was from Indiana. We met several that had taken the back track for the states homesick I presume let them go. . . .

MAY 13 . . . Henry has been no better to day. Soon after we stopped to night a man came along with a wheel barrow going to California he is a dutchmann He wheels his provisions and clothing all day and then stops where night overtakes him sleeps on the ground in the open air He eats raw meat and bread for his supper I think that he will get tired wheeling his way through the world by the time he gets to California. . . .

JUNE 16. We have not moved today our sick ones not able to go I went a few rods to a train this evening to see the sick There was two that were very sick The sickness on the road is alarming—most all proves fatal. . . .

Lydia Allen Rudd (1852)

Home Ties

Is there anything as horrible as starting on a trip? Once you're off, that's all right, but the last moments are earthquake and convulsion, and the feeling that you are a snail being pulled off your rock.

Anne Morrow Lindbergh (1973)

Houston, we have a problem. . . .

Astronaut James Lovell aboard Apollo 13 (1970)

Tom Lovell, The Heirloom *1976)*

Lost Travelers

We come together today to mourn the loss of seven brave Americans, to share the grief that we all feel and, perhaps in that sharing, to find the strength to bear our sorrow and the courage to look for the seeds of hope. . . . On the day of the disaster, our nation held a vigil by our television sets. In one cruel moment, our exhilaration turned to horror. . . .We learned again that this America . . . was built on heroism and noble sacrifice. It was built by men and women like our seven star voyagers, who answered a call beyond duty, who gave more than was expected or required, and who gave it with little thought of worldly reward.We think back to the pioneers of an earlier century, the sturdy souls who took their families and belongings and set out into the frontier of the American West. Often, they met with terrible hardship. Along the Oregon Trail you can still see the grave markers of those who fell on the way. But grief only steeled them to the journey ahead. Today, the frontier is space and the boundaries of human knowledge. Sometimes, when we reach for the stars, we fall short. But we must pick ourselves up again and press on despite the pain. Our nation is indeed fortunate that we can still draw on immense reservoirs of courage, character, and fortitude—that we are still blessed with heroes like those of the space shuttle *Challenger.*

Ronald Reagan (1986)

437

INSCRIPTION ON THE
STATUE OF LIBERTY

GIVE ME

YOUR TIRED,

YOUR POOR,

YOUR HUDDLED

MASSES

YEARNING

TO BREATHE

FREE. . . .

Emma Lazarus

(1883)

Alfred Stieglitz, The Steerage *(1907)*

Photographs taken about 1907 of Japanese immigrants in kimonos and American clothing.

The Moth and the Star

A young and impressionable moth once set his heart on a certain star. He told his mother about this and she counseled him to set his heart on a bridge lamp instead. "Stars aren't the thing to hang around," she said; "lamps are the thing to hang around." "You get somewhere that way," said the moth's father. "You don't get anywhere chasing stars." But the moth would not heed the words of either parent. Every evening at dusk when the star came out he would start flying toward it and every morning at dawn he would crawl back home worn out with his vain endeavor. One day his father said to him, "You haven't burned a wing in months, boy, and it looks to me as if you were never going to. All your brothers have been badly burned flying around street lamps and all your sisters have been terribly singed flying around house lamps. Come on, now, get out of here and get yourself scorched! A big strapping moth like you without a mark on him!" The moth left his father's house, but he would not fly around street lamps and he would not fly around house lamps. He went right on trying to reach the star, which was four and one-third light years, or twenty-five trillion miles, away. The moth thought it was just caught in the top branches of an elm. He never did reach the star, but he went right on trying, night after night, and when he was a very, very old moth he began to think that he really had reached the star and he went around saying so. This gave him a deep and lasting pleasure, and he lived to a great old age. His parents and his brothers and his sisters had all been burned to death when they were quite young.

Moral: Who flies afar from the sphere of our sorrow is here today and here tomorrow.

James Thurber (1940)

SPEED

In 200 miles
a tender painting
on the wind-

shield, not yet done,
in greeny yellows,
crystalline pinks,

a few smeared
browns. Fuselages
split on impact,

stuck, their juices
instantly dried. Spat-
tered flat out-

lines, superfine
strokes, tokens of
themselves flying,

frail engines
died in various
designs: mainly arrow-

shapes, wings gone,
bellies smitten
open, glaze and tincture

the wipers can't
erase. In 400 miles
a palette, thick

impasto; in 600
a palimpsest[1] the sun
bakes through. Stained

glass, not yet done
smiting the wind-
borne, speeds on.

May Swenson (1971)

---

1. **palimpsest** (pal'imp sest) *n.* writing surface that has been erased and written on again.

David Hockney, Pearblossom Hwy., 11–18th April 1986

Homesick Blues

DE RAILROAD BRIDGE'S
A SAD SONG IN DE AIR.
DE RAILROAD BRIDGE'S
A SAD SONG IN DE AIR.
EVER TIME DE TRAINS PASS
I WANTS TO GO SOMEWHERE. . . .

Langston Hughes (1926)

I BEEN WANDERIN'
EARLY AND LATE,
NEW YORK CITY
TO THE GOLDEN GATE,
AN' IT LOOKS LIKE
I'M NEVER GONNA CEASE MY WANDERIN.'

Folk song (20th century)

Jacob Lawrence, The Migration of the Negro series, No 1 (1940-41)

INDIAN BOARDING SCHOOL: THE RUNAWAYS

Home's the place we head for in our sleep.
Boxcars stumbling north in dreams
don't wait for us. We catch them on the run.
The rails, old lacerations that we love,
shoot parallel across the face and break
just under Turtle Mountains. Riding scars
you can't get lost. Home is the place they cross.

The lame guard strikes a match and makes the dark
less tolerant. We watch through cracks in boards
as the land starts rolling, rolling till it hurts
to be here, cold in regulation clothes.
We know the sheriff's waiting at midrun
to take us back. His car is dumb and warm.
The highway doesn't rock, it only hums
like a wing of long insults. The worn-down welts
of ancient punishments lead back and forth.

All runaways wear dresses, long green ones,
the color you would think shame was. We scrub
the sidewalks down because it's shameful work.
Our brushes cut the stone in watered arcs
and in the soak frail outlines shiver clear
a moment, things us kids pressed on the dark
face before it hardened, pale, remembering
delicate old injuries, the spines of names and leaves.

Louise Erdrich (1984)

SOMETIMES I GO ABOUT PITYING MYSELF,
AND ALL THE TIME
I AM BEING CARRIED ON GREAT WINDS
ACROSS THE SKY.

Chippewa

RESPONDING

1. Judging by these selections, what qualities are most important to the traveler?
2. In your opinion, which of these journeys have the qualities of a pilgrimage?
3. Which of these travelers seem to express the deepest truths about journeying?
4. Which of the images in this portfolio seem to reflect positive attitudes toward journeys? Which reflect negative attitudes?
5. Do you think travel makes people wiser? Why or why not?

Breaking the Mold

Beyond the Limits
Part One, pages 446–507

The Harlem Renaissance
Part Two, pages 508–550

THEMES IN AMERICAN LITERATURE

The Search for Equality
Theme Portfolio, pages 551–561

Although overdressed for the beach by today's standards, these "Gibson Girls," by popular illustrator Charles Dana Gibson (1867-1944), reflected a new, less sentimental image of American womanhood.

STRETCHING THE LIMITS

HISTORICAL OVERVIEW

In early rural America, women had often worked side by side with their husbands. As the economy changed in the mid-1800s, and at least middle-class women had more leisure, the expected role of a woman was ideal wife and mother, "an angel in the house" to serve as a model of virtue to her husband and children. The same period saw the rise and decline of the first women's rights movement, whose goals—including the right of women to own property, to higher education, and to vote—were still unrealized when the Civil War ended the reform impulse. A second women's movement occurred during the Progressive Era that began in the 1890s. This time the focus was women's suffrage—the right to vote. This time the reformers were successful, but not until 1920 when the 19th Amendment was passed.

Isadora Duncan was an American pioneer of modern dance in the early 1900s who rejected the formal, conventional technique of ballet and developed a new dance style based on nature and the complete freedom of movement.

Progressive Era reformers like Jane Addams opened settlement houses in city slums to combat poverty and improve housing, education, and health care. Here, a nurse climbs over rooftops of New York tenements to visit patients.

Although homemaking was still difficult on farms in the late 1800s, some women were resourceful in finding ways to make their lives easier. The woman pictured here has rigged a home-made washing machine.

Key Dates

1700s
Colonial law dictates that women are represented in society only by the males of the household.

1820s
Women are active outside the home as teachers and reformers.

1845
Margaret Fuller writes Woman in the Nineteenth Century, the first American feminist book.

1848
Seneca Falls Convention in New York discusses women's rights.

1890
National American Woman Suffrage Association is formed.

1920
The 19th Amendment passes.

In the late 1800s working women were confined to unskilled jobs in domestic service, factories, and "sweat shops." The few who could afford an education found work as teachers and nurses. The invention of the typewriter allowed women to enter the business world and by 1900 women outnumbered men in office jobs.

Suffragists often disagreed on how to get women the vote. Some supported a Constitutional amendment while others favored a state-by-state approach. Suffragists' tactics also varied from organizing petitions and parades to chaining themselves to the White House fence. When arrested they went on hunger strikes in jail and were force-fed by police.

Part One

Beyond the Limits

As the end of the 1800s approached, women began challenging the roles and rules that both defined and confined their gender. Feminists like Susan B. Anthony, Elizabeth Cady Stanton, and Sojourner Truth had been fighting for years to gain women's rights in education, the workplace, property ownership, and voting. Yet in every aspect of life there were still strict limits within which women were expected to live. In the following selections, you'll meet women who dared to step beyond society's limits.

🐚 **Multicultural Connection** While each of us is a part of one or more cultural groups, each person also finds ways to express her or his **individuality,** either within or beyond a society's expectations. How do the women in the following selections express their individuality?

Literature

Kate Chopin	**The Story of an Hour** ◆ short story	.450
Susan Glaspell	**Trifles** ◆ play	.455
Mary E. Wilkins Freeman	**The Revolt of "Mother"** ◆ short story	.468
Ida B. Wells-Barnett	*from* **Crusade for Justice** ◆ autobiography	.483
Edna St. Vincent Millay	**The Spring and the Fall** ◆ poem	.492
	On Thought in Harness ◆ poem	.493

Interdisciplinary Study Within Limits

The Uprising of Women ◆ history 495
Teaching by the Rules ◆ history 497
from For Her Own Good
    by Barbara Ehrenreich and Deirdre English ◆ science 498

Language History

The Language of Gender 500

Writing Workshop Expository Writing

Update: Women Then and Now 501

Beyond Print Visual Literacy

Looking at Photographs 506

The Story of an Hour

by Kate Chopin

Kate Chopin
1851–1904

Kate Chopin did not begin to write until she was thirty-six years old. A much sought-after belle of St. Louis society, Chopin married at nineteen and had six children. In 1879, her husband Oscar died suddenly of swamp fever. Financially independent and bored with her life as a society matron, Chopin began to write. For the most part, her writing was not well-received because of the unconventional behavior of her female characters. After she died, Chopin's works were essentially forgotten, then rediscovered during the women's movement of the late 1960s.

Building Background

Breaking New Ground When Chopin embarked on a literary career, she kept her writing a secret from her circle of friends. She was afraid that she would be criticized by a society that was unprepared to see women as professionals. In 1894, certain that she had found her true vocation, and equally certain that she understood the hidden desires of women of her time, Chopin created the character of Louise and wrote her short story, "The Story of an Hour."

Literary Focus

Irony is the contrast between what appears to be and what really is. In an ironic situation, an author presents a state of affairs that is the opposite of what is expected or what seems appropriate. Using a chart similar to the one below, note examples of irony in "The Story of an Hour."

Event	What is expected	What happens

Writer's Notebook

Free at Last? Have you ever dreamed of being completely free, with absolutely no responsibilities—nothing you *have* to do and nowhere you *have* to go? What are the advantages of this type of freedom? What are the disadvantages? In your notebook, write a paragraph that explains why you would or would not want to be completely free and on your own.

THE STORY OF AN HOUR

KATE CHOPIN

Knowing that Mrs. Mallard was afflicted with a heart trouble, great care was taken to break to her as gently as possible the news of her husband's death.

It was her sister Josephine who told her, in broken sentences; veiled hints that revealed in half concealing. Her husband's friend Richards was there, too, near her. It was he who had been in the newspaper office when intelligence of the railroad disaster was received, with Brently Mallard's name leading the list of "killed." He had only taken the time to assure himself of its truth by a second telegram, and had hastened to forestall[1] any less careful, less tender friend in bearing the sad message.

She did not hear the story as many women have heard the same, with a paralyzed inability to accept its significance. She wept at once, with sudden, wild abandonment,[2] in her sister's arms. When the storm of grief had spent itself she went away to her room alone. She would have no one follow her.

There stood, facing the open window, a comfortable, roomy armchair. Into this she sank, pressed down by a physical exhaustion that haunted her body and seemed to reach into her soul.

She could see in the open square before her house the tops of trees that were all aquiver with the new spring life. The delicious breath of rain was in the air. In the street below a peddler was crying his wares.[3] The notes of a distant song which someone was singing reached her faintly, and countless sparrows were twittering in the eaves.

There were patches of blue sky showing here and there through the clouds that had met and piled one above the other in the west facing her window.

She sat with her head thrown back upon the cushion of the chair, quite motionless, except when a sob came up into her throat and shook her, as a child who has cried itself to sleep continues to sob in its dreams.

She was young, with a fair, calm face, whose lines bespoke repression and even a certain strength. But now there was a dull stare in her eyes, whose gaze was fixed away off yonder on one of those patches of blue sky. It was not a glance of reflection, but rather indicated a suspension of intelligent thought.

---

1. **forestall** (fôr stôl′), *v.* prevent by acting first.
2. abandonment (ə ban′dən mənt), *n.* freedom from restraint.
3. **crying his wares**. Street peddlers often shouted out what they were selling as they walked down the street.

▲ How does the tone of this John Singer Sargent painting, *Repose* (1911), compare with the
tone of "The Story of an Hour"?

There was something coming to her and she was waiting for it, fearfully. What was it? She did not know; it was too subtle and elusive to name. But she felt it, creeping out of the sky, reaching toward her through the sounds, the scents, the color that filled the air.

Now her bosom rose and fell tumultuously.[4] She was beginning to recognize this thing that was approaching to possess her, and she was striving to beat it back with her will—as powerless as her two white slender hands would have been.

When she abandoned herself a little whispered word escaped her slightly parted lips. She said it over and over under her breath: "free, free, free!" The vacant stare and the look of terror that had followed it went from her eyes. They stayed keen and bright. Her pulses beat fast, and the coursing blood warmed and relaxed every inch of her body.

She did not stop to ask if it were or were not a monstrous joy that held her. A clear and exalted[5] perception enabled her to dismiss the suggestion as trivial.

She knew that she would weep again when she saw the kind, tender hands folded in death; the face that had never looked save with love upon her, fixed and gray and dead. But she saw beyond that bitter moment a long procession of years to come that would belong to her absolutely. And she opened and spread her arms out to them in welcome.

There would be no one to live for her during those coming years; she would live for herself. There would be no powerful will bending hers in that blind persistence with which men and women believe they have a right to impose a private will upon a fellow-creature. A kind intention or a cruel intention made the act seem no less a crime as she looked upon it in that brief moment of illumination.

And yet she had loved him—sometimes. Often she had not. What did it matter! What could love, the unsolved mystery, count for in face of this possession of self-assertion which she suddenly recognized as the strongest impulse of her being!

"Free! Body and soul free!" she kept whispering.

Josephine was kneeling before the closed door with her lips to the keyhole, imploring for admission. "Louise, open the door! I beg; open the door—you will make yourself ill. What are you doing, Louise? For heaven's sake open the door."

"Go away. I am not making myself ill." No; she was drinking in a very elixir[6] of life through that open window.

Her fancy was running riot along those days ahead of her. Spring days, and summer days, and all sorts of days that would be her own. She breathed a quick prayer that life might be long. It was only yesterday she had thought with a shudder that life might be long.

She arose at length and opened the door to her sister's importunities. There was a feverish triumph in her eyes, and she carried herself unwittingly[7] like a goddess of Victory. She clasped her sister's waist, and together they descended the stairs. Richards stood waiting for them at the bottom.

Someone was opening the front door with a latchkey. It was Brently Mallard who entered, a little travel-stained, composedly carrying his grip-sack and umbrella. He had been far from the scene of the accident, and did not even know there had been one. He stood amazed at Josephine's piercing cry; at Richards' quick motion to screen him from the view of his wife.

But Richards was too late.

When the doctors came they said she had died of heart disease—of joy that kills.

---

4. **tumultuously** (tü mul′chü əs lē), *adv.* violently.
5. **exalted** (eg zôl′təd), *adj.* noble; elevated.
6. **elixir** (i lik′sər), *n.* substance supposed to have the power of lengthening life indefinitely; cure-all.
7. **unwittingly** (un wit′ing lē), *adv.* not knowingly; unconsciously.

After Reading

Making Connections

Shaping Your Response

1. Does Louise Mallard deserve sympathy, or did she get what she deserved? Explain your opinion.

Analyzing the Story

2. How would you explain Louise's widely varied emotions in the story?

3. Find a paragraph in the story which seems to explain Louise's reaction. Analyze it carefully. Would you say it is talking about marriage, or sexism, or neither? Explain.

4. 👣 Why does Louise seem better able to express her **individuality** after she believes her husband has died?

Extending the Ideas

5. Bring "The Story of an Hour" up to the present. How might this story be different if it took place in modern times?

Literary Focus: Irony

Review the examples of **irony** you noted in your chart. Then choose one and explain why it is ironic. How does the situation—what really happens—differ from what seems appropriate or expected?

Vocabulary Study

abandonment
tumultuously
exalted
elixir
unwittingly

In your notebook, copy the chart shown here, providing a synonym and an antonym for each of the words.

	Synonym	Antonym
1. abandonment		
2. tumultuously		
3. exalted		
4. elixir		
5. unwittingly		

Expressing Your Ideas

Writing Choice

Writer's Notebook Update Has your attitude toward freedom changed after reading the selection? Write a paragraph that compares your thoughts about personal freedom and independence before and after reading the story.

Another Option

Reader's Theater Working in a small group, adapt "The Story of an Hour" as a **reader's theater play** and perform it for the rest of the class. Choose appropriate background music and costumes.

Trifles

by Susan Glaspell

Susan Glaspell
1876?–1948

In 1915, Susan Glaspell and her husband, George Cram Cook, organized a group of Provincetown, Massachusetts artists who produced several one-act plays in a shabby wharf theater. In 1916, playwright Eugene O'Neill and poet Edna St. Vincent Millay joined the group. Over the next seven years, Glaspell wrote one play after another, many of which focused on her favorite theme of escaping imprisoning environments in order to gain individual freedom. *Trifles* was first performed by the Provincetown Players in the summer of 1916.

Building Background

Producing *Trifles* Imagine that you are the director in charge of a class production of *Trifles*. While reading Glaspell's play, keep these questions in mind: What should your sets look like? What would be an appropriate musical score? What additional stage directions will you need to give your actors? Which of your classmates would be best suited to play the five characters?

Literary Focus

Plot is the sequence of interrelated actions and events that present and resolve a conflict. As the plot unfolds, often the conflict builds to an emotional or dramatic peak—the **turning point,** or climax, which is followed by a **resolution** or denouement.

Think about plot by doing a plot structure map for a mystery story or movie you've recently read or seen. Copy the plot structure map on a sheet of paper. At each of the five points on the map, write a sentence that explains the action.

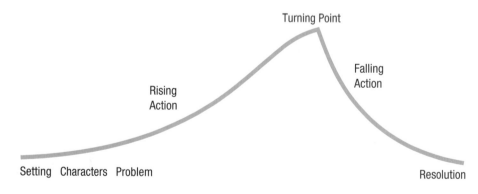

Writer's Notebook

Guilty or Innocent? In the play you're about to read, a woman has been accused of murdering her husband. Think of a trial that you've heard about recently. If you had been a member of the jury during that trial, would you have voted guilty or innocent? Why? In your notebook, write a paragraph that explains your verdict.

TRIFLES
SUSAN GLASPELL

SCENE: The kitchen in the now abandoned farmhouse of JOHN WRIGHT, *a gloomy kitchen, and left without having been put in order— unwashed pans under the sink, a loaf of bread outside the bread-box, a dish-towel on the table—other signs of incompleted work. At the rear the outer door opens and the* SHERIFF *comes in followed by the* COUNTY ATTORNEY *and* HALE. *The* SHERIFF *and* HALE *are men in middle life, the* COUNTY ATTORNEY *is a young man; all are much bundled up and go at once to the stove. They are followed by the two women—the* SHERIFF'S *wife first; she is a slight wiry[1] woman, a thin nervous face.* MRS. HALE *is larger and would ordinarily be called more comfortable looking, but she is disturbed now and looks fearfully about as she enters. The women have come in slowly, and stand close together near the door.*

COUNTY ATTORNEY (*rubbing his hands*). This feels good. Come up to the fire, ladies.

MRS. PETERS (*after taking a step forward*). I'm not—cold.

SHERIFF (*unbuttoning his overcoat and stepping away from the stove as if to mark the beginning of official business*). Now, Mr. Hale, before we move things about, you explain to Mr. Henderson just what you saw when you came here yesterday morning.

COUNTY ATTORNEY. By the way, has anything been moved? Are things just as you left them yesterday?

SHERIFF (*looking about*). It's just the same. When it dropped below zero last night I thought I'd better send Frank out this morning to make a fire for us—no use getting pneumonia with a big case on, but I told him not to touch anything except the stove—and you know Frank.

COUNTY ATTORNEY. Somebody should have been left here yesterday.

SHERIFF. Oh—yesterday. When I had to send Frank to Morris Center for that man who went crazy—I want you to know I had my hands full yesterday. I knew you could get back from Omaha by today and as long as I went over everything here myself—

COUNTY ATTORNEY. Well, Mr. Hale, tell just what happened when you came here yesterday morning.

HALE. Harry and I had started to town with a load of potatoes. We came along the road from my place and as I got here I said, "I'm going to see if I can't get John Wright to go in with me on a party telephone." I spoke to Wright about it once before and he put me off, saying folks talked too much anyway, and all he asked was peace and quiet—I guess you know about how much he talked himself; but I thought maybe if I went to the house and talked about it before his wife, though I said to Harry that I didn't know as what his wife wanted made much difference to John—

COUNTY ATTORNEY. Let's talk about that later, Mr. Hale. I do want to talk about that, but tell now just what happened when you got to the house.

HALE. I didn't hear or see anything; I knocked at the door, and still it was all quiet inside. I knew

---

1. **wiry** (wī′rē), *adj.* lean, strong, and tough.

they must be up, it was past eight o'clock. So I knocked again, and I thought I heard somebody say, "Come in." I wasn't sure, I'm not sure yet, but I opened the door—this door (*indicating the door by which the two women are still standing*) and there in that rocker—(*pointing to it*) sat Mrs. Wright.

(*They all look at the rocker.*)

COUNTY ATTORNEY. What—was she doing?

HALE. She was rockin' back and forth. She had her apron in her hand and was kind of—pleating it.

COUNTY ATTORNEY. And how did she—look?

HALE. Well, she looked queer.

COUNTY ATTORNEY. How do you mean—queer?

HALE. Well, as if she didn't know what she was going to do next. And kind of done up.

COUNTY ATTORNEY. How did she seem to feel about your coming?

HALE. Why, I don't think she minded—one way or other. She didn't pay much attention. I said, "How do, Mrs. Wright, it's cold, ain't it?" And she said, "Is it?" and went on kind of pleating at her apron. Well, I was surprised; she didn't ask me to come up to the stove, or to set down, but just sat there, not even looking at me, so I said, "I want to see John." And then she—laughed. I guess you would call it a laugh. I thought of Harry and the team outside, so I said a little sharp: "Can't I see John?" "No," she says, kind o' dull like. "Ain't he home?" says I. "Yes," says she, "he's home." "Then why can't I see him?" I asked her, out of patience. "'Cause he's dead," says she. *"Dead?"* says I. She just nodded her head, not getting a bit excited, but rockin' back and forth. "Why—where is he?" says I, not knowing what to say. She just pointed upstairs—like that (*himself pointing to the room above*). I got up, with the idea of going up there. I walked from there to here—then I says, "Why, what did he die of?" "He died of a rope round his neck," says she, and just went on pleatin' at her apron. Well, I went out and called Harry. I thought I might—

need help. We went upstairs and there he was lyin'—

COUNTY ATTORNEY. I think I'd rather have you go into that upstairs, where you can point it all out. Just go on now with the rest of the story.

HALE. Well, my first thought was to get that rope off. It looked . . . (*stops, his face twitches*) . . . but Harry, he went up to him, and he said, "No, he's dead all right, and we'd better not touch anything." So we went back downstairs. She was still sitting that same way. "Has anybody been notified?" I asked. "No," says she, unconcerned. "Who did this, Mrs. Wright?" said Harry. He said it business-like—and she stopped pleatin' of her apron. "I don't know," she says. "You don't *know?*" says Harry. "No," says she. "Weren't you sleepin' in the bed with him?" says Harry. "Yes," says she, "but I was on the inside." "Somebody slipped a rope round his neck and strangled him and you didn't wake up?" says Harry. "I didn't wake up," she said after him. We must 'a looked as if we didn't see how that could be, for after a minute she said, "I sleep sound." Harry was going to ask her more questions but I said maybe we ought to let her tell her story first to the coroner, or the sheriff, so Harry went fast as he could to Rivers' place, where there's a telephone.

COUNTY ATTORNEY. And what did Mrs. Wright do when she knew that you had gone for the coroner?

HALE. She moved from that chair to this one over here (*pointing to a small chair in the corner*) and just sat there with her hands held together and looking down. I got a feeling that I ought to make some conversation, so I said I had come in to see if John wanted to put in a telephone, and at that she started to laugh, and then she stopped and looked at me—scared. (*The* COUNTY ATTORNEY, *who has had his notebook out, makes a note.*) I dunno, maybe it wasn't scared. I wouldn't like to say it was. Soon Harry got back, and then Dr. Lloyd came, and you, Mr. Peters, and so

▲ In Susan Glaspell's play *Trifles* Mrs. Hale says she avoided the house because it wasn't "cheerful." Does the house in Bob Timberlake's *Tulip Quilt* (1972), have that same quality that made Mrs. Hale so uncomfortable? Why or why not?

▲ What do you think the woman in Thomas C. Eakins' painting, *Mother* (1903), is thinking about?

I guess that's all I know that you don't.

COUNTY ATTORNEY *(looking around).* I guess we'll go upstairs first—and then out to the barn and around there. *(To the* SHERIFF.*)* You're convinced that there was nothing important here—nothing that would point to any motive.

SHERIFF. Nothing here but kitchen things.

(The COUNTY ATTORNEY, *after again looking around the kitchen, opens the door of a cupboard closet. He gets up on a chair and looks on a shelf. Pulls his hand away, sticky.)*

COUNTY ATTORNEY. Here's a nice mess.

(The women draw nearer.)

MRS. PETERS *(to the other woman).* Oh, her fruit; it did freeze. *(To the* LAWYER.*)* She worried about that when it turned so cold. She said the fire'd go out and her jars would break.

SHERIFF. Well, can you beat the woman! Held for murder and worryin' about her preserves.

COUNTY ATTORNEY. I guess before we're through she may have something more serious than preserves to worry about.

HALE. Well, women are used to worrying over trifles.

(The two women move a little closer together.)

COUNTY ATTORNEY *(with the gallantry of a young politician).* And yet, for all their worries, what would we do without the ladies? (The women do not unbend. He goes to the sink, takes a dipperful of water from the pail and pouring it into a basin, washes his hands. Starts to wipe them on the roller-towel, turns it for a cleaner place.) Dirty towels! (Kicks his foot against the pans under the sink.) Not much of a housekeeper, would you say, ladies?

MRS. HALE *(stiffly).*[2] There's a great deal of work to be done on a farm.

COUNTY ATTORNEY. To be sure. And yet (with a little bow to her) I know there are some Dickson County farmhouses which do not have such roller towels.

(He gives it a pull to expose its full length again.)

---

2. **stiffly** (stif′lē), *adv.* not easy or natural in manner.

MRS. HALE. These towels get dirty awful quick. Men's hands aren't always as clean as they might be.

COUNTY ATTORNEY. Ah, loyal to your sex, I see. But you and Mrs. Wright were neighbors. I suppose you were friends, too.

MRS. HALE (*shaking her head*). I've not seen much of her of late years. I've not been in this house—it's more than a year.

COUNTY ATTORNEY. And why was that? You didn't like her?

MRS. HALE. I liked her all well enough. Farmers' wives have their hands full, Mr. Henderson. And then—

COUNTY ATTORNEY. Yes—?

MRS. HALE (*looking about*). It never seemed a very cheerful place.

COUNTY ATTORNEY. No—it's not cheerful. I shouldn't say she had the homemaking instinct.

MRS. HALE. Well, I don't know as Wright had, either.

COUNTY ATTORNEY. You mean that they didn't get on very well?

MRS. HALE. No, I don't mean anything. But I don't think a place'd be any cheerfuller for John Wright's being in it.

COUNTY ATTORNEY. I'd like to talk more of that a little later. I want to get the lay of things upstairs now.

(*He goes to the left, where three steps lead to a stair door.*)

SHERIFF. I suppose anything Mrs. Peters does'll be all right. She was to take in some clothes for her, you know, and a few little things. We left in such a hurry yesterday.

COUNTY ATTORNEY. Yes, but I would like to see what you take, Mrs. Peters, and keep an eye out for anything that might be of use to us.

MRS. PETERS. Yes, Mr. Henderson.

(*The women listen to the men's steps on the stairs, then look about the kitchen.*)

MRS. HALE. I'd hate to have men coming into my kitchen, snooping around and criticising.

(*She arranges the pans under sink which the* LAWYER *had shoved out of place.*)

MRS. PETERS. Of course it's no more than their duty.

MRS. HALE. Duty's all right, but I guess that deputy sheriff that came out to make the fire might have got a little of this on. (*Gives the roller towel a pull.*) Wish I'd thought of that sooner. Seems mean to talk about her for not having things slicked up when she had to come away in such a hurry.

MRS. PETERS (*who has gone to a small table in the left rear corner of the room, and lifted one end of a towel that covers a pan*). She had bread set.

(*Stands still.*)

MRS. HALE (*Eyes fixed on a loaf of bread beside the breadbox, which is on a low shelf at the other side of the room. Moves slowly toward it*). She was going to put this in there. (*Picks up loaf, then abruptly drops it. In a manner of returning to familiar things.*) It's a shame about her fruit. I wonder if it's all gone. (*Gets up on the chair and looks.*) I think there's some here that's all right, Mrs. Peters. Yes—here; (*Holding it toward the window*) this is cherries, too. (*Looking again.*) I declare I believe that's the only one. (*Gets down, bottle in her hand. Goes to the sink and wipes it off on the outside.*) She'll feel awful bad after all her hard work in the hot weather. I remember the afternoon I put up my cherries last summer.

(*She puts the bottle on the big kitchen table, center of the room. With a sigh, is about to sit down in the rocking-chair. Before she is seated realizes what chair it is; with a slow look at it, steps back. The chair which she has touched rocks back and forth.*)

MRS. PETERS. Well, I must get those things from the front room closet. (*She goes to the door at the right, but after looking into the other room, steps back.*) You coming with me, Mrs. Hale? You could help me carry them.

(*They go in the other room; reappear,* MRS. PETERS *carrying a dress and skirt,* MRS. HALE *following with a pair of shoes.*)

MRS. PETERS. My, it's cold in there.

(*She puts the clothes on the big table, and hurries to the stove.*)

MRS. HALE (*examining the skirt*). Wright was close.[3] I think maybe that's why she kept so much to herself. She didn't even belong to the Ladies' Aid. I suppose she felt she couldn't do her part, and then you don't enjoy things when you feel shabby. She used to wear pretty clothes and be lively, when she was Minnie Foster, one of the town girls singing in the choir. But that—oh, that was thirty years ago. This all you was to take in?

MRS. PETERS. She said she wanted an apron. Funny thing to want, for there isn't much to get you dirty in jail, goodness knows. But I suppose just to make her feel more natural. She said they was in the top drawer in this cupboard. Yes, here. And then her little shawl that always hung behind the door. (*Opens stair door and looks.*) Yes, here it is.

(*Quickly shuts door leading upstairs.*)

MRS. HALE (*abruptly moving toward her*). Mrs. Peters?

MRS. PETERS. Yes, Mrs. Hale?

MRS. HALE. Do you think she did it?

MRS. PETERS (*in a frightened voice*). Oh, I don't know.

MRS. HALE. Well, I don't think she did. Asking for an apron and her little shawl. Worrying about her fruit.

MRS. PETERS (*Starts to speak, glances up, where footsteps are heard in the room above. In a low voice*). Mr. Peters says it looks bad for her. Mr. Henderson is awful sarcastic in a speech and he'll make fun of her sayin' she didn't wake up.

MRS. HALE. Well, I guess John Wright didn't wake when they was slipping that rope under his neck.

MRS. PETERS. No, it's strange. It must have been done awful crafty and still. They say it was such a—funny way to kill a man, rigging it all up like that.

MRS. HALE. That's just what Mr. Hale said. There was a gun in the house. He says that's what he can't understand.

MRS. PETERS. Mr. Henderson said coming out that what was needed for the case was a motive; something to show anger, or—sudden feeling.

MRS. HALE (*who is standing by the table*). Well, I don't see any signs of anger around here. (*She puts her hand on the dish towel which lies on the table, stands looking down at the table, one half of which is clean, the other half messy.*) It's wiped to here. (*Makes a move as if to finish work, then turns and looks at loaf of bread outside the breadbox. Drops towel. In that voice of coming back to familiar things.*) Wonder how they are finding things upstairs. I hope she had it a little more red-up[4] there. You know, it seems kind of *sneaking*. Locking her up in town and then coming out here and trying to get her own house to turn against her!

MRS. PETERS. But Mrs. Hale, the law is the law.

MRS. HALE. I s'pose 'tis. (*Unbuttoning her coat.*) Better loosen up your things, Mrs. Peters. You won't feel them when you go out.

(MRS. PETERS *takes off her fur tippet, goes to hang it on hook at back of room, stands looking at the under part of the small corner table.*)

MRS. PETERS. She was piecing a quilt.

(*She brings the large sewing basket and they look at the bright pieces.*)

MRS. HALE. It's a log cabin pattern. Pretty, isn't it? I wonder if she was goin' to quilt it or just knot it?[5]

(*Footsteps have been heard coming down the stairs. The* SHERIFF *enters followed by* HALE *and the* COUNTY ATTORNEY.)

SHERIFF. They wonder if she was going to quilt it or just knot it!

(*The men laugh, the women look abashed.*)[6]

COUNTY ATTORNEY (*rubbing his hands over the stove*). Frank's fire didn't do much up there,

---

3. close (klōs), *adj.* private; reserved.
4. **red-up**, tidy, made-up.
5. **knot it**, a method of connecting the parts of a quilt.
6. abashed (ə basht′), *adj.* embarrassed; ashamed.

▲ List the feelings evoked by Albert Pinkham Ryder's painting *The Dead Bird* (1890–1900).
Are they the same as those evoked by the play? Explain.

did it? Well, let's go out to the barn and get that cleared up.

(The men go outside.)

MRS. HALE *(resentfully).* I don't know as there's anything so strange, our takin' up our time with little things while we're waiting for them to get the evidence. *(She sits down at the big table smoothing out a block with decision.)* I don't see as it's anything to laugh about.

MRS. PETERS *(apologetically).* Of course they've got awful important things on their minds.

(Pulls up a chair and joins MRS. HALE *at the table.)*

MRS. HALE *(examining another block).* Mrs. Peters, look at this one. Here, this is the one she was working on, and look at the sewing! All the rest of it has been so nice and even. And look at this! It's all over the place! Why, it looks as if she didn't know what she was about!

(After she has said this they look at each other, then start to glance back at the door. After an instant MRS. HALE *has pulled at a knot and ripped the sewing.)*

MRS. PETERS. Oh, what are you doing, Mrs. Hale?

MRS. HALE *(mildly).* Just pulling out a stitch or two that's not sewed very good. *(Threading a needle.)* Bad sewing always made me fidgety.

MRS. PETERS *(nervously).* I don't think we ought to touch things.

MRS. HALE. I'll just finish up this end. *(Suddenly stopping and leaning forward.)* Mrs. Peters?

MRS. PETERS. Yes, Mrs. Hale?

MRS. HALE. What do you suppose she was so nervous about?

MRS. PETERS. Oh—I don't know. I don't know as she was nervous. I sometimes sew awful queer when I'm just tired. (MRS. HALE *starts to say something, looks at* MRS. PETERS, *then goes on sewing.)* Well I must get these things wrapped up. They may be through sooner than we think. *(Pulling apron and other things together.)* I wonder where I can find a piece of paper, and string.

MRS. HALE. In that cupboard, maybe.

MRS. PETERS *(looking in cupboard).* Why, here's a bird-cage. *(Holds it up.)* Did she have a bird, Mrs. Hale?

MRS. HALE. Why, I don't know whether she did or not—I've not been here for so long. There was a man around last year selling canaries cheap, but I don't know as she took one; maybe she did. She used to sing real pretty herself.

Trifles **461**

MRS. PETERS (*glancing around*). Seems funny to think of a bird here. But she must have had one, or why would she have a cage? I wonder what happened to it.

MRS. HALE. I s'pose maybe the cat got it.

MRS. PETERS. No, she didn't have a cat. She's got that feeling some people have about cats—being afraid of them. My cat got in her room and she was real upset and asked me to take it out.

MRS. HALE. My sister Bessie was like that. Queer, ain't it?

MRS. PETERS (*examining the cage*). Why, look at this door. It's broke. One hinge is pulled apart.

MRS. HALE (*looking too*). Looks as if someone must have been rough with it.

MRS. PETERS. Why, yes.

(*She brings the cage forward and puts it on the table.*)

MRS. HALE. I wish if they're going to find any evidence they'd be about it. I don't like this place.

MRS. PETERS. But I'm awful glad you came with me, Mrs. Hale. It would be lonesome for me sitting here alone.

MRS. HALE. It would, wouldn't it? (*Dropping her sewing.*) But I tell you what I do wish, Mrs. Peters. I wish I had come over sometimes when *she* was here. I—(*looking around the room*)—wish I had.

MRS. PETERS. But of course you were awful busy, Mrs. Hale—your house and your children.

MRS. HALE. I could've come. I stayed away because it weren't cheerful—and that's why I ought to have come. I—I've never liked this place. Maybe because it's down in a hollow and you don't see the road. I dunno what it is, but it's a lonesome place and always was. I wish I had come over to see Minnie Foster sometimes. I can see now—

(*Shakes her head.*)

MRS. PETERS. Well, you mustn't reproach yourself, Mrs. Hale. Somehow we just don't see how it is with other folks until—something comes up.

MRS. HALE. Not having children makes less work—but it makes a quiet house, and Wright out to work all day, and no company when he did come in. Did you know John Wright, Mrs. Peters?

MRS. PETERS. Not to know him; I've seen him in town. They say he was a good man.

MRS. HALE. Yes—good; he didn't drink, and kept his word as well as most, I guess, and paid his debts. But he was a hard man, Mrs. Peters. Just to pass the time of day with him—(*Shivers.*) Like a raw wind that gets to the bone. (*Pauses, her eye falling on the cage.*) I should think she would 'a wanted a bird. But what do you suppose went with it?

MRS. PETERS. I don't know, unless it got sick and died.

(*She reaches over and swings the broken door, swings it again, both women watch it.*)

MRS. HALE. You weren't raised round here, were you? (MRS. PETERS *shakes her head.*) You didn't know—her?

MRS. PETERS. Not till they brought her yesterday.

MRS. HALE. She—come to think of it, she was kind of like a bird herself—real sweet and pretty, but kind of timid and—fluttery. How—she—did—change. (*Silence; then as if struck by a happy thought and relieved to get back to everyday things.*) Tell you what, Mrs. Peters, why don't you take the quilt in with you? It might take up her mind.

MRS. PETERS. Why, I think that's a real nice idea, Mrs. Hale. There couldn't possibly be any objection to it, could there? Now, just what would I take? I wonder if her patches are in here—and her things.

(*They look in the sewing basket.*)

MRS. HALE. Here's some red. I expect this has got sewing things in it. (*Brings out a fancy box.*) What a pretty box. Looks like something somebody would give you. Maybe her scissors are in here. (*Opens box. Suddenly puts her hand to her nose.*) Why—(MRS. PETERS *bends nearer, then turns her face away.*) There's something wrapped up in this piece of silk.

MRS. PETERS. Why, this isn't her scissors.

MRS. HALE (*lifting the silk*). Oh, Mrs. Peters—its—

(MRS. PETERS *bends closer.*)

MRS. PETERS. It's the bird.

MRS. HALE (*jumping up*). But, Mrs. Peters—look at it! Its neck! Look at its neck! It's all—other side *to*.

MRS. PETERS. Somebody—wrung—its—neck.

(*Their eyes meet. A look of growing comprehension, of horror. Steps are heard outside.* MRS. HALE *slips box under quilt pieces, and sinks into her chair. Enter* SHERIFF *and* COUNTY ATTORNEY. MRS. PETERS *rises.*)

COUNTY ATTORNEY (*as one turning from serious things to little pleasantries*). Well, ladies, have you decided whether she was going to quilt it or knot it?

MRS. PETERS. We think she was going to—knot it.

COUNTY ATTORNEY. Well, that's interesting, I'm sure. (*Seeing the birdcage.*) Has the bird flown?

MRS. HALE (*putting more quilt pieces over the box*). We think the—cat got it.

COUNTY ATTORNEY (*preoccupied*). Is there a cat?

(MRS. HALE *glances in a quick covert way at* MRS. PETERS.)

MRS. PETERS. Well, not *now*. They're superstitious, you know. They leave.

COUNTY ATTORNEY (*to* SHERIFF PETERS, *continuing an interrupted conversation*). No sign at all of anyone having come from the outside. Their own rope. Now let's go up again and go over it piece by piece. (*They start upstairs.*) It would have to have been someone who knew just the—

(MRS. PETERS *sits down. The two women sit there not looking at one another, but as if peering into something and at the same time holding back. When they talk now it is in the manner of feeling their way over strange ground, as if afraid of what they are saying, but as if they cannot help saying it.*)

MRS. HALE. She liked the bird. She was going to bury it in that pretty box.

MRS. PETERS (*in a whisper*). When I was a girl—my kitten—there was a boy took a hatchet, and before my eyes—and before I could get there—(*Covers her face an instant.*) If they hadn't held me back I would have—(*catches herself, looks upstairs where steps are heard, falters weakly*)—hurt him.

MRS. HALE (*with a slow look around her*). I wonder how it would seem never to have had any children around. (*Pause.*) No, Wright wouldn't like the bird—a thing that sang. She used to sing. He killed that, too.

MRS. PETERS (*moving uneasily*). We don't know who killed the bird.

MRS. HALE. I knew John Wright.

MRS. PETERS. It was an awful thing was done in this house that night, Mrs. Hale. Killing a man while he slept, slipping a rope around his neck that choked the life out of him.

MRS. HALE. His neck. Choked the life out of him.

(*Her hand goes out and rests on the bird-cage.*)

MRS. PETERS (*with rising voice*). We don't know who killed him. We don't *know*.

MRS. HALE (*her own feeling not interrupted*). If there'd been years and years of nothing, then a bird to sing to you, it would be awful—still, after the bird was still.

MRS. PETERS (*something within her speaking*). I know what stillness is. When we homesteaded in Dakota, and my first baby died—after he was two years old, and me with no other then—

MRS. HALE (*moving*). How soon do you suppose they'll be through, looking for the evidence?

MRS. PETERS. I know what stillness is. (*Pulling herself back.*) The law has got to punish crime, Mrs. Hale.

MRS. HALE (*not as if answering that*). I wish you'd seen Minnie Foster when she wore a white dress with blue ribbons and stood up there in the choir and sang. (*A look around the room.*) Oh, I *wish* I'd come over here once in a while! That was a crime! That was a crime! Who's going to punish that?

MRS. PETERS (*looking upstairs*). We mustn't—take on.

MRS. HALE. I might have known she needed help! I know how things can be—for women. I tell you, it's queer, Mrs. Peters. We live close together and we live far apart. We all go through the same things—it's all just a different kind of the same thing. (*Brushes her eyes, noticing the bottle of fruit, reaches out for it.*) If I was you I wouldn't tell her her fruit was gone. Tell her it *ain't.* Tell her it's all right. Take this in to prove it to her. She—she may never know whether it was broke or not.

MRS. PETERS (*Takes the bottle, looks about for something to wrap it in; takes petticoat from the clothes brought from the other room, very nervously begins winding this around the bottle. In a false voice*). My, it's a good thing the men couldn't hear us. Wouldn't they just laugh! Getting all stirred up over a little thing like a—dead canary. As if that could have anything to do with—with—wouldn't they *laugh!*

(*The men are heard coming down stairs.*)

MRS. HALE (*under her breath*). Maybe they would—maybe they wouldn't.

COUNTY ATTORNEY. No, Peters, it's all perfectly clear except a reason for doing it. But you know juries when it comes to women. If there was some definite thing. Something to show—something to make a story about—a thing that would connect up with this strange way of doing it—

(*The women's eyes meet for an instant. Enter* HALE *from outer door.*)

HALE. Well, I've got the team around. Pretty cold out there.

COUNTY ATTORNEY. I'm going to stay here a while by myself. (*To the* SHERIFF.) You can send Frank out for me, can't you? I want to go over everything. I'm not satisfied that we can't do better.

SHERIFF. Do you want to see what Mrs. Peters is going to take in?

(*The* LAWYER *goes to the table, picks up the apron, laughs.*)

COUNTY ATTORNEY. Oh, I guess they're not very dangerous things the ladies have picked out. (*Moves a few things about, disturbing the quilt pieces which cover the box. Steps back.*) No, Mrs. Peters doesn't need supervising. For that matter, a sheriff's wife is married to the law. Ever think of it that way, Mrs. Peters?

MRS. PETERS. Not—just that way.

SHERIFF (*chuckling*). Married to the law. (*Moves toward the other room.*) I just want you to come in here a minute, George. We ought to take a look at these windows.

COUNTY ATTORNEY. (*scoffingly*)[7] Oh, windows!

SHERIFF. We'll be right out, Mr. Hale.

(HALE *goes outside. The* SHERIFF *follows the* COUNTY ATTORNEY *into the other room. Then* MRS. HALE *rises, hands tight together, looking intensely at* MRS. PETERS, *whose eyes make a slow turn, finally meeting* MRS. HALE'S. *A moment* MRS. HALE *holds her, then her own eyes point the way to where the box is concealed. Suddenly* MRS. PETERS *throws back quilt pieces and tries to put the box in the bag she is wearing. It is too big. She opens box, starts to take bird out, cannot touch it, goes to pieces, stands there helpless. Sound of a knob turning in the other room.* MRS. HALE *snatches the box and puts it in the pocket of her big coat. Enter* COUNTY ATTORNEY *and* SHERIFF.)

COUNTY ATTORNEY (*facetiously*). Well, Henry, at least we found out that she was not going to quilt it. She was going to—what is it you call it, ladies?

MRS. HALE (*her hand against her pocket*). We call it—knot it, Mr. Henderson.

(*CURTAIN*)

---

7. **scoffingly** (skôf′ing lē), *adv.* mockingly; in a manner that makes fun to show one does not believe something.

After Reading

Making Connections

Shaping Your Response

1. As a class, take a vote: is Mrs. Wright guilty of murder? Discuss your theories.

Analyzing the Play

2. Why do you think this play is called *Trifles?*

3. How would you describe the sheriff's and the county attorney's attitude toward the two women?

4. Explain the significance of the canary.

5. How does Mrs. Peters's **character** change over the course of the play?

6. 🐾 What cultural norms and expectations do you think helped stifle Mrs. Wright's **individuality?**

Extending the Ideas

7. Assume for the moment that Mrs. Wright is guilty of murdering her husband. Would you call it a justifiable homicide? Why or why not?

8. Were Mrs. Peters and Mrs. Hale doing the right thing when they concealed the evidence they found? Explain your answer.

Literary Focus: Plot

On a **plot** structure map like the one on page 454, map the plot of *Trifles.* At each point on the map, write a sentence that explains the action in the play.

Vocabulary Study

Study the relationship of each of the following pairs of words; then choose another pair that has the same relationship.

wiry
stiffly
close
abashed
scoffingly

1. exercise : *wiry* : :
   a. meek : mild   b. education : wise
   c. anger : sadness   d. ugly : beauty

2. comfortably : *stiffly* : :
   a. funny : humorous   b. talkative : quiet
   c. neglect : failure   d. industrious : worker

3. *close* : private : :
   a. rich : wealthy   b. lake : river
   c. cold : hot   d. notorious : obscure

4. *abashed* : proud : :
   a. instruct : train   b. joke : laughter
   c. impregnable : fortress
   d. passionate : indifferent

5. *scoffingly* : mockingly : :
   a. impediment : hindrance
   b. sunlight : glare   c. hopefully : despairingly
   d. vibrant : colors

Expressing Your Ideas

Writing Choices

Writer's Notebook Update Review the paragraph that you wrote in your notebook before reading *Trifles.* What were some of your criteria for determining guilt or innocence? Write a paragraph that argues for or against Mrs. Wright's guilt. Be sure to support your opinion with evidence from the text.

Two Views of Farm Life In the late 1800s, folk art—with its emphasis on symmetry, pattern, and color—became extremely popular in America. *Mahantango Valley Farm* is considered a masterpiece of American folk art. Look carefully at this painting. Then write an **essay** that compares and contrasts this rendering of farm life to Glaspell's depiction of the Wrights's farm in *Trifles.*

Other Options

Performing *Trifles* Prepare a class production of *Trifles.* Begin by reviewing the production notes you kept while reading the play. Next, work with the rest of the class to assign roles. While the actors are learning their lines, others in the class should be working on set design, costume design, music, and publicity. When you've finished, give a performance of *Trifles* for another class, parents, or the whole school.

Going to Court Mrs. Wright is accused of murdering her husband. Working with your class, put on a **mock trial,** including a judge, a twelve-person jury, the accused, witnesses, and defense and prosecution teams.

Before Reading

The Revolt of "Mother"

by Mary E. Wilkins Freeman

Mary E. Wilkins Freeman
1852–1930

Mary Eleanor Wilkins Freeman grew up in a household dominated by women: her mother, grandmother, two aunts, and two cousins raised Mary and her sister Nan to honor the virtues of gentility, work, thrift, and above all else, self-sufficiency. It's not surprising, then, that Wilkins Freeman wrote mostly about women and the problems they faced in a society dominated by men. A recurring theme in her writing involves women looking inward—rather than to their husbands or fathers—to find the strength to overcome adversity. "The Revolt of 'Mother,'" is from Freeman's most famous collection of short stories, *A New England Nun, and Other Stories.*

Building Background

The Farmer's Wife Life on a farm was difficult in the 1800s—especially for women. From sunup to long past sundown, farm women toiled unceasingly in their homes and in the fields. They were responsible for raising and, at times, educating their children, as well as cooking, cleaning, milking, canning, and baking. At the time, of course, there was no electricity or indoor plumbing. So, even a simple load of laundry involved fetching pail after pail of water, heating the water on the cook stove, and then scrubbing one article of clothing at a time on a washboard. During harvest time, women were expected to join their husbands in the field, and keep up with the cooking, housework, and child care. Because their lives and the lives of their children depended on a productive farm with cash crops, farm wives worked endlessly, rarely taking the time to read, play music, or even socialize. In "The Revolt of 'Mother,'" Wilkins Freeman reveals what happens when a farm wife dares to take steps to make her life a little more comfortable.

Literary Focus

Foreshadowing At several points in "The Revolt of 'Mother,'" Wilkins Freeman uses foreshadowing—hints to the reader of what is to come. As you read the story, jot down examples of foreshadowing. You may want to consider these questions:

- What event or events is Wilkins Freeman foreshadowing?
- What is the effect of the foreshadowing?

Writer's Notebook

A Conflict of Your Own How do you go about resolving conflict? Are you the type of person to make your feelings known, or do you keep quiet in hopes that the problem will go away on its own? In your notebook, write about a disagreement you had with another person or group of people. With whom were you arguing? Why? How did you resolve the conflict?

The Revolt of "Mother"

MARY E. WILKINS FREEMAN

"Father!"

"What is it?"

"What are them men diggin' over there in the field for?"

There was a sudden dropping and enlarging of the lower part of the old man's face, as if some heavy weight had settled therein; he shut his mouth tight, and went on harnessing the great bay mare. He hustled the collar on to her neck with a jerk.

"Father!"

The old man slapped the saddle upon the mare's back.

"Look here, father, I want to know what them men are diggin' over in the field for, an' I'm goin' to know."

"I wish you'd go into the house, mother, an' 'tend to your own affairs," the old man said then. He ran his words together, and his speech was almost as inarticulate as a growl.

> "I wish you'd go into the house, mother, an' 'tend to your own affairs . . ."

But the woman understood; it was her most native tongue. "I ain't goin' into the house till you tell me what them men are doin' over there in the field," said she.

Then she stood waiting. She was a small woman, short and straight-waisted like a child in her brown cotton gown. Her forehead was mild and benevolent[1] between the smooth curves of gray hair; there were meek downward lines about her nose and mouth; but her eyes, fixed upon the old man, looked as if the meekness had been the result of her own will, never of the will of another.

They were in the barn, standing before the wide open doors. The spring air, full of the smell of growing grass and unseen blossoms, came in their faces. The deep yard in front was littered with farm wagons and piles of wood; on the edges, close to the fence and the house, the grass was a vivid green, and there were some dandelions.

The old man glanced doggedly at his wife as he tightened the last buckles on the harness. She looked as immovable to him as one of the

---

1. benevolent (bə nev′ə lənt), *adj.* kindly; charitable.

▲ After you've read the story, decide what the woman in George Schreiber's 1939 painting *From Arkansas* has in common with Sarah in "The Revolt of 'Mother.'"

rocks in his pasture-land, bound to the earth with generations of blackberry vines. He slapped the reins over the horse, and started forth from the barn.

"*Father!*" said she.

The old man pulled up. "What is it?"

"I want to know what them men are diggin' over there in that field for."

"They're diggin' a cellar, I s'pose, if you've got to know."

"A cellar for what?"

"A barn."

"A barn? You ain't goin' to build a barn over there where we was goin' to have a house, father?"

The old man said not another word. He hurried the horse into the farm wagon, and clattered out of the yard, jouncing as sturdily on his seat as a boy.

SUMMARIZE: From the description and dialogue, what can you infer about the personalities of the husband and wife?

The woman stood a moment looking after him, then she went out of the barn across a corner of the yard to the house. The house, standing at right angles with the great barn and a long reach of sheds and out-buildings, was infinitesimal[2] compared with them. It was scarcely as commodious[3] for people as the little boxes under the barn eaves were for doves.

A pretty girl's face, pink and delicate as a flower, was looking out of one of the house windows. She was watching three men who were digging over in the field which bounded the yard near the road line. She turned quietly when the woman entered.

"What are they digging for, mother?" said she. "Did he tell you?"

"They're diggin' for—a cellar for a new barn."

"Oh, mother, he ain't going to build another barn?"

"That's what he says."

A boy stood before the kitchen glass combing his hair. He combed slowly and painstakingly, arranging his brown hair in a smooth hillock over his forehead. He did not seem to pay any attention to the conversation.

"Sammy, did you know father was going to build a new barn?" asked the girl.

The boy combed assiduously.[4]

"Sammy!"

He turned, and showed a face like his father's under his smooth crest of hair. "Yes, I s'pose I did," he said, reluctantly.

"How long have you known it?" asked his mother.

" 'Bout three months, I guess."

"Why didn't you tell of it?"

"Didn't think 'twould do no good."

"I don't see what father wants another barn for," said the girl, in her sweet, slow voice. She turned again to the window, and stared out at the digging men in the field. Her tender, sweet face was full of a gentle distress. Her forehead was as bald and innocent as a baby's, with the light hair strained back from it in a row of curl-papers. She was quite large, but her soft curves did not look as if they covered muscles.

Her mother looked sternly at the boy. "Is he goin' to buy more cows?" said she.

The boy did not reply; he was tying his shoes.

"Sammy, I want you to tell me if he's goin' to buy more cows."

"I s'pose he is."

"How many?"

"Four, I guess."

His mother said nothing more. She went into the pantry, and there was a clatter of dishes. The boy got his cap from a nail behind the door, took an old arithmetic from the shelf, and started for school. He was lightly built, but clumsy. He went out of the yard with a curious

2. infinitesimal (in′fi nə tes′ə məl), *adj.* so small as to be almost nothing.
3. commodious (kə mō′dē əs), *adj.* spacious; roomy.
4. assiduously (ə sij′ŭ əs lē), *adv.* attentively; diligently.

spring in the hips, that made his loose home-made jacket tilt up in the rear.

The girl went to the sink, and began to wash the dishes that were piled up there. Her mother came promptly out of the pantry, and shoved her aside. "You wipe 'em," said she; "I'll wash. There's a good many this mornin'."

The mother plunged her hands vigorously into the water, the girl wiped the plates slowly and dreamily. "Mother," said she, "don't you think it's too bad father's going to build that new barn, much as we need a decent house to live in?"

Her mother scrubbed a dish fiercely. "You ain't found out yet we're women-folks, Nanny Penn," said she. "You ain't seen enough of men-folks yet to. One of these days you'll find it out, an' then you'll know that we know only what men-folks think we do, so far as any use of it goes, an' how we'd ought to reckon men-folks in with Providence, an' not complain of what they do any more than we do of the weather."

"I don't care; I don't believe George is anything like that, anyhow," said Nanny. Her delicate face flushed pink, her lips pouted softly, as if she were going to cry.

"You wait an' see. I guess George Eastman ain't no better than other men. You hadn't ought to judge father, though. He can't help it, 'cause he don't look at things jest the way we do. An' we've been pretty comfortable here, after all. The roof don't leak—ain't never but once—that's one thing. Father's kept it shingled right up."

"I do wish we had a parlor."

"I guess it won't hurt George Eastman any to come to see you in a nice clean kitchen. I guess a good many girls don't have as good a place as this. Nobody's ever heard me complain."

"I ain't complained either, mother."

"Well, I don't think you'd better, a good father an' a good home as you've got. S'pose your father made you go out an' work for your livin'? Lots of girls have to that ain't no stronger an' better able to than you be."

Sarah Penn washed the frying-pan with a conclusive[5] air. She scrubbed the outside of it as faithfully as the inside. She was a masterly keeper of her box of a house. Her one living-room never seemed to have in it any of the dust which the friction of life with inanimate matter produces. She swept, and there seemed to be no dirt to go before the broom; she cleaned, and one could see no difference. She was like an artist so perfect that he has apparently no art. Today she got out a mixing bowl and a board, and rolled some pies, and there was no more flour upon her than upon her daughter who was doing finer work. Nanny was to be married in the fall, and she was sewing on some white cambric and embroidery. She sewed industriously while her mother cooked, her soft milk-white hands and wrists showed whiter than her delicate work.

"We must have the stove moved out in the shed before long," said Mrs. Penn. "Talk about not havin' things, it's been a real blessin' to be able to put a stove up in that shed in hot weather. Father did one good thing when he fixed that stove-pipe out there."

Sarah Penn's face as she rolled her pies had that expression of meek vigor which might have characterized one of the New Testament saints. She was making mince-pies. Her husband, Adoniram Penn, liked them better than any other kind. She baked twice a week. Adoniram often liked a piece of pie between meals. She hurried this morning. It had been later than usual when she began, and she wanted to have a pie baked for dinner. However deep a resentment she might be forced to hold against her husband, she would never fail in sedulous[6] attention to his wants.

Nobility of character manifests[7] itself at loop-holes when it is not provided with large doors. Sarah Penn's showed itself today in flaky dishes of pastry. So she made the pies faithfully, while across the table she could see, when she glanced up from her work, the sight that rankled[8] in her

5. conclusive (kən klü′siv), *adj.* decisive; convincing.
6. sedulous (sej′ə ləs), *adj.* diligent; painstaking.
7. **manifest** (man′ə fest), *v.* show plainly; reveal; display.
8. **rankle** (rang′kəl), *v.* cause irritation or resentment.

patient and steadfast[9] soul—the digging of the cellar of the new barn in the place where Adoniram forty years ago had promised her their new house should stand.

The pies were done for dinner. Adoniram and Sammy were home a few minutes after twelve o'clock. The dinner was eaten with serious haste. There was never much conversation at the table in the Penn family. Adoniram asked a blessing, and they ate promptly, then rose up and went about their work.

Sammy went back to school, taking soft sly lopes out of the yard like a rabbit. He wanted a game of marbles before school, and feared his father would give him some chores to do. Adoniram hastened to the door and called after him, but he was out of sight.

"I don't see what you let him go for, mother," said he. "I wanted him to help me unload that wood."

Adoniram went to work out in the yard unloading wood from the wagon. Sarah put away the dinner dishes, while Nanny took down her curl-papers and changed her dress. She was going down to the store to buy some more embroidery and thread.

When Nanny was gone, Mrs. Penn went to the door. "Father!" she called.

"Well, what is it!"

"I want to see you jest a minute, father."

"I can't leave this wood nohow. I've got to git it unloaded an' go for a load of gravel afore two o'clock. Sammy had ought to helped me. You hadn't ought to let him go to school so early."

"I want to see you jest a minute."

"I tell ye I can't, nohow, mother."

"Father, you come here." Sarah Penn stood in the door like a queen; she held her head as if it bore a crown; there was the patience which makes authority royal in her voice. Adoniram went.

Mrs. Penn led the way into the kitchen, and pointed to a chair. "Sit down, father," said she; "I've got somethin' I want to say to you."

He sat down heavily; his face was quite stolid, but he looked at her with restive eyes. "Well, what is it, mother?"

"I want to know what you're buildin' that new barn for, father?"

"I ain't got nothin' to say about it."

"It can't be you think you need another barn?"

"I tell ye I ain't got nothin' to say about it, mother; an' I ain't goin' to say nothing'."

"Be you goin' to buy more cows?"

Adoniram did not reply; he shut his mouth tight.

"I know you be, as well as I want to. Now, father, look here"—Sarah Penn had not sat down; she stood before her husband in the humble fashion of a Scripture woman—"I'm goin' to talk real plain to you; I never have sence I married you, but I'm goin' to now. I ain't never complained, an' I ain't goin' to complain now, but I'm goin' to talk plain. You see this room here, father; you look at it well. You see there ain't no carpet on the floor, an' you see the paper is all dirty, an' droppin' off the walls. We ain't had no new paper on it for ten year, an' then I put it on myself, an' it didn't cost but ninepence a roll. You see this room, father; it's all the one I've had to work in an' eat in an' sit in sence we was married. There ain't another woman in the whole town whose husband ain't got half the means you have but what's got better. It's all the room Nanny's got to have her company in; an' there ain't one of her mates but what's got better, an' their fathers not so able as hers is. It's all the room she'll have to be married in. What would you have thought, father, if we had had our weddin' in a room no better than this? I was married in my mother's parlor, with a carpet on the floor, an' stuffed furniture, an' a mahogany card-table. An' this is all the room my daughter will have to be married in. Look here, father!"

Sarah Penn went across the room as though it were a tragic stage. She flung open a door and disclosed a tiny bedroom, only large enough for a bed and bureau, with a path between. "There,

---

9. **steadfast** (sted′fast′), *adj.* loyal and unwavering.

father," said she—"there's all the room I've had to sleep in forty year. All my children were born there—the two that died, an' the two that's livin'. I was sick with a fever there."

"I'm going to talk real plain to you; I never have sence I married you, but I'm goin' to now."

She stepped to another door and opened it. It led into the small, ill-lighted pantry. "Here," said she, "is all the buttery I've got—every place I've got for my dishes, to set away my victuals in, an' to keep my milk-pans in. Father, I've been takin' care of the milk of six cows in this place, an' now you're goin' to build a new barn, an' keep more cows, an' give me more to do in it."

She threw open another door. A narrow crooked flight of stairs wound upward from it. "There, father," said she, "I want you to look at the stairs that go up to them two unfinished chambers that are all the places our son an' daughter have had to sleep in all their lives. There ain't a prettier girl in town nor a more ladylike one than Nanny, an' that's the place she has to sleep in. It ain't so good as your horse's stall; it ain't so warm an' tight."

Sarah Penn went back and stood before her husband. "Now, father," said she, "I want to know if you think you're doin' right an' accordin' to what you profess. Here, when we was married, forty year ago, you promised me faithful that we should have a new house built in that lot over in the field before the year was out. You said you had money enough, an' you wouldn't ask me to live in no such place as this. It is forty year now, an' you've been makin' more money, an' I've been savin' of it for you ever since, an' you ain't built no house yet. You've built sheds an' cow-houses an' one new barn, an' now you're goin' to build another. Father, I want to know if you think it's right. You're lodgin' your dumb beasts better than you are your own flesh an' blood. I want to know if you think it's right."

"I ain't got nothin' to say."

"You can't say nothin' without ownin' it ain't right, father. An' there's another thing—I ain't complained; I've got along forty year, an' I s'pose I should forty more, if it wa'n't for that—if we don't have another house. Nanny she can't live with us after she's married. She'll have to go somewheres else to live away from us, an' it don't seem as if I could have it so, noways, father. She wa'n't ever strong. She's got considerable color, but there wa'n't ever any backbone to her. I've always took the heft of everything off her, an' she ain't fit to keep house an' do everything herself. She'll be all worn out inside of a year. Think of her doin' all the washin' an' ironin' an' bakin' with them soft white hands an' arms, an' sweepin'! I can't have it so, noways, father."

Mrs. Penn's face was burning; her mild eyes gleamed. She had pleaded her little cause like a Webster;[10] she had ranged from severity to pathos; but her opponent employed that obstinate silence which makes eloquence futile with mocking echoes. Adoniram arose clumsily.

"Father, ain't you got nothin' to say?" said Mrs. Penn.

"I've got to go off after that load of gravel. I can't stan' here talkin' all day."

"Father, won't you think it over, an' have a house built there instead of a barn?"

"I ain't got nothin' to say."

EVALUATE: Why do you suppose Adoniram refuses to respond to Sarah's questions?

Adoniram shuffled out. Mrs. Penn went into her bedroom. When she came out, her eyes were red. She had a roll of unbleached cotton cloth. She spread it out on the kitchen table,

10. **Webster,** Daniel Webster, Congressman and famous orator of the 1800s.

◄ Eric Sloan's *Sickle and Bucket* (1964) shows just a part of what is obviously a larger structure. The few details and objects tell a lot about what's not shown. What can you infer about the larger structure?

then; I can put it on. I guess you won't have no call to be ashamed of your belongin's."

"We might have the wedding in the new barn," said Nanny, with gentle pettishness.[12] "Why, mother, what makes you look so?"

Mrs. Penn had started, and was staring at her with a curious expression. She turned again to her work, and spread out a pattern carefully on the cloth.

"Nothin'," said she.

Presently Adoniram clattered out of the yard in his two-wheeled dump cart, standing as proudly upright as a Roman charioteer. Mrs. Penn opened the door and stood there a minute looking out; the halloos of the men sounded louder.

It seemed to her all through the spring months that she heard nothing but the halloos and the noises of saws and hammers. The new barn grew fast. It was a fine edifice for this little village. Men came on pleasant Sundays, in their meeting suits and clean shirt bosoms, and stood around it admiringly. Mrs. Penn did not speak of it, and Adoniram did not mention it to her,

and began cutting out some shirts for her husband. The men over in the field had a team to help them this afternoon; she could hear their halloos. She had a scanty pattern for the shirts; she had to plan and piece the sleeves.

Nanny came home with her embroidery, and sat down with her needlework. She had taken down her curl-papers, and there was a soft roll of fair hair like an auerole[11] over her forehead; her face was as delicately fine and clear as porcelain. Suddenly she looked up, and the tender red flamed all over her face and neck. "Mother," said she.

"What say?"

"I've been thinking—I don't see how we're goin' to have any—wedding in this room. I'd be ashamed to have his folks come if we didn't have anybody else."

"Mebbe we can have some new paper before

---

11. **aureole** (ôr′ē ōl), *n.* ring of light surrounding a figure or an object.
12. pettishness (pet′ish nəs), *n.* peevishness; crossness.

although sometimes, upon a return from inspecting it, he bore himself with injured dignity.

"It's a strange thing how your mother feels about the new barn," he said, confidentially, to Sammy one day.

Sammy only grunted after an odd fashion for a boy; he had learned it from his father.

The barn was all completed ready for use by the third week in July. Adoniram had planned to move his stock in on Wednesday; on Tuesday he received a letter which changed his plans. He came in with it early in the morning. "Sammy's been to the post-office," said he, "an' I've got a letter from Hiram." Hiram was Mrs. Penn's brother, who lived in Vermont.

"Well," said Mrs. Penn, "what does he say about the folks?"

"I guess they're all right. He says he thinks if I come up country right off there's a chance to buy jest the kind of a horse I want." He stared reflectively out of the window at the new barn.

Mrs. Penn was making pies. She went on clapping the rolling-pin into the crust, although she was very pale, and her heart beat loudly.

"I dun' know but what I'd better go," said Adoniram. "I hate to go off jest now, right in the midst of hayin', but the ten-acre lot's cut, an' I guess Rufus an' the others can git along without me three or four days. I can't get a horse round here to suit me, nohow, an' I've got to have another for all that wood-haulin' in the fall. I told Hiram to watch out, an' if he got wind of a good horse to let me know. I guess I'd better go."

"I'll get out your clean shirt an' collar," said Mrs. Penn calmly.

She laid out Adoniram's Sunday suit and his clean clothes on the bed in the little bedroom. She got his shaving-water and razor ready. At last she buttoned on his collar and fastened his black cravat.

Adoniram never wore his collar and cravat except on extra occasions. He held his head high, with a rasped dignity. When he was all ready, with his coat and hat brushed, and a lunch of pie and cheese in a paper bag, he hesitated on the threshold of the door. He looked at his wife, and his manner was defiantly apologetic. "*If* them cows come today, Sammy can drive 'em into the new barn," said he; "an' when they bring the hay up, they can pitch it in there."

"Well," replied Mrs. Penn.

Adoniram set his shaven face ahead and started. When he had cleared the doorstep, he turned and looked back with a kind of nervous solemnity. "I shall be back by Saturday if nothin' happens," said he.

"Do be careful, father," returned his wife.

She stood in the door with Nanny at her elbow and watched him out of sight. Her eyes had a strange, doubtful expression in them; her peaceful forehead was contracted. She went in, and about her baking again. Nanny sat sewing. Her wedding-day was drawing nearer, and she was getting pale and thin with her steady sewing. Her mother kept glancing at her.

"Have you got that pain in your side this mornin'?" she asked.

"A little."

Mrs. Penn's face, as she worked, changed, her perplexed forehead smoothed, her eyes were steady, her lips firmly set. She formed a maxim for herself, although incoherently with her unlettered thoughts. "Unsolicited opportunities are the guide-posts of the Lord to the new roads of life," she repeated in effect, and she made up her mind to her course of action.

"S'posin' I *had* wrote to Hiram," she muttered once, when she was in the pantry— "s'posin' I had wrote, an' asked him if he knew of any horse? But I didn't, an' father's goin' wa'n't none of my doin'. It looks like a providence." Her voice rang out quite loud at the last.

"What you talkin' about, mother?" called Nanny.

"Nothin'."

Mrs. Penn hurried her baking; at eleven o'clock it was all done. The load of hay from the west field came slowly down the cart track, and drew up at the new barn. Mrs. Penn ran out. "Stop!" she screamed—"stop!"

The men stopped and looked; Sammy upreared from the top of the load, and stared at his mother.

"Stop!" she cried out again. "Don't you put the hay in that barn; put it in the old one."

"Why, he said to put it in here," returned one of the hay-makers, wonderingly. He was a young man, a neighbor's son, whom Adoniram hired by the year to help on the farm.

"Don't you put the hay in the new barn; there's room enough in the old one, ain't there?" said Mrs. Penn.

"Room enough," returned the hired man, in his thick, rustic tones. "Didn't need the new barn, nohow, far as room's concerned. Well, I s'pose he changed his mind." He took hold of the horses' bridles.

Mrs. Penn went back to the house. Soon the kitchen windows were darkened, and a fragrance like warm honey came into the room.

Nanny laid down her work. "I thought father wanted them to put the hay into the new barn?" she said, wonderingly.

"It's all right," replied her mother.

Sammy slid down from the load of hay, and came in to see if dinner was ready.

"I ain't goin' to get a regular dinner today, as long as father's gone," said his mother. "I've let the fire go out. You can have some bread an' milk an' pie. I thought we could get along." She set out some bowls of milk, some bread and a pie on the kitchen table. "You'd better eat your dinner now," said she. "You might jest as well get through with it. I want you to help me afterward."

Nanny and Sammy stared at each other. There was something strange in their mother's manner.

Mrs. Penn did not eat anything herself. She went into the pantry, and they heard her moving dishes while they ate. Presently she came out with a pile of plates. She got the clothes-basket out of the shed, and packed them in it. Nanny and Sammy watched. She brought out cups and saucers, and put them in with the plates.

"What you goin' to do, mother?" inquired Nanny, in a timid voice. A sense of something unusual made her tremble, as if it were a ghost. Sammy rolled his eyes over his pie.

"You'll see what I'm goin' to do," replied Mrs. Penn. "If you're through, Nanny, I want you to go upstairs an' pack up your things; an' I want you, Sammy, to help me take down the bed in the bedroom."

"Oh, mother, what for?" gasped Nanny.

"You'll see."

During the next few hours a feat was performed by this simple, pious New England mother which was equal in its way to Wolfe's storming of the Heights of Abraham.[13] It took no more genius and audacity[14] of bravery for Wolfe to cheer his wondering soldiers up those steep precipices, under the sleeping eyes of the enemy, than for Sarah Penn, at the head of her children, to move all their little household goods into the new barn while her husband was away.

Nanny and Sammy followed their mother's instructions without a murmur; indeed, they were overawed.[15] There is a certain uncanny and superhuman quality about all such purely original undertakings as their mother's was to them. Nanny went back and forth with her light loads, and Sammy tugged with sober energy.

At five o'clock in the afternoon the little house in which the Penns had lived for forty years had emptied itself into the new barn.

Every builder builds somewhat for unknown purposes, and is in a measure a prophet.

The architect of Adoniram Penn's barn, while he designed it for the comfort of four-footed animals, had planned better than he knew for the comfort of humans. Sarah Penn saw at a glance its

---

13. **Wolfe's storming of the Heights of Abraham.** James Wolfe, a British general, scored a decisive victory against the French at Quebec in the Seven Years War (1765–1773). He had his soldiers climb the bluffs which were considered unscalable, taking the enemy by surprise.
14. **audacity** (ô das′ə tē), *n.* reckless daring; boldness.
15. **overawed** (ō′vər ôd′), *adj.* overcome with awe.

possibilities. These great box-stalls, with quilts hung before them, would make better bedrooms than the one she had occupied for forty years, and there was a tight carriage-room. The harness-room, with its chimney and shelves, would make a kitchen of her dreams. The great middle space would make a parlor, by-and-by, fit for a palace. Upstairs there was as much room as down. With partitions and windows, what a house would there be! Sarah looked at the row of stanchions[16] before the allotted space for cows, and reflected that she would have her front entry there.

At six o'clock the stove was up in the harness-room, the kettle was boiling, and the table set for tea. It looked almost as home-like as the abandoned house across the yard had ever done. The young hired man milked, and Sarah directed him calmly to bring the milk to the new barn. He came gaping, dropping little blots of foam from the brimming pails on the grass. Before the next morning he had spread the story of Adoniram Penn's wife moving into the new barn all over the little village. Men assembled in the store and talked it over, women with shawls over their heads scuttled into each other's houses before their work was done. Any deviation from the ordinary course of life in this quiet town was enough to stop all progress in it. Everybody paused to look at the staid, independent figure on the side track. There was a difference of opinion with regard to her. Some held her to be insane; some, of a lawless and rebellious spirit.

Friday the minister went to see her. It was in the forenoon, and she was at the barn door shelling peas for dinner. She looked up and returned his salutation with dignity, then she went on with her work. She did not invite him in. The saintly expression of her face remained fixed, but there was an angry flush over it.

The minister stood awkwardly before her, and talked. She handled the peas as if they were bullets. At last she looked up, and her eyes showed the spirit that her meek front had covered for a lifetime.

"There ain't no use talkin', Mr. Hersey," said she. "I've thought it all over an' over, an' I believe I'm doin' what's right. I've made it the subject of prayer, an' it's betwixt me an' the Lord an' Adoniram. There ain't no call for nobody else to worry about it."

Every builder builds somewhat for unknown purposes, and is in a measure a prophet.

"Well, of course, if you have brought it to the Lord in prayer, and feel satisfied that you are doing right, Mrs. Penn," said the minister, helplessly. His thin gray-bearded face was pathetic. He was a sickly man; his youthful confidence had cooled; he had to scourge himself up to some of his pastoral duties as relentlessly as a Catholic ascetic, and then he was prostrated by the smart.

"I think it's right jest as much as I think it was right for our forefathers to come over from the old country 'cause they didn't have what belonged to 'em," said Mrs. Penn. She arose. The barn threshold might have been Plymouth Rock from her bearing. "I don't doubt you mean well, Mr. Hersey," said she, "but there are things people hadn't ought to interfere with. I've been a member of the church for over forty year. I've got my own mind an' my own feet, an' I'm goin' to think my own thoughts an' go my own ways, an' nobody but the Lord is goin' to dictate to me unless I've a mind to have him. Won't you come in an' set down? How is Mis' Hersey?"

"She is well, I thank you," replied the minister. He added some more perplexed apologetic remarks; then he retreated.

He could expound the intricacies of every character study in the Scriptures, he was competent to grasp the Pilgrim Fathers and all historical innovators, but Sarah Penn was beyond

---

16. **stanchion** (stăn′chən), *n.* verticle post used to secure cattle in a stall.

him. He could deal with primal cases, but parallel ones worsted him. But, after all, although it was aside from his province, he wondered more how Adoniram Penn would deal with his wife than how the Lord would. Everybody shared the wonder. When Adoniram's four new cows arrived, Sarah ordered three to be put in the old barn, the other in the house shed where the cooking-stove had stood. That added to the excitement. It was whispered that all four cows were domiciled in the house.

Towards sunset on Saturday, when Adoniram was expected home, there was a knot of men in the road near the new barn. The hired man had milked, but he still hung around the premises. Sarah Penn had supper all ready. There were brown-bread and baked beans and a custard pie; it was the supper Adoniram loved on a Saturday night. She had a clean calico, and she bore herself imperturbably.[17] Nanny and Sammy kept close at her heels. Their eyes were large, and Nanny was full of nervous tremors. Still there was to them more pleasant excitement than anything else. An inborn confidence in their mother over their father asserted itself.

Sammy looked out of the harness-room window. "There he is," he announced, in an awed whisper. He and Nanny peeped around the casing. Mrs. Penn kept on about her work. The children watched Adoniram leave the new horse standing in the drive while he went to the house door. It was fastened. Then he went around to the shed. That door was seldom locked, even when the family was away. The thought how her father would be confronted by the cow flashed upon Nanny. There was a hysterical sob in her throat. Adoniram emerged from the shed and stood looking about in a dazed fashion. His lips moved; he was saying something, but they could not hear what it was. The hired man was peeping around a corner of the old barn, but nobody saw him.

Adoniram took the new horse by the bridle and led him across the yard to the new barn.

Nanny and Sammy slunk close to their mother. The barn doors rolled back, and there stood Adoniram, with the long mild face of the great Canadian farm horse looking over his shoulder.

Nanny kept behind her mother, but Sammy stepped suddenly forward, and stood in front of her.

Adoniram stared at the group. "What on airth you all down here for?" said he. "What's the matter over to the house?"

"We've come here to live, father," said Sammy. His shrill voice quavered out bravely.

"What"—Adoniram sniffed—"what is it smells like cookin'?" said he. He stepped forward and looked in the open door of the harness-room. Then he turned to his wife. His old bristling face was pale and frightened. "What on airth does this mean, mother?" he gasped.

"You come in here, father," said Sarah. She led the way into the harness-room and shut the door. "Now, father," said she, "you needn't be scared. I ain't crazy. There ain't nothin' to be upset over. But we've come here to live, an' we're goin' to live here. We've got jest as good a right here as new horses an' cows. The house wa'n't fit for us to live in any longer, an' I made up my mind I wa'n't goin' to stay there. I've done my duty by you forty year, an' I'm goin' to do it now; but I'm goin' to live here. You've got to put in some windows and partitions; an' you'll have to buy some furniture."

"Why, mother!" the old man gasped.

"You'd better take your coat off an' get washed—there's the wash-basin—an' then we'll have supper."

"Why, mother!"

Sammy went past the window, leading the new horse to the old barn. The old man saw him, and shook his head speechlessly. He tried to take off his coat, but his arms seemed to lack the power. His wife helped him. She poured some water into the tin basin, and put in a piece of soap. She got the comb and brush, and smoothed his thin gray

_____

17. **imperturbably** (im′pər tėr′bə bəl ē), _adv._ calmly.

How would you describe John Steuart Curry's depiction of farm life in *Wisconsin Landscape* (1938–1939). Is it idyllic? cozy? lonesome? Explain your interpretation.

hair after he had washed. Then she put the beans, hot bread, and tea on the table. Sammy came in, and the family drew up. Adoniram sat looking dazedly at his plate, and they waited.

"Ain't you goin' to ask a blessin', father?" said Sarah.

And the old man bent his head and mumbled.

All through the meal he stopped eating at intervals, and stared furtively[18] at his wife; but he ate well. The home food tasted good to him, and his old frame was too sturdily healthy to be affected by his mind. But after supper he went out, and sat down on the step of the smaller door at the right of the barn, through which he had meant his Jerseys to pass in stately file, but which Sarah designed for her front house door, and he leaned his head on his hands.

After the supper dishes were cleared away and the milk-pans washed, Sarah went out to him. The twilight was deepening. There was a clear green glow in the sky. Before them stretched the smooth

level of field; in the distance was a cluster of hay-stacks like the huts of a village; the air was very cool and calm and sweet. The landscape might have been an ideal one of peace.

Sarah bent over and touched her husband on one of his thin, sinewy shoulders. "Father!"

The old man's shoulders heaved; he was weeping.

"Why, don't do so, father," said Sarah.

"I'll—put up the—partitions, an'—everything you—want, mother."

Sarah put her apron up to her face; she was overcome by her own triumph.

Adoniram was like a fortress whose walls had no active resistance, and went down the instant the right besieging tools were used. "Why, mother," he said, hoarsely, "I hadn't no idee you was so set on't as all this comes to."

---

18. **furtively** (fèr′tiv lē), *adv.* done quickly and stealthily to avoid being noticed; secretly.

After Reading

Making Connections

Shaping Your
Response

1. As you read "The Revolt of 'Mother,'" did you find yourself applauding Sarah's actions or did you feel disapproving? Why?

Analyzing the
Story

2. Sarah had a lot of resentments about the new barn that she was at first willing to ignore. What do you think finally convinced her to take action?

3. Why do you suppose Adoniram agrees in the end to make the barn into a house?

4. Wilkins Freeman lamented that her characters in this story weren't realistic enough. Do you agree or disagree? Explain your answer.

5. ☻ For years Sarah never told her husband what she thought. Why do you suppose she was so reluctant to express needs and desires as an **individual?**

Extending the
Ideas

6. As a modern reader, if you could speak with Sarah and Adoniram, what would you say to them? Why?

7. You are writing a continuation of this story. Will things be different now between Sarah and Adoniram? Why or why not?

Literary Focus: Foreshadowing

When Nanny joked that she might have her wedding in the new barn Sarah "started, and was staring at her [Nanny] with a curious expression." Here Wilkins Freeman **foreshadows** Sarah's revolt by allowing the reader to see that an idea is forming in her mind. Choose another example of foreshadowing to study. Write a paragraph that explains the effect of the foreshadowing on the narrative. As you write, consider these questions:

- How does the example of foreshadowing set the stage for future events?

- Foreshadowing often builds **suspense** in stories. Does it have this effect in "The Revolt of 'Mother'"?

- How does the foreshadowing affect the **mood** of the story?

Vocabulary Study

assiduously
benevolent
commodious
conclusive
furtively
imperturbably
infinitesimal
pettishness
sedulous
steadfast

Choose the word from the list that best completes each sentence.

1. A ____ person is most likely to be forgiving.

2. If a problem is ____, it could be called insignificant.

3. The ____ new barn was much larger than the old house.

4. If your boss says you are working ____, she is complimenting you.

5. "Sarah Penn washed the frying pan with a ____ air" because she had made a decision.

6. A ____ person is most likely to be hard-working.

7. A person who is ____ is definitely not unstable.

8. Though Sarah Penn was upset, she never resorted to ____.

9. If he responds to the accusation ____, his response is calm.

10. A thief works ____ because he or she is afraid of being caught.

Expressing Your Ideas

Writing Choices

Writer's Notebook Update Before reading "The Revolt of 'Mother,'" you wrote about a disagreement you once had. Are there any similarities between how you resolved your argument and how Mother and Father resolved theirs? In your notebook, compare your methods of resolving a conflict to their methods.

Front Page News Sarah Penn's move from house to barn caused quite a stir in the community. Imagine you're a reporter assigned to cover the story for the local paper. Write a front-page **news story** that describes for your readers the Penns' move. Begin by "interviewing" Sarah, Nanny, Sammy, and Adoniram. Build your story around quotes from each character. You may also want to include in your story "reactions" from members of the community: Hiram, for example, or the minister, or one of the women in the town.

Spineless or Not? Twenty-some years after she wrote "The Revolt of 'Mother,'" Wilkins Freeman said in disgust, "The backbone of the best fiction is essential truth, and 'The Revolt of "Mother"' is perfectly spineless." Would you agree? Write a **letter** to Wilkins Freeman that responds to her comment that the story is "spineless."

Other Options

From Barn to Home Review the description of the new barn in "The Revolt of 'Mother.'" Imagine you are an architect assigned to make the **blueprints** for the work that needs to be done. How will you turn this barn into a home?

Does Art Imitate Life? Think back over the three selections you've just read: "The Story of an Hour," *Trifles,* and "The Revolt of 'Mother.'" What do the three main characters—Louise, Mrs. Wright, and Sarah Penn—have in common? In small groups, brainstorm a **list** of similarities between the three women. When you've finished, look carefully at your list. Based on these three stories, what generalizations can you make about nineteenth-century American women? Do you think that women of the time felt the same quiet desperation that Louise, Mrs. Wright, and Sarah Penn all seem to feel? Why or why not? If you like, broaden your discussion to include other fictional characters of the time—Aunt Georgiana from "A Wagner Matinée," for example, or Jo from *Little Women* or Lily from Edith Wharton's *House of Mirth.* Present your group's conclusions to the rest of the class.

Before Reading

from Crusade for Justice

by Ida B. Wells-Barnett

Ida B. Wells-Barnett
1862–1930

A courageous and determined woman, Ida B. Wells spent her life fighting for justice. Born in Mississippi, Wells witnessed at first-hand prejudice and discrimination against African Americans. In 1878, Wells's parents and youngest brother died during a yellow fever epidemic. Although she was only fourteen, Wells took on the responsibility of raising her six siblings. In 1892, a single event dramatically changed her life. Three Memphis men, all friends of hers, were lynched. These three men were accused of a crime, kidnapped by towns-people, and shot to death. Outraged by the violence, Wells began a national campaign against the practice of lynching.

Building Background

About Lynching Lynching means the killing, most often by hanging, of a person by a mob in defiance of law and order. During the last part of the 1800s, lynchings of African Americans had become almost commonplace. In 1892 alone, 230 African Americans were lynched. Sickened by the violence, Ida B. Wells began her antilynching campaign. She traveled the world telling her audiences about the brutality of lynching and gathering support for antilynching legislation. Wells's campaign and pressure from the public resulted in many states adopting laws against lynching, though the laws were not consistently enforced. In the selection you're about to read, Wells discusses the 1909 lynching of an African American man accused of murder.

Literary Focus

Tone is the author's relationship to his or her material, to the audience, or to both. As you read *Crusade for Justice,* try to get a sense of Wells's tone. In your notebook, jot down brief answers to these questions:

1. Would you say Wells's tone in this excerpt is formal or informal?
2. Does she take her subject matter seriously? How do you know?
3. What is her attitude toward the people responsible for James's lynching?
4. How does the African American community respond to James's lynching? Is Wells satisfied with this response? How do you know?

Writer's Notebook

To Be a Hero What's your definition of a hero? What qualities would you expect to see in a heroic person? In your notebook, make a list of what you believe are the characteristics of a hero.

CRUSADE FOR JUSTICE

Ida B. Wells-Barnett

Directly after the Springfield riot,[1] at the next session of the legislature, a law was enacted[2] which provided that any sheriff who permitted a prisoner to be taken from him and lynched should be removed from office. This bill was offered by Edward D. Green, who had been sent to Springfield to represent our race. Illinois had had not only a number of lynchings, but also a three days' riot at Springfield.

In due course of time the daily press announced that a lynching had taken place in Cairo, Illinois. The body of a white woman had been found in an alley in the residential district and, following the usual custom, the police immediately looked for a Negro. Finding a shiftless, penniless colored man known as "Frog" James, who seemed unable to give a good account of himself, according to police, this man was locked up in the police station and according to the newspapers a crowd began to gather around the station and the sheriff was sent for.

Mr. Frank Davis, the sheriff, after a brief conversation with the prisoner, took him to the railroad station, got on the train, and took him up into the woods accompanied by a single deputy. They remained there overnight. Next morning, when a mob had grown to great proportions, they too went up into the country and had no trouble in locating the sheriff and his prisoner. He was placed on a train and brought back to town, accompanied by the sheriff. The newspapers announced that as the train came to a standstill, some of the mob put a rope around "Frog's" neck and dragged him out of the train and to the most prominent[3] corner of the town, where the rope was thrown over an

---

1. **Springfield riot**. The Springfield riots were three days of racial violence against African Americans in Springfield, Illinois, during August of 1908. Shortly after the riots, Wells and Mary Church Terrell organized a conference in New York City to discuss the plight of African Americans everywhere. The conference led to the formation of the NAACP.
2. enact (en akt′), *v.* pass (a bill), giving it validity as law.
3. prominent (prom′ə nənt), *adj.* well-known or conspicuous.

electric light arch and the body hauled up above the heads of the crowd. . . .

When the news of this horrible thing appeared in the papers, immediately a meeting was called and a telegram sent to Governor Deneen demanding that the sheriff of Alexander County be dispossessed.[4] The newspapers had already quoted the governor as saying that he did not think it mandatory[5] on him to displace the sheriff. But when our telegram reached him calling attention to the law, he immediately ousted him by telegram.

This same law provided that after the expiration of a short time, the sheriff would have the right to appear before the governor and show cause why he ought to be reinstated. We had a telegram from Governor Deneen informing us that on the following Wednesday the sheriff would appear before him demanding reinstatement. Mr. Barnett[6] spent some time urging representative men of our race to appear before the governor and fight the sheriff's reinstatement. . . .

This information was given us at the dinner table by Mr. Barnett, and he wound up his recital of his fruitless efforts that Saturday afternoon to get someone to appear by saying, "And so it would seem that you will have to go to Cairo and get the facts with which to confront the sheriff next Wednesday morning. And your train leaves at eight o'clock." I objected very strongly because I had already been accused by some of our men of jumping in ahead of them and doing work without giving them a chance.

It was not very convenient for me to be leaving home at that time, and for once I was quite willing to let them attend to the job. Mr. Barnett replied that I knew it was important that somebody gather the evidence as well as he did, but if I was not willing to go, there was nothing more to be said. He picked up the evening paper and I picked up my baby and took her upstairs to bed. As usual I not only sang her to sleep but put myself to sleep lying there beside her.

I was awakened by my oldest child, who said, "Mother, Pa says it is time to go." "Go where?" I said. He said, "To take the train to Cairo." I said, "I told your father downstairs that I was not going. I don't see why I should have to go and do the work that the others refuse." My boy was only ten years old. He and the other children had been present at the dinner table when their father told the story. He stood by the bedside a little while and then said, "Mother if you don't go nobody else will."

I looked at my child standing there by the bed reminding me of my duty, and I thought of that passage of Scripture which tells of the wisdom from the mouths of babes and sucklings. I thought if my child wanted me to go that I ought not to fall by the wayside, and I said, "Tell daddy it is too late to catch the train now, that I'll go in the morning. It is better for me to arrive in Cairo after nightfall anyway."

CLARIFY: Why does Wells finally decide to go to Cairo?

Next morning all four of my children accompanied my husband and me to the station and saw me start on the journey. They were intensely interested and for the first time were willing to see me leave home.

I reached Cairo after nightfall, and was driven to the home of the leading A.M.E.[7] minister, just before he went into church for his evening service. I told him why I was there and asked if he could give me any help in getting the sentiment of the colored people and investigating facts. He said that they all believed that "Frog" James had committed that murder. I asked him if he

---

4. dispossess (dis′pə zes′), v. oust; deprive.
5. mandatory (man′də tôr′ē), adv. required by a command or order.
6. **Mr. Barnett**, Ferdinand L. Barnett, Ida B. Wells's husband.
7. **A. M. E.**, African Methodist Episcopal.

▲ This photo of Ida B. Wells-Barnett and her son, Charles Aked Barnett, was taken in 1896.

had anything upon which to base that belief. "Well," he said, "he was a worthless sort of fellow, just about the kind of a man who would do a trick like that. Anyhow, all of the colored people believe that and many of us have written letters already to the governor asking the reinstatement of the sheriff."

I sprang to my feet and asked him if he realized what he had done in condoning[8] the horrible lynching of a fellowman who was a member of his race. Did he not know that if they condoned the lynching of one man, the time might come when they would have to condone that of other men higher up, providing they were black?

I asked him if he could direct me to the home of some other colored persons; that I had been sent to see all of them, and it wouldn't be fair for me to accept reports from one man alone. He

---

8. condoning (kən dōn′ing), n. forgiving or overlooking.

This stamp was issued by the U.S. Postal Service on February 1, 1989. What do you think is the message the artist was trying to convey about Ida B. Wells? Explain. ➤

Ida B. Wells

25

Black Heritage USA

gave me the names of one or two others, and I withdrew. I had expected to stop at his home, but after he told me that I had no desire to do so. One of the men named was Will Taylor, a druggist, whom I had known in Chicago, and I asked to be directed to his place. . . .

EVALUATE: What is Wells's attitude toward the minister?

Mr. Taylor and I spent the day talking with colored citizens and ended with a meeting that night. . . .

The meeting was largely attended and in my statement to them I said I had come down to be their mouthpiece; that I correctly understood how hard it would be for those who lived there to take an active part in the movement to oust the sheriff; that we were willing to take the lead

in the matter but they must give me the facts; that it would be endangering the lives of other colored people in Illinois if we did not take a stand against the all too frequent lynchings which were taking place.

I went on to say that I came because I knew that they knew of my work against lynching for fifteen years past and felt that they would talk more freely to me and trust me more fully than they would someone of whom they knew nothing. I wanted them to tell me if Mr. Frank Davis had used his great power to protect the victim of the mob; if he had at any time placed him behind bars of the county jail as the law required; and if he had sworn in any deputies to help protect his prisoner as he was obliged by law to do until such time as he could be tried by due process of law. Although the meeting lasted for two hours, and although most of those present and speaking were friends of Frank Davis, some of whom had been deputy sheriffs in his office, not one of them could honestly say that Frank Davis had put his prisoner in the county jail or had done anything to protect him. I therefore offered a resolution to that effect which was almost unanimously adopted. . . .

Next morning before taking the train I learned of a Baptist ministers' meeting that was being held there and decided to attend for the purpose of having them pass the same resolution. I was told that it would do no good to make the effort and that it would delay me until midnight getting into Springfield. But I went, got an opportunity to speak, offered the resolution, told of the men who had sent letters to the governor, showed how that would confuse his mind as to the attitude of the colored people on the subject, and stated clearly that all such action would mean that we would have other lynchings in Illinois whenever it suited the mob anywhere.

I asked the adoption of the resolution passed the night before. There was discussion pro and con, and finally the moderator arose and said, "Brethren, they say an honest confession is good for the soul. I, too, am one of those men who have written to the governor asking Frank Davis's reinstatement. I knew he was a friend of ours; that the man who had taken his place has turned out all Negro deputies and put in Democrats, and I was told that when the mob placed the rope around "Frog" James's neck the sheriff tried to prevent them and was knocked down for his pains. But now that the sister has shown us plainly the construction that would be placed upon that letter, I want her when she appears before the governor tomorrow to tell him that I take that letter back and hereby sign my name to this resolution." By this time the old man was shedding tears. Needless to say the resolution went through without any further objections. . . .

I entered the room at ten o'clock that morning . . . On the other side of the room there was Frank Davis, and with him one of the biggest lawyers in southern Illinois, so I was afterward told, who was also a state senator.

There was the parish priest, the state's attorney of Alexander County, the United States land commissioner, and about half a dozen other representative white men who had journeyed from Cairo to give aid and comfort to Frank Davis in his fight for reinstatement.

The governor said that they had no precedent and that he would now hear the plea to be made by the sheriff; whereupon this big lawyer proceeded to present his petition for reinstatement and backed it up with letters and telegrams from Democrats and Republicans, bankers, lawyers, doctors, editors of both daily papers, and heads of women's clubs and of men's organizations. The whole of the white population of Cairo was evidently behind Frank Davis and his demand for reinstatement.

In addition to this there were read these letters from Negro ministers and colored politicians. Special emphasis was laid upon them. Just before reading one of them the state senator said, "Your Excellency, I have known the writer of this letter since I was a boy. He has such a standing for truth and veracity in the community that if he were to tell me that black was white I would believe him, and he, too, has written to ask that Frank Davis be reinstated.". . .

When the gentlemen had finished, Governor Deneen said, "I understand Mrs. Barnett is here to represent the colored people of Illinois." Not until that moment did I realize that the burden depended upon me. It so happened that Attorney A. M. Williams, a Negro lawyer of Springfield, having heard that I was in town, came over to the Capitol to invite me to his home for dinner. Finding me by myself, he immediately camped by my side and remained with me all through the ordeal. I was indeed thankful for this help, since never before had I been confronted with a situation that called for legal knowledge.

I began by reading the brief which Mr. Barnett prepared in due legal form. I then launched out to tell of my investigation in Cairo. Before I had gotten very far the clock struck twelve, and Springfield being a country town, everything stopped so people could go home to dinner, which was served in the middle of the day. I did not go with Mr. Williams to his home but urged him to do so.

I went to his office and stayed there, getting the balance of my address in shape. At two o'clock he came for me and we went back to the Capitol. I resumed the statement of facts I had found—of the meeting held Monday night and of the resolution passed there which stated Frank Davis had not put his prisoner in the county jail or sworn in deputies to protect him although he knew there was talk of mob violence. . . .

"But that is not all, Governor; I have here the signature of that leading Baptist minister who has been so highly praised to you. I went to his meeting yesterday and when I told him what a mistake it was to seem to condone the outrage on a human being by writing a letter asking for the reinstatement of a man who permitted it to be done, he rose and admitted he had sent the letter which has been read in your hearing, but having realized his mistake he wanted me to tell you that he endorsed the resolutions which I have here, and here is his name signed to them."

And then I wound up by saying, "Governor, the state of Illinois has had too many terrible lynchings within her borders within the last few years. If this man is sent back it will be an encouragement to those who resort to mob violence and will do so at any time, well knowing they will not be called to account for so doing. All the colored friends in Cairo are friends of Mr. Davis and they seem to feel that because his successor, a Democrat, has turned out all the Republican deputies, they owe their duty to the party to ask the return of a Republican sheriff. But not one of these, Mr. Davis's friends, would say that for one moment he had his prisoner in the county jail where the law demands that he should be placed or that he swore in a single deputy to help protect his life until he could be tried by law. It looked like encouragement to the mob to have the chief law officer in the county take that man up in the woods and keep him until the mob got big enough to come after him. I repeat, Governor, that if this man is reinstated, it will simply mean an increase of lynchings in the state of Illinois and an encouragement to mob violence."

When I had finished it was late in the afternoon . . . Mr. Williams said as we went down the steps, "Oh, the governor's going to send him back. I don't see how he can help it with such terrific pressure being brought to bear to have him to do so. But, by george, if I had time to dig up the law I would have furnished him so much of it that he wouldn't dare do so." I said, "We have done the best we could under the circumstances, and angels could do no more."

PREDICT: What will Governor Deneen decide to do?

The following Tuesday morning Governor Deneen issued one of the finest state papers that emanated from him during his whole eight years in the Capitol. The summary of his proclamation was that Frank Davis could not be reinstated because he had not properly protected the prisoner within his keeping and that lynch law could have no place in Illinois.

That was in 1909, and from that day until the present there has been no lynching in the state. Every sheriff, whenever there seem to be any signs of the kind, immediately telegraphs the governor for troops. And to Governor Deneen belongs the credit.

After Reading

Making Connections

Shaping Your Response

1. Ida B. Wells battled against a very serious injustice—that of the "lynch law." If you could write a letter to any person involved in this narrative, to whom would you write, and what would you want to say?

2. What three adjectives would you use to describe Wells? Explain your choices.

Analyzing the Autobiography

3. Why do you suppose Wells's husband thought it was so important for Wells to go to Cairo to investigate?

4. Wells's child finally convinced her that she should investigate the case. Why do you think he was successful in convincing her?

5. Many prominent African Americans in Cairo at first thought that Sheriff Davis should be reinstated. Why did Wells object to this so strongly?

6. Why do you suppose Wells gives credit to Governor Deneen for ending lynching in Illinois, rather than to herself or the other crusaders?

Extending the Ideas

7. If Ida B. Wells could visit the present time, what would she like about American society? What might she want to change?

8. As a class, brainstorm a list of contemporary people who are currently leading their own crusades for justice. What are some of the characteristics these people have in common?

9. In what ways would you say Ida B. Wells went "beyond the limits" of the traditional roles for women of her time?

Literary Focus: Tone

In this excerpt from her autobiography, Wells's **tone** is formal—she obviously takes the matter of the lynching seriously and expects her readers to do the same. Look back to the notes you kept about Wells's tone while reading the selection. At certain points in her writing, Wells reveals that she is dissatisfied with the response to the lynching. Of whom is she critical? Why? How does her tone reveal her feelings?

Vocabulary Study

Choose the word from the list that best completes each sentence.

enact
prominent
dispossess
mandatory
condoning

1. Wells believed that the African American community's ____ of the sheriff's actions would lead to more violence.

2. Wells was determined that lawmakers ____ legislation that would protect the rights of African Americans.

3. Several ____ townspeople argued that Sheriff Davis should be reinstated.

4. Wells believed that it was ____ that Davis be fired for his failure to protect the prisoner.

5. Governor Deneen decided to ____ Davis of his title as sheriff.

Expressing Your Ideas

Writing Choices

Writer's Notebook Update Would you call Ida B. Wells a hero? Why or why not? Review your list of characteristics for a heroic person. Are there any changes that you'd like to make to your list? In your notebook, write a short argument about whether or not Wells could be called a hero. Support your argument with evidence from the selection.

A Letter to James's Family Imagine that Wells followed up on her work in Illinois by locating "Frog" James's family. Draft a **letter** from Wells to his family that reveals her feelings about the lynching and explains her attitude toward the crusade for justice that followed. Before you begin your letter, decide on your **tone.** How emotional would Wells have been in a letter like this? Would she have allowed her anger to show?

Wells the Hero Use this episode from Wells's autobiography as the basis for a **short story** or **epic poem** with Wells as the hero. What does she have in common with traditional epic heroes?

Other Options

Ida B. Wells and the Governor . . . Today Arrange an imaginary meeting between Ida B. Wells and the current governor of your state. Working in pairs, brainstorm a **list** of the issues Wells might want to discuss with your governor. When you've finished your list, decide how the governor might respond to each of her points. With one person playing the role of Wells and the other playing the role of the governor, create a **dramatization** of their meeting in front of the class.

A Symbol of Wells's Crusade If you were to choose one object to symbolize Wells's crusade for justice in Illinois, what would it be? **Sketch** a picture of the object in your notebook. Include with your sketch a brief explanation of the object and how it is a symbol of Wells's crusade.

Before Reading

The Spring and the Fall
On Thought in Harness

by Edna St. Vincent Millay

Edna St. Vincent Millay
1892–1950

Born in Maine, Millay began writing verse at an early age—her mother taught her the form of a sonnet at age four. At age fourteen she published her first poem. Ten years later Millay moved to Greenwich Village in New York City and became the poetic voice of the "flaming youth" of the 1920s. Although she had some success as an actress and playwright, Millay is best remembered for her romantic poetry. She wrote about desire and death, about the self and the universe, and about the changeable emotions of rebellious youth.

Building Background

Reading Poetry When you read poetry, you do so in two ways: you read for meaning (what the poet is trying to say) and you read for structure (the poetic devices the poet uses to help illuminate meaning). Think for a moment about the poetry you've read. Which poems do you remember most vividly? List the titles on a sheet of paper. Next to each title, write a sentence that explains why the poem is memorable. Does the rhyme scheme or the structure of the poem help make it memorable? In groups, discuss what you think makes good poetry good. Make a list of the characteristics of good poetry.

Literary Focus

Rhythm and Rhyme The structure of a poem contributes to the poem's meaning. One aspect of a poem's structure, **rhythm,** is the way the poem sounds—the "beat" of the poem—when read aloud. **Rhyme** is the repetition of similar or identical sounds in the body of the poem. The pattern of rhyming words from line to line is called the **rhyme scheme** of the poem. As you read "The Spring and the Fall" and "On Thought in Harness," answer these questions:

• How should the poem sound when read aloud? Which syllables should be stressed?

• How does Millay set up her rhyme scheme? Which words rhyme? Do the rhyming words fall mostly at the ends of lines or at various places throughout the poem?

Writer's Notebook

Aspects of Love Draw a chart similar to the one shown here to list ten to fifteen words that you associate with the positive

Aspects of Love	
Positive	**Negative**

and negative aspects of love. For example, your chart may contain words like *joy, tenderness,* and *devotion,* as well as words like *betrayal, anguish,* and *sadness.* If you like, get together with some classmates and work on a group chart.

The Spring and the Fall

EDNA ST. VINCENT MILLAY

In the spring of the year, in the spring
     of the year,
I walked the road beside my dear.
The trees were black where the bark
     was wet.
I see them yet, in the spring of the year.
5 He broke me a bough[1] of the blossoming
     peach
That was out of the way and hard to reach.

In the fall of the year, in the fall of
     the year,
I walked the road beside my dear.
The rooks[2] went up with a raucous[3] trill.
10 I hear them still, in the fall of the year.
He laughed at all I dared to praise,
And broke my heart, in little ways.

Year be springing or year be falling,
The bark will drip and the birds be calling.
15 There's much that's fine to see and hear
In the spring of a year, in the fall of a year.
'Tis not love's going hurts my days,
But that it went in little ways.

---

1. bough (bou), *n.* one of the branches of a tree.
2. rook (rŭk), *n.* common European bird, closely
   resembling the crow.
3. raucous (rô′kəs), *adj.* hoarse; harsh sounding.

What is she doing? What is she thinking? Create a scenario for the women depicted in Theodore Robinson's *In the Garden* (1891). Use the poems for inspiration, if you wish.

On Thought in Harness

EDNA ST. VINCENT MILLAY

My falcon to my wrist
Returns
From no high air.
I sent her toward the sun that burns
5 Above the mist;
But she has not been there.

Her talons are not cold; her beak
Is closed upon no wonder;
Her head stinks of its hood, her feathers
    reek
10 Of me, that quake[1] at the thunder.

Degraded[2] bird, I give you back your eyes
    forever, ascend now whither you
    are tossed;
Forsake[3] this wrist, forsake this rhyme;
Soar, eat ether, see what has never been
    seen; depart, be lost,
But climb.

---

1. quake (kwāk), *v.* shake or tremble.
2. degraded (di grād′ ed), *adj.* lower in rank, honor, quality.
3. forsake (fôr sāk′), *v.* give up; abandon.

After Reading

Making Connections

Shaping Your Response

1. In your notebook, sketch a symbol that represents the poem "The Spring and the Fall." Do the same thing for "On Thought in Harness."

2. Which poem do you most identify with? Why?

Analyzing the Poems

3. What is the **tone** of "The Spring and the Fall"?

4. What do you think the falcon **symbolizes** in "On Thought in Harness"? Defend your choice with words from the poem.

Extending the Ideas

5. What happens when a person's thoughts are kept in harness? Would you agree that we must be allowed to "soar, eat ether, see what has never been seen"? Why?

Literary Focus: Rhyme and Rhythm

When you chart the **rhyme scheme** of a poem, you label the first rhyme *a,* the second rhyme *b,* the third rhyme *c,* and so on. Here is the rhyme scheme of the first stanza of "The Spring and the Fall":

> In the spring of the year, in the spring of the year, *a*
> I walked the road beside my dear. *a*
> The trees were black where the bark was wet. *b*
> I see them yet, in the spring of the year. *a*
> He broke me a bough of the blossoming peach *c*
> That was out of the way and hard to reach. *c*

The **rhythm**—or the **meter** of a poem is measured by the metrical **foot**. Each foot contains one accented syllable and one or more unaccented syllables. You can chart the rhythm of a poem by using a ˘ to mark the unaccented syllables and a ′ to mark the accented syllables, like this:

˘ ′ ˘ ˘ ′ ˘ ˘ ′   ˘ ˘ ′   ˘ ˘ ′ ˘ ′
My fal / con to / my wrist /   Re turns /   From no / high air. /

In your notebook, chart the rhyme scheme of one of the two Millay poems. Then chart the rhythm of the first stanza of "On Thought in Harness."

Vocabulary Study

bough
raucous
quake
degraded
forsake

Create a word web for each of the listed words. In the middle of the web, write the word, then add synonyms for the word at the spokes. An example has been done for you.

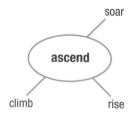

Beyond the Limits

Within Limits

History and Science Connections

During the late 1800s and early 1900s, women were expected to live within established limits of conduct. The following selections show the restrictions and attitudes women faced in their everyday lives.

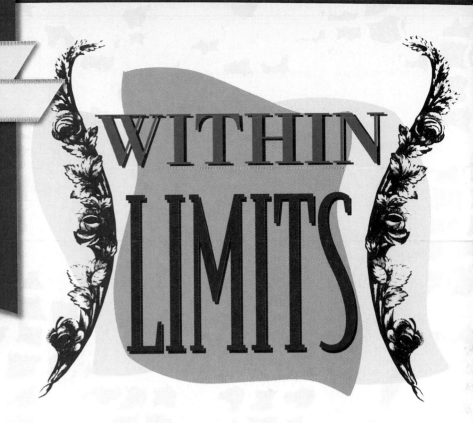

WITHIN LIMITS

The Uprising of Women

New York Times, May 5, 1912

On May 4, 1912, 10,000 women marched through New York City, demanding the right to vote. The following is the reaction of one man to the prospect of women voters.

We often hear the remark nowadays that women will get the vote, if they try hard enough andpersistently, and it is true that they will get it, and play havoc with it for themselves and society, if the men are not firm and wise enough, and, it may well be said, masculine enough to prevent them. The agitation has been on foot for many years. One does not need to be a profound student of biology to know that some women, a very small minority, have a natural inclination to usurp the social and civic function of men. But that is not true of a majority of the women in yesterday's parade, or of their thousands of sympathetic sisters who lacked the physical vigor, the courage, or the opportunity to join in the march. Their adherence to the cause is largely factitious, born of much agitation and much false theorizing. There are, however, unhappy creatures to whom the state of being a woman is naturally burdensome. Their influence would not count for so much if their less unhappy sisters, who have no real grievance against Mother Nature or society, would not give them countenance. There are numberless explanations of the conduct of otherwise nice and womanly women in this matter. There are few that can fairly be called "reasons."

We are told by some sages that education has made women discontented. It has made men discontented, too, for that matter. The equality of opportunity all men possess in this country has not allayed the discontent. There is no reason to suppose that the right to vote would allay feminine discontent. Granted the suffrage, they would demand all that the right implies. It is not possible to think of women as soldiers and sailors, police patrolmen, or firemen, although voters ought to fight if need be, but they would serve on juries and elect themselves if they could to executive offices and judgeships. Many of them are looking forward to an apportionment of high offices between the sexes. This may seem preposterous to some of the men who choose to smile complacently at the aggressiveness of the women's rights adherents, but it is true. It is a state of things these men will have to cope with before they die if they do not arouse themselves and do their duty now.

We have said that the ballot will secure to woman no right that she needs and does not now possess. That is a true statement, and we hold that it is not debatable. Woman is thoroughly protected by the existing laws. Her rights as a taxpayer, a holder of property, are not in danger. Her dower rights are scrupulously upheld in the probate courts. In her pursuit of all the privileges and duties of men, however, she is deliberately endangering many rights she now enjoys without legal sanction. She receives honors and privileges which the younger man will soon learn to withhold from her when she jostles him at the polls. It will be a sad day for society when woman loses the respect she now receives from all but the basest of men. Yet yesterday's parade demonstrates that she holds male

This 1869 Currier & Ives cartoon warns that voting would create masculine, aggressive women.

courtesy in slight regard, or would, if we were willing to regard the parade as a demonstration of the feelings and opinions of all our women.

Millions of men labor all their years to keep up a home, of which a woman is mistress. Poor enough the home may be, and the measure of toil its upkeep demands of the man may age him prematurely and deprive him of all the freedom which he instinctively desires. But most men throughout the civilized world have been doing their duty as husbands and fathers, as citizens, according to their lights. That the triumph of woman suffrage would tend quickly to change the point of view of these millions of plodding men is not to be doubted. If woman declares her independence, and forces the State to recognize it, the cry of the men will be "Let her uphold it and enjoy it as best she may." From the beginning "man that is born of woman" has been "of few days and full of trouble." Presumably he will continue to be born. Presumably he will continue to respect his mother, as Ishmael did. But with the opportunity afforded him by the refusal of woman to recognize his manhood as a title of supremacy in the world's affairs, he will be at pains to avoid some of the troubles which he has hitherto regarded as part of his heritage.

This we hold to be inevitable. Let the women who are not yet avowed suffragists consider it. Above all, let the complacent multitudes of men who have accepted the full responsibility of citizenship consider it. There were, at most, 10,000 women in yesterday's parade. If their cause triumphs there will be 700,000 women voters in this municipality. Have the 10,000 thought much about the measure of influence they would exert if the whole number voted under the control of their associations and environment as their intelligence impelled them to?

Teaching by the Rules

While women were struggling for career opportunities, teaching had long been an option for single women. Even so, women teachers had to live within strict limits.

Schoolteachers were expected to live up to saintly standards in private as well as public. About 1915, for example, Iva McDaniels, a schoolmarm for 15 years in one small Massachusetts community, came back after spending Thanksgiving with friends in a nearby town, to find that she had been fired for ignoring rules two and seven of those governing the conduct of female schoolteachers:

1. Do not get married.
2. Do not leave town at any time without school board permission.
3. Do not keep company with men.
4. Be home between the hours of 8 P.M. and 6 A.M.
5. Do not loiter downtown in ice cream stores.
6. Do not smoke.
7. Do not get into any carriage with any man except your father or brother.
8. Do not dress in bright colors.
9. Do not dye your hair.
10. Do not wear any dress more than two inches above the ankle.

WITHIN LIMITS

from

The Sexual Politics of Sickness

by Barbara Ehrenreich and Deirdre English

Corsets reduced women's waists by as much as fifteen inches, crushing and displacing ribs and internal organs in the process.

As middle- and upper-class women of the late 1800s found themselves with more leisure time and less to do, mysterious illnesses began taking over their lives. Doctors diagnosed the diseases using labels such as "neurasthenia," "dyspepsia," and "hysteria," and prescribed such cures as lying in bed several hours after every meal, staying indoors, and avoiding intellectual activity. This system kept the patients sick, the doctors wealthy, and women docile and frail.

The way [middle- and upper-class] woman was expected to live predisposed her to sickness, and sickness in turn predisposed her to continue to live as she was expected to. The delicate, affluent lady, who was completely dependent on her husband, set the sexual romanticist ideal of femininity for women of all classes.

Clear-headed feminists like Charlotte Perkins Gilman and Olive Schreiner saw a link between female invalidism and the economic situation of women in the upper classes. As they observed, poor women did not suffer from the syndrome. . . .

To Gilman's pragmatic mind, the affluent wife appeared to be a sort of tragic evolutionary anomaly, something like the dodo. She did not work; that is, there was no serious, productive work to do in the home, and the tasks which were left—keeping house, cooking and minding the children—she left as much as possible to the domestic help . . .

A successful man could have no better social ornament than an idle wife. Her delicacy, her culture, her childlike ignorance of the male world gave a man the "class" which money alone could not buy. A virtuous wife spent a hushed and peaceful life indoors, sewing, sketching, planning menus, and supervising the servants and children. The more adventurous might fill their leisure with shopping

feature such stories as "The Grave of My Friend" and "Song of Dying." Society ladies cultivated a sickly countenance by drinking vinegar in quantity or, more effectively, arsenic. The loveliest heroines were those who died young, like Beth in *Little Women,* too good and too pure for life in this world.

Meanwhile, the requirements of fashion insured that the well-dressed woman would actually be as frail and ornamental as she looked. The style of wearing tight-laced corsets, which was *de riguer* throughout the last half of the century, has to be ranked somewhere close to the old Chinese practice of foot-binding for its crippling effects on the female body. A fashionable woman's corsets exerted, on the average, twenty-one pounds of pressure on her internal organs, and extremes of up to eighty-eight pounds have been measured. (Add to this the fact that a well-dressed woman wore an average of thirty-seven pounds of street clothing in the winter months, of which nineteen pounds were suspended from her tortured waist.) Some of the short-term results of tight-lacing were shortness of breath, constipation, weakness, and a tendency to violent indigestion. Among the long-term effects were bent or fractured ribs [and] displacement of the liver . . .

The theories which guided the doctor's practice from the late nineteenth century to the early twentieth century held that woman's normal state was to be sick. This was not advanced as an empirical observation, but as physiological fact. Medicine had "discovered" that female functions were inherently pathological.

John Singer Sargent's 1889-90 portrait, *Miss Elsie Palmer,* idealizes the passivity and frailty of its female subject.

excursions, luncheons, balls, and novels. A "lady" could be charming, but never brilliant; interested, but not intense. . . . By no means was such a lady to concern herself with politics, business, international affairs, or the aching injustices of the industrial work world. . . .

If you have to be idle, you might as well be sick, and sickness, in turn, legitimates idleness. From the romantic perspective, the sick woman was not that far off from the ideal woman anyway. A morbid aesthetic developed, in which sickness was seen as a source of female beauty, and, beauty—in the high-fashion sense—was in fact a source of sickness. Over and over, nineteenth-century romantic paintings feature the beautiful invalid, sensuously dropping on her cushions, eyes fixed tremulously at her husband or physician, or already gazing into the Beyond. Literature aimed at female readers lingered on the romantic pathos of illness and death; popular women's magazines

Responding

1. Why do you think the writer of the *New York Times* article was so fearful at the prospect of women voters?

2. How would you explain the extraordinary amounts of sickness in women during this time period?

Language History

The Language of Gender

 That's one small step for man, one giant leap for mankind.

Astronaut Neil Armstrong made the above statement as he took the step that made him the first person ever to walk on the moon. When he made that famous statement, did he mean one small step for human beings, in general, or one small step for males? And whom was he including with the word *mankind*?

During the 1970s womens groups began to call attention to gender biases in American English. Feminists argued that American English needed reforming to eliminate sexist language. They wanted words like *mankind* to be replaced by more universal *humankind,* and to stop the generic use of *he* to indicate all people.

Many feminists argued that we should discontinue using *man* in words that also describe the professions or abilities of women. Women fight fires, they reasoned, so the term *fireman* is incorrect. Women deliver the mail, so *mailman* should be changed to *mail carrier, spokesman* should be *spokesperson,* and so on. For years the word *authoress* was used to describe a female writer. According to feminists, the *-ess* suffix has a minimizing or trivializing effect. An *authoress* performs the same job as an *author;* a *stewardess* performs the same job as a *steward.*

Much of the language considered to reflect gender biases is disappearing. We no longer use *sculptress* and *murderess* and are beginning to drop *hostess* for the more generic *host. Flight attendant* is now used in place of *steward* and *stewardess,* and those who write poetry or act are called poets and actors, regardless of their gender. Many women now use the generic title *Ms.* before their names rather than the *Mrs.* and *Miss* titles that differentiate between married and single women, with no parallel counterparts for men.

Most linguists believe that whenever we make changes in our language, we feel motivated to make accompanying changes in society. If we use words in our language that do not favor one gender over the other, then perhaps we are one step closer to achieving gender equality in other aspects of life.

Writing Workshop

Update: Women Then and Now

Assignment You have read about what life was like for women in the past. Now write about how things have changed.

WRITER'S BLUEPRINT

Product   An update on women's roles

Purpose   To explain how life has changed for women during the last century

Audience   Men and women from the turn of the century

Specs   To write a successful paper, you should:

❑ Imagine that you have the power to send news back in time. Today you are going to update people living in the year 1900 on how women's roles have changed since their time.

❑ Begin by orienting your audience in time and space. Introduce yourself, give the date and city, and briefly describe your setting—the place where you are writing this update.

❑ Go on to review women's roles at the turn of the century and update your audience on how things have changed since then. Focus on three of these aspects: marriage, motherhood, work, education, legal rights, or other aspects of your choice.

❑ Keep in mind the limits of your audience's knowledge, and give them the background they'll need to understand what you're telling them.

❑ Conclude by giving your opinion about the direction you think women's roles are taking and how you feel about this situation.

❑ Follow the rules of grammar, usage, spelling, and mechanics. Look closely at verb forms.

 PREWRITING

Chart women's roles. Working with a partner or small group, analyze the literature for information on women's roles at the turn of the century.

Organize your information in a chart similar to the one shown. Cover at least three of these aspects: marriage, motherhood, work, education, legal rights, or other aspects of your choice.

Turn of the Century	
Aspect	**Role**
Marriage	Submissive to husband. Life ruled by his decisions.

Research three aspects with your partner or small group. Consult history books, encyclopedias, and books on the women's movement for additional information about women's roles at the turn of the century. Also, research the state of women's roles today. Share your information and organize it in a change chart like the one shown.

Change Chart			
Aspect	**1900**	**How Things Have Changed**	**Background**
1. work	Women, as a rule, did not work outside the home.	Equal rights within the workplace and two-income families	—ERA and feminist movement —Girls encouraged to get education and seek careers

Try a quickwrite. From now on you'll be working on your own. Write for five or ten minutes. Use your change chart as a guide as you address these questions about the three aspects you chose:

- What direction do women's roles seem to be taking? Will there be more freedom in the future, or less?

- Do I approve of the direction in which things seem to be moving? Why or why not?

Plan your essay. Look back at your prewriting materials as you develop your writing plan. You might organize your notes in a plan like the one that follows.

- **Introduction** (orienting the audience)
  Who you are
  Date and city
  Description of setting

- **Body** (updating the audience on changes)
    First aspect
        —Conditions at the turn of the century
        —Conditions today
        —Background on how changes occurred
    Second aspect
    and so on . . .

- **Conclusion** (telling the audience how you feel)
    Direction women's roles are taking
    Your opinion about this direction

Consider your audience. Look back at your plan and prewriting notes and make a list of concepts and terms you are likely to use in your paper that would not be familiar to a turn-of-the-century audience, along with a brief definition of each term. For example, as you describe the room where you're writing, you might mention a computer and a TV, two items unknown to your audience. For more ideas on considering your audience, see the Revising Strategy in Step 3 of this lesson.

 DRAFTING

Before you draft, review your prewriting notes and writing plan. Then reread the Writer's Blueprint.

As you draft, don't worry about spelling or punctuation mistakes yet. Concentrate on getting the ideas from your writing plan down on paper. Here are some drafting tips.

- As you describe your setting, go beyond your immediate surroundings. Look out the window and mention things such as parking meters, street lamps, and automobiles (horseless carriages).

- Don't get bogged down in this introduction, though. Keep it brief—no more than a paragraph. Your purpose is to give your readers a taste of modern life, not an involved description and explanation.

 REVISING

Ask a partner to comment on your draft before you revise it. Use the checklist on the next page as a guide.

✔ Did I focus on three aspects related to women's roles?

✔ Did I express my opinion on the current direction of women's roles?

✔ Am I considering my audience as I write?

Revising Strategy

Orienting Your Audience

Because your audience is not from this century, you may need to clarify some of the language you use. As you revise your work, be on the look-out for any language that may be unfamiliar to your audience. Consider these options:

- Change the term to something the audience understands.

- Explain the term—but keep these explanations brief and simple. Give your audience the information they'll need to understand your train of thought. Don't overexplain.

Notice how the writer of the student model made changes with her audience in mind.

These changes in the household duties of women consequently

affect the role that females play in ~~parenting.~~ *bringing up their children* Whereas women were

previously expected to stay home with the children, this is not

always the case anymore. Children now often stay in day-care

centers ~~while the mother works.~~ *—places where small children are cared for while their parents are at work.*

STUDENT MODEL

4 EDITING

Ask a partner to review your revised draft before you edit. When you edit, look for errors in grammar, usage, spelling, and mechanics. Make sure you are using apostrophes correctly.

Editing Strategy

Using Apostrophes Correctly

When you edit your work, be on the lookout for problems with using apostrophes to form possessives. When you form possessive nouns, follow these rules:

FOR REFERENCE
For more information on using apostrophes correctly, see the Language and Grammar Handbook at the back of this text.

1. Add **'s** to form the possessive of most singular nouns (a woman**'s** courage, one generation**'s** problems).

2. Add only an apostrophe to form the possessive of plural nouns ending in **s** (twenty senators**'** votes, their wives**'** opinions).

3. Add **'s** to form the possessive of plural nouns that do not end in **s** (many women**'s** ideas, two children**'s** mothers).

5 PRESENTING

- Invite community leaders to your class to listen to some of your essays and present their own views.

- Include a time line with your paper, showing historical events that influenced women's roles from the turn of the century to the present.

COMPUTER TIP
Some word processing programs include a drawing program. If you have access to one, you could use it to make your time line.

6 LOOKING BACK

Self-evaluate. Look back at the Writer's Blueprint and give your paper a score on each point, from 6 (superior) to I (inadequate).

Reflect. Write answers to these questions.

✔ As you researched changes in women's roles, what did you discover about changes in men's roles?

✔ Imagine that a hundred years from now, students are asked to write the same update you did to an audience at the turn of the twentieth century about how women's roles have changed. Speculate about what such an update might say.

For Your Working Portfolio Add your update and reflection responses to your working portfolio.

Beyond Print

Looking at Photographs

Take a close look at the photograph of the woman on the right. What do you suppose her life was like? The photo represents an old world, far from the world you live in. Yet, you may have grandmothers or great-grandmothers who remember this world. Old photos can be a key to unlocking the past.

Exploring the Past

Use the photograph—or perhaps you have an old family photo or a photo you've found in a book that you'd rather use—to explore a world that no longer exists. Your photo should depict a time fifty or more years ago, and should have at least one person in it.

To begin, find two or more relatives, friends, or acquaintances who are old enough to remember life before World War II and are willing to be interviewed. Show them the photograph, and explain that you're trying to find out all you can about what life was like when the photo was taken. Ask questions like the following to get as much information as possible. If you are using a different photograph, you may have to adapt the questions.

Clothing Styles What time period do you think the woman's clothing belongs to? Did anyone you know—your mother or grandmother—dress like this woman? If so, describe the clothing. Was it comfortable? Was it easy to put on? What were the dresses made out of?

Situation Is this woman dressed up for a special occasion, or is she wearing everyday clothing? On what kind of an occasion might a photograph like this be taken? Do you know of any reason why she might be posed as she is, leaning on pillows with her eyes closed?

Objects Have you ever seen or owned furniture like the sofa in the picture? Does it bring back any memories? Do any of the objects in the photograph look familiar to you? What can you tell about them?

Larger Context What do you think life was like for the woman? What kinds of things might she have done for leisure? What kinds of responsibilities might she have had in the home? outside the home?

Personal Connection How was the life of your mother or grandmother different from your life? What kinds of stories, if any, did your mother and grandmother tell you when you were growing up?

After your interviews, share the information you've gathered with your classmates. The following activities are some ways you might try presenting your information.

Activity Options

Stepping Back in Time If members of your class used the same photograph, or at least photos from the same time period, form small groups of three to five students and share the information you gathered in your interviews. Analyze the combined information and give a group oral report about what life was like when the photo was taken.

A Voice from the Past Based on what you've learned from the photograph and from the interviews, create a personality for an individual in the photo. Create and perform a five-minute monologue in the character of the person you've invented. Include information about where you live, what you're doing in the photograph, and what your life is like.

Marcus Garvey

Marcus Garvey came to the U.S. in 1916 from Jamaica and organized the country's first important black nationalist movement. He formed the Universal Negro Improvement Association and his belief that blacks could only achieve equality by founding their own independent nation attracted much support in Harlem and other black communities.

A CULTURAL REVOLUTION

HISTORICAL OVERVIEW

In the 1920s, New York City's Harlem district, the largest African American community in the United States, also became a cultural magnet. African American actors, dancers, writers, painters, and musicians from around the country participated in an outburst of creativity that became known as the Harlem Renaissance. Many Harlem artists saw creativity as a force in their struggle against oppression, and desired to create uniquely African American traditions in the arts. Jazz rhythms, images from big-city life, and themes from African American history and folklore were important sources of inspiration. The individuals profiled here are just a few of those who made important contributions to the African American cultural revolution of the 1920s.

Duke Ellington

Edward "Duke" Ellington attracted world-wide attention as a jazz composer, pianist and band leader in the early 1900s. He went to New York in 1923 and quickly gained a reputation as an innovative band leader playing in clubs like Harlem's Cotton Club. To this day Ellington is regarded as one of the most significant figures in jazz history.

Aaron Douglas

Aaron Douglas was one of Harlem's most prominent visual artists in the 1920s. He came to New York in 1924 and quickly developed a unique style which reflected many different influences, including African sculpture and the works of European painters such as Gauguin, Picasso, and Matisse.

Langston Hughes

Langston Hughes was one of the first writers to accurately portray the African American experience in the U.S. through his poems, plays, and novels. He gained recognition as a major young poet of the Harlem Renaissance in the early 1920s and achieved national acclaim in 1926 with the publication of his first book, *The Weary Blues*.

Zora Neale Hurston

Novelist and folklorist Zora Neale Hurston arrived in New York in 1925 after studying at Howard University under Alaine Locke. She established herself as a figure of the Harlem Renaissance when she published short stories in the Harlem journal, Opportunity, and through her work with writers such as Langston Hughes, Claude McKay, and Jean Toomer.

Bessie Smith

Tennessee born Bessie Smith was a blues singer whose popularity in the 1920s earned her the title, "Empress of the Blues." After establishing a following in the South she went to New York in 1923 and recorded her first record, "Down Hearted Blues." It sold over a million copies and saved Columbia Records from bankruptcy. By 1927 she was the highest paid black artist in the world.

Key Dates

1916
African Americans migrate from the South to big cities in the North.

1920
Marcus Garvey organizes international convention of United Negro Improvement Association.

1921
Shuffle Along, an all-black musical, is Broadway hit.

1923
Jean Toomer's novel Cane is published.

1925
Alain Locke produces anthology of African American artists.

1926
Langston Hughes's The Weary Blues is published.

1927
Bessie Smith is world's highest paid black artist.

1929
Stock market crash signals start of the Great Depression and end of Harlem Renaissance.

Part Two

The Harlem Renaissance

In the 1920s, African American creativity sprang to the forefront of American culture in ways it never had before. An unprecedented number of African American writers were able to publish their works, African American artists flourished like never before, and blues singers and musicians gained national popularity. The capital of this creative burst of energy was New York City's Harlem, where artists, writers, musicians, and scholars gathered to share their ideas and encourage one another.

Multicultural Connection Family, social, cultural, and other **groups** help us define who we are and provide us with a sense of belonging. During the Harlem Renaissance, many African American artists, writers, and scholars were attempting to redefine what it meant to be part of the group called, at the time, "Negroes." What does each of the following works say about being part of this group?

Literature

James Weldon Johnson	**Harlem: The Culture Capital** ◆ essay	512
Arna Bontemps	**A Black Man Talks of Reaping** ◆ poem	524
Claude McKay	**If We Must Die** ◆ poem	525
Langston Hughes	**The Negro Speaks of Rivers** ◆ poem	526
Countee Cullen	**Harlem Wine** ◆ poem	526
Langston Hughes	**Youth** ◆ poem	527
Sterling A. Brown	**Ma Rainey** ◆ poem	528
Zora Neale Hurston	**How It Feels to Be Colored Me** ◆ essay	533

Interdisciplinary Study Harlem Renaissance Artists

Artworks by Meta Warrick Fuller, Richmond Barthé, Augusta Savage, Archibald J. Motley, Jr., Palmer Hayden, and Aaron Douglas ◆ fine art . .538

Tour Director Shows Off Harlem Treasures ◆ career connection 542

Writing Workshop Persuasive Writing

Calling All Artists 543

Beyond Print Effective Speaking

Speaking Your Mind 548

Before Reading

Harlem: The Culture Capital

by James Weldon Johnson

James Weldon Johnson
1871–1938

James Weldon Johnson's career took many paths. He practiced law, wrote popular show tunes with his brother Rosamond—their works also include "Lift Every Voice and Sing," the song that has become the African American national anthem, and campaign songs for Theodore Roosevelt—and served as consul to Venezuela and Nicaragua. Then, in 1920, Johnson began working for the National Association for the Advancement of Colored People. While at the NAACP, he acted as mentor to many young African American writers who moved to Harlem in the 1920s, offering encouragement, advice, and often a free meal or two as the writers worked to establish themselves in a new city.

Building Background

The Great Migration Before World War I, most African Americans lived in rural areas of the South, but with the onset of the war the flood of immigrants from Europe slowed to a trickle, many workers became soldiers, and suddenly northern industries were in desperate need of workers. What came to be known as the **Great Migration** began, as hundreds of thousands of African Americans left the South and moved to northern cities, where discriminatory laws and social restrictions were less severe than in the South, and where there were unprecedented opportunities for well-paying jobs. They moved to many of the large northern industrial centers—Chicago, Detroit, New York—but, whereas in other cities African Americans could generally find housing only in the older, more worn-down neighborhoods, New York City's Harlem was a good location filled with new apartment buildings, and it quickly became one of the largest predominately black communities in the world.

Literary Focus

Metaphor In his essay, "Harlem: The Culture Capital," Johnson uses metaphor to bring freshness and vitality to his writing. A metaphor is a comparison between two basically unlike things. "A copper sky" and "a heart of stone" are examples of metaphors. As you read "Harlem: The Culture Capital," see if you can spot three examples of metaphor.

Writer's Notebook

My Kind of Town What do you like best about your hometown? What would you say are its best features? In your notebook, write a paragraph that explains what you find most appealing about your hometown.

Harlem:
THE CULTURE CAPITAL

James Weldon Johnson

n the history of New York, the significance of the name Harlem has changed from Dutch to Irish to Jewish to Negro. Of these changes, the last has come most swiftly. Throughout colored America, from Massachusetts to Mississippi, and across the continent to Los Angeles and Seattle, its name, which as late as fifteen years ago had scarcely been heard, now stands for the Negro metropolis. Harlem is indeed the great Mecca[1] for the sight-seer, the pleasure-seeker, the curious, the adventurous, the enterprising, the ambitious and the talented of the whole Negro world; for the lure of it has reached down to every island of the Carib Sea and has penetrated even into Africa.

In the make-up of New York, Harlem is not merely a Negro colony or community, it is a city within a city, the greatest Negro city in the world. It is not a slum or a fringe, it is located in the heart of Manhattan and occupies one of the most beautiful and healthful sections of the city. It is not a "quarter" of dilapidated[2] tenements, but is made up of new-law apartments and handsome dwellings, with well-paved and well-lighted streets. It has its own churches, social and civic centers, shops, theaters and other places of amusement. And it contains more Negroes to the square mile than any other spot on earth. A stranger who rides up magnificent Seventh Avenue on a bus or in an automobile must be struck with surprise at the transformation which takes place after he crosses One Hundred and Twenty-fifth Street. Beginning there, the population suddenly darkens and he rides through twenty-five solid blocks where the passers-by, the shoppers, those sitting in restaurants, coming out of theaters, standing in doorways and looking out of windows are practically all Negroes; and then he emerges where the population as suddenly becomes white again. There is nothing just like it in any other city in the country, for there is no preparation for it; no change in the character of the houses and streets; no change, indeed, in the appearance of the people, except their color.

Negro Harlem is practically a development of the past decade, but the story behind it goes back a long way. There have always been colored people in New York. In the middle of the last century they lived in the vicinity of Lispenard, Broome and Spring Streets. When Washington Square and lower Fifth Avenue was the center of aristocratic life, the colored people, whose chief occupation was domestic service in the homes of the rich, lived in a fringe and were scattered in nests to the south, east and west of the square. As late as the '80s the major part of the colored population lived in Sullivan, Thompson, Bleecker, Grove, Minetta Lane and adjacent streets. It is curious to note that some of these nests still persist. In a number of the blocks of Greenwich Village and Little Italy may be found small groups of Negroes who have never lived in any other section of the city. By about 1890 the center of colored population had shifted to the upper Twenties and lower Thirties west of Sixth Avenue. Ten years later another considerable shift northward had been made to West Fifty-third Street.

The West Fifty-third Street settlement deserves some special mention because it ushered in a new phase of life among colored New Yorkers. Three rather well-appointed hotels were opened in the street and they quickly became the centers of a sort of fashionable life that hitherto had not existed. On Sunday evenings these hotels served dinner to music and attracted crowds of well-dressed diners. One of these hotels, The

◄ The photographs of James Van Der Zee vividly captured the Harlem Renaissance era. What impression of big city life is conveyed by this Van Der Zee photo, entitled *The Abyssinian Baptist Church* (1927)?

---

1. **Mecca** (mek′ə), a city in west Saudi Arabia; birthplace of Mohammed and spiritual center of Islam.
2. dilapidated (də lap′ə dā′tid), *adj.* fallen into ruin or disrepair.

▲ James Van Der Zee photographed his *Portrait of Couple with Raccoon Coats and Stylish Car* in 1932. What attitude toward wealth and luxury does this image convey?

Marshall, became famous as the headquarters of Negro talent. There gathered the actors, the musicians, the composers, the writers, the singers, dancers and vaudevillians. There one went to get a close-up of Williams and Walker, Cole and Johnson, Ernest Hogan, Will Marion Cook, Jim Europe, Aida Overton, and of others equally and less known. Paul Laurence Dunbar was frequently there whenever he was in New York. Numbers of those who love to shine by the light reflected from celebrities were always to be found. The first modern jazz band ever heard in New York, or, perhaps anywhere, was organized at The Marshall. It was a playing-singing-dancing orchestra, making the first dominant use of banjos, saxophones, clarinets and trap drums in combination, and was called The Memphis Students. Jim Europe was a member of that band, and out of it grew the famous Clef Club, of which he was the noted leader, and which for a long time monopolized the business of "entertaining" private parties and furnishing music for the new dance craze. Also in the Clef Club was "Buddy" Gilmore who originated trap drumming as it is now practised, and set hundreds of white men to juggling their sticks and doing acrobatic stunts while they manipulated a dozen other noise-making devices aside from their drums. A good many well-known white performers frequented The Marshall and for seven or eight years the place was one of the sights of New York.

The move to Fifty-third Street was the result of the opportunity to get into newer and better houses. About 1900 the move to Harlem began, and for the same reason. Harlem had been over-built with large, new-law apartment houses, but rapid transportation to that section was very in-adequate—the Lenox Avenue Subway had not yet been built—and landlords were finding difficulty in keeping houses on the east side of the section filled. Residents along and near Seventh Avenue were fairly well served by the Eighth Avenue Elevated. A colored man, in the real estate busi-ness at this time, Philip A. Payton, approached several of these landlords with the proposition[3] that he would fill their empty or partially empty houses with steady colored tenants. The sugges-tion was accepted, and one or two houses on One Hundred and Thirty-fourth Street east of Lenox Avenue were taken over. Gradually other houses were filled. The whites paid little attention to the movement until it began to spread west of Lenox Avenue; they then took steps to check it. They proposed through a financial organization, the Hudson Realty Company, to buy in all properties occupied by colored people and evict the tenants. The Negroes countered by similar methods. Payton formed the Afro-American Realty Com-pany, a Negro corporation organized for the pur-pose of buying and leasing houses for occupancy by colored people. Under this counter stroke the opposition subsided for several years.

But the continually increasing pressure of colored people to the west over the Lenox Avenue dead line caused the opposition to break out again, but in a new and more menacing form. Several white men undertook to organize all the white people of the community for the purpose of inducing financial institutions not to lend money or renew mortgages on properties occu-pied by colored people. In this effort they had considerable success, and created a situation which has not yet been completely overcome, a situation which is one of the hardest and most unjustifiable the Negro property owner in Harlem has to contend with. The Afro-American Realty Company was now defunct, but two or three col-ored men of means stepped into the breach. Philip A. Payton and J. C. Thomas bought two five-story apartments, dispossessed the white tenants and put in colored. J. B. Nail bought a row of five apartments and did the same thing. St. Philip's Church bought a row of thirteen apartment houses on One Hundred and Thirty-fifth Street, running from Seventh Avenue almost to Lenox.

The situation now resolved itself into an actual contest. Negroes not only continued to occupy available apartment houses, but began to purchase private dwellings between Lenox and Seventh Avenues. Then the whole movement, in the eyes of the whites, took on the aspect of an "invasion"; they became panic-stricken and began fleeing as from a plague. The presence of one colored family in a block, no mat-ter how well bred and orderly, was sufficient to precipitate[4] a flight. House after house and block after block was actually deserted. It was a great demonstration of human beings running amuck. None of them stopped to reason why they were doing it or what would happen if they didn't. The banks and lending companies holding mortgages on these deserted houses were compelled to take them over. For some time they held these houses vacant, preferring to do that and carry the charges than to rent or sell them to colored people. But values dropped and continued to drop until at the outbreak of the war in Europe property in the northern part of Harlem had reached the nadir.[5]

---

3. **proposition** (prop′ə zish′ən), *n*. what is offered to be considered; proposal.
4. **precipitate** (pri sip′ə tāt), *v*. hasten the beginning of; bring about suddenly.
5. **nadir** (nā′dər), *n*. lowest point.

In the meantime the Negro colony was becoming more stable; the churches were being moved from the lower part of the city; social and civic centers were being formed; and gradually a community was being evolved. Following the outbreak of the war in Europe Negro Harlem received a new and tremendous impetus. Because of the war thousands of aliens in the United States rushed back to their native lands to join the colors and immigration practically ceased. The result was a critical shortage in labor. This shortage was rapidly increased as the United States went more and more largely into the business of furnishing munitions and supplies to the warring countries. To help meet this shortage of common labor Negroes were brought up from the South. The government itself took the first steps, following the practice in vogue in Germany of shifting labor according to the supply and demand in various parts of the country. The example of the government was promptly taken up by the big industrial concerns, which sent hundreds, perhaps thousands, of labor agents into the South who recruited Negroes by wholesale. I was in Jacksonville, Fla., for a while at that time, and I sat one day and watched the stream of migrants passing to take the train. For hours they passed steadily, carrying flimsy suitcases, new and shiny, rusty old ones, bursting at the seams, boxes and bundles and impedimenta[6] of all sorts, including banjos, guitars, birds in cages and whatnot. Similar scenes were being enacted[7] in cities and towns all over that region. The first wave of the great exodus of Negroes from the South was on. Great numbers of these migrants headed for New York or eventually got there, and naturally the majority went up into Harlem. But the Negro population of Harlem was not swollen by migrants from the South alone; the opportunity for Negro labor exerted its pull upon the Negroes of the West Indies, and those islanders in the course of time poured into Harlem to the number of twenty-five thousand or more.

SUMMARIZE: How did World War I indirectly contribute to Harlem's population explosion?

These new-comers did not have to look for work; work looked for them, and at wages of which they had never even dreamed. And here is where the unlooked for, the unprecedented, the miraculous happened. According to all preconceived notions, these Negroes suddenly earning large sums of money for the first time in their lives should have had their heads turned; they should have squandered it in the most silly and absurd manners imaginable. Later, after the United States had entered the war and even Negroes in the South were making money fast, many stories in accord with the tradition came out of that section. There was the one about the colored man who went into a general store and on hearing a phonograph for the first time promptly ordered six of them, one for each child in the house. I shall not stop to discuss whether Negroes in the South did that sort of thing or not, but I do know that those who got to New York didn't. The Negroes of Harlem, for the greater part, worked and saved their money. Nobody knew how much they had saved until congestion made expansion necessary for tenants and ownership profitable for landlords, and they began to buy property. Persons who would never be suspected of having money bought property. The Rev. W. W. Brown, pastor of the Metropolitan Baptist Church, repeatedly made "Buy Property" the text of his sermons. A large part of his congregation carried out the injunction.[8] The church itself set an example by purchasing a magnificent brownstone church building on Seventh Avenue from a white

---

6. impedimenta (im ped/ə men/tə), *n. pl.* baggage, equipment, etc., which impedes movement or progress.
7. **enact** (en akt/), *v.* represent; act out.
8. injunction (in jungk/shən), *n.* an authoritative or emphatic order; command.

congregation. Buying property became a fever. At the height of this activity, that is, 1920–21, it was not an uncommon thing for a colored washerwoman or cook to go into a real estate office and lay down from one thousand to five thousand dollars on a house. "Pig Foot Mary" is a character in Harlem. Everybody who knows the corner of Lenox Avenue and One Hundred and Thirty-fifth Street knows "Mary" and her stand, and has been tempted by the smell of her pigsfeet, fried chicken and hot corn, even if he has not been a customer. "Mary," whose real name is Mrs. Mary Dean, bought the five-story apartment house at the corner of Seventh Avenue and One Hundred and Thirty-seventh Street at a price of $42,000. Later she sold it to the Y.W.C.A. for dormitory purposes. The Y.W.C.A. sold it recently to Adolph Howell, a leading colored undertaker, the price given being $72,000. Often companies of a half dozen men combined to buy a house—these combinations were and still are generally made up of West Indians—and would produce five or ten thousand dollars to put through the deal.

When the buying activity began to make itself felt, the lending companies that had been holding vacant the handsome dwellings on and abutting Seventh Avenue decided to put them on the market. The values on these houses had dropped to the lowest mark possible and they were put up at astonishingly low prices. Houses that had been bought at from $15,000 to $20,000 were sold at one-third those figures. They were quickly gobbled up. The Equitable Life Assurance Company held 106 model private houses that were designed by Stanford White. They are built with courts running straight through the block and closed off by wrought-iron gates. Every one of these houses was sold within eleven months at an aggregate[9] price of about two million dollars. Today they are probably worth about 100 percent more. And not only have private dwellings and similar apartments been bought but big elevator apartments have been taken over. Corporations have been organized for this

purpose. Two of these, The Antillian Realty Company, composed of West Indian Negroes, and the Sphinx Securities Company, composed of American and West Indian Negroes, represent holdings amounting to approximately $750,000. Individual Negroes and companies in the South have invested in Harlem real estate. About two years ago a Negro institution of Savannah, Ga., bought a parcel for $115,000 which it sold a month or so ago at a profit of $110,000.

I am informed by John E. Nail, a successful colored real estate dealer of Harlem and a reliable authority, that the total value of property in Harlem owned and controlled by colored people would at a conservative estimate amount to more than sixty million dollars. These figures are amazing, especially when we take into account the short time in which they have been piled up. Twenty years ago Negroes were begging for the privilege of renting a flat in Harlem. Fifteen years ago barely a half dozen colored men owned real property in all Manhattan. And down to ten years ago the amount that had been acquired in Harlem was comparatively negligible. Today Negro Harlem is practically owned by Negroes.

The question naturally arises, "Are the Negroes going to be able to hold Harlem?" If they have been steadily driven northward for the past hundred years and out of less desirable sections, can they hold this choice bit of Manhattan Island? It is hardly probable that Negroes will hold Harlem indefinitely, but when they are forced out it will not be for the same reasons that forced them out of former quarters in New York City. The situation is entirely different and without precedent. When colored people do leave Harlem, their homes, their churches, their investments and their businesses, it will be because the land has become so valuable they can no longer afford to live on it. But the date of another move northward is very far in the future.

_____

9. **aggregate** (ag′rə git), *adj.* total.

What will Harlem be and become in the meantime? Is there danger that the Negro may lose his economic status in New York and be unable to hold his property? Will Harlem become merely a famous ghetto, or will it be a center of intellectual, cultural and economic forces exerting an influence throughout the world, especially upon Negro peoples? Will it become a point of friction between the races in New York?

I think there is less danger to the Negroes of New York of losing out economically and industrially than to the Negroes of any large city in the North. In most of the big industrial centers Negroes are engaged in gang labor. They are employed by thousands in the stockyards in Chicago, by thousands in the automobile plants in Detroit; and in those cities they are likely to be the first to be let go, and in thousands, with every business depression. In New York there is hardly such a thing as gang labor among Negroes, except among the longshoremen, and it is in the longshoremen's unions, above all others, that Negroes stand on an equal footing. Employment among Negroes in New York is highly diversified;[10] in the main they are employed more as individuals than as non-integral parts of a gang. Furthermore, Harlem is gradually becoming more and more a self-supporting community. Negroes there are steadily branching out into new businesses and enterprises in which Negroes are employed. So the danger of great numbers of Negroes being thrown out of work at once, with a resulting economic crisis among them, is less in New York than in most of the large cities of the North to which Southern migrants have come.

SUMMARIZE: Why does Johnson believe that African Americans living in Harlem are in a better economic position than African Americans in other large cities?

These facts have an effect which goes beyond the economic and industrial situation. They have a direct bearing on the future character of Harlem and on the question as to whether Harlem will be a point of friction between the races in New York. It is true that Harlem is a Negro community, well defined and stable; anchored to its fixed homes, churches, institutions, business and amusement places; having its own working, business and professional classes. It is experiencing a constant growth of group consciousness and community feeling. Harlem is, therefore, in many respects, typically Negro. It has many unique characteristics. It has movement, color, gayety, singing, dancing, boisterous laughter and loud talk. One of its outstanding features is brass band parades. Hardly a Sunday passes but that there are several of these parades of which many are gorgeous with regalia and insignia. Almost any excuse will do—the death of an humble member of the Elks, the laying of a cornerstone, the "turning out" of the order of this or that. In many of these characteristics it is similar to the Italian colony. But withal, Harlem grows more metropolitan and more a part of New York all the while. Why is it then that its tendency is not to become a mere "quarter"?

I shall give three reasons that seem to me to be important in their order. First, the language of Harlem is not alien; it is not Italian or Yiddish; it is English. Harlem talks American, reads American, thinks American. Second, Harlem is not physically a "quarter." It is not a section cut off. It is merely a zone through which four main arteries of the city run. Third, the fact that there is little or no gang labor gives Harlem Negroes the opportunity for individual expansion and individual contacts with the life and spirit of New York. A thousand Negroes from Mississippi put to work as a gang in a Pittsburgh steel mill will for a long time remain a thousand Negroes from Mississippi. Under the conditions that prevail in New York they would all within six months become New Yorkers. The rapidity with which Negroes

10. **diversified** (də vėr′sə fīd), *adj.* varied.

become good New Yorkers is one of the marvels to observers.

These three reasons form a single reason why there is small probability that Harlem will ever be a point of race friction between the races in New York. One of the principal factors in the race riot in Chicago in 1919 was the fact that at that time there were 12,000 Negroes employed in gangs in the stockyards. There was considerable race feeling in Harlem at the time of the hegira[11] of white residents due to the "invasion," but that feeling, of course, is no more. Indeed, a number of the old white residents who didn't go or could not get away before the housing shortage struck New York are now living peacefully side by side with colored residents. In fact, in some cases white and colored tenants occupy apartments in the same house. Many white merchants still do business in thickest Harlem. On the whole, I know of no place in the country where the feeling between the races is so cordial[12] and at the same time so matter-of-fact and taken for granted. One of the surest safeguards against an outbreak in New York such as took place in so many Northern cities in the summer of 1919 is the large proportion of Negro police on duty in Harlem.

To my mind, Harlem is more than a Negro community; it is a large scale laboratory experiment in the race problem. The statement has often been made that if Negroes were transported to the North in large numbers the race problem with all of its acuteness and with new aspects would be transferred with them. Well, 175,000 Negroes live closely together in Harlem, in the heart of New York—75,000 more than live in any Southern city—and do so without any race friction. Nor is there any unusual record of crime. I once heard a captain of the 38th Police Precinct (the Harlem precinct) say that on the whole it was the most law-abiding precinct in the city. New York guarantees its Negro citizens the fundamental rights of American citizenship and protects them in the exercise of those rights. In

This 1927 photograph shows a policeman at the corner of Lenox Avenue and 135th Street in Harlem.

return the Negro loves New York and is proud of it, and contributes in his way to its greatness. He still meets with discriminations, but possessing the basic rights, he knows that these discriminations will be abolished.

I believe that the Negro's advantages and opportunities are greater in Harlem than in any other place in the country, and that Harlem will become the intellectual, the cultural and the financial center for Negroes of the United States, and will exert a vital influence upon all Negro peoples.

11. **hegira** (hej′ərə), *n*. departure; flight; journey.
12. **cordial** (kôr′jəl), *adj*. warm and friendly in manner.

After Reading

Making Connections

Shaping Your Response

1. You are designing a flag for the community James Weldon Johnson has described. What symbols will you use to capture the spirit of Harlem in the 1920s? Explain.

2. If someone asked you how Harlem became such an important African American community, what would you tell them in a few sentences?

Analyzing the Essay

3. What do you think was Johnson's **purpose** in writing this essay?

4. The population of Harlem grew tremendously during the 1920s. What seemed to be the main reasons people moved there?

5. What aspects of Harlem history and life seemed to interest Johnson the most? Explain your answer.

6. How would you describe the **tone** of Johnson's essay?

7. 👋 What kind of an attitude does Johnson project about being a member of his cultural **group?**

Extending the Ideas

8. With a group, make a list of the reasons why Johnson believed Harlem was a great place to live. Then make your own list of requirements for an ideal community. Are there any similarities between the two lists?

9. James Weldon Johnson was an important figure in the Harlem Renaissance. Which of the ideas in his essay do you think most appealed to the young African American writers and artists who studied his work? Explain your answer.

Literary Focus: Metaphor

Look back to the notes you made about Johnson's use of **metaphor** in his essay. Then choose one metaphor to examine more closely. On a sheet of paper, copy a metaphor from Johnson's essay that you found interesting. Then make an illustration of the literal meaning of the words. For example, at the top of page 517, Johnson says, "Buying property became a fever." To illustrate this metaphor, you might draw a line of people standing outside a real estate office with thermometers in their mouths. Then, compare the literal meaning of the words to the figurative meaning.

Vocabulary Study

dilapidated
proposition
precipitate
impedimenta
injunction
nadir
diversified
cordial
aggregate
hegira

Use the vocabulary words in the list to complete the paragraphs.

Real estate agents, writers, and others encouraged African Americans to move to Harlem in the 1910s and 20s, and the _(1)_ was tempting. While housing conditions in many urban black communities had reached the _(2)_, Harlem homes were new rather than _(3)_ and run-down. Race relations in New York City were comparatively _(4)_, although there had been a _(5)_ of white residents when African Americans began to move in.

The economic base of the community was _(6)_, due to the variety of people living there. Pastors directed parishioners to buy property, and many followed this _(7)_, so that the _(8)_ worth of African American-owned property was in the millions. In addition, a labor shortage during World War I was enough to _(9)_ the Great Migration, and thousands poured into Harlem, along with their suitcases, guitars, bird cages, and other _(10)_.

Expressing Your Ideas

Writing Choices

Writer's Notebook Update Review the paragraph that you wrote about your hometown before reading Johnson's essay. If you were to write an essay entitled "My Hometown: The Culture Capital," which aspects of your town would you write about? List them in your notebook.

The Perfect Narrator If you were to turn "Harlem: The Culture Capital" into a television documentary, whom would you choose to narrate? Write a **letter** to the narrator you've chosen, describing the documentary you want to produce. Be persuasive!

Another Option

Mapping Harlem Based on this map of Harlem, descriptions in the essay, and your own research and imagination, create an **illustrated map** of Harlem in the 1920s showing some of its major attractions. Your map should be larger and include more Harlem streets.

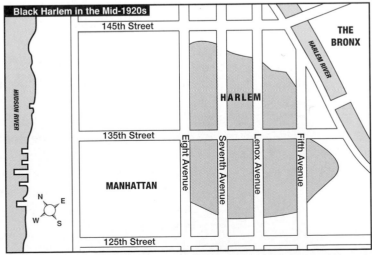

Harlem: The Culture Capital   **521**

Before Reading

A Black Man Talks of Reaping by Arna Bontemps

If We Must Die by Claude McKay

The Negro Speaks of Rivers by Langston Hughes

Harlem Wine by Countee Cullen

Youth by Langston Hughes

Ma Rainey by Sterling A. Brown

Building Background

A New Spirit In 1925, Alain Locke, an African American scholar, published a literature anthology called *The New Negro.* Many young African American writers read Locke's book and were so impressed that they followed his advice to move to Harlem. After they arrived in New York City, writers James Weldon Johnson and Claude McKay, among others, began sending letters to other black writers, encouraging *them* to move to Harlem. It was, recalls Arna Bontemps, an amazing, exhilarating period: "When acceptances from Harpers; Harcourt, Brace; Viking . . . and other front-line publishers began coming through in quick succession, the excitement among those of us who were writing was almost unbearable."

Literary Focus

Meter is the arrangement of beats, or accents, in a line of poetry. The meter of a poem is measured by **feet.** Each foot contains one accented syllable and one or more unaccented syllables. The most commonly used meter in English verse is known as **iambic.** An iamb consists of an unaccented syllable followed by an accented syllable /˘ ′/, as in the word *delight*. Claude McKay uses **iambic** meter in "If We Must Die":

> If we / must die, / O let / us no / bly die /
>
> So that / our pre / cious blood / may not / be shed /

Begin your study of meter by reading McKay's "If We Must Die" aloud. Then, in your notebook, copy two lines from the poem, marking the unaccented and accented syllables.

Writer's Notebook

A Bit of Style Each of the poets you're about to read has a distinctive poetic style. As you read the poems, keep track of any examples of poetic devices that you find. Before you begin, you may want to review literary devices such as *rhyme, repetition, alliteration,* and *onomatopoeia* in the Glossary of Literary Terms in the back of this book.

Arna Bontemps
1902–1973

Arna Bontemps once described the time he spent in Harlem as his "golden years"—an exciting time of house parties, pig's knuckles, bathtub gin, and above all else, excellent conversation. After writing his novel, *God Sends Sunday,* Bontemps left New York to pursue a teaching career. He spent his later years as Head Librarian and Director of University Relations at Fisk University.

Claude McKay
1889–1948

Claude McKay was born in Jamaica, and emigrated to the United States in 1912. His novel *Home to Harlem* was perhaps the first American best-selling novel by a black writer. McKay wrote with nostalgia for Jamaica, and about city life and social protest. His poem "If We Must Die" quickly became a rallying cry for change.

Langston Hughes
1902–1967

In 1925, while working at a hotel in Washington, D.C., Langston Hughes began to publish his poems, and eventually moved to Harlem. Over the next forty years, Hughes wrote a staggering amount of verse and traveled the United States and abroad giving public readings of his poetry. Because he was considered one of the most talented poets of the 1920s and 1930s, Hughes was often called the "poet laureate" of Harlem.

Countee Cullen
1903–1946

Countee Cullen was a novelist, essayist, and much-loved poet of the Harlem Renaissance. Cullen strongly opposed the belief that African American writers should limit themselves to African American themes, yet in much of his poetry he explores what he saw as the beauty, tenderness, and joy of African American life in Harlem.

Sterling A. Brown
1901–1989

Sterling A. Brown was an influential scholar of African American writing, as well as a prolific poet. As a scholar, Brown had two main interests: African American stereotypes in literature, and the African American folk tale tradition. For his poem "Ma Rainey," Brown used his knowledge of folklore to present a unique portrait of African Americans living in the rural South.

A BLACK MAN TALKS OF REAPING

Arna Bontemps

I have sown beside all waters in my day.
I planted deep, within my heart the fear
That wind or fowl would take the grain away.
I planted safe against this stark, lean year.

5 I scattered seed enough to plant the land
In rows from Canada to Mexico
But for my reaping only what the hand
Can hold at once is all that I can show.

Yet what I sowed and what the orchard yields
10 My brother's sons are gathering stalk and root,
Small wonder then my children glean[1] in fields
They have not sown, and feed on bitter fruit.

---

1. **glean** (glēn), *v.* gather (grain) left on a field by reapers.

IF WE MUST DIE

Claude McKay

If we must die, let it not be like hogs
Hunted and penned in an inglorious spot,
While round us bark the mad and hungry dogs,
Making their mock at our accursed[1] lot.
5   If we must die, O let us nobly die,
So that our precious blood may not be shed
In vain; then even the monsters we defy
Shall be constrained[2] to honor us though dead!
O kinsmen! we must meet the common foe!
10   Though far outnumbered let us show us brave,
And for their thousand blows deal one
        deathblow!
What though before us lies the open grave?
Like men we'll face the murderous, cowardly
        pack,
Pressed to the wall, dying, but fighting back!

This painting by Jacob Lawrence, panel no. 5 (1940–41) in his *Migration of the Negro* series, depicts one of the negative affects of cramped urban life. Many African Americans who moved north contracted tuberculosis. How would you compare the two treatments of death in this painting and in Claude McKay's poem?

---

1. **accursed** (ə kėr′sid), *adj.* hateful.
2. **constrain** (kən strān), *v.* force.

The Negro Speaks of Rivers

Langston Hughes

I've known rivers:
I've known rivers ancient as the world and older than
    the flow of human blood in human veins.

My soul has grown deep like the rivers.

5 I bathed in the Euphrates[1] when dawns were young.
I built my hut near the Congo and it lulled me to sleep.
I looked upon the Nile and raised the pyramids above it.
I heard the singing of the Mississippi when Abe Lincoln
    went down to New Orleans, and I've seen its muddy
10   bosom turn all golden in the sunset.

I've known rivers:
Ancient, dusky[2] rivers.

My soul has grown deep like the rivers.

---

1. **Euphrates** (yü frā′tēz), a river in southwest Asia.
   The Euphrates River flows through the area
   many believe was the birthplace or "cradle" of
   civilization.
2. dusky (dus′kē), *adj.* somewhat dark; dark-colored.

Harlem Wine

Countee Cullen

This is not water running here,
These thick rebellious streams
That hurtle[1] flesh and bone past fear
Down alleyways of dreams.

5 This is a wine that must flow on
Not caring how or where,
So it has ways to flow upon
Where song is in the air.

So it can woo an artful flute
10 With loose, elastic lips,
Its measurement of joy compute
With blithe,[2] ecstatic hips.

---

1. hurtle (hėr′tl), *v.* dash or drive
   violently.
2. blithe (blīᴛн), *adj.* happy; joyous.

Rise shine for thy light has come!

Youth

Langston Hughes

We have tomorrow
Bright before us
Like a flame.

Yesterday
5 A night-gone thing,
A sun-down name.

And dawn-today
Broad arch above the road
    we came.

We march!

▲ Describe the themes of this Aaron Douglas painting, *Rise Shine for Thy Light Has Come* (1932), and of Langston Hughes's poem, "Youth." Are they the same? Why or why not?

Ma Rainey

Sterling Brown

I

When Ma Rainey[1]
Comes to town,
Folks from anyplace
Miles aroun',
5 From Cape Girardeau,
Poplar Bluff,
Flocks in to hear
Ma do her stuff;
Comes flivverin'[2] in,
10 Or ridin' mules,
Or packed in trains,
Picknickin' fools. . . .
That's what it's like,
Fo' miles on down,
15 To New Orleans delta
An' Mobile town,
When Ma hits
Anywheres aroun'.

---

1. **Ma Rainey.** Gertrude "Ma" Rainey (1866–1939) was a former vaudeville entertainer who sang "weird" and "strange" music, which she eventually helped propel into national prominence as the classic blues.
2. **flivverin',** driving a flivver, slang for a small, cheap automobile, especially one that is no longer new.

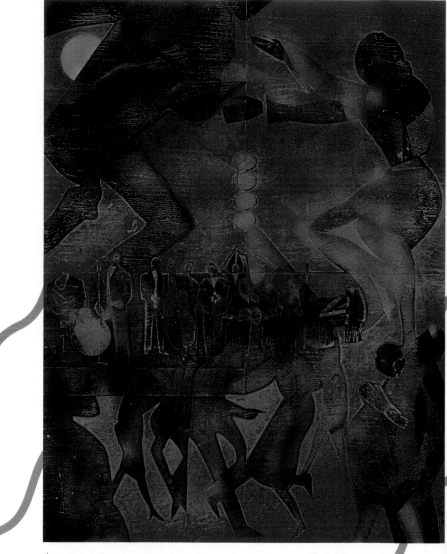

▲ Does this 1975 Romare Bearden work, *At the Savoy,* reflect the atmosphere described in Sterling Brown's poem, "Ma Rainey"? Explain your answer.

II

Dey comes to hear Ma Rainey from de little river settlements,
20 From blackbottom cornrows and from lumber camps;
Dey stumble in de hall, jes a-laughin' an' a-cacklin',
Cheerin' lak roarin' water, lak wind in river swamps.

An' some jokers keeps deir laughs a-goin' in de crowded aisles,
An' some folks sits dere waitin' wid deir aches an' miseries,
25 Till Ma comes out before dem, a-smilin' gold-toofed smiles
An' Long Boy ripples minors on de black an' yellow keys.

III

O Ma Rainey,
Sing yo' song;
Now you's back
30 Whah you belong,
Git way inside us,
Keep us strong. . . .
O Ma Rainey,
Li'l an' low;
35 Sing us 'bout de hard luck
Roun' our do';
Sing us 'bout de lonesome road
We mus' go. . . .

IV

I talked to a fellow, an' the fellow say,
40 "She jes' catch hold of us, somekindaway.
She sang Backwater Blues one day:

'It rained fo' days an' de skies was dark as night,
Trouble taken place in de lowlands at night.

'Thundered an' lightened an' the storm begin to roll
45 *Thousan's of people ain't got no place to go.*

'Den I went an' stood upon some high ol' lonesome hill
An' looked down on the place where I used to live.'

An' den de folks, dey natchally bowed dey heads an' cried,
Bowed dey heavy heads, shet dey moufs up tight an' cried,
50 An' Ma lef' de stage, an' followed some de folks outside."

Dere wasn't much more de fellow say:
She jes' gits hold of us dataway.

After Reading

Making Connections

Shaping Your Response

1. What musical piece would you choose to accompany an oral reading of each of these poems? Explain your choices.

2. Based on the poems you've read, which of the poets would you most want to invite to a poetry reading to be held in your school? Explain your choice.

Analyzing the Poems

3. What does the sowing and reaping **symbolize** in Bontemps's poem?

4. What emotional effect do you think McKay is trying to achieve with his poem?

5. Explain the **comparison** that Hughes makes between rivers and African heritage in "The Negro Speaks of Rivers."

6. How would you describe the **tone** of "Youth"?

7. What do you think the wine **symbolizes** in "Harlem Wine"?

8. Ma Rainey was one of the first blues singers to achieve national popularity. Based on the poem, how would you explain her popularity?

9. 👣 What kinds of shared **group** experiences do these poems both commemorate and celebrate?

Extending the Ideas

10. Which of the poems reminds you of a feeling or experience you have had? Explain your answer.

11. Compare Cullen's view of Harlem in "Harlem Wine" to Johnson's in "Harlem: The Culture Capital." Do they both see Harlem in the same way? Support your answer with examples from the literature.

Literary Focus: Meter

The **meter** of a poem can be regular or irregular. If the meter is regular, it follows a predictable pattern: / ˘ // ˘ //, for example. If the meter is irregular, its pattern is not as predictable. The meter of a poem will affect the poem's **tone.** A brisk meter can create a lighthearted, happy tone; a slow meter can create a more serious tone. Think again about the poems you've just read and then answer these questions about meter.

- Is the meter of "If We Must Die" regular or irregular?

- How does the meter of the poem contribute to its **tone?**

- How would you describe the meter of "The Negro Speaks of Rivers"? How is the meter in Hughes's poem different from the meter in McKay's poem?

Vocabulary Study

Choose the letter of the word that is the best synonym for each numbered vocabulary word. Use your Glossary if necessary.

blithe
constrain
hurtle
dusky
accursed

1. blithe   **a.** tired   **b.** annoyed   **c.** happy   **d.** nervous

2. constrain   **a.** choose   **b.** force   **c.** restrain   **d.** separate

3. hurtle   **a.** dash   **b.** fall   **c.** dive   **d.** carry

4. dusky   **a.** foggy   **b.** dark   **c.** shady   **d.** musty

5. accursed   **a.** enchanted   **b.** pledged   **c.** spoken   **d.** hateful

Expressing Your Ideas

Writing Choices

Writer's Notebook Update Using a poem you've just read as a model, try writing a few lines of poetry. Before you begin, decide on the subject of your poem. Then, review the notes you kept about poetic devices as you were reading the selections. Use at least two poetic devices in your poem.

Hidden Meaning What were some of the major themes, or main ideas, of the Harlem Renaissance? Copy the chart below on a piece of paper. Then, working in small groups, decide on a theme for each of the poems listed and then briefly state the theme on your chart. When you've finished, look carefully at your chart. What themes do some or all of these poems have in common? In a **paragraph,** explain some of the themes of the Harlem Renaissance.

Poem	Theme
A Black Man Talks of Reaping	
If We Must Die	
The Negro Speaks of Rivers	
Youth	
Harlem Wine	
Ma Rainey	

Other Options

The Birth of the Blues During the 1920s blues music began to gain national attention. Working with a small group, plan a 1920s **Blues Fest,** playing recordings for your class and telling about the singers.

From Poem to Art Use some form of **visual art** to capture the subject matter, theme, and emotions of one of the poems you've just read. You may want to draw a picture, or create a sculpture, or even choreograph a dance.

Becoming an Expert Prepare an **oral presentation** about the life and works of one of the poets you've just read. Begin your presentation with some biographical information about the poet. Discuss some interesting details about the poet's life, as well as the poet's role in the Harlem Renaissance. Then present some of the poet's major works, offering insight about recurring themes or subject matter.

Before Reading

How It Feels to Be Colored Me

by Zora Neale Hurston

Zora Neale Hurston
1891–1960

As a young girl growing up in southern Florida, Zora Neale Hurston loved to sit on the porch and listen in on adult "lying sessions" (daily exchanges of folk tales). Many years later, she used these stories in her own writing. Unlike other writers of the Harlem Renaissance, Hurston deliberately ignored issues of racism and discrimination in her writing. Instead, she chose to use her essays, short stories, and novels as a means of celebrating the vibrancy of African American life. Hurston spent the late 1920s and 1930s as an anthropologist, collecting and examining southern African American dialect, religious rituals, and folk tales.

Building Background

Hurston and the Harlem Renaissance At age thirty, Hurston moved to New York and became caught up in the Harlem Renaissance. She befriended other writers such as Claude McKay, Jean Toomer, and Langston Hughes and collaborated with them on various literary publications. Although her collections of folk tales were well-received by the public, she was criticized for failing to use her writing as a means of speaking out against racism and economic exploitation. Later, poet and critic Sterling Brown said that her writing about the rural South should have included, at the very least, "a few slave anecdotes that turn the tables on old marster" or "a bit of grumbling about hard work." This type of complaint about her writing made it difficult for Hurston to find publishers. By the time she died in 1960, her writing was essentially forgotten. In the 1970s, however, author Alice Walker rediscovered Hurston's works. Since Walker's rediscovery, Hurston's works have become hugely popular.

Literary Focus

Tone is the author's attitude toward his or her subject and audience. The tone of a piece of writing may be revealed by the author's word choice, the details included, or the arrangement of ideas and descriptions. As you read "How It Feels to Be Colored Me," make a few notes about Hurston's tone.

Writer's Notebook

Self-Esteem How necessary is self-esteem? Why is it important to feel good about yourself? Copy the web at the right in your log. At the end of each spoke, write an adjective that might describe a person who has high self-esteem. An example has been done for you.

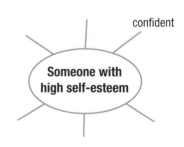

confident

Someone with high self-esteem

HOW IT FEELS TO BE COLORED ME

Zora Neale Hurston

I am colored but I offer nothing in the way of extenuating[1] circumstances except the fact that I am the only Negro in the United States whose grandfather on my mother's side was *not* an Indian chief.

I remember the very day that I became colored. Up to my thirteenth year I lived in the little Negro town of Eatonville, Florida. It is exclusively a colored town. The only white people I knew passed through going to or coming from Orlando. The native whites rode dusty horses, the Northern tourists chugged down the sandy village road in automobiles. The town knew the Southerners and never stopped chewing[2] when they passed. But the Northerners were something else again. They were peered at cautiously from behind curtains by the timid. The more venturesome[3] would come out on the porch to watch them go past and got just as much pleasure out of the tourists as the tourists got out of the village.

The front porch might seem a daring place for the rest of the town, but it was a gallery seat for me. My favorite place was atop the gate-post. Proscenium box[4] for a born first-nighter. Not only did I enjoy the show, but I didn't mind the actors knowing that I liked it. I usually spoke to them in passing. I'd wave at them and when they returned my salute, I would say something like this: "Howdy-do-well-I-thank-you-where-you-goin'?" Usually the automobile or the horse paused at this, and after a queer exchange of compliments, I would probably "go a piece of the way" with them, as we say in farthest Florida. If one of my family happened to come to the front in time to see me, of course negotiations would be rudely broken off. But even so, it is clear that I was the first

---

1. **extenuating** (ek sten′yü ā′ting), *adj.* making the seriousness of a fault seem less; partially excusing.
2. **chewing,** a reference to chewing sugar cane.
3. **venturesome** (ven′chər səm), *adj.* rash; daring.
4. **proscenium** (pro sē′nē əm) **box,** *n.* seating area in a theater directly in front of the stage.

"welcome-to-our-state" Floridian, and I hope the Miami Chamber of Commerce will please take notice.

During this period, white people differed from colored to me only in that they rode through town and never lived there. They liked to hear me "speak pieces" and sing and wanted to see me dance the parse-me-la, and gave me generously of their small silver for doing these things, which seemed strange to me for I wanted to do them so much that I needed bribing to stop. Only they didn't know it. The colored people gave me no dimes. They deplored any joyful tendencies in me, but I was their Zora neverthe-less. I belonged to them, to the nearby hotels, to the county—everybody's Zora.

But changes came in the family when I was thirteen, and I was sent to school in Jacksonville. I left Eatonville, the town of the oleanders, as Zora. When I disembarked from the river-boat at Jacksonville, she was no more. It seemed that I had suffered a sea-change. I was not Zora of Orange County any more, I was now a little colored girl. I found out in certain ways. In my heart as well as in the mirror, I became a fast brown—warranted not to rub or run.

But I am not tragically colored. There is no great sorrow dammed up in my soul, nor lurk-ing behind my eyes. I do not mind at all. I do not belong to the sobbing school of Negrohood who hold that nature has somehow given them a lowdown dirty deal and whose feelings are all hurt by it. Even in the helter-skelter skirmish[5] that is my life, I have seen that the world is to the strong regardless of a little pigmentation more or less. No, I do not weep at the world—I am too busy sharpening my oyster knife.[6]

Someone is always at my elbow reminding me that I am the granddaughter of slaves. It fails to register depression with me. Slavery is sixty years in the past. The operation was successful and the patient is doing well, thank you. The terrible struggle that made me an American out of a potential slave said "On

Ruby Green was a popular singer and nightclub entertainer in the late 1920s. What qualities does Green in James Chapin's 1928 painting, *Ruby Green Singing,* seem to have in common with Zora Neale Hurston in "How it Feels to Be Colored Me"? ➤

the line!" The Reconstruction said "Get set!"; and the generation before said "Go!" I am off to a flying start and I must not halt in the stretch to look behind and weep. Slavery is the price I paid for civilization, and the choice was not with me. It is a bully adventure and worth all that I have paid through my ancestors for it. No one on earth ever had a greater chance for glory. The world to be won and nothing to be lost. It is thrilling to think—to know that for any act of mine, I shall get twice as much praise and twice as much blame. It is quite exciting to hold the center of the national stage, with the spectators not knowing whether to laugh or to weep.

The position of my white neighbor is much more difficult. No brown specter pulls up a chair beside me when I sit down to eat. No dark ghost thrusts its leg against mine in bed. The game of keeping what one has is never so excit-ing as the game of getting.

I do not always feel colored. Even now I often achieve the unconscious Zora of Eatonville before the Hegira. I feel most colored when I am thrown against a sharp white background.

For instance at Barnard.[7] "Beside the waters of the Hudson"[8] I feel my race. Among the thou-sand white persons, I am a dark rock surged upon, and overswept, but through it all, I remain myself. When covered by the waters, I am; and the ebb but reveals me again.

---

5. skirmish (skėr′mish), *n.* minor conflict or contest.
6. **sharpening my oyster knife,** an allusion to the expression "the world is my oyster."
7. **Barnard,** New York college attended by Hurston.
8. **Beside the waters of the Hudson,** an allusion to the Bible's Psalm 137: "by the waters of Babylon." In Psalm 137, the Jewish people who were forced to leave Jerusalem mourn the loss of their beloved home.

Sometimes it is the other way around. A white person is set down in our midst, but the contrast is just as sharp for me. For instance, when I sit in the drafty basement that is The New World Cabaret with a white person, my color comes. We enter chatting about any little nothing that we have in common and are seated by the jazz waiters. In the abrupt way that jazz orchestras have, this one plunges into a number. It loses no time in circumlocutions, but gets right down to business. It constricts the thorax and splits the heart with its tempo and narcotic harmonies. This orchestra grows rambunctious,[9] rears on its hind legs and attacks the tonal veil with primitive fury, rending it, clawing it until it breaks through to the jungle beyond. I follow those heathen—follow them exultingly.[10] I dance wildly inside myself; I yell within, I whoop; I shake my assegai[11] above my head, I hurl it true to the mark *yeeeeooww!* I am in the jungle and living in the jungle way. My face is painted red and yellow and my body is painted blue. My pulse is throbbing like a war drum. I want to slaughter something—give pain, give death to what, I do not know. But the piece ends. The men of the orchestra wipe their lips and rest their fingers. I creep back slowly to the veneer we call civilization with the last tone and find the white friend sitting motionless in his seat, smoking calmly.

"Good music they have here," he remarks, drumming the table with his fingertips.

Music. The great blobs of red and purple emotion have not touched him. He has only heard what I felt. He is far away and I see him but dimly across the ocean and the continent that have fallen between us. He is so pale in his whiteness then and I am *so* colored.

t certain times I have no race, I am *me.* When I set my hat at a certain angle and saunter down Seventh Avenue, Harlem City, feeling as snooty as the lions in front of the Forty-second Street Library, for instance. So far

as my feelings are concerned, Peggy Hopkins Joyce[12] on the Boule Mich[13] with her gorgeous raiment, stately carriage, knees knocking together in a most aristocratic manner, has nothing on me. The cosmic Zora emerges. I belong to no race and no time. I am the eternal feminine with its string of beads.

I have no separate feeling about being an American citizen and colored. I am merely a fragment of the Great Soul that surges within the boundaries. My country, right or wrong.

Sometimes, I feel discriminated against, but it does not make me angry. It merely astonishes me. How *can* any deny themselves the pleasure of my company? It's beyond me.

But in the main, I feel like a brown bag of miscellany propped against a wall. Against a wall in company with other bags, white, red, and yellow. Pour out the contents, and there is discovered a jumble of small things priceless and worthless. A first-water diamond, an empty spool, bits of broken glass, lengths of string, a key to a door long since crumbled away, a rusty knife-blade, old shoes saved for a road that never was and never will be, a nail bent under the weight of things too heavy for any nail, a dried flower or two still a little fragrant. In your hand is the brown bag. On the ground before you is the jumble it held—so much like the jumble in the bags, could they be emptied, that all might be dumped in a single heap and the bags refilled without altering the content of any greatly. A bit of colored glass more or less would not matter. Perhaps that is how the Great Stuffer of bags filled them in the first place—who knows?

---

9. rambunctious (ram bungk′shəs), *adj.* wild and noisy.
10. exultingly (eg zult′ing lē), *adv.* happily; joyfully.
11. **assegai** (as′ə gī), *n.* short, broad-bladed spear of the Zulu people of southern Africa.
12. **Peggy Hopkins Joyce,** a famous American beauty of the 1920s.
13. **Boule Mich** (būl mēsh), a fashionable street in Paris.

After Reading

Making Connections

Shaping Your Response

1. If you were going to describe Zora Neale Hurston to a friend, what five adjectives would you use? Explain your choices.

Analyzing the Essay

2. What would you say is the **theme,** or main idea, of "How It Feels to Be Colored Me"? Write one sentence that summarizes Hurston's theme.

3. Reread the last paragraph of the essay. What point is Hurston making about people of different races through her **metaphor?**

4. How would you describe the **tone** of the essay?

5. ☝ Do you think Hurston identifies herself more strongly as an individual, or as a member of a **group?** Explain your answer.

Extending the Ideas

6. Based on her essay, what advice do you think Hurston might have for people living in today's society?

Vocabulary Study

Choose the word in the column on the right that most closely resembles the meaning of the word in the left column.

extenuating
venturesome
skirmish
exultingly
rambunctious

1. extenuating   a. joyfully
2. venturesome   b. rowdy
3. skirmish   c. excusing
4. exultingly   d. daring
5. rambunctious   e. conflict

Expressing Your Ideas

Writing Choices

Writer's Notebook Update Would you say Hurston has high self-esteem? Write a paragraph that discusses her sense of self.

How It Feels . . . Write a **paragraph** about yourself expressing "How It Feels to Be _____ Me." Fill in the blank with any adjective you wish.

Another Option

My Bag Apply Hurston's "brown bag" metaphor to your own life. What would the contents of your bag be like? Make a list of the items in your bag. Then, using a combination of your own drawings and images you've cut from newspapers and magazines, create a **collage** that reveals the contents of your bag.

An Artistic

Fine Art Connection

The extraordinary creativity of the writers and musicians associated with the Harlem Renaissance has tended to get more attention than the achievements of the many fine African American painters and sculptors of the period. Works by a few of the most important artists appear on these pages.

Archibald J. Motley, Jr.
Black Belt (1934)
The poet Countee Cullen observed that each artist had to "find his treasure where his heart lies." In his paintings, Motley chose to depict the vivid night life of big-city African American neighborhoods. What different light sources has the painter used to dramatize this scene?

538

Awakening

Meta Warrick Fuller
Talking Skull (1937)
Fuller emphasized African
cultural elements in her work.
What might this sculpture
be saying about the
relationship between the
individual and tradition?

Augusta Savage
Gamin (1929)
Using as a model a child she encountered near her studio, Savage created a lively, wistful portrait of a street urchin. What do you think is the principal emotional quality the sculptor has given to this child's face?

Palmer Hayden
Fétiche et Fleurs (1932–33)
Hayden incorporated examples of traditional African sculpture and weaving in this still life. What impact do these items have in the setting in which he has placed them?

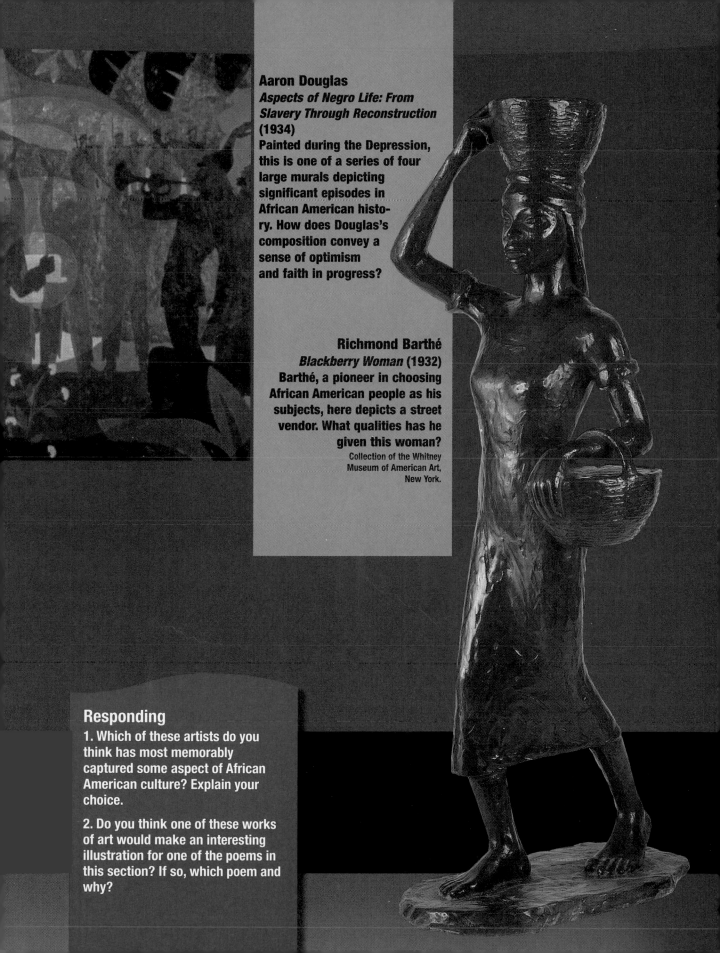

Aaron Douglas
Aspects of Negro Life: From Slavery Through Reconstruction (1934)
Painted during the Depression, this is one of a series of four large murals depicting significant episodes in African American history. How does Douglas's composition convey a sense of optimism and faith in progress?

Richmond Barthé
Blackberry Woman (1932)
Barthé, a pioneer in choosing African American people as his subjects, here depicts a street vendor. What qualities has he given this woman?
Collection of the Whitney Museum of American Art, New York.

Responding

1. Which of these artists do you think has most memorably captured some aspect of African American culture? Explain your choice.

2. Do you think one of these works of art would make an interesting illustration for one of the poems in this section? If so, which poem and why?

Career Connection

After the stock market crash of 1929, Harlem experienced many years of economic decline, and lost much of its reputation as a vibrant cultural center. Tour director and educator Larcelia Kebe is working to transform Harlem's image and rejuvenate the community.

Tour Director Shows Off

Harlem Treasures

In the fall of 1982 I started Harlem, Your Way! Tours Unlimited Incorporated. I was motivated to start my business because, first, I wanted to participate in the new Harlem Renaissance. Also, as an educator and administrator—I'm an elementary school principal—I looked at the very negative press Harlem had received for decades and I wanted to do something positive to dispel some of those negative images. Third, I wanted to let people know of the treasures here in Harlem.

We specialize in walking tours so that people can really see the community. A popular tour for New Yorkers is the Brownstone Tour and Workshop. I had bought and started restoring a brownstone myself in 1982. I did all the wrong things. So I take people on a tour of four or five restored brownstones in the neighborhood, and the owners talk about their homes. Afterwards we come back to my house for a workshop. Building inspectors, attorneys, architects, and designers speak. The workshops put participants closer to their dream of owning a brownstone.

Most of my clients on other kinds of tours are Europeans. Gospel tours are popular with them. They've heard of the music and want to listen to it and experience the worship service themselves. Services in European churches are not so participatory. But at a service at a Baptist church here in Harlem, the people clap, shout, talk, sing— they feel the spirit and participate.

We have a lot of history here. We have the Jumel mansion on a tour. General Washington conducted some battles of the Revolutionary War from there. The mansion is important to Harlem's history, but the furnishings are being removed and taken to museums. This is happening to several of our historical sites. The community is fighting against this.

I give a Black History Walking Tour of Harlem in February. Another special tour is A Look at the World of Malcolm X.

I feel very strongly about circulating money in the community. My guides are people of color from the community. We try to stop at local restaurants.

Many of us are hopeful about the future of Harlem. Many positive things are happening.

Larcelia Kebe

Responding

1. Why do you suppose it is so important to Larcelia Kebe to hire guides from the community and stop at local restaurants?

2. Imagine you are going to take a Harlem, Your Way! tour. What kind of tour do you want to take, and what do you want to see and do?

Writing Workshop

Calling All Artists

Assignment During the Harlem Renaissance, Harlem artists wrote to encourage other talented artists from around the country to come join them. Now put yourself in the position of one of these Harlem artists.

WRITER'S BLUEPRINT

Product	A persuasive letter
Purpose	To encourage another artist to come to Harlem
Audience	A person living during the Harlem Renaissance who is skilled in one of the fine arts
Specs	As the writer of an effective letter, you should:

❏ Choose an African-American artist (painter, sculptor, writer, dancer, musician, etc.) who actually lived in Harlem during the Harlem Renaissance. You will write your letter as if you were this artist.

❏ Choose another artist living elsewhere to write to: a well-known artist who actually lived during this era, or a fictitious African-American artist you create.

❏ Compose a letter in which you try to persuade this artist to move to Harlem. Write in a tone suitable to your reader, a fellow artist you have met once, briefly. Emphasize the advantages of Harlem's thriving arts community, economic opportunities, exciting night life, and other advantages. Use examples of real people, places, and activities to strengthen your case, including quotations from the literature.

❏ Anticipate reasons why someone might not want to move to Harlem, and counter them with logical arguments.

❏ Close by stressing what a welcome addition this artist would be to the arts community of Harlem.

❏ Follow the rules of grammar, usage, spelling, and mechanics. Avoid confusing adjectives with adverbs.

PREWRITING

Review the literature to find at least six reasons, along with quotes to back them up, that you could use to convince an artist to move to Harlem during the Harlem Renaissance. Gather more background information from other sources, including history books, documentary films, and artists' biographies. Record the information in a chart like this.

Reasons To Move	Quote (Source)
Harlem most advantageous place for Negroes in the whole country	". . .the Negro's advantages and opportunities are greater in Harlem than in any other place in the country, . . ." ("Harlem: The Cultural Capital")

LITERARY SOURCE
"I believe that the Negro's advantages and opportunities are greater in Harlem and that Harlem will become the intellectual, the cultural and the financial center for Negroes of the United States. . . ."
from "Harlem: The Cultural Capital" by James Weldon Johnson

Anticipate possible objections that your reader might raise about leaving home and moving to Harlem. List two or three objections along with a counterargument that addresses each one.

Choose a real artist whose role you will play as the letter writer. Then choose an artist to be the recipient of your letter. This could be either a real person or a character you make up. Review your chart for ideas. Gather more information on this artist from writings by and about him or her.

OR . . .
Before you make notes, act out a telephone conversation in which you try to convince another artist (played by a partner) to move to Harlem.

Plan your letter by making notes in an outline like the one shown. Use the standard form for a friendly letter, as shown on in the Language and Grammar Handbook at the end of this text.

- **Introduction**
  Who you are
  Why you are writing
- **First reason to move to Harlem**
  Quotes or examples from the literature
- **Second reason to move to Harlem**
  and so on . . .
- **Possible objections and counterarguments**
- **Conclusion**
  Why this artist would be a welcome addition to the Harlem arts community

2 DRAFTING

Before you draft, review your prewriting notes and writing plan, as well as the Writer's Blueprint.

As you draft, keep your plan and the Writer's Blueprint at hand. Here are some tips to help you get started.

- Open with a dramatic description of a Harlem street scene. Imagine that you are there in Harlem. What do you see? How do you feel? Try to convey your enthusiasm to your reader with vivid descriptions.

- Open with a friendly greeting that establishes a warm but respectful tone. (For more information on establishing an appropriate tone, see the Revising Strategy in Step 3 of this lesson.)

3 REVISING

Exchange drafts with a partner. Taking the role of the artist who received your partner's letter, write back:

> Dear ____,
>
> Your letter did/did not convince me to come to Harlem because ____.
>
> The best reason you gave was ____.
>
> You anticipated that I would object to moving to Harlem because ____. However, you overcame the objection by saying ____.
>
> I thought your tone was
> just right   too formal   too informal
>
> Sincerely,

Revising Strategy

Using Appropriate Tone

As you reread your letter, consider how well its tone suits your audience and purpose. Aim to be enthusiastic and friendly, but not be too informal. These examples show how you can modify tone through word choice and sentence structure.

INAPPROPRIATE: bossy, disrespectful
Hey, you have <u>got</u> to head to Harlem and check out the art scene here . . .

INAPPROPRIATE: formal, pretentious
It is my pleasure to acquaint you with the advantages inherent in the environs of our fair city . . .

APPROPRIATE: warm, but respectful
I would like to invite you to join our thriving arts community here in Harlem . . .

Notice how the writer of the paragraph below revised her writing to make it more respectful.

> ○   *I feel that if you and your wife take the time to consider Harlem's* ᴿ
>   ∧ ~~Now that you've heard what I have to say, you've just got to~~
> *many advantages, you'll find yourself heading our way.*
> ~~head north and join us. Any other decision would be ridiculous!~~ ᵍ
>
> ○   Speaking from personal experience, I can tell you that Harlem is an
>
>   incredible place to live. If I can provide any more information, just
>
> ○   let me know. Hope to hear from you soon!

4 EDITING

Ask a partner to review your revised draft before you edit. When you edit, watch for errors in grammar, usage, spelling, and mechanics. Make sure you haven't confused adjectives and adverbs.

Editing Strategy

Using Adjectives and Adverbs Correctly

Remember that adjectives modify nouns and that adverbs modify verbs, adjectives, and other adverbs. If you're unsure whether to use an adjective or an adverb, look at the word being modified.

FOR REFERENCE
For more information on adjectives and adverbs, see the Language and Grammar Handbook at the back of this text.

Don't write:	You could <u>live</u> quite <u>happy</u> here.
Write:	You could <u>live</u> quite <u>happily</u> here.
Don't write:	The <u>bakeries</u> down the street smell <u>deliciously</u>.
Write:	The <u>bakeries</u> down the street smell <u>delicious</u>.
Don't write:	The artists here are <u>real supportive</u>.
Write:	The artists here are <u>really supportive</u>.

PRESENTING

Consider these ideas for presenting your letter:

• Read your letters to each other in a small group and discuss reasons you found most persuasive and why.

• Design a poster that incorporates ideas from your letter.

LOOKING BACK

Self-evaluate. Look back at the Writer's Blueprint and give yourself a score on each item, from 6 (superior) to 1 (inadequate).

Reflect. Think about what you learned from writing your letter as you write answers to these questions:

✔ What are some persuasive techniques that you used in this assignment that you might use in your personal life?

✔ Do you think you would have liked living in Harlem during this period if you had been an African-American artist? Why or why not?

For Your Working Portfolio Add your persuasive letter and your reflection responses to your working portfolio.

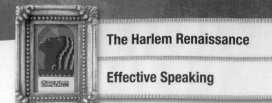
Beyond Print

Speaking Your Mind

In this Harlem Renaissance section you've seen the ideas of some of the most famous African Americans of the time expressed in the form of essays, poetry, and art. Another important way to communicate ideas is to give a speech. When giving a speech, the following strategies can help you capture and keep your audience's attention:

Rehearse Practice your speech out loud more than once. Not only does practice help you become more familiar with your material, it lets you try out different gestures and different kinds of vocal emphasis.

Get organized If you spend the first minute or so shuffling your notes, your audience may get bored and stop paying attention. Get everything in order before you walk to the front of the classroom or the stage.

Stand up straight Good posture actually helps you project your voice better. Stand on both feet so that you are balanced. If there is a desk or podium you may grasp it—lightly—but *don't* lean your weight on it.

Look at your audience Talk to your audience, not to your notes, the podium, or the floor. Pick one person and direct a sentence or two right at her or him; then pick another and another, and so on.

Speak loudly and clearly Your speech is worthless if your audience can't hear you. Try to project your voice to the back wall of the room.

Avoid meaningless vocalisms It's tempting to fill in moments of silence with *Ummm* or *Uhhh,* which may be distracting to an audience. You may not be able to avoid these altogether, but try.

Make simple, meaningful gestures While making some gestures is preferable to standing stock still, keep your gestures simple and natural.

Activity Option

Sharing Your Thoughts Choose one of the essays, poems, or artworks from this Harlem Renaissance section to react to in a five-minute speech. Explain why you like or dislike the work, what you think the artist's message is, and, if appropriate, whether you agree with the artist. Use the strategies listed above.

Multicultural Connections

Individuality

Part One: Beyond the Limits The women in this literature convey through their actions the importance of being able to express one's individuality, whether the surrounding community or culture supports such expression or not. Mrs. Mallard in "The Story of an Hour" and Mrs. Wright in *Trifles* are victims of suppressed individuality. Sarah in "The Revolt of 'Mother'" finally takes matters into her own hands after years of suppressing her own thoughts and desires, and Ida B. Wells stands up for what she believes is right even when everyone around her seems to think she's wrong.

■ Which of these women do you think is most effective in coping with forces that suppress individuality? The least effective?

Group

Part Two: The Harlem Renaissance One of the great legacies of the Harlem Renaissance was to revitalize and reassert the strength, creativity, and pride in being African American. The artists and writers of the Harlem Renaissance helped forge a new group identity while expressing their individual talents as well. James Weldon Johnson celebrates Harlem as "the greatest Negro city in the world," Claude McKay's poem proclaims the honor and necessity of fighting back against oppressors, and Langston Hughes, Countee Cullen, and Zora Neale Hurston offer hope for the future.

■ How do you think the work of the artists and writers of this period affected and influenced African Americans across the United States?

Activities

1. Why is it sometimes hard to just "be yourself"? Considering the experiences of the women in the "Beyond the Limits" selections, along with your own experiences, work with a group to create a chart of forces in society that discourage individuality. For each "force," list a recommendation that can be used to preserve individuality.

2. What family, social, community, and cultural groups are you part of? Choose one of the groups you identify with and tell about it, including the impact the group has had on your life.

549

Independent and Group Projects

Media

All About the Author Choose one of the writers in this unit and create a five-minute audio or video biography, focusing on the life or career of that person or on the lasting impact of her or his work. Or, use the multimedia capabilities of a computer to create your mini-biography. You will have to do some research to find additional images and perhaps writings or quotations. Include music, sound effects, and exciting graphics as appropriate.

Writing

Quiz Exchange Working with a partner, write a thirty-question quiz that tests students' knowledge of the literature in Unit 5. Ask questions that test knowledge of important themes, events, characters, and so on, rather than minor details. When you've finished writing your questions, write an answer key with suggested responses. Trade your quiz with a partner's, and see how many of his or her questions you can answer.

Entertainment

Harlem Renaissance: The Game Create a board game, trivia game, video game or any other kind of game you wish that focuses on one or more aspects of the Harlem Renaissance. The purpose of the game, along with having fun, should be to educate the players about the personalities and events of the Harlem Renaissance.

Art

I SEE What You Mean The authors and poets in this unit use words to express their thoughts and feelings. Pick a selection that had a particular impact on you and translate the words into images. Create a collage of pictures, photographs, and objects that you feel convey the sentiments of the writer. Explain your collage to your class.

The SEARCH *for* EQUALITY

THEMES IN AMERICAN LITERATURE

for EQUALITY

Ralph Waldo Emerson once observed that the schoolyard boast "I'm as good as you be," contained the essence of the Declaration of Independence. Human equality is the first of the "self-evident" truths recognized by the Declaration. Of course, the society that produced this document was still a very unequal one, with few civil rights for women and none for American Indians or enslaved African Americans. America's subsequent history has been a struggle to expand our notions of equality to include all Americans.

The right of citizens of the United States to vote shall not be denied or abridged by the United States or by any state on account of race, color, or previous condition of servitude.

15th Amendment (1870)

The right of citizens of the United States to vote shall not be denied or abridged by the United States or by any state on account of sex.

19th Amendment (1920)

The right of citizens of the United States, who are eighteen years or older, to vote shall not be denied or abridged by the United States or by any state on account of age.

26th Amendment (1971)

WE HOLD THESE TRUTHS TO BE SELF-EVIDENT: THAT ALL MEN ARE CREATED EQUAL; THAT THEY ARE ENDOWED BY THEIR CREATOR WITH CERTAIN UNALIENABLE RIGHTS; THAT AMONG THESE ARE LIFE, LIBERTY, AND THE PURSUIT OF HAPPINESS.

Thomas Jefferson, The Declaration of Independence (1776)

We hold these truths to be self-evident: that all men and women are created equal . . . .

Elizabeth Cady Stanton, Seneca Falls Declaration of Sentiments (1848)

George Caleb Bingham, Stump Speaking. *Done in the early 1850s, this is one of a series of paintings by Bingham depicting a local election in Missouri.*

No novelty in the United States struck me more vividly during my stay here than the equality of conditions. It is easy to see the immense influence of this basic fact on the whole course of society. It gives a particular turn to public opinion and a particular twist to the laws, new maxims to those who govern and particular habits to the governed.

Alexis de Tocqueville, Democracy in America *(1835)*

What, then, is the American, this new man? He is neither an European nor the descendent of an European; hence that strange mixture of blood, which you will find in no other country. I could point out to you a family whose grandfather was an Englishman, whose wife was Dutch, whose son married a French woman, and whose present four sons have four wives of different nations. . . . Here individuals of all nations are melted into a new race of men, whose labors and posterity will one day cause great changes in the world.

Hector St. Jean de Crèvecoeur,
Letters from an American Farmer *(1782)*

OH, FREEDOM!

Oh, Freedom!
Oh, Freedom!
Oh, Freedom over me!
And before I'd be a slave,
I'd be buried in my grave,
And go home to my Lord and be
free! . . .

African American Spiritual (late 1800s)

FOLLOW THE DRINKING GOURD

When the sun comes back and the first quail calls,
Follow the drinking gourd.1
The old man is a-waitin' for to carry you to freedom
If you follow the drinking gourd.

CHORUS
Follow the drinking gourd,
Follow the drinking gourd,
For the old man is a-waitin' for to carry you to freedom
If you follow the drinking gourd.

The riverbank will make a mighty good road,
The dead trees will show you the way,
And left foot, peg foot, travelling on
Just you follow the drinking gourd.

Now the river ends between two hills,
Follow the drinking gourd.
And there's another river on the other side,
Follow the drinking gourd.

Where the little river meets the great big river,
Follow the drinking gourd.
The old man is a-waitin' for to carry you to freedom,
If you follow the drinking gourd.

African American spiritual (mid–1800s)

1. **the drinking gourd,** dialect variant for the
constellation also known as the Big Dipper,
used by runaway slaves to guide them north.

The Price of Freedom

Lewis Douglass, son of reformer Frederick Douglass, served with the 54th Massachusetts Regiment, the first African American unit recruited by the Union. Lewis Douglass wrote to his wife after the 54th had been involved on July 18, 1863 in a bloody assault on Fort Wagner, a Confederate battery defending Charleston, South Carolina.

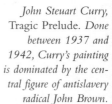

John Steuart Curry, Tragic Prelude. *Done between 1937 and 1942, Curry's painting is dominated by the central figure of antislavery radical John Brown.*

My dear Amelia:

I have been in two fights, and am unhurt. I am about to go in another I believe tonight. Our men fought well on both occasions. The last was desperate. We charged that terrible battery on Morris island known as Fort Wagner, and were repulsed. . . . Jacob Carter is missing, Charles Reason wounded, Charles Whiting, Charles Creamer all wounded.

I escaped unhurt from amidst that perfect hail of shot and shell. It was terrible. I need not particularize, the papers will give a better [account] than I have time to give. My thoughts are with you often, you are as dear as ever, be good to remember it as I no doubt you will. As I said before, we are on the eve of another fight and I am very busy and have just snatched a moment to write you. I must necessarily be brief. Should I fall in the next fight killed or wounded I hope I fall with my face to the foe.

This regiment has established its reputation as a fighting regiment, not a man flinched, though it was a trying time. Men fell all around me. A shell would explode and clear a space of twenty feet. Our men would close up again, but it was no use, we had to retreat, which was a very hazardous undertaking. How I got out of that fight alive I cannot tell, but I am here.

My Dear girl I hope to see you again. I must bid you farewell should I be killed. Remember if I die I die in a good cause. I wish we had a hundred thousand colored troops we would put an end to this war.

Good Bye to all. Your own loving—Write soon—

Lewis

"THERE ARE NO LAUNDRIES IN CHINA"

The Chinese laundryman does not learn his trade in China; there are no laundries in China. The women there do the washing in tubs and have no washboards or flat irons. . . .

The reason why so many Chinese go into the laundry business is because it requires little capital and is one of the few opportunities that are open. Men of other nationalities who are jealous of the Chinese, because he is a more faithful worker than one of their own people, have raised such a great outcry about Chinese cheap labor that they have shut him out of working on farms or in factories or building railroads or making streets or digging sewers. He cannot practice any trade, and his opportunities to do business are limited to his own countrymen. So he opens a laundry. . . .

There is no reason for the prejudice against the Chinese. The cheap labor cry was always a falsehood. Their labor was never cheap, and is not cheap now. It has always commanded the highest market price. But the trouble is that the Chinese are such excellent and faithful workers that bosses will have no others when they can get them.

Chinese immigrant (1903)

Washington and Du Bois Debate

The wisest among my race understand that the agitation of questions of social equality is the extremest folly, and that progress in the enjoyment of all the privileges that will come to us must be the result of severe and constant struggle rather than of artificial forcing. No race that has anything to contribute to the markets of the world is long in any degree ostracized. It is important and right that all privileges of the law be ours, but it is vastly more important that we be prepared for the exercise of those privileges. The opportunity to earn a dollar in a factory just now is worth infinitely more than the opportunity to spend a dollar in an opera-house.

Booker T. Washington (1895)

This is an age of unusual economic development, and Mr. Washington's program naturally takes an economic cast, becoming a gospel of Work and Money to such an extent as apparently almost completely to overshadow the higher aims of life. . . . Mr. Washington's program practically accepts the alleged inferiority of the Negro race. . . .

In other periods of intensified prejudice all the Negro's tendency to self-assertion has been called forth; at this period a policy of submission is advocated. In the history of all other races and peoples the doctrine preached at such crises has been that manly self-respect is worth more than lands and houses, and that a people who voluntarily surrender such respect, or cease striving for it, are not worth civilizing.

W. E. B. Dubois (1903)

In her autobiography The Promised Land, *Mary Antin, a Russian Jew who came to Boston in 1894, emphasized the importance of education in the immigrants' search for equality in their new home.*

Education was free. That subject my father had written about repeatedly, as comprising his chief hope for us children, the essence of American opportunity, the treasure no thief could touch, not even misfortune or poverty. It was the one thing he was able to promise us when he sent for us; surer, safer than bread or shelter. . . .

The apex of my civic pride and personal contentment was reached on the bright September morning when I entered the public school. . . .

Father himself conducted us to school. He would not have delegated that job to the President of the United States. He had awaited the day with impatience equal to mine, and the visions he saw as he hurried us over the sun-flecked pavements transcended all my dreams. Almost his first act on landing on American soil, three years before, had been his application for naturalization. He had taken the remaining steps in the process with eager promptness, and at the earliest moment allowed by the law, he became a citizen of the United States. It is true that he had left home in search of bread for his hungry family, but he went blessing the necessity that drove him to America.

The boasted freedom of the New World meant to him far more than the right to reside, travel, and work wherever he pleased; it meant the freedom to speak his thought, to throw off the shackles of superstition, to test his own fate, unhindered by political or religious tyranny. . . .

If education, culture, the higher life were shining things to be worshipped from afar, he had still a means left whereby he could draw one step nearer to them. He could send his children to school, to learn all those things that he knew by fame to be desirable. The common school[1] at least, perhaps high school; for one or two, perhaps even college! His children should be students, should fill his house with books and intellectual company; and thus he would walk by proxy in the Elysian fields[2] of liberal learning. As for the children themselves, he knew no surer way to their advancement and happiness.

So it was with a heart full of longing and hope that my father led us to school on that first day. He took long strides in his eagerness, the rest of us running and hopping to keep up.

At last the four of us stood around the teacher's desk; and my father, in his impossible English, gave us over in her charge, with some broken word of his hopes for us that his swelling heart could no longer contain. I venture to say that Miss Nixon was struck by something uncommon in the group we made, something outside of Semitic[3] features and the abashed manner of the alien. . . .

I think Miss Nixon guessed what my father's best English could not convey. I think she divined that by the simple act of delivering our school certificates to her he took possession of America.

---

1. **common school,** elementary school.
2. **Elysian** (ə lē′zən) **Fields,** paradise in classical mythology.
3. **Semitic,** Jewish.

WHICH SIDE ARE YOU ON?

Come all of you good workers,
Good news to you I'll tell
Of how the good old union
Has come in here to dwell.

Chorus:
Which side are you on?
Which side are you on?
Which side are you on?
Which side are you on?

My daddy was a miner
And I'm a miner's son,
And I'll stick with the union
Till every battle's won.

They say in Harlan County[1]
There are no neutrals there;
You'll either be a union man
Or a thug for J. H. Blair.[2]

Oh, workers, can you stand it?
Oh, tell me how you can.
Will you be a lousy scab[3]
Or will you be a man?

Don't scab for the bosses,
Don't listen to their lies.
Us poor folks haven't got a chance
Unless we organize.

Florence Reece (1931)

"RAISE LESS CORN AND MORE HELL!"

Mary Elizabeth Lease was a Populist famous for her fiery speeches to farmers.

This is a nation of inconsistencies. The Puritans fleeing from oppression became oppressors. We fought England for our liberty and put chains on four millions of blacks. We wiped out slavery and by our tariff laws and national banks began a system of white wage slavery worse than the first. Wall Street owns the country. It is no longer a government of the people, by the people, and for the people, but a government of Wall Street, by Wall Street, and for Wall Street. The great common people of this country are slaves, and monopoly is the master. . . . Money rules, and our . . . laws are the output of a system, which clothes rascals in robes and honesty in rags.

Mary Elizabeth Lease (1890)

This anti-labor cartoon by Frederick Opper appeared in 1887.

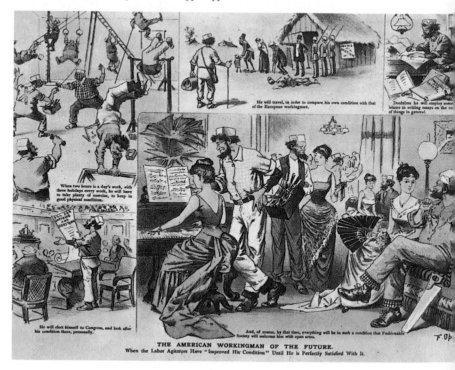

THE AMERICAN WORKINGMAN OF THE FUTURE.
When the Labor Agitators Have "Improved His Condition" Until He is Perfectly Satisfied With It.

---

1. **Harlan County.** Kentucky's Harlan County was the scene of bitter and frequently violent labor disputes between coal-mine operators and miners.
2. **J. H. Blair,** High Sheriff of Harlan County.
3. **scab,** non-union worker brought in to break a strike.

Paul Davis, poster

I am 34 years old and I try to organize for the United Farm Workers. . . . But until two years ago, my world was still very small. I would read all these things in the papers about Cesar Chavez[1] and I would denounce him because I still had that thing about becoming a first-class patriotic citizen. . . . It wasn't until Chavez came to Salinas[2] where I was working in the fields, that I saw what a beautiful man he was. I went to this rally, I still intended to stay with the company. But something—I don't know—I was close to the workers. They couldn't speak English and wanted me to be their spokesman in favor of going on strike. I don't know—I just got caught up with it all, the beautiful feeling of solidarity.

Roberto Acuna (early 1970s)

1. **Cesar Chavez** (1927–1993), Chicano labor organizer who founded the United Farm Workers in 1962.

2. **Salinas,** a city in west central California.

To separate [minority children] from others of similar age and qualifications solely because of their race generates a feeling of inferiority as to their status in the community that may affect their hearts and minds in a way unlikely ever to be undone. . . .

We conclude that in the field of public education, the doctrine of "separate but equal" has no place. . . .

U.S. Supreme Court, Brown *decision*

Jim Domke, The Indian and the Buffalo *(date?)*

RETURN TO WOUNDED KNEE

In early 1973, a group of American Indians seized the tiny town of Wounded Knee, South Dakota, site of an 1890 massacre of hundreds of Sioux by U.S. cavalry, to dramatize Indian grievances.

On February 27, 1973, we stood on the hill where the fate of the old Sioux Nation, Sitting Bull's and Crazy Horse's[1] nation, had been decided, and where we, ourselves, came face to face with our fate. . . . We all felt the presence of the spirits of those lying close by in the long ditch,[2] wondering whether we were about to join them, wondering when the marshals would arrive. . . . The young men tied eagle feathers to their braids, no longer unemployed kids, juvenile delinquents, or winos, but warriors.

Mary Crow Dog (1973)

No one can make you feel inferior without your consent.

Eleanor Roosevelt (1937)

---

1. **Sitting Bull** (1834–1890), **Crazy Horse** (1849–1877), Sioux leaders who defeated General Custer in 1876 at the Battle of Little Big Horn.

2. **ditch,** mass grave where the bodies of those killed at Wounded Knee in 1890 are buried.

AFFIRMATIVE ACTION: PRO AND CON

Perhaps the most divisive civil rights issue of the recent past has been affirmative action. Do such policies represent a correction of past injustice or are they "reverse discrimination"? The following passages argue for and against affirmative action.

The founding tenet of racism is that blacks are inferior, particularly when it comes to intellectual capability. And an underpinning of racism has been an all-out cultural onslaught on the self-esteem of blacks, to transform them from assertive and self-sufficient human beings into dependents, mere extensions of the will of the whites who choose to use them.

Affirmative action, even weakly and spottily deployed, opens doors of opportunity that would otherwise be slammed tight. As a result, the country is better and stronger. It surely is one of the most effective antidotes to the widespread habit of undervaluing the capacities of minorities and women. It also serves as a counterbalance to the tendency to overvalue, as a recruitment tool, the effectiveness and fairness of old-boy networks. . . .

Roger Wilkins (1990)

I think one of the most troubling effects of racial preferences for blacks is a kind of demoralization. Under affirmative action, the quality that earns us preferential treatment is an implied inferiority. However this inferiority is explained—and it is easily enough explained by the myriad deprivations that grew out of our oppression—it is still inferiority. There are explanations and then there is the fact. And the

fact must be borne by the individual as a condition apart from the explanation. . . .

I believe another liability of affirmative action comes from the fact that it indirectly encourages blacks to exploit their own past victimization. Like implied inferiority, victimization is what justifies preference, so that to receive the benefits of preferential treatment one must, to some extent, become invested in the view of one's self as a victim. In this way, affirmative action nurtures a victim-focused identity in blacks and sends us the message that there is more power in our past suffering than in our present achievements.

Shelby Steele (1990)

RESPONDING

1. Contrast the different visions of politics expressed in the paintings Stump Speaking *(page 553) and* Tragic Prelude *(page 555).*
2. Do you agree with Booker T. Washington (page 556) that in the search for equality, economic power must come first? Why or why not?
3. Do you think that an immigrant father today would have the same confidence as Mr. Antin (page 557) that American public education would ensure his children's future success? Why or why not?
4. In your opinion, are quota systems designed to increase minority representation in higher education and the work force fair? Why or why not?
5. Is American society today moving toward greater equality among its citizens or greater inequality? Explain.

Modern Dilemmas

Lost in a Crowd
Part One, pages 564–631

The Strength of Tradition
Part Two, pages 632–713

Between

HISTORICAL OVERVIEW

The idealism that had prompted America's entry into World War I, "the war to end wars," was largely exhausted by 1920. The new decade saw a retreat from reform, a return to isolationism, and an outburst of unrestrained self-indulgence that earned the period the nickname "the Roaring '20s." Following the stock market crash of 1929, America suffered through the Great Depression, an economic crisis unparalleled in U.S. history. By the mid-1930s, some of the worst privation had been eased by the social welfare programs of President Franklin D. Roosevelt's New Deal, but full economic recovery did not take place until America's entry into World War II provided full employment. On the right are a few famous individuals and characteristic social types from the social scene of the 1920s and 1930s.

REVIVALIST

Cheering Prohibition, evangelist Billy Sunday declared, "Hell will be forever for rent."

ANARCHISTS

Radicals Sacco and Vanzetti (rear) were executed for murder after a questionable trial.

GANGSTER

"Machine Gun" Kelly (shown with his wife) was a notorious bank robber in the 1930s.

the Wars

WORK-IS-WHAT-I
WANT-AND-NOT-CHARITY
WHO-WILL-HELP-ME-
GET-A-JOB-7 YEARS-
IN-DETROIT-NO-MONEY
SENT-AWAY-FURNISH-
BEST-OF-REFERENCES
PHONE-RANDOLPH-2 3 1 ROOM #59.

Key Dates

1918
World War I ends.

1919
Prohibition goes into effect.

1920
First commercial radio broadcast.

1925
John Scopes tried for teaching evolution in public school.

1927
Charles Lindbergh flies nonstop from New York to Paris; Sacco and Vanzetti executed.

1929
Stock market crashes.

1932
Franklin D. Roosevelt elected President.

1933
Unemployment reaches its peak.

1941
United States enters World War II.

HERO
Charles Lindbergh's solo flight from New York to Paris was the greatest '20s publicity stunt.

FLAPPER
Silent screen star Clara Bow was one of the glamour queens of the 1920s.

ATHLETE
Preeminent golfer of the '20s, Bobby Jones won 3 U.S. Open titles during the decade.

UNEMPLOYED
In the early 1930s, more than 20 percent of the U.S. work force was jobless.

Part One

Lost in a Crowd

The face of the United States began changing at a faster rate than ever before between World War I and World War II. The growth of industrialization attracted people to the cities, and the jazz age ushered in new music, new language, and new values. Changes happened so rapidly that some people found themselves lost in an increasingly urbanized and impersonal society.

Multicultural Connection Each person has a unique **perspective** on the world and on society. As you read the following selections, notice how the main characters react to the society in which they find themselves. How do their perspectives differ from those of the people around them, and what causes them to see things differently?

Literature

T. S. Eliot	**The Love Song of J. Alfred Prufrock** ◆ poem	...568
Edwin Arlington Robinson	**Richard Cory** ◆ poem	.576
E. E. Cummings	**l(a** ◆ poem	.577
Ernest Hemingway	**In Another Country** ◆ short story	.580
F. Scott Fitzgerald	**Winter Dreams** ◆ short story	.586
Richard Wright	*from* **Black Boy** ◆ autobiography	.605
Katherine Anne Porter	**The Jilting of Granny Weatherall** ◆ short story	.611

Interdisciplinary Study The Roaring Twenties

The Younger Generation Runs Wild ◆ pop culture 620
Roaring Twenties Glossary ◆ pop culture 622

Language History

What's New in Language 624

Writing Workshop Expository Writing

Analyzing Alienation 625

Beyond Print Technology

The Wonders of Word Processing 631

Before Reading

The Love Song of J. Alfred Prufrock

by T. S. Eliot

T. S. Eliot
1888–1965

After graduating from Harvard, T. S. Eliot studied in France and England, and eventually became a British subject. His writing career was encouraged by Ezra Pound, poet and the acting foreign editor for *Poetry* magazine, which first published "The Love Song of J. Alfred Prufrock" in 1915. The poem reflects Eliot's feeling that modern people are shallow, their lives spiritually empty. This theme continued in Eliot's poetry until his conversion to the Anglican Church where he rediscovered faith, which he felt was the answer to the meaninglessness of modern life. In 1948 Eliot was awarded the Nobel Prize for literature.

Building Background

A Pessimistic View of the World The years during and after World War I were times of drastic social change. Industry, geared up during war time, was booming. People out to get rich quick were investing heavily in the stock market. For some citizens, eager to forget the war, it was a time to party—the "Roaring Twenties." For others, disillusioned with the war and post-war politics, it was a time to abandon the United States. Many writers and artists, including T. S. Eliot, became expatriates, living and working in Europe. It was during this time that T. S. Eliot wrote some of his most famous poems.

Literary Focus

Allusion If a news article says an investment banker has a "Midas touch," the reporter is alluding to King Midas of Greek mythology, who turned everything he touched to gold. The reporter is using a kind of shorthand to say that the banker is good at making money. A reference like this to a person, thing, event, situation, or aspect of culture, real or fictional, past or present, is an allusion. Before you read "The Love Song of J. Alfred Prufrock," find out about these topics so that you understand the allusions T. S. Eliot makes in the poem: Dante's *Inferno,* Michelangelo, John the Baptist, Lazarus, Shakespeare's characters Hamlet and Polonius, and Shakespeare's play *Twelfth Night.*

Writer's Notebook

I Should Have Said . . . J. Alfred Prufrock, the main character in the poem, is mulling over a social situation. He feels uncomfortable, and he can't say what he wants to say. Before reading the poem, think of a time when you have felt uncomfortable in a social situation. List similes or metaphors that describe how you were feeling at that time. For example, if you ran into a famous athlete and you didn't know what to say, you might describe the occasion this way: "My voice crackled like radio static and my hands shook like a washing machine in the spin cycle."

The Love Song of J. Alfred Prufrock

T. S. ELIOT

S'io credesse che mia riposta fosse
A persona che mai tornasse al mondo,
Questa fiamma staria senza piu scosse.
Ma perciocche giammai di questo fondo
Non torno vivo alcun, s' i' odo il vero,
Senza tema d' infamia ti rispondo.

Let us go then, you and I,
When the evening is spread out against the sky
Like a patient etherised upon a table;
Let us go, through certain half-deserted streets,
5 The muttering retreats
Of restless nights in one-night cheap hotels
And sawdust restaurants with oyster-shells:
Streets that follow like a tedious argument
Of insidious intent
10 To lead you to an overwhelming question . . .
Oh, do not ask, "What is it?"
Let us go and make our visit.

In the room the women come and go
Talking of Michelangelo.

15   The yellow fog that rubs its back upon the window-panes,
The yellow smoke that rubs its muzzle on the window-panes
Licked its tongue into the corners of the evening,
Lingered upon the pools that stand in drains,
Let fall upon its back the soot that falls from chimneys,
20 Slipped by the terrace, made a sudden leap,
And seeing that it was a soft October night,
Curled once about the house, and fell asleep.

Epigraph *S'io credesse . . . ti rispondo,* "If I believed my answer were being made to one who could ever return to the world, this flame would gleam no more; but since, if what I hear is true, never from this abyss [Hell] did living man return, I answer thee without fear of infamy." (Dante, *Inferno* XXVII, 61-66)

3 etherised (ē′thə rīzd′), *adj.* unconscious from ether fumes. Ether was used to anesthetize patients during operations.

8 tedious (tē′dē əs), *adj.* long and tiring, boring, wearisome.

13–14 **In the room . . . Michelangelo.** These lines refer to the women at the tea party which Prufrock is attending. The great Renaissance artist Michelangelo is the topic of their chatter.

▲ How would you describe the situation in Philip Evergood's 1927 painting, *Tea for Two*? What does it have in common with Prufrock's situation?

And indeed there will be time
For the yellow smoke that slides along the street,
25 Rubbing its back upon the window-panes;
There will be time, there will be time
To prepare a face to meet the faces that you meet;
There will be time to murder and create,
And time for all the works and days of hands
30 That lift and drop a question on your plate;
Time for you and time for me,
And time yet for a hundred indecisions,
And for a hundred visions and revisions,
Before the taking of a toast and tea.

35   In the room the women come and go
Talking of Michelangelo.

And indeed there will be time
To wonder, "Do I dare?" and, "Do I dare?"
Time to turn back and descend the stair,
40 With a bald spot in the middle of my hair—
[They will say: "How his hair is growing thin!"]
My morning coat, my collar mounting firmly to the chin,
My necktie rich and modest, but asserted by a simple pin—
[They will say: "But how his arms and legs are thin!"]
45 Do I dare
Disturb the universe?
In a minute there is time
For decisions and revisions which a minute will reverse.

For I have known them all already, known them all:—
50 Have known the evenings, mornings, afternoons,
I have measured out my life with coffee spoons;
I know the voices dying with a dying fall
Beneath the music from a farther room.
    So how should I presume?

55 And I have known the eyes already, known them all—
The eyes that fix you in a formulated phrase,
And when I am formulated, sprawling on a pin,
When I am pinned and wriggling on the wall,
Then how should I begin
60 To spit out all the butt-ends of my days and ways?
    And how should I presume?

32 indecision (in′di sizh′ən),
n. tendency to delay or
hesitate.

42 **morning coat,** a man's
coat that tapers from the
front waist downward
toward tails at the back,
worn for formal daytime
dress.

57 formulated (fôr′myə lāt-
əd), adj. reduced to a formula; expressed in a for-
mula. These lines suggest
that Prufrock has been
scrutinized like an insect
that has been classified
and mounted for display.

And I have known the arms already, known them all—
Arms that are braceleted and white and bare
[But in the lamplight, downed with light brown hair!]
65 Is it perfume from a dress
That makes me so digress?
Arms that lie along a table, or wrap about a shawl.
    And should I then presume?
    And how should I begin?

     . . . . .

70 Shall I say, I have gone at dusk through narrow streets
And watched the smoke that rises from the pipes
Of lonely men in shirt-sleeves, leaning out of windows? . . .

    I should have been a pair of ragged claws
Scuttling across the floors of silent seas.

     . . . . .

75 And the afternoon, the evening, sleeps so peacefully!
Smoothed by long fingers,
Asleep . . . tired . . . or it malingers,
Stretched on the floor, here beside you and me.
Should I, after tea and cakes and ices,
80 Have the strength to force the moment to its crisis?
But though I have wept and fasted, wept and prayed,
Though I have seen my head [grown slightly bald] brought in
    upon a platter,
I am no prophet—and here's no great matter;
I have seen the moment of my greatness flicker,
85 And I have seen the eternal Footman hold my coat, and snicker,
And in short, I was afraid.

    And would it have been worth it, after all,
After the cups, the marmalade, the tea,
Among the porcelain, among some talk of you and me,
90 Would it have been worth while,
To have bitten off the matter with a smile,
To have squeezed the universe into a ball
To roll it toward some overwhelming question,
To say: "I am Lazarus, come from the dead,
95 Come back to tell you all, I shall tell you all"—
If one, settling a pillow by her head,
    Should say: "That is not what I meant at all.
    That is not it, at all."

66 digress (dī gres′), *v.* turn aside from the main subject; to ramble.

77 malinger (mə ling′gər), *v.* pretend to be sick in order to avoid work.

81–83 But though . . . no great matter. These lines allude to John the Baptist. King Herod had him beheaded and presented the head on a platter at his stepdaughter Salome's request.

94–95 "I am Lazarus . . . tell you all." The biblical Lazarus lay dead in his tomb for four days until Jesus restored him to life.

And would it have been worth it, after all,
100 Would it have been worth while,
After the sunsets and the dooryards and the sprinkled streets,
After the novels, after the teacups, after the skirts that trail along
       the floor—
And this, and so much more?—
It is impossible to say just what I mean!
105 But as if a magic lantern threw the nerves in patterns on a
       screen:
Would it have been worth while
If one, settling a pillow or throwing off a shawl,
And turning toward the window, should say:
     "That is not it at all,
110   That is not what I meant, at all."

     . . . . .

No! I am not Prince Hamlet, nor was meant to be;
Am an attendant lord, one that will do
To swell a progress, start a scene or two,
Advise the prince; no doubt an easy tool,
115 Deferential, glad to be of use,
Politic, cautious, and meticulous;
Full of high sentence, but a bit obtuse;
At times, indeed, almost ridiculous—
Almost, at times, the Fool.

120   I grow old . . . I grow old . . .
I shall wear the bottoms of my trousers rolled.

   Shall I part my hair behind? Do I dare to eat a peach?
I shall wear white flannel trousers, and walk upon the beach.
I have heard the mermaids singing, each to each.

125   I do not think that they will sing to me.

   I have seen them riding seaward on the waves
Combing the white hair of the waves blown back
When the wind blows the water white and black.

   We have lingered in the chambers of the sea
130 By sea-girls wreathed with seaweed red and brown
Till human voices wake us, and we drown.

111 **Prince Hamlet,** the hero of William Shakespeare's play *Hamlet,* who set out to prove that his uncle had murdered his father. Here Prufrock envisions himself as playing a minor character rather than the lead.

115 deferential (def′ə ren′-shəl), *adj.* showing respect for the judgment, opinion, wishes of another.

116 politic (pol′ə tik), *adj.* wise in looking out for one's own interests.

116 meticulous (mə tik′yə-ləs), *adj.* extremely care-ful about details.

117 obtuse (əb tüs′), *adj.* slow in understanding.

After Reading

Making Connections

Shaping Your Response

1. In your log, write three words that you think describe J. Alfred Prufrock. Share your words with your classmates.

2. Tea parties and morning coats are no longer in fashion. Describe where you might find a modern J. Alfred Prufrock and what he might be wearing.

Analyzing the Poem

3. Explain the extended **metaphor** that begins with line 15.

4. What do you think the fog **symbolizes** in J. Alfred Prufrock's life?

5. The words in the **epigraph** to the poem are spoken by Guido da Montefeltro, whom Dante encounters in his imaginary journey through hell. Guido is suffering eternal torment for his sins; he tells his story to Dante on the assumption that Dante, like himself, can never leave hell. In what respect is Prufrock's song likewise the confession of a soul in torment? What kinds of torment might he be suffering?

6. What kind of "overwhelming question" do you think Prufrock is trying to ask? Explain why you think so.

7. 👣 Does Prufrock's **perspective** on society seem to differ from the people around him? Explain your answer.

Extending the Ideas

8. Select one of the following common phrases or use one of your own choosing and explain how it relates to J. Alfred Prufrock.

   - All form and no substance

   - On the outside looking in

   - Make up your mind

Literary Focus: Allusion

Writers use **allusions** to make their literature richer and more meaningful. By referring to another piece of literature or a historical character, the author makes a connection between what he or she is writing about and a familiar topic. Choose one of the allusions T. S. Eliot makes in "The Love Song of J. Alfred Prufrock," and find out its source and context. To what is the allusion referring? What connection is Eliot trying to make between Prufrock and the allusion?

deferential
politic
meticulous
obtuse
tedious
etherised
formulated
digress
malinger
indecision

Vocabulary Study

J. Alfred Prufrock uses these adjectives to describe himself: *deferential, politic, meticulous,* and *obtuse.* These words from the poem also relate to Prufrock and his life: *tedious, etherised, formulated, digress, malinger* and *indecision.* Write your own sentences using each of the listed words to describe Prufrock and his behavior. For example, Prufrock also says that he is *ridiculous.* You might write, "It is *ridiculous* that J. Alfred Prufrock worries about which way to part his hair."

Expressing Your Ideas

Writing Choices

Writer's Notebook Update Compare J. Alfred Prufrock's discomfort in a social situation with the incident you wrote about in your notebook. Then imitate T. S. Eliot's poetic style and write a poem about your experience. Try to include either a simile or a metaphor in your poem.

Diagnosis Needed What is Prufrock's problem? Write a **diagnosis** of his condition, and then write a **prescription** for his treatment that you think will help him overcome his problem.

What Matters? Everyone has different priorities in life. Look at the list below of things people value. Rank them according to the value you place on each, from most to least important. Then be J. Alfred Prufrock and rank them as you think he would. Compare the **rankings** and write a **paragraph** comparing your priorities to Prufrock's.

- job satisfaction
- social standing
- personal appearance
- wealth
- friends
- health
- education
- family

Other Options

Picture It J. Alfred Prufrock jumbles ideas and images together as he reflects on his life and his behavior. Make a **collage** using photographs and quotations from the poem to depict his inner turmoil.

Make a CD Cover T. S. Eliot himself made a recording of "The Love Song of J. Alfred Prufrock." Imagine the recording is going to be rereleased as a CD. Your job is to design the **CD cover.** It should not only catch the attention of the CD shopper, but also express the theme of the poem.

Learn About the Times Writers are influenced by the times and the places in which they live. "The Love Song of J. Alfred Prufrock" was first published in 1915, and T. S. Eliot lived in England. What was going on in the world then? Who was in power in England? What were the social standards of the day? Research what life was like in England at this time in history, and present a report to the class. Your report might be in the form of a **speech** or a **display,** or you may want to work in groups to **dramatize** some of the events and the society of the time.

Before Reading

Richard Cory by Edwin Arlington Robinson
I(a by E. E. Cummings

Edwin Arlington Robinson
1869–1935

President Theodore Roosevelt gave the young struggling poet Edward Arlington Robinson a "job" at the Custom House in New York. All Robinson had to do was show up, and then he could go home and write. By the time President Taft came into office, Robinson's poetry was famous.

E. E. Cummings
1894–1962

E. E. Cummings is famous for his innovative writing style. His name, like his poetry, sometimes appears without capitalization, but his legal name always remained capitalized, according to the E. E. Cummings Society, and it should appear that way in print.

Building Background

Variety in Poetry Both Edwin Arlington Robinson and E. E. Cummings grew up in New England and studied at Harvard. Both are highly acclaimed American poets. However, the similarities end there. Their poetic styles differ greatly. Robinson is traditional; Cummings is an innovator. Robinson's poems are matter-of-fact in their language; Cummings's poems are like puzzles to be taken apart and reassembled. Cummings, when asked to define poetry, said, "Poetry is what's different." He once wrote, "The day of the spoken lyric is past. The poem which has at last taken its place does not sing itself; it builds itself, three dimensionally, gradually, subtly, in the consciousness of the experiencer." As you read "Richard Cory" and "I(a," enjoy each poet's style and look for a common theme.

Literary Focus

Shapely Poetry Concrete poetry must be seen as well as heard because a concrete poem has a shape that is related to its subject. To hear and not see the shape of a concrete poem or the way the words are fragmented would be to miss most of the meaning. "I(a" by E. E. Cummings is an example of concrete poetry. What do you see when you look at the poem on the page? How does the shape contribute to its meaning?

Writer's Notebook

Both Edwin Arlington Robinson and E. E. Cummings explore similar themes in their poems. Before reading the poems, make a chart in which you list words that you might use to write about sadness and loneliness. Then list visual images that you might use to express that theme. Examples are provided.

Words	Images
• silent	• A person trapped in a doorless and windowless room
• depression	
• empty	

Richard Cory

Edwin Arlington Robinson

Whenever Richard Cory went downtown,
    We people on the pavement looked at him:
He was a gentleman from sole to crown,[1]
    Clean-favored, and imperially[2] slim.

5 And he was always quietly arrayed,[3]
    And he was always human when he talked;
But still he fluttered pulses when he said,
    "Good morning," and he glittered when
      he walked.

And he was rich—yes, richer than a king—
10   And admirably schooled in every grace:
In fine, we thought that he was everything
    To make us wish that we were in his place.

So on we worked, and waited for the light,
    And went without the meat, and cursed
      the bread;
15 And Richard Cory, one calm summer night,
    Went home and put a bullet through
      his head.

---

1. **crown** (kroun), *n.* the top part of a hat.
2. **imperially** (im pir′ē əl ē), *adv.* majestically, magnificently.
3. **array** (ə rā′), *v.* dress in fine clothes.

How does J. Krans's 1895 statue, *Tinsmith,* reflect the
physical appearance and emotional state of Richard
Cory in Edwin Arlington Robinson's poem? ➤

l(a

E. E. Cummings

l(a

le
af
fa

ll

s)
one
l
iness

▲ Georgia O'Keeffe's painting, *Brown and Tan Leaves* (1928), uses the same subject matter—fallen leaves—as does Cummings's poem. Would you say the painting and poem also share a similar theme? Why or why not?

After Reading

Making Connections

Shaping Your Response

1. You and a classmate are two of the "people on the pavement." What would you say to each other about Cory and his death? Perform a dialogue for the class.

2. What scene did you visualize as you read E. E. Cummings's "l(a"?

Analyzing the Poems

3. Do you think the **ironic** ending of "Richard Cory" makes it a better poem than it would have been otherwise? Explain your answer.

4. What possible **motive** might Cory have had for killing himself?

5. What about a falling leaf makes it a suitable **symbol** for loneliness?

6. "l(a" and "Richard Cory" are very different in their poetic style. What do the two poems have in common?

Extending the Ideas

7. If Richard Cory had confided his troubles to you before he went home that summer night, what advice might you have given to him?

Literary Focus: Concrete Poetry

Shape adds meaning to **concrete poetry.** Discuss how the shape of "l(a" contributes to its meaning. Then find other examples of concrete poetry to share with the class. How does the shape of each poem add to its meaning? "Seal" by William Jay Smith, which can be found in *A Green Place: Modern Poems* (Delacorte Press, 1982), and "Forsythia" by Mary Ellen Solt, which can be found in *A Book of Women Poets from Antiquity to Now* (Schocken Books, 1980), are both good examples of concrete poems. After the discussion, compose an original poem that uses shape to convey an idea.

Expressing Your Ideas

Writing Choice

Writer's Notebook Update Develop one of the images you listed into a poem, either using Robinson's or Cummings's style.

Another Option

Character Portraits What did Richard Cory look like? Edwin Arlington Robinson gives you clues about his character's appearance and personality. Read several other poems from Edwin Arlington Robinson's *Tilbury Town.* Draw pictures of how you visualize the characters in those poems. Copy the poems and make a **scrapbook** of the poems and the portraits.

Before Reading

In Another Country

by Ernest Hemingway

Ernest Hemingway
1899–1961

After serving in an American ambulance unit and an Italian combat unit in World War I, Ernest Hemingway became a newspaper correspondent in France. There he met F. Scott Fitzgerald, who helped Hemingway get his works published. Hemingway described his writing this way: "I always try to write on the principle of the iceberg. There is seven-eighths of it underwater for every part that shows. Anything you know, you can eliminate and it only strengthens your iceberg. It is the part that doesn't show. If a writer omits something because he does not know it, then there is a hole in the story." In addition to writing, Hemingway enjoyed fishing, boxing, hunting in Africa, and watching bullfights. A dramatic figure to the end, he died of a self-inflicted gunshot wound.

Building Background

World War I World War I began in 1914 when a Serbian nationalist assassinated the heir to the Austrian-Hungarian throne. Many European countries took sides, as you can see in the map. The United States tried to remain neutral, but two events eventually brought the U.S into the war. Tsar Nicholas of Russia was deposed from his throne, and it looked like Russia would soon be abandoning their war effort. The next day, Germany sank three American merchant ships. In April of 1917, Congress declared war. Germany finally admitted defeat and signed an armistice on November 11, 1918.

Literary Focus

Mood As you read "In Another Country," look for the details Hemingway uses to describe the setting and characters. What effect do these details have on the overall feeling—or mood—of the work?

Writer's Notebook

Rx: Hope The wounded soldiers in the story are receiving medical treatment. Write about the importance of *hope* to successful recovery.

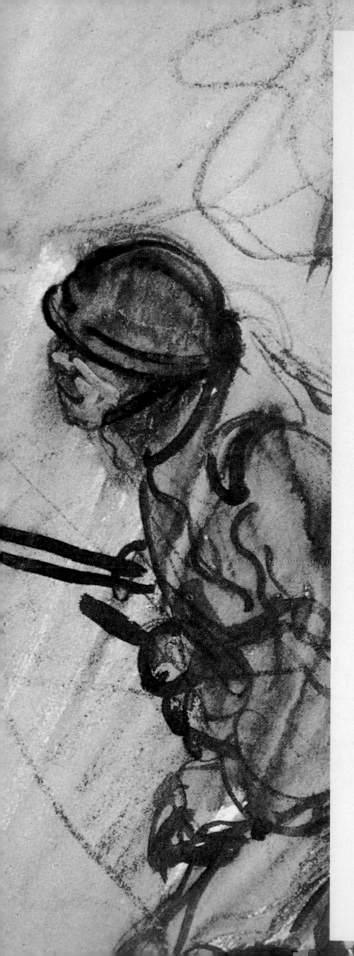

In Another Country

Ernest Hemingway

In the fall the war[1] was always there, but we did not go to it any more. It was cold in the fall in Milan and the dark came very early. Then the electric lights came on, and it was pleasant along the streets looking in the windows. There was much game[2] hanging outside the shops, and the snow powdered in the fur of the foxes and the wind blew their tails. The deer hung stiff and heavy and empty, and small birds blew in the wind and the wind turned their feathers. It was a cold fall and the wind came down from the mountains.

We were all at the hospital every afternoon, and there were different ways of walking across the town through the dusk to the hospital. Two of the ways were alongside canals, but they were long. Always, though, you crossed a bridge across a canal to enter the hospital. There was a choice of three bridges. On one of them a woman sold roasted chestnuts. It was warm, standing in front of her charcoal fire, and the chestnuts were warm afterward in your pocket. The hospital was very old and very beautiful, and you entered through a gate and walked across a courtyard and out a gate on the other side. There were usually funerals starting from the courtyard. Beyond the old hospital were the

---

1. **the war,** World War I (1914–1918).
2. game (gām), *n.* wild animals, birds, or fish hunted or caught for sport or food.

new brick pavilions,[3] and there we met every afternoon and were all very polite and interested in what was the matter, and sat in the machines that were to make so much difference.

The doctor came up to the machine where I was sitting and said: "What did you like best to do before the war? Did you practice a sport?"

I said: "Yes, football."

"Good," he said. "You will be able to play football again better than ever."

My knee did not bend and the leg dropped straight from the knee to the ankle without a calf, and the machine was to bend the knee and make it move as in riding a tricycle. But it did not bend yet, and instead the machine lurched when it came to the bending part. The doctor said: "That will all pass. You are a fortunate young man. You will play football again like a champion."

In the next machine was a major who had a little hand like a baby's. He winked at me when the doctor examined his hand, which was between two leather straps that bounced up and down and flapped the stiff fingers, and said: "And will I too play football, captain-doctor?" He had been a very great fencer,[4] and before the war the greatest fencer in Italy.

The doctor went to his office in the back room and brought a photograph which showed a hand that had been withered[5] almost as small as the major's, before it had taken a machine course, and after was a little larger. The major held the photograph with his good hand and looked at it very carefully. "A wound?" he asked.

"An industrial accident," the doctor said.

"Very interesting, very interesting," the major said, and handed it back to the doctor.

"You have confidence?"

"No," said the major.

There were three boys who came each day who were about the same age I was. They were all three from Milan, and one of them was to be a lawyer, and one was to be a painter, and one had intended to be a soldier, and after we were finished with the machines, sometimes we walked back together to the Café Cova, which was next door to the Scala.[6] We walked the short way through the communist quarter because we were four together. The people hated us because we were officers, and from a wineshop someone called out, *"A basso gli ufficiali!"*[7] as we passed. Another boy who walked with us sometimes and made us five wore a black silk handkerchief across his face because he had no nose then and his face was to be rebuilt. He had gone out to the front from the military academy and been wounded within an hour after he had gone into the front line for the first time. They rebuilt his face, but he came from a very old family and they could never get the nose exactly right. He went to South America and worked in a bank. But this was a long time ago, and then we did not any of us know how it was going to be afterward. We only knew then that there was always the war, but that we were not going to it anymore.

We all had the same medals, except the boy with the black silk bandage across his face, and he had not been at the front long enough to get any medals. The tall boy with a very pale face who was to be a lawyer had been a lieutenant of Arditi[8] and had three medals of the sort we each had only one of. He had lived a very long time with death and was a little detached.[9] We were all a little detached, and there was nothing that held us together except that we met every afternoon at the hospital. Although, as we walked to the Cova through the tough part of town, walking in the

---

3. **pavilion** (pə vil′yən), *n.* one of a group of buildings forming a hospital.
4. **fencer** (fens′er), *n.* sword fighter.
5. wither (wiᴛн′ər), *v.* shrivel.
6. **the Scala,** La Scala, Milan's world-famous opera house.
7. *"a basso gli ufficiali!"* Down with the officers! *[Italian]*
8. **Arditi,** an elite group of volunteers which served as storm troops of the Italian infantry.
9. detached (di tacht′), *adj.* reserved, aloof.

dark, with light and singing coming out of the wineshops, and sometimes having to walk into the street when the men and women would crowd together on the sidewalk so that we would have had to jostle them to get by, we felt held together by there being something that had happened that they, the people who disliked us, did not understand.

SUMMARIZE: Why were the men detached?

We ourselves all understood the Cova, where it was rich and warm and not too brightly lighted, and noisy and smoky at certain hours, and there were always girls at the tables and the illustrated papers on a rack on the wall. The girls at the Cova were very patriotic, and I found that the most patriotic people in Italy were café girls—and I believe they are still patriotic.

The boys at first were very polite about my medals and asked me what I had done to get them. I showed them the papers, which were written in very beautiful language and full of *fratellanza* and *abnegazione*,[10] but which really said, with the adjective removed, that I had been given the medals because I was an American. After that their manner changed a little toward me, although I was their friend against outsiders. I was a friend, but I was never really one of them after they had read the citations,[11] because it had been different with them and they had done very different things to get their medals. I had been wounded, it was true; but we all knew that being wounded, after all, was really an accident. I was never ashamed of the ribbons, though, and sometimes after cocktail hour, I would imagine myself having done all the things they had done to get their medals; but walking home at night through the empty streets with the cold wind and all the shops closed, trying to keep near the street lights, I knew that I would never have

done such things, and I was very much afraid to die, and often lay in bed at night by myself, afraid to die and wondering how I would be when I went back to the front again.

The three with the medals were like hunting hawks; and I was not a hawk, although I might seem a hawk to those who had never hunted; they, the three, knew better and so we drifted apart. But I stayed good friends with the boy who had been wounded his first day at the front, because he would never know now how he would have turned out; so he could never be accepted either, and I liked him because I thought perhaps he would not have turned out to be a hawk either.

The major, who had been the great fencer, did not believe in bravery, and spent much time while we sat in the machines correcting my grammar. He had complimented me on how I spoke Italian, and we talked together very easily. One day I had said that Italian seemed such an easy language to me that I could not take a great interest in it; everything was so easy to say. "Ah, yes," the major said. "Why, then, do you not take up the use of grammar?" So we took up the use of grammar, and soon Italian was such a difficult language that I was afraid to talk to him until I had the grammar straight in my mind.

The major came very regularly to the hospital. I do not think he ever missed a day, although I am sure he did not believe in the machines. There was a time when none of us believed in the machines, and one day the major said it was all nonsense. The machines were new then and it was we who were to prove them. It was an idiotic idea, he said, "a theory, like another." I had not learned my grammar, and he said I was a stupid impossible disgrace, and he was a fool to have bothered with me. He was a small man and he sat straight up in his chair with his right hand

---

10. *fratellanza* (frä tel län′zä) and *abnegazione* (äb′nä gä-tzyō′ne), brotherhood and self-denial. *[Italian]*
11. citation (sī tā′shən), *n.* honorable mention for bravery in war.

thrust into the machine and looked straight ahead at the wall while the straps thumped up and down with his fingers in them.

EVALUATE: Why do you think the major continued his daily treatment if he didn't believe in the machines?

"What will you do when the war is over if it is over?" he asked me. "Speak grammatically!"

"I will go to the States."

"Are you married?"

"No, but I hope to be."

"The more of a fool you are," he said. He seemed very angry. "A man must not marry."

"Why, Signor Maggiore?"[12]

"Don't call me 'Signor Maggiore.'"

"Why must not a man marry?"

"He cannot marry. He cannot marry," he said angrily. "If he is to lose everything, he should not place himself in a position to lose that. He should not place himself in a position to lose. He should find things he cannot lose."

He spoke very angrily and bitterly, and looked straight ahead while he talked.

"But why should he necessarily lose it?"

"He'll lose it," the major said. He was looking at the wall. Then he looked down at the machine and jerked his little hand out from between the straps and slapped it hard against his thigh. "He'll lose it," he almost shouted. "Don't argue with me!" Then he called to the attendant who ran the machines. "Come and turn this damned thing off."

He went back into the other room for the light treatment and massage. Then I heard him ask the doctor if he might use his telephone and he shut the door. When he came back into the room, I was sitting in another machine. He was wearing his cape and had his cap on, and he came directly toward my machine and put his arm on my shoulder.

"I am so sorry," he said, and patted me on the shoulder with his good hand. "I would not be rude. My wife has just died. You must forgive me."

"Oh——" I said, feeling sick for him. "I am so sorry."

He stood there biting his lower lip. "It is very difficult," he said. "I cannot resign[13] myself."

He looked straight past me and out through the window. Then he began to cry. "I am utterly unable to resign myself," he said, and choked. And then crying, his head up looking at nothing, carrying himself straight and soldierly, with tears on both his cheeks and biting his lips, he walked past the machines and out the door.

The doctor told me that the major's wife, who was very young and whom he had not married until he was definitely invalided out of the war, had died of pneumonia. She had been sick only a few days. No one expected her to die. The major did not come to the hospital for three days. Then he came at the usual hour, wearing a black band on the sleeve of his uniform. When he came back, there were large framed photographs around the wall, of all sorts of wounds before and after they had been cured by the machines. In front of the machine the major used were three photographs of hands like his that were completely restored. I do not know where the doctor got them. I always understood we were the first to use the machines. The photographs did not make much difference to the major because he only looked out of the window.

---

12. **Signor Maggiore,** (sē′nyôr maj jô′re) Mr. Major. *[Italian]* In Italy it is a sign of respect to prefix an officer's name with *Signor.*

13. resign (ri zīn′), *v.* submit quietly; accept without complaint.

After Reading

Making Connections

Shaping Your Response

1. As you read "In Another Country," for which character did you have the most sympathy? Why?

Analyzing the Story

2. How does Hemingway show the loneliness of each man?

3. What do you think is the **theme** of the story?

4. Cite examples from the story that illustrate Hemingway's terse, understated **style.** Explain how this style is suited to Hemingway's theme.

Extending the Ideas

5. J. Alfred Prufrock and Richard Cory are both unhappy, lonely men. Compare their isolation to that of the soldiers in "In Another Country."

Vocabulary Study

Study the relationship of each of the following pairs of words in capital letters; then choose another pair that has the same relationship.

detached
wither
resign
citation
game

1. DEPRESSION : DETACHED : : **a.** sad : happy **b.** close : aloof **c.** virus : cold **d.** illness : cure

2. SWELL : WITHER : : **a.** bloat : shrink **b.** grape : raisin **c.** large : enormous **d.** exaggeration : silence

3. RESIGN : YIELD : : **a.** go : stop **b.** quit : apply **c.** assign : report **d.** grieve : mourn

4. CITATION : WAR : : **a.** grades : report card **b.** honorable mention : runner-up **c.** trophy : tournament **d.** medal : hero

5. DEER : GAME : : **a.** rabbit : trap **b.** hawk : predator **c.** horse : donkey **d.** tame : wild

Expressing Your Ideas

Mood Adjustment How does the mood of Childe Hassam's painting *Allies Day, May 1917* differ from the mood of "In Another Country"? Write an **analysis** describing the techniques and images the artist used to create the painting's mood.

Before Reading

Winter Dreams

by F. Scott Fitzgerald

F. Scott Fitzgerald
1896–1940

F. Scott Fitzgerald wrote his novel *The Great Gatsby* while attending college at Princeton. He never finished college, but his writing brought him fame and fortune. After the success of his novel *This Side of Paradise,* Fitzgerald married Zelda Sayre, and the two took a rollercoaster ride through the Jazz Age, both at home and abroad. Both drank and partied too much, and they spent money lavishly. Their fortunes changed drastically during the Great Depression. Zelda's mental illness became unmanageable, and she was institutionalized. Fitzgerald's work was no longer popular, and he wrote screenplays in Hollywood until his early death.

Building Background

Do-Wacka-Do-Wacka-Do After the terrible years of World War I, people were ready to celebrate. Because of advances made in technology and the passage of fair labor laws, people had more leisure time. In spite of Prohibition (1919), which made making and selling alcoholic beverages illegal, "speakeasies"—private clubs where people could drink, listen to music, and dance—sprang up all over the country. Jazz blossomed as a musical style, and people danced the Charleston and the Black Bottom Rag. Henry Ford's affordable automobile made the society mobile. The thriving new movie industry created instant celebrities and fashions. Bobbed hair and flapper dresses became the rage. This was the time in which F. Scott Fitzgerald wrote, and it is the setting for "Winter Dreams."

Literary Focus

Character An author acquaints us with a **character** by describing his or her physical appearance, personality, behavior, thoughts, feelings, and speech. As you read "Winter Dreams," collect evidence to help you characterize Dexter Green and Judy Jones. Make a chart for each of them to organize your observations.

Character: _____

Appearance	Behavior	Speech	Thoughts

Writer's Notebook

Talk, Talk, Talk The use of dialogue makes fiction more realistic. Listen to people speaking to one another. Record bits of conversations in your notebook. Add the necessary dialogue tags to identify the speakers and to describe how they are speaking. "T. J. whispered," is an example of a dialogue tag. As you read "Winter Dreams," notice how F. Scott Fitzgerald uses dialogue to bring his characters to life.

Winter Dreams

F. Scott Fitzgerald

I

Some of the caddies were poor as sin and lived in one-room houses with a neurasthenic cow in the front yard, but Dexter Green's father owned the second best grocery store in Black Bear—the best one was "The Hub," patronized by the wealthy people from Sherry Island—and Dexter caddied only for pocket money.

In the fall when the days became crisp and gray, and the long Minnesota winter shut down like the white lid of a box, Dexter's skis moved over the snow that hid the fairways of the golf course. At these times the country gave him a feeling of profound melancholy— it offended him that the links should lie in enforced fallowness, haunted by ragged sparrows for the long season. It was dreary, too, that on the tees where the gay colors fluttered in summer there were now only the desolate sandboxes, knee-deep covered in crusted ice. When he crossed the hills the wind blew cold as misery, and if the sun was out he tramped with his eyes squinted up against the hard dimensionless glare.

In April the winter ceased abruptly.[1] The snow ran down into Black Bear Lake scarcely tarrying for the early golfers to brave the season with red and black balls. Without elation, without an interval of moist glory, the cold was gone.

Dexter knew that there was something dismal about this Northern spring, just as he knew there was something gorgeous about the fall. Fall made him clinch his hands and tremble and repeat idiotic sentences to himself, and make brisk abrupt gestures of command to imaginary audiences and armies. October filled him with hope which November raised to a sort of ecstatic triumph, and in this mood the fleeting brilliant impressions of the summer at Sherry Island were ready grist to his mill. He became a golf champion and defeated Mr. T. A. Hedrick in a marvelous match played a hundred times over the fairways of his imagination, a match each detail of which he changed about untiringly—sometimes he won with almost laughable ease, sometimes he came up magnificently from behind. Again, stepping from a Pierce-Arrow automobile, like Mr. Mortimer Jones, he strolled frigidly into the lounge of the Sherry Island Golf Club—or perhaps, surrounded by an admiring crowd, he gave an exhibition of fancy diving from the springboard of the club raft. . . . Among those who watched him in open-mouthed wonder was Mr. Mortimer Jones.

And one day it came to pass that Mr. Jones—himself and not his ghost—came up to Dexter with tears in his eyes and said that Dexter was the —— —— best caddy in the club, and wouldn't he decide not to quit if Mr. Jones made it worth his while, because every other —— —— caddy in the club lost one ball a hole for him—regularly—

"No sir," said Dexter decisively,[2] "I don't want to caddy anymore." Then, after a pause: "I'm too old."

"You're not more than fourteen. Why the devil did you decide just this morning that you wanted to quit? You promised that next week you'd go over to the state tournament with me."

"I decided I was too old."

Dexter handed in his "A Class" badge, collected what money was due him from the caddy master, and walked home to Black Bear Village.

"The best —— —— caddy I ever saw," shouted Mr. Mortimer Jones over a drink that afternoon. "Never lost a ball! Willing! Intelligent! Quiet! Honest! Grateful!"

The little girl who had done this was eleven—beautifully ugly as little girls are apt to be who are destined after a few years to be inexpressibly lovely and bring no end of misery to a great number of men. The spark, however, was perceptible. There was a general ungodliness in the way her lips twisted down at the corners when she smiled, and in the—Heaven help us!—in the almost passionate quality of her eyes. Vitality is born early in such women. It was utterly in evidence now, shining through her thin frame in a sort of glow.

She had come eagerly out on to the course at nine o'clock with a white linen nurse and five small new golf clubs in a white canvas bag which the nurse was carrying. When Dexter first saw her, she was standing by the caddy house, rather ill at ease and trying to conceal the fact by engaging her nurse in an obviously unnatural conversation graced by startling and irrelevant grimaces from herself.

"Well, it's certainly a nice day, Hilda," Dexter heard her say. She drew down the corners of her mouth, smiled, and glanced furtively[3] around,

---

1. **abruptly** (ə brupt′lē), *adv.* unexpectedly.
2. **decisively** (di sī′siv lē), *adj.* firmly, expressing no question or doubt.
3. **furtively** (fėr′tiv lē), *adv.* stealthily; secretly.

her eyes in transit falling for an instant on Dexter.

Then to the nurse:

"Well, I guess there aren't very many people out here this morning, are there?"

The smile again—radiant, blatantly[4] artificial—convincing.

"I don't know what we're supposed to do now," said the nurse looking nowhere in particular.

"Oh, that's all right. I'll fix it up."

Dexter stood perfectly still, his mouth slightly ajar. He knew that if he moved forward a step, his stare would be in her line of vision—if he moved backward, he would lose his full view of her face. For a moment he had not realized how young she was. Now he remembered having seen her several times the year before—in bloomers.

Suddenly, involuntarily,[5] he laughed, a short abrupt laugh—then, startled by himself, he turned and began to walk quickly away.

"Boy!"

Dexter stopped.

"Boy——"

Beyond question he was addressed. Not only that, but he was treated to that absurd smile, that preposterous smile—the memory of which at least a dozen men were to carry into middle age.

"Boy, do you know where the golf teacher is?"

"He's giving a lesson."

"Well, do you know where the caddy master is?"

"He isn't here yet this morning."

"Oh." For a moment this baffled her. She stood alternately on her right and left foot.

"We'd like to get a caddy," said the nurse. "Mrs. Mortimer Jones sent us out to play golf, and we don't know how without we get a caddy."

Here she was stopped by an ominous glance from Miss Jones, followed immediately by the smile.

"There aren't any caddies here except me," said Dexter to the nurse, "and I got to stay here in charge until the caddy master gets here."

"Oh."

Miss Jones and her retinue now withdrew, and at a proper distance from Dexter became involved in a heated conversation, which was concluded by Miss Jones taking one of the clubs and hitting it on the ground with violence. For further emphasis she raised it again and was about to bring it down smartly upon the nurse's bosom, when the nurse seized the club and twisted it from her hands.

"You little mean old *thing!*" cried Miss Jones wildly.

Another argument ensued. Realizing that the elements of the comedy were implied in the scene, Dexter several times began to laugh, but each time restrained the laugh before it reached audibility. He could not resist the monstrous conviction that the little girl was justified in beating the nurse.

The situation was resolved by the fortuitous appearance of the caddy master, who was appealed to immediately by the nurse.

"Miss Jones is to have a little caddy, and this one says he can't go."

"Mr. McKenna said I was to wait here till you came," said Dexter quickly.

"Well, he's here now." Miss Jones smiled cheerfully at the caddy master. Then she dropped her bag and set off at a haughty mince toward the first tee.

"Well?" The caddy master turned to Dexter. "What you standing there like a dummy for? Go pick up the young lady's clubs."

"I don't think I'll go out today," said Dexter.

"You don't——"

"I think I'll quit."

The enormity of his decision frightened him. He was a favorite caddy, and the thirty dollars a month he earned through the summer were not to be made elsewhere around the lake. But he had received a strong emotional shock, and his perturbation required

---

4. **blatantly** (blāt′nt lē), *adv.* obviously or flagrantly.

5. **involuntarily** (in vol′ən ter′ə lē), *adv.* in a manner that is not of one's own free will.

a violent and immediate outlet.

It is not so simple as that, either. As so frequently would be the case in the future, Dexter was unconsciously dictated to by his winter dreams.

CLARIFY: Why did Dexter suddenly quit his caddy job?

II

Now, of course, the quality and the seasonability of these winter dreams varied, but the stuff of them remained. They persuaded Dexter several years later to pass up a business course at the State university—his father, prospering now, would have paid his way—for the precarious advantage of attending an older and more famous university in the East, where he was bothered by his scanty funds. But do not get the impression, because his winter dreams happened to be concerned at first with musings on the rich, that there was anything merely snobbish in the boy. He wanted not association with glittering things and glittering people—he wanted the glittering things themselves. Often he reached out for the best without knowing why he wanted it—and sometimes he ran up against the mysterious denials and prohibitions in which life indulges. It is with one of those denials and not with his career as a whole that this story deals.

He made money. It was rather amazing. After college he went to the city from which Black Bear Lake draws its wealthy patrons. When he was only twenty-three and had been there not quite two years, there were already people who liked to say: "Now *there's* a boy——" All about him rich men's sons were peddling bonds precariously,[6] or investing patrimonies precariously, or plodding through the two dozen volumes of the "George Washington Commercial Course," but Dexter borrowed a thousand dollars on his college degree and his

confident mouth, and bought a partnership in a laundry.

It was a small laundry when he went into it, but Dexter made a specialty of learning how the English washed fine woolen golf stockings without shrinking them, and within a year he was catering to the trade that wore knickerbockers.[7] Men were insisting that their Shetland[8] hose and sweaters go to his laundry, just as they had insisted on a caddy who could find golf balls. A little later he was doing their wives' lingerie as well—and running five branches in different parts of the city. Before he was twenty-seven he owned the largest string of laundries in his section of the country. It was then that he sold out and went to New York. But the part of his story that concerns us goes back to the days when he was making his first big success.

When he was twenty-three, Mr. Hart—one of the gray-haired men who like to say "Now there's a boy"—gave him a guest card to the Sherry Island Golf Club for a weekend. So he signed his name one day on the register, and that afternoon played golf in a foursome with Mr. Hart and Mr. Sandwood and Mr. T. A. Hedrick. He did not consider it necessary to remark that he had once carried Mr. Hart's bag over this same links, and that he knew every trap and gully with his eyes shut—but he found himself glancing at the four caddies who trailed them, trying to catch a gleam or gesture that would remind him of himself, that would lessen the gap which lay between his present and his past.

It was a curious day, slashed abruptly with fleeting, familiar impressions. One minute he had the sense of being a trespasser—in the next he was impressed by the tremendous superiority

---

6. **precariously** (pri ker′ē əs lē), *adv.* insecurely; uncertainly.
7. **knickerbockers,** full breeches gathered and banded just below the knee.
8. **Shetland,** made from the wool of Shetland sheep.

he felt toward Mr. T. A. Hedrick, who was a bore and not even a good golfer anymore.

Then, because of a ball Mr. Hart lost near the fifteenth green, an enormous thing happened. While they were searching the stiff grasses of the rough, there was a clear call of "Fore!" from behind a hill in their rear. And as they all turned abruptly from their search a bright new ball sliced abruptly over the hill and caught Mr. T. A. Hedrick in the abdomen.

"By Gad!" cried Mr. T. A. Hedrick, "they ought to put some of these crazy women off the course. It's getting to be outrageous."

A head and a voice came up together over the hill:

"Do you mind if we go through?"

"You hit me in the stomach!" declared Mr. Hedrick wildly.

"Did I?" The girl approached the group of men. "I'm sorry. I yelled 'Fore!'"

Her glance fell casually on each of the men—then scanned the fairway for her ball.

"Did I bounce into the rough?"

It was impossible to determine whether this question was ingenuous or malicious. In a moment, however, she left no doubt, for as her partner came up over the hill she called cheerfully:

"Here I am! I'd have gone on the green except that I hit something."

As she took her stance for a short mashie[9] shot, Dexter looked at her closely. She wore a blue gingham dress, rimmed at throat and shoulders with a white edging that accentuated her tan. The quality of exaggeration, of thinness, which had made her passionate eyes and down-turning mouth absurd at eleven, was gone now. She was arrestingly beautiful. The color in her cheeks was centered like the color in a picture—it was not a "high" color, but a sort of fluctuating and feverish warmth, so shaded that it seemed at any moment it would recede and disappear. This color and the mobility of her mouth gave a continual impression of flux, of intense life, of passionate vitality—balanced only partially by the sad luxury of her eyes.

She swung her mashie impatiently[10] and without interest, pitching the ball into a sand pit on the other side of the green. With a quick, insincere smile and a careless "Thank you!" she went on after it.

"That Judy Jones!" remarked Mr. Hedrick on the next tee, as they waited—some moments—for her to play on ahead. "All she needs is to be turned up and spanked for six months and then to be married off to an old-fashioned cavalry captain."

"My, she's good-looking!" said Mr. Sandwood, who was just over thirty.

"Good-looking!" cried Mr. Hedrick contemptuously,[11] "she always looks as if she wanted to be kissed! Turning those big cow eyes on every calf in town!"

It was doubtful if Mr. Hedrick intended a reference to the maternal instinct.

"She'd play pretty good golf if she'd try," said Mr. Sandwood.

"She has no form," said Mr. Hedrick solemnly.

"She has a nice figure," said Mr. Sandwood.

"Better thank the Lord she doesn't drive a swifter ball," said Mr. Hart, winking at Dexter.

*L*ater in the afternoon the sun went down with a riotous swirl of gold and varying blues and scarlets, and left the dry, rustling night of western summer. Dexter watched from the veranda of the Golf Club, watched the even overlap of the waters in the little wind, silver molasses under the harvest moon. Then the moon held a finger to her lips and the lake became a clear pool, pale and quiet. Dexter put on his bathing suit and swam out to the farthest raft, where he stretched dripping on the wet canvas of the springboard.

There was a fish jumping and a star shining and the lights around the lake were gleaming.

---

9. **mashie,** a kind of golf club.
10. impatiently (im pā′shənt lē), *adv.* crossly; in a manner showing a lack of patience.
11. contemptuously (kən temp′chū əs lē), *adv.* scornfully.

Over on a dark peninsula a piano was playing the songs of last summer and of summers before that—songs from *Chin-Chin* and *The Count of Luxemburg* and *The Chocolate Soldier*[12]— and because the sound of a piano over a stretch of water had always seemed beautiful to Dexter, he lay perfectly quiet and listened.

The tune the piano was playing at that moment had been gay and new five years before when Dexter was a sophomore at college. They had played it at a prom once when he could not afford the luxury of proms, and he had stood outside the gymnasium and listened. The sound of the tune precipitated in him a sort of ecstasy, and it was with that ecstasy he viewed what happened to him now. It was a mood of intense appreciation, a sense that, for once, he was magnificently attuned to life and that everything about him was radiating a brightness and a glamor he might never know again.

A low, pale oblong detached itself suddenly from the darkness of the Island, spitting forth the reverberate sound of a racing motorboat. Two white streamers of cleft water rolled themselves out behind it and almost immediately the boat was beside him, drowning out the hot tinkle of the piano in the drone of its spray. Dexter raising himself on his arms was aware of a figure standing at the wheel, of two dark eyes regarding him over the lengthening space of water—then the boat had gone by and was sweeping in an immense and purposeless circle of spray round and round in the middle of the lake. With equal eccentricity one of the circles flattened out and headed back toward the raft.

"Who's that?" she called, shutting off her motor. She was so near now that Dexter could see her bathing suit, which consisted apparently of pink rompers.

The nose of the boat bumped the raft, and as the latter tilted rakishly, he was precipitated toward her. With different degrees of interest they recognized each other.

"Aren't you one of those men we played through this afternoon?" she demanded.

He was.

"Well, do you know how to drive a motorboat? Because if you do, I wish you'd drive this one so I can ride on the surfboard behind. My name is Judy Jones"—she favored him with an absurd smirk—rather, what tried to be a smirk, for, twist her mouth as she might, it was not grotesque, it was merely beautiful—"and I live in a house over there on the Island, and in that house there is a man waiting for me. When he drove up at the door, I drove out of the dock because he says I'm his ideal."

There was a fish jumping and a star shining and the lights around the lake were gleaming. Dexter sat beside Judy Jones and she explained how her boat was driven. Then she was in the water, swimming to the floating surfboard with a sinuous crawl. Watching her was without effort to the eye, watching a branch waving or a sea gull flying. Her arms, burned to butternut, moved sinuously among the dull platinum ripples, elbow appearing first, casting the forearm back with a cadence of falling water, then reaching out and down, stabbing a path ahead.

They moved out into the lake; turning, Dexter saw that she was kneeling on the low rear of the now uptilted surfboard.

"Go faster," she called, "fast as it'll go."

Obediently he jammed the lever forward and the white spray mounted at the bow. When he looked around again, the girl was standing up on the rushing board, her arms spread wide, her eyes lifted toward the moon.

"It's awful cold," she shouted. "What's your name?"

He told her.

"Well, why don't you come to dinner tomorrow night?"

His heart turned over like the flywheel of the boat, and, for the second time, her casual whim gave a new direction to his life.

---

12. *Chin-Chin . . . Soldier,* popular musicals and light operas of the day.

Next evening while he waited for her to come downstairs, Dexter peopled the soft deep summer room and the sun porch that opened from it with the men who had already loved Judy Jones. He knew the sort of men they were—the men who when he first went to college had entered from the great prep schools with graceful clothes and the deep tan of healthy summers. He had seen that, in one sense, he was better than these men. He was newer and stronger. Yet in acknowledging to himself that he wished his children to be like them, he was admitting that he was but the rough, strong stuff from which they eternally sprang.

When the time had come for him to wear good clothes, he had known who were the best tailors in America, and the best tailors in America had made him the suit he wore this evening. He had acquired that particular reserve peculiar to his university, that set it off from other universities. He recognized the value to him of such a mannerism and he had adopted it; he knew that to be careless in dress and manner required more confidence than to be careful. But carelessness was for his children. His mother's name had been Krimslich. She was a Bohemian of the peasant class and she had talked broken English to the end of her days. Her son must keep to the set patterns.

At a little after seven Judy Jones came downstairs. She wore a blue silk afternoon dress, and he was disappointed at first that she had not put on something more elaborate. This feeling was accentuated when, after a brief greeting, she went to the door of a butler's pantry and pushing it open called: "You can serve dinner, Martha." He had rather expected that a butler would announce dinner, that there would be a cocktail. Then he put these thoughts behind him as they sat down side by side on a lounge and looked at each other.

"Father and Mother won't be here," she said thoughtfully.

J.C. Leyendecker was an illustrator whose Arrow Collar and shirt ads made him famous in the early 1900s. The illustrations for F. Scott Fitzgerald's "Winter Dreams" are examples of Leyendecker's work. ➤

He remembered the last time he had seen her father, and he was glad the parents were not to be here tonight—they might wonder who he was. He had been born in Keeble, a Minnesota village fifty miles farther north, and he always gave Keeble as his home instead of Black Bear Village. Country towns were well enough to come from if they weren't inconveniently in sight and used as footstools by fashionable lakes.

They talked of his university, which she had visited frequently during the past two years, and of the nearby city which supplied Sherry Island with its patrons, and whither Dexter would return next day to his prospering laundries.

EVALUATE: How does the grown-up Judy compare to Dexter's recollection of her as a child?

During dinner she slipped into a moody depression which gave Dexter a feeling of uneasiness. Whatever petulance she uttered in her throaty voice worried him. Whatever she smiled at—at him, at a chicken liver, at nothing—it disturbed him that her smile could have no root in mirth, or even in amusement. When the scarlet corners of her lips curved down, it was less a smile than an invitation to a kiss.

Then, after dinner, she led him out on the dark sun porch and deliberately changed the atmosphere.

"Do you mind if I weep a little?" she said.

"I'm afraid I'm boring you," he responded quickly.

"You're not. I like you. But I've just had a terrible afternoon. There was a man I cared about,

and this afternoon he told me out of a clear sky that he was poor as a church mouse. He'd never even hinted it before. Does this sound horribly mundane?"

"Perhaps he was afraid to tell you."

"Suppose he was," she answered. "He didn't start right. You see, if I'd thought of him as poor—well, I've been mad about loads of poor men, and fully intended to marry them all. But in this case, I hadn't thought of him that way, and my interest in him wasn't strong enough to survive the shock. As if a girl calmly informed her fiancé that she was a widow. He might not object to widows, but——

"Let's start right," she interrupted herself suddenly. "Who are you, anyhow?"

For a moment Dexter hesitated. Then:

"I'm nobody," he announced. "My career is largely a matter of futures."

"Are you poor?"

"No," he said frankly,[13] "I'm probably making more money than any man my age in the Northwest. I know that's an obnoxious remark, but you advised me to start right."

There was a pause. Then she smiled and the corners of her mouth drooped and an almost imperceptible sway brought her closer to him, looking up into his eyes. A lump rose in Dexter's throat, and he waited breathless for the

---

13. **frankly** (frangk lē), *adv.* openly; expressing one's thoughts, opinions, and feelings freely.

experiment, facing the unpredictable compound that would form mysteriously from the elements of their lips. Then he saw—she communicated her excitement to him, lavishly, deeply, with kisses that were not a promise but a fulfillment. They aroused in him not hunger demanding renewal but surfeit[14] that would demand more surfeit . . . kisses that were like charity, creating want by holding back nothing at all.

It did not take him many hours to decide that he had wanted Judy Jones ever since he was a proud, desirous little boy.

IV

It began like that—and continued, with varying shades of intensity, on such a note right up to the denouement.[15] Dexter surrendered a part of himself to the most direct and unprincipled personality with which he had ever come in contact. Whatever Judy wanted, she went after with the full pressure of her charm. There was no divergence of method, no jockeying for position or premeditation of effects—there was a very little mental side to any of her affairs. She simply made men conscious to the highest degree of her physical loveliness. Dexter had no desire to change her. Her deficiencies were knit up with a passionate energy that transcended and justified them.

When, as Judy's head lay against his shoulder that first night, she whispered, "I don't know what's the matter with me. Last night I thought I was in love with a man and tonight I think I'm in love with you——"—it seemed to him a beautiful and romantic thing to say. It was the exquisite excitability that for the moment he controlled and owned. But a week later he was compelled to view this same quality in a different light. She took him in her roadster to a picnic supper, and after supper she disappeared, likewise in her roadster, with another man. Dexter became enormously upset and was scarcely able to be decently civil to the other people present. When she assured him that she had not kissed the other man, he knew she was lying—yet he was glad that she had taken the trouble to lie to him.

He was, as he found before the summer ended, one of a varying dozen who circulated about her. Each of them had at one time been favored above all others—about half of them still basked in the solace of occasional sentimental revivals. Whenever one showed signs of dropping out through long neglect, she granted him a brief honeyed hour, which encouraged him to tag along for a year or so longer. Judy made these forays upon the helpless and defeated without malice, indeed half unconscious that there was anything mischievous in what she did.

When a new man came to town, everyone dropped out—dates were automatically cancelled.

The helpless part of trying to do anything about it was that she did it all herself. She was not a girl who could be "won" in the kinetic sense—she was proof against cleverness, she was proof against charm; if any of these assailed her too strongly, she would immediately resolve the affair to a physical basis, and under the magic of her physical splendor the strong as well as the brilliant played her game and not their own. She was entertained only by the gratification of her desires and by the direct exercise of her own charm. Perhaps from so much youthful love, so many youthful lovers, she had come, in self-defense, to nourish herself wholly from within.

Succeeding Dexter's first exhilaration came restlessness and dissatisfaction. The helpless ecstasy of losing himself in her was opiate rather than tonic. It was fortunate for his work during the winter that those moments of ecstasy came infrequently. Early in their acquaintance it had seemed for a while that there was a deep and spontaneous mutual attraction—that first August, for example—three days of long evenings on her dusky veranda, of strange wan kisses through the late afternoon, in shadowy alcoves or behind the

14. **surfeit** (sûr′fit), *n.* overindulgence.
15. **denouement** (dā′nü mänt′), *n.* solution of a plot in a story, play, situation, etc.

protecting trellises of the garden arbors, of mornings when she was fresh as a dream and almost shy at meeting him in the clarity of the rising day. There was all the ecstasy of an engagement about it, sharpened by his realization that there was no engagement. It was during those three days that, for the first time, he had asked her to marry him. She said "maybe some day," she said "kiss me," she said "I'd like to marry you," she said "I love you"— she said—nothing.

The three days were interrupted by the arrival of a New York man who visited at her house for half September. To Dexter's agony, rumor engaged them. The man was the son of the president of a great trust company. But at the end of a month it was reported that Judy was yawning. At a dance one night she sat all evening in a motorboat with a local beau, while the New Yorker searched the club for her frantically. She told the local beau that she was bored with her visitor, and two days later he left. She was seen with him at the station, and it was reported that he looked very mournful indeed.

On this note the summer ended. Dexter was twenty-four, and he found himself increasingly in a position to do as he wished. He joined two clubs in the city and lived at one of them. Though he was by no means an integral part of the stag lines at these clubs, he managed to be on hand at dances where Judy Jones was likely to appear. He could have gone out socially as much as he liked—he was an eligible young man, now, and popular with downtown fathers. His confessed devotion to Judy Jones had rather solidified his position. But he had no social aspirations and rather despised the dancing men who were always on tap for the Thursday or Saturday parties and who filled in at dinners with the younger married set. Already he was playing with the idea of going East to New York. He wanted to take Judy Jones with him. No disillusion as to the world in which she had grown up could cure his illusion as to her desirability.

Remember that—for only in the light of it can what he did for her be understood.

Eighteen months after he first met Judy Jones, he became engaged to another girl. Her name was Irene Scheerer, and her father was one of the men who had always believed in Dexter. Irene was light-haired and sweet and honorable, and a little stout, and she had two suitors whom she pleasantly relinquished when Dexter formally asked her to marry him.

Summer, fall, winter, spring, another summer, another fall—so much he had given of his active life to the incorrigible lips of Judy Jones. She had treated him with interest, with encouragement, with malice, with indifference, with contempt. She had inflicted on him the innumerable little slights and indignities possible in such a case—as if in revenge for having ever cared for him at all. She had beckoned him and yawned at him and beckoned him again and he had responded often with bitterness and narrowed eyes. She had brought him ecstatic happiness and intolerable agony of spirit. She had caused him untold inconvenience and not a little trouble. She had insulted him, and she had ridden over him, and she had played his interest in her against his interest in his work—for fun. She had done everything to him except to criticize him—this she had not done—it seemed to him only because it might have sullied the utter indifference she manifested and sincerely felt toward him.

When autumn had come and gone again, it occurred to him that he could not have Judy Jones. He had to beat this into his mind but he convinced himself at last. He lay awake at night for a while and argued it over. He told himself the trouble and pain she had caused him, he enumerated her glaring deficiencies as a wife. Then he said to himself that he loved her, and after a while he fell asleep. For a week, lest he imagine her husky voice over the telephone or her eyes opposite him at lunch, he worked hard and late, and at night he went to his office and plotted out his years.

At the end of a week he went to a dance and cut in on her once. For almost the first time since they had met he did not ask her to sit out with him or tell her that she was lovely. It hurt him that she did not miss these things—that was all. He was not jealous when he saw that there was a new man tonight. He had been hardened against jealousy long before.

He stayed late at the dance. He sat for an hour with Irene Scheerer and talked about books and about music. He knew very little about either. But he was beginning to be master of his own time now, and he had a rather priggish notion that he—the young and already fabulously successful Dexter Green—should know more about such things.

That was in October, when he was twenty-five. In January, Dexter and Irene became engaged. It was to be announced in June, and they were to be married three months later.

The Minnesota winter prolonged itself interminably, and it was almost May when the winds came soft and the snow ran down into Black Bear Lake at last. For the first time in over a year Dexter was enjoying a certain tranquility of spirit. Judy Jones had been in Florida, and afterward in Hot Springs, and somewhere she had been engaged, and somewhere she had broken it off. At first, when Dexter had definitely given her up, it had made him sad that people still linked them together and asked for news of her, but when he began to be placed at dinner next to Irene Scheerer, people didn't ask him about her anymore—they told him about her. He ceased to be an authority on her.

May at last. Dexter walked the streets at night when the darkness was damp as rain, wondering that so soon, with so little done, so much of ecstasy had gone from him. May one year back had been marked by Judy's poignant, unforgivable yet forgiven turbulence—it had been one of those rare times when he fancied she had grown to care for him. That old penny's worth of happiness he had spent for this bushel of content. He knew that Irene would be no more than a curtain spread behind him, a hand moving among gleaming teacups, a voice calling to children . . . fire and loveliness were gone, the magic of nights and the wonder of the varying hours and seasons . . . slender lips, down-turning, dropping to his lips and bearing him up into a heaven of eyes. . . . The thing was deep in him. He was too strong and alive for it to die lightly.

In the middle of May when the weather balanced for a few days on the thin bridge that led to deep summer, he turned in one night at Irene's house. Their engagement was to be announced in a week now—no one would be surprised at it. And tonight they would sit together on the lounge at the University Club and look on for an hour at the dancers. It gave him a sense of solidity to go with her—she was so sturdily popular, so intensely "great."

CLARIFY: What does Dexter like about Irene Scheerer?

He mounted the steps of the brownstone house and stepped inside.

"Irene," he called.

Mrs. Scheerer came out of the living room to meet him.

"Dexter," she said. "Irene's gone upstairs with a splitting headache. She wanted to go with you but I made her go to bed."

"Nothing serious, I——"

"Oh, no. She's going to play golf with you in the morning. You can spare her for just one night, can't you, Dexter?"

Her smile was kind. She and Dexter liked each other. In the living room he talked for a moment before he said good night.

Returning to the University Club, where he had rooms, he stood in the doorway for a moment and watched the dancers. He leaned against the doorpost, nodded at a man or two—yawned.

"Hello, darling."

The familiar voice at his elbow startled him. Judy Jones had left a man and crossed the room to him—Judy Jones, a slender enameled doll in cloth of gold: gold in a band at her head, gold in two slipper points at her dress's hem. The fragile glow of her face seemed to blossom as she smiled at him. A breeze of warmth and light blew through the room. His hands in the pockets of his dinner jacket tightened spasmodically.[16] He was filled with a sudden excitement.

"When did you get back?" he asked casually.

"Come here and I'll tell you about it."

She turned and he followed her. She had been away—he could have wept at the wonder of her return. She had passed through enchanted streets, doing things that were like provocative music. All mysterious happenings, all fresh and quickening hopes, had gone away with her, come back with her now.

She turned in the doorway.

"Have you a car here? If you haven't, I have."

"I have a coupé."

In then, with a rustle of golden cloth. He slammed the door. Into so many cars she had stepped—like this—like that—her back against the leather, so—her elbow resting on the door—waiting. She would have been soiled long since had there been anything to soil her—except herself—but this was her own self outpouring.

With an effort he forced himself to start the car and back into the street. This was nothing, he must remember. She had done this before, and he had put her behind him, as he would have crossed a bad account from his books.

He drove slowly downtown, and, affecting abstraction, traversed the deserted streets of the business section, peopled here and there where a movie was giving out its crowd or where consumptive or pugilistic youth lounged in front of pool halls. The clink of glasses and the slap of hands on the bars issued from saloons, cloisters of glazed glass and dirty yellow light.

She was watching him closely and the silence was embarrassing, yet in this crisis he could find no casual word with which to profane the hour.

At a convenient turning he began to zigzag back toward the University Club.

"Have you missed me?" she asked suddenly.

"Everybody missed you."

He wondered if she knew of Irene Scheerer. She had been back only a day—her absence had been almost contemporaneous with his engagement.

"What a remark!" Judy laughed sadly—without sadness. She looked at him searchingly. He became absorbed in the dashboard.

"You're handsomer than you used to be," she said thoughtfully. "Dexter, you have the most rememberable eyes."

He could have laughed at this, but he did not laugh. It was the sort of thing that was said to sophomores. Yet it stabbed at him.

"I'm awfully tired of everything, darling." She called everyone darling, endowing the endearment with careless, individual camaraderie. "I wish you'd marry me."

The directness of this confused him. He should have told her now that he was going to marry another girl, but he could not tell her. He could as easily have sworn that he had never loved her.

"I think we'd get along," she continued, on the same note, "unless probably you've forgotten me and fallen in love with another girl."

Her confidence was obviously enormous. She had said, in effect, that she found such a thing impossible to believe, that if it were true he had merely committed a childish indiscretion—and probably to show off. She would forgive him, because it was not a matter of any moment but rather something to be brushed aside lightly.

"Of course, you could never love anybody but me," she continued, "I like the way you love me. Oh, Dexter, have you forgotten last year?"

"No, I haven't forgotten."

"Neither have I!"

---

16. **spasmodically** (spaz mod′ik lē), *adv.* in a manner characterized by sudden, involuntary contractions of a muscle or muscles.

Was she sincerely moved—or was she carried along by the wave of her own acting?

"I wish we could be like that again," she said, and he forced himself to answer:

"I don't think we can."

"I suppose not. . . . I hear you're giving Irene Scheerer a violent rush."

There was not the faintest emphasis on the name, yet Dexter was suddenly ashamed.

"Oh, take me home," cried Judy suddenly; "I don't want to go back to that idiotic dance—with those children."

Then, as he turned up the street that led to the residence district, Judy began to cry quietly to herself. He had never seen her cry before.

The dark street lightened, the dwellings of the rich loomed up around them, he stopped his coupé in front of the great white bulk of the Mortimer Joneses' house, somnolent, gorgeous, drenched with the splendor of the damp moonlight. Its solidity startled him. The strong walls, the steel of the girders, the breadth and beam and pomp of it were there only to bring out the contrast with the young beauty beside him. It was sturdy to accentuate her slightness—as if to show what a breeze could be generated by a butterfly's wing.

He sat perfectly quiet, his nerves in wild clamor, afraid that if he moved, he would find her irresistibly in his arms. Two tears had rolled down her wet face and trembled on her upper lip.

"I'm more beautiful than anybody else," she said brokenly, "why can't I be happy?" Her moist eyes tore at his stability—her mouth turned slowly downward with an exquisite sadness: "I'd like to marry you if you'll have me, Dexter. I suppose you think I'm not worth having, but I'll be so beautiful for you, Dexter."

A million phrases of anger, pride, passion, hatred, tenderness fought on his lips. Then a perfect wave of emotion washed over him, carrying off with it a sediment of wisdom, of convention, of doubt, of honor. This was his girl who was speaking, his own, his beautiful, his pride.

Would this 1913 ad by J.C. Leyendecker best portray Dexter with Judy or with Irene? Explain your choice. ➤

"Won't you come in?" He heard her draw in her breath sharply.

Waiting.

"All right," his voice was trembling, "I'll come in."

V

It was strange that neither when it was over nor a long time afterward did he regret that night. Looking at it from the perspective of ten years, the fact that Judy's flare for him endured just one month seemed of little importance. Nor did it matter that by his yielding he subjected himself to a deeper agony in the end and gave serious hurt to Irene Scheerer and to Irene's parents, who had befriended him. There was nothing sufficiently pictorial about Irene's grief to stamp itself on his mind.

Dexter was at bottom hard minded. The attitude of the city on his action was of no importance to him, not because he was going to leave the city, but because any outside attitude on the situation seemed superficial. He was completely indifferent to popular opinion. Nor, when he had seen that it was no use, that he did not possess in himself the power to move fundamentally or to hold Judy Jones, did he bear any malice toward her. He loved her, and he would love her until the day he was too old for loving—but he could not have her. So he tasted the deep pain that is reserved only for the strong, just as he had tasted for a little while the deep happiness.

Even the ultimate falsity of the grounds upon which Judy terminated the engagement that she did not want to "take him away" from Irene—Judy who had wanted nothing else—did not revolt him. He was beyond any revulsion or any amusement.

He went East in February with the intention of selling out his laundries and settling in New York—but the war came to America in March and changed his plans. He returned to the West, handed over the management of the business to his partner, and went into the first officers' training camp in late April. He was one of those young thousands who greeted the war with a certain amount of relief, welcoming the liberation from webs of tangled emotion.

VI

This story is not his biography, remember, although things creep into it which have nothing to do with those dreams he had when he was young. We are almost done with them and with him now. There is only one more incident to be related here, and it happens seven years farther on.

It took place in New York, where he had done well—so well that there were no barriers too high for him. He was thirty-two years old, and, except for one flying trip immediately after the war, he had not been West in seven years. A man named Devlin from Detroit came into his office to see him in a business way, and then and there this incident occurred, and closed out, so to speak, this particular side of his life.

"So you're from the Middle West," said the man Devlin with careless curiosity. "That's funny—I thought men like you were probably born and raised on Wall Street. You know—wife of one of my best friends in Detroit came from your city. I was an usher at the wedding."

Dexter waited with no apprehension of what was coming.

"Judy Simms," said Devlin with no particular interest; "Judy Jones she was once."

"Yes, I knew her." A dull impatience spread over him. He had heard, of course, that she was married—perhaps deliberately he had heard no more.

"Awfully nice girl," brooded Devlin meaninglessly, "I'm sort of sorry for her."

▲ In what ways does this man from an Arrow Collar advertisement by J.C. Leyendecker (1919) resemble Dexter Green at the end of the story?

"Why?" Something in Dexter was alert, receptive, at once.

"Oh, Lud Simms has gone to pieces in a way. I don't mean he ill-uses her, but he drinks and runs around——"

"Doesn't she run around?"

"No. Stays at home with her kids."

"Oh."

"She's a little too old for him," said Devlin.

"Too old!" cried Dexter. "Why, man, she's only twenty-seven."

He was possessed with a wild notion of rushing out into the streets and taking a train to Detroit. He rose to his feet spasmodically.

"I guess you're busy," Devlin apologized quickly. "I didn't realize——"

"No, I'm not busy," said Dexter, steadying his voice. "I'm not busy at all. Not busy at all. Did you say she was—twenty-seven? No, I said she was twenty-seven."

"Yes, you did," agreed Devlin dryly.

"Go on, then. Go on."

"What do you mean?"

"About Judy Jones."

Devlin looked at him helplessly.

"Well, that's—I told you all there is to it. He treats her like the devil. Oh, they're not going to get divorced or anything. When he's particularly outrageous she forgives him. In fact, I'm inclined to think she loves him. She was a pretty girl when she first came to Detroit."

A pretty girl! The phrase struck Dexter as ludicrous.

"Isn't she—a pretty girl anymore?"

"Oh, she's all right."

"Look here," said Dexter, sitting down suddenly. "I don't understand. You say she was a 'pretty girl' and now you say she's 'all right.' I don't understand what you mean—Judy Jones wasn't a pretty girl, at all. She was a great beauty. Why, I knew her. She was——"

Devlin laughed pleasantly.

"I'm not trying to start a row," he said. "I think Judy's a nice girl and I like her. I can't understand how a man like Lud Simms could fall madly in love with her, but he did." Then he added: "Most of the women like her."

Dexter looked closely at Devlin, thinking wildly that there must be a reason for this, some insensitivity in the man or some private malice.

"Lots of women fade just like *that,*" Devlin snapped his fingers. "You must have seen it happen. Perhaps I've forgotten how pretty she was at her wedding. I've seen her so much since then, you see. She has nice eyes."

A sort of dullness settled down upon Dexter. For the first time in his life he felt like getting very drunk. He knew that he was laughing loudly at something Devlin had said, but he did not know what it was or why it was funny. When, in a few minutes, Devlin went he lay down on his lounge and looked out the window at the New York skyline into which the sun was sinking in dull lovely shades of pink and gold.

He had thought that having nothing else to lose he was invulnerable at last—but he knew that he had just lost something more, as surely as if he had married Judy Jones and seen her fade away before his eyes.

The dream was gone. Something had been taken from him. In a sort of panic he pushed the palms of his hands into his eyes and tried to bring up a picture of the waters lapping on Sherry Island and the moonlit veranda, and gingham on the golf links and the dry sun and the gold color of her neck's soft down. And her mouth damp to his kisses and her eyes plaintive with melancholy and her freshness like new fine linen in the morning. Why, these things were no longer in the world! They had existed and they existed no longer.

For the first time in years the tears were streaming down his face. But they were for himself now. He did not care about mouth and eyes and moving hands. He wanted to care, and he could not care. For he had gone away and he could never go back anymore. The gates were closed, the sun was gone down, and there was no beauty but the gray beauty of steel that withstands all time. Even the grief he could have borne was left behind in the country of illusion, of youth, of the richness of life, where his winter dreams had flourished.

"Long ago," he said, "long ago, there was something in me, but now that thing is gone. Now that thing is gone, that thing is gone. I cannot cry. I cannot care. That thing will come back no more."

After Reading

Making Connections

Shaping Your Response

1. Would you want Judy Jones for a friend? Why or why not?

2. What do you think makes Judy Jones so appealing to Dexter Green?

Analyzing the Story

3. When Dexter gave up caddying, he was "unconsciously dictated to by his *winter dreams*." Why do you think these words are the title of the story, and what do you think the title means?

4. Why do you think Dexter tells Judy that "I'm probably making more money than any man my age in the Northwest"?

5. Why do you think Dexter becomes engaged to Irene Scheerer?

6. After Dexter hears about Judy Jones Simms from a business associate, he is bereft. "The dream was gone. Something had been taken from him." What do you think Dexter has lost?

Extending the Ideas

7. Would Dexter have been happier if he had married Irene? Explain your answer.

8. ☝ Compare Dexter Green's **perspective** on life to your own. What kinds of things are most important to Dexter, and are his values the same as or different than yours?

Literary Focus: Character

Use the charts you made to write a gossip-column article describing Dexter Green and Judy Jones.

Vocabulary Study

Complete each sentence with the adverb from the list that matches the context of the sentence.

decisively
spasmodically
blatantly
precariously
contemptuously
furtively
involuntarily
impatiently
abruptly
frankly

1. Dexter couldn't wait to have Judy as his wife. "I absolutely have to marry Judy," Dexter said to himself ____.

2. Mr. Scheerer—Irene's father—scorned Dexter's attentions to Judy, and eyed Dexter ____ as he escorted Judy out of the club.

3. Judy obviously did not love Dexter, and lied ____ when she told him that she wanted to marry him.

4. Mr. Mortimer Jones seemed to have little control over his movements, and gripped his golf club ____.

5. Dexter's uncertain feelings for Irene were ____ balanced against his infatuation with Judy Jones.

6. Dexter didn't want anyone to see him looking, so he glanced ____ around the room to see if anyone noticed him leaving with Judy.

7. Without warning, Judy stopped the speedboat ____, almost hitting the raft.

8. Dexter couldn't help himself, and he laughed ____ when young Judy called him "Boy!"

9. Judy Jones was quite certain she wanted to leave when she said ____, "Let's escape from this boring party right now."

10. "To answer your question, Judy, I'm making a lot of money," said Dexter ____, expressing himself freely.

Expressing Your Ideas

Writing Choices

Writer's Notebook Update Reread the dialogue you recorded in your notebook. Then try your hand at writing your own realistic dialogue. Imagine that Dexter runs into Irene Scheerer the summer after their break-up. Write a conversation that they might have.

Take a Peek Although Judy Jones doesn't seem introspective, perhaps she kept a diary. Be Judy and write six **diary entries**—one to follow each of the six sections of the story.

Art Imitates Life Much of F. Scott Fitzgerald's writing is autobiographical. Find out more about his life and make a **chart** listing the similarities between the characters and events in "Winter Dreams" and F. Scott Fitzgerald's life.

Similarities	
Events in "Winter Dreams"	Events in Fitzgerald's life

Other Options

The Jazz Age Work with a small group to research the roots of jazz as a musical style and define it. Then find recordings of famous jazz musicians of the 1920s. Give an **oral report** and play some of the recordings for the class.

The Roaring Twenties What were the highlights of the 1920s? Create a **multimedia report** showing the fashions of the day, the major political events, entertainment trends, famous people, and so on.

Women of the Jazz Age At the time this story took place, men did not generally consider women their equals. Make a **list of quotations** from the story that represent attitudes toward women. For example, Mr. Hedrick says of Judy, "All she needs is to be turned up and spanked for six months and then to be married off to an old-fashioned cavalry captain."

Before Reading

from Black Boy

by Richard Wright

Richard Wright
1908–1960

All four of Richard Wright's grandparents were born into slavery. His father was a sharecropper who deserted the family when Wright was five, and his mother fell ill and was eventually paralyzed. Wright and his brother were passed from relative to orphanage to relative until, at age fifteen, he went out on his own. After moving about the country, he eventually went to New York to pursue his writing career. Wright's most famous book, *Native Son,* was published in 1940, followed by *Black Boy* in 1944. Wright continued writing and traveled extensively, later moving his family to France to escape the racial discrimination they encountered in the United States.

Building Background

Set the Scene *Black Boy* is the autobiographical account of Richard Wright's life. The incident in this excerpt occurred when Wright was in the eighth grade at Smith Robertson Junior High School in Jackson, Mississippi. Wright and his mother lived with his grandmother, a strict Seventh-Day Adventist. For Wright's family poverty was a way of life. Keeping food on the table and the rent paid were the primary goals. There was no time for "foolish dreams" like writing. Racial discrimination was enforced by law. Ambition was not rewarded. In spite of this hostile environment, the seeds of Wright's future career as a writer began to grow.

Literary Focus

Look Who's Talking Dialogue, the conversation between two or more people in a literary work, can serve many purposes. It can help to characterize both the speaker and those spoken about, it can create a mood or atmosphere, it can move the plot forward, and it can develop a theme. As you read this excerpt from *Black Boy,* think about the purposes of the dialogue. What does it contribute to the story of Wright's life?

Writer's Notebook

What's In a Name? Richard Wright was bored, so he decided to write a story. He wrote it in three days and gave it a title that really caught the reader's eye. In your notebook jot down several plot ideas that you might like to develop into a story. Then write an eye-catching title that you think would be appropriate for each idea.

FROM

Black BOY

RICHARD WRIGHT

The eighth grade days flowed in their hungry path and I grew more conscious of myself; I sat in classes, bored, wondering, dreaming. One long dry afternoon I took out my composition book and told myself that I would write a story; it was sheer idleness that led me to it. What would the story be about? It resolved itself into a plot about a villain who wanted a widow's home and I called it *The Voodoo of Hell's Half-Acre.* It was crudely atmospheric, emotional, intuitively psychological, and stemmed from pure feeling. I finished it in three days and then wondered what to do with it.

The local Negro newspaper! That's it . . . I sailed into the office and shoved my ragged composition book under the nose of the man who called himself the editor.

"What is that?" he asked.

"A story," I said.

"A news story?"

"No, fiction."

"All right. I'll read it," he said.

He pushed my composition book back on his desk and looked at me curiously, sucking at his pipe.

"But I want you to read it *now,*" I said.

He blinked. I had no idea how newspapers were run. I thought that one took a story to an editor and he sat down then and there and read it and said yes or no.

"I'll read this and let you know about it tomorrow," he said.

I was disappointed; I had taken time to write it and he seemed distant and uninterested.

"Give me the story," I said, reaching for it.

He turned from me, took up the book and read ten pages or more.

"Won't you come in tomorrow?" he asked. "I'll have it finished then."

I honestly relented.[1]

"All right," I said. "I'll stop in tomorrow."

I left with the conviction[2] that he would not read it. Now, where else could I take it after he had turned it down? The next afternoon, en route to my job, I stepped into the newspaper office.

"Where's my story?" I asked.

"It's in galleys," he said.

"What's that?" I asked; I did not know what galleys were.

"It's set up in type," he said. "We're publishing it."

"How much money will I get?" I asked, excited.

"We can't pay for manuscript," he said.

"But you sell your papers for money," I said with logic.

"Yes, but we're young in business," he explained.

"But you're asking me to *give* you my story, but you don't *give* your papers away," I said.

He laughed.

"Look, you're just starting. This story will put your name before our readers. Now, that's something," he said.

---

1. **relent** (ri lent′), *v.* give in.
2. **conviction** (kən vik′shən), *n.* firm belief, certainty.

"But if the story is good enough to sell to your readers, then you ought to give me some of the money you get from it," I insisted.

He laughed again and I sensed that I was amusing him.

"I'm going to offer you something more valuable than money," he said. "I'll give you a chance to learn to write."

I was pleased, but I still thought he was taking advantage of me.

"When will you publish my story?"

"I'm dividing it into three installments," he said. "The first installment appears this week. But the main thing is this: Will you get news for me on a space rate basis?"

"I work mornings and evenings for three dollars a week," I said.

"Oh," he said. "Then you better keep that. But what are you doing this summer?"

"Nothing."

"Then come to see me before you take another job," he said. "And write some more stories."

A few days later my classmates came to me with baffled eyes, holding copies of the *Southern Register* in their hands.

"Did you really write that story?" they asked me.

"Yes."

"Why?"

"Because I wanted to."

"Where did you get it from?"

"I made it up."

"You didn't. You copied it out of a book."

"If I had, no one would publish it."

"But what are they publishing it for?"

"So people can read it."

"Who told you to do that?"

"Nobody."

"Then why did you do it?"

"Because I wanted to," I said again.

They were convinced that I had not told them the truth. We had never had any instruction in literary matters at school; the literature of the nation or the Negro had never been mentioned. My schoolmates could not understand why anyone would want to write a story; and, above all, they could not understand why I had called it *The Voodoo of Hell's Half-Acre*. The mood out of which a story was written was the most <u>alien</u>[3] thing conceivable to them. They looked at me with new eyes, and a distance, a suspiciousness came between us. If I had thought anything in writing the story, I had thought that perhaps it would make me more acceptable to them, and now it was cutting me off from them more completely than ever.

At home the effects were no less disturbing. Granny came into my room early one morning and sat on the edge of my bed.

"Richard, what is this you're putting in the papers?" she asked.

"A story," I said.

"About what?"

"It's just a story, granny."

"But they tell me it's been in three times."

"It's the same story. It's in three parts."

"But what is it about?" she insisted.

I <u>hedged</u>,[4] fearful of getting into a religious argument.

"It's just a story I made up," I said.

"Then it's a lie," she said.

"Oh, Christ," I said.

"You must get out of this house if you take the name of the Lord in vain," she said.

"Granny, please . . . I'm sorry," I pleaded. "But it's hard to tell you about the story. You see, granny, everybody knows that the story isn't true, but . . ."

"Then why write it?" she asked.

"Because people might want to read it."

"That's the Devil's work," she said and left.

My mother also was worried.

"Son, you ought to be more serious," she said. "You're growing up now and you won't be able to get jobs if you let people think that

---

3. alien (ā′lyən), *adj.* strange; foreign.
4. hedge (hej), *v.* avoid giving a direct answer.

◄ What thoughts, moods, or emotions do you think are portrayed in Hughie Lee Smith's, *Portrait of a Boy* (1938)? Explain your answer.

you're weak-minded. Suppose the superintendent of schools would ask you to teach here in Jackson, and he found out that you had been writing stories?"

I could not answer her.

"I'll be all right, mama," I said.

Uncle Tom, though surprised, was highly critical and contemptuous.[5] The story had no point, he said. And whoever heard of a story by the title of *The Voodoo of Hell's Half-Acre*? Aunt

5. **contemptuous** (kən temp′chü əs), *adj.* showing the feeling that a person, act, or thing is mean, low, or worthless.

Addie said that it was a sin for anyone to use the word "hell" and what was wrong with me was that I had nobody to guide me. She blamed the whole thing upon my upbringing.

In the end I was so angry that I refused to talk about the story. From no quarter, with the exception of the Negro newspaper editor, had there come a single encouraging word. It was rumored that the principal wanted to know why I had used the word "hell." I felt that I had committed a crime. Had I been conscious of the full extent to which I was pushing against the current of my environment, I would have been frightened altogether out of my attempts at writing. But my reactions were limited to the attitude of the people about me, and I did not speculate or generalize.

I dreamed of going north and writing books, novels. The North symbolized to me all that I had not felt and seen; it had no relation whatever to what actually existed. Yet, by imagining a place where everything was possible, I kept hope alive in me. But where had I got this notion of doing something in the future, of going away from home and accomplishing something that would be recognized by others? I had, of course, read my Horatio Alger[6] stories, my pulp stories, and I knew my Get-Rich-Quick Wallingford series from cover to cover, though I had sense enough not to hope to get rich; even to my naive[7] imagination that possibility was too remote. I knew that I lived in a country in which the aspirations[8] of black people were limited, marked-off. Yet I felt that I had to go somewhere and do something to redeem my being alive.

I was building up in me a dream which the entire educational system of the South had been rigged to stifle. I was feeling the very thing that the state of Mississippi had spent millions of dollars to make sure that I would never feel; I was becoming aware of the thing that the Jim Crow laws[9] had been drafted and passed to keep out of my consciousness; I was acting on impulses that southern senators in the nation's capital had striven to keep out of Negro life; I was beginning to dream the dreams that the state had said were wrong, that the schools had said were taboo.[10]

Had I been articulate[11] about my ultimate aspirations, no doubt someone would have told me what I was bargaining for; but nobody seemed to know, and least of all did I. My classmates felt that I was doing something that was vaguely wrong, but they did not know how to express it. As the outside world grew more meaningful, I became more concerned, tense; and my classmates and my teachers would say: "Why do you ask so many questions?" Or: "Keep quiet."

I was in my fifteenth year; in terms of schooling I was far behind the average youth of the nation, but I did not know that. In me was shaping a yearning[12] for a kind of consciousness, a mode of being that the way of life about me had said could not be, must not be, and upon which the penalty of death had been placed. Somewhere in the dead of the southern night my life had switched onto the wrong track and, without my knowing it, the locomotive of my heart was rushing down a dangerously steep slope, heading for a collision, heedless of the warning red lights that blinked all about me, the sirens and the bells and the screams that filled the air.

---

6. **Horatio Alger** (1834–1899), American author of a series of inspirational books for boys.
7. naive (nä ēv′), *adj.* not sophisticated.
8. aspiration (as′ pə rā′shən), *n.* a longing; ambition.
9. **Jim Crow laws.** "Jim Crow" was a term used by many whites to refer to African Americans. In the late 1800s and early 1900s many Southern states passed laws, called Jim Crow laws, mandating segregation by race in schools, public places, and so on.
10. taboo (tə bü′), *adj.* prohibited; banned.
11. articulate (är tik′yə lit), *adj.* able to put one's thoughts into words easily and clearly.
12. yearning (yėr′ning), *n.* strong desire; longing.

After Reading

Making Connections

Shaping Your Response

1. What would you say to young Richard Wright if he were in your class and got a story published in the local newspaper?

Analyzing the Autobiography

2. How does Wright **characterize** the editor of the *Southern Register?*

3. Richard Wright, disappointed by people's response to his first story, attempts to justify their reactions. Why does he think they don't appreciate his writing?

4. ☝ Why do you think young Wright's **perspective** on life is so different from that of his family and peers?

Extending the Ideas

5. If Richard Wright were a fifteen-year-old now writing his first story, how do you think his life might be different?

Vocabulary Study

Answer these questions about Richard Wright. Refer to the Glossary if necessary to find the meanings of the italicized vocabulary words.

naive
taboo
relent
aspiration
articulate
contemptuous
alien
hedge
conviction
yearning

1. How is Richard Wright *naive* in thinking that publishing his story will benefit him?

2. What kind of language is *taboo* in Granny's house?

3. Should the editor *relent* and pay Richard Wright for his story?

4. What was Richard Wright's main *aspiration?*

5. Why was being *articulate* not valued in Wright's community?

6. What was it about Wright's story that provoked such a *contemptuous* response by his family?

7. Why was becoming a writer an *alien* ambition in Wright's school?

8. Wright had to *hedge* when his grandmother asked what his story was about. Why?

9. Explain Wright's *conviction* about the educational system he experienced.

10. Describe the *yearning* Wright began to feel when he was fifteen.

Expressing Your Ideas

Writer's Notebook Update Choose one of the ideas you selected and develop it into a **story outline.** Think of two titles for the story, one that is outrageous, like "The Voodoo of Hell's Half Acre," and another that is more subtle.

Before Reading

The Jilting of Granny Weatherall

by Katherine Anne Porter

Katherine Anne Porter
1890–1980

Katherine Anne Porter, born in Texas and the great-great-great granddaughter of Daniel Boone, is best known for her short stories. As she said, "As soon as I learned to form letters on paper, at about three years, I began to write stories, and this has been the basic and absorbing occupation, the intact line of my life. . . ." Although she had been writing for many years, Porter didn't try to have anything published until she was thirty, and her first collection of short stories, *Flowering Judas,* wasn't published until she was forty. She took twenty-two years to complete her only novel, *The Ship of Fools.* Porter also worked at a newspaper in Chicago, played bit parts in movies, and studied Aztec and Mayan art in Mexico.

Building Background

Slipping Away In a famous elegy, the poet Dylan Thomas offered this advice to his dying father: "Do not go gentle into that good night." Rather, Thomas urged his father to "rage" against death. Granny Weatherall would have approved of this response to dying. "The Jilting of Granny Weatherall" is the story of a dying woman who is reminiscing about her life. Her memories are not logical or chronological but are free associations. As Granny slips between the reality of her sickroom in her daughter's house and the rooms of her past, the events of her life unfold. As you read her story, look for the transitions between reality and memory. Notice when Granny cannot leave her dreams for reality.

Literary Focus

Stream of Consciousness Katherine Anne Porter reveals Granny Weatherall's character by presenting the illogical, random flow of her thoughts, sensations, memories, emotions, and mental associations without any attempt at explanation. This writing technique is called **stream of consciousness.**

Writer's Notebook

Describe the Feeling Granny Weatherall is hovering between life and death, the past and the present. She can see and hear, but she's not completely there. Katherine Anne Porter uses figurative language to describe her semiconscious state. For example, Porter writes of Granny, "Her bones felt loose, and floated around in her skin, and Doctor Harry floated like a balloon around the foot of the bed." The time between sleep and waking is another example of a semiconscious state. How do you feel when you first wake up? In your notebook, use figurative language to express how you feel in that time between sleep and wakefulness.

The JILTING OF GRANNY WEATHERALL

Katherine Anne Porter

She flicked her wrist neatly out of Doctor Harry's pudgy careful fingers and pulled the sheet up to her chin. The brat ought to be in knee breeches. Doctoring around the country with spectacles on his nose! "Get along now, take your schoolbooks and go. There's nothing wrong with me."

Doctor Harry spread a warm paw like a cushion on her forehead where the forked green vein danced and made her eyelids twitch. "Now, now, be a good girl, and we'll have you up in no time."

"That's no way to speak to a woman nearly eighty years old just because she's down. I'd have you respect your elders, young man."

"Well, Missy, excuse me." Doctor Harry patted her cheek. "But I've got to warn you, haven't I? You're a marvel,[1] but you must be careful or you're going to be good and sorry."

"Don't tell me what I'm going to be. I'm on my feet now, morally speaking. It's Cornelia. I had to go to bed to get rid of her."

Her bones felt loose, and floated around in her skin, and Doctor Harry floated like a balloon around the foot of the bed. He floated and pulled down his waistcoat and swung his glasses on a cord. "Well, stay where you are, it certainly can't hurt you."

"Get along and doctor your sick," said Granny Weatherall. "Leave a well woman alone. I'll call for you when I want you. . . . Where were you forty years ago when I pulled through milkleg and double pneumonia? You weren't even born. Don't let Cornelia lead you on," she shouted, because Doctor Harry appeared to float up to the ceiling and out. "I pay my own bills, and I don't throw my money away on nonsense!"

She meant to wave good-by, but it was too much trouble. Her eyes closed of themselves, it was like a dark curtain drawn around the bed. The pillow rose and floated under her, pleasant as a hammock in a light wind. She listened to the leaves rustling outside the window. No, somebody was swishing newspapers; no, Cornelia and Doctor Harry were whispering together. She leaped broad awake, thinking they whispered in her ear.

"She was never like this, *never* like this!" "Well, what can we expect?" "Yes, eighty years old. . . ."

Well, and what if she was? She still had ears. It was like Cornelia to whisper around doors. She always kept things secret in such a public way. She was always being tactful and kind. Cornelia was dutiful; that was the trouble with her. Dutiful and good: "So good and dutiful," said Granny, "that I'd like to spank her." She saw herself spanking Cornelia and making a fine job of it.

---

1. **marvel** (mär′vəl), *n.* something wonderful; an astonishing thing.

"What'd you say, Mother?" Granny felt her face tying up in hard knots. "Can't a body think, I'd like to know?"

"I thought you might want something."

"I do. I want a lot of things. First off, go away and don't whisper."

She lay and drowsed, hoping in her sleep that the children would keep out and let her rest a minute. It had been a long day. Not that she was tired. It was always pleasant to snatch a minute now and then. There was always so much to be done, let me see: tomorrow.

Tomorrow was far away and there was nothing to trouble about. Things were finished somehow when the time came; thank God there was always a little margin over for peace: then a person could spread out the plan of life and tuck in the edges orderly. It was good to have everything clean and folded away, with the hair brushes and tonic bottles sitting straight on the white embroidered linen: the day started without fuss and the pantry shelves laid out with rows of jelly glasses and brown jugs and white stone-china jars with blue whirligigs and words painted on them: coffee, tea, sugar, ginger, cinnamon, allspice: and the bronze clock with the lion on top nicely dusted off. The dust that lion could collect in twenty-four hours! The box in the attic with all those letters tied up, well, she'd have to go through that tomorrow. All those letters—George's letters and John's letters and her letters to them both—lying around for the children to find afterward made her uneasy. Yes, that would be tomorrow's business. No use to let them know how silly she had been once.

> **EVALUATE:** Why doesn't Granny Weatherall want her children to find her old love letters?

While she was rummaging[2] around, she found death in her mind and it felt clammy and unfamiliar. She had spent so much time preparing for death there was no need for bringing it up again.

Let it take care of itself now. When she was sixty, she had felt very old, finished, and went around making farewell trips to see her children and grandchildren, with a secret in her mind: This is the very last of your mother, children! Then she made her will and came down with a long fever. That was all just a notion like a lot of other things, but it was lucky too, for she had once and for all got over the idea of dying for a long time. Now she couldn't be worried. She hoped she had better sense now. Her father had lived to be one hundred and two years old and had drunk a noggin of strong hot toddy[3] on his last birthday. He told the reporters it was his daily habit, and he owed his long life to that. He had made quite a scandal and was very pleased about it. She believed she'd just plague[4] Cornelia a little.

"Cornelia! Cornelia!" No footsteps, but a sudden hand on her cheek. "Bless you, where have you been?"

"Here, Mother."

"Well, Cornelia, I want a noggin of hot toddy."

"Are you cold, darling?"

"I'm chilly, Cornelia. Lying in bed stops the circulation. I must have told you that a thousand times."

Well, she could just hear Cornelia telling her husband that Mother was getting a little childish and they'd have to humor[5] her. The thing that most annoyed her was that Cornelia thought she was deaf, dumb, and blind. Little hasty glances and tiny gestures tossed around her and over her head saying, "Don't cross her, let her have her way, she's eighty years old," and she sitting there as if she lived in a thin glass cage. Sometimes Granny almost made up her mind to pack up and move back to her own house where nobody

---

2. **rummage** (rum′ij), v. search thoroughly by moving things about.
3. **noggin of hot toddy,** a small cup of a drink made from an alcoholic beverage, hot water, sugar, and spices.
4. **plague** (plāg), v. annoy or bother.
5. **humor** (hyü′mər), v. give in to the whims of a person; indulge.

List five adjectives that describe this woman in Grant Wood's painting, *Victorian Survivor* (1931). Which of those words, if any, could also describe Granny Weatherall? ➤

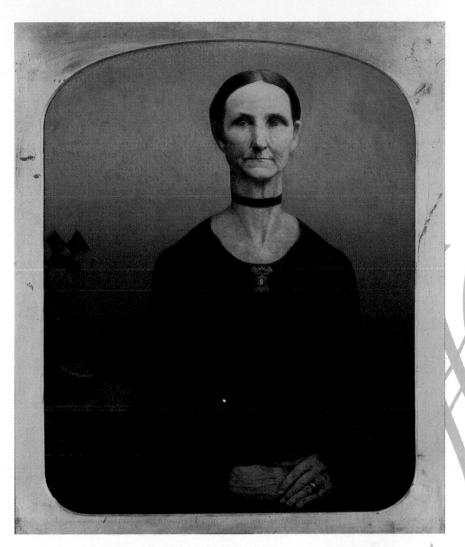

could remind her every minute that she was old. Wait, wait, Cornelia, till your own children whisper behind your back!

In her day she had kept a better house and had got more work done. She wasn't too old yet for Lydia to be driving eighty miles for advice when one of the children jumped the track, and Jimmy still dropped in and talked things over: "Now, Mammy, you've a good business head, I want to know what you think of this? . . ." Old. Cornelia couldn't change the furniture around without asking. Little things, little things! They had been so sweet when they were little. Granny wished the old days were back again with the children young and everything to be done over. It had been a hard pull, but not too much for her. When she thought of all the food she had cooked, and all the clothes she had cut and sewed, and all the gardens she had made—well, the children showed it. There they were, made out of her, and they couldn't get away from that. Sometimes she wanted to see John again and point to them and say, Well, I didn't do so badly, did I? But that would have to wait. That was for tomorrow. She used to think of him as a man, but now all the children were older than their father, and he would be a child beside her if she saw him now. It seemed strange and there was something wrong in the idea. Why, he couldn't possibly recognize her. She had fenced in a hundred acres once, digging the postholes herself and clamping the wires with just a Negro boy to help. That changed a woman. John would be looking for a young woman with the peaked Spanish comb in her hair and the painted fan. Digging postholes changed a woman. Riding country roads in the winter when women had their babies was another thing: sitting up nights with sick horses and sick Negroes and sick children and hardly ever losing one. John, I hardly ever lost one of them! John would see that in a minute, that would be something he could understand, she wouldn't have to explain anything!

CLARIFY: How could the children be older than their father?

◄ What emotions or feelings are conveyed in Stephen Arnold Douglas Volk's painting, *After the Reception* (1887)?

and moving up the hill like an army of ghosts. Soon it would be at the near edge of the orchard, and then it was time to go in and light the lamps. Come in, children, don't stay out in the night air.

Lighting the lamps had been beautiful. The children huddled up to her and breathed like little calves waiting at the bars in the twilight. Their eyes followed the match and watched the flame rise and settle in a blue curve, then they moved away from her. The lamp was lit, they didn't have to be scared and hang on to Mother anymore. Never, never, nevermore. God, for all my life I thank Thee. Without Thee, my God, I could never have done it. Hail, Mary, full of grace.[6]

I want you to pick all the fruit this year and see that nothing is wasted. There's always someone who can use it. Don't let good things rot for want of using. You waste life when you waste good food. Don't let things get lost. It's bitter to lose things. Now, don't let me get to thinking, not when I am tired and taking a little nap before supper. . . .

The pillow rose about her shoulders and pressed against her heart and the memory was being squeezed out of it: oh, push down the

It made her feel like rolling up her sleeves and putting the whole place to rights again. No matter if Cornelia was determined to be everywhere at once, there were a great many things left undone on this place. She would start tomorrow and do them. It was good to be strong enough for everything, even if all you made melted and changed and slipped under your hands, so that by the time you finished you almost forgot what you were working for. What was it I set out to do? she asked herself intently, but she could not remember. A fog rose over the valley, she saw it marching across the creek swallowing the trees

---

6. *Hail, Mary, full of grace,* the opening line of a Catholic prayer.

pillow, somebody: it would smother her if she tried to hold it. Such a fresh breeze blowing and such a green day with no threats in it. But he had not come, just the same. What does a woman do when she has put on the white veil and set out the white cake for a man and he doesn't come? She tried to remember. No, I swear he never harmed me but in that. He never harmed me but in that . . . and what if he did? There was the day, the day, but a whirl of dark smoke rose and covered it, crept up and over into the bright field where everything was planted so carefully in orderly rows. That was hell, she knew hell when she saw it. For sixty years she had prayed against remembering him and against losing her soul in the deep pit of hell, and now the two things were mingled in one and the thought of him was a smoky cloud from hell that moved and crept in her head when she had just got rid of Doctor Harry and was trying to rest a minute. Wounded vanity,[7] Ellen, said a sharp voice in the top of her mind. Don't let your wounded vanity get the upper hand of you. Plenty of girls get jilted.[8] You were jilted, weren't you? Then stand up to it. Her eyelids wavered and let in streamers of blue-gray light like tissue paper over her eyes. She must get up and pull the shades down or she'd never sleep. She was in bed again and the shades were not down. How could that happen? Better turn over, hide from the light, sleeping in the light gave you nightmares. "Mother, how do you feel now?" and a stinging wetness on her forehead. But I don't like having my face washed in cold water!

Hapsy? George? Lydia? Jimmy? No, Cornelia, and her features were swollen and full of little puddles. "They're coming, darling, they'll all be here soon." Go wash your face, child, you look funny.

Instead of obeying, Cornelia knelt down and put her head on the pillow. She seemed to be talking but there was no sound. "Well, are you tongue-tied? Whose birthday is it? Are you going to give a party?"

Cornelia's mouth moved urgently[9] in strange shapes. "Don't do that, you bother me, daughter."

"Oh, no, Mother. Oh, no. . . ."

Nonsense. It was strange about children. They disputed[10] your every word. "No what, Cornelia?"

"Here's Doctor Harry."

"I won't see that boy again. He just left five minutes ago."

"That was this morning, Mother. It's night now. Here's the nurse."

"This is Doctor Harry, Mrs. Weathcrall. I never saw you look so young and happy!"

"Ah, I'll never be young again—but I'd be happy if they'd let me lie in peace and get rested."

She thought she spoke up loudly, but no one answered. A warm weight on her forehead, a warm bracelet on her wrist, and a breeze went on whispering, trying to tell her something. A shuffle of leaves in the everlasting hand of God. He blew on them and they danced and rattled. "Mother, don't mind, we're going to give you a little hypodermic." "Look here, daughter, how do ants get in this bed? I saw sugar ants yesterday." Did you send for Hapsy too?

It was Hapsy she really wanted. She had to go a long way back through a great many rooms to find Hapsy standing with a baby on her arm. She seemed to herself to be Hapsy also, and the baby on Hapsy's arm was Hapsy and himself and herself, all at once, and there was no surprise in the meeting. Then Hapsy melted from within and turned flimsy as gray gauze and the baby was a gauzy shadow, and Hapsy came up close and said, "I thought you'd never come," and looked at her very searchingly and said, "You haven't changed a bit!" They leaned forward to

---

7. **vanity** (van′ə tē), *n.* too much pride in one's looks, abilities, and so on.
8. **jilt,** *v.* cast off a lover or sweetheart after giving encouragement.
9. **urgently** (ėr′jənt lē), *adv.* in a manner demanding immediate attention.
10. **dispute** (dis pyūt′), *v.* argue; disagree with.

The Jilting of Granny Weatherall **615**

kiss, when Cornelia began whispering from a long way off, "Oh, is there anything you want to tell me? Is there anything I can do for you?"

Yes, she had changed her mind after sixty years and she would like to see George. I want you to find George. Find him and be sure to tell him I forgot him. I want him to know I had my husband just the same and my children and my house like any other woman. A good house too and a good husband that I loved and fine children out of him. Better than I hoped for even. Tell him I was given back everything he took away and more. Oh, no, oh, God, no, there was something else besides the house and the man and the children. Oh, surely they were not all? What was it? Something not given back. . . . Her breath crowded down under her ribs and grew into a monstrous frightening shape with cutting edges; it bored up into her head, and the agony was unbelievable: Yes, John, get the doctor now, no more talk, my time has come.

> **EVALUATE:** Why does Granny Weatherall make this contradictory statement: "Find him and be sure to tell him I forgot him"? What does she want?

When this one was born, it should be the last. The last. It should have been born first, for it was the one she had truly wanted. Everything came in good time. Nothing left out, left over. She was strong, in three days she would be as well as ever. Better. A woman needed milk in her to have her full health.

"Mother, do you hear me?"

"I've been telling you——"

"Mother, Father Connolly's here."

"I went to Holy Communion only last week. Tell him I'm not so sinful as all that."

"Father just wants to speak to you."

He could speak as much as he pleased. It was like him to drop in and inquire about her soul as if it were a teething baby, and then stay on for a cup of tea and a round of cards and gossip. He

always had a funny story of some sort, usually about an Irishman who made his little mistakes and confessed them, and the point lay in some absurd thing he would blurt out in the confessional showing his struggles between native piety and original sin. Granny felt easy about her soul. Cornelia, where are your manners? Give Father Connolly a chair. She had her secret comfortable understanding with a few favorite saints who cleared a straight road to God for her. All as surely signed and sealed as the papers for the new Forty Acres. Forever . . . heirs and assigns forever. Since the day the wedding cake was not cut, but thrown out and wasted. The whole bottom dropped out of the world, and there she was blind and sweating with nothing under her feet and the walls falling away. His hand had caught her under the breast, she had not fallen, there was the freshly polished floor with the green rug on it, just as before. He had cursed like a sailor's parrot and said, "I'll kill him for you." Don't lay a hand on him, for my sake leave something to God. "Now, Ellen, you must believe what I tell you. . . ."

So there was nothing, nothing to worry about any more, except sometimes in the night one of the children screamed in a nightmare, and they both hustled out shaking and hunting for the matches and calling, "There, wait a minute, here we are!" John, get the doctor now, Hapsy's time has come. But there was Hapsy standing by the bed in a white cap. "Cornelia, tell Hapsy to take off her cap. I can't see her plain."

Her eyes opened very wide and the room stood out like a picture she had seen somewhere. Dark colors with the shadows rising toward the ceiling in long angles. The tall black dresser gleamed with nothing on it but John's picture, enlarged from a little one, with John's eyes very black when they should have been blue. You never saw him, so how do you know how he looked? But the man insisted the copy was perfect, it was very rich and handsome. For a picture, yes, but it's not my husband. The table by the bed had a linen cover and a candle and a crucifix. The light was blue from Cornelia's silk lampshades.

No sort of light at all, just frippery. You had to live forty years with kerosene lamps to appreciate honest electricity. She felt very strong and she saw Doctor Harry with a rosy nimbus around him.

"You look like a saint, Doctor Harry, and I vow that's as near as you'll ever come to it."

"She's saying something."

"I heard you, Cornelia. What's all this carrying on?"

"Father Connolly's saying——"

Cornelia's voice staggered and bumped like a cart in a bad road. It rounded corners and turned back again and arrived nowhere. Granny stepped up in the cart very lightly and reached for the reins, but a man sat beside her and she knew him by his hands, driving the cart. She did not look in his face, for she knew without seeing, but looked instead down the road where the trees leaned over and bowed to each other and a thousand birds were singing a Mass. She felt like singing too, but she put her hand in the bosom of her dress and pulled out a rosary, and Father Connolly murmured Latin in a very solemn[11] voice and tickled her feet.[12] My God, will you stop that nonsense? I'm a married woman. What if he did run away and leave me to face the priest by myself? I found another a whole world better. I wouldn't have exchanged my husband for anybody except St. Michael himself, and you may tell him that for me with a thank you in the bargain.

Light flashed on her closed eyelids, and a deep roaring shook her. Cornelia, is that lightning? I hear thunder. There's going to be a storm. Close all the windows. Call the children in. . . . "Mother, here we are, all of us." "Is that you, Hapsy?" "Oh, no, I'm Lydia. We drove as fast as we could." Their faces drifted above her, drifted away. The rosary fell out of her hands and Lydia put it back. Jimmy tried to help, their hands fumbled together, and Granny closed two fingers around Jimmy's thumb. Beads wouldn't do, it must be something alive. She was so amazed her thoughts ran round and round. So, my dear Lord, this is my death and I wasn't even thinking about it. My children have come to see me die. But I can't, it's not time. Oh, I always hated surprises. I wanted to give Cornelia the amethyst set—Cornelia, you're to have the amethyst set, but Hapsy's to wear it when she wants, and, Doctor Harry, do shut up. Nobody sent for you. Oh, my dear Lord, do wait a minute. I meant to do something about the Forty Acres, Jimmy doesn't need it and Lydia will later on, with that worthless husband of hers. I meant to finish the altar cloth and send six bottles of wine to Sister Borgia for her dyspepsia. I want to send six bottles of wine to Sister Borgia, Father Connolly, now don't let me forget.

Cornelia's voice made short turns and tilted over and crashed. "Oh, Mother, oh, Mother, oh, Mother. . . ."

"I'm not going, Cornelia. I'm taken by surprise. I can't go."

You'll see Hapsy again. What about her? "I thought you'd never come." Granny made a long journey outward, looking for Hapsy. What if I don't find her? What then? Her heart sank down and down, there was no bottom to death, she couldn't come to the end of it. The blue light from Cornelia's lampshade drew into a tiny point in the center of her brain, it flickered and winked like an eye, quietly it fluttered and dwindled.[13] Granny lay curled down within herself, amazed and watchful, staring at the point of light that was herself; her body was now only a deeper mass of shadow in an endless darkness and this darkness would curl around the light and swallow it up. God, give a sign!

For the second time there was no sign. Again no bridegroom and the priest in the house. She could not remember any other sorrow because this grief wiped them all away. Oh, no, there's nothing more cruel than this—I'll never forgive it. She stretched herself with a deep breath and blew out the light.

---

11. **solemn** (sol′əm), *adj.* done with form and ceremony.
12. ***Father Connolly . . . feet,*** The priest is administering the sacrament for the dying, which includes anointing the hands and feet.
13. **dwindle** (dwin′dl), *v.* shrink; diminish.

After Reading

Making Connections

Shaping Your Response

1. Imagine the story as a movie or television special. Explain who you would cast in each part and how you would handle the scenes from Granny's past.

2. Granny is not fully conscious at the end of the story. If she were, what might she have discussed with Father Connolly before her death?

3. 👋 Describe Cornelia as characterized from Granny's **perspective.** Do you think this characterization is accurate?

Analyzing the Story

4. Why is Granny's last name appropriate?

5. Why do you think the author reveals the facts about the jilting in a **flashback** instead of giving the information straightforwardly and then ending her story?

6. Granny Weatherall reacted to being jilted by pushing the memory deep into her subconscious and working hard. How might she have avoided carrying her emotional sorrow to her deathbed?

Extending the Ideas

7. Compare Katherine Anne Porter's portrayal of death to Emily Dickinson's in "Because I could not stop for Death" on page 357. How are the two portrayals similar and different?

Literary Focus: Stream of Consciousness

Granny Weatherall's freely flowing thoughts and memories are presented through a technique called **stream of consciousness.** This random flow of mental associations without any attempt at explanation suggests both the vagueness and confusion and also the moments of clarity that characterize Granny. Cite passages where Granny is completely lucid, where she is clearly reliving the past, and where she is in the present but doesn't realize what is happening to her.

Clearly in the present	Clearly in the past	Confused

Vocabulary Study

Answer these questions about Granny Weatherall. Refer to the Glossary for help with the italicized words.

marvel
rummage
plague
humor
vanity
jilt
dispute
dwindle
urgently
solemn

1. Why is Granny Weatherall described as a *marvel?*
2. Why didn't Granny want Cornelia, Lydia, or Jimmy to *rummage* in the attic?
3. How does Granny *plague* Cornelia?
4. How does Cornelia *humor* her mother?
5. Does Granny consider *vanity* a virtue or a vice?
6. How did her fiancé *jilt* Granny Weatherall?
7. With whom did Granny seem to *dispute* the most?
8. What seemed to *dwindle* as Granny Weatherall's family gathered around her?
9. What did Granny *urgently* want to tell her children?
10. Why was Father Connolly speaking in a *solemn* voice?

Expressing Your Ideas

Writing Choices

Writer's Notebook Update How did you describe the way you feel when you begin to wake up? Did you use comparisons to express the feeling? Copy the most vivid comparisons used by Katherine Anne Porter to describe Granny's state of consciousness into your notebook. Share the passages with the class.

The Dear Departed Father Connolly knew Granny Weatherall much of her life. Write a fitting **eulogy** about Granny for Father to deliver at her funeral.

Other Options

Oh, Mother . . . Cornelia has been caring for her sick mother, and she has been at her bedside all day. What details will she tell her brother Jimmy and her sister Lydia about her mother's last day? Be Cornelia and tell them about it.

Pieces of a Life Make a paper "**patchwork quilt**" representing the significant events, people, and things in Granny Weatherall's life. Using 4″ x 4″ squares of colored paper, create the individual quilt squares and then fasten them together with staples or tape.

Hallucinations Can you visualize the scenes that Granny Weatherall describes? Reread the descriptions of Dr. Harry's first visit ("Her bones . . . ," p. 611), of her wedding day ("Such a fresh . . . ," p. 615), and of her death ("The blue light . . . ," p. 617). Choose one of these three otherworldly scenes and illustrate it.

Alone in a Crowd

The Roaring Twenties

Pop Culture Connection

The excitement and terror of World War I left a lasting impression on the minds of a whole generation of young Americans. Traditional values and codes of behavior seemed outdated to 1920s youth, and their new ways shocked their elders. In the following passage from his book, *Only Yesterday*, Frederick Lewis Allen describes the new enemy that had invaded American society.

THE YOUNGER GENERATION Runs Wild

by Frederick Lewis Allen

The war [World War I] had not long been over when cries of alarm from parents, teachers, and moral preceptors began to rend the air. For the boys and girls just growing out of adolescence were making mincemeat of [the moral] code.

The dresses that the girls—and for that matter most of the older women—were wearing seemed alarming enough. In July, 1920, a fashion writer reported in the *New York Times* that "the American woman . . . has lifted her skirts far beyond any modest limitation," which was another way of saying that the hem was now all of nine inches above the ground. It was freely predicted that skirts would come down again in the winter of 1920–1921, but instead they climbed a few scandalous inches farther. The flappers wore thin dresses, short-sleeved and occasionally (in the evening) sleeveless; some of the wilder young things rolled their stockings below their knees, revealing to the shocked eyes of virtue a fleeting glance of shin-bones and knee-cap; and many of them were visibly using cosmetics. "The intoxication of rouge," earnestly explained Dorothy Speare in *Dancers in the Dark,* "is an insidious vintage known to more girls than mere man can ever believe." Useless for frantic parents to insist that no lady did such things; the answer was that the daughters of ladies were doing it, and even retouching their masterpieces in public. Some of them, further-more, were abandoning their corsets. "The men won't dance with you if you wear a corset," they were quoted as saying.

The current mode in dancing created still more consternation. Not the romantic violin but the barbaric saxophone now dom-inated the orchestra, and to its passionate crooning and wailing the fox-trotters moved in what the editor of the Hobart College

Herald disgustedly called a "syncopated embrace." No longer did even an inch of space separate them; they danced as if glued together, body to body, cheek to cheek. Cried the *Catholic Telegraph* of Cincinnati in righteous indignation, "The music is sensuous, the embracing of partners—the female only half dressed—is absolutely indecent; and the motions—they are such as may not be described, with any respect for propriety, in a family newspaper. Suffice it to say that there are certain houses appropriate for such dances; but those houses have been closed by law." . . .

It was not until F. Scott Fitzgerald, who had hardly grad-uated from Princeton and ought to know what his generation were doing, brought out *This Side of Paradise* in April, 1920, that fathers and mothers realized fully what was afoot and how long it had been going on . . . . "None of the Victorian mothers—and most of the mothers were Victorian—had any idea how casually their daughters were accustomed to be kissed," wrote Fitzgerald. ". . . Amory saw girls doing things that even in his memory would have been impossible: eating three-o'clock, after-dance suppers in impossible cafés, talking of every side of life with an air half of earnestness, half of mockery, yet with a furtive excitement that Amory considered stood for a real moral let-down. But he never realized how widespread it was until he saw the cities between New York and Chicago as one vast juvenile intrigue." The book caused a shudder to run

down the national spine; did not Mr. Fitzgerald represent one of his well-nurtured heroines as brazenly confessing, "I've kissed dozens of men. I suppose I'll kiss dozens more" . . .

It was incredible. It was abominable. What did it all mean? Was every decent standard being thrown over? Mothers read the scarlet words and wondered if they themselves "had any idea how often their daughters were accustomed to be kissed." . . . But no, this must be an exaggerated account of the misconduct of some especially depraved group. Nice girls couldn't behave like that and talk openly about passion. But in due course other books appeared to substantiate the findings of Mr. Fitzgerald; *Dancers in the Dark, The Plastic Age, Flaming Youth.* Magazine articles and newspapers reiterat-ed the scandal. To be sure, there were plenty of communities where nice girls did not, in actual fact, "behave like that"; and even in the more sophisticated urban centers there were plenty of girls who did not. Nevertheless, there was enough fire beneath the smoke of these sensational revelations to make the Problem of the Younger Generation a topic of anxious discussion from coast to coast.

Responding

1. Do you think the older generation was overreacting to the youth of the 1920s? Why or why not?

2. How do the concerns of today's parents compare with those of the older generation in the 1920s?

Pop Culture Connection

The new ways of the 1920s called for a new vocabulary. The younger generation considered the established ways of their elders to be nonsense, and invented creative new ways to say "nonsense." Their exuberance and easy attitude toward life were reflected in their words as well. The following list includes some of the terms coined during this era.

Roaring Twenties

DRUGSTORE COWBOY

ALARM CLOCK – a persistent worrier; a chaperone.

ALL WET – wrong; arguing a mistaken notion.

AND HOW! – yes, indeed!

APPLESAUCE – a term of derogation; nonsense.

BADGE – police officer.

BALLOON SOUP – empty talk, nonsense; same as applesauce.

BALONEY – nonsense, same as applesauce and balloon soup.

BEE'S KNEES – a marvelous person or thing.

BIG CHEESE – an important, influential person.

BLIND DATE – a date with an unknown person of the opposite sex.

BOOK WORM – a person who spends much time reading or studying.

BRAWL – a wild party or celebration.

BREEZER – an open-topped car.

BUM RAP – a false accusation or conviction.

BUNK – nonsense (a shortened form of *bunkum*, which is also spelled *buncombe*, from the name of a North Carolina county whose representative in Congress from 1819–1821 kept making long-winded and pointless speeches "for Buncombe").

CAKE – a male flirt.

CARRY A TORCH – to love someone who does not return one's affections.

CAT'S MEOW – anything first-rate; similar to bee's knees.

CHEATERS – eyeglasses.

COPACETIC – very good, excellent.

CRACKERS – crazy or eccentric.

Glossary

CRUSH – a sudden romantic feeling for another person.

DAD – fellow; friend.

DRUGSTORE COWBOY – a fashionably dressed young man who hangs around public places trying to pick up young women.

FAN THE AIR – to chatter; gossip.

FLAPPER – a young woman of the 1920s who dressed unconventionally – with short skirts and rolled stockings – and behaved with considerable freedom.

FLAT TIRE – a boring person.

FRAME – to make someone seem guilty through false evidence.

GATECRASHER – a person who attends parties and other events without an invitation.

GUSSIE UP – to dress up.

HEEBIE-JEEBIES – a nervous feeling; the jitters.

HEP – informed; wise.

HOOCH – bootleg liquor (from Hoochinoo, an Alaskan Indian tribe who made liquor).

JAKE – fine, okay (commonly used in the phrase "everything's jake").

JALOPY – an old automobile.

KEEN – excellent; wonderful.

LOUNGE LIZARD – a ladies' man.

MAIN DRAG – the busiest or chief street of a city or town.

PINCH – to arrest.

REAL McCOY, THE – the real thing; the genuine article (comes either from a Scottish clan leader named MacKay; a boxer named Kid McCoy, who had a rival with the same name; or a bootlegger named McCoy who did not dilute his liquor).

RITZY – smart; stylish (from *Ritz,* the name of the palatial hotels founded by César Ritz, 1850–1918, Swiss-born hotel manager).

RUN-AROUND – evasion or indefinite postponement of an action, especially in response to a request.

SCRAM – to leave at once (from scramble).

SPEAKEASY – a saloon or bar illegally selling alcohol.

SPIFFY – having a smart, elegantly fashionable appearance.

SWELL – excellent; first-rate.

WHOOPEE – boisterous, jovial fun.

Responding

1. Which of these terms have endured the test of time and are still used today?

2. What are some modern-day equivalents to these terms and expressions? What new words and phrases would be included in a "modern age" glossary?

Language History

What's New in Language

 Slang is language that rolls up its sleeves, spits on its hands, and goes to work.

When poet Carl Sandburg made the above statement, what did he mean by *slang?* What is slang, and who comes up with slang words? Actually, no one is quite sure where the term *slang* came from. Slang is an informal, highly colloquial part of any spoken language. Many slang words become firmly embedded in the standard language; others are used for a time and then fall out of fashion.

Some slang used in American English comes from foreign languages. The word *nosh* comes from the Hebrew word *noshen* and is slang for snack. Other slang words come from jargon used by groups such as the military, government bureaucracies, musicians, scientists, athletes, and so on. From music we have *jazzed;* from sports we have *saved by the bell* and *kick-off;* from medicine we have *psycho, stressed,* and *stressed out.*

Much of the slang used in American English comes from subgroups within our society. Among the most prolific in creating slang are the young. For years teenagers have coined new words and phrases to describe their emotions and attitudes: a tired student might be called *wiped, whipped,* or *washed;* a nauseated child might *heave, ralph, puke,* or *purge* at any moment.

For the most part, slang words are "in" one generation and out the next. Those who were young in the 1920s and 30s might call something that's great *the bees knees* or *the cat's pajamas,* phrases that probably don't mean much to the young of today. Some slang goes in and out of vogue. *Groovy* is a word that has fallen in and out of favor, depending on the whims of the young. Some slang, though, remains current for generations. *Cool* is still cool, *hip* is still hip, and *bogus* is still used exactly the same way it was used a hundred years ago.

Writing Workshop

Analyzing Alienation

Assignment You have read stories and poems about alienation. Now examine the causes and effects of this alienation.

WRITER'S BLUEPRINT

Product	A cause-effect essay
Purpose	To analyze a character's alienation
Audience	People who have read the literature
Specs	As the writer of a successful essay, you should:

❏ Choose a character from one of the selections in this part as your subject. Open with an intriguing description of your character in action that in some way signals his or her alienation. This introduction should draw your readers into your essay and make them eager to read on.

❏ Then make a thesis statement which, in a nutshell, states your views on the chief causes of this character's alienation. Consider both internal causes, such as the character's personality, and external causes, such as other people and the nature of society itself.

❏ Tell what this character does, says, thinks, and feels that signals his or her alienation.

❏ Elaborate on the causes mentioned in your thesis statement. Support your conclusions and opinions with specific details from the selection, including quotations where appropriate.

❏ Finally, return to your thesis statement and conclude by restating it in a way that reflects new insights you've gained from writing this essay.

❏ Follow the rules of grammar, usage, spelling, and mechanics. Be sure to use commas correctly.

 STEP **1** PREWRITING

Analyze alienation. In a group, discuss characters from the literature, current books, or movies who seem disillusioned or detached from their own social worlds. What do they do and say that signals their alienation?

How do they feel? (See the Literary Source.) Formulate an explanation of the term *alienation* that goes beyond a dictionary definition.

Try a quickwrite. For five minutes or so, describe a time you yourself felt alienated. Concentrate on your feelings, your actions and reactions, and the causes and effects of your alienation.

Choose the character you'll focus on and reread the selection. Find examples of things the character does and says that signal alienation, and list them in a chart. The examples here are for the soldier in Hemingway's "In Another Country."

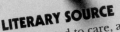
What Character Does and Says	How This Signals Alienation
lies in bed wondering how he will be when he gets back to front	shows he's unsure of himself, has lost confidence in his courage
"We were all a little detached. . . ."	

Chart causes of your character's alienation with examples from the selection.

Internal causes	External causes	Specific details and quotations
afraid to die in war. . .	got medals but hadn't risked his life . . .	". . . it had been different with them and they had done very different things to get their medals."

Develop an intriguing opening. You'll want to start by showing your character in action in a way that signals alienation and makes your audience want to read on. Here are some suggestions:

- Start right off with your character in action. Don't explain anything yet, just describe him or her. For example: "The soldier lies in bed looking up at the cracks in the ceiling as if they were far-off constellations in the night sky, distant and cold."

- Start by speaking directly to the reader, as if the two of you were standing together watching the character in action. For example: "See that man there lying in that hospital bed? Look at his expression. What does it tell you about . . . ?"

Compose your thesis statement—your assertion, which the rest of your essay will develop. It should:

- consist of a sentence or two

- assert a claim you intend to prove (the chief causes of your character's alienation)

- be limited and specific enough to serve as the guiding force for your essay

Ask a partner to look over your thesis statement and comment on how well it meets the three objectives listed above. Then comment on your partner's statement. See Step 3 of this lesson.

Plan your essay. Organize your thoughts in a plan like the one shown. (You'll have to wait until you've actually drafted the Introduction and Body before you can make notes on the Conclusion.)

- **Introduction**
  Description of character in action
  Thesis statement (chief causes of alienation)

- **Body**
  Description of alienation (with support from selection)
  —What character says
  —What character does
  —What character thinks
  —What character feels
  Chief causes (with support from selection)
  —Internal
  —External

- **Conclusion**
  Fresh insights gained from writing

OR . . .
First, make a time line of key moments in the story and jot down notes about how those moments reflect the causes of the character's alienation. Use these notes to help you make your plan.

STEP *2* DRAFTING

Before you write, gather together your prewriting materials and reread the Writer's Blueprint.

As you draft, keep returning to your thesis statement. You may need to revise it from time to time as you move along.

Ask a partner for comments on your draft before you revise it. Pay special attention to the thesis statement.

Revising Strategy

Revising a Thesis Statement

Your thesis statement must be sufficiently limited and specific. Here is an example of the development of a thesis statement (based on Hemingway's "In Another Country"):

Thesis Statement	Sufficiently Limited and Specific?
The soldier's alienation is caused by a variety of factors.	Unworkable. Way too broad and general. The writer needs to define what "a variety of factors" means.
The alien world that surrounds the soldier makes him feel lost and detached from society.	Better. "The alien world that surrounds the soldier" is a bit more specific and limited, but still too vague.
The unfriendly and wounded people who populate the world are the chief causes of the soldier's alienation.	Workable. The writer now has something definite to fasten on—the "unfriendly and wounded people." The rest of the essay can focus on these people, the chief contributors to his alienation.

Notice how the writer of this student model has revised his thesis statement to make it more limited and specific.

STUDENT MODEL

When people do not think like their peers, they sometimes become alienated because they are misunderstood and viewed as being dangerous. In the story "Black Boy" by Richard Wright, ~~Richard~~ *Richard's desire to be and do more than people told him that he was capable of doing alienates him from his* ~~is alienated from his family and friends because they believe he is~~ *family and friends.* ~~different from them.~~

4 EDITING

Ask a partner to review your revised draft before you edit. When you edit, watch for errors in grammar, usage, spelling, and mechanics. Pay special attention to errors with commas.

Editing Strategy

Using Commas Correctly

Use commas to avoid, not cause, confusion. Take care to use a comma when it's needed for sense—and not to add needless commas that end up confusing the reader. For example:

No commas needed: Some people want to live their lives, in a way that they consider, to be dangerous.

Edited: Some people want to live their lives in a way that they consider to be dangerous.

Commas needed: In the first instance I've mentioned because Richard yearns to see the world outside of his home town Jackson he loses the support of his family and friends.

Edited: In the first instance I've mentioned, because Richard yearns to see the world outside of his home town, Jackson, he loses the support of his family and friends.

Notice how the writer of the student model made corrections with commas to avoid confusion. Look for these same kinds of comma-confusion errors when you edit your writing.

> **FOR REFERENCE**
> More rules for using commas can be found in the Language and Grammar Handbook at the back of this text.

> Richard's family and friends cannot understand him. His dreams~~,~~ of becoming a writer~~,~~ reach past Jackson into new places where he believes he can encounter new things‸ things that will broaden and deepen his experience. Richard dreams of going to the North‸ a place where he feels that anything is possible.

STUDENT MODEL

5 PRESENTING

Consider these ideas for presenting your paper.

- Meet with students in your class who chose the same character you did. Read your essays to each other and compare your conclusions.

- Find at least two other students who each wrote about different characters, and form a small group. Make a list of the causes of each character's alienation. Then draw some conclusions about what causes alienation. Make a poster to illustrate these causes, and share it with the class.

6 LOOKING BACK

Self-evaluate. What grade would *you* give your paper? Look back at the Writer's Blueprint and give yourself a score on each item, from 6 (superior) to 1 (inadequate).

Reflect. Think about what you learned from writing your essay as you write answers to these questions:

✔ What did you learn about alienation by writing this paper? Will you do or react to anything differently as a result of exploring this topic? Why or why not?

✔ In what ways are your feelings or the feelings of today's youth similar to or different from the feelings expressed in the literature you read?

For Your Working Portfolio Add your essay and your reflection responses to your working portfolio.

Beyond Print

The Wonders of Word Processing

When Ernest Hemingway was a young writer struggling to make a living in Paris, a suitcase full of his manuscripts was lost on a train. Since Hemingway had no other copies, he lost several years' worth of work. Today, thanks to word processing programs, writers can save their work on a hard drive or file server, back it up on floppy disks, and print it out as hard copy.

The true power of word processors, however, lies not in their ability to preserve documents, but in their ability to make writing easier and more efficient. The following tips can help you make the most of the word processor you use:

- When you're working on a rough draft, don't worry about mistakes. Correcting, moving, and editing text can be done later, so let yourself go and *just write!*

- Use the spelling checker on your word processor, but proofread your work as well. Why? Be cause they spill checker wood knot find any miss steaks in this sentience, that's way. Are you convinced?

- Save your documents frequently as you work, since power outages and system errors can wipe out unsaved work. Back up important documents by putting a copy on a server or on an extra floppy disk.

- Limit your use of fonts. Use different font styles like outline, shadow, bold, and italic only when needed. Too many fonts can make a document confusing to read.

- Learn how to use word-processing tools such as automatic page numbers, footnotes, centered headings, and even charts and graphs.

Activity Options

Word-Processed Homework If you've never done this before, try to compose your next writing assignment entirely on the computer.

How-To Handbook Spend some time exploring all of the capabilities of your word processing program, then write a user-friendly "User's Guide." Create the handbook, of course, using your word processor, then share it with your classmates.

The STRENGTH of TRADITION

HISTORICAL OVERVIEW

In the early 1900s, the impact of movies, radio, magazines, and advertising was to homogenize American culture. Despite this tendency, regional cultural traditions that emphasized the unique characteristics of different parts of the country thrived in the period between World War I and World War II. The regionalist ideal was expressed by Southern poet Allen Tate: "Only a return to the provinces, to the small, self-contained centers of life, will put the all-destroying abstraction America to rest." During the Great Depression of the 1930s, a number of New Deal programs, notably the Works Progress Administration (WPA), funded a wide variety of regional cultural projects. Among the WPA programs were the Federal Writers Project, the Federal Arts Projects, and the Federal Theatre Project, which supported a wide variety of regional cultural efforts.

The Far West

The Grapes of Wrath by John Steinbeck, which describes the migration of Dust Bowl farmers to California, is a classic of 20th century American regionalism. Migrant life was also recorded by photographer Dorothea Lange.

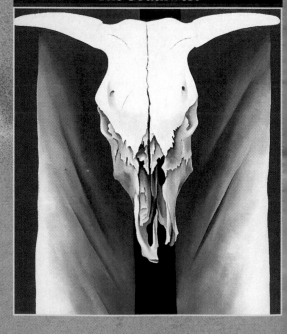

The Southwest

In the late 1920s Georgia O'Keeffe began painting the mountains, flowers, cloud forms, and bleached bones of desert animals in a monumental style that combines realism and abstraction.

The Midwest

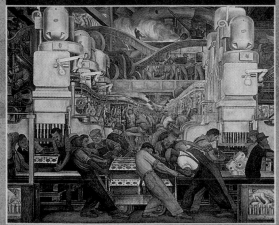

The industrial Midwest is celebrated in Diego Rivera's *Detroit Industry* (1932-33).

In works such as *North of Boston*, poet Robert Frost evoked the landscapes and folkways of rural New England. This area was also the subject of many of the paintings of Edward Hopper such as *Corn Hill* (1930).

New England

Appalachia

In a series of recordings beginning in the later 1920s, the Carter Family preserved the musical culture of the Appalachian region.

In novels and stories set in his fictional Yoknapatawpha County, William Faulkner vividly recreated rural Mississippi. Writers such as Tennessee Williams, Flannery O'Connor, and Eudora Welty demonstrated the continuing strength of regionalism in Southern literature.

The South

Key Dates

1927
The Carter Family begins recording Appalachian music.

late 1920s
Georgia O'Keeffe begins painting in the Southwest.

1933
Diego Rivera completes mural Detroit Industry.

mid 1930s
Dust Bowl develops in Great Plains.

1935
Works Progress Administration established.

mid 1930s
Dorothea Lange begins photographing migrant farmers.

late 1930s
Federal Writers Project supports regional culture.

1939
The Grapes of Wrath *is published.*

Part Two

The Strength of Tradition

While American society was rapidly changing between the wars, many individuals found strength in maintaining the traditions and customs of their cultures and regions. Particularly in rural America, people resisted the changes caused by rapid industrialization, and chose to hold on to the wisdom and ways of older generations.

🐾 **Multicultural Connection** The way we communicate with each other depends a lot on our individual experiences and our cultural backgrounds. In the following selections, notice how **communication** styles differ between the individuals and groups depicted. What in these selections leads to successful communication, and what causes communication to break down?

Literature

Robert Frost	**Stopping by Woods on a Snowy Evening** ◆ poem	..636
	Mending Wall ◆ poem	.637
	Birches ◆ poem	.639
William Faulkner	**The Tall Men** ◆ short story	.644
Thomas S. Whitecloud	**Blue Winds Dancing** ◆ essay	.658
Eudora Welty	**A Worn Path** ◆ short story	.667
John Steinbeck	**The Leader of the People** ◆ short story	.676
Tennessee Williams	**Lord Byron's Love Letter** ◆ play	.690

Interdisciplinary Study Life on the Home Front

New Opportunities for African Americans and Women:
Sybil Lewis ◆ history .699
Children of the Home Front: Sheril Jankovsky Cunning ◆ history ...700
Japanese Americans are "Relocated": Henry Murakami ◆ history 702

Writing Workshop Expository Writing

Point-Counterpoint .704

Beyond Print Critical Thinking

Propaganda .710

Before Reading

Stopping by Woods on a Snowy Evening
Mending Wall
Birches

by Robert Frost

Robert Frost
1874–1963

Born in San Francisco, ten-year-old Robert Frost moved with his mother and sister to his grandfather's farm in Massachusetts following his father's death. For twenty years, while farming, teaching, and working in a bobbin factory, Frost was a mostly unknown and unsuccessful poet. Then in 1912 he made a big decision. Frost sold the farm and moved with his wife and four children to England. There he could "write and be poor without further scandal in the family." Two books of Frost's poetry were published in England, *A Boy's Will* in 1913 and *North of Boston* in 1914. When Frost returned to the United States, he was famous. This Yankee farmer/poet won the Pulitzer Prize four times.

Building Background

Think Yankee What do you visualize when you think of New England? Rocky farmland? cold, snowy winters? rutted roads? deep woods? wild Atlantic waters? Robert Frost was a Yankee; his home was New England. His poems are populated with tough, hard-working people whose words are spare. Although Frost is sometimes considered a regional writer because he wrote about the New England landscape as well as the customs, dress, and speech of its people, his poems are rich in universal meanings. As you read these three poems by Robert Frost, reflect on how his insights relate to you today.

Literary Focus

Blank Verse At times Robert Frost's poems sound almost as if the poet were chatting with you. To achieve this natural sound, Frost often uses **blank verse,** which is unrhymed iambic pentameter. Each unrhymed line has five feet or ten syllables, the first syllable in each pair unaccented and the second accented. A line of blank verse sounds like this: ta Dum ta Dum ta Dum ta Dum ta Dum. Notice the rhythm in the first two lines of "Birches."

> When I see birches bend to left and right
>
> Across the lines of straighter darker trees

Now look ahead at the first few lines of "Mending Wall" and "Stopping by Woods on a Snowy Evening." Which one is written in blank verse? How do you know?

Writer's Notebook

Your Backdrop Good writers write about what they know, and Robert Frost is no exception. A New England farmer at heart, Frost uses the New England landscape and Yankee farmers as a backdrop for his reflections on life. What things in your surroundings inspire you? Look around and then jot down some possible topics.

STOPPING BY WOODS ON A SNOWY EVENING

ROBERT FROST

Whose woods these are I think I know.
His house is in the village, though;
He will not see me stopping here
To watch his woods fill up with snow.

5 My little horse must think it queer
To stop without a farmhouse near
Between the woods and frozen lake
The darkest evening of the year.

He gives his harness bells a shake
10 To ask if there is some mistake.
The only other sound's the sweep
Of easy wind and downy flake.

The woods are lovely, dark, and deep,
But I have promises to keep,
15 And miles to go before I sleep,
And miles to go before I sleep.

▲ This barn which stood isolated from other farm buildings was the inspiration for Eric Sloane's painting, *Hill Farm Barn.* Could the stone wall in his painting resemble one that may have inspired Robert Frost's poem, "Mending Wall"? Why or why not?

MENDING WALL

ROBERT FROST

Something there is that doesn't love a wall,
That sends the frozen-ground-swell under it
And spills the upper boulders in the sun,
And makes gaps even two can pass abreast.
5 The work of hunters is another thing:
I have come after them and made repair
Where they have left not one stone on a stone,
But they would have the rabbit out of hiding,
To please the yelping dogs. The gaps I mean,

10 No one has seen them made or heard them made,
   But at spring mending-time we find them there.
   I let my neighbor know beyond the hill;
   And on a day we meet to walk the line
   And set the wall between us once again.
15 We keep the wall between us as we go.
   To each the boulders that have fallen to each.
   And some are loaves and some so nearly balls
   We have to use a spell to make them balance:
   "Stay where you are until our backs are turned!"
20 We wear our fingers rough with handling them.
   Oh, just another kind of outdoor game,
   One on a side. It comes to little more:
   There where it is we do not need the wall:
   He is all pine and I am apple orchard.
25 My apple trees will never get across
   And eat the cones under his pines, I tell him.
   He only says, "Good fences make good neighbors."
   Spring is the mischief in me, and I wonder
   If I could put a notion in his head:
30 "*Why* do they make good neighbors? Isn't it
   Where there are cows? But here there are no cows.
   Before I built a wall I'd ask to know
   What I was walling in or walling out,
   And to whom I was like to give offense.
35 Something there is that doesn't love a wall,
   That wants it down." I could say "Elves" to him,
   But it's not elves exactly, and I'd rather
   He said it for himself. I see him there,
   Bringing a stone grasped firmly by the top
40 In each hand, like an old-stone savage armed.
   He moves in darkness as it seems to me,
   Not of woods only and the shade of trees.
   He will not go behind his father's saying,
   And he likes having thought of it so well
45 He says again, "Good fences make good neighbors."

What would you say is the appeal of birch trees that would inspire a painting like Neil Welliver's *The Birches* (1977) or a poem like Robert Frost's "Birches"? ➤

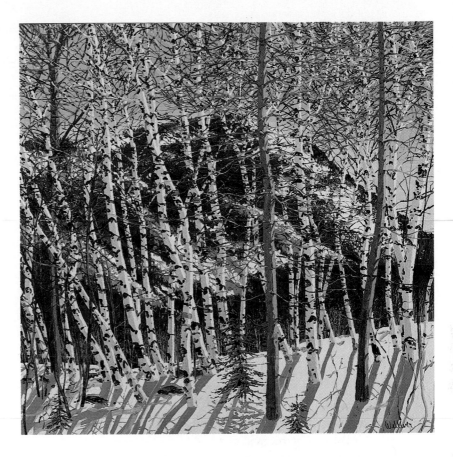

BIRCHES

ROBERT FROST

When I see birches bend to left and right
Across the lines of straighter darker trees,
I like to think some boy's been swinging them.
But swinging doesn't bend them down to stay
5 As ice storms do. Often you must have seen them
Loaded with ice a sunny winter morning
After a rain. They click upon themselves
As the breeze rises, and turn many-colored
As the stir cracks and crazes their enamel.
10 Soon the sun's warmth makes them shed crystal shells
Shattering and avalanching on the snow crust—
Such heaps of broken glass to sweep away
You'd think the inner dome of heaven had fallen.
They are dragged to the withered bracken[1] by the load,

---

1. **bracken** (brak′ən), *n.* a large, coarse fern common
   on hillsides, in woods, etc.

15 And they seem not to break; though once they are bowed
So low for long, they never right themselves:
You may see their trunks arching in the woods
Years afterwards, trailing their leaves on the ground
Like girls on hands and knees that throw their hair
20 Before them over their heads to dry in the sun.
But I was going to say when Truth broke in
With all her matter of fact about the ice storm,
I should prefer to have some boy bend them
As he went out and in to fetch the cows—
25 Some boy too far from town to learn baseball,
Whose only play was what he found himself,
Summer or winter, and could play alone.
One by one he subdued his father's trees
By riding them down over and over again
30 Until he took the stiffness out of them,
And not one but hung limp, not one was left
For him to conquer. He learned all there was
To learn about not launching out too soon
And so not carrying the tree away
35 Clear to the ground. He always kept his poise
To the top branches, climbing carefully
With the same pains you use to fill a cup
Up to the brim, and even above the brim.
Then he flung outward, feet first, with a swish,
40 Kicking his way down through the air to the ground.
So was I once myself a swinger of birches.
And so I dream of going back to be.
It's when I'm weary of considerations,
And life is too much like a pathless wood
45 Where your face burns and tickles with the cobwebs
Broken across it, and one eye is weeping
From a twig's having lashed across it open.
I'd like to get away from earth awhile
And then come back to it and begin over.
50 May no fate willfully misunderstand me
And half grant what I wish and snatch me away
Not to return. Earth's the right place for love:
I don't know where it's likely to go better.
I'd like to go by climbing a birch tree,
55 And climb black branches up a snow-white trunk
Toward heaven, till the tree could bear no more,
But dipped its top and set me down again.
That would be good both going and coming back.
One could do worse than be a swinger of birches.

After Reading

Making Connections

Shaping Your Response

1. Which of the three Frost poems do you like the best? Why?

2. Two opposing opinions are expressed in "Mending Wall": "Good fences make good neighbors" and "Something there is that doesn't love a wall." Which opinion do you hold? Why? Survey the class to see whether your classmates agree.

Analyzing the Poems

3. What examples of **alliteration,** the repetition of initial sounds *(lovely, ladies),* can you find in "Stopping by Woods on a Snowy Evening"?

4. What effect does the **repetition** in the last two lines of "Stopping by Woods on a Snowy Evening" have?

5. How does the speaker in "Mending Wall" **characterize** his neighbor?

6. What **images, metaphors,** and **similes** describe the effect of ice storms on birches in the poem "Birches"?

7. How would you describe the **mood** of "Birches" in lines 43–47?

Extending the Ideas

8. Compare the three Frost poems. Do they have a common **theme?** Explain your answer.

9. Robert Frost writes about a stone fence, a traveler in a snowy woods, and a stand of birches. What three things characteristic of your geographic region could you substitute for Frost's topics?

10. 🐾 In "Mending Wall," two neighbors repair a wall between their property. What kinds of metaphorical walls sometimes impede **communication** between people? How can such "walls" be torn down?

Literary Focus: Blank Verse

Robert Frost uses **blank verse,** but he occasionally alternates iambic pentameter with other rhythms to convey a conversational quality. Read "Birches" aloud. In which line does Frost begin to deviate from iambic pentameter? In which line does he return to it? What would you say is the effect of the variations in rhythm in this poem?

Expressing Your Ideas

Writing Choices

Writer's Notebook Update Choose one of the topics you listed in your Writer's Notebook. Then write ten lines of blank verse about it. For example, if you have chosen *school* as one of your topics, you might begin with this line: "Today I got to school at eight o'clock." You may vary the rhythm occasionally to keep the verse from becoming monotonous.

Childhood Pastimes The speaker in "Birches" was a swinger of birches as a boy. What was your favorite pastime as a child? Were you a skipper of stones, a comic book kid, or something else? Write a **description** of your childhood pastime.

Local Poetry Who is your local poet laureate? Find out more about a poet from your community, state, or region at a library or bookstore. Then write a short **report** on the poet's life and work.

Other Options

Step into the Poem Choose one of the three Frost poems to present to the class. Prepare a **dramatic reading** of the poem, or you might try memorizing it.

Don't Fence Me In Your neighbors are circulating a petition to take down all the fences in your community. However, an opposition group is forming to keep the fences up and add more! Which side will you take? Prepare your arguments and then **debate** a classmate with an opposing viewpoint.

New England Scenes Find and play for the class parts of a **recording** of either of the following works for orchestra by American composers: *Three Places in New England* by Charles Ives or *New England Triptych* by William Schuman. Have your classmates draw what they visualize as they listen.

Before Reading

The Tall Men

by William Faulkner

William Faulkner
1897–1962

Like Robert Frost, William Faulkner is often considered a regionalist. Born near Oxford, Mississippi, he spent most of his life there. He began by writing poetry and then a novel about World War I. Writer Sherwood Anderson, who was a roommate of Faulkner's in New Orleans, convinced him to write about "that little patch up there in Mississippi where you started from." Following Anderson's advice, Faulkner created Yoknapatawpha County, Mississippi, and peopled it with unforgettable characters. Some of the Yoknapatawpha novels are *Sartoris, The Sound and the Fury, As I Lay Dying,* and *Sanctuary.* Faulkner won the Nobel Prize for literature in 1950.

Building Background

A "New Deal" for Farmers When President Franklin Roosevelt took office in 1933, the United States was on the verge of economic collapse. Neither business nor agriculture had recovered from the stock market crash of 1929. To help farmers, Roosevelt's administration implemented the Agricultural Adjustment Act (AAA). Based on the economic principle of supply and demand—when an item is scarce, the price will rise, and when plentiful, the price will fall—the AAA sought to control the supply of crops in the country by paying farmers cash subsidies to *not* plant certain crops, thereby driving up prices. The McCallum family, the farmers in "The Tall Men," chose not to participate in the farm subsidy program.

Literary Focus

Characterization The method an author uses to develop his or her characters is called **characterization.** A writer may describe a character's appearance, personality, behavior, thoughts, feelings, or speech. *Flat characters* are one-dimensional and lacking in complexity. *Round characters* are multi-faceted, with realistic emotions and behavior. Choose one of the main characters in "The Tall Men," and find story passages that show examples of Faulkner's methods of characterization.

Writer's Notebook

Skillet or Fry Pan? To establish the setting of the rural South in the 1940s and to develop his characters, William Faulkner uses **dialect.** Dialect is a form of speech characteristic of a particular region or group. For example, one of the characters in Faulkner's story refers to a *demijohn,* a kind of bottle. Another character says, "This here ain't hurt none to speak of since I got a-holt of this *johnny-jug.*" Do you or the people in your area have names for things that are different from names used in other areas? In your notebook, write words, phrases, or expressions that you think might be dialect.

Dorothea Lange was an influential documentary photographer who is renowned for her photographs of destitute victims of the Great Depression of the 1930s. This 1938 photograph is from Lange's collection.

THE TALL MEN

William Faulkner

They passed the dark bulk of the cotton gin. Then they saw the lamplit house and the other car, the doctor's coupé, just stopping at the gate, and they could hear the hound baying.

"Here we are," the old deputy marshal said.

"What's that other car?" the younger man said, the stranger, the state draft[1] investigator.

"Doctor Schofield's," the marshal said. "Lee McCallum asked me to send him out when I telephoned we were coming."

"You mean you warned them?" the investigator said. "You telephoned ahead that I was coming out with a warrant for these two evaders? Is this how you carry out the orders of the United States Government?"

The marshal was a lean, clean old man who chewed tobacco, who had been born and lived in the county all his life.

"I understood all you wanted was to arrest these two McCallum boys and bring them back to town," he said.

> **CLARIFY: Why does the state investigator intend to arrest the McCallum boys?**

"It was!" the investigator said. "And now you have warned them, given them a chance to run. Possibly put the Government to the expense of hunting them down with troops. Have you forgotten that you are under a bond yourself?"

"I ain't forgot it," the marshal said. "And ever since we left Jefferson I been trying to tell you something for you not to forget. But I reckon it will take these McCallums to impress that on you. . . . Pull in behind the other car. We'll try to find out first just how sick whoever it is that is sick is."

The investigator drew up behind the other car and switched off and blacked out his lights. "These people," he said. Then he thought, *But this doddering, tobacco-chewing old man is one of them, too, despite the honor and pride of his office, which should have made him different.* So he didn't speak it aloud, removing the keys and getting out of the car, and then locking the car itself, rolling the windows up first, thinking, *These people who lie about and conceal the ownership of land and property in order to hold relief jobs which they have no intention of performing, standing on their constitutional rights against having to work, who jeopardize[2] the very job itself through petty and transparent subterfuge to acquire a free mattress which they intend to attempt to sell; who would relinquish[3]*

---

1. **draft,** *n.* selection of persons for some special purpose. Soldiers are supplied to the army by draft during periods of war.
2. **jeopardize** (jɛpʹər dīz), *v.* put in danger; risk.
3. **relinquish** (ri lingʹkwish), *v.* give up; let go.

even the job, if by so doing they could receive free food and a place, any rathole, in town to sleep in; who, as farmers, make false statements to get seed loans which they will later misuse, and then react in loud vituperative outrage and astonishment when caught at it. And then, when at long last a suffering and threatened Government asks one thing of them in return, one thing simply, which is to put their names down on a selective-service[4] list, they refuse to do it.

The old marshal had gone on. The investigator followed, through a stout paintless gate in a picket fence, up a broad brick walk between two rows of old shabby cedars, toward the rambling and likewise paintless sprawl of the two-story house in the open hall of which the soft lamplight glowed and the lower story of which, as the investigator now perceived, was of logs.

H e saw a hall full of soft lamplight beyond a stout paintless gallery running across the log front, from beneath which the same dog which they had heard, a big hound, came booming again, to stand foursquare facing them in the walk, bellowing, until a man's voice spoke to it from the house. He followed the marshal up the steps onto the gallery. Then he saw the man standing in the door, waiting for them to approach—a man of about forty-five, not tall, but blocky, with a brown, still face and horseman's hands, who looked at him once, brief and hard, and then no more, speaking to the marshal, "Howdy, Mr. Gombault. Come in."

"Howdy, Rafe," the marshal said. "Who's sick?"

"Buddy," the other said. "Slipped and caught his leg in the hammer mill this afternoon."

"Is it bad?" the marshal said.

"It looks bad to me," the other said. "That's why we sent for the doctor instead of bringing him in to town. We couldn't get the bleeding stopped."

"I'm sorry to hear that," the marshal said. "This is Mr. Pearson." Once more the investigator found the other looking at him, the brown eyes still, courteous enough in the brown face,

the hand he offered hard enough, but the clasp quite limp, quite cold. The marshal was still speaking. "From Jackson. From the draft board." Then he said, and the investigator could discern[5] no change whatever in his tone: "He's got a warrant for the boys."

The investigator could discern no change whatever anywhere. The limp hard hand merely withdrew from his, the still face now looking at the marshal. "You mean we have declared war?"

"No," the marshal said.

"That's not the question, Mr. McCallum," the investigator said. "All required of them was to register. Their numbers might not even be drawn this time; under the law of averages, they probably would not be. But they refused—failed, anyway—to register."

"I see," the other said. He was not looking at the investigator. The investigator couldn't tell certainly if he was even looking at the marshal, although he spoke to him, "You want to see Buddy? The doctor's with him now."

"Wait," the investigator said. "I'm sorry about your brother's accident, but I——" The marshal glanced back at him for a moment, his shaggy gray brows beetling, with something at once courteous yet a little impatient about the glance, so that during the instant the investigator sensed from the old marshal the same quality which had been in the other's brief look. The investigator was a man of better than average intelligence; he was already becoming aware of something a little different here from what he had expected. But he had been in relief work in the state several years, dealing almost exclusively with country people, so he still believed he knew them. So he looked at the old marshal, thinking, *Yes. The same sort of people, despite the office, the authority and responsibility which should have changed him.*

---

4. **selective service,** compulsory military service of persons selected from the general population according to age, physical fitness, etc.

5. **discern** (də zėrn′), *v.* perceive the difference between two or more things.

Thinking again, *These people. These people.* "I intend to take the night train back to Jackson," he said. "My reservation is already made. Serve the warrant and we will——"

"Come along," the old marshal said. "We are going to have plenty of time."

PREDICT: What does Mr. Pearson, the investigator from the draft board, expect the McCallums to be like? What do you expect them to be like?

So he followed—there was nothing else to do—fuming and seethe,[6] attempting in the short length of the hall to regain control of himself in order to control the situation, because he realized now that if the situation were controlled, it would devolve upon him to control it; that if their departure with their prisoners were expedited,[7] it must be himself and not the old marshal who would expedite it. He had been right. The doddering old officer was not only at bottom one of these people, he had apparently been corrupted anew to his old, inherent, shiftless sloth and unreliability merely by entering the house. So he followed in turn, down the hall and into a bedroom; whereupon he looked about him not only with amazement but with something very like terror. The room was a big room, with a bare unpainted floor, and besides the bed, it contained only a chair or two and one other piece of old-fashioned furniture. Yet to the investigator it seemed so filled with tremendous men cast in the same mold as the man who had met them that the very walls themselves must bulge. Yet they were not big, not tall, and it was not vitality, exuberance, because they made no sound, merely looking quietly at him where he stood in the door, with faces bearing an almost identical stamp of kinship—a thin, almost frail old man of about seventy, slightly taller than the others; a second one, white-haired, too, but otherwise identical with the man who had met them at the door; a third one about the same age as the man who had met them, but with something delicate in his face and something tragic and dark and wild in the same dark eyes; the two absolutely identical blue-eyed youths; and lastly the blue-eyed man on the bed over which the doctor, who might have been any city doctor, in his neat city suit, leaned—all of them turning to look quietly at him and the marshal as they entered. And he saw, past the doctor, the slit trousers of the man on the bed and the exposed, bloody, mangled leg, and he turned sick, stopping just inside the door under that quiet, steady regard while the marshal went up to the man who lay on the bed, smoking a cob pipe, a big, old-fashioned, wicker-covered demijohn, such as the investigator's grandfather had kept his whisky in, on the table beside him.

"Well, Buddy," the marshal said, "this is bad."

"Ah, it was my own damn fault," the man on the bed said. "Stuart kept warning me about that frame I was using."

"That's correct," the second old one said.

Still the others said nothing. They just looked steadily and quietly at the investigator until the marshal turned slightly and said, "This is Mr. Pearson. From Jackson. He's got a warrant for the boys."

Then the man on the bed said, "What for?"

"That draft business, Buddy," the marshal said.

"We're not at war now," the man on the bed said.

"No," the marshal said. "It's that new law. They didn't register."

"What are you going to do with them?"

"It's a warrant, Buddy. Swore out."

"That means jail."

"It's a warrant," the old marshal said. Then the investigator saw that the man on the bed was watching him, puffing steadily at the pipe.

"Pour me some whisky, Jackson," he said.

---

6. **seethe** (sēтн), *v.* be excited; be disturbed.

7. **expedite** (ekʹspə dīt), *v.* do or perform quickly.

"No," the doctor said. "He's had too much already."

"Pour me some whisky, Jackson," the man on the bed said. He puffed steadily at the pipe, looking at the investigator. "You come from the Government?" he said.

"Yes," the investigator said. "They should have registered. That's all required of them yet. They did not——" His voice ceased,[8] while the seven pairs of eyes contemplated him, and the man on the bed puffed steadily.

...the seven pairs of eyes contemplated him ...

"We would have still been here," the man on the bed said. "We wasn't going to run." He turned his head. The two youths were standing side by side at the foot of the bed. "Anse, Lucius," he said.

To the investigator it sounded as if they answered as one, "Yes, father."

"This gentleman has come all the way from Jackson to say the Government is ready for you. I reckon the quickest place to enlist will be Memphis. Go upstairs and pack."

The investigator started, moved forward, "Wait!" he cried.

But Jackson, the eldest, had forestalled him. He said, "Wait," also, and now they were not looking at the investigator. They were looking at the doctor.

"What about his leg?" Jackson said.

"Look at it," the doctor said. "He almost amputated it himself. It won't wait. And he can't be moved now. I'll need my nurse to help me, and some ether, provided he hasn't had too much whisky to stand the anesthetic too. One of you can drive to town in my car. I'll telephone——"

"Ether?" the man on the bed said. "What for? You just said yourself it's pretty near off now. I could whet up one of Jackson's butcher knives and finish it myself, with another drink or two. Go on. Finish it."

"You couldn't stand any more shock," the doctor said. "This is whisky talking now."

"Shucks," the other said. "One day in France we was running through a wheat field and I saw the machine gun, coming across the wheat, and I tried to jump it like you would jump a fence rail somebody was swinging at your middle, only I never made it. And I was on the ground then, and along toward dark that begun to hurt, only about that time something went whang on the back of my helmet, like when you hit a anvil, so I never knowed nothing else until I woke up. There was a heap of us racked up along a bank outside a field dressing station, only it took a long time for the doctor to get around to all of us, and by that time it was hurting bad. This here ain't hurt none to speak of since I got a-holt of this johnny-jug. You go on and finish it. If it's help you need, Stuart and Rafe will help you. . . . Pour me a drink, Jackson."

This time the doctor raised the demijohn and examined the level of the liquor. "There's a good quart gone," he said. "If you've drunk a quart of whisky since four o'clock, I doubt if you could stand the anesthetic. Do you think you could stand it if I finished it now?"

"Yes, finish it. I've ruined it; I want to get shut of it."[9]

The doctor looked about at the others, at the still, identical faces watching him. "If I had him in town, in the hospital, with a nurse to watch him, I'd probably wait until he got over this first shock and got the whisky out of his system. But he can't be moved now, and I can't stop the bleeding like this, and even if I had ether or a local anesthetic——"

"Shucks," the man on the bed said. "God never made no better local nor general comfort or anesthetic neither than what's in this johnny-jug. And this ain't Jackson's leg nor Stuart's nor

8. cease (sēs), *v.* come to an end or stop.
9. **get shut of it,** colloquial expression meaning "get rid of it," or "get it over with."

▲ Do these tenant farmers in Dorothea Lange's 1937 photograph fill the picture the way the "tremendous men" encountered by the investigator filled Buddy's room in William Faulkner's story, "The Tall Men"? Why or why not?

Rafe's nor Lee's. It's mine. I done started it; I reckon I can finish cutting it off any way I want to."

But the doctor was still looking at Jackson. "Well, Mr. McCallum?" he said. "You're the oldest."

But it was Stuart who answered. "Yes," he said. "Finish it. What do you want? Hot water, I reckon."

"Yes," the doctor said. "Some clean sheets. Have you got a big table you can move in here?"

"The kitchen table," the man who had met them at the door said. "Me and the boys——"

"Wait," the man on the bed said. "The boys won't have time to help you." He looked at them again. "Anse, Lucius," he said.

Again it seemed to the investigator that they answered as one, "Yes, father."

"This gentleman yonder is beginning to look impatient. You better start. Come to think of it, you won't need to pack. You will have uniforms in a day or two. Take the truck. There won't be nobody to drive you to Memphis and bring the truck back, so you can leave it at the Gayoso Feed Company until we can send for it. I'd like for you to enlist into the old Sixth Infantry, where I used to be. But I reckon that's too much to hope, and you'll just have to chance where they send you. But it likely won't matter, once you are in. The Government done right by me in my day, and it will do right by you. You just enlist wherever they want to send you, need you, and obey your sergeants and officers until you find out how to be soldiers. Obey them, but remember your name and don't take nothing from no man. You can go now."

"Wait!" the investigator cried again; again he started, moved forward into the center of the room. "I protest this! I'm sorry about Mr. McCallum's accident. I'm sorry about the whole business. But it's out of my hands and out of his hands now. This charge, failure to register according to law, has been made and the warrant issued. It cannot be evaded[10] this way. The course of the action must be completed before any other step can be taken. They should have thought of this when these boys failed to register. If Mr. Gombault refuses to serve this warrant, I will serve it myself and take these men back to Jefferson with me to answer this charge as made. And I must warn Mr. Gombault that he will be cited[11] for contempt."

The old marshal turned, his shaggy eyebrows beetling again, speaking down to the investigator as if he were a child, "Ain't you found out yet that me or you neither ain't going nowhere for a while?"

"What?" the investigator cried. He looked about at the grave faces once more contemplating him with that remote and speculative[12] regard. "Am I being threatened?" he cried.

"Ain't anybody paying any attention to you at all," the marshal said. "Now you just be quiet for a while, and you will be all right, and after a while we can go back to town."

So he stopped again and stood while the grave, contemplative faces freed him once more of that impersonal and unbearable regard, and saw the two youths approach the bed and bend down in turn and kiss their father on the mouth, and then turn as one and leave the room, passing him without even looking at him. And sitting in the lamplit hall beside the old marshal, the bedroom door closed now, he heard the truck start up and back and turn and go down the road, the sound of it dying away, ceasing, leaving the still, hot night—the Mississippi Indian summer, which had already outlasted half of November—filled with the loud last shrilling of the summer's cicadas, as though they, too, were aware of the imminent season of cold weather and of death.

CLARIFY: What do Anse and Lucius intend to do, and why is this upsetting to Mr. Pearson?

"I remember old Anse," the marshal said pleasantly, chattily, in that tone in which an adult addresses a strange child. "He's been dead fifteen-sixteen years now. He was about sixteen when the old war broke out, and he walked all the way to Virginia to get into it. He could have enlisted and fought right here at home, but his ma was a Carter, so wouldn't nothing do him but to go all the way back to Virginia to do his fighting, even though he hadn't never seen Virginia before himself; walked all the way back to a land he hadn't never ever seen before and enlisted in Stonewall Jackson's army and stayed in it all through the Valley, and right up to Chancellorsville, where them Carolina boys shot Jackson by mistake, and right on up to that morning in 'Sixty-five when Sheridan's cavalry blocked the road from Appomattox to the Valley, where they might have got away again. And he walked back to Mississippi with just about what he had carried away with him when he left, and he got married and built the first story of this house—this here log story we're in right now—and started getting them boys—Jackson and Stuart and Raphael and Lee

---

10. **evade** (i vād′), *v.* avoid by cleverness; elude.
11. **cite** (sīt), *v.* summon officially to appear in court.
12. **speculative** (spek′yə lā′tiv), *adj.* reflective.

Jackson and Stuart and Raphael and Lee and Buddy.

"Buddy come along late, late enough to be in the other war, in France in it. You heard him in there. He brought back two medals, an American medal and a French one, and no man knows till yet how he got them, just what he done. I don't believe he even told Jackson and Stuart and them. He hadn't hardly got back home, with them numbers on his uniform and the wound stripes and them two medals, before he had found him a girl, found her right off, and a year later them twin boys was born, the livin', spittin' image of old Anse McCallum. If old Anse had just been about seventy-five years younger, the three of them might have been thriblets. I remember them—two little critters exactly alike, and wild as spikehorn bucks, running around here day and night both with a pack of coon dogs until they got big enough to help Buddy and Stuart and Lee with the farm and the gin, and Rafe with the horses and mules, when he would breed and raise and train them and take them to Memphis to sell, right on up to three, four years back, when they went to the agricultural college for a year to learn more about whiteface cattle.

"That was after Buddy and them had quit raising cotton. I remember that too. It was when the Government first begun to interfere with how a man farmed his own land, raised his cotton. Stabilizing[13] the price, using up the surplus, they called it, giving a man advice and help, whether he wanted it or not. You may have noticed them boys in yonder tonight; curious folks almost, you might call them. That first year, when county agents come out here and tried to explain it to Buddy and Lee and Stuart, explaining how they would cut down the crop, but that the Government would pay farmers the difference, and so they would actually be better off than trying to farm by themselves.

"'Why, we're much obliged,' Buddy says.

'But we don't need no help. We'll just make the cotton like we always done; if we can't make a crop of it, that will just be our lookout and our loss, and we'll try again.'

"So they wouldn't sign no papers nor no cards nor nothing. They just went on and made the cotton like old Anse had taught them to; it was like they just couldn't believe that the Government aimed to help a man whether he wanted help or not, aimed to interfere with how much of anything he could make by hard work on his own land, making the crop and ginning it right here in their own gin, like they had always done, and hauling it to town to sell, hauling it all the way into Jefferson before they found out they couldn't sell it because, in the first place, they had made too much of it and, in the second place, they never had no card to sell what they would have been allowed. So they hauled it back. The gin wouldn't hold all of it, so they put some of it under Rafe's mule shed and they put the rest of it right here in the hall where we are setting now, where they would have to walk around it all winter and keep themselves reminded to be sho and fill out that card next time.

...they just couldn't believe that the Government aimed to help a man whether he wanted help or not ...

"Only next year they didn't fill out no papers neither. It was like they still couldn't believe it, still believed in the freedom and liberty to make or break according to a man's fitness and will to work, guaranteed by the Government that old Anse had tried to tear in two once and failed, and

---

13. **stabilize** (stā′bə līz), *v.* prevent changes in, hold steady.

▲ This photograph shows cotton waiting to be processed at a cotton gin near Orangeburg, South Carolina.

admitted in good faith he had failed and taken the consequences, and that had give Buddy a medal and taken care of him when he was far away from home in a strange land and hurt.

"So they made that second crop. And they couldn't sell it to nobody neither because they never had no cards. This time they built a special shed to put it under, and I remember how in that second winter Buddy come to town one day to see Lawyer Gavin Stevens. Not for legal advice how to sue the Government or somebody into buying the cotton, even if they never had no card for it, but just to find out why. 'I was for going ahead and signing up for it,' Buddy says.

'If that's going to be the new rule. But we talked it over, and Jackson ain't no farmer, but he knowed father longer than the rest of us, and he said father would have said no, and I reckon now he would have been right.'

"So they didn't raise any more cotton; they had a plenty of it to last a while—twenty-two bales, I think it was. That was when they went into whiteface cattle, putting old Anse's cotton land into pasture, because that's what he would have wanted them to do if the only way they could raise cotton was by the Government telling them how much they could raise and how much they could sell it for, and where, and when, and then pay them for not doing the work they didn't do. Only even when they didn't raise cotton, every year the county agent's young fellow would come out to measure the pasture crops they planted so he could pay them for that, even if they never had no not-cotton to be paid for. Except that he never measured no crop on this place. 'You're welcome to look at what we are doing,' Buddy says. 'But don't draw it down on your map.'

"'But you can get money for this,' the young fellow says. 'The Government wants to pay you for planting all this.'

"'We are aiming to get money for it,' Buddy says. 'When we can't, we will try something else. But not from the Government. Give that to them that want to take it. We can make out.'

"And that's about all. Them twenty-two bales of orphan cotton are down yonder in the gin right now, because there's room for it in the gin now because they ain't using the gin no more. And them boys grew up and went off a year to the agricultural college to learn right about whiteface cattle, and then come back to the rest of them—these here curious folks living off here to themselves, with the rest of the world all full of pretty neon lights burning night and day both, and easy, quick money scattering itself around everywhere for any man to grab a little, and every man with a shiny new automobile already wore out and throwed away and the new one delivered before the first one was even paid for, and everywhere a fine loud grabble and snatch of AAA and WPA[14] and a dozen other three-letter reasons for a man not to work. Then this here draft comes along, and these curious folks ain't got around to signing that neither, and you come all the way up from Jackson with your paper all signed and regular, and we come out here, and after a while we can go back to town. A man gets around, don't he?"

"Yes," the investigator said. "Do you suppose we can go back to town now?"

"No," the marshal told him in that same kindly tone, "not just yet. But we can leave after a while. Of course you will miss your train. But there will be another one tomorrow."

He rose, though the investigator had heard nothing. The investigator watched him go down the hall and open the bedroom door and enter and close it behind him. The investigator sat quietly, listening to the night sounds and looking at the closed door until it opened presently and the marshal came back, carrying something in a bloody sheet, carrying it gingerly.

"Here," he said. "Hold it a minute."

"It's bloody," the investigator said.

"That's all right," the marshal said. "We can wash when we get through." So the investigator took the bundle and stood holding it while he watched the old marshal go back down the hall and on through it and vanish and return presently with a lighted lantern and a shovel. "Come along," he said. "We're pretty near through now."

The investigator followed him out of the house and across the yard, carrying gingerly the bloody, shattered, heavy bundle in which it still seemed to him he could feel some warmth of life, the marshal striding on ahead, the lantern swinging against his leg, the shadow of his striding scissoring and enormous along the earth, his voice still coming back over his shoulder, chatty and cheerful, "Yes, sir. A man gets around and he sees a heap; a heap of folks in a heap of situations. The trouble is, we done got into the habit of confusing the situations with the folks. Take yourself, now," he said in that same kindly tone, chatty and easy; "you mean all right. You just went and got yourself all fogged up with rules and regulations. That's our trouble. We done invented ourselves so many

14. **AAA** and **WPA,** Agricultural Adjustment Act, which paid farmers to reduce their crops, and the Works Progress Administration, which created public service projects in order to employ people and restore their self-respect. Both programs were instituted under President Franklin D. Roosevelt to help bring the country out of the Great Depression.

alphabets and rules and recipes that we can't see anything else; if what we see can't be fitted to an alphabet or a rule, we are lost. We have come to be like critters doctor folks might have created in laboratories, that have learned how to slip off their bones and guts and still live, still be kept alive indefinite and forever maybe even without even knowing the bones and the guts are gone. We have slipped our backbone; we have about decided a man don't need a backbone any more; to have one is old-fashioned. But the groove where the backbone used to be is still there, and the backbone has been kept alive, too, and someday we're going to slip back onto it. I don't know just when nor just how much of a wrench it will take to teach us, but someday."

SUMMARIZE: Describe the marshal's view of what has happened to people.

They had left the yard now. They were mounting a slope; ahead of them the investigator could see another clump of cedars, a small clump, somehow shaggily formal against the starred sky. The marshal entered it and stopped and set the lantern down and, following with the bundle, the investigator saw a small rectangle of earth enclosed by a low brick coping. Then he saw the two graves, or the headstones—two plain granite slabs set upright in the earth.

"Old Anse and Mrs. Anse," the marshal said. "Buddy's wife wanted to be buried with her folks. I reckon she would have been right lonesome up here with just McCallums. Now, let's see." He stood for a moment, his chin in his hand; to the investigator he looked exactly like an old lady trying to decide where to set out a shrub. "They was to run from left to right, beginning with Jackson. But after the boys was born, Jackson and Stuart was to come up here by their pa and ma, so Buddy could move up some and make room. So he will be about here." He moved the lantern nearer and took up the shovel. Then he saw the investigator still holding the bundle. "Set it down," he said. "I got to dig first."

"I'll hold it," the investigator said.

"Nonsense, put it down," the marshal said. "Buddy won't mind."

So the investigator put the bundle down on the brick coping and the marshal began to dig, skillfully and rapidly, still talking in that cheerful, interminable voice, "Yes, sir. We done forgot about folks. Life has done got cheap, and life ain't cheap. Life's a pretty durn valuable thing. I don't mean just getting along from one WPA relief check to the next one, but honor and pride and discipline that make a man worth preserving, making him of any value. That's what we got to learn again. Maybe it takes trouble, bad trouble, to teach it back to us; maybe it was the walking to Virginia because that's where his ma come from, and losing a war and then walking back, that taught it to old Anse. Anyway, he seems to learned it, and to learned it good enough to bequeath it to his boys. Did you notice how all Buddy had to do was to tell them boys of his it was time to go, because the Government had sent them word? And how they told him good-by? Growned men kissing one another without hiding and without shame. Maybe that's what I am trying to say. . . . There," he said. "That's big enough."

He moved quickly, easily; before the investigator could stir, he had lifted the bundle into the narrow trench and was covering it, covering it as rapidly as he had dug, smoothing the earth over it with the shovel. Then he stood up and raised the lantern—a tall, lean old man, breathing easily and lightly.

"I reckon we can go back to town now," he said.

After Reading

Making Connections

Shaping Your Response

1. The marshal never comes right out and tells the state draft investigator what he thinks of him and his arrest warrant. If he had, what do you think he would have said to Mr. Pearson?

2. Do you think the marshal did the right thing by letting the McCallum boys drive off and enlist in Memphis? Explain your opinion.

Analyzing the Story

3. What does the italicized type signal in the story?

4. What are the major **conflicts?**

5. Reread the description of the McCallum men on page 648. Why do you think the story is called "The Tall Men"?

6. Why do you think the McCallums refused to take any kind of government assistance?

7. Marshal Gombault says, "We have slipped our backbone; we have about decided a man don't need a backbone any more; to have one is old-fashioned." What do you think he means?

8. ☝ How would you explain the difference in **communication** styles between Mr. Pearson and the others?

Extending the Ideas

9. The McCallum boys broke the law by not registering for the draft, and yet their intentions seemed to be good. Should the law give such people second chances? Why or why not?

10. The McCallums didn't always agree with the government's policies. Are there any laws or policies you'd like to see changed? With a group, brainstorm and write a list of ways you might try to change such laws and policies.

Literary Focus: Characterization

Characterization is the method an author uses to acquaint readers with his or her characters. Are the main characters in "The Tall Men" round or flat characters? Choose one and make a list of adjectives that describe him. Next to each adjective, jot down or describe a passage from the story that illustrates that personal attribute.

Vocabulary Study

On a piece of paper, write the verb that best completes each sentence. Use the Glossary if you need help.

cease
cite
discern
evade
expedite
jeopardize
relinquish
seethe
stabilize
speculative

1. The doctor attempted to ____ the patient's blood pressure.

2. Mr. Pearson wondered when the hounds' barking would ____.

3. The McCallum family refused to ____ control of their cotton crop to the government.

4. When there is a military draft, draft evaders ____ their future because they are breaking the law.

5. The McCallums did not intend to ____ military service; they didn't see the point in registering for the draft when there wasn't a war.

6. It will ____ the registration process if you bring current identification.

7. As time passed, the state draft investigator became less rigid and more ____ about why the men didn't register for the draft.

8. Could Mr. Pearson ____ the difference between the letter of the law and the spirit of the law?

9. Mr. Pearson intended to ask a judge to ____ the marshal for contempt.

10. Mr. Pearson began to ____ when he realized the marshal's intent to save the McCallum boys from arrest.

Expressing Your Ideas

Writing Choices

Writer's Notebook Update Review the examples of dialect that you wrote in your notebook. Then create a character who might use that dialect and write a monologue for him or her.

Respectfully Submitted As a government employee, Mr. Pearson would probably have to write a report about the McCallum boys to submit to his superior. What do you suppose he would write in order to explain why he did not arrest them? What version of the story will he tell? Assume that you are Pearson and write a **report** for the McCallum file.

Other Options

Farm Subsidies Research the history of farm subsidies. Why did the government institute them? How do they work? How have they changed over the years? How do they affect the nation's economy? Prepare an **oral report** summarizing your research on the topic.

Reader's Theater Select a scene from "The Tall Men" that would make a good **reader's theater production.** Assign the parts of the narrator and characters, rehearse the scene, and present it to the class.

Before Reading

Blue Winds Dancing

by Thomas S. Whitecloud

Thomas S. Whitecloud
1914–1972

Thomas S. Whitecloud was born in New York. His father was a Chippewa Indian and his mother was white. His parents divorced when Whitecloud's father, who had a law degree from Yale, decided to return to the Lac du Flambeau Reservation and live with the Chippewa people. Whitecloud began working when he was ten, and he held a variety of jobs: farm worker, truck driver, and boxer, to name a few. He flunked out of the University of New Mexico, but eventually graduated from the University of Redlands in California. It was during this time that he wrote "Blue Winds Dancing," which won first prize in a Phi Beta Kappa essay contest. He went on to earn his medical degree and practiced medicine in the military as an Indian Service physician and in private practice.

Building Background

Who Am I? As a child of two different cultures, Thomas Whitecloud grew up in two different worlds. The customs and values of his relatives on the Lac du Flambeau Reservation were quite different from those he encountered at school and on the job. While he was attending school, Whitecloud missed his family, his community, and his people's ways and values. Discouraged and homesick, Whitecloud followed an impulse to hop a freight train and go home for Christmas. This essay recounts his trip back home and his reflections on the differences between white and American Indian society.

Literary Focus

Imagery "And there is a fall wind blowing in my heart." This line from Thomas Whitecloud's essay makes the reader feel a chill, brisk wind. Whitecloud uses **imagery,** descriptions that appeal to the senses, throughout "Blue Winds Dancing." In this case, the image is figurative. A wind isn't really blowing in his heart; his heart feels restless because he is homesick. As you read the essay, look for other sensory images. Which are literal and which are figurative? To which sense does each appeal: sight, hearing, touch (or motion), taste, or smell? Use a chart like this to record the images from the essay.

Image	Sense to Which It Appeals

Writer's Notebook

Culture Shock Imagine this scene: You are far away from home, living with people in a culture different from your own, and today is an important family day. Maybe it is your birthday or a holiday. Take three minutes to write about how you feel, and what you miss most about home.

Blue Winds Dancing

Thomas S. Whitecloud

There is a moon out tonight. Moon and stars and clouds tipped with moonlight. And there is a fall wind blowing in my heart. Ever since this evening, when against a fading sky I saw geese wedge southward. They were going home. . . . Now I try to study, but against the pages I see them again, driving southward. Going home.

Across the valley there are heavy mountains holding up the night sky, and beyond the mountains there is home. Home, and peace, and the beat of drums, and blue winds dancing over snow fields. The Indian lodge will fill with my people, and our gods will come and sit among them. I should be there then. I should be at home.

But home is beyond the mountains, and I am here. Here where fall hides in the valleys, and winter never comes down from the mountains. Here where all the trees grow in rows; the palms stand stiffly by the roadsides, and in the groves the orange trees line in military rows, and endlessly bear fruit. Beautiful, yes; there is always beauty in order, in rows of growing things! But it is the beauty of captivity. A pine fighting for existence on a windy knoll is much more beautiful.

In my Wisconsin, the leaves change before the snows come. In the air there is the smell of wild rice and venison cooking; and when the winds come whispering through the forests, they carry the smell of rotting leaves. In the evenings, the loon calls, lonely; and birds sing their last songs before leaving. Bears dig roots and eat late fall berries, fattening for their long winter sleep. Later, when the first snows fall, one awakens in the morning to find the world white and beautiful and clean. Then one can look back over his trail and see the tracks following. In the woods there are tracks of deer and snowshoe rabbits, and long streaks where partridges slide to alight. Chipmunks make tiny footprints on the limbs; and one can hear squirrels busy in hollow trees, sorting acorns. Soft lake waves wash the shores, and sunsets burst each evening over the lakes, and make them look as if they were afire.

That land which is my home! Beautiful, calm—where there is no hurry

▲ After you've finished the story, come back to this image, Richard Red Owl's acrylic, *Lost in Dance* (1994). Does it match the mood of the end of "Blue Winds Dancing"? Why or why not?

to get anywhere, no driving to keep up in a race that knows no ending and no goal. No classes where men talk and talk, and then stop now and then to hear their own words come back to them from the students. No constant peering into the maelstrom[1] of one's mind; no worries about grades and honors; no hysterical preparing for life until that life is half over; no anxiety about one's place in the thing they call Society.

I hear again the ring of axes in deep woods, the crunch of snow beneath my feet. I feel again the smooth velvet of ghost-birch bark. I hear the rhythm of the drums. . . . I am tired. I am weary of trying to keep up this bluff of being civilized. Being civilized means trying to do everything you don't want to, never doing anything you want to. It means dancing to the strings of custom and tradition; it means living in houses and never knowing or caring who is next door. These civilized white men want us to be like them—always dissatisfied, getting a hill and wanting a mountain.

Then again, maybe I am not tired. Maybe I'm licked. Maybe I am just not smart enough to grasp these things that go to make up civilization. Maybe I am just too lazy to think hard enough to keep up.

Still, I know my people have many things that civilization has taken from the whites. They know how to give; how to tear one's piece of meat in two and share it with one's brother. They know how to sing—how to make each man his own songs and sing them; for their music they do not have to listen to other men singing over a radio. They know how to make things with their hands, how to shape beads into design and make a thing of beauty from a piece of birch bark.

But we are inferior. It is terrible to have to feel inferior; to have to read reports of intelligence tests, and learn that one's race is behind. It is terrible to sit in classes and hear men tell you that your people worship sticks of wood—that your gods are all false, that the Manitou[2] forgot your people and did not write them a book.

I am tired. I want to walk again among the ghost-birches. I want to see the leaves turn in autumn, the smoke rise from the lodgehouses, and to feel the blue winds. I want to hear the drums; I want to hear the drums and feel the blue whispering winds.

There is a train wailing into the night. The trains go across the mountains. It would be easy to catch a freight. They will say he has gone back to the blanket; I don't care. The dance at Christmas. . . .

There is a train wailing into the night. . . . It would be easy to catch a freight.

A bunch of bums warming at a tiny fire talk politics and women and joke about the Relief and the WPA[3] and smoke cigarettes. These men in caps and overcoats and dirty overalls living on the outskirts of civilization are free, but they pay the price of being free in civilization. They are outcasts. I remember a sociology professor lecturing on adjustment to society; hobos and prostitutes and criminals are individuals who never adjusted, he said. He could learn a lot if he came and listened to a bunch of bums talk. He would learn that work and a woman and a place to hang his hat are all the ordinary man wants. These are all he wants, but other men are not content to let him want only these. He must be taught to want radios and automobiles and a new suit every spring. Progress would stop if he did not want these things. I listen to hear if there is any talk of communism or socialism in the hobo jungles. There is none. At best there is a sort of disgusted philosophy about life. They

---

1. **maelstrom** (māl′strəm), *n.* a turbulent whirlpool.
2. **Manitou** (man′ə tü), Great Spirit; deity.
3. **Relief** and **the WPA,** "Relief" refers to the Civil Works Administration (CWA), a forerunner of the Works Progress Administration (WPA). Both were federal jobs projects to help the unemployed during the Depression.

seem to think there should be a better distribution of wealth, or more work, or something. But they are not rabid about it. The radicals[4] live in the cities.

I find a fellow headed for Albuquerque, and talk road-talk with him. "It is hard to ride fruit cars. Bums break in. Better to wait for a cattle car going back to the Middle West, and ride that." We catch the next east-bound and walk the tops until we find a cattle car. Inside, we crouch near the forward wall, huddle, and try to sleep. I feel peaceful and content at last. I am going home. The cattle car rocks. I sleep.

Morning and the desert. Noon and the Salton Sea, lying more lifeless than a mirage under a somber sun in a pale sky. Skeleton mountains rearing on the skyline, thrusting out of the desert floor, all rock and shadow and edges. Desert. Good country for an Indian reservation. . . .

Yuma and the muddy Colorado. Night again, and I wait shivering for the dawn.

Phoenix. Pima country. Mountains that look like cardboard sets on a forgotten stage. Tucson. Papago country. Giant cacti that look like petrified hitchhikers along the highways. Apache country. At El Paso my road-buddy decides to go on to Houston. I leave him, and head north to the mesa country. Las Cruces and the terrible Organ Mountains, jagged peaks that instill fear and wondering. Albuquerque. Pueblos along the Rio Grande. On the boardwalk there are some Indian women in colored sashes selling bits of pottery. The stone age offering its art to the twentieth century. They hold up a piece and fix the tourists with black eyes until, embarrassed, he buys or turns away. I feel suddenly angry that my people should have to do such things for a living. . . .

Santa Fe trains are fast, and they keep them pretty clean of bums. I decide to hurry and ride passenger coaltenders. Hide in the dark, judge the speed of the train as it leaves, and then dash out, and catch it. I hug the cold steel wall of the tender and think of the roaring fire in the engine ahead, and of the passengers back in the dining car reading their papers over hot coffee. Beneath me there is blur of rails. Death would come quick if my hands should freeze and I fall. Up over the Sangre De Cristo range, around cliffs and through canyons to Denver. Bitter cold here, and I must watch out for Denver Bob. He is railroad bull who has thrown bums from fast freights. I miss him. It is too cold, I suppose. On north to the Sioux country.

Small towns lit for the coming Christmas. On the streets of one I see a beam-shouldered young farmer gazing into a window filled with shining silver toasters. He is tall and wears a blue shirt buttoned, with no tie. His young wife by his side looks at him hopefully. He wants decorations for his place to hang his hat to please his woman. . . .

Northward again. Minnesota, and great white fields of snow; frozen lakes, and dawn running into dusk without noon. Long forests wearing white. Bitter cold, and one night the northern lights.[5] I am nearing home.

I reach Woodruff at midnight. Suddenly I am afraid, now that I am but twenty miles from home. Afraid of what my father will say, afraid of being looked on as a stranger by my own people. I sit by a fire and think about myself and all the other young Indians. We just don't seem to fit in anywhere—certainly not among the whites, and not among the older people. I think again about the learned sociology professor and his professing. So many things seem to be clear now that I am away from school and do not have to worry about some man's opinion of my ideas. It is easy to think while looking at dancing flames.

Morning. I spend the day cleaning up, and buying some presents for my family with what is

---

4. **radical** (rad′ə kəl), *n*. person favoring extreme changes or reforms.
5. **northern lights,** aurora borealis; streamers or bands of light appearing in the sky at night, especially in polar regions.

left of my money. Nothing much, but a gift is a gift, if a man buys it with his last quarter. I wait until evening, then start up the track toward home.

Christmas Eve comes in on a north wind. Snow clouds hang over the pines, and the night comes early. Walking along the railroad bed, I feel the calm peace of snowbound forests on either side of me. I take my time; I am back in a world where time does not mean so much now. I am alone; alone but not nearly so lonely as I was back on the campus at school. Those are never lonely who love the snow and the pines; never lonely when the pines are wearing white shawls and snow crunches coldly underfoot. In the woods I know there are the tracks of deer and rabbit; I know that if I leave the rails and go into the woods I shall find them. I walk along feeling glad because my legs are light and my feet seem to know that they are home. A deer comes out of the woods just ahead of me, and stands silhouetted on the rails. The North, I feel, has welcomed me home. I watch him and am glad that I do not wish for a gun. He goes into the woods quietly, leaving only the design of his tracks in the snow. I walk on. Now and then I pass a field, white under the night sky, with houses at the far end. Snow comes from the chimneys of the houses, and I try to tell what sort of wood each is burning by the smoke; some burn pine, others aspen, others tamarack. There is one from which comes black coal smoke that rises lazily and drifts out over the tops of the trees. I like to watch houses and try to imagine what might be happening in them.

Just as a light snow begins to fall, I cross the reservation boundary; somehow it seems as though I have stepped into another world. Deep woods in a white-and-black winter night. A faint trail leading to the village.

The railroad on which I stand comes from a city sprawled by a lake—a city with a million people who walk around without seeing one another; a city sucking the life from all the country around; a city with stores and police and intellectuals and criminals and movies and apartment houses; a city with its politics and libraries and zoos.

I cross the reservation boundary; somehow it seems as though I have stepped into another world.

Laughing, I go into the woods. As I cross a frozen lake I begin to hear the drums. Soft in the night the drums beat. It is like the pulse beat of the world. The white line of the lake ends at a black forest, and above the trees the blue winds are dancing.

I come to the outlying houses of the village. Simple box houses, etched black in the night. From one or two windows soft lamp light falls on the snow. Christmas here, too, but it does not mean much; not much in the way of parties and presents. Joe Sky will get drunk. Alex Bodidash will buy his children red mittens and a new sled. Alex is a Carlisle man, and tries to keep his home up to white standards. White standards. Funny that my people should be ever falling farther behind. The more they try to imitate whites the more tragic the result. Yet they want us to be imitation white men. About all we imitate well are their vices.

The village is not a sight to instill pride, yet I am not ashamed; one can never be ashamed of his own people when he knows they have dreams as beautiful as white snow on a tall pine.

Father and my brother and sister are seated around the table as I walk in. Father stares at me for a moment, then I am in his arms, crying on his shoulder. I give them the presents I have brought, and my throat tightens as I watch my sister save carefully bits of red string from the packages. I hide my feelings by wrestling with my brother when he strikes my shoulder in token of affection. Father looks at me, and I know he has many questions, but he seems to know why I have come. He tells me to go on alone to the lodge, and he will follow.

I walk along the trail to the lodge, watching the northern lights forming in the heavens. White waving ribbons that seem to pulsate[6] with the rhythm of the drums. Clean snow creaks beneath my feet, and a soft wind sighs through the trees, singing to me. Everything seems to say "Be happy! You are home now—you are free. You are among friends—we are your friends; we, the trees, and the snow, and the lights." I follow the trail to the lodge. My feet are light, my heart seems to sing to the music, and I hold my head high. Across white snow fields blue winds are dancing.

Before the lodge door I stop, afraid. I wonder if my people will remember me. I wonder—"Am I Indian, or am I white?" I stand before the door a long time. I hear the ice groan on the lake, and remember the story of the old woman who is under the ice, trying to get out, so she can punish some runaway lovers. I think to myself, "If I am white I will not believe that story; if I am Indian, I will know that there is an old woman under the ice." I listen for a while, and I know that there is an old woman under the ice. I look again at the lights, and go in.

Inside the lodge there are many Indians. Some sit on benches around the walls, others dance in the center of the floor around a drum. Nobody seems to notice me. It seems as though I were among a people I have never seen before. Heavy women with long black hair. Women with children on their knees—small children that watch with intent black eyes the movements of the dancers, whose small faces are solemn and serene.[7] The faces of the old people are serene, too, and their eyes are merry and bright. I look at the old men. Straight, dressed in dark trousers and beaded velvet vests, wearing soft moccasins.

Dark, lined faces intent on the music. I wonder if I am at all like them. They dance on, lifting their feet to the rhythm of the drums, swaying lightly, looking upward. I look at their eyes, and am startled at the rapt[8] attention to the rhythm of the music.

The dance stops. The men walk back to the walls, and talk in low tones or with their hands. There is little conversation, yet everyone seems to be sharing some secret. A woman looks at a small boy wandering away, and he comes back to her.

Strange, I think, and then remember. These people are not sharing words—they are sharing a mood. Everyone is happy. I am so used to white people that it seems strange so many people could be together without someone talking. These Indians are happy because they are together, and because the night is beautiful outside, and the music is beautiful. I try hard to forget school and white people, and be one of these—my people. I try to forget everything but the night, and it is a part of me; that I am one with my people and we are all a part of something universal. I watch eyes, and see now that the old people are speaking to me. They nod slightly, imperceptibly, and their eyes laugh into mine. I look around the room. All the eyes are friendly; they all laugh. No one questions my being here. The drums begin to beat again, and I catch the invitation in the eyes of the old men. My feet begin to lift to the rhythm, and I look out beyond the walls into the night and see the lights. I am happy. It is beautiful. I am home.

---

6. **pulsate** (pul′sāt), *v.* beat; throb.
7. **serene** (sə rēn′), *adj.* peaceful, calm.
8. **rapt** (rapt), *adj.* so busy thinking of or enjoying one thing that one does not know what else is happening.

After Reading

Making Connections

Shaping Your Response

1. What three words would you use to describe Thomas Whitecloud at the beginning of the essay? at the end?

2. Can you visualize the California orange groves, or the scenes passing by Whitecloud from the train, or the Wisconsin winter? Choose a descriptive passage from the essay and prepare to read it for the class.

Analyzing the Essay

3. What do you think the "blue winds" that Whitecloud mentions might **symbolize?**

4. Describe the **conflict** that is tormenting Whitecloud. How is it resolved?

5. 🐾 How would you describe the **communication** style Whitecloud encounters when he is back home on the reservation?

6. **Summarize** the most striking differences Whitecloud presents between his American Indian friends and relatives on the reservation and the society in which he is living.

Extending the Ideas

7. 🐾 Many students today live in two cultures that are sometimes in conflict. In a small group, brainstorm ways your school might help ease this conflict.

8. Whitecloud describes being civilized as "trying to do everything you don't want to, never doing anything you want to. It means dancing to the strings of custom and tradition; it means living in houses and never knowing or caring who is next door . . . always dissatisfied, getting a hill and wanting a mountain." Decide whether you agree or disagree, then come up with your own definition of *civilization*.

Literary Focus: Imagery

As you read "Blue Winds Dancing," could you picture Whitecloud's home and the sights he saw as he traveled thousands of miles to get there? Reread the first five paragraphs of the text, or choose another section and discuss the images you listed in the chart you completed during reading. As you discuss each image, determine whether it is literal or figurative.

Vocabulary Study

On your paper, answer the following questions. Use your Glossary for help with the italicized words.

maelstrom
serene
radical
rapt
pulsate

1. Thomas S. Whitecloud referred to the "*maelstrom* of one's mind." Where would you be if you were in an actual *maelstrom*?

2. Would a *serene* person be likely to laugh hysterically, smile peacefully, or cry uncontrollably?

3. Whitecloud says that the bums he encounters are upset about the distribution of wealth in the United States, but they aren't radicals. What is an antonym for *radical*?

4. The music in the lodge held the Indians' *rapt* attention. What has that effect on you?

5. Whitecloud could feel his heart *pulsate* as he neared his home. What is a synonym for *pulsate*?

Expressing Your Ideas

Writing Choices

Writer's Notebook Update Reread your notebook entry reflecting on how you would feel if you were living in another culture on a special holiday in your own culture. Now expand this into an essay.

Why? Whitecloud's father "has many questions" when his son returns home, but he doesn't ask them. Write a **list of questions** that you think he might have wanted to ask.

Your Home in Winter Thomas Whitecloud writes about his Wisconsin home in winter. Write about your home in winter. What can you see, hear, smell, and feel as you walk out-of-doors? Write a **description** of the scene, using vivid images.

Other Options

Educate Your Classmates The people at Whitecloud's school didn't seem to understand his heritage. Find out more about your culture and its history, and prepare an **oral presentation** that contains things your classmates might benefit from knowing.

Impressions of Home Walk around your neighborhood and **photograph** some scenes typical of the area. Display them, along with photos by other class members.

Which Way Is It? Whitecloud started his trip in Redlands, California, and his destination was the reservation near Woodruff, Wisconsin. Using information from the essay, trace the route he took to get home for the holidays, and create your own **map** for a bulletin board display.

Before Reading

A Worn Path

by Eudora Welty

Eudora Welty
born 1909

"One day I saw a solitary old woman. . . . She was walking. I saw her at middle distance, in a winter country landscape, and watched her slowly make her way across my line of vision. That sight of her made me write the story," wrote Eudora Welty about her inspiration for "A Worn Path." Welty, like Faulkner, was from Mississippi, and many of her stories are set in the South. Born in Jackson, she attended the University of Wisconsin and then went to New York to study journalism. When she returned to Jackson, she worked as a photographer for the Works Progress Administration (WPA). Her first collection of stories, *A Curtain of Green,* was published in 1941.

Building Background

A Country Mile, and Then Some How far do you have to travel to shop or go to a restaurant? How do you get there—by walking, driving, or taking public transportation? And how long does it take? Phoenix Jackson, the main character in "A Worn Path," is an old, frail woman who lives in the backwoods of Mississippi. She has no car, there is no public transportation, and she lives miles from town. Wooded hills surround her house; beyond that are fields of cotton and corn. The path that leads from her house to town is one she has traveled many times.

Literary Focus

Inferences Writers don't spell out everything. Readers must make inferences, or draw reasonable conclusions based on clues provided by a writer. Such inferences may or may not be accurate, but good readers make them, and adjust their conclusions if necessary. As you read "A Worn Path," make some inferences about Phoenix and her trip from the information provided.

Writer's Notebook

A Sensory Experience Eudora Welty writes descriptions that appeal to all of the senses. For example, a cane's tapping is "like the chirping of a solitary bird" (sound), and ". . . cones dropped as light as feathers" (touch or motion). Before you read "A Worn Path," write in your notebook a list of sensory words, phrases, or sentences that describe the route you take to school.

EUDORA WELTY

It was December—a bright frozen day in the early morning. Far out in the country there was an old Negro woman with her head tied in a red rag, coming along a path through the pine-woods. Her name was Phoenix Jackson. She was very old and small and she walked slowly in the dark pine shadows, moving a little from side to side in her steps, with the balanced heaviness and lightness of a pendulum in a grandfather clock. She carried a thin, small cane made from an umbrella, and with this she kept tapping the frozen earth in front of her. This made a grave and persistent noise in the still air, that seemed meditative like the chirping of a solitary little bird.

She wore a dark striped dress reaching down to her shoe tops, and an equally long apron of bleached sugar sacks, with a full pocket: all neat and tidy, but every time she took a step she might have fallen over her shoelaces, which dragged from her unlaced shoes. She looked straight ahead. Her eyes were blue with age. Her skin had a pattern all its own of numberless branching wrinkles and as though a whole little tree stood in the middle of her forehead, but a golden color ran underneath, and the two knobs of her cheeks were illumined by a yellow burning under the dark. Under the red rag her hair came down on her neck in the frailest of ringlets, still black, and with an odor like copper.

Now and then there was a quivering in the thicket. Old Phoenix said, "Out of my way, all you foxes, owls, beetles, jack rabbits, coons and wild animals! . . . Keep out from under these feet, little bobwhites. . . . Keep the big wild hogs out of my path. Don't let none of those come running my direction. I got a long way." Under her small black-freckled hand her cane, limber as a buggy whip, would switch at the bush as if to rouse up any hiding things.

On she went. The woods were deep and still. The sun made the pine needles almost too bright to look at, up where the wind rocked. The cones dropped as light as feathers. Down in the hollow[1] was the mourning dove—it was not too late for him.

The path ran up a hill. "Seem like there is chains about my feet, time I get this far," she said, in the voice of argument old people keep to use with themselves. "Something always take a hold of me on this hill—pleads I should stay."

After she got to the top, she turned and gave a full, severe look behind her where she had come. "Up through pines," she said at length. "Now down through oaks."

Her eyes opened their widest, and she started down gently. But before she got to the bottom of the hill a bush caught her dress.

Her fingers were busy and intent, but her skirts were full and long, so that before she could pull them free in one place they were caught in another. It was not possible to allow the dress to tear. "I in the thorny bush," she said. "Thorns, you doing your appointed work. Never want to let folks pass, no sir. Old eyes thought you was a pretty little *green* bush."

Finally, trembling all over, she stood free, and after a moment dared to stoop for her cane.

---

1. **hollow** (hol′ō), *n.* a low place between hills.

Writer and photographer Eudora Welty is especially known for her fictionalized accounts of life in rural Mississippi and her photographs taken during the 1930s. The story, "A Worn Path," and its accompanying photograph, *A woman of the 'thirties,* are examples of her work.

"Sun so high!" she cried, leaning back and looking, while the thick tears went over her eyes. "The time getting all gone here."

At the foot of this hill was a place where a log was laid across the creek.

"Now comes the trial," said Phoenix.

Putting her right foot out, she mounted the log and shut her eyes. Lifting her skirt, leveling her cane fiercely before her, like a festival figure in some parade, she began to march across. Then she opened her eyes and she was safe on the other side.

"I wasn't as old as I thought," she said.

But she sat down to rest. She spread her skirts on the bank around her and folded her hands over her knees. Up above her was a tree in a pearly cloud of mistletoe. She did not dare to close her eyes, and when a little boy brought her a plate with a slice of marble cake on it she spoke to him. "That would be acceptable," she said. But when she went to take it there was just her own hand in the air.

So she left that tree, and had to go through a barbed-wire fence. There she had to creep and crawl, spreading her knees and stretching her fingers like a baby trying to climb the steps. But she talked loudly to herself; she could not let her dress be torn now, so late in the day, and she could not pay for having her arm or leg sawed off if she got caught fast where she was.

At last she was safe through the fence and risen up out in the clearing. Big dead trees, like black men with one arm, were standing in the purple stalks of the withered cotton field. There sat a buzzard.

"Who you watching?"

In the furrow[2] she made her way along.

"Glad this not the season for bulls," she said, looking sideways, "and the good Lord made his snakes to curl up and sleep in the winter. A pleasure I don't see no two-headed snake coming around that tree, where it come once. It took a while to get by him, back in the summer."

She passed through the old cotton and went into a field of dead corn. It whispered and shook and was taller than her head. "Through the maze now," she said, for there was no path.

Then there was something tall, black, and skinny there, moving before her.

At first she took it for a man. It could have been a man dancing in the field. But she stood still and listened, and it did not make a sound. It was silent as a ghost.

"Ghost," she said sharply, "who be you the ghost of? For I have heard of nary death close by."

But there was no answer—only the ragged dancing in the wind.

She shut her eyes, reached out her hand, and touched a sleeve. She found a coat and inside that an emptiness, cold as ice.

"You scarecrow," she said. Her face lighted. "I ought to be shut up for good," she said with laughter. "My senses is gone. I too old. I the oldest people I ever know. Dance, old scarecrow," she said, "while I dancing with you."

She kicked her foot over the furrow, and with mouth drawn down, shook her head once or twice in a little strutting way. Some husks blew down and whirled in streamers about her skirts.

Then she went on, parting her way from side to side with the cane, through the whispering field. At last she came to the end, to a wagon track where the silver grass blew between the red ruts. The quail were walking around like pullets, seeming all dainty and unseen.

"Walk pretty," she said. "This the easy place. This the easy going."

She followed the track, swaying through the quiet bare fields, through the little strings of trees silver in their dead leaves, past cabins silver from weather, with the doors and windows boarded shut, all like old women under a spell sitting there. "I walking in their sleep," she said, nodding her head vigorously.

---

2. **furrow** (fėr′ō), *n.* a long, narrow track cut in the earth by a plow.

In a ravine[3] she went where a spring was silently flowing through a hollow log. Old Phoenix bent and drank. "Sweet gum makes the water sweet," she said, and drank more. "Nobody know who made this well, for it was here when I was born."

The track crossed a swampy part where the moss hung as white as lace from every limb. "Sleep on, alligators, and blow your bubbles." Then the track went into the road.

Deep, deep the road went down between the high green-colored banks. Overhead the live oaks met, and it was dark as a cave.

A black dog with a lolling tongue came up out of the weeds by the ditch. She was meditating, and not ready, and when he came at her she only hit him a little with her cane. Over she went in the ditch, like a little puff of milkweed.

Down there, her senses drifted away. A dream visited her, and she reached her hand up, but nothing reached down and gave her a pull. So she lay there and presently went to talking. "Old woman," she said to herself, "that black dog came up out of the weeds to stall you off, and now there he sitting on his fine tail, smiling at you."

A white man finally came along and found her—a hunter, a young man, with his dog on a chain.

"Well, Granny!" he laughed. "What are you doing there?"

"Lying on my back like a June bug waiting to be turned over, mister," she said, reaching up her hand.

He lifted her up, gave her a swing in the air, and set her down. "Anything broken, Granny?"

"No sir, them old dead weeds is springy enough," said Phoenix, when she had got her breath. "I thank you for your trouble."

"Where do you live, Granny?" he asked, while the two dogs were growling at each other.

"Away back yonder, sir, behind the ridge. You can't even see it from here."

"On your way home?"

"No sir, I going to town."

"Why, that's too far! That's as far as I walk when I come out myself, and I get something for my trouble." He patted the stuffed bag he carried, and there hung down a little closed claw. It was one of the bobwhites, with its beak hooked bitterly to show it was dead. "Now you go on home, Granny!"

"I bound to go to town, mister," said Phoenix. "The time come around."

He gave another laugh, filling the whole landscape. "I know you old colored people! Wouldn't miss going to town to see Santa Claus!"

But something held old Phoenix very still. The deep lines in her face went into a fierce and different radiation. Without warning, she had seen with her own eyes a flashing nickel fall out of the man's pocket onto the ground.

"How old are you, Granny?" he was saying.

"There is no telling, mister," she said, "no telling."

Then she gave a little cry and clapped her hands and said, "Git on away from here, dog! Look! Look at that dog!" She laughed as if in admiration. "He ain't scared of nobody. He a big black dog." She whispered, "Sic him!"

"Watch me get rid of that cur," said the man. "Sic him, Pete! Sic him!"

Phoenix heard the dogs fighting, and heard the man running and throwing sticks. She even heard a gunshot. But she was slowly bending forward by that time, further and further forward, the lids stretched down over her eyes, as if she were doing this in her sleep. Her chin was lowered almost to her knees. The yellow palm of her hand came out from the fold of her apron. Her fingers slid down and along the ground under the piece of money with the grace and care they would have in lifting an egg from under a setting hen. Then she slowly straightened up, she stood erect, and the nickel was in her apron pocket. A bird flew by. Her lips

---

3. **ravine** (rə vēn′), *n.* a long, deep, narrow gorge eroded by running water.

moved. "God watching me the whole time. I come to stealing."

The man came back, and his own dog panted about them. "Well, I scared him off that time," he said, and then he laughed and lifted his gun and pointed it at Phoenix.

She stood straight and faced him.

"Doesn't the gun scare you?" he said, still pointing it.

"No, sir, I seen plenty go off closer by, in my day, and for less than what I done," she said, holding utterly still.

He smiled, and shouldered the gun. "Well, Granny," he said, "you must be a hundred years old, and scared of nothing. I'd give you a dime if I had any money with me. But you take my advice and stay home, and nothing will happen to you."

"I bound to go on my way, mister," said Phoenix. She inclined her head in the red rag. Then they went in different directions, but she could hear the gun shooting again and again over the hill.

She walked on. The shadows hung from the oak trees to the road like curtains. Then she smelled wood-smoke, and smelled the river, and she saw a steeple and the cabins on their steep steps. Dozens of little black children whirled around her. There ahead was Natchez shining. Bells were ringing. She walked on.

In the paved city it was Christmas time. There were red and green electric lights strung and criss-crossed everywhere, and all turned on in the day-time. Old Phoenix would have been lost if she had not distrusted her eyesight and depended on her feet to know where to take her.

She paused quietly on the sidewalk where people were passing by. A lady came along in the crowd, carrying an armful of red-, green-, and silver-wrapped presents; she gave off perfume like the red roses in hot summer, and Phoenix stopped her.

"Please, missy, will you lace up my shoe?" She held up her foot.

"What do you want, Grandma?"

"See my shoe," said Phoenix. "Do all right for out in the country, but wouldn't look right to go in a big building."

"Stand still then, Grandma," said the lady. She put her packages down on the sidewalk beside her and laced and tied both shoes tightly.

"Can't lace 'em with a cane," said Phoenix. "Thank you, missy. I doesn't mind asking a nice lady to tie up my shoe, when I gets out on the street."

Moving slowly and from side to side, she went into the big building, and into a tower of steps, where she walked up and around and around until her feet knew to stop.

She entered a door, and there she saw nailed up on the wall the document that had been stamped with the gold seal and framed in the gold frame, which matched the dream that was hung up in her head.

"Here I be," she said. There was a fixed and ceremonial stiffness over her body.

"A charity case, I suppose," said an attendant who sat at the desk before her.

But Phoenix only looked over her head. There was sweat on her face, the wrinkles in her skin shone like a bright net.

"Speak up, Grandma," the woman said. "What's your name? We must have your history, you know. Have you been here before? What seems to be the trouble with you?"

Old Phoenix only gave a twitch to her face as if a fly were bothering her.

"Are you deaf?" cried the attendant.

But then the nurse came in.

"Oh, that's just old Aunt Phoenix," she said. "She doesn't come for herself—she has a little grandson. She makes these trips just as regular as clockwork. She lives away back off the Old Natchez Trace." She bent down. "Well, Aunt Phoenix, why don't you just take a seat? We won't keep you standing after your long trip." She pointed.

The old woman sat down, bolt upright in the chair.

"Now, how is the boy?" asked the nurse.

Old Phoenix did not speak.

"I said, how is the boy?"

But Phoenix only waited and stared straight ahead, her face very solemn and withdrawn into rigidity.

"Is his throat any better?" asked the nurse. "Aunt Phoenix, don't you hear me? Is your grandson's throat any better since the last time you came for the medicine?"

With her hands on her knees, the old woman waited, silent, erect and motionless, just as if she were in armor.

"You mustn't take up our time this way, Aunt Phoenix," the nurse said. "Tell us quickly about your grandson, and get it over. He isn't dead, is he?"

At last there came a flicker and then a flame of comprehension across her face, and she spoke.

"My grandson. It was my memory had left me. There I sat and forgot why I made my long trip."

"Forgot?" The nurse frowned. "After you came so far?"

Then Phoenix was like an old woman begging a dignified forgiveness for waking up frightened in the night. "I never did go to school, I was too old at the Surrender,[4] she said in a soft voice. "I'm an old woman without an education. It was my memory fail me. My little grandson, he is just the same, and I forgot it in the coming."

"Throat never heals, does it?" said the nurse, speaking in a loud, sure voice to old Phoenix. By now she had a card with something written on it, a little list. "Yes. Swallowed lye. When was it?—January—two-three years ago——"

Phoenix spoke unasked now. "No, missy, he not dead, he just the same. Every little while his throat begin to close up again, and he not able to swallow. He not get his breath. He not able to help himself. So the time come around, and I go on another trip for the soothing medicine."

"All right. The doctor said as long as you came to get it, you could have it," said the nurse. "But it's an obstinate case."

"My little grandson, he sit up there in the house all wrapped up, waiting by himself," Phoenix went on. "We is the only two left in the world. He suffer and it don't seem to put him back at all. He got a sweet look. He going to last. He wear a little patch quilt and peep out holding his mouth open like a little bird. I remembers so plain now. I not going to forget him again, no, the whole enduring time. I could tell him from all the others in creation."

"All right." The nurse was trying to hush her now. She brought her a bottle of medicine. "Charity," she said, making a check mark in a book.

Old Phoenix held the bottle close to her eyes, and then carefully put it into her pocket.

"I thank you," she said.

"It's Christmas time, Grandma," said the attendant. "Could I give you a few pennies out of my purse?"

"Five pennies is a nickel," said Phoenix stiffly.

"Here's a nickel," said the attendant.

Phoenix rose carefully and held out her hand. She received the nickel and then fished the other nickel out of her pocket and laid it beside the new one. She stared at her palm closely, with her head on one side.

Then she gave a tap with her cane on the floor.

"This is what come to me to do," she said. "I going to the store and buy my child a little windmill they sells, made out of paper. He going to find it hard to believe there such a thing in the world. I'll march myself back where he waiting, holding it straight up in this hand."

She lifted her free hand, gave a little nod, turned around, and walked out of the doctor's office. Then her slow step began on the stairs, going down.

---

4. **the Surrender,** the surrender of the Confederate Army to the Union Army at Appomattox on April 9, 1865.

After Reading

Making Connections

Shaping Your
Response

1. What do you think was the most difficult part of the trip for Phoenix? Why?

2. What would you like to say to the hunter on Phoenix's behalf?

Analyzing the
Story

3. What **character** traits does Phoenix Jackson reveal on her solitary trek?

4. What "worn paths"—both literal and **metaphorical**—do you find in this story?

5. **Local color** writing is based on characters, plots, and settings that could not be transplanted to another geographical area without damaging their authenticity. Does this story qualify as local color writing in your opinion? Explain.

6. A phoenix is a mythical bird that dies consumed in flames and then rises again from the ashes, fresh and beautiful, to begin a new life. Do you think that Phoenix is an appropriate name for the main character in this story? Why or why not?

Extending the
Ideas

7. Think of ordinary people you have known or heard about who have done extraordinary things out of love for their families, friends, or even strangers. Describe one of them and his or her extraordinary act.

Literary Focus: Inference

A reasonable conclusion drawn about the behavior of a character or the meaning of an event is an **inference.** Not until the end of the story do you know why Phoenix is attempting this long and difficult journey. And even she forgets and has to be reminded by the nurse!

1. What can you infer about the relationship of Phoenix and her grandson from her plan to buy the paper windmill?

2. When Phoenix enters the medical office, "she saw nailed up on the wall the document framed in the gold frame, which matched the dream that was hung up in her head." What inferences can you draw about the nature of this document and what it means to Phoenix?

Expressing Your Ideas

Writing Choices

Writer's Notebook Update Compare the sensory words, phrases, and sentences you wrote in your log with those of your classmates. Reflect on a trip that you make every day. What are the sights, sounds, and smells that you experience on that route? Write a **descriptive paragraph** that makes your routine trip sound unusual.

Return of the Hunter Imagine that you are the hunter who meets Phoenix and helps her to her feet. You have returned home and are telling your family about the encounter with the old woman. In a **narrative** of a page or two, try to capture the relaxed, conversational tone that the man would probably use. Before you begin writing, reread that section of the story to review what happened and what was said.

Your Point of View Some readers feel that "A Worn Path" would be somehow "better" if Phoenix's grandson were dead. Others are sure the boy must be alive. Still others think it makes no difference to the story. Write an **essay** of at least four paragraphs for a literary magazine in which you support one of these three positions. Consider the purpose of Phoenix's trip, her devotion and single-mindedness, the outcome of the story, and the irony that the boy's death would provide.

Other Options

Turn Right, Then Left What if Phoenix cannot make the next trip for the medicine? She gives you the directions so that you can go in her place. Make a **map** of the path from Phoenix's place to the doctor's office so that you can find your way.

Obstacle Game Review the story and **list** all of the hazards Phoenix Jackson encountered on this trip or on other trips she has taken along this path. Then design a **board game** with the object of the game to get Phoenix from her home on the Natchez Trace to the doctor's office. Make the board and any cards or game pieces you might need.

A Path of Pictures Work with a group and select the most memorable scenes along the path. Each of you choose one scene, illustrate it, and provide a quote from the story as a caption. Display the **illustrations** for your class.

Before Reading

The Leader of the People

by John Steinbeck

John Steinbeck
1902–1968

"If there is a magic in story writing, and I am convinced that there is, no one has ever been able to reduce it to a recipe that can be passed from one person to another," wrote John Steinbeck in a letter to one of his professors at Stanford University. Born in Salinas, California, Steinbeck struggled through the early days of the Depression working as a hod-carrier, surveyor, and fruit picker. As a writer, he populated his stories and novels with poor and working-class people. However, his characters, such as those in *Of Mice and Men* and *The Grapes of Wrath*, which won a Pulitzer Prize, show a love for life and a dignity that goes beyond their humble circumstances.

Building Background

The End of the Trail The discovery of gold in 1848 and the Homestead Act in 1862, with the promise of free land, enticed thousands of people to Oregon and California. Artists and writers glorified these pioneers. But once these pioneers began to move across the land, the West changed. Buffalo hunters killed off most of the herds, altering forever the lives of the Plains Indians. Broken treaties and government mandates forced Indians off their lands and onto reservations. The "Wild West" didn't last long—soon the frontier was officially declared closed and the pioneers were stopped in their tracks by the Pacific Ocean.

South Pass through Rocky Mts. discovered.	First emigrants follow the Oregon Trail.	Gold discovered in California.	California becomes a state.	Homestead Act is passed.	Transcontinental railroad completed.	Indian Appropriation Act makes Indians wards of the nation.	Barbed wire invented.
1824	1832	1848	1850	1862	1869	1871	1873

Literary Focus

Setting The time and place in which the action of a narrative takes place is the setting. "The Leader of the People" takes place on a ranch in Salinas, California, sometime in the 1920s or 1930s. Before you begin reading the story, find Salinas on a map. What is the countryside around it like? How close is it to the ocean? As you read, notice how Steinbeck describes the setting. Ask yourself: What effect does the setting have on the mood of the story? How does it help to reveal character? Does it affect the plot in any way?

Writer's Notebook

All in the Family In your notebook, jot down the first words you think of when you hear each of these phrases describing family relationships: father–son, father–daughter, father-in-law–son-in-law, husband–wife, and grandfather–grandson.

The Leader of the People **675**

JOHN STEINBECK

The Leader

O n Saturday afternoon Billy Buck, the ranch hand, raked together the last of the old year's haystack and pitched small forkfuls over the wire fence to a few mildly interested cattle. High in the air small clouds like puffs of cannon smoke were driven eastward by the March wind. The wind could be heard whishing in the brush on the ridge crests, but no breath of it penetrated down into the ranch cup.

The little boy, Jody, emerged[1] from the house eating a thick piece of buttered bread. He saw Billy working on the last of the haystack. Jody tramped down scuffling his shoes in a way he had been told was destructive to good shoe leather. A flock of white pigeons flew out of the black cypress tree as Jody passed, and circled the tree and landed again. A half-grown tortoise-shell cat leaped from the bunkhouse porch, galloped on stiff legs across the road, whirled and galloped back again. Jody picked up a stone to help the game along, but he was too late, for the cat was under the porch before the stone could be discharged. He threw the stone into the cypress tree and started the white pigeons on another whirling flight.

Arriving at the used-up haystack, the boy leaned against the barbed-wire fence. "Will that be all of it, do you think?" he asked.

The middle-aged ranch hand stopped his careful raking and stuck his fork into the ground. He took off his black hat and smoothed down his

---

1. **emerge** (i mėrj′), *v.* come into view; come out.

Does David DeMatteo's painting of the Santa Ynez Valley in California depict a place where you'd like to live? Why or why not? ➤

of the People

hair. "Nothing left of it that isn't soggy from ground moisture," he said. He replaced his hat and rubbed his dry leathery hands together.

"Ought to be plenty mice," Jody suggested.

"Lousy with them," said Billy. "Just crawling with mice."

"Well, maybe, when you get all through, I could call the dogs and hunt the mice."

"Sure, I guess you could," said Billy Buck. He lifted a forkful of the damp ground hay and threw it into the air. Instantly three mice leaped out and burrowed frantically under the hay again.

Jody sighed with satisfaction. Those plump, sleek, arrogant mice were doomed. For eight months they had lived and multiplied in the haystack. They had been immune from cats, from traps, from poison, and from Jody. They had grown smug in their security, overbearing and fat. Now the time of disaster had come; they would not survive another day.

Billy looked up at the top of the hills that surrounded the ranch. "Maybe you better ask your father before you do it," he suggested.

"Well, where is he? I'll ask him now."

"He rode up to the ridge ranch after dinner. He'll be back pretty soon."

Jody slumped against the fence post. "I don't think he'd care."

As Billy went back to his work he said ominously, "You'd better ask him anyway. You know how he is."

Jody did know. His father, Carl Tiflin, insisted upon giving permission for anything that was done on the ranch, whether it was important or not. Jody sagged farther against the post until he was sitting on the ground. He looked up at the little puffs of wind-driven cloud. "Is it like to rain, Billy?"

"It might. The wind's good for it, but not strong enough."

"Well, I hope it don't rain until after I kill those damn mice." He looked over his shoulder to see whether Billy had noticed the mature profanity. Billy worked on without comment.

Jody turned back and looked at the side-hill where the road from the outside world came down. The hill was washed with lean March sunshine. Silver thistles, blue lupins and a few poppies bloomed among the sage bushes. Halfway up the hill Jody could see Doubletree Mutt, the black dog, digging in a squirrel hole. He paddled for a while and then paused to kick bursts of dirt out between his hind legs, and he dug with an earnestness which belied the knowledge he must have had that no dog had ever caught a squirrel by digging in a hole.

*S*uddenly, while Jody watched, the black dog stiffened, and backed out of the hole and looked up the hill toward the cleft in the ridge where the road came through. Jody looked up too. For a moment Carl Tiflin on horseback stood out against the pale sky and then he moved down the road toward the house. He carried something white in his hand.

The boy started to his feet. "He's got a letter," Jody cried. He trotted away toward the ranch house, for the letter would probably be read aloud and he wanted to be there. He reached the house before his father did, and ran in. He heard Carl dismount from his creaking saddle and slap the horse on the side to send it to the barn where Billy would unsaddle it and turn it out.

Jody ran into the kitchen. "We got a letter!" he cried.

His mother looked up from a pan of beans. "Who has?"

"Father has. I saw it in his hand."

Carl strode into the kitchen then, and Jody's mother asked, "Who's the letter from, Carl?"

He frowned quickly. "How did you know there was a letter?"

She nodded her head in the boy's direction. "Big-Britches Jody told me."

Jody was embarrassed.

His father looked down at him contemptuously. "He *is* getting to be a Big-Britches," Carl said. "He's minding everybody's business but his own. Got his big nose into everything."

Mrs. Tiflin relented a little, "Well, he hasn't enough to keep him busy. Who's the letter from?"

Carl still frowned on Jody. "I'll keep him busy if he isn't careful." He held out a sealed letter. "I guess it's from your father."

Mrs. Tiflin took a hairpin from her head and slit open the flap. Her lips pursed judiciously. Jody saw her eyes snap back and forth over the lines. "He says," she translated, "he says he's going to drive out Saturday to stay for a little while. Why, this is Saturday. The letter must have been delayed." She looked at the postmark. "This was mailed day before yesterday. It should have been here yesterday." She looked up questioningly at her husband, and then her face darkened angrily. "Now what have you got that look on you for? He doesn't come often."

Carl turned his eyes away from her anger. He could be stern with her most of the time, but when occasionally her temper arose, he could not combat it.

"What's the matter with you?" she demanded again.

In his explanation there was a tone of apology Jody himself might have used. "It's just that he talks," Carl said lamely. "Just talks."

"Well, what of it? You talk yourself."

"Sure I do. But your father only talks about one thing."

"Indians!" Jody broke in excitedly. "Indians and crossing the plains!"

Carl turned fiercely on him. "You get out, Mr. Big-Britches! Go on, now! Get out!"

Jody went miserably out the back door and closed the screen with elaborate quietness. Under the kitchen window his shamed, downcast eyes fell upon a curiously shaped stone, a stone of such fascination that he squatted down and picked it up and turned it over in his hands.

The voices came clearly to him through the open kitchen window. "Jody's damn well right," he heard his father say. "Just Indians and crossing the plains. I've heard that story about how the horses got driven off about a thousand times. He just goes on and on, and he never changes a word in the things he tells."

When Mrs. Tiflin answered, her tone was so changed that Jody, outside the window, looked up from his study of the stone. Her voice had become soft and explanatory. Jody knew how her face would have changed to match the tone. She said quietly, "Look at it this way, Carl. That was the big thing in my father's life. He led a wagon train clear across the plains to the coast, and when it was finished, his life was done. It was a big thing to do, but it didn't last long enough. Look!" she continued, "it's as though he was born to do that, and after he finished it, there wasn't anything more for him to do but think about it and talk about it. If there'd been any farther west to go, he'd have gone. He's told me so himself. But at last there was the ocean. He lives right by the ocean where he had to stop."

> ## *He led a wagon train clear across the plains to the coast, and when it was finished, his life was done.*

She had caught Carl, caught him and entangled him in her soft tone.

"I've seen him," he agreed quietly. "He goes down and stares off west over the ocean." His voice sharpened a little. "And then he goes up to the Horseshoe Club in Pacific Grove, and he tells people how the Indians drove off the horses."

She tried to catch him again. "Well, it's everything to him. You might be patient with him and pretend to listen."

Carl turned impatiently away. "Well, if it gets too bad, I can always go down to the bunkhouse and sit with Billy," he said irritably. He walked through the house and slammed the front door after him.

Jody ran to his chores. He dumped the grain to the chickens without chasing any of them. He gathered the eggs from the nests. He trotted into the house with the wood and interlaced it so carefully in the wood-box that two armloads seemed to fill it to overflowing.

His mother had finished the beans by now. She stirred up the fire and brushed off the stove top with a turkey wing. Jody peered[2] cautiously at her to see whether any rancor toward him remained. "Is he coming today?" Jody asked.

"That's what his letter said."

"Maybe I better walk up the road to meet him."

Mrs. Tiflin clanged the stove lid shut. "That would be nice," she said. "He'd probably like to be met."

"I guess I'll just do it then."

Outside, Jody whistled shrilly to the dogs. "Come on up the hill," he commanded. The two dogs waved their tails and ran ahead. Along the roadside the sage had tender new tips. Jody tore off some pieces and rubbed them on his hands until the air was filled with the sharp wild smell. With a rush the dogs leaped from the road and yapped into the brush after a rabbit. That was the last Jody saw of them, for when they failed to catch the rabbit, they went back home.

Jody plodded on up the hill toward the ridge top. When he reached the little cleft where the road came through, the afternoon wind struck him and blew up his hair and ruffled his shirt. He looked down on the little hills and ridges below and then out at the huge green Salinas Valley.[3] He could see the white town of Salinas

---

2. **peer** (pēr), *v.* look closely to see clearly.
3. **Salinas Valley,** an agriculturally rich valley in California.

far out in the flat and the flash of its windows under the waning sun. Directly below him, in an oak tree, a crow congress had convened.[4] The tree was black with crows all cawing at once. Then Jody's eyes followed the wagon road down from the ridge where he stood, and lost it behind a hill, and picked it up again on the other side. On that distant stretch he saw a cart slowly pulled by a bay horse. It disappeared behind the hill. Jody sat down on the ground and watched the place where the cart would reappear again. The wind sang on the hilltops and the puffball clouds hurried eastward.

Then the cart came into sight and stopped. A man dressed in black dismounted from the seat and walked to the horse's head. Although it was so faraway, Jody knew he had unhooked the checkrein, for the horse's head dropped forward. The horse moved on, and the man walked slowly up the hill beside it. Jody gave a glad cry and ran down the road toward them. The squirrels bumped along off the road, and a roadrunner flirted its tail and raced over the edge of the hill and sailed out like a glider.

Jody tried to leap into the middle of his shadow at every step. A stone rolled under his foot and he went down. Around a little bend he raced, and there, a short distance ahead, were his grandfather and the cart. The boy dropped from his unseemly running and approached at a dignified walk.

The horse plodded stumble-footedly up the hill and the old man walked beside it. In the lowering sun their giant shadows flickered darkly behind them. The grandfather was dressed in a black broadcloth suit and he wore kid congress gaiters and a black tie on a short, hard collar. He carried his black slouch hat in his hand. His white beard was cropped close and his white eyebrows overhung his eyes like

▲ Arthur Rothstein's 1939 photograph is of Frank Lotta, an old-time cowpuncher. What might this man and Grandfather in Steinbeck's story have in common?

mustaches. The blue eyes were sternly merry. About the whole face and figure there was a granite dignity, so that every motion seemed an impossible thing. Once at rest, it seemed the old man would be stone, would never move again. His steps were slow and certain. Once made, no step could ever be retraced; once headed in a direction, the path would never bend nor the pace increase nor slow.

When Jody appeared around the bend, Grandfather waved his hat slowly in welcome, and he called, "Why, Jody! Come down to meet me, have you?"

Jody sidled[5] near and turned and matched

4. **convene** (kən vēn′), v. meet for some purpose.
5. **sidle** (sī′dl), v. move sideways.

his step to the old man's step and stiffened his body and dragged his heels a little. "Yes, sir," he said. "We got your letter only today."

"Should have been here yesterday," said Grandfather. "It certainly should. How are all the folks?"

"They're fine, sir." He hesitated and then suggested shyly, "Would you like to come on a mouse hunt tomorrow, sir?"

"Mouse hunt, Jody?" Grandfather chuckled. "Have the people of this generation come down to hunting mice? They aren't very strong, the new people, but I hardly thought mice would be game for them."

"No, sir. It's just play. The haystack's gone. I'm going to drive out the mice to the dogs. And you can watch, or even beat the hay a little."

The stern, merry eyes turned down on him. "I see. You don't eat them, then. You haven't come to that yet."

Jody explained, "The dogs eat them, sir. It wouldn't be much like hunting Indians, I guess."

"No, not much—but then later, when the troops were hunting Indians and shooting children and burning teepees, it wasn't much different from your mouse hunt."

They topped the rise and started down into the ranch cup, and they lost the sun from their shoulders. "You've grown," Grandfather said. "Nearly an inch, I should say."

"More," Jody boasted. "Where they mark me on the door, I'm up more than an inch since Thanksgiving even."

Grandfather's rich throaty voice said, "Maybe you're getting too much water and turning to pith and stalk. Wait until you head out, and then we'll see."

Jody looked quickly into the old man's face to see whether his feelings should be hurt, but there was no will to injure, no punishing nor putting-in-your-place light in the keen blue eyes. "We might kill a pig," Jody suggested.

"Oh, no! I couldn't let you do that. You're just humoring me. It isn't the time and you know it."

"You know Riley, the big boar, sir?"

"Yes. I remember Riley well."

"Well, Riley ate a hole into that same haystack, and it fell down on him and smothered him."

"Pigs do that when they can," said Grandfather.

"Riley was a nice pig, for a boar, sir. I rode him sometimes, and he didn't mind."

A door slammed at the house below them, and they saw Jody's mother standing on the porch waving her apron in welcome. And they saw Carl Tiflin walking up from the barn to be at the house for the arrival.

The sun had disappeared from the hills by now. The blue smoke from the house chimney hung in flat layers in the purpling ranch cup. The puffball clouds, dropped by the falling wind, hung listlessly in the sky.

Billy Buck came out of the bunkhouse and flung a washbasin of soapy water on the ground. He had been shaving in midweek, for Billy held Grandfather in reverence, and Grandfather said that Billy was one of the few men of the new generation who had not gone soft. Although Billy was in middle age, Grandfather considered him a boy. Now Billy was hurrying toward the house too.

When Jody and Grandfather arrived, the three were waiting for them in front of the yard gate.

Carl said, "Hello, sir. We've been looking for you."

Mrs. Tiflin kissed Grandfather on the side of his beard, and stood still while his big hand patted her shoulder. Billy shook hands solemnly, grinning under his straw mustache. "I'll put up your horse," said Billy, and he led the rig away.

Grandfather watched him go, and then, turning back to the group, he said as he had said a hundred times before, "There's a good boy. I knew his father, old Mule-tail Buck. I never knew why they called him Mule-tail except he packed mules."

Mrs. Tiflin turned and led the way into the house. "How long are you going to stay, Father? Your letter didn't say."

"Well, I don't know. I thought I'd stay about two weeks. But I never stay as long as I think I'm going to."

In a short while they were sitting at the white oilcloth table eating their supper. The lamp with the tin reflector hung over the table. Outside the dining-room windows the big moths battered softly against the glass.

Grandfather cut his steak into tiny pieces and chewed slowly. "I'm hungry," he said. "Driving out here got my appetite up. It's like when we were crossing. We all got so hungry every night we could hardly wait to let the meat get done. I could eat about five pounds of buffalo meat every night."

"It's moving around does it," said Billy. "My father was a government packer. I helped him when I was a kid. Just the two of us could about clean up a deer's ham."

"I knew your father, Billy," said Grandfather. "A fine man he was. They called him Mule-tail Buck. I don't know why, except he packed mules."

"That was it," Billy agreed. "He packed mules."

Grandfather put down his knife and fork, and looked around the table. "I remember one time we ran out of meat——" His voice dropped to a curious low singsong, dropped into a tonal groove the story had worn for itself. "There was no buffalo, no antelope, not even rabbits. The hunters couldn't even shoot a coyote. That was the time for the leader to be on the watch. I was the leader, and I kept my eyes open. Know why? Well, just the minute the people began to get hungry they'd start slaughtering the team oxen. Do you believe that? I've heard of parties that just ate up their draft cattle. Started from the middle and worked toward the ends. Finally they'd eat the lead pair, and then the wheelers. The leader of a party had to keep them from doing that."

In some manner a big moth got into the room and circled the hanging kerosene lamp. Billy got up and tried to clap it between his hands. Carl struck with a cupped palm and caught the moth and broke it. He walked to the window and dropped it out.

"As I was saying," Grandfather began again, but Carl interrupted him. "You'd better eat some more meat. All the rest of us are ready for our pudding."

Jody saw a flash of anger in his mother's eyes. Grandfather picked up his knife and fork. "I'm pretty hungry, all right," he said. "I'll tell you about that later."

When supper was over, when the family and Billy Buck sat in front of the fireplace in the other room, Jody anxiously watched Grandfather. He saw the signs he knew. The bearded head leaned forward; the eyes lost their sternness and looked wonderingly into the fire; the big lean fingers laced themselves on the black knees.

"I wonder," he began, "I just wonder whether I ever told you how those thieving Piutes drove off thirty-five of our horses."

"I think you did," Carl interrupted. "Wasn't it just before you went up into the Tahoe country?"

Grandfather turned quickly toward his son-in-law. "That's right. I guess I must have told you that story."

"Lots of times," Carl said cruelly, and he avoided his wife's eyes. But he felt the angry eyes on him, and he said, "'Course I'd like to hear it again."

Grandfather looked back at the fire. His fingers unlaced and laced again. Jody knew how he felt, how his insides were collapsed and empty. Hadn't Jody been called a Big-Britches that very afternoon? He arose to heroism and opened himself to the term Big-Britches again. "Tell about Indians," he said softly.

Grandfather's eyes grew stern again. "Boys always want to hear about Indians. It was a job for men, but boys want to hear about it. Well, let's see. Did I ever tell you how I wanted each wagon to carry a long iron plate?"

Everyone but Jody remained silent. Jody said, "No. You didn't."

"Well, when the Indians attacked, we always put the wagons in a circle and fought from between the wheels. I thought that if every wagon carried a long plate with rifle holes, the

What interpretation of "westering" does Samuel Colman present in his 1872 painting, *Ships of the Plains?* Does he focus on the difficulties or on the grandeur of "westering"?

men could stand the plates on the outside of the wheels when the wagons were in the circle and they would be protected. It would save lives and that would make up for the extra weight of the iron. But of course the party wouldn't do it. No party had done it before and they couldn't see why they should go to the expense. They lived to regret it, too."

Jody looked at his mother, and knew from her expression that she was not listening at all. Carl picked at a callus on his thumb and Billy Buck watched a spider crawling up the wall.

Grandfather's tone dropped into its narrative groove again. Jody knew in advance exactly what words would fall. The story droned on, speeded up for the attack, grew sad over the wounds, struck a dirge at the burials on the great plains. Jody sat quietly watching Grandfather. The stern blue eyes were detached. He looked as though he were not very interested in the story himself.

When it was finished, when the pause had been politely respected as the frontier of the story, Billy Buck stood up and stretched and hitched his trousers. "I guess I'll turn in," he said. Then he faced Grandfather. "I've got an old powder horn and a cap and ball pistol down to the bunkhouse. Did I ever show them to you?"

Grandfather nodded slowly. "Yes, I think you did, Billy. Reminds me of a pistol I had when I was leading the people across." Billy stood politely until the little story was done, and then he said, "Good night," and went out of the house.

> *A race of giants had lived then, fearless men, men of a staunchness unknown in this day.*

Carl Tiflin tried to turn the conversation then. "How's the country between here and Monterey? I've heard it's pretty dry."

"It is dry," said Grandfather. "There's not a drop of water in the Laguna Seca. But it's a long pull from '87. The whole country was powder then, and in '61 I believe all the coyotes starved to death. We had fifteen inches of rain this year."

"Yes, but it all came too early. We could do with some now." Carl's eye fell on Jody. "Hadn't you better be getting to bed?"

Jody stood up obediently. "Can I kill the mice in the old haystack, sir?"

"Mice? Oh! Sure, kill them all off. Billy said there isn't any good hay left."

Jody exchanged a secret and satisfying look with Grandfather. "I'll kill every one tomorrow," he promised.

Jody lay in his bed and thought of the impossible world of Indians and buffaloes, a world that had ceased to be forever. He wished he could have been living in the heroic time, but he knew he was not of heroic timber. No one living now, save possibly Billy Buck, was worthy to do the things that had been done. A race of giants had lived then, fearless men, men of a staunchness unknown in this day. Jody thought of the wide plains and of the wagons moving across like centipedes. He thought of Grandfather on a huge white horse, marshaling the people. Across his mind marched the great phantoms, and they marched off the earth and they were gone.

He came back to the ranch for a moment, then. He heard the dull rushing sound that space and silence make. He heard one of the dogs, out in the doghouse, scratching a flea and bumping his elbow against the floor with every stroke. Then the wind arose again and the black cypress groaned and Jody went to sleep.

He was up half an hour before the triangle sounded for breakfast. His mother was rattling the stove to make the flames roar when Jody went through the kitchen. "You're up early," she said. "Where are you going?"

"Out to get a good stick. We're going to kill the mice today."

"Who is 'we'?"

"Why, Grandfather and I."

"So you've got him in it. You always like to have someone in with you in case there's blame to share."

"I'll be right back," said Jody. "I just want to have a good stick ready for after breakfast."

He closed the screen door after him and went out into the cool blue morning. The birds were noisy in the dawn and the ranch cats came down from the hill like blunt snakes. They had been hunting gophers in the dark, and although the four cats were full of gopher meat, they sat in a semicircle at the back door and mewed piteously for milk. Doubletree Mutt and Smasher moved sniffing along the edge of the brush, performing the duty with rigid ceremony, but when Jody whistled, their heads jerked up and their tails waved. They plunged down to him, wriggling their skins and yawning. Jody patted their heads seriously, and moved on to the weathered scrap pile. He selected an old broom handle and a short piece of inch-square scrap wood. From his pocket he took a shoelace and tied the ends of the sticks loosely together to make a flail. He whistled his new weapon through the air and struck the ground experimentally, while the dogs leaped aside and whined with apprehension.

Jody turned and started down past the house toward the old haystack ground to look over the field of slaughter, but Billy Buck, sitting patiently on the back steps, called to him, "You better come back. It's only a couple of minutes till breakfast."

Jody changed his course and moved toward the house. He leaned his flail against the steps. "That's to drive the mice out," he said. "I'll bet they're fat. I'll bet they don't know what's going to happen to them today."

"No, nor you either," Billy remarked philosophically, "nor me, nor anyone."

Jody was staggered by this thought. He knew it was true. His imagination twitched away from the mouse hunt. Then his mother came out on the back porch and struck the triangle, and all thoughts fell in a heap.

Grandfather hadn't appeared at the table when they sat down. Billy nodded at his empty chair. "He's all right? He isn't sick?"

"He takes a long time to dress," said Mrs. Tiflin. "He combs his whiskers and rubs up his shoes and brushes his clothes."

Carl scattered sugar on his mush. "A man that's led a wagon train across the plains has got to be pretty careful how he dresses."

Mrs. Tiflin turned on him. "Don't do that, Carl! Please don't!" There was more of threat than of request in her tone. And the threat irritated Carl.

"Well, how many times do I have to listen to the story of the iron plates, and the thirty-five horses? That time's done. Why can't he forget it, now it's done?" He grew angrier while he talked, and his voice rose. "Why does he have to tell them over and over? He came across the plains. All right! Now it's finished. Nobody wants to hear about it over and over."

The door into the kitchen closed softly. The four at the table sat frozen. Carl laid his mush spoon on the table and touched his chin with his fingers.

Then the kitchen door opened and Grandfather walked in. His mouth smiled tightly and his eyes were squinted. "Good morning," he said, and he sat down and looked at his mush dish.

Carl could not leave it there. "Did—did you hear what I said?"

Grandfather jerked a little nod.

"I don't know what got into me, sir. I didn't mean it. I was just being funny."

Jody glanced in shame at his mother, and he saw that she was looking at Carl, and that she wasn't breathing. It was an awful thing that he was doing. He was tearing himself to pieces to talk like that. It was a terrible thing to him to retract a word, but to retract it in shame was infinitely worse.

Grandfather looked sidewise. "I'm trying to get right side up," he said gently. "I'm not being mad. I don't mind what you said, but it might be true, and I would mind that."

"It isn't true," said Carl. "I'm not feeling well this morning. I'm sorry I said it."

"Don't be sorry, Carl. An old man doesn't see things sometimes. Maybe you're right. The crossing is finished. Maybe it should be forgotten, now it's done."

Carl got up from the table. "I've had enough to eat. I'm going to work. Take your time, Billy!" He walked quickly out of the dining room. Billy gulped the rest of his food and followed soon after. But Jody could not leave his chair.

"Won't you tell any more stories?" Jody asked.

"Why, sure I'll tell them, but only when—I'm sure people want to hear them."

"I like to hear them, sir."

"Oh! Of course you do, but you're a little boy. It was a job for men, but only the little boys like to hear about it."

Jody got up from his place. "I'll wait outside for you, sir. I've got a good stick for those mice."

He waited by the gate until the old man came out on the porch. "Let's go down and kill the mice now," Jody called.

"I think I'll just sit in the sun, Jody. You go kill the mice."

"You can use my stick if you like."

"No, I'll just sit here a while."

Jody turned disconsolately away, and walked down toward the old haystack. He tried to whip up his enthusiasm with thoughts of the fat juicy mice. He beat the ground with his flail. The dogs coaxed and whined about him, but he could not go. Back at the house he could see Grandfather sitting on the porch, looking small and thin and black.

Jody gave up and went to sit on the steps at the old man's feet.

"Back already? Did you kill the mice?"

"No, sir. I'll kill them some other day."

The morning flies buzzed close to the ground, and the ants dashed about in front of the steps. The heavy smell of sage slipped down the hill. The porch boards grew warm in the sunshine.

Jody hardly knew when Grandfather started to talk. "I shouldn't stay here, feeling the way I do." He examined his strong old hands. "I feel as though the crossing wasn't worth doing." His eyes moved up the side-hill and stopped on a motionless hawk perched on a dead limb. "I tell those old stories, but they're not what I want to tell. I only know how I want people to feel when I tell them.

"It wasn't the Indians that were important, nor adventures, nor even getting out here. It was a whole bunch of people made into one big crawling beast. And I was the head. It was westering and westering. Every man wanted something for himself, but the big beast that was all of them wanted only westering. I was the leader, but if I hadn't been there, someone else would have been the head. The thing had to have a head.

"Under the little bushes the shadows were black at white noonday. When we saw the mountains at last, we cried—all of us. But it wasn't getting here that mattered, it was movement and westering.

"We carried life out here and set it down the way those ants carry eggs. And I was the leader. The westering was as big as God, and the slow steps that made the movement piled up and piled up until the continent was crossed.

"Then we came down to the sea, and it was done." He stopped and wiped his eyes until the rims were red. "That's what I should be telling instead of stories."

When Jody spoke, Grandfather stared and looked down at him. "Maybe I could lead the people some day," Jody said.

The old man smiled. "There's no place to go. There's the ocean to stop you. There's a line of old men along the shore hating the ocean because it stopped them."

"In boats I might, sir."

"No place to go, Jody. Every place is taken. But that's not the worst—no, not the worst. Westering has died out of the people. Westering isn't a hunger any more. It's all done. Your father is right. It is finished." He laced his fingers on his knee and looked at them.

Jody felt very sad. "If you'd like a glass of lemonade, I could make it for you."

Grandfather was about to refuse, and then he saw Jody's face. "That would be nice," he said. "Yes, it would be nice to drink a lemonade."

Jody ran into the kitchen where his mother was wiping the last of the breakfast dishes. "Can I have a lemon to make a lemonade for Grandfather?"

His mother mimicked—⁶ "And another lemon to make a lemonade for you."

"No, ma'am. I don't want one."

"Jody! You're sick!" Then she stopped suddenly. "Take a lemon out of the cooler," she said softly. "Here, I'll reach the squeezer down to you."

6. **mimic** (mim′ik), *v.* make fun of by imitating.

After Reading

Making Connections

Shaping Your Response

1. Write five adjectives that you think describe Jody. Then do the same thing for Carl Tiflin, Mrs. Tiflin, and Grandfather.

2. Being a parent isn't easy, and some people are better at it than others. Where would you place Carl Tiflin on this "parent performance scale"? Where would you place Mrs. Tiflin? Explain.

poor   **excellent**

Analyzing the Story

3. Why do you think Jody doesn't believe himself to be "of heroic timber"?

4. What **character** traits show through in Jody's interactions with the adults in his life?

5. What can you **infer** is the reason for the change in Jody's attitude about killing mice?

6. At the beginning of the story Jody sees his grandfather as a "giant shadow." Near the end of the story, Jody sees his grandfather looking "small and thin." How would you explain this change in Jody's perception?

Extending the Ideas

7. The westward movement was over long before your grandparents were born. What were the major events that took place during their young adulthood that made a lasting impression on them?

Literary Focus: Setting

The time (year, season, and time of day) and place in which the action of a narrative occurs is called **setting.**

- What effect does the setting have on the mood of the story?
- How does setting help to reveal character?
- Does the setting affect the plot in any way?

Vocabulary Study

convene
emerge
mimic
peer
sidle

Work with a small group to pantomime each of the action verbs at the left, and have the class identify the verb. As a follow-up, write original sentences using the verbs.

Expressing Your Ideas

Writing Choices

Writer's Notebook Update Did the words you associated with different family relationships fit the Tiflin family? Enlarge and copy the following diagram into your notebook. On the arrows write **sentences** that explain how the characters relate to each other. A sample sentence is provided here.

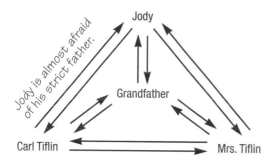

Jody

Jody is almost afraid of his strict father.

Grandfather

Carl Tiflin

Mrs. Tiflin

Other Options

Read On With a partner, write an **annotated bibliography** of selected Steinbeck works. If possible, display a collection of his books in the classroom along with the bibliography.

At the Movies *The Red Pony,* from which "The Leader of the People" is taken, was made into a film. With a partner, view the film and **review** it orally for the class.

Campfire Conversation Study the William Ranney painting *The Old Scout's Tale.* What do you suppose they are discussing? Make up names for the characters in the painting and imagine a **conversation** that they might be having about the trip west. With a group of classmates perform the conversation for the rest of the class.

What I Want to Know If you could talk to Jody's grandfather about his experience, what would you ask him? Make a **list of questions** that you would ask about traveling across the country in a covered wagon.

Before Reading

Lord Byron's Love Letter

by Tennessee Williams

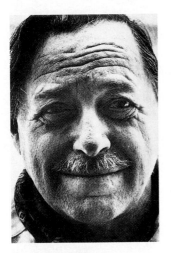

Tennessee Williams
1911–1983

Because his traveling salesman father was away much of the time, Thomas Lanier Williams lived in Columbus, Mississippi, in the home of his maternal grandparents. Later, however, the family moved to St. Louis. The children had trouble adjusting to city life, and to their father who often drank and gambled. Thomas found an escape in writing. After graduating from college, he moved to New York to write professionally, publishing his works as "Tennessee" Williams, a name he chose because his paternal ancestors were some of the original settlers of Tennessee. Williams is best known for his plays, which are filled with Southern romantics who cannot adjust to the modern South.

Building Background

How Scandalous! Strikingly handsome, with a reputation for wickedness and free thought, the English Romantic poet Lord Byron embodied in his life and in his writings the figure subsequently known as the "Byronic hero": a moody, turbulent individual, self-exiled from society after exhausting all possibilities of human excitement, and tormented by remorse over secret sins committed in the past.

Enjoying his role as the favorite of London society, Byron gained the reputation of being one who was "mad, bad, and dangerous to know." He dressed as he felt a poet should and cultivated a deliberately mysterious air. After several love affairs, he married the nobly born, very proper Annabella Milbanke. After one year of marriage, his wife returned to her parents with their newborn daughter. The circumstances of the separation scandalized English society and led to Byron's decision, in 1816, to leave England for good. Byron went to Greece, where he committed his money and energies to the Greek's war of liberation from Turkish rule until his death from illness on April 19, 1824, at the age of thirty-six.

Literary Focus

Diction In *Lord Byron's Love Letter,* Tennessee Williams includes characters from different walks of life. One way that Williams contrasted these characters was through diction, his choice of words and phrases. As you read the play, notice the language used by each character.

Writer's Notebook

Fraud! A *con artist* is someone who gains a person's confidence and then swindles him or her out of money. For example, there are con artists who pose as tradesmen and prey on elderly homeowners by collecting money for making unnecessary home repairs. Preview the characters and the setting of *Lord Byron's Love Letter.* In your notebook predict which of the characters might be a con artist and what you think the "con" might involve.

LORD BYRON'S
Love Letter

TENNESSEE WILLIAMS

CHARACTERS

THE SPINSTER
THE OLD WOMAN
THE MATRON
THE HUSBAND

(SCENE: The parlor of a faded old residence in the French Quarter of New Orleans in the late nineteenth century. The shuttered doors of the room open directly upon the sidewalk and the noise of the Mardi Gras[1] festivities can be faintly distinguished. The interior is very dusky. Beside a rose-shaded lamp, the SPINSTER,[2] a woman of forty, is sewing. In the opposite corner, completely motionless, the OLD WOMAN sits in a black silk dress. The doorbell tinkles.)

SPINSTER *(rising).* It's probably someone coming to look at the letter.

OLD WOMAN *(rising on her cane).* Give me time to get out.

(She withdraws gradually behind the curtains. One of her claw-like hands remains visible, holding a curtain slightly open so that she can watch the visitors. The SPINSTER opens the door and the MATRON, a middle-aged woman, walks into the room.)

SPINSTER. Won't you come in?

MATRON. Thank you.

SPINSTER. You're from out of town?

MATRON. Oh, yes, we're all the way from Milwaukee. We've come for Mardi Gras, my husband and I. *(She suddenly notices a stuffed canary in its tiny pink cage.)* Oh, this poor little bird in such a tiny cage! It's much too small to keep a canary in!

SPINSTER. It isn't a live canary.

OLD WOMAN *(from behind the curtain).* No. It's stuffed.

MATRON. Oh. *(She self-consciously touches a stuffed bird on her hat.)* Winston is out there dilly-dallying on the street, afraid he'll miss the parade. The parade comes by here, don't it?

SPINSTER. Yes, unfortunately it does.

MATRON. I noticed your sign at the door. Is it true that you have one of Lord Byron's love letters?

SPINSTER. Yes.

MATRON. How very interesting! How did you get it?

SPINSTER. It was written to my grandmother, Irénée Marguerite de Poitevent.

---

1. **Mardi Gras** (mär′dē grä′), the last day before Lent; Shrove Tuesday. It is celebrated with parades and festivities.
2. **spinster** (spin′stər), *n.* an older, unmarried woman.

▲ Audrey Flack's painting, *Truman's Teachers* (1964), was inspired by a magazine photograph. How might this painting portray the women differently than a photograph would?

MATRON. How very interesting! Where did she meet Lord Byron?

SPINSTER. On the steps of the Acropolis³ in Athens.

MATRON. How very, very interesting! I didn't know that Lord Byron was ever in Greece.

SPINSTER. Lord Byron spent the final years of his turbulent⁴ life in Greece.

OLD WOMAN *(still behind the curtains)*. He was exiled⁵ from England!

SPINSTER. Yes, he went into voluntary exile from England.

OLD WOMAN. Because of scandalous gossip in the Regent's court.

SPINSTER. Yes, involving his half-sister!

OLD WOMAN. It was false—completely.

SPINSTER. It was never confirmed.

OLD WOMAN. He was a passionate man but not an evil man.

---

3. **Acropolis** (ə krop′ə lis), the high, fortified part of Athens on which the Parthenon was built.
4. **turbulent** (tėr′byə lənt), stormy; tempestuous.
5. **exile** (eg′zīl), *v.* banish; force to leave one's country or home.

SPINSTER. Morals are such <u>ambiguous</u>[6] matters, I think.

MATRON. Won't the lady behind the curtains come in?

SPINSTER. You'll have to excuse her. She prefers to stay out.

MATRON (*stiffly*). Oh, I see. What was Lord Byron doing in Greece, may I ask?

OLD WOMAN (*proudly*). *Fighting for Freedom!*

SPINSTER. Yes, Lord Byron went to Greece to join the force that fought against the infidels.[7]

OLD WOMAN. He gave his life in defense of the universal cause of freedom!

MATRON. What was that, did she say?

SPINSTER (*repeating automatically*). He gave his life in defense of the universal cause of freedom.

MATRON. Oh, how very interesting!

OLD WOMAN. Also he swam the Hellespont.[8]

SPINSTER. Yes.

OLD WOMAN. And burned the body of the poet Shelley, who was drowned in a storm on the Mediterranean with a volume of Keats in his pocket!

MATRON (*incredulously*). Pardon?

SPINSTER (*repeating*). And burned the body of the poet Shelley who was drowned in a storm on the Mediterranean with a volume of Keats in his pocket.

MATRON. Oh. How very, very interesting! Indeed, I'd like so much to have my husband hear it. Do you mind if I just step out for a moment to call him in?

SPINSTER. Please do.

(*The* MATRON *steps out quickly, calling,* "Winston! Winston!")

OLD WOMAN (*poking her head out for a moment*). Watch them carefully! Keep a sharp eye on them!

SPINSTER. Yes. Be still.

(*The* MATRON *returns with her* HUSBAND *who has been drinking and wears a paper cap sprinkled with confetti.*)

MATRON. Winston, remove that cap. Sit down on the sofa. These ladies are going to show us Lord Byron's love letter.

SPINSTER. Shall I proceed?

MATRON. Oh, yes. This—uh—is my husband—Mr. Tutwiler.

SPINSTER (*coldly*). How do you do.

MATRON. I am *Mrs.* Tutwiler.

SPINSTER. Of course. Please keep your seat.

MATRON (*nervously*). He's been—celebrating a little.

OLD WOMAN (*shaking the curtain that conceals her*). Ask him please to be careful with his cigar.

SPINSTER. Oh, that's all right, you may use this bowl for your ashes.

OLD WOMAN. Smoking is such an unnecessary habit!

HUSBAND. Uh!

MATRON. This lady was telling us how her grandmother happened to meet Lord Byron. In Italy, wasn't it?

SPINSTER. No.

OLD WOMAN (*firmly*). In Greece, in Athens, on the steps of the Acropolis! We've mentioned that *twice,* I believe. Ariadne, you may read them a passage from the journal first.

SPINSTER. Yes.

OLD WOMAN. But please be careful what you choose to read!

(*The* SPINSTER *has removed from the secretary a volume wrapped in tissue and tied with ribbon.*)

SPINSTER. Like many other young American girls of that day and this, my grandmother went to Europe.

OLD WOMAN. The year before she was going to be presented to society!

MATRON. How old was she?

OLD WOMAN. Sixteen! Barely sixteen! She was very beautiful too! Please show her the picture, show these people the picture! It's in the front of the journal.

(*The* SPINSTER *removes the picture from the book and*

---

6. **ambiguous** (am big′yü əs), having several possible interpretations; lacking definiteness.
7. **infidel** (in′fə dəl), *n.* person who does not accept a particular faith.
8. **Hellespont** (hel′i spont), ancient name for the Dardanelles, the strait in Northwest Turkey which connects the Sea of Marmara with the Aegean Sea.

hands it to the MATRON.)

MATRON *(taking a look).* What a lovely young girl. (*Passing it to her* HUSBAND.) Don't you think it resembles Agnes a little?

HUSBAND. Uh!

OLD WOMAN. Watch out! Ariadne, you'll have to *watch* the man. I believe he's been drinking. I *do* believe that he's been——

HUSBAND. *(truculently).* Yeah? What is she saying back there?

MATRON *(touching his arm warningly).* Winston! Be quiet.

SPINSTER *(quickly).* Near the end of her tour, my grandmother and her aunt went to Greece, to study the classic remains of the oldest civilization.

OLD WOMAN *(correcting).* The oldest *European* civilization.

SPINSTER. It was an early morning in April of the year eighteen hundred and——

OLD WOMAN. Twenty-seven!

SPINSTER. Yes. In my grandmother's journal she mentions——

OLD WOMAN. Read it, read it, *read* it.

MATRON. Yes, *please* read it to us.

SPINSTER. I'm trying to find the place, if you'll just be patient.

MATRON. Certainly, excuse me. *(She punches her* HUSBAND *who is nodding.)* Winston!

SPINSTER. Ah, here it is.

OLD WOMAN. Be *careful!* Remember where to *stop* at, Ariadne!

SPINSTER. Shhh! *(She adjusts her glasses and seats herself by the lamp.)* "We set out early that morning to inspect the ruins of the Acropolis. I know I shall never forget how extraordinarily pure the atmosphere was that morning. It seemed as though the world were not very old, but very, very young, almost as though the world had been newly created. There was a taste of earliness in the air, a feeling of freshness, exhilarating my senses, exalting my spirit. How shall I tell you, dear Diary, the way the sky looked? It was almost as though I had moistened the tip of

my pen in a shallow bowl full of milk, so delicate was the blue in the dome of the heavens. The sun was barely up yet, a tentative breeze disturbed the ends of my scarf, the plumes of the marvelous hat which I had bought in Paris and thrilled me with pride whenever I saw them reflected! The papers that morning, we read them over our coffee before we left the hotel, had spoken of possible war, but it seemed unlikely, unreal: nothing was real, indeed, but the spell of golden antiquity and rose-colored romance that breathed from this fabulous city."

OLD WOMAN. Skip that part! Get on to where she meets him!

SPINSTER. Yes . . . *(She turns several pages and continues.)* "Out of the tongues of ancients, the lyrical voices of many long-ago poets who dreamed of the world of ideals, who had in their hearts the pure and absolute image—"

OLD WOMAN. *Skip* that part! Slip down to where——

SPINSTER. Yes! *Here! Do* let us manage without any more *interruptions!* "The carriage came to a halt at the foot of the hill and my aunt, not being too well——"

OLD WOMAN. She had a sore throat that morning.

SPINSTER. "—preferred to remain with the driver while I undertook the rather steep climb on foot. As I ascended the long and crumbling flight of old stone steps——"

OLD WOMAN. Yes, yes, that's the place! *(The* SPINSTER *looks up in annoyance. The* OLD WOMAN's *cane taps impatiently behind the curtains.)* Go *on,* Ariadne!

SPINSTER. "I could not help observing continually above me a man who walked with a barely perceptible limp—"

OLD WOMAN *(in hushed wonder).* Yes—Lord Byron!

SPINSTER. "—and as he turned now and then to observe beneath him the lovely Panorama——"

OLD WOMAN. Actually he was watching the girl behind him.

SPINSTER. *(sharply).* Will you please let me finish!

(There is no answer from behind the curtains, and she continues to read.) "I was irresistibly impressed by the unusual nobility and refinement of his features!"

(She turns a page.)

OLD WOMAN. The handsomest man that ever walked the earth!

(She emphasizes the speech with three slow but loud taps of her cane.)

SPINSTER *(flurriedly).* "The strength and grace of his throat, like that of a statue, the classic outlines of his profile, the sensitive lips and the slightly dilated nostrils, the dark lock of hair that fell down over his forehead in such a way that——"

OLD WOMAN *(tapping her cane rapidly).* Skip that, it goes on for pages!

SPINSTER. ". . . When he had reached the very summit[9] of the Acropolis he spread out his arms in a great, magnificent gesture like a young god. Now, thought I to myself, Apollo[10] has come to earth in modern dress."

OLD WOMAN. Go on, skip that, get on to where she *meets* him!

SPINSTER. "Fearing to interrupt his poetic trance, I slackened[11] my pace and pretended to watch the view. I kept my look thus carefully averted[12] until the narrowness of the steps compelled[13] me to move close by him."

OLD WOMAN. Of course he pretended not to see she was coming!

SPINSTER. "Then finally I faced him."

OLD WOMAN. Yes!

SPINSTER. "Our eyes came together!"

OLD WOMAN. Yes! Yes! That's the part!

SPINSTER. "A thing which I don't understand had occurred between us, a flush as of recognition swept through my whole being! Suffused[14] my——"

OLD WOMAN. Yes . . . Yes, that's the part!

SPINSTER. "'Pardon me,' he exclaimed, 'you have dropped your glove!' And indeed to my surprise I found that I had, and as he returned it to me, his fingers ever so lightly pressed the cups of my palm."

OLD WOMAN *(hoarsely).* Yes!

(Her bony fingers clutch higher up on the curtain, the other hand also appears, slightly widening the aperture.)

SPINSTER. "Believe me, dear Diary, I became quite faint and breathless, I almost wondered if I could continue my lonely walk through the ruins. Perhaps I stumbled, perhaps I swayed a little. I leaned for a moment against the side of a column. The sun seemed terribly brilliant, it hurt my eyes. Close behind me I heard that voice again, almost it seemed I could feel his breath on my——"

OLD WOMAN. Stop *there!* That will be quite enough!

(The SPINSTER closes the journal.)

MATRON. Oh, is that all?

OLD WOMAN. There's a great deal more that's not to be read to people.

MATRON. Oh.

SPINSTER. I'm sorry. I'll show you the letter.

MATRON. How nice! I'm dying to see it! Winston? *Do sit up!*

(He has nearly fallen asleep. The SPINSTER produces from the cabinet another small packet which she unfolds. It contains the letter. She hands it to the MATRON, who starts to open it.)

OLD WOMAN. Watch out, watch *out,* that woman can't *open* the letter!

SPINSTER. No, no, please, you mustn't. The contents of the letter are strictly private. I'll hold it over here at a little distance so you can see the writing.

OLD WOMAN. Not too close, she's holding up her glasses!

(The MATRON quickly lowers her lorgnette.)

SPINSTER. Only a short while later Byron was killed.

MATRON. How did he die?

---

9. **summit** (sum′it), *n.* the highest point; top.
10. **Apollo** (ə pol′ō), the Greek god of the sun. Apollo was considered the highest type of youthful, manly beauty.
11. **slacken** (slak′ən), *v.* become slower.
12. **averted** (ə vėrt′əd), *adj.* turned away or turned aside.
13. **compel** (kəm pel′), *v.* drive or urge with force.
14. **suffuse** (sə fyüz′), *v.* overspread.

◄ Does the style of Sandra Burshell's 1994 pastel, *Tranquil Corner,* match the atmosphere of the parlor in the play? Why or why not?

MATRON. Tch-tch-tch! How dreadful! I think that was foolish of her.

(The cane taps furiously behind the curtains.)

SPINSTER. You don't understand. When a life is completed, it ought to be put away. It's like a sonnet. When you've written the final couplet, why go on any further? You only destroy the part that's already written!

OLD WOMAN. Read them a poem, the sonnet your grandmother wrote to the memory of Lord Byron.

SPINSTER. Would you be interested?

MATRON. We'd adore it—truly!

SPINSTER. It's called "Enchantment."

MATRON *(she assumes a rapt[15] expression). Aahhh!*

SPINSTER *(reciting).*

Un saison enchanté! I mused, Beguiled
Seemed Time herself, her erstwhile errant ways
Briefly forgotten, she stayed here and smiled,
Caught in a net of blue and golden days.

OLD WOMAN. Not blue and golden—gold and *azure*[16] days!

SPINSTER.

Caught in a net—of gold and azure days!

But I lacked wit to see how lightly shoon
Were Time and you, to vagrancy so used——

OLD WOMAN. He was killed in action, defending the cause of freedom!

(This is uttered so strongly the HUSBAND *starts.)*

SPINSTER. When my grandmother received the news of Lord Byron's death in battle, she retired from the world and remained in complete seclusion for the rest of her life.

---

15. **rapt** (rapt), *adj.* so busy thinking of or enjoying one thing that one does not know what else is happening.
16. **azure** (azh'ər), *adj.* the clear blue color of the unclouded sky.

(The OLD WOMAN *begins to accompany in a hoarse undertone. Faint band music can be heard.)*

That by the touch of one October moon
From summer's tranquil[17] spell you might be
    loosed!

OLD WOMAN *(rising stridently with intense feeling above the* SPINSTER'S *voice).*

Think you love is writ on my soul with chalk,
To be washed off by a few parting tears?

Then you know not with what slow step I walk.
The barren way of those hibernal years—

My life a vanished interlude, a shell
Whose walls are your first kiss—and last
    farewell!

(The band, leading the parade, has started down the street, growing rapidly louder. It passes by like the heedless, turbulent years. The HUSBAND, *roused from his stupor,[18] lunges to the door.)*

MATRON. What's that, what's that? The *parade?*

(The HUSBAND *slaps the paper cap on his head and rushes for the door.)*

HUSBAND *(at the door).* Come on, Mama, you'll
    miss it!

SPINSTER *(quickly).* We usually accept—you under-
    stand?—a small sum of money, just anything
    that you happen to think you can spare.

OLD WOMAN. Stop him! He's gone outside!

(The HUSBAND *has escaped to the street. The band blares through the door.)*

SPINSTER *(extending her hand).* Please—a dollar . . .

OLD WOMAN. *Fifty cents!*

SPINSTER. Or a *quarter!*

MATRON *(paying no attention to them).* Oh, my
    goodness—*Winston!* He's *disappeared* in the
    crowd! Winston—*Winston! Excuse* me! *(She
    rushes out onto the door sill.) Winston!* Oh, my
    goodness gracious, he's off again!

SPINSTER *(quickly).* We usually accept a little
    money for the display of the letter. Whatever
    you feel that you are able to give. As a matter
    of fact it's all that we have to *live* on!

OLD WOMAN *(loudly).* One dollar!

SPINSTER. Fifty cents—or a quarter!

MATRON *(oblivious,[19] at the door).* Winston! *Winston!*
    Heavenly days. *Good-bye!*

(She rushes out on the street. The SPINSTER *follows to the door and shields her eyes from the light as she looks after the* MATRON. *A stream of confetti is tossed through the doorway into her face. Trumpets blare. She slams the door shut and bolts it.)*

SPINSTER. *Canaille!* . . . *Canaille!*

OLD WOMAN. Gone? Without paying? *Cheated* us? *(She parts the curtains.)*

SPINSTER. *Yes*—the *canaille!*[20]

(She fastidiously plucks the thread of confetti from her shoulder. The OLD WOMAN *steps from behind the curtain, rigid with anger.)*

OLD WOMAN. Ariadne, my letter! You've dropped
    my letter! Your grandfather's letter is lying
    on the floor!

---

17. **tranquil** (trang′kwəl), *adj.* calm; peaceful.
18. **stupor** (stü′pər), *n.* a dazed condition.
19. **oblivious** (ə bliv′ē əs), *adj.* not mindful; unaware.
20. **canaille** (kə nēl′), riffraff, scoundrel.

After Reading

Making Connections

Shaping Your Response

1. Poll the class to see who believes the letter was from Lord Byron and who believes it was a fake. Ask your classmates to explain their opinions.

2. If you could have a part in this play, which would you choose? Why?

Analyzing the Play

3. What do you think the curtain that the old woman hides behind **symbolizes?**

4. Notice the **diction** in the play. Whose words are the most poetic? Whose are the least poetic?

5. How would you describe the **characters** of the spinster and the old woman?

6. How would you **characterize** the Tutwilers?

7. Ariadne calls Mrs. Tutwiler a *canaille,* or scoundrel. Who do *you* think is a *canaille* in this play, and why?

Extending the Ideas

8. Lord Byron was a romantic hero in his day. He was handsome, athletic, artistic, and notorious. Describe someone you would consider to be a contemporary romantic hero.

Vocabulary Study

Choose the response that best answers the question or completes the sentence.

azure
stupor
exile
suffuse
averted
turbulent
ambiguous
compel
tranquil
oblivious

1. What might the old woman describe as *azure?*

    a. Lord Byron's hair   **b.** the Grecian sky   **c.** clumps of grass

2. Mr. Tutwiler was in a *stupor.* Which word best describes his state?

    a. tranquil   **b.** turbulent   **c.** oblivious

3. A *tranquil* home would be:

    a. peaceful and calm   **b.** buzzing with excitement   **c.** untidy

4. Lord Byron chose to *exile* himself from England and would never ____.

    a. leave   **b.** complain   **c.** return

5. You can tell that Mr. Tutwiler is *oblivious* to the conversation, because he:

    a. likes parades   **b.** pays no attention   **c.** despises Lord Byron

6. Which of the following would definitely <u>not</u> be described as *turbulent?*

    a. the parade   **b.** the old woman's mood
    c. Mr. Tutwiler's interest in the letter

7. The ladies may have noticed Mrs. Tutwiler ____ with embarrassment at her husband's behavior.

  a. *suffuse* **b.** *averted* **c.** *compel*

8. The young woman glimpsed Lord Byron through ____ eyes.

  a. *suffuse* **b.** *averted* **c.** *compel*

9. An *ambiguous* message is:

  a. unclear **b.** clear **c.** silent

10. The best synonym for "force" is:

  a. *suffuse* **b.** *averted* **c.** *compel*

Expressing Your Ideas

Writing Choices

Writer's Notebook Update Imagine that the police received a complaint about the two women, and a police officer had to visit them to check out the situation. Write a scene for the three characters expressing what you think might be said in such a confrontation.

Williams at His Best Either read a copy of *The Glass Menagerie* by Tennessee Williams, or watch a videotape of the movie adaptation. Write a **comparison** of it and *Lord Byron's Love Letter.*

More About Lord Byron The Building Background article preceding the play provides a brief biography of Lord Byron. To round out your knowledge of this romantic poet, research his life and write your own **biographical account.**

Other Options

In His Own Words Although the play is titled *Lord Byron's Love Letter,* the audience doesn't hear one word written by Lord Byron. Work with a small group of students and read some of Lord Byron's poetry or letters. Practice reading them aloud, and then present an **oral interpretation** of them to the class.

Tourist Trap Imagine that the New Orleans Chamber of Commerce has gotten complaints about the old woman and the spinster for running a "scam." Would you as a chamber member vote to allow them to continue their business or put a stop to it? Choose your position, prepare an **oral argument,** and present your argument to the class.

The Play's the Thing Plays are meant to be performed, not read silently. Work with a small group of students and perform *Lord Byron's Love Letter.* Depending on the available recording equipment and class time, produce either a live **performance,** a videotaped production, or an audiotaped "radio play."

The Strength of Tradition

Life on the Home Front

History Connection
World War II began for the United States on December 7, 1941, when Japan attacked Pearl Harbor. The war's effects on Americans at home were as diverse as the people themselves. The following pages relate some of these home front experiences.

Recruitment posters urged women to "roll up their sleeves" and join the work force to aid the war effort. By 1944 more than a third of the nation's workers were women.

New Opportunities for African Americans and Women

Sybil Lewis

The need for more industrial workers provided new and better paying jobs for many African Americans and women. Sybil Lewis details some of the economic and social changes of the time.

Had it not been for the war I don't think blacks would be in the position they are now. The war and defense work gave black people opportunities to work on jobs they never had before. It gave them opportunity to do things they never experienced before.

Celebrated in posters and in a song (called "Rosie the Riveter"), riveting was one of the best-known war jobs for women. Here the woman on the left "sets" whlle the woman on the right "bucks" rivets in a defense plant.

They made more money and began to experience a different lifestyle. Their expectations changed. Money will do that. You could sense that they would no longer be satisfied with the way they had lived before.

When I got my first paycheck, I'd never seen that much money before, not even in the bank, because I'd never been in a bank too much. I don't recall exactly what it was in the aircraft plant, but it was more than three hundred dollars a month, and later, in the shipyard, it was even more.

To be able to buy what you wanted, your clothing and shoes, all this was just a different way of life.

When I first got my paycheck I bought everything that I thought I had ever wanted, but in particular I bought shoes. I wore a large size as a child and I could never be fitted properly for shoes. The woman I worked for in Oklahoma wore beautiful shoes, and I remember thinking then that when I got a chance to make some money I was going to buy shoes first. So my first paycheck I bought

mostly shoes. And it felt very good. To be honest, today I still buy more shoes than anything else.

Other experiences I had during the war were important, too, like having to rivet with a white farm girl from Arkansas and both of us having to relate to each other in ways that we had never experienced before. Although we had our differences we both learned to work together and talk together. We learned that despite our hostilities and resentments we could open up to each other and get along. As I look back

CHILDREN OF THE HOME FRONT

SHERIL JANKOVSKY CUNNING

The world turned upside down for the children of the home front. Many of their families were broken up as fathers and older brothers went off to war. In the following excerpt Sheril Jankovsky Cunning talks about growing up during the war.

As a child growing up during the war in Long Beach, California, I lived constantly with the fear we might be invaded or bombed. We lived only three blocks from the beach,

and before the war started we would walk down there with our mother and play in the waves and sand. But during the war the whole coast was blocked off from civilian use. All along the bluffs, they set up giant antiaircraft artillery and camouflage netting which to a small child appeared to be several stories high. You couldn't see the ocean anymore. All you could see was the guns and camouflage.

We also had air raid alerts which made the possibility of invasion seem very real. Because Pearl Harbor had been bombed and California was the Pacific and close to the Japanese, we felt we could have a surprise air attack at any minute.

My father was the block air raid warden. I'll never forget the fear I felt as he went out during air raid alert and left the family huddled in the hallway. The sirens would go off, the searchlights would sweep the sky, and Daddy would don his gas mask and his big hard hat and goggles and go out to protect the neighborhood.

Although we had blackout curtains, my parents didn't really trust them not to leak light. So we sat in a hall closet with all the doors closed in order to be able to have the lights on. We had a wind-up Victrola which we'd take in there with us. My mother would sing to us to keep up our spirits. But we couldn't help being afraid for our father. And afraid for ourselves.

now I feel that experience was meaningful to me and meaningful to her. She learned that Negroes were people, too, and I saw her as a person also, and we both gained from it.

I also saw in California that black women were working in jobs that I had never seen in the South, not only defense work but working in nice hotels as waitresses, working in the post office, doing clerical work. So I realized there were a lot of things women could do besides housework. I saw black people accepted in the school system and accepted in other kinds of jobs that they had not been accepted in before. It's too bad it took a war to motivate people to move here to want to make more of their lives, but if it had not been for the war offering better jobs and opportunities, some people would have never left the South. They would have had nothing to move for.

After I graduated from college I returned to California and started applying for civil-service jobs. Had it not been for the war I probably would have ended up a schoolteacher in rural Oklahoma, but the impact of the war changed my life, gave me an opportunity to leave my small town and discover there was another way of life. It financed my college education and opened my eyes to opportunities I could take advantage of when the war was over.

Our prime protector was out protecting someone else. It gave us the feeling of being abandoned. The searchlights and sirens struck great fear in our hearts and yet it was exciting.

Many of our games involved war themes. We made hideouts and plans (and alternate plans) in the event Long Beach would be invaded or bombed. My sister and I planned for situations in which we might be like the poor, starving children of Europe we saw in the news-reels, living without parents, in rags, in bombed-out buildings. We were convinced

Children participated wholeheartedly in supporting the nation's war effort by collecting recyclables such as scrap metal which eventually found its way into war machinery.

that if attacked only children would survive and all adults would be killed.

We had a back closet that we figured was the safest place in the house to hide in case of invasion. My mother stored all her old clothes in there in big rubber garment bags. We figured that nobody would find us behind those bags. But just in case they did, we kept a bottle of ketchup in the closet. We were going to douse ourselves with it and lie there as if we had already been bloodied and killed, so that they would walk away and not stick their bayonets into us.

What was funny is we always thought it would be the Germans who would invade. Although Japan was on the other side of that ocean out there in our front yard, we had very strong visions of storm troopers in big boots invading our shores. The Japanese were going to bomb us, but it was the Nazis who were going to open that closet door and see two little dead girls. I'm sure that came from the newsreels and *Life* magazine. *Life* came every week to deliver the war to our doorstep and replenish our fear.

The war also brought my first experience of death. I remember the day that we got the news that my cousin was killed when his troopship was torpedoed. Yet there were so many stories and movies around about someone coming back after being declared dead that I thought, Well, maybe they'll discover Jimmy alive someday. My mother tried to make me realize. "No, Jimmy is really dead. He was in the middle of the ocean. There isn't going to be any finding Jimmy." And I remember her crying, saying things like "He was so young, he never hurt anybody, and he never had a chance to grow up and be a man." It was a long time after the war before I gave up my hope that he would return.

JAPANESE AMERICANS ARE "RELOCATED"

HENRY MURAKAMI

In 1942, 110,000 people of Japanese ancestry were sent to internment camps across the western United States. In the following excerpt, Henry Murakami remembers the events endured by his family.

After Pearl Harbor we were ordered not to go out fishing. We put away all the nets, tied the boats, and all you had to do was stay home and watch what was going on. It was worse than terrible. You could do nothing. Day after day you just had to stay around the house, and that's all.

On February 11, I was outside the house, holding my year-and-a-half daughter in my arms. And a big flock of tall American men came around. One of them had a piece of paper in his hand, and he started asking me who lives where, where is this man, and so on. So I said, "What is this?" and he said, "We're just asking a few questions." I asked, "Is my name on the list?" And he asked, "What's your name?" So I told him. He was checking the names, and he found it. So right there he said, "You come with us for just a little while and you'll come right back." I called my wife and she came on the porch and I asked the FBI man if I could go in and put my shoes on. I had no socks, just Japanese slippers. And the FBI man said, "No, you don't need to change. You'll come right back." I believed what they said. I couldn't argue. So I handed the baby to my wife and I went with them.

They took us to the immigration office in San Pedro. We were there two days and two nights, then they put us all in old trains. Two days and two nights more we traveled. No window, all closed; you couldn't look outside. And suddenly the trains stopped and the guards said, "Get out." We came out, and all you could see was white, noth-

This painting, *Boys With Kite* (1944), was created by the non-Japanese wife of a detainee who chose to accompany her husband into the relocation camps.

ing but white. You couldn't even see houses or buildings. Just snow. They said eight feet high. And we found out it was Bismarck, North Dakota, and it was twenty-nine degrees below zero, and I was walking on the snow in my bare feet and slippers.

They took us to Fort Lincoln, and we had to go to the mess hall where hundreds of people were standing in line. You know how hard it is to stand only fifteen or twenty minutes in cold like that? Within a week I had frostbite. I couldn't walk anymore.

Why? We hadn't done anything wrong. We obeyed the laws. None of us were spies. We didn't know anything about those things. But we were all arrested because we carried fishermen's licenses.

After I was at Fort Lincoln a few weeks I received a letter from my wife that she had

forty-eight hours' notice to evacuate from the island. She was eight months pregnant and there was nothing she could do. So she abandoned everything. Pregnant and with four children, how much could she carry? So she took the children and one suitcase and they all went to the camp the government had built at the Santa Anita Racetrack.

They were there about sixty days, then they were sent to Manzanar. In July I was sent to Manzanar and joined my family, and my new son who was born in May. And we were really joyous . . .

After the war I came back to California, but I couldn't fish anymore. I had no gear to start with. I had no money. How could I go back to fishing? None of the old Japanese fishermen ever went back.

My own loss I can say, was $55,000 or more. Minimum. In 1940 I bought three new sets of nets. One was for tuna, one for mackerel, and one for sardines. The mackerel and sardine nets each cost $15,000; the tuna net cost about $25,000, because it had all heavyweight webbings. I worked so hard to pay for them. I bought everything by cash. I didn't like that credit business.

Each of the nets we kept in a big flatbed truck on the street where we lived. The day I was arrested I saw with my own eyes my three sets of nets sitting on the flatbeds. I saw them. When we were sent to Fort Lincoln I asked the FBI men about my nets. They said, "Don't worry. Everything is going to be taken care of." But I never saw the nets again, nor my brand-new 1941 Plymouth, nor our furniture. It all just disappeared. I lost everything. But I don't blame anyone. It was a war. We had nothing to do with the war, but we were its victims.

Responding

1. How were the experiences of the individuals similar? Different?

2. How do you think wartime experiences affected the lives of women, African Americans, and Japanese Americans after the war?

Writing Workshop

Point-Counterpoint

Assignment Write an essay in which you compare and contrast differing points of view about the same issue, based on one of the selections in this part of the unit.

WRITER'S BLUEPRINT

Product   A comparison/contrast essay
Purpose   To analyze and evaluate differing points of view
Audience   People who've read the literature
Specs   To write a successful essay, you should:

❑ Choose one of these topics:

—differing points of view about fences and neighbors in "Mending Wall"

—differing points of view about the law in "The Tall Men" (for example, the investigator's and the deputy's)

—another topic of your choice involving differing points of view, drawn from one of the selections

❑ Begin your paper by identifying the issue and describing the two differing points of view in the selection that you've chosen to deal with. Use quotations to illustrate each point of view. Take care to signal comparisons and contrasts.

❑ Go on to discuss your own reactions to each point of view. Illustrate your reactions with specific examples from experiences in your own life.

❑ Conclude with a summary of the merits of each point of view. Then tell which point of view you favor and why.

❑ Follow the rules of grammar, usage, spelling, and mechanics. Punctuate quotations from literature correctly.

Review the literature selections to identify differing points of view about the same issue. Note that *differing* doesn't necessarily mean *opposite.* Characters may disagree on some aspects of an issue and agree on others. Just be sure that the two points of view show significant differences. When you finish, look over your notes and choose your topic: the issue and the differing points about it held by two characters.

Compare and contrast the two points of view you chose. Reread the selection closely to find examples of similarities and differences. Include at least two quotations for each character. These quotations should show why your characters firmly believe in the views they hold. Record your examples in a Venn diagram. In the overlapping area in the middle, list aspects of the issue that both characters agree on, as in the example that follows.

Issue: Whether good fences make good neighbors

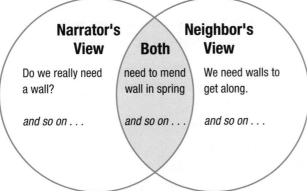

LITERARY SOURCE
"My apple trees will never get across/And eat the cones under his pines, I tell him./He only says, 'Good fences make good neighbors'"
from "Mending Wall" by Robert Frost

Walk in someone else's shoes. Refer to your Venn diagram and try to see each character's point of view. Write for five minutes as if you were one of the characters expressing your point of view. Then switch roles and do the same for the other character.

Notice how the writer of the student model on the next page captured one character's point of view from "The Tall Men."

OR . . .
With a partner listening, take on one character's point of view and improvise what the character would say if asked to explain his or her position. Then try it again as the other character you've chosen.

The investigator is dead serious about the law. He doesn't want to give an inch. He plays it by the book, as the TV cops say, always on the lookout for violators. He thinks people ought to live up to their legal obligations no matter what, and if they don't, they ought to suffer the consequences.

List the merits of each position. Use your quickwrite as a guide. Consider each point of view in a positive light and make a list of reasons why someone might take that position.

Formulate your own opinion. Look over your list of reasons in favor of each point of view and jot down notes on your reactions. Think of experiences you've had in your own life and complete these sentences:

A time in my life when I was confronted with this issue was when _____.

My point of view about the issue at that time was _____.

The way I feel about it now is _____.

Then ask yourself: *Which point of view comes closer to my own position?* Explain your decision to a partner, discuss it, and take notes on your discussion.

Plan your essay, using a three-part outline like the one shown.

- **Introduction**
  The issue
  The first point of view
      —Quotations from the text
  The second point of view
      —Quotations from the text

- **Body**
  Reactions to first point of view
      —examples from your own experience
  Reactions to second point of view
      —examples from your own experience

- **Conclusion**
  Merits of first point of view
  Merits of second point of view
  Which one you favor
  Why

Ask a partner to review your plan.

✔ Have I described two differing points of view presented in a selection?

✔ Do my quotations illustrate and support my claims?

✔ Do I demonstrate which point of view I prefer?

Use your partner's comments to help you revise your plan.

STEP ## 2 DRAFTING

Before you draft, review the Writer's Blueprint and your prewriting materials. Be sure your plan takes into account each point in the blueprint.

As you draft, consider these ideas:

- Write your introduction as if it were being spoken by two characters from the selection who hold differing points of view, with each character making a brief statement that summarizes his or her position on the issue. Then write the rest of the essay in your own voice.

- Write your introduction by relating an incident from your own experience when you dealt with the issue at hand.

- Remember that your audience is familiar with the selection, so don't spend a lot of time summarizing the plot. Get right to the heart of the issue and stay there.

- Be sure you state comparisons and contrasts clearly. See the Revising Strategy in Step 3 of this lesson.

STEP ## 3 REVISING

Ask a partner for comments on your draft before you revise it.

✔ Have I used specific examples to illustrate each point of view?

✔ Have I concluded with a summary of the merits of each point of view and an explanation of which one I favor and why?

✔ Do I state comparisons and contrasts clearly?

Revising Strategy

Signalling Comparisons and Contrasts

When you look over your draft, look for words and phrases like the ones listed below. You can use them to signal similarities (comparisons) and differences (contrasts) between the two points of view. Use them to make it easier for your readers to follow your train of thought.

Comparison Words	Contrast Words
like, likewise, just as, as, also, both, similarly, in the same way, as well, compared with	unlike, however, otherwise, although, but, yet, still, on the other hand, in contrast, even though

Notice how the writer of the student model has added a comparison-contrast signal during revision.

In this story the investigator represents what a police officer should be like in today's society. He is a strict, hard core, "don't mess with me" type of guy. He will obey the law and make sure that the law is obeyed. *On the other hand,* The deputy marshal represents a humanitarian officer. He is an officer who cares about the law but *also* cares about the well being of the criminals more.

STUDENT MODEL

4 EDITING

Ask a partner to review your revised draft before you edit. When you edit, look for errors in grammar, usage, spelling, and mechanics. Look closely for errors in punctuating quotations from literature.

Editing Strategy

FOR REFERENCE
More information about punctuating literary quotations can be found in the Language and Grammar Handbook in the back of this text.

Punctuating Quotations from Literature

The way you punctuate a quotation depends on the length of the quoted material. For short quotations (less than 4 lines of prose or 3 lines of poetry), enclose the quoted material in quotation marks and run it in. For longer quotations, instead of using quotation marks, set the quoted material off by indenting it from the left margin:

The narrator drives home his view of the wall as a

barrier in the following passage:

    And on a day we meet to walk the line

    And set the wall between us once again.

    We keep the wall between us as we go.

    To each the boulders that have fallen to each.

COMPUTER TIP
Many word processors allow you to indent text by changing the margins for individual paragraphs without using tabs. Consult your manual to find out how.

STEP 5 PRESENTING

- Find other classmates who wrote about the same selection as you. Read your essays aloud and discuss your points of view.

- Design a bumper sticker that promotes the point of view you favor.

STEP 6 LOOKING BACK

Self-evaluate. Look back at the Writer's Blueprint and give yourself a score for each item, from 6 (superior) to 1 (inadequate).

Reflect. Write about how your own point of view did or did not change during the writing of this essay.

For Your Working Portfolio Add your comparison/contrast essay and your reflection responses to your working portfolio.

Beyond Print

Propaganda

What do you think of when you hear the term *propaganda?* Propaganda is a systematic effort to spread opinions or beliefs. Often people have negative associations with the word *propaganda,* but it is really just a tool with which to convince or motivate people, and can be used for both good causes and bad.

The trouble with propaganda is that it often distorts reality. It may take very complex issues and oversimplify them, dividing them into categories of good and evil. It also tends to exploit people's emotions and insecurities, for instance, making people feel threatened when they may not be in real danger, or making them feel they are lacking something and need to buy a certain product to make up for it.

Propaganda surrounds you every day. It is your job to be able to analyze the message the propaganda is attempting to deliver, then choose whether or not you agree. Start by analyzing the World War II poster on the facing page.

Analyzing the Poster

Initial Response What is your first reaction to the poster? What feelings do you associate with the images? Are they positive, negative, or both?

Analyzing the Figures The two hands represent the United States' two major enemies during World War II. The hand in the upper right has Nazi Germany's swastika symbol on it, and the one on the bottom left has a sun, a symbol Japan uses on its flag. What do the portrayal of the two hands say about the two countries and their intentions?

Whom would you say the mother and baby are supposed to be? What qualities do they portray? What do their facial expressions suggest? Looking at the figures symbolically, what do you think the hands symbolize? What might the woman and baby symbolize?

Analyzing the Message What is this poster telling its viewers? Victory bonds were bonds individuals could buy to help fund the war effort. What does the poster suggest will happen if the viewers do *not* buy victory bonds?

Evaluating the Propaganda In what ways does the poster reflect reality? distort reality? Do you agree with the poster's message? Is it furthering a worthy cause? Explain.

Activity Option

Today's Propaganda Today's world is filled with propaganda—on television, radio, billboards, pamphlets, books, even on the Internet. It comes in the form of advertisements, political materials, public service announcements, and so on. Choose a piece of propaganda to analyze for your classmates. Tell your initial response, what is going on in the piece, what the message is, and your opinion of the effectiveness and worth of the message.

Multicultural Connections

Perspective

Part One: Lost in a Crowd J. Alfred Prufrock attends a tea-party, but from his perspective it almost seems more like an ordeal than an enjoyable social event. From the perspective of those around him Richard Cory has all that life has to offer, yet in the end it's clear that he has miseries others cannot see. Granny Weatherall's perspective drifts in and out of reality as her death approaches.

■ Which of the selections in this section provide the most interesting perspective, or way of looking at things? Explain your choice.

Communication

Part Two: The Strength of Tradition The way individuals communicate depends a great deal on their cultural background. The narrator and the neighbor in Frost's "Mending Wall" communicate over a wall. The McCallums in "The Tall Men" communicate as much through glances and gestures as through words. When Thomas Whitecloud returns to his home in Wisconsin, he notices his community's habit of communicating welcome and acceptance without words. The differences in communication styles between the two women and their guests provide humor in *Lord Byron's Love Letter.*

■ What are the greatest obstacles to communication in this section, and how are these obstacles overcome?

Activities

Work in small groups on the following activities.

1. Often two people can have very different impressions of the same thing. For instance, to someone who likes thrills, riding a roller-coaster could be a great time, whereas to someone who is afraid of heights, it could be a nightmare. In your group, think of times when a difference in perspectives led to a misunderstanding. Choose one of the situations to dramatize.

2. Society has rules and customs about how to communicate when on the phone, in a library, online, writing a letter, in a movie theater, talking to an authority figure, to a baby, and so on. Make a list of as many situations as you can think of that call for a particular style of communication. Compare lists with the rest of your class.

Independent and Group Projects

Writing

Disillusionment When someone or something has not lived up to our expectations, this can cause disillusionment. Look back over the selections by T. S. Eliot, Edwin Arlington Robinson, Ernest Hemingway, and F. Scott Fitzgerald. Why are the characters they have created disillusioned? In an essay, compare and contrast how each author has treated this theme.

Entertainment

Literary Pursuits In this unit you have been introduced to some of the most famous American writers of the twentieth century. Use your knowledge of the writers and the literature presented in this unit to create a "Literary Pursuits" game. Create categories that you would like to develop like "Expatriate Writers," "Regional Writers," "Memorable Characters," "Famous Lines," and so on. Then write ten questions for each category, each question on a separate index card. Make up rules of play for the game, and play it in class.

Geography

Mapping the Literary Scene Make a literary map showing the areas of the United States that the writers in this unit described. Begin by tracing a U.S. map, then highlight the states, cities, and locales that the authors wrote about. Make feature boxes on the margin of the map that describe each author and the memorable regional characters that he or she wrote about. Alternatively, you can use software to create the literary map and author/region cards.

Drama

Be the Writer Hal Holbrook, a well-known actor, has toured the country performing as writer Mark Twain. Choose one of the writers in this unit that you would like to become and create a monologue to present to the class. As part of the production, create a costume, set a scene, and provide appropriate background music. Your monologue should include autobiographical information as well as a discussion of the stories or poetry you have written. As a finale, read a favorite passage from one of your writer's stories or poems.

Years of Change

Person to Person
Part One, pages 716–789

In the Midst of Struggle . . .
Part Two, pages 790–859

POSTWAR CULTURE

HISTORICAL OVERVIEW

In the 15 years following World War II, America experienced huge changes. A postwar baby boom created the future audience for the youth culture of the 1950s and '60s. The landscape was altered by interstate highways, suburban subdivisions, drive-in theaters, and shopping malls. Television changed the way Americans entertained themselves, and eventually how they saw themselves and the world. The increasing dominance of the American economy by large corporations created affluence but also left many workers feeling anonymous and powerless. There was a pervasive feeling of complacency, symbolized by the comfortable families seen on television, but also an under-current of revolt that appeared in Beatnik literature, movies about teenage rebels, and rock 'n' roll.

SPUTNIK I

When the Soviets beat the United States into space by launching a satellite in 1957, Americans criticized the direction of the U.S. economy and the quality of American education.

JACKIE ROBINSON

Baseball finally lived up to its nickname of "the national pastime" in 1947 when Jackie Robinson became the first African American to play in the major leagues.

JACK KEROUAC

Beatnik writer Jack Kerouac celebrated nonconformity and criticized the consumer culture of the 1950s in novels like *On the Road*.

OZZIE AND HARRIET

Serious family problems were remote from the comfortable, suburban version of domestic life presented in the 1950s by TV situation comedies like *Ozzie and Harriet.*

ELVIS PRESLEY

In the mid–1950s, rock 'n' roll music became a craze as teenagers went wild for such stars as Elvis Presley, whose recording of "Heartbreak Hotel" became the best-selling record in America in 1956.

MARILYN MONROE

With the feminist movement of the 1960s still in the future, the most visible image of women in the postwar period remained glamorous Hollywood stars like Marilyn Monroe.

Key Dates

1947
Major league baseball is racially integrated.

1952
Eisenhower is elected President.

1953
Two out of three American homes have television.

1955
"Rock Around the Clock" is the first rock 'n' roll hit.

1956
Congress approves interstate highway system.

1957
Kerouac's On the Road *is published; Soviet Union launches* Sputnik I.

1960
Presidential campaign debates between candidates John F. Kennedy and Richard M. Nixon are televised.

Part One

Person to Person

The way Americans relate with one another—among family members, friends, acquaintances, and even the way we relate to ourselves—has long been a source of inspiration for American writers. The following selections each provide insights into different kinds of person-to-person relationships.

Multicultural Connection Our cultural heritage—including our family, community, and customs—can affect our **interactions** with others. In which of the following selections do cultural factors enhance the person-to-person interactions, and in which do they seem to inhibit or complicate interactions?

Literature

Flannery O'Connor	The Life You Save May Be Your Own	
	◆ short story	720
Tillie Olsen	I Stand Here Ironing ◆ short story	732
John Updike	Separating ◆ short story	742
Maxine Hong Kingston	*from* The Woman Warrior	
	◆ essay	754
Alice Walker	Everyday Use ◆ short story	760
Sylvia Plath	Mirror ◆ poem	771
Elizabeth Bishop	One Art ◆ poem	772
Nikki Giovanni	Legacies ◆ poem	773
Sam Hamod	Leaves ◆ poem	774
Alma Luz Villanueva	To Jesus Villanueva, with Love ◆ poem	775

Interdisciplinary Study Television Comes of Age

Life After Television by John Brooks ◆ pop culture 779
What's on TV? ◆ pop culture 781

Writing Workshop Persuasive Writing

You Be the Judge 784

Beyond Print Media Literacy

Looking at Television 789

Before Reading

The Life You Save May Be Your Own

by Flannery O'Connor

Flannery O'Connor
1925–1964

Flannery O'Connor once said, "Whenever I'm asked why Southern writers particularly have a penchant for writing about freaks, I say it is because we are still able to recognize one." O'Connor was born in Savannah, Georgia. Educated in convent schools, her religious upbringing had a profound impact on her writing, and the theme of salvation is explored throughout her works. O'Connor attended Georgia State College for Women and the State University of Iowa. Her first novel and most famous single work, *Wise Blood,* was published in 1952. She won a National Book Award in 1972 for *The Complete Stories.* In 1950, O'Connor was diagnosed with lupus. She died at the age of thirty-nine.

Building Background

Who Is Being Saved? ". . . she could tell, even from a distance, that he was a tramp and no one to be afraid of." That is Mrs. Lucynell Crater's first impression of Mr. Shiftlet as he approaches her home. But things are not what they seem in O'Connor's stories, which often contain deep psychological complexities. Critic C. Hugh Holman wrote that "Flannery O'Connor's world is the world of people rendered grotesque by their inability to satisfy their spiritual hungers." As you read "The Life You Save May Be Your Own," make some inferences about the characters and their motives. Is Mr. Shiftlet a complex character, or is he entirely predictable? Is Mrs. Crater shrewd or naive?

Literary Focus

Diction Flannery O'Connor's fiction is distinguished by her careful choice of words. Consider Mr. Shiftlet's name, for example. The name sounds almost like the word *shiftless.* What clue might this give you about his character? This thoughtful choice of words and phrases, which considers both the connotative and denotative meanings of words as well as levels of usage, is called **diction.**

Writer's Notebook

Good and Evil Much of literature through the ages deals with the conflict between good and evil. The Biblical accounts of Adam and Eve and the serpent and of Cain's murder of Abel are just the beginning. In your writer's notebook, write examples of stories, novels, movies, television shows, and even video games that you have read, seen, or played that deal with good versus evil. Explain how good and evil are portrayed in these examples.

THE LIFE YOU SAVE MAY BE YOUR OWN

Flannery O'Connor

The old woman and her daughter were sitting on their porch when Mr. Shiftlet came up their road for the first time. The old woman slid to the edge of her chair and leaned forward, shading her eyes from the piercing sunset with her hand. The daughter could not see far in front of her and continued to play with her fingers. Although the old woman lived in this desolate[1] spot with only her daughter and she had never seen Mr. Shiftlet before, she could tell, even from a distance, that he was a tramp and no one to be afraid of. His left coat sleeve was folded up to show that there was only half an arm in it and his gaunt[2] figure listed slightly to the side as if the breeze were pushing him. He had on a black town suit and a brown felt hat that was turned up in the front and down in the back and he carried a tin tool box by a handle. He came on, at an amble, up her road, his face turned toward the sun which appeared to be balancing itself on the peak of a small mountain.

The old woman didn't change her position until he was almost into her yard; then she rose with one hand fisted on her hip. The daughter, a large girl in a short blue organdy dress, saw him all at once and jumped up and began to stamp and point and make excited speechless sounds.

Mr. Shiftlet stopped just inside the yard and set his box on the ground and tipped his hat at her as if she were not in the least afflicted; then he turned toward the old woman and swung the hat all the way off. He had long black slick hair that hung flat from a part in the middle to beyond the tips of his ears on either side. His face descended in forehead for more than half its length and ended suddenly with his features just balanced over a jutting steel-trap jaw. He seemed to be a young man but he had a look of

1. **desolate** (des′ə lit), *adj.* deserted.
2. **gaunt** (gônt), *adj.* very thin and bony.

composed dissatisfaction as if he understood life thoroughly.

"Good evening," the old woman said. She was about the size of a cedar fence post and she had a man's gray hat pulled down low over her head.

The tramp stood looking at her and didn't answer. He turned his back and faced the sunset. He swung both his whole and his short arm up slowly so that they indicated an expanse of sky and his figure formed a crooked cross. The old woman watched him with her arms folded across her chest as if she were the owner of the sun, and the daughter watched, her head thrust forward and her fat helpless hands hanging at the wrists. She had long pink-gold hair and eyes as blue as a peacock's neck.

He held the pose for almost fifty seconds and then he picked up his box and came on to the porch and dropped down on the bottom step. "Lady," he said in a firm nasal voice, "I'd give a fortune to live where I could see me a sun do that every evening."

"Does it every evening," the old woman said and sat back down. The daughter sat down too and watched him with a cautious sly look as if he were a bird that had come up very close. He leaned to one side, rooting in his pants pocket, and in a second he brought out a package of chewing gum and offered her a piece. She took it and unpeeled it and began to chew without taking her eyes off him. He offered the old woman a piece but she only raised her upper lip to indicate she had no teeth.

M̲r. Shiftlet's pale sharp glance had already passed over everything in the yard—the pump near the corner of the house and the big fig tree that three or four chickens were preparing to roost in—and had moved to a shed where he saw the square rusted back of an automobile. "You ladies drive?" he asked.

"That car ain't run in fifteen years," the old woman said. "The day my husband died, it quit running."

"Nothing is like it used to be, lady," he said. "The world is almost rotten."

"That's right," the old woman said. "You from around here?"

"Name Tom T. Shiftlet," he murmured, looking at the tires.

"I'm pleased to meet you," the old woman said. "Name Lucynell Crater and daughter Lucynell Crater. What you doing around here, Mr. Shiftlet?"

He judged the car to be about a 1928 or '29 Ford. "Lady," he said, and turned and gave her his full attention, "lemme tell you something. There's one of these doctors in Atlanta that's taken a knife and cut the human heart—the human heart," he repeated, leaning forward, "out of a man's chest and held it in his hand," and he held his hand out, palm up, as if it were slightly weighted with the human heart, "and

studied it like it was a day-old chicken, and, lady," he said, allowing a long significant pause in which his head slid forward and his clay-colored eyes brightened, "he don't know no more about it than you or me."

"That's right," the old woman said.

"Why, if he was to take that knife and cut into every corner of it, he still wouldn't know no more than you or me. What you want to bet?"

"Nothing," the old woman said wisely. "Where you come from, Mr. Shiftlet?"

He didn't answer. He reached into his pocket and brought out a sack of tobacco and a package of cigarette papers and rolled himself a cigarette, expertly with one hand, and attached it in a hanging position to his upper lip. Then he took a box of wooden matches from his pocket and struck one on his shoe. He held the burning match as if he were studying the mystery of flame while it traveled dangerously toward his skin. The daughter began to make loud noises and to point to his hand and shake her finger at him, but when the flame was just before touching him, he leaned down with his hand cupped over it as if he were going to set fire to his nose and lit the cigarette.

He flipped away the dead match and blew a stream of gray into the evening. A sly look came over his face. "Lady," he said, "nowadays, people'll do anything anyways. I can tell you my name is Tom T. Shiftlet and I come from Tarwater, Tennessee, but you never have seen me before: how you know I ain't lying? How you know my name ain't Aaron Sparks, lady, and I come from Singleberry, Georgia, or how you know it's not George Speeds and I come from Lucy, Alabama, or how you know I ain't Thompson Bright from Toolafalls, Mississippi?"

"I don't know nothing about you," the old woman muttered, irked.[3]

"Lady," he said, "people don't care how they lie. Maybe the best I can tell you is, I'm a man; but listen, lady," he said and paused and made

---

3. **irked** (ėrkd), *adj.* disgusted, annoyed.

his tone more ominous still, "what is a man?"

The old woman began to gum a seed. "What you carry in that tin box, Mr. Shiftlet?" she asked.

"Tools," he said, put back. "I'm a carpenter."

"Well, if you come out here to work, I'll be able to feed you and give you a place to sleep but I can't pay. I'll tell you that before you begin," she said.

There was no answer at once and no particular expression on his face. He leaned back against the two-by-four that helped support the porch roof. "Lady," he said slowly, "there's some men that some things mean more to them than money." The old woman rocked without comment, and the daughter watched the trigger that moved up and down in his neck. He told the old woman then that all most people were interested in was money, but he asked what a man was made for. He asked her if a man was made for money, or what. He asked her what she thought she was made for but she didn't answer, she only sat rocking and wondered if a one-armed man could put a new roof on her garden house. He asked a lot of questions that she didn't answer. He told her that he was twenty-eight years old and had lived a varied life. He had been a gospel singer, a foreman on the railroad, an assistant in an undertaking parlor, and he had come over the radio for three months with Uncle Roy and his Red Creek Wranglers. He said he had fought and bled in the Arm Service of his country and visited every foreign land and that everywhere he had seen people that didn't care if they did a thing one way or another. He said he hadn't been raised thataway.

A fat yellow moon appeared on the branches of the fig tree as if it were going to roost there with the chickens. He said that a man had to escape to the country to see the world whole and that he wished he lived in a desolate place like this where he could see the sun go down every evening like God made it to do.

"Are you married or are you single?" the old woman asked.

There was a long silence. "Lady," he asked finally, "where would you find you an innocent woman today? I wouldn't have any of this trash I could just pick up."

The daughter was leaning very far down, hanging her head almost between her knees, watching him through a triangular door she had made in her overturned hair; and she suddenly fell in a heap on the floor and began to whimper. Mr. Shiftlet straightened her out and helped her get back in the chair.

"Is she your baby girl?" he asked.

"My only," the old woman said, "and she's the sweetest girl in the world. I wouldn't give her up for nothing on earth. She's smart too. She can sweep the floor, cook, wash, feed the chickens, and hoe. I wouldn't give her up for a casket of jewels."

"No," he said kindly, "don't ever let any man take her away from you."

"Any man come after her," the old woman said, "'ll have to stay around the place."

Mr. Shiftlet's eye in the darkness was focused on a part of the automobile bumper that glittered in the distance. "Lady," he said, jerking his short arm up as if he could point with it to her house and yard and pump, "there ain't a broken thing on this plantation that I couldn't fix for you, one-arm jackleg or not. I'm a man," he said with a sullen[4] dignity, "even if I ain't a whole one. I got," he said, tapping his knuckles on the floor to emphasize the immensity of what he was going to say, "a moral intelligence!" and his face pierced out of the darkness into a shaft of doorlight and he stared at her as if he were astonished himself at this impossible truth.

The old woman was not impressed with the phrase. "I told you you could hang around and

> . . . there's some men that some things mean more to them than money.

---

4. **sullen** (sul′ən), *adj.* showing resentment; somber.

work for food," she said, "if you don't mind sleeping in that car yonder."

"Why listen, Lady," he said with a grin of delight, "the monks of old slept in their coffins!"

"They wasn't as advanced as we are," the old woman said.

EVALUATE: Based on their conversations, what do you think Mrs. Crater wants from Mr. Shiftlet? What do you think Mr. Shiftlet wants from Mrs. Crater?

The next morning he began on the roof of the garden house while Lucynell, the daughter, sat on a rock and watched him work. He had not been around a week before the change he had made in the place was apparent. He had patched the front and back steps, built a new hog pen, restored a fence, and taught Lucynell, who was completely deaf and had never said a word in her life, to say the word *bird*. The big rosy-faced girl followed him everywhere, saying "Burrttddt ddbirrrttdt," and clapping her hands. The old woman watched from a distance, secretly pleased. She was ravenous[5] for a son-in-law.

Mr. Shiftlet slept on the hard narrow back seat of the car with his feet out the side window. He had his razor and a can of water on a crate that served him as a bedside table and he put up a piece of mirror against the back glass and kept his coat neatly on a hanger that he hung over one of the windows.

In the evenings he sat on the steps and talked while the old woman and Lucynell rocked violently in their chairs on either side of him. The old woman's three mountains were black against the dark blue sky and were visited off and on by various planets and by the moon after it had left the chickens. Mr. Shiftlet pointed out that the reason he had improved this plantation was because he had taken a personal interest in it. He said he was even going to make the automobile run.

He had raised the hood and studied the mechanism and he said he could tell that the car had been built in the days when cars were really built. You take now, he said, one man puts in one bolt and another man puts in another bolt and another man puts in another bolt so that it's a man for a bolt. That's why you have to pay so much for a car: you're paying all those men. Now if you didn't have to pay for but one man, you could get you a cheaper car and one that had had a personal interest taken in it, and it would be a better car. The old woman agreed with him that this was so.

Mr. Shiftlet said that the trouble with the world was that nobody cared, or stopped and took any trouble. He said he never would have been able to teach Lucynell to say a word if he hadn't cared and stopped long enough.

"Teach her to say something else," the old woman said.

"What you want her to say next?" Mr. Shiftlet asked.

The old woman's smile was broad and toothless and suggestive. "Teach her to say 'sugarpie,' " she said.

Mr. Shiftlet already knew what was on her mind.

CLARIFY: What is on Mrs. Crater's mind?

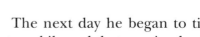

The next day he began to tinker with the automobile and that evening he told her that if she would buy a fan belt, he would be able to make the car run.

The old woman said she would give him the money. "You see that girl yonder?" she asked, pointing to Lucynell who was sitting on the floor a foot away, watching him, her eyes blue even in the dark. "If it was ever a man wanted to take her away, I would say, 'No man on earth is going to take that sweet girl of mine away from me!' but if he was to say, 'Lady, I don't want to take her away, I want her right here,' I would say, 'Mister, I don't blame you none. I wouldn't pass

_____

5. **ravenous** (rav′ə nəs), *adj.* very hungry; greedy.

▲ Does the setting in Aaron Bohrod's painting, *Landscape Near Chicago* (1934), remind you of Mrs. Crater's place? Why or why not?

up a chance to live in a permanent place and get the sweetest girl in the world myself. You ain't no fool,' I would say."

"How old is she?" Mr. Shiftlet asked casually.

"Fifteen, sixteen," the old woman said. The girl was nearly thirty but because of her innocence it was impossible to guess.

"It would be a good idea to paint it too," Mr. Shiftlet remarked. "You don't want it to rust out."

"We'll see about that later," the old woman said.

The next day he walked into town and returned with the parts he needed and a can of gasoline. Late in the afternoon, terrible noises issued from the shed and the old woman rushed out of the house, thinking Lucynell was somewhere having a fit. Lucynell was sitting on a chicken crate, stamping her feet and screaming, "Burrrddttt! bddurrddtttt!" but her fuss was drowned out by the car. With a volley of blasts it emerged from the shed, moving in a fierce and stately[6] way. Mr. Shiftlet was in the driver's seat, sitting very erect. He had an expression of serious modesty on his face as if he had just raised the dead.

That night, rocking on the porch, the old

6. stately (stāt′lē), *adj.* having dignity; imposing; majestic.

woman began her business at once. "You want you an innocent woman, don't you?" she asked sympathetically. "You don't want none of this trash."

"No'm, I don't," Mr. Shiftlet said.

"One that can't talk," she continued, "can't sass you back or use foul language. That's the kind for you to have. Right there," and she pointed to Lucynell sitting cross-legged in her chair, holding both feet in her hands.

"That's right," he admitted. "She wouldn't give me any trouble."

"Saturday," the old woman said, "you and her and me can drive into town and get married."

Mr. Shiftlet eased his position on the steps.

"I can't get married right now," he said. "Everything you want to do takes money and I ain't got any."

"What you need with money?" she asked.

"It takes money," he said. "Some people'll do anything anyhow these days, but the way I think, I wouldn't marry no woman that I couldn't take on a trip like she was somebody. I mean take her to a hotel and treat her. I wouldn't marry the Duchesser Windsor,[7] he said firmly, "unless I could take her to a hotel and give her something good to eat.

"I was raised thataway and there ain't a thing I can do about it. My old mother taught me how to do."

"Lucynell don't even know what a hotel is," the old woman muttered. "Listen here, Mr. Shiftlet," she said, sliding forward in her chair, "you'd be getting a permanent house and a deep well and the most innocent girl in the world. You don't need no money. Lemme tell you something: there ain't any place in the world for a poor disabled friendless drifting man."

The ugly words settled in Mr. Shiftlet's head like a group of buzzards in the top of a tree. He didn't answer at once. He rolled himself a cigarette and lit it and then he said in an even voice, "Lady, a man is divided into two parts, body and spirit."

> . . . the spirit, lady, is like a automobile: always on the move, always. . . .

The old woman clamped her gums together.

"A body and a spirit," he repeated. "The body, lady, is like a house: it don't go anywhere; but the spirit, lady, is like a automobile: always on the move, always. . . ."

"Listen, Mr. Shiftlet," she said, "my well never goes dry and my house is always warm in the winter and there's no mortgage on a thing about this place. You can go to the courthouse and see for yourself. And yonder under that shed is a fine automobile." She laid the bait carefully. "You can have it painted by Saturday. I'll pay for the paint."

In the darkness, Mr. Shiftlet's smile stretched like a weary snake waking up by a fire. After a second he recalled himself and said, "I'm only saying a man's spirit means more to him than anything else. I would have to take my wife off for the weekend without no regards at all for cost. I got to follow where my spirit says to go."

"I'll give you fifteen dollars for a weekend trip," the old woman said in a crabbed voice. "That's the best I can do."

"That wouldn't hardly pay for more than the gas and the hotel," he said. "It wouldn't feed her."

"Seventeen-fifty," the old woman said. "That's all I got so it isn't any use you trying to milk me. You can take a lunch."

Mr. Shiftlet was deeply hurt by the word *milk*. He didn't doubt that she had more money sewed up in her mattress, but he had already told her he was not interested in her money. "I'll make that do," he said and rose and walked off without treating with her further.

On Saturday the three of them drove into town in the car that the paint had barely dried on and Mr. Shiftlet and Lucynell were married

---

7. **Duchesser Windsor.** The Duchess of Windsor was a member of the British royal family.

in the Ordinary's office while the old woman witnessed. As they came out of the courthouse, Mr. Shiftlet began twisting his neck in his collar. He looked morose[8] and bitter as if he had been insulted while someone held him. "That didn't satisfy me none," he said. "That was just something a woman in an office did, nothing but paper and blood tests. What do they know about my blood? If they was to take my heart and cut it out," he said, "they wouldn't know a thing about me. It didn't satisfy me at all."

"It satisfied the law," the old woman said sharply.

"The law," Mr. Shiftlet said and spit. "It's the law that don't satisfy me."

He had painted the car dark green with a yellow band around it just under the windows. The three of them climbed in the front seat and the old woman said, "Don't Lucynell look pretty? Looks like a baby doll." Lucynell was dressed up in a white dress that her mother had uprooted from a trunk and there was a Panama hat on her head with a bunch of red wooden cherries on the brim. Every now and then her placid[9] expression was changed by a sly isolated little thought like a shoot of green in the desert. "You got a prize!" the old woman said.

Mr. Shiftlet didn't even look at her.

They drove back to the house to let the old woman off and pick up the lunch. When they were ready to leave, she stood staring at the window of the car, with her fingers clenched around the glass. Tears began to seep sideways out of her eyes and run along the dirty creases in her face. "I ain't ever been parted with her for two days before," she said.

Mr. Shiftlet started the motor.

"And I wouldn't let no man have her but you because I seen you would do right. Goodby, Sugarbaby," she said, clutching at the sleeve of the white dress. Lucynell looked straight at her and didn't seem to see her there at all. Mr. Shiftlet eased the car forward so that she had to move her hands.

SUMMARIZE: How would you describe the change that has come over Mr. Shiftlet?

The early afternoon was clear and open and surrounded by pale blue sky. Although the car would go only thirty miles an hour, Mr. Shiftlet imagined a terrific climb and dip and swerve that went entirely to his head so that he forgot his morning bitterness. He had always wanted an automobile but he had never been able to afford one before. He drove very fast because he wanted to make Mobile by nightfall.

Occasionally he stopped his thought long enough to look at Lucynell in the seat beside him. She had eaten the lunch as soon as they were out of the yard and now she was pulling the cherries off the hat one by one and throwing them out the window. He became depressed in spite of the car. He had driven about a hundred miles when he decided that she must be hungry again and at the next small town they came to, he stopped in front of an aluminum-painted eating place called The Hot Spot and took her in and ordered her a plate of ham and grits. The ride had made her sleepy and as soon as she got up on the stool, she rested her head on the counter and shut her eyes. There was no one in The Hot Spot but Mr. Shiftlet and the boy behind the counter, a pale youth with a greasy rag hung over his shoulder. Before he could dish up the food, she was snoring gently.

"Give it to her when she wakes up," Mr. Shiftlet said. "I'll pay for it now."

The boy bent over her and stared at the long pink-gold hair and the half-shut sleeping eyes. Then he looked up and stared at Mr. Shiftlet. "She looks like an angel of Gawd," he murmured. "Hitchhiker," Mr. Shiftlet explained. "I can't wait. I got to make Tuscaloosa."

The boy bent over again and very carefully

---

8. morose (mə rōs′), *adj.* gloomy; sullen; ill-humored.
9. placid (plas′id), *adj.* pleasantly calm or peaceful.

touched his finger to a strand of the golden hair and Mr. Shiftlet left.

He was more depressed than ever as he drove on by himself. The late afternoon had grown hot and sultry[10] and the country had flattened out. Deep in the sky a storm was preparing very slowly and without thunder as if it meant to drain every drop of air from the earth before it broke. There were times when Mr. Shiftlet preferred not to be alone. He felt too that a man with a car had a responsibility to others and he kept his eye out for a hitchhiker. Occasionally he saw a sign that warned: "Drive carefully. The life you save may be your own."

The narrow road dropped off on either side into dry fields and here and there a shack or a filling station stood in a clearing. The sun began to set directly in front of the automobile. It was a reddening ball that through his windshield was slightly flat on the bottom and top. He saw a boy in overalls and a gray hat standing on the edge of the road and he slowed the car down and stopped in front of him. The boy didn't have his hand raised to thumb the ride, he was only standing there, but he had a small cardboard suitcase and his hat was set on his head in a way to indicate that he had left somewhere for good. "Son," Mr. Shiftlet said, "I see you want a ride."

The boy didn't say he did or he didn't but he opened the door of the car and got in, and Mr. Shiftlet started driving again. The child held the suitcase on his lap and folded his arms on top of it. He turned his head and looked out the window away from Mr. Shiftlet. Mr. Shiftlet felt oppressed. "Son," he said after a minute, "I got the best old mother in the world so I reckon you only got the second best."

The boy gave him a quick dark glance and then turned his face back to the window.

"It's nothing so sweet," Mr. Shiftlet continued, "as a boy's mother. She taught him his first prayers at her knee, she gave him love when no other would, she told him what was right and what wasn't, and she seen that he done the right thing. Son," he said, "I never rued[11] a day in my life like the one I rued when I left that old mother of mine."

The boy shifted in his seat but he didn't look at Mr. Shiftlet. He unfolded his arms and put one hand on the door handle.

"My mother was a angel of Gawd," Mr. Shiftlet said in a very strained voice. "He took her from heaven and giver to me and I left her." His eyes were instantly clouded over with a mist of tears. The car was barely moving.

The boy turned angrily in the seat. "You go to the devil!" he cried. "My old woman is a flea bag and yours is a stinking polecat!" and with that he flung the door open and jumped out with his suitcase into the ditch.

Mr. Shiftlet was so shocked that for about a hundred feet he drove along slowly with the door still open. A cloud, the exact color of the boy's hat and shaped like a turnip, had descended over the sun, and another, worse looking, crouched behind the car. Mr. Shiftlet felt that the rottenness of the world was about to engulf him. He raised his arm and let it fall again to his breast. "Oh Lord!" he prayed. "Break forth and wash the slime from this earth!"

The turnip continued slowly to descend. After a few minutes there was a guffawing peal of thunder from behind, and fantastic raindrops, like tin can tops, crashed over the rear of Mr. Shiftlet's car. Very quickly he stepped on the gas and with his stump sticking out the window he raced the galloping shower into Mobile.

---

10. **sultry** (sul′trē), *adj.* hot, close, and moist.
11. **rue** (rü), *v.* to feel regret or remorse.

Making Connections

Shaping Your Response

1. Where would you place Lucynell, Mrs. Crater, and Mr. Shiftlet on this continuum of good and evil? Explain your choices.

```
good                                              evil
```

2. In your opinion, whose life is referred to in the title of the story?

Analyzing the Story

3. How would you describe Mrs. Crater's attitude toward her daughter?

4. What is Mr. Shiftlet's main goal in the story? List details and **figurative language** that reveal his goal.

5. What is Mrs. Crater's main goal? Cite instances in which she tries to achieve that goal.

6. Select two or three passages from the story that you feel are especially effective in contributing to the **mood** of the selection. Consider the **imagery,** details and description, **setting,** evocative phrases, and anything else that Flannery O'Connor uses to create the atmosphere and feeling of the story. Explain the significance of your chosen passages.

7. How can you reconcile the content of Mr. Shiftlet's prayer at the end of the story with his abandonment of Lucynell?

8. In general, how would you describe the **interactions** between Mrs. Crater and Mr. Shiftlet?

Extending the Ideas

9. Rather than marriage to Mr. Shiftlet, what would you propose as an alternative plan for Lucynell's future?

Literary Focus: Diction

Diction, the author's choice of words and phrases, helps to develop the character of Mr. Shiftlet and of Mrs. Crater. Mr. Shiftlet likes to impress people with his talk. For example, he explains that he fought and bled in the "Arm Service" of his country, a play on words that calls to mind his missing arm. Mrs. Crater is less subtle in her attempts to snare Mr. Shiftlet for her daughter. "Are you married or are you single?" she asks. Find other examples of diction in the story that help characterize Mr. Shiftlet and Mrs. Crater.

Vocabulary Study

Match each vocabulary word from the first column with an antonym from the second column. Use the Glossary or a dictionary for help. You will use one answer twice.

desolate
gaunt
irked
morose
placid
ravenous
rue
stately
sullen
sultry

1. placid
2. sullen
3. gaunt
4. desolate
5. sultry
6. irked
7. rue
8. ravenous
9. morose
10. stately

a. pleased
b. satiated
c. appreciate
d. chilly
e. populous
f. frantic
g. stout
h. undignified
i. cheerful

Expressing Your Ideas

Writing Choices

Writer's Notebook Update Is Mr. Shiftlet evil? Mrs. Crater? You listed literature, movies, television shows, and video games that deal with the conflict of good versus evil. Do you want to add this story to the list? Write a paragraph explaining whether and how you think this story develops the conflict between good and evil.

Part Two Imagine Mrs. Crater's dismay when the new Mr. and Mrs. Shiftlet fail to return home from their honeymoon. Write a **continuation of the story** explaining what Mrs. Crater does next and what ultimately happens to Lucynell and Mr. Shiftlet.

Other Options

Wedding Portrait Mr. Shiftlet and Lucynell did not have wedding photographs taken. Imagine that you are a portrait artist. Make a **color drawing** of the bride and bridegroom on their wedding day. Under the pictures, write the quotes that guided you.

Sheriff's Report When Shiftlet and Lucynell did not return, Mrs. Crater probably reported the incident to the local sheriff. Work with a classmate to create a **dialogue** between Mrs. Crater and the sheriff, including an explanation about Lucynell, Mr. Shiftlet, and the wedding. Perform your dialogue for the class.

Before Reading

I Stand Here Ironing

by Tillie Olsen

Tillie Olsen
born 1913

Tillie Olsen began writing her first novel when she was nineteen, but put it aside after her marriage to Jack Olsen and the birth of their four daughters. For twenty years there was no time for writing. In addition to caring for her family, Olsen worked as a typist in San Francisco. She never lost her desire to write, however, and was able to begin writing again when she earned a creative writing fellowship to Stanford University in 1956. A Ford grant enabled her to quit her office job in 1959 and write full time. *Tell Me a Riddle,* which includes "I Stand Here Ironing," was published in 1961 when Olsen was forty-eight. Olsen has taught at Amherst, Stanford, MIT, and the University of Massachusetts.

Building Background

Doing the Best I Can Parenthood is often idealized in magazine ads and television shows: a beautiful, well-dressed, young woman cuddles a cherubic, smiling child in a beautifully furnished home. In the background, painting the baby's room, is the handsome, loving, attentive father. Reality is often very different. Interview your own or other parents about the difficulties and rewards of parenting. Work with a partner to develop questions to ask them. After the interviews are completed, discuss the parents' responses in class, and make a chart recording the most difficult and most rewarding parts of being a parent.

Parenthood	
Most Difficult	Most Rewarding

Literary Focus

Interior Monologue "I Stand Here Ironing" is told entirely through the narrator's thoughts, or stream of consciousness, as she reviews crucial events in her daughter Emily's life. One technique for presenting stream of consciousness is **interior monologue,** the recording of the emotional experiences of a character. The reader is made aware of the character's private thoughts, which are never spoken aloud. As you read "I Stand Here Ironing," decide whether this is an effective technique for the story.

Writer's Notebook

Childhood Memories Emily, the narrator's daughter, is a high school student. Before you begin reading her mother's reflections on Emily's childhood, talk to family members about your childhood. What do they remember about you at various ages? Write about some of these events in your notebook.

I STAND HERE IRONING

TILLIE OLSEN

I stand here ironing, and what you asked me moves tormented back and forth with the iron.

"I wish you could manage the time to come in and talk with me about your daughter. I'm sure you can help me understand her. She's a youngster who needs help and whom I'm deeply interested in helping."

"Who needs help." Even if I came, what good would it do? You think because I am her mother I have a key, or that in some way you could use me as a key? She has lived for nineteen years. There is all that life that has happened outside of me, beyond me.

CLARIFY: To whom do you think the narrator is responding?

And when is there time to remember, to sift, to weigh, to estimate, to total? I will start and there will be an interruption and I will have to gather it all together again. Or I will become engulfed with all I did or did not do, with what should have been and what cannot be helped.

She was a beautiful baby. The first and only one of our five that was beautiful at birth. You do not guess how new and uneasy her tenancy in her now-loveliness. You did not know her all those years she was thought homely,[1] or see her poring over her baby pictures, making me tell her over and over how beautiful she had been—and would be, I would tell her—and was now, to the seeing eye. But the seeing eyes were few or nonexistent. Including mine.

I nursed her. They feel that's important nowadays. I nursed all the children, but with her, with all the fierce rigidity of first motherhood, I did like the books then said. Though her cries battered me to trembling and my breasts ached with swollenness, I waited till the clock decreed.

Why do I put that first? I do not even know if it matters, or if it explains anything.

She was a beautiful baby. She blew shining bubbles of sound. She loved motion, loved light, loved color and music and textures. She would lie on the floor in her blue overalls, patting the surface so hard in ecstasy[2] her hands and feet would

---

1. **homely** (hōm′lē), *adj.* not good-looking; plain.
2. **ecstasy** (ek′stə sē), *n.* condition of very great joy; overwhelming delight.

▲ Does the mood of Edgar Degas's painting, *Woman Ironing* (1892), resemble that of the story? Explain.

blur. She was a miracle to me, but when she was eight months old, I had to leave her daytimes with the woman downstairs, to whom she was no miracle at all, for I worked or looked for work and for Emily's father, who "could no longer endure" (he wrote in his goodbye note) "sharing want with us."

I was nineteen. It was the pre-relief, pre-WPA[3] world of the depression. I would start running as soon as I got off the streetcar, running up the stairs, the place smelling sour, and awake or asleep to startle awake, when she saw me, she would break into a clogged weeping that could not be comforted, a weeping I can yet hear.

After a while I found a job hashing[4] at night so I could be with her days, and it was better. But it came to where I had to bring her to his family and leave her.

It took a long time to raise the money for her fare back. Then she got chicken pox, and I had to wait longer. When she finally came, I hardly knew her, walking quick and nervous like her father, looking like her father, thin, and dressed in a shoddy red that yellowed her skin and glared at the pockmarks. All the baby loveliness gone.

She was two. Old enough for nursery school they said, and I did not know then what I know now—the fatigue of the long day, and the lacerations of group life in the nurseries that are only parking places for children.

Except that it would have made no difference if I had known. It was the only place there was. It was the only way we could be together, the only way I could hold a job.

And even without knowing, I knew. I knew the teacher was evil because all these years it has curdled into my memory, the little boy hunched in the corner, her rasp, "Why aren't you outside, because Alvin hits you? That's no reason, go out, scaredy." I knew Emily hated it even if she did not clutch and implore[5] "Don't go, Mommy" like the other children, mornings.

She always had a reason why we should stay home. Momma, you look sick. Momma, I feel sick. Momma, the teachers aren't there today, they're sick. Momma, there was a fire there last night. Momma, it's a holiday today, no school, they told me.

But never a direct protest, never rebellion. I think of our others in their three-, four-year-oldness—the explosions, the tempers, the denunciations, the demands—and I feel suddenly ill. I put the iron down. What in me demanded that goodness in her? And what was the cost, the cost to her of such goodness?

The old man living in the back once said in his gentle way: "You should smile at Emily more when you look at her." What *was* in my face when I looked at her? I loved her. There were all the acts of love.

It was only with the others I remembered what he said, and it was the face of joy, and not of care or tightness or worry I turned to them— too late for Emily. She does not smile easily, let alone almost always as her brothers and sisters do. Her face is closed and somber,[6] but when she wants, how fluid. You must have seen it in her pantomimes; you spoke of her rare gift for comedy on the stage that rouses a laughter out of the audience so dear they applaud and applaud and do not want to let her go.

Where does it come from, that comedy? There was none of it in her when she came back to me that second time, after I had had to send her away again. She had a new daddy now to learn to love, and I think perhaps it was a better time.

CLARIFY: How did the narrator's life change at this point in time?

Except when we left her alone nights, telling ourselves she was old enough.

"Can't you go some other time, Mommy, like

---

3. **relief, WPA,** relief programs established to help the poor and unemployed during the Great Depression.
4. **hashing,** a slang term for waitressing.
5. implore (im plôr′), *v.* beg or pray earnestly for.
6. somber (som′bər), *adj.* melancholy; dismal.

tomorrow?" she would ask. "Will it be just a little while you'll be gone? Do you promise?"

The time we came back, the front door open, the clock on the floor in the hall. She rigid awake. "It wasn't just a little while. I didn't cry. Three times I called you, just three times, and then I ran downstairs to open the door so you could come faster. The clock talked loud. I threw it away; it scared me when it talked."

She said the clock talked loud again that night when I went to the hospital to have Susan. She was delirious with the fever that comes before red measles, but she was fully conscious all the week I was gone and the week after we were home, when she could not come near the new baby or me.

She did not get well. She stayed skeleton thin, not wanting to eat, and night after night she had nightmares. She would call for me, and I would rouse from exhaustion to sleepily call back, "You're all right, darling—go to sleep—it's just a dream" and if she still called, in a sterner voice, "now go to sleep Emily, there's nothing to hurt you." Twice, only twice, when I had to get up for Susan anyhow, I went in to sit with her.

Now, when it is too late (as if she would let me hold and comfort her like I do the others), I get up and go to her at once at her moan or restless stirring. "Are you awake, Emily? Can I get you something?" And the answer is always the same: "No, I'm all right, go back to sleep, Mother."

They persuaded me at the clinic to send her away to a convalescent home in the country where "she can have the kind of food and care you can't manage for her, and you'll be free to concentrate on the new baby." They still send children to that place. I see pictures on the society page of sleek young women planning affairs to raise money for it, or dancing at the affairs, or decorating Easter eggs or filling Christmas stockings for the children.

They never have a picture of the children, so I do not know if the girls still wear those gigantic red bows and the ravaged looks on the every other Sunday when parents can come to visit "unless otherwise notified"—as we were notified the first six weeks.

Oh, it is a handsome place, green lawns and tall trees and fluted flower beds. High up on the balconies of each cottage the children stand, the girls in their red bows and white dresses, the boys in white suits and giant red ties. The parents stand below shrieking up to be heard and the children shriek down to be heard, and between them the invisible wall "Not to Be Contaminated by Parental Germs or Physical Affection."

There was a tiny girl who always stood hand in hand with Emily. Her parents never came. One visit she was gone. "They moved her to Rose Cottage," Emily shouted in explanation. "They don't like you to love anybody here."

She wrote once a week, the labored writing of a seven-year-old. "I am fine. How is the baby. If I write my leter nicly I will have a star. Love." There never was a star. We wrote every other day, letters she could never hold or keep but only hear read—once. "We simply do not have room for children to keep any personal possessions," they patiently explained when we pieced one Sunday's shrieking together to plead how much it would mean to Emily, who loved so to keep things, to be allowed to keep her letters and cards.

They don't like you to love anybody here.

Each visit she looked frailer. "She isn't eating," they told us. (They had runny eggs for breakfast or mush with lumps, Emily said later; I'd hold it in my mouth and not swallow. Nothing ever tasted good, just when they had chicken.)

It took us eight months to get her released home, and only the fact that she gained back so little of her seven lost pounds convinced the social worker.

◄ What do you think is the relationship between the girl in Raphael Soyer's painting, *The Brown Sweater* (1952), and the woman and children in the background? Explain your thoughts.

should look a chubby blonde replica of Shirley Temple.[7] The doorbell sometimes rang for her, but no one seemed to come and play in the house or be a best friend. Maybe because we moved so much.

There was a boy she loved painfully through two school semesters. Months later she told me how she had taken pennies from my purse to buy him candy. "Licorice was his favorite and I brought him some every day, but he still liked Jennifer better'n me. Why, Mommy?" The kind of question for which there is no answer.

School was a worry to her. She was not glib or quick in a world where glibness and quickness were easily confused with ability to learn. To her overworked and exasperated teachers she was an overconscientious "slow learner" who kept trying to catch up and was absent entirely too often.

I used to try to hold and love her after she came back, but her body would stay stiff, and after a while she'd push away. She ate little. Food sickened her, and I think much of life too. Oh, she had physical lightness and brightness, twinkling by on skates, bouncing like a ball up and down, up and down, over the jump rope, skimming over the hill; but these were momentary.

She fretted about her appearance, thin and dark and foreign-looking at a time when every little girl was supposed to look or thought she

I let her be absent, though sometimes the illness was imaginary. How different from my now-strictness about attendance with the others. I wasn't working. We had a new baby, I was home anyhow. Sometimes, after Susan grew old enough, I would keep her home from school, too, to have them all together.

---

7. **Shirley Temple,** a child movie star of the thirties who had curly blonde hair and a round, dimpled face.

Mostly Emily had asthma, and her breathing, harsh and labored, would fill the house with a curiously tranquil sound. I would bring the two old dresser mirrors and her boxes of collections to her bed. She would select beads and single earrings, bottle tops and shells, dried flowers and pebbles, old postcards and scraps, all sorts of oddments; then she and Susan would play Kingdom, setting up landscapes and furniture, peopling them with action.

Those were the only times of peaceful companionship between her and Susan. I have edged away from it, that poisonous feeling between them, that terrible balancing of hurts and needs I had to do between the two, and did so badly, those earlier years.

Oh, there are conflicts between the others too, each one human, needing, demanding, hurting, taking—but only between Emily and Susan, no, Emily toward Susan, that corroding resentment. It seems so obvious on the surface, yet it is not obvious. Susan, the second child, Susan, golden- and curly-haired and chubby, quick and articulate and assured, everything in appearance and manner Emily was not. Susan, not able to resist Emily's precious things, losing or sometimes clumsily breaking them; Susan telling jokes and riddles to company for applause, while Emily sat silent (to say to me later: that was *my* riddle, Mother, I told it to Susan); Susan, who for all the five years' difference of age was just a year behind Emily in developing physically.

EVALUATE: Why do you think Emily resents Susan more than the other children?

I am glad for that slow physical development that widened the difference between her and her contemporaries, though she suffered over it. She was too vulnerable for that terrible world of youthful competition, of preening and parading, of constant measuring of yourself against every other, of envy, "If I had that copper hair," "If I had that skin. . . ." She tormented herself enough about not looking like the others, there was enough of the unsureness, the having to be conscious of words before you speak, the constant caring—what are they thinking of me?—without having it all magnified by the merciless physical drives.

Ronnie is calling. He is wet and I change him. It is rare there is such a cry now. That time of motherhood is almost behind me when the ear is not one's own but must always be racked and listening for the child cry, the child call. We sit for a while and I hold him, looking out over the city spread in charcoal with its soft aisles of light. *"Shoogily,"* he breathes and curls closer. I carry him back to bed, asleep. *Shoogily.* A funny word, a family word, inherited from Emily, invented by her to say: *comfort.*

In this and other ways she leaves her seal, I say aloud. And startle at my saying it. What do I mean? What did I start to gather together, to try and make coherent? I was at the terrible, growing years. War years. I do not remember them well. I was working, there were four smaller ones now, there was not time for her. She had to help be a mother, and housekeeper, and shopper. She had to set her seal. Mornings of crisis and near hysteria trying to get lunches packed, hair combed, coats and shoes found, everyone to school or child care on time, the baby ready for transportation. And always the paper scribbled on by a smaller one, the book looked at by Susan then mislaid, the homework not done. Running out to that huge school where she was one, she was lost, she was a drop; suffering over her unpreparedness, stammering and unsure in her classes.

There was so little time left at night after the kids were bedded down. She would struggle over books, always eating (it was in those years she developed her enormous appetite that is legendary in our family), and I would be ironing, or preparing food for the next day, or writing V-mail[8] to Bill, or tending the baby. Sometimes,

---

8. **V-mail,** mail converted to microfilm and sent to and from soldiers in World War II.

to make me laugh, or out of her despair, she would imitate happenings or types at school.

I think I said once: "Why don't you do something like this in the school amateur shows?" One morning she phoned me at work, hardly understandable through the weeping: "Mother, I did it. I won, I won; they gave me first prize; they clapped and clapped and wouldn't let me go."

Now suddenly she was Somebody, and as imprisoned in her difference as she had been in her anonymity.[9]

She began to be asked to perform at other high schools, even in colleges, then at city and statewide affairs. The first one we went to, I only recognized her that first moment when thin, shy, she almost drowned herself into the curtains. Then: Was this Emily? the control, the command, the convulsing and deadly clowning, the spell, then the roaring, stamping audience, unwilling to let this rare and precious laughter out of their lives.

Afterward: You ought to do something about her with a gift like that—but without money or knowing how, what does one do? We have left it all to her, and the gift has as often eddied inside, clogged and clotted, as been used and growing.

She is coming. She runs up the stairs two at a time with her light, graceful step, and I know she is happy tonight. Whatever it was that occasioned your call did not happen today.

"Aren't you ever going to finish the ironing, Mother? Whistler[10] painted his mother in a rocker. I'd have to paint mine standing over an ironing board." This is one of her communicative nights, and she tells me everything and nothing as she fixes herself a plate of food out of the icebox.

She is so lovely. Why did you want me to come in at all? Why were you concerned? She will find her way.

She starts up the stairs to bed. "Don't get *me* up with the rest in the morning," "But I thought you were having midterms." "Oh, those," she comes back in, kisses me, and says quite lightly, "in a couple of years when we'll all be atom-dead, they won't matter a bit."

She has said it before. She *believes* it. But because I have been dredging the past, and all that compounds a human being is so heavy and meaningful to me, I cannot endure it tonight.

I will never total it all. I will never come in to say: She was a child seldom smiled at. Her father left me before she was a year old. I had to work away from her her first six years when there was work, or I sent her home and to his relatives. There were years she had care she hated. She was dark and thin and foreign-looking in a world where the prestige went to blondness and curly hair and dimples; she was slow where glibness was prized. She was a child of anxious, not proud, love. We were poor and could not afford for her the soil of easy growth. I was a young mother, I was a distracted mother. There were other children pushing up, demanding. Her younger sister seemed all that she was not. There were years she did not let me touch her. She kept too much in herself; her life has been such she had to keep too much in herself. My wisdom came too late. She has much to her and probably little will come of it. She is a child of her age, of depression, of war, of fear.

Let her be. So all that is in her will not bloom—but in how many does it? There is still enough left to live by. Only help her to know—help make it so there is cause for her to know—that she is more than this dress on the ironing board, helpless before the iron.

---

9. anonymity (an/ə nim/ə tē), *n.* condition or quality of being unknown, nameless.
10. **Whistler,** James McNeill Whistler (1834–1903), an American painter and etcher who is best known for his painting which shows his mother sitting in a rocking chair.

After Reading

Making Connections

Shaping Your Response

1. If you could change one part of Emily's childhood to make it easier for her, what part would you change? Why?

Analyzing the Story

2. Describe the **setting** of "I Stand Here Ironing."

3. Which of the events could the narrator have changed to make Emily's childhood better, and which were beyond her control? Explain.

4. Explain the narrator's wish for her daughter: "Only help her to know—help make it so there is cause for her to know—that she is more than this dress on the ironing board, helpless before the iron."

Extending the Ideas

5. In your opinion, are single mothers in today's society better off than the narrator was? Explain your response.

6. What do you think Emily will be doing in ten years? Explain why you think so.

Literary Focus: Interior Monologue

Interior monologue is a technique for presenting a character's stream of consciousness or private thoughts. Keeping in mind the story, answer these questions:

- What is the advantage of reading a character's uncensored thoughts?
- Do you find this technique for relating a story appealing? Why or why not?

Vocabulary Study

Analogies express relationships. Notice the relationships between these pairs of words.

MOVEMENT : PANTOMIME : : WORDS : DIALOGUE

Movement is the means of expression for *pantomime,* just as *words* are the means of expression for *dialogue.*

Use the vocabulary words in the list to complete the following analogies on your paper. Refer to your Glossary for help.

**anonymity
ecstasy
homely
implore
somber**

1. FAME : MOVIE STAR : : ____ : moviegoer
2. GIVE : DONATE : : beg : ____
3. ROSE BUSH : BEAUTIFUL : : crabgrass : ____
4. ORANGE : VIVID : : gray : ____
5. FEAR : TERROR : : happiness : ____

Expressing Your Ideas

Writing Choices

Writer's Notebook Update Review the childhood stories that you recorded in your notebook. Choose a particularly vivid one, and describe it in a short essay.

Developing Character Anne Frank wrote the following words in her diary. "[Daddy] said: 'All children must look after their own upbringing.' Parents can only give good advice or put them on the right paths, but the final forming of a person's character lies in [his or her] own hands." Analyze this viewpoint in an **essay,** thinking not only about your own experiences but the way you might bring up children of your own.

Susan's Point of View "I Stand Here Ironing" is told from Emily's mother's point of view. Other characters might describe Emily differently. Write a **description** of her from her younger sister Susan's point of view.

Other Options

The Ideal Childhood Prepare and deliver a **speech** on what childhood ought to be. Imagine that your audience is a segment of national television viewers, even though you will be delivering your speech for your class. Consider finding some quotes about childhood and including them in your essay.

Growing Up With several partners, prepare an **oral reading** of parts of "I Stand Here Ironing," with each reader choosing a section that recounts Emily's different ages. The first reader might begin with paragraph five and read through paragraph eleven. The next reader would then begin with paragraph twelve, and so on.

The Stand-up Comic Emily's mother mentions the child actress Shirley Temple, who was popular when Emily was growing up. Examine this picture of her, then rent or borrow a Shirley Temple movie on videotape and watch it. Invent a **routine** that Emily might use in her stand-up comedy act relating to Shirley Temple, and perform it for the class.

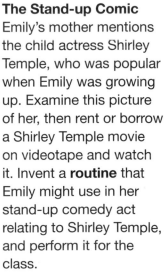

Separating

by John Updike

John Updike
born 1932

John Updike says the goal of his writing is "to transcribe middleness with all its grits, bumps, and anonymities, in all its fullness of satisfaction and mystery." He grew up in Pennsylvania, and went to Harvard, where he was the editor of the Harvard *Lampoon.* His work includes poetry, short stories, essays, and novels, and the topic of much of his work is life in the suburbs. His most famous books are the novels in the series about car salesman Harry "Rabbit" Angstrom. The third book in the series, *Rabbit Is Rich,* won a Pulitzer Prize, an American Book Award, and a commendation from the National Book Critics circle.

Building Background

Till Death Us Do Part The institutions of marriage and family have changed dramatically in the last twenty-five years. This graph, taken from information in *Fatherless America* by David Blankenhorn, illustrates the change in family structure for children in the United States. Updike records the human side of these statistics in "Separating."

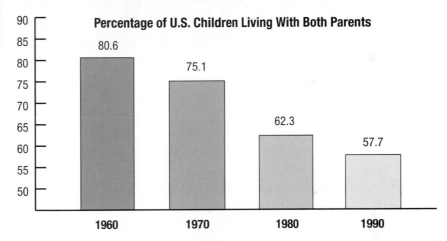

Percentage of U.S. Children Living With Both Parents

Year	Percentage
1960	80.6
1970	75.1
1980	62.3
1990	57.7

Literary Focus

Point of View The vantage point from which an author tells a story is called **point of view.** This vantage point is established through an author's choice of narrator. A story may be related by a character (*first-person point of view*) or by a narrator who does not participate in the action (*third-person point of view*). The third-person narrator may be *omniscient*—that is, able to see into the thoughts of all of the characters; *limited*—confined to a single character's perceptions; or *objective,* describing only what can be seen. As you read "Separating," identify the point of view used by John Updike.

Writer's Notebook

Prime Time Families Do television shows portray realistic family situations? Should they? In your notebook jot down the names of some television shows in which the characters are family members. Then note which ones you think portray a realistic family situation.

JOHN UPDIKE

The day was fair. Brilliant. All that June the weather had mocked the Maples' internal misery with solid sunlight—golden shafts and cascades of green in which their conversations had wormed unseeing, their sad murmuring selves the only stain in Nature. Usually by this time of the year they had acquired tans; but when they met their elder daughter's plane on her return from a year in England they were almost as pale as she, though Judith was too dazzled by the sunny opulent jumble of her native land to notice. They did not spoil her homecoming by telling her immediately. Wait a few days, let her recover from jet lag, had been one of their formulations, in that string of gray dialogues—over coffee, over cocktails, over Cointreau[1]—that had shaped the strategy of their dissolution, while the earth performed its annual stunt of renewal unnoticed beyond their closed windows. Richard had thought to leave at Easter; Joan had insisted they wait until the four children were at last assembled, with all exams passed and ceremonies attended, and the bauble of summer to console them. So he had drudged away, in love, in dread, repairing screens, getting the mowers sharpened, rolling and patching their new tennis court.

The court, clay, had come through its first winter pitted and wind-swept bare of redcoat. Years ago the Maples had observed how often, among their friends, divorce followed a dramatic home improvement, as if the marriage were making one last effort to live; their own worst crisis had come amid the plaster dust and exposed plumbing of a kitchen renovation. Yet, a summer ago, as canary-yellow bulldozers gaily churned a grassy, daisy-dotted knoll into a muddy plateau, and a crew of pigtailed young men raked and tamped clay into a plane, this transformation did not strike them as ominous, but festive in its impudence; their marriage

SEPARATING

could rend the earth for fun. The next spring, waking each day at dawn to a sliding sensation as if the bed were being tipped, Richard found the barren tennis court—its nets and tapes still rolled in the barn—an environment congruous with his mood of purposeful desolation, and the crumbling of handfuls of clay into cracks and holes (dogs had frolicked on the court in a thaw; rivulets[2] had eroded trenches) an activity suitably elemental and interminable.[3] In his sealed heart he hoped the day would never come.

Now it was here. A Friday. Judith was reacclimated; all four children were assembled before jobs and camps and visits again scattered them. Joan thought they should be told one by one. Richard was for making an announcement at the table. She said, "I think just making an announcement is a cop-out. They'll start quarreling and playing to each other instead of focusing. They're

---

1. **Cointreau** (kwôn′trō′), brand name of an expensive orange-flavored liquor.
2. **rivulet** (riv′yə lit), *n.* a very small stream.
3. **interminable** (in tèr′mə nə bəl), *adj.* unceasing; endless.

▲ Does Fairfield Porter's 1962 painting, *A Day Indoors,* portray a feeling of separation or separateness? Explain your answer.

each individuals, you know, not just some corporate obstacle to your freedom."

"OK, OK. I agree." Joan's plan was exact. That evening, they were giving Judith a belated welcome-home dinner, of lobster and champagne. Then, the party over, they, the two of them, who nineteen years before would push her in a baby carriage along Fifth Avenue to Washington Square, were to walk her out of the house, to the bridge across the salt creek, and tell her, swearing her to secrecy. Then Richard Jr., who was going directly from work to a rock concert in Boston, would be told, either late when he returned on the train or early Saturday morning before he went off to his job; he was seventeen and employed as one of a golf-course maintenance crew. Then the two younger children, John and Margaret, could, as the morning wore on, be informed.

He and Joan stood as a thin barrier between the children and the truth.

"Mopped up, as it were," Richard said.

"Do you have any better plan? That leaves you the rest of Saturday to answer any questions, pack, and make your wonderful departure."

"No," he said, meaning he had no better plan, and agreed to hers, though to him it showed an edge of false order, a hidden plea for control, like Joan's long chore lists and financial accountings and, in the days when he first knew her, her too-copious lecture notes. Her plan turned one hurdle for him into four—four knife-sharp walls, each with a sheer blind drop on the other side.

All spring he had moved through a world of insides and outsides, of barriers and partitions. He and Joan stood as a thin barrier between the children and the truth. Each moment was a partition, with the past on one side and the future on the other, a future containing this unthinkable *now*. Beyond four knifelike walls a new life for him waited vaguely. His skull cupped a secret, a white face, a face both frightened and soothing, both strange and known, that he wanted to shield from tears, which he felt all about him, solid as the sunlight. So haunted, he had become obsessed with battening down the house against his absence, replacing screens and sash cords, hinges and latches—a Houdini[4] making things snug before his escape.

The lock. He had still to replace a lock on one of the doors of the screened porch. The task, like most such, proved more difficult than he had imagined. The old lock, aluminum frozen by corrosion, had been deliberately rendered obsolete by manufacturers. Three hardware stores had nothing that even approximately matched the mortised hole its removal (surprisingly easy) left.

Another hole had to be gouged, with bits too small and saws too big, and the old hole fitted with a block of wood—the chisels dull, the saw rusty, his fingers thick with lack of sleep. The sun poured down, beyond the porch, on a world of neglect. The bushes already needed pruning, the windward side of the house was shedding flakes of paint, rain would get in when he was gone, insects, rot, death. His family, all those he would lose, filtered through the edges of his awareness as he struggled with screw holes, splinters, opaque instructions, minutiae of metal.

Judith sat on the porch, a princess returned from exile. She regaled them with stories of fuel shortages, of bomb scares in the Underground,[5] of Pakistani workmen loudly lusting after her as she walked past on her way to dance school. Joan came and went, in and out of the house, calmer than she should have been, praising his struggles with the lock as if this were one more and not the

---

4. **Houdini** (hū dē′nē), Harry (1874–1926), American magician known for his famous escapes from locked places.
5. **Underground,** the subway system in London.

last of their long succession of shared chores. The younger of his sons for a few minutes held the rickety screen door while his father clumsily hammered and chiseled, each blow a kind of sob in Richard's ears. His younger daughter, having been at a slumber party, slept on the porch hammock through all the noise—heavy and pink, trusting and forsaken. Time, like the sunlight, continued relentlessly; the sunlight slowly slanted. Today was one of the longest days. The lock clicked, worked. He was through. He had a drink; he drank it on the porch, listening to his daughter. "It was so sweet," she was saying, "during the worst of it, how all the butchers and bakery shops kept open by candlelight. They're all so plucky and cute. From the papers, things sounded so much worse here—people shooting people in gas lines, and everybody freezing."

Richard asked her, "Do you still want to live in England forever?" *Forever:* the concept, now a reality upon him, pressed and scratched at the back of his throat.

"No," Judith confessed, turning her oval face to him, its eyes still childishly far apart, but the lips set as over something succulent[6] and satisfactory. "I was anxious to come home. I'm an American." She was a woman. They had raised her; he and Joan had endured together to raise her, alone of the four. The others had still some raising left in them. Yet it was the thought of telling Judith—the image of her, their first baby, walking between them arm in arm to the bridge —that broke him. The partition between his face and the tears broke. Richard sat down to the celebratory meal with the back of his throat aching; the champagne, the lobster seemed phases of sunshine; he saw them and tasted them through tears. He blinked, swallowed, croakily joked about hay fever. The tears would not stop leaking through; they came not through a hole that could be plugged but through a permeable spot in a membrane, steadily, purely, endlessly, fruitfully. They became, his tears, a shield for himself against these others—their faces, the fact of their assembly, a last time as innocents, at a table where

he sat the last time as head. Tears dropped from his nose as he broke the lobster's back; salt flavored his champagne as he sipped it; the raw clench at the back of his throat was delicious. He could not help himself.

His children tried to ignore his tears. Judith, on his right, lit a cigarette, gazed upward in the direction of her too energetic, too sophisticated exhalation; on her other side, John earnestly bent his face to the extraction of the last morsels—legs, tail segments—from the scarlet corpse. Joan, at the opposite end of the table, glanced at him surprised, her reproach displaced by a quick grimace, of forgiveness, or of salute to his superior gift of strategy. Between them, Margaret, no longer called Bean, thirteen and large for her age, gazed from the other side of his pane of tears as if into a shop window at something she coveted—at her father, a crystalline heap of splinters and memories. It was not she, however, but John who, in the kitchen, as they cleared the plates and carapaces[7] away, asked Joan the question: *"Why is Daddy crying?"*

Richard heard the question but not the murmured answer. Then he heard Bean cry, "Oh, no-oh!"—the faintly dramatized exclamation of one who had long expected it.

John returned to the table carrying a bowl of salad. He nodded tersely at his father and his lips shaped the conspiratorial words "She told."

"Told what?" Richard asked aloud, insanely.

The boy sat down as if to rebuke[8] his father's distraction with the example of his own good manners. He said quietly, "The separation."

Joan and Margaret returned; the child, in Richard's twisted vision, seemed diminished in size, and relieved, relieved to have had the bogeyman at last proved real. He called out to her—the

---

6. **succulent** (suk′yə lənt), *adj.* full of juice, juicy.
7. **carpace** (kar′ə pās), *n.* bony shell of an amimal such as a lobster.
8. **rebuke** (ri byük′), *v.* express disapproval of.

distances at the table had grown immense—"You knew, you always knew," but the clenching at the back of his throat prevented him from making sense of it. From afar he heard Joan talking, levelly, sensibly, reciting what they had prepared: it was a separation for the summer, an experiment. She and Daddy both agreed it would be good for them; they needed space and time to think; they liked each other but did not make each other happy enough, somehow.

Judith, imitating her mother's factual tone, but in her youth off-key, too cool, said, "I think it's silly. You should either live together or get divorced."

... THEY LIKED EACH OTHER BUT DID NOT MAKE EACH OTHER HAPPY ENOUGH, SOMEHOW.

Richard's crying, like a wave that has crested and crashed, had become tumultuous; but it was overtopped by another tumult, for John, who had been so reserved, now grew larger and larger at the table. Perhaps his younger sister's being credited with knowing set him off. "Why didn't you *tell* us?" he asked, in a large round voice quite unlike his own. "You should have *told* us you weren't getting along."

Richard was startled into attempting to force words through his tears. "We *do* get along, that's the trouble, so it doesn't show even to us—" *That we do not love each other* was the rest of the sentence; he couldn't finish it.

Joan finished for him, in her style. "And we've always, *especially*, loved our children."

John was not mollified. "What do you care about *us?*" he boomed. "We're just little things you *had.*" His sisters' laughing forced a laugh from him, which he turned hard and parodistic. "Ha ha *ha.*" Richard and Joan realized simultaneously that the child was drunk, on Judith's homecoming champagne. Feeling bound to

keep the center of the stage, John took a cigarette from Judith's pack, poked it into his mouth, let it hang from his lower lip, and squinted like a gangster.

"You're not little things we had," Richard called to him. "You're the whole point. But you're grown. Or almost."

The boy was lighting matches. Instead of holding them to his cigarette (for they had never seen him smoke; being "good" had been his way of setting himself apart), he held them to his mother's face, closer and closer, for her to blow out. Then he lit the whole folder—a hiss and then a torch, held against his mother's face.

Prismed by tears, the flame filled Richard's vision; he didn't know how it was extinguished. He heard Margaret say, "Oh stop showing off," and saw John, in response, break the cigarette in two and put the halves entirely into his mouth and chew, sticking out his tongue to display the shreds to his sister.

Joan talked to him, reasoning—a fountain of reason, unintelligible. "Talked about it for years . . . our children must help us . . . Daddy and I both want . . ." As the boy listened, he carefully wadded a paper napkin into the leaves of his salad, fashioned a ball of paper and lettuce, and popped it into his mouth, looking around the table for the expected laughter. None came. Judith said, "Be mature," and dismissed a plume of smoke.

Richard got up from this stifling table and led the boy outside. Though the house was in twilight, the outdoors still brimmed with light, the lovely waste light of high summer. Both laughing, he supervised John's spitting out the lettuce and paper and tobacco into the pachysandra. He took him by the hand—a square gritty hand, but for its softness a man's. Yet, it held on. They ran together up into the field, past the tennis court. The raw banking left by the bulldozers was dotted with daisies. Past the court and a flat stretch where they used to play family baseball stood a

Could the child in Fairfield Porter's painting, *Under the Elms* (1971-1972) portray any of the children in the story? Why or why not? ➤

soft green rise glorious in the sun, each weed and species of grass distinct as illumination on parchment. "I'm sorry, so sorry," Richard cried. "You were the only one who ever tried to help me with all the damn jobs around this place."

Sobbing, safe within his tears and the champagne, John explained. "It's not just the separation, it's the whole crummy year. I *hate* that school, you can't make any friends, the history teacher's a scud."[9]

They sat on the crest of the rise, shaking and warm from their tears but easier in their voices, and Richard tried to focus on the child's sad year—the weekdays long with homework, the weekends spent in his room with model airplanes, while his parents murmured down below, nursing their separation. How selfish, how blind, Richard thought; his eyes felt scoured. He told his son, "We'll think about getting you transferred. Life's too short to be miserable."

They had said what they could, but did not want the moment to heal, and talked on, about the school, about the tennis court, whether it would ever again be as good as it had been that first summer. They walked to inspect it and pressed a few more tapes more firmly down. A little stiltedly, perhaps trying now to make too much of the moment, Richard led the boy to the spot in the field where the view was best, of the metallic blue river, the emerald marsh, the scattered islands velvety with shadow in the low light, the white bits of beach far away. "See," he said. "It goes on being beautiful. It'll be here tomorrow."

"I know," John answered, impatiently. The moment had closed.

Back in the house, the others had opened some white wine, the champagne being drunk,

---

9. **scud,** a slang term for an undesirable teacher.

and still sat at the table, the three females, gossiping. Where Joan sat had become the head. She turned, showing him a tearless face, and asked, "All right?"

"We're fine," he said, resenting it, though relieved, that the party went on without him.

In bed she explained, "I couldn't cry I guess because I cried so much all spring. It really wasn't fair. It's your idea, and you made it look as though I was kicking you out."

"I'm sorry," he said. "I couldn't stop. I wanted to but couldn't."

"You *didn't* want to. You loved it. You were having your way, making a general announcement."

"I love having it over," he admitted. "God, those kids were great. So brave and funny." John, returned to the house, had settled to a model airplane in his room, and kept shouting down to them, "I'm OK. No sweat." "And the way," Richard went on, cozy in his relief, "they never questioned the reasons we gave. No thought of a third person. Not even Judith."

"That *was* touching," Joan said.

He gave her a hug. "You were great too. Very reassuring to everybody. Thank you." Guiltily, he realized he did not feel separated.

"You still have Dickie to do," she told him. These words set before him a black mountain in the darkness; its cold breath, its near weight affected his chest. Of the four children, his elder son was most nearly his conscience. Joan did not need to add, "That's one piece of your dirty work I won't do for you."

"I know. I'll do it. You go to sleep."

Within minutes, her breathing slowed, became oblivious and deep. It was quarter to midnight. Dickie's train from the concert would come in at one-fourteen. Richard set the alarm for one. He had slept atrociously[10] for weeks. But whenever he closed his lids some glimpse of the last hours scorched them—Judith exhaling toward the ceiling in a kind of aversion. Bean's mute staring, the sunstruck growth in the field where he and John had rested. The mountain before him moved closer, moved within him; he

was huge, momentous. The ache at the back of his throat felt stale. His wife slept as if slain beside him. When, exasperated by his hot lids, his crowded heart, he rose from bed and dressed, she awoke enough to turn over. He told her then, "Joan, if I could undo it all, I would."

"Where would you begin?" she asked. There was no place. Giving him courage, she was always giving him courage. He put on shoes without socks in the dark. The children were breathing in their rooms, the downstairs was hollow. In their confusion they had left lights burning. He turned off all but one, the kitchen overhead. The car started. He had hoped it wouldn't. He met only moonlight on the road; it seemed a diaphanous[11] companion, flickering in the leaves along the roadside, haunting his rearview mirror like a pursuer, melting under his headlights. The center of town, not quite deserted, was eerie at this hour. A young cop in uniform kept company with a gang of T-shirted kids on the steps of the bank. Across from the railroad station, several bars kept open. Customers, mostly young, passed in and out of the warm night, savoring summer's novelty. Voices shouted from cars as they passed; an immense conversation seemed in progress. Richard parked and in his weariness put his head on the passenger seat, out of the commotion and wheeling lights. It was as when, in the movies, an assassin grimly carries his mission through the jostle of a carnival—except the movies cannot show the precipitous, palpable slope you cling to within. You cannot climb back down; you can only fall. The synthetic fabric of the car seat, warmed by his cheek, confided to him an ancient, distant scent of vanilla.

A train whistle caused him to lift his head. It was on time; he had hoped it would be late. The slender draw-gates descended. The bell of approach tingled happily. The great metal body, horizontally fluted, rocked to a stop, and sleepy

---

10. **atrociously** (ə trō′shes lē), *adv.* shockingly badly.
11. **diaphanous** (dī af′ə nəs), *adj.* transparent.

teenagers disembarked, his son among them. Dickie did not show surprise that his father was meeting him at this terrible hour. He sauntered to the car with two friends, both taller than he. He said "Hi" to his father and took the passenger's seat with an exhausted promptness that expressed gratitude. The friends got in the back, and Richard was grateful; a few more minutes' postponement would be won by driving them home.

RICHARD HAD FEARED THAT HIS TEARS WOULD RETURN AND CHOKE HIM . . .

He asked, "How was the concert?"

"Groovy," one boy said from the back seat.

"It was OK," Dickie said, moderate by nature, so reasonable that in his childhood the unreason of the world had given him headaches, stomachaches, nausea. When the second friend had been dropped off at his dark house, the boy blurted, "Dad, my eyes are killing me with hay fever! I'm out there cutting that grass all day!"

"Do we still have those drops?"

"They didn't do any good last summer."

"They might this." Richard swung a U-turn on the empty street. The drive home took a few minutes. The mountain was here, in his throat. "Richard," he said, and felt the boy, slumped and rubbing his eyes, go tense at his tone, "I didn't come to meet you just to make your life easier. I came because your mother and I have some news for you, and you're a hard man to get ahold of these days. It's sad news."

"That's OK." The reassurance came out soft, but quick, as if released from the tip of a spring.

Richard had feared that his tears would return and choke him, but the boy's manliness set an example, and his voice issued forth steady and dry. "It's sad news, but it needn't be tragic news, at least for you. It should have no practical effect on your life, though it's bound to have an emotional effect. You'll work at your job, and go back to school in September. Your mother and I are really proud of what you're making of your life; we don't want that to change at all."

"Yeah," the boy said lightly, on the intake of his breath, holding himself up. They turned the corner; the church they went to loomed like a gutted fort. The home of the woman Richard hoped to marry stood across the green. Her bedroom light burned.

"Your mother and I," he said, "have decided to separate. For the summer. Nothing legal, no divorce yet. We want to see how it feels. For some years now, we haven't been doing enough for each other, making each other as happy as we should be. Have you sensed that?"

"No," the boy said. It was an honest, unemotional answer: true or false in a quiz.

Glad for the factual basis, Richard pursued, even garrulously, the details. His apartment across town, his utter accessibility, the split vacation arrangements, the advantages to the children, the added mobility and variety of the summer. Dickie listened, absorbing. "Do the others know?"

"Yes."

"How did they take it?"

"The girls pretty calmly. John flipped out; he shouted and ate a cigarette and made a salad out of his napkin and told us how much he hated school."

His brother chuckled. "He did?"

"Yeah. The school issue was more upsetting for him than Mom and me. He seemed to feel better for having exploded."

"He did?" The repetition was the first sign that he was stunned.

"Yes. Dickie, I want to tell you something. This last hour, waiting for your train to get in, has been about the worst of my life. I hate this. *Hate* it. My father would have died before doing it to me." He felt immensely lighter, saying this. He had dumped the mountain on the boy. They were home. Moving swiftly as a shadow, Dickie was out of the car, through the bright kitchen. Richard called after him, "Want a glass of milk or anything?"

"No thanks."

"Want to call the course tomorrow and say you're too sick to work?"

IN HIS FATHER'S EAR HE MOANED ONE WORD, THE CRUCIAL, INTELLIGENT WORD: WHY?

"No, that's all right." The answer was faint, delivered at the door to his room; Richard listened for the slam that went with a tantrum. The door closed normally, gently. The sound was sickening.

Joan had sunk into that first deep trough of sleep and was slow to awake. Richard had to repeat, "I told him."

"What did he say?"

"Nothing much. Could you go say good-night to him? Please."

She left their room, without putting on a bathrobe. He sluggishly changed back into his pajamas and walked down the hall. Dickie was already in bed, Joan was sitting beside him, and the boy's bedside clock radio was murmuring music. When she stood, an inexplicable light—the moon?—outlined her body through the nightie. Richard sat on the warm place she had indented on the child's narrow mattress. He asked him, "Do you want the radio on like that?"

"It always is."

"Doesn't it keep you awake? It would me."

"No."

"Are you sleepy?"

"Yeah."

"Good. Sure you want to get up and go to work? You've had a big night."

"I want to."

Away at school this winter he had learned for the first time that you can go short of sleep and live. As an infant he had slept with an immobile, sweating intensity that had alarmed his baby sitters. In adolescence he had often been the first of the four children to go to bed. Even now, he would go slack in the middle of a television show, his sprawled legs hairy and brown. "OK. Good boy. Dickie, listen. I love you so much, I never knew how much until now. No matter how this works out, I'll always be with you. Really."

Richard bent to kiss an averted face but his son, sinewy, turned and with wet cheeks embraced him and gave him a kiss, on the lips, passionate as a woman's. In his father's ear he moaned one word, the crucial,[12] intelligent word: *"Why?"*

Why. It was a whistle of wind in a crack, a knife thrust, a window thrown open on emptiness. The white face was gone, the darkness was featureless. Richard had forgotten why.

---

12. **crucial** (krü′shəl), *adj.* very important; critical.

After Reading

Making Connections

Shaping Your Response

1. Does the story "Separating" strike you as realistic or unrealistic? Explain your opinion.

Analyzing the Story

2. Choose a passage that you think is a good example of Updike's ability to describe emotion, and explain how he achieves this.

3. How would you **characterize** Richard? Joan? Use details from the story to support your descriptions.

4. What do you think is the basic **conflict** in the story?

5. 👣 Describe the **interactions** between the characters in this story. Would you say they communicate well with each other or not? Explain your answer.

Extending the Ideas

6. Do you think the Maples will go through with a divorce, or do you think they will reconcile? Be prepared to support your opinion with information from the story.

7. How do you think the children will be affected by the absence of their father?

Literary Focus: Point of View

Point of View is the vantage point from which a story is told. A story may be told from first- or third-person point of view, and a third-person narrator may be omniscient, limited, or objective. Answer the following questions about the story:

- Is the narrator in this story able to see into the minds of all the characters?

- Is the point of view limited to a single character's perceptions?

- Does the narrator describe only what can be seen, without any attempt to describe emotions or reactions?

- Who is the narrator and from what point of view is the story told?

Vocabulary Study

Select the vocabulary word from the list that best completes each sentence about "Separating."

atrociously
crucial
diaphanous
rebuke
rivulet

1. The back yard could be seen through the _____ window curtains.
2. Richard slept _____ for weeks, waking often in the middle of the night.
3. Dickie's question "Why?" served to _____ his father's explanation.
4. Richard's tears gathered to form a _____ on his face.
5. The Maples felt that giving their children a sense of security in spite of the separation was _____ to their well-being.

Expressing Your Ideas

Writing Choices

Writer's Notebook Update Use a Venn diagram to compare one of the TV families you wrote about in your notebook to the Maple family. In what ways are the families alike? How are they different? What kind of interactions take place? Which family is portrayed more sympathetically? more realistically? Use the information in the diagram to write a comparison-contrast paragraph.

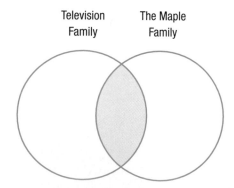

Television Family   The Maple Family

For Better or for Worse Make lists of things that you think help to keep a marriage together and the things that lead to divorce. Then write an **essay** presenting your viewpoint on marriage and the causes of divorce.

Other Options

Graphing Trends How has the divorce rate in the U.S. changed since 1900? Work with a small group and look up the data on divorce rates in the United States in an almanac. Then convert the data that you find in table form into a **bar graph** or a **line graph** to show the trend in divorce over the years. Discuss with your group possible reasons for the trends you find, then present your ideas to the class.

The Kids Talk Back Create a **monologue** for one of the children in the story. Have the character tell the parents his or her thoughts and feelings about the separation, including any hopes, fears, and suggestions. Perform the monologue for the class. Be sure to introduce the character in some way so your classmates will know which character is speaking.

Before Reading

from The Woman Warrior

by Maxine Hong Kingston

Maxine Hong Kingston
born 1940

Maxine Hong Kingston was born in Stockton, California, to a Chinese American father and a Chinese mother. School was a struggle for her because she had difficulties speaking and understanding English, and she was not familiar with the culture of the other students. This clash of cultures and her attempts to reconcile her Chinese heritage with her American upbringing are explored in her autobiography, *The Woman Warrior,* which is about the women in her family. Kingston learned the stories of her female ancestors from her mother's "talking story," or oral history. A companion book, *China Men,* chronicles the history of the men in her family.

Building Background

Imagine the Scene You are five years old, and it is your first day of school. The school building is intimidating, and so is the strange person standing at the front of the classroom. The loud, happy children all around you are not the least bit comforting, either. Most look different from you, dress different from you, and speak different from you. To begin the day, the teacher writes her name on the chalkboard. It is a puzzle to you. The letters are meaningless squiggles, nothing at all like the alphabet you know. This is a situation faced by many children in the United States whose first language is not English as they enter American schools for the first time. In the following essay, Maxine Hong Kingston describes her childhood experiences as she adjusted to this situation.

Literary Focus

Symbolism An object or event that represents something else is called a symbol. Frequently, a symbol will stand for an abstract idea or concept. For example, a lighted candle might stand for the memory of someone who has died. To determine whether something is a symbol, ask yourself whether the author stresses a particular idea or image or equates something concrete with something abstract. In the excerpt you are about to read from *The Woman Warrior,* Maxine Hong Kingston's mother says that she cut her daughter's frenum, a membrane just below the tongue, when the daughter was a child. As you read this excerpt, decide what abstract quality this concrete act might **symbolize,** or stand for, in the author's life.

Writer's Notebook

Way Back When . . . Maxine Hong Kingston shares some of her kindergarten experiences in *The Woman Warrior.* What do you remember about your kindergarten or first-grade experiences? Who was your teacher? Who were your classmates? What did you do on a typical day? What were your most favorite and least favorite activities? In your notebook write about a memorable experience.

THE WOMAN WARRIOR

MAXINE HONG KINGSTON

Long ago in China, knot-makers tied string into buttons and frogs, and rope into bell pulls. There was one knot so complicated that it blinded the knot-maker. Finally an emperor outlawed this cruel knot, and the nobles could not order it anymore. If I had lived in China, I would have been an outlaw knot-maker.

Maybe that's why my mother cut my tongue. She pushed my tongue up and sliced the frenum.[1] Or maybe she snipped it with a pair of nail scissors. I don't remember her doing it, only her telling me about it, but all during childhood I felt sorry for the baby whose mother waited with scissors or knife in hand for it to cry—and then, when its mouth was wide open like a baby bird's, cut. The Chinese say "a ready tongue is an evil."

I used to curl up my tongue in front of the mirror and tauten[2] my frenum into a white line, itself as thin as a razor blade. I saw no scars in my mouth. I thought perhaps I had had two frena, and she had cut one. I made other children open their mouths so I could compare theirs to mine. I saw perfect pink membranes stretching into precise edges that looked easy enough to cut. Sometimes I felt very proud that my mother committed such a powerful act upon me. At other times I was terrified—the first thing my mother did when she saw me was to cut my tongue.

"Why did you do that to me, Mother?"

"I told you."

"Tell me again."

"I cut it so you would not be tongue-tied. Your tongue would be able to move in any language. You'll be able to speak languages that are completely different from one another. You'll be able to pronounce anything. Your frenum looked too tight to do those things, so I cut it."

"But isn't 'a ready tongue an evil'?"

"Things are different in this ghost country."[3]

"Did it hurt me? Did I cry and bleed?"

"I don't remember. Probably."

She didn't cut the other children's. When I asked cousins and other Chinese children whether their mothers had cut their tongues loose, they said, "What?"

"Why didn't you cut my brothers' and sisters' tongues?"

"They didn't need it."

"Why not? Were theirs longer than mine?"

"Why don't you quit blabbering and get to work?"

If my mother was not lying she should have cut more, scraped away the rest of the frenum skin, because I have a terrible time talking. Or she should not have cut at all, tampering[3] with my speech. When I went to kindergarten and had to speak English for the first time, I became silent. A dumbness—a shame—still cracks my voice in two, even when I want to say "hello" casually, or ask an easy question in front of the check-out counter, or ask directions of a bus driver. I stand frozen, or I hold up the line with the complete, grammatical sentence that comes squeaking out at impossible length. "What did you say?" says the cab driver, or "Speak up," so I have to perform again, only weaker the second time. A telephone call makes my throat bleed

---

1. frenum (frē′nəm), *n.* fold of membrane beneath the tongue.
2. tauten (tôt′n), *v.* tighten.
3. **ghost country.** Chinese immigrants commonly referred to white Americans as *ghosts.*
4. tamper (tam′pər), *v.* meddle improperly.

Artist Tomie Arai once explained that a central character in Asian American art is "the sojourner, forever foreign, uprooted and marginal . . ." Does her 1988 silkscreen, *Laundryman's Daughter,* reflect that idea? If so, how?

and takes up that day's courage. It spoils my day with self-disgust when I hear my broken voice come skittering out into the open. It makes people wince to hear it. I'm getting better, though. Recently I asked the postman for special-issue stamps; I've waited since childhood for postmen to give me some of their own accord. I am making progress, a little every day.

My silence was thickest—total—during the three years that I covered my school paintings with black paint. I painted layers of black over houses and flowers and suns, and when I drew on the blackboard, I put a layer of chalk on top. I was making a stage curtain, and it was the moment before the curtain parted or rose. The teachers called my parents to school, and I saw they had

The Woman Warrior 755

been saving my pictures, curling and cracking, all alike and black. The teachers pointed to the pictures and looked serious, talked seriously too, but my parents did not understand English. ("The parents and teachers of criminals were executed," said my father.) My parents took the pictures home. I spread them out (so black and full of possibilities) and pretended the curtains were swinging open, flying up, one after another, sunlight underneath, mighty operas.

During the first silent year I spoke to no one at school, did not ask before going to the lavatory, and flunked kindergarten. My sister also said nothing for three years, silent in the playground and silent at lunch. There were other quiet Chinese girls not of our family, but most of them got over it sooner than we did. I enjoyed the silence. At first it did not occur to me I was supposed to talk or to pass kindergarten. I talked at home and to one or two of the Chinese kids in class. I made motions and even made some jokes. I drank out of a toy saucer when the water spilled out of the cup, and everybody laughed, pointing at me, so I did it some more. I didn't know that Americans don't drink out of saucers.

I liked the Negro students (Black Ghosts) best because they laughed the loudest and talked to me as if I were a daring talker too. One of the Negro girls had her mother coil braids over her ears Shanghai-style like mine; we were Shanghai[5] twins except that she was covered with black like my paintings. Two Negro kids enrolled in Chinese school, and the teachers gave them Chinese names. Some Negro kids walked me to school and home, protecting me from the Japanese kids, who hit me and chased me and stuck gum in my ears. The Japanese kids were noisy and tough. They appeared one day in kindergarten, released from concentration camp,[6] which was a tic-tac-toe mark, like barbed wire, on the map.

It was when I found out I had to talk that school became a misery, that the silence became a misery. I did not speak and felt bad each time that I did not speak. I read aloud in the first grade, though, and heard the barest whisper with little squeaks come out of my throat. "Louder," said the teacher, who scared the voice away again. The other Chinese girls did not talk either, so I knew the silence had to do with being a Chinese girl.

Reading out loud was easier than speaking because we did not have to make up what to say, but I stopped often, and the teacher would think I'd gone quiet again. I could not understand "I." The Chinese "I" has seven strokes, intricacies.[7] How could the American "I," assuredly[8] wearing a hat like the Chinese, have only three strokes, the middle so straight? Was it out of politeness that this writer left off strokes the way a Chinese has to write her own name small and crooked? No, it was not politeness; "I" is a capital and "you" is a lower-case. I stared at that middle line and waited so long for its black center to resolve[9] into tight strokes and dots that I forgot to pronounce it. The other troublesome word was "here," no strong consonant to hang on to, and so flat, when "here" is two mountainous ideographs.[10] The teacher, who had already told me every day how to read "I" and "here," put me in the low corner under the stairs again, where the noisy boys usually sat.

When my second grade class did a play, the whole class went to the auditorium except the Chinese girls. The teacher, lovely and Hawaiian, should have understood about us, but instead left us behind in the classroom. Our voices were too soft or nonexistent,[11] and our parents never signed the permission slips anyway. They never

---

5. **Shanghai** (shang′hī′), seaport in Eastern China.
6. **concentration camp,** refers to the internment camps in the U.S. where Japanese Americans were imprisoned during World War II.
7. **intricacy** (in′trə kə sē), *n.* intricate nature or condition; complexity.
8. **assuredly** (ə shŭr′əd lē), *adv.* confidently, boldly.
9. **resolve** (ri zolv′), *v.* break into parts or components.
10. **ideograph** (id′ē ə graf), *n.* a graphic symbol that represents a thing or an idea directly, without representing the sounds of the word for the thing or idea.
11. **nonexistent** (non′ig zis′tənt), *adj.* having no being or existence.

signed anything unnecessary. We opened the door a crack and peeked out, but closed it again quickly. One of us (not me) won every spelling bee, though.

I remember telling the Hawaiian teacher, "We Chinese can't sing 'land where our fathers died.'" She argued with me about politics, while I meant because of curses. But how can I have that memory when I couldn't talk? My mother says that we, like the ghosts, have no memories.

After American school, we picked up our cigar boxes, in which we had arranged books, brushes, and an inkbox neatly, and went to Chinese school, from 5:00 to 7:30 P.M. There we chanted together, voices rising and falling, loud and soft, some boys shouting, everybody reading together, reciting together and not alone with one voice. When we had a memorization test, the teacher let each of us come to his desk and say the lesson to him privately, while the rest of the class practiced copying or tracing. Most of the teachers were men. The boys who were so well behaved in the American school played tricks on them and talked back to them. The girls were not mute.[12] They screamed and yelled during recess, when there were no rules; they had fistfights. Nobody was afraid of children hurting themselves or of children hurting school property. The glass doors to the red and green balconies with the gold joy symbols were left wide open so that we could run out and climb the fire escapes. We played capture-the-flag in the auditorium, where Sun Yat-sen[13] and Chiang Kai-shek's[14] pictures hung at the back of the stage, the Chinese flag on their left and the American flag on their right. We climbed the teak[15] ceremonial chairs and made flying leaps off the stage. One flag headquarters was behind the glass door and the other on stage right. Our feet drummed on the hollow stage. During recess the teachers locked themselves up in their office with the shelves of books, copybooks, inks from China. They drank tea and warmed their hands at a stove. There was no play supervision. At recess we had the school to ourselves, and also we could roam as far as we could go—downtown, Chinatown stores, home—as long as we returned before the bell rang.

At exactly 7:30 the teacher again picked up the brass bell that sat on his desk and swung it over our heads, while we charged down the stairs, our cheering magnified in the stairwell. Nobody had to line up.

Not all of the children who were silent at American school found voice at Chinese school. One new teacher said each of us had to get up and recite in front of the class, who was to listen. My sister and I had memorized the lesson perfectly. We said it to each other at home, one chanting, one listening. The teacher called on my sister to recite first. It was the first time a teacher had called on the second-born to go first. My sister was scared. She glanced at me and looked away. I looked down at my desk. I hoped that she could do it because if she could, then I would have to. She opened her mouth and a voice came out that wasn't a whisper, but it wasn't a proper voice either. I hoped that she would not cry, fear breaking up her voice like twigs underfoot. She sounded as if she were trying to sing through weeping and strangling. She did not pause or stop to end the embarrassment. She kept going until she said the last word, and then she sat down. When it was my turn, the same voice came out, a crippled animal running on broken legs. You could hear splinters in my voice, bones rubbing jagged against one another. I was loud, though. I was glad I didn't whisper. There was one little girl who whispered.

---

12. **mute** (myūt), *adj.* not making any sound; silent.
13. **Sun Yat-sen** (sŭn′ yät′sen′), (1866–1925) Chinese revolutionary leader and statesman who worked to establish the republic of China.
14. **Chiang Kai-shek,** (chyäng′ kī′shek′), (1886–1975) Chinese general and political leader, president of Nationalist China in 1948, and of its government on Taiwan from 1950 to 1975.
15. **teak** (tēk), *n.* made of hard, durable, yellowish-brown wood from a large tree that grows in the East Indies.

After Reading

Making Connections

Shaping Your
Response

Analyzing the
Autobiography

Extending the
Ideas

1. If you were the young Kingston's teacher, what would you have done to try to encourage her to speak?

2. ✋ What factors inhibit young Kingston's **interactions** with others?

3. What is the **irony** in the notion that Kingston's mother cut her frenum to free her tongue?

4. What do you think Kingston means when she says she would be an "outlaw knot maker"?

5. How have schools changed since Kingston's schooling in the 1940s to accommodate students whose home language is not English?

Vocabulary Study

Choose the word least related in meaning to the vocabulary word.

frenum
teak
tamper
mute
tauten
assuredly
nonexistent
ideograph
intricacy
resolve

1. *frenum*   a. tongue   b. palate   c. forehead
2. *teak*   a. oak   b. mahogany   c. brass
3. *tamper*   a. ignore   b. meddle   c. interfere
4. *mute*   a. dumb   b. deaf   c. silent
5. *tauten*   a. cut   b. stretch   c. tighten
6. *assuredly*   a. confidently   b. carefully   c. certainly
7. *nonexistent* a. imaginary   b. real   c. unreal
8. *ideograph*   a. photograph   b. pictograph   c. symbol
9. *intricacy*   a. simplification b. entanglement   c. complication
10. *resolve*   a. divide   b. separate   c. disappear

Expressing Your Ideas

Writing Choice

Writer's Notebook Update As a child, were you ever in a situation where being too quiet or talking too much got you into trouble? Write a list of rules telling when it's best to talk and when it's best to be silent.

Another Option

California, Here I Come Research the immigration of Chinese people to California in the first half of the 1900s. Make a **graph** showing the immigration trends, and prepare a **map** of California that shows the major destinations of the immigrants.

Before Reading

Everyday Use

by Alice Walker

Alice Walker
born 1944

Alice Walker was born in Eatonton, Georgia, the eighth child of sharecroppers. When she was eight, Walker was blinded in her right eye as a result of a BB gun accident. This incident left her physically and emotionally scarred, and it was at this time that she turned to journal writing. From the late 1960s to the mid-1970s she taught writing and African American studies at a number of universities. In her poetry, short stories, novels, and essays she often focuses on the themes of racism and sexism, and her main characters are usually African American women, as in her novel *The Color Purple,* which won a Pulitzer Prize and was made into a movie.

Building Background

Forty Acres and a Mule Although the Emancipation Proclamation freed all enslaved African Americans, daily life was not much changed for them in the South after the Civil War. Land-reform plans which promised to give former slaves "40 acres and a mule" did not materialize. Many former slaves stayed on the plantations as laborers. Others worked as sharecroppers, farming a plot of land for the owner in exchange for part of the crops. Still others worked in factories springing up in the South, getting paid very low wages. Opportunities were better in the North and in the West. The industrial boom, along with slowed immigration, that accompanied World War I offered African Americans unprecedented opportunities for employment. The price of this economic gain, however, often included leaving behind relatives and friendships, as well as rural traditions and ways of living.

Literary Focus

Figurative Language Figurative language is the use of words apart from their ordinary, literal meanings to add freshness or vitality to a piece of writing. Some common figures of speech are **hyperbole, simile,** and **metaphor.** Hyperbole is obvious exaggeration: "The noise of the jack hammer was so loud it could have awakened the dead." A simile is a comparison using *like* or *as:* "The trees lined the driveway like soldiers standing at attention." A metaphor is an implied comparison: "She wept a storm of tears." As you read "Everyday Use," look for examples of figurative language.

Writer's Notebook

That Certain Something If you could choose one item from your childhood home to take with you when you move out, what would it be? In your log write a description of the object you would choose, and explain its significance to you.

EVERYDAY USE

Alice Walker

I will wait for her in the yard that Maggie and I made so clean and wavy yesterday afternoon. A yard like this is more comfortable than most people know. It is not just a yard. It is like an extended living room. When the clay is swept clean as a floor and the fine sand around the edges lined with tiny, irregular grooves, anyone can come and sit and look up into the elm tree and wait for the breezes that never come inside the house.

Maggie will be nervous until after her sister goes: she will stand hopelessly in corners, homely and ashamed of the burn scars down her arms and legs, eyeing her sister with a mixture of envy and awe. She thinks her sister has held life always in the palm of one hand, that "no" is a word the world never learned to say to her.

You've no doubt seen those TV shows where the child who has "made it" is confronted,[1] as a surprise, by her own mother and father, tottering in weakly from backstage. (A pleasant surprise, of course: What would they do if parent and child came on the show only to curse out and insult each other?) On TV mother and child embrace and smile into each other's faces. Sometimes the mother and father weep, the child wraps them in her arms and leans across the table to tell how she would not have made it without their help. I have seen these programs.

Sometimes I dream a dream in which Dee and I are suddenly brought together on a TV program of this sort. Out of a dark and softseated limousine I am ushered into a bright room filled with many people. There I meet a smiling, gray, sporty man like Johnny Carson who shakes my hand and tells me what a fine girl I have. Then we are on the stage and Dee is embracing me with tears in her eyes. She pins on my dress a large orchid, even though she has told me once that she thinks orchids are tacky flowers.

In real life I am a large, big-boned woman with rough, man-working hands. In the winter I wear flannel nightgowns to bed and overalls during the day. I can kill and clean a hog as mercilessly as a man. My fat keeps me hot in zero weather. I can work outside all day, breaking ice to get water for washing; I can eat pork liver cooked over the open fire minutes after it comes steaming from the hog. One winter I knocked a bull calf straight in the brain between the eyes with a sledgehammer and had the meat hung up to chill before nightfall. But of course all this does not show on television. I am the way my daughter would want me to be: a hundred pounds lighter, my skin like an uncooked barley pancake. My hair glistens in the hot, bright lights. Johnny Carson has much to do to keep up with my quick and witty tongue.

But that is a mistake. I know even before I wake up. Who ever knew a Johnson with a quick tongue? Who can even imagine me looking a strange white man in the eye? It seems to me I have talked to them always with one foot raised in flight, with my head turned in whichever way is farthest from them. Dee, though. She would always look anyone in the eye. Hesitation was no part of her nature.

"How do I look, Mama?" Maggie says, showing

---

1. **confront** (kən frunt′), *v.* bring face to face; place before.

▲ What details in Hubert Shuptrine's 1985 portrait, *Mama Agnes,* match the story?

just enough of her thin body enveloped in pink skirt and red blouse for me to know she's there, almost hidden by the door.

"Come out into the yard," I say.

Have you ever seen a lame animal, perhaps a dog run over by some careless person rich enough to own a car, sidle up to someone who is ignorant enough to be kind to him? That is the way Maggie walks. She has been like this, chin on chest, eyes on ground, feet in shuffle, ever since the fire that burned the other house to the ground.

Dee is lighter than Maggie, with nicer hair and a fuller figure. She's a woman now, though sometimes I forget. How long ago was it that the other house burned? Ten, twelve years? Sometimes I can still hear the flames and feel Maggie's arms sticking to me, her hair smoking and her dress falling off her in little black paper flakes. Her eyes seemed stretched open, blazed open by the flames reflected in them. And Dee. I see her standing off under the sweet gum tree she used to dig gum out of; a look of concentration on her face as she watched the last dingy gray board of the house fall in toward the red-hot brick chimney. Why don't you do a dance around the ashes? I'd wanted to ask her. She had hated the house that much.

I used to think she hated Maggie, too. But that was before we raised the money, the church and me, to send her to Augusta to school. She used to read to us without pity; forcing words, lies, other folks' habits, whole lives upon us two, sitting trapped and ignorant underneath her voice. She washed us in the river of make-believe, burned us with a lot of knowledge we didn't necessarily need to know. Pressed us to her with the serious way she read, to shove us away at just the moment, like dimwits, we seemed about to understand.

Dee wanted nice things. A yellow organdy[2] dress to wear to her graduation from high school; black pumps to match a green suit she'd

made from an old suit somebody gave me. She was determined to stare down any disaster in her efforts. Her eyelids would not flicker for minutes at a time. Often I fought off the temptation to shake her. At sixteen she had a style of her own—and knew what style was.

I never had an education myself. After second grade the school was closed down. Don't ask me why: in 1927 colored asked fewer questions than they do now. Sometimes Maggie reads to me. She stumbles along good-naturedly but can't see well. She knows she is not bright. Like good looks and money, quickness passed her by. She will marry John Thomas (who has mossy teeth in an earnest face), and then I'll be free to sit here and I guess just sing church songs to myself. Although I never was a good singer. Never could carry a tune. I was always better at a man's job. I used to love to milk till I was hooked in the side in '49. Cows are soothing and slow and don't bother you, unless you try to milk them the wrong way.

I have deliberately turned my back on the house. It is three rooms, just like the one that burned, except the roof is tin; they don't make shingle roofs any more. There are no real windows, just some holes cut in the sides, like the portholes in a ship, but not round and not square, with rawhide holding the shutters up on the outside. This house is in a pasture, too, like the other one. No doubt when Dee sees it she will want to tear it down. She wrote me once that no matter where we "choose" to live, she will manage to come see us. But she will never bring her friends. Maggie and I thought about this and Maggie asked me, "Mama, when did Dee ever *have* any friends?"

She had a few. Furtive[3] boys in pink shirts hanging about on washday after school. Nervous

> At sixteen she had a style of her own—and knew what style was.

---

2. **organdy** (ôr′gən dē′), *n.* a fine, thin, stiff, transparent material, used for dresses, curtains, etc.

3. **furtive** (fėr′tiv), *adj.* sly, stealthy.

girls who never laughed. Impressed with her they worshipped the well-turned phrase, the cute shape, the scalding humor that erupted like bubbles in lye. She read to them.

When she was courting Jimmy T, she didn't have much time to pay to us, but turned all her fault-finding power on him. He *flew* to marry a cheap city girl from a family of ignorant flashy people. She hardly had time to recompose herself.

When she comes I will meet—but there they are!

Maggie attempts to make a dash for the house, in her shuffling way, but I stay her with my hand. "Come back here," I say. And she stops and tries to dig a well in the sand with her toe.

PREDICT: What do you think the reunion between the narrator and her daughter Dee will be like?

It is hard to see them clearly through the strong sun. But even the first glimpse of leg out of the car tells me it is Dee. Her feet were always neat-looking, as if God himself had shaped them with a certain style. From the other side of the car comes a short, stocky man. Hair is all over his head a foot long and hanging from his chin like a kinky mule tail. I hear Maggie suck in her breath. "Uhnnnh," is what it sounds like. Like when you see the wriggling end of a snake just in front of your foot on the road. "Uhnnnh."

Dee next. A dress down to the ground, in this hot weather. A dress so loud it hurts my eyes. There are yellows and oranges enough to throw back the light of the sun. I feel my whole face warming from the heat waves it throws out. Earrings gold, too, and hanging down to her shoulders. Bracelets dangling and making noises when she moves her arm up to shake the folds of the dress out of her armpits. The dress is loose and flows, and as she walks closer, I like it. I hear Maggie go "Uhnnnh" again. It is her sister's hair. It stands straight up like the wool

on a sheep. It is black as night and around the edges are two long pigtails that rope about like small lizards disappearing behind her ears.

"Wa-su-zo-Tean-o!" she says, coming on in that gliding way the dress makes her move. The short, stocky fellow with the hair to his navel is all grinning and he follows up with "Asalamalakim,[4] my mother and sister!" He moves to hug Maggie but she falls back, right up against the back of my chair. I feel her trembling there and when I look up I see the perspiration falling off her chin.

"Don't get up," says Dee. Since I am stout it takes something of a push. You can see me trying to move a second or two before I make it. She turns, showing white heels through her sandals, and goes back to the car. Out she peeks next with a Polaroid. She stoops down quickly and lines up picture after picture of me sitting there in front of the house with Maggie cowering behind me. She never takes a shot without making sure the house is included. When a cow comes nibbling around the edge of the yard she snaps it and me and Maggie *and* the house. Then she puts the Polaroid in the back seat of the car, and comes up and kisses me on the forehead.

Meanwhile Asalamalakim is going through motions with Maggie's hand. Maggie's hand is as limp as a fish, and probably as cold, dispite the sweat, and she keeps trying to pull it back. It looks like Asalamalakim wants to shake hands but wants to do it fancy. Or maybe he don't know how people shake hands. Anyhow, he soon gives up on Maggie.

"Well," I say. "Dee."

"No, Mama," She says. "Not 'Dee,' Wangero Leewanika Kemanjo!"

"What happened to 'Dee'?" I wanted to know.

"She's dead," Wangero said. "I couldn't bear

---

4. **Wa-su-zo-Tean-o! . . . Asalamalakim!** Black Muslim greetings.

it any longer, being named after the people who oppress[5] me."

CLARIFY: Why did Dee change her name?

"You know as well as me you was named after your aunt Dicie," I said. Dicie is my sister. She named Dee. We called her "Big Dee" after Dee was born.

"But who was *she* named after?" asked Wangero.

"I guess after Grandma Dee," I said.

"And who was she named after?" asked Wangero.

"Her mother," I said, and saw Wangero was getting tired. "That's about as far back as I can trace it," I said. Though, in fact, I probably could have carried it back beyond the Civil War through the branches.

"Well," said Asalamalakim, "there you are."

"Uhnnnh," I heard Maggie say.

"There I was not," I said, "before 'Dicie' cropped up in our family, so why should I try to trace it that far back?"

He just stood there grinning, looking down on me like somebody inspecting a Model A car. Every once in a while he and Wangero sent eye signals over my head.

"How do you pronounce this name?" I asked.

"You don't have to call me by it if you don't want to," said Wangero.

"Why shouldn't I?" I asked. "If it's what you want us to call you, we'll call you."

"I know it might sound awkward at first," said Wangero.

"I'll get used to it," I said. "Ream it out again."

Well, soon we got the name out of the way. Asalamalakim had a name twice as long and three times as hard. After I tripped over it two or three times he told me to just call him Hakim-a-barber. I wanted to ask him was he a barber, but I didn't really think he was, so I didn't ask.

"You must belong to those beef-cattle peoples down the road," I said. They said "Asalamalakim" when they met you, too, but they didn't shake hands. Always too busy: feeding the cattle, fixing the fences, putting up salt-lick shelters, throwing down hay. When the white folks poisoned some of the herd the men stayed up all night with rifles in their hands. I walked a mile and a half just to see the sight.

Hakim-a-barber said, "I accept some of their doctrines,[6] but farming and raising cattle is not my style." (They didn't tell me, and I didn't ask, whether Wangero [Dee] had really gone and married him.)

We sat down to eat and right away he said he didn't eat collards[7] and pork was unclean. Wangero, though, went on through the chitlins[8] and corn bread, the greens and everything else. She talked a blue streak over the sweet potatoes. Everything delighted her. Even the fact that we still used the benches her daddy made for the table when we couldn't afford to buy chairs.

"Oh, Mama!" she cried. Then turned to Hakim-a-barber. "I never knew how lovely these benches are. You can feel the rump prints," she said, running her hands underneath her and along the bench. Then she gave a sigh and her hand closed over Grandma Dee's butter dish. "That's it!" she said. "I knew there was something I wanted to ask you if I could have." She jumped up from the table and went over in the corner where the churn stood, the milk in it clabber[9] by now. She looked at the churn and looked at it.

"This churn top is what I need," she said. "Didn't Uncle Buddy whittle it out of a tree you all used to have?"

"Yes," I said.

---

5. **oppress** (ə pres′), *v.* keep down unjustly or by cruelty.
6. **doctrine** (dok′trən), *n.* a principle taught by a church, nation, or group of persons; belief.
7. **collards** (kol′ərds), *n.* the fleshy leaves of the kale plant, cooked as greens.
8. **chitlins, chitterlings** (chit′linz), *n.* parts of the small intestines of pigs, calves, etc., cooked as food.
9. **clabber** (klab′ər), *n.* thick, sour milk.

"Uh huh," she said happily. "And I want the dasher,[10] too."

"Uncle Buddy whittle that, too?" asked the barber.

Dee (Wangero) looked up at me.

"Aunt Dee's first husband whittled the dash," said Maggie so low you almost couldn't hear her. "His name was Henry, but they called him Stash."

"Maggie's brain is like an elephant's," Wangero said, laughing. "I can use the churn top as a centerpiece for the alcove[11] table," she said, sliding a plate over the churn, "and I'll think of something artistic to do with the dasher."

When she finished wrapping the dasher the handle stuck out. I took it for a moment in my hands. You didn't even have to look close to see where hands pushing the dasher up and down to make butter had left a kind of sink in the wood. In fact, there were a lot of small sinks; you could see where thumbs and fingers had sunk into the wood. It was beautiful light yellow wood, from a tree that grew in the yard where Big Dee and Stash had lived.

fter dinner Dee (Wangero) went to the trunk at the foot of my bed and started rifling through it. Maggie hung back in the kitchen over the dishpan. Out came Wangero with two quilts. They had been pieced by Grandma Dee and then Big Dee and me had hung them on the quilt frames on the front porch and quilted them. One was in the Lone Star pattern. The other was Walk Around the Mountain. In both of them were scraps of dresses Grandma Dee had worn fifty and more years ago. Bits and pieces of Grandpa Jarrell's paisley shirts. And one teeny faded blue piece, about the size of a penny matchbox, that was from Great Grandpa Ezra's uniform that he wore in the Civil War.

"Mama," Wangero said sweet as a bird. "Can I have these old quilts?"

▲ List five words that describe the physical features of the scene in this painting, *Gilley's House* (about 1976), by Bob Timberlake. Then list another five that describe the feeling you get from this painting. Are your lists similar or different from each other?

I heard something fall in the kitchen, and a minute later the kitchen door slammed.

"Why don't you take one or two of the others?" I asked. "These old things was just done by me and Big Dee from some tops your grandma pieced before she died."

"No," said Wangero. "I don't want those. They are stitched around the borders by machine."

---

10. **dasher** (dash′ər), *n.* device for stirring the cream in a churn.
11. alcove (al′kōv), *n.* a small room opening out of a larger room.

"That'll make them last better," I said.

"That's not the point," said Wangero. "These are all pieces of dresses Grandma used to wear. She did all this stitching by hand. Imagine!" She held the quilts securely in her arms, stroking them.

"Some of the pieces, like those lavender ones, come from old clothes her mother handed down to her," I said, moving up to touch the quilts. Dee (Wangero) moved back just enough so that I couldn't reach the quilts. They already belonged to her.

"Imagine!" she breathed again, clutching them closely to her bosom.

"The truth is," I said, "I promised to give them quilts to Maggie, for when she marries John Thomas."

She gasped like a bee had stung her.

"Maggie can't appreciate these quilts!" she said. "She'd probably be backward enough to put them to everyday use."

"I reckon she would," I said. "God knows I been saving 'em for long enough with nobody using 'em. I hope she will!" I didn't want to bring up how I had offered Dee (Wangero) a quilt when she went away to college. Then she had told me they were old-fashioned, out of style.

"But they're *priceless!*" she was saying now, furiously; for she had a temper. "Maggie would put them on the bed and in five years they'd be in rags. Less than that!"

"She can always make some more," I said. "Maggie knows how to quilt."

Dee (Wangero) looked at me with hatred. "You just will not understand. The point is these quilts, *these* quilts!"

"Well," I said, stumped. "What would *you* do with them?"

"Hang them," she said. As if that was the only thing you *could* do with quilts.

Maggie by now was standing in the door. I could almost hear the sound her feet made as they scraped over each other.

"She can have them, Mama," she said, like somebody used to never winning anything, or having anything reserved for her. "I can 'member Grandma Dee without the quilts."

I looked at her hard. She had filled her bottom lip with checkerberry snuff and it gave her face a kind of dopey, hangdog look. It was Grandma Dee and Big Dee who taught her how to quilt herself. She stood there with her scarred hands hidden in the folds of her skirt. She looked at her sister with something like fear but wasn't mad at her. This was Maggie's portion. This was the way she knew God to work.

When I looked at her like that something hit me in the top of my head and ran down to the soles of my feet. Just like when I'm in church and the spirit of God touches me and I get happy and shout. I did something I never had done before: hugged Maggie to me, then dragged her on into the room, snatched the quilts out of Miss Wangero's hands and dumped them into Maggie's lap. Maggie just sat there on the bed with her mouth open.

"Take one or two of the others," I said to Dee.

But she turned without a word and went out to Hakim-a-barber.

"You just don't understand," she said, as Maggie and I came out to the car.

"What don't I understand?" I wanted to know.

"Your heritage," she said. And then she turned to Maggie, kissed her, and said, "You ought to try to make something of yourself, too, Maggie. It's really a new day for us. But from the way you and Mama still live you'd never know it."

She put on some sunglasses that hid everything above the tip of her nose and her chin.

Maggie smiled; maybe at the sunglasses. But a real smile, not scared. After we watched the car dust settle I asked Maggie to bring me a dip of snuff. And then the two of us sat there just enjoying, until it was time to go in the house and go to bed.

After Reading

Making Connections

Shaping Your Response

1. Write five adjectives that you would use to describe Dee. Then write five adjectives to describe the narrator and five to describe Maggie.

Analyzing the Story

2. What is the significance of the title "Everyday Use"?

3. What do you think is the purpose of Dee's visit with her mother and sister? Explain.

4. What do you think the narrator realizes about herself during her argument with Dee over the quilts?

5. 👣 How does cultural heritage play a part in the **interactions** between Dee and her family?

Extending the Ideas

6. Dee is an ambitious person. Explain when, in your opinion, ambition is a good quality and when it is a bad quality.

Literary Focus: Figurative Language

Skim the story to find examples of similes, metaphors, and hyperbole. Make a chart like the one below in your notebook and add to it as you find examples of each kind of figure of speech.

Similes	Metaphors	Hyperbole
yard like an extended living room (p. 760)		

Vocabulary Study

Study the relationship between the first word pair for each item, then choose the word that completes the second pair so that it expresses a similar relationship.

furtive
organdy
alcove
doctrine
oppress

1. photogenic : model : : *furtive* : ____
   a. photographer   b. farmer   c. spy   d. writer

2. burlap : homely : : *organdy* : ____
   a. corduroy   b. beautiful   c. ugly   d. cozy

3. cove : lake : : *alcove* : ____
   a. river   b. room   c. neighborhood   d. porch

4. rule : school : : *doctrine* : ____
   a. belief   b. education   c. medicine   d. religion

5. lower : raise : : *oppress* : ____
   a. elevate   b. repress   c. compress   d. enslave

Expressing Your Ideas

Writing Choices

Writer's Notebook Update Families have significant material things, like the item you described in your notebook, but one intangible thing that families have is their name. Write a paragraph explaining the significance of your name—both your given name and your family name. If you, like Dee, don't like your name, write about the name you would like to have, and why you would like it.

Don't Stop Now Alice Walker has written several volumes of short stories, including *In Love and Trouble: Stories of Black Women* and *You Can't Keep a Good Woman Down*. Choose another story written by Walker, read it, and write a **summary** of it.

Other Options

Maggie Speaks Maggie doesn't say much during the course of the story. Work with a partner to create a **dialogue** that Maggie might have with her fiancé, John Thomas, discussing the events of the day. Take on the roles of the two characters and perform your dialogue for the class.

Stitching Up History One of the quilts Dee wanted was in the Lone Star pattern like the one pictured here. Research the history of quilt patterns in the United States. Some are simple blocks of cloth, and others are made with complicated designs and intricate stitchwork. Create a **quilt square,** either on graph paper or with cloth, and explain to your class the significance of the pattern. Or, use your imagination to create an **original quilt design** on paper or with cloth. Be sure to title your design.

Before Reading

Mirror by Sylvia Plath
One Art by Elizabeth Bishop
Legacies by Nikki Giovanni

Leaves by Sam Hamod
To Jesus Villanueva, with Love by Alma Luz Villanueva

Building Background

Deep Thoughts Introspection is the art of looking within one's heart and soul and reflecting on what is there. *Who is important to me? What is important to me? What should I do? How should I behave?* All of these are questions we ask ourselves in introspective moments. The five poems you are about to read are different in tone, form, and style, but each is the result of the poet's introspection about a relationship in his or her life.

Literary Focus

Personification Just as the mirror in "Snow White" comes alive and speaks, the mirror in Sylvia Plath's poem "Mirror" tells about the woman who looks into it. This technique of attributing human qualities to nonhuman or nonliving things is called **personification.** As you read "Mirror," note details that make this technique effective for conveying the meaning of the poem. What relationship is explored in this poem?

Writer's Notebook

Poetic License Poets take some liberties with language. They may disregard the rules of punctuation, grammar, or capitalization to achieve the effect they desire. They may or may not impose a rhythm and/or rhyme on their words. Before reading the following poems, copy a favorite short poem into your notebook. Does the poet take any liberties with the conventions of language? As you read the five poems that follow, try to answer these questions:

- Which of the poems disregard the conventions of capitalization and punctuation?

- Which of the poems are more structured?

- Which poems use conversational language or colloquial speech in them?

- What difference do these things make?

Sylvia Plath
1932–1963

When her father died suddenly when she was eight, Sylvia Plath began writing poetry as "a new way of being happy." She won a Fulbright scholarship to Cambridge University, where she met and married English poet Ted Hughes. She battled chronic depression her whole life, and killed herself at the age of thirty-one.

Elizabeth Bishop
1911–1979

Elizabeth Bishop's father died when she was eight months old, and her mother was committed to a mental institution in 1916. She was raised by relatives. After college, Bishop made a trip to Europe that whetted her appetite for adventure. A later two-week trip to Brazil stretched into a fifteen-year stay. Bishop's poetry won many awards, among them the Pulitzer Prize and the National Book Award.

Nikki Giovanni
born 1943

Nikki Giovanni enrolled in Fisk University when she was sixteen. When she was suspended for leaving the campus without permission to visit her sick grandmother, she quit college, disgusted with the rigid rules. She later returned to Fisk and began to write poetry. She presently teaches at Virginia Polytechnic and State University.

Sam Hamod
born 1936

Born in his parents' boardinghouse in Gary, Indiana, Lebanese American poet Sam Hamod has said, "My earliest recollections are of my father, mother, and maternal grandfather, plus a lot of guys who roomed at the hotel and ate with us—gandy dancers, railroad firemen and engineers, open-hearth workers—everything—and from every nationality in the world." Hamod is currently a professor of English at Howard University.

Alma Luz Villanueva
born 1944

In her poetry, novels, and short stories, Villanueva relates her experiences as a woman in a male-dominated society, as part of an extended family, as a mother of four, and as a Chicana in a white society. Her novel, *The Ultraviolet Sky,* won an American Book Award in 1989. She teaches at the University of California at Santa Cruz.

What do you think is happening in George Tooker's painting, *Mirror II* (1963)? Write an explanation that tells your view of the relationship between the young woman, the old woman, and the mirror. ➤

Mirror

Sylvia Plath

I am silver and exact. I have no preconceptions.[1]
Whatever I see I swallow immediately
Just as it is, unmisted by love or dislike.
I am not cruel, only truthful—
5 The eye of a little god, four-cornered.
Most of the time I meditate[2] on the opposite wall.
It is pink, with speckles. I have looked at it so long
I think it is a part of my heart. But it flickers.
Faces and darkness separate us over and over.

10 Now I am a lake. A woman bends over me,
Searching my reaches for what she really is.
Then she turns to those liars, the candles or the moon.
I see her back, and reflect it faithfully.
She rewards me with tears and an agitation of hands.
15 I am important to her. She comes and goes.
Each morning it is her face that replaces the darkness.
In me she has drowned a young girl, and in me an old woman
Rises toward her day after day, like a terrible fish.

---

1. **preconception** (prē′kən sep′shən), *n.* idea or opinion formed beforehand.
2. **meditate** (med′ə tāt), *v.* engage in deep and serious thought.

One Art

Elizabeth Bishop

The art of losing isn't hard to master;
so many things seem filled with the intent
to be lost that their loss is no disaster.

Lose something every day. Accept the fluster
5 of lost door keys, the hour badly spent.
The art of losing isn't hard to master.

Then practice losing farther, losing faster:
places, and names, and where it was you meant
to travel. None of these will bring disaster.

10 I lost my mother's watch. And look! my last, or
next-to-last, of three loved houses went.
The art of losing isn't hard to master.

I lost two cities, lovely ones. And, vaster,
some realms I owned, two rivers, a continent.
15 I miss them, but it wasn't a disaster.

—Even losing you (the joking voice, a gesture
I love) I shan't have lied. It's evident[1]
the art of losing's not too hard to master
though it may look like (*Write* it!) like disaster.

---

1. **evident** (ev′ə dənt), *adj.* easy to see or understand.

Legacies

Nikki Giovanni

her grandmother called her from the
     playground
    "yes, ma'am"
    "i want chu to learn how to make rolls,"
     said the old
woman proudly
5 but the little girl didn't want
to learn how because she knew
even if she couldn't say it that
that would mean when the old one died
     she would be less
dependent on her spirit so
10 she said
    "i don't want to know how to make
     no rolls"
with her lips poked out
and the old woman wiped her hands on
her apron saying "lord
15   these children"
and neither of them ever
said what they meant
and i guess nobody ever does

▲ What feeling would you say the artist, Lois Mailou Jones, has
captured in her 1943 oil painting, *Jennie?* How does the work
convey the feeling?

Leaves

Hamod

FOR DAVID, LAURA, AND SALLY

Tonight, Sally and I are making stuffed
grapeleaves, we get out a package, it's
drying out, I've been saving it in the freezer, it's
one of the last things my father ever picked in this
5 life—they're over five years old
and up till now
we just kept finding packages of them in the
freezer, as if he were still picking them
somewhere   packing them
10 carefully to send us
making sure they didn't break into pieces.

* * *

"To my Dar Garnchildn
Davd and Lura
from Thr Jido"
15 twisted on tablet paper
between the lines
in this English lettering
hard for him even to print,
I keep this small torn record,
20 this piece of paper stays in the upstairs storage,
one of the few pieces of American
my father ever wrote. We find his Arabic letters
all over the place, even in the files we find
letters to him in English, one I found from Charles Atlas[1]
25 telling him, in 1932,
"Of course, Mr. Hamod, you too can build
your muscles like mine . . ."

* * *

Last week my mother told me, when I was
asking why I became a poet, "But don't you remember,
30 your father made up poems, don't you remember him
singing in the car as we drove—those were poems."
Even now, at night, I sometimes
get out the Arabic grammar book
though it seems so late.

---

1. **Charles Atlas,** a famous bodybuilder.

What effect do the colors in Fatima Del Real's 1988 painting, *Tacos Sabrosos,* have on the mood of the painting? ➤

To Jesus Villanueva, with Love

Alma Luz Villanueva

my first vivid memory of you
mamacita,
we made tortillas together
yours, perfect and round
5 mine, irregular and fat
we laughed
and named them: *ose, pajarito, gatito.*[1]
my last vivid memory of you
      (except for the very last
10   sacred memory
      i won't share)
mamacita
beautiful, thick, long, gray hair
the eyes gone sad
15 with flashes of fury
when they wouldn't let you
have your chilis, your onions, your peppers
      —what do these damned gringos[2]
            know of *my* stomach?—
so when I came to comb
20 your beautiful, thick, long, gray hair

as we sat for hours
(it soothed you
my hand
on your hair)
25 I brought you your chilis, your onions,
            your peppers.
and they'd always catch you
because you'd forget
and leave it lying open.
they'd scold you like a child
30 and you'd be embarrassed like a child
silent, repentant,[3] angry
and secretly waiting for my visit, the new
            supplies
we laughed at our secret

---

1. *ose, pajarito, gatito,* the Spanish words for bear (oso), little bird, little cat.
2. *gringos,* Spanish word for English-speaking people.
3. repentant (ri pen′tənt), *adj.* feeling regret; sorry for wrongdoing.

we always laughed
35   you and I
you never could understand
the rules
at clinics, welfare offices, schools
any of it.
40 I did.
you lie. you push. you get.
I learned to do all this by
the third clinic day of being persistently[4]
sent to the back of the line by 5 in the
      afternoon
45 and being so close to done by 8 in the
      morning.
so my lungs grew larger
and my voice got louder
and a doctor consented
to see an old lady,
50 and the welfare would give you the money
and the landlady would remember to
      spray for cockroaches
and the store would charge the food till
      the check came
and the bank might cash the check if I got
      the nice man this time
and I'd order hot dogs and Cokes for us
55 at the old "Crystal Palace" on Market
      Street
and we'd sit on the steps
by the rear exit, laughing
      you and I

mamacita,
60 I remember you proudly at Christmas
time, church at midnight services:
you wear a plain black dress
your hair down, straight and silver
(you always wore it up
65 tied in a kerchief,
knotted to the side)
your face shining, your eyes clear,
your vision intact.

you play Death.
70 you are Death.
you quote long stanzas from a poem
      I've long
forgotten;
even fitful babies hush
such is the power of your voice,
75 your presence
fills us all.
the special, pregnant
silence.
eyes and hands lifted up
80 imploringly and passionately
the vision and power
offered to us,
eyes and hands cast down
it flows through you
85 to us,
a gift.

your daughter, my mother
told me a story I'd never
heard before;
90   you were leaving Mexico
      with your husband and two
      older children, pregnant
      with my mother.
      the U.S. customs officer
95   undid everything you so
      preciously packed, you
      took a sack, blew it up
      and when he asked about
      the contents of the sack,
100   well, you popped it with
      your hand and shouted
      MEXICAN AIR!

aiiiiiiiiii mamacita, Jesus,
I won't forget my visions and reality.
105 to lie, to push, to get
just isn't
enough.

---

4. **persistently** (pər sis′tənt lē), *adv.* continually.

After Reading

Making Connections

Shaping Your Response

1. Which one of these five poems had the greatest impact on you? Why?

2. If you were to associate emotions with these poems, what would they be? Make a chart like the one shown here in your notebook and fill it in. Be prepared to explain your choices.

Poem	Emotion
"Mirror"	
"One Art"	

Analyzing the Poems

3. What relationship does the poem "The Mirror" explore?

4. Describe the **tone** of the first five stanzas of "One Art." How does it change in the last stanza?

5. What do you learn about Hamod's father from each stanza of "Leaves"?

6. What is the **point of view** of each poem?

7. 👆 Describe the person-to-person **interactions** discussed in each poem.

Extending the Ideas

8. The poems by Hamod, Villanueva, and Giovanni all portray memorable relationships. If you were to write a poem describing a relationship that you have, who would it be about? What is special about that relationship?

Literary Focus: Personification

The mirror in the poem "Mirror" is **personified,** or given human attributes. Reread the first stanza and list all the phrases that describe what human things the mirror does.

Vocabulary Study

Answer the following questions. Use the Glossary for help with the italicized vocabulary words.

meditate
evident
preconception
repentant
persistently

1. What does the narrator of "One Art" *meditate* about?

2. What fact is *evident* near the end of the poem about the woman described in "Mirror"?

3. Describe a common *preconception* about aging.

4. What words might a *repentant* person say to someone he or she has harmed?

5. If a patient calls the doctor *persistently,* does he or she call occasionally, reluctantly, or constantly?

Expressing Your Ideas _____

Writing Choices

Writer's Notebook Update Choose one of the five poems in this section and write an analysis of it. Discuss the form of the poem and any special techniques used by the poet. Consider the point of view, the use of dialect or colloquial speech, figurative language, rhythm, and rhyme, and tell how these things might relate to the poem's meaning.

A Tribute Hamod, Giovanni, and Villanueva each wrote a poem as a tribute to a close relative. Choose a family member or friend that you would like to honor. Either write an original **poem** or a **personal narrative** telling an anecdote about your relationship.

Other Options

Voices of the Twentieth Century Go to the library and find another poem by one of these five poets, or choose a poem by a different twentieth-century poet. Work with a small group to present a **poetry reading** of several poems.

Picture the Poem What do you visualize when you read each of these poems? Choose one of the poems and create an **illustration** that captures the emotions represented in the poem and presents the setting.

Cultural Legacies Hamod's father came from Lebanon and Villanueva's grandmother came from Mexico. Choose one of these countries and research its history, geography, and culture, and look into the lives of Americans whose ancestors came from that country. Either present an **oral report** to the class or create a **hyperstudio report** presenting your findings.

Pop Culture Connection

The most dramatic cultural change in America in the 1950s was the rapid growth of television. In 1950, only 5 million American families had a TV. By the middle of the decade televisions could be found in 32 million homes.

The most striking thing about the arrival of television on the American scene was certainly the almost apocalyptic suddenness with which it became a fully established part of our national life, complete with a huge audience and an established minority opposition, affecting not only all our other communications media and the whole world of our popular arts but also our manners, morals, habits, ways of thinking.

Life After Television

John Brooks

Children have been one of the most enthusiastic portions of television's mass audience since its arrival in the early 1950s.

By comparison, the much chronicled automobile revolution earlier in the century had been [very gradual]. . . . As late as 1948 there were still fewer than 20 TV stations on the air, and only 172,000 families had receiving sets. Then the explosion began. During 1949 and 1950 sets were installed at a rate sometimes as high as a quarter of a million a month. In June, 1950, there were more than 100 stations operating in 38 states; coaxial cable, the device by which reception is extended beyond a station's normal range and network broadcasting is made possible, reached along the East Coast from Boston to Richmond, and westward as far as Milwaukee and St. Louis; and the census of that year found 5 million families with TV sets in the house.

What happened next is already history. Set ownership rose at a rate of roughly 5 million a year during the 1950s. Here, surely, was something totally unprecedented in world history. Neither in this nation nor in any other had anything like 5 million families per year ever acquired for the first time any wholly new thing of any sort. . . .

There were moments in the late Fifties, when television had become all-pervasive and yet still retained the sheen of a new toy, when it seemed almost to bring our national life to a halt. The year 1954 saw the "TV dinner" make its appearance; it also saw the city of Toledo make the astonishing discovery that water consumption rose startlingly during certain three-minute periods that turned out to be the time of commercials during popular programs. In a small town that I know of, at certain hours no one was to be seen in the streets; the stores and restaurants were almost deserted, and a strange hush fell; and even a telephone call was generally answered curtly and with ill grace. No one could be very much surprised at the results of a national survey made by Westinghouse Electric shortly after the beginning of the 1960s. More man-hours per year in the United States, Westinghouse found, were being spent watching TV than were spent working for pay. . . .

Almost as sudden as the arrival of TV was the emergence of the critical counterattack. . . . In particular, the attacks had been, and continued to be, focused on the effects on children, an audience so numerous and so devoted that some TV men say they constitute, collectively, a virtual tyranny dictating the timing and nature of programming. Does the child . . . who sits mesmerized in front of the screen 20 or 30 hours a week, suffer any lasting effects from the experience? Are the eyes damaged? Does the violence of the programs predispose to a life of crime? Does the passivity of the act of watching damage initiative? While none of these charges has been definitely proved, none has been definitely proved false. A report to the American Academy of Pediatrics in the fall of 1964 declared that excessive television watching can lead to a specific physical sickness—the "tired-child syndrome," characterized by fatigue, headache, loss of appetite, and vomiting, and curable only by abstinence from television. Nor is excessive exposure to such hazards an exclusively American phenomenon; a United Nations study published in 1965 showed that childhood TV-watching habits in Japan and England are about the same as here.

What's on TV?

What were so many Americans watching with such devotion during the 1950s? Many of the new programs were adapted from radio shows and vaudeville comedy, while others struck out in new directions, taking advantage of the abilities of the new TV medium. The following are a few of the shows that left their mark on the '50s.

SITUATION COMEDIES

In 1951 film and radio comedienne Lucille Ball tried out the new medium with a television sit-com featuring her as the wacky wife of a Cuban bandleader played by her real-life husband Desi Arnaz. *I Love Lucy* was among the most successful programs in television history, remaining the number one show on TV throughout the early '50s and appearing in syndicated reruns ever since.

Television has never paid much attention to working-class America. A notable exception was *The Honeymooners,* a sit-com set in the run-down apartment of bus driver Ralph Cramden and his wife Alice. This program, starring Jackie Gleason as Ralph, began as a popular comedy sketch on Gleason's variety program and later became a series in its own right. While not as successful as an independent program, it remains one of the best remembered sit-coms of the 1950s.

QUIZ AND GAME SHOWS

Quiz programs and game shows had long been featured on radio. But radio's *$64 Question* underwent a huge inflation in moving to television in the summer of 1955. TV's *$64,000 Question* was an overnight hit. As a recent history of television observes, "The appeal of seeing ordinary people sweating through complex questions to reach huge sums of money was enormous." In the late 1950s a scandal erupted concerning rigging of the big-money quiz shows and their popularity abruptly waned.

One of the best known TV game shows was *What's My Line?*, where a celebrity panel attempted to guess the occupations of the contestants. The wit of regular panelists such as actress Arlene Francis proved engaging and *What's My Line?* ran for 18 seasons.

Journalist Edward R. Murrow became famous for his dramatic radio news broadcasts from wartime London. On November 18, 1951, he premiered his television news program, *See It Now,* with a striking demonstration of the potential of the new medium, showing simultaneous live shots of both the Atlantic and Pacific Ocean and commenting that "no journalistic age was ever given a weapon for truth with quite the scope of this fledgling television." Murrow's style of television journalism proved its worth in 1954, when he used it to expose the smear tactics of anticommunist crusader Senator Joseph McCarthy.

Responding

1. Does TV have the same impact on society today that it had back in the 50s? Why or why not?

2. Early criticism of TV warned that it could become "the opiate of the people" and "would corrupt the morals of the young." Looking back, were the concerns of TV critics valid? What new criticisms have been sounded about TV?

Writing Workshop

You Be the Judge

Assignment In their stories in this part of the unit, Tillie Olson, John Updike, Alice Walker, and Maxine Hong Kingston write about person-to-person relationships. Which author created the most true-to-life relationship? You be the judge.

WRITER'S BLUEPRINT

Product	A literary critique
Purpose	To present convincingly your views on how a fiction writer makes a person-to-person relationship seem true-to-life
Audience	People who have read the literature
Specs	As the writer of an effective critique, you should:

❑ Establish your own criteria for what makes a relationship in a story seem true-to-life and then, based on these criteria, decide which person-to-person relationship in the four stories is most realistic.

❑ Begin your written critique by declaring your choice and describing the criteria you used in making it.

❑ Go on to describe this relationship and explain why you consider it the most realistic. Support your position with quotations from the stories.

❑ Anticipate reasons why others might disagree, and provide counter-arguments.

❑ Conclude with a summary of your main points and a strong statement of support for your choice, using an authoritative tone that demands serious consideration. Write in the active voice.

❑ Follow the rules of grammar for correct usage, spelling, and mechanics. Pay special attention to the comparative forms of adjectives and adverbs.

1 PREWRITING

Establish criteria for a realistic relationship. Ask yourself: *What makes the writing about this relationship realistic?* Review the Olson, Updike, Walker, and Kingston stories and make notes on details that seem true-to-life. Organize your notes into a chart like the one shown.

Realistic Details

Story/Characters	Characterization	Dialogue	Actions
"I Stand Here Ironing" —Emily's mother and Emily	". . . and she tells me everything and nothing . . ." (Superficial conversation is like this.)	" ' . . . I did it. I won, I won . . .' " (repeating things when you get excited)	mother does everyday chore of ironing

Now look over your chart and draw conclusions. These conclusions will become your criteria for judgment. Here is part of one student's list:

STUDENT MODEL

○
○
○

> **Characterization:** All four stories involve characters who have problems communicating. In real life, that happens a lot. One person says one thing and the other person hears something else. The result is they never quite connect.
>
> **Dialogue:** The characters in these stories speak like real people do. For example,

LITERARY SOURCE

"This is one of her communicative nights, and she tells me everything and nothing as she fixes herself a plate of food out of the icebox."
from "I Stand Here Ironing" by Tillie Olsen

Discuss your criteria. With a small group, discuss each other's criteria for realistic writing about relationships. Use group members' comments and observations to help you revise and sharpen your criteria.

Make your judgment. Using the criteria you've developed, rank each relationship somewhere on the following scale. Your highest-ranked relationship is the one you'll present.

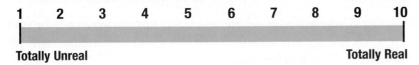

| 1 | 2 | 3 | 4 | 5 | 6 | 7 | 8 | 9 | 10 |

Totally Unreal   **Totally Real**

Revisit the story you chose and make more detailed notes on characterization, setting, dialogue, and plot.

Listen to opposing viewpoints and prepare counter-arguments. Meet with a group of classmates who've chosen a different relationship and discuss your differing viewpoints. Listen carefully to your classmates' reasons for choosing a different relationship, and make notes on counter-arguments you'll be providing in your critique.

Plan your essay. Organize your thoughts in a three-part outline like the one shown:

- **Introduction**
    Your choice
    Your criteria

- **Body**
    Description of the relationship
    Why it's the most realistic
        —characterization (with supporting details and quotations)
        —dialogue (with supporting details and quotations)
        —actions (with supporting details and quotations)
    Reasons others might disagree
    Counter-arguments

- **Conclusion**
    Summary of main points from body
    Closing statement of support for your choice

OR . . .
In addition to taking notes on each opposing viewpoint, complete this written statement: I disagree with your choice because ____.

STEP  DRAFTING

Start writing. As you draft, concentrate on developing a persuasive argument. The following tips may help you get started:

- Begin your critique with a quote from the story that you feel exemplifies realistic writing about a relationship. Then state your choice.

- When you finish the introduction and body, pause and review. Check your main points against the points listed in the Conclusion part of your plan. You may find that your main points have changed. If so, revise the last part of your plan before writing the conclusion.

- Approach your critique as you would a formal argument or debate. Write in a strong, persuasive tone in the active voice. See the Revising Strategy in Step 3 of this lesson.

3 REVISING

Ask a partner for comments on your draft before you revise it. Pay special attention to writing in the active voice.

Revising Strategy

Writing in the Active Voice

Verbs in the active voice express action done *by* the subject of the sentence, while verbs in the passive voice show action done *to* the subject. In general, the active voice makes writing clearer, more concise, and more forceful. For example:

Passive: A descriptive language was created by Emily.

Active: Emily created her own descriptive language.

As you revise, check to see that you're writing in the active voice. Notice how this writer made his critique more forceful and direct by changing passive-voice sentences to the active voice.

○ ~~Nothing was suspected by~~ the eldest daughter, Judith, and so *suspected nothing*
~~she continued to be protected by~~ her family. They recalled pushing *continued to protect her*

○ her in a carriage nineteen years earlier.

4 EDITING

Ask a partner to review your revised draft before you edit. As you edit, pay special attention to the comparative forms of adjectives and adverbs.

Editing Strategy

FOR REFERENCE
You'll find more rules for using comparative forms of adjectives and adverbs in the Language and Grammar Handbook at the back of this text.

Comparative Forms of Adjectives and Adverbs

Avoid the common mistake of using "more" or "less" with adjectives or adverbs that are already in the comparative form. For example:

Incorrect: Her burdens were <u>more bigger</u> when Emily was small.
Correct: Her burdens were <u>bigger</u> when Emily was small.

Incorrect: Ronnie's crying during the night occurs <u>less oftener</u> now.
Correct: Ronnie's crying during the night occurs <u>less often</u> now.

STEP 5 PRESENTING

- Read your critique aloud to a small group of classmates who chose different relationships, and discuss the similarities among the criteria you each chose. Come up with a list of criteria for fiction which portrays a realistic relationship that you all agree on and turn it into a poster to be displayed in the classroom.

- Work up a short TV-style thumbs-up thumbs-down discussion in which you and a classmate, as literary critics, describe your disagreements over one of the selections, and present your discussion to the class.

STEP 6 LOOKING BACK

Self-evaluate. Look back at the Writer's Blueprint and give yourself a score on each point, from 6 (superior) to 1 (inadequate).

Reflect. Think about what you learned from writing your critique as you write answers to these questions.

✔ Looking back at the stories, which relationship was least true-to-life? Explain why.

✔ Think about the relationships you have in your own life. Which one do you feel is the most important and why?

For Your Working Portfolio Add your critique and your reflection responses to your working portfolio.

Beyond Print

Looking at Television

Why do some TV shows bomb, while others return to entertain us year after year? The best shows maintain a life of their own in reruns and videos even after they're canceled. What makes them last?

Some of the shows you read about from the fifties—shows like *I Love Lucy* and *The Honeymooners*—are still popular in reruns today. *M*A*S*H*, a series about a medical unit in the Korean War, lasted longer than the actual Korean War did. In the eighties shows like *The Cosby Show* and *Cheers* were memorable, while more recent hits like *Roseanne, The Simpsons, Seinfeld, Friends,* and *E.R.* came back season after season. Why do some last while others fail? To unravel this TV mystery, analyze your favorite television program using the following criteria:

Characters What makes the characters so interesting? Why are viewers willing to spend time with them week after week? Consider personality, lifestyle, sense of humor, commitment, zaniness, and appearance.

Themes Why are the weekly stories so interesting to viewers? What universal human conditions does the show manage to describe? What interesting and unusual twists does the show depict? How do the stories develop? How do the beginnings, middles, and endings make viewers feel satisfied?

Composition and Editing What does the show look like? What do viewers see that is both comfortable and interesting? How does the show keep moving? How are transitions handled? Describe the overall visual appeal of the show.

Other Criteria Apply any other criteria you feel is important to a successful, long term television show.

Activity Option

Your Analysis Share your analysis of your favorite television program with classmates. If it's a relatively new program, use your analysis to convince classmates of the potential of the show to become a classic. Unfortunately, only time can prove you right, but in a few years you may find yourself to be a great predictor of quality television.

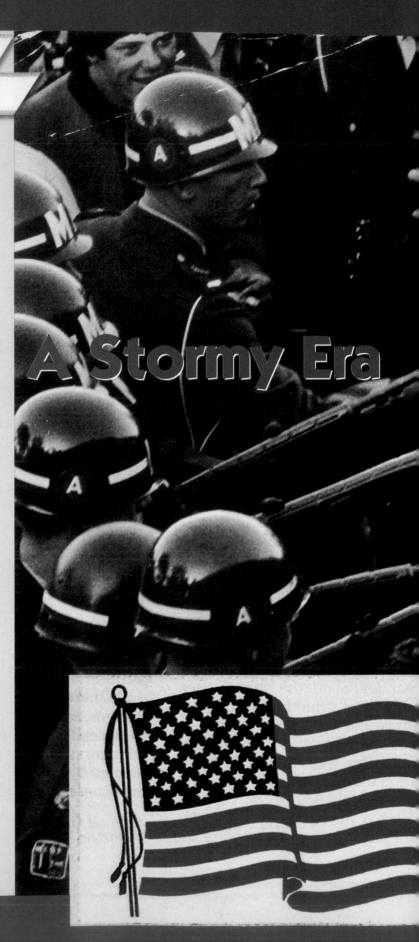

A Stormy Era

HISTORICAL OVERVIEW

The period from the mid-1950s to the mid-1970s was a political, social, and cultural watershed for the United States, as Americans found themselves challenged by a variety of issues. At home, inspired by the African American civil rights movement, a variety of groups, including women, American Indians, and Latinos sought greater freedom and equality. Internationally, U. S. involvement in the Southeast Asian country of Vietnam resulted in America's longest and most divisive war, producing stalemate on the battlefield and protest at home. Beginning with the assassination of President Kennedy, violence haunted American politics during this period. But it was also a hopeful time, in which many Americans felt that by coming together with optimism and good will they could change their society.

An anti-war protest and a popular pro-war bumper sticker reflect two views of the Vietnam War. ➤

AMERICA: LOVE IT OR LEAVE IT

Key Dates

1954
Supreme Court outlaws racially segregated schools.

1955
Montgomery bus boycott begins.

1962
Cesar Chavez organizes United Farm Workers.

1963
Civil rights march on Washington, D.C. takes place. President Kennedy assassinated.

1966
National Organization for Women founded.

1968
Martin Luther King, Jr., assassinated. Anti-war protests mark Democratic Convention.

1970
First Earth Day observed.

1973
American Indians occupy Wounded Knee.

1975
United States withdraws from Vietnam.

Part Two

In the Midst of Struggle . . .

The 1960s and '70s proved to be very turbulent decades for the United States as African Americans began to demand the rights they fought for in the Civil War but were never fully granted; as young Americans began protesting a war they didn't understand or support and yet were forced, if drafted, to fight; as women began demanding equal opportunities in the workplace and in society. The following selections describe individuals in the midst of these struggles.

 Multicultural Connection In times of great social upheaval, individuals often find themselves in the position of having to make difficult **choices.** As they are caught between society's expectations and personal convictions, note the kinds of choices the individuals in the following selections face.

Literature

Lorraine Hansberry   *from* **To Be Young, Gifted and Black**
◆ autobiographical essay 794

Martin Luther King, Jr.   *from* **Letter from a Birmingham Jail** ◆ letter . .800

Malcolm X   *from* **The Autobiography of Malcolm X**
◆ autobiography 806

Tim O'Brien   **On the Rainy River** ◆ short story 812

Nguyên Qúi Dú'c   *from* **Where the Ashes Are** ◆ autobiography . .828

Estela Portillo Trambley   **Village** ◆ short story 838

Interdisciplinary Study   Time of Turmoil: 1955–1975

The Pace of Change ◆ history 846

Language History

Euphemisms: Polite and Deadly Language 851

Writing Workshop   Narrative Writing

Reflecting on the Sixties 852

Beyond Print   Technology

Multimedia Presentations 857

Before Reading

To Be Young, Gifted and Black

by Lorraine Hansberry

Lorraine Hansberry
1930–1965

Lorraine Hansberry's mother and father were both political activists determined to fight racism. When she was eight years old, her family moved to an all-white neighborhood on Chicago's South Side to fight racial segregation. Angry neighbors threw bricks and stones at the family's new home. When the lower courts ordered the family to move, Hansberry's father took their case to the U.S. Supreme Court. In the famous *Hansberry* v. *Lee* decision, the Court declared that neighborhood segregation was unconstitutional. In *To Be Young, Gifted and Black,* Hansberry discusses her family's political activism and the effect it had on her life.

Building Background

Hansberry's Legacy When Lorraine Hansberry died of cancer at age 34, she left behind three file cabinets of manuscripts. One of her last notes read: "If anything should happen—before 'tis done—may I trust that all commas and periods will be placed and someone will complete my thoughts. . . . This last should be the least difficult—since there are so many who think as I do . . . " After she died, Hansberry's husband, Robert Nemiroff, gathered together many of these manuscripts and published them under the title *To Be Young, Gifted and Black.*

Literary Focus

Point of View In literature, a story is told by a narrator from a particular point of view, or vantage point. The story may be related by a character in his or her own words *(first-person point of view)* or by a narrator who is not a character and stands anonymously outside the action *(third-person point of view).* The third-person point of view may be either *omniscient* (able to see into the minds of all characters), *limited* (confined to a single character's perspective), or *objective* (a factual, eyewitness account).

Copy the chart below. Fill it in with examples from your reading of each type of point of view. Then, after you've read "To Be Young, Gifted and Black," identify the point of view that is used.

Point of View	Selection Name	What You Know About the Narrator
first-person		
third-person *omniscient*		
third-person *limited*		
third-person *objective*		

Writer's Notebook

Family Ideals In her essay Hansberry mentions the ideals and attitudes her parents instilled in their children. In your notebook, make a list of the ideals you would like to instill in your children someday.

To Be
YOUNG, GIFTED AND BLACK

Lorraine Hansberry

What do the individual details and faces in Romare Bearden's 1969 collage, *Black Manhattan* remind you of? Jot down any words or thoughts the images call to mind, then write a statement about why you think Romare Bearden brought these images together in his collage. ➤

Chicago: Southside Summers

1 For some time now—I think since I was a child—I have been possessed of the desire to put down the stuff of my life. That is a commonplace impulse, apparently, among persons of massive self-interest; sooner or later we all do it. And, I am quite certain, there is only one internal quarrel: how much of the truth to tell? How much, how much, how much! It *is* brutal, in sober uncompromising moments, to reflect on the comedy of concern we all enact when it comes to our precious images!

Even so, when such vanity as propels the writing of such memoirs is examined, certainly one would wish at least to have some boast of social serviceability on one's side. I shall set down in these pages what shall seem to me to be the truth of my life and essences . . . which are to be found, first of all, on the Southside of Chicago, where I was born. . . .

2 All travelers to my city should ride the elevated trains that race along the back ways of Chicago. The lives you can look into!

I think you could find the tempo of my people on their back porches. The honesty of their living is there in the shabbiness. Scrubbed porches that sag and look their danger. Dirty gray wood steps. And always a line of white and pink clothes scrubbed so well, waving in the dirty wind of the city.

My people are poor. And they are tired. And they are determined to live.

Our Southside is a place apart: each piece of our living is a protest.

3 I was born on May 19, 1930, the last of four children.

Of love and my parents there is little to be written: their relationship to the children was utilitarian.[1] We were fed and housed and dressed and outfitted with more cash than our associates and that was all. We were also vaguely taught certain vague absolutes: that we were better than no one but infinitely superior to everyone; that we were the products of the proudest and most mistreated of the races of man; that there was nothing enormously difficult about life; that one *succeeded* as a matter of course.

Life was not a struggle—it was something that one *did*. One won an argument because, if facts gave out, one invented them—with color! The only sinful people in the world were dull people. And, above all, there were two things which were never to be betrayed: the family and the race. But of love, there was nothing ever said.

If we were sick, we were sternly, impersonally and carefully nursed and doctored back to health. Fevers, toothaches were attended to with urgency and importance; one always felt *important* in my family. Mother came with a tray to your room with the soup and Vick's salve or gave the enemas in a steaming bathroom. But we were not fondled, any of us—head held to breast, fingers about that head—until we were grown, all of us, and my father died.

At his funeral I at last, in my memory, saw my mother hold her sons that way, and for the first time in her life my sister held me in her arms I think. We were not a loving people: we were passionate in our hostilities and affinities,[2] but the caress embarrassed us.

We have changed little. . . .

4 Seven years separated the nearest of my brothers and sisters and myself; I wear, I am sure, the earmarks of that familial station to this day. Little has been written or thought to my knowledge about children who

---

1. **utilitarian** (yŭ til′ə ter′ē ən), *adj.* designed for usefulness rather than beauty.
2. **affinity** (ə fin′ə tē), *n.* attraction to people or things.

occupy that place: the last born separated by an uncommon length of time from the next youngest. I suspect we are probably a race apart.

The last born is an object toy which comes in years when brothers and sisters who are seven, ten, twelve years older are old enough to appreciate it rather than poke out its eyes. They do not mind diapering you the first two years, but by the time you are five you are a pest that has to be attended to in the washroom, taken to the movies, and "sat with" at night. You are not a person—you are a nuisance who is not particular fun anymore. Consequently, you swiftly learn to play alone. . . .

5 My childhood Southside summers were the ordinary city kind, full of the street games which other rememberers have turned into fine ballets these days, and rhymes that anticipated what some people insist on calling modern poetry:

Oh, Mary Mack, Mack, Mack
With the silver buttons, buttons, buttons
All down her back, back, back.
She asked her mother, mother, mother
For fifteen cents, cents, cents
To see the elephant, elephant, elephant
Jump the fence, fence, fence.
Well, he jumped so high, high, high
'Til he touched the sky, sky, sky
And he didn't come back, back, back
'Til the Fourth of Ju—ly, ly, ly!

I remember skinny little Southside bodies by the fives and tens of us panting the delicious hours away:

"May I?"

And the voice of authority: "Yes, you may— you may take one giant step."

One drew in all one's breath and tightened one's fist and pulled the small body against the heavens, stretching, straining all the muscles in the legs to make—one giant step.

It is a long time. One forgets the reason for the game. (For children's games are always explicit in their reasons for being. To play is to win something. Or not to be "it." Or to be high pointer, or outdoer or, sometimes—just *the winner*. But after a time one forgets.)

Why was it important to take a small step, a teeny step, or the most desired of all—one GIANT step?

A giant step to *where*?

6 Evenings were spent mainly on the back porches where screen doors slammed in the darkness with those really very special summertime sounds. And, sometimes, when Chicago nights got too steamy, the whole family got into the car and went to the park and slept out in the open on blankets. Those were, of course, the best times of all because the grownups were invariably reminded of having been children in the South and told the best stories then. And it was also cool and sweet to be on the grass and there was usually the scent of freshly cut lemons or melons in the air. Daddy would lie on his back, as fathers must, and explain about how men thought the stars above us came to be and how far away they were.

I never did learn to believe that anything could be as far away as *that*. Especially the stars. . . .

7 The man that I remember was an educated soul, though I think now, looking back, that it was as much a matter of the physical bearing of my father as his command of information and of thought that left that impression upon me. I know nothing of the "assurance of kings" and will not use that metaphor on account of it. Suffice it to say that my father's enduring image in my mind is that of a man whom kings might have imitated and properly created their own flattering descriptions of. A man who always seemed to be doing something brilliant and/or unusual to such an extent that to be doing something brilliant and/or unusual was the way I assumed fathers behaved.

He digested the laws of the State of Illinois and put them into little booklets. He invented complicated pumps and railroad devices. He could talk at length on American history and private enterprise (to which he utterly subscribed). And he carried his head in such a way that I was quite certain that there was nothing he was afraid of. Even writing this, how profoundly it shocks my inner sense to realize suddenly that *my father,* like all men, must have known *fear.* . . .

8   April 23, 1964

To the Editor,
The *New York Times:*

With reference to civil disobedience and the Congress of Racial Equality stall-in:

. . . My father was typical of a generation of Negroes who believed that the "American way" could successfully be made to work to democratize the United States. Thus, twenty-five years ago, he spent a small personal fortune, his considerable talents, and many years of his life fighting, in association with NAACP[3] attorneys, Chicago's "restrictive[4] covenants"[5] in one of this nation's ugliest ghettos.

That fight also required that our family occupy the disputed property in a hellishly hostile "white neighborhood" in which, literally, howling mobs surrounded our house. One of their missiles almost took the life of the then eight-year-old signer of this letter. My memories of this "correct" way of fighting white supremacy in America include being spat at, cursed, and pummeled[6] in the daily trek to and from school. And I also remember my desperate and courageous mother, patrolling our house all night with a loaded German luger, doggedly guarding her four children, while my father fought the respectable part of the battle in the Washington court.

The fact that my father and the NAACP "won" a Supreme Court decision, in a now famous case which bears his name in the lawbooks, is—ironically—the sort of "progress" our satisfied friends allude to when they presume[7] to deride[8] the more radical means of struggle. The cost, in emotional turmoil, time and money, which led to my father's early death as a permanently embittered exile in a foreign country when he saw that after such sacrificial efforts the Negroes of Chicago were as ghetto-locked as ever, does not seem to figure in their calculations.

That is the reality that I am faced with when I now read that some Negroes my own age and younger say that we must now lie down in the streets, tie up traffic, do whatever we can—take to the hills with guns if necessary—and fight back. Fatuous[9] people remark these days on our "bitterness." Why, of course we are bitter. The entire situation suggests that the nation be reminded of the too little noted final lines of Langston Hughes's[10] mighty poem.

What happens to a dream deferred?
Does it dry up
Like a raisin in the sun?
Or fester like a sore—
And then run?
Does it stink like rotten meat?
Or crust and sugar over—
Like a syrupy sweet?
Maybe it just sags
Like a heavy load.

Or does it explode?

Sincerely,

Lorraine Hansberry

---

3. **NAACP**, National Association for the Advancement of Colored People.
4. restrictive (ri strik′tiv), *adj.* confining; limiting.
5. covenant (kuv′ə nənt), *n.* solemn agreement; compact.
6. pummel (pum′əl), *v.* strike or beat; beat with the fists.
7. presume (pri züm′), *v.* dare; take liberties.
8. deride (di rīd′), *v.* scorn; ridicule.
9. fatuous (fach′ü əs), *adj.* stupid but self-satisfied.
10. **Langston Hughes's mighty poem,** refers to "Harlem," later published under the title "Dream Deferred."

After Reading

Making Connections

Shaping Your Response

1. Which events in Hansberry's life can you relate to the most? Explain your answer.

Analyzing the Essay

2. Would you say Hansberry is proud of her upbringing? Explain.

3. What connection do you think Hansberry makes between Langston Hughes's poem, "A Dream Deferred," and her experiences?

Extending the Ideas

4. From your experience or observation, write a brief summary indicating how you think race relations have changed since Hansberry's time.

Vocabulary Study

Use the vocabulary words in the list to complete the paragraph.

presume
restrictive
covenant
pummel
deride

Lorraine Hansberry's father spent much of his life fighting a discriminatory __(1)__ of Chicago's housing laws. To protest the __(2)__ policy, the Hansberrys moved to an all-white neighborhood. Neighbors would routinely taunt, curse, and __(3)__ the Hansberry children. Thinking back on her experiences, Hansberry wonders how critics have the nerve to __(4)__ the more radical means of protest. How can they __(5)__ to criticize if they've never been the victim of racial injustice?

Expressing Your Ideas

Picture Yourself Look carefully at Hansberry's self-portrait. Why do you suppose she chose to use the classified section of a newspaper as a background for her sketch? What would you choose as a backdrop for your own self-portrait? A shopping bag? The cover of a sports magazine? An art museum brochure? Sketch a **self-portrait,** using paper of your choice. Include an explanation of your composition.

Before Reading

from **Letter from a Birmingham Jail** by Martin Luther King, Jr.
from **The Autobiography of Malcolm X**

Martin Luther King, Jr.
1928–1968

When he was 26 years old, Martin Luther King, Jr. led a successful boycott of the Montgomery, Alabama city bus line to protest discrimination against African American riders. King spent the next 11 years leading nonviolent protest against racism. Four years after he won the 1964 Nobel Peace Prize, King was assassinated. On his tombstone is a line from his famous "I Have a Dream" speech: "Free at last, free at last, thank God Almighty, I'm free at last."

Malcolm X
1925–1965

When he was 21 years old, Malcolm Little, later known as Malcolm X, was imprisoned for burglary. While in prison he adopted the beliefs of the Nation of Islam, which preached the separation of the races. After his release, Malcolm acted as a spokesperson for the Nation of Islam until he began to question their separatist beliefs. In 1965 he was assassinated. Three men, including two members of the Nation of Islam, were sentenced to life in prison for Malcolm's murder.

Building Background

The Civil Rights Movement How much do you know about the Civil Rights Movement of the 1950s and 1960s? As a class, work together to complete the chart below. Elect a secretary to copy the chart on the board and keep notes about your class discussion. Use the "What We Want to Find Out" column to keep track of events that you need to research. After you finish reading the selections, return to your class chart to make corrections or additions as necessary.

Event	What We Know	What We Want to Find Out
1. *Brown* v. *Board of Education*		
2. Rosa Parks arrested		
3. Sit-ins at lunch counters		
4. The March on Washington		
5. "I Have a Dream" Speech		
6. The Nation of Islam		
7. "Black Power" movement		

Literary Focus

Allusion An allusion is a reference to a person, thing, event, situation, or aspect of culture. Allusions may be drawn from art, myth, literature, history, religion, or any aspect of culture. For example, in "Letter from a Birmingham Jail," King makes an allusion to the Apostle Paul and the journey he embarks upon in order to preach the gospel of Jesus Christ. As you read "Letter from a Birmingham Jail," watch for more examples of allusion. List each example in your notebook.

Writer's Notebook

Two Crusaders for Justice How was King's crusade different from Malcolm X's? Make some notes about King's and Malcolm X's struggles for freedom in your notebook.

Letter from a Birmingham Jail

DR. MARTIN LUTHER KING, JR.

By 1963, Dr. Martin Luther King, Jr. and other civil rights leaders had grown tired of waiting for President John F. Kennedy to take action on issues concerning civil rights for African Americans. King and his associates organized massive demonstrations to protest racial discrimination in Birmingham, Alabama. Police used dogs and fire hoses to drive back the peaceful protesters, many of whom were children. King, among others, was jailed for his participation in the protest. While in prison, King wrote a letter to the citizens of Birmingham. In his letter, King responds to the opinion of several Alabama clergymen that the battle for integration should take place in the courts, rather than on the streets.

My Dear Fellow Clergymen,

While confined here in the Birmingham city jail, I came across your recent statement calling our present activities "unwise and untimely." Seldom, if ever, do I pause to answer criticism of my work and ideas. If I sought to answer all of the criticisms that cross my desk, my secretaries would be engaged in little else in the course of the day, and I would have no time for constructive work. But since I feel that you are men of genuine good will and your criticisms are sincerely set forth, I would like to answer your statement in what I hope will be patient and reasonable terms.

I think I should give the reason for my being in Birmingham, since you have been influenced by the argument of "outsiders coming in." I have the honor of serving as president of the Southern Christian Leadership Conference, an organization operating in every southern state, with headquarters in Atlanta, Georgia. We have some eighty-five affiliate organizations all across the South—one being the Alabama Christian Movement for Human Rights. Whenever necessary and possible we share staff, educational and financial resources with our affiliates. Several months ago our local affiliate here in Birmingham invited us to be on call to engage in a nonviolent

This is a section of Don Miller's *King Mural* which was unveiled on the first national celebration of Dr. Martin Luther King, Jr.'s birthday on January 20, 1986. The mural depicts some of the significant people and events in King's life and is exhibited at the King Memorial Library in Washington, D.C. ➤

direct-action program if such were deemed necessary. We readily consented and when the hour came we lived up to our promises. So I am here, along with several members of my staff, because we were invited here. I am here because I have basic organizational ties here.

Beyond this, I am in Birmingham because injustice is here. Just as the eighth-century prophets left their little villages and carried their "thus saith the Lord" far beyond the boundaries of their hometowns; and just as the Apostle Paul left his little village of Tarsus and carried the gospel of Jesus Christ to practically every hamlet and city of the Graeco-Roman world, I too am compelled to carry the gospel of freedom beyond my particular hometown. Like Paul, I must constantly respond to the Macedonian call for aid.

Injustice anywhere is a threat to justice everywhere.

Moreover, I am cognizant of the interrelatedness of all communities and states. I cannot sit idly by in Atlanta and not be concerned about what happens in Birmingham. Injustice anywhere is a threat to justice everywhere. We are caught in an inescapable network of mutuality, tied in a single garment of destiny. Whatever affects one directly affects all indirectly. Never again can we afford to live with the narrow, provincial "outside agitator" idea. Anyone who lives in the United States can never be considered an outsider anywhere in this country.

You deplore the demonstrations that are presently taking place in Birmingham. But I am sorry that your statement did not express a similar concern for the conditions that brought the demonstrations into being. I am sure that each of you would want to go beyond the superficial social analyst who looks merely at effects, and does not grapple with underlying causes. I would not hesitate to say that it is unfortunate that so-called demonstrations are taking place in Birmingham at this time, but I would say in more emphatic terms that it is even more unfortunate that the white power structure of this city left the Negro community with no other alternative.

In any nonviolent campaign there are four basic steps: (1) collection of the facts to determine whether injustices are alive, (2) negotiation, (3) self-purification, and (4) direct action. We have gone through all of these steps in Birmingham. There can be no gainsaying[1] of the fact that racial injustice engulfs this community.

Birmingham is probably the most thoroughly segregated city in the United States. Its ugly record of police brutality is known in every section of this country. Its unjust treatment of Negroes in the courts is a notorious reality. There have been more unsolved bombings of Negro homes and churches in Birmingham than any city in this nation. These are the hard, brutal and unbelievable facts. On the basis of these conditions Negro leaders sought to negotiate with the city fathers. But the political leaders consistently refused to engage in good faith negotiation.

Then came the opportunity last September to talk with some of the leaders of the economic community. In these negotiating sessions certain promises were made by the merchants—such as the promise to remove the humiliating racial signs from the stores. On the basis of these promises Rev. Shuttlesworth and the leaders of the Alabama Christian Movement for Human Rights agreed to call a moratorium[2] on any type of demonstrations. As the weeks and months unfolded we realized that we were the victims of a broken promise. The signs remained. Like so many experiences of the past we were

---

1. **gainsay** (gān′sā′), *v.* deny; contradict.
2. **moratorium** (môr′ə tôr′ē əm), *n.* temporary cessation of action on any issue.

confronted with blasted hopes, and the dark shadow of a deep disappointment settled upon us. So we had no alternative except that of preparing for direct action, whereby we would present our very bodies as a means of laying our case before the conscience of the local and national community. We were not unmindful of the difficulties involved. So we decided to go through a process of self-purification. We started having workshops on nonviolence and repeatedly asked ourselves the questions, "Are you able to accept blows without retaliating?" "Are you able to endure the ordeals of jail?" We decided to set our direct-action program around the Easter season, realizing that with the exception of Christmas, this was the largest shopping period of the year. Knowing that a strong economic withdrawal program would be the by-product of direct action, we felt that this was the best time to bring pressure on the merchants for the needed changes. Then it occurred to us that the March election was ahead and so we speedily decided to postpone action until after election day. When we discovered that Mr. Connor was in the run-off, we decided again to postpone action so that the demonstrations could not be used to cloud the issues. At this time we agreed to begin our nonviolent witness the day after the run-off.

This reveals that we did not move irresponsibly into direct action. We too wanted to see Mr. Connor defeated; so we went through postponement after postponement to aid in this community need. After this we felt that direct action could be delayed no longer.

You may well ask, "Why direct action? Why sit-ins, marches, etc.? Isn't negotiation a better path?" You are exactly right in your call for negotiation. Indeed, this is the purpose of direct action. Nonviolent direct action seeks to create such a crisis and establish such creative tension that a community that has constantly refused to negotiate is forced to confront the issue. It seeks so to dramatize the issue that it can no longer be ignored. I just referred to the creation of tension as a part of the work of the nonviolent resister. This may sound rather shocking. But I must confess that I am not afraid of the word *tension*. I have earnestly worked and preached against violent tension, but there is a type of constructive nonviolent tension that is necessary for growth. Just as Socrates felt that it was necessary to create a tension in the mind so that individuals could rise from the bondage of myths and half-truths to the unfettered realm of creative analysis and objective appraisal, we must see the need of having nonviolent gadflies[3] to create the kind of tension in society that will help men to rise from the dark depths of prejudice and racism to the majestic heights of understanding and brotherhood. So the purpose of the direct action is to create a situation so crisis-packed that it will inevitably open the door to negotiation. We, therefore, concur with you in your call for negotiation. Too long has our beloved Southland been bogged down in the tragic attempt to live in monologue rather than dialogue.

One of the basic points in your statement is that our acts are untimely. Some have asked, "Why didn't you give the new administration time to act?" The only answer that I can give to this inquiry is that the new administration must be prodded about as much as the outgoing one before it acts. We will be sadly mistaken if we feel that the election of Mr. Boutwell will bring the millennium to Birmingham. While Mr. Boutwell is much more articulate and gentle than Mr. Connor, they are both segregationists, dedicated to the task of maintaining the status quo. The hope I see in Mr. Boutwell is that he will be reasonable enough to see the futility of massive resistance to desegregation. But he will not see this without pressure from the devotees of civil rights. My friends, I must say to you that we have not made a single gain in civil rights without determined legal and nonviolent pressure. History is

---

3. **gadfly** (gad′flī), *n.* person who goads others to action with irritating or annoying remarks.

the long and tragic story of the fact that privileged groups seldom give up their privileges voluntarily. Individuals may see the moral light and voluntarily give up their unjust posture; but as Reinhold Niebuhr has reminded us, groups are more immoral than individuals.

We know through painful experience that freedom is never voluntarily given by the oppressor; it must be demanded by the oppressed. Frankly, I have never yet engaged in a direct action movement that was "well-timed," according to the timetable of those who have not suffered unduly from the disease of segregation. For years now I have heard the word "Wait!" It rings in the ear of every Negro with a piercing familiarity. This "Wait" has almost always meant "Never." It has been a tranquilizing thalidomide,[4] relieving the emotional stress for a moment, only to give birth to an ill-formed infant of frustration. We must come to see with the distinguished jurist of yesterday that "justice too long delayed is justice denied." We have waited for more than 340 years for our constitutional and God-given rights. The nations of Asia and Africa are moving with jet-like speed toward the goal of political independence, and we still creep at horse and buggy pace toward the gaining of a cup of coffee at a lunch counter. I guess it is easy for those who have never felt the stinging darts of segregation to say, "Wait." But when you have seen vicious mobs lynch your mothers and fathers at will and drown your sisters and brothers at whim; when you have seen hate-filled policemen curse, kick, brutalize and even kill your black brothers and sisters with impunity;[5] when you see the vast majority of your twenty million Negro brothers smothering in an airtight cage of poverty in the midst of an affluent society; when you suddenly find your tongue twisted and your speech stammering as you seek to explain to your six-year-old daughter why she can't go to the public amusement park that has just been advertised on television, and see tears welling up in her little eyes when she is told that Funtown is closed to colored children, and see the depressing clouds of inferiority begin to form in her little mental sky, and see her begin to distort her little personality by unconsciously developing a bitterness toward white people; when you have to concoct an answer for a five-year-old son asking in agonizing pathos:[6] "Daddy, why do white people treat colored people so mean?"; when you take a cross-country drive and find it necessary to sleep night after night in the uncomfortable corners of your automobile because no motel will accept you; when you are humiliated day in and day out by nagging signs reading "white" and "colored"; when your first name becomes "nigger" and your middle name becomes "boy" (however old you are) and your last name becomes "John," and when your wife and mother are never given the respected title "Mrs."; when you are harried by day and haunted by night by the fact that you are a Negro, living constantly at tiptoe stance never quite knowing what to expect next, and plagued with inner fears and outer resentments; when you are forever fighting a degenerating[7] sense of "nobodiness"; then you will understand why we find it difficult to wait. There comes a time when the cup of endurance runs over, and men are no longer willing to be plunged into an abyss of injustice where they experience the blackness of corroding[8] despair. I hope, sirs, you can understand our legitimate and unavoidable impatience. . . .

You spoke of our activity in Birmingham as extreme. At first I was rather disappointed that fellow clergymen would see my nonviolent efforts as those of the extremist. I started thinking about

---

4. **thalidomide** (thə lid′ə mīd′), *n.* drug formerly used as a sedative, discontinued after it was found to cause malformation of the fetus in early pregnancy.
5. **impunity** (im pyü′nə tē), *n.* freedom from punishment.
6. **pathos** (pā′thos), *n.* quality that arouses a feeling of pity or sadness.
7. **degenerating** (di jen′ə rāt′ing), *adj.* worsening.
8. **corroding** (kə rōd′ing), *adj.* eating away gradually.

the fact that I stand in the middle of two opposing forces in the Negro community. One is a force of complacency[9] made up of Negroes who, as a result of long years of oppression, have been so completely drained of self-respect and a sense of "somebodiness" that they have adjusted to segregation, and, of a few Negroes in the middle class who, because of a degree of academic and economic security, and because at points they profit by segregation, have unconsciously become insensitive to the problems of the masses. The other force is one of bitterness and hatred, and comes perilously close to advocating violence. It is expressed in the various black nationalist groups that are springing up over the nation, the largest and best known being Elijah Muhammad's[10] Muslim movement. This movement is nourished by the contemporary frustration over the continued existence of racial discrimination. It is made up of people who have lost faith in America, who have absolutely repudiated[11] Christianity, and who have concluded that the white man is an incurable "devil." I have tried to stand between these two forces, saying that we need not follow the "do-nothingism" of the complacent or the hatred and despair of the black nationalist. There is the more excellent way of love and nonviolent protest. I'm grateful to God that, through the Negro church, the dimension of nonviolence entered our struggle. If this philosophy had not emerged, I am convinced that by now many streets of the South would be flowing with floods of blood. And I am further convinced that if our white brothers dismiss as "rabble-rousers" and "outside agitators" those of us who are working through the channels of nonviolent direct action and refuse to support our nonviolent efforts, millions of Negroes, out of frustration and despair, will seek solace and security in black nationalist

...freedom is never voluntarily given by the oppressor; it must be demanded by the oppressed.

ideologies, a development that will lead inevitably to a frightening racial nightmare.

Oppressed people cannot remain oppressed forever. The urge for freedom will eventually come. This is what happened to the American Negro. Something within has reminded him of his birthright of freedom; something without has reminded him that he can gain it. Consciously and unconsciously, he has been swept in by what the Germans call the *Zeitgeist*,[12] and with his black brothers of Africa, and his brown and yellow brothers of Asia, South America and the Caribbean, he is moving with a sense of cosmic urgency toward the promised land of racial justice. Recognizing this vital urge that has engulfed the Negro community, one should readily understand public demonstrations. The Negro has many pent-up resentments and latent frustrations. He has to get them out. So let him march sometime; let him have his prayer pilgrimages to the city hall; understand why he must have sit-ins and freedom rides. If his repressed emotions do not come out in these nonviolent ways, they will come out in ominous[13] expressions of violence. This is not a threat; it is a fact of history. So I have not said to my people "get rid of your discontent." But I have tried to say that this normal and healthy discontent can be channelized through the creative outlet of nonviolent direct action.

---

9. **complacency** (kəm plā′sn sē), *n.* self-satisfaction; a sense of security.
10. **Elijah Muhammad** (i lī′jə mú ham′əd), leader of the Nation of Islam, advocated racial separation and was in favor of establishing an African American nation within the borders of the United States.
11. **repudiate** (ri pyŭ′dē āt), *v.* refuse to accept; reject.
12. ***Zeitgeist*** (tsīt′gīst′), *n.* the characteristic thought or feeling of a period of time; spirit of the age.
13. **ominous** (om′ə nəs), *adj.* unfavorable; threatening.

The
Autobiography
of
Malcolm X

Malcolm X

In 1963 Alex Haley approached Malcolm X with the idea of collaborating on writing an autobiography of Malcolm's life. Malcolm agreed to the project, though he was reluctant at first. In The Autobiography of Malcolm X, *first published in 1964, Malcolm details the story of his life and reveals why he chose to become a spokesperson for African Americans. The selection that follows is an excerpt from the last section of his autobiography.*

On the streets, after my speeches, in the faces and the voices of the people I met—even those who would pump my hands and want my autograph—I would feel the wait-and-see attitude. I would feel—and I understood—their uncertainty about where I stood. Since the Civil War's "freedom" the black man has gone down so many fruitless paths. His leaders, very largely, had failed him. The religion of Christianity had failed him. The black man was scarred, he was cautious, he was apprehensive.

I understood it better now than I had before. In the Holy World, away from America's race problem, was the first time I ever had been able to think clearly about the basic divisions of white people in America, and how their attitudes and their motives related to, and affected Negroes. In my thirty-nine years on this earth, the Holy City of Mecca had been the first time I had ever stood before the Creator of All and felt like a complete human being.

In that peace of the Holy World—in fact, the very night I have mentioned when I lay awake surrounded by snoring brother pilgrims—my mind took me back to personal memories I would have thought were gone forever . . . as far back, even, as when I was just a little boy, eight or nine years old. Out behind our house, out in the country from Lansing, Michigan, there was an old, grassy "Hector's Hill," we called it—which may still be there. I remembered there in the Holy World how I used to lie on the top of Hector's Hill, and look up at the sky, at the clouds moving over me, and daydream, all kinds of things. And then, in a funny contrast of recollections, I remembered how years later, when I was in prison, I used to lie on my cell bunk—this would be especially when I was in solitary: what we convicts called "The Hole"—and I would picture myself talking to large crowds. I don't have any idea why such previsions came to me. But they did. To tell that to anyone then would have sounded crazy. Even I

◄ What qualities does Gordon Parks's 1963 photograph of Malcolm X portray?

didn't have, myself, the slightest inkling. . . .

In Mecca, too, I had played back for myself the twelve years I had spent with Elijah Muhammad as if it were a motion picture. I guess it would be impossible for anyone ever to realize fully how complete was my belief in Elijah Muhammad. I believed in him not only as a leader in the ordinary *human* sense, but also I believed in him as a *divine* leader. I believed he had no human weaknesses or faults, and that, therefore, he could make no mistakes and that he could do no wrong. There on a Holy World hilltop, I realized how very dangerous it is for people to hold any human being in such esteem, especially to consider anyone some sort of "divinely guided" and "protected" person.

My thinking had been opened up wide in Mecca. In the long letters I wrote to friends, I tried to convey to them my new insights into the American black man's struggle and his problems, as well as the depths of my search for truth and justice.

"I've had enough of someone else's propaganda," I had written to these friends. "I'm for truth, no matter who tells it. I'm for justice, no matter who it is for or against. I'm a human being first and foremost, and as such I'm for whoever and whatever benefits humanity *as a whole.*"

Largely, the American white man's press refused to convey that I was now attempting to teach Negroes a new direction. With the 1964 "long, hot summer" steadily producing new incidents, I was constantly accused of "stirring up Negroes." Every time I had another radio or television microphone at my mouth, when I was asked about "stirring up Negroes" or "inciting violence," I'd get hot.

"It takes no one to stir up the sociological dynamite that stems from the unemployment, bad housing, and inferior education already in the ghettoes. This explosively criminal condition has existed for so long, it needs no fuse; it fuses itself; it spontaneously combusts from within itself. . . ."

They called me "the angriest Negro in

America." I wouldn't deny that charge. I spoke exactly as I felt. "I *believe* in anger. The Bible says there is a *time* for anger." They called me "a teacher, a fomenter[1] of violence." I would say point blank, "That is a lie. I'm not for wanton violence, I'm for justice. I feel that if white people were attacked by Negroes—if the forces of law prove unable, or inadequate, or reluctant to protect those whites from those Negroes— then those white people should protect and defend themselves from those Negroes, using arms if necessary. And I feel that when the law fails to protect Negroes from whites' attack, then those Negroes should use arms, if necessary, to defend themselves."

"Malcolm X Advocates Armed Negroes!"

What was wrong with that? I'll tell you what was wrong. I was a black man talking about physical defense against the white man. The white man can lynch and burn and bomb and beat Negroes—that's all right: "Have patience" . . . "The customs are entrenched" . . . "Things are getting better."

Well, I believe it's a crime for anyone who is being brutalized to continue to accept that brutality without doing something to defend himself. If that's how "Christian" philosophy is interpreted, if that's what Gandhian[2] philosophy teaches, well, then, I will call them criminal philosophies.

I tried in every speech I made to clarify my new position regarding white people—"I don't speak against the sincere, well-meaning, good white people. I have learned that there *are* some. I have learned that not all white people are racists. I am speaking against and my fight is against the white *racists*. I firmly believe that Negroes have the right to fight against these racists, by any means that are necessary." . . .

Sometimes, I have dared to dream to myself that one day, history may even say that my voice—which disturbed the white man's smugness,[3] and his arrogance, and his complacency—that my voice helped to save America from a grave, possibly even a fatal catastrophe.

The goal has always been the same, with the approaches to it as different as mine and Dr. Martin Luther King's non-violent marching, that dramatizes the brutality and the evil climate of this country today, it is anybody's guess which of the "extremes" in approach to the black man's problem might *personally* meet a fatal catastrophe first—"non-violent" Dr. King, or so-called "violent" me.

Anything I do today, I regard as urgent. No man is given but so much time to accomplish whatever is his life's work. My life in particular never has stayed fixed in one position for very long. You have seen how throughout my life, I have often known unexpected drastic changes.

I am only facing the facts when I know that any moment of any day, or any night, could bring me death. This is particularly true since the last trip that I made abroad. I have seen the nature of things that are happening, and I have heard things from sources which are reliable.

To speculate about dying doesn't disturb me as it might some people. I never have felt that I would live to become an old man. Even before I was a Muslim—when I was a hustler in the ghetto jungle, and then a criminal in prison, it always stayed on my mind that I would die a violent death. In fact, it runs in my family. My father and most of his brothers died by violence—my father because of what he believed in. To come right down to it, if I take the kind of things in which I believe, then add to that the kind of temperament that I have, plus the one hundred per cent dedication I have to whatever I believe in—these are ingredients which make it just about impossible for me to die of old age. . . .

---

1. **fomenter** (fō men′ər), *n.* one who stirs up trouble.
2. **Gandhian** (gän′dē n), a reference to Mohandas Gandhi, Hindu leader of India, known for his policies of passive resistance in gaining reforms.
3. **smugness** (smug′nes), *n.* overly pleased with one's own goodness, cleverness, respectability, etc.

After Reading

Making Connections

Shaping Your
Response

1. How convincing is King in his argument for *non-violent* protest? Use the scale below to rate his argument. Explain your rating.

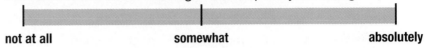

not at all   somewhat   absolutely

2. How convincing is Malcolm X in his argument for *violence as necessary?* Use the scale below to rate his argument. Explain.

not at all   somewhat   absolutely

Analyzing the
Selections

3. In your own words, explain King's concerns about black nationalist groups such as Elijah Muhammad's Muslim movement.

4. How is the **tone** of King's writing different from the tone of Malcolm X's writing? Support your interpretation of tone with examples from the two selections.

5. Why do you think Malcolm X speaks so critically of the "white man's press"?

6. King and Malcolm X struggled against the same injustices, yet made different **choices** about how to best fight injustices. How do you think they arrived at such different approaches?

Extending the
Ideas

7. What do you imagine King's response to Malcolm X's essay might have been? Malcolm X's response to King's letter?

8. Malcolm X was called "the angriest Negro in America." Describe a time you were angry about an injustice.

Literary Focus: Allusion

When you see an **allusion** in a work, first be certain you understand the reference. Sometimes research will be required. Then decide on the effect of the allusion. Why would the author want to make reference to this person, thing, event, or culture? As an example, consider again King's allusion to the Apostle Paul. With this allusion, King implies to his audience—a group of clergymen—that he too has a mission, and that he is compelled to spread the word of the Civil Rights Movement in the same way that the Apostle Paul was compelled to spread the word of Jesus Christ. Choose another allusion in "Letter from a Birmingham Jail" to examine carefully. Explain the allusion, including its effect.

Vocabulary Study

Using your Glossary if necessary, choose the word that is most nearly the same as the numbered vocabulary word.

gainsay
impunity
pathos
degenerating
repudiate
corroding
ominous
fomenter
smugness
complacency

1. gainsay   **a.** agree   **b.** contradict   **c.** acknowledge
2. impunity   **a.** punishment   **b.** confine   **c.** exemption
3. pathos   **a.** sadness   **b.** fury   **c.** progressive
4. degenerating   **a.** improving   **b.** creating   **c.** worsening
5. repudiate   **a.** reject   **b.** repeat   **c.** redo
6. corroding   **a.** gnawing   **b.** concealing   **c.** influencing
7. ominous   **a.** threatening   **b.** noisy   **c.** ugly
8. fomenter   **a.** foe   **b.** instigator   **c.** detractor
9. smugness   **a.** happiness   **b.** conceit   **c.** resentment
10. complacency   **a.** contentment   **b.** joy   **c.** worry

Expressing Your Ideas

Writing Choices

Writer's Notebook Update Now that you've read the excerpts from "Letter from a Birmingham Jail" and *The Autobiography of Malcolm X,* you may want to make some changes to what you've written in your notebook. Review the notes you made about King and Malcolm X, and decide which leader you agree with most.

Leader to Leader Martin Luther King and Malcolm X both had distinctive ways of expressing themselves. Create a one-page **dialogue** between the two leaders, using "Letter from a Birmingham Jail" and *The Autobiography of Malcolm X* as models for each man's style. Before you begin, choose the topic for their dialogue. For example, you may decide to have the two leaders speak to each other about the use of violence in the fight for racial justice. Team with a partner to perform your dialogue for the class.

Other Options

Telling Their Stories You are the producer of a **television special,** focusing on the lives and times of Dr. Martin Luther King, Jr. and Malcolm X. Working in small groups, prepare for your show. You'll need biographical information about both men, as well as an understanding of their work and philosophies. Plan some visuals for the show, either art of your own creation or art that you find in a library. Write a script for your show including quotes from their writings, then videotape your show. Play the video for your class.

Musical Accompaniment What music would you choose to accompany an oral reading of King's letter? of Malcolm X's autobiography? Choose two different **musical accompaniments** for the selections. Play the music for the class, offering a brief explanation for your choices.

Before Reading

On the Rainy River

by Tim O'Brien

Tim O'Brien
born 1946

Born in Austin, Minnesota, Tim O'Brien was drafted to serve in Vietnam immediately following his graduation from college. He served for two years as a soldier with the United States infantry. When he returned home from the war, O'Brien began to write about his experiences. In his writing about the war, O'Brien explores the human element of the conflict in Vietnam—the fear, the confusion, and the isolation that many of the soldiers who served in Vietnam experienced. "On the Rainy River" (a chapter from his 1990 book, *The Things They Carried*) is narrated by a character named Tim O'Brien, who the author says is not himself. According to O'Brien, "On the Rainy River" is a **fictional memoir** of a tumultuous time in American history.

Building Background

The Vietnam War In the Vietnam War, which lasted from the mid-1950s until 1975, Communist-ruled North Vietnam fought to take control of non-Communist South Vietnam. The United States government feared that if one Southeast Asian nation fell to the Communists, other nations would fall as well. As a result, the U. S. government sent financial assistance to the government of South Vietnam. Later, when it seemed that South Vietnam might collapse, President Lyndon Johnson ordered combat troops to Vietnam. The Vietnam War caused tremendous controversy in the United States. Many Americans, especially young people, staged protests against the war. Many of those who were drafted to serve in Vietnam refused to go and sought refuge in countries such as Canada. In the story you're about to read, a young man struggles with the question of what to do after he is drafted to fight in Vietnam.

Literary Focus

Dialogue Conversation between two or more people in a literary work is called **dialogue**. Dialogue can serve many purposes, among them:

- characterization, both of those speaking and of those spoken about;
- the creation of mood or atmosphere;
- the advancement of plot;
- the development of theme.

As you read "On the Rainy River," watch for the dialogue between the two main characters. What does their dialogue reveal about their characters? What can you learn about the theme from the dialogue?

Writer's Notebook

Making Decisions Before reading "On the Rainy River," think about a time in your life when you've had to make a tough decision. In your notebook, write how you felt about the decision. Then make a list of the people in your life who influenced your decision. Did you do what *you* wanted to do, or did you do what others thought you should do? Why?

ON THE RAINY RIVER

Tim O'Brien

This is one story I've never told before. Not to anyone. Not to my parents, not to my brother or sister, not even to my wife. To go into it, I've always thought, would only cause embarrassment for all of us, a sudden need to be elsewhere, which is the natural response to a confession. Even now, I'll admit, the story makes me squirm. For more than twenty years I've had to live with it, feeling the shame, trying to push it away, and so by this act of remembrance, by putting the facts down on paper, I'm hoping to relieve at least some of the pressure on my dreams. Still, it's a hard story to tell. All of us, I suppose, like to believe that in a moral emergency we will behave like the heroes of our youth, bravely and forthrightly, without thought of personal loss or discredit. Certainly that was my conviction back in the summer of 1968. Tim O'Brien: a secret hero. The Lone Ranger. If the stakes ever became high enough—if the evil were evil enough, if the good were good enough—I would simply tap a secret reservoir of courage that had been accumulating inside me over the years. Courage, I seemed to think, comes to us in finite quantities, like an inheritance, and by being frugal and stashing it away and letting it earn interest, we steadily increase our moral capital in preparation for that day when the account must be drawn down. It was a comforting theory. It dispensed with all those bothersome little acts of daily courage; it offered hope and grace to the repetitive coward; it justified the past while amortizing[1] the future.

In June of 1968, a month after graduating from Macalester College, I was drafted to fight a war I hated. I was twenty-one years old. Young, yes, and politically naive, but even so the

---

1. **amortize** (am'ər tīz), *v.* set aside quantities of money at regular intervals, to accumulate a larger sum.

▲ What kind of mood, thoughts, or feelings do you think the young man in this painting, *Bellamy 9* (1988), is experiencing? How does artist Glenn Priestly convey his state of mind?

American war in Vietnam seemed to me wrong. Certain blood was being shed for uncertain reasons. I saw no unity of purpose, no consensus on matters of philosophy or history or law. The very facts were shrouded in uncertainty: Was it a civil war? A war of national liberation or simple aggression? Who started it, and when, and why? What really happened to the USS *Maddox* on that dark night in the Gulf of Tonkin? Was Ho Chi Minh[2] a Communist stooge, or a nationalist savior, or both, or neither? What about the Geneva Accords?[3] What about SEATO[4] and the Cold

2. **Ho Chi Minh** (hō′chē′min′), Communist president of North Vietnam from 1954 to 1969.
3. **Geneva Accords.** In 1954, France and the Democratic Republic of Vietnam agreed to divide Vietnam into two parts: the north was given to the communists, and the south was given to the Saigon government. Under the terms of the agreement, the country was to be reunified in 1956.
4. **SEATO,** the Southeast Asia Treaty Organization, formed in 1954. SEATO brought Thailand, Pakistan, and the Philippines into alliance with the United States, Britain, France, Australia, and New Zealand. SEATO was formed for defense against aggression in southeastern Asia and the southwestern Pacific.

War? What about dominoes?[5] America was divided on these and a thousand other issues, and the debate had spilled out across the floor of the United States Senate and into the streets, and smart men in pinstripes could not agree on even the most fundamental matters of public policy. The only certainty that summer was moral confusion. It was my view then, and still is, that you don't make war without knowing why. Knowledge, of course, is always imperfect, but it seemed to me that when a nation goes to war it must have reasonable confidence in the justice and imperative of its cause. You can't fix your mistakes. Once people are dead, you can't make them undead.

In any case those were my convictions,[6] and back in college I had taken a modest stand against the war. Nothing radical, no hothead stuff, just ringing a few doorbells for Gene McCarthy,[7] composing a few tedious, uninspired editorials for the campus newspaper. Oddly, though, it was almost entirely an intellectual activity. I brought some energy to it, of course, but it was the energy that accompanies almost any abstract endeavor; I felt no personal danger; I felt no sense of an impending crisis in my life. Stupidly, with a kind of smug removal[8] that I can't begin to fathom, I assumed that the problems of killing and dying did not fall within my special province.

The draft notice arrived on June 17, 1968. It was a humid afternoon, I remember, cloudy and very quiet, and I'd just come in from a round of golf. My mother and father were having lunch out in the kitchen. I remember opening up the letter, scanning the first few lines, feeling the blood go thick behind my eyes. I remember a sound in my head. It wasn't thinking, just a silent howl. A million things all at once—I was too *good* for this war. Too smart, too compassionate, too everything. It couldn't happen. I was above it. I had the world licked—Phi Beta Kappa and summa cum laude[9] and president of the student body and a full-ride scholarship for grad studies at Harvard. A mistake, maybe—a foul-up in the paperwork. I was no soldier. I hated Boy Scouts. I hated camping out. I hated dirt and tents and mosquitoes. The sight of blood made me queasy, and I couldn't tolerate authority, and I didn't know a rifle from a slingshot. I was a *liberal:* If they needed fresh bodies, why not draft some back-to-the-stone-age hawk? Or some dumb jingo in his hard hat and Bomb Hanoi button, or one of LBJ's[10] pretty daughters, or Westmoreland's[11] whole handsome family—nephews and nieces and baby grandson. There should be a law, I thought. If you support a war, if you think it's worth the price, that's fine, but you have to put your own precious fluids on the line. You have to head for the front and hook up with an infantry unit and help spill the blood. And you have to bring along your wife, or your kids, or your lover. A *law,* I thought.

I remember the rage in my stomach. Later it burned down to a smoldering self-pity, then to numbness. At dinner that night my father asked what my plans were.

"Nothing," I said. "Wait."

I spent the summer of 1968 working in an Armour meat-packing plant in my hometown of Worthington, Minnesota. The plant specialized in pork products, and for eight hours a day I stood on a quarter-mile assembly line—more properly, a disassembly line—removing blood clots from the necks of dead pigs. My job title, I believe, was Declotter. After slaughter, the

---

5. **dominoes,** supporters of the war believed that if South Vietnam fell under Communist control, other countries would also fall "like a row of dominoes."
6. conviction (kən vik′shən), *n.* firmly held belief.
7. **Gene McCarthy.** Senator Eugene McCarthy was an early candidate in the 1968 presidential elections. He spoke out strongly against the war in Vietnam.
8. removal (ri mü′vəl), *n.* emotional distance.
9. **Phi Beta Kappa and summa cum laude,** honors for outstanding students.
10. **LBJ,** Lyndon Baines Johnson, President of the United States from 1963 to 1969.
11. **Westmoreland,** General William Westmoreland, commander of the U. S. ground troops in South Vietnam.

hogs were decapitated, split down the length of the belly, pried open, eviscerated,[12] and strung up by the hind hocks on a high conveyer belt. Then gravity took over. By the time a carcass reached my spot on the line, the fluids had mostly drained out, everything except for thick clots of blood in the neck and upper chest cavity. To remove the stuff, I used a kind of water gun. The machine was heavy, maybe eighty pounds, and was suspended from the ceiling by a heavy rubber cord. There was some bounce to it, an elastic up-and-down give, and the trick was to maneuver the gun with your whole body, not lifting with the arms, just letting the rubber cord do the work for you. At one end was a trigger; at the muzzle end was a small nozzle and a steel roller brush. As a carcass passed by, you'd lean forward and swing the gun up against the clots and squeeze the trigger, all in one motion, and the brush would whirl and water would come shooting out and you'd hear a quick splattering sound as the clots dissolved into a fine red mist. It was not pleasant work. Goggles were a necessity, and a rubber apron, but even so it was like standing for eight hours a day under a lukewarm blood-shower. At night I'd go home smelling of pig. It wouldn't go away. Even after a hot bath, scrubbing hard, the stink was always there—like old bacon, or sausage, a dense greasy pig-stink that soaked deep into my skin and hair. Among other things, I remember, it was tough getting dates that summer. I felt isolated; I spent a lot of time alone. And there was also that draft notice tucked away in my wallet.

In the evenings I'd sometimes borrow my father's car and drive aimlessly around town, feeling sorry for myself, thinking about the war and the pig factory and how my life seemed to be collapsing toward slaughter. I felt paralyzed. All around me the options seemed to be narrowing, as if I were hurtling down a huge black funnel, the whole world squeezing in tight. There was no happy way out. The government had ended most graduate school deferments; the waiting lists for the National Guard and Reserves were impossibly long; my health was solid; I didn't qualify for CO[13] status—no religious grounds, no history as a pacifist. Moreover, I could not claim to be opposed to war as a matter of general principle. There were occasions, I believed, when a nation was justified in using military force to achieve its ends, to stop a Hitler or some comparable evil, and I told myself that in such circumstances I would've willingly marched off to the battle. The problem, though, was that a draft board did not let you choose your war.

Beyond all this, or at the very center, was the raw fact of terror. I did not want to die. Not ever. But certainly not then, not there, not in a wrong war. Driving up Main Street, past the courthouse and the Ben Franklin store, I sometimes felt the fear spreading inside me like weeds. I imagined myself dead. I imagined myself doing things I could not do—charging an enemy position, taking aim at another human being.

Beyond all this . . . was the raw fact of terror. I did not want to die.

At some point in mid-July I began thinking seriously about Canada. The border lay a few hundred miles north, an eight-hour drive. Both my conscience and my instincts were telling me to make a break for it, just take off and run like hell and never stop. In the beginning the idea seemed purely abstract, the word Canada printing itself out in my head; but after a time I could see particular shapes and images, the sorry details of my own future—a hotel room in Winnipeg, a battered old suitcase, my father's eyes as I tried to explain myself over the telephone. I could almost hear his voice, and my mother's. Run, I'd think. Then I'd think, Impossible. Then a second later I'd think, *Run.*

12. **eviscerate** (i vis′ə rāt′) *v.* remove the internal organs.
13. **CO,** conscientious objector: person with moral or religious objections to serving in the armed forces.

It was a kind of schizophrenia. A moral split. I couldn't make up my mind. I feared the war, yes, but I also feared exile. I was afraid of walking away from my own life, my friends and my family, my whole history, everything that mattered to me. I feared losing the respect of my parents. I feared the law. I feared ridicule and censure.[14] My hometown was a conservative little spot on the prairie, a place where tradition counted, and it was easy to imagine people sitting around a table down at the old Gobbler Café on Main Street, coffee cups poised, the conversation slowly zeroing in on the young O'Brien kid, how the damned sissy had taken off for Canada. At night, when I couldn't sleep, I'd sometimes carry on fierce arguments with those people. I'd be screaming at them, telling them how much I detested their blind, thoughtless, automatic acquiescence[15] to it all, their simple-minded patriotism, their prideful ignorance, their love-it-or-leave-it platitudes,[16] how they were sending me off to fight a war they didn't understand and didn't want to understand. I held them responsible. By God, yes, I *did*. All of them—I held them personally and individually responsible—the polyestered Kiwanis boys, the merchants and farmers, the pious churchgoers, the chatty housewives, the PTA and the Lions club and the Veterans of Foreign Wars and the fine upstanding gentry out at the country club. They didn't know Bao Dai from the man in the moon. They didn't know history. They didn't know the first thing about Diem's[17] tyranny, or the nature of Vietnamese nationalism, or the long colonialism of the French—this was all too damned complicated, it required some reading—but no matter, it was a war to stop the Communists, plain and simple, which was how they liked things, and you were a treasonous[18] sissy if you had second thoughts about killing or dying for plain and simple reasons.

I was bitter, sure. But it was so much more than that. The emotions went from outrage to terror to bewilderment to guilt to sorrow and then back again to outrage. I felt a sickness inside me. Real disease.

Most of this I've told before, or at least hinted at, but what I have never told is the full truth. How I cracked. How at work one morning, standing on the pig line, I felt something break open in my chest. I don't know what it was. I'll never know. But it was real, I know that much, it was a physical rupture—a cracking-leaking-popping feeling. I remember dropping my water gun. Quickly, almost without thought, I took off my apron and walked out of the plant and drove home. It was midmorning, I remember, and the house was empty. Down in my chest there was still that leaking sensation, something very warm and precious spilling out, and I was covered with blood and hog-stink, and for a long while I just concentrated on holding myself together. I remember taking a hot shower. I remember packing a suitcase and carrying it out to the kitchen, standing very still for a few minutes, looking carefully at the familiar objects all around me. The old chrome toaster, the telephone, the pink and white Formica on the kitchen counters. The room was full of bright sunshine. Everything sparkled. My house, I thought. My life. I'm not sure how long I stood there, but later I scribbled out a short note to my parents.

What it said, exactly, I don't recall now. Something vague. Taking off, will call, love Tim.

drove north.

It's a blur now, as it was then, and all I remember is a sense of high velocity and the feel of the steering wheel in my hands. I was

---

14. **censure** (sen′shər), *n.* expression of disapproval.
15. **acquiescence** (ak′wē es′ns), *n.* consent given without making objections; assent.
16. **platitude** (plat′ə tüd), *n.* dull or commonplace remark, especially one given out solemnly as if it were fresh and important.
17. **Bao Dai** (bou′dī′) . . . **Diem** (zīem). Bao Dai was Vietnam's last emperor who was deposed in 1955. Ngo Dinh Diem became president, then refused to allow the South Vietnamese to vote to reunify Vietnam.
18. **treasonous** (trē′zn əs), *adj.* traitorous; involving betrayal of one's country.

riding on adrenaline.[19] A giddy feeling, in a way, except there was the dreamy edge of impossibility to it—like running a dead-end maze—no way out—it couldn't come to a happy conclusion and yet I was doing it anyway because it was all I could think of to do. It was pure flight, fast and mindless. I had no plan. Just hit the border at high speed and crash through and keep on running. Near dusk I passed through Bemidji, then turned northeast toward International Falls. I spent the night in the car behind a closed-down gas station a half mile from the border. In the morning, after gassing up, I headed straight west along the Rainy River, which separates Minnesota from Canada, and which for me separated one life from another. The land was mostly wilderness. Here and there I passed a motel or bait shop, but otherwise the country unfolded in great sweeps of pine and birch and sumac. Though it was still August, the air already had the smell of October, football season, piles of yellow-red leaves, everything crisp and clean. I remember a huge blue sky. Off to my right was the Rainy River, wide as a lake in places, and beyond the Rainy River was Canada.

For a while I just drove, not aiming at anything, then in the late morning I began looking for a place to lie low for a day or two. I was exhausted, and scared sick, and around noon I pulled into an old fishing resort called the Tip Top Lodge. Actually it was not a lodge at all, just eight or nine tiny yellow cabins clustered on a peninsula that jutted northward into the Rainy River. The place was in sorry shape. There was a dangerous wooden dock, an old minnow tank, a flimsy tar paper boathouse along the shore. The main building, which stood in a cluster of pines on high ground, seemed to lean heavily to one side, like a cripple, the roof sagging toward Canada. Briefly, I thought about turning around, just giving up, but then I got out of the car and walked up to the front porch.

The man who opened the door that day is the hero of my life. How do I say this without sounding sappy? Blurt it out—the man saved me. He offered exactly what I needed, without questions, without any words at all. He took me in. He was there at the critical time—a silent, watchful presence. Six days later, when it ended, I was unable to find a proper way to thank him, and I never have, and so, if nothing else, this story represents a small gesture of gratitude twenty years overdue.

The man who opened the door that day is the hero of my life.

Even after two decades I can close my eyes and return to that porch at the Tip Top Lodge. I can see the old guy staring at me. Elroy Berdahl: eighty-one years old, skinny and shrunken and mostly bald. He wore a flannel shirt and brown work pants. In one hand, I remember, he carried a green apple, a small paring knife in the other. His eyes had the bluish gray color of a razor blade, the same polished shine, and as he peered up at me I felt a strange sharpness, almost painful, a cutting sensation, as if his gaze were somehow slicing me open. In part, no doubt, it was my own sense of guilt, but even so I'm absolutely certain that the old man took one look and went right to the heart of things—a kid in trouble. When I asked for a room, Elroy made a little clicking sound with his tongue. He nodded, led me out to one of the cabins, and dropped a key in my hand. I remember smiling at him. I also remember wishing I hadn't. The old man shook his head as if to tell me it wasn't worth the bother.

"Dinner at five-thirty," he said. "You eat fish?"

"Anything," I said.

Elroy grunted and said, "I'll bet."

---

19. **adrenaline** (ə dren′l ən), *n.* hormone which speeds up the heartbeat and thereby increases bodily energy.

We spent six days together at the Tip Top Lodge. Just the two of us. Tourist season was over, and there were no boats on the river, and the wilderness seemed to withdraw into a great permanent stillness. Over those six days Elroy Berdahl and I took most of our meals together. In the mornings we sometimes went out on long hikes into the woods, and at night we played Scrabble or listened to records or sat reading in front of his big stone fireplace. At times I felt the awkwardness of an intruder, but Elroy accepted me into his quiet routine without fuss or ceremony. He took my presence for granted, the same way he might've sheltered a stray cat—no wasted sighs or pity—and there was never any talk about it. Just the opposite. What I remember more than anything is the man's willful, almost ferocious silence. In all that time together, all those hours, he never asked the obvious questions: Why was I there? Why alone? Why so preoccupied?[20] If Elroy was curious about any of this, he was careful never to put it into words.

My hunch, though, is that he already knew. At least the basics. After all, it was 1968, and guys were burning draft cards, and Canada was just a boat ride away. Elroy Berdahl was no hick. His bedroom, I remember, was cluttered with books and newspapers. He killed me at the Scrabble board, barely concentrating, and on those occasions when speech was necessary he had a way of compressing large thoughts into small, cryptic packets of language. One evening, just at sunset, he pointed up at an owl circling over the violet-lighted forest to the west.

"Hey, O'Brien," he said. "There's Jesus."

The man was sharp—he didn't miss much. Those razor eyes. Now and then he'd catch me staring out at the river, at the far shore, and I could almost hear the tumblers clicking in his head. Maybe I'm wrong, but I doubt it.

One thing for certain, he knew I was in desperate trouble. And he knew I couldn't talk about it. The wrong word—or even the right word—and I would've disappeared. I was wired and jittery. My skin felt too tight. After supper one evening I vomited and went back to my cabin and lay down for a few moments and then vomited again; another time, in the middle of the afternoon, I began sweating and couldn't shut it off. I went through whole days feeling dizzy with sorrow. I couldn't sleep; I couldn't lie still. At night I'd toss around in bed, half awake, half dreaming, imagining how I'd sneak down to the beach and quietly push one of the old man's boats out into the river and start paddling my way toward Canada. There were times when I thought I'd gone off the psychic edge. I couldn't tell up from down, I was just falling, and late in the night I'd lie there watching weird pictures spin through my head. Getting chased by the Border Patrol—helicopters and searchlights and barking dogs—I'd be crashing through the woods, I'd be down on my hands and knees—people shouting out my name—the law closing in on all sides—my hometown draft board and the FBI and the Royal Canadian Mounted Police. It all seemed crazy and impossible. Twenty-one years old, an ordinary kid with all the ordinary dreams and ambitions, and all I wanted was to live the life I was born to—a mainstream life—I loved baseball and hamburgers and cherry Cokes—and now I was off on the margins of exile, leaving my country forever, and it seemed so impossible and terrible and sad.

I'm not sure how I made it through those six days. Most of it I can't remember. On two or three afternoons, to pass some time, I helped Elroy get the place ready for winter, sweeping down the cabins and hauling in the boats, little chores that kept my body moving. The days were cool and bright. The nights were very dark. One morning the old man showed me how to split and stack firewood, and for several hours we just worked in silence out behind his house. At one point, I remember, Elroy put down his maul and looked at me for a long time, his lips

---

20. **preoccupied** (prē ok′yə pīd), *adj.* absorbed; engrossed.

Review some of the descriptions of Elroy Berdahl. Do you envision a man like the one in Doug Brega's portrait, *Emerson* (1986)? Why or why not?

drawn as if framing a difficult question, but then he shook his head and went back to work. The man's self-control was amazing. He never pried. He never put me in a position that required lies or denials. To an extent, I suppose, his reti-cence[21] was typical of that part of Minnesota, where privacy still held value, and even if I'd been walking around with some horrible defor-mity—four arms and three heads—I'm sure the old man would've talked about everything except those extra arms and heads. Simple politeness was part of it. But even more than that, I think, the man understood that words were insufficient. The problem had gone beyond discussion. During that long summer I'd been over and over the various arguments, all the pros and cons, and it was no longer a question that could be decided by an act of pure reason. Intellect had come up against emotion. My conscience told me to run, but some irra-tional and powerful force was resisting, like a weight pushing me toward the war. What it came down to, stupidly, was a sense of shame. Hot, stupid shame. I did not want people to think badly of me. Not my parents, not my brother and sister, not even the folks down at the Gobbler Café. I was ashamed to be there at the Tip Top Lodge. I was ashamed of my con-science, ashamed to be doing the right thing.

Some of this Elroy must've understood. Not the details, of course, but the plain fact of crisis.

Although the old man never confronted me about it, there was one occasion when he came close to forcing the whole thing out into the open. It was early evening, and we'd just fin-ished supper, and over coffee and dessert I asked him about my bill, how much I owed so far. For a long while the old man squinted down at the tablecloth.

"Well, the basic rate," he said, "is fifty bucks a night. Not counting meals. This makes four nights, right?"

I nodded. I had three hundred and twelve dollars in my wallet.

Elroy kept his eyes on the tablecloth. "Now that's an on-season price. To be fair, I suppose we should knock it down a peg or two." He leaned back in his chair. "What's a reasonable number, you figure?"

"I don't know," I said. "Forty?"

"Forty's good. Forty a night. Then we tack on food—say another hundred? Two hundred sixty total?"

"I guess."

He raised his eyebrows. "Too much?"

"No, that's fair. It's fine. Tomorrow, though . . . I think I'd better take off tomorrow."

Elroy shrugged and began clearing the table. For a time he fussed with the dishes, whistling to himself as if the subject had been settled. After a second he slapped his hands together.

"You know what we forgot?" he said. "We for-got wages. Those odd jobs you done. What we have to do, we have to figure out what your time's worth. Your last job—how much did you pull in an hour?"

"Not enough," I said.

"A bad one?"

"Yes. Pretty bad."

Slowly then, without intending any long ser-mon, I told him about my days at the pig plant. It began as a straight recitation of the facts, but before I could stop myself I was talking about the blood clots and the water gun and how the smell had soaked into my skin and how I couldn't wash it away. I went on for a long time. I told him about wild hogs squealing in my dreams, the sounds of butchery, slaughterhouse sounds, and how I'd sometimes wake up with that greasy pig-stink in my throat.

When I was finished, Elroy nodded at me.

"Well, to be honest," he said, "when you first showed up here, I wondered about all that. The aroma, I mean. Smelled like you was awful damned fond of pork chops." The old man almost smiled. He made a snuffling sound, then

---

21. **reticence** (ret′ə səns), *n.* tendency to be silent or say little; reserved in speech.

sat down with a pencil and a piece of paper. "So what'd this crud job pay? Ten bucks an hour? Fifteen?"

"Less."

Elroy shook his head. "Let's make it fifteen. You put in twenty-five hours here, easy. That's three hundred seventy-five bucks total wages. We subtract the two hundred sixty for food and lodging, I still owe you a hundred and fifteen."

He took four fifties out of his shirt pocket and laid them on the table.

"Call it even," he said.

"No."

"Pick it up. Get yourself a haircut."

The money lay on the table for the rest of the evening. It was still there when I went back to my cabin. In the morning, though, I found an envelope tacked to my door. Inside were the four fifties and a two-word note that said EMERGENCY FUND.

The man knew.

Looking back after twenty years, I sometimes wonder if the events of that summer didn't happen in some other dimension, a place where your life exists before you've lived it, and where it goes afterward. None of it ever seemed real. During my time at the Tip Top Lodge I had the feeling that I'd slipped out of my own skin, hovering a few feet away while some poor yo-yo with my name and face tried to make his way toward a future he didn't understand and didn't want. Even now I can see myself as I was then. It's like watching an old home movie: I'm young and tan and fit. I've got hair—lots of it. I don't smoke or drink. I'm wearing faded blue jeans and a white polo shirt. I can see myself sitting on Elroy Berdahl's dock near dusk one evening, the sky a bright shimmering pink and I'm finishing up a letter to my parents that tells what I'm about to do and why I'm doing it and how sorry I am that I'd never found the courage to talk to them about it. I ask them not to be angry. I try to explain some of my feelings, but there aren't enough words, and so I just say that it's a thing that has to be done. At the end

of the letter I talk about the vacations we used to take up in this north country, at a place called Whitefish Lake, and how the scenery here reminds me of those good times. I tell them I'm fine. I tell them I'll write again from Winnipeg or Montreal or wherever I end up.

On my last full day, the sixth day, the old man took me out fishing on the Rainy River. The afternoon was sunny and cold. A stiff breeze came in from the north, and I remember how the little fourteen-foot boat made sharp rocking motions as we pushed off from the dock. The current was fast. All around us, I remember, there was a vastness to the world, an unpeopled rawness, just the trees and the sky and the water reaching out toward nowhere. The air had the brittle scent of October.

For ten or fifteen minutes Elroy held a course upstream, the river choppy and silver-gray, then he turned straight north and put the engine on full throttle. I felt the bow lift beneath me. I remember the wind in my ears, the sound of the old outboard Evinrude. For a time I didn't pay attention to anything, just feeling the cold spray against my face, but then it occurred to me that at some point we must've passed into Canadian waters, across that dotted line between two different worlds, and I remember a sudden tightness in my chest as I looked up and watched the far shore come at me. This wasn't a daydream. It was tangible and real. As we came in toward land, Elroy cut the engine, letting the boat fishtail lightly about twenty yards off shore. The old man didn't look at me or speak. Bending down, he opened up his tackle box and busied himself with a bobber and a piece of wire leader, humming to himself, his eyes down.

It struck me then that he must've planned it. I'll never be certain, of course, but I think he meant to bring me up against the realities, to guide me across the river and to take me to the edge and to stand a kind of vigil as I chose a life for myself.

I remember staring at the old man, then at my hands, then at Canada. The shoreline was dense with brush and timber. I could see tiny red berries on the bushes. I could see a squirrel up in one of the birch trees, a big crow looking at me from a boulder along the river. That close—twenty yards—and I could see the delicate latticework of the leaves, the texture of the soil, the browned needles beneath the pines, the configurations of geology and human history. Twenty yards. I could've done it. I could've jumped and started swimming for my life. Inside me, in my chest, I felt a terrible squeezing pressure. Even now, as I write this, I can still feel that tightness. And I want you to feel it—the wind coming off the river, the waves, the silence, the wooded frontier. You're at the bow of a boat on the Rainy River. You're twenty-one years old, you're scared, and there's a hard squeezing pressure in our chest.

What would you do?

Would you jump? Would you feel pity for yourself? Would you think about your family and your childhood and your dreams and all you're leaving behind? Would it hurt? Would it feel like dying? Would you cry, as I did?

I tried to swallow it back. I tried to smile, except I was crying.

Now, perhaps, you can understand why I've never told this story before. It's not just the embarrassment of tears. That's part of it, no doubt, but what embarrasses me much more, and always will, is the paralysis that took my heart. A moral freeze: I couldn't decide, I couldn't act, I couldn't comport[22] myself with even a pretense of modest human dignity.

All I could do was cry. Quietly, not bawling, just the chest-chokes.

At the rear of the boat Elroy Berdahl pretended not to notice. He held a fishing rod in his hands, his head bowed to hide his eyes. He kept humming a soft, monotonous little tune. Everywhere, it seemed, in the trees and water and sky, a great worldwide sadness came pressing down on me, a crushing sorrow, sorrow like

I had never known it before. And what was so sad, I realized, was that Canada had become a pitiful fantasy. Silly and hopeless. It was no longer a possibility. Right then, with the shore so close, I understood that I would not do what I should do. I would not swim away from my hometown and my country and my life. I would not be brave. That old image of myself as a hero, as a man of conscience and courage, all that was just a threadbare pipe dream. Bobbing there on the Rainy River, looking back at the Minnesota shore, I felt a sudden swell of helplessness come over me, a drowning sensation, as if I had toppled overboard and was being swept away by the silver waves. Chunks of my own history flashed by. I saw a seven-year-old boy in a white cowboy hat and a Lone Ranger mask and a pair of holstered six-shooters; I saw a twelve-year-old Little League shortstop pivoting to turn a double play; I saw a sixteen-year-old kid decked out for his first prom, looking spiffy in a white tux and a black bow tie, his hair cut short and flat, his shoes freshly polished. My whole life seemed to spill out into the river, swirling away from me, everything I had ever been or ever wanted to be. I couldn't get my breath; I couldn't stay afloat; I couldn't tell which way to swim. A hallucination, I suppose, but it was as real as anything I would ever feel. I saw my parents calling to me from the far shoreline. I saw my brother and sister, all the townsfolk, the mayor and the entire Chamber of Commerce and all my old teachers and girlfriends and high school buddies. Like some weird sporting event: everybody screaming from the sidelines, rooting me on—a loud stadium roar. Hotdogs and popcorn—stadium smells, stadium heat. A squad of cheerleaders did cartwheels along the banks of the Rainy River; they had megaphones and pompoms and smooth brown thighs. The crowd swayed left and right. A marching band played fight songs. All my aunts and uncles were there, and

----

22. **comport** (kəm pôrt′), *v.* conduct (oneself) in a certain manner; behave.

▲ How would you describe the mood of Ken Moylan's 1995 painting, *Boundary Lake?* Is it the
same as, or does it contrast with, the mood of the story?

Abraham Lincoln, and Saint George, and a nine-year-old girl named Linda who had died of a brain tumor back in fifth grade, and several members of the United States Senate, and a blind poet scribbling notes, and LBJ, and Huck Finn, and Abbie Hoffman, and all the dead soldiers back from the grave, and the many thousands who were later to die—villagers with terrible burns, little kids without arms or legs— yes, and the Joint Chiefs of Staff were there, and a couple of popes, and a first lieutenant named Jimmy Cross, and the last surviving veteran of the American Civil War, and Jane Fonda dressed up as Barbarella, and an old man sprawled beside a pigpen, and my grandfather, and Gary Cooper, and a kind-faced woman carrying an umbrella and a copy of Plato's *Republic,* and a million ferocious citizens waving flags of all shapes and colors—people in hard hats, people in headbands—they were all whooping and chanting and urging me toward one shore or the other. I saw faces from my distant past and distant future. My wife was there. My unborn daughter waved at me, and my two sons hopped up and down, and a drill sergeant named Blyton sneered and shot up a finger and shook his head. There was a choir in bright purple robes. There was a cabbie from the Bronx. There was a slim young man I would one day kill with a hand grenade along a red clay trail outside the village of My Khe.

The little aluminum boat rocked softly beneath me. There was the wind and the sky.

I tried to will myself overboard.

I gripped the edge of the boat and leaned forward and thought, *Now.*

I did try. It just wasn't possible.

All those eyes on me—the town, the whole universe—and I couldn't risk the embarrassment. It was as if there were an audience to my life, that swirl of faces along the river, and in my head I could hear people screaming at me. Traitor! they yelled. Turncoat! I felt myself blush. I couldn't tolerate it. I couldn't endure the mockery, or the disgrace, or the patriotic ridicule. Even in my imagination, the shore just twenty yards away, I couldn't make myself be brave. It had nothing to do with morality. Embarrassment, that's all it was.

And right then I submitted.

I would go to the war—I would kill and maybe die—because I was embarrassed not to.

That was the sad thing. And so I sat in the bow of the boat and cried.

It was loud now. Loud, hard crying.

Elroy Berdahl remained quiet. He kept fishing. He worked his line with the tips of his fingers, patiently, squinting out at his red and white bobber on the Rainy River. His eyes were flat and impassive. He didn't speak. He was simply there, like the river and the late-summer sun. And yet by his presence, his mute watchfulness, he made it real. He was the true audience. He was a witness, like God, or like the gods, who look on in absolute silence as we live our lives, as we make our choices or fail to make them.

"Ain't biting," he said.

Then after a time the old man pulled in his line and turned the boat back toward Minnesota.

I don't remember saying goodbye. That last night we had dinner together, and I went to bed early, and in the morning Elroy fixed breakfast for me. When I told him I'd be leaving, the old man nodded as if he already knew. He looked down at the table and smiled.

At some point later in the morning it's possible that we shook hands—I just don't remember—but I do know that by the time I'd finished packing the old man had disappeared. Around noon, when I took my suitcase out to the car, I noticed that his old black pickup truck was no longer parked in front of the house. I went inside and waited for a while, but I felt a bone certainty that he wouldn't be back. In a way, I thought, it was appropriate. I washed up the breakfast dishes, left his two hundred dollars on the kitchen counter, got into the car, and drove south toward home.

The day was cloudy. I passed through towns with familiar names, through the pine forests and down to the prairie, and then to Vietnam, where I was a soldier, and then home again. I survived, but it's not a happy ending. I was a coward. I went to the war.

After Reading

Making Connections

Shaping Your Response

1. Was O'Brien a coward? Why or why not?

2. If you'd been faced with O'Brien's decision to either run or go to war, what would you have done?

Analyzing the Story

3. How would you describe the **tone** of "On the Rainy River"?

4. Why do you think O'Brien calls Elroy Berdahl the hero of his life?

5. Why do you suppose Berdahl never questions O'Brien about his reasons for being at the Tip Top Lodge?

6. 👣 What forces influence O'Brien as he tries to make the right **choice?**

7. How do you think O'Brien would define the word "courage"?

Extending the Ideas

8. In "On the Rainy River," O'Brien explores the concept of patriotism. Explain your definition of patriotism.

Literary Focus: Dialogue

What does the **dialogue** between O'Brien and Berdahl reveal about their characters? Choose two conversations between O'Brien and Berdahl to examine more closely. Write a paragraph that explains what you learn about the two characters from what they say.

Vocabulary Study

conviction
acquiescence
removal
preoccupied
reticence
censure
comport
platitude
treasonous
adrenaline

Write a letter from the character Tim O'Brien to the draft board that summarizes his feelings about the Vietnam War. Use the vocabulary words in the list in your letter. Consult your Glossary as necessary.

Expressing Your Ideas

Writing Choices

Writer's Notebook Update Before you read "On the Rainy River," you wrote about an important decision you once made. In one or two paragraphs, write a comparison between the decision the character O'Brien made and the decision you made. How did each of you arrive at your decisions?

A Letter from Vietnam Imagine you are O'Brien. You've been shipped out to the steamy jungles of Vietnam. Write a **letter** home, telling your parents about the war, about your experiences. What will you talk about in your letter? What will your tone be like? Will you be bitter? Will you be upbeat? Will you reveal your fear, or will you put up a brave front?

Berdahl's Perspective O'Brien isn't able to say much about Berdahl, and is only able to make a few guesses about what he is thinking. What do *you* think Berdahl's opinion of O'Brien is? If Berdahl had been keeping a journal, what might he have written about O'Brien? Write three **diary entries** for Berdahl, one for the first night of O'Brien's stay, one for the night after O'Brien refuses to take Berdahl's money, and one for the night after O'Brien leaves.

The Things He Carried "On the Rainy River" is a chapter from the author Tim O'Brien's book, *The Things They Carried.* The title of the book refers to the things a soldier takes into combat—not necessarily all physical items like weapons, but also intangibles such as fear, confusion, and memories. Working in small groups, make a **list** of the tangible and intangible things your group thinks the character O'Brien might have carried with him to Vietnam. Present your list to the rest of the class, explaining each item.

Other Options

O'Brien's Approval Rating When he's on the boat, O'Brien has a vision of a crowd of people watching him. Choose one of the historical figures or events mentioned and research information about it. Give an **oral report** of your findings, including visual prompts such as maps, charts, or photos.

Designer for a Day You are a graphic designer assigned to create a **poster** that promotes the Hollywood film *On the Rainy River.* What will you draw that will capture the interest of the movie-going public? Using a piece of tag board, create your poster. When you've finished your art, add a few lines of text—whatever you think will best promote the film.

Looking Back Do some in-depth **interviews** about the Vietnam War. Ask family members, neighbors, and teachers about their opinions of the war. Did they support the war in Vietnam? Why or why not? In retrospect, do they think the Vietnam War needed to be fought? As a class, write a list of at least ten interview questions, and then each student can interview up to five people. Capture your interviews on video camera, and then play the tape for your class. Your class may also want to compile the survey results on a **chart.**

Before Reading

from **Where the Ashes Are**

by Nguyên Qúi Dú'c

Nguyên Qúi Dú'c
born 1959

Nguyên Qúi Dú'c was born to an upper-class Vietnamese family. His mother was a school principal; his father was a high-ranking civil servant in the South Vietnamese government. During the Tet offensive, Dú'c's father was seized by the Vietcong and imprisoned for sixteen years. Dú'c's mother, no longer allowed to teach school, began selling noodles in the street. At age eighteen, Dú'c moved to the United States where he eventually became a reporter for National Public Radio. In his first book, *Where the Ashes Are,* Dú'c describes the profound effect the Vietnam War had on his family.

Building Background

The Tet Offensive In late January of 1968, during the Vietnamese holiday of Tet, the Vietcong attacked all the major cities in South Vietnam simultaneously. Most of the people of South Vietnam were caught off-guard by the Tet offensive because they believed the holiday of Tet would be held sacred and a cease-fire agreement would be honored by the government of North Vietnam. The destruction of lives and property during Tet was overwhelming; thousands of civilians were killed or made homeless, and entire cities were leveled. In his autobiography, Nguyên Qúi Dú'c—who was nine years old in 1968—describes the terrifying days of the Tet offensive.

Literary Focus

Imagery Nguyên Qúi Dú'c uses imagery—word pictures that appeal to any of the senses—to bring vividness to the frightening scenes he describes. Imagery may appeal to the reader's sense of sight, hearing, taste, smell, or motor activity (motion or feeling). Using a web similar to the one below, make some notes about Dú'c's use of imagery as you read his story.

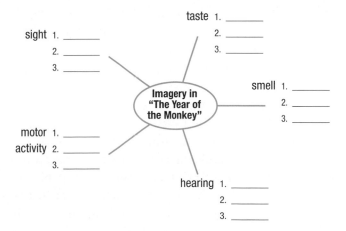

Writer's Notebook

In your notebook, make a list of the words and images that you associate with war and its affects on people and property.

Where the Ashes Are

Nguyên Qúi Dú'c

"Wake up, wake up!" my mother shouted. "We've got to get out of here! How can you sleep through all this?" She pulled the covers off me, handed me my clothes, and rushed out of the room.

"Wait!" I cried out, throwing off my pajamas. One leg in and one out of my dark blue school trousers, I stumbled over to my sister Dieu-Hà's room. My mother was yelling, "Are you deaf? Get out! We're going downstairs!"

It was five in the morning. Explosions and gunfire echoed through the high-ceilinged rooms of the government guest house. Arched corridors surrounded the twenty bedrooms on the second floor of the massive French-style mansion. My parents had taken the master suite at the end of the hall while my two sisters and I had large rooms next to one another. We had arrived at the end of January 1968, two days before the lunar New Year. Our family were the only guests in the building. Rather than having us stay at my grandfather's small house, my father felt we would be safer at the guest house, where extra platoons of local soldiers had been assigned to protect him. He also preferred the guest house because it was built along the bank of the river in Hue, the old imperial city, and away

This photograph by William Albert Allard shows South Vietnamese refugees arriving in Hong Kong in 1979. What do their expressions and body language relate about what they're experiencing?

from the town's noisy center. The nearby train station was defunct,[1] since the war had disrupted all but a few railway lines.

For many years my father had been working for the government of South Viet Nam. Assigned to central Viet Nam as a civilian deputy to the military governor, he was based in Dà Nang, a coastal town just over an hour's drive from Hue. He sent us to visit his parents there regularly, especially at holidays. He came along on this holiday visit—for the lunar New Year, Tet, in 1968.

Although my father had been warned about a possible escalation[2] in the fighting, he said to my mother: "There's a ceasefire. It's New Year's. We'll be safe." But he abandoned his plan to drive and instead arranged for a flight to Hue. We'd landed at the Phú Bài airport in midafternoon.

SUMMARIZE: What possible dangers does the visit present? Why does the family decide to proceed with the visit?

The road into town had been taken over by an endless convoy of tanks and army trucks transporting U.S. soldiers, most likely toward Khe Sanh, an American base that had been under siege for several months. Along with a few other civilian cars, small trucks, and innumerable[3] motorcycles, we inched our way toward Hue. I kept looking out the car window, glimpsing rice fields here and there. Mostly, though, the view was blocked by the olive green steel of tanks and trucks.

My mother sought to distract us. "You kids are going to be spoiled this year. I bet your grandparents will have lots of treats for you. But I want you to behave."

Settled in at the guest house, on the second night of our stay my mother and sisters and I fell asleep just after twelve, insulated by its thick walls and heavy curtains. Endless rounds of firecrackers went off as the people of Hue celebrated the arrival of Tet. No one knew that along with the Year of the Monkey, the dreaded Viet Cong soldiers had also arrived. No one could tell when the firecrackers stopped and the gunfire began.

Dieu-Hà and I followed my mother into my other sister's room. Dieu-Qùynh had buried herself under a pile of blankets. Ma shook her. "Come on, we're going downstairs!" As she started to rifle through Dieu-Qùynh's drawers, grabbing clothes for her to change into, she said to Dieu-Hà and me, "Go see if your father's downstairs, and stay with him!"

We rushed down the corridors toward the double staircase. Its marble steps formed a half-circle framed by an intricately[4] carved banister. A bullet shattered a porthole as we skipped down the steps. Dieu-Hà screamed. Pieces of glass and marble flew by. We raced past the elephant tusks in the huge vestibule and toward the reception hall. A chilly wind blew through the huge room. Someone had opened the drapes and shutters of the dozens of windows rising from knee level to ten feet above my head, each framing a view of the River of Perfume, Sông Hu'o'ng.

In the somber light I could make out dark foliage swaying by the riverbank as a coat of morning mist rose above the water. Nature paints winter scenes in Hue in shades of gray, but this morning I could see rapid bursts of orange and red fire coming from behind the bushes. A flare shot out from the far distance. Exploding with a thud, it hung from a small parachute and cast a brilliant midday light over a large area of the river as it floated down. Rockets exploded across the burning sky and fell to the ground in rapid succession. Deafened, Dieu-Hà and I dove

---

1. **defunct** (di fungkt′), *adj.* no longer in use.
2. **escalation** (es′kə lā′shən), *n.* act of increasing or expanding rapidly in stages.
3. **innumerable** (i nü′mər ə bəl), *adj.* too many to count.
4. **intricately** (in′trə kit lē), *adv.* elaborately.

behind an antique cabinet at the end of the room. My father had been nowhere in sight.

That night he had stayed up late to read a French book that contrasted two warriors: North Viet Nam's famed general Võ Nguyên Giáp and William Westmoreland, commander of the U.S. ground troops in South Viet Nam. Just before four o'clock Cha[5] had left his bed and gone up to the rooftop terrace, where he marveled at the red and green tracers flying across the sky like shooting stars. Despite his interest in the generals, he had little understanding of the role of flares and tracers as tools of warfare. They were simply a beautiful sight as they burst over the night sky.

"Your father's still up there. Been on that roof an hour! He'll get killed!" Ma wailed as she came down the staircase. Seeing the open windows, she took us into a chamber behind the reception room. "Where's Dieu-Quỳnh?" she exclaimed. "She was just on the stairs with me!"

In the midst of the gunfire and explosions, my sister had gone back to bed—a mad thing to do, since bullets were now flying indoors. By 1968, however, most of what Dieu-Quỳnh did was irrational. For four years she had been showing signs of mental illness. Ordering Dieu-Hà and me to sit still, my mother dashed back upstairs. A bullet came through Dieu-Quỳnh's room, hitting the lamp on her bedstand. Sparks flew in all directions. Ma grabbed my older sister by the wrist and led her downstairs, calling out to my father all the while.

"We shouldn't worry too much," he said in his usual unruffled tone when he entered the room a few minutes later. When he had finally left the roof, he went downstairs to look for the butler, then into an office off the living room. "I called the provincial office; they say the fighting is far away."

"Look out the windows!" my mother shot back.

"I did," Cha replied, still calm and composed. "Our soldiers are still at their posts." From the rooftop he had been able to see men in green surrounding the guest house.

We gathered together, crouching on the floor. No one spoke. My father glanced at the spacious desk and heavy armchairs, hoping to hide behind the furniture until the gunfire died down.

Between explosions came the sound of someone knocking at the front door. My parents put out their arms. We sat still. The pounding grew louder. After a moment of hesitation, Ma stood up. "It's our soldiers," she declared. "Come on!" My sisters followed her through the reception area to the vestibule. As my father and I reached the door to the reception room, we heard her scream.

My father led me back to the office in the back, locking the door behind him as quietly as possible. We went to the desk, and I held his hand as we lowered ourselves behind it. My father didn't know what else to do. Spotting a steel safe in the corner of the room, he went over to open it, then without a word closed it again. Not even a nine-year-old boy could fit inside.

"I have a young son in the house," my mother was explaining to the intruders in the vestibule, Viet Cong soldiers in olive green uniforms. They wore no insignia or badges that showed affiliation[6] or rank. Whether because of the darkness or distance, his poor eyesight, or his unfamiliarity with military matters, my father had mistaken them for our own Southern Republican Army troops.

One of the soldiers now threatened to shoot anyone still hiding in the house. "Tell us where everyone is and you'll be safe, Sister," he assured my mother.

"Please, please don't hurt us, please!" she begged. "Just let me go find my son."

Cha groped behind the heavy dark green drapes along the office wall, where a set of double doors opened onto a hallway. We tiptoed through the hall to the doors that led outside. My father

---

5. **Cha,** Father. *[Vietnamese]*
6. **affiliation** (ə fil/ē ā/shən) *n.* association or connection with a group or organization.

motioned me out first, then carefully closed the doors behind him. I ran down the steps and turned toward the hedges that separated the guest house grounds from the riverbank. "Hey, boy!" someone cried. I turned. A Viet Cong soldier sitting cross-legged pointed his rifle at me. I ran back to my father.

Back in the hallway inside the house, Cha quietly approached each door to the offices surrounding the reception area. A gun muzzle protruded from one, and we backed off. The doorway to yet another office also had a gun muzzle poking out from it. There was no escape.

Out in the courtyard it was still dark. Dozens of people in nightclothes shivered in the early morning dampness. Slowly the soldiers separated families from one another. The guest house was to be used as a temporary holding center. More people were brought into the courtyard. A disheveled[7] Frenchman of about thirty entered the area barefooted, a trench coat thrown on over his pajamas. Hands clasped together, he tried to explain his situation to two Viet Cong soldiers. "De Gaulle, Ho Chí Minh,[8] *amis,*" he kept saying. "Friends."

The two Viet Cong waved him away. One of them shouted, *"Không biet tieng dâu!"*[9] They did not speak any foreign languages.

"They're regular soldiers," my father whispered to a man next to him, whose crisp white shirt was tucked into pajama trousers. "Such a strong northern accent."

"You're right," the man whispered back. "The way they call everybody 'Sister' and 'Brother' is strange." The men and women before us were not part of the so-called National Liberation Front[10] within South Viet Nam. Ho Chí Minh was now sending in troops from the North for an outright offensive, a full invasion.

In the confusion our family took refuge in a small temple just off the grounds of the guest house. Searching through his wallet, my father took out all his business cards and hid them under a mat. "Just say you're a teacher," whispered my mother.

CLARIFY: Why does Dú'c's father want to hide his identity from the soldiers?

He never had the chance. When a Viet Cong woman found us in the temple a little more than an hour later, she jabbed her index finger into his chest. "You, Brother, I know who you are," she said. "The Party and the Revolution will be generous to all those willing to confess their crimes against the People."

"The Party" could only be the Communist party headquartered in Hà Noi. The enemy's arm had now reached into the heart of Hue. "Don't lie!" the woman continued. Putting her finger up to my father's nose, she said, "Brother, we know—you're the general staying in this house. Such opulence.[11] We'll take care of you."

We lost track of the time as the soldiers sorted out all the people gathered in front of the guest house. At last, however, they accepted my father's protestations that he was not a general but a government functionary. He and the other men were taken inside the mansion. Women and children were sent to a neighboring building, down into a long rectangular basement with extremely thick walls and a single narrow door at one end. The rocket explosions had ceased, but the sound of gunfire continued. We had become accustomed to it and no longer jumped at the bursts from automatic weapons. Ten families followed each other below ground. I ended up leading the way into the darkness.

---

7. **disheveled** (də shev′əld), *adj.* rumpled; disordered.
8. **De Gaulle, Ho Chi Minh.** Charles de Gaulle was president of France from 1959 to 1969. Ho Chi Minh was president of North Vietnam from 1954 to 1969.
9. *Không biet tieng dâu,* I do not speak any foreign languages. *[Vietnamese]*
10. **National Liberation Front,** a political organization formed by the Vietcong in South Vietnam.
11 opulence (op′yə ləns), *n.* wealth; riches.

"Go to the far end. Go!" my mother urged me, and made sure that Dieu-Quỳnh stayed with us. She knew that, on capturing a town, the Communists would use residents as workers to support military operations. Women would be sent to look for food, or nurse the wounded. If not required to take up arms themselves, men would have to gather the wounded and the dead. Dieu-Quỳnh, a tall girl of eighteen, was at risk of being drafted for such service. Turning to the family behind her, my mother explained. "My daughter is ill. A big girl, but not all that wise." It was an explanation she would feel compelled to repeat often in the next days. I finally settled for a spot below a minuscule[12] window with iron bars. In the damp, cavernous basement, the tiny hole let in a faint ray of the light that signaled the first day of the Year of the Monkey.

Throughout that day and most of the next night the adults carried on a whispered debate, trying to make sense out of what had happened. "They can't win," the guest house chauffeur pronounced. "I bet they'll retreat soon. The Americans will bomb, and our troops will rescue us in a few days." My mother listened dispassionately. She sighed often, and refused to eat any of the food the family next to us offered. Busy with their prisoners in the mansion, the soldiers left us alone.

On our second day of captivity, a female voice shouted into the basement. "Mrs. Dai! Is there a Mrs. Dai down there?" My mother picked her way toward the door. "Your husband's up in the house. He wants to see you," the voice announced. My mother went up alone, warning me to keep my sister Dieu-Quỳnh from wandering out. During the night, Dieu-Quỳnh had been difficult, continually demanding hot water. For the last year or so she had been obsessed with matters of hygiene, compulsively washing her hands as well as any household utensils before she would use them. Finally realizing that this was a luxury, she now sat silent and withdrawn. I asked Dieu-Hà to stay with her, then went to sit at the door to wait for my mother.

The guns had gone quiet at some point without anyone noticing. More soldiers had arrived in the compound and were now setting up a crude hospital. A stretched-out army poncho served as an awning, sheltering three bamboo cots that had been shoved together. The soldiers put a mat of woven branches and leaves on top of the cots, enlarging the surface to accommodate five wounded men. Looking like pallbearers carrying a white porcelain coffin, three young men and a woman in civilian clothes brought in an ancient French bathtub. They filled the tub half full of water, warning us not to use it. No one seemed to be in charge, yet a lot of orders were being issued. Sitting by the door of the basement, I watched the men and women from the North. From the way they handled the everyday artifacts of city life, they must have spent years in the jungle. One came with a beer can with a pull tab on its top. He shook it, hearing the sound of sloshing liquid inside. When he pulled the tab and the beer exploded, he threw the can on the ground and ran away. "It's a grenade! A grenade!" he yelled. I dared not laugh.

Later, I watched two men struggle to start a motorized tricycle. They tried to push it, but the gears were engaged. They gave up after a while and walked away. Half an hour later they came back on two bicycles whose frames had been lashed together with branches, with which they were hauling a few bags of New Year's food: cakes of sticky rice stuffed with pork and green beans and wrapped in banana leaves. I was wondering who the food was for when my mother came back. "What are you doing here?" she asked, roughing up my hair. "We're going up to see your father in a while." She did not sound excited. After checking on my sisters, she set about looking for food for my father.

"Ma, what are they going to do with him?" I asked. I repeated the question again and again,

---

12. **minuscule** (mi nus′kyūl), *adj.* extremely small.

but my mother would only shake her head; finally she responded, "Oh, he'll be all right. They said all he needed was a few days of re-education. They're taking him somewhere, but he'll be back."

Taken where? Would we be rescued first? Would they let him go? I didn't think she knew the answers to my questions. I tugged at her sleeve. "Ma, what's 're-education'?"

She glanced at the wounded Viet Cong lying beneath the poncho. "It's like school, that's all. Now help me with this pot."

Spoiled since her youth by household servants, my mother had rarely gone near a kitchen. Now she was cooking a big pot of rice she had secured from a woman in the basement. The Viet Cong had set up a few clay burners and gave us some coal. Other than the rice, there was nothing to cook. We ate it with pickled leeks and cucumber, which normally accompanied fancier foods during Tet. The rice tasted of the river water my mother had used to cook it in. The Viet Cong had allowed her only a small amount of water from the bathtub to take to my father. She was happy to have cleaner water for him to drink—until she tasted it. It smelled of Mercurochrome, the red disinfectant common in Viet Nam. The soldiers had used the water to wash the wounds of injured men, then poured back unused portions, now laced with Mercurochrome. She found a tiny bit of tea to steep in the water and packed some rice into a big bowl for my father.

I sensed that my father was happy to see us, but his face showed no such emotion. He took the woven basket Ma handed him, which contained a towel, two T-shirts, and a pair of pants she had found on her previous trip to the guest house to see him. "There's no need—you will be well provided for," a Viet Cong cadre[12] said. "You'll be in re-education for just a short time. Now that the region is liberated, you'll be allowed to come back soon."

In the big hall across from the master suite, my father kept caressing my head. I couldn't think of much to say. Some prisoners crouched along the wall, watching us. Others were curled up on the floor like shrimps. My mother gave my father the bowl of rice and the tea. I waited to see if he could taste the Mercurochrome, but I couldn't tell from his expression.

I glanced around my parents' bedroom. It had been turned upside down. The book my father had been reading about Giáp and Westmoreland still lay by his bed. My mother's jewelry and toilet case had had a hole gashed through it with a crude knife.

"Your mother will take you over to your grandparents' in a few days," Cha said. "I'll be back after a time."

Later, sometime past midnight, Communist soldiers took my father and a dozen other men away. Standing on a stool with my mother at my side, I watched through the tiny basement window. A rope was hooked through my father's elbows and tied behind his back, while his wrists were bound together in front of his chest. He was also tied to the man in front of him. It would be sixteen years before I saw him again.

---

12. **cadre** (kad′rē), *n.* persons trained for organizing or expanding an organization such as a political party.

After Reading

Making Connections

Shaping Your Response

1. What three questions would you like to ask Dú'c about the events he describes?

Analyzing the Autobiography

2. What adjectives would you use to describe Dú'c's mother?

3. Why do you think Dú'c hesitates to reveal to his father how frightened he feels?

4. Describe Dú'c's narrative **style.** Would you call him an *emotional* or a *dispassionate* narrator? Why?

Extending the Ideas

5. Compare Dú'c's writing to Tim O'Brien's "On the Rainy River." In what ways are the two selections similar? In what ways are they different?

6. After arriving in the United States, what do you think Dú'c might have wanted to tell the American people about the Vietnam War? Explain.

Literary Focus: Imagery

Look over the notes you took about Dú'c's use of **imagery.** What effect does the imagery have on his story? Now try using imagery in your own writing. Write a **paragraph** that describes an incident in your own life. In your paragraph, use a series of images that appeal to the different senses. Then give your paragraph to a classmate to read. Can your classmate spot the imagery in your writing?

Vocabulary Study

From the lettered word list below, choose a word that is most nearly the opposite of each numbered vocabulary word. Use your Glossary if necessary.

escalation
defunct
affiliation
intricately
opulence

1. escalation
2. defunct
3. affiliation
4. intricately
5. opulence

a. separateness
b. poverty
c. decrease
d. viable
e. simply

Expressing Your Ideas

Writing Choices

Writer's Notebook Update Review the list of words and images that you associate with war. Then use these words and images in a two- or three-stanza poem about war.

Write a Review Write a **review** of the excerpt for a literary magazine. In your review, explain how you think Dú'c's memoir is relevant today, more than thirty years after the Vietnam War's end.

The Young Author Do a **character study** of Dú'c, the nine-year-old boy. Begin by listing everything you know about him. Describe his personality, his place in the family, and his attitude toward the war. What do you think his life was like before the war? Is he strong enough to help care for the family after his father is taken away? When you've finished your notes, write a short personality sketch of Dú'c.

Other Options

On Stage As a class, do a **stage production** of the excerpt from *Where the Ashes Are.* Divide yourselves into several small groups, with each group responsible for one part of the production: actors, set designers, script, playbill, costumes, music, and so on. You may also want to choose a narrator who will give background information to your audience.

Bulletin Board Art Using sketches of your own, pictures you've cut from magazines, and captions that you generate on a computer, create a **bulletin board display** that reflects the action—and emotions—of Dú'c's story.

Why Did We Leave Vietnam? General William Westmoreland, whom Dú'c mentions in his memoir, was furious when the United States began its withdrawal of troops from Vietnam. In 1976 Westmoreland said, "Press and television . . . created an aura not of victory but of defeat and timid officials in Washington listened more to the media than to their own representatives on the scene." [Westmoreland: *A Soldier Reports,* 1976.] Was Westmoreland correct? Why *did* the United States abandon its efforts in Vietnam? Was it because it was an "unwinnable" war, or was it because the American public, through protest, forced the United States government to back out? In small groups, research the question. Then divide your group into two teams and prepare to **debate** the issue in front of the class.

Before Reading

Village

by Estela Portillo Trambley

Estela Portillo Trambley
born 1936

Estela Portillo Trambley was born in El Paso, Texas. Raised primarily by her grandparents, Portillo Trambley returned to her parents at age twelve, then was married just out of high school. She earned a Bachelor's degree in English in 1956 and a Master's degree in English in 1978, both from the University of Texas at El Paso. Her book *Rain of Scorpions and Other Writings,* first published in 1975, is generally recognized as the first work of fiction published by a Chicana, or Mexican American woman. Portillo Trambley recently revised this collection, rewriting some of the stories and adding several new ones under the title *Rain of Scorpions and Other Stories.* "Village" is one of the new stories that appears in this collection.

Building Background

American Troops in Vietnam In 1965, the United States government began sending combat troops to Vietnam. Three years later, there were close to 540,000 U.S. troops stationed in Vietnam. Most of the Vietnam War was fought in the jungle. Soldiers lived in makeshift huts or army tents and usually tried to set up camp in jungle clearings. The jungles of Vietnam are hot and humid places, full of biting and stinging insects. Excursions into the jungle were extremely difficult and often unbearably uncomfortable. Although American troops stationed in Vietnam lived with the constant fear of an attack by the Vietcong, they were also bored and homesick a great deal of the time. "Some GI's," wrote Cathleen Cordova, who worked as a club director in Vietnam in 1968 and 1969, "say this war could have, and should have, been won by now if it weren't for the politicians meddling in military matters. Others are opposed to the war and don't think we should be here. . . . Actually, the majority of the guys aren't concerned with issues, moral judgments or politics. Most of them are young guys who didn't want to come here, and they just want to get out in one piece." By the time the United States pulled out of Vietnam in 1973, 58,000 American men and women had been killed.

Literary Focus

Theme The theme of a literary work is its underlying main idea. A theme may be directly stated but is more often implied. Plot, characters, tone, and setting all contribute to theme. As you read "The Village," try to get a sense of the theme. What point is the author making? In your notebook, jot down examples of dialogue, description, and action that contribute to the story's theme.

Writer's Notebook

The Controversy at Home The Vietnam War caused a tremendous amount of controversy in the United States. In your notebook, list some of the reasons why you think the Vietnam War was so controversial. Why did people protest the war? Why were many soldiers reluctant to fight this war?

VILLAGE

ESTELA PORTILLO TRAMBLEY

Rico stood on top of a bluff overlooking Mai Cao.[1] The whole of the wide horizon was immersed in a rosy haze. His platoon was returning from an all night patrol. They had scoured the area in a radius of thirty-two miles, following the length of the canal system along the delta, furtively on the lookout for an enemy attack. On their way back, they had stopped to rest, smoke, drink warm beer after parking the carryalls[2] along the edge of the climb leading to the top of the bluff. The hill was good cover, seemingly safe.

Harry was behind him on the rocky slope. Then the sound of thunder overhead. It wasn't thunder, but a squadron of their own helicopters on the usual run. Rico and Harry sat down to watch the planes go by. After that, a stillness, a special kind of silence. Rico knew it well, the same kind of stillness that was part of him back home, the kind of stillness that makes a man part of his world—river, clearing, sun, wind. The stillness of a village early in the morning—barrio[3] stillness, the first stirrings of life that come with dawn. Harry was looking down at the village of Mai Cao.

"Makes me homesick . . ." Harry lighted a cigarette.

Rico was surprised. He thought Harry was a city dude. Chicago, no less. "I don't see no freeway or neon lights."

"I'm just sick of doing nothing in this damned war."

No action yet. But who wanted action? Rico had been transformed into a soldier, but he knew he was no soldier. He had been trained to kill the enemy in Vietnam. He watched the first curl of smoke coming out of one of the chimneys. They were the enemy down there. Rico didn't believe it. He would never believe it. Perhaps because there had been no confrontation with Viet Cong soldiers or village people. Harry flicked away his cigarette and started down the slope. He turned, waiting for Rico to follow him. "Coming?"

"I'll be down after a while."

"Suit yourself." Harry walked swiftly down the bluff, his feet carrying with them the dirt yieldings in a flurry of small pebbles and loose earth. Rico was relieved. He needed some time by himself, to think things out. But Harry was right. To come

The title of the 1984 painting on the facing page by Rachael Romero is *He Who Feels It Knows It.* Explain what you think this means. Could the same title apply to Rico in the story? Why or why not?

---

1. **Mai Cao** (mī kou′).
2. **carryall** (kar′ē ôl), *n.* enclosed truck-like vehicle.
3. **barrio** (bär′ē ō), *n.* in the United States, a section of a city inhabited chiefly by Spanish-speaking people.

across an ocean just to do routine checks, to patrol ground where there was no real danger . . . it could get pretty bad. The enemy was hundreds of miles away. The enemy! He remembered the combat bible—kill or be killed. Down a man—the lethal lick: a garotte[4] strangling is neater and more quiet than the slitting of a throat; grind your heel against a face to mash the brains. Stomp the rib cage to carve the heart with bone splinters. Kill . . .

Hey, who was kidding who? They almost made him believe it back at boot camp in the States. In fact, only a short while ago, only that morning he had crouched down along the growth following a mangrove[5] swamp, fearing an unseen enemy, ready to kill. Only that morning. But now, looking down at the peaceful village with its small rice field, its scattered huts, something had struck deep, something beyond the logic of war and enemy, something deep in his guts.

He had been cautioned. The rows of thatched huts were not really peoples' homes, but "hootches," makeshift temporary stays built by the makeshift enemy. But then they were real enemies. There were too many dead Americans to prove it. The hootches didn't matter. The people didn't matter. These people knew how to pick up their sticks and go. Go where? Then how many of these villages had been bulldozed? Flattened by gunfire? Good pyre[6] for napalm,[7] these Vietnamese villages. A new kind of battleground.

Rico looked down and saw huts that were homes, clustered in an intimacy that he knew well. The village of Mai Cao was no different than Valverde, the barrio where he had grown up. A woman came out of a hut, walking straight and with a certain grace, a child on her shoulder. She was walking toward a stream east of the slope. She stopped along the path and looked up to say something to the child. It struck him again, the feeling a bond—people all the same everywhere.

The same scent from the earth, the same warmth from the sun, a woman walking with a child—his mother, Trini. His little mother who had left Tarahumara country and crossed the Barranca del Cobre, taking with her the seeds from the hills of Batopilas,[8] withstanding suffering, danger—for what? A dream—a piece of ground in the land of plenty, the United States of America. She had waded across the Rio Grande from Juarez, Mexico, to El Paso, Texas, when she felt the birth pangs of his coming. He had been born a citizen because his mother had had a dream. She had made the dream come true—an acre of river land in Valverde, on the edge of the border. His mother, like the earth and the sun, mattered. The woman with the child on her shoulder mattered. Every human life in the village mattered. He knew this not only with the mind but with the heart.

Rico remembered a warning from combat training, from the weary, wounded soldiers who had fought and killed and survived, soldiers sent to Saigon, waiting to go home. His company had been flown to Saigon before being sent to the front. And this was the front, villages like Mai Cao. He felt relieved knowing that the fighting was hundreds of miles away from the people in Mai Cao—but the warning was still there:

Watch out for pregnant women with machine guns. Toothless old women are experts with the knife between the shoulders. Begging children with hidden grenades, the unseen VC hiding in the hootches—village people were not people; they were the enemy. The woman who knew the child on her shoulder, who knew the path to the

---

4. **garotte** (gə rōt′), *n.* a cord or wire used for strangling.
5. **mangrove** (mang′grōv), *n.* tropical trees or shrubs that have branches that send down many roots which look like additional trunks.
6. **pyre** (pīr), *n.* large pile of burnable material.
7. **napalm** (nā′päm), *n.* jellied gasoline used for making incendiary bombs and in flamethrowers.
8. **Tarahumara** (tär′ä hä mär′ä) . . . **Barranca del Cobre** (bä rän′ka del kō′brä) . . . **Batopilas** (bä′tō pē′läs); places in Mexico.

door, who knew the coming of the sun—she was the enemy.

It was a discord[9] not to be believed by instinct or intuition. And Rico was an Indian, the son of a Tarahumara chieftain. Theirs was a world of instinct and intuitive decisions. Suddenly he heard the sounds of motors. He looked to the other side of the slope, down to the road where the carryalls had started queuing[10] their way back to the post. Rico ran down the hill to join his company.

In his dream, Sergeant Keever was shouting, "Heller, heller . . ." Rico woke with a start. It wasn't a dream. The men around him were scrambling out of the pup tent. Outside, most of the men were lining up in uneven formation. Rico saw a communiqué[11] in the sergeant's hand. Next to Keever was a lieutenant from communications headquarters. Keever was reading the communiqué:

"Special mission 72 . . . for Company C, platoon 2, assigned at 22 hours. Move into the village of Mai Cao, field manual description— hill 72. Destroy the village."

No! It was crazy. Why? Just words on a piece of paper. Keever had to tell him why. There had to be a reason. Had the enemy come this far? It was impossible. Only that morning he had stood on the slope. He caught up with Keever, blurting out, "Why? I mean—why must we destroy it?"

Sergeant Keever stopped in his tracks and turned steel blue eyes at Rico. "What you say?"

"Why?"

"You just follow orders, savvy?"[11]

"Are the Viet Cong . . ."

"Did you hear me? You want trouble, Private?"

"There's people . . ."

"I don't believe you, soldier. But OK. Tell you as much as I know. We gotta erase the village in case the Viet Cong come this way. That way they won't use it as a stronghold. Now move . . ."

Keever walked away from him, his lips tight in some kind of disgust. Rico did not follow this

time. He went to get his gear and join the men in one of the carryalls. Three carryalls for the assault—three carryalls moving up the same road. Rico felt the weight and hardness of his carbine. Now it had a strange, hideous meaning. The machine guns were some kind of nightmare. The mission was to kill and burn and erase all memories. Rico swallowed a guilt that rose from the marrow—with it, all kinds of fear. He had to do something, something to stop it, but he didn't know what. And with all these feelings, a certain reluctance to do anything but follow orders. In the darkness, his lips formed words from the anthem, "My country, 'tis of thee . . ."

They came to the point where the tree lines straggled between two hills that rose darkly against the moon. Rico wondered if all the men were of one mind—one mind to kill. . . . Was he a coward? No! It was not killing the enemy that his whole being was rejecting, but firing machine guns into a village of sleeping people . . . people. Rico remembered only the week before, returning from their usual patrol, the men from the company had stopped at the stream, mingling with the children, old men, and women of the village. There had been an innocence about the whole thing. His voice broke the silence in the carryall, a voice harsh and feverish. "We can get the people out of there. Help them evacuate . . ."

"Shut up." Harry's voice was tight, impatient.

The carryalls traveled through tall, undulant grass following the dirt road that led to the edge of the bluff. It was not all tall grass. Once in a while trees appeared again, clumped around scrub bushes. Ten miles out the carryalls stopped. It was still a mile's walk to the bluff in the darkness, but they had to avoid detection. Sergeant Keever was leading the party. Rico,

---

9. **discord** (dis′kôrd), *n.* lack of harmony; contradiction.
10. **queue** (kyū), *v.* follow in a line.
10. **communiqué** (kə myü′nə kā′), *n.* official communication.
11. **savvy** (sav′ē), *v.* slang for understand.

almost at the rear, knew he had to catch up to him. He had to stop him. Harry was ahead of him, a silent black bundle walking stealthily through rutted ground to discharge his duty. For a second, Rico hesitated. That was the easy thing to do—to carry out his duty—to die a hero, to do his duty blindly and survive. Hell, why not? He knew what happened to men who backed down in battle. But he wasn't backing down. Hell, what else was it? How often had he heard it among the gringos[12] in his company?

"You Mexican? Hey, you Mexicans are real fighters. I mean, everybody knows Mexicans have guts . . ."

A myth perhaps. But no. He thought of the old guys who had fought in World War II. Many of them were on welfare back in the barrio. But, man! Did they have medals! He had never seen so many purple hearts. He remembered old Toque, the wino, who had tried to pawn his medals to buy a bottle. No way, man. They weren't worth a nickel.

He quickly edged past Harry, pushing the men ahead of him to reach the sergeant. He was running, tall grass brushing his shoulder, tall grass that swayed peacefully like wheat. The figure of Sergeant Keever was in front of him now. There was a sudden impulse to reach out and hold him back. But the sergeant had stopped. Rico did not touch him but whispered hoarsely, desperately in the dark. "Let's get the people out—evacuate . . ."

"What the hell . . ." Keever's voice was ice. He recognized Rico and hissed, "Get back to your position, soldier, or I'll shoot you myself."

Rico did as he was told, almost unaware of the men around him. But at a distance he heard something splashing in the water of the canal, in his nostrils the smell of sweet burnt wood. He looked toward the clearing and saw the cluster of huts bathed in moonlight. In the same moonlight, he saw Keever giving signals. In the gloom, he saw the figures of the men carrying machine guns. They looked like dancing grasshoppers as they ran ahead to position themselves on the bluff. He felt like yelling, "For Christ's sake! Where is the enemy?"

The taste of blood in his mouth—he suddenly realized he had bitten his quivering lower lip. As soon as Sergeant Keever gave the signal, all sixteen men would open fire on the huts—machine guns, carbines—everything would be erased. No more Mai Cao. The execution of duty without question, without alternative. They were positioned on the south slope, Sergeant Keever up ahead, squatting on his heels, looking at his watch. He raised himself, after a quick glance at the men. As Sergeant Keever raised his hand to give the signal for attack, Rico felt the cold metallic deadness of his rifle. His hands began to tremble as he released the safety catch. Sergeant Keever was on the rise just above him. Rico stared at the sergeant's arm, raised, ready to fall—the signal to fire. The cross-fire was inside Rico, a heavy dosed tumult[13]—destroy the village, erase all memory. There was ash in his mouth. Once the arm came down, there was no turning back.

In a split second, Rico turned his rifle at a forty-degree angle and fired at the sergeant's arm. Keever half turned with the impact of the bullet, then fell to his knees. In a whooping whisper the old-timer soldier blew out the words, "That . . . —get him." He got up and signaled the platoon back to the carryalls as two men grabbed Rico, one hitting him on the side of his head with the butt of his rifle. Rico felt the sting of the blow as they pinned his arm back and forced him to walk the path back to the carryall. He did not resist. There was a lump in his throat, and he blinked back tears, tears of relief. The memory of the village would not be erased. Someone shouted in the dark, "They're on to us. There's an old man with a lantern and others coming out of the hootches . . ."

---

12. **gringo** (gring′gō), *n.* a term in Spanish, often considered offensive, for a foreigner, especially an American or Englishman.
13. **tumult** (tŭ′mult), *n.* emotional disturbance.

"People—just people . . ." Rico whispered, wanting to shout it, wanting to tell them that he had done the right thing. But the heaviness that filled his senses was the weight of the truth. He was a traitor—a maniac. He had shot his superior in a battle crisis. He was being carried almost bodily back to the truck. He glanced at the thick brush along the road, thinking that somewhere beyond it was a rice field, and beyond that a mangrove swamp. There was a madman inside his soul that made him think of rice fields and mangrove swamps instead of what he had done. Not once did he look up. Everyone around him was strangely quiet and remote. Only the sound of trudging feet.

In the carryall, the faces of the men sitting around Rico were indiscernible[14] in the dark, but he imagined their eyes, wide, confused, peering through the dark at him with a wakefulness that questioned what he had done. Did they know his reason? Did they care? The truck suddenly lurched. Deep in the gut, Rico felt a growing fear. He choked back a hysteria rising from the diaphragm. The incessant bumping of the carryalls as they moved unevenly on the dirt road accused him, too. He looked up into a night sky and watched the moon eerily weave in and out of tree branches. The darkness was like his fear. It had no solutions.

Back on the post, Sergeant Keever and a medic passed by Rico, already handcuffed, without any sign of recognition. Sergeant Keever had already erased him from existence. The wheels of justice would take their course. Rico had been placed under arrest, temporarily shackled to a cot in one of the tents. Three days later he was moved to a makeshift bamboo hut, with a guard in front of the hut at all times. His buddies brought in food like strangers, awkward in their silence, anxious to leave him alone. He felt like some kind of poisonous bug. Only Harry came by to see him after a week.

"You dumb jerk, were you on locoweed?" Harry asked in disgust.

"I didn't want people killed, that's all."

"Hell that's no reason, those chinks aren't even—even . . ."

"Even what?" Rico demanded. He almost screamed it a second time. "Even what?"

"Take it easy, will you? You better go for a section 8." Harry was putting him aside like everyone else. "They're sending you back to the States next week. You'll have to face Keever sometime this afternoon. I thought I'd better let you know."

"Thanks." Rico knew the hopelessness of it all. There was still the nagging question he had to ask. "Listen, nobody tells me anything. Did you all go back to Mai Cao? I mean, is it still there?"

"Still there. Orders from headquarters to forget it. The enemy were spotted taking an opposite direction. But nobody's going to call you a hero, you understand? What you did was crud. You're no soldier. You'll never be a soldier."

Rico said nothing to defend himself. He began to scratch the area around the steel rings on his ankles. Harry was scowling at him. He said it again, almost shouting, "I said, you'll never be a soldier."

"So?" There was soft disdain[15] in Rico's voice.

"You blew it, man. You'll be locked up for a long, long time."

"Maybe . . ." Rico's voice was without concern.

"Don't you care?"

"I'm free inside, Harry." Rico laughed in relief. "Free . . ."

Harry shrugged, peering at Rico unbelievingly, then turned and walked out of the hut.

---

14. **indiscernible** (in′də zėr′nə bəl), *adj.* not distinguishable; imperceptible.

15. **disdain** (dis dān′), *n.* a feeling of scorn.

After Reading

Making Connections

Shaping Your
Response

1. If you could be the hand of fate, how would you change the events of this story?

2. As a class, take a vote: Is Rico a traitor to his platoon? Be prepared to explain your opinion.

Analyzing the
Story

3. What bothers Rico about the orders to level the village?

4. ☝ Why does Rico make a **choice** that is different from that of his comrades?

5. Why do you suppose Keever ignores Rico after he has been placed under arrest?

6. Explain what you think Rico means when he says, "I'm free inside."

Extending the
Ideas

7. Compare Rico's feelings about the Vietnam War to the character Tim O'Brien's feelings. How are they similar and different?

8. Now Rico is back in the United States. If there were another chapter to this story, what would happen to Rico?

Literary Focus: Theme

What is the **theme,** or main idea, of "Village"? Write a sentence that explains the theme, and list the clues you found in the text that helped reveal the theme. Keep in mind that elements such as plot, character, dialogue, and setting can all contribute to the theme.

Vocabulary Study

Study the relationship of each of the following pairs of words, then choose another pair that has the same relationship.

**pyre
discord
tumult
indiscernable
disdain**

1. BRANCH : PYRE :: **a.** dream : snore **b.** water : fire
c. transient : permanent **d.** raindrop : flood

2. DISCORD : CONFLICT :: **a.** unremitting : boredom
b. ostentatious : opulent **c.** prodigious : tiny **d.** talented : cellist

3. DISTURBANCE : TUMULT :: **a.** politician : power **b.** wise : foolish
c. anger : shout **d.** horror : terror

4. INDISCERNIBLE : FEATURES :: **a.** superfluous : needed
b. corpulent : physique **c.** transgression : infraction
d. accurate : correct

5. SCORN : DISDAIN :: **a.** disorganized : orderly **b.** vengeful : bully
c. ethereal : music **d.** exhort : urge

Expressing Your Ideas

Writing Choices

Writer's Notebook Update Based on the list you made of some of the reasons why the Vietnam War caused so much controversy in the United States and on your reading of Portillo Trambley's short story, write a summary of the controversy that could be included in an encyclopedia entry about the Vietnam War under the heading "Vietnam War: Dissent and Protest." Your summary should be no longer than one paragraph.

Recent Revelations In 1995, Robert McNamara, former United States Secretary of Defense under President Johnson, revealed that as early as 1967 he had concluded that the Vietnam War was unwinnable and that the combat strategies he had helped design were "wrong, terribly wrong." McNamara says in his 1995 autobiography, *In Retrospect,* that he deeply regrets United States involvement in Vietnam. Imagine that you are Rico. Write a **letter** to McNamara explaining why you agree or disagree with him.

Other Options

Vietnam Today Working with a partner, prepare a **presentation** of today's Vietnam, using maps and other visual aids as necessary. In your presentation, include an explanation of current diplomatic relations between the United States and Vietnam.

Divergent Viewpoints In "Village," Rico sees Mai Cao in two different ways. At times he views the village as a quiet, innocent place. At other times he attempts to see the village as his fellow soldiers do—a place of "begging children with hidden grenades, the unseen VC hiding in the hootches . . ." Divide a large piece of paper into two sections. On the left hand side of the paper, make a **sketch** of the village that represents the way Rico sees it. On the right-hand side, make a sketch of the village that represents the way Rico has been *ordered* to see it.

A Memorial The Vietnam Veterans Memorial in Washington, D.C. includes two black granite walls inscribed with the names of all Americans who died in the Vietnam War, or who remained classified as missing in action when the walls were built. If you were asked to create a Vietnam Veterans Memorial for your town, what would it be? Sketch your memorial. Include with your design an explanation of the materials you would use. Then write an inscription for a plaque that might accompany the memorial.

The Pace of Change

History Connection

The pace of social change accelerated dramatically in the 1960s and 1970s. Below and on the following pages is a time line charting some of the most memorable events that occurred during this time of turmoil.

1955

Rosa Parks is arrested in Montgomery, Alabama after refusing to surrender her seat on a city bus to a white passenger. Her indictment prompts African American leaders to form the Montgomery Improvement Association to challenge segregation in public transportation. The group chooses Martin Luther King, Jr. as its leader and organizes a boycott of the city buses.

1956

The U.S. Supreme Court outlaws segregation on buses, ending the Montgomery bus boycott. Boycotters return to riding the buses and for the first time receive the right to first-come, first-served seating, and African American men are hired as drivers. The success of the Montgomery boycott leads to boycotts in other cities in the South.

1957

Arkansas Governor Orval Faubus orders National Guardsmen to prevent 9 African American students from entering previously all-white Central High School in Little Rock, Arkansas. A court order forces Gov. Faubus to admit the students and President Eisenhower sends U.S. army troops to maintain order.

1960

College and high school students begin staging peaceful demonstrations known as sit-ins, in which they sit at segregated lunch counters and refuse to leave until served. Trained not to fight back when harassed or attacked, these protesters endure beatings and arrests but are successful at desegregating some lunch counters and other public facilities. The success of early sit-ins leads to a movement that spreads to cities across the South during the early part of the decade. Other forms of nonviolent protest emerge such as Freedom Rides on interstate buses and mass freedom marches.

1962

During the fall, federal troops are sent to Oxford, Mississippi when a large mob of whites riots in violent protest against the admission of African American student James Meredith to the University of Mississippi.

1963

In June NAACP leader Medger Evers is shot to death in Jackson, Mississippi.

1963

During the summer civil rights leader A. Philip Randolph organizes the March on Washington for Jobs and Freedom. On August 28 more than 250,000 people gather at the Lincoln Memorial where Dr. Martin Luther King, Jr., delivers his "I Have a Dream" speech.

1962

Folk singer Bob Dylan writes the song "Blowin' in the Wind," which becomes an unofficial anthem of the civil rights movement.

I have a dream...

we HeLL no won't go!

1965

U.S. involvement in Vietnam increases as President Johnson orders sustained bombing of North Vietnam and the deployment of the first American combat troops. Claiming that it would be dishonorable not to come to the aid of South Vietnam, President Johnson begins an escalation of American forces that commits nearly 200,000 troops by year's end, and continues for the next three years.

1965

Labor leader Cesar Chavez and the National Farm Workers Association join with Filipino grape pickers to strike against growers' unfair wage practices. The strike, which quickly gains national attention and becomes known as "La Causa" or the Cause, lasts 3 years when Chavez, in an effort to heighten public awareness of the workers' cause, initiates a nation-wide boycott of table grapes. The boycott helps end the strike in 1970.

1966

The National Organization for Women (NOW) forms to pressure the Equal Employment Opportunity Commission to enforce a law prohibiting sex discrimination. With its president, Betty Friedan—author of *The Feminine Mystique,* a book that three years earlier charged society's institutions with conditioning women to believe they could become nothing other than housewives and mothers—the group pledges to "bring women into full participation in the mainstream of American society . . . now."

1967

The protest movement against the Vietnam War grows with more marches, sit-ins, and demonstrations against U.S. presence in Vietnam. American men— eligible to be drafted into the army at the age of 18—publicly tear up or burn their draft cards. Renowned pediatrician Dr. Benjamin Spock and poet Allen Ginsburg are among more than 500 arrested at an antiwar protest in New York. A poll at year's end reveals for the first time that most Americans believe that getting involved in Vietnam was a mistake.

Sisterhood is Power

1968

The police, FBI, and CIA infiltrate meetings of antiwar protest organizers and use information to disrupt planned demonstrations. In Chicago, some 10,000 antiwar protesters converge in August to demonstrate at the Democratic National Convention. Chicago's Mayor Richard J. Daley orders 12,000 police and 5000 National Guardsmen to prevent protesters from disturbing the convention. Violence erupts as demonstrators break through police barriers and police attack protesters.

1968

African American athletes consider boycotting the summer Olympic Games in Mexico City to protest racism in the United States. Although the boycott is canceled, U.S. Olympic champions Tommie Smith and John Carlos make their own protest at the medals ceremony when they bow their heads and raise black-gloved fists during the playing of their national anthem. Their Black Power salute prompts the international Olympic committee to force the U.S. committee to suspend the two runners from the team.

1969

Nearly 500,000 members of America's counterculture —a social revolt that developed earlier in the decade among young people mostly opposed to the Vietnam War, individualism, and capitalism, and in favor of communal living—unite for the Woodstock Music and Art Fair in New York. The three day festival becomes a symbol of solidarity for a generation in revolt against "the establishment." Several months later, in contrast to the peaceful atmosphere of Woodstock, violence disrupts a free concert at the Altamont Speedway in California and a man is murdered by a member of the Hell's Angels—a motorcycle gang hired to keep order at the concert.

1970

President Nixon announces that U.S. forces have launched a surprise attack on Vietnamese communists' military headquarters in Cambodia. The announcement reignites the antiwar movement. National student strikes are organized and students close down college campuses across the nation. Four students are killed at Kent State University, Ohio, by National Guardsmen called in to enforce martial law.

4 dead in Ohio

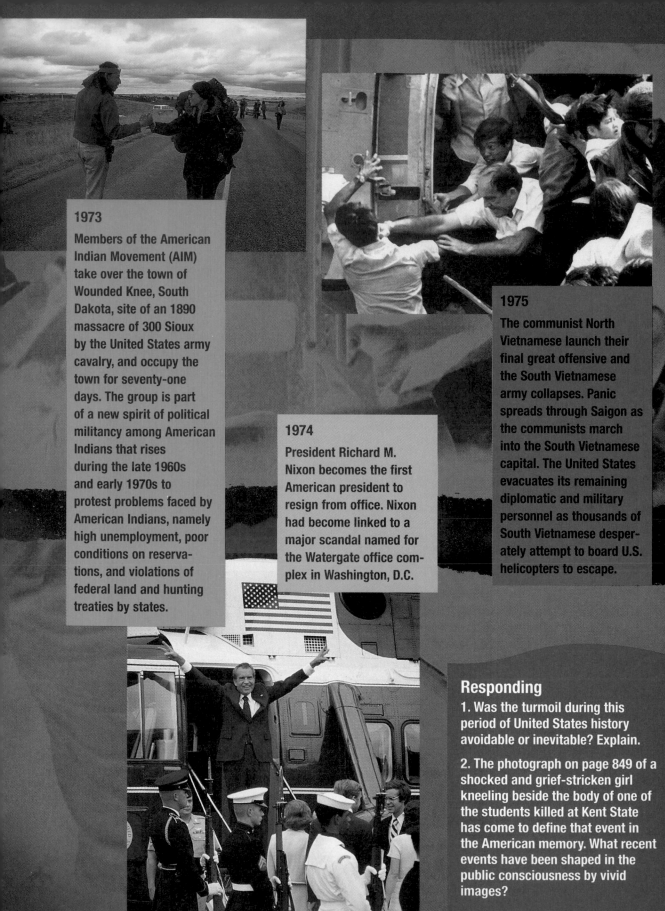

1973

Members of the American Indian Movement (AIM) take over the town of Wounded Knee, South Dakota, site of an 1890 massacre of 300 Sioux by the United States army cavalry, and occupy the town for seventy-one days. The group is part of a new spirit of political militancy among American Indians that rises during the late 1960s and early 1970s to protest problems faced by American Indians, namely high unemployment, poor conditions on reservations, and violations of federal land and hunting treaties by states.

1974

President Richard M. Nixon becomes the first American president to resign from office. Nixon had become linked to a major scandal named for the Watergate office complex in Washington, D.C.

1975

The communist North Vietnamese launch their final great offensive and the South Vietnamese army collapses. Panic spreads through Saigon as the communists march into the South Vietnamese capital. The United States evacuates its remaining diplomatic and military personnel as thousands of South Vietnamese desperately attempt to board U.S. helicopters to escape.

Responding

1. Was the turmoil during this period of United States history avoidable or inevitable? Explain.

2. The photograph on page 849 of a shocked and grief-stricken girl kneeling beside the body of one of the students killed at Kent State has come to define that event in the American memory. What recent events have been shaped in the public consciousness by vivid images?

850

Language History

Euphemisms: Polite and Deadly Language

 As for your criticism of our pacification, you are right that war is devastating. But we are doing everything we can to limit that.

At first glance, one hardly notices that this quote by President Lyndon Johnson is talking about the violent death of American soldiers and others in Vietnam. During wars, government and military leaders use many euphemisms—mild or indirect expressions used in place of harsh, direct ones—to direct their own attention, as well as the public's, away from the brutal reality of war.

In the early years of the Vietnam War the U.S. government referred to the fighting in Vietnam as a *police action* to avoid calling it war. The Pentagon coined many euphemisms designed to obscure what was really happening in Vietnam. Mercenaries—soldiers serving for pay in a foreign army—were known as *civilian irregular defense soldiers*, refugees were *ambient noncombatant personnel*, and dead civilians were called *collateral damage*. Spraying an area with machine-gun fire was known as *reconnaissance by fire;* a *traumatic amputation* occurred when a soldier's arm or leg was blown off. Perhaps most chilling of all: *aluminum transfer containers* was the term for coffins used to transport dead soldiers home.

Soldiers stationed in Vietnam used euphemisms as a way of protecting themselves from the difficulty of their mission. A *birdfarm* was an aircraft carrier loaded with weapons. A Vietcong (enemy) soldier was a *hard-hat* and a Vietnamese home was called a *hooch*.

Euphemisms don't only occur during times of war, of course. Whenever there's an unpleasant task to do, you can be sure euphemisms will be created to describe it. Whereas in the past companies might *fire* or *lay off* employees, today they are more likely to *down-size*. A politician may not admit to wanting to raise taxes, but may see a need for *revenue enhancement*. The danger in euphemisms, of course, is that they shield us from realities that we are sometimes better off confronting head-on, and may lull us into doing nothing when we should be taking action.

Writing Workshop

Reflecting on the Sixties

Assignment Work in a small group to explore the 1960s.

WRITER'S BLUEPRINT

Product	An interview
Purpose	To present personal reflections on the 1960s by someone who lived during that era
Audience	Anyone with an interest in the 1960s
Specs	As the creators of a successful interview, your group should:

❑ Choose someone born before 1945 who is willing to be interviewed about the 1960s.

❑ Research and prepare interview questions about personalities, events, and issues of the 1960s. Then interview your subject, focusing on his or her personal reflections about the personalities, events, and issues from your research.

❑ Begin your paper by introducing your subject. Give background on who the person is now, and who the person was then. Then write your interview, using a mix of descriptive details, paraphrases, and direct quotations.

❑ Conclude by telling whether you would have liked to have lived during the 1960s and why.

❑ Follow the rules of grammar, usage, spelling, and mechanics. Take care to punctuate quotations correctly.

STEP **1** PREWRITING

Choose your subject. Brainstorm a list of people born before 1945 who are well-known to members of your group. When you make your choice, be sure to contact him or her right away and arrange for a live interview. (See the Or . . . option at the bottom of the next page.)

Review the literature in this part of the unit, as well as the Interdisciplinary Study, to start developing interview questions. What events, issues, and personalities from the 1960s do the authors focus on? In a group, brainstorm ideas and organize them in a chart like this one:

1960s		
Events	**Issues**	**Personalities**
Vietnam War	—U.S. and French involvement in Vietnam —U.S. citizens' reactions to involvement in Vietnam	Diem

Research the 1960s. Consult other sources to add to your chart. Consider books; magazine and newspaper articles; 1960s TV shows, movies, and music; online sources; and other people you know who lived during the era. Along the way, gather together photographs and other illustrations from magazines and newspapers of the time to use when you present your interview.

Develop interview questions. Working as a group, develop a list of interview questions that focus on those issues, events, and personalities that your research indicates are the most interesting and prominent. Here are some tips:

- Write each question on a separate piece of paper to give plenty of room to take notes on the answers.

- If you know your subject has detailed knowledge about a particular issue, plan to ask a number of questions about it. (See the first Or . . . option.)

- Include questions that focus on your subject's background: who he or is now (occupation, interests, accomplishments), and who he or she was then, in the 1960s. You'll need this information when you draft your introduction.

OR . . .
Give your subject an idea of the topics you plan to focus on and ask him or her for some initial reactions. Use these reactions to help you formulate your questions.

Interview your subject. Be on time and be prepared. If your subject agrees, take his or her picture to use when you present the interview. If you plan to tape-record the interview, be sure you have your subject's permission beforehand. Here are more interview tips:

- Tape-record the interview, if you can, to ensure the accuracy of the information and of the direct quotes you will use.

- Whether you tape the interview or not, take careful notes.

OR . . .
If your subject can't be interviewed in person, arrange to conduct the interview by phone. A third option is to submit a list of questions by mail first and then follow up with a phone interview.

- Although it's important to prepare your questions in advance, listen carefully to the answers. Don't focus so intently on asking the next question on your list that you fail to ask the follow-up questions that will add the necessary detail and depth to enrich the interview.

- Make notes on your subject's appearance and mannerisms.

OR . . .
If you've taped the interview, edit the actual tape before you draft. Eliminate extraneous information and rearrange the order to create a smooth narrative flow. Then write your draft from this edited tape.

STEP 2 DRAFTING

Draft the introduction. Be sure to include background information about who your subject is now (occupation, interests, accomplishments), and who your subject was then, in the 1960s.

Draft the interview. Use a format that mixes descriptive details about the subject's appearance and mannerisms, paraphrases of what was said, and direct quotations. For example:

 paraphrase

We asked if he'd ever seen the Beatles in person. He ran a hand through

his salt and pepper hair and furrowed his brow, then raised a hand in the air.

"Once, yes," he said. "It was in my college days—in Chicago." He smiled at the

thought, lowering his arm and settling back in his chair. "Let's see now . . ."

descriptive detail   direct quotation

STUDENT MODEL

Look ahead to the Revising Strategy in Step 3 of this lesson for tips on when to paraphrase material and when to quote directly.

Draft the conclusion. Separately, complete this sentence:

From our research and interview I get the impression that I would/would not like to have lived then because _____.

Then share your impressions and draft your conclusion.

STEP 3 REVISING

Ask another group to comment on your draft before you revise it. Use the checklist on the next page as a guide.

✔ Did we start by introducing our subject, then and now?

✔ Does our interview focus on issues, events, and personalities of the 1960s?

✔ Have we presented our interview as a mix of descriptive details, paraphrases, and direct quotations?

Revising Strategy

When to Quote Directly and When to Paraphrase

A paraphrase is a summary of what was said (I asked him what happened next), while a direct quotation gives the speaker's exact words ("We got into the car"). Paraphrases are used to move the interview along smoothly and to lead into—set up—direct quotations. For example:

> We asked Eddie for more details about the rally. At first he couldn't recall anything and we talked about how hard it is to remember things you haven't thought about in a long while. Then a thought came to him. "Yes, now I remember," he said. "Things started to get scary when the protesters began chanting. . . ."

STUDENT MODEL

Look back at your draft and see if you can move things along more smoothly by mixing paraphrases and direct quotations.

4 EDITING

Ask another group to review your revised draft before you edit. When you edit, look for errors in grammar, usage, spelling, and mechanics. Look at each sentence to make sure you are punctuating direct quotations correctly.

Editing Strategy

FOR REFERENCE
For more information on punctuating direct quotations, see the Language and Grammar Handbook at the back of this text.

Punctuating Direct Quotations

Follow these rules for punctuating direct quotations:

- If a quotation is uninterrupted, put quotation marks only at the beginning and end of the entire quotation, no matter how many sentences are in it: "No, I don't think so. I'd like to, though."

- If a quotation is interrupted by a speaker tag or some other words that are not part of the actual quotation, use a separate set of quotation marks for each part: "No, I don't think so," he said. "I'd like to, though."

COMPUTER TIP
If you do a magazine article presentation, plan your layout in advance and format your text so that it wraps around and along the sides of your illustrations.

5 PRESENTING

- Turn your materials into a magazine article, with captioned visuals, including a photograph of your subject. (See the Computer Tip.)

- Present a copy of your written material to your subject.

6 LOOKING BACK

Self-evaluate. What grade would *you* give your paper? Look back at the Writer's Blueprint and give yourself a score on each point, from 6 (superior) to 1 (inadequate).

Reflect. Think about what you've learned from writing this interview as you write answers to these questions.

✔ How does what you know of life in the 1960s compare with life today? What are some similarities? some differences?

✔ What are some lessons you learned about the art of interviewing? Next time you conduct an interview, what will you do differently?

For Your Working Portfolio Add your interview and reflection responses to your working portfolio.

Beyond Print

Multimedia Presentations

You are living in an age in which modern technology—computers, VCRs, CD ROMs, and programs with multimedia capabilities—can transform traditional reports and speeches into exciting media events. Whenever you use a combination of media to communicate to an audience, you are making a multimedia presentation. This includes speeches, posters, slides, video, projected images, graphs, recordings, or even skits.

The computer is a powerful tool in producing any multimedia presentation. You can hook up the computer to a projection unit in order to use the program during an oral presentation and provide animation, special effects, sound, and video. You might engage your audience with an interactive program in which viewers manipulate the type and order of information they receive by clicking a button.

Since each piece of media you add makes the presentation more complex, be thoughtful and organized in preparing your materials. Save only the most important information for posters or computer screens. Avoid materials that are cluttered or confusing.

Here are some hints for using multimedia in oral presentations.

- Use pictures and music that will supplement the information, not distract the audience.

- Use large type (for readability) and important heads (for emphasis) in projections. Present additional details orally or in handouts.

- Use concise, clear, and correctly spelled text.

- Plan, organize, and practice presenting your material.

- Project your voice so that everyone can hear.

Activity Option

- Prepare a multimedia presentation on one of the topics or famous personalities you've encountered in this section. Prepare a speech; then add one or more other media. You might use, for example, a slide, picture, or video footage from the Vietnam War, a recording of a speech by Malcolm X or King, or music from the 1960s.

Multicultural Connections

Interactions

Part One: Person to Person Cultural factors influence the way people interact. In "I Stand Here Ironing," society's attempts to help the mother seem only to further alienate her from her daughter. Tension over different cultural values cause trouble for Dee and her mother in "Everyday Use." Young Maxine Hong Kingston's cultural heritage makes her interactions with teachers and other students difficult.

■ In which selections does cultural heritage—in the forms of family, community, and customs—seem to support and enhance positive interactions between people?

Choices

Part Two: In the Midst of Struggle . . . How we make choices is influenced both by our cultures of origin and the society around us. Lorraine Hansberry's father chose to fight for racial integration, even when it put his own family in danger. In "On the Rainy River," Tim O'Brien's personal convictions told him that the war in Vietnam was wrong, but community pressure was so strong that he chose to go to war anyway. Rico in "Village" was caught between the army, personal convictions, and his cultural heritage as he made his choices.

■ Which individual in this section do you think faced the most difficult choices? Explain.

Activities

Work in small groups on the following activities.

1. Choose the selection from Part One that you think presents the *worst* example of interactions between people. Do a dramatization of the selection, but, during the dramatization, stop the action in places where your group thinks the interactions could be improved, and explain what the people should have done instead.

2. Making the right choice can be tough sometimes. Choose an issue of interest to your group that involves a personal choice. Some examples of issues might be drug use, joining a gang, standing up against injustice, and so on. Make a list of the cultural and social pressures that help individuals make the right choice, and those that lead individuals in the wrong direction.

Independent and Group Projects

Art

The Essence of the Work Of all the works in Unit 7, which one had the greatest impact on you? Choose the piece that you thought was the most powerful and create a visual work of art that expresses your thoughts or impressions of the literature. Choose any medium you wish—sculpture, collage, painting, drawing, and so on. Exhibit your work in the classroom. Can your classmates tell which piece of literature your artwork relates to?

Music

Music of the Era Many of the musicians who were popular in the 1960s and early 1970s tried to capture the social upheaval of the times in their music. Artists such as the Beatles, the Rolling Stones, Bob Dylan, and Joan Baez sang about the Vietnam War, race relations, and the anger that many young people felt toward the "establishment." Working with a partner, put together an audio montage that you feel best reflects the Vietnam War era. Play them for your class and analyze the lyrics, telling how they relate to the issues of the times.

Drama

Sneak Preview Working with a group of students, create a video "sneak preview" of Unit 7, as if to capture the interest of students who have not yet read the literature. Choose some of the highlights of the literature—your favorite scenes from stories, poems, and so on, and present them in the form of a video. You may want to read the passages dramatically, or actually dramatize some scenes. Include some of your own thoughts and impressions about the works in Unit 7 as well. You may wish to include music and art in your video.

Multimedia

The Author's Life Choose one of the authors from this unit to research. Gather information about the author's life and times, most well-known works, motivation for writing, and so on. Present your information in a hypertext report, using pictures, sound, and text, if possible.

American Voices Today

Citizens of Tomorrow
Pages 862–954

THEMES IN AMERICAN LITERATURE

The Media
Theme Portfolio, pages 955–965

HISTORICAL OVERVIEW

Building Unity on Diversity

Throughout our history, Americans have balanced forces of unity and diversity in building our society. Too much emphasis on uniformity can lead to political repression, like the McCarthyism of the 1950s. Too much divisiveness and Americans fear that the structure of their society is crumbling, as many feared during the radical 1960s. Today as in the past, Americans recognize that diversity brings both cultural richness and social problems; while the search for unity—for common American ideals—remains an elusive but necessary goal. Issues such as bilingual education, affirmative action, and immigration policy must be addressed in ways that build unity on diversity if the structure of our society is to remain sound in the 21st century. The young people shown here reflect the multicultural future of America.

If you are [Mexican American], inside you, around you, you feel the Indian and Spanish cultures. I am both these cultures.
Tito, age 14

The greatest pressure for black students is that we must achieve athletically to be recognized. . . . This is discouraging to students who go unrecognized but achieve in other areas such as fine arts, industrial arts, and the sciences.
Camille, age 17

My family have become citizens of the United States. We don't believe in nationalism. I was born in Iran . . . so we are Persians, we are Americans, but we are also citizens of the world.
Marjan, age 19

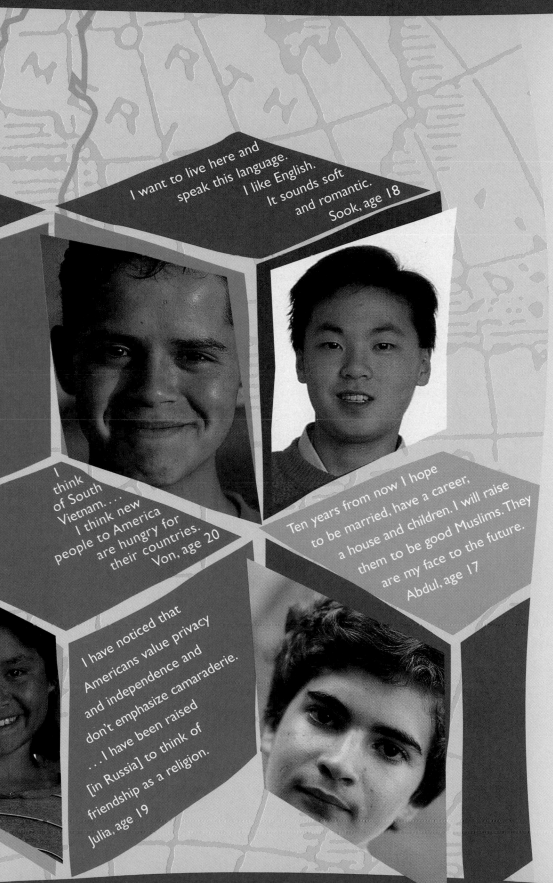

I want to live here and speak this language. I like English. It sounds soft and romantic.
Sook, age 18

I think of South Vietnam.... I think new people to America are hungry for their countries.
Von, age 20

Ten years from now I hope to be married, have a career, a house and children. I will raise them to be good Muslims. They are my face to the future.
Abdul, age 17

I have noticed that Americans value privacy and independence and don't emphasize camaraderie. ...I have been raised [in Russia] to think of friendship as a religion.
Julia, age 19

Key Dates

1980s
Majority of U.S. immigrants are from Asia and Latin America.

1990
Second observance of Earth Day takes place.

1992
500th anniversary of Columbus's landing in the New World.

1993
Toni Morrison wins the Nobel Prize for literature.

2000
Projections estimate 20 percent of Americans will be over 65.

2006
Projections estimate Hispanics will be largest U.S. minority.

2050
Projections estimate only half of U.S. population will be of European background.

Citizens of Tomorrow

Americans are facing a new century and a new millennium. The following selections present a cross-section of the lives and experiences of a changing America, and offer important insights for the citizens of tomorrow.

🐾 **Multicultural Connection** How does **cultural change** play a part in the lives of characters in the following selections, and how do they cope with change?

Literature

Anne Tyler	**Teenage Wasteland** ◆ short story	866
Garrison Keillor	**Gary Keillor** ◆ short story	876
Sandra Cisneros	**Salvador Late or Early** ◆ short story	888
Martín Espada	**Coca-Cola and Coco Frío** ◆ poem	893
Cathy Song	**Lost Sister** ◆ poem	894
Barbara Kingsolver	**Naming Myself** ◆ poem	896
Ana Castillo	**Red Wagons** ◆ poem	898
Amy Tan	**Mother Tongue** ◆ essay	902
Sherman Alexie	**This Is What It Means to Say Phoenix, Arizona** ◆ short story	911
T. Coraghessan Boyle	**Top of the Food Chain** ◆ short story	923
Pam Houston	**A Blizzard Under Blue Sky** ◆ short story	930
August Wilson	**The Janitor** ◆ play	936

Interdisciplinary Study A Glimpse Into the Future

The Way We Will Be ◆ futurist connection	939
Future Technology ◆ futurist connection	940
Future Fashions ◆ futurist connection	942
The Changing Face of America ◆ career connection	944

Language History

Computerese	945

Writing Workshop Narrative Writing

Poetic Insights	946

Beyond Print Critical Thinking

Analyzing Advertising	951

Before Reading

Teenage Wasteland

by Anne Tyler

Anne Tyler
born 1941

Anne Tyler grew up in North Carolina, attended Duke University in Raleigh and Columbia University in New York, and in 1963 married Taghi Mohammed Modarressi, a psychiatrist and writer. They and their two daughters settled in Baltimore, Maryland in 1967. Baltimore has been the setting for most of Tyler's novels. The family is at the center of Tyler's fiction, and her quirky characters endure the crises in their lives. Tyler's novels are both popular and critically acclaimed. *Dinner at the Homesick Restaurant* (1982) was nominated for the Pulitzer Prize, and *Breathing Lessons* (1988) won it. *The Accidental Tourist* (1985), which was made into a movie starring William Hurt, won the National Book Critics Circle Award.

Building Background

You're the Parent Imagine you are a parent, and your teenage son or daughter is having problems in school. Your child's grades have been steadily slipping, he or she has been caught skipping classes, and you suspect your child is smoking or drinking. What should you, as a parent, do when you see these signs of trouble? As a class, brainstorm ways to cope with these problems. Use a web like the one shown to record your ideas.

Best ways to cope with your teenage son or daughter's problems.

Literary Focus

Mood "When I opened the door after school, I was greeted with the tempting aroma of chocolate chip cookies cooling on the counter and the pleasant chatter of my mother playing with my twin brothers at the kitchen table." The preceding sentence establishes a cozy, cheerful mood. The kitchen setting is warm and inviting. The image of a mother playing with her children is heartwarming. The sensory description of the aroma of baking cookies is appealing, and the connotation associated with baking cookies—that of dispensing love—adds to the overall mood. In addition, the choice of words—*greeted, tempting aroma,* and *pleasant chatter*—contributes to the cheerful mood. As you read "Teenage Wasteland," identify the mood of the story and notice how Anne Tyler establishes that mood.

Writer's Notebook

Heart to Heart Once again, you're the parent, and your teenager is having problems in school—getting bad grades, cutting classes, smoking, drinking, and so on. You just can't seem to talk to each other, so you try a different route—you write a letter. What will you say to your teenager to try to make a difference in his or her life? Write your letter in your notebook.

TEENAGE WASTELAND

Anne Tyler

He used to have very blond hair—almost white—cut shorter than other children's so that on his crown a little cowlick always stood up to catch the light. But this was when he was small. As he grew older, his hair grew darker, and he wore it longer—past his collar even. It hung in lank, taffy-colored ropes around his face, which was still an endearing face, fine-featured, the eyes an unusual aqua blue. But his cheeks, of course, were no longer round, and a sharp new Adam's apple jogged in his throat when he talked.

In October, they called from the private school he attended to request a conference with his parents. Daisy went alone; her husband was at work. Clutching her purse, she sat on the principal's couch and learned that Donny was noisy, lazy, and disruptive, always fooling around with his friends, and he wouldn't respond in class.

In the past, before her children were born, Daisy had been a fourth-grade teacher. It shamed her now to sit before this principal as a parent, a delinquent parent, a parent who struck Mr. Lanham, no doubt, as unseeing or uncaring. "It isn't that we're not concerned," she said. "Both of us are. And we've done what we could, whatever we could think of. We don't let him watch TV on school nights. We don't let him talk on the phone till he's finished his homework. But he tells us he doesn't *have* any homework or he did it all in study hall. How are we to know what to believe?"

From early October through November, at Mr. Lanham's suggestion, Daisy checked Donny's assignments every day. She sat next to him as he worked, trying to be encouraging, sagging inwardly as she saw the poor quality of everything he did—the sloppy mistakes in math, the illogical leaps in his English themes, the history questions left blank if they required any research.

Daisy was often late starting supper, and she couldn't give as much attention to Donny's younger sister. "You'll never guess what happened at . . ." Amanda would begin, and Daisy would have to tell her, "Not now, honey."

By the time her husband Matt came home, she'd be snappish. She would recite the day's hardships—the fuzzy instructions in English, the botched history map, the morass[1] of unsolvable algebra equations. Matt would look surprised and confused, and Daisy would gradually wind down. There was no way, really, to convey how exhausting all this was.

In December, the school called again. This time, they wanted Matt to come as well. She and Matt had to sit on Mr. Lanham's couch like two bad children and listen to the news: Donny had improved only slightly, raising a D in history to a C, and a C in algebra to a B-minus. What was worse, he had developed new problems. He had cut classes on a least three occasions. Smoked in the furnace room. Helped Sonny Barnett break

---

1. **morass** (mə ras'), *n.* a difficult situation; puzzling mess.

What is the boy feeling in Alex Katz's 1972 painting, *Ada and Vincent in the Car?* What is the woman feeling? What clues from the painting support your ideas?

into a freshman's locker. And last week, during athletics, he and three friends had been seen off the school grounds; when they returned, the coach had smelled beer on their breath.

Daisy and Matt sat silent, shocked. Matt rubbed his forehead with his fingertips. Imagine, Daisy thought, how they must look to Mr. Lanham: an overweight housewife in a cotton dress and a too-tall, too-thin insurance agent in a baggy, frayed suit. Failures, both of them—the kind of people who are always hurrying to catch up, missing the point of things that everyone else grasps at once. She wished she'd worn nylons instead of knee socks.

It was arranged that Donny would visit a psychologist for testing. Mr. Lanham knew just the person. He would set this boy straight, he said.

When they stood to leave, Daisy held her stomach in and gave Mr. Lanham a firm, responsible handshake.

Donny said the psychologist was a jackass and the tests were really dumb; but he kept all three of his appointments, and when it was time for the follow-up conference with the psychologist and both parents, Donny combed his hair and seemed unusually sober and subdued. The psychologist said Donny had no serious emotional problems. He was merely going through a difficult period in his life. He required some academic help and a better sense of self-worth. For this reason, he was suggesting a man named Calvin Beadle, a tutor with considerable psychological training.

In the car going home, Donny said he'd be damned if he'd let them drag him to some stupid fairy tutor. His father told him to watch his language in front of his mother.

That night, Daisy lay awake pondering the term "self-worth." She had always been free with her praise. She had always told Donny he had talent, was smart, was good with his hands. She had made a big to-do over every little gift he gave her. In fact, maybe she had gone too far, although, Lord knows, she had meant every word. Was that his trouble?

She remembered when Amanda was born.

Donny had acted lost and bewildered. Daisy had been alert to that, of course, but still, a new baby keeps you so busy. Had she really done all she could have? She longed—she ached—for a time machine. Given one more chance, she'd do it perfectly—hug him more, praise him more, or perhaps praise him less. Oh, who can say . . .

The tutor told Donny to call him Cal. All his kids did he said. Daisy thought for a second that he meant his own children, then realized her mistake. He seemed too young, anyhow, to be a family man. He wore a heavy brown handlebar mustache. His hair was as long and stringy as Donny's, and his jeans as faded. Wire-rimmed spectacles slid down his nose. He lounged in a canvas director's chair with his fingers laced across his chest, and he casually, amiably[2] questioned Donny, who sat upright and glaring in an armchair.

"So they're getting on your back at school," said Cal. "Making a big deal about anything you do wrong."

"Right," said Donny.

"Any idea why that would be?"

"Oh, well, you know, stuff like homework and all," Donny said.

"You don't do your homework?"

"Oh well, I might do it sometimes but not just exactly like they want it." Donny sat forward and said, "It's like a prison there, you know? You've got to go to every class, you can never step off the school grounds."

"You cut classes sometimes?"

"Sometimes," Donny said, with a glance at his parents.

Cal didn't seemed perturbed.[3] "Well," he said, "I'll tell you what. Let's you and me try working together three nights a week. Think you could handle that? We'll see if we can show that school of yours a thing or two. Give it a month; then if you don't like it, we'll stop. If *I* don't like it, we'll stop. I mean, sometimes people just don't get along, right? What do you say to that?"

"Okay," Donny said. He seemed pleased.

"Make it seven o'clock till eight, Monday, Wednesday, and Friday," Cal told Matt and Daisy. They nodded. Cal shambled to his feet, gave them a little salute, and showed them to the door.

This was where he lived as well as worked, evidently. The interview had taken place in the dining room, which had been transformed into a kind of office. Passing the living room, Daisy winced at the rock music she had been hearing, without registering it, ever since she had entered the house. She looked in and saw a boy about Donny's age lying on a sofa with a book. Another boy and a girl were playing Ping-Pong in front of the fireplace. "You have several here together?" Daisy asked Cal.

"Oh, sometimes they stay on after their sessions, just to rap. They're a pretty sociable group, all in all. Plenty of goof-offs like young Donny here."

He cuffed Donny's shoulder playfully. Donny flushed and grinned.

Climbing into the car, Daisy asked Donny, "Well? What did you think?"

But Donny had returned to his old evasive[4] self. He jerked his chin toward the garage. "Look," he said. "He's got a basketball net."

Now on Mondays, Wednesdays, and Fridays, they had supper early—the instant Matt came home. Sometimes, they had to leave before they were really finished. Amanda would still be eating her dessert. "Bye, honey. Sorry," Daisy would tell her.

Cal's first bill sent a flutter of panic through Daisy's chest, but it was worth it, of course. Just look at Donny's face when they picked him up: alight and full of interest. The principal telephoned Daisy to tell her how Donny had improved. "Of course, it hasn't shown up in his

---

2. **amiably** (ā′mē ə blē), *adv.* in a pleasant and agreeable way.
3. **perturbed** (pər tėrbd′), *adj.* uneasy or troubled.
4. **evasive** (i vā′siv), *adj.* tending or trying to avoid by cleverness; misleading.

grades yet, but several of the teachers have noticed how his attitude's changed. Yes sir, I think we're onto something here."

At home, Donny didn't act much different. He still seemed to have a low opinion of his parents. But Daisy supposed that was unavoidable—part of being fifteen. He said his parents were too "controlling"—a word that made Daisy give him a sudden look. He said they acted like wardens. On weekends, they enforced a curfew. And any time he went to a party, they always telephoned first to see if adults would be supervising. "For God's sake!" he said. "Don't you trust me?"

"It isn't a matter of trust, honey . . ." But there was no explaining to him.

His tutor called one afternoon. "I get the sense," he said, "that this kid's feeling . . . underestimated, you know? Like you folks expect the worst of him. I'm thinking we ought to give him more rope."

"But see, he's still so suggestible," Daisy said. "When his friends suggest some mischief—smoking or drinking or such—why, he just finds it very hard not to go along with them."

"Mrs. Coble," the tutor said, "I think this kid is hurting. You know? Here's a serious, sensitive kid, telling you he'd like to take on some grown-up challenges, and you're giving him the message that he can't be trusted. Don't you understand how that hurts?"

"Oh," said Daisy.

"It undermines his self-esteem—don't you realize that?"

"Well, I guess you're right," said Daisy. She saw Donny suddenly from a whole new angle: his pathetically poor posture, that slouch so forlorn[5] that his shoulders seemed about to meet his chin . . . oh, wasn't it awful being young? She'd had a miserable adolescence herself and had always sworn no child of hers would ever be that unhappy.

They let Donny stay out later, they didn't call ahead to see if the parties were supervised, and they were careful not to grill him about his evening. The tutor had set down so many rules! They were not allowed any questions at all about any aspect of school, nor were they to speak with his teachers. If a teacher had some complaint, she should phone Cal. Only one teacher disobeyed—the history teacher, Miss Evans. She called one morning in February. "I'm a little concerned about Donny, Mrs. Coble."

"Oh, I'm sorry, Miss Evans, but Donny's tutor handles these things now . . ."

"I always deal directly with the parents. You are the parent," Miss Evans said, speaking very slowly and distinctly. "Now, here is the problem. Back when you were helping Donny with his homework, his grades rose from a D to a C, but now they've slipped back, and they're closer to an F."

"They are?"

"I think you should start overseeing his homework again."

She saw Donny suddenly from a whole new angle . . .

"But Donny's tutor says . . ."

"It's nice that Donny has a tutor, but you should still be in charge of his homework. With you, he learned it. Then he passed his tests. With the tutor, well, it seems the tutor is more of a crutch. 'Donny,' I say, 'a quiz is coming up on Friday. Hadn't you better be listening instead of talking?' 'That's okay, Miss Evans,' he says. 'I have a tutor now.' Like a talisman![6] I really think you ought to take over, Mrs. Coble."

"I see," said Daisy. "Well, I'll think about that. Thank you for calling."

Hanging up, she felt a rush of anger at Donny. A talisman! For a talisman, she'd given up all luxuries, all that time with her daughter, her evenings at home!

She dialed Cal's number. He sounded muzzy.

---

5. **forlorn** (fôr lôrn′), *adj.* wretched in feeling or looks; unhappy.

6. **talisman** (tal′is mən), *n.* anything that acts as a charm.

"I'm sorry I woke you," she told him, "but Donny's history teacher just called. She says he isn't doing well."

"She should have dealt with me."

"She wants me to start supervising his homework again. His grades are slipping."

"Yes," said the tutor, "but you and I both know there's more to it than mere grades, don't we? I care about the *whole* child—his happiness, his self-esteem. The grades will come. Just give them time."

When she hung up, it was Miss Evans she was angry at. What a narrow woman!

It was Cal this, Cal that, Cal says this, Cal and I did that. Cal lent Donny an album by the Who. He took Donny and two other pupils to a rock concert. In March, when Donny began to talk endlessly on the phone with a girl named Miriam, Cal even let Miriam come to one of the tutoring sessions. Daisy was touched that Cal would grow so involved in Donny's life, but she was also a little hurt, because she had offered to have Miriam to dinner and Donny had refused. Now he asked them to drive her to Cal's house without a qualm.

This Miriam was an unappealing girl with blurry lipstick and masses of rough red hair. She wore a short, bulky jacket that would not have been out of place on a motorcycle. During the trip to Cal's she was silent, but coming back, she was more talkative. "What a neat guy, and what a house! All those kids hanging out, like a club. And the stereo playing rock . . . gosh, he's not like a grown-up at all! Married and divorced and everything, but you'd think he was our own age."

"Mr. Beadle was married?" Daisy asked.

"Yeah, to this really controlling lady. She didn't understand him a bit."

"No, I guess not," Daisy said.

Spring came, and the students who hung around at Cal's drifted out to the basketball net above the garage. Sometimes, when Daisy and Matt arrived to pick up Donny, they'd find him there with the others—spiky and excited, jittering on his toes beneath the backboard. It was staying light much longer now, and the neighboring fence cast narrow bars across the bright grass. Loud music would be spilling from Cal's windows. Once it was the Who, which Daisy recognized from the time that Donny had borrowed the album. "*Teenage Wasteland,*" she said aloud, identifying the song, and Matt gave a short, dry laugh. "It certainly is," he said. He'd misunderstood; he thought she was commenting on the scene spread before them. In fact, she might have been. The players looked like hoodlums, even her son. Why, one of Cal's students had recently been knifed in a tavern. One had been shipped off to boarding school in midterm; two had been withdrawn by their parents. On the other hand, Donny had mentioned someone who'd been studying with Cal for five years. "Five years!" said Daisy. "Doesn't anyone ever stop needing him?"

Donny looked at her. Lately, whatever she said about Cal was read as criticism. "You're just feeling competitive," he said. "And controlling."

She bit her lip and said no more.

In April, the principal called to tell her that Donny had been expelled. There had been a locker check, and in Donny's locker they found five cans of beer and half a pack of cigarettes. With Donny's previous record, this offense meant expulsion.

Daisy gripped the receiver tightly and said, "Well, where is he now?"

"We've sent him home," said Mr. Lanham. "He's packed up all his belongings, and he's coming home on foot."

Daisy wondered what she would say to him. She felt him looming closer and closer, bringing this brand-new situation that no one had prepared her to handle. What other place would take him? Could they enter him in a public school? What were the rules? She stood at the living room window, waiting for him to show up. Gradually, she realized that he was taking too long. She checked the clock. She stared up the street again.

When an hour had passed, she phoned the school. Mr. Lanham's secretary answered and told her in a grave, sympathetic voice that yes, Donny Coble had most definitely gone home. Daisy called her husband. He was out of the office. She went back to the window and thought a while, and then she called Donny's tutor.

"Donny's been expelled from school," she said, "and now I don't know where he's gone. I wonder if you've heard from him?"

There was a long silence. "Donny's with me, Mrs. Coble," he finally said.

"With you? How'd he get there?"

"He hailed a cab, and I paid the driver."

"Could I speak to him, please?"

There was another silence. "Maybe it'd be better if we had a conference," Cal said.

"I don't *want* a conference. I've been standing at the window picturing him dead or kidnapped or something, and now you tell me you want a—"

"Donny is very, very upset. Understandably so," said Cal. "Believe me, Mrs. Coble, this is not what it seems. Have you asked Donny's side of the story?"

"Well, of course not, how could I? He went running off to you instead."

"Because he didn't feel he'd be listened to."

"But I haven't even—"

"Why don't you come out and talk? The three of us," said Cal, "will try to get this thing in perspective."

"Well, all right," Daisy said. But she wasn't as reluctant as she sounded. Already, she felt soothed by the calm way Cal was taking this.

Cal answered the doorbell at once. He said, "Hi, there," and led her into the dining room. Donny sat slumped in a chair, chewing the knuckle of one thumb. "Hello, Donny," Daisy said. He flicked his eyes in her direction.

"Sit here, Mrs. Coble," said Cal, placing her opposite Donny. He himself remained standing, restlessly pacing. "So," he said.

Daisy stole a look at Donny. His lips were swollen, as if he'd been crying.

After you've finished reading the entire story, decide where in the story this painting, *Ada Behind the Screen Door* (1985) by Alex Katz, best fits. Explain your answer.

"You know," Cal told Daisy, "I kind of expected something like this. That's a very punitive school you've got him in—you realize that. And any half-decent lawyer will tell you they've violated his civil rights. Locker checks! Where's their search warrant?"

"But if the rule is—" Daisy said.

"Well, anyhow, let him tell you his side."

She looked at Donny. He said, "It wasn't my fault. I promise."

"They said your locker was full of beer."

"It was a put-up job! See, there's this guy that doesn't like me. He put all these beers in my locker and started a rumor going, so Mr. Lanham ordered a locker check."

"What was the boy's name?" Daisy asked.

"Huh?"

"Mrs. Coble, take my word, the situation is not so unusual," Cal said. "You can't imagine how vindictive[7] kids can be sometimes."

"What was the boy's *name*," said Daisy, "so that I can ask Mr. Lanham if that's who suggested he run a locker check."

"You don't believe me," Donny said.

"And how'd this boy get your combination in the first place?"

"Frankly," said Cal, "I wouldn't be surprised to learn the school was in on it. Any kid that marches to a different drummer, why, they'd just love an excuse to get rid of him. The school is where I lay the blame."

"Doesn't *Donny* ever get blamed?"

"Now, Mrs. Coble, you heard what he—"

"Forget it," Donny told Cal. "You can see she doesn't trust me."

Daisy drew in a breath to say that of course she trusted him—a reflex. But she knew that bold-faced, wide-eyed look of Donny's. He had worn that look when he was small, denying some petty misdeed with the evidence plain as day all around him. Still, it was hard for her to accuse him outright. She temporized and said, "The only thing I'm sure of is that they've kicked you out of school, and now I don't know what we're going to do."

"We'll fight it," said Cal.

"We can't. Even you must see we can't."

"I could apply to Brantly," Donny said.

Cal stopped his pacing to beam down at him. "Brantly! Yes. They're really onto where a kid is coming from, at Brantly. Why, *I* could get you into Brantly. I work with a lot of their students."

Daisy had never heard of Brantly, but already she didn't like it. And she didn't like Cal's smile, which struck her now as feverish and avid[8]—a smile of hunger.

On the fifteenth of April, they entered Donny in a public school, and they stopped his tutoring sessions. Donny fought both decisions bitterly. Cal,

surprisingly enough, did not object. He admitted he'd made no headway with Donny and said it was because Donny was emotionally disturbed.

Donny went to his new school every morning, plodding off alone with his head down. He did his assignments, and he earned average grades, but he gathered no friends, joined no clubs. There was something exhausted and defeated about him.

The first week in June, during final exams, Donny vanished. He simply didn't come home one afternoon, and no one at school remembered seeing him. The police were reassuring, and for the first few days, they worked hard. They combed Donny's sad, messy room for clues; they visited Miriam and Cal. But then they started talking about the number of kids who ran away every year. Hundreds, just in this city. "He'll show up, if he wants to," they said. "If he doesn't, he won't."

Evidently, Donny didn't want to.

It's been three months now and still no word. Matt and Daisy still look for him in every crowd of awkward, heartbreaking teenage boys. Every time the phone rings, they imagine it might be Donny. Both parents have aged. Donny's sister seems to be staying away from home as much as possible.

At night, Daisy lies awake and goes over Donny's life. She is trying to figure out what went wrong, where they made their first mistake. Often, she finds herself blaming Cal, although she knows he didn't begin it. Then at other times she excuses him, for without him, Donny might have left earlier. Who really knows? In the end, she can only sigh and search for a cooler spot on the pillow. As she falls asleep, she occasionally glimpses something in the corner of her vision. It's something fleet and round, a ball—a basketball. It flies up, it sinks through the hoop, descends, lands in a yard littered with last year's leaves and striped with bars of sunlight as white as bones, bleached and parched and cleanly picked.

---

7. **vindictive** (vin dik′tiv), *adj.* feeling a strong tendency toward revenge.
8. **avid** (av′id), *adj.* extremely eager; greatly desirous.

After Reading

Making Connections

Shaping Your Response

1. Cal seems to think Donny is a sensitive, misunderstood youngster who needs more trust and freedom. Daisy seems to think Donny needs more guidance and discipline. With which character do you agree? Explain your answer.

2. Why do you think Donny ran away?

Analyzing the Story

3. What do you think is the significance of the title "Teenage Wasteland"?

4. Notice how Tyler **characterizes** the two Coble parents during the second meeting with the principal. What are these two characters like, and how might their personalities be affecting Donny?

5. Why do you think Daisy and Matt Coble listen to Cal's advice even though it contradicts what they think is the right way to raise Donny?

6. Identify the **point of view** used in the story and explain why you think Tyler chose to use that point of view.

7. This story leaves a lot of questions unanswered. Why do you think Tyler chose to leave Donny's story unresolved?

Extending the Ideas

8. Who do you think is responsible for the behavior of a teenager, the teenager, the teachers, or the parents? Explain your reasoning.

9. 🐾 Times changed between Daisy Coble's teenage years and Donny's. How would you describe the changes that happened in the culture at large during this period?

Literary Focus: Mood

Anne Tyler uses details about the characters and the settings in "Teenage Wasteland" to establish the **mood** of the story. Describe what you think is the mood of the story, and then make a list of details that help to create that mood.

Vocabulary Study

Choose the pair of words that best expresses a relationship similar to that of the numbered pair.

forlorn
morass
amiably
talisman
vindictive

1. RABBIT'S FOOT : TALISMAN : : **a.** lucky : unlucky **b.** black cat : misfortune **c.** mouse : rodent **d.** toe : foot

2. FORLORN : UNHAPPY : : **a.** miserable : happy **b.** placid : calm **c.** lonely : contented **d.** misery : company

3. VINDICTIVE : PERSONALITY : : **a.** glove : mitten **b.** revenge : anger **c.** strong : handsome **d.** brown : eyes

4. AMIABLY : CHAT : : **a.** quickly : move **b.** yell : shout **c.** whisper : talk **d.** dutifully : faithfully

5. MORASS : CONFUSION : : **a.** messy : bedroom **b.** reconstruction : devastation **c.** simple : complex **d.** catastrophe : destruction

Expressing Your Ideas

Writing Choices

Writer's Notebook Update If you were Donny's parents, what would you have done differently to help him get on the right track? Based on what you'd do and say as a parent, write a note of advice to the Coble parents.

Tying Up Loose Ends Write a **sequel** to this story that resolves some of the questions left at the end of the story. Why was Donny so unhappy, and why was he behaving so badly? Who was helping him most, his parents or Cal? Why did he run away? Where did he go, and what became of him? Share your story sequel with the class.

School Policy How should a school handle a student who is having problems like Donny's? In a group, write a **policy handbook** you think schools should use as a guide for dealing with students like Donny.

Other Options

A Telling Conversation With a partner, create a **dialogue** between Cal and Donny in one of their tutoring sessions that reveals the personalities of both characters. Perform your dialogue for the class.

Background Music Anne Tyler alludes to music that was popular with teenagers in the past. What contemporary music do you think represents teenage life today? Prepare a **musical program** of contemporary songs about teenage life, play the songs for the class, and explain why you chose them.

Literature About Teens Stories and novels about teenagers and their problems abound. Choose a novel or short story about teenage life, read it, and present an **oral critique** to the class telling whether or not the selection is an accurate representation of teen life.

Before Reading

Gary Keillor

by Garrison Keillor

Garrison Keillor
born 1942

"That's the news from Lake Wobegon, where all the women are strong, the men are good-looking, and all the children are above average." That line is how Garrison Keillor closes his national radio show, "A Prairie Home Companion," during which he tells the weekly news about Lake Wobegon's imaginary residents. Although he is now known as *Garrison*, he was actually christened *Gary*. He changed his name when he submitted poetry to his junior high school newspaper. "It was in a school and at a time when boys didn't write poetry . . . I was trying to hide behind a name that meant strength and 'don't give me a hard time about this.'" Keillor's story, "Gary Keillor," is a fictionalized account of the author's youth.

Building Background

A Slice of Life in the Fifties The 1950s were prosperous years in the United States. Dwight D. Eisenhower, better known as Ike, was President. Men and women who had served in World War II came home, attended college on the G.I. Bill, got good jobs, married and started families, and moved into the new subdivisions which were springing up all over the country. The baby boom had begun. On the entertainment scene, movies were still popular, and television, a relatively new invention, was finding its way into homes throughout the country. By the mid-1950s rock-and-roll music had become popular, and Elvis Presley was the king of rock-and-roll. Fashion in the fifties was formal compared to fashion today; no one except a farmer or rancher would dream of wearing blue jeans. It was during this decade that the young Garrison Keillor grew up.

Literary Focus

Hyperbole When you say, "Traffic was so slow it took forever to get home," you are using hyperbole, or exaggeration, to cause a humorous, satiric, dramatic, or sentimental effect. It didn't really take *forever;* you are just being dramatic. Garrison Keillor uses hyperbole for humorous effect in his story. As you read "Gary Keillor," note as many examples as you can of hyperbole.

Writer's Notebook

What's So Funny? Think of the funniest thing that you have ever seen or that has happened to you. What made the incident funny? Now think of a way to describe the incident so that someone else will think it is funny too. Write your humorous description in your notebook.

Gary Keillor

GARRISON KEILLOR

When I was sixteen years old, I stood six feet two inches tall and weighed a hundred and forty pounds. I was intense and had the metabolism of a wolverine. I ate two or three lunches a day and three full dinners at night, as my family sat around the kitchen table and observed, and I cleaned off their plates too when they had poor appetites or were finicky. There was no food I disliked except muskmelon, which smelled rotten and loathsome. Everything else I ate. (It was Minnesota so we didn't have seafood, except fish sticks, of course.) I was a remarkable person. I was a junior in high school, Class of 1960. I was smart, so smart that poor grades didn't bother me in the slightest; I considered them no reflection on my intelligence. I read four books a week, and I sometimes walked home from school, all twelve miles, so I could relive favorite chapters out loud, stride along the shoulder of the highway past the potato farms, and say brilliant and outrageous things, and

sing in a big throbbing voice great songs like "Til There Was You" and "Love Me Tender."

I had no wish to sing in front of an audience, songs were a private thing with me. I was an intense person, filled with powerful feelings, and I assumed that I would live alone for the rest of my life, perhaps in a monastery, silent, swishing around in a cassock, my heart broken by a tragic love affair with someone like Natalie Wood, my life dedicated to God.

I was a lucky boy. I had learned this two years before on a car trip to Colorado. My Uncle Earl and Aunt Myrna drove there that summer—he had been stationed in Colorado Springs during the war—along with my cousins Gordon and Mel, and I got to go too. I won that trip by dropping over to their house and being extremely nice. I'd say, "Here, let me wash those dishes." I'd say, "Boy, I'm sure in a mood to mow a lawn." And then she'd offer me a glass of nectar and a piece of angel food cake and I'd eat it and say, "Boy, I was looking at *National Geographic* the other night and they had a big article on Colorado. It was so interesting. Just the different rock formations and things. I don't see how people can look at those mountains and not know there's a God." And she'd smile at me, a good boy who mowed lawns and whose faith was pure, and I got to go. Of course my brothers and sisters were fit to be tied. "How come he gets to go? We never get to go. Oh no, we have to stay here all summer and work in the garden while he goes riding out to Colorado." They just didn't get it. Trips to Colorado don't fall in your lap. You've got to go out and earn Colorado.

We took off on the trip, and I was a very good passenger. I sat in the favored front seat between my aunt and uncle, looking at the scenery for hours, no stains on my clothes, my face clean, a good strong bladder, never got carsick, and had a subtle[1] sideways technique for picking my nose—you'd never see it even if you looked straight at me. Far off, the mountains appeared, shining on the horizon for almost a whole day, and then we rose up into them—

---

1. **subtle** (sut′l), *adj.* so fine or delicate as to elude observation or analysis.

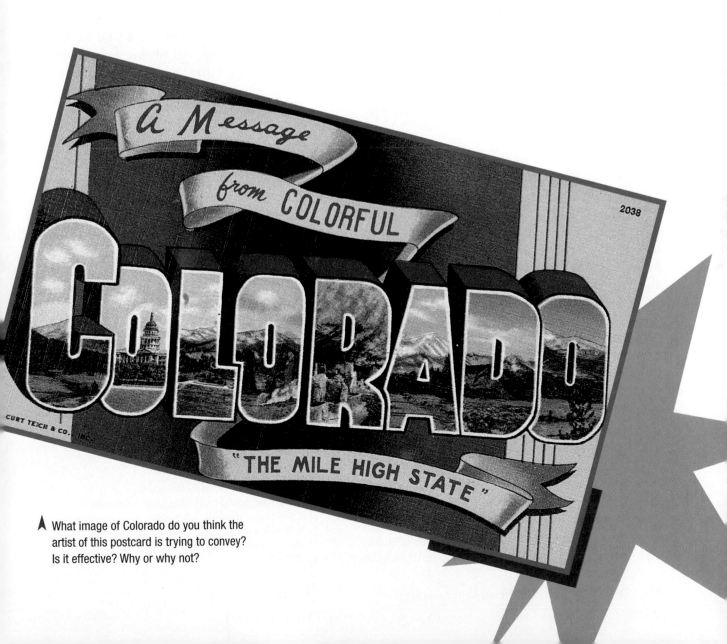

▲ What image of Colorado do you think the artist of this postcard is trying to convey? Is it effective? Why or why not?

snowcapped peaks, like the last scene in a western in which justice and romance prevail,[2] and when we reached Denver (*EL. 5280,* the sign said, exactly a mile), we ate dinner at a Chinese restaurant and my fortune cookie said: "You are enterprising[3]—take advantage of it." Well, there it was in a nutshell.

The mountains were startling in their whiteness and steepness, the valleys dark in the late afternoon, the peaks glittering in pure sunlight, beautiful stands of light gray-green aspen floating like fog, and my aunt took a picture of me with trees and mountains behind me. Just me, tall and intense. You would never guess I was from Minnesota. I thought, "This is my lucky picture. I'll keep it the rest of my life."

I had been in love with Dede for two years, in an intense and secret way.

My family lived in the country, along the Mississippi River between Minneapolis and Tryon, and I attended New Tryon High School, which was bulging under a tidal wave of children from new subdivisions on the other side of the river, places with names like Riverview Estates and Woodlawn and Forest Hills. Our side, South Tryon Township, along the West River Road, was still rural, truck farms, and scattered houses on big rolling tracts, and we West River Roaders were the cream of the school. The editor of the school paper, *The Beacon,* Elaine Eggert, was one of us; so were the stars of the debate team and the speech team, three of the class officers, and the chairperson of the spring talent show, Dede Petersen, who rode on my bus.

I had been in love with Dede for two years, in an intense and secret way. She had bouncy blonde hair and wore soft sweaters, plaid skirts, penny loafers and knee socks. One winter day I wrote her a fourteen-page letter (single-spaced) saying that she was my ideal of womanhood, a person of pure taste, excellent judgment, stunning beauty, and natural intelligence, a woman to whom I could pledge myself in a spiritual friendship that would last forever no matter what. If the friendship should turn into physical love, good, and if not, fine. We would be friends for the rest of our lives, our souls communing over vast distances.

I did not, after long thought, give her the letter. I guessed that she might laugh at it and also that her boyfriend Bill Swenson might pound me into the ground. He was an intense person too.

One afternoon riding home on the bus, sitting behind her, I heard her complain to her pal Marcy about the miseries of planning the April talent show. Bill Swenson would be in it, lip-synching "All Shook Up,"[4] and he was terrific, but there wasn't much other talent around, nothing compared to last year, when all those guys sang "Bali Hai" with the coconuts on their chests, and the skit about school lunch when the kids pretended to vomit and out came green confetti, and of course last year there had been Barbara Lee. Barbara Lee was the most talented person ever to graduate from our school. She danced, she sang, she did the splits, she played the marimba. She was Broadway bound, no doubt about it.

I leaned forward and said, "Well, I think we have lots of talent." Oh? like who, for example? she said. I said, "Well, I could do something." *You?* she said. "Or I could get together with some other kids and we could do a skit." *Like what?* she said. I said, "Oh, I don't know. Something about the school burning down. It all depends."

---

2. prevail (pri vāl′), *v.* win out; triumph.
3. enterprising (en′tər prī′zing), *adj.* showing initiative and readiness to undertake a project or venture.
4. **"All Shook Up,"** a rock-and-roll song made famous by singer Elvis Presley, who was popular in the 1950s and 1960s.

"That doesn't sound funny to me," she said. Marcy didn't think it was funny either.

What burned my toast was her saying *"You?"* when I volunteered to be in her talent show. I was only being helpful, I was not claiming to be another Barbara Lee. I had no interest in the stage at all until I heard her incredulity and amusement— *"You?"*—and then I was interested in being interested. A spiritual friendship with Dede was out of the question, if she thought I was the sort of guy you could say *"You?"* to.

No one in our family sang or performed for entertainment, only for the glory of God and only in groups, never solo. We were Christian people; we did not go in for show. But I was an intense young man. Intensity was my guiding principle. And when I thought about joining that monastery after Natalie Wood rejected me and spending my life in the woodshop making sturdy chairs and tables, I thought that perhaps I ought to get in the talent show at New Tryon High first, get a whiff of show business before I gave my life to God.

It was one of those ugly and treacherous springs in the Midwest, when winter refuses to quit, like a big surly[5] drunk who heads for home and then staggers back for another round and a few more songs that everyone has heard before. It was cold and wet, and we sat day after day in dim airless classrooms, the fluorescent lights turned on at midday, the murky sky and bare trees filling the big classroom windows, pools of oil-slicked rain in the parking lot, the grass in front dead, the Stars and Stripes hanging limp and wet like laundry. In plane geometry, I was lost in the wilderness, had been lost since Christmas, and in history, we were slogging through World War I, and in English class, we were memorizing poems. "These are treasures you will carry with you forever," said Miss Rasmussen, a big woman in a blue knit suit. In her wanderings around the classroom as she talked about poetry and metaphor, she often stopped in the aisle and stood looming above me, her voice overhead, her hand resting on my desk, her puffy white hand and red knuckles and short ringless fingers. Her stopping there indicated, I knew, her fondness for me. I was the only student of hers who wrote poems. She had even suggested that I memorize and recite one of my own poems. I declined. Part of the memorization assignment was reciting the poem in front of the class. My poems were far too intense and personal to be said out loud in front of people. I was memorizing Whitman's elegy on the death of Abraham Lincoln, "O Captain! My Captain!" I walked home through the rain one cold day crying out, "O Captain! my Captain! our fearful trip is done, / The ship has weather'd every rack, the prize we sought is won."

One day a fuel oil truck backed into our driveway and got stuck in the mud and the driver put it into forward gear and got dug in deeper. He gunned it in reverse and gunned it forward and rocked the truck loose and pulled forward and unwound his hose and started filling our fuel oil tank, but meanwhile he had left deep ruts in my mother's garden and the front yard. She was home alone, washing clothes. She heard the grinding and roaring from down in the laundry room and came outdoors to find her garden dug up and the tulips and irises destroyed, and the driver looked at her and said, "You ought to do something about your driveway." Not a word of apology, acted like it was the driveway's fault. My mother was the quietest, politest person ever, she felt that raising your voice indicated a flawed character, but she put her hands on her hips and said, "Mister, if you can't figure out how to drive a truck, then they oughta find you a job you'd be able to handle." And she told him to get out and she would be sending the company a bill for the flower garden. And he did. And she did. And the company sent us a check and an apology from the general manager, a Harold L. Bergstrom.

---

5. **surly** (sėr/lē), *adj.* bad-tempered.

It was the first time in my memory that my mother had fought back and raised her voice to a stranger, a watershed[6] moment for me. I heard the story from our neighbor, Mr. Couture, and I admired her so much for standing up to the jerk and defending our family's honor. Her principles had always told her to be quiet and polite and turn the other cheek and never make trouble, but there comes a time to let go of principle and do the right thing. To me, this seemed to open the door to show business.

And then, about a week before the talent show, suddenly I was in. The real power behind the show wasn't Dede, it was Miss Rasmussen, my teacher, the adviser to the talent show, and the day I stood before the class and recited "O Captain! My Captain!" she told Dede to put me in the show. The next day, Miss Rasmussen had me stand up in class and recite it again. It was one of the finest pieces of oral interpretation she had ever seen, she said. She sat in a back corner of the room, her head bowed, her eyes closed, as I stood in front and with dry mouth launched the Captain's ship again, and she did not see the kids smirking and gagging and retching and pulling long invisible skeins of snot from their nostrils and when my Captain died and I got to "O the bleeding drops of red, / Where on the deck my Captain lies, / Fallen cold and dead," they rolled their eyes and clutched at their hearts and died. Then, when she stood up, her eyes moist, and clapped, they all clapped too. "Wasn't that good!" she cried. "You really liked it, didn't you! Oh, I'm glad you did! He's going to recite it in the talent show, too! Won't that be nice!" A couple of boys in front clapped their hands over their mouths and pretended to lose their lunch. They seemed to speak for most of the class.

So I was in the talent show, which I wanted to be, but with an inferior piece of material. I suggested to Miss Rasmussen that "O Captain! My Captain!" might not be right for the talent show audience, that maybe I could find a humorous poem, and she said, "Oh, it'll be just fine," not realizing the gravity[7] of the situation. "Never give up on beauty," she said. "Never compromise your standards out of fear that someone may not understand." Teachers were full of useless advice like that.

I tried not to think about "O Captain." I experimented with combing my hair a new way, with the part on the right. I was handsome at certain angles, I thought, and a right-hand part would emphasize a good angle. I stood at the bathroom mirror, a small mirror in my hand, and experimented holding my head cocked back and aimed up and to the right, a pose favored by seniors in their graduation pictures, which looked good from either side, and reciting "O Captain" with my head at that angle. I had good skin except when it flared up, which it did two days before the show, and it took a long time to repair the damage. There were six children in our family and only one bathroom, but I spent fifteen minutes behind a locked door doing surgery and applying alcohol and cold packs and skin-toned cream. The little kids stood banging on the door, pleading to use the toilet. I said, "Well, how bad do you have to go?" I was the one in show business, after all.

So I was in the talent show, which I wanted to be, but with an inferior piece of material.

I worked on "O Captain" so that every line was set in my head. I recited it to myself in the mirror ("O Captain! O Captain! the fateful day is done, / Your blemishes have disappeared, the skin you sought is won") and for my mother, who said I was holding my head at an unnatural angle, and then, the Friday night before the show, I recited it at a

---

6. **watershed** (wô′tər shed′), *n.* point at which a notable change takes place.
7. **gravity** (grav′ə tē), *n.* serious or critical character; importance.

party at Elaine Eggert's house, and there my interpretation of "O Captain! My Captain!" took a sharp turn toward the English stage.

Miss Rasmussen loved a recording of Sir John Gielgud reading "Favourites of English Poetry" and she played it once for our class, a whole hour of it, and from that day, all the boys in the class loved to do English accents. A little lisp, endless dramatic pauses, fruity inflections including shrill birdlike tones of wonderment, and instead of the vowel *o* that delicious English *aaoooww,* a bleating sound not found anywhere in American speech. In the cafeteria, when my friend Ralph Moody came to the table where all of us West River Road rats sat, he stood holding his tray, peering down at us and the welter of milk cartons and comic books and ice cream wrappers and uneaten macaroni-cheese lunches, and after a long pause he cried "Aaaaoooooww," with a shudder, a great man forced to sit among savages. So at the party, surrounded by kids from the debate team and the newspaper, the cream of West River Road society, when Elaine had said for the sixth time, "Do the poem you're going to do on Monday," I reached back for Ralph's *Aaoooww* and did "O Captain" as Sir John might have done it:

Aoowww Cap-tin, myyyyy Cap-tin,

aower————feeah-fool twip eez done!

Th' sheep has wethah'd————eviddy rack!

th' priiiiiiize we sot————————eez won!

But—————— aaaooooooooowwwww

th' bleeeeeeeding drrrops————of rrred——

wheahhhh————

on th' deck————

myyyy Captin liiiiiiiies————————

fallin————————

caaaooooowwwld—————————

and——————————————————ded!

It was a good party poem. I recited it in the basement, and then everyone upstairs had to come down and hear it, and then Elaine had to call up a friend of hers in the city and I did it on the phone. It got better. "Miss Rasmussen is going to burst a blood vessel," said Elaine. She was a true rebel, despite the editorials she wrote extolling the value of team play and school spirit. I was starting to see some of the virtues in her that I had previously imagined in Dede Petersen.

Bill Swenson had worked for weeks on "All Shook Up," and he looked cool and capable backstage before the curtain went up. His hair was slicked down, he wore heavy eye makeup, and he was dressed in a white suit with gold trim, without a single wrinkle in it. He stood, holding his arms out to the sides, avoiding wrinkling, and practiced moving his lips to "A-wella bless my soul, what'sa wrong with me? I'm itching like a man on a fuzzy tree." Dede knelt, shining his black shoes.

He pretended to be surprised to see me. "What are you doing here? You running the p.a. or what?"

I told him I would be in the show, reciting a poem by Walt Whitman.

"Who? Twitman?" No. Whitman, I said.

"Well, I'm glad I don't have to follow that," he said, with heavy sarcasm. He glanced at my outfit, brown corduroy pants, a green plaid cotton shirt, a charcoal gray sweater vest, and said, "You better change into your stage clothes though."

"These are my stage clothes," I said.

"Oh," he said, his eyebrows raised. "Oh." He smiled. "Well, good luck." He did not know how much luck I had. I had my lucky picture in my pocket, the one of me in the mountains.

Dede brushed his forehead with face powder and poofed up his hair. She gave him a light kiss on the lips. "You're going to be great," she said. He smiled. He had no doubt about that. She had put him high on the program, right after "America the Beautiful," a dramatic choral reading from *Antigone,* a solo trumpet rendition[8] of "Nobody Knows the Trouble I've Seen," and a medley of Rodgers and Hammerstein songs performed on the piano by Cheryl Ann Hansen. Then Bill would electrify the crowd with "All Shook Up," and then I would do "O Captain."

He was Mr. Cool. After Cheryl Ann Hansen's interminable medley, which kids clapped and cheered for only because they knew that her mother had recently died of cancer, Bill grinned at Dede and bounced out on stage and yelled, "Helllll-ooo baby!" in a Big Bopper voice, and the audience clapped and yelled "Helllloo baby!" and he yelled, "You knowwwwwwww what I like!" and he was a big hit in the first five seconds. He

8. **rendition** (ren dish'ən), *n.* a performance of a musical score or dramatic piece.

◀ This photograph of Elvis Presley was taken by Bob Verlin in 1956, the same year Presley achieved national recognition with his best-selling record, "Heartbreak Hotel."

said it again, "Hellllllllooo baby!" and the audience yelled back, "Hellllllllloo baby!" And then Dede carefully set the phonograph needle on the record of "All Shook Up" and Elvis's hoody voice blasted out in the auditorium and Bill started shimmying across the stage and tossing his head like a dustmop. "My friends say I'm acting queer as a bug, I'm in love—huh! I'm all shook up," and on the *huh* he stuck both arms in the air and threw his hip to the left, *huh,* and the audience sang along on the "hmm hmm hmm—oh—yeah yeah"—he was the star of the show right there. Dede ran to look out through a hole in the curtain, leaving me standing by the record player. She was so thrilled, she hopped up and down and squealed.

I could see part of him out there, his white suit hanging loose, the red socks flashing, him pulling out the red satin hanky and tossing it into the audience, *hmmm hmmm hmmm oh yeah yeah,* and at the end the whole auditorium stood up and screamed. He came off stage bright with sweat, grinning, and went back out and made three deep bows, and threw his hip, *huh,* and came off and Dede wiped his face with a towel and kissed him, and the audience was still screaming and whistling and yelling, "More! More!" and right then Bill made his fateful decision. He went out and did his other number.

It was "Vaya con Dios" by the Conquistadores. Dede put the needle down and the guitars throbbed, and the audience clapped, but Bill hadn't worked as hard on "Vaya con Dios" as on "All Shook Up" and his lips didn't synch very well, but the main problem was that "Vaya con Dios" was "Vaya con Dios," and after "All Shook Up" it seemed like a joke, especially since the Conquistadores were a trio and Bill wasn't. Kids started to laugh, and Bill got mad—perhaps "Vaya con Dios" meant a lot to him personally—and his grim face and his clenched fists made "Vaya con Dios" seem even zanier. Dede ran to the hole in the curtain to see where the hooting and light booing were coming from, and there, standing by the record player,

I thought I would help poor Bill out by lightly touching the record with my finger and making the music go flat and sour for a moment.

It was miraculous, the effect this had, like pressing a laugh button. I touched the black vinyl rim and the music warbled, and fifty feet away, people erupted[9] in fits of happiness. I did it again. How wonderful to hear people laugh! and to be able to give them this precious gift of laughter so easily. Then I discovered a speed control that let me slow it down and speed it up. The singers sounded demented,[10] in love one moment, carsick the next. The audience thought this was a stitch. But Bill sort of went to pieces. One prime qualification for a show business career, I would think, is the ability to improvise[11] and go with the audience, but Bill Swenson did not have that ability. Here he was, rescued from his drippy encore, magically transformed into comedy, and he was too rigid to recognize what a hit he was. His lips stopped moving. He shook his fist at someone in the wings, perhaps me, and yelled a common vulgar expression at someone in the crowd, and wheeled around and walked off.

I didn't care to meet him, so I walked fast right past him onto the stage, and coming out of the bright light into the dark, he didn't see me until I was out of reach. There was still some heavy booing when I arrived at the microphone, and I made a deep English-actor type of bow, with princely flourishes and flutters, and they laughed, and then they were mine all the way. I held on to them for dear life for the next two minutes. I sailed into "O Captain," in my ripest and fruitiest accent, with roundhouse gestures, outflung arms, hand clapped to the forehead ————I cried:

AOOWWW CAP-TIN, MYYYYY CAP-TIN,

---

9. erupt (i rupt′), *v.* burst forth.
10. demented (di men′tid), *adj.* insane; crazy.
11. improvise (im′prə vīz), *v.* make up on the spur of the moment; perform without preparation.

AOWER————————FEEAH-FOOL TWIP EEZ DONE!

TH' SHEEP HAS WETHAH'D————————EVIDDY

    RACK!

TH' PRIIIIIIIZE WE SOT————————EEZ WON!

BUT————— —————AAAAOOOOOOOWWWWW

TH' BLLEEEEEEEDING DRRROPS—————————

OF RRRED—————————

WHEAHH—————————

ON TH' DECK—————————

BEEEL SWEN-SON LIIIIIIIIES—————————

FALLIN—————————

CAAAOOOOWWWLD

—————————AND—————————

—————DED!

It wasn't a kind or generous thing to do, but it was successful, especially the "AAAAAOOOO-OOOWWWWW" and also the part about Bill Swenson, and at the end there was shouting and whistling and pandemonium,[12] and I left the stage with the audience wanting more, but I had witnessed the perils of success, and did not consider an encore. "Go out and take a bow," said Miss Rasmussen, and out I went, and came back off. Dede and Bill were gone. Dede was not feeling well, said Miss Rasmussen.

I watched the rest of the show standing at the back of the auditorium. The act after me was a girl from the wrong side of the river who did a humorous oral interpretation entitled "Granny on the Phone with Her Minister." The girl had painted big surprise eyebrows and a big red mouth on her so we would know it was comedy, and as the sketch went on, she shrieked to remind us that it was humorous. The joke was that Granny was hard-of-hearing and got the words wrong. Then came an accordionist, a plump young man named David Lee, Barbara's cousin, who was a little overambitious with "Lady of Spain" and should have left out two or three of the variations, and a tap dancer who tapped to a recording of "Nola" and who made the mistake of starting the number all over again after she had made a mistake. I enjoyed watching these dogs, strictly from a professional point of view. And then the choir returned to sing "Climb Every Mountain," and then Miss Rasmussen stood and spoke about the importance of encouraging those with talent and how lucky we should feel to have them in our midst to bring beauty and meaning to our lives. And then the lights came up, and my classmates piled into the aisles and headed for the door and saw me standing in back, modest me, looking off toward the stage. Almost every one of them said how good I was as they trooped past—clapped my shoulder, said, hey, you were great, you should've done more, that was funny—and I stood and patiently endured their attention until the auditorium was empty and then I went home.

"You changed the poem a little," Miss Rasmussen said the next day. "Did you forget the line?" "Yes," I said. "Your voice sounded funny," she said. I told her I was nervous. "Oh well," she said, "they seemed to like it anyway."

"Thank you," I said, "thank you very much."

---

12. **pandemonium** (pan′də mō′nē əm), *n.* wild disorder or lawless confusion.

After Reading

Making Connections

Shaping Your Response

1. How would you describe the young Gary Keillor? Write five adjectives that you would use to tell about him. Then write five adjectives each to describe Bill Swenson, Dede Peterson, and Miss Rasmussen.

2. Choose what you think is the most humorous part of the story and prepare to read it to the class.

Analyzing the Story

3. Gary Keillor describes himself as *intense*. What do you think he means by that?

4. One way that Garrison Keillor introduces humor into his writing is by relating humorous incidents. Find several examples.

5. What is the **point of view** in "Gary Keillor"? How would the selection be different if it were told from another point of view?

6. What does the picture of Gary in Colorado seem to **symbolize** to him?

Extending the Ideas

7. Compare the **tone** of "Teenage Wasteland" to that of "Gary Keillor." How would you explain the differences?

8. If you were to write about a humorous incident that took place at your high school, what would it be?

Literary Focus: Hyperbole

Garrison Keillor's use of hyperbole, or obvious exaggeration, is one of the reasons his story is so funny. Make a list of examples of his use of hyperbole. Then, find examples of hyperbole in other sources, either from magazine or newspaper cartoons, or from jokes or tall tales. Share one of your examples with the class.

Vocabulary Study

demented
enterprising
erupt
gravity
improvise
prevail
pandemonium
rendition
subtle
surly

Use the vocabulary words in the list to complete these statements that Bill Swenson and Miss Rasmussen might have made about Gary Keillor.

"That Gary Keillor is __(1)__," said Bill Swenson, the Elvis impersonator, in a __(2)__ voice. "I could strangle him for ruining my __(3)__ of 'Vaya con Dios.' Did you hear the laughter __(4)__ when the music slowed down and then speeded up? That idiot had better steer clear of me!"

"Well," said Miss Rasmussen, "Gary Keillor's sense of humor is not exactly __(5)__. First of all the __(6)__ young man decided to improve the talent show. He turned a serious song into a comedy by varying the speed on the record player. Needless to say, the audience loved it, and __(7)__ broke out in the auditorium. Although the poor lip synch performer was ready to attack Gary, cooler heads were able to __(8)__ . The lip synch performer left in a huff. I don't think Gary realized the __(9)__ of the situation. Anyway, Gary then proceeded to his talent show number, a reading of a famous poem. He began to __(10)__ on his delivery, and he had the audience in stitches. What a comedian!"

Expressing Your Ideas

Writing Choices

Writer's Notebook Update Reread the humorous incident you recorded in your log before reading "Gary Keillor." How could you improve your narrative? Does it need more colorful descriptions? Could you use exaggeration for humorous effect? Revise your humorous narrative to make it even funnier. Write the final draft in your notebook.

Tune In Check out one of Garrison Keillor's recordings of his radio show, "A Prairie Home Companion," from your library. Listen to several episodes and then write a **summary** of your favorite show.

Yearbook Signing Gary Keillor was quite a character. What do you think that Elaine Eggert, one of Gary's West River Road buddies, might have written in his yearbook at the end of this year? What would Bill Swanson write? Dede Peterson? Miss Rasmussen? Be these characters and write **notes** to Gary in his yearbook.

Other Options

It's All in the Delivery Find a copy of Walt Whitman's poem "O Captain! My Captain!", about the death of Abraham Lincoln. Prepare an **oral interpretation** of the poem to present to the class. Choose whether you would like to present it as Miss Rasmussen would like it, as Gary Keillor performed it for the talent show, or an original interpretation.

High School Happenings Telling a funny story requires different skills than writing one. Imagine that your high school has a radio show and you are the host. Prepare a three- to five- minute **"humor spot"** about things you have observed around your school. Tape your show and then play the tape for the class.

Lively Allusions Throughout his narrative Garrison refers to songs and singers that were popular in the 1950s. If you are familiar with the songs, his story is even funnier. Do some research and find recordings of as many of the songs as you can. Work with a partner to make an **oral presentation** explaining the origins of the songs and playing parts of each of them.

Before Reading

Salvador Late or Early

by Sandra Cisneros

Sandra Cisneros
born 1954

The daughter of a Mexican father and a Chicana mother, Sandra Cisneros studied writing at Loyola University in Chicago, and then went to the University of Iowa for graduate school. As she listened to her classmates in the Iowa Writer's Workshop describe their childhood homes as part of an assignment, Cisneros realized that their middle and upper class childhoods were nothing like her experiences as an urban Chicana. As she once said, "I'm trying to write the stories that haven't been written. I feel like a cartographer. I'm determined to fill a literary void." Some of her books are *The House on Mango Street, My Wicked, Wicked Ways,* and *Woman Hollering Creek and Other Stories.*

Building Background

The Author's Heritage More than eighteen million Mexican Americans currently live in the United States. The long, rich history which intertwines the countries and peoples of Mexico and the United States began in 1540 when the Spanish explorer Coronado marched into what is now New Mexico. Mexicans, descendants of both European explorers and Indians, settled in many areas of the Southwest as well as parts of the Midwest. Often lumped together with other Spanish-speaking peoples, the children of Mexican Americans created the word *Chicano* (*Chicana* for the feminine form) to define themselves. Sandra Cisneros, the author of "Salvador Late or Early," shares the experiences of Chicano life in her prose and her poetry.

Literary Focus

Figurative Language Sandra Cisneros writes both poetry and prose, and her poetic talents spill over into her fiction. She uses figurative language, the use of words apart from their ordinary, literal meanings, to add freshness, conciseness, and vitality to her writing. For example, she describes homes as being "the color of bad weather," which not only brings to mind a dark, dreary color, but also creates a feeling of uneasiness. As you read "Salvador Late or Early," notice how Cisneros uses figurative language to create a vivid picture of Salvador's life.

Writer's Notebook

On the Economic Edge What images come to mind when you think of the word *poverty?* What is life like for families who are struggling to get by? Before reading "Salvador Late or Early," write down your impressions of what it means to live in poverty.

Salvador
Late or Early

Sandra Cisneros

Salvador with eyes the color of caterpillar, Salvador of the crooked hair and crooked teeth, Salvador whose name the teacher cannot remember, is a boy who is no one's friend, runs along somewhere in that vague direction where homes are the color of bad weather, lives behind a raw wood doorway, shakes the sleepy brothers awake, ties their shoes, combs their hair with water, feeds them milk and corn flakes from a tin cup in the dim dark of the morning.

Salvador, late or early, sooner or later arrives with the string of younger brothers ready. Helps his mama, who is busy with the business of the baby. Tugs the arms of Cecilio, Arturito, makes them hurry, because today, like yesterday, Arturito has dropped the cigar box of crayons, has let go the hundred little fingers of red, green, yellow, blue, and nub of black sticks that tumble and spill over and beyond the asphalt puddles until the crossing-guard lady holds back the blur of traffic for Salvador to collect them again.

Salvador inside that wrinkled shirt, inside the throat that must clear itself and apologize each time it speaks, inside that forty-pound body of boy with its geography of scars, its history of hurt, limbs stuffed with feathers and rags, in what part of the eyes, in what part of the heart, in that cage of the chest where something throbs with both fists and knows only what Salvador knows, inside that body too small to contain the hundred balloons of happiness, the single guitar of grief, is a boy like any other disappearing out the door, beside the schoolyard gate, where he has told his brothers they must wait. Collects the hands of Cecilio and Arturito, scuttles off dodging the many schoolyard colors, the elbows and wrists crisscrossing, the several shoes running. Grows small and smaller to the eye, dissolves into the bright horizon, flutters in the air before disappearing like a memory of kites.

In the image at the right, why do you think Antonio Bernis combined real objects with painted images in his 1974 mixed-media work, *Juanito en la Laguna?* How would you describe the effect of the combined materials?

After Reading

Making Connections

Shaping Your Response

1. If you were going to illustrate this story, what images and materials would you use? Describe your illustration.

Analyzing the Story

2. Sandra Cisneros paints a vivid picture of her **character** Salvador in only three paragraphs. Describe his appearance and personality.

3. What do you think is the significance of the title, "Salvador Late or Early"?

4. In some ways "Salvador Late or Early" seems like a story, and in other ways it seems like a poem. What elements does it have in common with each of these **genres?**

Extending the Ideas

5. Salvador has a lot of responsibility for a young boy. What tasks or chores do you think 10- or 12-year-old children should have?

Expressing Your Ideas

Writing Choices

Writer's Notebook Update Review your thoughts about poverty that you described in your notebook. Would you say Salvador's family is impoverished or not? Write a paragraph explaining your thoughts about Salvador's family.

Best Friends With a partner, create a best friend for Salvador. Then create and perform a **dialogue** between the two, allowing Salvador to share his thoughts about his family, his school, and his life.

Other Options

Show-and-Tell Imagine you are Arturito. You must tell about a family member for "show and tell." Give a short **speech** to the class about Salvador as you think Arturito might.

A Portrait of Salvador Create a likeness of Salvador in the form of a **painting,** a **papier-mâché or clay sculpture,** or a **drawing.** In your creation, try to capture the personality and mood Cisneros has caught in her story.

Before Reading

Coca-Cola and Coco Frío by Martín Espada

Lost Sister by Cathy Song

Naming Myself by Barbara Kingsolver

Red Wagons by Ana Castillo

Building Background

The Shadows of the Past What convergence of experiences has made you the person you are today? We are each a product of our past, both of our childhood and of our family heritage. The narrators of the poems in this section each examine something in his or her past that has made a difference in some way. Think about the influences in your life—people, places, and events. Use a pie chart to apportion the impact of each influence on your life. For example, the young girl in the Unit 7 poem "Legacies" (page 773), looking back as an adult, might apportion her pie chart this way. Be prepared to discuss your chart in class.

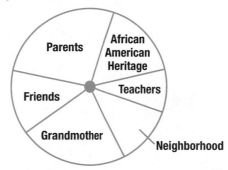

Literary Focus

Theme The deeper, underlying meaning of a poem is its theme. A theme is usually not stated explicitly, but is implied. Also, a theme of a poem is not its subject but rather an observation about that subject. For example, the subject of the poem "Legacies" on page 773 is a grandmother's desire to teach her granddaughter how to make biscuits. One statement of its theme might be, "Family members express their love in different ways." As you read the four poems that follow, think about what you think is the theme of each one.

Writer's Notebook

Who Are You? If you were the topic of a poem, what words might a poet use to accurately express your individuality? In your notebook make a list of five nouns, five verbs, five adjectives, and five adverbs that could be used in the poem about you.

Martín Espada
born 1957

Martín Espada is a tenant lawyer in Boston, and he also teaches classes in Latino poetry at local colleges and universities. Born in Brooklyn, New York, of Puerto Rican and Jewish parentage, Espada writes mostly about working class people, many of them immigrants. His poetry collections include *The Immigrant Iceboy's Bolero* (1982), *Trumpets from the Islands of Their Eviction* (1987), *Rebellion Is a Circle of a Lover's Hands* (1990), and *City of Coughing and Dead Radiators* (1993).

Cathy Song
born 1955

"Lost Sister" is taken from Cathy Song's poetry collection *Picture Bride,* which won the Yale Series of Younger Poets Award in 1982. In the title poem Song reveals some of her family history. Her grandmother was a mail-order bride—a "picture bride"—from Korea who was sent for by Song's grandfather in Hawaii. Song herself was born and raised in Honolulu, Hawaii. Her poetry reflects the tug-of-war between the cultural ties to Asia and life in modern Hawaii.

Barbara Kingsolver
born 1955

Although Barbara Kingsolver studied to be a biologist, she always loved writing. She began writing short stories and essays as a child and has kept a personal journal since she was eight. Her books include the novels *The Bean Trees* (1988), *Animal Dreams* (1990), and *Pigs in Heaven* (1993); a short story collection, *Homeland and Other Stories* (1989); nonfiction works; and a poetry collection called *Another America* (1994). Most of Kingsolver's writing features characters who are struggling to survive economically, psychologically, or politically.

Ana Castillo
born 1953

Born in Chicago of Mexican American parents, Ana Castillo's professional training is in art education and social science. In addition to writing, Castillo also dances, and she sometimes performs her poetry set to music. Her poetry collections include *Otro Canto* (1977), *The Invitation* (1979), *Pajaros Enganosos* (1983), and *Women Are Not Roses* (1984). She has also published a collection called *My Father Was a Toltec* (1995), in which the poem "Red Wagons" appears.

Coca-Cola and Coco Frío

MARTÍN ESPADA

◄ Which Puerto Rico do you think this painting, *Merengue in Boca Chica* (1983) by Rafael Ferrer, most resembles—the one where aunts serve Coca-Cola, or the one that enjoys Coco Frío? Explain your answer.

On his first visit to Puerto Rico,
island of family folklore,
the fat boy wandered
from table to table
5 with his mouth open.
At every table, some great-aunt
would steer him with cool spotted hands
to a glass of Coca-Cola.
One even sang to him, in all the English
10 she could remember, a Coca-Cola jingle
from the forties. He drank obediently, though
he was bored with this potion, familiar
from soda fountains in Brooklyn.

Then, at a roadside stand off the beach,
the fat boy

15 opened his mouth to coco frío, a coconut
chilled, then scalped by a machete
so that a straw could inhale the clear milk.
The boy tilted the green shell overhead
and drooled coconut milk down his chin;
20 suddenly, Puerto Rico was not Coca-Cola
or Brooklyn, and neither was he.

For years afterward, the boy marveled at
an island
where the people drank Coca-Cola
and sang jingles from World War II
25 in a language they did not speak,
while so many coconuts in the trees
sagged heavy with milk, swollen
and unsuckled.

Coca-Cola and Coco Frío   **893**

Lost Sister

CATHY SONG

1.

In China,
even the peasants
named their first daughters,
Jade—
5 the stone that in the far fields
could moisten the dry season,
could make men move mountains
for the healing green of the inner hills,
glistening like slices of winter melon.

10 And the daughters were grateful:
they never left home.
To move freely was a luxury
stolen from them at birth.
Instead, they gathered patience,
15 learning to walk in shoes
the size of teacups,
without breaking—
the arc of their movements
as dormant[1] as the rooted willow,
20 as redundant[2] as the farmyard hens.
But they travelled far
in surviving,
learning to stretch the family rice,
to quiet the demons,
25 the noisy stomachs.

2.

There is a sister
across the ocean,
who relinquished her name,
diluting jade green
30 with the blue of the Pacific.
Rising with a tide of locusts,
she swarmed with others
to inundate[3] another shore.

In America,
35 there are many roads
and women can stride along with men.

But in another wilderness,
the possibilities,
the loneliness,
40 can strangulate like jungle vines.
The meager[4] provisions and sentiments
of once belonging:
fermented[5] roots, mahjong[6] tiles and fire crackers;
cannot shake away the ghosts,
45 sets but a flimsy household
in a forest of nightless cities.
A giant snake rattles above,
spewing black clouds into your kitchen.
Dough faced landlords
50 slip in and out of your keyholes,
making claims you don't understand,
tapping into your communication systems
of laundry lines and restaurant chains.
You find you need China:
55 your one fragile identification,
a jade link
handcuffed to your wrist.

You remember your mother
who walked for centuries,
60 footless—
and like her,
you have left no footprints,
but only because
there is an ocean inbetween,
65 the unremitting[7] space of your rebellion.

---

1. **dormant** (dôr′mənt), *adj.* in a state of rest or inactivity.
2. **redundant** (ri dun′dənt), *adj.* needlessly repetitive.
3. **inundate** (in′un dāt), *v.* overspread as if with a flood.

---

4. **meager** (mē′gər), *adj.* poor or scanty; sparse.
5. **fermented** (fər ment′əd), *adj.* chemically changed by yeast, enzymes, or bacteria changing sugars to alcohol.
6. **mahjong** (mä′zhong′), *n.* game played with tiles.
7. **unremitting** (un′ri mit′ing), *adj.* never stopping.

618—906
SACRAMENTO

▲ In this painting, *Tang Ren Jie* (1988) by Hung Lui, what story might the artist be trying to tell? Who is the woman in the center, where and when is she living, and what is her relationship to the boat, the traditionally dressed woman, and the numbers?

Naming Myself

Barbara Kingsolver

I have guarded my name as people
in other times kept their own clipped hair,
believing the soul could be scattered
if they were careless.

5 I knew my first ancestor.
His legend. I have touched
his boots and moustache, the grandfather
whose people owned slaves and cotton.
He was restless in Virginia
10 among the gentleman brothers, until
one peppered, flaming autumn he stole a horse,
rode over the mountains to marry
a leaf-eyed Cherokee.
The theft was forgiven but never
15 the Indian blood. He lost his family's name
and invented mine, gave it fruit and seeds.
I never knew the grandmother.
Her photograph has ink-thin braids
and buttoned clothes, and nothing that she
    was called.

20 I could shed my name in the middle of life,
the ordinary thing, and it would flee
along with childhood and dead grandmothers
to that Limbo[1] for discontinued maiden names.[2]

But it would grow restless there.
25 I know this. It would ride over leaf smoke
    mountains
and steal horses.

---

1. **Limbo** (lim′bō), *n.* the dwelling place of souls kept
   from Heaven; place for persons and things forgotten,
   cast aside, or out of date.
2. **maiden name,** a woman's surname before her marriage.

Poniendome un Nombre

Barbara Kingsolver

He protegido mi nombre como la gente
de otras épocas guardaba mechones de su
    cabello,
creyendo que el alma podía fugarse
si no tenían cuidado.

5 Conocí a mi primer antepasado.
Su leyenda. He tocado
sus botas y el mostacho, el abuelo
cuya familia era dueña de esclavos y algodón.
Se sentía inquieto en Virginia
10 entre sus hermanos aristócratas, hasta que
un otoño llameante robó un caballo,
y galopó sobre las montañas para desposar
a una cheroki de ojos en forma de hojas.
El robo fue perdonado, pero nunca
15 la sangre indígena. Perdió el nombre de
    familia
e inventó el mío, le dió frutos y semillas.
Nunca conocí a la abuela.
Su fotografía tiene delgadas trenzas color tinta
y ropas abotonadas, y ningún nombre por
    el cual se le conociera.

20 Podría deshacerme de mi nombre en la mitad
    de la vida,
la cosa más común, y desaparecería
junto con la niñez y las abuelas muertas
hacia ese limbo creado para los nombres
    de soltera fuera de circulación.

Pero se inquietaría allí.
25 Lo sé. Cabalgaría sobre montañas con humo
    de hojas
para robar caballos.

▲ What story might Jaune Quick-To-See
Smith be telling in her 1992
composition *Red Horse?*

R ED W AGONS

Ana Castillo

c. 1958

In grammar school primers[1]
the red wagon
was for children
pulled along
5 past lawns on a sunny day.
Father drove into
the driveway. "Look,
Father, look!"
Silly Sally pulled Tim
10 on the red wagon.

Out of school,
the red wagon carried
kerosene cans
to heat the flat.[2]
15 Father pulled it to the gas
station
when he was home
and if there was money.

If not, children went to bed
20 in silly coats
silly socks; in the morning
were already dressed
for school.

---

1. **primer** (prim′ər), *n.* a first book in reading.
2. **flat** (flat), *n.* apartment.

After Reading

Making Connections

Shaping Your Response

1. Choose one of the poems and write three questions you would like to ask the narrator.

2. What sensory image do you recall most vividly from these poems? Cite the lines that created the **imagery.**

Analyzing the Poems

3. **Summarize** what astonished the boy in "Coca-Cola and Coco Frío."

4. Explain the **comparison** that Ana Castillo develops in "Red Wagons."

5. In "Lost Sister" the narrator says that even Chinese peasants named their first daughters "Jade." What is **ironic** about this?

6. **Compare** the two places described in "Lost Sister."

7. What example of **personification** can you find in "Naming Myself"?

8. **Summarize** the narrator's reasons for keeping her maiden name.

9. 👣 Choose two of the four poems and explain the **changes** the characters experience. Tell how cultural heritage plays a part in or is effected by the changes.

Extending the Ideas

10. 👣 The United States has in the past been called a "melting pot" because it has received many peoples from different lands who then become "Americans." Think about the notion of "assimilation," or becoming part of a larger group. What do you think are the advantages and disadvantages of assimilation? Cite examples from the poems to support your opinions.

Literary Focus: Theme

Think about the underlying meaning of each of the poems. Then complete the following chart by stating the subject and writing a statement of theme for each poem. Do any of the poems share common themes?

Poem	Subject	Statement of Theme
"Coca-Cola and Coco Frío"		
"Lost Sister"		
"Red Wagons"		
"Naming Myself"		

Vocabulary Study

Write the word from the list that could replace the italicized word or words in each sentence.

dormant
meager
inundate
redundant
unremitting

1. My comment about Puerto Rico was *repetitious* because Ana already answered the teacher's question.

2. The flower seed was *inactive* throughout the winter, but began to grow in the spring.

3. Radio and television broadcasts *bombard* their audiences with commercials.

4. Dinner was usually a *small* portion of potatoes and corn.

5. The anxiety caused by the loss of family support and cultural familiarity is *constant* for many people who emigrate to the United States.

Expressing Your Ideas

Writing Choices

Writer's Notebook Update Use the words that you wrote in your writer's notebook to write a poem about yourself. It can be rhymed or unrhymed, long or short. If you are not the poetic type, write a descriptive paragraph about yourself.

You Can't Judge a Book by Its Cover
Sometimes a book will have a subtitle that further explains the book's topic. For example, an autobiography by a basketball referee entitled *The Last Word* might have the subtitle *I Make the Calls.* Write informative **subtitles** for the four poems you have just read.

Other Options

Meeting of Minds In groups of four, find out all you can about the four authors in this cluster, including becoming familiar with their other works. Then, based on what you learn, dramatize a **panel discussion** between the four, discussing what they think it means to be American in today's multicultural society.

Conversing on the Net Imagine that two of the narrators or characters from these poems have found each other on a bulletin board or newsgroup of the Internet and begin writing to each other. What will they say to each other? With a partner, choose two of the poem's personalities and write a series of **electronic mail messages** to and from each other. Be sure to use the information in the poems as a basis for your discussion.

Before Reading

Mother Tongue

by Amy Tan

Amy Tan
Born 1952

Amy Tan was born in Oakland, California, to parents who had recently emigrated from China. Tan won her first literary contest when she was eight. She has since worked as a consultant, writer, editor, and publisher. Tan comments on her writing: "The kind of writing I do is very dream-like. . . . I focus on a specific image, and that image takes me into a scene. Then I begin to see the scene and I ask myself, "What's to your right? What's to your left? and I open up into this fictional world . . . and let it go where it wants to go, wherever the characters want to go." Tan's latest work of fiction is *The Hundred Secret Senses* (1995).

Building Background

What Languages Do You Speak? In "Mother Tongue," the essay you are about to read, Amy Tan talks about "all the Englishes" she grew up with. Analyze the Englishes that you use. Think about how you speak to your parents, your teachers, your friends, and younger children. Do the vocabularies differ? How about the sentence structure and grammar you use? Does your family have ethnic words or expressions infused into its English? For example, does your grandmother call a scarf a *babushka,* or is your uncle referred to as *tío?* Does your English have a regional flavor—a Texas twang, a Chicago accent, or a Southern drawl? Tape-record or make a written transcript of three short conversations between you and an adult non-family member, between you and a friend, and between you and a family member. How do the Englishes that you use compare to each other?

Literary Focus

Denotation and Connotation Words not only have denotations, or literal meanings, but also connotations, or emotional associations. For example, in the phrase *mother tongue,* the denotative meaning of the word *mother* is: "derived from one's mother; native." However, the word may also connote feelings of warmth and goodness. As you read the essay, notice the connotations of the words *broken* and *limited* as Tan uses them to describe her mother's English.

Writer's Notebook

Know Your Audience Imagine that you are supposed to present a report to the class about contemporary music and provide taped examples. During the middle of your report, the audiotape breaks, ruining your presentation. How would you write about the situation in a letter to your brother who is away at college? How would you write about it if you were writing to the manufacturer of the audiotape? Choose one of these situations and write a sample letter in your notebook.

Mother Tongue

Amy Tan

I AM NOT a scholar of English or literature. I cannot give you much more than personal opinions on the English language and its variations in this country or others.

I am a writer. And by that definition, I am someone who has always loved language. I am fascinated by language in daily life. I spend a great deal of my time thinking about the power of language—the way it can evoke an emotion, a visual image, a complex idea, or a simple truth. Language is the tool of my trade. And I use them all—all the Englishes I grew up with.

Recently, I was made keenly aware of the different Englishes I do use. I was giving a talk to a large group of people, the same talk I had already given to half a dozen other groups. The nature of the talk was about my writing, my life, and my book, *The Joy Luck Club*. The talk was going along well enough, until I remembered one major difference that made the whole talk sound wrong. My mother was in the room.

This 1991 work by Pacita Abad is titled *How Mali Lost Her Accent*. Based on the details in the work, what else do you think Mali may have lost, and what does she seem to have gained? ➤

And it was perhaps the first time she had heard me give a lengthy speech, using the kind of English I have never used with her. I was saying things like, "The intersection of memory upon imagination" and "There is an aspect of my fiction that relates to thus-and-thus"—a speech filled with carefully wrought grammatical phrases, burdened, it suddenly seemed to me, with nominalized forms, past perfect tenses, conditional phrases, all the forms of standard English that I had learned in school and through books, the forms of English I did not use at home with my mother.

CLARIFY: What difference does having her mother in the audience make to Amy Tan?

Just last week, I was walking down the street with my mother, and again I found myself conscious of the English I was using, the English I do use with her. We were talking about the price of new and used furniture and I heard myself saying this: "Not waste money that way." My husband was with us as well, and he didn't notice any switch in my English. And then I realized why. It's because over the twenty years we've been together I've often used that same kind of English with him, and sometimes he even uses it with me. It has become our language of intimacy, a different sort of English that relates to family talk, the language I grew up with.

So you'll have some idea of what this family talk I heard sounds like, I'll quote what my mother said during a recent conversation which I videotaped and then transcribed.[1] During this conversation, my mother was talking about a political gangster in Shanghai who had the same last name as her family's, Du, and how the gangster in his early years wanted to be adopted by her family, which was rich by comparison. Later, the gangster became more powerful, far richer than my mother's family, and one day showed up at my mother's wedding to pay his respects. Here's what she said in part:

"Du Yusong having business like fruit stand. Like off the street kind. He is Du like Du Zong—but not Tsung-ming Island people. The local people call putong, the river east side, he belong to that side local people. That man want to ask Du Zong father take him in like become own family. Du Zong father wasn't look down on him, but didn't take seriously, until that man big like become a mafia. Now important person, very hard to inviting him. Chinese way, came only to show respect, don't stay for dinner. Respect for making big celebration, he shows up. Mean gives lots of respect. Chinese custom. Chinese social life that way. If too important won't have to stay too long. He come to my wedding. I didn't see, I heard it. I gone to boy's side, they have YMCA dinner. Chinese age I was nineteen."

You should know that my mother's expressive command of English belies[2] how much she actually understands. She reads the *Forbes* report, listens to *Wall Street Week*, converses daily with her stockbroker, reads all of Shirley MacLaine's books with ease—all kinds of things I can't begin to understand. Yet some of my friends tell me they understand 50 percent of what my mother says. Some say they understand 80 to 90 percent. Some say they understand none of it, as if she were speaking pure Chinese. But to me, my mother's English is perfectly clear, perfectly natural. It's my mother tongue. Her language, as I hear it, is vivid, direct, full of observation and imagery. That was the language that helped shape the way I saw things, expressed things, made sense of the world.

LATELY, I'VE BEEN GIVING more thought to the kind of English my mother speaks. Like others, I have described it to people as "broken" or "fractured" English. But I wince when I say that. It has always bothered me that I can think of no way to describe it other than "broken," as if it were damaged and needed to be fixed, as if

---

1. **transcribe** (tran skrīb′), *v.* set down in writing.
2. **belie** (bi lī), *v.* give a false idea of; misrepresent.

it lacked a certain wholeness and soundness. I've heard other terms used, "limited English," for example. But they seem just as bad, as if everything is limited, including people's perceptions of the limited English speaker.

. . . to me, my mother's English is perfectly clear, perfectly natural. It's my mother tongue.

I know this for a fact, because when I was growing up, my mother's "limited" English limited *my* perception of her. I was ashamed of her English. I believed that her English reflected the quality of what she had to say. That is, because she expressed them imperfectly, her thoughts were imperfect. And I had plenty of empirical evidence to support me: the fact that people in department stores, at banks, and at restaurants did not take her seriously, did not give her good service, pretended not to understand her, or even acted as if they did not hear her.

My mother has long realized the limitations of her English as well. When I was fifteen, she used to have me call people on the phone to pretend I was she. In this guise, I was forced to ask for information or even to complain and yell at people who had been rude to her. One time it was a call to her stockbroker in New York. She had cashed out her small portfolio[3] and it just so happened we were going to go to New York the next week, our very first trip outside California. I had to get on the phone and say in an adolescent voice that was not very convincing, "This is Mrs. Tan."

And my mother was standing in the back whispering loudly, "Why he don't send me check, already two weeks late. So mad he lie to me, losing me money."

And then I said in perfect English, "Yes, I'm getting rather concerned. You had agreed to send the check two weeks ago, but it hasn't arrived."

Then she began to talk more loudly. "What he want. I come to New York tell him front of his boss, you cheating me?" And I was trying to calm her down, make her be quiet, while telling the stockbroker, "I can't tolerate any more excuses. If I don't receive the check immediately, I am going to have to speak to your manager when I'm in New York next week." And sure enough, the following week there we were in front of this astonished stockbroker, and I was sitting there red-faced and quiet, and my mother, the real Mrs. Tan, was shouting at his boss in her impeccable[4] broken English.

EVALUATE: How can Amy Tan's mother's English be both "broken" and "impeccable"?

We used a similar routine just five days ago, for a situation that was far less humorous. My mother had gone to the hospital for an appointment, to find out about a benign brain tumor a CAT scan had revealed a month ago. She said she had spoken very good English, her best English, no mistakes. Still, she said, the hospital did not apologize when they said they had lost the CAT scan and she had come for nothing. She said they did not seem to have any sympathy when she told them she was anxious to know the exact diagnosis, since her husband and son had both died of brain tumors. She said they would not give her any more information until the next time and she would have to make another appointment for that. So she said she would not leave until the doctor called her daughter. She wouldn't budge. And when the doctor finally called her daughter, me, who spoke in perfect English—lo and behold—we had assurances the CAT scan would be found, promises that a

---

3. **portfolio** (pôrt fō′lē ō), *n.* holdings in the form of stocks, bonds, etc.
4. **impeccable** (im pek′ə bəl), *adj.* free from fault; irreproachable.

conference call on Monday would be held, and apologies for any suffering my mother had gone through for a most regrettable mistake.

I think my mother's English almost had an effect on limiting my possibilities in life as well. Sociologists and linguists probably will tell you that a person's developing language skills are more influenced by peers. But I do think that the language spoken in the family, especially in immigrant families which are more insular,[5] plays a large role in shaping the language of the child. And I believe that it affected my results on achievement tests, IQ tests, and the SAT. While my English skills were never judged as poor, compared to math, English could not be considered my strong suit. In grade school I did moderately well, getting perhaps B's, sometimes B-pluses, in English and scoring perhaps in the sixtieth or seventieth percentile on achievement tests. But those scores were not good enough to override the opinion that my true abilities lay in math and science, because in those areas I achieved A's and scored in the ninetieth percentile or higher.

This was understandable. Math is precise: there is only one correct answer. Whereas, for me at least, the answers on English tests were always a judgment call, a matter of opinion and personal experience. Those tests were constructed around items like fill-in-the-blank sentence completion, such as, "Even though Tom was _____, Mary thought he was _____." And the correct answer always seemed to be the most bland combinations of thoughts, for example, "Even though Tom was shy, Mary thought he was charming," with the grammatical structure "even though" limiting the correct answer to some sort of semantic opposites, so you wouldn't get answers like, "Even though Tom was foolish, Mary thought he was ridiculous." Well, according to my mother, there were very few limitations as to what Tom could have been and what Mary might have thought of him. So I never did well on tests like that.

The same was true with word analogies, pairs of words in which you were supposed to find some sort of logical, semantic[6] relationship—for example, "*Sunset* is to *nightfall* as _____ is to _____." And here you would be presented with a list of four possible pairs, one of which showed the same kind of relationship: *red* is to *stoplight, bus* is to *arrival, chills* is to *fever, yawn* is to *boring*. Well, I could never think that way. I knew what the tests were asking, but I could not block out of my mind the images already created by the first pair, *"sunset* is to *nightfall"*—and I would see a burst of colors against a darkening sky, the moon rising, the lowering of a curtain of stars. And all the other pairs of words—red, bus, stoplight, boring—just threw up a mass of confusing images, making it impossible for me to sort out something as logical as saying: "A sunset precedes nightfall" is the same as "a chill precedes a fever." The only way I would have gotten that answer right would have been to imagine an associative situation, for example, my being disobedient and staying out past sunset, catching a chill at night, which turns into feverish pneumonia as punishment, which indeed did happen to me.

. . . the correct answer always seemed to be the most bland . . .

I HAVE BEEN THINKING about all this lately, about my mother's English, about achievement tests. Because lately I've been asked, as a writer, why there are not more Asian Americans represented in American literature. Why are there so few Asian Americans enrolled in creative writing programs? Why do so many Chinese students go into engineering? Well, these are broad sociological questions I can't begin to

---

5. insular (in′sə lər), *adj.* standing alone like an island; isolated.
6. semantic (sə man′tik), *adj.* having to do with the meaning of words.

answer. But I have noticed in surveys—in fact, just last week—that Asian students, as a whole, always do significantly better on math achievement tests than in English. And this makes me think that there are other Asian American students whose English spoken in the home might also be described as "broken" or "limited." And perhaps they also have teachers who are steering them away from writing and into math and science, which is what happened to me.

SUMMARIZE: How does Amy Tan think her "mother tongue" affected her academically?

Fortunately, I happen to be rebellious in nature and enjoy the challenge of disproving assumptions made about me. I became an English major my first year in college, after being enrolled as pre-med. I started writing nonfiction as a freelancer the week after I was told by my former boss that writing was my worst skill and I should hone[7] my talents toward account management.

But it wasn't until 1985 that I finally began to write fiction. And at first I wrote using what I thought to be wittily crafted sentences, sentences that would finally prove I had mastery over the English language. Here's an example from the first draft of a story that later made its way into *The Joy Luck Club,* but without this line: "That was my mental quandary[8] in its nascent[9] state." A terrible line, which I can barely pronounce.

Fortunately, for reasons I won't get into today, I later decided I should envision a reader for the stories I would write. And the reader I decided upon was my mother, because these were stories about mothers. So with this reader in mind—and in fact she did read my early drafts—I began to write stories using all the Englishes I grew up with: the English I spoke to my mother, which for lack of a better term might be described as "simple"; the English she used with me, which for lack of a better term might be described as "broken"; my translation of her Chinese, which could certainly be described as "watered down"; and what I imagined to be her translation of her Chinese if she could speak in perfect English, her internal language, and for that I sought to preserve the essence, but neither an English nor a Chinese structure. I wanted to capture what language ability tests can never reveal: her intent, her passion, her imagery, the rhythms of her speech and the nature of her thoughts.

Fortunately, I happen to be rebellious in nature . . .

Apart from what any critic had to say about my writing, I knew I had succeeded where it counted when my mother finished reading my book and gave me her verdict: "So easy to read."

---

7. **hone** (hōn), *v.* to perfect or make more effective.
8. **quandary** (kwon′dər ē), *n.* state of perplexity or uncertainty; dilemma.
9. **nascent** (nas′nt), *adj.* in the process of coming into existence; emerging.

After Reading

Making Connections

Shaping Your Response

1. What five adjectives would you use to describe Amy Tan's mother?

2. Can you understand Tan's mother? Retell her story about Du Yusong in your own words.

Analyzing the Essay

3. **Summarize** the point that Tan is trying to make about language.

4. How does Tan's childhood perception of her mother differ from her adult perception?

5. Describe either the New York stockbroker or the hospital personnel and their treatment of Tan's mother.

6. Compare the words that Tan's mother uses to tell Amy what to tell the stockbroker over the phone to the words Amy uses in the conversation. How would you describe the difference?

Extending the Ideas

7. Amy Tan refers to the "power of language." Do you see language as powerful? Explain.

8. What advice would you give to people about communicating with people whose first language is not English?

Literary Focus: Denotation and Connotation

Review the paragraph in which Amy Tan describes her mother's English. Why does she have a problem with referring to it as "broken" or "limited" or "fractured"?

Vocabulary Study

Amy Tan would hate this exercise; however, you are probably an expert on analogies by now. Use the list of vocabulary words to complete each analogy. One word will be used twice.

portfolio
transcribe
impeccable
insular
quandary
semantic
belie
hone
nascent

1. recipe : cookbook : : stock : _____
2. imperfect : flawed : : perfect : _____
3. behavior : psychological : : words : _____
4. peninsula : connected : : island : _____
5. scene : photograph : : speech : _____
6. answer : question : : certainty : _____
7. knife : sharpen : : talent : _____
8. deception : misperception : : hide : _____
9. tree : mature : : seedling : _____
10. outgoing : social : : shy : _____

Expressing Your Ideas

Writing Choices

Writer's Notebook Update When you write a letter, you have a very specific audience in mind. Review the letter you wrote before reading the essay by Amy Tan. How did you tailor your language to fit the recipient of your letter, either a college-aged sibling or a manufacturer? Write a paragraph explaining how the letter you didn't write would be different from the letter you did write.

Thumbs Up, Thumbs Down Borrow or rent a copy of the movie version of Amy Tan's book *The Joy Luck Club.* Watch it and then write a **movie review** to post in your classroom.

Another Option

A Trip to China Amy Tan didn't visit China until she was an adult. She said of her visit, "As soon as my feet touched China, I became Chinese." If you were to visit China, what would you like to see? Using a travel guide and a map, and any other resources you can find about China, create a **travel brochure**— including a daily itinerary of cities and sights as well as photographs—that advertises the China trip you would like to take.

Before Reading

This Is What It Means to Say Phoenix, Arizona

by Sherman Alexie

Sherman Alexie
born 1966

Writer Sherman Alexie explains, "I am a Spokane/Coeur d'Alene Indian from Wellpinit, Washington, where I live on the Spokane Indian Reservation. Everything I do now, writing and otherwise, has its origin in that." Alexie attended Gonzaga University and received a B.A. from Washington State University in 1991. He has written a number of books of poetry: *The Business of Fancy Dancing* (1992), *I Would Steal Horses* (1992), *Old Shirts and New Skins* (1993), and *First Indian on the Moon* (1993). The story "This Is What It Means to Say Phoenix, Arizona" is taken from his collection of short stories, *The Lone Ranger and Tonto Fistfight in Heaven* (1993).

Building Background

Reservation Life The Spokane and Coeur d'Alene Indians originally lived along the river valleys on the Columbia Plateau, which is bordered on the east by the Rocky Mountains and on the west by the Cascade Mountains. After the Coeur d'Alene War in 1858 they were forced to live on reservations. With the best lands reserved for white settlers, railroads, and mining interests, the Indians on the reservations were left with few means of economic self-sufficiency. Poverty, despair, and alcoholism are some of the problems that the reservation system has created. This is the reality of reservation life about which Sherman Alexie writes.

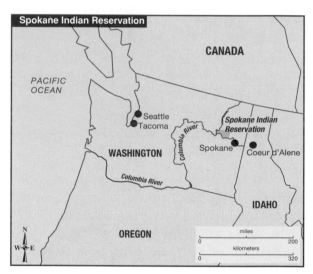

Literary Focus

Flashback Flashbacks are interruptions in a narrative that show events that happened previously. As you read "This Is What It Means to Say Phoenix, Arizona," notice each flashback and reflect on why the author chooses to include it.

Writer's Notebook

Growing Up The two main characters in the story you are about to read are childhood friends who grew apart. In your notebook write about a childhood friend of yours. What did he or she look like? What did you enjoy doing together? Are you still friends? Write a paragraph about it.

THIS IS WHAT IT MEANS TO SAY PHOENIX, ARIZONA

SHERMAN ALEXIE

Just after Victor lost his job at the BIA,[1] he also found out that his father had died of a heart attack in Phoenix, Arizona. Victor hadn't seen his father in a few years, only talked to him on the telephone once or twice, but there still was a genetic[2] pain, which was soon to be pain as real and immediate as a broken bone.

Victor didn't have any money. Who does have money on a reservation, except the cigarette and fireworks salespeople? His father had a savings account waiting to be claimed, but Victor needed to find a way to get to Phoenix. Victor's mother was just as poor as he was, and the rest of his family didn't have any use at all for him. So Victor called the Tribal Council.

"Listen," Victor said. "My father just died. I need some money to get to Phoenix to make arrangements."

"Now, Victor," the council said. "You know we're having a difficult time financially."

"But I thought the council had special funds set aside for stuff like this."

"Now, Victor, we do have some money available for the proper return of tribal members' bodies. But I don't think we have enough to bring your father all the way back from Phoenix."

"Well," Victor said. "It ain't going to cost all that much. He had to be cremated.[3] Things were kind of ugly. He died of a heart attack in his trailer and nobody found him for a week. It was really hot, too. You get the picture."

"Now, Victor, we're sorry for your loss and the circumstances. But we can really only afford to give you one hundred dollars."

"That's not even enough for a plane ticket."

"Well, you might consider driving down to Phoenix."

"I don't have a car. Besides, I was going to drive my father's pickup back up here."

"Now, Victor," the council said. "We're sure there is somebody who could drive you to Phoenix. Or is there somebody who could lend you the rest of the money?"

"You know there ain't nobody around with that kind of money."

"Well, we're sorry, Victor, but that's the best we can do."

Victor accepted the Tribal Council's offer. What else could he do? So he signed the proper papers, picked up his check, and walked over to the Trading Post to cash it.

While Victor stood in line, he watched Thomas Builds-the-Fire standing near the magazine rack, talking to himself. Like he always did. Thomas was a storyteller that nobody wanted to listen to. That's like being a dentist in a town where everybody has false teeth.

Victor and Thomas Builds-the-Fire were the same age, had grown up and played in the dirt

---

1. **BIA,** Bureau of Indian Affairs.
2. genetic (jə net′ik), *adj.* having to do with origin and natural growth.
3. cremate (krē′māt), *v.* to burn a dead body to ashes.

together. Ever since Victor could remember, it was Thomas who always had something to say.

Once, when they were seven years old, when Victor's father still lived with the family, Thomas closed his eyes and told Victor this story: "Your father's heart is weak. He is afraid of his own family. He is afraid of you. Late at night he sits in the dark. Watches the television until there's nothing but that white noise. Sometimes he feels like he wants to buy a motorcycle and ride away. He wants to run and hide. He doesn't want to be found."

Thomas Builds-the-Fire had known that Victor's father was going to leave, knew it before anyone. Now Victor stood in the Trading Post with a one-hundred-dollar check in his hand, wondering if Thomas knew that Victor's father was dead, if he knew what was going to happen next.

Just then Thomas looked at Victor, smiled, and walked over to him.

"Victor, I'm sorry about your father," Thomas said.

"How did you know about it?" Victor asked.

"I heard it on the wind. I heard it from the birds. I felt it in the sunlight. Also, your mother was just in here crying."

"Oh," Victor said and looked around the Trading Post. All the other Indians stared, surprised that Victor was even talking to Thomas. Nobody talked to Thomas anymore because he told the same damn stories over and over again. Victor was embarrassed, but he thought that Thomas might be able to help him. Victor felt a sudden need for tradition.

"I can lend you the money you need," Thomas said suddenly. "But you have to take me with you."

"I can't take your money," Victor said. "I mean, I haven't hardly talked to you in years. We're not really friends anymore."

"I didn't say we were friends. I said you had to take me with you."

"Let me think about it."

Victor went home with his one hundred dollars and sat at the kitchen table. He held his head in his hands and thought about Thomas Builds-the-Fire, remembered little details, tears and scars, the bicycle they shared for a summer, so many stories.

Thomas Builds-the-Fire sat on the bicycle, waited in Victor's yard. He was ten years old and skinny. His hair was dirty because it was the Fourth of July.

"Victor," Thomas yelled. "Hurry up. We're going to miss the fireworks."

After a few minutes, Victor ran out of his house, jumped the porch railing, and landed gracefully on the sidewalk.

"And the judges award him a 9.95, the highest score of the summer," Thomas said, clapped, laughed.

"That was perfect, cousin," Victor said. "And it's my turn to ride the bike."

Thomas gave up the bike and they headed for the fairgrounds. It was nearly dark and the fireworks were about to start.

"You know," Thomas said. "It's strange how us Indians celebrate the Fourth of July. It ain't like it was *our* independence everybody was fighting for."

"You think about things too much," Victor said. "It's just supposed to be fun. Maybe Junior will be there."

"Which Junior? Everybody on this reservation is named Junior."

And they both laughed.

The fireworks were small, hardly more than a few bottle rockets and a fountain. But it was enough for two Indian boys. Years later, they would need much more.

Afterwards, sitting in the dark, fighting off mosquitoes, Victor turned to Thomas Builds-the-Fire.

"Hey," Victor said. "Tell me a story."

Thomas closed his eyes and told this story: "There were these two Indian boys who wanted to be warriors. But it was too late to be warriors in the old way. All the horses were gone. So the two Indian boys stole a car and drove to the city. They parked the stolen car in front of the police station and then hitchhiked back home to the

Artist James Bama refers to his painting, *A Sioux Indian,* as showing "a guy who would like to have exploits like Crazy Horse and do brave and courageous things but has no vehicle for doing it anymore." How do the painting's images convey that sentiment?

reservation. When they got back, all their friends cheered and their parents' eyes shone with pride. *You were very brave,* everybody said to the two Indian boys. *Very brave.*"

"Ya-hey," Victor said. "That's a good one. I wish I could be a warrior."

"Me, too," Thomas said.

They went home together in the dark, Thomas on the bike now, Victor on foot. They walked through shadows and light from streetlamps.

"We've come a long ways," Thomas said. "We have outdoor lighting."

"All I need is the stars," Victor said. "And besides, you still think about things too much."

They separated then, each headed for home, both laughing all the way.

Victor sat at his kitchen table. He counted his one hundred dollars again and again. He knew he needed more to make it to Phoenix and back. He knew he needed Thomas Builds-the-Fire. So he put his money in his wallet and opened the front door to find Thomas on the porch.

"Ya-hey, Victor," Thomas said. "I knew you'd call me."

Thomas walked into the living room and sat down on Victor's favorite chair.

"I've got some money saved up," Thomas said. "It's enough to get us down there, but you have to get us back."

"I've got this hundred dollars," Victor said. "And my dad had a savings account I'm going to claim."

"How much in your dad's account?"

"Enough. A few hundred."

"Sounds good. When we leaving?"

When they were fifteen and had long since stopped being friends, Victor and Thomas got into a fistfight. That is, Victor was really drunk and beat Thomas up for no reason at all. All the other Indian boys stood around and watched it happen. Junior was there and so were Lester, Seymour, and a lot of others. The beating might

have gone on until Thomas was dead if Norma Many Horses hadn't come along and stopped it.

"Hey, you boys," Norma yelled and jumped out of her car. "Leave him alone."

If it had been someone else, even another man, the Indian boys would've just ignored the warnings. But Norma was a warrior. She was powerful. She could have picked up any two of the boys and smashed their skulls together. But worse than that, she would have dragged them all over to some tipi, and made them listen to some elder tell a dusty old story.

The Indian boys scattered, and Norma walked over to Thomas and picked him up.

"Hey, little man, are you okay?" she asked.

Thomas gave her a thumbs up.

"Why they always picking on you?"

Thomas shook his head, closed his eyes, but no stories came to him, no words or music. He just wanted to go home, to lie in his bed and let his dreams tell his stories for him.

Thomas Builds-the-Fire and Victor sat next to each other in the airplane, coach section. A tiny white woman had the window seat. She was busy twisting her body into pretzels. She was flexible.

"I have to ask," Thomas said, and Victor closed his eyes in embarrassment.

"Don't," Victor said.

"Excuse me, miss," Thomas asked. "Are you a gymnast or something?"

"There's no something about it," she said. "I was first alternate on the 1980 Olympic team."

"Really?" Thomas asked.

"Really."

"I mean, you used to be a world-class athlete?" Thomas asked.

"My husband still thinks I am."

Thomas Builds-the-Fire smiled. She was a mental gymnast, too. She pulled her leg straight up against her body so that she could've kissed her kneecap.

"I wish I could do that," Thomas said.

Victor was ready to jump out of the plane. Thomas, that crazy Indian storyteller with ratty old braids and broken teeth, was flirting with a beautiful Olympic gymnast. Nobody back home on the reservation would ever believe it.

"Well," the gymnast said. "It's easy. Try it."

Thomas grabbed at his leg and tried to pull it up into the same position as the gymnast. He couldn't even come close, which made Victor and the gymnast laugh.

"Hey," she asked. "You two are Indian, right?"

"Full-blood," Victor said.

"Not me," Thomas said. "I'm half magician on my mother's side and half clown on my father's."

They all laughed.

"What are your names?" she asked.

"Victor and Thomas."

"Mine is Cathy. Pleased to meet you all."

The three of them talked for the duration of the flight. Cathy the gymnast complained about the government, how they screwed the 1980 Olympic team by boycotting.[4]

"Sounds like you all got a lot in common with Indians," Thomas said.

Nobody laughed.

After the plane landed in Phoenix and they had all found their way to the terminal, Cathy the gymnast smiled and waved good-bye.

"She was really nice," Thomas said.

"Yeah, but everybody talks to everybody on airplanes," Victor said. "It's too bad we can't always be that way."

"You always used to tell me I think too much," Thomas said. "Now it sounds like you do."

"Maybe I caught it from you."

"Yeah."

Thomas and Victor rode in a taxi to the trailer where Victor's father died.

"Listen," Victor said as they stopped in front of the trailer. "I never told you I was sorry for beating you up that time."

"Oh, it was nothing. We were just kids and you were drunk."

"Yeah, but I'm still sorry."

"That's all right."

Victor paid for the taxi and the two of them

stood in the hot Phoenix summer. They could smell the trailer.

"This ain't going to be nice," Victor said. "You don't have to go in."

"You're going to need help."

Victor walked to the front door and opened it. The stink rolled out and made them both gag. Victor's father had lain in that trailer for a week in hundred-degree temperatures before anyone found him. And the only reason anyone found him was because of the smell. They needed dental records to identify him. That's exactly what the coroner said. They needed dental records.

"Oh, man," Victor said. "I don't know if I can do this."

"Well, then don't."

"But there might be something valuable in there."

"I thought his money was in the bank."

"It is. I was talking about pictures and letters and stuff like that."

"Oh," Thomas said as he held his breath and followed Victor into the trailer.

When Victor was twelve, he stepped into an underground wasp nest. His foot was caught in the hole, and no matter how hard he struggled, Victor couldn't pull free. He might have died there, stung a thousand times, if Thomas Builds-the-Fire had not come by.

"Run," Thomas yelled and pulled Victor's foot from the hole. They ran then, hard as they ever had, faster than Billy Mills, faster than Jim Thorpe,[5] faster than the wasps could fly.

Victor and Thomas ran until they couldn't breathe, ran until it was cold and dark outside, ran until they were lost and it took hours to find

---

4. **boycott** (boi′kot), *v.* to abstain from using, buying, participating, or dealing with to express protest.

5. **Billy Mills . . . Jim Thorpe,** both U.S. Olympians, both American Indians, Thorpe won gold medals in 1912 and Mills in 1964.

their way home. All the way back, Victor counted his stings.

"Seven," Victor said. "My lucky number."

Victor didn't find much to keep in the trailer. Only a photo album and a stereo. Everything else had that smell stuck in it or was useless anyway.

"I guess this is all," Victor said. "It ain't much."

"Better than nothing," Thomas said.

"Yea, and I do have the pickup."

"Yeah," Thomas said. "It's in good shape."

"Dad was good about that stuff."

"Yeah, I remember your dad."

"Really?" Victor asked. "What do you remember?"

Thomas Builds-the-Fire closed his eyes and told this story: "I remember when I had this dream that told me to go to Spokane, to stand by the Falls in the middle of the city and wait for a sign. I knew I had to go there but I didn't have a car. Didn't have a license. I was only thirteen. So I walked all the way, took me all day, and I finally made it to the Falls. I stood there for an hour waiting. Then your dad came walking up. *What the hell are you doing here?* he asked me. I said, *Waiting for a vision.* Then your father said, *All you're going to get here is mugged.* So he drove me over to Denny's, bought me dinner, and then drove me home to the reservation. For a long time I was mad because I thought my dreams had lied to me. But they didn't. Your dad was my vision. *Take care of each other* is what my dreams were saying. *Take care of each other.*"

Victor was quiet for a long time. He searched his mind for memories of his father, found the good ones, found a few bad ones, added it all up, and smiled.

"My father never told me about finding you in Spokane," Victor said.

"He said he wouldn't tell anybody. Didn't want me to get in trouble. But he said I had to watch out for you as part of the deal."

"Really?"

"Really. Your father said you would need the help. He was right."

"That's why you came down here with me, isn't it?" Victor asked.

"I came because of your father."

Victor and Thomas climbed into the pickup, drove over to the bank, and claimed the three hundred dollars in the savings account.

Thomas Builds-the-Fire could fly.

Once, he jumped off the roof of the tribal school and flapped his arms like a crazy eagle. And he flew. For a second, he hovered,[6] suspended above all the other Indian boys who were too smart or too scared to jump.

"He's flying," Junior yelled, and Seymour was busy looking for the trick wires or mirrors. But it was real. As real as the dirt when Thomas lost altitude[7] and crashed to the ground.

He broke his arm in two places.

"He broke his wing," Victor chanted, and the other Indian boys joined in, made it a tribal song.

"He broke his wing, he broke his wing, he broke his wing," all the Indian boys chanted as they ran off, flapping their wings, wishing they could fly, too. They hated Thomas for his courage, his brief moment as a bird. Everybody has dreams about flying. Thomas flew.

One of his dreams came true for just a second, just enough to make it real.

Victor's father, his ashes, fit in one wooden box with enough left over to fill a cardboard box.

"He always was a big man," Thomas said.

Victor carried part of his father and Thomas carried the rest out to the pickup. They set him down carefully behind the seats, put a cowboy hat on the wooden box and a Dodgers cap on the cardboard box. That's the way it was supposed to be.

"Ready to head back home," Victor asked.

"It's going to be a long drive."

"Yeah, take a couple days, maybe."

"We can take turns," Thomas said.

---

6. **hover** (huv′ər), *v.* hang fluttering or suspended in air.
7. **altitude** (al′tə tüd), *n.* height above the earth's surface.

"Okay," Victor said, but they didn't take turns. Victor drove for sixteen hours straight north, made it halfway up Nevada toward home before he finally pulled over.

"Hey, Thomas," Victor said. "You got to drive for a while."

"Okay."

Thomas Builds-the-Fire slid behind the wheel and started off down the road. All through Nevada, Thomas and Victor had been amazed at the lack of animal life, at the absence of water, of movement.

"Where is everything?" Victor had asked more than once.

Now when Thomas was finally driving they saw the first animal, maybe the only animal in Nevada. It was a long-eared jackrabbit.

"Look," Victor yelled. "It's alive."

Thomas and Victor were busy congratulating themselves on their discovery when the jackrabbit darted out into the road and under the wheels of the pickup.

"Stop the damn car," Victor yelled, and Thomas did stop, backed the pickup to the dead jackrabbit.

"Oh man, he's dead," Victor said as he looked at the squashed animal.

"Really dead."

"The only thing alive in this whole state and we just killed it."

"I don't know," Thomas said. "I think it was suicide."

Victor looked around the desert, sniffed the air, felt the emptiness and loneliness, and nodded his head.

"Yeah," Victor said. "It had to be suicide."

"I can't believe this," Thomas said. "You drive for a thousand miles and there ain't even any bugs smashed on the windshield. I drive for ten seconds and kill the only living thing in Nevada."

"Yeah," Victor said. "Maybe I should drive."

"Maybe you should."

Thomas Builds-the-Fire walked through the corridors of the tribal school by himself. Nobody wanted to be anywhere near him because of all those stories. Story after story.

Thomas closed his eyes and this story came to him: "We are all given one thing by which our lives are measured, one determination. Mine are the stories which can change or not change the world. It doesn't matter which as long as I continue to tell the stories. My father, he died on Okinawa in World War II, died fighting for this country, which had tried to kill him for years. My mother, she died giving birth to me, died while I was still inside her. She pushed me out into the world with her last breath. I have no brothers or sisters. I have only my stories which came to me before I even had the words to speak. I learned a thousand stories before I took my first thousand steps. They are all I have. It's all I can do."

Thomas Builds-the-Fire told his stories to all those who would stop and listen. He kept telling them long after people had stopped listening.

Victor and Thomas made it back to the reservation just as the sun was rising. It was the beginning of a new day on earth.

"Good morning," Thomas said.

"Good morning."

The tribe was waking up, ready for work, eating breakfast, reading the newspaper, just like everybody else does. Willene LeBret was out in her garden wearing a bathrobe. She waved when Thomas and Victor drove by.

"Crazy Indians made it," she said to herself and went back to her roses.

Victor stopped the pickup in front of Thomas Builds-the-Fire's HUD[8] house. They both yawned, stretched a little, shook dust from their bodies.

"I'm tired," Victor said.

"Of everything," Thomas added.

They both searched for words to end the journey. Victor needed to thank Thomas for his

8. **HUD,** Housing and Urban Development, a department of the U.S. government.

help, for the money, and make the promise to pay it all back.

"Don't worry about the money," Thomas said. "It don't make any difference anyhow."

"Probably not, enit?"

"Nope."

Victor knew that Thomas would remain the crazy storyteller who talked to dogs and cats, who listened to the wind and pine trees. Victor knew that he couldn't really be friends with Thomas, even after all that had happened. It was cruel but it was real. As real as the ashes, as Victor's father, sitting behind the seats.

"I know how it is," Thomas said. "I know you ain't going to treat me any better than you did before. I know your friends would give you too much trouble."

Victor was ashamed of himself. Whatever happened to the tribal ties, the sense of community? The only real thing he shared with anybody was a bottle and broken dreams. He owed Thomas something, anything.

"Listen," Victor said and handed Thomas the cardboard box which contained half of his father. "I want you to have this."

Thomas took the ashes and smiled, closed his eyes, and told this story: "I'm going to travel to Spokane Falls one last time and toss these ashes into the water. And your father will rise like a salmon, leap over the bridge, over me, and find his way home. It will be beautiful. His teeth will shine like silver, like a rainbow. He will rise, Victor, he will rise."

Victor smiled.

"I was planning on doing the same thing with my half," Victor said. "But I didn't imagine my father looking anything like a salmon. I thought it'd be like cleaning the attic or something. Like letting things go after they've stopped having any use."

"Nothing stops, cousin," Thomas said. "Nothing stops."

Thomas Builds-the-Fire got out of the pickup and walked up his driveway. Victor started the pickup and began the drive home.

"Wait," Thomas yelled suddenly from his porch. "I just got to ask one favor."

Victor stopped the pickup, leaned out the window, and shouted back. "What do you want?"

"Just one time when I'm telling a story somewhere, why don't you stop and listen?" Thomas asked.

"Just once?"

"Just once."

Victor waved his arms to let Thomas know that the deal was good. It was a fair trade, and that was all Victor had ever wanted from his whole life. So Victor drove his father's pickup toward home while Thomas went into his house, closed the door behind him, and heard a new story come to him in the silence afterwards.

> ▲ What is the mood of Laurie Brown's 1984 photo-series, *Journey Foretold, Launa Niguel, California?* Choose five adjectives that describe the work's mood, then tell whether the same five could apply to the story.

After Reading

Making Connections

Shaping Your
Response

1. Which of the two men would you prefer for a friend, Victor or
   Thomas? Why?

2. If you had to choose a section from this story for a dramatic reading,
   which section would you choose? Explain your choice.

Analyzing the
Story

3. This story can be seen as being about two journeys, one real and one
   spiritual. Describe the journeys.

4. Why do you think people don't listen to Thomas Builds-the-Fire's
   stories anymore?

5. Why do you think Thomas Builds-the-Fire wanted to accompany
   Victor to Phoenix?

Extending the
Ideas

6. Is Victor's reason for not being friends with Thomas valid in your
   opinion? Why or why not?

7. Do you think that Victor's life will change after his journey to claim the
   body of his father? Explain your answer.

Literary Focus: Flashback

Skim the story to find all of the flashbacks that Sherman Alexie uses
to reveal the relationship of the two main characters. Make a map of
the story showing the "detours" for the flashbacks. Your map might
begin like this.

Plot:

> Victor's father
> dies. Victor tries
> to get to Phoenix.

Flashbacks:

> Young Thomas
> and Victor cele-
> brate the Fourth
> of July.

Vocabulary Study

Use the vocabulary words in the list to complete the sentences below on a separate sheet of paper.

altitude
genetic
boycott
hover
cremate

1. The plane began to lose _____ as it approached Phoenix.

2. There were no _____ ties between Victor and Thomas.

3. Thomas planned to _____ around Victor's front door waiting to be asked to go along to Phoenix.

4. The authorities had to _____ the body of Victor's father.

5. The gymnast's chance for fame was ruined when the U.S. decided to _____ the 1980 Olympic Games.

Expressing Your Ideas

Writing Choices

Writer's Notebook Update Reread the writer's notebook entry about your childhood friend. Then think about your current friends. Consider what it is that makes a person a friend. Write an **explanatory paragraph** discussing the qualities that you value in a friendship.

In Loving Memory Write a **sermon** or **speech** that might be given at a memorial service for Victor's father by Thomas Builds-the-Fire.

Plateau Tribes Choose the Spokane Indians, the Coeur d'Alene Indians, or another Columbia River Plateau tribe and learn about the pre-reservation tribal history, customs, leaders, and economy. Write a **research report** describing the information you discover.

Other Options

Tell a Story Read another one of the stories about reservation life from Sherman Alexie's collection *The Lone Ranger and Tonto Fistfight in Heaven.* Prepare a **retelling** of the story to present to the class.

Scene 1, Take 1 Because of all of the flashbacks, this story would make a better movie than a play. If you were the screenwriter converting this story to a movie script, how many different sets would you have to describe for the director? Draw an **illustration** of one of the sets you would need for the production.

Heart to Heart Give Thomas Builds-the-Fire some advice. Should he continue telling stories or not? Why? Work with a friend and prepare a **conversation** that Victor might have with Thomas giving him helpful advice. Act out the dialogue for the class.

Top of the Food Chain

by T. Coraghessan Boyle

T. Coraghessan Boyle
born 1948

T. Coraghessan Boyle once said, "I would like to be a guy like [Kurt] Vonnegut for my generation, who could wake up people a little bit and show them that literature is fun and entertaining, and also serious at the same time." His writing career began in college at the State University of New York at Potsdam when he took an elective class in creative writing. He now teaches creative writing at the University of Southern California and writes both short stories and novels. One of his recent novels, *The Road to Wellville* (1993), was also made into a movie.

Building Background

Which Way to Borneo? Borneo is a large island southwest of the Philippines. Part or all of three different countries are included within the borders of the island. Brunei, the smallest of the three, is on the north coast of Borneo. It is an independent oil-rich sultanate, which means that the country is ruled by a sultan, an Islamic sovereign. Below Brunei are two states belonging to Malaysia, Sabah and Sarawak. South of these Malaysian states is Kaliman-tan, a region belonging to the Republic of Indonesia. This equatorial island, once colonized by the British, Portuguese, and Dutch, has a tropical climate and is cov-ered with rugged mountains and large areas of rain forest. The rain forests of Borneo and other places in the world are important to the ecosystem of the planet. Locate Borneo on the map.

Literary Focus

Hyperbole "Top of the Food Chain" is a **satire,** and T. Coraghessan Boyle uses hyperbole, or obvious exaggeration, to create satiric humor. As you read the story, look for examples of hyperbole.

Writer's Notebook

Environmental Impact In your opinion, how well are human beings managing the resources of the natural environment? In your note-book, make a list of concerns that you have about the future of our environment.

TOP of the FOOD CHAIN

T. Coraghessan Boyle

THE THING WAS, WE HAD A LITTLE PROBLEM WITH THE INSECT vector[1] there, and believe me, your tamer stuff, your malathion and pyrethrum[2] and the rest of the so-called environmentally safe products, didn't begin to make a dent in it, not a dent, I mean it was utterly useless—we might as well have been spraying Chanel No. 5[3] for all the good it did. And you've got to realize these people were literally covered with insects night and day—and the fact that they hardly wore any clothes just compounded the problem. Picture if you can, gentlemen, a naked two-year-old boy so black with flies and mosquitoes it looks like he's wearing long johns, or the young mother so racked with the malarial shakes she can't even lift a Diet Coke to her lips—it was pathetic, just pathetic, like something out of the Dark Ages. . . . Well, anyway, the decision was made to go with DDT. In the short term. Just to get the situation under control, you understand.

Yes, that's right, Senator, DDT: dichlorodiphenyl-trichloro-ethane.

---

1. **vector** (vek′tər), *n.* organism that transmits disease germs, such as a mosquito or a tick.
2. **malathion and pyrethrum** (mal′ə thī′ on, pī rē′-thrəm), *n.* insecticides.
3. **Chanel No. 5** a brand of perfume.

YES, I'M AWARE OF THAT FACT, sir. But just because *we* banned it domestically,[4] under pressure from the bird-watching contingent[5] and the hopheads down at the EPA, it doesn't necessarily follow that the rest of the world—especially the developing world—was about to jump on the bandwagon. And that's the key here, Senator, "developing." You've got to realize this is Borneo we're talking about here, not Port Townsend or Enumclaw. These people don't know from square one about sanitation, disease control, pest eradication[6]—or even personal hygiene, if you want to come right down to it. It rains 120 inches a year, minimum. They dig up roots in the jungle. They've still got headhunters along the Rajang River, for God's sake.

And please don't forget they *asked* us to come in there, practically begged us—and not only the World Health Organization but the Sultan of Brunei and the government in Sarawak too. We did what we could to accommodate them and reach our objective in the shortest period of time and by the most direct and effective means. We went to the air. Obviously. And no one could have foreseen the consequences, no one, not even if we'd gone out and generated a hundred environmental impact statements—it was just one of those things, a freak occurrence, and there's no defense against that. Not that I know of, anyway . . .

CLARIFY: What is the problem that the speaker was asked to address, and what is the solution that he undertook?

CATERPILLARS? YES, SENATOR, that's correct. That was the first sign: caterpillars.

But let me backtrack a minute here. You see, out in the bush they have these roofs made of thatched palm leaves—you'll see them in the towns too, even in Bintulu or Brunei—and they're really pretty effective, you'd be surprised. A hundred and twenty inches of rain, they've got to figure a way to keep it out of the hut, and for centuries, that was it. Palm leaves. Well, it was about a month after we sprayed for the final time and I'm sitting at my desk in the trailer thinking about the drainage project at Kuching, enjoying the fact that for the first time in maybe a year I'm not smearing mosquitoes all over the back of my neck, when there's a knock at the door. It's this elderly gentleman, tattooed from head to toe, dressed only in a pair of running shorts—they love those shorts, by the way, the shiny material and the tight machine-stitching, the whole country, men and women both, they can't get enough of them . . . Anyway, he's the headman of the local village and he's very excited, something about the roofs— *atap,* they call them. That's all he can say, *atap, atap,* over and over again.

It's raining of course. It's always raining. So I shrug into my rain slicker, start up the 4x4, and go have a look. Sure enough, all the *atap* roofs are collapsing, not only in his village but throughout the target area. The people are all huddled there in their running shorts, looking pretty miserable, and one after another roofs keep falling in, it's bewildering, and gradually I realize the headman's diatribe[7] has begun to feature a new term I was unfamiliar with at the time—the word for caterpillar, as it turns out, in the Iban dialect. But who was to make the connection between three passes with the crop duster and all these staved-in roofs?

Our people finally sorted it out a couple of weeks later. The chemical, which, by the way, cut down the number of mosquitoes exponentially,[8]

---

4. **domestically** (də mes′tik lē), *adv.* having to do with one's own country; not foreign.
5. **contingent** (kən tin′jənt), *n.* a group that is a part of another group.
6. **eradication** (i rad′ə kā′shən), *n.* complete destruction or elimination.
7. **diatribe** (dī′ə trib), *n.* a bitter, abusive criticism or denunciation.
8. **exponentially** (ek′spō nen′shəl lē), *adv.* in a way that involves unknown or variable quantities as exponents. In everyday use, if objects decrease *exponentially,* they decrease dramatically in number.

had the unfortunate side effect of killing off this little wasp—I've got the scientific name for it somewhere in my report here, if you're interested—that preyed on a type of caterpillar that in turn ate palm leaves. Well, with the wasps gone, the caterpillars hatched out with nothing to keep them in check and chewed the roofs to pieces, which was unfortunate, we admit it, and we had a real cost overrun on replacing those roofs with tin . . . but the people were happier, I think, in the long run, because, let's face it, no matter how tightly you weave those palm leaves, they're just not going to keep the water out like tin. Of course, nothing's perfect, and we had a lot of complaints about the rain drumming on the panels, people unable to sleep, and what have you . . .

YES SIR, THAT'S CORRECT—THE flies were next.
Well, you've got to understand the magnitude of the fly problem in Borneo, there's nothing like it to compare it with, except maybe a garbage strike in New York. Every minute of every day you've got flies everywhere, up your nose, in your mouth, your ears, your eyes, flies in your rice, your Coke, your Singapore sling, and your gin rickey. It's enough to drive you to distraction, not to mention the diseases these things carry, from dysentery to typhoid to cholera and back round the loop again. And once the mosquito population was down, the flies seemed to breed up to fill in the gap—Borneo wouldn't be Borneo without some damned insect blackening the air.

Of course, this was before our people had tracked down the problem with caterpillars and the wasps and all of that, so we'd figured we'd had a big success with the mosquitoes, why not a series of ground sweeps, mount a fogger in the back of a Suzuki Brat, and sanitize the huts, not to mention the open sewers, which as you know are nothing but a breeding ground for flies, chiggers, and biting insects of every sort—at least it was an error of commission rather than omission. At least we were trying.

I watched the flies go down myself. One day they were so thick in the trailer I couldn't even *find* my paperwork, let alone attempt to get through it, and the next they were collecting on the windows, bumbling around like they were drunk. A day later they were gone. Just like that. From a million flies in the trailer to none . . .

Well, no one could have foreseen that, Senator.

The geckos ate the flies, yes. You're all familiar with geckos, I assume, gentlemen? These are the lizards you've seen during your trips to Hawaii, very colorful, patrolling the houses for roaches and flies, almost like pets, but of course they're wild animals, never lose sight of that, and just about as unsanitary as anything I can think of, except maybe the flies.

Yes, well don't forget, sir, we're viewing this with twenty-twenty hindsight, but at the time no one gave a thought to geckos or what they ate—they were just another fact of life in the tropics. Mosquitoes, lizards, scorpions, leeches—you name it, they've got it. When the flies began piling up on the windowsills like drift, naturally the geckos feasted on them, stuffing themselves till they looked like sausages crawling up the walls. Whereas before they moved so fast you could never be sure you'd seen them, now they waddled across the floor, laid around in the corners, clung to the air vents like magnets—and even then no one paid much attention to them till they started turning belly-up in the streets. Believe me, we confirmed a lot of things there about the buildup of these products as you move up the food chain and the efficacy[9]—or lack thereof—of certain methods, no doubt about that . . .

EVALUATE: How did the speaker compound the problems he created?

---

9. **efficacy** (ef′ə kə sē), *n.* power to produce the effect wanted; effectiveness.

A This 1993 illustration of T. Coraghessan Boyle's story was done by Caty Bartholomew.
Do you think the artist has done a good job matching the tone of "Top of the Food Chain"?

 **THE CATS? THAT'S WHERE IT GOT** sticky, really sticky. You see, nobody really lost sleep over a pile of dead lizards—though we did tests routinely and the tests confirmed what we'd expected, that is, the product had been concentrated in the geckos because of the number of contaminated flies they consumed. But lizards are one thing and cats are another. These people really have an affection for their cats—no house, no hut, no matter how primitive, is without at least a couple of them. Mangy-looking things, long-legged and scrawny, maybe, not at all the sort of animal you'd see here, but there it was: they

loved their cats. Because the cats were functional, you understand—without them, the place would be swimming in rodents inside of a week.

You're right there, Senator, yes—that's exactly what happened.

You see, the cats had a field day with these feeble geckos—you can imagine, if any of you have ever owned a cat, the kind of joy these animals must have experienced to see their nemesis,[10] this ultra-quick lizard, and it's just barely creeping across the floor like a bug. Well, to make a long story short, the cats ate up every dead and dying gecko in the country, from snout to tail, and then the cats began to die . . . which to my mind would have been no great loss if it wasn't for the rats. Suddenly there were rats everywhere—you couldn't drive down the streets without running over half a dozen of them at a time. They fouled the grain supplies, fell in the wells and died, bit infants as they slept in their cradles. But that wasn't the worst, not by a long shot. No, things really went down the tube after that. Within the month we were getting scattered reports of bubonic plague,[11] and of course we tracked them all down and made sure the people got antibiotics, but still we lost a few and the rats kept coming . . .

It was my plan, yes. I was brainstorming one night, rats scuttling all over the trailer like something out of a cheap horror film, the villagers in a panic over the threat of the plague and the stream of nonstop hysterical reports from the interior—people were turning black, swelling up, and bursting, that sort of thing—well, as I say, I came up with a plan, a stopgap, not perfect, not cheap, but at this juncture, I'm sure you will agree, something had to be done.

PREDICT: What plan do you think the speaker has come up with? If you were in his place, what might you propose?

We wound up going as far as Australia for some of the cats, cleaning out the S.P.C.A.

facilities and what have you, though we rounded most of them up in Indonesia and Singapore—approximately 14,000 in all. And yes, it cost us—cost us up-front purchase money and aircraft fuel and pilots' overtime and all the rest of it—but we really felt there was no alternative. It was like all nature had turned against us.

And yet, all things considered, we made a lot of friends for the U.S.A. the day we dropped the cats, and you should have seen them, gentlemen, the little parachutes and harnesses we'd tricked up, 14,000 of them, cats in every color of the rainbow, cats with one ear, no ears, half a tail, three-legged cats, cats that could have taken pride of show in Springfield, Massachusetts, and all of them twirling down out of the sky like great big oversized snowflakes . . .

IT WAS SOMETHING. IT was really something.

Of course, you've all seen the reports. There were other factors we hadn't counted on, adverse[12] conditions in the paddies and manioc fields—we don't to this day know what predatory species were inadvertently[13] killed off by the initial sprayings, it's just a mystery—but the weevils and whatnot took a pretty heavy toll on the crops that year, and by the time we dropped the cats, well—the people were pretty hungry, and I suppose it was inevitable that we lost a good proportion of them right then and there. But we've got a CARE program going there now and something hit the rat population—we still don't know what, a virus we think—and the geckos, they tell me, are making a comeback.

So what I'm saying is it could be worse, and to every cloud a silver lining, wouldn't you agree, gentlemen?

---

10. **nemesis** (nem′ə sis), *n.* an unbeatable rival.
11. **bubonic plague** (byŭ bon′ik plāg), *n.* a very serious contagious disease, usually carried to human beings by fleas from rats or squirrels.
12. **adverse** (ad vèrs′), *adj.* unfavorable; harmful.
13. **inadvertently** (in′ad vèrt′nt lē), *adv.* in an inattentive, careless, or negligent way.

After Reading

Shaping Your Response

Analyzing the Story

Extending the Ideas

Making Connections

1. If you were the speaker's boss and had to write a job performance report on his work in Borneo, what would you say?

2. What is the significance of the title "Top of the Food Chain"?

3. How would you **characterize** the speaker of the story?

4. The purpose of **satire** is to instruct or inform. What do you think is the message of Boyle's satirical story "Top of the Food Chain"?

5. What role, if any, do you think the United States should play in the internal affairs of other nations?

Vocabulary Study

diatribe
vector
adverse
efficacy
inadvertently
eradication
domestically
contingent
nemesis
exponentially

Use the listed vocabulary words to make a "Top of the Food Chain" crossword puzzle. On a piece of graph paper, map out your puzzle with five words down and five across. Then, as clues, write sentences that relate to the story, leaving a blank in each where the vocabulary word fits in the sentence. Trade with a partner and see if you can solve each other's puzzles.

Expressing Your Ideas

Writing Choices

Writer's Notebook Update Choose one of the environmental concerns that you listed in your writer's notebook. Write what you know about the problem and explain the progress, if any, that is being made toward solving it.

Congressional Report You are one of the members of the congressional committee listening to the speaker's report on his activities in Borneo. Write a **report** summarizing the results of those activities and making recommendations for the future of the project in Borneo.

Another Option

What's for Dinner? The ecological balance in Borneo was upset when the speaker attempted to solve the insect problem there. Make an **illustrated diagram** of the food chains that he weakened in his misguided attempts to improve the living conditions on the island.

Before Reading

A Blizzard Under Blue Sky

by Pam Houston

Pam Houston
born 1962

Born and raised in New Jersey, Pam Houston graduated with a B.A. from Denison University. After her graduation she took a cross-country bicycle trip with a friend and wound up in Colorado. There, in order to follow modern-day cowboys, she threw herself into mastering all kinds of outdoor activities. She has worked as a horse trainer, ski instructor, hunting guide, and rafting guide. In addition, she found time to complete her Ph.D. at the University of Utah. She currently writes during the winter and works as a river guide in the summer. She married a former safari guide from South Africa. The story you are about to read is taken from Houston's first book, *Cowboys Are My Weakness* (1992).

Building Background

More Than Just the Blues People often say that they are "depressed." More often than not, they are just suffering from a normal "down" mood. Usually these everyday "blues" evaporate by themselves. More severe depression may be caused by a chemical imbalance and usually requires medical attention. The depressed person may feel numb, may not want to get out of bed in the morning, may exhibit symptoms of physical illness, and may become irritable and unable to concentrate. People can overcome less severe depression by giving themselves special treats, by doing intense physical activity, by keeping busy with challenging tasks, or by getting outside of themselves by helping others. The main character of "A Blizzard Under Blue Sky" tries a new activity to help her overcome her depression.

Literary Focus

Setting Where and when a story takes place is its setting. Setting can help establish mood, reveal character, and affect the development of the plot. For example, "The Devil and Tom Walker" (page 240) takes place outside of Boston in a swamp in the year 1727. The dismal, dreary setting creates an ominous mood. The setting of "A Worn Path" (page 667), the rural countryside of Mississippi, reveals the character of Phoenix Jackson, the old woman who conquers the landscape to get medicine for her grandson. As you read "A Blizzard Under Blue Sky," note the details that describe the setting. Also, determine what effect, if any, the setting has on the mood, character development, and plot of the story.

Writer's Notebook

'Tis the Season Weather plays a big part in the story you are about to read. What is it like where you live during each of the four seasons? Are you mired in mud or socked in by heavy fog in spring? Are you parched by droughts or cooled by mountain breezes in the summer? In your notebook, write a list of descriptive phrases telling what your area of the country is like during your favorite season.

A Blizzard
UNDER BLUE SKY

Pam Houston

The doctor said I was clinically depressed. It was February, the month in which depression runs rampant[1] in the inversion-cloaked Salt Lake Valley and the city dwellers escape to Park City, where the snow is fresh and the sun is shining and everybody is happy, except me. In truth, my life was on the verge[2] of more spectacular and satisfying discoveries than I had ever imagined, but of course I couldn't see that far ahead. What I saw was work that wasn't getting done, bills that weren't getting paid, and a man I'd given my heart to weekending in the desert with his ex.

The doctor said, "I can give you drugs."

I said, "No way."

She said, "The machine that drives you is broken. You need something to help you get it fixed."

I said, "Winter camping."

She said, "Whatever floats your boat."

One of the things I love the most about the natural world is the way it gives you what's good for you even if you don't know it at the time. I had never been winter camping before, at least not in the high country, and the weekend I chose to try and fix my machine was the same weekend the air mass they called the Alaska Clipper showed up. It was thirty-two degrees below zero in town on the night I spent in my snow cave. I don't know how cold it was out on Beaver Creek. I had listened to the weather forecast, and to the advice of my housemate, Alex, who was an experienced winter camper.

"I don't know what you think you're going to prove by freezing to death," Alex said, "but if you've got to go, take my bivvy sack;[3] it's warmer than anything you have."

"Thanks," I said.

"If you mix Kool-Aid with your water it won't freeze up," he said, "and don't forget lighting paste for your stove."

"Okay," I said.

"I hope it turns out to be worth it," he said, "because you are going to freeze your butt."

When everything in your life is uncertain, there's nothing quite like the clarity and precision of fresh snow and blue sky. That was the first thought I had on Saturday morning as I stepped away from the warmth of my truck and let my skis slap the snow in front of me. There was no wind and no clouds that morning, just still air and cold sunshine. The hair in my nostrils froze almost immediately. When I took a deep breath, my lungs only filled up halfway.

I opened the tailgate to excited whines and whimpers. I never go skiing without Jackson and

---

1. **rampant** (ram′pənt), *adj.* unrestrained; unchecked.
2. **verge** (vėrj), *n.* the point at which something begins or happens; brink.
3. **bivvy sack** a bag designed to contain a sleeping bag and protect it from wind and water.

▲ Describe your personal reaction to Paul Ladnier's *Grandy Snow Scene.* Does it make you want to step into the picture, or does it make you feel glad that you aren't there?

Hailey; my two best friends, my yin and yang[4] of dogs. Some of you might know Jackson. He's the oversized sheepdog-and-something-else with the great big nose and the bark that will shatter glass. He gets out and about more than I do. People I've never seen before come by my house daily and call him by name. He's all grace, and he's tireless; he won't go skiing with me unless I let him lead. Hailey is not so graceful, and her body seems in constant indecision when she runs. When we ski she stays behind me, and on the downhills she tries to sneak rides on my skis.

The dogs ran circles in the chest-high snow while I inventoried my backpack one more time to make sure I had everything I needed. My sleeping bag, my Thermarest, my stove, Alex's bivvy sack, matches, lighting paste, flashlight, knife. I brought three pairs of long underwear—tops and bottoms—so I could change once before I went to

bed, and once again in the morning, so I wouldn't get chilled by my own sweat. I brought paper and pen, and Kool-Aid to mix with my water. I brought Mountain House chicken stew and some freeze-dried green peas, some peanut butter and honey, lots of dried apricots, coffee and Carnation instant breakfast for morning.

Jackson stood very still while I adjusted his backpack. He carries the dog food and enough water for all of us. He takes himself very seriously when he's got his pack on. He won't step off the trail for any reason, not even to chase rabbits, and he gets nervous and angry if I do. That morning he was impatient with me. "Miles to go, Mom," he said over his shoulder. I

---

4. **yin and yang,** elements in Chinese philosophy representing opposing forces. The phrase is used to describe complementary opposites.

snapped my boots into my skis and we were off.

There are not too many good things you can say about temperatures that dip past twenty below zero, except this: They turn the landscape into a crystal palace and they turn your vision into Superman's. In the cold thin morning air the trees and mountains, even the twigs and shadows, seemed to leap out of the background like a 3-D movie, only it was better than 3-D because I could feel the sharpness of the air.

I have a friend in Moab who swears that Utah is the center of the fourth dimension, and although I know he has in mind something much different and more complicated than sub-zero weather, it was there, on that ice-edged morning, that I felt on the verge of seeing something more than depth perception in the brutal clarity of the morning sun.

As I kicked along the first couple of miles, I noticed the sun crawling higher in the sky and yet the day wasn't really warming, and I wondered if I should have brought another vest, another layer to put between me and the cold night ahead.

It was utterly quiet out there, and what minimal noise we made intruded on the morning like a brass band: the squeaking of my bindings, the slosh of the water in Jackson's pack, the whoosh of nylon, the jangle of dog tags. It was the brass line and percussion to some primal⁵ song, and I kept wanting to sing to it, but I didn't know the words.

Jackson and I crested the top of a hill and stopped to wait for Hailey. The trail stretched out as far as we could see into the meadow below us and beyond, a double track and pole plants carving through softer trails of rabbit and deer.

"Nice place," I said to Jackson, and his tail thumped the snow underneath him without sound.

We stopped for lunch near something that looked like it could be a lake in its other life, or maybe just a womb-shaped meadow. I made peanut butter and honey sandwiches for all of us, and we opened the apricots.

"It's fabulous here," I told the dogs. "But so far it's not working."

There had never been anything wrong with my life that a few good days in the wilderness wouldn't cure, but there I sat in the middle of all those crystal-coated trees, all that diamond-studded sunshine, and I didn't feel any better. Apparently clinical depression was not like having a bad day, it wasn't even like having a lot of bad days, it was more like a house of mirrors, it was like being in a room full of one-way glass.

"Come on, Mom," Jackson said. "Ski harder, go faster, climb higher."

Hailey turned her belly to the sun and groaned.

"He's right," I told her. "It's all we can do."

After lunch the sun had moved behind our backs, throwing a whole different light on the path ahead of us. The snow we moved through stopped being simply white and became translucent,⁶ hinting at other colors, reflections of blues and purples and grays. I thought of Moby Dick, you know, the whiteness of the whale, where white is really the absence of all color, and whiteness equals truth, and Ahab's search is finally futile, as he finds nothing but his own reflection.

"Put your mind where your skis are," Jackson said, and we made considerably better time after that.

The sun was getting quite low in the sky when I asked Jackson if he thought we should stop to build the snow cave, and he said he'd look for the next good bank. About one hundred yards down the trail we found it, a gentle slope with eastern exposure that didn't look like it would cave in under any circumstances. Jackson started to dig first.

Let me make one thing clear. I knew only slightly more about building snow caves than Jackson, having never built one, and all my knowledge coming from disaster tales of winter camping fatalities. I knew several things *not* to

---

5. **primal** (prī′məl), *adj.* of early times; first; primeval.
6. **translucent** (tran slü′snt), *adj.* letting light through without being transparent.

do when building a snow cave, but I was having a hard time knowing what exactly to do. But Jackson helped, and Hailey supervised, and before too long we had a little cave built, just big enough for three. We ate dinner quite pleased with our accomplishments and set the bivvy sack up inside the cave just as the sun slipped away and dusk came over Beaver Creek.

The temperature, which hadn't exactly soared during the day, dropped twenty degrees in as many minutes, and suddenly it didn't seem like such a great idea to change my long underwear. The original plan was to sleep with the dogs inside the bivvy sack but outside the sleeping bag, which was okay with Jackson the super-metabolizer, but not so with Hailey, the couch potato. She whined and wriggled and managed to stuff her entire fat body down inside my mummy bag, and Jackson stretched out full-length on top.

One of the unfortunate things about winter camping is that it has to happen when the days are so short. Fourteen hours is a long time to lie in a snow cave under the most perfect of circumstances. And when it's thirty-two below, or forty, fourteen hours seems like weeks.

I wish I could tell you I dropped right off to sleep. In truth, fear crept into my spine with the cold and I never closed my eyes. Cuddled there, amid my dogs and water bottles, I spent half of the night chastising[7] myself for thinking I was Wonder Woman,[8] not only risking my own life but the lives of my dogs, and the other half trying to keep the numbness in my feet from crawling up to my knees. When I did doze off, which was actually more like blacking out than dozing off, I'd come back to my senses wondering if I had frozen to death, but the alternating pain and numbness that started in my extremities and worked its way into my bones convinced me I must still be alive.

It was a clear night, and every now and again I would poke my head out of its nest of down and nylon to watch the progress of the moon across the sky. There is no doubt that it was the longest and most uncomfortable night of my life.

But then the sky began to get gray, and then it began to get pink, and before too long the sun was on my bivvy sack, not warm, exactly, but holding the promise of warmth later in the day. And I ate apricots and drank Kool-Aid-flavored coffee and celebrated the rebirth of my fingers and toes, and the survival of many more important parts of my body. I sang "Rocky Mountain High" and "If I Had a Hammer," and yodeled and whistled, and even danced the two-step with Jackson and let him lick my face. And when Hailey finally emerged from the sleeping bag a full hour after I did, we shared a peanut butter and honey sandwich and she said nothing ever tasted so good.

We broke camp and packed up and kicked in the snow cave with something resembling glee.

I was five miles down the trail before I realized what had happened. Not once in that fourteen-hour night did I think about deadlines, or bills, or the man in the desert. For the first time in many months I was happy to see a day beginning. The morning sunshine was like a present from the gods. What really happened, of course, is that I remembered about joy.

I know that one night out at thirty-two below doesn't sound like much to those of you who have climbed Everest or run the Iditarod[9] or kayaked to Antarctica, and I won't try to convince you that my life was like the movies where depression goes away in one weekend, and all of life's problems vanish with a moment's clear sight. The simple truth of the matter is this: On Sunday I had a glimpse outside of the house of mirrors, on Saturday I couldn't have seen my way out of a paper bag. And while I was skiing back toward the truck that morning, a wind came up behind us and swirled the snow around our bodies like a blizzard under blue sky. And I was struck by the simple perfection of the snowflakes, and startled by the hopefulness of sun on frozen trees.

7. chastise (cha stīz′), v. criticize severely; rebuke.
8. **Wonder Woman,** a comic book heroine.
9. **Iditarod,** a famous Alaskan dog-sled race.

A Blizzard Under Blue Sky　　**933**

After Reading

Making Connections

Shaping Your
Response

1. If the main character had asked you to accompany her on her camping trip, would you have gone? Why or why not?

Analyzing the
Story

2. Describe the narrator, the main **character** in the story.

3. Why do you think Houston chose a **first-person narrator?**

4. What was it about the winter camping trip that proved to be therapeutic for the narrator?

Extending the
Ideas

5. What do you know about the causes and remedies of depression from sources in the mass media?

Vocabulary Study

Which item in the group following each vocabulary word is *least* related to the numbered word?

**translucent
chastise
verge
primal
rampant**

1. *translucent*   **a.** sunglasses   **b.** tin foil   **c.** stained glass

2. *chastise*   **a.** comment   **b.** scold   **c.** rebuke

3. *verge*   **a.** beginning   **b.** brink   **c.** ending

4. *primal*   **a.** ancient   **b.** modern   **c.** original

5. *rampant*   **a.** diamonds   **b.** rumors   **c.** epidemic

Expressing Your Ideas

Writing Choices

Writer's Notebook Update Using the phrases you wrote in your writer's notebook about your favorite season, write a prose description of your part of the country during that season.

Wish You Were Here Write **postcard messages** that the narrator might have sent to her housemate, her therapist, and her ex-boyfriend.

Other Options

Sunny and Cold You are the meteorologist for a Salt Lake City television station. Prepare a **weather report** for the nightly news show predicting the weather for the day the narrator is to leave on her camping trip. Videotape your weather report and present it to the class.

Brrrr! Research winter camping and present an **oral report** explaining any special supplies or clothing that winter campers need. Also, explain the dangers involved in winter camping.

Before Reading

The Janitor

by August Wilson

August Wilson
born 1945

When August Wilson was sixteen he was accused of passing off his sister's schoolwork as his own. He left school and never returned. Wilson continued his education independently at the local library while holding various jobs to support himself. During this time he began writing poetry. In 1968 he founded the Black Horizons Theatre Company in St. Paul, Minnesota. He describes himself as "a cultural nationalist . . . trying to raise consciousness through theater." In 1982 Wilson wrote his first play, *Jitney,* and others followed, including *Ma Rainey's Black Bottom* (1985), *Fences* (1986), *Joe Turner's Come and Gone* (1988), *The Piano Lesson* (1990), and *Two Trains Running* (1992).

Building Background

Expert Advice If you were to attend a National Conference on Youth, which of these experts would you like to see on the program, and what topic would you like to hear each discuss? Copy a chart like the following into your writer's notebook and fill it in. In which three topics and experts are you and your classmates most interested?

Expert	Topic
teacher	
psychologist	
athletic coach	
doctor	
parent	
police officer	
other (specify)	

Literary Focus

Allusion A reference to a person, thing, event, or aspect of culture is called an allusion. Allusions may be drawn from art, myth, literature, history, religion, or any other aspect of culture. Can you explain the allusions in these sentences?

- Carl thought he was another Babe Ruth when he stepped up to the plate.
- My chemistry teacher has a Jekyll-Hyde personality.
- It's hotter than Hades in here!

Writer's Notebook

America's Youth If you could give a five-minute speech that would be heard by young people all across America, what would you say? Write your ideas in your notebook.

The Janitor

AUGUST WILSON

A hotel ballroom. Sam enters, pushing a broom near the lectern.[1] He stops and reads the sign hanging across the ballroom.

Sam. NATIONAL . . . CONFERENCE . . . ON . . . YOUTH. (*He nods his approval and continues sweeping. He gets an idea, stops, and approaches the lectern. He clears his throat and begins to speak. His speech is delivered with the literacy[2] of a janitor. He chooses his ideas carefully. He is a man who has approached life honestly, with both eyes open.*) I want to thank you all for inviting me here to speak about youth. See . . . I's fifty-six years old and I knows something about youth. The first thing I knows . . . is that youth is sweet before flight . . . its odor is rife[3] with speculation, and its resilience[4]—that means bounce back—is remarkable. But it's that sweetness that we victims of. All of us. Its sweetness . . . and its flight. One of them fellows in that Shakespeare stuff said, "I'm not what I am." See. He wasn't like Popeye. This fellow had a different understanding. "I am not what I am." Well, neither are you. You are just what you have been . . . whatever you are now. But what you are now ain't what you gonna become . . . even though it is with you now . . . it's inside you now this instant. Time . . . see, this is how you get to this . . . Time ain't changed. It's just moved. Or maybe it ain't moved . . . maybe it just changed. It don't matter. We are all victims of the sweetness of youth and the time of its flight.

See . . . just like you I forgot who I am. I forgot what happened first. But I know the river I step into now . . . is not the same river I stepped into twenty years ago. See, I know that much. But I have forgotten the name of the river . . . I have forgotten the name of the gods . . . and like everybody else I have tried to fool them with my dancing . . . and guess at their faces. It's the same with everybody. We don't have to mention no names. Ain't nobody innocent. We are all victims of ourselves. We have all had our hand in the soup . . . and made the music play just so.

See now . . . this is what I call wrestling with Jacob's angel. You lay down at night and that angel come to wrestle with you. When you wrestling with that angel, you bargaining for your future. See. And what you need to bargain with is that sweetness of youth. So . . . to the youth of the United States I says . . . don't spend that sweetness too fast! 'Cause you gonna need it. See. I's fifty-six years old and I done found that out. But it's all the same. It all comes back on you . . . just like sowing

---

1. **lectern** (lek′tərn), *n.* a reading desk or stand.
2. **literacy** (lit′ər ə sē), *n.* ability to read and write.
3. **rife** (rīf), *adj.* full; abounding.
4. **resilience** (ri zil′ē əns), *n.* power of springing back; resilient quality or nature; elasticity.

▲ What personality traits would you say artist Hubert Shuptrine has captured in his 1976 painting, *Study of Williams?*

and reaping.[5] Down and out ain't nothing but being caught up in the balance of what you put down. If you down and out and things ain't going right for you . . . you can bet you done put down a payment on your troubles. Now you got to pay up on the balance. That's as true as I'm standing here. Sometimes you can't see it like that. The last note on Gabriel's horn always gets lost when you get to realizing you done heard the first. So, it's just like—

Mr. Collins (*entering*). Come on, Sam . . . let's quit wasting time and get this floor swept. There's going to be a big important meeting here this afternoon.

Sam. Yessuh, Mr. Collins. Yessuh. (*He goes back to sweeping, as the lights go down to black.*)

---

5. **reap** (rēp), *v.* to gather a crop.

After Reading

Making Connections

1. If you had heard Sam speak, what questions would you want to ask him?

2. **Characterize** Sam, the main character in this play.

3. Sam speaks to an empty ballroom. What do you think the empty ballroom might **symbolize,** if anything?

4. What do you think Sam means when he says, " . . . the river I step into now is not the river I stepped into twenty years ago"?

5. What advice do you think Sam might give to Salvador of "Salvador Late or Early" or Donny from "Teenage Wasteland"?

Literary Focus: Allusion

Sam's speech is rich with **allusions.** Working in groups, find the allusions that he uses and try to track down their sources.

Vocabulary Study

lectern
literacy
reap
resilience
rife

Complete the paragraph using the listed vocabulary words.

Sam, the janitor, is __(1)__ with ideas he would like to express to today's youth. Although his __(2)__ level is not as high as other experts on youth, when he approaches the __(3)__ and speaks to the empty auditorium, his wisdom begins to show. He emphasizes that the __(4)__ of youth does not last forever, and that what one sows in one's youth, one will __(5)__ in later life.

Expressing Your Ideas ———

Writing Choices

Writer's Notebook Update Reread your ideas for the speech to America's youth from your writer's notebook. Is there anything you would like to add or delete after reflecting on the topic? After organizing your thoughts, write a speech about youth to deliver to your class.

Stop and Reflect How do you feel about your youth? Is it as sweet as Sam says it is? Reflect on what you treasure about your youth and what aspects of youth you are anxious to leave behind. Write a **journal entry** reflecting your thoughts.

Futurist Connection

As we begin a new millennium, America's eyes are turned toward the future. What will life be like as the twenty-first century progresses? The following pages explore possibilities for America's future, both serious and frivolous.

African Americans
Their ranks will almost double, from 32 million to 62 million.

Hispanics
Their numbers will more than triple, from 24 million to 81 million.

THE WAY WE WILL BE

By midcentury [the year 2050], seemingly small changes in birth, immigration, and mortality rates will have changed dramatically the way America looks. Here's a preview:

Age
The median age will climb from 33.4 years to 39.3, and senior citizens will make up almost 21 percent of the population, compared with just 13 percent today. Americans also will live longer than today's average of 75.8 years. A baby born in 2050 can expect to be around for 82.1 years.

Population
In the United States, it will have grown from 255 million to 383 million. World population will nearly double to 10 billion, from 5.6 billion today.

Whites
Their numbers will remain roughly the same, rising from 191 million now to 202 million in 2050, but they will drop from 75 percent of the population to just 53 percent.

Asians
The fastest-growing group by far, they will jump from 8.5 million to 41 million.

The Jetsons, a cartoon first aired in the early 1960s, is still popular today in reruns. It features a family living in the distant future, whose lives are surrounded by technological wonders. ➤

DREAM OR NIGHTMARE?

FUTURE TECHNOLOGY

One thing's nearly certain about the future: technology will advance by leaps and bounds. Will technology help us solve present problems, and make our lives easier and more comfortable? Or will it exacerbate our problems and add new ones we haven't yet imagined? The following articles discuss the advantages and drawbacks of life in a technological age.

Waking Up in 2025: A Scenario

It is November 28, 2025: You wake up at 7 A.M. and your biometric bed checks your vital signs. "The old blood pressure is a little high this morning, my friend," the bed warns in a soothing tone. You step into the shower, and the showerhead automatically adjusts from your father-in-law's 6-foot, 4-inch, 240-pound frame to your slimmer body; the spray is rousingly forceful. You listen attentively as the shower room's personal information system reports on the overnight stock activity from Tokyo. As the shower douses you with antibacterial suds, you ask the information system for a quick personality assessment from the psychotherapeutic expert system you installed. "Hey, relax! Try to image a sun-drenched beach," you're advised. "You'll be able to handle that marketing presentation much better."

You smile, thinking about the fun you had on your last vacation in Hawaii as the shower's heat jet blasts you dry. The robotic closet-valet brings out your color-coordinated, temperature-sensitive business suit, and you quickly dress. As you leave your bedroom, you sense the temperature going down behind you and the lights turning off automatically.

You peek into the kids' room to make sure they've transmitted their homework to school and have gotten dressed for their teleclass, which they "attend" for three hours in your home's media room during what used to be a long Thanksgiving holiday.

You are now ready to face an average workday in the twenty-first century.

The Armored Cocoon

As the world grows more complicated, stressful, and dangerous, we are turning our homes into bunkers, cozy sanctuaries in which we can set up alarm systems, pull down the blinds, and imagine ourselves safe from the threats outside. A man's home was once his castle; today it has become an armored cocoon.

Technology has made this retreat from reality possible. A telephone call brings nearly all the essentials of life—from footwear to pizza—right to our doorstep. Computer games and home video supply entertainment on demand. Now a new technology, virtual reality, could send us ever deeper into our cocoons—or inspire us to emerge, like butterflies, and explore the world.

Virtual reality's power lies in its ability to simulate an alternative universe. The tiny monitors inside a virtual reality helmet depict three-dimensional computer graphics of a landscape that shifts as you turn your head. Sophisticated hand controls let you move about and manipulate objects in this artificial world. Virtual reality allows users to immerse themselves in environs they might never otherwise visit—or which exist only in the mind of a software designer. Armchair adventurers can explore the ocean bottom or visit an imaginary planet, and risk nothing more than eye strain.

The danger is that, as conditions outside our windows worsen, virtual reality may seem more appealing than reality itself. Why spend hundreds of dollars per family member to visit the Grand Canyon—fighting crowds of pushy tourists and spending the night in a grungy motel—when a computer will create a clean, quiet Virtual Canyon in the comfort of your humble abode? Especially when the computerized version lets you adjust the canyon's color scheme to suit your personal tastes? Virtual reality gives us another excuse to stay home, thereby depriving us of the social interactions that are so vital to our humanity.

Even if virtual reality doesn't supplant the physical world, it may well divert us from solving real world problems. Many of us have become addicted to video games; virtual reality's realism could make it the technological equivalent of a narcotic. We can't save the environment or fight crime if we're constantly donning a helmet and escaping to another universe.

Of course, any technological development has both positive and negative impacts. Nuclear weapons threaten us with unprecedented annihilation, but fear of their use has probably prevented several bloody conventional wars from occurring. Millions of us let our minds atrophy in front of the boob tube each night—but television also brings us valuable news shows and documentaries.

Perhaps instead of isolating us from the outside world, virtual reality will stimulate our imaginations. It is easy to think of intriguing educational applications for this technology. Instead of describing the French Revolution to school kids, we will be able to take them to 18th century Paris and let them experience it "firsthand." In college physics classes, a virtual Albert Einstein might teach relativity. Used as a mental launching pad, virtual reality might inspire us to climb off our couch and see the world— to break out of our armored cocoon.

At NASA Ames, scientist Rick Jacoby controls the movements of a virtual robot.

Future Fashions

Future Fashions

On the lighter side of the future, what will Americans be wearing by the middle of the 2000s? Film director Tim Burton and designer Donna Karan were asked to imagine what the fashion of the future might look like. The following are their visions of tomorrow's fashions.

Donna Karan believes that in the future clothing will merge with communications. "The future of fashion will focus on technology— in fabric and personal electronics," she says. Her basic "catsuit" clothing design, made of course from the latest temperature-sensitive fabrics, are enhanced by high-tech accessories, including an "info-wrist" that contains both a Filofax and a videophone.

SOLAR BAND

UNI-

THERMAL CATSUIT

INFO-

-WRIST

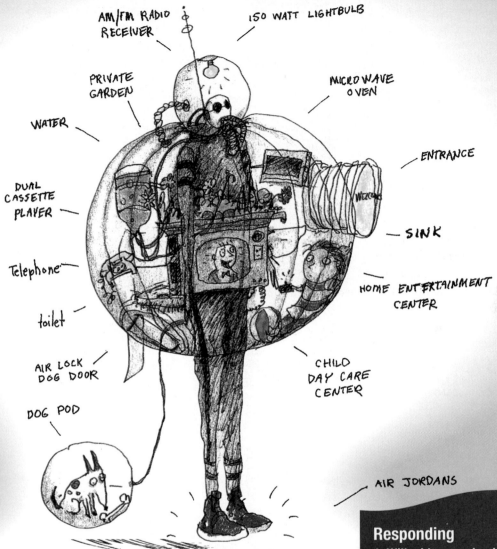

AM/FM RADIO RECEIVER

150 WATT LIGHTBULB

PRIVATE GARDEN

MICROWAVE OVEN

WATER

ENTRANCE

DUAL CASSETTE PLAYER

SINK

Telephone

HOME ENTERTAINMENT CENTER

toilet

AIR LOCK DOG DOOR

CHILD DAY CARE CENTER

DOG POD

AIR JORDANS

Tim Burton envisions a future in which our apparel will protect us from a toxic environment. This is how he explains his creation: "The bubble holds oxygen. There's a microwave, and a child has his own area to watch TV. There's an entrance chamber so you can hold hands on a date." You may recognize the all-purpose clothing underneath—it's a jogging suit.

Responding

1. Will widespread, advanced tcchnologies help or hinder us in the 21st century? Respond to the two articles you read, giving your thoughts and opinions.

2. What do you think Americans will be wearing in the 2050s? Make your own sketch of tomorrow's fashions, including an explanation.

3. The environment, technology, isolation, population growth, crime, poverty—which of these (or come up with your own) do you think will be the most important issue of the 21st century? Explain your answer.

Career Connection

How will increasing cultural diversity affect American society? Raul José Lopez has a unique perspective on this question. As Senior Vice President and Director of Syndicated Research at Strategy Research Corporation in Miami, Lopez has made it his career to keep tabs on the diverse Spanish-speaking peoples known as Hispanic Americans, who, combined, make up one of the fastest-growing groups in the United States.

Most immigrant groups in the past have been quickly absorbed into the 'melting pot' of America, but this phenomenon has not had the same influence on Hispanics. Many factors are responsible for this, including the proximity of the countries of origin, the increasing ease of communication and travel, the availability of media outlets (television, radio, magazines, and newspapers) in Spanish, and an increased focus on racial and ethnic pride in the United States in general.

The Changing Face of America

by Raul José Lopez

A ccording to projections of the U.S. Bureau of the Census, Hispanic Americans will become the largest minority group in the United States, surpassing the Non-Hispanic Black population around the year 2006. By the year 2010 Hispanics will represent 13.5 percent of the total U.S. population, and by the year 2050, the total combined minorities of Hispanics, Non-Hispanic Blacks, and Asians will represent nearly half of the total population. Thus, by 2050 nearly one out of every two people in the United States will be a member of a minority group.

I have personally seen the changes here in Miami, a city with over 1.3 million Hispanics. When I went to high school, the ethnic mix in my school was roughly 35% Black, 35% Hispanic, and 30% White Non-Hispanic. That same high school today is 65% Hispanic, 25% Black, and 10% White Non-Hispanic.

The changes in the population have led to lifestyle changes for persons living in markets with large Hispanic populations. Bilingualism has become a virtual necessity rather than a simple advantage. The interaction of the cultures has seen both English and Spanish incorporate new words. Many Hispanic American children and teens in Miami speak a combination of both languages. Further, the mixing of the cultures has affected many lifestyle factors including the food people eat, the way people dress, and their forms of entertainment.

Responding

How has cultural diversity affected your life—in education, food, dress, entertainment, personal relationships, or other ways? List as many instances as you can in which America's cultural diversity has touched your life.

Language History

Computerese

 Although some grammarians undoubtedly abhor the use of the word *interface* as a verb, nowadays it's quite common to hear that people who don't get on well with each other don't interface as they should.

This observation, in a recent article by computer expert Edward Swart, suggests the extent to which our language has been affected by computers. The term *computerese* refers to the technical vocabulary and other jargon used by people who work with computers. This term dates from the latter half of the 1950s. In the last 50 years, this word and hundreds of others associated with computers have become part of American English.

One of the strengths of the English language is the ease with which it accommodates new words. In the 400 years since the first English speakers arrived in the Western Hemisphere American English has absorbed words from a great variety of sources: American Indian languages (see page 45), the foreign languages spoken by successive waves of immigrants (page 422), dialect and slang (page 624), government, the military (page 851), science and technology, fine art, and popular culture. One major recent source of new words for American English has been the computer.

Many of these words are used largely by people working with computers and are first employed generally in their technical senses. These words include such terms as *hypertext, cursor, database, download, hard drive, internet,* and *modem.* However, as computers assume an ever larger role in people's lives, the language associated with them comes into ever more general use in contexts that have nothing to do with computers, as Swart notes above.

Writing Workshop

Poetic Insights

Assignment Among the characters in this part of the unit, which one stands out for you? Which one moves you most, interests you most? Answer these questions with a poem.

WRITER'S BLUEPRINT

Product	A poem
Purpose	To gain insight into a character
Audience	People who have read the literature
Specs	As the writer of a successful poem, you should:

❑ Choose a character from the literature you feel strongly about and write a poem about him or her.

❑ Imagine that this character could somehow read your finished poem. In it, try to give this character some real insight into his or her true self. You don't have to address the poem directly to the character ("You . . ."), but you might.

❑ Use either free verse or rhyme, whichever works best for you.

❑ Use imagery and figures of speech to dramatize your insights.

❑ Use punctuation suitable for the kind of poem you're writing. Make sure everything is spelled correctly.

OR . . .
Discuss these characters with a partner or small group. Listen to their choices and to their reactions to your choices. Use what you learn to help you choose the character you'll be focusing on.

STEP  PREWRITING

Choose a character. Review the literature in this part of the unit and choose three characters who stand out for you. Take a few minutes and jot down what it is about each character that makes him or her stand out. When you finish, look over your notes and choose the character who interests you most.

Profile your character. Go back over the selection in which your character appears and take insightful notes on him or her. Use an outline like the one shown. For your character you may want to use a different set of categories. These categories will occur to you as you review the selection. Look for quotes from the selection to illustrate your insights.

Pam Houston from "A Blizzard Under Blue Sky"

- **Skills, Strengths**
  —sensitive, a sharp observer of life: Hailey's body "seems in constant indecision when she runs"
  —resourceful: knows little about snow caves but builds one herself
  and so on . . .

- **Problems, Weaknesses**
  —"When everything in your life is uncertain"
  —"The doctor said I was clinically depressed."
  and so on . . .

- **Likes**
  —"the natural world" because it "gives you what's good for you"
  —her two dogs, Jackson and Hailey
  and so on . . .

- **Dislikes**
  —the everyday, workaday world that deeply depresses her
  and so on . . .

Make comparisons to supply yourself with ideas for imagery and figures of speech you might use in your poem. Finish a sentence like this one for each of the boldfaced words and phrases, and for any other people, places, or things that might lead to vivid, lively comparisons:

If (my character) were a _____ (he, she) would be _____ because
_____ .

> **OR . . .**
> In addition to making comparisons, design a coat of arms with images and symbols (animals, flowers, colors, designs, etc.) that you feel reflect the essence of your character.

    emotion, time of day, season, piece of furniture, jewel, plant, song, body of water, color, building

For example: If Pam were an animal, she would be a butterfly because during her camping trip she emerges from her cocoon of depression.

Try a quickwrite. First, look over your comparisons and character profile and circle the ten words or phrases that stand out most. Then write for five minutes about your character, focusing on as many of your circled items as you have time for. Write quickly, getting your ideas down as fast as they come to you. On the next page is part of one student's quickwrite.

Donny is a mess. He is a candle burning at both ends. On one end he feels burned. Hurt. On the other end, he burns others. Hurts them. And all the while he hurts himself. He keeps thinking that other people are somehow responsible for his problems. He can't seem to see that his biggest enemy is himself.

STUDENT MODEL

Plan your poem. Look back at your prewriting materials and jot down answers to these questions:

✔ What are some important words and phrases I'll want to focus on?

✔ What are some images and figures of speech I might use?

✔ What shape will my poem take? Will I break it into stanzas?

✔ Will I use rhyme or free verse?

STEP 2 DRAFTING

Start writing. Concentrate on getting your ideas down on paper. Use your prewriting materials as guides. Here are some drafting tips.

- Don't forget that your primary objective is to give insight into your character's true self.

- Be vivid and specific. Use imagery and figures of speech to lift your writing from the ordinary and everyday to the extraordinary and poetic. See the Revising Strategy in Step 3 of this lesson.

- When you finish, look back at what you've written and give your poem an appropriate title.

STEP 3 REVISING

Exchange drafts with a partner before you revise. Mark the words, phrases, and figures of speech from your partner's poem that are most memorable to you. Then, beneath your partner's poem, complete this sentence:

The insights you provide into your character's personality are _____.

Revising Strategy

Using Imagery and Figures of Speech

Don't just state your insights in a literal manner. Dramatize them with imagery and figures of speech. As you revise, look for places where an image or a figure of speech could bring an idea to life. For example:

Idea Stated Literally	Idea Dramatized
You have made things difficult for yourself	For the road you have chosen now Is nothing but bumps and ditches
He said your parents/had made life a game of survival for you	He said/you were an eagle/and you had wings/and your parents were the hunters

The image of a bumpy road brings the idea of *difficult* to life. The metaphor of an eagle being hunted brings the idea of *a game of survival* to life. Notice how the writer of the student model used imagery to bring ideas to life.

You live in a ~~place~~ *wasteland*

Of seemingly unending ~~misery~~ *emotional storms*

The ~~problems~~ *storm damage* can be ~~solved~~ *repaired*

Provided you ~~help.~~ *do the cleanup.*

STUDENT MODEL

EDITING

Ask a partner to review your revised draft before you edit. When you edit, look for errors in grammar, usage, spelling, and mechanics. Look over each line to make sure there are no careless spelling errors. See the Editing Strategy on the next page.

Editing Strategy

Avoiding Careless Spelling Mistakes

We often misspell familiar words because we overlook them—words like these:

know	now	I'm	outside	where
our	which	their	Christmas	to
we're	don't	let's	friends	they

These mistakes make us look bad. If we could learn too notice these mistakes, we'd catch them. (Did you catch the misspelling in that last sentence?) Reading your work aloud and focusing on one line at a time are both good methods for proofreading for careless spelling mistakes. See the Computer Tip for more advice.

COMPUTER TIP

If your computer has a spell checker, use it—but don't rely on it to give you perfect spelling. A spell checker won't catch a mistake like substituting *too* for *to*. Proofread your writing carefully for spelling.

STEP 5 PRESENTING

- Create a poetry portrait by drawing a border around your poem as if you were making a picture frame for it. In this border, draw images and symbols from your poem.

- Make a cover sheet with graphics that reflect the essence of the character you describe in your poem.

STEP 6 LOOKING BACK

Self-evaluate. Look back at the Writer's Blueprint and evaluate your paper on each point, from 6 (superior) to 1 (inadequate).

Reflect. Think about what you've learned from writing this poem as you write responses to these items.

✔ In what ways is the character like you? different from you?

✔ Look back at the "Make comparisons" prewriting activity and write some comparison sentences about yourself.

For Your Working Portfolio Add your poem and reflection responses to your working portfolio.

Beyond Print

Analyzing Advertising

Wait! Before you read any further, take a look at the image below. Jot down the first fifteen words or phrases that come to mind as you look at it.

t can't explain funk.

Victoria Johnson

Your list of words may look something like: *freedom, graceful, funky, young, strong, independent, freethinker, athletic, attitude,* and so on. Or it may not. But chances are you didn't include a lot of words and phrases like: *gym shoes, price, quality, materials, endurance, arch support,* and so on.

This advertisement is for athletic shoes, but that's not really what the ad is selling. Rather it's carefully constructed to sell a feeling, an attitude, a mind-set. The advertiser hopes that, unconsciously, the viewer will associate the product with the feeling so that, in a sense, buying the product is like buying the feeling.

A Closer Look

Now look at the ad again and analyze it. Start by thinking about the following concepts:

Symbolism Ads have only the split second you're looking at them to get their point across, so they often let symbols tell the story. Consider the ad on this page. What might a dancer symbolize? What message may be contained in her position—seemingly soaring through the air with arms flung out and arched above her? What might the colorful, wacky hat and sunglasses suggest? What is the advertiser trying to say through the contrast between the dancer's small, graceful, colorless body and the large, colorful, untied shoes?

Target Audience Advertisers carefully consider the age, income level, even gender and ethnic background of the people they think are most likely to buy the product. To what group do you think the ad on the previous page is targeted? Explain why you think so.

Medium Ads are everywhere—on television, radio, billboards, magazines, newspapers, trucks, even on the Internet. The medium an advertiser chooses depends on the advertiser's budget, as well as on the message and the target audience. For instance, if an advertiser wants to convince people to ride subways, a good place to advertise might be on billboards where those who are stuck in rush-hour traffic can read them.

Copy Words used in an ad are called *copy*. Often copy is kept to a minimum—perhaps even a slogan, if it's printed, or a jingle (song) if it's on radio or TV—so the audience can remember it easily. Why do you think the ad on the previous page uses the phrase, "You can't explain funk"? How do these words relate to the images, to the message or feel of the ad, and to the target audience?

Activity Options

A Critical View Choose an advertisement to analyze. What images does the ad include, and what might they symbolize? What overall feeling or message is the ad trying to convey? What is the medium, and why was it chosen? Who is the target audience? What copy is included, and why? Share your analysis with the class.

Shoe on the Other Foot Now you're the advertiser. You are selling a shoe. Decide whether it is a woman's or man's shoe, or both; an athletic, casual, or dress shoe; an expensive or economical shoe. Now plan an advertising campaign. Consider carefully your message, target audience, and medium. Create a TV commercial, magazine ad, radio jingle, or poster (billboard) for your product.

Multicultural Connections

Change

Citizens of Tomorrow The Coble parents in "Teenage Wasteland" watch their son Donny change into someone they cannot understand or help. Gary Keillor's attitude changes when his mother stands up for their family, a "watershed moment" that seems to him to "open the door to show business." Generations of tradition were interrupted when "a sister . . . relinquished her name" in "Lost Sister." A winter camping expedition changes the narrator's outlook in "A Blizzard Under Blue Sky," and Sam in *The Janitor* reminds the youth of America that, "what you are now ain't what you gonna become." These are just some of the instances of change you have encountered in "Citizens of Tomorrow."

■ Based on the changes you've encountered in this unit, would you say that change is good, bad, or both? Explain, using examples from the literature.

Activities

Work in small groups on the following activities.

1. Do we change society or does society change us? Choose one of these views and make a list of reasons that led your group to its conclusion. Your reasons should include specific examples of individuals or events, past or present, that support your group's position. Compare your ideas with those of other groups.

2. Discuss changes that your group thinks need to occur at your school or in your community. Pick one that the group feels is the most important and brainstorm possible solutions for the problem. Write an editorial to a school or community newspaper that explains your proposed change, why you think it's necessary, and what you think will need to occur for the change to happen. Read your editorial to the class before sending it.

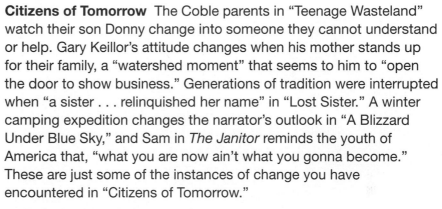

REFRESHMENTS 7up

Independent and Group Projects

Writing

Looking Ahead Donny, Gary, Salvador, the boy in "Coca-Cola and Coco Frío," the woman in "Lost Sister," the character in "Top of the Food Chain," Victor, Thomas, the narrator in "A Blizzard Under Blue Sky": What will all of these characters be doing twenty years from now? What will the world they are living in then be like? Write a short paragraph for each of these characters, telling how their lives have progressed. Compare your future scenarios with those of other students.

Drama

Shared Wisdom Sam in *The Janitor* has a lot to say to the young people of today. Working with a partner, choose one of the other characters in this unit and pair him or her up with Sam. Create and present a conversation between Sam and the character in which the character confides in Sam some of his or her concerns and thoughts, and Sam shares the wisdom he has acquired through years of thoughtful living.

Geography

Where in the World is Borneo? Many of the selections in this unit mention a specific place. In a group, list all of the places mentioned in the works. Divide the places up among the group members. Locate the places on a map and do some research into each place's history, climate, and peoples. Present the information to the class in the form of a labeled world map, and take turns telling about the places.

Entertainment

Quiz Show In a group, create your own television quiz show by gathering bits and facts about the people and events from the Unit 8 literature. You will ask volunteer contestants from your classroom audience questions about the characters, events, settings, and so on, and assign points for each correct answer. Or, you may want to have students guess letters to fill in phrases from the literature, Wheel-of-Fortune style. Have fun with your quiz show: create an appropriate set, choose a good show host, and provide real or imaginary "fabulous prizes" as incentives for your contestants.

THE
MEDIA

THEMES
IN AMERICAN
LITERATURE

THE MEDIA

From the days of Benjamin Franklin's best-selling publication *Poor Richard's Almanac* in the mid-1700s to the Internet today, Americans have been enthusiastic users of an extraordinary variety of communication and entertainment media: books, newspapers, magazines, advertising, movies, radio, television, computers. The media have informed and misinformed, shaped and distorted, amused and annoyed Americans from the beginning.

PHOTOGRAPHERS LIKE THESE HAVE HOUNDED CELEBRITIES IN THE 20TH CENTURY AND HELPED CREATE THE FRENZIED ATMOSPHERE SURROUNDING "MEDIA EVENTS."

Ballyhoo and Media Blitz

In the future, everyone will be world-famous for fifteen minutes.

ANDY WARHOL (1968)

In Only Yesterday, *his social history of the 1920s, Frederick Lewis Allen describes the origins of what was known then as "ballyhoo" and might now be described as a "media blitz."*

I t was the tragedy of Floyd Collins, perhaps, which gave the clearest indication up to that time of the unanimity with which the American people could be excited over a quite unimportant event if only it were dramatic enough.

Floyd Collins was an obscure young Kentuckian who had been exploring an underground passage five miles from Mammoth Cave. . . . Some 125 feet from daylight he was caught by a cave-in which pinned his foot under a huge rock. . . . Only a few people might have heard of Collins's predicament if W. B. Miller of the *Louisville Courier-Journal* had not been slight of stature, daring, and an able reporter. Miller wormed his way down the slippery, tortuous passageway to interview Collins, became engrossed in the efforts to rescue the man, described them in vivid dispatches—and to his amazement found that the whole country was turning to watch the struggle. Collins's plight contained those elements of dramatic suspense and individual conflict with fate which make a great news story, and every city editor, day after day, planted it on page one. When Miller arrived at Sand Cave he had found only three men at the entrance. . . . A fortnight later there was a city of a hundred or more tents there and the milling crowds had to be restrained by barbed-wire barriers and State troops with drawn bayonets; and on February 17, 1925, even *The New York Times* gave a three-column page-one headline to the news of the dénouement:

Find Floyd Collins Dead in Cave Trap on 18th Day; Lifeless at Least 24 Hours; Foot Must Be Amputated to Get Body Out

Within a month, as Charles Merz later reminded readers of the *New Republic,* there was a cave-in in a North Carolina mine in which 71 men were caught and 53 actually lost. It attracted no great notice. It was "just a mine disaster." . . .

FREDERICK LEWIS ALLEN (1931)

A recent account of a media blitz surrounding a tragic event was reported in the following article from The New York Times *on television coverage of the earthquake that struck Los Angeles on January 14, 1994.*

There's always a positive media spin for tragedy. In Los Angeles, it is that a city racked by racial and class divisions has come together after the earthquake. On TV and in the papers we are told how African-Americans, Latinos, Asians, Middle Easterners, and Anglos have laid down their arms—literal and rhetorical— to pitch in and help their neighbors. But the truth is that even in disaster, the fault lines that divide L.A. are there for all to see.

Take the way the city's two largest ethnic groups have responded. The quake thrust Anglo suburbia into an unaccustomed dramatic role: when the shaking stopped, neighbors spilled into the streets, offering each other gallons of water, flashlights, words of reassurance. Normally, the brick walls between their homes are so high that neighbors rarely speak, much less borrow sugar. Now, with all those bricks in dusty piles on the sidewalks, people greet each other like long-lost relatives.

A world away in the Latino immigrant barrios, such solidarity is the survival mechanism of daily life. The firetrap apartment buildings have the thinnest of walls. Trained for disaster by war and poverty in their native countries, residents see tragedy as inevitable as a heart attack, a car accident or a stray bullet. After the quake, there was more resignation in the barrios than chaos or hysteria; once again tragedy had struck and once again it had to be overcome. . . .

On the morning of the quake, in the pancaked parking lot of the Northridge Fashion Mall, Salvador Peña, an immigrant from El Salvador, was trapped beneath tons of concrete. He was saved because the street sweeper he was driving around at 4:30 A.M. protected him from falling debris like a steel womb. Live on TV, firefighters worked for hours before freeing him. Throughout the ordeal, rescuers assured us, the man was in good spirits, although few could be sure what he was saying since only one spoke Spanish.

Yes, this rescue assured us, good will can guide us through tragedy. . . .

RUBÉN MARTÍNEZ (1994)

"Yellow Journalism" and the Spanish-American War

In the late 1890s, two New York newspapers, Joseph Pulitzer's World *and William Randolph Hearst's* Journal, *were engaged in a circulation war. As part of their effort to attract readers, the two papers vied with each other in publishing lurid stories about Spanish atrocities in Cuba. This sensationalistic "yellow journalism" (from the name of a* World *comic strip, "The Yellow Kid") helped feed the war fever in the United States that led to the outbreak of the Spanish-American War in 1898. In the following passage, a correspondent who covered the war defends "yellow journalism."*

It has been said by those calm students of human events who were untroubled by the cries of oppressed Cuba, that the war between the United States and Spain was the work of "yellow newspapers"—that form of American journalistic energy which is not content merely to print a daily record of history, but seeks to take part in events as an active and sometimes decisive agent. . . . As one of the multitude who served in that crusade of "yellow journalism" . . . I can bear witness to the martyrdom of men who suffered all but death—and some, even death itself—in those days of darkness.

It may be that a desire to sell their newspapers influenced some of the "yellow editors," just as a desire to gain votes inspired some of the political orators. But

that was not the chief motive; for if ever any human agency was thrilled by the consciousness of its moral responsibility, it was "yellow journalism" in the never-to-be-forgotten months before the outbreak of hostilities, when the masterful Spanish minister at Washington seemed to have the influence of every government in the world behind him in his effort to hide the truth and strangle the voice of humanity. . . .

If the war against Spain is justified in the eyes of history, then "yellow journalism" deserves its place among the most useful instrumentalities of civilization. It may be guilty of giving the world a lopsided view of a few things and ignoring others, it may offend the eye by typographical violence, it may sometimes proclaim its own deeds too loudly; but it has never deserted the cause of the poor and downtrodden; it has never taken bribes,—and that is more than can be said of its most conspicuous critics.

One of the accusations against "yellow journalism" is that it steps outside of the legitimate business of gathering news and commenting upon it—that it acts. It is argued that a newspaper which creates events and thus creates news, cannot, in human nature, be a fair witness.

There is a grain of truth in this criticism; but it must not be forgotten that the very nature of journalism enables it to act in the very heart of events at critical moments and with knowledge not possessed by the general public; that what is everybody's business and the business of nobody in particular, is the journalist's business.

JAMES CREELMAN (1901)

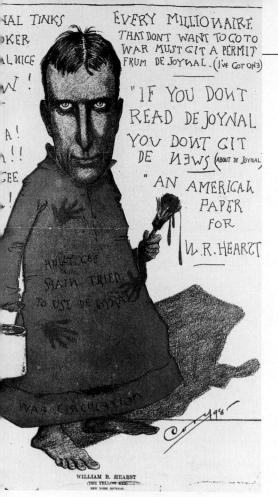

THIS CARTOON SHOWS NEWSPAPER
PUBLISHER WILLIAM RANDOLPH
HEARST AS "THE YELLOW KID."

Nast Attacks
Boss Tweed

*In the years after the Civil War, Thomas
Nast (1840–1902) became America's
most influential political cartoonist. Nast's
cartoons helped overthrow William Marcy
"Boss" Tweed (1828–1878), leader of a
group of corrupt politicians who controlled
the government of New York City in the
1860s and early 1870s. Tweed himself
admitted their effectiveness: "I don't care
a straw for your newspaper articles. My
constituents don't know how to read, but
they can't help seeing them . . . pictures."*

A GROUP OF VULTURES
WAITING FOR THE
STORM TO "BLOW
OVER"— "LET US PREY"

THE NEWSSTAND

A newsstand is a good introduction to the popular mythology of a culture. The one at left was photographed in 1938 by John Vauhon in Omaha, Nebraska. The supermarket tabloids above are contemporary.

Bigfoot
Captured!

Elvis is Alive!

*World War II
Bomber Found
on Moon!*

63-year-old
Mom Gives
Birth to
Alien Twins!

Fanzines

While much of the media has become more and more high-tech, one determinedly low-tech media phenomenon of recent years is the fanzine (short for "fan magazine" and abbreviated still further to zine or 'zine). Zines are generally addressed to small audiences of enthusiasts (typical print runs are usually fewer than 2,000 copies) and deal with a bewildering variety of subjects from the serious to the trivial. Diseased Pariah News, for example, gives a sardonically humorous view of living with AIDS; The I Hate Brenda Newsletter is devoted to attacking former Beverly Hills 90210 star Shannen Doherty. The basic point of zines is to give their creators a voice. A sampling of fanzines is shown below.

My zine is just about me. . . . about how I wanted to be a famous writer and about all the other stuff that occupied my narcissistic little mind. Hair trouble. My crush on Danny Bonaduce. My sinus problems.

PAGAN KENNEDY,
CREATOR OF *PAGAN'S HEAD*
(1995)

TALK
SHOWS

Talk shows are radio or television programs where the famous or just outrageous are allowed to spout their views on a chosen topic, the more controversial the better (for ratings if not for the moral tone of the proceedings). Among the most famous talk show hosts are radio's Rush Limbaugh and television's Oprah Winfrey.

[Talk shows] are on to something. The frayed edges should be cut off. These shows have great relevance to tens of millions, but sometimes the moral message is obscured by a burlesque theater.

GERALDO RIVERA (1995)

Video Games

Among the most popular forms of interactive media are

video games, played on television screens or video monitors

hooked up to a microcomputer system. A sampling of video

games is shown below.

T h e
I n t e r n e t

Perhaps the most dramatic event in recent media history has been the rapid development of the Internet, a worldwide network of linked computers that offer users access to a tremendous range of information and services. The home page for the Smithsonian Institution Internet site appears above.

RESPONDING

1. In your opinion, what are the most important characteristics of a "media event"?
2. What examples of "yellow journalism" (page 958) can you find in the media today?
3. What is your favorite headline from a supermarket tabloid?
4. In general, do you think radio and TV talk shows serve a useful purpose? Why or why not?
5. Should there be any attempt to control the content of material in video games or on the Internet? Why or why not?

Glossaries, Handbooks, and Indexes

Glossary of Literary Terms 968

Glossary of Vocabulary Words 975

Language and Grammar Handbook 985

Index of Skills and Strategies 1003

Index of Fine Art and Artists 1011

Index of Authors and Titles 1013

Text Acknowledgments 1015

Illustration Acknowledgments 1017

Glossary of Literary Terms

Words within entries in SMALL CAPITAL LETTERS refer to other entries in the Glossary of Literary Terms.

alliteration (ə lit′ə rā′shən), the REPETITION of consonant sounds at the beginnings of words or within words, particularly in accented syllables. It can be used to reinforce meaning, unify thought, or create a musical effect.

> *S*inuous *s*outhward and *s*inuous northward
>   the *sh*immering band
> Of the *s*and-beach *f*astens the *fr*inge of
>   the marsh to the *f*olds of the land.
>   Lanier, from "The Marshes of Glynn"

allusion (ə lü′zhən), a brief reference to a person, event, place, real or fictitious, or to a work of art.

analogy (ə nal′ə jē), a comparison made between two basically different things. Frequently an unfamiliar object or idea will be explained through comparison to a familiar one.

anastrophe (ə nas′trə fē) See INVERSION.

antagonist (an tag′ə nist), a character in a story or play who opposes the chief character or PROTAGONIST. In Freeman's "The Revolt of 'Mother'" (page 468), "Father" is the antagonist.

aphorism See MAXIM.

apostrophe (ə pos′trə fē), a figure of speech in which an absent person, an abstract concept, or an inanimate object is directly addressed. Melville addresses an inaminate object, the Shenandoah Valley, in "The Portent" (page 308):

> Hanging from the beam,
>   Slowly swaying (such the law),
> Gaunt the shadow on your green,
>   Shenandoah.

assonance (as′n əns), the REPETITION of similar vowel sounds followed by different consonant sounds in stressed syllables or words. *Hate* and *great* are examples of rhyme; *hate* and *sail* are examples of assonance.

autobiography See BIOGRAPHY.

ballad, a NARRATIVE song or poem passed on in the oral tradition. It often makes use of REPETITION and DIALOGUE. "El Corrido de Gregorio Cortez" (page 398) is a ballad.

biography, an account of a person's life written by someone else. AUTOBIOGRAPHY is the story of a person's life written by the person who lived it.

blank verse, unrhymed IAMBIC PENTAMETER:
> *See the first four lines of "Birches" (page 639).*

cacophony (ka kof′ə nē), a succession of harsh, discordant sounds in either poetry or prose, used to achieve a specific effect. Note the harsh, somewhat explosive sounds in these lines:

> Too much horrified to speak,
> They can only shriek, shriek,
>   Out of tune,
> In a clamorous appealing to the mercy of the fire,
> In a mad expostulation with the deaf and frantic
>   fire. . . .
>
>   Poe, from "The Bells"

characterization, the methods an author uses to develop a character. A character's physical traits and personality may be described, as in the first two paragraphs of "A Worn Path" (page 667); a character's speech and behavior may be presented, as in "The Life You Save May Be Your Own" (page 720); or the thoughts and feelings of a character may be shown, as in "The Jilting of Granny Weatherall" (page 611). Characters can be described as either round or flat. A round character is fully developed and exhibits a variety of human traits. A flat character displays few, if any, distinguishing features.

climax, the decisive point in a story or play when the problem must be resolved in one way or another. In "The Leader of the People" (page 676), the climax comes when Grandfather, after overhearing an angry Carl Tiflin, realizes that no one but Jody wants to hear his stories of westering anymore. Not every story or play has a dramatic climax. Sometimes a character may simply resolve a problem in his or her mind.
> *See also PLOT.*

comedy, a play written primarily to amuse the audience. Comic writing often appeals to the intellect, and the comic mode has often been used to "instruct" the audience about the follies of certain social conventions and human foibles.

concrete poetry, poetry in which the appearance of the poem on the page suggests the subject of the poem. "1(a" on page 577 is a concrete poem that sugests a falling leaf.

conflict, the struggle between two opposing forces. The four basic kinds of conflict are these: 1. a person against another person or ANTAGONIST, as in *Trifles* (page 455); 2. a person against nature, as in "Top of the Food Chain" (page 923); 3. a person against society, as in the excerpt from *Crusade for Justice* (page 483); and 4. two elements within a person struggling for mastery, as in Tim O'Brien's "On the Rainy River (page 812).

See also PLOT.

connotation, the emotional associations surrounding a word, as opposed to the word's literal meaning or DENOTATION. Some connotations are fairly universal, others quite personal. The author of "Leaves" (page 774) explores the many personal connotations of grape leaves and pieces of paper with his father's writing on them.

consonance, the repetition of consonant sounds that are preceded by different vowel sounds.

> The autu*mn*-ti*m*e has co*m*e;
> On woods that drea*m* of bloo*m*. . . .
> > Whittier, from "My Triumph"

Consonance is an effective device for linking sound, MOOD, and meaning. In the lines above, the *m* sounds contribute to a drowsy feeling.

couplet, a pair of rhyming lines with identical METER. See "The Spring and the Fall" (page 492).

denotation the strict, literal meaning of a word.

See also CONNOTATION.

denouement (dä′nü män′), the RESOLUTION of the PLOT. The word is derived from a French word meaning "to untie."

dialect, a form of speech characteristic of a particular region or class, differing from the standard language in pronunciation, vocabulary, and grammatical form. "Ma Rainey" (page 528) is partly written in dialect.

dialogue, conversation between two or more people in a literary work. Dialogue can help develop CHARACTERIZATION of those speaking and those spoken about, create MOOD, advance PLOT, and develop THEME.

diary, a record of daily happenings written by a person for his or her own use. The diary makes up in immediacy and frankness what it lacks in artistic shape and coherence. Examples are the excerpts from *The Diary* of *Samuel Sewall* (page 56) and from Mary Chesnut's diary (page 302).

See also JOURNAL *and* MEMOIR.

diction, the author's choice of words and phrases in a literary work. This choice involves both the CONNOTATION and DENOTATION of a word, as well as levels of usage. In "The Devil and Tom Walker," (page 240) Irving refers to Mrs. Tom Walker as "a tall termagant," a choice of words that reveals something about Irving as well as about Walker's wife, whom another writer might have chosen to describe as a common scold.

drama, a literary work in verse or prose, written to be acted, that tells a story through the speech and actions of the characters.

dramatic convention, any of several devices that the audience accepts as reality in a dramatic work. For instance, the audience accepts that an interval between acts may represent hours, days, weeks, months, or years; or that a bare stage may be a meadow or an inner room.

dramatic irony See IRONY.

dramatic monologue (mon′l ôg), a LYRIC poem in which the speaker addresses someone whose replies are not recorded. Sometimes the one addressed seems to be present, sometimes not. "The Love Song of J. Alfred Prufrock" (page 568) is a dramatic monologue.

epigram, any short, witty VERSE or saying, often ending with a wry twist.

> Let us all be happy and live within our means,
> Even if we have to borrow the money to do it with.
> > Artemus Ward

Compare with MAXIM *and* PROVERB.

epigraph, a motto or quotation at the beginning of a book, poem, or chapter, often indicating the THEME. An example is found at the beginning of "The Love Song of J. Alfred Prufrock" (page 568).

epiphany (i pif′ə nē), a moment of enlightenment in which the underlying truth or the meaning of something is suddenly made clear. In O'Brien's "On the Rainy River"(page 812), that moment comes when he realizes that going to Canada to escape the draft is no longer a possibility for him.

essay, a composition that presents a personal viewpoint. An essay may present a viewpoint through formal analysis and argument, as in the excerpt from "Civil Disobedience" (page 231) or it may be more informal in style, as in "Harlem: The Culture Capital" (page 512).

exposition, the beginning of a work of fiction, particularly a play, in which the author sets the atmosphere and TONE, explains the SETTING, introduces the characters, and provides the reader with any other information needed in order to understand the PLOT. The exposition in Miller's *The Crucible* appears on pages 64-66.

extended metaphor, a comparison that is developed at great length, often through a whole work or a great part of it. "A Black Man Talks of Reaping" by Arna Bontemps (page 524) contains an extended metaphor, with *sowing* and *planting* representing the efforts of black people and *reaping* representing the meager rewards for black people, rewards that others mostly glean.

falling action, the RESOLUTION of a dramatic PLOT, which takes place after the CLIMAX.

fantasy, a work that takes place in an unreal world or concerns incredible characters or employs fictional scientific principles. Though it does not take place in an unreal world, Hawthorne's "Dr. Heidegger's Experiment" (page 276) has other elements of fantasy.

See also SCIENCE FICTION.

fiction, a type of literature that tells about imaginary people and happenings. NOVELS and SHORT STORIES are fiction.

figurative language, language used in a nonliteral way to express a suitable relationship between essentially unlike things in order to furnish new effects or fresh insights. When Twain writes that a frog whirled in the air "like a doughnut," he is using a figure of speech or figurative language. The more common figures of speech are APOSTROPHE, SIMILE, METAPHOR, PERSONIFICATION, HYPERBOLE, METONYMY, and SYNECDOCHE.

flashback, interruption of the narrative to show an episode that happened before that particular point in the story. Alexie's "This Is What It Means to Say Phoenix, Arizona" (page 911) contains several flashbacks.

foil, a character whose traits are the opposite of those of another character, and who thus points out the strengths or weaknesses of the other character. Dee and Maggie are foils in Walker's "Everyday Use" (page 644).

folk literature, a type of early literature that was passed orally from generation to generation, and only written down later. The authorship of folk literature is unknown. Folk literature includes MYTHS, FABLES, BALLADS, and LEGENDS. "How the World Was Made" (page 6) is folk literature.

folklore, the customs, proverbs, legends, superstitions, songs, and tales of a people or nation.

Literature often borrows elements from folklore. The old legend (common to the folklore of many countries) of someone who strikes a bargain with the devil is incorporated by Irving into "The Devil and Tom Walker" (page 240).

foot, a group of syllables in verse usually consisting of one accented syllable and one or more unaccented syllables. A foot may occasionally, for variety, have two accented syllables (a spondee) or two unaccented syllables. In the following lines the feet are separated by slanted lines.

> At mid-/night, in/the month/of June.
> I stand/beneath/the mys-/tic moon.
>
> Poe, from "The Sleeper"

The most common line lengths are five feet (PENTAMETER), four feet (tetrameter), and three feet (trimeter). The lines above are iambic tetrameter.

See also RHYTHM.

foreshadowing, a hint given to the reader of what is to come. In "The Revolt of 'Mother'" (page 468), mother's revolt is foreshadowed from the moment her husband reveals that a new barn instead of a house is being built.

free verse, a type of poetry that differs from conventional verse forms in being "free" from a fixed pattern of METER and RHYME, but using RHYTHM and other poetic devices. Walt Whitman (page 360) was the first recognized poet to use free verse extensively.

genre (zhän′rə), a form or type of literary work. DRAMA, the NOVEL, the SHORT STORY, and the poem are all genres. Subheadings under these types are also called genres: the mystery, the myth, and fantasy, for example.

hero, the central character in a NOVEL, SHORT STORY, DRAMA, or other work of fiction. When the central character is a woman, she is sometimes called a *heroine.* The term *hero,* however, can be used to refer to both males and females.

historical narrative, a nonfiction prose account of real people, places, and events, such as Bradford's *Of Plymouth Plantation* (page 31).

hyperbole (hī pėr′bə lē), great exaggeration. The effect may be serious or comic. American folklore abounds with hyperbole, such as the story about the man who was so stingy that he stood on one foot at a time to avoid wearing out his shoes. There is hyperbole in "The Jumping Frog of Calaveras County" (page 390) by Mark Twain.

iamb (ī′amb), a two-syllable metrical FOOT consisting of an unaccented syllable followed by an accented syllable, as in the word *until.*

idiom, an expression whose meaning cannot be understood from the ordinary meanings of the words in it. To "smell a rat" indicates suspicion and to "get cold feet" describes an unwillingness to do something; both are idioms.

imagery, the sensory details that provide vividness in a literary work and tend to arouse emotions in a reader that abstract language does not. Houston's "A Blizzard Under Blue Sky" (page 930) contains many sensory details.

inference, a reasonable conclusion about the behavior of a character or the meaning of an event, drawn from the limited information presented by the author. After reading "In Another Country" by Hemingway (page 580), one might infer that this is a story about human isolation and that the physical wounds of the soldiers symbolize the emotional scars of alienation.

interior monologue, a technique used by writers to present the stream of consciousness of a fictional character, either directly by presenting what is passing through the character's mind or indirectly by the author's selection of and comments upon the character's thoughts. Olsen's "I Stand Here Ironing" (page 732) consists entirely of interior monologue.

inversion A reversal of the usual order of the parts of a sentence, primarily for emphasis or to achieve a certain RHYTHM or RHYME. In this example both lines contain inversion.

> In a branch of a willow hid
> Sings the evening Caty-did. . . .
> > Freneau, from "To a Caty-Did"

irony, the term used to describe a contrast between what appears to be and what really is. In *verbal irony,* the intended meaning of a statement or work is different from (often the opposite of) what the statement or work literally says. *Understatement,* in which an idea is expressed less emphatically than it might be, is a form of verbal irony often used for humorous or cutting effect. In "Gary Keillor" (page 876), Garrison Keillor uses understatement when he comments on two talent show acts by his fellow classmates: "I enjoyed watching these dogs, strictly from a professional point of view." *Irony of situation* refers to an occurrence that is contrary to what is expected or intended, as in "Richard Cory"

(page 576). *Dramatic irony* refers to a situation in which events or facts not known to a character on stage or in a fictional work are known to another character and the audience or reader.

legend, a story handed down from the past, often associated with some period in the history of a people. A legend differs from a MYTH in having some historical truth and often less of the supernatural. There are many legends about Pocohantas but relatively little is actually known about her.

local color, a type of regional writing that focuses on a particular locale and the peculiarities of speech, dress, custom, and landscape that make it distinctive. Willa Cather is a writer who explores the effects that setting has on character.

lyric, a poem, usually short, that expresses some basic emotion or state of mind. It usually creates a single impression and is highly personal. It may be rhymed or unrhymed. "One Art" (page 772) fulfills the qualifications of a lyric.

maxim, a brief saying embodying a moral, such as "Eat not to dullness: drink not to elevation" [Benjamin Franklin]. It is also called an aphorism.

memoir (mem′wär), a form of AUTOBIOGRAPHY that is more concerned with personalities, events, and actions of public importance than with the private life of the writer, for example the excerpt from Ulysses S. Grant's *Memoirs* (page 322).

metaphor, a figure of speech that makes a comparison, without *like* or *as,* between two basically unlike things. This comparison may be stated (She was a stone) or implied (Her stony silence filled the room).
(See also SIMILE and FIGURATIVE LANGUAGE.)

meter, the pattern of stressed and unstressed syllables in POETRY.
See also RHYTHM and FOOT.

metonymy (mə ton′ə mē), a figure of speech in which a specific word naming an object is substituted for another word with which it is closely associated, as when the term "city hall" is used to refer to a mayor, or "the bench" is used to refer to persons who sit as judges.

monologue, an extended speech given by one speaker. It differs from a SOLILOQUY, which is the extended speech of a character on stage who is in effect talking to himself or herself and expressing inner thoughts aloud.

mood, the overall atmosphere or prevailing emotional aura of a work. Words such as *mysterious, hypnotic, dreamlike, vibrant,* and *nostalgic* can be used to describe mood.

See TONE *for a comparison.*

moral, the lesson or inner meaning to be learned from a FABLE, TALE, or other story.

motivation, the process of presenting a convincing cause for the actions of a character in a dramatic or fictional work in order to justify those actions. Motivation usually involves a combination of external events and the character's psychological traits. In "The Life You Save May Be Your Own" (page 720), Mr. Shiftlet's agreeing to marry Lucynell seems plausible, given his interest in acquiring Mrs. Crater's car.

myth, a traditional story connected with the religion of a people, usually attempting to account for something in nature. "How the World Was Made" (page 6) can be described as a myth.

narrative, a story or account of an event or a series of events. It may be either fictional or true and told in poetry or prose.

narrative poetry, a poem that tells a story or recounts a series of events. It may be either long or short. BALLADS are types of narrative poetry.

narrator, the teller of a story. The teller may be a character in the story, as in O'Brien's "On the Rainy River" (page 812); an anonymous voice outside the story, as in Welty's "A Worn Path" (page 667); or the author, as in the excerpt from Kingston's *Woman Warrior* (page 754). A narrator's attitude toward his or her subject can range from one of indifference to one of extreme conviction and feeling.

See also PERSONA *and* POINT OF VIEW.

nonfiction, any writing that is not FICTION; any type of prose that deals with real people and happenings. BIOGRAPHY and history are types of nonfiction. The excerpt from Bradford's *Of Plymouth Plantation* (page 31) is nonfiction.

novel, a long work of NARRATIVE prose fiction dealing with characters, situations, and SETTINGS that imitate those of real life. Among the authors in this text who have written novels are Nathaniel Hawthorne, Mark Twain, Ernest Hemingway, Richard Wright, Eudora Welty, and Amy Tan.

novella, a story that is longer than a SHORT STORY usually is, but shorter than a NOVEL.

onomatopoeia (on′ə mat′ə pē′ə), a word or words used in such a way that the sound imitates the sound of the thing spoken of. Some single words in which sound suggests meaning are *hiss, smack, buzz,* and *hum.*

parable, a brief fictional work that concretely illustrates an abstract idea or teaches some lesson. It differs from a FABLE in that its characters are generally people rather than animals.

paradox, a statement, often metaphorical, that seems to be self-contradictory but that has valid meaning, as in Thoreau's statement from *Walden*: "I never found the companion that was so companionable as solitude."

pentameter a metrical line of five feet.

> O star/of morn-/ing and/of lib-/erty!
> O bring-/er of/the light,/whose splen-/dor shines
> Above/the dark-/ness of/the Ap-/pennines,
> Forerun-/ner of/the day/that is/to be!
> Longfellow, from *Divina Commedia*

persona (pər sō′nə), the mask or voice of the author or the author's creation in a particular work. T. S. Eliot is the author of "The Love Song of J. Alfred Prufrock" (page 568), but the persona is Prufrock, through whom Eliot speaks. In "The Devil and Tom Walker" (page 240), Irving has assumed a voice or persona, gently ironic, somewhat indulgent, in telling the story.

personification, the representation of abstractions, ideas, animals, or inanimate objects as human beings by endowing them with human qualities. Death is personified in Dickinson's "Because I Could Not Stop for Death" (page 357). Personification is one kind of FIGURATIVE LANGUAGE.

play See DRAMA.

plot, a series of happenings in a literary work.

poetry, a type of literature that creates an emotional response by the imaginative use of words patterned to produce a desired effect through RHYTHM, sound, and meaning. Poetry may be rhymed or unrhymed. Some forms of poetry are the ODE, LYRIC, SONNET, BALLAD, and ELEGY.

point of view, the vantage point from which an author presents the actions and characters of a story. The story may be related by a character (the *first-person* point of view), as in Hemingway's "In Another Country" (page 580); or the story may be told by a NARRATOR who does not participate in the action (the *third-person* point of view). Further, the third-person narrator may be *omniscient* (om nish′nt)—able to see into the minds of all characters. A third-person narrator may be *limited*—confined to a single character's perceptions, as in Welty's "A Worn Path" (page 667). An author who describes only what can be seen, like a newspaper reporter, is said to use an *objective* or *dramatic* point of view.

protagonist (prō tag′ə nist), the leading character in a literary work.

proverb, a short, wise saying, often handed down from the past, that expresses a truth or a shrewd observation about life. "Haste makes waste" is an example.

pun, a play on words; a humorous use of a word where it can have different meanings (fly/fly), or of two or more words with the same or nearly the same sound but different meanings (meat/meet).

realism, a way of representing life that emphasizes ordinary people in everyday experiences. Much of the work of Welty (page 666) and Hemingway (page 579) has realistic aspects.

refrain, the REPETITION of one or more lines in each STANZA of a poem.

repetition, a poetic device in which a sound, word, or phrase is repeated for style and emphasis, as in Bishop's "One Art" (page 772), in which she repeats the words *lost* and *losing.*

resolution, events that follow the climax of a PLOT in which the complications of the plot are resolved.

rhyme, the exact repetition of sounds in at least the final accented syllables of two or more words.

rhyme scheme, any pattern of end rhyme in a STANZA. For purposes of study, the pattern is labeled as shown, with the first rhyme and all words rhyming with it labeled *a,* the second rhyme and all words rhyming with it labeled *b,* and so on.

And what is so rare as a day in June?	*a*
Then, if ever, come perfect days;	*b*
Then Heaven tries earth if it be in tune	*a*
And over it softly her warm ear lays:	*b*
Whether we look, or whether we listen,	*c*
We hear life murmur, or see it glisten;	*c*

Lowell, from *The Vision of Sir Launfal*

rhythm, the arrangement of stressed and unstressed sounds into patterns in speech or writing. Rhythm, or METER, may be regular, or it may vary within a line or work.

rising action, the part of a PLOT that leads up to the CLIMAX. In rising action, the complication caused by the CONFLICT of opposing forces is developed.

romanticism, a type of literature that, unlike REALISM, tends to portray the uncommon. It tends to deal with extraordinary people in unusual settings having unusual experiences. There is often an emphasis on the past and on nature. American romanticism is usually identified with Washington Irving, Nathaniel Hawthorne, Herman Melville, Emily Dickinson, and Walt Whitman, among others, during a period of about 1830–1865.

satire, the technique that employs wit to ridicule a subject, usually some social institution or human foible, with the intention of inspiring reform. IRONY and sarcasm are often used in writing satire, and PARODY is closely related. "Top of the Food Chain" by T. Coraghessan Boyle (page 923) is a satire on bureaucratic responses to and explanations for environmental crises.

scansion (skan′shən), the marking off of lines of POETRY into feet and indicating the stressed and unstressed syllables.

See RHYTHM and FOOT.

science fiction, a fictional literary work that uses scientific and technological facts and hypotheses as a basis for stories about such subjects as extraterrestrial beings, adventures in the future or on other planets, and travel through time. Science fiction is a form of FANTASY.

sermon, a written version of a speech on some aspect of religion, morality, conduct, or the like. Edwards's "Sinners in the Hands of an Angry God" (page 58) is a famous sermon.

setting, the time (both time of day and period in history) and place in which the action of a NARRATIVE occurs. The setting may be suggested through DIALOGUE and action, or it may be described by the NARRATOR or one of the characters. Setting contributes strongly to the MOOD, atmosphere, and plausibility of a work. The detailed, precise description of the swamp in "The Devil and Tom Walker" (page 240), for example, convinces us that if the devil is ever going to appear, he will do so in this fiendish setting.

short story, a short prose NARRATIVE that is carefully crafted and usually tightly constructed. The short story form developed in the 1800s.

simile a figure of speech involving a direct comparison, using *like* or *as,* between two basically unlike things that have something in common.

soliloquy (sə lil′ə kwē), a DRAMATIC CONVENTION that allows a character alone on stage to speak his or her thoughts aloud. If someone else is on stage but cannot hear the character's words, the soliloquy becomes an *aside.*
Compare with DRAMATIC MONOLOGUE.

sonnet, a LYRIC poem with a traditional form of fourteen iambic PENTAMETER lines. Sonnets fall into two groups, according to their RHYME SCHEMES. "If We Must Die" (page 525) is an example of a Shakespearean sonnet. The rhyme scheme of a Shakespearean sonnet is *abab cdcd efef gg.* Another type of sonnet is called Italian or Petrarchan, after a fourteenth century Italian poet named Petrarch. Its rhyme scheme is usually *abbaabba cdecde.* Both types have fourteen lines.

sound devices, the choice and arrangement of words to please the ear and suit meaning. RHYME, RHYTHM, ASSONANCE, ONOMATOPOEIA, and ALLITERATION are examples of sound devices.

speaker, the person who is speaking in a poem, as in Eliot's "The Lovesong of J. Alfred Prufrock" (page 568).

stage directions, directions given by the author of a play to indicate the action, costumes, SETTING, arrangement of the stage, and so on. For examples of stage directions, see Miller's *The Crucible* (page 62), where they are in italic type.

stanza, a group of lines set off to form a division in a poem and sometimes linked with other stanzas by RHYME.

stereotype a conventional character, PLOT, or SETTING that possesses little or no individuality. Such situations, characters, or settings are usually predictable. Examples of literary stereotypes include the dead body in the library, the wandering lone hero, or aliens who terrorize a city.

stream of consciousness, the recording or re-creation of a character's flow of thought. Raw images, perceptions, and memories come and go in seemingly random fashion, much as they do in people's minds. Actually the author orders these images and perceptions, however, as in Porter's "The Jilting of Granny Weatherall" (page 611).

style, the distinctive handling of language by an author. It involves the specific choices made with regard to DICTION, syntax, FIGURATIVE LANGUAGE, and so on. For a comparison of two different styles, see Hemingway's "In Another Country" (page 580) and Tyler's "Teenage Wasteland" (page 866).

symbol, a concrete image used to designate an abstract quality or concept. A military medal may be a symbol of bravery, a dove a symbol of peace. Often the title of a work or a repeated image is a clue to symbolic meaning. See, for example, Ana Castillo's "Red Wagons" (page 898).

synecdoche (si nek′də kē), a figure of speech in which a part stands for the whole, as in "hired hands." *Hands* (the part) stands for the whole (those who do manual labor; those who work with their hands). The term also refers to a figurative expression in which the whole stands for a part, as in "call the law." *Law* (the whole) represents the police (a part of the whole system of law).

tale, a simple prose or verse NARRATIVE, either true or fictitious. Twain's "The Celebrated Jumping Frog of Calaveras County" (page 390) is a tale.

theme, the underlying meaning of a literary work. A theme may be directly stated but more often is implied. The topic of Hawthorne's "Dr. Heidegger's Experiment" (page 276) is the experiment involving a miraculous water, but the theme concerns vanity. Not every work has a theme.

tone, the author's attitude, either stated or implied, toward his or her subject matter and toward the audience. Cabeza de Vaca's tone (page 14) is sometimes matter-of-fact, sometimes wondering. Satanta's tone (page 403) is firm and forthright.

tragedy, dramatic or NARRATIVE writing in which the main character suffers disaster after a serious and significant struggle, but faces his or her downfall in such a way as to attain heroic stature.

verse, in its most general sense, a synonym for POETRY. Verse may also be used to refer to poetry carefully composed as to RHYTHM and RHYME SCHEME, but of inferior literary value.

Glossary of Vocabulary Words

a hat	ī ice	ü rule
ā age	o hot	ch child
ä far	ō open	ng long
â care	ô order, all	sh she
e let	oi oil	th thin
ē equal	ou out	ŦH then
ė term	u cup	zh measure
i it	ù put	

ə { a in about
e in taken
i in pencil
o in lemon
u in circus }

abandonment (ə ban′dən mənt), *n.* freedom from restraint.

abashed (ə basht′), *adj.* embarrassed; ashamed.

abdicate (ab′də kāt), *v.* give up or relinquish formally.

abet (ə bet′), *v.* urge or assist in any way.

abolitionist (ab′ə lish′ə nist), *n.* person who advocates doing away with an institution or custom, such as slavery.

abruptly (ə brupt′lē), *adv.* unexpectedly.

accost (ə kost′), *v.* approach and speak to.

accursed (ə kėr′sid), *adj.* hateful.

acquiescence (ak′wē es′ns), *n.* consent given without objections; assent.

adrenaline (ə dren′l ən), *n.* hormone which speeds up the heartbeat and thereby increases bodily energy and resistance to fatigue.

adverse (ad vėrs′), *adj.* unfavorable; harmful.

affidavit (af′ə dā′vit), *n.* statement written down and sworn to be true, usually before an authorized official.

affiliation (ə fil′ē ā′shən) *n.* association or connection with a group or organization.

affirm (ə fėrm′), *v.* declare positively to be true.

afford (ə fôrd′), *v.* manage to give or spare.

aggregate (ag′rə git), *adj.* total.

agitated (aj′ə tāt əd), *adj.* disturbed; very upset.

alcove (al′kōv), *n.* a small room opening out of a larger room.

alien (ā′lyən), *adj.* strange; foreign.

alight (ə līt′), *v.* descend and lightly settle.

altitude (al′tə tüd), *n.* height above the earth's surface.

ambiguous (am big′yü əs), having several possible interpretations; lacking definiteness.

ameliorate (ə mē′lyə rāt), *v.* to make better or improve something.

amiably (ā′mē ə blē), *adv.* in a pleasant and agreeable way.

anguish (ang′gwish), *n.* great suffering.

anonymity (an′ə nim′ə tē), *n.* condition or quality of being unknown, nameless.

append (ə pend′), *v.* attach as a supplement.

aptly (apt′lē), *adv.* intelligently.

arbitrary (är′bə trer′ē), *adj.* based on one's own wishes, notions, or will.

arduous (är′jü əs), *adj.* hard to do.

articulate (är tik′yə lit), *adj.* able to put one's thoughts into words easily and clearly.

aspiration (as′pə rā′shən), *n.* a longing; ambition.

assiduously (ə sij′ü əs lē), *adv.* attentively; diligently.

assuredly (ə shùr′əd lē), *adv.* confidently, boldly.

atrociously (ə trō′shes lē), *adv.* shockingly badly.

audaciously (ô dā′shəs lē), *adv.* in a bold or impudent manner.

avarice (av′ər is), *n.* greed.

averted (ə vėrt′əd), *adj.* turned away or turned aside.

avid (av′id), *adj.* extremely eager.

azure (azh′ər), *adj.* the clear blue color of the unclouded sky.

barbarous (bär′bər əs), *adj.* not civilized; savage.

barren (bar′ən), *adj.* infertile or sterile; empty.

begrudge (bi gruj′), v. be reluctant to give or allow (something).

beguile (bi gīl′), v. entertain; amuse. Also deceive; delude.

belie (bi lī′), v. give a false idea of; misrepresent.

benevolent (bə nev′ə lənt), adj. kindly; charitable; wishing to promote the happiness of others.

bestow (bi stō′), v. give as a gift.

blatantly (blāt′nt lē), adv. obviously or flagrantly.

blithe (blīᴛʜ), adj. happy and cheerful; joyous.

bough (bou), n. one of the branches of a tree.

boycott (boi′kot), v. to abstain from using, buying, participating, or dealing with to express protest.

breaker (brā′kər), n. wave that breaks into foam on the shore, rocks, etc.

buxom (buk′səm), adj. attractively and healthily plump.

callow (kal′ō), adj. young and inexperienced.

capitulate (kə pich′ə lāt), v. surrender.

cardinal points (kärd′n əl points), n. pl. the four main points of a compass.

cavity (kav′ə tē), n. hollow place; hole.

cease (sēs), v. come to an end or stop.

censure (sen′shər), n. expression of disapproval; criticism.

cessation (se sā′shən), n. a ceasing, stopping.

chalice (chal′is), n. a cup-shaped blossom of a flower.

chaotic (kā ot′ik), adj. very confused; completely disordered.

charnel (chär′nl), adj. deathlike; ghastly.

chastise (cha stīz′), v. criticize severely; rebuke.

citation (sī tā′shən), n. honorable mention for bravery in war.

cite (sīt), v. summon officially to appear in court.

close (klōs), adj. private; reserved.

cognizance (kog′nə zəns), n. awareness.

commodious (kə mō′dē əs), adj. spacious; roomy.

compel (kəm pel′), v. drive or urge with force.

compensate (kom′pən sāt), v. make an equal return.

complacency (kəm plā′sn sē), n. a self-satisfaction; a sense of security.

comport (kəm pôrt′), v. conduct (oneself) in a certain manner; behave.

conclusive (kən klü′siv), adj. decisive; convincing.

condoning (kən dōn′ing), n. forgiving or overlooking.

conjecture (kən jek′chər), n. formation of opinion without sufficient evidence or proof.

conjurer (kon′jər ər), n. person who practices magic.

consanguinity (kon′sang gwin′ə tē), n. relationship by descent from the same parent or ancestor.

constrain (kən strān′), v. force; compel.

contempt (kən tempt′), n. open disrespect for the rules or decisions of a court of law.

contemptuous (kən temp′chü əs), adj. showing the feeling that a person, act, or thing is mean, low, or worthless.

contemptuously (kən temp′chü əs lē), adv. scornfully.

contention (kən ten′shən), n. struggle; competition.

contingent (kən tin′jənt), n. a group that is a part of another group.

convene (kən vēn′), v. meet for some purpose.

conviction (kən vik′shən), n. firmly-held belief, certainty.

coquetry (kō′kə trē), n. flirting.

cordial (kôr′jəl), adj. strengthening; stimulating; also warm and friendly in manner.

cornice (kôr′nis), n. an ornamental molding along the top of a wall, pillar, building, etc.

corroborate (kə rob′ə rāt′), v. confirm; support.

corroding (kə rōd′ing), adj. eating away gradually.

countenance (koun′tə nəns), n. expression of the face.

covenant (kuv′ə nənt), n. solemn agreement; compact.

craven (krā′vən), adj. cowardly.

cremate (krē′māt), v. to burn a dead body to ashes.

crimson (krim′zən), adj. a deep red.

crucial (krü′shəl), adj. very important; critical.

decisively (di sī′siv lē), adj. firmly, expressing no question or doubt.

deference (def′ər əns), n. respect.

deferential (def′ə ren′shəl), adj. showing respect for the judgment, opinion, wishes of another.

defilement (di fīl′mənt), n. an act of dishonoring.

defunct (di fungkt′), adj. no longer in use.

degenerating (di jen′ə rāt′ing), adj. worsening; showing a decline.

degraded (di grād′ed), adj. lower in rank, honor, quality.

demeanor (di mē′nər), n. way a person looks and acts, manner.

demented (di men′tid), adj. insane; crazy.

demur (di mėr′), v. show disapproval or dislike, take exception, object.

deposition (dep′ə zish′ən), n. testimony, especially a sworn statement in writing.

deprivation (dep′rə vā′shən), n. act of depriving; loss.

deride (di rīd′), v. scorn; ridicule.

desolate (des′ə lit), adj. deserted.

detached (di tacht′), adj. reserved, aloof.

diaphanous (dī af′ə nəs), adj. transparent.

diatribe (dī′ə trīb), n. a bitter, abusive criticism or denunciation.

digress (dī gres′), v. turn aside from the main subject; to ramble.

dilapidated (də lap′ə dā′tid), adj. fallen into ruin or disrepair.

diligent (dil′ə jənt), adj. hard-working; industrious.

discern (də zėrn′), v. perceive the difference between two or more things.

discerning (də zėrn′ing), adj. seeing clearly, perceiving the difference between two or more things.

disciplined (dis′ə plind), adj. well-trained.

discord (dis′kôrd), n. lack of harmony; contradiction.

disdain (dis dān′), n. a feeling of scorn.

disfigure (dis fig′yər), v. spoil the appearance of.

disposition (dis′pə zish′ən), n. one's habitual ways of acting toward others or of thinking about things; one's nature or attitude.

dispossess (dis′pə zes′), v. oust; deprive.

dispute (dis pyüt′), v. argue; disagree with.

dissemble (di sem′bəl), v. hide (one's real feelings, thoughts, plans, etc.); conceal one's motives.

dissipation (dis′ə pā′shən), n. a scattering in different directions.

diversified (də vėr′sə fīd), adj. varied.

doctrine (dok′trən), n. a principle taught by a church, nation, or group of persons; belief.

domestically (də mes′tik lē), adv. having to do with one's own country; not foreign.

dominion (də min′yən), n. power or right of governing.

dormant (dôr′mənt), adj. in a state of rest or inactivity.

dusky (dus′kē), adj. somewhat dark; dark-colored.

dwindle (dwin′dl), v. shrink; diminish.

eccentricity (ek′sen tris′ə tē), n. oddity; peculiarity.

ecstasy (ek′stə sē), *n.* condition of very great joy; overwhelming delight.

effaced (ə fāsd′), *adj.* rubbed out; blotted out; wiped out.

efficacy (ef′ə kə sē), *n.* power to produce the effect wanted; effectiveness.

elixir (i lik′sər), *n.* substance supposed to have the power of lengthening life indefinitely; cure-all.

emancipate (i man′sə pāt), *v.* release from slavery or restraint; set free.

emblem (em′bləm), *n.* object or symbol that represents an idea.

emerge (i mėrj′), *v.* come into view; come out.

eminent (em′ə nənt), *adj.* above most others; outstanding; distinguished.

enact (en akt′), *v.* pass (a bill), giving it validity as law.

enfranchisement (en fran′chīz mənt), *n.* the rights of citizenship, especially the right to vote.

enterprise (en′tər prīz), *n.* any undertaking, project, or venture.

enterprising (en′tər prī′zing), *adj.* showing initiative and readiness to undertake a project or venture.

entreaty (en trē′tē), *n.* an earnest request or appeal.

eradication (i rad′ə kā′shən), *n.* complete destruction or elimination.

erupt (i rupt′), *v.* burst forth.

escalation (es′kə lā′shən), *n.* act of being increasing or expanding something rapidly in stages.

etherised (ē′thə rīzd′), *adj.* unconscious from ether fumes.

evade (i vād′), *v.* avoid by cleverness; elude.

evasive (i vā′siv), *adj.* tending or trying to evade.

evident (ev′ə dənt), *adj.* easy to see or understand.

exalted (eg zôl′təd), *adj.* noble; elevated.

excommunication (ek′skə myü′nə kā′shən), *n.* a formal cutting off from membership in the church.

excruciatingly (ek skrü′shē ā′ting lē), *adv.* very painfully; torturously.

exile (eg′zīl), *v.* banish; force to leave one's country or home.

expedite (ek′spə dīt), *v.* do or perform quickly.

exponentially (ek′spō nen′shəl lē), *adv.* in a way that involves unknown or variable quantities as exponents. In everyday use, if objects decrease exponentially, they decrease dramatically in number.

extenuating (ek sten′yü ā′ting), *adj.* making the seriousness of a fault seem less; partially excusing.

exuberant (eg zü′bər ənt), *adj.* abounding in health and good spirits.

exultingly (eg zult′ing lē), *adv.* happily; joyfully.

fathom (faтн′əm), *n.* unit for measuring depth of water; a fathom is six feet.

fetch (fech), *v.* go to another place and bring back.

foeman (fō′mən), *n.* enemy in war; adversary.

fomenter (fō ment′ər), *n.* one who stirs up trouble or rebellion.

forbear (fôr bar′), *v.* hold back; keep from doing.

foreboding (fōr bō′ding), *n.* feeling that something bad is going to happen.

forlorn (fôr lôrn′), *adj.* wretched in feeling or looks; unhappy.

formidable (fôr′mə də bəl), *adj.* hard to overcome.

formulated (fôr′myə lāt əd), *adj.* reduced to a formula; expressed in a formula.

forsake (fôr sāk′), *v.* give up; abandon.

founder (foun′dər), *v.* fill with water and sink.

frankly (frangk′lē), *adv.* openly; expressing one's thoughts, opinions, and feelings freely.

frenum (frē′nəm), *n.* fold of membrane beneath the tongue.

furtive (fėr′tiv), *adj.* sly, stealthy.

furtively (fėr′tiv lē), *adv.* done quickly and stealthily to avoid being noticed; secretly.

futile (fyü′tl), *adj.* not successful, useless.

gainsay (gān′sā′), *v.* deny; contradict.

game (gām), *n.* wild animals, birds, or fish hunted or caught for sport or food.

gangling (gang′gling), *adj.* thin, tall, and awkward.

garret (gar′it), *n.* a space in a house just below a sloping roof.

garrulous (gar′ə ləs), *adj.* talkative.

gaunt (gônt), *adj.* very thin and bony.

genetic (jə net′ik), *adj.* having to do with origin and natural growth.

gentry (jen′trē), *n.* people belonging to the upper class of society.

gravity (grav′ə tē), *n.* serious or critical character; importance.

guile (gīl), *n.* crafty deceit, sly tricks, cunning.

gyration (jī rā′shən), *n.* a circular or spiral motion; whirling.

harass (har′əs, hə ras′), *v.* trouble by repeated attacks; harry.

hedge (hej), *v.* avoid giving a direct answer.

hegira (hej′ərə), *n.* departure; flight; journey.

helm (helm), *n.* the steering apparatus of a ship.

hinder (hin′dər), *v.* get in the way; make difficult.

hindrance (hin′drəns), *n.* person or thing that hinders; an obstacle.

homely (hōm′lē), *adj.* not good-looking; plain.

hone (hōn), *v.* to perfect or make more effective.

horizon (hə rī′zn), *n.* line where the earth and sky seem to meet.

hover (huv′ər), *v.* hang fluttering or suspended in air.

humiliate (hyü mil′ē āt), *v.* cause to feel ashamed.

humor (hyü′mər), *v.* give in to the whims of a person; indulge.

hurtle (hėr′tl), *v.* dash or drive violently.

hypocrite (hip′ə krit), *n.* person who is not sincere.

ideograph (id′ē ə graf), *n.* a graphic symbol that represents a thing or an idea directly, without representing the sounds of the word for the thing or idea.

imbibe (im bīb′), *v.* absorb; drink in.

immortality (im′ôr tal′ə tē), *n.* life without death, a living forever.

impassible (im pas′ə bəl), *adj.* not expressing feeling or emotion.

impatiently (im pā′shənt lē), *adv.* crossly; in a manner showing a lack of patience.

impeccable (im pek′ə bəl), *adj.* free from fault; irreproachable.

impedimenta (im ped′ə men′tə), *n.* pl. baggage, equipment, etc., which impedes movement or progress.

imperturbably (im′pər tėr′bə blē), *adv.* calmly.

impious (im pī′əs), *adj.* not showing reverence to God; wicked; profane.

implicate (im′plə kāt), *v.* show to have a part or be connected; involve.

implore (im plōr′), *v.* beg or pray earnestly for.

importune (im′pôr tün′), *v.* ask urgently or repeatedly.

imprecation (im′prə kā′shən), *n.* curse.

impregnable (im preg′nə bəl), *adj.* able to resist attack.

improvise (im′prə vīz), *v.* make up on the spur of the moment; perform without preparation.

impunity (im pyü′nə tē), *n.* freedom from punishment.

inadvertently (in′əd vėrt′nt lē), *adv.* in an inattentive, careless, or negligent way.

inconsistency (in′kən sis′tən sē), *n.* act that is lacking in agreement, harmony.

indecision (in′di sizh′ən), *n.* tendency to delay or hesitate.

indeterminate (in′di tėr′mə nit), *adj.* not definite or fixed.

indictment (in dīt′mənt), *n.* accusation.

indignant (in dig′nənt), *adj.* angry at something unworthy, unjust, unfair.

indiscernible (in′də zėr′nə bəl), *adj.* not distinguishable; imperceptible.

ineffable (in ef′ə bəl), *adj.* too great to be described in words.

ineptly (in ept′lē), *adv.* in an awkward or clumsy manner.

infamous (in′fə məs), *adj.* well-known, but with a very bad reputation.

infinitesimal (in′fi nə tes′ə məl), *adj.* so small as to be almost nothing.

infirmity (in fėr′mə tē), *n.* sickness, illness.

injunction (in jungk′shən), *n.* an authoritative or emphatic order; command.

insidious (in sid′ē əs), *adj.* wily; sly.

insular (in′sə lər), *adj.* standing alone like an island; isolated.

insuperable (in sü′pər ə bəl), *adj.* unable to overcome.

interminable (in tėr′mə nə bəl), *adj.* unceasing; endless.

interminableness (in tėr′mə nə bəl nes), *n.* end-lessness.

interminably (in tėr′mə nə blē), *adv.* endlessly.

intricacy (in′trə kə sē), *n.* intricate nature or con-dition; complexity.

intricately (in′trə kit lē), *adv.* elaborately.

inundate (in′un dāt), *v.* overspread as if with a flood.

involuntarily (in vol′ən ter′ə lē), *adv.* in a manner that is not of one's own free will.

irked (ėrkd), *adj.* disgusted, annoyed.

jeopardize (jep′ər dīz), *v.* put in danger; risk.

jilt, *v.* cast off a lover or sweetheart after giving encouragement.

jocularity (jok′yə lar′ə tē), *n.* with a jocular (funny, joking) quality.

jubilant (jü′bə lənt), *adj.* joyful.

laudable (lo′də bəl), *adj.* worthy of praise.

lectern (lek′tərn), *n.* a reading desk or stand.

literacy (lit′ər ə sē), *n.* ability to read and write.

loathsomeness (lōŦH′səm nəs), *n.* cause of dis-gust.

maelstrom (māl′strəm), *n.* a turbulent whirlpool.

magnanimity (mag′nə nim′ə tē), *n.* nobility of soul or mind.

maize (māz), *n.* corn.

malign (mə līn′), *adj.* evil; injurious.

malinger (mə ling′gər), *v.* pretend to be sick in order to avoid work.

mandatory (man′də tôr′ē), *adv.* required by a command or order.

martinet (märt′n et′), *n.* a person who upholds and enforces very strict discipline.

marvel (mär′vəl), *n.* something wonderful; an astonishing thing.

massive (mas′iv), *adj.* bulky and heavy; huge.

meager (mē′gər), *adj.* poor or scanty; sparse.

meanly (mēn′lē), *adv.* of a small-minded nature.

meditate (med′ə tāt), *v.* engage in deep and seri-ous thought.

melancholy (mel′ən kol′ē), *adj.* sad; gloomy.

menacingly (men′is ing lē), *adv.* in a threatening manner.

mendicant (men′də kənt), *n.* beggar.

mentor (men′tər), *n.* a wise and trusted advisor.

meticulous (mə tik′yə ləs), *adj.* extremely careful about details.

mimic (mim′ik), *v.* make fun of by imitating.

morass (mə ras′), *n.* a difficult situation; puzzling mess.

morose (mə rōs′), *adj.* gloomy; sullen; ill-humored.

mute (myüt), *adj.* not making any sound; silent.

myriad (mir′ē əd), *n.* a very great number; countless; innumerable.

nadir (nā′dər), *n.* lowest point.

naive (nä ēv′), *adj.* not sophisticated.

nascent (nā′snt), *adj.* in the process of coming into existence; emerging.

nemesis (nem′ə sis), *n.* an unbeatable rival.

nominal (nom′ə nəl), *adj.* in name only.

nonexistent (non′ig zis′tənt), *adj.* having no being or existence.

notorious (nō tōr′ē əs), *adj.* well-known, especially for something bad.

obeisance (ō bē′sns), *n.* show of deference or respect.

oblivious (ə bliv′ē əs), *adj.* not mindful; unaware.

obscure (əb skyùr′), *adj.* not well known; attracting no notice.

obsequious (əb sē′kwē əs), *adj.* polite or obedient from hope of gain.

obstinate (ob′stə nit), *adj.* not giving in; stubborn.

obtuse (əb tüs′), *adj.* slow in understanding.

ominous (om′ə nəs), *adj.* unfavorable; threatening.

oppress (ə pres′), *v.* keep down unjustly or by cruelty.

opulence (op′yə ləns), *n.* wealth; riches.

organdy (ôr′gən dē′), *n.* a fine, thin, stiff, transparent material, used for dresses, curtains, etc.

ostentation (os′ten tā′shən), *n.* display intended to impress others.

pallor (pal′ər), *n.* lack of normal color from fear, illness, or death.

pandemonium (pan′də mō′nē əm), *n.* wild disorder or lawless confusion.

parched (pärcht), *adj.* hot and dry; thirsty.

parochial (pə rō′kē əl), *adj.* narrowly restricted.

parsimony (pär′sə mō′nē), *n.* extreme economy; stinginess.

pathos (pā′thos), *n.* quality that arouses a feeling of pity or sadness.

peer (pēr), *v.* look closely to see clearly.

perfidy (pėr′fə dē), *n.* being false to a trust; base treachery.

peril (per′əl), *n.* chance of harm or loss.

perjury (pėr′jər ē), *n.* crime of willfully giving false testimony or withholding evidence while under oath.

perplexed (pər pleksd′), *adj.* puzzled; bewildered.

persecuted (pėr′sə kyüt əd), *adj.* oppressed because of one's principles or beliefs.

persistently (pər sis′tənt lē), *adv.* continually.

pestilential (pes′tl en′shəl), *adj.* causing or likely to cause disease or death.

pettishness (pet′ish nəs), *n.* peevishness; crossness.

placid (plas′id), *adj.* pleasantly calm or peaceful.

plague (plāg), *v.* annoy or bother.

platitude (plat′ə tüd), *n.* dull or commonplace remark, especially one give out solemnly as if it were fresh and important.

plunder (plun′dər), *v.* rob.

poignant (poi′nyənt), *adj.* very distressing; deeply felt.

politic (pol′ə tik), *adj.* wise in looking out for one's own interests.

portfolio (pôrt fō′lē ō), *n.* holdings in the form of stocks, bonds, etc.

postponement (pōst pōn′mənt), *n.* delay.

precariously (pri kar′ē əs lē), *adv.* insecurely; uncertainly.

Glossary of Vocabulary Words   **981**

precipitate (pri sip'ə tāt), *v.* hasten the beginning of; bring about suddenly.

precipitation (pri sip'ə tā'shən), *n.* a hurrying.

preconception (prē'kən sep'shən), *n.* idea or opinion formed beforehand.

predilection (pred'ə lek'shən), *n.* a liking; preference.

premeditation (prē'med ə tā'shən), *n.* previous deliberation or planning.

preoccupied (prē ok'yə pīd), *adj.* absorbed; engrossed.

presage (pres'ij), *v.* give warning of.

presume (pri züm'), *v.* dare; take liberties.

prevail (pri vāl'), *v.* to be great in strength or influence; triumph.

prevalent (prev'ə lənt), *adj.* widespread; common.

primal (prī'məl), *adj.* of early times; first; primeval.

prismatic (priz mat'ik), *adj.* varied in color; brilliant.

profoundly (prə found'lē), *adv.* deeply felt; very greatly.

prominent (prom'ə nənt), *adj.* well-known or conspicuous.

propitious (prə pish'əs), *adj.* favorable.

proposition (prop'ə zish'ən), *n.* what is offered to be considered; proposal.

prosecutor (pros'ə kyü'tər), *n.* the lawyer in charge of the government's case against an accused person.

prostrate (pros'trāt), *v.* to bow down low in submission, worship, or respect.

prowess (prou'is), *n.* bravery; daring.

pulsate (pul'sāt), *v.* beat; throb.

pummel (pum'əl), *v.* strike or beat; beat with the fists.

pursue (pər sü'), *v.* follow to catch, chase.

pyre (pīr), *n.* large pile of burnable material.

quake (kwāk), *v.* shake or tremble.

quandary (kwon'drē), *n.* state of perplexity or uncertainty; dilemma.

radical (rad'ə kəl), *n.* person favoring extreme changes or reforms.

rambunctious (ram bungk'shəs), *adj.* wild and noisy.

rampant (ram'pənt), *adj.* unrestrained; unchecked.

rapt (rapt), *adj.* so busy thinking of or enjoying one thing that one does not know what else is happening.

raucous (rô'kəs), *adj.* hoarse; harsh sounding.

ravenous (rav'ə nəs), *adj.* very hungry; greedy.

reap (rēp), *v.* to gather a crop.

rebuke (ri byük'), *v.* express disapproval of.

recommence (rē kə mens'), begin again.

recusant (ri kyü'sənt), *n.* one who refuses to submit or comply.

redundant (ri dun'dənt), *adj.* needlessly repetitive.

reiterated (rē it'ə rāt'əd), *adj.* repeated.

relent (ri lent'), *v.* give in.

relinquish (ri ling'kwish), *v.* give up; let go.

remonstrate (ri mon'strāt), *v.* reason in protest.

removal (ri mü'vəl), *n.* a degree of distance; remoteness.

render (ren'dər), *v.* give in return; give; do.

rendition (ren dish'ən), *n.* a performance of a musical score or dramatic piece.

repentant (ri pen'tənt), *adj.* feeling regret; sorry for wrongdoing.

reprieve (ri prēv'), *n.* delay in carrying out a punishment, especially the death penalty.

repudiate (ri pyü'dē āt), *v.* refuse to accept; reject.

resign (ri zīn'), *v.* submit quietly; accept without complaint.

resilience (ri zil′ē əns), *n.* power of springing back; resilient quality or nature; elasticity.

resolute (rez′ə lüt), *adj.* determined; firm.

resolve (ri zolv′), *v.* break into parts or components.

restrictive (ri strik′tiv), *adj.* confining; limiting.

retaliation (ri tal′ē ā′shən), *n.* pay back for a wrong, injury, etc.

reticence (ret′ə səns), *n.* tendency to be silent or say little; reserved in speech.

reverential (rev′ə ren′shəl), *adj.* feeling deeply respectful, mixed with wonder.

rife (rīf), *adj.* full; abounding.

rivulet (riv′yə lit), *n.* a very small stream.

robust (rō bust′), *adj.* strong and healthy, sturdy.

rue (rü), *v.* to feel regret or remorse.

rummage (rum′ij), *v.* search thoroughly by moving things about.

scoff (skof), *v.* to show one does not believe something; mock.

scoffingly (skôf′ing lē), *adv.* mockingly; in a manner that makes fun to show one does not believe something.

scruple (skrü′pəl), *n.* a feeling of uneasiness that keeps a person from doing something.

sedulous (sej′ə ləs), *adj.* diligent; painstaking.

seethe (sēᴛH), *v.* be excited; be disturbed.

semantic (sə man′tik), *adj.* having to do with the meaning of words.

serene (sə rēn′), *adj.* peaceful, calm.

sidle (sī′dl), *v.* move sideways.

skirmish (skėr′mish), *n.* minor conflict or contest.

smartly (smärt′lē), *adv.* in a lively, keen way.

smugness (smug′nes), *n.* overly pleased with one's own goodness, cleverness, respectability, etc.

solace (sol′is), *v.* to give comfort or relief.

solemn (sol′əm), *adj.* done with form and ceremony.

somber (som′bər), *adj.* melancholy; dismal.

spasmodically (spaz mod′ik lē), *adv.* in a manner characterized by sudden, involuntary contractions of a muscle or muscles.

speculative (spek′yə lā′tiv), *adj.* reflective.

stabilize (stā′bə līz), *v.* prevent changes in, hold steady.

stately (stāt′lē), *adj.* having dignity; imposing; majestic.

steadfast (sted′fast′), *adj.* loyal and unwavering.

stealthily (stelth′ə lē), *adv.* secretly; slyly.

stern (stėrn), *n.* rear part of a ship or boat.

stiffly (stif′lē), *adv.* not easy or natural in manner.

stigma (stig′mə), *n.* mark of disgrace.

stupor (stü′pər), *n.* a dazed condition.

subtle (sut′l), *adj.* so fine or delicate as to elude observation or analysis.

subtlety (sut′l tē), *n.* fine-drawn distinction, refinement of reasoning.

suffuse (sə fyüz′), *v.* overspread.

sullen (sul′ən), *adj.* showing resentment; somber.

sultry (sul′trē), *adj.* hot, close, and moist.

superfluous (sù pėr′flü əs), *adj.* more than is needed.

superlative (sə pėr′lə tiv), *adj.* of the highest kind; above all others; supreme.

surly (sėr′lē), *adj.* bad-tempered.

surmise (sər mīz′), *v.* infer or guess.

suspiciously (sə spish′əs lē), *adv.* in a mistrustful manner.

taboo (tə bü′), *adj.* prohibited; banned.

talisman (tal′is mən), *n.* anything that acts as a charm.

tamper (tam′pər), *v.* meddle improperly.

tauten (tôt′n), *v.* tighten.

teak (tēk), *n.* made of hard, durable, yellowish-brown wood from a large tree that grows in the East Indies.

tedious (tē′dē əs), *adj.* long and tiring, boring, wearisome.

thistle (this′əl), *n.* any of various composite plants with prickly stalks and leaves.

tranquil (trang′kwəl), *adj.* calm; peaceful.

transcribe (tran skrīb′), *v.* set down in writing.

transient (tran′shənt), *adj.* passing soon; fleeting.

translucent (tran slü′snt), *adj.* letting light through without being transparent.

transpire (tran spīr′), *v.* pass off or send off moisture in the form of vapor, through a membrane or surface, as from the human body or from leaves.

treacherous (trech′ər əs), *adj.* not reliable.

treasonous (trē′zn əs), *adj.* traitorous; involving betrayal of one's country.

trepidation (trep′ə dā′shən), *n.* nervous dread; fear.

tumult (tü′mult), *n.* emotional disturbance.

tumultuously (tü mul′chü əs lē), *adv.* violently.

turbulent (tėr′byə lənt), stormy; tempestuous.

unalienable (un ā′lyə nə bəl), *adj.* permanent; non-transferable.

unremitting (un′ri mit′ing), *adj.* never stopping; persistent.

unwittingly (un wit′ing lē), *adv.* not knowingly; unconsciously.

urgently (ėr′jənt lē), *adv.* in a manner demanding immediate attention.

usurpation (yü′zər pā′shən), *n.* the seizing and holding of the places or powers of another by force or without right.

vanity (van′ə tē), *n.* too much pride in one's looks, abilities, and so on.

vault (vôlt), *n.* something like an arched roof.

vector (vek′tər), *n.* organism that transmits disease germs, such as a mosquito or a tick.

vengeance (ven′jəns), *n.* revenge.

venturesome (ven′chər səm), *adj.* rash; daring.

veracious (və rā′shəs), *adj.* truthful.

verge (vėrj), *n.* the point at which something begins or happens; brink.

vile (vīl), *adj.* very bad; foul, disgusting, obnoxious.

vindicate (vin′də kāt), *v.* justify or support.

vindictive (vin dik′tiv), *adj.* feeling a strong tendency toward revenge.

visage (viz′ij), *n.* face, appearance or aspect.

wiry (wī′rē), *adj.* lean, strong, and tough.

wither (wiŦH′ər), *v.* shrivel.

wrath (rath), *n.* very great anger; rage.

yearning (yėr′ning), *n.* strong desire; longing.

Language and Grammar Handbook

A

accept, except The similarity in sound causes these words to be confused. *Accept* means "to take or receive; consent to receive; say yes to." It is always a verb. *Except* is most commonly used as a preposition meaning "but."

◆ She did not hear the story as many women have heard the same, with a paralyzed ability to *accept* it.
from "The Story of an Hour" by Kate Chopin

◆ She sat . . . quite motionless, *except* when a sob came up . . .
from "The Story of an Hour" by Kate Chopin

active and passive voice A verb is said to be in the active voice when its subject is the doer of the action, and in the passive voice when its subject is the receiver of the action. A passive verb is a form of the verb *be* plus the past particple of the verb: *is written, had been written, will be written,* and so on.

ACTIVE: Jessica prepared dinner for the family.

PASSIVE: Dinner for the family was prepared by Jessica.

Active verbs are more natural, direct, and forceful than passive verbs. Passive verbs are useful and effective, however, when the doer of the action is unknown, unimportant, or obvious, or when special emphasis is wanted for the receiver of the action:

◆ Without elation, without an interval of moist glory, the cold was gone.
from "Winter Dreams" by F. Scott Fitzgerald

◆ Evenings were spent mainly on the back porches. . . .
from "To Be Young, Gifted and Black" by Lorraine Hansberry

adjective Adjectives are modifiers that describe nouns and pronouns and make their meaning more exact. Adjectives tell *what kind, which one,* or *how many.*

What kind:	*dusty* road	*red* bird	*brick* house
Which one:	*this* game	*that* person	*those* players
How many:	*five* weeks	*few* spectators	*many* ducks

See also **comparative forms of adjectives and adverbs.**

adverb Adverbs modify verbs, adjectives, or other adverbs. They tell *how, when,* or *where* about verbs.

How:	quickly	courageously	slowly
When:	soon	now	tomorrow
Where:	here	there	near

See also **comparative forms of adjectives and adverbs.**

affect, effect *Affect* is a verb. It is most frequently used to mean "to influence." *Effect* is mainly used as a noun meaning "result" or "consequence."

◆ . . . seeing wise Seneca was so *affected* with sailing a few miles on the coast of his own Italy, as he affirmed, that he had rather remain. . . .
from *Of Plymouth Plantation* by William Bradford

◆ At home the *effects* were no less disturbing.
from *Black Boy* by Richard Wright

agreement
1. subject-verb agreement

a. Most compound subjects joined by *and* or *both . . . and* are plural and are followed by plural verbs.

◆ The old woman and her daughter were sitting on their porch when Mr. Shiftlet came up their road for the first time.
from "The Life You Save May Be Your Own" by Flannery O'Connor

b. A compound subject joined by *or, either . . . or,* or *neither . . . nor* is followed by a verb that agrees in number with the closer subject.

Neither Josie nor the Riveras drive a van.

Neither the Riveras nor Josie drives a van.

Problems arise when it isn't obvious what the subject is. The following rules should help you with some of the most troublesome situations.

c. Phrases or clauses coming between the subject and the verb do not affect the subject-verb agreement.

◆ The helpless part of trying to do anything about it was that she did it all herself.
from "Winter Dreams" by F. Scott Fitzgerald

d. Singular verbs are used with singular indefinite pronouns—*each, every, either, neither, anyone, anybody, one, everyone, everybody, someone, somebody, nobody, no one.*

◆ Nobody seems to notice me.
from "Blue Winds Dancing" by Thomas S. Whitecloud

e. Plural indefinite pronouns take plural verbs. They are *both, few, many,* and *several.*

Many of the football players sleep on the way home.

f. The indefinite pronouns *all, any, most, none,* and *some* can be either singular or plural depending on their meaning in a sentence.

<u>Singular</u>
All the neighborhood *was* dark.
Most of the night *was* calm.
None of the shopping *is* done.

<u>Plural</u>
All the streets *were* snowy.
Most of the cars *were* stuck.
None of the groceries *are* here.

g. The verb agrees with the subject regardless of the number of the predicate complement (after a form of a linking verb).

His one *dislike was* cats.
Cats were his one dislike.

h. Unusual word order does not affect agreement; the verb generally agrees with the subject, whether the subject follows or precedes it:

◆ In me was shaping a yearning for a kind of consciousness, a mode of being that the way of life about me had said could not be. . . .
from *Black Boy* by Richard Wright

In informal English, you may often hear sentences like "There's a sandwich and a cold drink for you on the counter." *There's* is a contraction for "There is." Technically, since the subject is a sandwich and a cold drink, the verb should be plural and the sentence should begin, "There are . . ." Since this may sound strange, you may want to revise the sentence to something like "A sandwich and a cold drink are on the counter." Be especially careful of sentences beginning with *There;* be sure the verb agrees with the subject.

◆ There were times when I thought I'd gone off the psychic edge.
from "On the Rainy River" by Tim O'Brien

◆ There is an incessant influx of novelty into the world, and yet we tolerate incredible dullness.
from *Walden* by Henry David Thoreau

2. Pronoun-antecedent agreement.

a. An antecedent is a word, clause, or phrase to which a pronoun refers. The pronoun agrees with its antecedent in person, number, and gender.

antec.   pron.
Alma will tell me if she can go.

antec.   pron.
The actors knew that the audience was filled with their relatives.

b. Singular pronouns are generally used to refer to the indefinite pronouns *one, anyone, each, either, neither, everybody, everyone, somebody, someone, nobody,* and *no one.*

antec. pron.
Has somebody lost her jacket?

antec. pron.
No one remembered his ticket.

The second sentence poses problems. It is clearly plural in meaning, and "everybody" may not refer to men only. To avoid the latter problem, you could write "No one remembered his or her ticket." This solution is clumsy and wordy, though. Sometimes it is best to revise:

No students remembered their tickets.

HINT: If you can use the word *ready* alone, without changing the meaning of the sentence, *all ready* is the one to use.

all ready, already *All ready* is an adjective phrase meaning "quite ready." *Already* is an adverb of time.

We are packed and *all ready* to go.

♦ . . . he lost consciousness and was as one *already* dead.
from "An Occurrence at Owl Creek Bridge" by Ambrose Bierce

NOTE: The spelling *alright* is not accepted in either formal or informal writing.

all right *All right* is used both as an adjective and as an adverb.

♦ "I'm pretty hungry, *all right*," he said. "I'll tell you about that later."
from "The Leader of the People" by John Steinbeck

ambiguity An ambiguous sentence is one that has two or more possible meanings. The most common causes of ambiguity are these:

1. misplaced modifiers Misplaced modifiers, because of their position in a sentence, do not clearly modify the word they are intended to modify. They are also often a source of humor that the writer does not intend.

Ambiguous: The tourists saw the tower on the bus.
Clear: The tourists on the bus saw the tower.
Clear: On the bus, the tourists saw the tower.

2. incomplete comparisons

Ambiguous: Seiko likes sushi as much as Eric.
Clear: Seiko likes sushi as much as Eric does.

amount, number *Amount* is used to refer to nouns which name things that can be measured or weighed; *number* is used in referring to nouns which name things that can be counted.

large amount of wood   large number of jewels
small amount of cloth   small number of books

NOTE: An apostrophe is not used in forming other plurals or in the possessive form of personal pronouns: "The tickets are theirs."

apostrophe (') An apostrophe is used in possessive words, both singular and plural, and in contractions. It is also used to form the plurals of letters and numbers.

men's league	Teresa's bracelet	can't
A's and *B*'s	6's and 7's	wasn't

Apostrophes may be used to indicate places in words in which the speaker does not pronounce certain sounds.

◆ "They're digging a cellar, I *s'pose,* if you've got to know."
from "The Revolt of 'Mother'" by Mary E. Wilkins Freeman

appositive Apposition means, literally, a "putting beside." An appositive is a noun or phrase that follows a noun and identifies or explains it more fully. It is usually set off by commas or dashes.

◆ Mr Frank Davis, *the sheriff,* . . .
from *Crusade for Justice* by Ida B. Wells-Barnett

If, however, the appositive is used to specify a particular person or thing, it is not set off.

◆ . . . and burned the body of the poet *Shelley* who was drowned in a storm . . .
from *Lord Byron's Love Letter* by Tennessee Williams

as, like. *See* **like, as.**

awhile, a while *Awhile* (one word) is an adverb; use two words when *while* is a noun in a prepositional phrase.

◆ Stop and rest *awhile.*

◆ For a *while* I just drove, not aiming at anything. [*While* is object of the preposition *for.*]
from "On the Rainy River" by Tim O' Brien

B

bad, badly In formal English and in writing, *bad* (the adjective) is used to modify a noun or pronoun and is used after a linking verb. *Badly* (the adverb) modifies a verb.

◆ . . . though he knew it was *bad* for him, . . . [adjective used with linking verb *was*]
from "The First Seven Years" by Bernard Malamud

◆ She wanted to see John again and point to them and say, Well, I didn't do so *badly,* did I?
from "The Jilting of Granny Weatherall" by Katherine Anne Porter

HINT: To check yourself, mentally eliminate the first term. You would never say "between we," you would say "between us," us being the objective form of the pronoun we.

between you and me After prepositions such as *between,* use the objective form of the personal pronouns: between you and **me,** between you and **her,** between you and **him,** between you and **us,** between you and **them.**

The run-off will be between you and him.

◆ Those were the only times of peaceful companionship between her and Susan.

from "I Stand Here Ironing" by Tillie Olsen

capitalization

C

1. Capitalize all proper nouns and adjectives.

Proper Nouns	Proper Adjectives
Canada	Canadian
China	Chinese
Victoria	Victorian

2. Capitalize people's names and titles.

General Powell	Uncle Jack	Grandma
Justice Ginsburg	Bishop Clark	Senator Hanrahan
Ms. Sarah Stoner	Dr. Fernandez	

3. Capitalize the names of ethnic groups, languages, religions, revered persons, deities, religious bodies, buildings, and writings. Also capitalize any adjectives made from these names.

Indo-European	Buddha	Grace Lutheran Church
German	Catholicism	the Bible
Islam	Allah	

NOTE: Do not capitalize directions of the compass or adjectives that indicate direction: Front Street runs north and south. The weather map showed showers in the northwest.

4. Capitalize geographical names (except for articles and prepositions) and any adjectives made from these names.

Australia	Tampa Bay	the Red Arrow Highway
Gila River	Danish pastry	Zion National Park
Straits of Mackinac	Spanish rice	
the Rockies	Southern accent	
Arctic Circle	Gettysburg	

NOTE: Earth, sun, and moon are not capitalized unless used with the names of other planets: Is Venus closer to the Sun than Saturn? The earth revolves around the sun.

5. Capitalize the names of structures, organizations, and bodies in the universe.

the Capitol	the House of Representatives
Carnegie Hall	the United Way
the Eiffel Tower	Neptune
the Cubs	the Milky Way

6. Capitalize the names of historical events, times, and documents.

the Hundred Years' War	the Elizabethan Period
the Treaty of Versailles	the Emancipation Proclamation

7. Capitalize the names of months, days, holidays, and time abbreviations.

February	Sunday
Thanksgiving	A.M. P.M.

8. Capitalize the first letters in sentences, lines of poetry, and direct quotations.

◆ Because I could not stop for Death—
He kindly stopped for me
   by Emily Dickinson

◆ "If you see this boy," said the ballerina, "do not—I repeat, do not—try to reason with him."
   from "Harrison Bergeron" by Kurt Vonnegut, Jr.

9. Capitalize certain parts of letters and outlines.

Dear Mrs. Moore,   Sincerely yours,

I. Early types of automobiles
   A. Gasoline powered
      1. Haynes
      2. Ford
      3. Other makes
   B. Steam powered
   C. Electric cars

10. Capitalize the first, last, and all other important words in titles.

book	Dickens's *Great Expectations*
newspaper	story in the *Washington Post*
play and movie	starred in *Showboat*
television series	liked *Murphy Brown*
short story	read "The Monkey's Paw"
music (long)	saw *The Pirates of Penzance*
music (short)	sang "Swing Low, Sweet Chariot"
work of art	Winslow Homer's *Breezing Up*
magazine	*Seventeen* magazine

See also **Italics.**

clause A clause is a group of words that has a subject and a verb. A clause is independent when it can stand alone and make sense. A dependent clause has a subject and a verb, but when it stands alone it is incomplete, and the reader is left wondering about the meaning.

Independent Clause

s   v
Richard Wright wrote *Black Boy.*

Dependent Clause

s   v
Because Richard Wright wrote *Black Boy.*

Language and Grammar Handbook   **991**

collective nouns A collective noun is one that though singular in form names a group of people or things.

    committee   mob   team   class

When a collective noun means the group taken as a whole, use a singular verb and pronoun. When individual members of a group are meant, use a plural verb and pronoun.

    The <u>class should bring its</u> petition to the study hall at noon.

    The <u>committee were</u> still in disgreement about <u>their</u> purpose.

colon (:) A colon is often used to explain or clarify what has preceded it.

◆ She said it over and over under her breath: "free, free, free!"
    from "The Story of an Hour" by Kate Chopin

◆ An old wish returned to haunt the shoemaker: that he had a son instead of a daughter, . . .
    from "The First Seven Years" by Bernard Malamud

A colon is also used after phrases that introduce a list or quotation.

◆ In any nonviolent campaign there are four basic steps: (1) collection of the facts to determine whether injustices are alive, (2) negotiations, (3) self-purification, and (4) direct action.
    from "Letter from a Birmingham Jail" by Martin Luther King, Jr.

◆ The doctor came up to the machine where I was sitting and said: "What did you like best to do before the war?" . . .
    from "In Another Country" by Ernest Hemingway

comma (,) Commas are used to show a pause or separation between words and word groups in sentences, to avoid confusion in sentences, to separate items in addresses, in dialogue, and in figures.

NOTE: If the items in a series are all separated by a word like *and,* no comma is necessary: Dolphins and whales and seals were the main attractions.

1. Use a comma between items in a series. Words, phrases, and clauses in a series are separated by commas.

◆ He had been a gospel singer, a foreman on the railroad, an assistant in an undertaking parlor, and he had come over the radio for three months . . .
    from "The Life You Save May Be Your Own" by Flannery O'Connor

2. Use a comma after certain introductory words and groups of words such as clauses and prepositional phrases of five words or more.

◆ No, somebody was swishing newspapers; no, Cornelia and Doctor Harry were whispering together.
    from "The Jilting of Granny Weatherall" by Katherine Anne Porter

3. Use a comma to set off nouns in direct address. The name or title by which persons (or animals) are addressed is called a noun of direct address.

◆ "Lady," he said in a firm nasal voice, "I'd give a fortune to live where I could see me a sun do that every evening."
from "The Life You Save May Be Your Own" by Flannery O'Connor

◆ "Certainly, my dear madam, certainly!"
from "Dr. Heidegger's Experiment" by Nathaniel Hawthorne

4. Use commas to set off interrupting elements and appositives. Any phrase or clause that interrupts the flow of a sentence is often set off by commas. Parenthetical expressions like *of course, after all, to be sure, on the other hand, I suppose,* and *as you know;* and words like *yes, no, oh,* and *well* are all set off by commas.

◆ The daughter, a large girl in a short blue organdy dress, saw him all at once and jumped up and began to stamp and point and make excited speechless sounds.
from "The Life You Save May Be Your Own" by Flannery O'Connor

NOTE: No comma is used when the connecting words are *so that:*

5. Use a comma before a coordinating conjunction *(and, but, for, or, nor, yet, so)* in a compound sentence.

◆ The world will little note nor long remember what we say here, but it can never forget what they did here.
from "The Gettysburg Address" by Abraham Lincoln

6. Use a comma after a dependent clause that begins a sentence. Do not use a comma before a dependent clause that follows the independent clause.

◆ Though the attack was very mild, he lay in bed for three weeks.
from "The First Seven Years" by Bernard Malamud

7. Use commas in punctuating dialogue. *See* **dialogue.**

comma splice *See* **run-on.**

comparative forms of adjectives and adverbs To show a greater degree of the quality or characteristic named by an adjective or adverb, *-er* or *-est* is added to the word or *more* or *most* is put before it.

Positive: Arnetta is sensitive.

Comparative: Arnetta is more sensitive than Sue.

Superlative: Arnetta is the most sensitive person in the office.

More and *most* are generally used with longer adjectives and adverbs, and with all adverbs ending in *-ly.*

Positive: The documentary was interesting.

Comparative: This documentary was more interesting than the one we saw last week.

Superlative: That documentary was the most interesting one I've ever seen.

See also **modifiers.**

conjunction A conjunction is a word that links one part of a sentence to another. It can join words, phrases, or entire sentences. Coordinating conjunctions *(and, but, for, yet, or, nor, so)* connect words, phrases, and clauses of equal value. Subordinating conjunctions *(after, because, so that, unless, while,* and so on) connect dependent, or subordinate, clauses with main clauses.

Coordinating	Subordinating
rose *and* fell	Sara worked quickly *until* the
She came yesterday,	dishes were done.
but left today.	

D **dangling modifiers** A modifier that has no word in a sentence which it can modify is said to be dangling. The italicized words in the first sentence seem, illogically, to modify *concert.*

Dangling: *Seated in the balcony,* the concert sounded magnificent.

Revised: The concert sounded magnificent to the audience seated in the balcony.

dash (—) A dash is used to indicate a sudden break or change of thought in a sentence:

◆ And yet she had loved him—sometimes.
   from "The Story of an Hour" by Kate Chopin

dialogue Dialogue is often used to enliven many types of writing. Notice the punctuation, capitalization, and paragraphing of the following passage.

◆ "What is that? he asked.
"A story," I said.
"A news story?"
"No, fiction."
"All right, I'll read it," he said.
He pushed my composition book back on his desk and looked at me curiously, sucking at his pipe.
   "But I want you to read it *now,*" I said.
      from *Black Boy* by Richard Wright

See also **quotation marks.**

direct address *See* **Comma Rule 3**

E **ellipsis (. . .)** An ellipsis is used to indicate that words (or sentences or paragraphs) have been omitted. An ellipsis consists of three dots, but if the omitted portion would have completed the sentence, a fourth dot is added for the period.

◆ "Well, what can we expect" "Yes, eighty years old. . . ."
from "The Jilting of Granny Weatherall" by Katherine Anne Porter

◆ She was too vulnerable for that terrible world of youthful competition, of preening and parading, of constant measuring of yourself against every other, of envy, "If I had that copper hair," "If I had that skin. . . ."
from "I Stand Here Ironing" by Tillie Olsen

exclamation point (!) An exclamation mark is used at the end of an exclamatory sentence—one that shows excitement or strong emotion. Exclamation points can also be used with strong interjections.

◆ "Free! Body and soul free!" she kept whispering.
from "The Story of an Hour" by Kate Chopin

See also **quotation marks.**

fewer, less *See* **less, fewer**

F **fragment** *See* **sentence fragment.**

friendly letter form A typical form for a friendly letter contains five parts: the heading, which provides the writer's address and the date, the greeting, the body of the letter, the closing, and the signature. Note the sample below.

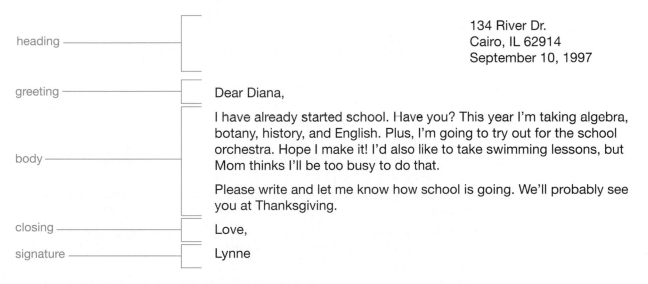

heading

134 River Dr.
Cairo, IL 62914
September 10, 1997

greeting

Dear Diana,

body

I have already started school. Have you? This year I'm taking algebra, botany, history, and English. Plus, I'm going to try out for the school orchestra. Hope I make it! I'd also like to take swimming lessons, but Mom thinks I'll be too busy to do that.

Please write and let me know how school is going. We'll probably see you at Thanksgiving.

closing

Love,

signature

Lynne

G **gerund** A verb form ending in *-ing* that is used as a noun.

◆ It means *dancing* to the strings of custom and tradition; it means *living* in houses and never knowing or caring who is next door.
from "Blue Winds Dancing" by Thomas S. Whitecloud

good, well *Good* is used as an adjective to modify a noun or pronoun. Do not use it to modify a verb. *Well* is usually used as an adverb to modify a verb.

◆ But I stayed *good* friends with the boy who had been wounded. . . .
from "In Another Country" by Ernest Hemingway

◆ And as for the decks and upper works, they would caulk them as *well* as they could . . .
from *Of Plymouth Plantation* by William Bradford

HINT: When you are referring to health, use *well* if the meaning is "not ill." "I am quite well, thank you." If the meaning is "pleasant" or "in good spirits," use *good*. "I feel good today."

H **hopefully** This is often used to mean "it is hoped" or "I hope," as in the following sentence, "*Hopefully,* I can relieve at least some of the pressure." However in formal writing, avoid this usage.

◆ I'm hoping to relieve at least some of the pressure on my dreams.
from "On the Rainy River" by Tim O'Brien

however Words like *however, moreover, nevertheless, therefore, consequently,* etc. (known as conjunctive adverbs) require special punctuation. If the word comes within a clause, it is generally set off by commas:

◆ Tom Walker, however, was not a man to be troubled. . . .
from "The Devil and Tom Walker" by Washington Irving

If the conjunctive adverb separates two independent clauses, a semicolon is used preceding the word. If it begins a sentence, a comma is used after it:

◆ He did not argue; however, as the days went by . . .
from "The First Seven Years" by Bernard Malamud

I **infinitive** The infinitive is the simple form of the verb, usually preceded by *to.* Infinitives are used as nouns, adjectives, or adverbs. In the following sentence, each infinitive acts as a noun:

◆ *To play* is *to win* something.
from "To Be Young, Gifted and Black" by Lorraine Hansberry

interjection An interjection is a word or phrase used to express strong emotion.

◆ Never lost a ball! Willing! Intelligent! Quiet! Honest! Grateful!
from "Winter Dreams" by F. Scott Fitzgerald

italics Italic type is used to indicate titles of whole works such as books, magazines, newspapers, plays, films, and so on. It is also used to indicate foreign words and phrases, or to emphasize a word.

◆ . . . perished usually at the *autos-da-fé*, and one of those had been held. . . .
from "The Pit and the Pendulum" by Edgar Allan Poe

See also **Capitalization Rule 10** for titles that are italicized.

its, it's *Its* is the possessive form of the personal pronoun *it; it's* is the contraction meaning "it is."

lay, lie This verb pair presents problems because, in addition to the similarity between the words, the past tense of *lie* is *lay.* The verb *to lay,* means "to put or place something somewhere." The verb *to lie* means "to rest" or "to be at rest."

Present	Past	Past Participle	Present Participle
lay	laid	(has) laid	(is) laying
lie	lay	(has) lain	(is) lying

Notice how the verbs are used in the following sentences:

◆ Special emphasis was laid upon them. [Stress was placed on them.]
from *Crusade for Justice* by Ida B. Wells

◆ . . . he lay perfectly quiet and listened. [He rested quietly.]
from "Winter Dreams" by F. Scott Fitzgerald

less, fewer Use less to refer to amount or quantity (things that are measured). Use fewer to refer to number (to things that are counted).

less heat	fewer houses
less work	fewer jobs
less poverty	fewer scholarships

M **media** *Media* is the plural of *medium.* Many people use a singular verb when referring to the mass media. In formal writing it is best to use a plural verb.

All the media *are* focused on the trial.

misplaced modifier *See* **ambiguity.**

modifier A modifier is a word or group of words that restrict, limit, or make more exact the meaning of other words. The modifiers of nouns and pronouns are usually adjectives, participles, adjective phrases, and adjective clauses. The modifiers of verbs, adjectives, and adverbs are adverbs, adverb phrases, and adverb clauses. In the following example, the italicized words modify the words in bold-face type.

◆ **Moving** *slowly* and from *side to side,* she went into the *big* **building,** and into a tower of steps where she **walked** *up* and *around* . . .
from "A Worn Path" by Eudora Welty

See also **comparative forms of adjectives and adverbs; dangling modifiers.**

NOTE: In formal English the correct way to respond to a question such as, "Who's there?" is "It is I." This sounds too formal in some situations, however. While it is not correct to say, "It's them," 'It's him," "It's us," or "It's her," "It's me" is generally accepted as standard usage.

NOTE: *Lied* refers only to not telling the truth: "The jury was convinced that the defendent lied."

myself (and **himself, herself,** and **so on**) Be careful not to use *myself* and the other reflexive and intensive pronouns when you simply need to use the personal pronoun *I* or its objective form *me.*

> Incorrect: Robert called Evan and myself into the office.

> Correct: Robert called Evan and me into the office.

HINT: When trying to decide which pronoun to use, remember that you would not say, "Myself is going to the game." You would use *I.* Use *I* with a compound subject, too.

Reflexive pronouns reflect the action of the verb back to the subject. An intensive pronoun adds emphasis to the noun or pronoun just named.

◆ ". . . with which I amuse myself here in my study."
  from "Dr. Heidegger's Experiment" by Nathaniel Hawthorne

◆ Even I didn't have, myself, the slightest inkling . . .
  from *The Autobiography of Malcolm X* by Malcolm X and Alex Haley

N

noun A noun is a word that names a person, place, thing, or idea. Most nouns are made plural by adding *-s* or *-es* to the singular. When you are unsure about a plural form, check a dictionary.

P

parallel construction Items in a sentence that are of equal importance should be expressed in parallel (or similar) forms. These can take the form of noun phrases, verb phrases, infinitive phrases, and prepositional phrases:

◆ I've got my own mind an' my own feet, an' I'm goin' to think my own thoughts an' go my own ways, an' nobody but the Lord is goin' to dictate to me unless I've a mind to have him.
  from "The Revolt of 'Mother'" by Mary E. Wilkins Freeman

◆ She had treated him with interest, with encouragement, with malice, with indifference, with contempt.
  from "Winter Dreams" by F. Scott Fitzgerald

◆ Nobody was smarter than anybody else. Nobody was better looking than anybody else. Nobody was stronger or quicker than anybody else.
  from "Harrison Bergeron" by Kurt Vonnegut, Jr.

parentheses ( ) Parentheses are used to enclose words that interrupt or add explanation to a sentence. They are also used to enclose references to page numbers, chapters, or dates. Punctuation marks that belong to the sentence come after the parentheses, not before.

◆ Now, when it is too late (as if she would let me hold and comfort her like I do the others), I get up and go to her at once at her moan or restless stirring.
  from "I Stand Here Ironing" by Tillie Olsen

participle A participle is a verb form used in forming various tenses of verbs. The present participle ends in *-ing:* growing. The past participle usually ends in *-ed, -t, -d, -en,* or *-n: scared, wept, said, risen, grown.* Participles are also used as adjectives, modifying nouns and pronouns.

◆ White *waving* ribbons that seem to pulsate with the rhythm of the drums.
from "Blue Winds Dancing" by Thomas S. Whitecloud

plagiarism Using the words, ideas, or expressions of others as if they were your own is called plagiarism. Plagiarism problems usually grow from the following circumstances: l. copying a passage from a source without giving credit; 2. paraphrasing a source so closely that only a few words or phrases are changed; 3. using someone else's ideas without giving credit. In a short paper credit is usually given directly in the text. In a longer piece of writing, you will need to footnote your sources.

possessive case The possessive case is formed in various ways. For singular nouns and indefinite pronouns, add an apostrophe and -s:

my *brother's* car   *no one's* notebook   *everybody's* children

For plural nouns ending in an -s, add only an apostrophe:

the *doctors'* offices   the *babies'* shoes   the *teachers'* rooms

If the plural is irregular and does not end in -s, add an apostrophe and then an -s: women's clothing.

prepositions Prepositions are words such as *about, between, during, from, in, of, over, under, until,* and *with* that show the relationship between a noun or pronoun and some other word in a sentence.

prepositional phrase Prepositional phrases are groups of words that begin with a preposition and end with a noun or pronoun (the object of the preposition). These phrases act as modifiers and create vivid pictures for the reader. Notice the prepositional phrases in the following sentence:

◆ The investigator followed, *through a stout paintless gate in a picket fence, past a broad brick walk between two rows of shabby cedars, toward the rambling and likewise paintless sprawl of the two-story house in the open hall* of which the soft lamplight glowed and the lower story of which, as the investigator now perceived, was of logs.
from "The Tall Men" by William Faulkner

pronoun A pronoun is a word used instead of a noun to designate a person or object. Subject pronouns are used as subjects of sentences. Object pronouns can be used as direct objects, indirect objects, or objects of prepositions.

When a pronoun is used as the subject, it is in the nominative case. When a pronoun is used as an object, it is in the objective case.

HINT: When you are uncertain about whether to use a subject pronoun or an object pronoun, take out the first pronoun to test the sentence. (You wouldn't say "Me played yesterday" or "Tom asked I to stay.")

Subject Pronouns			Object Pronouns		
Singular: I	you	he, she, it	me	you	him, her, it
Plural: we	you	they	us	you	them

He and I played yesterday   Tom asked her and me to stay.

Q

quotation marks (" ") Quotation marks enclose a speaker's words. They are also used to enclose some titles. When you use someone's words in your writing, use the following rules:

1. Enclose all quoted words within quotation marks.

> Thomas Jefferson wrote, "All men are created equal."

2. Introductory and explanatory expressions *(he said, I replied)* are set off by a comma, or if they interrupt a sentence, by two commas.

3. Periods and commas are always put inside quotation marks. Semicolons are put outside quotation marks.

> "I've read several of his poems," he said, "and liked them."

4. A question mark or exclamation point is put inside the quotation mark if it applies only to the quoted matter, outside if it applies to the complete sentence that contains the quotation.

> Didn't Thomas Jefferson write "The Declaration of Independence"?

5. When both the sentence and the quotation ending the sentence are questions or exclamations, only one mark is used—inside the quotation marks.

> Who wrote "What Was It?"

6. A long quoted passage is often presented without quotation marks and indented instead, sometimes in smaller type.

See also **dialogue.**

R

real, really *Real* is used as an adjective, and *really* is used as an adverb.

> We couldn't tell the *real* diamond from the fake one.

> Our vacation was *really* great. [not "real great"]

run-on sentence A run-on sentence occurs when there is only a comma (known as a comma splice) or no punctuation between two independent clauses. Separate the clauses into two complete sentences, join them with a semicolon, or use a comma and a coordinating conjunction

> Run-On: Anita saw the play, then she wrote a review.
> Correct: Anita saw the play. Then she wrote a review.
> Correct: Anita saw the play; then she wrote a review.
> Correct: Anita saw the play, and then she wrote a review.

Often, in narrative writing, authors purposely choose to use run-ons for effect, as in the following passage:

◆ Although, as we walked to the Cova through the tough part of town, walking in the dark, with light and singing coming out of the wineshops, and sometimes having to walk into the street when the men and women would crowd together on the sidewalk so that we would have had to jostle them to get by, we felt held together by there being something that had happened that they, the people who disliked us, did not understand.

    from "In Another Country" by Ernest Hemingway

See also **stringy sentences.**

S

semicolon (;) Use this punctuation mark to separate the two parts of a compound sentence when they are not joined by a comma and a conjunction.

◆ Adoniram did not reply; he shut his mouth tight.

    from "The Revolt of 'Mother'" by Mary E. Wilkins Freeman

sentence fragment A fragment often occurs when one sentence is finished, but another thought occurs to the writer and that thought is written and punctuated as a complete sentence. Experienced writers often use fragments for effect as in the following passage.

◆ Northward again. Minnesota, and great white fields of snow; frozen lakes, and dawn running in dusk without noon. Long forests wearing white. Bitter cold, and one night the northern lights.

    from "Blue Winds Dancing" by Thomas S. Whitecloud

stringy sentences A stringy sentence is one in which several independent clauses are strung together with *and.* Since all the ideas seem to be treated equally, a reader may have difficulty seeing how they are related. Correct a stringy sentence by breaking it into individual sentences or changing some of the independent clauses into subordinate clauses or phrases.

Stringy sentence: Saturday morning I have to take my brother to his music lesson and pick up some dry cleaning and then I'm supposed to let Mom have the car so she can shop and I guess I'll have to walk or hitch a ride to football practice.

Corrected: Saturday morning I have to take my brother to his music lesson and pick up some dry cleaning. Since I'm supposed to let Mom have the car so she can shop, I guess I'll have to walk or hitch a ride to football practice.

T

titles *See* **Capitalization Rules 2** *and* **10.**

V

verb A verb is a word that tells about an action or a state of being. The form or tense of the verb tells whether the action occurred in the past, the present, or the future.

verb shifts in tense Use the same tense to show two or more actions that occur at the same time.

Incorrect: She *went* [past] to the mall with friends and she *buys* [present] a sweater and earrings.

Correct: She *went* [past] to the mall with friends and she *bought* [present] a sweater and earrings.

When the verb in the main clause is in the present tense, the verb in the subordinate clause is in whatever tense expresses the meaning intended.

Mr. Washington *thinks* that the dinner *was* a success.

voice *See* **active and passive voice.**

who, whom Use *who* as the subject of a sentence or clause. *Whom* is used as a direct object or the object of a preposition.

◆ The doctor told me that the major's wife, *who* was very young and *whom* he had not married until he was definitely invalided out of the war, had died of pnuemonia.
   from "In Another Country" by Ernest Hemingway

who's, whose *Who's* is a contraction meaning "who is"; *whose* is a possessive.

◆ "Howdy, Rafe," the marshal said. "*Who's* sick?"
   from "The Tall Men" by William Faulkner

◆ . . . in her eyes, *whose* gaze was fixed . . .
   from "The Story of an Hour" by Kate Chopin

your, you're *Your* is the possessive form of the personal pronoun *you*; *you're* is a contraction meaning "you are."

◆ "Is she *your* baby girl?" he asked.
   from "The Life You Save May Be Your Own" by Flannery O' Connor

◆ "Tom, *you're* come for," . . .
   from "The Devil and Tom Walker" by Washington Irving

Index of Skills and Strategies

Literary Genres, Terms, and Techniques

Alliteration, 267, 307, 367, 522, 641, 968

Allusion, 187, 225, 234, 238, 567, 573, 799, 809, 886, 935, 938, 968

Analogy, 968

Anastrophe. *See* Inversion.

Antagonist, 968

Aphorism. *See* Maxim.

Apostrophe, 968

Assonance, 267, 968

Autobiography, 14, 22, 31, 34, 162, 322, 358, 418, 483, 604, 794, 806, 828, 876, 902, 968

Ballad, 398, 968

Blank verse, 635, 641, 968

Cacaphony, 968

Cataloging, 360, 368

Character, 19, 28, 87, 103, 161, 167, 250, 251, 252, 265, 266, 273, 284, 285, 291, 295, 320, 395, 404, 406, 414, 465, 480, 507, 566, 578, 585, 602, 609, 618, 625–630, 641, 643, 655, 673, 687, 697, 713, 751, 785, 789, 811, 873, 890, 928, 934, 938, 946–947, 968

Climax, 103, 454, 968

Comedy, 968

Comic relief, 751, 920

Conclusion, 319

Concrete poetry, 578

Conflict, 87, 103, 134, 655, 664, 751, 968

Connotation, 901, 908, 969

Consonance, 969

Copy, 952

Couplet, 969

Creation story, 5, 6, 11

Denotation, 901, 908, 969

Denouement, 454, 969

Dialect, 389, 395, 422, 643, 778, 969

Dialogue, 585, 604, 785, 811, 825, 969

Diary entry, 56, 60, 302, 306, 434, 436, 969. *See also* Journal.

Diction, 689, 697, 719, 729, 969

Drama, 62, 88, 103, 104, 122, 134, 454, 455, 690, 936, 969

Dramatic convention, 969

Dramatic irony, *See* Irony.

Epigram, 969

Epigraph, 573, 969

Epiphany, 969

Essay, 170, 222, 226, 231, 512, 533, 754, 902, 969

Euphemism, 851

Exaggeration. *See* Hyperbole

Exposition, 969

Extended metaphor, 358, 777, 970

Falling Action, 970

Fantasy, 970

Faust legend, 239

Fiction, 970

Figurative language, 103, 221, 224, 327, 331, 610, 619, 657, 729, 759, 767, 778, 887, 949, 970. *See also* Hyperbole, Metaphor, Simile.

Flashback, 311, 319, 618, 910, 920, 970

Foil, 970

Folk tale, 6, 18, 239, 250, 532

Folk literature, 970

Folklore, 970

Foot, 494, 522, 970

Foreshadowing, 275, 284, 467, 480, 970

Free verse, 367, 970

Genre, 890, 970

Hero, 490, 970

Historical document, 178, 325

Historical narrative, 971

Horror story, 252, 253, 276, 286–287, 290, 291

Humor, 250, 389, 395, 396, 875, 885

Hyperbole, 221, 389, 759, 767, 875, 885, 922, 970

Iambic meter, 522, 635, 641, 971

Idiom, 971

Imagery, 11, 21, 28, 39, 175, 234, 265, 338, 360, 367, 368, 373, 404, 550, 575, 578, 584, 641, 657, 664, 729, 827, 835, 947, 949, 971

Inference, 666, 673, 971

Interior monologue, 731, 739, 971

Introspection, 769

Inversion, 971

Irony, 167, 307, 373, 376, 449, 453, 578, 758, 899, 971

Journal, 56, 225, 434, 436. *See also* Diary.

Legend, 239, 971

Letter, 183, 184, 800

Local color, 673, 971

Maxim, 183, 187, 971

Memoir, 971

Metaphor, 55, 221, 250, 331, 358, 511, 520, 537, 567, 573, 641, 673, 759, 767, 777, 971

Meter, 367, 373, 494, 522, 530, 635, 641, 971

Metonymy, 971

Monologue, 731, 739, 971

Mood, 39, 252, 265, 266, 273, 274, 293, 294, 347, 480, 579, 584, 641, 675, 687, 729, 811, 865, 873, 890, 972

Moral, 972

Motivation, 972

Myth, 972

Narrative, 972

Narrative poetry, 972

Narrator, 13, 19, 39, 741, 751, 793, 835, 934, 972. *See also* Point of view.

Nonfiction, 972

Novel, 972

Novella, 972

Onomatopoeia, 267, 307, 522, 972

Oral tradition, 5, 6, 9, 10, 158

Origin story, 5, 6, 11

Pantomime, 739

Parable, 972

Paradox, 11, 30, 972

Paraphrase, 60, 855

Parody, 274

Pentameter, 635, 641, 972

Persona, 972

Personification, 331, 353, 358, 769, 777, 899, 972

Petition, 186

Play. *See* Drama.

Plot, 250, 251, 266, 291, 295, 319, 395, 454, 465, 675, 687, 811, 972

Poetic license, 769

Poetry, 11, 267, 268, 273, 307, 308, 310, 353, 354, 357, 358, 360, 361, 362, 364, 367, 369, 370, 371, 372, 374, 375, 376, 400, 491, 492, 493, 494, 522, 524–529, 525, 526, 527, 528, 530, 531, 568, 575, 576, 577, 578, 635, 636, 637, 639, 769, 771, 772, 773, 774, 775, 893, 894, 896, 897, 898, 899, 972

Point of view, 13, 19, 319, 364–365, 372, 374–375, 404, 674, 704–709, 740, 741, 751, 777, 793, 873, 972

Protagonist, 973

Proverb, 973

Pun, 973

Realism, 973

Refrain, 973

Repetition, 193, 195, 196, 238, 267, 273, 307, 310, 342, 367, 522, 641, 973

Resolution, 454, 973

Rhetorical question, 193, 195

Rhyme, 267, 274, 307, 367, 373, 491, 494, 522, 778, 948, 973

Rhyme scheme, 491, 494, 973

Rhythm, 274, 404, 491, 494, 641, 778, 973

Rising Action, 454, 973

Romanticism, 218–219, 220, 221, 973

Satire, 923, 928, 973

Scansion, 973

Science fiction, 973

Sermon, 58, 973

Setting, 250, 252, 265, 266, 274, 284, 291, 338, 501, 675, 687, 729, 739, 778, 929, 973

Shapely poetry, 575

Short story, 239, 240, 253, 276, 312, 390, 407, 450, 468, 580, 586, 605, 611, 645, 658, 667, 676, 720, 732, 742, 760, 812, 838, 866, 888, 911, 930, 973

Simile, 55, 331, 567, 641, 759, 767, 974

Slang, 624

Soliloquy, 974

Song, 9, 10, 886

Sonnet, 974

Sound device, 267, 273, 307, 310, 974

Spatial order, 425

Speaker, 974

Speech, 33, 172, 237, 304, 306

Stage directions, 974

Stanza, 974

Stereotype, 39, 239, 250, 405, 974

Stream of consciousness, 610, 618, 731, 739, 974

Style, 30, 39, 169, 175, 292–293, 295, 321, 404, 522, 584, 810, 974

Suspense, 267, 275, 284, 311, 320, 480

Symbolism, 138, 157, 250, 267, 310, 358, 360, 372, 490, 494, 520, 530, 573, 578, 641, 664, 697, 710, 753, 885, 938, 951–952, 974

Synedoche, 974

Tale, 974. *See also* Folk Tale, Narrative.

Theme, 5, 11, 61, 103, 121, 134, 160, 239, 266, 369, 372, 376, 428, 531, 537, 574, 577, 584, 641, 713, 789, 811, 837, 844, 891, 899, 974

Thesis, 627, 628

Title, 304–305, 319, 372, 465, 602, 604, 609, 655, 729, 767, 826, 838, 890, 928

Tone, 39, 44, 138, 177, 182, 187, 193, 195, 234, 236, 250, 273, 301, 303, 372, 397, 404, 451, 482, 489, 490, 494, 520, 530, 532, 537, 545, 546, 777, 809, 825, 974

Tragedy, 974

Turning point, 454. *See also* Climax.

Verse, 974. *See also* Poetry.

Writing Forms, Modes, and Processes

Audience, 55, 142, 143, 144, 182, 503, 504, 707, 901, 909, 952

Creative writing, 12, 29, 46–50, 103, 135, 142, 149, 168, 176, 238, 251, 252, 266, 273, 274, 285, 310, 320, 321, 326, 331, 359, 368, 372, 376, 381–384, 396, 405, 415, 481, 490, 531, 574, 578, 603, 604, 609, 619, 656, 698, 713, 730, 752, 825, 826, 874, 886, 900, 934, 946–950

Descriptive writing, 29, 103, 221, 224, 235, 252, 266, 267, 273, 274, 331, 360, 372, 396, 481, 490, 532, 537, 545, 574, 584, 602, 610, 642, 665, 666, 674, 740, 759, 826, 836, 875, 891, 900, 910, 929, 934, 951

Drafting, 48, 144, 177, 195, 293, 341, 382, 425, 503, 545, 627, 631, 707, 786–787, 854, 948

Editing, 49–50, 146, 196–197, 294–295, 319, 342–343, 383–384, 426, 504–505, 546–547, 629, 631, 708–709, 788, 855–856, 949–950

Expository/informative writing, 19, 20, 29, 39, 40, 55, 60, 103, 121, 161, 239, 251, 266, 267, 284, 338–343, 381–384, 405, 423–426, 429, 449, 453, 454, 466, 480, 481, 501–505, 625–630, 657, 704–709, 730, 752, 768, 836, 890, 900, 921, 928, 938, 953

Forms
  analysis, 584
  art review, 584
  autobiographical incident, 490, 713. *See also* Diary entry, Journal.
  biography, 320, 698, 836
  blank verse, 642
  character sketch, 836
  consumer complaint, 901
  continuation, 730
  critique, 784–789
  dialogue, 103, 135, 149, 168, 202, 251, 321, 368, 373, 376, 490, 578, 585, 603, 688, 730, 810, 874, 890, 921, 954
  diary entry, 20, 55, 103, 301, 415, 603, 826

epic poem, 490

essay, 193–198, 405, 466, 501–505, 521, 625–630, 665, 674, 705–709, 740, 752

eulogy, 619, 921

gossip column, 602

guidelines, 157

handbook, 874

horror story, 266

humor, 740, 875, 886

interview, 224, 826, 852–856

itinerary, 909

journal, 147, 326, 359, 368, 938

letter, 39, 40, 121, 135, 285, 319, 331, 381–384, 405, 429, 481, 489, 490, 521, 543–547, 825, 826, 845, 865, 874, 901, 909

monologue, 656, 752

movie review, 688, 909

newspaper editorial, 29, 135, 953

news story, 251, 481

origin story, 12

outline, 225, 238, 609

pamphlet, 176

paraphrase, 60, 175, 358, 855

persuasive speech, 193–198

play, 453. *See also* Dramatization, in Speaking, Listening, Viewing section of Index.

poem, 12, 29, 274, 310, 359, 360, 368, 372, 376, 574, 578, 778, 836, 900, 946–950

proposal, 423–426

questions, 193, 195, 550, 665, 688, 713, 731, 810, 826, 853, 855, 899, 948

quiz, 550

report, 338–343, 642, 656, 921, 928

research report, 338–343, 921

review, 182, 584, 688, 836, 909

rules, 758

saturation research paper, 338–343

scene, 698

sequel, 874

sermon, 55, 147, 921

short story, 396, 490, 730

story plot, 320, 604

subtitle, 900

summary, 20, 168, 194, 285, 367, 381, 404, 415, 537, 768, 798, 845

want ad, 20

weather report, 934

Looking Back, 50, 147, 198, 295, 343, 384, 426, 505, 547, 630, 709, 788, 856, 950

Narrative writing, 19, 46–50, 121, 168, 292–295, 306, 319, 320, 321, 341, 347, 359, 368, 396, 415, 507, 537, 574, 603, 642, 674, 698, 713, 730, 778, 826, 836, 845, 852–856, 874, 886, 901, 909, 910, 928, 934, 938, 946–950

Paragraphs, 12, 103, 121, 331, 396, 466, 531, 537, 574, 674, 698, 730, 752, 768, 825, 835, 890, 900, 909, 921

Personal expression, 5, 12, 13, 20, 29, 30, 40, 55, 60, 103, 121, 135, 149, 157, 161, 168, 169, 175, 176, 177, 182, 183, 221, 224, 225, 235, 236, 238, 239, 251, 266, 267, 275, 285, 306, 307, 320, 321, 331, 353, 360, 372, 376, 381–384, 449, 453, 467, 491, 511, 537, 602, 610, 635, 642, 657, 665, 673, 674, 675, 707, 731, 740, 752, 753, 759, 778, 809, 811, 826, 835, 875, 891, 900, 929. *See also* Personal response, in Reading/Thinking Strategies section of Index.

Persuasive/argumentative writing, 21, 29, 39, 121, 135, 142, 169, 173, 176, 183, 187, 193–198, 235, 331, 405, 423–426, 466, 490, 521, 543–547, 784–789, 865

Presenting, 50, 147, 198, 295, 343, 384, 426, 505, 547, 630, 709, 788, 856, 950

Prewriting, 47, 143, 194–195, 292–293, 339–341, 345, 381–382, 424, 501–503, 544, 625–627, 705–707, 785–786, 852–854, 946–948

Proofreading/editing. *See* Editing.

Purpose, 46, 134, 142, 193, 292, 338, 381, 423, 501, 543, 550, 625, 704, 784, 852, 946. *See also* Setting purpose, in Reading/Thinking Strategies section of Index.

Quickwrite, 143, 194, 340, 382, 502, 626, 947–948

Revising, 48, 144–145, 196, 294, 320, 341–342, 383, 425, 503–504, 545–546, 628, 707–708, 787, 854–855, 948–949

Working Portfolio, 50, 147, 198, 295, 343, 384, 426, 505, 547, 630, 709, 788, 856, 950

Writer's Blueprint, 46, 142, 193, 292, 338, 381, 423, 501, 543, 625, 704, 784, 852, 946

Writer's Notebook, 5, 12, 13, 20, 21, 29, 30, 40, 55, 60, 103, 135, 157, 176, 177, 182, 183, 221, 224, 225, 235, 236, 239, 251, 252, 266, 267, 274, 275, 285, 301, 306, 307, 311, 320, 321, 327, 331, 389, 396, 397, 405, 406, 415, 449, 453, 454, 466, 467, 481, 482, 490, 491, 532, 537, 567, 574, 579, 585, 603, 604, 609, 610, 619, 635, 643, 656, 657, 665, 666, 674, 689, 799, 810, 811, 826, 827, 835, 837, 845, 875, 886, 891, 900, 901, 909, 922, 928, 929, 934, 935, 938

family and home, 161, 168, 353, 511, 521, 675, 688, 741, 752, 759, 768, 793, 865, 874, 887, 890

good and evil, 61, 121, 719, 730

memories, 731, 740, 753, 758, 910, 921

poetry, 310, 353, 359, 360, 368, 369, 372, 373, 376, 522, 531, 575, 578, 642, 769, 778

■

Reading/Thinking Strategies

Active reading model, xxvi–xxxv

Bias and propaganda, 30, 61, 87, 121, 239, 702–703, 710–711

Cause and effect, 11, 103, 221, 326, 453, 480, 494, 520, 625–630, 729, 751

Clarify, xxvii, 11, 23, 24, 28, 39, 60, 87, 121, 134, 166, 167, 228, 230, 244, 282, 317, 412, 484, 589, 596, 613, 645, 650, 724, 732, 734, 764, 832, 904, 908, 912, 924, 934, 938

Comparison/contrast, 11, 19, 39, 55, 60, 63, 87, 103, 121, 134, 175, 182, 183, 201, 224, 238, 250, 265, 273, 284, 285, 289, 293, 294, 301, 306, 310, 319, 320, 327, 331, 358, 367, 369, 385, 388, 395, 396, 404, 406, 414, 415, 421, 428, 429, 453, 465, 480, 481, 520, 530, 561, 566, 573, 575, 578, 584, 618, 619, 620, 641, 674, 691, 697, 698, 703, 704–709, 713, 739, 752, 765, 799, 826, 835, 844, 885, 890, 899, 901, 947

Comprehension. See Cause and effect, Comparison/contrast, Details, Drawing conclusions, Inferring, Main idea, Visualizing.

Connect, xxvii, 5, 11, 19, 28, 39, 60, 87, 103, 121, 134, 160, 163, 167, 175, 182, 187, 224, 234, 238, 250, 265, 273, 284, 306, 310, 319, 326, 331, 358, 367, 372, 376, 404, 414, 453, 465, 480, 489, 494, 507, 520, 530, 537, 573, 578, 584, 602, 609, 618, 641, 655, 664, 673, 687, 697, 729, 739, 751, 758, 767, 777, 798, 809, 825, 835, 844, 873, 885, 890, 899, 908, 920, 928, 934, 938

Critical response. See Clarify, Connect, Evaluate, Predict, Question, Summarize.

Details, 19, 28, 39, 60, 167, 234, 252, 265, 301, 347, 358, 474, 618, 619, 729, 739, 751, 809, 825, 844, 873, 920, 928, 929, 934

Drawing conclusions, 39, 60, 121, 134, 167, 187, 224, 250, 275, 295, 319, 414, 453, 480, 481, 489, 501, 503, 578, 655, 729, 739, 751, 825, 844, 873, 953. See also Inferring.

Evaluate, xxvii, 19, 39, 50, 60, 87, 103, 121, 134, 147, 150, 160, 164, 167, 175, 182, 187, 194, 198, 201, 215, 224, 234, 238, 245, 250, 283, 284, 295, 310, 343, 367, 372, 384, 395, 404, 410, 426, 430, 443, 465, 473, 480, 486, 505, 530, 537, 547, 549, 561, 578, 583, 592, 602, 612, 616, 618, 620, 630, 655, 664, 674, 687, 697, 698, 706, 709, 712, 724, 737, 741, 751, 777, 783, 788, 789, 809, 825, 835, 844, 850, 856, 873, 890, 905, 908, 920, 925, 928, 943, 950, 953

Images, 11, 234, 252, 265, 338, 367, 368, 424, 550, 575, 578, 584, 641, 657, 664, 729, 890, 899

Inferring, 60, 103, 121, 134, 160, 167, 175, 187, 234, 250, 265, 273, 284, 306, 310, 326, 331, 367, 372, 376, 404, 414, 453, 474, 489, 506, 507, 520, 537, 573, 602, 609, 666, 673, 674, 687, 719, 767, 798, 809, 825, 826, 835, 836, 844, 885, 908, 920, 928. See also Drawing conclusions

Main idea, 5, 11, 19, 28, 39, 87, 103, 537, 655. See also Theme, in Literary Genres, Terms, and Techniques section of Index.

Personal response, xxxv, 11, 13, 19, 20, 28, 29, 39, 43, 44, 51, 60, 87, 103, 121, 134, 136, 141, 160, 167, 175, 182, 190, 191, 215, 224, 234, 238, 250, 265, 273, 284, 289, 290, 295, 306, 310, 319, 326, 331, 333, 336, 337, 358, 367, 369, 372, 376, 380, 395, 404, 414, 417, 421, 429, 430, 443, 453, 465, 480, 489, 494, 499, 506–507, 520, 530, 537, 541, 542, 549, 561, 573–574, 584, 602, 609, 618,

620, 623, 641, 655, 664, 673, 687, 697, 703, 710–711, 729, 739, 751, 758, 767, 777, 783, 798, 809, 825, 835, 844, 850, 859, 873, 885, 890, 899, 908, 920, 928, 931, 934, 938, 943, 944. See also Personal expression, in Writing Forms, Modes, and Processes section of Index

Predict, xxvii, 19, 28, 60, 121, 239, 265, 275, 280, 284, 295, 347, 367, 453, 480, 488, 489, 530, 537, 573, 602, 609, 618, 647, 655, 656, 689, 729, 730, 739, 751, 763, 789, 809, 844, 886, 920, 927, 939–944, 954

Prereading. See Previewing

Previewing, 5, 13, 21, 30, 55, 61, 157, 161, 169, 177, 183, 221, 225, 239, 252, 267, 275, 301, 307, 327, 353, 360, 369, 373, 397, 406, 449, 454, 482, 491, 511, 532, 575, 579, 585, 604, 610, 635, 657, 666, 675, 689, 719, 753, 769, 811, 827, 859, 875, 887, 891, 901, 929

Question, xxvii, 43, 48, 50, 136, 144, 145, 190, 191, 196, 198, 224, 239, 243, 246, 289, 290, 294, 295, 301, 306, 313, 333, 336, 337, 339, 341, 343, 380, 397, 425, 443, 499, 504, 505, 550, 584, 703, 707, 769, 787, 938

Reader response. See Personal response.

Sequence, 319, 910

Setting purpose, 5, 30, 51, 55, 61, 134, 135, 143, 169, 221, 252, 275, 306, 482, 520, 550, 604

Summarize, xxvii, 20, 28, 87, 168, 194, 277, 285, 314, 318, 331, 367, 381, 404, 415, 465, 470, 516, 518, 537, 582, 654, 655, 664, 727, 798, 825, 830, 845, 899, 907, 908, 928

Using prior knowledge, 30, 58, 182, 311, 501, 934

Visualizing, 235, 250, 265, 376, 425, 494, 520, 578, 619, 635, 664, 778

Vocabulary and Study Skills

Analogies, 160, 465, 584, 739, 767, 844, 874, 909

Annotated bibliography, 688. *See also* Works cited list.

Antonyms, 40, 251, 285, 319, 404, 453, 730, 835

Charts
Building Background, 30, 731, 799, 891, 935
Literary Focus, 55, 267, 307, 373, 449, 585, 618, 767, 793
Making Connections, 284, 367, 777, 899
Multicultural Connections, 201
Vocabulary Study, 404, 453
Writer's Notebook, 236, 275, 491, 575
Writing Choices, 238, 531, 603
Writing Workshop, 47, 143–144, 194, 293, 382, 502, 544, 626, 785, 853

Classifying, 367

Coined terms, 622–623

Computers, 151, 344–345, 426, 505, 550, 709, 713, 859, 950

Continuums, 376, 729. *See also* Rating scales.

Diagrams, 424, 688

Events chains. See Time lines

Graphic organizers. *See* Charts, Graphs, Venn diagrams, Webs.

Graphs, 741

Language History, 45, 192, 291, 422, 500, 624, 851, 945

Library, 343, 344, 345, 426, 642, 778, 810

Maps 5, 13, 21, 157, 521, 579, 910, 920, 922. *See also* Creating art, in Speaking, Listening, and Viewing section of Index.

Pronunciation, 192, 274, 295, 395, 689, 697, 719, 729

Rankings, 574, 786

Rating scales, 19, 175, 234, 376, 395, 687, 729, 784, 809

Reference books, 146, 176, 192, 197, 306, 339

Research, 20, 29, 40, 151, 176, 235, 266, 326, 338–343, 344–345, 405, 415, 430, 502, 544, 573, 574, 603, 642, 656, 698, 705, 758, 778, 799, 810, 826, 836, 853, 859, 886, 900, 921, 938

Slang, 624

Source cards, 340

Synonyms, 60, 160, 182, 224, 285, 306, 310, 319, 404, 453, 531, 810, 900

Time lines, 47, 347, 397, 405, 505, 550, 675, 846–850

Venn diagrams, 167, 273, 414, 705, 752

Vivid language, 49, 103, 221, 293, 338. *See also* Figurative language, in Literary Genres, Terms, and Techniques section of Index.

Vocabulary Study, 12, 20, 28, 40, 60, 87, 103, 121, 135, 160, 168, 176, 182, 187, 224, 235, 251, 265, 274, 285, 306, 310, 319, 326, 331, 359, 368, 372, 376, 396, 404, 415, 465, 480, 490, 494, 521, 531, 537, 574, 584, 602–603, 609, 619, 656, 665, 687, 697–698, 730, 739, 752, 758, 767, 778, 798, 810, 825, 835, 844, 874, 885, 900, 909, 921, 928, 934, 938

Webs, 252, 266, 306, 353, 358, 494, 532, 688, 827, 865

Works cited list, 343. *See also* Annotated bibliography.

Grammar, Usage, Mechanics, and Spelling

Active and passive voice, 787, 985

Adjectives, 167, 233, 361, 395, 489, 532, 537, 547, 574, 613, 655, 687, 767, 788, 835, 885, 891, 908, 915, 985

Adverbs, 547, 602–603, 788, 891, 985

Agreement, 986

Ambiguity, 988

Amount/Number, 988

Apostrophes, 505, 989

Appositive, 989

Awkward writing, 145

Capitalization, 990

Clause, 991

Collective nouns, 992

Colon, 992

Commas, 629, 992

Comma splice. *See* Sentences, run-ons.

Comparative forms of adjectives and adverbs, 993

Comparison/contrast words, 708

Conjunctions, 384, 708, 994

Dangling modifiers, 994

Dash, 994

Dialogue, 994

Direct Address, 994

Direct quotations, 709, 856

Ellipses, 995

Exclamation point, 995

Friendly letter form, 995

Gerund, 996

Infinitive, 996

Interjection, 996

Italics, 996

Modifier, 997

Nouns, 891, 998

Parallel construction, 998

Parenthesis, 998

Participle, 998

Person, 13, 19, 46, 338

Plagiarism, 999

Possessives, 505, 999

Prepositions, 999

Prepostional phrases, 999

Pronouns, 46, 146, 197, 999

Quotation marks, 709, 856, 1000

Run-on sentences. *See* Sentences, run-ons.

Semicolons, 293, 1001

Sentences, 175, 251, 293, 331
fragment, 1001
run-ons, 383–384, 1000
stringy, 1001

Spatial order, 425

Spelling, 192, 295, 950
homophones, 426
spell checkers, 426, 631, 950

Tense, 50, 338, 1002

Usage and spelling problems
accept/except, 985

affect/effect, 986
all ready/already, 988
all right, 988
as/like, 989
awhile/a while, 989
bad/badly, 989
between you and me, 990
fewer/less, 995
hopefully, 996
however, 996
it's/its, 426, 997
lie/lay, 997
less/fewer, 997
media, 997
myself, 998
real/really, 1000
who/whom, 1002
who's/whose, 1002
your/you're, 426, 1002
Verbs, 293, 687, 891, 1001

■

Speaking, Listening, and Viewing

Analyzing art, xxviii, 6–7, 10,
   24–25, 29, 31, 51, 58, 63, 159,
   168, 173, 178–179, 199–200,
   215, 226–227, 233, 237, 241,
   268, 288–289, 296–297, 303,
   320, 323, 356, 359, 361, 371,
   374–375, 385, 391, 400,
   408–409, 411, 451, 457, 458,
   461, 466, 469, 474, 479,
   492–493, 525, 527, 528,
   534–535, 561, 569, 576, 577,
   613, 614, 639, 659, 676–677,
   683, 695, 710–711, 721, 725,
   733, 747, 761, 773, 798,
   838–839, 871, 896–897,
   914–915, 931
   composition, 222, 385, 428,
   889
   critical viewing, 15, 18, 34–35,
   57, 141, 165, 184, 256–257,
   260–261, 266, 304–305,
   308–309, 354–355, 363,
   364–365, 385, 486, 512–513,
   607, 637, 688, 691, 736, 743,
   755, 765, 771, 775, 813, 819,
   823, 867, 877, 895, 902–903,
   913, 937

   See also Looking at
   photographs, in Media and
   Technology section of Index.
Beyond Print
   Analyzing Advertising (critical
   thinking), 951–952
   Electronic Research
   (technology), 344–345
   Looking at Art (visual literacy), 51
   Looking at Heroes (visual liter-
   acy), 199–200
   Looking at Horror Movies
   (media literacy), 296–297
   Looking at Photographs (visual
   literacy), 506–507
   Looking at Television (critical
   viewing), 789
   Multimedia Presentations (tech-
   nology), 857
   Propaganda (critical thinking),
   710–711
   Reading a Painting (visual literacy), 385
   Speaking the Language of
   Technology (technology),
   148–149
   Speaking Your Mind (effective
   speaking), 548
   Watching Westerns (media literacy), 427–428
   The Wonders of Word
   Processing (technology), 631
Collaborative learning, 11, 12, 29,
   40, 48, 49, 50, 144, 146, 147,
   150, 151, 160, 168, 194, 196,
   198, 200, 201, 202, 224, 238,
   251, 266, 274, 284, 285, 293,
   294, 295, 310, 320, 326, 331,
   339, 341, 342, 346, 347, 368,
   381–382, 383, 385, 396, 404,
   405, 415, 424–425, 426, 429,
   430, 453, 465, 466, 481, 489,
   490, 491, 501–502, 503, 504,
   505, 507, 520, 531, 546, 547,
   549, 550, 574, 578, 625–626,
   628, 629, 630, 655, 664, 688,
   697, 698, 707, 708, 709, 712,
   713, 730, 731, 740, 752, 768,
   778, 785, 786, 787, 788, 799,
   810, 826, 835, 836, 845, 853,
   854, 855, 858, 859, 874, 886,

   890, 900, 921, 928, 938, 948,
   949, 953, 954
Creating art, 51, 151, 202, 859
   blueprints, 481
   bumper stickers, 709
   cartoons, 168, 376, 389
   charts, 12, 29, 40, 934
   collages, 200, 359, 368,
   381–384, 537, 550, 574
   comic strips, 376
   costumes, 430, 453, 713
   diagrams, 424, 928
   dioramas, 168
   displays, 343, 531, 574
   drawings, 20, 60, 274, 297, 372,
   428, 537, 578, 730, 890
   dust jacket design, 359
   games, 347, 396, 550, 674, 713
   graphs, 40, 752, 758
   illustrations, 29, 151, 251, 285,
   376, 415, 520, 619, 674, 778,
   921, 928
   maps, 151, 168, 306, 430, 521,
   665, 674, 713, 758, 845, 934,
   954
   mobiles, 12
   models, 359, 426
   murals, 550
   paintings, 320, 428, 890
   papier-maché, 537, 890
   posters, 12, 547, 630, 826
   quilts, 619, 768
   scenery, 415
   scrapbooks, 578
   sculptures, 274, 531, 890
   silhouettes, 273
   sketches, 235, 396, 414, 415,
   428, 490, 494, 798, 836, 845,
   934
   T-shirt design, 359
Debate, 20, 177, 326, 430, 642,
   836
Discussion, 238, 250, 293, 304,
   331, 347, 405, 481, 547, 578,
   752, 799, 900
Dramatization, 201, 346, 574, 712,
   858, 900, 953
   comedy, 740
   dialogue, 149, 168, 202, 251,
   368, 490, 578, 688, 730, 768,
   810, 874, 890, 921, 954

dramatic readings, 182, 274, 310, 642, 740, 920
plays, 453, 466, 656, 698, 836
quiz show, 954
radio humor, 886
radio plays, 295, 698
reader's theater, 251, 453, 656
reenactments, 150, 168, 326
retelling, 921
television commercials, 198, 285, 952
trials, 135, 235, 466
Effective listening, 19, 28, 51, 103, 121, 134, 135, 167, 175, 176, 187, 198, 224, 234, 238, 250, 265, 310, 331, 453, 602, 655, 739, 758, 844, 909, 938
Effective speaking, 29, 40, 251, 274, 521, 548, 752
contest, 295
storytelling, 12
Evaluating art, 380, 385, 405
Exhibiting art, 266, 384, 423–426, 859, 926
Interviews, 224, 430, 506, 507, 731, 826, 852–856
Media Literacy, 296–297, 427–428. *See also* Media and Technology section of Index.
Movie review, 688, 909
Multimedia presentations, 151, 295, 310, 368, 550, 603, 713, 857, 859
Music, 273, 274, 295, 531, 603, 642, 859
background music, 310, 453, 530, 713, 810, 874
dance, 531
opera, 415
program, 874
song, 11, 886
Oral essay, 740
Oral reports, 29, 121, 151, 176, 235, 266, 306, 320, 405, 430, 507, 531, 603, 656, 665, 778, 826, 845, 874, 934
Reading aloud, 12, 147, 160, 396, 709, 713
poetry, 310, 358, 359, 530, 641, 642, 698, 778, 886
Relating art to literature, xxviii, 6–7,

14–15, 31, 57, 159, 165, 173, 178, 184, 202, 226–227, 241, 256–257, 260–261, 266, 289, 303, 308–309, 320, 356, 359, 361, 364–365, 374–375, 377–380, 391, 405, 411, 451, 457, 461, 466, 469, 492–493, 525, 527, 528, 531, 534–535, 541, 561, 569, 576, 577, 584, 592–593, 598–599, 600, 613, 637, 639, 649, 659, 668, 680, 683, 695, 721, 725, 733, 747, 761, 773, 819, 838–839, 871, 889, 914–915, 926
Relating art to personal experience, 222, 233, 328–329, 385, 400
Slide show, 368
Speech, 40, 160, 193, 237, 328, 331, 347, 396, 403, 507, 548, 574, 857, 890, 921, 938
extemporaneous, 936
motivational, 135, 301, 302, 306
persuasive, 173, 175, 202, 238, 698
proposal, 426
Television documentaries/specials, 20, 151, 202, 521, 810
Visual Literacy, 51, 199–200, 385, 506–507

Interdisciplinary Connections

Architecture, 481
Art, 12, 51, 218–219, 289, 377–380, 538–541. See also Analyzing art, in Speaking, Listening, and Viewing section of Index
Career Connection, 190, 337, 542, 944
Economics, 643, 759
Futurist Connection, 939–943
Geography, 5, 13, 21, 157, 306, 386, 641, 665, 675, 713, 778, 909, 910, 922, 954
Health, 290, 332–333
History, 2–4, 52–54, 154–156, 218–220, 265, 291, 298–300, 350–351, 386–388, 397, 422,

432–443, 446–448, 500, 508–510, 552, 564–566, 624, 632–634, 716–717, 790–791, 790–792, 851, 945. See also Interdisciplinary Study
Interdisciplinary Study
American Visionaries, 377–380
An Appetite for Fright, 286–290
An Artistic Awakening, 538–542
Behind the Lines, 332–337
Frontier Adventures and Tragedies, 416–421
A Glimpse into the Future, 939–944
The Great Exchange, 41–44
Life on the Home Front, 699–703
Mass Hysteria, 136–141
The Quest for Freedom, 188–191
The Roaring Twenties, 620–623
Television Comes of Age, 779–783
Time of Turmoil, 846–850
Within Limits, 495–499
Language, 10, 44, 45, 60, 192, 422, 500, 622–623, 624, 753, 758, 851, 901, 908, 945
Media, 286–287, 290, 955–965
Multicultural Connections, 150, 188, 201, 346, 429, 549, 712, 858, 953. See also Multicultural Awareness and Appreciation section of Index.
Music, 310, 508–509
Pop culture, 286–288, 620–623, 779
Science, 11, 136, 148–149, 275, 332–333, 376, 498–499, 922, 928. See also Media and Technology section of Index.
Social studies, 41–43, 44, 137

Multicultural Awareness and Appreciation

Change, 187, 201, 236, 268, 300, 306, 331, 346, 350–351, 489, 500, 501–505, 502, 506–507, 550, 624, 632–634, 655, 687, 741, 758, 798, 846–850, 939–944, 953

Choice, 156, 160, 167, 175, 187, 201, 285, 792, 809, 811, 825, 844, 858

Communication, 40, 51, 388, 395, 400, 404, 429, 634, 641, 655, 664, 712, 751, 908

Cultural awareness, 5, 6, 9, 10, 12, 13, 19, 20, 34–35, 156, 295, 298–299, 300, 310, 352, 388, 404, 405, 520, 657, 665, 778, 910, 943, 944

Exploring similarities, 6, 11, 40, 275, 388, 421, 481, 520, 531, 551–561, 705

Groups, 2–3, 5, 9, 10, 19, 21, 39, 45, 54, 55, 58, 87, 103, 134, 150, 156, 157, 160, 161, 167, 187, 188–189, 236, 266, 268, 298–299, 306, 327, 331, 336–337, 388, 404, 422, 430, 446–447, 448, 481, 482, 489, 500, 501, 508–509, 510, 511, 520, 521, 522–523, 530, 532, 537, 538, 549, 551–561, 603, 624, 634, 699–703, 758, 759, 811, 827, 837, 846–850, 887, 899, 910, 921, 939

Individuality, 134, 192, 218, 220, 221, 222, 224, 225, 234, 239, 266, 307, 311, 321, 346, 352, 353, 360, 373, 448, 453, 465, 480, 539, 549, 634, 891

Interaction, 4, 19, 24–25, 34–35, 39, 41–44, 150, 161, 265, 306, 321, 353, 405, 467, 687, 718, 729, 751, 752, 758, 767, 777, 858

Perspectives, 43, 151, 252, 260–261, 265, 300, 306, 319, 339, 347, 352, 358, 364–365, 367, 369, 372, 374–375, 376, 381–382, 429, 530, 566, 573, 602, 609, 618, 712

Recognizing/respecting differences, 2–3, 11, 30, 39, 40, 54, 60, 138–139, 194, 198, 224, 266, 298–299, 326, 353, 360, 369, 388, 414, 421, 422, 500, 566, 574, 603, 634, 657, 664, 705, 712, 753, 786, 811, 827, 837, 845, 846–850, 891, 901, 929, 943

Special themes

The Journey, 431–443

The Media, 955–965

The Search for Equality, 551–561

The Wilderness, 203–215

Symbols, 138, 139, 157, 267, 268, 326, 490, 520, 710

Tradition, 5, 12, 54, 157, 448, 467, 489, 539, 620, 632–633, 699–703, 712, 741, 759, 891

Values, 20, 28, 30, 40, 52–53, 54, 55, 60, 61, 87, 103, 134, 138–139, 156, 159, 166, 167, 175, 187, 194, 199–200, 201, 218, 222, 224, 237, 250, 251, 252, 266, 284, 285, 298–299, 300, 306, 310, 327, 328–329, 331, 352, 353, 381–382, 406, 427, 430, 443, 448, 449, 465, 467, 480, 481, 482, 489, 500, 532, 537, 574, 602, 603, 620, 689, 710–711, 739, 752, 767, 811, 826, 837, 846–850, 859, 921, 953

■

Media and Technology

Animation, 396

Audiotaping, 359, 550, 698, 853, 886, 901

Camera angles, 296

Color, 296, 385

Compact disks, 344, 574

Computers, 148–149, 151, 297, 344–345, 426, 503, 505, 550, 631, 709, 713, 778, 836, 857, 859, 950

Computer talk, 945

Editing, 296, 789

Electronic mail, 900

Electronic research, 344–345

Evaluating media, 198, 741, 779–782, 789, 952

Internet, 345, 711

Inventions, 234

Lighting, 296

Looking at ads, 198, 299, 424, 598–599, 600, 951–952

Looking at movies, 139, 250, 286–287, 290, 296–297, 312–313, 320, 415, 427–428, 454, 688, 698, 740

Looking at photographs, 506–507, 512–513, 514, 644, 649, 652, 665, 668, 680, 691, 730, 740, 806–807, 828–829, 850, 882

Looking at television, 239, 250, 779–783, 789

Multimedia presentations, 151, 295, 310, 368, 550, 603, 713, 857, 859

Music, 295, 296, 310, 531, 550, 603, 642, 810

Sound effects, 295, 296, 550

Special effects, 286–287, 297

Technology, 148–149, 218, 297, 344–345, 350–351, 422, 447, 503, 631, 857, 940–941

Video games, 347

Videotaping, 20, 151, 202, 238, 285, 343, 347, 550, 698, 826, 859, 934

Index of Fine Arts & Artists

Abad, Pacita, How Mali Lost Her Accent, 903

Albright, Ivan, That Which I Should Have Done I Did Not Do, 289

Allard, William Albert, photograph of Vietnamese refugees, 828–829

Alston, Charles, Walking, 444–445

American Indian art (anonymous), Kachina doll, 10

Angell, Tony, Transformation, 268

Arai, Tomie, Laundryman's Daughter, 755

Audubon, John James, House Wren, 359

Bama, James, Portrait of a Sioux, ii; A Sioux Indian, 913

Barralet, John James, Sacred to the Memory of Washington, 200

Barthé, Richmond, Blackberry Woman, 541

Bartholomew, Caty, illustration for "Top of the Food Chain," 926

Beals, Jessie Tarbox, A Short Cut Over the Roofs of the Tenements, 446

Beard, William Holbrook, The Lost Balloon, 380

Bearden, Romare, At the Savoy, 528; Black Manhattan, 794

Beneker, Gerrit A., Man Are Square, 222

Benton, Thomas Hart, The Boy, 433

Bernis, Antonio, Juanito en la Laguna, 889

Bierstadt, Albert, Niagara Falls, 209; A View of the Rocky Mountains, 218–219

Bingham, George Caleb, The Jolly Flatboatmen, 361; Stump Speaking, 553

Blyth, Benjamin, portrait of Abigail Adams, 184

Bohrod, Aaron, Landscape Near Chicago, 725

Borglum, Gutzon, Mount Rushmore, 199

Brega, Doug, Emerson, 819

Brooke, Richard Norris, Furling the Flag, 323

Brown, Laurie, Journey Foretold, Laguna Niguel, California, 914–915

Burchfield, Charles, Song of the Red Bird, 206

Burshell, Sandra, Tranquil Corner, 695

Cassatt, Mary, At the Opera, 411

Catlin, George, River Bluffs, 1320 Miles above St. Louis, 205

Chapin, James, Ruby Green Singing, 535

Church, Frederic Edwin, Our Banner in the Sky, 377

Colman, Samuel, Ships of the Plains, 683

Copley, John Singleton, Mrs. Ezekial Goldthwait, 279

Coxe, Reginald Cleveland, The Coming Wind, 374–375

Curry, John Steuart, Wisconsin Landscape, 479; Tragic Prelude, 554–555

Dali, Salvador, The Persistence of Memory, 320

Davis, Paul, Viva Chavez, 559

Degas, Edgar, Woman Ironing, 733

Del Real, Tacos Sabrosos, 775

DeMatteo, David, painting of the Santa Ynez Valley, 676–677

Deming, Edwin W., Braddock's Defeat, July 9, 1755, 165

Domke, Jim, The Indian and the Buffalo, 560

Douglas, Aaron, Rise Shine for Thy Light Has Come, 527; Aspects of Negro Life: From Slavery Through Reconstruction, 540–541

Dunn, Harvey, The Homesteader's Wife, 408–409

Dunn, John Gibson, The Pledge, 244

Eakins, Thomas, Mother, 458

English art (anonymous), portrait of Richard Mather, 58; frontier cabin, 210

Evergood, Philip, Tea for Two, 569

Field, Erastus Salisbury, Historical Monument of the American Republic, 379

Flack, Audrey, Truman's Teachers, 691

Folk art (anonymous), Mahatango Valley Farm, 466

French, Daniel Chester, bust of Ralph Waldo Emerson, 218

Friedrich, Caspar David, Woman at the Window, 355

Fuller, Meta Warrick, Talking Skull, 538–539

Gibson, Charles Dana, drawing of bathing beauties, 446

Goings, Ralph, Hot-Fudge Sundae, 714–715

Halsall, William Formby, Mayflower in Plymouth Harbor, 31

Hassam, Childe, Allies Day, May 1917, 584

Hayden, Palmer, Fétiche et Fleurs, 540

Hicks, Edward, The Falls of Niagara, 208

Hockney, David, Peachblossom Hwy., 11–18th April, 1986, 440–441

Hopper, Edward, Nighthawks, 562–563; Corn Hill, 633

Hovenden, Thomas, The Last Moments of John Brown, 309

Hoy, Carol, Dead Pine Over Canyonlands, 212

Hung Lui, Tang Ren Jie, 895

Jackson, Billy Morrow, Philo Bound, 240–241; The Interloper, 721

Johnson, Herbert, National Park cartoon, 213

Johnson, Sargent, Forever Free, 237

Jones, Lois Mailou, Jennie, 773

Katz, Alex, Ada and Vincent in the Car, 867; Ada Behind the Screen Door, 871

King, Charles Bird, Young Omahaw, War Eagle, Little Missouri, and Pawnees, 1

Krans, J., Tinsmith, 576

Ladnier, Paul, Grandy Snow Scene, 931

Lange, Dorothea, photographs, 633, 644, 649, 652

Larrain, Gilles, photomontage, 371

Lawrence, Jacob, Migration of the Negro series, Panel No. 1, 442; Panel No. 55, 525

Leyendecker, J. C., illustrations, 586, 593, 599, 600

Lovell, Tim, The Heirloom, 437

Lynch, Laura, Oak Street Beach, 860–861

Matteson, T. H., Trial of George Jacobs, August 5, 1692, 57

Mayer, Frank Blackwell, Independence (Squire Jack Porter), 216–217

McRae, John, Raising the Liberty Pole, 179

Miller, Don, King Mural, 800

Monet, Claude, Garden at Vétheuil, 365

Motley, Jr., Archibald J., Black Belt, 538

Moylan, Ken, Boundary Lake, 823

Munch, Edvard, The Scream, 266

Nast, Thomas, A Group of Vultures Waiting for the Storm to Blow Over—"Let Us Prey," 959

O'Keeffe, Georgia, Brown and Tan Leaves, 577; Cow's Skull: Red, White, and Blue, 632

O'Sullivan, Timothy, photograph of dead at Gettysburg, 304–305

Opper, Frederick, The American Working Man of the Future, 558

Parks, Gordon, portrait of Malcolm X, 806

Paxson, E. S., Lewis and Clark at Three Forks, 154

Peale, Charles Willson, George Washington at the Battle of Trenton, 199; James Peale (The Lamplight Portrait), 277

Phillips, Laura, illustration of frogs with sneakers, 391

Porter, Elliot, photograph of Walden Pond, 227

Porter, Fairfield, A Day Indoors, 743; Under the Elms, 747

Priestly, Glen, Bellamy 9, 813

Pyle, Howard, The Nation Makers, 173

Red Owl, Richard, Lost in the Dance, 659

Remington, Frederic, Cabeza de Vaca in the Desert, 15; Downing the Nigh Leader, 404

Rickard, Jolene, Two Canoes, 35

Riggs, Robert, The Slave Ship, 24–25

Rimmer, William, Flight and Pursuit, 378

Rivera Diego, Detroit Industry, 633

Robinson, Theodore, In the Garden, 492–493

Romero, Rachael, He Who Feels It Knows It, 839

Rothstein, Arnold, photograph of cowboy Frank Lotta, 680

Ryder, Albert Pinkham, The Race Track, or Death on a Pale Horse, 378; The Dead Bird, 461

Sargent, John Singer, Repose, 451; Miss Elsie Palmer, 499

Satty, Wilfried, illustrations for "The Pit and the Pendulum," 253, 257, 261

Savage, Augusta, Gamin, 540

Savage, Edward, The Washington Family, 200

Schreiber, George, From Arkansas, 469

Shuptrine, Hubert, Mama Agnes, 761

Sloane, Eric, Sickle and Bucket, 474; Hill Farm Barn, 637

Smith, Hughie Lee, Portrait of a Boy, 607

Smith, Jane Quick-to-See, Red Horse, 896–897

Smith, William A. , illustration of Walt Whitman, 363

Soyer, Raphael, The Brown Sweater, 736

Steiglitz, Alfred, The Steerage, 438

Theodore, Gentilz, Camp of the Lipans, 18

Timberlake, Bob, Tulip Quilt, 457; Gilley's House, 765

Tooker, George, Government Bureau, 141; Mirror II, 771

Two Arrows, Tom, Creation Legend, 7

Ufer, Walter, Where the Desert Meets the Mountains, 348–349

Van Der Zee, James, The Abyssian Baptist Church, 512; Portrait of Couple with Raccoon Coats and Stylish Car, 514

Van Vechten, Carl, portrait of Zora Neale Hurston, 509

Vauhon, John, photograph of newsstand in Omaha, Nebraska, 1938, 960–961

Vedder, Elihu, The Lair of the Sea Serpent, 379

Verelst, John, portrait of Sa Ga Yeath Qua Piet Tow, 159

Verlin, Bob, photograph of Elvis Presley, 882

Volk, Stephen Arnold Douglas, After the Reception, 614

Von Blaas, E., The Miser, 247

Walcutt, William, Pulling Down the Statue of George III, 152–153

Walker, James, Gauchos in a Horse Corral, 398

Wallace, Isaac, Portrait of a Chinese Man, 400

Welliver, Neil, The Birches, 639

Welty, Eudora, A woman of the 'thirties, 668

Wood, Grant, Victorian Survivor, 613

Wyeth, Andrew, Trodden Weeds, 233

Wyeth, Jamie, And Then into the Deep Gorge, 356

Index of Authors and Titles

Acuna, Roberto, 559
Adams, Abigail, 183
Ain't I a Woman?, 237
Alcott, Louisa May, 334
Alexie, Sherman, 910
Allen, Frederick Lewis, 620, 956
from American Crisis, The, 170
Antin, Mary, 557
Attack on Fort Sumter, The, 302
from Autobiography of Benjamin Franklin, The, 162
from Autobiography of Malcolm X, The, 806
Barish, Ellen Blum, 290
Bates, Katherine Lee, 215
Because I could not stop for Death, 357
Before They Got Thick, 18
from Behind the Blue and the Gray, 332
Bierce, Ambrose, 311
Bigmouth, Percy, 13
Birches, 639
Bird Came Down the Walk, A, 357
Bird, Isabella, 211
Bishop, Elizabeth, 770
from Black Boy, 605
Black Hawk, 418
from Black Hawk, an Autobiography, 418
Black Man Talks of Reaping, A, 524
Blizzard Under Blue Sky, A, 930
Blue Winds Dancing, 658
Bontemps, Arna, 522
Boyle, T. Coraghessan, 922
Bradford, William, 30, 206
Brooks, John, 779
Brown, Sterling A., 522
Bryant, William Cullen, 211
Cabeza de Vaca, Álvar Núñez, 13
Canassatego, 30
Carson, Rachel, 213
Castillo, Ann, 892
Cather, Willa, 406
Celebrated Jumping Frog of Calaveras County, The, 390
Chavez, Cesar, 435
Chesnut, Mary, 301
Chopin, Kate, 449
Cisneros, Sandra, 887
from Civil Disobedience, 231
from "Co. Aytch," 335

Coca-Cola and Coco-Frío, 893
Cole, Thomas, 208
Corrido de Gregorio Cortez, El, 398
Crane, Stephen, 373
Creelman, James, 958
Créveçoeur, Hector St. Jean de, 553
Crow Dog, Mary, 560
Crucible, The, 62
from Crusade for Justice, 483
Cullen, Countee, 522
Cummings, E. E., 575
Cunning, Sheril Jankovsky, 700
from Danse Macabre, 288
Declaration of Independence, The, 178
Dekanawidah, 157
Devil and Tom Walker, The, 240
from Diary of Samuel Sewall, The, 56
Dickinson, Emily, 353
Douglass, Frederick, 327
Douglass, Lewis, 554
from Down the Santa Fe Trail, 421
Dr. Heidegger's Experiment, 276
Dream Song, 9
DuBois, W. E. B., 556
Dú'c, Nyuyên Qúi, 827
Dunbar, Paul Laurence, 369
Edwards, Jonathan, 60
Ehrenreich, Barbara, 498
Eliot, T. S., 567
Emerson, Ralph Waldo, 221
English, Deirdre, 498
Equiano, Olaudah, 321
Erdrich, Louise, 443
Erikson, Erik H., 208
Espada, Martín, 892
Everyday Use, 760
Fable for Tomorrow, A, 213
Farewell Order to the Army of Northern Virginia, 325
Faulkner, William, 633, 643
Fitzgerald, F. Scott, 585
Follow the Drinking Gourd, 554
from For Her Own Good, 498
Franklin, Benjamin, 161
Freeman, Mary E. Wilkins, 467
Frost, Robert, 205, 633, 635
Gary Keillor, 876
Gettysburg Address, The, 304
Gift Outright, The, 205
Giovanni, Nikki, 770

Glaspell, Susan, 454
Gold Mountain Poems, 400
Grant, Ulysses S., 321
Guthrie, Woody, 207
Hall, Prince, 183
Hamod, Sam, 770
Hansberry, Lorraine, 793
Harlem Wine, 526
Harlem: The Culture Capital, 512
Harris, Eddy, 433
Hawthorne, Nathaniel, 275
Hemingway, Ernest, 579
Henry, Patrick, 169
Home Ties, 436
Homesick Blues, 442
from Hospital Sketches, 334
Houston, Pam, 929
How It Feels to Be Colored Me, 533
How the World Was Made, 6
Hughes, Langston, 442, 509, 522
Hurston, Zora Neale, 509, 532
I Have Killed the Deer, 10
I Hear America Singing, 361
I Saw a Man Pursuing the Horizon, 375
I Stand Here Ironing, 732
If We Must Die, 525
In Another Country, 580
Indian Boarding School: The Runaways, 443
from Interesting Narrative of the Life of Olaudah Equiano, The, 22
from Iroquois Constitution, The, 158
Irving, Washington, 239
James, William, 210
Janitor, The, 936
Jeffers, Robinson, 215
Jefferson, Thomas, 177, 552
Jemison, Mary, 30
Jilting of Granny Weatherall, The, 611
Johnson, James Weldon, 511
Kebe, Larcelia, 542
Keillor, Garrison, 875
King, Martin Luther, Jr., 799
King, Stephen, 288
Kingsolver, Barbara, 892
Kingston, Maxine Hong, 753
Knight, Sarah Kemble, 434
Kuralt, Charles, 212
l(a, 577
Lazarus, Emma, 438
Leader of the People, The 676

Lease, Mary Elizabeth, 558
Least Heat Moon, William, 433
Leaves, 774
Lee, Robert E., 321
Legacies, 773
from Letter from a Birmingham Jail, 800
Letter to John Adams, 184
from Letters from an American Farmer, 553
from Life of Mary Jemison, The, 34
Life You Save May Be Your Own, The, 720
Lincoln, Abraham, 301, 432
Lindbergh, Anne Morrow, 436
Locke, John, 204
Lopez, Raul José, 944
Lord Byron's Love Letter, 690
Lost, 205
Lost Sister, 894
Love Song of J. Alfred Prufrock, The, 568
Ma Rainey, 528
Magoffin, Susan Shelby, 421
Malcolm X, 799
Man Said to the Universe, A, 375
Martínez, Rubén, 957
McCunn, Ruthanne Lum, 420
McKay, Claude, 522
Melville, Herman, 307
Mending Wall, 637
Millay, Edna St. Vincent, 491
Miller, Arthur, 61, 138
Mirror, 771
Mississippi Solo, 433
Momaday, N. Scott, 432
Moth and the Star, The, 440
Mother Tongue, 902
Much Madness is divinest Sense, 354
Murakami, Henry, 702
My Heart Feels Like Bursting, 403
Naming Myself, 896
Negro Speaks of Rivers, The, 526
Night Journey, 432
O'Brien, Tim, 811
O'Connor, Flannery, 719
Occurrence at Owl Creek Bridge, An, 312
from Of Plymouth Plantation, 31
Offer of Help, 33
Oh Freedom!, 554
Olsen, Tillie, 731
On the Rainy River, 812

On Thought in Harness, 493
One Art, 772
Paine, Thomas, 169
Paredes, Américo, 397
Park Ranger Brings the Civil War to Life, 337
from Personal Memoirs of U. S. Grant, 322
Petition to the Massachusetts General Assembly, 186
Pit and the Pendulum, The, 253
Plath, Sylvia, 770
Poe, Edgar Allan, 252
Portent, The, 308
Porter, Katherine Anne, 610
Prairies, The, 211
from Promised Land, The, 557
Raven, The, 268
Ray, Delia, 332
Reagan, Ronald, 437
Red Wagons, 898
Reece, Florence, 558
from Relación, La, 14
Reminiscences of My Life in Camp, 336
Return, 214
Revolt of "Mother," The, 468
Richard Cory, 576
Robinson, Edwin Arlington, 575
Roethke, Theodore, 432
Rowlandson, Mary, 206
Rudd, Lydia Allen, 436
Salvador Late or Early, 888
Satanta, 397
from Self-Reliance, 222
Separating, 742
Setting Out, The, 432
Sewall, Samuel, 55
Shiloh, 308
from Sinners in the Hands of an Angry God, 58
Song of the Sky Loom, 204
Song, Cathy, 892
Soul selects her own Society, The, 354
from Speech in the Virginia Convention, 172
Speed, 440
Spring and the Fall, The, 492
Stanton, Elizabeth Cady, 552
Steele, Shelby, 561
Steinbeck, John, 435, 633, 675
Stopping by Woods on a Snowy Evening, 636
Story of an Hour, The, 450

Swenson, May, 440
Sympathy, 370
Tall Men, The, 644
Tan, Amy, 901
Taylor, Susie King, 336
Tecumseh, 207
Teenage Wasteland, 866
There Was a Child Went Forth, 364
This Is What It Means to Say Phoenix, Arizona, 911
This is my letter to the World, 354
This Land Is Your Land, 207
This Newly Created World, 9
Thoreau, Henry David, 225
from Thousand Pieces of Gold, 420
Thurber, James, 440
from To Be Young, Gifted and Black, 794
To Jesus Villanueva, with Love, 775
To the Maiden, 374
Top of the Food Chain, 923
Trambley, Estela Portillo, 837
Trifles, 455
Truth, Sojourner, 236
Turner, Frederick Jackson, 211
Twain, Mark, 389, 433
Tyler, Anne, 865
Updike, John, 741
Village, 838
Villanueva, Alma Luz, 770
Wagner Matinée, A, 407
Wagoner, David, 205
from Walden, 226
Walker, Alice, 759
Washington, Booker T., 556
Watkins, Sam R., 335
Wayfarer, The, 374
We Wear the Mask, 371
Wells-Barnett, Ida B., 482
Welty, Eudora, 666
What Is the Grass?, 362
from What the Black Man Wants, 328
from Where the Ashes Are, 828
Which Side Are You On?, 558
Whitecloud, Thomas S., 657
Whitman, Walt, 360
Wilkins, Roger, 561
Williams, Tennessee, 689
Wilson, August, 935
Winter Dreams, 586
from Woman Warrior, The, 754
Worn Path, A, 667
Wright, Richard, 604
Youth, 527

Acknowledgments

continued from page iv

335 From *"Co. Aytch": A Side Show of the Big Show* by Sam R. Watkins, with a new Introduction by Roy P. Basler, pages 109–11. Copyright © 1962 by Macmillan Publishing Company. Reprinted by permission of Simon & Schuster Inc. **354–357** "Much Madness is divinest Sense," "The Soul selects her own Society," "This is my letter to the World," "A Bird came down the Walk" and "Because I could not stop for Death" by Emily Dickinson. Reprinted by permission of the publishers and the Trustees of Amherst College from *The Poems of Emily Dickinson,* Thomas H. Johnson, ed., Cambridge, Mass.: The Belknap Press of Harvard University Press, Copyright 1951, 1955, 1979, 1983 by the President and Fellows of Harvard College. **398** From *With His Pistol in His Hand: A Border Ballad and its Hero* by Américo Paredes, Copyright 1958, renewed 1986. By permission of the author and the University of Texas Press. **400** "Gold Mountain Poems" from *Songs of Gold Mountain: Cantonese Rhymes from San Francisco Chinatown* by Marlon K. Hom. Reprinted by permission of the University of California Press and the author. **420** From "Eleven" from *Thousand Pieces of Gold* by Ruthanne Lum McCunn, pages 105–108 and 109–110. Copyright © 1981 by Ruthanne Lum McCunn. Reprinted by permission of Beacon Press. **421** From *Down the Santa Fe Trail and into Mexico: The Diary of Susan Shelby Magoffin 1846–1857,* edited by Stella M Drumm, pages 37–39. Copyright 1926 by Yale University Press. Reprinted by permission of Yale University Press. **432** "The Setting Out" by N. Scott Momaday. Reprinted by permission. **432** "Night Journey" by Theodore Roethke from *The collected Poems of Theodore Roethke.* Copyright 1940 by Theodore Roethke. Reprinted by permission of Doubleday, a division of Bantam Doubleday Dell Publishing Group, Inc. **433** From *Blue Highways* by William Least Heat Moon. Copyright © 1982 by William Least Heat Moon. First appeared in *The Atlantic Monthly.* By permission of Little, Brown and Company in association with the Atlantic Monthly Press. **433** From Chapter 1 from *Mississippi Solo: A River Quest* by Eddy L. Harris, pages 1–2. Copyright © 1988 by Eddy L. Harris. Reprinted by permission of Lyons & Buford Publishers. **435** Excerpt from *The Grapes of Wrath* by John Steinbeck. Used by permission of Viking Penguin, a division of Penguin Books USA, Inc. **435** "Peregrinacion, Penitencia, Revolucion" by Cesar E. Chavez. Reprinted by permission of the Cesar E. Chavez Foundation. For additional information about Cesar E. Chavez and the UFW, please contact the Cesar E. Chavez Foundation, P.O. Box 62, Keene, CA 93531, (815) 882-5571, ext. 256. **436** Excerpt from *Diary of an Overland Journey* by Lydia Rudd. This item is reproduced by permission of The Huntington Library, San Marino, California. **440** "Speed" by May Swenson (Originally published in *The New Yorker*) from *Nature: Poems of Old and New.* Copyright © 1994 by The Literary Estate of May Swenson. Reprinted by permission of Houghton Mifflin Company. All rights reserved. **440** "The Moth and the Star" by James Thurber from *Fables for Our Time* (HarperCollins). Copyright © 1940 by James Thurber. Copyright © 1968 by Rosemary A. Thurber. Reprinted by permission of Rosemary A. Thurber. **442** "Homesick Blues" from *The Dream Keeper and Other Poems* by Langston Hughes. Reprinted by permission of the publisher. **442** "Indian Boarding School: The Runaways" from *Jacklight* by Louise Erdrich. Copyright © 1984 by Louise Erdrich. Reprinted by permission of Henry Holt and Company, Inc. **483** From *Crusade for Justice: The Autobiography of Ida B. Wells,* edited by Alfreda M. Duster. Copyright 1970 by the University of Chicago. Reprinted by permission. **492–493** "The Spring and the Fall" and "On Thought in Harness" by Edna St. Vincent Millay from *Collected Poems* (HarperCollins). Copyright 1923, 1934, 1951, © 1962 by Edna St. Vincent Millay and Norma Millay Ellis. Reprinted by permission of Elizabeth Barnett, Literary Executor. **498** From *Complaints and Disorders: The Sexual Politics of Sickness* by Barbara Ehrenreich and Deirdre English. Reprinted by permission. **512** "Harlem: The Culture Capital" by James Weldon Johnson from *The New Negro,* edited by Alain Locke. With introduction by Arnold Rampersad, pages 301–311. **526** "Harlem Wine" by Countee Cullen. Reprinted by permission. **527** "Youth" from *The Dream Keeper and Other Poems* by Langston Hughes. Copyright 1932 by Alfred A. Knopf, Inc. and renewed © 1960 by Langston Hughes. Reprinted by permission of the publisher. **528** "Ma Rainey" by Sterling A. Brown from *The Collected Poems of Sterling A. Brown,* edited by Michael S. Harper. Copyright 1932 by Harcourt Brace & Company. Copyright renewed © 1960 by Sterling A. Brown. Reprinted by permission of HarperCollins Publishers, Inc. **533** "How It Feels to Be Colored Me" by Zora Neale Hurston. Reprinted by permission of Lucy Ann Hurston. **558** From "Which Side Are You On?," words by Florence Reece. Copyright 1946 by Stormking Music Inc. Reprinted by permission of Stormking Music Inc. All rights reserved. **559** Studs Turkel, *Working.* New York, N.Y.: Random House, Inc. **560** Mary Crow Dog, *Lakota Woman.* Grove Weidenfeld, 1990. **568** "The Love Song of J. Alfred Prufrock: from *Collected Poems 1909–1962* by T.S. Eliot. Reprinted by permission of Faber & Faber Ltd. **577** "1(a" by E.E. Cummings from *Complete Poems: 1904–1962,* edited by George J. Firmage. Copyright © 1958, 1986, 1991 by the Trustees for the E.E. Cummings Trust. Reprinted by permission of Liveright Publishing Corporation. **580** "In Another Country" by Ernest Hemingway, from *Men Without Women.* Copyright 1927 Charles Scribner's Sons; copyright renewed 1955 Ernest Hemingway. Reprinted with the permission of Charles Scribner's Sons and Jonathan Cape Ltd. **586** "Winter Dreams" reprinted (with slight deletions) with permission of Scribner, and imprint of Simon & Schuster, Inc., from *All the Sad Young Men* by F. Scott Fitzgerald. Copyright 1922 by Metropolitan Publications, Inc. Copyright renewed 1950 by Frances Scott Fitzgerald Lanahan. **605** From *Black Boy* by Richard Wright. Copyright 1937, 1942, 1944, 1945 by Richard Wright. Copyright renewed © 1973 by Ellen Wright. Reprinted by permission of HarperCollins Publishers, Inc. **611** "The Jilting of Granny Weatherall" in *Flowering Judas and Other Stories,* copyright 1930 and renewed 1958 by Katherine Anne Porter, reprinted by permission of Harcourt Brace & Company. **620** From Chapter Five, "The Revolution In Manners and Morals" from *Only Yesterday: An Informal History of the Nineteen-Twenties* by Frederick Lewis Allen, pages 89–92. Copyright 1931 by Frederick Lewis Allen. Copyright renewed © 1959 by Agnes Rogers Allen. Reprinted by permission of HarperCollins Publishers, Inc. **636, 637, 639** "Stopping By Woods On A Snowy Evening," "Mending Wall," and "Birches" from *the Poetry of Robert Frost* edited by Edward Connery Lathem. Copyright © 1962 by Holt, Rinehart, and Winston, Inc. Reprinted by permission of Henry Holt and Company, Inc., the Estate of Robert Frost, and Jonathan Cape, Ltd. **644** "The Tall Men" from *Collected Stories of William Faulkner* by William Faulkner. Copyright 1941 and renewed © 1969 by Estelle Faulkner and Jill Faulkner Summers. Reprinted by permission of Random House, Inc. **658** "Blue Winds Dancing" by Thomas S. Whitecloud in *Scribner's Magazine,* Vol. CIII. Copyright 1938 Charles Scribner's Sons; copyright renewed. Reprinted by permission of Charles Scribner's Sons, and imprint of Macmillan Publishing Company. **667** "A Worn Path" from *A Curtain of Green and Other Stories,* copyright 1941 and renewed 1969 by Eudora Welty, reprinted by permission of Harcourt Brace & Company. **676** "The Leader of the People" from *The Red Pony* by John Steinbeck. Copyright 1933, 1937, 1938, renewed © 1961, 1965, 1966 by John Steinbeck. Reprinted by permission of Viking Penguin, a division of Penguin Books USA Inc. **690** *Lord Byron's Love Letter* by Tennessee Williams. Reprinted by permission. **699, 700, 702** From *The Homefront: America During World War II* by Mark Jonathan Harris, Franklin D. Mitchell, and Steven J. Schechter, pages 69–70, 109–111, 251–252. Copyright © 1984 by Mark Jonathan Harris, Franklin D. Mitchell, and Steven J. Schechter. Reprinted by permission of The Putnam Publishing Group. **720** "The Life You Save May Be Your Own" from *A Good Man is Hard to Find and Other Stories* by Flannery O'Connor. Copyright 1953 by Flannery O'Connor and renewed © 1981 by Regina O'Connor. Reprinted by permission of Harcourt Brace & Company. **732** "I Stand Here Ironing" from *Tell Me a Riddle* by Tillie Olsen, introduction by John Leonard. Copyright © 1956, 1957, 1960, 1961 by Tillie Olsen. Reprinted by permission of Delacorte Press/Seymour Lawrence, a division of Bantam Doubleday Dell Publishing Group, Inc. **742** "Separating" from *Problems and Other Stories* by John Updike. Copyright © 1979 by John Updike. Reprinted by permission of Alfred A.

Knopf, Inc. **754** From *The Woman Warrior: Memoirs of a Girlhood Among Ghosts* by Maxine Hong Kingston. Copyright © 1975, 1976 by Maxine Hong Kingston. Reprinted by permission of the author. **760** "Everyday Use" from *In Love & Trouble: Stories of Black Women* by Alice Walker. Copyright © 1973 by Alice Walker. Reprinted by permission of Harcourt Brace & Company. **771** "Mirror" from *Crossing the Water* by Sylvia Plath. Reprinted by permission of HarperCollins Publishers, Inc. and Faber & Faber Ltd. **772** "One Art" by Elizabeth Bishop from *The Complete Poems 1927–1979.* Copyright © 1979, 1983 by Alice Helen Methfessel. Reprinted by permission of Farrar, Straus & Giroux, Inc. **773** "Legacies" from *My House* by Nikki Giovanni. Copyright © by Nikki Giovanni. Reprinted by permission of William Morrow and Company, Inc. **774** "Leaves" by Hamod from *Dying With the Wrong Name: New and Selected Poems* 1958–1979 (Smyrna-Anthe Press, New York, N.Y.). Copyright © 1980 by Hamod. Reprinted by permission of the author. **775** From *Blood Root* by Alma Villanueva (Place of Herons Press). Copyright © 1977 by Alma Luz Villanueva. By permission of the author. **779** Abridged from *The Great Leap: The Past Twenty-Five Years in America* by John Brooks. Copyright © 1966 by John Brooks. Reprinted by permission of Harper & Row, Publishers, Inc. and Harold Ober Associates Inc. **794** "Chicago: Southside Summers" from *To Be Young, Gifted and Black: Lorrainne Hansberry in Her Own Words* (A Prentice-Hall Publication), adapted by Robert Nemiroff, pages 17–21. Copyright © 1969 by Robert Nemiroff & Robert Nemiroff as Executor of the Estate of Lorraine Hansberry. Reprinted by permission of Simon & Schuster Inc. **797** "Dream Deferred" from *The Panther and the Lash* by Langston Hughes. Copyright 1951 by Langston Hughes. Reprinted by permission of Alfred A. Knopf, Inc. **800** From "Letter from a Birmingham Jail" by Dr. Martin Luther King, Jr. Reprinted by permission. **806** From Chapter Nineteen 1965 from *The Autobiography of Malcolm X* by Malcolm X, with the assistance of Alex Haley, introduction by M.S. Handler, Epilogue by Alex Haley, pages 364–367 and 377–378. Copyright © 1964 by Alex Haley and Malcolm X. Copyright © 1965 by Alex Haley and Betty Shabazz. Reprinted by permission of Random House, Inc. **812** Adapted from "On the Rainy River" from *The Things They Carried* by Tim O'Brien. Copyright © 1990 by Tim O'Brien. Reprinted by permission of Houghton Mifflin Company/Seymour Lawrence. All rights reserved. **828** From "The Year of the Monkey" from *Where the Ashes Are: The Odyssey of a Vietnamese Family* by Nguyên Qúi Dúʼc. Reprinted by permission of Addison-Wesley Publishing Company, Inc. **838** "The Village by Estela Portillo. Copyright © 1989 by Estela Portillo. Reprinted by permission of the author. **866** "Teenage Wasteland" by Anne Tyler from *Seventeen Magazine,* November 1983, pages 145 and 167–169. Copyright © 1983 by Martín Espada. Reprinted by permission of W. W. Norton & Company, Inc. **876** "Gary Keillor" from *The Book of Guys* by Garriosn Keillor, pages 175–192. Reprinted by permission. **888** "Salvador Late or Early" from *Woman Hollering Creek: and Other Stories* by Sandra Cisneros. Published by Vintage Books, a division of Random House, Inc., New York and originally in hardcover by Random House, Inc. Copyright © 1991 by Sandra Cisneros. Reprinted by permission of Susan Bergholz Literary Services, New York. **893** "Coca-Cola and Coco Frío" from *City of Coughing and Dead Radiators* by Martín Espada, pages 26–27. Copyright © 1993 by Martín Espada. Reprinted by permission of W. W. Norton & Company, Inc. **894** "Lost Sister" from *Picture Bride* by Cathy Song. Reprinted by permission. **896** "Naming Myself" ("Poniendome Un Nombre") from *Another America (Otra América)* by Barbara Kingsolver, with Spanish Translations by Rebeca Cates, pages 56–57. Copyright © 1992 by Barbara Kingsolver. Reprinted with permission of Seal Press. **898** "Red Wagons" from *My Father Was a Toltec: And Selected Poems* by Ana Castillo, page 5. Reprinted by permission. **902** "Mother Tongue" by Amy Tan, first published in *The Threepenny Review*. Reprinted by permission. **911** Adaptation of "This Is What It Means to Say Phoenix, Arizona" from *The Lone Ranger and Tonto Fistfight in Heaven* by Sherman Alexie. Reprinted by permission. **923** "Top of the Food Chain," Copyright © 1993 by T. Coraghessan Boyle, from *Without a Hero* by T. Coraghessan Boyle. Used by permission of Viking Penguin, a division of Penguin Books USA Inc. **930** "A Blizzard Under Blue Sky: from *Cowboys Are My Weakness* by Pam Houston, pages 133–139. Copyright © 1992 by Pam Houston. Reprinted by permission of W. W. Norton & Company, Inc. **936** *The Janitor* by August Wilson. Copyright © 1985 by August Wilson. Reprinted by permission of the author. **939** "The Way We Will Be" from *U.S. News & World Report*, Oct. 25, 1993, vol. 115, No. 16, page 71. Copyright © 1993 by U.S. News & World Report. Reprinted by permission of U.S. News & World Report. **941** "Waking Up in 2025: A Scenario" from *The Futurist,* November–December 1994, page 38. Copyright G 1994 by World Future Society. Reprinted by permission of World Future Society, 7910 Woodmont Avenue, Suite 450, Bethesda, MD 20814. **942** "The Armored Cacoon" by Faith Popcorn from *Psychology Today,* Jan./Feb. 1995. Reprinted by permission. **956** From *Only Yesterday: An Informal History of the Nineteen-Twenties,* page 193–195. Reprinted by permission. **957** "1 Quake, 2 Worlds" by Rubén Martínez from *The New York Times,* January 20, 1994. Reprinted by permission.

■

Illustrations

Unless otherwise acknowledged, all photographs are the property of Scott, Foresman and Company. Page abbreviations are as follows: (t)top, (c)center, (b)bottom, (l)left, (r)right.

cover & frontispiece The Greenwich Workshop, Inc. Courtesy of The Greenwich Workshop, Inc., Shelton, CT (detail) on cover only **ii** The Greenwich Workshop, Inc. Courtesy of The Greenwich Workshop, Inc., Shelton, CT **viii** Charles Bird King, "Young Omahaw, War Eagle, Little Missouri and Pawnees"/National Museum of American Art, Washington, D. C./Art Resource **x** William Walcutt, "Pulling Down the Statue of George III," Private Collection **xii** National Museum of American Art, Washington, D. C./Art Resource **xix** Ralph Goings/O. K. Harris Gallery **xvii** Edward Hopper, "Nighthawks," Art Institute of Chicago/Superstock, Inc. **xvii** Robert Marcus Collection **0–1** Charles Bird King, "Young Omahaw, War Eagle, Little Missouri and Pawnees"/National Museum of American Art, Washington, D. C./Art Resource **1, 52, 54, 136, 142, 148** (icon) Delaware Art Museum **1, 2, 4, 41, 46, 51** (icon) Ohio Historical Society **3** Stock Montage, Inc. **7–8(c)** Philbrook Museum of Art, Tulsa, Oklahoma **9** Willard Clay **10** Jerry Jacka **12(br & tc)** Courtesy, Virginia Historical Society, Richmond **12(bcr& 13b)** Los Angeles County Museum of Art **12(bcl & 13t)** Historical Society of Pennsylvania **12(bl&cr)** National Archives of Canada, Ottawa **13** Granger Collection, New York **18** San Antonio Museum Association **21** Granger Collection, New York **24–25** Life Picture Service/Time-Warner Inc. **29** American Antiquarian Society **31** Pilgrim Society, Plymouth, Massachusetts **35** Jolene Rickard, "Two Canoes," 1987, color photograph collage, 28 x 17 inches, The M. & T. Bank Collection at the Burchfield Penney Art Center, Buffalo State College, Buffalo, New York **41(tobacco)** Arents Collection/New York Public Library, Astor, Lenox and Tilden Foundations, (pig) Library of Congress **42** Mireille Votter/Woodfin Camp & Associates **43** Bancroft Library, University of California, Berkeley **52–53** David Hiser/Photographers/Aspen, Inc. **52–53** Cynthia Clampitt **55(t)** Corbis-Bettmann Archive **55(b)** Granger Collection, New York **57** Peabody and Essex Museum **58** Massachusetts Historical Society **61** UPI/Corbis-Bettmann **68–132** Joan Marcus **137** U. S. Army photo **138(tr&br)** Archive Photos **138(bl)** Granger Collection **138(tl), 139(tl)** UPI/Corbis-Bettmann **139(tr)** Archive Photos **140** AP/Wide World **141** Metropolitan Museum of Art, New York, George A. Hearn Fund, 1956 **150** Charles Bird King, "Young Omahaw, War Eagle, Little Missouri and Pawnees"/National Museum of American Art, Washington, D. C./Art Resource **151(b)** Jerry Jacka **151(t)** Joan Marcus **152–153** William Walcutt, "Pulling Down the Statue of George III," Private Collection **153, 154, 156, 188, 193, 199(icon)** Tsing-Fang Chen, "Independence and Freedom," (detail)/Lucia Gallery, New York City/Superstock, Inc. **154(b)** The Fine Arts Museums of San Francisco, Gift of Mrs. Eleanor Martin **154(t)** Montana Historical Society **154–155** map, Diana Cole **154–155** title, Janice Clark **155(b)** Granger Collection **155(c)** New York Public Library, Astor, Lenox and Tilden Foundations **155(t)** Albany Institute of History & Art, New York **159** National Archives of Canada, Ottawa **161** Philadelphia Museum of Art, The Mr. and Mrs. Wharton Sinkler Collection **165** State Historical Society of Wisconsin, Museum Collection **169(b)** Corbis-Bettmann Archive **169(t)** National Portrait Gallery,

London **173** Collection of the Brandywine River Museum, Purchased through a grant from the Mabel Pew Myrin Trust **177** Independence National Parks & Monument Association/Eastern National Parks & Monuments Association **178–179** Library of Congress **184** Massachusetts Historical Society **188(r)** Library of Congress **188(c)** Robert Frerck/Odyssey Productions **188(l)** Schomburg Center for Research in Black Culture, New York Public Library **189(b)** S. Ferry/Gamma-Liaison **189(tr)** Charlie Cole/Sipa Press **189(tl)** UPI/Bettmann **190** Smithsonian Institution **191** Courtesy of Petty Officer Maureen Sims **199(b)** Yale University Art Gallery **200(b)** Courtesy, The Henry Francis du Pont Winterthur Museum **200(t)** National Gallery of Art, Washington, D. C., Andrew Mellon Collection **201** William Walcutt, "Pulling Down the Statue of George III," Private Collection **202(b)** State Historical Society of Wisconsin, Museum Collection **202(t)** Library of Congress **205** National Museum of American Art, Smithsonian Institution, Gift of Mrs. Joseph Harrison, Jr./Art Resource **206** Private Collection, Photograph Courtesy of Kennedy Galleries Inc., New York **209** Gilcrease Institute of American History & Art, Tulsa **210** The Hudson Bay Co. **212** Courtesy Carol Hoy **213** National Park Service History Collection, Harper's Ferry Center, Harper's Ferry, West Virginia **216–217** National Museum of American Art, Washington, D. C./Art Resource **217, 298, 300, 332, 338, 344(icon)** Library of Congress **218(r)** Metropolitan Museum of Art, Gift of the Sculptor, 1906 (07.101) **218(l)** New York Public Library, Astor, Lenox and Tilden Foundations **218–219** title, Marilyn Reaves (for Eliza Schultz Lettering Design) **219(b)** Smithsonian Institution **219(cr)** Library of Congress **219(cl)** New Hampshire Historical Society **219(t)** White House Collection/Superstock, Inc. **221** George Eastman House **222** Private Collection **225** Concord Free Public Library **227** Elliot Porter **233** *Trodden Weed* by Andrew Wyeth, Tempera on panel, 1951. Collection of Mr. and Mrs. Andrew Wyeth, copyright 1995 by Andrew Wyeth **236** Sophia Smith Collection, Smith College **237** San Francisco Museum of Modern Art, Gift of Mrs. E. D. Lederman **239** Sleepy Hollow Restorations **240–241** Illinois State Museum **244** Indianapolis Museum of Art, Gift of Mrs. Morris Clark **247** Culver Pictures Inc. **252** Manuscripts Dept/Lilly Library, Indiana University, Bloomington, IN **266** National Gallery, Oslo, Norway/Superstock, Inc. **268** Courtesy of Tony Angell **275** Essex Institute, Salem, MA **277** Detroit Institute of Arts, Gift of Dexter M. Ferry, Jr. **279** Bequest of John T. Bowen, in memory of Eliza M. Bowen, Courtesy, Museum of Fine Arts, Boston **286(bl&br)** Kobal Collection **286(t)** Photofest **286–289** sky background, Sarah Marciniak **286–287** title, Janice Clark **287(br)** From the Collection of the Memory Shop **287(t&bl)** Kobal Collection **289** Courtesy of the Art Institute of Chicago **290** Universal Pictures **297** Photofest **298(b)** National Portrait Gallery/Transfer from the National Gallery of Art, Washington, D. C./Gift of Andrew W. Mellon **298–299(b)** St. Louis Museum of Art **298–299** Library of Congress **298(t)** The Metropolitan Museum of Art, Gift of I. N. Phelps Stokes, Edward S. Hawes, Alice Mary Hawes, Marian Augusta Hawes, 1937. (37.14.2) **299(t)** Stowe Day Foundation **301(b)** Library of Congress **301(t)** Granger Collection, New York **303** *Harpers Weekly*, May, 1861 **304–305(b)** Library of Congress **304–305(t)** National Archives **307** Corbis-Bettmann Archive **309** Metropolitan Museum of Art, Gift of Mr. and Mrs. Carl Stoecker, 1897 **311** Corbis-Bettmann Archive **312(inset)** British Film Institute **312** Yukimasa Hirota/Photonica **317(inset)** Lester Glassner Collection **317** Yukimasa Hirota/Photonica **320** Dali, Salvador, THE PERSISTENCE OF MEMORY. 1931. Oil on canvas, 9–1/2 x 13". Collection, The Museum of Modern Art, New York. Given anonymously. Photograph © The Museum of Modern Art, New York. **321(all)** Library of Congress **323** West Point Museum, United States Military Academy **325(r)** Chris Nelson **325(l)** Fort Ward Museum, City of Alexandria, VA **328** Library of Congress **332** Museum of the Confederacy, Richmond, Virginia, photograph by Katherine Wetzel Museum of the Confederacy **333** National Archives **334** Courtesy of the Louise May Alcott Memorial Association **335** Collection of Mr. & Mrs. Franklin Fulton **337** Courtesy of Dennis Kelly **348–349** Walter, Ufer, "Where the Desert Meets the Mountain," The Anschutz Collection **349, 386, 388, 416, 423, 427(icon)** Library of Congress **349, 350, 352, 377, 381, 385(icon)** Culver Collections/Superstock, Inc. **350(tl)** Berry-Hill Galleries, New York **350(bl), 351(bl)** Library of Congress **350(br)** Edison Historic Site, National Park Service **350(t)** Museum of the City of New York **351(br)** Chicago Historical Society **351(c)** International Ladies Garment Workers Union Labor Management Documentation Center, Cornell University **351(t)** Brown Brothers **353** Trustees of Amherst College **355** National Gallery, Berlin/Superstock, Inc. **356** James Wyeth **360** Pennsylvania Academy of Fine Arts **361** Terra Museum of American Art **363** John Hancock Financial Services **364** Superstock, Inc. **369** Corbis-Bettmann Archive **370** "Photo Icon" by Gilles Larrain **373** Newark Public Library photo **374–375** Private Collection **377–380** background art, Cybele Grandjean **377** Terra Museum of American Art, Daniel J. Terra Collection, 1992.27 **378(b)** Museum of Fine Arts, Boston, Bequest of Miss Edith Nichols **378(t)** Cleveland Museum of Art, Purchase from the J. H. Wade Fund **379(b)** Museum of Fine Arts, Springfield, MA, The Morgan Wesson Memorial Collection **379(t)** Museum of Fine Arts, Boston, Bequest of Thomas G. Appleton **380** National Museum of American Art, Washington, D. C./Art Resource **386** map, Diane Cole **386(b)** Photograph courtesy History Division, Los Angeles County Museum of Natural History **386(c)** Union Pacific Museum Collection **386(t)** National Archives/Photo: Jonathan Wallen **387(b)** From *A Pictographic History of the Oglala Sioux*, The University of Nebraska Press **387(c)** Clara McDonald Williamson, "The Old Chisholm Trail," The Roland P. Murdock Collection, Wichita Art Museum, Wichita, Kansas **387(tr)** Union Pacific Museum Collection **387(tl)** Private Collection **388** Library of Congress **389(t)** North Wind Picture Archives

391 Laura Phillips/Bernstein & Andriulli **398** Gilcrease Museum of American Art, Tulsa, OK **400** Library of Congress **403** Smithsonian Institution **405** Museum of Western Art, Denver **406** Willa Cather Pioneer Memorial Collection/Nebraska State Historical Society **408–409** South Dakota Memorial Art Center Collection, Brookings **411** Museum of Fine Arts, Boston **416(b)** William Franklin McMahon **416(t)** Historical Pictures Service/Stock Montage, Inc. **417(br)** Western History Department/Denver Public Library **417(bl)** Western History Collections, University of Oklahoma Library **417(tr)** Library of Congress **417(tl)** California State Archives **419** The Thomas Gilcrease Institute of American History and Art, Tulsa, Oklahoma **419** Superstock, Inc. **420** Idaho State Historical Society **428** Everett Collection, Inc. **429** John Hancock Financial Services **430(b)** South Dakota Memorial Art Center Collection, Brookings **430(t)** Gilcrease Museum of American Art, Tulsa, OK **433** Jack and Pearl Resnick Collection **437** The Greenwich Workshop, Inc., Trumbull, CT **438** Philadelphia Museum of Art: Given by Carl Zigrosser **439(all)** Akita Collection **440–441** Courtesy David Hockney **442** Phillips Collection, Washington, D. C. **444–445** Charles Alston, "Walking," Sydney Smith Gordon Collection **445, 508, 510, 538, 543, 548(icon)** Aaron Douglas, "Rise, Shine for Thy Light Has Come," 1932/The Gallery of Art, Howard University, Washington, D. C. **445, 446, 448, 495, 501, 506(icon)** Claude Monet, "Woman With a Parasol," (detail), Musee D'Orsay, Paris/A. K. G., Berlin/Superstock, Inc. **446–447** Library of Congress **446(br)** Museum of the City of New York **446(t)** Old Life **446(bl)** Underwood/Corbis-Bettmann **447(b)** Library of Congress **447(t)** J. C. Allen & Sons **449** Missouri Historical Society **451** National Gallery of Art, Washington, D.C., Gift of Curt H. Reisinger **454** AP/Wide World **457** © Bob Timberlake **458** National Museum of American Art, Washington/Art Resource **461** The Phillips Collection, Washington, D. C. **466** Edgar William & Bernice Chrysler Garbisch Collection/National Gallery of Art, Washington, D. C. **467** Granger Collection, New York **469** Shelden Swope Art Museum, Terre Haute **474** Eric Sloan **479** Metropolitan Museum of Art, George A. Hearn Fund, 1942 **482** University of Chicago Library **486** U. S. Postal Service **491** Courtesy of Vassar College **492–493** Thyssen-Bornemisza Museum, Madrid/Art Resource **495(icon)** Musee D'Orsay, Paris/A. K. G., Berlin/Superstock, Inc. **496** Museum of the City of New York, Harry T. Peters Collection **498** Culver Pictures Inc. **499** Colorado Springs Fine Arts Center **502–503** Edward Hopper, "Nighthawks," Art Institute of Chicago/Superstock, Inc. **508(b)** AP/Wide World **508(t)** Dr. E. David Cronin, University of Wisconsin **509(tl)** Beinecke Rare Book and Manuscript Library, Yale University **509(br)** Globe Photos, Inc. **509(bl)** The estate of Carl Van Vechten, Joseph Solomon, executor **509(tr)** Schomburg Center for Research in Black Culture, New York Public Library, Astor, Lenox and Tilden Foundations **511** National Portrait Gallery, Smithsonian Institution/Art Resource **512, 514** Photograph by James Van Der Zee, Courtesy of Donna Van Der Zee **517, 523(c)** Corbis-Bettmann **523(b)** New York Times **523(tc)** Schomburg Center for Research in Black Culture, New York Public Library **523(t)** AP/Wide World **525** Phillips Collection, Washington, D. C. **527** The Gallery of Art, Howard University, Washington, D. C. **528** Courtesy Estate of Romare Howard Bearden **532** Courtesy The Estate of Carl Van Vechten **535** Norton Gallery of Art, West Palm Beach, Florida 1932/The Gallery of Art, Howard University, Washington, D. C. **538–539** Museum of Afro American Art, Boston **538(l)** Hampton University Museum, Hampton, VA **540(r)** Museum of African American Art **540(l)** National Museum of American Art, Smithsonian Institution, Gift of Benjamin and Olya Margolin/Art Resource **540–541** Schomburg Center for Research in Black Culture, New York Public Library **541** Whitney Museum of American Art, New York **553** Boatmen's National Bank of St. Louis **554–555** Courtesy Kansas State House **558** New York State Historical Association, Cooperstown **559** Paul Davis **560** National Geographic Society **563, 564, 566, 620(icon)** Grant Wood, "American Gothic," (detail), © 1996 Grant Wood/VAGA/Superstock, Inc. **563, 564, 566, 620, 625, 631(icon)** Edvard Munch, "The Scream," (detail), National Gallery, Oslo, Norway/A. K. G., Berlin/Superstock, Inc. **564–565** diorama, Diane Cole **564–565(background)** Holland McCombs **564(br)** Holland McCombs **564(t)** Brown Brothers **564(bl)** Library of Congress **565(r)** Detroit News **565(cr)** Culver Pictures Inc. **565(cl)** Culver Pictures Inc. **565(l)** Library of Congress **567** AP/Wide World **569** Private Collection **575(b)** Corbis-Bettmann Archive **575(t)** Corbis-Bettmann Archive **576** Private Collection **577** Private Collection **579** UPI/Corbis-Bettmann **580** Heerers Museum, Vienna **584** National Gallery of Art, Washington, D. C./Superstock, Inc. **585** Ivan Massar/Black Star **586, 593, 599, 600** Courtesy, Cluett, Peabody & Co., Inc. **604** AP/Wide World **607** Vaga, New York, NY **610** Jill Krementz **613** Carnegie-Stout Public Library **614** Minneapolis Institute of Arts **620** Culver Pictures Inc. **623(b)** AP/Wide World **623(t)** Old Life **632(b)** Metropolitan Museum of Art, New York, Alfred Stieglitz Collection, 1952 (52.203) **632(t)** Library of Congress **633(br)** Country Music Foundation Library and Media Center, Nashville **633(tl)** Detroit Institute of Arts, Gift of the Edsel B. Ford Fund **635** Dartmouth College **637** Eric Sloane **639** Metropolitan Museum of Art, Gift of Dr. and Mrs. Robert E. Carroll, 1979. (1979.138.2) **643** Bern Keating/Black Star **644, 647** The Oakland Museum of California, The City of Oakland, Gift of Paul B. Taylor **659** © Richard Red Owl **666** Jill Krementz **668** Eudora Welty Collection, Mississippi Department of Archives and History **676–677** Courtesy David DeMatteo **680** Library of Congress **683** Superstock, Inc. **688** Private Collection **689** NPA **691** Courtesy of Audrey Flack **695** Courtesy of Sandra Burshell **699(b)** Schomburg Center for Research in Black Culture, New York Public Library **699(t)** National Archives **701** AP/Wide World **714–715** Ralph Goings/O. K. Harris Gallery **715, 790, 792, 846, 852, 857(icon)** UPI/Corbis-Bettmann **715, 716, 718, 779, 784,**

789(icon) Superstock, Inc. 716(b) Fred DeWitt/Time-Warner Inc. 716(c) Brown Brothers 716(t) Sovfoto 717(tr&b) & Superstock, Inc. 717(tl) CBS 719 AP/Wide World 720–721 Courtesy Billy Morrow Jackson 725 Collection of the Whitney Museum of American Art, Purchase 731 AP/Wide World 733 Walker City Art Gallery, Liverpool/Superstock, Inc. 736 Collection of Whitney Museum of American Art, Purchase, and gift of Gertrude Vanderbilt Whitney, by exchange 741 Michael Chikiris 743 Parrish Art Museum, Southampton, NY 747 The Pennsylvania Academy of the Fine Arts, Gift of Mrs. Fairfield Porter 753 © Franco Salmoiraghi 755 Courtesy Tomie Arai 759 AP/Wide World Photos 761 Copyright © 1985 by S. Hill Corporation. All rights reserved. Used with permission. 765 The Bob Timberlake Gallery, Lexington, North Carolina 770(tc) Courtesy HarperCollins Publishers 770(t) Courtesy Farrar, Straus and Giroux, Photo: Thomas Victor 770(bc) Courtesy Nikki Giovanni 771 Photo by Wilfredo Q. Castano 771 Addison Gallery of American Art, Phillips Academy, Andover, Massachusetts, Gift of R. H. Donnelley Erdman (PA.1956) 773 The Howard University Gallery of Art, Washington, D. C. 775 Courtesy Fatima Del Real 779 Brown Brothers 781(l&r) Everett Collection, Inc. 782(t&b) Photofest 783 CBS News 790–791 Bernie Boston/*Washington Evening Star* 793 Nat Fein/New York Herald Tribune 794 Art and Artifacts Division, Schomburg Center for Research in Black Culture, New York Public Library 801 Courtesy Martin Luther King Memorial Library, Washington, D. C. 806 UPI/Corbis-Bettmann 811 AP/Wide World 813 Gerold-Wunderlich Gallery, New York 819 Courtesy of the artist 823 Thomas Barry Fine Arts, Minneapolis 828–829 William Albert Allard/ © National Geographic Society Image Collection 837 Courtesy Achilles Studio 839 Courtesy Rachael Romero 845 Susan Meiselas/Magnum Photos 846 UPI/Corbis-Bettmann 847(t) AP/Wide World 848(br) Owen Franken/Stock Boston 848(bl) James Pickerell/Black Star 848(tr) Peter Amft 848(tl) Bob Fitch/Black Star 849(b) John P. Filo 849(c) UPI/Corbis-Bettmann 849(t) Elliott Landy/Magnum Photos 850(tl) Michael Abramson/Black Star 850(b) Alex Webb/Magnum Photos 850(tr) UPI/Thai Khad Chuon/Corbis-Bettmann 858 Ralph Goings/O. K. Harris Gallery 859(b) Gerold-Wunderlich Gallery, New York 859(t) Art and Artifacts Division, Schomburg Center for Research in Black Culture, New York Public Library 860–861 Robert Marcus Collection 861, 862, 864, 939, 946, 951(icon) Diana Ong, "Family Unit," (detail)/Superstock, Inc. 862–863(b) Jack Parsons 862(bl) Ernst A. John 863(br) Lawrence Migdale 863(tr) David R. Frazier 865 Jerry Bauer 867 Hirshhorn Museum and Sculpture Garden, Smithsonian Institution, The Joseph H. Hirshhorn Bequest, 1981, photograph by Lee Stalsworth 871 Marlborough Fine Art Ltd. 875 AP/Wide World 877 © Curt Teich Postcard Archives, Lake County (IL) Museum 882 Bob Verlin/Monkmeyer Press Photo Service, Inc. 887 Rubin Guzman 889 Private Collection, Courtesy of Ruth Benzacar Galeria de Arte, Buenos Aires 892(bc) Courtesy HarperCollins Publishers, Photo: Steven L. Hopp 892(b) Courtesy W. W. Norton, Photo: Barbara Seyda 892(tc) L. Tom 893 Metropolitan Museum of Art, Purchase, Anonymous Gift, 1984 (1984.2) 895 Collection of Dr. Connie Christine Wheeler, Photography by Oren Slor 896–897 Steinbaum Krauss Gallery 898 Mary MacDonald 903 Courtesy Pacita Abad 910 Courtesy HarperPerennial, Photo: Rex Rystedt 913 The Greenwich Workshop, Inc., Trumbull, CT 914–915 Collection of the Oakland Museum of California, Burden Fund 922 Courtesy Viking Press, Photo: Pablo Campos 923–927 animals, Ralph Creaseman 926 Courtesy Caty Bartholomew 929 Courtesy W. W. Norton 931 Gallery Contemporanea, Jacksonville, FL/Superstock, Inc. 935 AP/Wide World 937 Copyright © 1976 by Hubert Shuptrine. All rights reserved. Used with permission 939 Superstock, Inc. 940–941(background) Superstock, Inc. 940 Everett Collection, Inc. 941 Roger Ressmeyer © 1995 Corbis 942 Donna Karan 943 Tim Burton 944 Courtesy Raul Jose Lopez 953 Robert Marcus Collection 954(b) Collection of Dr. Connie Christine Wheeler, Photography by Oren Slor 954(t) Copyright © 1976 by Hubert Shuptrine. All rights reserved. Used with permission 956 Photoworld/FPG International Corp. 959(t) Culver Pictures Inc. 960–961 Library of Congress 963(t&b) Kevin Horan.

Handlettering by Eliza Schulte.

Electronic Illustrations by Bruce Burdick, Lena Checroun, Scott J. Jordan, Steven Kiecker, and Gwen Plogman.